April 18–23, 2015
Seoul, Republic of Korea

Association for Computing Machinery

Advancing Computing as a Science & Profession

SIGCHI

CHI 2015
CROSSINGS

CHI 2015

Proceedings of the

33rd Annual CHI Conference on Human Factors in Computing Systems

Sponsored by:

ACM SIGCHI

Supported by:

Samsung, Golfzon, Google, Microsoft, NAVER, SK Planet, AutoDesk, Daumkakao, Disney Research, FuturePlay, Hyundai Motor Group, Language Grid, LG, NSF, Adobe Systems, H9Works, Yonsei University, KIPFA, and Samsung Art & Design Institute

Association for
Computing Machinery

Advancing Computing as a Science & Profession

The Association for Computing Machinery
2 Penn Plaza, Suite 701
New York, New York 10121-0701

Notice to Past Authors of ACM-Published Articles
ACM intends to create a complete electronic archive of all articles and/or other material previously published by ACM. If you have written a work that has been previously published by ACM in any journal or conference proceedings prior to 1978, or any SIG Newsletter at any time, and you do NOT want this work to appear in the ACM Digital Library, please inform permissions@acm.org, stating the title of the work, the author(s), and where and when published.

ISBN: 978-1-4503-3145-6 (Digital)

ISBN: 978-1-4503-3774-8 (Print)

Additional copies may be ordered prepaid from:

ACM Order Department
PO Box 30777
New York, NY 10087-0777, USA

Phone: 1-800-342-6626 (USA and Canada)
+1-212-626-0500 (Global)
Fax: +1-212-944-1318
E-mail: acmhelp@acm.org
Hours of Operation: 8:30 am – 4:30 pm ET

Printed in the USA

From the General and Technical Program Chairs

Welcome to CHI 2015, the premier international forum for human-computer interaction (HCI). In its early days, HCI focused on optimizing interactions between a user and a computer. Today, computers pervade our world, impacting our lives in varied and subtle ways. By never focusing solely on technology itself but always on innovations and their effects throughout human lives, HCI has increasingly come to mean *human-centered innovation.*

The theme for the conference this year is *CROSSINGS* which represents our excitement about crossing into Asia and also reflects CHI's core principle of crossing disciplines, crossing people and technology, crossing research and business, crossing physical and digital, … crossing you and me.

This year's conference brings CHI to Asia for the first time in its 33-year history, continuing the SIGCHI commitment to making CHI a truly international community. The city of Seoul represents one of many innovation centers in Asia and provides a fantastic opportunity to showcase groundbreaking content from across the region. In addition to an exciting technical program, we are holding four special symposia devoted to breakthrough insights and innovations from the Chinese, Japanese and ASEAN research communities.

The exciting keynote program features speakers who will bring fresh perspectives to CHI including Dean ***Lou Yongqi*** of Tongji University, China, a prominent global thinker on social and sustainable design; Executive VP ***Donghoon Chang***, MFA, head of Samsung Electronic's design strategy; Senior Research Fellow ***David Min***, PhD, head of the Software Center at LG Electronics; and ***PSY***, the media record breaker and innovator discussing creative methods and the impact of social media on to cross cultural boundaries.

CHI is honored this year to be the forum chosen by the recipient of one of ACM's top awards, the Athena Lecturer Award, ***Susan T. Dumais*** who developed novel algorithms and interfaces for interactive retrieval that have made it easier for people to find, use and make sense of information. She will present insights from her experiences at a special keynote session at the conference.

CHI 2015 includes two days of focused workshops and four days of technical content, including CHI's prestigious technical program, with 16 parallel sessions of rigorously reviewed research Papers, engaging Panels, Case Studies and Special Interest Groups (SIGs), an extensive Course program and invited talks from SIGCHI's award winners: Leysia Palen, Jean Scholtz, Michel Beaudouin-Lafon, Jim Hollan, Susan Dray and the new inductees to the CHI Academy.

We also host student research, design, and game competitions, and last-minute SIGs for discussing current topics. The popular alt.chi forum entered its tenth year of provocation to the HCI community. Interactivity's hands-on demonstrations showcase the best of interactive technology and innovation. The program also highlights more than 200 Work-In-Progress posters. Evening events include the CHI 2015 conference reception, Sponsors and University events, local performances and the Job Fair. Across all tracks, CHI received over 2800 submissions and accepted nearly 1000 that will appear in the ACM Digital Library.

We are deeply indebted to an enormous number of volunteers, without whom CHI 2015 would not be possible, including over 3800 reviewers, over 200 senior members of the program committee, nearly 100 members of the CHI 2015 conference organization committee and, of course, the more than 180 student volunteers. We are also deeply grateful to the ongoing support of the Korean HCI society who demonstrated incredible hospitality by moving their own conference's time and location to make room for

CHI in Seoul and who provided tremendous resources from their membership to support CHI logistically and in attracting novel content from around Asia.

We hope you will see fresh insights, strengthen connections and find new collaborators in Asia. *Above all, we hope you enjoy this unique experience of CHI 2015!*

General Conference Chairs

Bo Begole
Huawei, USA

Jinwoo Kim
Yonsei University, Korea

Technical Program Chairs

Kori Inkpen
Microsoft Research, USA

Woontack Woo
KAIST, Korea

From ACM SIGCHI's President and Vice President for Conferences

SIGCHI is proud to sponsor the premier annual conference in the field of human-computer interaction. We are extremely grateful to the CHI 2015 Conference Chairs Jinwoo Kim and Bo Begole, to Technical Program Chairs Woontack Woo and Kori Inkpen, and to their wonderful crew, who succeeded to build an impressive program and experience.

CHI 2015 is in Seoul, Korea, the first CHI ever in Asia. CHI started in Gaithersburg, MD, USA, in March 1982. That first conference in Gaithersburg drew over 900 attendees, and since then CHI, with the official name: "ACM Conference on Human Factors in Computing Systems" moved to annual, originally moving between the USA and Canada. Starting with 1993 CHI traveled between locations in Europe and North America. This year is another big step forward, made possible thanks to the Korean HCI Society that helped understand and navigate the local context, that moved its annual conference 3 months earlier to December 2014, and at the same time supported CHI's Technical Program meeting.

CHI has continued to grow and broaden its range of topics and contributing disciplines: the founding psychologists and software engineers began to meet new visions from ethnography, sociology, communication sciences and arts, among others. Relevant industries, as well as research institutes and academia, showed an increasing — and often long-lasting — interest and involvement (through volunteers and through sponsorship for conference expenses). This year's Conference Committee truly succeeded in crossing borders of all kind, providing new and unique opportunities for all participants to meet something entirely different.

CHI is an ideal forum for people to meet formally as well as informally, to exchange knowledge and views, to share experiences, and to learn. The CHI conference brings together professionals from research and practice; people from industry, academia, and from government; long-term veterans of HCI, young professionals and students; all in an environment designed to encourage interaction. We invite you to actively participate in that interaction: introduce yourself to people, interact with presenters and speakers, renew old friendships and make new ones

CHI is organized on behalf of ACM's Special Interest Group on Computer-Human Interaction (SIGCHI), an international community of professionals who share an interest in the many diverse facets of HCI. SIGCHI is committed both to advancing the field of HCI, to facilitate exchange of information within the SIGCHI community, and to support students to enter the domain.

The CHI conference is arguably the single most visible activity of SIGCHI, but we also sponsor and support a wide range of specialized conferences and workshops in areas ranging from interactive systems design to user interface technology to computer-supported cooperative work to "intelligent" user interfaces. Visit the SIGCHI website at **http://www.sigchi.org** to find our conference schedule, listing upcoming as well as past conferences.

SIGCHI and ACM produce some of the most respected publications in the field. All members receive interactions, a highly-acclaimed magazine covering the broad field of HCI and user interface design. ACM Transactions on Computer-Human Interactions (ToCHI), now in its 21st year, is our flagship journal – a quarterly publication with the top-quality archival research aimed at researchers and those translating research into practice.

SIGCHI is truly an international organization, with around 40 local chapters and 3 student chapters in 25 countries on 6 continents. We encourage all SIGCHI members to join their local chapter — or if there isn't one in your area, we would love to help you create one. And don't forget virtual communities! SIGCHI hosts dozens of electronic mailing lists on topics ranging from HCI and the Web, to HCI educations, to public policy and beyond. Those lists range from dozens of subscribers to thousands, and are an excellent way to keep up with the field and with friends and colleagues.

Finally, on behalf of ACM SGICHI, we again want to thank the conference committee and all of the hundreds of volunteers who make this conference possible. Their work makes this a rewarding experience for all of us.

Gerrit C. van der Veer
SIGCHI President

John "Scooter" Morris
SIGCHI Vice-President for Conferences

About SIGCHI

CHI 2015 is sponsored by ACM's Special Interest Group on Computer-Human Interaction (ACM SIGCHI). ACM, the Association for Computing Machinery, is an educational and scientific society uniting the world's computing educators, researchers, and professionals to inspire dialogue, share resources, and address the field's challenges. ACM strengthens the profession's collective voice through strong leadership, promotion of the highest standards, and recognition of technical excellence. ACM supports the professional growth of its members by providing opportunities for life-long learning, career development, and professional networking. ACM offers its more than 100,000 worldwide members cutting edge technical information through world class journals and magazines, dynamic special interest groups, and globally recognized conferences.

Visit www.acm.org for more information about the ACM.

SIGCHI is the premier international society for professionals, academics, and students who are interested in human-computer interaction (HCI). We provide a forum for the discussion of all aspects of HCI through our conferences, including our flagship CHI conference, publications, web sites, email discussion groups, and other services. We advance education in HCI through courses, workshops, and outreach, and we promote informal access to a wide range of individuals and organizations involved in HCI. Members can be involved in HCI-related activities with others in their region through local SIGCHI chapters. Come to the SIGCHI Town Hall meeting on Wednesday, April 22, at 12:50 to 14:30 in Room 308 or visit **www.sigchi.org** to learn more about SIGCHI.

Membership Information

Please contact ACM's Member Services Dept.
Online: **www.acm.org**
Tel: +1-800-342-6626 (USA/Canada)
+1-212-626-0500 (International)
Fax: +1-212-944-1318
Email: acmhelp@acm.org

Write:

Association for Computing Machinery, Inc.
General Post Office
P.O. Box 30777
New York, NY 10087-0777, USA

CHI 2015 Papers and Notes Chairs' Welcome

The CHI Papers and Notes programme is continuing to grow and this year! We are pleased that CHI continues to be the leading conference for research in human-computer interaction.

This year we considered more than 2120 submissions, ~600 of which were notes. This represents a continuation of ~4% annual growth in submissions. We accepted 486 submissions (~23%): 379 papers and 107 notes.

The CHI review process demands a tremendous amount of work from all areas of the human-computer interaction community. As co-chairs of the process, we are amazed at the ability of the community to organize itself to accomplish this task. We would like to thank the 2809 individual reviewers for their careful consideration of these papers. Every submission received at least three external reviews.

We also deeply appreciate the huge amount of time donated to this process by the 225-member program committee, who paid their own way to attend the face-to-face program committee meeting, an event larger than most ACM conferences.

We are proud of the work of the CHI 2015 program committee and hope that you enjoy these papers and notes, which represent the best research in human-computer interaction.

CHI 2015 Paper and Notes Chairs

Andy Cockburn
University of Canterbury

Janna McGrenere
University of British Columbia

Table of Contents

Supporting Change in Developing Countries

Privacy, Security & Interruptions

Making & Sharing Assistive Technologies

Matching & Facilitating Social Interactions

Collaborative Tables, Walls & Rooms

Session Chair: Harald Reiterer, *University of Konstanz, Germany*

The Value of Things

Session Chair: Mark Blythe, *Northumbria University, UK*

Phones for more than Just Talking & Text

Session Chair: Naomi Yamashita, *NTT Communication Science Laboratories, Japan*

Search & Recommendations

Session Chair: Susan Dumais, *Microsoft Research, USA*

Kids Haptic, Wearable, Tangible Learning

Session Chair: Shuli Gilutz, *Interdisciplinary Center (IDC) Herzliya, Israel*

Motivation & Participation

Session Chair: Meredith Morris, *Microsoft Research, USA*

Sustainability & Recycling

Session Chair: Adrian Clear, *Lancaster University, UK*

The Value of the Village in Caregiving

Session Chair: Lena Mamykina, *Columbia University, USA*

1135 Effects of Public Commitments and Accountability in a Technology-Supported Physical Activity Intervention
Sean A. Munson, *University of Washington*
Erin Krupka, Caroline Richardson, Paul Resnick, *University of Michigan*

1145 Rare World: Towards Technology for Rare Diseases
Haley MacLeod, Kim Oakes, Danika Geisler, *Indiana University*
Kay Connelly, *Indiana University, Bloomington*
Katie Siek, *Indiana University*

1155 Looking for Respite and Support: Technological Opportunities for Spousal Caregivers
Matthieu Tixier, Myriam Lewkowicz, *Troyes University of Technology*

1159 Barriers and Negative Nudges: Exploring Challenges in Food Journaling
Felicia Cordeiro, Daniel A. Epstein, *University of Washington*
Edison Thomaz, *Georgia Institute of Technology*
Elizabeth Bales, *University of Washington*
Arvind K. Jagannathan, Gregory D. Abowd, *Georgia Institute of Technology*
James Fogarty, *University of Washington*

I Like What I See - Interface Aesthetics

Session Chair: Simon Bowen, *Newcastle University, UK*

1163 Computation of Interface Aesthetics
Aliaksei Miniukovich, Antonella De Angeli, *University of Trento*

1173 Patina Engraver: Visualizing Activity Logs as Patina in Fashionable Trackers
Moon-Hwan Lee, Seijin Cha, Tek-Jin Nam, *Korea Advanced Institute of Science and Technology*

1183 Real-time Guidance Camera Interface to Enhance Photo Aesthetic Quality
Yan Xu, Joshua Ratcliff, *Intel Labs*
James Scovell, *Intel Corporation*
Gheric Speiginer, *Georgia Institute of Technology*
Ronald Azuma, *Intel Labs*

1187 Infographic Aesthetics: Designing for the First Impression
Lane Harrison, *Tufts University*
Katharina Reinecke, *University of Michigan*
Remco Chang, *Tufts University*

1191 ISOTYPE Visualization – Working Memory, Performance, and Engagement with Pictographs
Steve Haroz, *Northwestern University*
Robert Kosara, *Tableau Software*
Steven L. Franconeri, *Northwestern University*

Supporting Creativity through UX Design

Session Chair: Luciano Gamberini, *University of Padova, Italy*

1201 *GEM-NI:* A System for Creating and Managing Alternatives in Generative Design
Loutfouz Zaman, *York University*
Wolfgang Stuerzlinger, *Simon Fraser University*
Christian Neugebauer, *University of Applied Sciences Bonn-Rhein-Sieg*
Robert Woodbury, Maher Elkhaldi, Naghmi Shireen, *Simon Fraser Univeristy*
Michael Terry, *University of Waterloo*

1211 Motif: Supporting Novice Creativity through Expert Patterns
Joy Kim, *Stanford University*
Mira Dontcheva, *Adobe Research*
Wilmot Li, *Adobe Systems*
Michael S. Bernstein, *Stanford University*
Daniela Steinsapir, *Adobe Research*

1221 DesignScape: Design with Interactive Layout Suggestions
Peter O'Donovan, *University of Toronto & Adobe Research*
Aseem Agarwala, *Adobe Research*
Aaron Hertzmann, *University of Toronto & Adobe Research*

1225 Using Game Principles in UX Research: A Board Game for Eliciting Future User Needs
Karin Slegers, *KU Leuven & iMinds*
Sanne Ruelens, *iMinds & VUB*
Jorick Vissers, *Social Spaces & KU Leuven/iMinds*
Pieter Duysburgh, *iMinds & VUB*

Smartwatch Interaction

Session Chair: Daniel Ashbrook, *Rochester Institute of Technology, USA*

1229 Investigating the Information Transfer Efficiency of a 3x3 Watch-back Tactile Display
Jaeyeon Lee, Jaehyun Han, Geehyuk Lee, *Korea Advanced Institute of Science and Technology*

1233 SplitBoard: A Simple Split Soft Keyboard for Wristwatch-sized Touch Screens
Jonggi Hong, Seongkook Heo, *Korea Advanced Institute of Science and Technology*
Poika Isokoski, *KAIST & University of Tampere*
Geehyuk Lee, *Korea Advanced Institute of Science and Technology*

1237 Beats: Tapping Gestures for Smart Watches
Ian Oakley, DoYoung Lee, MD. Rasel Islam, *Ulsan National Institute of Science and Technology*
Augusto Esteves, *University of Madeira*

Tangible Interactions

Session Chair: Otmar Hilliges, *ETH Zurich, Switzerland*

New Evaluation Approaches

Session Chair: David England, *Liverpool John Moores University, UK*

Evaluating Crowdsourcing

Session Chair: Bongwon Suh, *Seoul National University, Republic of Korea*

Smart Smartphone Authentication

Session Chair: Andrea Bianchi, *Sungkyunkwan University, Republic of Korea*

Healthcare Bias, Engagement & Adaptation

Session Chair: Tae-Jung Yun, *Samsung Electronics, Republic of Korea*

Storytelling in InfoVis

Session Chair: Charles Perin, *INRIA Saclay, France*

Grip, Move & Tilt: Novel Interaction

Session Chair: Jessica Cauchard, *Stanford University, USA*

DIY Healthcare: Apps & Wearables

Session Chair: David Coyle, *University College Dublin*

Social Embodied Interaction

Session Chair: Gina Venolia, *Microsoft Research, USA*

Innovation in Theories & Products

Session Chair: Volker Wulf, *University of Siegen, Germany*

Design and 3D Object Fabrication

Session Chair: David Kim, *Microsoft Research, UK*

Understanding & Extending Touch Interfaces

Session Chair: Theophanis Tsandilas, *INRIA, France*

Sharing & Collaboration @ Work

Session Chair: Steven Drucker, *Microsoft Research, USA*

Families and Their Use of Technology

Session Chair: Jennifer Marlow, *Carnegie Mellon University, USA*

Understanding Crowdwork in Many Domains

Session Chair: Uichin Lee, *Korea Advanced Institute of Science and Technology, South Korea*

Player Performance & Experience in Games

Neighborhoods & Disadvantaged Communities

Enhanced Security with Passwords & CAPTCHAs

Accessibility at Home & on The Go

Interactive & Multi-Surface Maps

Session Chair: Brent Hecht, *University of Minnesota, USA*

Robot Personalities

Session Chair: Malte Jung, *Cornell University, USA*

Mid-Air Gestures and Interaction

Session Chair: Yang Li, *Google Research, USA*

MOOCS & e-Learning

Session Chair: Juho Kim, *Massachusetts Institute of Technology, USA*

Understanding Gamers

Session Chair: Toni-Jan Keith Monserrat, *National University of Singapore, Singapore*

Bridging Communities

Session Chair: Edward Cutrell, *Microsoft Research India, India*

Gender & Technology

Session Chair: Antonella De Angeli, *University of Trento, Italy*

CHI 2015 Organization

General Conference Chairs
Jinwoo Kim, *Yonsei University, Korea*
Bo Begole, *Huawei, USA*

Technical Program

Technical Program Chairs
Woontack Woo, *KAIST, Korea*
Kori Inkpen, *Microsoft Research, USA*

Papers
Andy Cockburn, *University of Canterbury, New Zealand*
Joanna McGrenere, *University of British Columbia, Canada*
Jun Rekimoto, *University of Toyko, Japan*

Case Studies
Danielle Cooley, *DGCooley Consulting, USA*
Joonhwan Lee, *Seoul National University, Korea*

Courses
Regina Bernhaupt, *ICS-IRIT, France*
Matt Jones, *Swansea University, UK*

Interactivity
Julie Rico Williamson, *University of Glasgow, UK*
Juhyun Eune, *Seoul National University, Korea*

Video Showcase
Jinwook Seo, *Seoul National University, Korea*
Rodrigo de Oliveira, *Google, USA*

SIGs
Enrico Rukzio, *Ulm University, Germany*
Simone Barbosa, *PUC-Rio, Brazil*

Doctoral Consortium
Si-Jung "Jun" Kim, *University of Central Florida, USA*
Jaime Teevan, *Microsoft Research, USA*
Sue Fussell, *Cornell University, USA*

Workshops
Juergen Steimle, *Max Planck Institute for Informatics, Germany*
Bongshin Lee, *Microsoft Research, USA*

Works in Progress
Shamsi Iqbal, *Microsoft Research, USA*
Shaun Lawson, *University of Lincoln, UK*
Shendong Zhao, *National University of Singapore, Singapore*

Student Research Competition
Seungyon "Claire" Lee, *Google, USA*
Geehyuk Lee, *KAIST, Korea*

Student Design Competition
Youn-Kyung Lim, *KAIST, Korea*
Anirudha Joshi, *ITT Bombay, India*

Student Game Competition
Floyd Muller, *RMIT University, Australia*
Alessandro Canossa, *Northeastern University, USA*
Soojin Jun, *Yonsei University, Korea*

alt.chi
Silvia Lindtner, *University of California, Irvine, USA*
Morgan Ames, *Intel, USA*
Henry Duh, *University of Tasmania, Australia*

TOCHI Papers
Jeffrey Nichols, *IBM Research, USA*

Best of CHI Awards
Mark Billinghurst, *University of Canterbury, New Zealand*

Panels
Khai Truong, *University of North Carolina, Charlotte, USA*
Elaine M. Huang, *University of Zurich, Switzerland*

Conference Theme Chair
Kyle Hyunsuk Kim, *Hongik University, Korea*

Industry Liaison
Garett Dworman, *TecEd, USA*

Operations

Chair's Assistant
Yoojin Lee, *Yonsei University, Korea*

Chair's Assistant
Nik Martelaro, *Stanford University, USA*

Student Volunteer
Jon Haber, *University of Calgary, Canada*
Siroberto Scerbo, *Virginia Tech, USA*
Jieun Wee, *Seoul National University, Korea*

Technology Liaisons
Sara Drenner, *University of Minnesota-Twin Cities, USA*
Scooter Morris, *University of California, San Francisco, USA*

Webmaster
Juho Kim, *MIT, USA*
TJ Monserrat, *National University of Singapore, Singapore*

Social Media
Max Wilson, *Nottingham University, UK*
Kwangsu Cho, *Sungkyunkwan University, Korea*

Data Managerment
Max Van Kleek, *University of Southampton, UK*
BoYu Gao, *Konkuk University, Korea*

Proceedings
Deana Brown, *Georgia Tech, USA*
Jaejeung Kim, *KAIST, Korea*

Infrastructure Accessibility Chair
Jongbae Kim, *Yonsei University, Korea*

Digital Accessibility Chair
Jeff Bigham, *University of Rochester, USA*

Scheduling
Christophe Hurter, *ENAC, France*
Juho Kim, *MIT, USA*

Mobile Apps
Stephen Oney, *Carnegie Mellon University, USA*
Eiji Hayashi, *Carnegie Mellon University, USA*
Jason Wiese, *Carnegie Mellon University, USA*
Célia Martinie, *Université Paul Sabatier, France*

Video Previews
Fanny Chevalier, *INRIA, France*
Stéphane Huo, *Université Paris-Sud, France*

Posters
Hyun Joo Song, *Seoul National University, Korea*

Translations
Sue Fussell, *Cornell University, USA*
Naomi Yamashita, *NTT, Japan*

Local Hospitality
Junho Choi, *Yonsei University, Korea*

Sponsors, Exhibits & Recruitment
Carol Klyver, *Foundations of Excellence, USA*

Registration
Yvonne Lopez, *Executive Events, Inc. USA*
Brooke Daley, *Executive Events, Inc. USA*

PCS Liaisons
Max van Kleek, *University of Southampton, UK*
Carol Klyver, *Foundations of Excellence, USA*
Scooter Morris, *University of California, San Francisco, USA*

RIMES: Embedding Interactive Multimedia Exercises in Lecture Videos

Juho Kim[1,2] Elena L. Glassman[1,2] Andrés Monroy-Hernández[1] Meredith Ringel Morris[1]
[1]Microsoft Research, Redmond, WA, USA
[2]MIT CSAIL, Cambridge, MA, USA
{juhokim, elg}@mit.edu {andresmh, merrie}@microsoft.com

ABSTRACT
Teachers in conventional classrooms often ask learners to express themselves and show their thought processes by speaking out loud, drawing on a whiteboard, or even using physical objects. Despite the pedagogical value of such activities, interactive exercises available in most online learning platforms are constrained to multiple-choice and short answer questions. We introduce RIMES, a system for easily authoring, recording, and reviewing interactive multimedia exercises embedded in lecture videos. With RIMES, teachers can prompt learners to record their responses to an activity using video, audio, and inking while watching lecture videos. Teachers can then review and interact with all the learners' responses in an aggregated gallery. We evaluated RIMES with 19 teachers and 25 students. Teachers created a diverse set of activities across multiple subjects that tested deep conceptual and procedural knowledge. Teachers found the exercises useful for capturing students' thought processes, identifying misconceptions, and engaging students with content.

Author Keywords
Educational videos; online education; interactive exercises.

ACM Classification Keywords
H.5.1. Multimedia Information Systems: Video

INTRODUCTION
Lecture videos are gaining popularity in traditional classrooms, with many teachers using online lectures as supplementary materials, or even "flipping" their classes by assigning lecture videos to watch at home and spending class time for hands-on exercises and discussions [29]. Such blended learning models (e.g., flipped classrooms [29] and Small Private Online Courses (SPOCs) [13]) as well as online-only classes leverage videos specifically created for the course, accessible as open educational resources (OER) (e.g., MIT OpenCourseWare [ocw.mit.edu]), or available on large-scale online learning platforms that have garnered the attention of millions of learners recently [24,30] (e.g., Khan Academy, YouTube, and Massive Open Online Courses (MOOCs) [6]).

Most online video lecture systems, however, only provide disconnected and passive learning experiences. Lectures are commonly captured as videos, but interactive components that promote deeper understanding in classrooms – speaking out loud, drawing on a whiteboard, or using physical objects – are often lost. Furthermore, while videos and assessments are two of the primary features on online platforms [18], these components are often separate, potentially causing a cognitive overhead for students in linking information [22]. Many online computer programming courses include interactive coding exercises, but assessments in most other subject areas are constrained to multiple-choice and short answer questions that lack the interactivity and expressiveness common in classroom activities. Supporting richer modalities and activities for lecture videos requires significant technical expertise and resources that most teachers do not have.

Education research shows that higher interactivity in a video improves learning [35], and constructive and active learning (e.g., working out an answer in steps) outperforms passive learning (e.g., watching a video) [9]. Enabling multiple modalities such as drawing, moving, and speaking, in addition to typing, can provide learners with more opportunities for expressing ideas and learning deeply.

We introduce RIMES (Rich Interactive Multimedia Exercise System), a system for authoring, recording, and reviewing interactive multimedia exercises embedded in video lectures. The system's authoring interface allows teachers to create and embed these exercises in videos produced with Office Mix [officemix.com], a free plug-in for PowerPoint that turns slides into online videos with voice and webcam recordings of the presenter.

RIMES offers a new and expressive exercise widget for Office Mix, allowing for richer and more open-ended exercises than traditional quizzes. While watching the video, and without leaving their web browser, students are prompted to record their own responses, using their webcam, microphone, and inking (via mouse, touch, or stylus). Finally, RIMES aggregates all the students' responses in a gallery that lets teachers get an overview of all submissions as well as replay individual responses.

CHI 2015, April 18 - 23 2015, Seoul, Republic of Korea
Copyright is held by the owner/author(s). Publication rights licensed to ACM.
ACM 978-1-4503-3145-6/15/04…$15.00
http://dx.doi.org/10.1145/2702123.2702186

We evaluated the RIMES system and its workflow with 19 middle and high school teachers who authored video lectures with RIMES exercises, and 25 middle and high school students who recorded their responses to those same exercises. We also hired crowd workers on Amazon's Mechanical Turk to answer the exercises, simulating larger gallery sizes. Finally, the teachers returned to the lab to review the responses using the RIMES gallery.

Teachers created a wide variety of RIMES exercises across multiple subjects (math, sciences, English, and history), modalities (drawing, audio, and video), and question types (asking for open-ended responses, step-by-step explanations, and visual representations). Teachers reported that the system was effective at helping them identify misconceptions, capturing students' thought processes, and engaging students through formative assessment.

This paper makes the following contributions:

- A workflow for authoring, recording, and reviewing multimedia responses inside educational videos.
- A working prototype that implements the workflow as an extension to PowerPoint's Office Mix.
- A lab study with teachers and students showing how RIMES might be applied to the classroom.

BACKGROUND AND RELATED WORK

Previous research on the value of interactive exercises and the technologies that support them was instrumental in the development of RIMES.

Pedagogical Benefits of In-Video, Interactive Exercises

Constructivism and active learning theories emphasize the importance of the learner's active role in engaging with the learning material and the learning process: *"Students do more than just listen: They must read, write, discuss, or be engaged in solving problems"* [5]. Examples of active learning activities include group discussions, short written exercises, learning by teaching, and reacting to a video. Previous research has shown the pedagogical benefits of active learning over traditional lectures [14,27]. A meta-analysis of hundreds of research studies, dubbed ICAP [9], found that learning increases as engagement increases. For instance, simply watching a video is a *passive* activity, while answering in-video quizzes and open-ended exercises can promote *active* and *constructive* learning. ICAP ranked these activities as follows (from most to least learning impact): Interactive > Constructive > Active > Passive.

Another form of constructive learning is *self-explanation*, an activity that prompts learners to explain their answers and thinking [10]. It increases learning by encouraging students to make inferences and adjust mental models. A surprising research finding is that the learning benefits of self-explanations hold even without the presence of a teaching expert or any performance feedback [10]. Moreover, research has shown that these learning benefits extend to multimedia learning environments [34]. In terms of modality for explanation, students self-explained more frequently when asked to speak than when asked to type [16]. RIMES supports written and verbal self-explanations.

Previous research has also shown that interactive videos supporting random access and self-paced browsing improve learning [35] and task performance [17]. Tutored Videotape Instruction [15] reported improved learning when pausing videos every few minutes for discussion. RIMES supports such interactive activities for online videos. VITAL [26] allows students to clip and annotate on video segments, and further embed them in multimedia essays. While VITAL enables adding videos to an activity, RIMES takes an opposite approach by enabling adding activity to a video.

Systems Supporting Interactive Online Learning

Many existing online learning platforms support in-video quizzes for flipped classrooms and MOOCs. Khan Academy [khanacademy.org] links supplementary videos to practice problems, and EDpuzzle [edpuzzle.com] and eduCanon [educanon.com] allow inserting quizzes into any video. MOOC platforms such as Udacity [udacity.com], Coursera [coursera.org], and edX [edx.org] commonly pause the video every few minutes and ask short questions to engage learners and test learning. Previous research has attempted to integrate video, comments, and assessments in a single view [22]. Short answer prompts for online learning have been shown to help learners self-correct misconceptions when asked to explain anomalies [33], and engage learners in tutorial videos while collaboratively summarizing them [31]. RIMES extends these systems by supporting rich media responses rather than multiple-choice or typed short answer questions. RIMES also captures the problem-solving process rather than just the outcome.

Some classroom technologies have used inking to support open-ended, freeform responses from students. Classroom Presenter [1] and Ubiquitous Presenter [32], for example, allow teachers and students to use digital ink on slides and share the annotated slides. Classroom Learning Partner [19] interprets handwritten answers and aggregates them into equivalent classes for built-in question types. These systems share many design goals with our work, but they are designed for use in traditional lecture settings; RIMES incorporates inking into asynchronous video learning, and allows teachers to author inking-oriented activities.

Recent systems in "learning at scale" settings attempt to support modalities beyond multiple-choice questions, such as open-ended short answers [3,7] and essay writing [21]. Improving social learning support is another thread of active research, via discussion forums, peer feedback and grading [25], chat rooms [11], and live video discussions [8]. RIMES contributes to this area of work with a new type of rich activity, namely recorded multimedia responses.

DESIGN GOALS

This work aims to support more interactive and expressive exercises inside lecture videos. To discover the needs and challenges teachers have in using videos, we participated in a three-hour workshop at a local school with nine teachers (for grades 6–12) and three technical staff. They were asked to create lecture videos using the Office Mix plugin for PowerPoint, which turns slides into lesson videos with voice and video recordings per slide as well as exercise widgets such as multiple-choice or short answer questions. Observations and interviews with the teachers and the staff, as well as our review of prior research, led to the following high-level goals that informed the design of RIMES:

Capture the thought process. Multiple-choice or short answer questions are great for quickly aggregating responses, but they only capture the final outcome of the student's thought process. Teachers noted that simply checking against the right answer is not enough to ensure that students understand the material. Students might have answered correctly without really knowing why, or they might have missed one last trivial step when answering incorrectly. Teachers noted that in classrooms they walk around to listen to group discussions, and ask students to show their work in paper- or whiteboard-based exercises. However, for lecture videos that are not live, capturing the problem solving process is difficult.

Enable multiple input modalities. Many teachers found existing in-video exercises to be limiting, as they only allow students to type text or select from a pre-populated list. Some exercises naturally lend themselves to demonstrating, speaking, or drawing, most of which teachers use only inside classrooms. For flipped classrooms or purely online classes, supporting additional input modalities can enable more diverse and expressive exercises.

Support customizable, open-ended exercises. Many teachers mentioned that they would like to add interactive exercises to their videos or import external exercises, but they found the integration cost to be high. They often had specific requirements for tailoring exercises to their classes. Teachers expressed the need for adding their own commentary or exercises inside videos, which are not currently supported by most existing environments.

Make it easy to integrate into existing practice. While many teachers wanted to use videos in their classes, they pointed out having limited time to adopt new technologies. Only a few had experience editing and publishing videos, which suggests it is important for a video lecture system to work with what teachers are already familiar with. RIMES augments PowerPoint, a common lecture-delivery tool used by many teachers, to minimize integration issues.

RIMES: RICH INTERACTIVE MULTIMEDIA EXERCISE SYSTEM FOR LECTURE VIDEOS

This section introduces RIMES, a system for teachers to author and manage multimedia exercises inside lecture videos, and for students to record their own responses while watching the videos. The following scenario illustrates a use case and a process for working with RIMES exercises.

Usage Scenario

Allison is a middle school teacher looking to flip her English lecture on subject-verb matching. Rather than assigning a lecture video for her students to watch as homework, she wants to embed interactive exercises into her video. She expects to get students more excited about the material, and identify model answers and common misconceptions she can address during class time.

After deciding to add an interactive exercise after the slide with an example of a compound subject, Allison inserts a RIMES exercise into a blank slide; the slide now displays the RIMES authoring interface. She types in the instruction *("Record yourself as you identify the subject and the verb of each sentence. Circle the subject in green and the verb in red.")*, and uploads an image file of the sentences to show as the background. She records her lecture using the default features of Office Mix and publishes the video. She shares the web link to the video with her students.

Bobby, a student in Allison's class, opens the video link from a tablet computer at his house. As he watches the video, the video pauses after the compound subject example, and asks him to identify the subject and verb from two example sentences by drawing on them and voice-recording his answer. After reflecting for a while, he clicks "Record." He uses his finger to circle the subject in green and the verb in red, and verbally describes the rationale behind his selections. He clicks on "Stop" to submit his response. The video then advances to the next slide.

Allison opens the RIMES gallery interface before class to review all students' responses. By visually scanning thumbnails of all the responses (sentences marked up with green and red ink), she is happy with the overall quality of the answers. But she notices a few incorrect answers, and clicks on one submitted by Ryan to listen to his response. The player plays back Ryan's voice and pen strokes. Allison discovers that Ryan did not correctly understand the compound subject because he said, *"a subject should be a noun..."* Browsing the gallery, she finds that two other students made the same mistake and notes to remind students of this common error in the next class.

Authoring

The RIMES authoring interface (Figure 1) lets the teacher embed a custom RIMES exercise into any slide. Inserting a RIMES object in PowerPoint renders the authoring interface directly into the current slide. It contains the following options for customizing the exercise:

- **Instructions**: the text prompt that students see when the video pauses and the RIMES exercise pops up.
- **Time limit**: the expected maximum length of a student response, useful for students in planning their response and for bounding media storage needs.
- **Input mode**: a student response can use any combination of video, audio, and drawing. Available

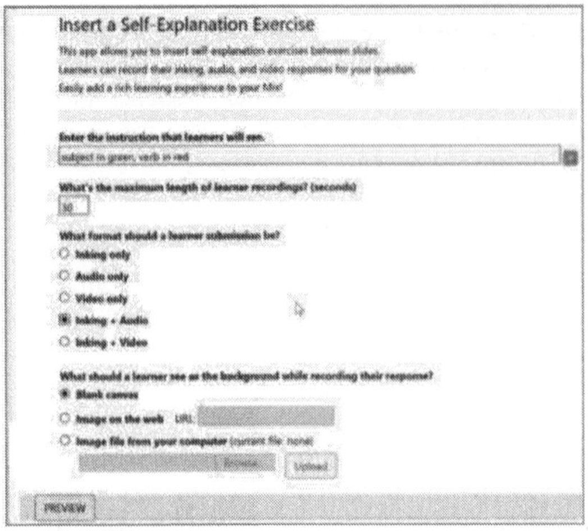

Figure 1. The RIMES authoring interface allows the teacher to create and customize RIMES exercises by directly editing a PowerPoint slide.

modes are: "Inking only," "Audio only," "Video only," "Inking + Audio," and "Inking + Video."

- **Background image**: an optional background image that students can reference or mark on. The teacher can add a link to any web image, or upload their own.

The teacher can click on a "Preview" button within the RIMES slide to check what the recording view will look like for students. The teacher can move between the preview and edit modes to update the exercise. Once a video including a RIMES exercise is published, the RIMES exercise is part of the video playback sequence. The video automatically pauses when the play control reaches the slide with the RIMES exercise. The Office Mix tool already supports the video publication and playback environment.

Recording

While watching a video, students are prompted to record their own response using video, audio, and/or drawing when they encounter a RIMES slide (Figure 2). They can explain their solution using multiple modalities inside a web browser without having to install any plugins.

The recording interface starts capturing any of the enabled modalities (video, audio, drawing) once the student clicks the "Record" button. When inking is enabled, the sidebar shows a palette for changing the pen size and color. The student can use touch or a stylus if available, or a mouse if not. When video is enabled, the student sees a visual preview in real-time. When the student is done recording, she clicks "Stop." She is given options to either re-record or submit. Once she submits, the submission dialog box opens, asking her to rate how confident she is about her response and how helpful the RIMES exercise was. The teacher can refer to these scores when reviewing students' responses, as research suggests that self-efficacy and confidence are effective indicators of learning [2].

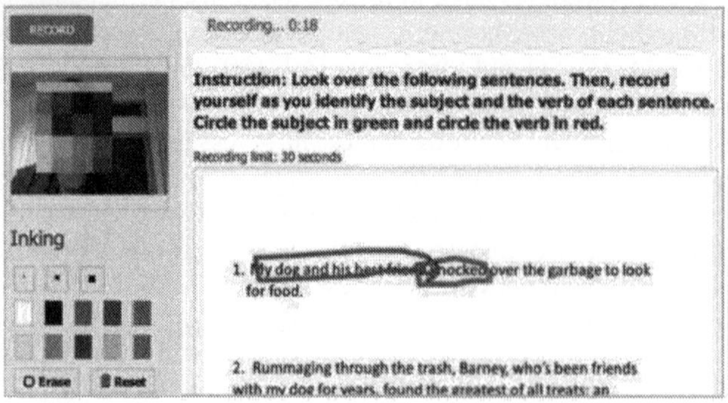

Figure 2. The RIMES recording interface in a web browser. The student's face is blurred from the screenshot for privacy.

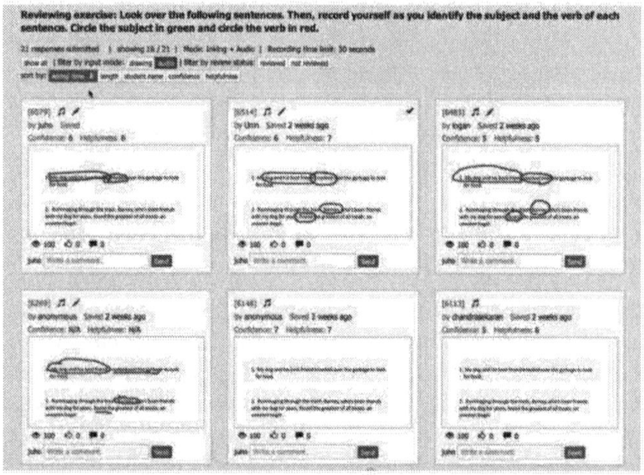

Figure 3. The RIMES reviewing interface shows a gallery of all responses to a RIMES exercise. Various sorting and filtering options help the teacher with the reviewing process.

Once a recording is submitted, the RIMES backend post-processes each recording for improved navigation in the gallery. It detects responses with silent audio or no pen input, and labels them as "no audio" or "no inking," respectively.

Reviewing

The gallery for each RIMES exercise (Figure 3) is automatically populated as the students submit their responses. The gallery renders each response in a card-style layout, and displays thumbnails of the final drawing canvas or video recording if available, student name, helpfulness and confidence ratings, recorded length, and captured input modes. The gallery is designed to support the following use cases: 1) get a quick overview of all student responses, 2) easily identify model answers and misconceptions, and 3) replay a particular student's response to better understand his thought process. The specific gallery features are:

- **Sorting**: the teacher can sort all responses using various sorting options, such as submission timestamp, recording length, student name, and students' self-reported confidence and helpfulness ratings. These options help teachers prioritize their reviewing order.

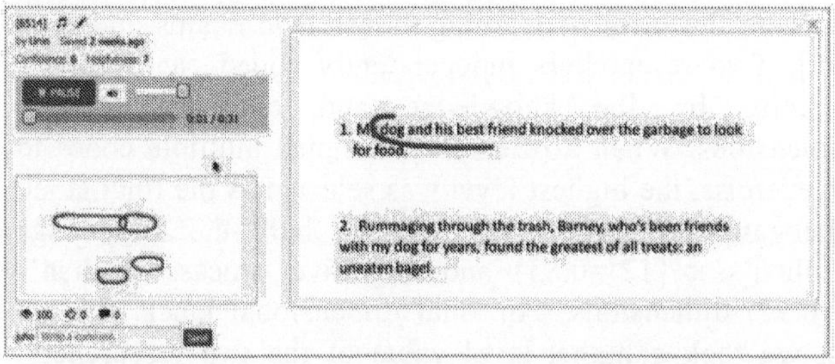

Figure 4. Clicking on a response in the gallery opens the player, letting the teacher synchronously replay the captured video, audio, or inking stroke sequences.

- **Filtering**: the teacher can selectively view responses that match certain filtering criteria. Available options include input mode (e.g., selecting "drawing" displays all responses that include pen strokes), and review status (e.g., selecting "not reviewed" displays all responses that the teacher has not yet played).
- **Playback** (Figure 4): the teacher can replay the process in which a response was recorded. Based on the input modes captured, the player provides a synchronized playback of all modalities used in a response.
- **Social interactions**: the teacher can either "like" or leave comments for each response, both as feedback to students and as a note to herself. Students given access to the gallery can read comments and reply as well.

Implementation

We implemented RIMES using standard web technologies: HTML5, CSS3, and JavaScript. For audio and video recording, the WebRTC protocol is used. To reduce the network bandwidth required in recording, canvas strokes are not captured as video but as JSON with per-stroke timestamp, action type, and action coordinates. The canvas playback reads the JSON and replays the strokes in animation, using the *requestAnimationFrame* method.

We implemented our conceptual workflow for managing multimedia in-video exercises in the context of PowerPoint and Office Mix. The general idea can be implemented for other video platforms (e.g., YouTube) with simple player customizations for RIMES. The authoring interface is a Microsoft Office application, which uses the *labs.js* [labsjs.blob.core.windows.net/sdk/index.html] library. This library allows a standalone web application to be recognized by PowerPoint. This integration allows the RIMES authoring interface to open inside PowerPoint, and the recording interface to open RIMES exercises inside the Office Mix player on its portal [officemix.com].

EVALUATION: TESTING THE RIMES WORKFLOW

We conducted a three-part user study to evaluate the three-stage RIMES workflow end-to-end. We designed our study to allow us to address the following questions:

Teaching Subject	Count
Math	7
English	5
Science	4
Social Science	3
Technology & Computers	4

Teaching Grade	6	7	8	9	10	11	12
Count	4	4	4	9	8	8	8

Table 1. Subjects and grades taught by the 19 teachers in Study 1. Multiple responses were allowed.

- **Authoring**: can teachers create a variety of RIMES exercises spanning multiple subjects, input modes, and question types?
- **Recording**: can students effectively record their responses to a teacher's RIMES exercise?
- **Reviewing**: can teachers browse students' responses to their RIMES exercises to get an overview of responses, identify model answers and misconceptions, and understand students' thought processes?

STUDY 1. TEACHERS AUTHOR RIMES EXERCISES

The first study focused on the RIMES creation experience.

Participants

We recruited 19 middle and high school teachers (13 female, 5 male, 1 preferred not to specify, mean age=49, σ=11, max=68, min=27, T1-T19) from a large, U.S. metropolitan area. They had 21 years of teaching experience on average, with 14 of them teaching at a public school and 5 at a private school at the time the study was conducted. Subjects and grades they teach spanned a wide range (Table 1). Ten teachers indicated that they had made instructional videos before, using software such as Camtasia, Adobe Premiere, and iMovie. Seven indicated that they had flipped their classrooms before. In a 5-point scale question (1: not familiar, 5: very familiar), most teachers said they were familiar with PowerPoint (mean=3.8, σ=0.6). Five had prior experience with Office Mix. Participants were offered a gratuity for their time.

Procedure

Each study session was a three-hour workshop in which teachers were asked to create one or two educational videos using RIMES and Office Mix inside PowerPoint. We asked them to bring in their own existing slides as initial materials to create a realistic lecture video. Teachers were provided with a Windows tablet, webcam, external mouse, and stylus pen. An external microphone was available upon request for improved audio quality.

The session started with a pre-questionnaire asking participants about demographic information as well as teaching and technical experiences. After a tutorial on using

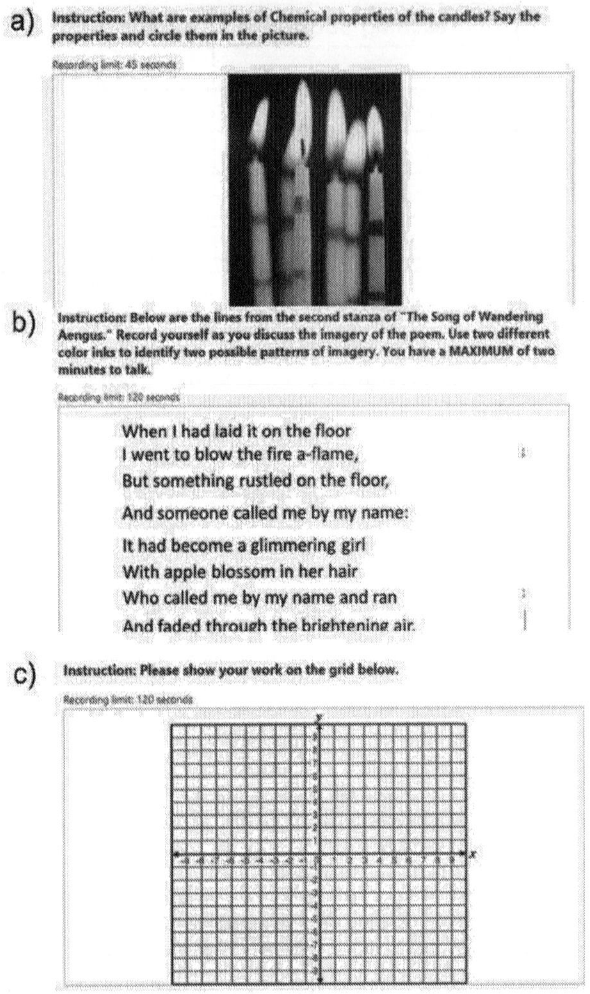

Figure 5. Example RIMES exercises teachers created in Study 1: a) explain chemical properties of a candle while circling relevant parts, b) use color marking to identify imagery patterns in a poem, c) draw a graph on a chart grid.

Office Mix and authoring RIMES exercises, teachers spent two hours creating videos. We asked them to make short videos (five minutes or shorter) and to include at least one RIMES exercise in each video they created. Researchers provided technical support when requested. After publishing each video to the Office Mix portal, teachers were asked to indicate the self-rated quality and target grade level of their video. The session concluded with a questionnaire about the pedagogical implications and usability of the RIMES tool.

After all sessions were complete, researchers manually selected one video and one RIMES exercise in the video from each teacher to assign to students in the second study. For a deeper understanding of the RIMES exercises created, researchers coded all RIMES exercises by subject area, as well as by the knowledge type and the level of cognitive process they test, using the revised version of Bloom's Taxonomy [20]. The original Bloom's Taxonomy [4] and the revised version [20] are commonly used frameworks to evaluate the level of learning assessed in exams and tests [36]. Two researchers independently coded each RIMES exercise by the knowledge and cognitive process dimensions. When a researcher assigned multiple codes to an exercise, the highest level was selected as the final label. Inter-rater reliability was high for both the knowledge (Cohen's κ [12]=0.83) and cognitive process (Cohen's κ=0.72) dimensions. For final dimensional labels (Figure 6), we took a higher-level value of the two researchers' labels when they did not match.

Results

The 19 teachers created 36 videos and 69 RIMES exercises (mean=1.9 videos per teacher, σ=1.4). The videos were, on average, 3.6 minutes long (σ=2.4), and had 10.4 slides (σ=5.3). Teachers used a background image in 41% of the RIMES exercises (28/69), such as a chart area for math, text to analyze for English, and a photo for science (Figure 5).

The RIMES exercises spanned multiple subjects, input modes, and knowledge and cognitive processes. Subject areas in the exercises included math (e.g., "Use substitution to solve the following system."), science (e.g., "Draw a picture of an organism showing one or more of the characteristics of life."), English (e.g., "When do we use capitalization?"), and history (e.g., "Explain why murdering a king was considered a disruption of order in the Renaissance world.").

Teachers added inking to a vast majority of RIMES exercises (60/69), while audio (37/69) and video (12/69) were used less frequently. The most common input mode was inking combined with audio (33/69), which gave students an opportunity to verbally explain their answer while drawing on a canvas or background image.

A qualitative analysis of the exercises using the revised Bloom's taxonomy reveals that the RIMES exercises require knowledge and cognitive processes beyond factual knowledge and rote memorization. In the knowledge dimension (Figure 6, top), only 23% of the exercises focused on factual knowledge, while 43% tested conceptual knowledge and 30% procedural knowledge. In the cognitive process dimension (Figure 6, bottom), *Remember* (e.g., "What three keys do we use to take a screenshot?"), the lowest level process, comprised 14%, while many exercises addressed higher-level processes such as *Understand* (30%, e.g., "Why did the regular coke sink and the diet coke float? What ideas do you have to explain this phenomenon?"), *Apply* (25%, e.g., "In the space below, please show your work that will allow you to find the weight of one math book."), and *Create* (17%, e.g., "Sketch a picture that represents how a Renaiassance [sic] person would see the relationship between a star, a flower and a mole."). In the ICAP model [9], RIMES exercises mostly fall under the Constructive and Active categories beyond Passive.

Teachers' responses to RIMES were mostly positive. On a 7-point Likert scale (1: strongly disagree, 7: strongly agree), teachers found the RIMES recording interface to be easy (6.3) and enjoyable to use (6.4). They thought they were able to effectively add RIMES exercises (6.5), and most were willing to use it in the future (6.7). Many thought the rich media support could lead to a better understanding of students' thought processes: *"I really like that students can draw or respond to my prompts orally. I think that will really give me a window into their thinking."* [T19]

All but two teachers agreed that RIMES exercises would be pedagogically valuable. Teachers compared RIMES exercises against multiple-choice or short answer questions: *"Given multiple choice, many students just guess instead of working out a solution. Many of my students don't feel comfortable answering short answer options in a Math class. RIMES just works better."* [T3]

STUDY 2. STUDENTS RECORD RESPONSES

The second study was designed to test the recording interface, see students' reactions to RIMES, and collect responses for the teachers to review in the next phase.

Participants

We invited 25 middle and high school students from a large, U.S. metropolitan area to our lab (15 female, 9 male, 1 preferred not to specify, mean age=14.7, σ=1.4, max=17, min=13, S1-S25). Nine indicated that their teachers occasionally assign videos to watch at home. Participants were offered a gratuity for their time.

Procedure

In a one-hour session, students first answered a pre-questionnaire that obtained demographic information and feedback on students' video learning experiences. Researchers then gave a tutorial on the Office Mix video player and the RIMES recording interface, giving students a chance to practice recording. Students were provided with a Windows tablet, webcam, external mouse, and stylus pen.

Students then watched two videos created by teachers in Study 1. We ensured that students' grade level matched the target audience level of the exercise, which the teachers specified a priori. While watching each video, students recorded their responses to RIMES exercises as they encountered them. Depending on the remaining time, 21 out of 25 students had a chance to look at the gallery interface and shared their thoughts on social interactions around student responses. The session concluded with a post-questionnaire on the usability of the recording interface and students' reaction to sharing their responses with other students and seeing others' responses.

Supplemental Turker Responses

We additionally recruited crowd workers on Mechanical Turk to record responses to the RIMES exercises. Although most Turkers were adults and beyond the target age range for most of the RIMES exercises, we used Mechanical Turk for two reasons. First, we wanted to test the usability of the recording interface with remote users who have diverse computing environments (Turkers used their own

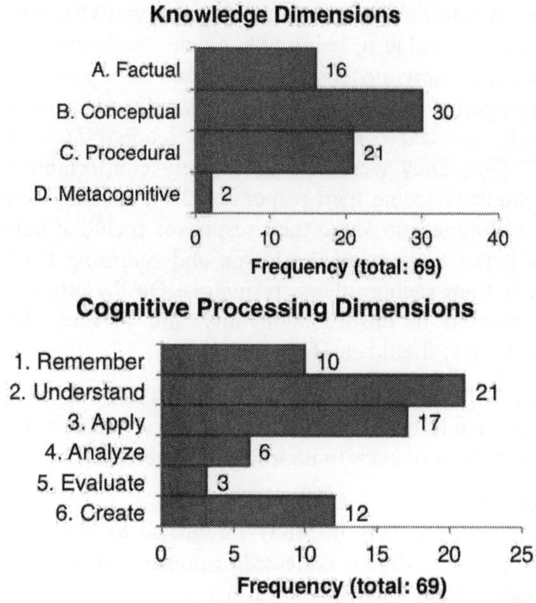

Figure 6. Frequency of RIMES exercises' knowledge (top) and cognitive process (bottom) dimensions using the revised Bloom's Taxonomy [20].

computers and input devices for recording responses). Second, we wanted to populate the gallery for each RIMES exercise with the number of responses comparable to that of a real classroom (20–30), which the 25 in-lab students watching two videos each could not fully populate. We created a total of 574 HITs (30.2 per RIMES exercise), with an average hourly wage of $8.98 over the course of 10 days. HIT instructions told Turkers they would need to watch a provided educational video and complete any exercises within the video. The HIT also included a few brief demographic questions, which showed that 46% of the Turkers were 24 or younger, 62% had a college degree or higher level of education, and 47% were female.

Results

Students' comments about the recording experience were generally positive. When questioned using a 7-point Likert scale (1: strongly disagree, 7: strongly agree), students found the recording interface to be easy (5.5) and somewhat enjoyable (4.8) to use. S1 commented, *"I liked being able to interact in the lesson, rather than just taking notes or listening."* They thought they could effectively add their responses (5.9), found the exercises to be engaging (5.5), and were willing to use the interface in the future (5.4). Many found the high interactivity of RIMES exercises helpful: *"It made sure you could actually learn it and if you were paying attention or not."* [S10] On the other hand, several students found self-recording to be awkward, the time limit to be too short (e.g., *"the time limits made it sometimes hard to complete your full thought and drawing"* [S14]), and the canvas size to be too small.

When asked about sharing responses with others in 4-point scale questions (1: not at all, 4: highly interested), students expressed interest in seeing other responses (3.0), nothing that they saw value in being able to see *"different ways of solving the same problem"* [S19], and comparing their answer against others: *"If some had similar ideas to mine, or what they did better than me so I could learn from them."* [S3] They were also moderately comfortable with other students seeing their responses (2.7). Primary reasons for a willingness to share their responses included helping others better understand the lesson and returning the help they got from seeing others' responses. On the other hand, some wanted to ensure anonymity and privacy, which future designs should carefully address.

STUDY 3. TEACHERS REVIEW RESPONSES

The final study tested the gallery interface, where teachers reviewed the responses to their RIMES exercises.

Procedure

The same 19 teachers in Study 1 returned to the lab after about 10 days to review collected responses to their RIMES exercises. They used the RIMES gallery interface, populated with 20 to 30 responses to one of their RIMES exercises submitted by both the Study 2 students and Turkers. After a tutorial on the interface, teachers freely explored the gallery, spending 10 to 20 minutes reviewing the responses while thinking aloud. A post-questionnaire asked teachers about the usability of the gallery interface, as well as how it might support their teaching practices.

Results

We asked teachers how often they would be willing to create videos and use RIMES in them. All 19 teachers indicated they would be willing to use RIMES: 10 for every video, 6 no more than once a week, and 3 no more than once a month. Of the 10 who answered every video, 2 said they want to make a video every day, 6 every week, and 2 every month. While lab study responses may introduce the Hawthorne effect, teachers acknowledged the need for and value of interactive exercises, and many asked when RIMES would be publically available.

On 5-point Likert scale questions (1: strongly disagree, 5: strongly agree) about the gallery experience, teachers rated the gallery interface as easy to use (4.8), useful (4.5), and interesting (4.3). We organize additional findings by the three key goals the gallery supported:

Get an overview

Teachers thought the gallery made it easy to get an overview of student responses (4.3). T4 described, *"I like that all responses are on a single page and viewable without having to click anything."*

Identify good answers and misconceptions

Using the gallery, teachers answered that they were able to identify good answers (4.4) and misconceptions (4.2), and that it was easy to compare and contrast multiple responses (4.1). Because many teachers mentioned that finding time to review many lengthy responses could be a practical barrier to applying RIMES in their classrooms, it is encouraging that most teachers felt the gallery interface helped them quickly identify noticeable ones. T9 said, *"I liked how quickly [sic] it was to get a sense of student understanding and misunderstanding."* Many teachers applied sorting by helpfulness and confidence and paid special attention to those with low self-ratings: *"Sorting by helpfulness and confidence let me immediately identify people who thought they were struggling."* [T8]

Understand the thought process

Teachers replied that the gallery helped them understand students' thought processes (4.2). A common review strategy was to first skim all the responses to get an overview and pick a few noteworthy ones (normally outliers, such as incorrect, long, or visually different answers) for a detailed playback: *"The ability to see the time-lapse of the drawing helped me understand the thinking behind the drawings."* [T12]

Some teachers identified *why* the student reached the final answer. In a math exercise on functions that asked students to find outputs to various input values (shown below),

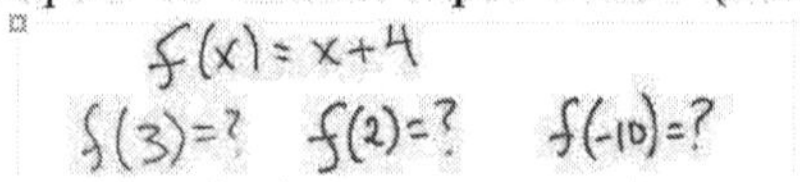

the teacher played back a response with incorrect answers (6, 4, and -20 instead of 7, 6, and -6, shown below).

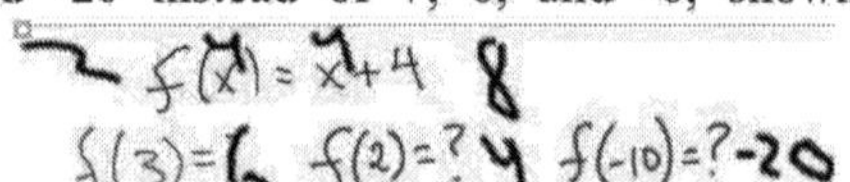

While listening to the student's explanation, T18 said, *"Aha! This student thought this function doubles the input based on his test with f(4) that gave him 8. That's why he doubled all inputs. This is a common mistake students make when they first learn about functions."* In the gallery, there were a couple other responses that had this set of incorrect answers (shown below).

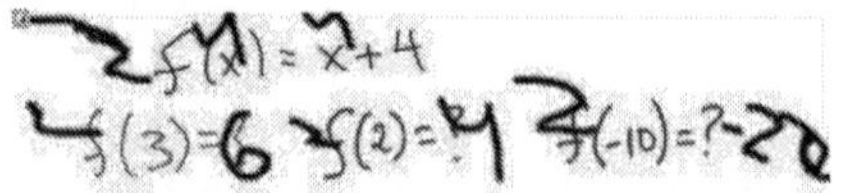

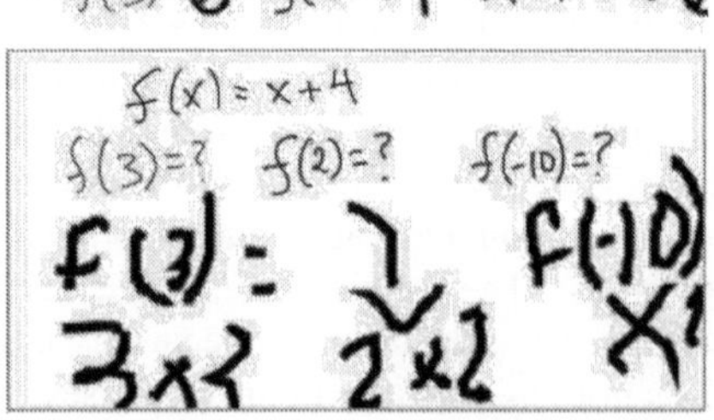

T5 described the benefit of the playback, *"I believe that by listening to the responses of each student we truly get a realistic view of student understanding of concepts presented. It will definitely help teachers to know which students need assistance in understanding the concept."*

DISCUSSION AND FUTURE WORK

We discuss several practical issues surrounding RIMES, including the choice of input, real-life applications, and the limitations of our findings.

Input Modes

The multiple input modes in RIMES serve complementary purposes, thus expanding the spectrum of exercises possible with RIMES. Drawing (inking) helped students visualize their thinking, and enabled richer, more expressive descriptions not possible with typing: *"[Drawing] made obvious what students imagined in their heads about the material and the ideas."* [T12] Audio-recording open-ended explanations *"forces the kids to be clear and articulate,"* [T18] and works better for certain students: *"There are always kids who do better [than writing] while explaining w/ audio."* [T8] Several teachers who required video recording appreciated that students' facial expression and body language were captured. A student in a physics exercise instructed to calculate kinetic energy showed his calculator screen in the video, to which T7 reacted, *"This is very nice as a teacher because this is where many errors are made."* Video, however, did not work for everyone. Some students expressed concern about anonymity and recording anxiety. Both for audio and video, several teachers indicated the difficulty of reviewing them, because they are more tedious to review than static answers that lend themselves to easy skimming.

Possible Applications of RIMES

When asked about the potential practical applications of RIMES, teachers suggested that RIMES would be beneficial for flipped classrooms, SPOCs [13], remedial lectures, or make-up lectures for students who missed a day. RIMES can also be useful in identifying and helping struggling students: *"I would also have a follow-up set of slides for remediation if needed for those students still having difficulty."* [T7] Distance learning and online-only classes can adopt RIMES, with frequent in-video exercises and recording opportunities increasing student engagement.

Rather than replacing existing summative assessment (e.g., tests) and easy-to-grade quizzes (e.g., multiple-choice questions), teachers indicated they would use RIMES as a formative assessment tool, through which they could refine their lectures and provide qualitative feedback to students [28]. Many teachers mentioned that they would not want to assign grades to RIMES responses for this reason.

Challenges in Adopting RIMES

We share challenges and design lessons for future designers and practitioners. Firstly, students' experience needs to be carefully designed because of recording anxiety, different preferences in input modalities, and preferences for socially sharing their response. Supporting re-recording, preview, and multiple input modes in RIMES mitigated some of these challenges. Also, teachers felt that RIMES exercises are more suitable for formative assessment, indicating that RIMES should be used in conjunction with other assessment tools. Giving guidance on how teachers can effectively use RIMES is another challenge; creating online galleries where teachers can share successful activities and re-use others' exercises will be important to adoption.

Limitations

Our evaluation used a mixed-methods approach, combining many data sources: questionnaires, observations, think-alouds, interviews, and qualitative analysis of RIMES artifacts. While this subjective data helped us answer how teachers and students would use and react to RIMES, it lacks conclusive evidence that RIMES leads to meaningful pedagogical improvements. Future work will incorporate quantitative measures such as click logs or learning gains.

A limitation of the study is that we recruited paid adult crowd workers to simulate online learners. While teachers confirmed that the responses were not noticeably different from what they normally see in their classes, this setup might have missed response patterns unique to the original target population. Also, due to practical recruiting constraints, the age-appropriate students we recruited for the lab portion of the study were not necessarily in the regular class of the teacher whose lecture they viewed. The dynamics of response recording and reviewing may vary when teachers and students interact on a regular basis. Since continuous feedback plays an important role in learning [23], and many teachers left comments for students using the gallery, a follow-up study focusing on feedback on RIMES would be valuable. We aim to publicly release RIMES, which may help us understand engagement and interaction dynamics not observed in the lab study.

FUTURE WORK

We plan to investigate the impact of using RIMES in classrooms in a longer-term, live deployment. Research questions include: How do the lab study findings translate to real teacher practices? How do the different interactivity and exercise types affect students' learning? How to help teachers save time in reviewing and providing feedback?

Future work will explore ways for students to interact with other students' responses to increase potential peer learning benefits. We also plan to support the collaborative RIMES experience in which multiple students record their discussion or outcomes achieved from teamwork.

CONCLUSION

We introduced RIMES, a system that allows teachers to easily create interactive multimedia exercises embedded within online lecture videos. Students can record audio, video, and ink-based answers from their web browsers, and teachers can efficiently review the responses. A three-part evaluation with 6th – 12th grade teachers and students found that the RIMES interface and workflow were usable and compelling. The teachers created exercises for a diverse array of subjects, involving diverse knowledge and cognitive processing dimensions. These studies illustrated how RIMES could facilitate creating online lectures that move beyond passive learning and simple assessments. RIMES presents a model for designing usable tools that empower teachers and students to create engaging and interactive content for online learning.

ACKNOWLEDGMENTS
The authors would like to thank Anoop Gupta, Kurt Berglund, Sasa Junuzovic, and the Office Mix team for their feedback and support.

REFERENCES
1. Anderson, R., Anderson, R., Davis, P., et al. Classroom presenter: Enhancing interactive education with digital ink. *Computer 40*, 9 (2007), 56–61.
2. Bandura, A. Self-efficacy: toward a unifying theory of behavioral change. *Psychological review 84*, 2 (1977).
3. Basu, S., Jacobs, C., and Vanderwende, L. Powergrading: a Clustering Approach to Amplify Human Effort for Short Answer Grading. *TACL 1*, (2013), 391–402.
4. Bloom, B. S. and Krathwohl, D.R. Taxonomy of educational objectives: The classification of educational goals. Handbook I: Cognitive domain. (1956).
5. Bonwell, C. C. and Eison, J.A. *Active Learning: Creating Excitement in the Classroom. 1991 ASHE-ERIC Higher Education Reports.* ERIC, 1991.
6. Breslow, L., Pritchard, D.E., DeBoer, J., Stump, G.S., Ho, A.D., and Seaton, D.T. Studying learning in the worldwide classroom: Research into edX's first MOOC. *Research & Practice in Assessment 8*, (2013), 13–25.
7. Brooks, M., Basu, S., Jacobs, C., and Vanderwende, L. Divide and correct: using clusters to grade short answers at scale. *Learning at Scale '14*, ACM (2014), 89–98.
8. Cambre, J., Kulkarni, C., Bernstein, M.S., and Klemmer, S.R. Talkabout: small-group discussions in massive global classes. *Learning at Scale '14*, ACM (2014).
9. Chi, M.T. Active-constructive-interactive: A conceptual framework for differentiating learning activities. *Topics in Cognitive Science 1*, 1 (2009), 73–105.
10. Chi, M.T., Bassok, M., Lewis, M.W., Reimann, P., and Glaser, R. Self-explanations: How students study and use examples in learning to solve problems. *Cognitive science 13*, 2 (1989), 145–182.
11. Coetzee, D., Fox, A., Hearst, M.A., and Hartmann, B. Chatrooms in MOOCs: All Talk and No Action. *Learning at Scale '14*, ACM (2014), 127–136.
12. Cohen, J. A coefficient of agreement for nominal scales. *Educational and Psychological Measurement 20*, (1960), 37–46.
13. Fox, A. From MOOCs to SPOCs. *Communications of the ACM 56*, 12 (2013), 38–40.
14. Freeman, S., Eddy, S.L., McDonough, M., et al. Active learning increases student performance in science, engineering, and mathematics. *PNAS 111*, 23 (2014).
15. Gibbons, J.F. Tutored Videotape Instruction. (1977).
16. Hausmann, R.G. and Chi, M.H. Can a computer interface support self-explaining. *Cognitive Technology 7*, 1 (2002), 4–14.
17. Kim, J., Nguyen, P.T., Weir, S., Guo, P.J., Miller, R.C., and Gajos, K.Z. Crowdsourcing Step-by-step Information Extraction to Enhance Existing How-to Videos. *CHI'14*, ACM (2014), 4017–4026.
18. Kizilcec, R.F., Piech, C., and Schneider, E. Deconstructing Disengagement: Analyzing Learner Subpopulations in Massive Open Online Courses. *LAK'13*, ACM (2013), 170–179.
19. Koile, K., Chevalier, K., Rbeiz, M., et al. Supporting Feedback and Assessment of Digital Ink Answers to In-class Exercises. *IAAI'07*, (2007), 1787–1794.
20. Krathwohl, D.R. A revision of Bloom's taxonomy: An overview. *Theory into practice 41*, 4 (2002), 212–218.
21. Markoff, J. Essay-grading software offers professors a break. *The New York Times Apr. 4, 2013*, (2013).
22. Monserrat, T.-J.K.P., Li, Y., Zhao, S., and Cao, X. L.IVE: An Integrated Interactive Video-based Learning Environment. *CHI'14*, ACM (2014), 3399–3402.
23. Mory, E.H. Feedback research revisited. *Handbook of research on educational communications and technology 2*, (2004), 745–783.
24. Noer, M. One Man, One Computer, 10 Million Students: How Khan Academy Is Reinventing Education. *Forbes*, Nov. 19, 2012 (2012).
25. Piech, C., Huang, J., Chen, Z., Do, C., Ng, A., and Koller, D. Tuned models of peer assessment in MOOCs. *arXiv preprint arXiv:1307.2579*, (2013).
26. Preston, M., Campbell, G., Ginsburg, H., et al. Developing New Tools for Video Analysis and Communication to Promote Critical Thinking. *EdMedia'05*, (2005), 4357–4364.
27. Prince, M. Does Active Learning Work? A Review of the Research. *J. of Engineering Education 93*, 3 (2004).
28. Sadler, D.R. Formative assessment and the design of instructional systems. *Instructional science 18*, 2 (1989).
29. Sams, A. and Bergmann, J. Flip your classroom: Reach every student in every class every day. *International Society for Technology in Education (ISTE)*, (2012).
30. Shumski, D. MOOCs by the numbers: How do EdX, Coursera and Udacity stack up? *Education Dive August 15, 2013*, (2013).
31. Weir, S., Kim, J., Gajos, K.Z., and Miller, R.C. Learnersourcing Subgoal Labels for How-to Videos. *CSCW'15*, ACM (2015).
32. Wilkerson, M., Griswold, W.G., and Simon, B. Ubiquitous presenter: increasing student access and control in a digital lecturing environment. *ACM SIGCSE Bulletin 37*, 1 (2005), 116–120.
33. Williams, J.J., Kovacs, G., Walker, C., Maldonado, S., and Lombrozo, T. Learning Online via Prompts to Explain. *CHI EA'14*, ACM (2014), 2269–2274.
34. Wylie, R. and Chi, M.T. 17 The Self-Explanation Principle in Multimedia Learning. *The Cambridge Handbook of Multimedia Learning*, (2014), 413.
35. Zhang, D., Zhou, L., Briggs, R.O., and Nunamaker Jr, J.F. Instructional video in e-learning: Assessing the impact of interactive video on learning effectiveness. *Information & Management 43*, 1 (2006), 15–27.
36. Zheng, A.Y., Lawhorn, J.K., Lumley, T., and Freeman, S. ASSESSMENT: Application of Bloom's Taxonomy Debunks the "MCAT Myth." *Science 319*, 5862 (2008).

A Framework for Automatically Generating Interactive Instructional Scaffolding

Eleanor O'Rourke[1], Erik Andersen[2], Sumit Gulwani[3], Zoran Popović[1]
[1]Center for Game Science, Computer Science & Engineering, University of Washington
[2]Department of Computer Science, Cornell University [3]Microsoft Research Redmond
{eorourke, zoran}@cs.washington.edu, eland@cs.cornell.edu, sumitg@microsoft.com

ABSTRACT
Interactive learning environments such as intelligent tutoring systems and software tutorials often teach procedures with step-by-step demonstrations. This instructional scaffolding is typically authored by hand, and little can be reused across problem domains. In this work, we present a framework for generating interactive tutorials from an algorithmic representation of the problem-solving thought process. Given a set of mappings between programming language constructs and user interface elements, we step through this algorithm line-by-line to trigger visual explanations of each step. This approach allows us to automatically generate tutorials for *any* example problem that can be solved with this algorithm. We describe two prototype implementations in the domains of K-12 mathematics and educational games, and present results from two user studies showing that educational technologists can author thought-process procedures and that generated tutorials can effectively teach a new procedure to students.

Author Keywords
Computational education; scaffolding; authoring tools.

ACM Classification Keywords
H.5.0. Information Interfaces and Presentation: General

INTRODUCTION
Procedural knowledge is required for a wide range of human activities, from cooking to mathematics to using software applications. Many of the concepts taught in interactive learning environments like cognitive tutors, educational games, and software tutorials are procedural in nature. Some procedures, such as opening a file in a text editor, are simple. Others, such as long division, involve complex control flow structures like loops and conditionals. Teaching complex procedures in interactive learning environments presents many challenges.

One effective method of teaching procedures is by providing scaffolding that helps students solve problems that would otherwise be beyond their reach [11, 27]. While there are many different approaches to scaffolding learning, interactive learning environments typically use step-by-step demonstrations, tailored progressions of practice problems, and individual feedback to support students. Intelligent tutoring systems provide student with adaptive sequences of problems and personalized hints [4, 10, 26], and software tutorials often use step-by-step demonstrations to teach procedural tasks [6, 14].

While interactive scaffolding is effective, this type of content is often time-consuming to create because it must be authored by hand [1, 12]. As a result, many researchers have explored methods of generating interactive explanations automatically [2, 6, 7, 9, 12, 13]. While these approaches have significantly reduced the amount of effort required to author scaffolding, they often apply to only one application domain or require the designer to write separate content for each example problem. In some domains, such as K-12 mathematics, we may want to demonstrate a procedure for a large number of practice problems and produce multiple different types of scaffolding. Ideally, we would like an application-independent method of explaining a given procedure for *any* example problem.

In this paper, we introduce a new framework for automatically generating interactive tutorials to teach the entire space of problems that can be solved with a given procedure. In our framework, an educational technologist encodes the problem-solving thought process as an algorithm and provides a mapping between programming language constructs and visual objects in the user interface. By stepping through this algorithm line-by-line, we automatically generate visual explanations for each step. This approach has a number of advantages. Given a set of mappings and an encoded algorithm, our framework automatically produces tutorials for any example problem in the domain. Furthermore, our framework naturally supports the creation of many different types of interactive scaffolding, including problem progressions, just-in-time feedback, and fading worked-out examples.

We demonstrate the generality of our approach by showing how it applies to two distinct problem-solving domains: a K-12 mathematics application and an educational game. Through a user study with fifth-grade students, we show that our generated tutorials can produce learning gains similar to those of a human teacher. We also show that that educational technologists can encode an algorithm to explain subtraction in just a few hours. We believe this approach can greatly improve the process of authoring interactive scaffolding, particularly in domains with large numbers of practice problems.

CHI 2015, April 18 - 23, 2015, Seoul, Republic of Korea
Copyright 2015 ACM 978-1-4503-3145-6/15/04$15.00
http://dx.doi.org/10.1145/2702123.2702580

RELATED WORK

Researchers have explored many methods of designing and authoring interactive instructional materials to teach procedural knowledge through computer applications. In this section, we provide an overview of existing work in two domains: intelligent tutoring systems and software tutorials.

Intelligent Tutoring Systems

Intelligent tutoring systems (ITS) are applications that emulate one-on-one tutoring with a human teacher [4, 10, 26]. These systems teach procedural concepts using personalized progressions of practice problems and contextual feedback [26], and they have been shown to produce learning gains in classroom studies [15]. While ITSs have great potential, they have not been widely adopted because they are expensive to build [10]. It has been estimated that 200-300 hours of expert design is needed to produce one hour of ITS content [1].

Researchers have explored many methods of reducing tutor authoring effort. Brawner et al. provide design recommendations for authoring tools, highlighting the importance of domain-independent methods [8]. Sottilare describes efforts to develop a Generalized Intelligent Framework for Tutors based around a standard ontology for representing knowledge [24]. Stamper et al. developed the Hint Factory to make it easier to add ITS-style interaction to existing educational software by using Markov decision processes to automatically generate contextual hints from past student data [25].

Others have focused on reducing the expertise required to author content for an intelligent tutoring system. Blessing et al. developed a cognitive model SDK that allows authors to edit rule hierarchies through a user interface to reduce the need for programming expertise [7]. Aleven et al. developed the Cognitive Tutor Authoring Tools (CTAT) to allow designers to create example-tracing tutors without programming [2]. With CTAT, designers demonstrate correct and incorrect procedures for an example problem to create a "behavior graph" that can be generalized to tutor multiple isomorphic problems. CTAT has been shown to reduce development costs by a factor of 4 to 8 [2]. Olsen et al. extended CTAT to support the authoring of collaborative ITSs built around collaborative scripts [18]. We take a different approach to improving the scaffolding authoring process. Rather than designing tools to reduce the expertise required to author tutors, we aim to maximize the content that programmers can create.

Software Tutorials

Since many tasks in software applications involve following procedures, there is a body of research in software usability that explores methods of teaching procedural knowledge. This work has shown that step-by-step tutorials are effective instructional tools, especially when they provide interactive elements such as stencils [14], videos that track the user's progress [20], and interface highlighting [6].

While step-by-step tutorials are effective, authoring this content can be time-consuming [6, 12, 21]. To address this issue, some researchers have focused on improving the quality of video tutorials, since these are comparatively low-cost to create. Pongnumkul et al. developed Pause-and-Play, a system that links events in a video to user events in the target application, pausing the tutorial when the user lags behind [20]. Others have focused on adapting existing tutorials for new domains. Ramesh et al. developed ShowMeHow, a system that automatically transfers step-by-step tutorials between similar applications such as Photoshop and GIMP [21].

Researchers have also explored methods for generating tutorials automatically [9, 12]. One approach is to generate tutorials directly from user demonstrations of a procedural task. Grabler et al. developed a system for automatically generating text and image tutorials from demonstrations in an instrumented version of GIMP [12]. Chi et al. developed MixT, which automatically generates mixed media tutorials with both text and video from user demonstrations in Photoshop [9]. While these systems produce tutorials automatically, they only work for specific domains like image manipulation, and the tutorials cannot always be applied to new problems. Furthermore, these systems only support linear procedures. In contrast, our framework supports complex non-linear procedures, applies to multiple domains, and can generate tutorials for any example problem that can be solved by the procedure.

Another approach is to generate tutorials that show users how to recreate an artifact in a user application. For example, Harms et al. augment a programming environment to automatically generate stencil-based instructions from code snippets [13], and Li et al. automatically generate tutorials to recreate AutoCAD drawings [16]. These systems can automatically produce tutorials for multiple example problems, but provide little control over how the tutorial teaches the procedure. In educational domains, it is important to teach students by describing the problem-solving thought process.

The work that relates most closely to ours is the DocWizards system by Bergman et al., which learns a procedure from multiple user demonstrations [6]. The DocWizards interface exposes a human-readable version of the learned procedure so a new user can step through it line-by-line. At each step, the current line is highlighted and the widget involved in the next action is circled in the user interface. While the DocWizards system uses an algorithmic representation of a procedure to automatically generate tutorials, it was not designed to explain the thought process. The learner is expected to read and understand $if - else$ statements, which significantly reduces the usability of this system. Furthermore, the procedure must be demonstrated on many distinct problems to create an accurate underlying algorithm, and the complexity of the procedures that can be represented is limited.

FRAMEWORK DESIGN

We present a new framework for generating step-by-step tutorials to teach procedural knowledge. In our framework, an educational technologist encodes the problem-solving thought process as an algorithm. Using a domain-independent interpreter, we step through this algorithm line-by-line. We explain each line using a set of mappings between programming language constructs and visual objects in the user interface, provided by the educational technologist. This approach allows us to automatically explain any problem that can be solved with the procedure. Figure 1 shows this workflow.

Algorithm 1 Given as input a 2D array $table$ containing a minuend p, represented as a set of digits $p_0, p_1, ..., p_m$ located in cells (0,0) to (0, m), and a subtrahend q, represented as a set of digits $q_0, q_1, ..., q_n$ in cells (1,$m-n$) to (1, m), subtract:

```
procedure SUBTRACT(table)
    for each column in table.GetColsFromRight() do
        top := column.GetCell(0)
        bottom := column.GetCell(1)
        if bottom.NotEmpty() then
            if top.value < bottom.value then
                borrow := table.LeftOf(top)
                while borrow.value == 0 do
                    borrow := table.LeftOf(borrow)
                end while
                borrow.value := borrow.value − 1
                while borrow.NotNextTo(top) do
                    borrow := table.RightOf(borrow)
                    borrow.value := 9
                end while
                top.value := top.value + 10
            end if
            result := column.GetCell(2)
            result.value := top.value − bottom.value
        else
            result := column.GetCell(2)
            result.value := top.value
        end if
    end for
end procedure
```

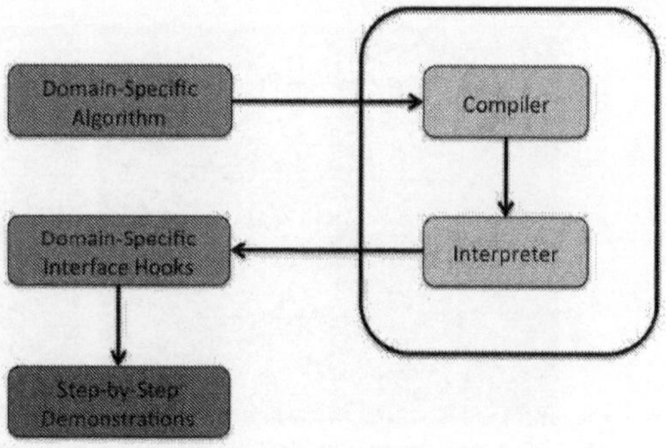

Figure 1. The framework workflow. A domain-specific TPL algorithm representing the problem-solving thought process is given as input, compiled, and then passed to the interpreter. The interpreter steps through the algorithm line-by-line and throws events, which are passed to the domain-specific interface hooks, which generate visual explanations.

Event	Interface Hook
Put variable in context	Interface Highlighting
Remove variable from context	Interface Highlighting
Execute assignment statement	Textual Explanation
Execute conditional statement	Textual Explanation
Execute loop statement	Textual Explanation
Execute return statement	Textual Explanation

Table 1. The type of interface hook used to explain each type of event.

Thought Process Language

To complete a procedural task, a student must follow a certain thought process to decide when to perform each action. A simple procedure may be a list of actions to be executed in order, while a complex procedure will require the student to choose which steps to execute based on features of the current problem. To solve a subtraction problem, for example, the student needs to decide whether or not to borrow by comparing the top and bottom digits in a column.

We encode this problem-solving thought process in a language we call the Thought Process Language (TPL). The TPL algorithm for subtraction is given in Algorithm 1. This algorithm solves all single-digit and multi-digit subtraction problems. TPL constructs are standard to many programming languages, and are not a contribution of this paper. TPL includes basic primitives like variables and constants, as well as expressions that can include integer operators ($+$, $-$, $*$, $/$) or Boolean operators ($<$, $>$, $==$, $!=$). TPL has three types of statements: assignments, conditionals, and loops (for, while, do-while, for-each). TPL is based on object-oriented programming languages and also supports objects, object fields, and object methods. Additionally, TPL includes functions and a procedure can reference multiple sub-procedures.

Compiler and Interpreter

We generate explanations for a given problem by stepping through the TPL algorithm line-by-line like a debugger. To accomplish this, we use a compiler and an interpreter that are designed to be reused across applications. The TPL algorithm is compiled and passed into the interpreter, which maintains information about the set of variables that are currently stored in memory. As the interpreter executes each line, it broadcasts events about this state, such as when new variables are put into context, when statements are executed, and when sub-procedures return. A full list of the events thrown by the interpreter is given in Table 1. Each event contains relevant information like the name of the variable, the programming language object associated with the executed statement, or the name of the sub-procedure that was called. These events are passed to domain-specific interface hook functions, which generate and display visual explanations.

Interface Hooks

To explain the events that are broadcast by the interpreter, we use domain-specific functions called *interface hooks* that map events to visual explanations in the user interface. We use two types of visual explanations: textual descriptions and interface highlighting. The explanation used for each type of interpreter event is shown in Table 1. Authoring interface hook functions involves writing code that is similar to what a developer would write to create problem-specific tutorials for an application, but our framework allows this code to be re-used to explain any problem in the given domain.

Textual Explanations

Textual explanations are commonly used to teach procedural tasks in both software tutorials and intelligent tutoring systems [9, 26]. We use text to describe assignment statements, return statements, loops, and conditionals. To display a textual explanation in our framework, we first automatically generate the explanation and then display it in the user interface.

We generate explanation text in a completely application-independent manner using information that is encoded within the TPL algorithm itself. We use templates to convert lines of TPL code into textual explanations. A template is a single-sentence string that describes a certain type of statement, for example a conditional statement. To generate the explanation for a line of code, we fill the appropriate template with the

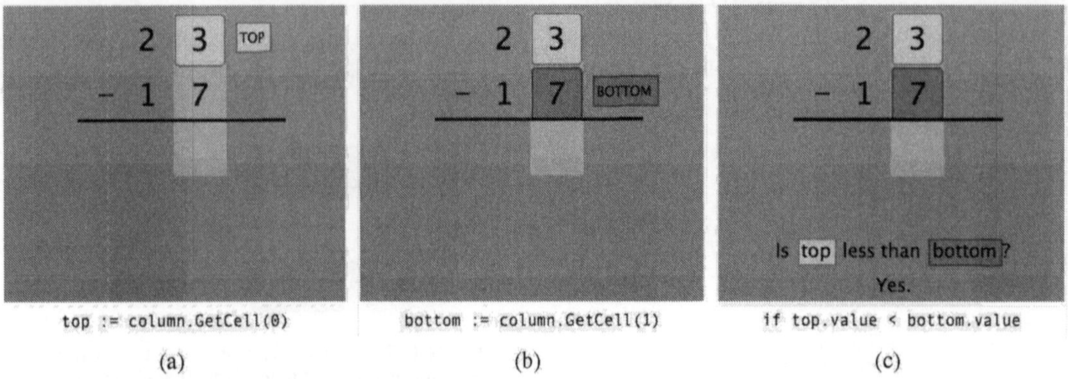

Figure 2. Examples of the explanations generated for the subtraction procedure. Figure (a) shows the explanation of the assignment of a variable called *top* to the top cell in a column. Figure (b) shows the explanation of the assignment of a variable called *bottom* to the bottom cell. Since the variable *top* is still in scope it remains highlighted. Figure (c) shows the explanation of the condition statement that determines whether borrowing is needed.

names of the variables, properties, or functions that are used in that line. The template library includes 20 explanation templates, which are designed to be reused across applications.

Figure 2 shows explanations generated for the subtraction procedure in Algorithm 1. Assignment statements are explained using the name of the assigned variable, so the code $top := column.GetCell(0)$ in line 3 is explained with the text "Top". To explain the conditional statement $if\ top.value < bottom.value$ in line 6, we fill in the conditional template "<explain boolean expression> <explain boolean result>". We populate the boolean expression template "Is <variable one> less than <variable two>?" to get "Is top less than bottom? <boolean result>." Finally, we fill the boolean result template with either "Yes" or "No" based on whether the expression evaluates to true or false. This produce the final explanation "Is top less than bottom? Yes."

To display the generated textual explanations in the user interface, our framework relies on application-specific interface hook functions. One interface hook function must be written for each location in the user interface where the designer wants to display text. As a result, the number of interface hooks required is highly dependent on the complexity of the domain. For the subtraction example, text is displayed in two locations. One interface hook function displays text next to a grid cell when a variable is assigned to a cell, and another displays text below the problem for all other types of programming language statements.

Interface Highlighting

We provide context to our textual explanations by highlighting visual objects in the user interface, an approach that is used in many effective software tutorials [6, 14]. Our goal is to highlight the set of interface objects that are relevant to the current steps in the procedure, without overwhelming the student by highlighting too many objects at once. To accomplish this, we determine highlighting based on the scope of variables within the procedure context.

Most imperative languages have a sense of *variable scope*, or the context in which a variable is defined and can be referenced. A variable that is defined within a branch of a conditional statement, like the $borrow$ variable in the subtraction procedure, will only be in scope while that branch is executing. We draw a connection between variable scope and working memory, declaring that the objects a student needs to keep in working memory while executing a procedure are equivalent to the variables that are currently in scope. We use the scope of variables to determine whether the visual representations of those objects should be highlighted.

To highlight objects in the user interface, our framework relies on application-specific interface hook functions. One interface hook function must be written for each type of object defined as a variable in the TPL algorithm. In the subtraction example, we define four variables: top, $bottom$, $borrow$, and $result$. All four of the variables are grid cell objects, so in this example we use one interface hook function that highlights arbitrary grid cells in the user interface. Using this interface hook function, our system highlights the objects referenced by the top and $bottom$ variables while they are in context, as shown in Figure 2(b). Variables defined in the TPL algorithm must refer to visual objects in the user interface, however we have found that all variables do have visual representations in the procedures we implemented for our prototype systems.

Authoring Process

This framework utilizes domain-independent components where possible to reduce authoring effort. To apply this framework to a new application, an educational technologist first integrates the domain-independent compiler, interpreter, and explanation templates into their code base. Then, the developer writes interface hook functions that display textual explanations and highly visual objects in the user interface. Finally, the developer writes algorithms in TPL that encode the problem-solving thought process for each procedure to be taught. Note that the interface hook functions are only written once for a given application, and can then be used to explain multiple TPL algorithms. For example, in our grid mathematics prototype, one set of interface hooks can be used to explain a broad range of K-12 math procedures such as subtraction, long division, and fraction multiplication. The number of interface hooks required for a given application will depend highly on the complexity of the problem domain.

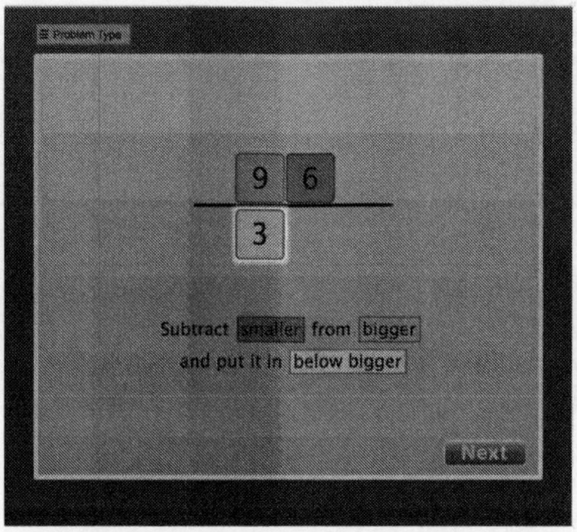

Figure 3. Screenshot of the grid mathematics application, set up to explain a greatest common factor problem with Euclid's Algorithm. The user can switch to a new procedure using the "Problem Type" menu bar.

PROTOTYPE IMPLEMENTATIONS

Our framework for automatically generating step-by-step demonstrations can theoretically be used to explain any deterministic procedural process. However, it is more appropriate for some domains than others. This approach is most effective in rich domains where many problem types can be represented through a single interface. The framework is also best suited to complex procedures with loops and branching. This represents a wide variety of problem-solving domains in K-12 education. In this section, we demonstrate how the framework applies to two distinct domains: a K-12 mathematics application and an educational game. Both applications are written in ActionScript 3, so we implemented our Thought Process Language, Compiler, and Interpreter in AS3 as well. Through these prototypes, we show that our framework can produce instructional materials for a variety of procedures and tasks without any problem-specific design.

K-12 Grid Mathematics

The domain of grid mathematics includes all problems that can be solved on a two-dimensional grid. This covers a large portion of K-12 math, including addition, subtraction, long division, prime factorization, fraction arithmetic, and even algebra. For this prototype, we implemented a general-purpose grid math application that can display a wide variety of problem types. Figure 3 shows the application interface displaying a greatest common factor problem. Users can select the desired procedure using the "Problem Type" drop-down menu. Step-by-step demonstrations for each procedure are provided for a progression of increasingly complex problems. Users step through the explanations by clicking the "next" button.

We wrote three interface hooks for this application: one that highlights an arbitrary grid cell, one that displays an explanation next to an arbitrary grid cell, and one that displays an explanation under the problem. These three simple functions can explain a large variety of procedures. For this prototype, we implemented three TPL procedures: a subtraction procedure, a multiplication procedure, and a procedure for Euclid's algorithm to find the greatest common factor of two numbers.

For each TPL procedure, our prototype can automatically generate explanations for a massive number of problems. For example, there are 55 million unique four-digit subtraction problems. Some are simple, while others require borrowing or borrowing across zero. Each type of problem is solved with a different set of steps, which is represented by a trace through our TPL algorithm. Four-digit subtraction is covered with 73 unique traces. It would require a lot of effort to author tutorials for each type of problem individually. Our approach allows us to explain all problem types automatically.

Educational Puzzle Game

Our second prototype is an educational puzzle game that is solved with a highly complex procedure. We chose this application to show how our approach scales to domains that require students to make complex decisions. *Refraction* was designed to teach fraction concepts to elementary school students. To play, the user interacts with a grid containing laser sources and target spaceships, as shown in Figure 4. The goal is to satisfy target spaceships by splitting the laser into the correct fractional amounts. The player uses pieces to change the laser direction and split the laser into fractional parts.

The most complex levels of *Refraction* cannot be solved with a deterministic procedure; heuristic search is sometimes required. For this prototype, we wrote a TPL procedure that covers the subset of *Refraction* levels that can be solved deterministically. This procedure is still much more complex than any of the grid math procedures implemented for our first prototype. It consists of 80 lines of TPL code and can solve thousands of distinct *Refraction* levels.

We wrote 27 interface hooks to explain the problem-solving process for *Refraction*. One set of functions highlights the following objects in the interface: pieces, arrays of pieces, spaceships, grid cells, grid columns or rows, spaceship fractions, laser fractions, and cardinal directions. Other functions display textual explanations that point to those same visual objects. The code we wrote in these interface hooks is very similar to the code *Refraction* developers wrote to author the game's original introductory tutorials. As a result, the authoring effort was similar to the effort required to write level-specific tutorials. However, with this approach, our functions can be used to explain any level solved by our TPL algorithm.

The textual explanations are automatically generated using explanation templates, as described in the Framework Design section. To effectively describe the complex procedure used to solve *Refraction* levels, we encoded explanations within the variable names themselves. For example, the explanation shown in Figure 4(a) was generated from the assignment of a variable named *theShipNeedsThisMuchPower*. The explanation shown in Figure 4(b) was generated from a conditional statement that calls the function $areTheseTwoValuesEqual$. By encoding textual explanations directly in the TPL algorithm's variable and function names, we can automatically generate detailed walkthroughs for any game level that can be solved by our TPL algorithm. This could improve the process of authoring tutorials and hints for educational games; previous research shows that this process can be challenging and time-consuming [19].

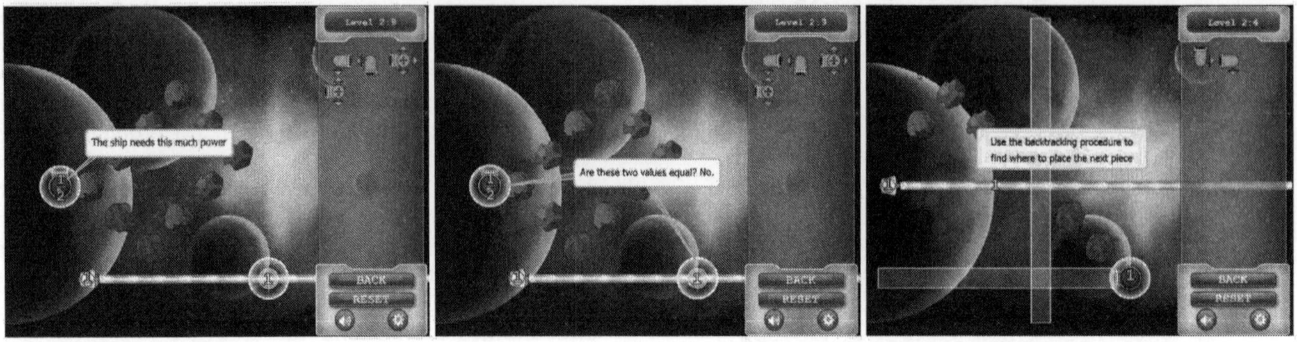

(a) (b) (c)

Figure 4. Screenshots of the *Refraction* prototype. To play, the student moves pieces from the bin on the right to the grid to bend and split the laser. Figure (a) shows an explanation of an assignment statement generated by our system. The text is generated from the variable name. Figure (b) shows an explanation of a conditional statement generated by our system. Figure (c) shows a summary explanation for the backtracking sub-procedure.

SCAFFOLDING MODALITIES

A central benefit of our authoring framework is that it naturally supports the creation of many different types of interactive instructional scaffolding, in addition to the step-by-step explanations described thus far. In this section, we show how our framework can be extended to produce tutorial progressions, just-in-time feedback, and fading worked examples.

Tutorial Progressions

The optimal amount of information to provide students as they work to master a new procedure varies throughout the learning process. Reigeluth and Stein argue that educators should introduce the simplest version of a new task first, and then give students progressively more complex tasks that build on the original task [22]. For novices, it is therefore desirable to minimize cognitive load by starting with simple problems that can be solved with the most straightforward procedures. For example, when introducing a simple subtraction problem like $15 - 3$, we would not mention the procedure for borrowing because it is not needed in this problem.

To produce explanations with the ideal level of detail automatically, we trace the TPL algorithm for the given problem before generating the explanations to determine which statements should be explained and which should be skipped. For each statement that branches, like a loop or a conditional, we track whether the branching behavior of this statement varies during the execution of the algorithm for the current problem. If the statement always executes the same branch, for example if the "borrowing" conditional in subtraction never evaluates to true, we skip the explanation for that statement because it is not required for the current problem.

As a student masters portions of a complex algorithm, less explanation is required. For example, an algorithm for solving linear equations will include addition and subtraction as sub-procedures. However, since students studying algebra have already mastered these procedures, it is not necessary to step through them in detail. Our approach naturally supports multiple levels of explanation granularity. If the designer indicates that a sub-procedure should be summarized rather than explained in detail for a given problem, we automatically generate a summary explanation by fusing information stored in the procedure's comments. To author a sub-procedure summary, the designer writes a header comment with a high-level description of the procedure, and indicates which variables should be highlighted by adding the comment $//explain$ to the end of the assignment statement for that variable. Figure 4(c) shows the summary explanation for the backtracking procedure in *Refraction*, which is used to determine where the next piece should be placed on the grid.

A key advantage of these techniques for producing appropriate explanations is that they build on recent work on automatically generating problem progressions for procedural tasks from an algorithmic representation of the procedure [3]. By combining our framework with these approaches, it would be possible use the TPL encoding of a procedure to automatically produce a lesson that introduces practice problems in order of increasing complexity and explains each one with an appropriate level of detail. This would remove the need to author both practice problems and their explanations by hand.

Just-in-Time Feedback

Another effective method of scaffolding learning is by providing students with feedback just as it is needed. Human tutors often give hints and suggestions when students make mistakes. Personalized hints are a central component of most cognitive tutors [26] and studies show that students perform better when these tutors provide hints [4]. Our framework naturally supports of interactive just-in-time feedback.

To show how we can generate interactive feedback directly from our step-by-step demonstrations, we created a "feedback mode" in each of our prototype applications. In this mode, the application waits for a user action and responds with a message if the action is incorrect. To author just-in-time feedback, the designer adds the comment $//action$ to each line in the TPL algorithm that modifies the user interface. For example, for the subtraction procedure in Algorithm 1, this comment would be added to lines 11, 16, 19, and 22, all of which set the value of a grid cell to a new number.

While running in "feedback mode", the interpreter executes the TPL algorithm silently, without displaying any explanations, until it reaches a line with an $//action$ comment. Then,

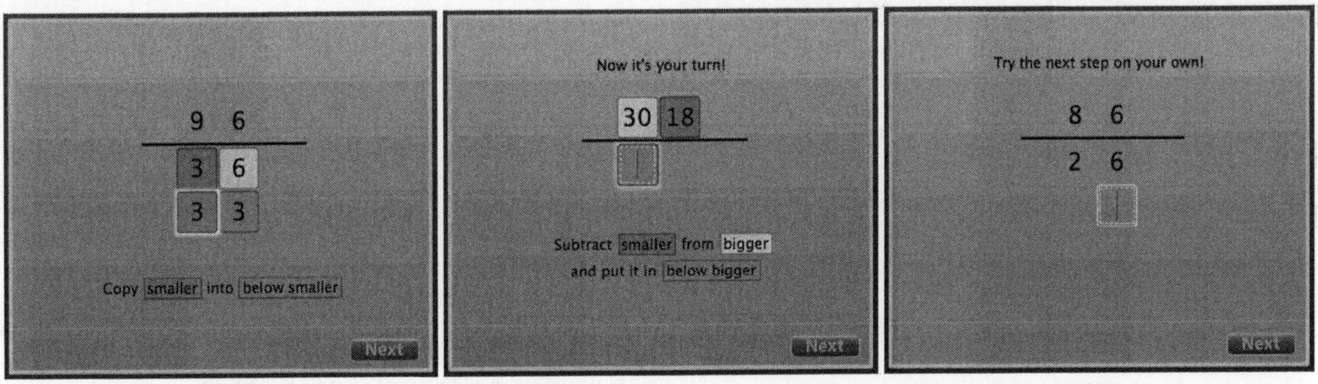

(a) (b) (c)

Figure 5. Screenshots of the progression for Euclid's Algorithm that gradually fades between step-by-step explanations and independent problem solving. Figure (a) shows a full demonstration, Figure (b) shows the system asking the student to perform one step with help, and Figure (c) shows independent problem solving with just-in-time feedback.

the system waits until the user performs an action. If the user action does not match the expected action, then the user has made a mistake. The designer can define how many incorrect tries the students can make before the correct steps are explained. If the student exhausts all of their attempts, the interpreter reverts the incorrect action, backtracks to the previous $//action$ comment, and displays a step-by-step demonstration of the steps the student should have made between their last correct action and their mistake.

This approach allows us to leverage the power of the interpreter to provide just-in-time feedback that directly targets student mistakes with minimal authoring effort.

Fading Worked-Out Examples

The typical method for teaching procedures begins with a full demonstration of the procedure and ends with the student solving problems without help. One limitation of this approach is that the transition between demonstrations and independent problem solving is often abrupt; students observe a teacher demonstration on the board and then solve worksheet problems without help. Some researchers have suggested that scaffolding should be used to smooth this transition [5, 23]. Renkl et al. describe a method where some steps of a procedure are demonstrated while other steps are completed by the student. By gradually reducing the number of demonstrated steps, the student eventually learns to solve the problem without help. They found that this type of gradual fading improved student performance on near-transfer tasks [23].

Initial studies that explore the effectiveness of fading worked-out examples have all used explanations and fading that were authored by hand for each problem [17]. Melis et al. have explored methods of automatically generating and adapting fading examples within the context of the ActiveMath intelligent tutoring system [17], but this approach does not generalize to other interactive learning environments or domains. Our approach naturally facilitates fading worked-out examples across multiple application domains.

We extended our framework to support fading in both of our prototype applications. To author fading for a given example, the designer indicates in the problem definition which actions in the TPL algorithm should be demonstrated and which should be performed by the student. Actions can also be fast-forwarded to focus more directly on a new part of the procedure. By defining whether each action in the TPL algorithm should be explained, performed by the user, or fast-forwarded, we can automatically create scaffolding that provides that level of fading. Figure 3 shows three different levels of fading that we created for Euclid's Algorithm in the grid math application. In Figure 5(a) the procedure is fully explained, in Figure 5(b) the student is given instructions but must complete the step on their own, and in Figure 5(c) the student solves the problem independently and receives just-in-time feedback in response to any mistakes.

The current design of our framework requires the designer to define which actions should be explained, fast-forwarded, and completed by the student for each problem. However, it could be extended further to produce faded progressions automatically. Gradual fading between worked-out examples and independent problem solving has great potential to support students as they learn new procedures, however this content is time-intensive to author and therefore difficult to study. We hope this new approach to authoring faded progressions can reduce the barrier to using and studying this technique.

USER EVALUATION

To gain a better understanding of the process of authoring scaffolding using our framework and the quality of the generated explanations, we conducted two user studies: one with educational technologists and one with fifth-grade students.

TPL Authoring User Study

The process of authoring step-by-step demonstrations with our framework consists of two parts: writing interface hook functions for the problem domain and writing a TPL algorithm for each procedure to be taught. In this study, we specifically examine the process of authoring TPL algorithms. To generate effective explanations, a TPL algorithm must abstract information into conditional blocks so that it is only explained when needed, and use variable names that describe

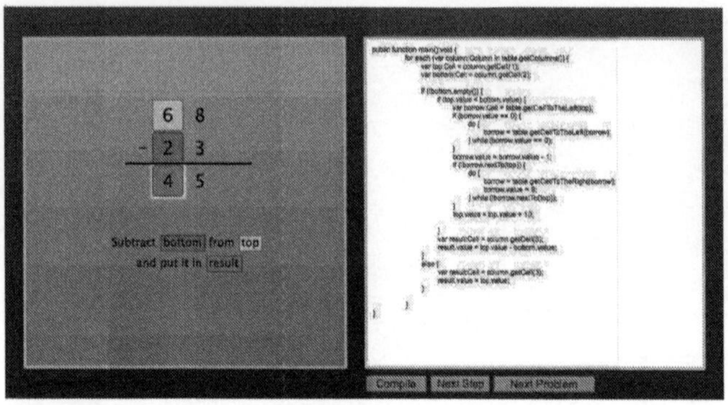

Figure 6. Screenshot of the authoring version of the grid mathematics application used in the authoring user study. Users can write Thought Process Language procedures in the panel to the right and step through the explanations they produce.

the human thought process. This requires an unusual programming style that could be challenging for authors. In contrast, authoring interface hooks requires standard programming and design skills. We were therefore most interested in evaluating whether educational technologists can learn the unique skill set required to write effective TPL algorithms.

To evaluate the process of writing TPL algorithms, we conducted a small-scale user study with three educational technologists recruited through our institution. All three participants were professional developers of educational applications with no expertise in designing instructional content. We asked participants to write a TPL procedure for subtracting one to three digit numbers that supported borrowing. We developed an authoring version of the grid mathematics application for this study, which included a code-editing panel as shown in Figure 6. To author the step-by-step demonstrations, participants wrote their TPL procedure in the code panel, clicked “Compile”, and stepped through the procedure for a set of provided example problems. We gave the participants a brief overview of the system before they began the task, and provided a few resources. This included documentation for the classes that their TPL procedures could reference, descriptions of the system's interface hooks, and an example procedure for Euclid's Algorithm.

All three participants produced TPL algorithms that solved the set of example problems we provided. They spent between 2.5 and 4 hours on the task in total, a reasonable amount of time considering that their procedures could explain all three-digit subtraction problems. The explanations generated by their algorithms provided clear descriptions of the subtraction procedure, although two participants included extra steps such as counting the number of columns rather than looping over them. Most interestingly, the authors each described a slightly different thought process for solving subtraction problems, displaying our framework's ability to support multiple types of explanations. All three participants iterated on their procedures extensively during the authoring process, and were able to learn effective ways of expressing the thought process using the feedback provided by the generated explanations themselves. This shows that educational technologists are able to learn to encode the problem-solving thought process to produce high-quality step-by-step tutorials without extensive training.

While we have not formally evaluated the process of authoring interface hook functions, we found it to be straightforward for our example implementations. This process requires standard programming and design skills, and a familiarity with the target application. The effort required to author the interface hooks is highly dependent on the complexity of the application: we wrote three interface hooks for the grid math prototype and 27 for Refraction. Furthermore, interface hooks are only implemented once per problem domain, while TPL is written for each procedure to be taught.

Student User Study

The textual explanations generated by our framework are phrased slightly differently than hand-authored explanations due to the format of the underlying algorithm. We were therefore interested in evaluating whether the generated explanations can effectively teach students a new procedure. To explore this question, we collaborated with an elementary school math teacher to conduct a user study with two of his fifth-grade classes. We chose to teach Euclid's Algorithm for finding the greatest common factor of two integers because this is a procedure that is rarely taught in schools; the teacher we worked with was not familiar with the procedure.

We created two computer lessons to teach Euclid's Algorithm using our grid math prototype. One lesson displayed step-by-step demonstrations of the procedure for three example problems, and then provided a set of 18 practice problems with just-in time feedback. The second lesson presented the same 21 problems in the same order, but faded gradually between demonstrations and independent problem solving. We compared these two computer-based lessons to a traditional lesson given by the math teacher to see how the automatically-generated explanations compared to human explanations.

The Euclid's Algorithm lesson was conducted during a 50-minute math period. The first class received the traditional lesson, and the second class was split into two groups who received the two computer-based lessons. In both classes, the teacher began by giving an identical five-minute overview of factors and greatest common factors. Next, students had 10 minutes to work on a paper pre-test with three greatest common factor problems. One problem could be solved by listing the factors of each number and selecting the greatest common one, but the other two problems were designed to be difficult to solve without using Euclid's Algorithm.

After finishing the pre-test, the first class was given a traditional 25-minute lesson by their teacher. We asked him to teach Euclid's Algorithm as he would teach any new procedure, but had him introduce the same set of 21 example problems in the same order as in the computer lessons. The teacher demonstrated the procedure for two example problems on the white board, and then asked students to work on the 19 practice problems on their own while he answered questions and worked with individual students. The second class moved to computers after completing the pre-test at their desks. Half of the students, randomly chosen, logged into a lesson with demonstrations and practice problems, while the other have logged into a lesson that faded between the demonstrations and practice problems. The students were given 15 minutes to interact with the system after logging in.

After the lessons, students went back to their desks to take the paper post-test. This test used the same three questions as the pre-test, given in a different order. We chose to use the same questions to be sure that the tests were of equal difficulty. Students were given 10 minutes to work on the post-test.

Results

We collected data from 28 students, and were given informed consent for participation by the students, their parents, their teacher, and their school principal. Of these students, 18 received the traditional lesson, 5 received the computer lesson with just-in-time feedback, and 5 received the computer lesson with fading worked-out examples. Due to a server issue we lost data from several students in the computer class, hence the smaller number of participants in these conditions.

We used non-parametric statistics in our analysis because the students' scores on the pre- and post-tests were non-normally distributed. We found that overall, scores improved between the pre- and post-test. We used a Wilcoxon rank sums test to measure the effect of *test* (either pre or post) on scores, showing that students performed significantly better on the post-test (Z=-3.80, p<0.0001), with a median of 2.5 questions correct out of three, compared to 0 correct on the pre-test. We also calculated a learning gain for each student by taking the difference between their pre- and post-test scores, and found that the median learning gain was 1 point.

Next, we used a Kruskal-Wallis test to determine whether *condition* had any impact on students' scores. There was no significant difference in pre-test scores (χ^2=3.11, *n.s.*). Students in the traditional lesson condition got a median of 1 problem correct, compared to 0 for the two computer lesson conditions. There was also no significant difference in post-test scores (χ^2=3.11, *n.s.*); students in the traditional lesson condition got a median of 3 problems correct, compared to 2 problems correct for students in the fading computer lesson, and 1 problem correct for students in the just-in-time feedback computer lesson. Finally, *condition* had no significant impact on learning gains (χ^2=0.01 *n.s.*). Students in all three conditions had a median learning gain of 1 point.

Our results show that students who received the two computer lessons had learning gains roughly equivalent to those who received the traditional lesson. Only two students did not use Euclid's Algorithm to solve the post-test problems, one in the traditional lesson condition and one in the just-in-time feedback condition. This shows that the generated explanations were able to effectively convey a new procedure to students, even over a very short period of time. Students had less time-on-task and no help from their teacher with the computer lessons, but still performed equally well on the post-test.

While these results are promising, our sample size is small and we only looked at one TPL algorithm in this study. In future work, it would be valuable to conduct a more thorough experiment that focuses on the student experience. This would help us gain a better understanding of the strengths and weaknesses of our automatically generated explanations.

CONCLUSION

In this work, we present a new framework for automatically generating interactive scaffolding to teach the entire space of problems that can be solved with a given procedure. We encode the problem-solving thought process as an algorithm and use this model to generate explanations. This approach has a number of advantages. Given a small set of mappings between programming language constructs and visual objects in the user interface, we can produce tutorials for any Thought Process Language procedure that can be applied in the application. Furthermore, this framework naturally facilitates the authoring of problem progressions that introduce information gradually, just-in-time feedback, and scaffolding that fades between demonstrations and independent problem solving.

We demonstrate the generality of our approach by showing how the framework applies to two distinct problem-solving domains: a K-12 math application and an educational game. For each prototype, we authored interface hooks and TPL algorithms that produce in-depth explanations for problem-solving procedures in that domain. We also conduced an authoring user study to determine whether educational technologists can effectively encode a problem-solving procedure in our Thought Process Language. All three participants produced high-quality TPL procedures to explain subtraction in a reasonable amount of time. Finally, we conducted a user study with fifth grade students to determine whether the explanations generated by our framework can effectively teach a new procedure. This study showed that students who received computer lessons had similar learning gains to students who received a traditional lesson from their math teacher.

Our new approach for authoring interactive instructional scaffolding is designed to maximize the content that educational technologists with programming expertise can create. The authoring effort required to write interface hooks and TPL algorithms will not be not justified in all domains. However, our framework has incredible potential in domains where we would like to generate scaffolding for a wide variety of example problems. Perhaps most importantly, this approach naturally supports the creation of a variety of different types of instructional scaffolding, including problem progressions, just-in-time feedback, and fading worked-out examples. Since these types of scaffolding are costly to produce, many important questions about the relative effectiveness of different scaffolding methods remain unanswered. We hope that this framework will be used to improve tutorial authoring and also expand our understanding of effective scaffolding design.

ACKNOWLEDGMENTS

We would like to thank our study participants, the creators of *Refraction*, and Craig Connor for his work on the grid mathematics prototype. This work was supported by the Office of Naval Research grant N00014-12-C-0158, the Bill and Melinda Gates Foundation grant OPP1031488, the Hewlett Foundation grant 2012-8161, Adobe, and Microsoft.

REFERENCES

1. Aleven, V., McLaren, B. M., Sewall, J., and Koedinger, K. R. The cognitive tutor authoring tools (CTAT): preliminary evaluation of efficiency gains. In *International Conference on Intelligent Tutoring Systems*, ITS'06 (2006), 61–70.
2. Aleven, V., Mclaren, B. M., Sewall, J., and Koedinger, K. R. A new paradigm for intelligent tutoring systems: Example-tracing tutors. *Int. J. Artif. Intell. Ed. 19*, 2 (Apr. 2009), 105–154.
3. Andersen, E., Gulwani, S., and Popović, Z. A trace-based framework for analyzing and synthesizing educational progressions. In *CHI* (2013), 773–782.
4. Anderson, J. R., Corbett, A. T., Koedinger, K. R., and Pelletier, R. Cognitive tutors: Lessons learned. *The Journal of the Learning Sciences 4*, 2 (1995), 167–207.
5. Atkinson, R. K., Renkl, A., and Merrill, M. M. Transitioning from Studying Examples to Solving Problems: Effects of Self-Explanation Prompts and Fading Worked-Out Steps. *Journal of Educational Psychology 95*, 4 (2003), 774–83.
6. Bergman, L., Castelli, V., Lau, T., and Oblinger, D. Docwizards: A system for authoring follow-me documentation wizards. In *UIST* (2005), 191–200.
7. Blessing, S. B., Gilbert, S. B., Ourada, S., and Ritter, S. Authoring model-tracing cognitive tutors. *International Journal of Artificial Intelligence in Education 19*, 2 (2009), 189 – 210.
8. Brawner, K., Holden, H., Goldberg, B., and Sottilare, R. Recommendations for modern tools to author tutoring systems. In *The Interservice/Industry Training, Simulation & Education Conference (I/ITSEC)* (2012).
9. Chi, P.-Y., Ahn, S., Ren, A., Dontcheva, M., Li, W., and Hartmann, B. MixT: automatic generation of step-by-step mixed media tutorials. In *UIST* (2012), 93–102.
10. Corbett, A., Koedinger, K. R., and Anderson, J. R. Intelligent tutoring systems. In *Handbook of Human-Computer Interaction, Second Edition*, M. Helander, T. K. Landauer, and P. Prahu, Eds. Elsevier Science, Amsterdam, 1997, 849–874.
11. Glazewski, K. D., and Ertmer, P. A. Scaffolding disciplined inquiry in problem-based learning environments. *International Journal of Learning 12*, 6 (2005), 297–306.
12. Grabler, F., Agrawala, M., Li, W., Dontcheva, M., and Igarashi, T. Generating photo manipulation tutorials by demonstration. In *ACM SIGGRAPH* (2009), 66:1–66:9.
13. Harms, K. J., Cosgrove, D., Gray, S., and Kelleher, C. Automatically generating tutorials to enable middle school children to learn programming independently. In *International Conference on Interaction Design and Children*, IDC '13 (2013), 11–19.
14. Kelleher, C., and Pausch, R. Stencils-based tutorials: Design and evaluation. In *CHI* (2005), 541–550.
15. Koedinger, K. R., Anderson, J. R., Hadley, W. H., and Mark, M. A. Intelligent tutoring goes to school in the big city. *International Journal of Artificial Intelligence in Education 8* (1997), 30–43.
16. Li, W., Zhang, Y., and Fitzmaurice, G. Tutorialplan: Automated tutorial generation from cad drawings. In *IJCAI*, F. Rossi, Ed., IJCAI/AAAI (2013), 2020–2027.
17. Melis, E., Goguadze, G., and Saarl, U. D. Towards adaptive generation of faded examples. In *International Conference on Intelligent Tutoring Systems , LNCS*, Springer- Verlag (2004), 762–771.
18. Olsen, J., Belenky, D., Aleven, V., Rummel, N., Sewall, J., and Ringenberg, M. Authoring tools for collaborative intelligent tutoring system environments. In *Intelligent Tutoring Systems* (2014), 523–528.
19. O'Rourke, E., Ballweber, C., and Popović, Z. Hint systems may negatively impact performance in educational games. In *Proceedings of Learning @ Scale*, L@S '14 (2014), 51–60.
20. Pongnumkul, S., Dontcheva, M., Li, W., Wang, J., Bourdev, L., Avidan, S., and Cohen, M. F. Pause-and-play: automatically linking screencast video tutorials with applications. In *UIST* (2011), 135–144.
21. Ramesh, V., Hsu, C., Agrawala, M., and Hartmann, B. Showmehow: Translating user interface instructions between applications. In *UIST* (2011), 127–134.
22. Reigeluth, C. M., and Stein, F. S. The elaboration theory of instruction. In *Instructional Design Theories and Models: An Overview of their Current States*, Lawrence Erlbaum (Hillsdale, NJ, 1983).
23. Renkl, A., Atkinson, R. K., Maier, U. H., and Staley, R. From example study to problem solving: Smooth transitions help learning. *Journal of Experimental Education 70*, 4 (2002), 293–315.
24. Sottilare, R. A. Considerations in the development of an ontology for a generalized intelligent framework for tutoring. In *International Defense & Homeland Security Simulation Workshop in Proceedings of the I3M Conference* (2012), 19–25.
25. Stamper, J., Barnes, T., Lehmann, L., and Croy, M. The hint factory: Automatic generation of contextualized help for existing computer aided instruction. In *Proceedings of the 9th International Conference on Intelligent Tutoring Systems Young Researchers Track* (2008), 71–78.
26. VanLehn, K. The behavior of tutoring systems. *International Journal of Artificial Intelligence in Education 16* (2006), 227–265.
27. Wood, D., Bruner, J., and Ross, G. The role of tutoring in problem solving. *Journal of Child Psychology and Psychiatry 17* (1976), 89–100.

Mudslide: A Spatially Anchored Census of Student Confusion for Online Lecture Videos

Elena L. Glassman[1,2] **Juho Kim**[1,2] **Andrés Monroy-Hernández**[1] **Meredith Ringel Morris**[1]

[1]Microsoft Research, Redmond, WA, USA
[2]MIT CSAIL, Cambridge, MA, USA
{juhokim, elg}@mit.edu {andresmh, merrie}@microsoft.com

ABSTRACT
Educators have developed an effective technique to get feedback after in-person lectures, called "muddy cards." Students are given time to reflect and write the "muddiest" (least clear) point on an index card, to hand in as they leave class. This practice of assigning end-of-lecture reflection tasks to generate explicit student feedback is well suited for adaptation to the challenge of supporting feedback in online video lectures. We describe the design and evaluation of Mudslide, a prototype system that translates the practice of muddy cards into the realm of online lecture videos. Based on an in-lab study of students and teachers, we find that spatially contextualizing students' muddy point feedback with respect to particular lecture slides is advantageous to both students and teachers. We also reflect on further opportunities for enhancing this feedback method based on teachers' and students' experiences with our prototype.

Author Keywords
Flipped classrooms; lecture feedback; online lecture videos

ACM Classification Keywords
H.5.m. Information interfaces and presentation: Misc.

INTRODUCTION
Teachers are finding "flipped classrooms" increasingly attractive and feasible [12]. In a flipped classroom, students watch lectures outside of class and do more active learning activities within class. Some teachers flip their classrooms using educational videos from services like Khan Academy [khanacademy.org], Coursera [coursera.org], or edX [edx.org], while others create their own video lectures using tools like Camtasia [techsmith.com] or Office Mix [officemix.com]. One drawback of online lectures is that teachers no longer have access to many traditional signals of student confusion (such as facial expressions or raised hands).

Educators have developed an effective technique to get feedback about in-person lectures, called "muddy cards" [18] or "One-Minute Papers" [11,22]. These are index cards that teachers give to students at the end of a lecture. Students are given time to reflect and write the "muddiest" (least clear) point on the index card to hand in as they leave. The teacher then adjusts the next day's activities based on students' common confusion points. The aggregation of the responses in the index cards is often a time-consuming process [11,18].

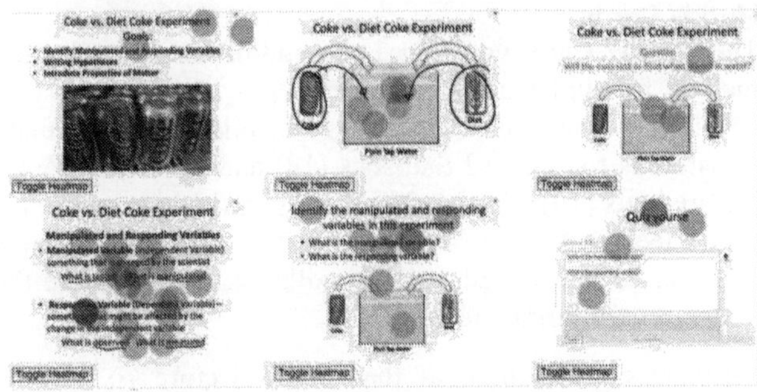

Figure 1. Mudslide Teacher Interface: slides presented in the lecture video, with muddy points generated by students that can be clicked to view descriptions of confusion. Red muddy points indicate that the author found the lecture confusing. Gray muddy points are created by those who rated the lecture as not confusing overall.

This practice of assigning end-of-lecture reflection tasks to generate explicit student feedback seems well suited for adaptation to the challenge of supporting feedback on online video lectures. In this paper, we describe the design and evaluation of Mudslide, a prototype system that translates the practice of "muddy cards" into the realm of online lecture videos. Mudslide provides timely feedback where real-time feedback, i.e., students' raised hands, is absent. Figure 1 shows Mudslide's teacher interface.

After discussing related work, we describe how we adapt the workflow for soliciting and summarizing muddy points to online lecture technologies, and we present Mudslide, our instantiation of this concept. We then describe a three-stage evaluation of Mudslide, in which students used the tool to give feedback on lecture videos and teachers viewed and reflected on this feedback. Our findings indicate that spatially contextualizing students' muddy point feedback with respect to particular lecture slides is advantageous to

CHI 2015, April 18 - 23 2015, Seoul, Republic of Korea

ACM 978-1-4503-3145-6/15/04...$15.00
http://dx.doi.org/10.1145/2702123.2702304

both students and teachers; Mudslide's workflow demonstrates a simple yet effective method for incorporating new types of student feedback into online educational experiences.

RELATED WORK

We first discuss the traditional Muddy Card educational method that inspired our system design. We then discuss literature on the role of confusion in learning. Finally, we reflect on status quo techniques for gathering student feedback from online lectures.

Muddy Cards

The Muddy Card workflow is an end-of-lecture reflection method for students that has been deployed in a variety of traditional educational settings, from middle school math classrooms to Harvard Statistics [18] and MIT Aero/Astro lecture halls [10]. The Muddy Card workflow is simple: (1) give a lecture, (2) ask students to write what confused them most on an index card, and (3) collect and summarize the responses for further action.

Responses are written at the end of lecture so that by engaging with the material through reflection, students experience benefits like increased retention of the material [2,9]. The Muddy Card workflow turns that engagement into a signal for teachers to learn from and act on, such as by revising their own lectures for future class sections and/or addressing common points of confusion at the start of the next lecture.

While the workflow is simple, the exact prompt used has an impact on the quality of responses. Mosteller [18] observed that asking, *"What do you want to know more about?"* produced answers in his classroom that often just referred back to the key points of the lecture. However, asking a variant of, *"What was the muddiest point in the lecture?"* promoted specific, relevant, and concrete responses describing what students wanted to know more about.

Muddy cards can take a few minutes of students' time at the end of lecture; the demands on teachers' time, however, can be somewhat larger. For instance, after every lecture, Professor Harwood spent 30 minutes or less reviewing Muddy Cards from his ~250-person chemistry class [11]. Professor Mosteller spent 30 to 45 minutes summarizing the most common responses from his ~50 person class, which he then handed back to students, with clarifications [18].

Beneficial Confusion

Confusion is part of the learning process. Craig et al. [6] observed a positive correlation between confusion and learning. This supports Piaget's theory that cognitive disequilibrium, experienced as confusion, may trigger learning: the creation or restructuring of knowledge schema [13]. However, D'Mello et al. [8] notes that, to be beneficial, confusion must be appropriately resolved. Mudslide aims to expose students' confusion within online lecture videos, so teachers can appropriately resolve it.

Gathering Feedback on Online Lecture Videos

When students asynchronously view lecture materials online, gathering feedback about whether the lecture was understood or how to improve it for future viewers is not straightforward. Explicit polling is one option; applications like InstFeedback [instfeedback.com] could be used as a virtual Muddy Card. However, the resulting answers are shown as a simple list. This would not address the time-consuming nature of reading and summarizing muddy points in the existing Muddy Card workflow.

Alternatively, teachers can observe online students' confusion by monitoring discussion forums. Discussion forums are a standard feature of many online lecture platforms (e.g., Coursera, Udacity). Researchers have also experimented with novel discussion forum features and formats for educational purposes, such as Nota Bene [24] and WebAnn [4], which are in-place collaborative annotation tools that create a forum within the margins of assigned class reading material. While useful, forums do not necessarily serve as a census of confusion by which teachers can prioritize the development of additional clarifying material. Even with a mechanism for "upvoting" others' questions, it is not clear how many passive student "lurkers" benefit from a teacher answering a particular question. In addition, the bar for participation in forums can be high: students may need to read multiple threads before discovering that their question has not already been asked and answered, and not all feel comfortable posting. This may be reflected in the low forum participation rates observed in massively open online courses (MOOCs): in edX's first offering of "Circuits and Electronics," only 3% of enrolled students participated in the discussion forum [3].

Students' interactions with educational videos can also be an implicit source of feedback. With VidWiki [7], students spatially and temporally annotate lecture videos to correct errors and translate or clarify text for themselves and others. LectureScape [14] converts the log files of students' interactions with lecture videos in MOOCs into a heatmap of viewing activity along the video timeline. Teachers may be able to infer trouble spots, but the explicit reasons for emergent patterns, such as rewatching, are not known.

Voyant [23] and CrowdCrit [17] demonstrate that crowds, given appropriate structure, can generate feedback for content authors. Non-expert or remote crowds created spatially anchored structured feedback specifically for visual designers. However, the feedback-providers were not students; their role is evaluative rather than reflective. Our system and evaluation focus on how spatially anchored, reflective student feedback can be produced and interpreted in the context of online educational lecture videos.

MUDSLIDE

Mudslide is a prototype system that incorporates ideas from the Muddy Card technique into a feedback system for online lecture videos. The overall system design is minimalistic and general; to use Mudslide, a teacher simply supplies a folder of lecture slide images used in their video (video key frames could be used as an alternative in scenarios where a teacher does not use lecture slides). Mudslide uses this data to create an online, interactive slide gallery, with separate student and teacher interfaces accessible at different URLs. The teacher sends students the student URL for a lecture's Mudslide gallery to visit after viewing an online lecture (for a more seamless experience, the URL could be incorporated into the lecture itself as a link at the end of the video or within a hosting platform's forum area). Mudslide is implemented with the Django web framework, using Python 2.7, HTML5, CSS3, JavaScript, and the d3.js library.

Design Goals

In creating Mudslide, we had four design goals, inspired by our review of the literature and by a formative three-hour workshop at a local school with nine teachers (for grades 6 – 12) and three technical staff in which teachers discussed their current practices and concerns with respect to flipping their classrooms while making lecture videos with Office Mix [officemix.com].

- **G1:** Encourage students to reflect on the entire lecture.
- **G2:** Encourage students to provide specific feedback (not just "this lecture was confusing").
- **G3:** Provide a fast and intuitive way for students to give feedback.
- **G4:** Allow teachers to quickly interpret student feedback, even with large class sizes or multiple classrooms.

Toward fulfilling these goals, we modify the freeform responses from the traditional Muddy Card workflow into a two-step process for students at the end of a lecture: (1) indicate the region on a particular slide that represents the muddiest point and (2) provide a typed explanation of why that point was confusing. Since students do not see others' annotations before making their own, their independent judgments may represent a more accurate census of post-lecture confusion than forums [20].

By preserving this reflection as an end-of-lecture activity, we fulfill design goal **G1**: to support students' pedagogically valuable reflection on the lecture as a whole, and their comprehension of each component. Submitted muddy points represent *unresolved* confusion at the end of lecture. Showing the set of lecture slides as the interface to allow students to specify their feedback further supports this reflection by providing a visual reminder of the entire lecture's contents.

Constraining students to generate a spatial anchor for each textual muddy point description is intended to fulfill design goal **G2**: helping students generate specific, concrete comments and questions. It is also a feature intended to fulfill design goal **G3**: to give students a fast and intuitive mechanism for describing muddy points. Rather than explaining both where and why they were confused, they can simply point to where they were confused and then use text to explain why.

The spatial anchors for muddy points are the key to creating a visual summary for teachers, intended to fulfill design goal **G4**: reducing the muddy-point processing burden on teachers. Rather than reading through a list of purely textual muddy points, teachers can first glance at the distribution of spatially anchored muddy points across their lecture slides to assess trouble spots quickly. Many teachers in our workshop teach the same material to multiple classrooms over the course of a day, and could send a single lecture video to many more students than fit in a single classroom.

Student Interface

After watching an online lecture and then clicking the Mudslide URL the teacher provided, students see a gallery of thumbnails of the lecture's slides, laid out chronologically. Atop the gallery are instructions stating, "Double-click on *exactly where* this lecture is most confusing. *The exact location of your click will be shown to the teacher.* You may double-click on multiple confusing points, if you wish." Double-clicking anywhere on a slide's thumbnail places a small, semi-translucent circle at that point (Figure 2). After placing a circle, a dialogue box appears (Figure 3) asking the student to explain why that point was unclear. If the student clicks "Cancel" or fails to provide an explanation, the circle is removed. A separate button, beneath the thumbnail gallery, can clear all of that student's muddy points.

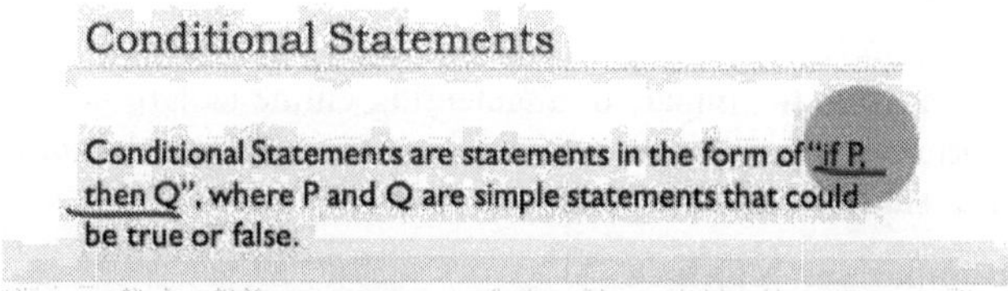

Figure 2. In this example, a student has clicked on the region of a slide stating "if P," creating a red muddy point indicator.

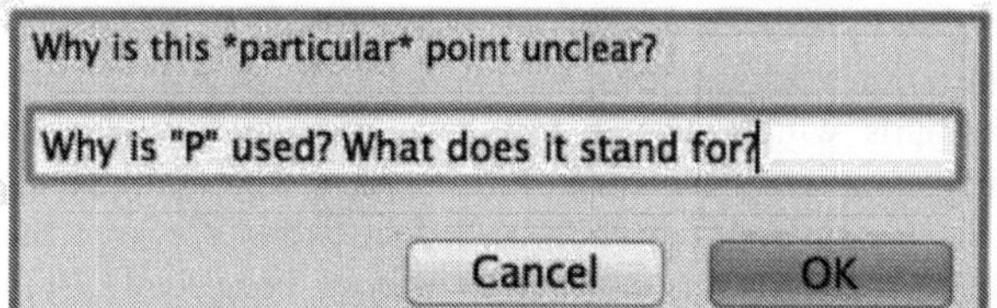

Figure 3. After spatially selecting a muddy point (Figure 2), the student is prompted to provide a specific explanation of why she found that section of the lesson confusing.

Before submitting, students must rate the lecture by choosing one of four choices to complete the following statement: "This lecture was: [extremely confusing | moderately confusing | slightly confusing | not confusing]." After rating the lecture's overall clarity and marking up the slides with one or more muddy point(s), the student clicks the "Submit to Teacher" button below the last lecture slide.

Teacher Interface

The teacher's Mudslide URL directs her to a page that aggregates and summarizes all of the students' feedback. As shown in Figure 1, the defining feature of the teacher interface is an interactive heatmap formed by overlaying the accumulated semi-transparent muddy points on the gallery of lecture slide thumbnails. To save teachers time, the slide with the largest number of muddy points is featured, with its heatmap, at the top of the gallery.

The teacher can click on any spot on the heatmap; clicks within the boundary of one or more circles trigger a pop-up displaying the text of the corresponding muddy point descriptions. A button allows the teacher to toggle the heatmap on and off in case the circles overlap enough to block the text, figure, or equation underneath. To see all comments for a slide at once, the teacher can click a button that "flips" the slide over to reveal a scrollable list of all muddy comments associated with that slide.

By visually differentiating comments by the confusion level of their creator, teachers can investigate trouble spots in their lecture as a function of both the volume of comments and the severity of confusion. Mudslide can differentially color-code points in the heatmap based on students' holistic confusion rating–for example, in Figure 1, points submitted by students who rated the lecture overall as "not confusing" are shown in gray, rather than red. Beneath the gallery, we list the raw muddy point descriptions, ordered by slide, as well as a Word Tree [21] and histogram representation of the same textual data.

EVALUATION

To measure the impact of augmenting online lecture videos with muddy point feedback, we ran a multi-stage, lab-based user study.

Comparison Interface

As a baseline for comparison, we implemented a research prototype implementing the original Muddy Card workflow. Since the original workflow has no spatial anchors for muddy points, we replaced the gallery of slide thumbnails with a simple text input box in the baseline student interface. The text box is a simple digital metaphor for a physical index card collected in class. We kept the look and feel of the teacher interfaces consistent. Both teacher interfaces had a list of raw comments and summary text representations (histograms and Word Trees); only Mudslide had an interactive heatmap. Since the baseline raw comments have no associated slide, they are ordered by how confusing the student rated the lecture.

We included this baseline interface to allow us to evaluate how spatial anchoring affects students' perceptions of the feedback process, the nature of the feedback provided, and teachers' ability to interpret the feedback. In the analysis that follows, a "muddy card" is the collection of muddy points described by a student in either interface.

Stage 1. Teachers Create Lecture Videos

We recruited 19 teachers (13 female) from a U.S. metropolitan region, 14 from public schools, and five from private schools. The teachers (T1-T19) all taught at the middle or high school level (U.S. grades 6–12), and taught a variety of subjects, including math, science, English, and history. Ten of the 19 participating teachers indicated that they had made instructional videos before, using software such as Camtasia, Adobe Premiere, and iMovie. Seven indicated that they had flipped their classrooms before. In a 5-point Likert scale question (1-not familiar, 5-very familiar), most teachers said that they were familiar with PowerPoint (mean=3.8, σ=0.6). Five had prior experience with Office Mix. The teachers were offered a gratuity to come to our lab for a three-hour session. The teachers were told that they would be preparing video lectures, and each brought PowerPoint files of two of their existing classroom lectures to serve as seed material for their videos.

We provided each teacher with a tablet computer, stylus, webcam, and microphone to use during the study. After completing a questionnaire about personal demographics and any relevant experiences with video lectures, we conducted a tutorial on how to transform their PowerPoint slides into video lectures using Office Mix, a free PowerPoint add-in [officemix.com]. The teachers used the remaining session time to create one or two video lectures based on the slides they brought with them; we instructed them to limit the length of each video to about five minutes (to bound student viewing time in stage 2 of the study).

The teachers made a total of 36 videos. For each video, we asked them to specify the target grade level(s), and to identify what they thought the most confusing point of the lecture might be for students. From the 36 videos, we chose one video authored by each teacher (19 total) for the next stage of the study, based on length, quality, and clarity.

Stage 2. Students Generate Muddy Points

We invited 25 middle and high school students (15 female) from a U.S. metropolitan area to our lab (mean age=14.7, max=17, min=13). Each session lasted one hour, and the participants were offered a gratuity for their time. Due to practical constraints, these students were not the members of the 19 teachers' regular classes.

We matched each student (S1-S25) to two of the lecture videos produced in the first stage of the study based on the students' grade level. We also attempted to balance the matching of videos to students so that each video had a similar number of students view it (25 students x 2 videos viewed = 50 viewings divided by 19 available videos = a target of showing each video to 2 – 3 of the students). Students were provided with a tablet computer, mouse, and stylus. We first gave them a questionnaire about their familiarity with online lecture videos, followed by a tutorial on how to view videos using the Office Mix video player. We then demonstrated the features of Mudslide's student interface on a sample set of slides.

Students then completed the following routine twice: (1) watch the assigned lecture video, (2) submit muddy point(s) with the assigned student interface, and (3) complete a survey about their experience. Students were permitted to refer back to the video when composing their muddiest points, if desired. We encouraged students to pick the "least clear" point(s) if they felt that the lecture was clear overall. This stage followed a counter-balanced, within-subjects experimental design. Each student used both the baseline and Mudslide student interfaces once over the course of the session. After the first video, half the students saw the Mudslide student interface, and half saw the baseline.

At the end of the session, the students each filled out a final survey, in which they explicitly compared the baseline and Mudslide student interfaces. The Mudslide student interface was identified by its affordance for pointing and clicking on slides, while the baseline student interface was identified by its text box. Neither interface was ever referred to by a name. Twenty-one of the students completed the study with spare time remaining; we showed these students the Mudslide teacher interface to get formative opinions on whether viewing other students' confusion points was potentially valuable.

The teacher interface is designed to aggregate muddy points from a large or multiple classroom-sized viewer pool. Since time constraints made it impractical to generate a classroom-sized viewer pool of students for each of the teachers' 19 videos, we also hired workers on Amazon's Mechanical Turk service ("Turkers") to view each video and create muddy cards using either the Mudslide or baseline interface. The HITs were completed over ten days with an average hourly wage of $9.04. Based on demographic information requested in the HIT, 34% of muddy cards were composed by Turkers under 25, 37% by women, and 62% by those with at least a college degree.

Stage 3. Teachers View Muddy Points

The same 19 teachers from stage 1 returned to the lab for a second session approximately one week later, for one hour. Teachers first reviewed the video we chose from the one or two videos they produced during their first session. Then they were told how muddy points were generated for their lecture videos in each interface. Mudslide was referred to as the point-and-click interface, while the baseline was referred to as the free-response interface.

Teachers were given a quick tutorial of how to read the four components present in the teacher interfaces: the heatmap (Mudslide only), raw comments, histogram of frequent words, and Word Tree. Then, teachers saw (1) the muddy points generated and visualized with the baseline interface and (2) the muddy points generated and visualized in the Mudslide interfaces. The order of which interface each teacher saw first was counterbalanced across all teachers.

Teachers explored each interface themselves for approximately ten minutes while talking aloud to an experimenter taking notes. Their task during this time was to fill out a questionnaire about their impressions. After having seen both interfaces, teachers filled out an additional questionnaire asking for explicit comparisons between the two interfaces. As part of that survey, the experimenter reminded the teachers of their prediction about the muddiest point of their lecture videos (which they had made at the end of stage 1). They were then asked to reflect on the difference between what they had predicted and what they observed in students' muddy points. The lead author analyzed students' and teachers' free-text questionnaire responses for common themes using an iterative open coding approach; categories were not mutually exclusive.

RESULTS

Stage 1: Teachers Create Lecture Videos

The teachers made a total of 36 videos, which had a mean length of 3.6 minutes (σ=2.4), and 10.4 slides (σ=5.3). The 19 videos selected for stage 2 covered a range of topics, such as "Characteristics of Life," "Energy and Matter," "Six Traits of Writing," and "Resumes: How to Make Yourself Look Good."

Stage 2: Students Generate Muddy Points

Nine of the 25 student participants indicated that their teachers at least occasionally assign videos to watch at home. Those nine students were then asked to describe what they do not like about watching lecture videos. Two students described the frustration of not being able to immediately ask a question. Five students complained that lecture videos could be too long or repetitive compared to reading a textbook. The remaining two students were frustrated by videos that were overwhelming, required pre-requisites they did not have, or used unfamiliar terms. When these nine students had questions triggered by an assigned lecture video, they relied on a combination of emailing their teacher (55%), using a search engine (55%), waiting for the next day's class (33%), or asking their friends (11%).

When reviewing the baseline and Mudslide student interfaces separately, students did not find either interface significantly more tedious or difficult to use, nor did they perceive a difference in the ease of remembering muddy points from the lecture. However, when asked which interface students preferred, 21 of the 25 students preferred the Mudslide student interface, and only four of the 25 students preferred the baseline interface.

Baseline Student Interface

Two main themes emerged from students' free responses describing their likes, dislikes, and wishes for the baseline interface. First, there is the freedom of the text box. 24% of students specifically mentioned how easy it was to review the video and simply type up their muddy points in the text box. This ease of use is perhaps especially true when muddy points are inherently non-spatial: *"It was easy to describe simple things such as voice volume or clarity of speech."* [S15] 36% of students liked that they *"could write down whatever [they] wanted"* [S10] to *"fully explain"* [S4] the muddiest point with *"a detailed reason."* [S22] An additional student [S14] appreciated that muddy points were not tied to a specific slide.

This freedom had costs, as well. When asked what they did not like about the baseline interface, 28% of the students specifically mentioned the difficulty or tedium of expressing the muddiest point only through text *"instead of just pointing to it."* [S3] The same student [S15] who extolled the simplicity of writing about *"simple things,"* like voice volume, observed that the text box alone is not suitable for more complex material: *"Advanced scenarios were very difficult to explain and say what about them was confusing."* When also considering what they wished for in this interface, 20% described a desire to anchor their comments to a particular slide or part of a slide, as is possible in the Mudslide interface.

24% of students specifically disliked not having thumbnails or wished for thumbnails of slides. Students were able to revisit the lecture video, but it *"was much easier to provide the muddiest moment when I had the visual cues to help remind me what they were."* [S4] As a final note, one student added, *"This method* [baseline UI] *of giving feedback was similar to the ones I've used in the past for lecture videos, so I was more accustomed to it, but I do not like it much."* [S2]

Mudslide Student Interface

When students wrote about their likes, dislikes, and wishes for the Mudslide student interface, the dominant two themes were ease and exactness. 44% of students described the system as easy to understand and use. 28% of students mentioned their appreciation for the exactness with which they could discuss the muddiest points: *"I really liked this method of entering the muddiest point. I could easily show the instructor the area where I was confused with pretty accurate precision"* [S4] and *"Very efficient, easy to show exactly what was confusing"* [S15]. Only 24% of students did not express appreciation for the system's ease or exactness in their response.

Requiring a spatial anchor for each muddy point affected the process of commenting on non-spatial aspects of the video. 16% of students described wanting to "point" to a moment in time or to what was being said over the slide, instead of the text or images on the slide. Without any summary representation of the audio as a timeline or transcript, students reported clicking somewhere on the slide containing the muddy voice-over, but could not be any more spatially specific than that. One student remarked that this was especially problematic when teachers spent a long time talking over a slide with little information on it.

The intentional constraint that every muddy point submitted had to be associated with a location on a slide caused frustration for the 8% of students who reported difficulty composing any muddy point. This task is not trivial: *"You had to come up with something very relevant and specific to the slides you were clicking on"* [S10]. One student, stuck, admitted to picking an arbitrary point.

While the simple click-and-describe muddy point submission process was clear and easy, it did not allow for students to indicate just how large or small the region on the slide they were "pointing" to was. 20% of students specifically complained that they could not add arrows or highlight large areas, even whole slides, at once.

Muddy Points Generated

To assess whether the student interface affected the type and quality of the muddy points generated by these students, two raters independently scored the muddy points generated by the 25 students. Since students were allowed to describe multiple muddy points in the baseline text box, each rater independently parsed how many muddy points the students' freeform textual response contained, and the category each parsed muddy point fell into. The categories chosen were Question, Description of Confusion or Complaint, Suggestion, Appreciation, and No Substance. Each parsed muddy point was given a single category. We defined comments of "no substance" as those comments containing no suggestions, questions, descriptions of confusion, complaints, or statements of appreciation. An example would be: "Nothing was confusing."

The raters also each marked muddy points as (1) either spatial (i.e., relating to an object on the slide) or non-spatial (i.e., relating to a non-spatial issue like volume), and (2) either specific (i.e., relating to a particular section or slide) or holistic (i.e., relating to the entire lecture). The same process was applied to the spatially anchored textual responses from the Mudslide student interface.

While one student's response in the baseline interface was lost, the 24 remaining freeform responses were parsed into 42 and 36 muddy points, respectively, by the independent raters. On the subset of 19 students' freeform responses that were parsed by both raters into the same number of muddy points, the categorical label agreement on that subset of 30 muddy points across raters was high (Scott's pi of 0.92) [16]. Of the 31 spatially anchored textual responses provided by the 25 students, the raters independently both parsed 32 muddy points (only one textual response had two muddy points contained within it). On those 32 parsed muddy points, the categorical label agreement was also high enough to be considered consistent (Scott's pi of 0.70) [16]. To merge their ratings, we took the sum of their respective category counts. Regardless of the interface used, students appropriately channeled the majority of muddy points into the intended categories of Questions and Confusions/Complaints. However, when using the Mudslide student interface, fewer students submitted muddy points of no substance (two-sided Fisher exact probability test, $p < 0.05$). Insubstantial muddy points like "Nothing was unclear" or "I was confused" are something that teachers mentioned as being uninformative.

The same raters coded muddy points as either spatial or non-spatial with a Cohen's κ [5] of 0.57 and 0.59 for the baseline and Mudslide interfaces, respectively. The raters coded muddy points as either specific or holistic with a Cohen's κ of 0.70 and 0.26 for the baseline and Mudslide interfaces, respectively. Agreement was fair or better, by a commonly cited scale [1], so we proceeded to test whether the interfaces had a significant effect on the specificity and spatial nature of muddy points. The total number of spatial comments (averaged across both raters) submitted with the Mudslide student interface was not significantly different than the analogous statistic for the baseline (one-tailed Fisher exact probability test). The same is true for specific comments. Across both interfaces, roughly a third of muddy points referred to a non-spatial aspect of the lecture video. A possibly overlapping third of muddy points across both interfaces refer to the lecture as a whole, rather than a specific part.

Students' Reactions to the Mudslide Teacher Interface

Twenty-one students had time left over within their session to explore the Mudslide teacher interface. Specifically, they explored the Mudslide teacher interface for the same lecture video for which they used the Mudslide student interface. On a 5-point Likert scale question (1-strongly disagree, 5-strongly agree) students felt that the Mudslide heatmap was easy to use (4.9, σ=0.4) and easy to understand (4.8, σ=0.6). Students disagreed with statements describing the heatmap as not useful (2.1, σ=1.1) and not interesting (2.0, σ=1.1). Students were comfortable with the idea of other students viewing their anonymous muddy points (4.3, σ=0.7) and strongly agreed with the statement "I like seeing other people's anonymous muddy points." (4.8, σ=0.5)

Students' free responses about the Mudslide heatmap flesh out these Likert scale ratings and contribute several additional themes. When asked what they learned while interacting with the heatmap, 52% of the 21 students specifically mentioned appreciating the opportunity to see the ideas of others. 29% of students appreciated the perspective they gained when seeing others' muddy points that were different from their own: *"I learned what others are confused about which helped with my personal analysis of potential energy"* [S25]. Finally, 33% expressed reassurance that, as one student wrote, *"people shared my thoughts on the muddiest section"* [S19].

When asked what they liked about the heatmap, the same theme of appreciating the access to everyone else's responses came through even more clearly: 86% of student responses mentioned this as a benefit. The remaining 14% use the space to describe the visual clarity or ease of use, e.g., *"Easy to see hotspots of problems."* [S15] When asked what they did not like about the heatmap, 43% listed nothing. Another third of students gave design requests, including the improvement of the slide's visibility beneath the heatmap and better filtering for or aggregation of similar muddy points.

Stage 3: Teachers View Muddy Points

In stage 3, teachers viewed the feedback generated by the 25 middle and high school students and the online crowd workers. The Mudslide teacher interface was populated with an average of 45.3 muddy cards (σ=16.7, min=24, max=94) from Turkers and 1.4 (σ=1.0, min=0, max=4) muddy cards from students per lecture video. The heatmaps generated for each lecture video were varied in appearance, depending on factors like the total number of muddy points (viewers had to specify at least one muddy point, but could specify as many as they liked if they found multiple parts of the lecture confusing), the number of slides in the lecture, and the information density on each slide. For example, the lecture video with the fewest slides introduced the concept of kinetic energy; the lecture contained only two slides, the second of which was quite information-dense, containing several equations. This lecture received 106 muddy points – three from three students, and 103 from 65 crowd workers. Shown in Figure 4, the vast majority, 93%, were on the second slide, and in particular were concentrated specifically over two of the eight equations on that slide, clearly indicating to the teacher which particular equations were not sufficiently explained in the video.

A different pattern of muddy points occurred in a lecture explaining how to set up a particular type of scientific experiment, which contained thirteen slides and received 60 muddy points (two from one student, and 58 from 39 crowd workers). On this lecture, the muddy points were more distributed across all slides, yet a clear plurality of points, 19, fell on a slide about the definitions of manipulated and responding variables (see Figure 1). In this case, the points were not clustered in one distinct sub-area within the slide, but the teacher could see that the text of these comments all reflected a similar theme relevant to the slide as a whole, e.g., *"Confusion over manupulated [sic] variable and responding variable."* As expressed during a session talk-aloud, the Mudslide design was in line with teachers' goals regarding feedback: *"If a student says, 'this is confusing' generally, I can't really help them. This way (with the heatmap), we can train them to be able to explain their confusion more clearly, which is something we try to teach."* [T1, paraphrased]

Over half of the teachers (53%) did not anticipate what the muddiest point of the lecture would be, indicating that muddy point feedback offers perspectives that are not easy

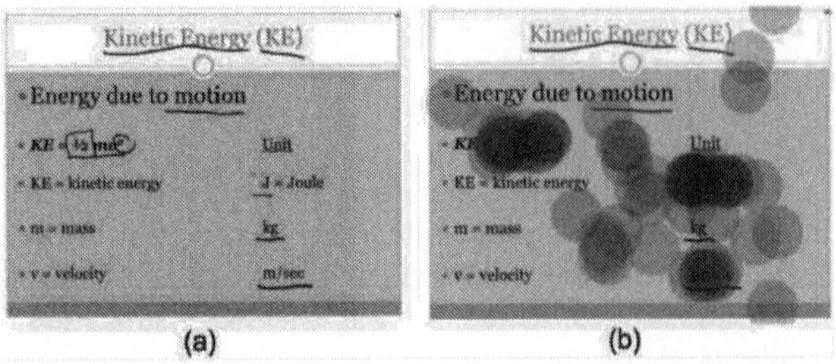

Figure 4 (a) Final slide in a video lecture on Kinetic Energy. (b) Students' and Turkers' muddy points, clustered around the KE equation, many of which are asking why there is a ½ or why velocity is squared, and around the symbol for Joule (J), asking for its definition. The teacher can now create targeted, data-driven clarifications.

for teachers to anticipate. Teachers' ability to foresee what might confuse students may depend on whether their online videos are watched by an audience comprised of unfamiliar viewers (as in our evaluation scenario) or a set of known students. Even without knowing the students and Turkers, teachers expressed excitement about the potential of rapid feedback (*"LOVE the heat map!"* [T6]).

Muddy Points as Formative Assessment for Teachers

Teachers also saw muddy cards submitted by students written out as free-form responses. The baseline teacher interface displayed 30 (σ=0) muddy cards from Turkers and 1.3 (σ=0.9, min=0, max=3) muddy cards from students per lecture video. The number of Turker-produced muddy cards collected per lecture is less in the baseline condition but still comparable to typical classroom(s). After seeing both teacher interfaces, an older, partially retired teacher reflected on muddy points' utility for helping teachers improve their own skills: *"Since these days teachers have to collect portfolio information, the reflection they might be able to do on the effectiveness of a lecture could be greatly enhanced by this tool. By the same token, teachers might be intimidated by the feedback and reject or repress it or not want administrators to see it. Might be wonderful for peer reflection groups like CFG (Critical Friends Group)."* [T12] This teacher points out that tools like Mudslide could double as a formative assessment tool [19] for teachers, through which they could refine their lectures, in addition to directly helping students.

T12's musings proved accurate–during stage 3: teachers' emotional reactions to muddy points on their own lectures split teachers into two groups, one that interpreted the feedback constructively (~85%) and one that felt that their skills were not accurately reflected in the feedback from viewers who were not their actual students (~15%). The first group interpreted the feedback as a way to learn more about what worked and did not work in their lecture, and to learn about their teaching style in general. For example, *"What I thought was entertaining was, in fact, confusing. Analogies were too silly. The repetition of [the comment] 'This was a strange lecture' definitely makes me reflect on how I present information"* [T14]. Another teacher, faced with a hotspot of muddy points on one particular slide about dependent and independent variables within an example of an experiment, reflected that she would *"provide examples of identifying variables from other experiments"* [T2]. Another teacher, also looking at the heatmap, noted: *"I could see where my weaknesses were in the presentation, easily"* [T5]. However, the second, smaller group of teachers perceived the confusion as caused only by viewers' missing prerequisites. After the study, one teacher expressed concern that their ability to teach was being evaluated unfairly, as if the volume and character of the muddy points were directly related to their teaching ability.

After seeing both the baseline and Mudslide teacher interfaces, teachers reflected on how the muddy points affected their perception and design of their video lectures. On a 5-point Likert scale question (1-strongly disagree, 5-strongly agree), teachers expressed a strong (4.4, σ=0.7) desire to make changes to their lectures after seeing the muddy points. The muddy points changed their perceptions of the clarity of their lectures (4.2, σ=0.9). In spite of their presumably constrained time, teachers agreed with the statement, "I would make time to review this feedback from students during a typical day" (3.9, σ=0.7).

Teachers rated their agreement with statements explicitly comparing the baseline with Mudslide, e.g., "The feedback I got from the point-and-click responses was *more useful* than the feedback I got from students' free responses." The opposite statement, that the students' free responses were more useful than the point-and-click responses, was also included, to make the overall perceived bias of the survey neutral between the two interfaces. These opposing statements were not adjacent to each other, and were interspersed with other 5-point Likert scale questions about the interfaces. The same was done for statements explicitly comparing which interface "gave me a better sense of my students' confusion."

By the two-sided Wilcoxon rank sum test, Mudslide was rated significantly more useful ($W = 262, p < 0.05$) and gave teachers "a better sense of students' confusion" ($W = 293, p < 0.001$) than the baseline. These significance findings are backed up by teachers' questionnaire responses, such as, *"[The Mudslide UI] allowed me to see EXACTLY [emphasis theirs] where the kids were confused while [the baseline] method was more vague"* [T3]. However, teachers still noted some drawbacks; in the baseline interface, *"the students provided information about the pace and tone quality of the lecture that were not evident in the point and click feedback [Mudslide] web page"* [T12].

Comparing Visualizations of Muddy Points

We asked teachers to rank the four visualizations of muddy points available to them across the two interfaces (note that the heatmap was only available for muddy points collected with the Mudslide student interface). Each visualization was assigned a 4 for every time it was ranked 1st, a 3 for 2nd, etc., so that higher averages correspond to better rankings. The average rank given to the heatmap (3.4) and raw comment (3.3) visualizations of muddy points were both greater than the average rank of the Word Tree (1.9) and histogram (1.4) visualizations. A Friedman test revealed a significant effect ($p < 0.001$). Post-hoc two-sided Wilcoxon rank sum tests showed a significant difference between both the heatmap and the raw comments and the lower ranked Word Tree and histogram ($17.5<W<32.5$, $p < 0.001$).

The heatmap was repeatedly praised by teachers as a time-saver: *"I found that the heatmap was much better for a quick at a glance view, and I could literally zoom in on problem areas. If I had more time I'd prefer the comments in text form but I am pretty sure that doesn't happen very often..."* [T8] An average of 50 muddy points were generated per video lecture, so it was not prohibitive to skim every muddy point available, but it was not necessarily fast. Another teacher wrote, *"Reading through all of this takes a while. I think it may be helpful occasionally but it's not something I'd want all the time"* [T8].

When justifying their visualization rankings, 53% of teachers mentioned either the specificity of spatial annotations or the speed of visually identifying trouble spots as major advantages of the Mudslide teacher interface. Without the spatial organization offered in Mudslide, it was *"hard to just jump to a confusion point visually, you have to sort it out"* [T1]. On the other end of the utility spectrum, *"The word tree and histogram are interesting, but not that useful to me,"* another teacher [T2] wrote, echoing the sentiment of many others.

DISCUSSION

Student and teacher feedback from our study indicates that Muddy Card-inspired feedback can be a valuable addition to online video lectures. Taking advantage of the visual nature of the video medium by allowing students to anchor their muddy points spatially rather than merely typing a free-text response, seems like a particularly promising approach–this approach was preferred by students, resulting in fewer comments lacking substance, and enabled teachers to get a quick gestalt of a class's feedback via a heatmap representation.

Although Mudslide's visual point-and-click interface was suggestive of spatially-oriented feedback, many students nonetheless provided feedback on non-spatial and/or holistic aspects of the lecture. Providing visual representations of audio tracks (such as a graph of audio levels over time) or other meta-data about a lecture may be a valuable enhancement to our design. Although the simple circle-based representation of muddy points employed by Mudslide was effective, exploring ways to allow students to specify regions of varied shapes and sizes while preserving the simplicity of the specification process and the ease of creating a glance-able heatmap for teachers is a design challenge worth considering.

In our study, the students watching the videos were not members of the producing teachers' regular classes. In many "flipping" scenarios, students watch content produced by teachers they do not have an ongoing relationship with (e.g., a teacher may use a video by a well-known expert on a particular subject), so our study design is a reasonable facsimile of that scenario. However, in other flipping scenarios, a teacher may show her class self-produced videos–her knowledge of the students' backgrounds and prior contexts, and their knowledge of her teaching style may change the nature of the videos themselves and/or the type and interpretation of comments. The teachers' comments in the final stage of our study indicated that they found the feedback (from both the students and Turkers) to be similar to the types of feedback they get from their regular students, indicating that this may not be a large confound; however, investigating whether Mudslide-inspired feedback systems for familiar teacher-student sets necessitate different affordances than those for unfamiliar sets is an interesting avenue for future investigation.

Investigating whether Mudslide-like interactions would be a valuable feedback mechanism for MOOCs, whose viewership may be orders of magnitude larger than the classroom-flipping scenario we focused on, is also a valuable area for further study. Text summarization features, such as Word Trees and histograms, may be more valued by MOOC instructors than the teachers in our scenarios, as skimming individual comments becomes less feasible when thousands of students provide muddy points. Enabling filtering of the heatmap (perhaps allowing the teacher to remove points corresponding to certain confusion levels, or to students meeting certain criteria such as grades on prior class assignments, or perhaps based on tags that students could be encouraged to associate with their comments) may also become important to retaining its value as a tool for quick insights in a MOOC scenario.

Although traditional Muddy Cards are meant for the teacher's attention, students expressed interest in seeing others' muddy points. In our current design, a teacher could choose to send his URL for the Mudslide interface to the class if he wished to offer his students this experience. Considering how the muddy-point viewing interface might be redesigned specifically for this peer-oriented scenario (which may require higher standards for language blacklisting, privacy guarding, etc.) is another potential avenue of future study. This scenario might be particularly relevant for MOOCs, where peer-based interactions sometimes supplant teacher interactions for reasons of scalability [15].

Assumptions and Limitations

We drew inspiration from literature and interviews about traditional lectures, but we designed Mudslide for short, slide-based, video lectures. Mudslide was not thoroughly tested on different scales of lecture length or number of muddy points. We are exploring Mudslide's flexibility.

CONCLUSION

As teachers increasingly flip some or all of their classes by assigning students to view videos that they or other instructors have created as a homework activity [12], there is a need to capture signals about students' understanding of these videos. We identified an opportunity for interaction design by observing that the paper-based Muddy Card technique is well suited to adaptation to online video lectures. Our Mudslide prototype enhances the muddy card concept by taking advantage of the visual nature of video lectures to enable spatially anchored feedback; students preferred this to free-form feedback, and produced higher quality comments with this interface. The spatial nature of the feedback made glance-able confusion heatmaps possible, which teachers found valuable and more efficient to interpret than a list of free-form comments. Mudslide provides a simple, yet valuable, interface for enriching online video lectures by providing a way for students to efficiently and specifically express their confusion to instructors.

ACKNOWLEDGMENTS

The authors would like to thank Anoop Gupta, Kurt Berglund, Sasa Junuzovic, and the Office Mix team for their feedback and support.

REFERENCES

1. Altman, D.G. *Practical statistics for medical research.* CRC Press, 1990.
2. Angelo, T.A. and Cross, K.P. *Classroom assessment techniques.* 1993.
3. Breslow, L., Pritchard, D.E., DeBoer, J., Stump, G.S., Ho, A.D., and Seaton, D.T. Studying learning in the worldwide classroom: Research into edX's first MOOC. *Research & Practice in Assessment 8*, (2013), 13–25.
4. Brush, A.J.B., Bargeron, D., Grudin, J., Borning, A., and Gupta, A. Supporting Interaction Outside of Class: Anchored Discussions vs. Discussion Boards. *CSCL 2002*, International Society of the Learning Sciences (2002), 425–434.
5. Cohen, J. A Coefficient of Agreement for Nominal Scales. *Educational and Psychological Measurement 20*, 1 (1960), 37–46.
6. Craig, S., Graesser, A., Sullins, J., and Gholson, B. Affect and learning: an exploratory look into the role of affect in learning with AutoTutor. *Journal of Educational Media 29*, 3 (2004), 241–250.
7. Cross, A., Bayyapunedi, M., Ravindran, D., Cutrell, E., and Thies, W. VidWiki: Enabling the Crowd to Improve the Legibility of Online Educational Videos. *Proceedings of the 17th ACM Conference on Computer Supported Cooperative Work & Social Computing*, ACM (2014), 1167–1175.
8. D'Mello, S., Lehman, B., Pekrun, R., and Graesser, A. Confusion can be beneficial for learning. *Learning and Instruction 29*, (2014), 153–170.
9. Freeman, S., Eddy, S.L., McDonough, M., et al. Active learning increases student performance in science, engineering, and mathematics. *PNAS 111*, 23 (2014), 8410–8415.
10. Hall, S.R. Teaching By Questioning. *MIT Aero-Astro Annual*, 2003, 29–35.
11. Harwood, W.S. The one-minute paper: a communication tool for large lecture classes. *J. Chemical Education 73*, 3 (1996), 229.
12. Herreid, C.F. and Schiller, N.A. Case studies and the flipped classroom. *J. College Science Teaching 42*, 5 (2013), 62–66.
13. Kibler, J. Cognitive Disequilibrium. In S. Goldstein and J.A. Naglieri, eds., *Encyclopedia of Child Behavior and Development.* Springer US, 2011, 380–380.
14. Kim, J., Guo, P.J., Cai, C.J., Li, S.-W.D., Gajos, K.Z., and Miller, R.C. Data-Driven Interaction Techniques for Improving Navigation of Educational Videos. *UIST 2014.*
15. Kulkarni, C., Wei, K.P., Le, H., et al. Peer and self assessment in massive online classes. *ACM Trans. on Computer-Human Interaction 20*, 6 (2013), 33.
16. Lombard, M., Snyder-Duch, J., and Bracken, C.C. Practical resources for assessing and reporting intercoder reliability in content analysis research projects. *Retrieved April 19*, (2004), 2004.
17. Luther, K., Pavel, A., Wu, W., et al. CrowdCrit: crowdsourcing and aggregating visual design critique. *CSCW 2014*, ACM (2014), 21–24.
18. Mosteller, F. The 'Muddiest Point in the Lecture'as a feedback device. *On Teaching and Learning: J. Harvard-Danforth Center 3*, (1989), 10–21.
19. Sadler, D.R. Formative assessment and the design of instructional systems. *Instructional science 18*, 2 (1989), 119–144.
20. Surowiecki, J. *The wisdom of crowds.* Random House LLC, 2005.
21. Wattenberg, M. and Viegas, F.B. The Word Tree, an Interactive Visual Concordance. *IEEE Transactions on Visualization and Computer Graphics 14*, 6 (2008), 1221–1228.
22. Wilson, R.C. Improving faculty teaching: Effective use of student evaluations and consultants. *J. Higher Education*, (1986), 196–211.
23. Xu, A., Huang, S.-W., and Bailey, B. Voyant: generating structured feedback on visual designs using a crowd of non-experts. *CSCW 2014*, ACM (2014), 1433–1444.
24. Zyto, S., Karger, D., Ackerman, M., and Mahajan, S. Successful classroom deployment of a social document annotation system. *CHI 2012*, ACM (2012), 1883–1892.

Making Software Tutorial Video Responsive

Cuong Nguyen
Portland State University
Portland, OR 97207-0751
cuong3@pdx.edu

Feng Liu
Portland State University
Portland, OR 97207-0751
fliu@cs.pdx.edu

ABSTRACT
Tutorial videos are widely available to help people use software. These videos, however, are viewed by users as captured and offer little direct interaction between users and software. This paper presents a video navigation method that allows users to interact with software tutorial video as if they were using the software. To make the tutorial video responsive, our method records the user interaction events like mouse click and drag during capturing the video. Our method then analyzes, selects, and visualizes these user interaction events at the event locations. When a user directly interacts with an event visualization, our method automatically navigates to the proper video frame to provide the visual feedback as if the software were responding to the user input. Thus, our method provides the experience of "interacting" with the software through directly manipulating the tutorial video. Our study shows our method can better help users follow tutorial videos to complete tasks than the baseline timeline interface.

Author Keywords
Video Navigation and Browsing; Software Tutorial Video

ACM Classification Keywords
H.5.2 Information Interfaces and Presentation: User Interfaces

INTRODUCTION
Tutorial videos are widely employed to help people use software. These tutorial videos are often produced by screen capturing the software-use workflow. When watching a software tutorial video, users often need to frequently navigate to relevant frames to recall parameters, check results, or skip certain steps [12]. These navigation goals are important for users to understand the operations and perform them using the software; however, the classic timeline-based players do not suit these navigation goals very well. Using the timeline for video navigation, users need to focus on two different locations: the timeline and the video content simultaneously. It is often slow to locate frames of interest. More importantly, the timeline interface does not provide direct interaction between users and software. It does not support users to directly work with the software through the software interface and does not provide the visual feedback to the user input from the software. That

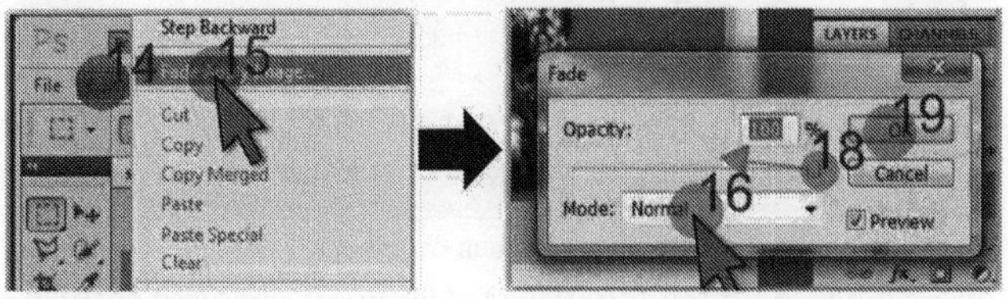

Figure 1. Responsive tutorial video navigation. When a user clicks Event 15, our system navigates to the proper frame that shows a dialog to respond to the user input.

is, the tutorial video is not responsive with the timeline interface. These problems can compromise the user's performance in learning to use the software from the tutorial video.

This paper presents a method that makes a software tutorial video responsive to the user input and allows users to navigate the tutorial video as if they were using the software[1]. To make the tutorial video responsive, our method records the user interaction with the software when screen-capturing the tutorial author's software-use process. Our method then analyzes these interaction events and selects the relevant ones at the current frame. These events are finally visualized close to the event locations, such as buttons and menu items. Users can navigate the tutorial video by directly interacting with the event visualization as if they were interacting with the software. Figure 1 shows an example of a user navigating a *Photoshop* tutorial video. In the current frame, our system displays the relevant events 14 and 15. Event 15 indicates that the tutorial author clicked the menu item *Fade Apply Image*. When watching this tutorial video, a user clicks Event 15 and our system automatically navigates to the frame that provides the visual feedback to the user input as if *Photoshop* is responding to the user input. Here the *Fade* dialog window appears after Event 15 is clicked which is exactly what happened after the tutorial author clicked *Fade Apply Image*.

This responsive tutorial video navigation method has advantages over timeline methods in that it merges two processes together: navigating a software tutorial video and using the software. Moreover, this method allows users to quickly reach frames of interest by directly "interacting" with the software through interacting with the event visualization. Our study shows that our method can better help users follow tutorial videos to complete tasks than timeline interfaces.

RELATED WORK
The timeline interface has been enhanced with event visualization to better support software tutorial video navigation. Some methods detect and display tool invocation events on timeline [1, 11, 12] and can help users quickly find frames of

[1]`http://graphics.cs.pdx.edu/project/tutorDMVN`

CHI 2015, April 18–23, 2015, Seoul, Republic of Korea.

http://dx.doi.org/10.1145/2702123.2702209

Figure 2. System overview.

interest based on the tool usage. *Chronicle* captures software workflow histories and visualizes them on timeline to support workflow exploration in a tutorial video [7]. *Toolscape* explores crowdsourcing to display step-by-step instructions on timeline [9]. Instead of enhancing timeline, our work visualizes user interaction events right in the video window where these events actually happen and allows users to navigate the tutorial video through these in-context event visualization as if they were directly interacting with the software.

Direct manipulation video navigation, which allows users to navigate a video by dragging an object of interest along its motion trajectory [5, 6, 8], has been extended to assist software tutorial video navigation. Denoue *et al.* developed a text-based tutorial video navigation method that enables users to directly select text content and scroll text in the video as if they were using a text viewer [4]. The *Waken* video player [1] displays tooltips and menus when a user hovers on corresponding tool icons in the video and allows the user to directly click on an icon to search for moments in the video when that tool was used in a separated side panel. Our work is inspired by these methods and further extends direct manipulation video navigation to develop a responsive software tutorial video navigation method. Our method automatically navigates to the proper frame to provide the visual feedback as if the software were responding to the user input, providing a navigation experience of directly using the software.

RESPONSIVE SOFTWARE TUTORIAL VIDEO

Our software tutorial video navigation method consists of two components: *event processing* that captures, analyzes, and visualizes user interaction events in the tutorial video and *user interface* that supports users to directly interact with the visualized events as if they were using the software.

Figure 2 shows an overview of our system. Our system has a video window and a timeline. Unlike timeline video players, our system depicts a selected set of user interaction events like mouse click and drag as visual annotations and overlays them on their corresponding software interface elements, such as buttons and menu items. These events are color-coded and labeled to convey the temporal order. The set of selected events are dynamically adjusted to provide enough information of the tutorial video around the current frame while not cluttering the screen and overwhelming users. The event annotations help users understand the operations performed and the order in which they happen. Users can navigate the video to events of interest by directly interacting with their annotations in the video window. When users click or drag on a software interface element hinted by an event, our system automatically navigates to the proper frame as if the software were responding. For example, clicking the *File* menu on top of the screen will show a drop down menu, or dragging along the arrow will gradually show the brush motion. Note, while our system visualizes the event order, users can click and navigate to any event without necessarily respecting the order. The capability of non-linear navigation provided by our system allows users to quickly locate frames of interest.

Event Processing

Our system records the events of user interaction with the software when screen-capturing the tutorial author's software-use process. Our system currently focuses on mouse activities, namely click and drag. Click events are often used to invoke a tool or select an object and drag events are often used for complex operations like drawing or adjusting parameters. Each extracted event contains the event label (click or drag) and its corresponding trigger location (x, y) and time t. We find that these two interaction events can already capture a range of user interactions with software. More interaction events will be included in future. These events can be gathered using publicly available APIs [3] or through computer vision analysis of the captured tutorial video [1].

Event Analysis and Selection

A software tutorial video often carries a large number of user interaction events. At each frame, visualizing all the events will clutter the video content and overwhelm users. Therefore, our system only selects relevant events to visualize.

Temporal event culling. In software tutorial videos, users often do not need to see all the interaction events in the video at once to perform learning tasks. They often watch a tutorial video for a few seconds, pause, and then switch to the software to perform the operations they just watched [12]. Thus, the interaction events in the local temporal interval around the current frame often provide users enough learning information since they are directly related to the software-using task that users will perform using the software. Therefore, at any video frame, we limit the number of events that will be finally visualized to be 10 in the time interval around the current frame. This time interval is dynamically adjusted to always include at most 10 events at any time. We empirically find that 10 events can already provide users with enough cues for learning the use of the software, while avoiding cluttering the video window and overwhelming users.

Relevant event selection. At each frame, our system displays the current events as well as some past and future events. In this way, the visual annotations of some events will overlay software interface elements that are invisible at the current frame. As illustrated in Figure 3 (b), Event 41 and 42 in the dialog box are still visible after the dialog box disappears later on. These events appear *out of context* and can confuse users. Our system displays an event annotation only if its context is visible. The event context is defined as the visual content around the event location when it is triggered, such as the

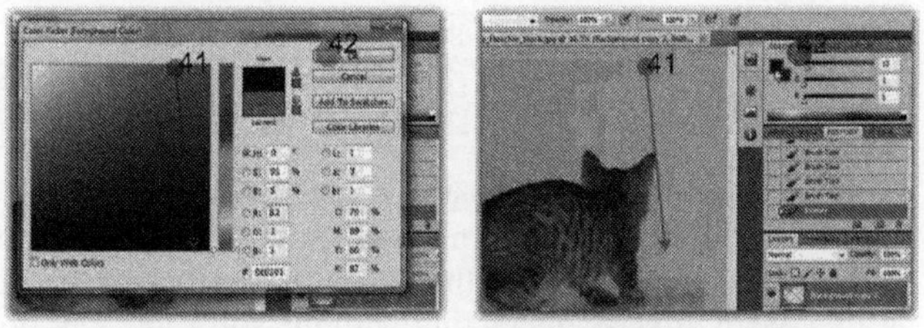

(a) Frame 2632 (b) Frame 2657

Figure 3. Relevant event selection. Event 41 and 42 are in context in (a), but are out of context in (b) where the dialog window disappears.

software interface elements and the image that a user draws on. This task cannot be simply achieved by checking whether the event is triggered at the current frame or not as some event context lasts for an extended amount of time.

We use a visual template matching algorithm to determine if an event context is visible or not. Specifically, we take the pixel patch centered at the event location in the frame when the event is triggered and compare it with the corresponding patch centered at the same location in the current frame. The pixel patch for a click event is a 20×20 window centered at the event location. The pixel patch for a drag event is the bounding box around the dragging path. We use the template matching algorithm in *OpenCV* to compute the similarity between two pixel patches. If the matching score is no less than 0.6, we consider the event context is visible.

In software tutorial videos, some interface elements may change states or appearances when being clicked or dragged. This may cause problems if we only compare the pixel patch in the current frame with that in the event-triggered frame. To address this problem, we also consider frames that contain other states of the event such as idle, hover, and pressed. For each event, we take the event-triggered frame as the pressed-state frame. We search back in the video to find its corresponding hover-state and idle-state frames. These frames are also used for template matching. The maximum matching score between any of these frames and the current frame is used to determine the visibility of an event annotation.

Data adjustment. Sometimes, consecutive mouse activities may occur at nearly the same location [10]. When these events are visualized, their visual annotations will overlap with each other. Our system detects these spatially co-located events and offset their coordinates so that their annotations are separated horizontally by at least 5 pixels. Multiple events can also be triggered in a short time, but at different locations, we merge these events as a single drag event to simplify the visualization and make navigation of these events easier.

Event Visualization

We use graphical annotations to visualize the selected user interaction events. The annotations provide users with navigation cues to quickly locate frames of interest and help them understand the operations performed in the tutorial video. Figure 2 shows the annotations of the click and drag events in our system. Similar to DemoWiz [3], we annotate a click event as a circle centered at the event location and a drag event as a straight arrow that connects the starting and ending point of the path. The start of the arrow is annotated as a circle and the end is annotated as an arrow-head. For the drag event, we uniformly map the frames along the arrow so that users can drag along the arrow to mimic the drag operation in the tutorial video and obtain the corresponding instantaneous feedback, as detailed later. We choose not to visualize the drag event as the exact dragging path to simplify the annotation for both clear visualization and easy navigation. As reported in direct manipulation video navigation research [2], a complex path needs to be simplified for users to drag easily.

To convey the event order, we label each event with a unique number and render it next to the event. We also color-code each event such that the past and future events are rendered in blue and red, respectively.

User Interaction

Our system supports users to directly interact with the event annotations to navigate a software tutorial video as if they were interacting with the software. This is achieved by replicating the software behavior by automatically navigating to a target video frame where the software responds to the user action. Such a target frame is available in the tutorial video after an event is triggered.

We pre-process the event data to find the target frame of each event. For each event, we measure the difference between the event-triggered frame and the following frames. We compute the difference between two frames by counting the number of pixels that are different between two frames. We select the target frame as the frame with the highest difference value within the next 10 frames after the event was triggered. This target frame shows the software's response to the event. For example, the target frame of a right click event on the canvas in *Photoshop* brings in a drop down menu.

After a user clicks an event annotation in the video window, our system calculates and selects the event with the closest spatio-temporal distance to the click location. Then, the video is navigated to the associated target frame of that event, creating an illusion that the software is responding to the user interaction. For example, when watching a tutorial video showing the use of the Gaussian Blur tool in *Photoshop*, the user may want to locate the frame where the tool's dialog box is presented to recall its settings. Instead of scrubbing the timeline in a video player, the user can quickly locate the frame with the dialog box by invoking the same set of operations as in *Photoshop*. That is, the user clicks on the *Filter* menu, then clicks *Blur*, and finally invokes the dialog box by clicking *Gaussian Blur*. Each step is fast and intuitive because the user is guided by the annotated events and can easily click these events to navigate to the desired video segment.

Our system also supports direct scrubbing along the arrow annotation of a drag event to allow a user to mimic the dragging user input. When a user is dragging along the arrow, our system will automatically navigate to the following frames to provide the instantaneous feedback.

EVALUATION

We conducted a preliminary user study in our lab to evaluate how our responsive video navigation method supports users to navigate tutorial videos. We compared our method with a classic timeline interface (*Timeline*).

We asked participants to learn from software tutorial videos to perform two tasks, one using *Excel* and the other using *Photoshop*. We captured and narrated two videos for our study. The *Excel* video (1.85 minutes) shows how to create a column chart, correct its entries, and relocate the chart legends. The *Photoshop* video (1.83 minutes) shows how to apply the *Emboss Filter*, *Apply Image*, and *Fade* tools on an image. The video frame size is 860×546 pixels. We used a desktop PC with two 23-inch monitors, a speaker, a standard mouse and keyboard. Similar to a previous study [12], we displayed the video player in one monitor and the actual software in another one to minimize the effects of the limited screen space.

We used a between-subjects design to avoid the strong learning effect from having a participant perform the same task aided by two methods. 12 users from the university campus participated in our study. Their majors include Computer Science, Accounting, Arts, etc. Their ages range from 18 to 28 years. These participants were randomly assigned to one of the two methods, resulting in 6 participants per method.

Before the study, we showed the final results of the tasks and asked participants if they could produce exactly the same results using the software. All participants responded that they were not sure how to perform the tasks and would need the tutorial videos although about half of them are familiar with *Photoshop* and *Excel*. They were trained to navigate tutorial videos using the method that they would use. The training session used a practice video that lasts 46 seconds and shows how to use some tools in *Photoshop*. These tools are different than those used in the *Photoshop* tutorial video in the formal study. Participants then proceeded to perform the *Excel* and *Photoshop* task. They were told to complete the task with the software as fast and as accurate as possible. Participants click the start and end buttons to record the task completion time.

Results. As reported in Table 1, participants were faster using our method to complete both tasks than *Timeline*. We analyzed the task completion time with an independent-samples t-test. The difference between our method and *Timeline* in the *Excel* task is not statistically significant ($p = 0.34$) and that in the *Photoshop* task is statistically significant ($p < 0.02$).

The subjective feedback shows that most participants who used our method consider that having the tutorial video respond to the user input like a software is very intuitive and helps them easily find frames of interest. They felt that our method helps them perform the tasks faster in the software as they can practice the interactions beforehand in the video.

Limitations. For a long video with a large number of events, it is difficult for our method to provide a concise summary of all the events at once although our method can enable users to quickly navigate through it by directly interacting with the event visualizations. Moreover, our method currently only captures mouse click and drag events. We will incorporate more user interaction events like keyboard inputs in future.

CONCLUSION

This paper presented a dedicated method for software tutorial video navigation. Our method captures user interaction events and visualizes a set of appropriately selected events in the event locations. Our method allows users to navigate a tutorial video and mimic the captured user interactions as if they were directly interacting with the software. Our preliminary study showed that our responsive video navigation method enables users to follow tutorial videos to complete software-use tasks quickly.

	Excel: mean	std	*Photoshop*: mean	std
Timeline	211.0	78.6	218.6	28.8
Ours	177.8	19.5	155.6	45.9

Table 1. The task completion time (in seconds).

Acknowledgments. Figure 2 and 3 use cat images from Pixabay user wilkernet and DevianArt user Oliver Pietern under a Creative Commons license. This work was supported by NSF IIS-1344163, CNS-1205746 and CNS-1218589.

REFERENCES

1. Banovic, N., Grossman, T., Matejka, J., and Fitzmaurice, G. Waken: reverse engineering usage information and interface structure from software videos. In *ACM UIST* (2012), 83–92.
2. Brockly, C. Evaluation of direct manipulation techniques for in-scene video navigation. *Master's thesis, RWTH Aachen University* (2009).
3. Chi, P., Lee, B., and Drucker, S. DemoWiz: re-performing software demonstrations for a live presentation. In *ACM CHI* (2014), 1581–1590.
4. Denoue, L., Carter, S., Cooper, M., and Adcock, J. Real-time direct manipulation of screen-based videos. In *IUI Companion* (Mar. 2013), 43–44.
5. Dragicevic, P., Ramos, G., Bibliowitcz, J., Nowrouzezahrai, D., Balakrishnan, R., and Singh, K. Video browsing by direct manipulation. In *ACM CHI* (2008), 237–246.
6. Goldman, D. B., Gonterman, C., Curless, B., Salesin, D., and Seitz, S. M. Video object annotation, navigation, and composition. In *ACM UIST* (2008), 3–12.
7. Grossman, T., Matejka, J., and Fitzmaurice, G. Chronicle: capture, exploration, and playback of document workflow histories. In *UIST* (2010), 143–152.
8. Karrer, T., Weiss, M., Lee, E., and Borchers, J. Dragon: a direct manipulation interface for frame-accurate in-scene video navigation. In *CHI* (2008), 247–250.
9. Kim, J., Nguyen, P., Weir, S., and Guo, P. Crowdsourcing step-by-step information extraction to enhance existing how-to videos. In *ACM CHI* (2014), 4017–4026.
10. Lafreniere, B., Grossman, T., and Fitzmaurice, G. Investigating the feasibility of extracting tool demonstrations from in-situ video content. In *ACM CHI* (2014), 4007–4016.
11. Matejka, J., Grossman, T., and Fitzmaurice, G. Ambient help. In *ACM CHI* (2011), 2751–2760.
12. Pongnumkul, S., Dontcheva, M., Li, W., and Wang, J. Pause-and-play: automatically linking screencast video tutorials with applications. In *ACM UIST* (2011).

Gaze-Based Annotations for Reading Comprehension

Shiwei Cheng, Zhiqiang Sun
Zhejiang University of Technology
swc@zjut.edu.cn

Lingyun Sun
Zhejiang University
sunly@zju.edu.cn

Kirsten Yee, Anind K. Dey
Carnegie Mellon University
anind@ cs.cmu.edu

ABSTRACT
We study eye gaze movement behavior during paper reading and generate a series of annotations from a user's reading features: gray shading to indicate reading speed, borders to indicate frequency of re-reading, and lines to indicate transitions between sections of a document. Through a user study, we validate that our *SocialReading* system that shares teachers' gaze data for an academic paper can improve students' reading comprehension of that paper.

Author Keywords
Eye Tracking; Fixation; Social Computing.

ACM Classification Keywords
H.5.m. Information interfaces and presentation (e.g., HCI): Miscellaneous.

INTRODUCTION
People often create manual annotations when reading physical books and documents. The annotations not only help them with identifying or remembering some important, interesting or hard to read passages, but can also supply them who re-read, or others who read, the same book or document with deeper understanding [4,9]. Digital annotations for a document can also be useful, *e.g.*, highlights of important passages that are shared with other readers who may share interests. Hence there is the potential for a reader to take advantage of previous readers' experiences and understand a document through a more focused reading process and with greater efficiency. Markitup [4] is a crowdsourced reading tool that projects digital annotations on artifacts, such as physical books. This enables individuals to read and annotate in a collaborative environment and benefit from the knowledge in a social context. However, such a tool uses specialized hardware, limiting deployment and usage.

Traditional manual annotations also have limitations. For example, highlighting a sentence or making a comment takes some manual physical and cognitive effort and cannot reveal readers' visual attention behaviors (*e.g.*, whether the reader just scanned the page or did a focused deep read). In contrast, gaze data can indicate people's visual attention, and visualizations of gaze data can be used as a new kind of annotation. Text 2.0 framework [1] creates annotations from a user's gaze data in real time, such as displaying or highlighting figures when the user gazes at related text descriptions. Others have used eye tracking to monitor what and how many words users read and to detect the type of document being read [6, 7]. Eye tracker and OCR (optical character recognition) techniques have been used to determine which lines users read or skim, to generate document-level annotations (*e.g.*, reading duration) automatically [3]. However, leveraging gaze-based annotations to improve reading comprehension has not been explored.

In this context, we contribute an exploration of gaze-based annotations that visualize visual attention features such as reading speed. We conducted a study of our *SocialReading* system in which we share teachers' (experts) gaze-based annotations with students (non-experts). Although teachers sometimes have different reading patterns due to their expertise and experience (*e.g.*, skip sections), we validated that viewing the teacher's annotations resulted in increased similarities in the reading patterns of students, and improved students' comprehension of the reading material.

GAZE-BASED ANNOTATIONS

Reading-related measures
For this work, we explored visual attention with academic papers and defined each title (or subtitle), paragraph (including references), and figure as an area of interest (AOI). The remaining areas were mostly blank and only infrequently viewed, and therefore we did not code them in our study. Then we record raw gaze data located in each AOI, and analyze them to obtain different measures. Reading-related measures, such as reading speed and reading count, are the most discriminative features for distinguishing very comprehensible from barely comprehensible text passages [2]. Inspired by this research, we define two reading-related measures: (1) Intra-AOI measures: reading speed for a single AOI (a specific part of a document); reading count (frequency) for each AOI. (2) Inter-AOI measures: switching frequency between two AOIs. It can indicate tight semantic relationships among different parts of a document, and is a useful navigation aid for active reading [9].

Reading speed on each AOI
Reading speed can reflect reading interest; for example, users may glance at some boring or well-understood parts of a document and go through them quickly. We denote reading speed for each AOI as the ratio of *saccade length* and *dwell time*. Here *saccade length* is the sum of the

CHI 2015, April 18 - 23 2015, Seoul, Republic of Korea

http://dx.doi.org/10.1145/2702123.2702271

lengths of all saccades on the current AOI including both regression (*i.e.*, back tracking) and skimming saccades (*i.e.*, forward tracking) that can help a reader achieve a better understanding of the information [2, 10]. If the *dwell time* on the current AOI is longer than a predefined *Intra-AOI threshold* (*e.g.*, 1s), we record the reading speed over this period of dwell time, because a short dwell time often means these are spurious glances and not helpful for reading. For example, users will often scroll up and down in a document browser. During this process, their gaze will be located in several AOIs for very short durations, with little specific reading activity occurring. We not only use the threshold to exclude this "noisy" data, but also use it to adjust the visualization results. For example, reducing the *Intra-AOI threshold* will visualize more AOIs to highlight low reading speed, and it may be distracting, causing readers to focus on more parts of the paper than necessary.

Reading count for each AOI

We denote the reading count for each AOI as the number of times a user's gaze returns to that AOI after a period of time of gazing elsewhere (longer than the *Intra-AOI threshold*). It can indicate difficult passages that need to be re-read [8].

Switching frequency

We denote switching frequency as the number of times a user's gaze switches between two AOIs. Here we define "Source AOI" and "Target AOI". If the user's gaze is located in one AOI for longer than the *Intra-AOI threshold*, the AOI is the source AOI; then if the gaze moves to another AOI and remains there for longer than the threshold, that AOI is the target AOI. This helps us filter the data, in this case, for spurious switching. For example, when a user focuses on an AOI, her gaze will unconsciously shift to other AOIs (visual distractors that may attract bottom-up attention [5], *e.g.*, a salient title located nearby) for a short while and then switch back. In addition, two AOIs have tight relationships will be close to each other. So, if the duration time between the gazes departing the source AOI and arriving at the target AOI is lower than a predefined threshold (*Inter-AOI threshold*, *e.g.*, 10s), we indicate that these AOIs are related and increase the switching frequency between these two AOIs by one. Note that we also filter out natural transitions from one paragraph to the next paragraph in the paper, except for cycles where the reader goes back and forth between adjacent paragraphs.

Visual Encodings

We propose the following gaze visualizations to encode the reading-related measures: (1) Gray shading for reading speed: indicates how quickly a user reads a specific AOI (darker indicates faster). (2) Border for reading count: indicates how many times a user focuses on an AOI. Thicker borders around an AOI, indicates a higher reading count for that AOI. (3) Transition line for switching frequency: indicates how many times the user switched between reading two different AOIs. A thicker line indicates more switches between the two connected AOIs. Color indicates links between different pairs of AOIs.

PROTOTYPE SYSTEM

We built our *SocialReading* system using an SMI™ iViewX RED eye tracker and its SDK to record users' gaze data when reading the paper. We auto-calculated our gaze measures, and projected the gaze data onto the corresponding AOIs as annotations (Figure 1).

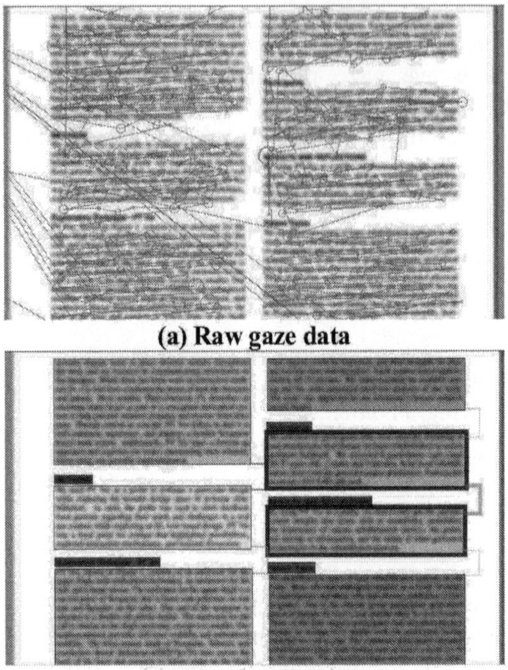

(a) Raw gaze data

(b) Our visualizations

Figure 1. Screenshots of our gaze annotation system.

Raw gaze data is shown in Figure 1(a): the red solid circles represent fixation points, and the red lines connecting them represent the saccades. Figure 1(b) shows the corresponding gaze annotations: gray shade of each paragraph indicates reading speed (lighter means slower), border width indicates reading count (thicker is higher), and colored semi-transparent lines that link two paragraphs indicate gaze switching frequency (thicker is higher). Parameters of the visualization can be configured by the viewer, such as thresholds, transparency, hiding/displaying different visualization layers, to enable the best visual effects. For example, we hide the fixation points and saccades (raw data), and allow users to view our 3 visualization types.

USER STUDY

Participants

Our study has two kinds of participants, two faculty members (one female and one male, ages between 35 and 45, with similar academic backgrounds and expertise) and 30 students (11 females, 19 males, aged between 18 and 37 years, M=24.8, SD=4.6) all from our local participant pool. None of them had any visual impairment. All participants were native English speakers, and had similar backgrounds in HCI. Each student read at least one academic paper every week. We conducted a reading pre-test to screen out student participants who read a 2-page academic paper very quickly (*e.g.*, < 6 min) or slowly (*e.g.*, > 30 min). These checks were performed to identify any obvious differences in reading experiences and general reading abilities.

Apparatus

We used the SMI™ iViewX RED desk-mounted eye tracker (gaze sampling rate was configured to 60Hz) to record gaze data. Its operating distance (between user's gaze and monitor screen) is about 40 to 50cm. In this context, we measured an average accuracy of 0.5 degrees. We selected one academic 4-page paper from the SIGCHI archives for participants to read, because it had clear and compact logic structure and layout, which made it easy to measure and visualize gaze data. It was shown on a 21-inch LCD screen with a resolution of 1680×1050.

Procedure

Faculty member participants read the paper first with no time limit. After reading, each wrote a brief summary of the paper, and answered a questionnaire to assess their reading comprehension. We also recorded their gaze data during their reading process, and visualize them as annotations. A between-subject user study design was chosen to investigate the effect of gaze-based annotations on students' reading comprehension. Hence, student participants were divided into two groups randomly, and then some group members were swapped to balance age and gender. All students read the same paper that the faculty read. There was no time limit, so that each student could read at her own natural reading speed. The students in the control group did so without any annotation. Those in the experimental group received the annotations based on faculty members' gaze data. After paper reading, we used both objective and subjective measures to evaluate students' reading comprehension. Students were asked to answer the comprehension questions about the paper by recalling what they read (objective measure). Each student was also asked to write a brief summary of the paper, and the summary was evaluated by faculty members for reading comprehension quality (subjective measure).

Results

Expert gaze annotations help non-experts improve their comprehension performance

In the questionnaire, there were 5 *fact-finding* (multiple-choice) comprehension questions, whose answers could be found at related sections of the paper. For example, one question was "what is the paper's main contribution", and the answer was in the Introduction. Correct answers were given a score of 1, for a total possible score of 5. A Mann-Whitney U test showed a significant difference in the scores for the control group (M=3.0, SD=1.3) and experimental group (M=3.9, SD=0.8); U=61.0, $p<0.05$.

We asked 2 faculty participants to independently evaluate student summary quality with a 5-point rating (1 is the worst, and 5 is the best). They evaluated the students' summaries similarly, and we averaged their ratings. A Mann-Whitney U test showed a significant difference in the ratings for the control (M=2.2, SD=1.3) and experimental groups (M=3.4, SD=1.2); U=54.0, $p<0.05$.

Expert gaze annotations influence non-experts

Our 4-page test paper had 77 AOIs (AOI1 to AOI77), but 23 were very tiny, in which little gaze data was captured (*e.g.*,titles/subtitles), or were less important for reading comprehension (*e.g.*, references). Accordingly, an analysis comparing the reading similarity (*e.g.*, reading speed) across *all* AOIs for our two conditions (control and experimental group), did not reveal any significant results. To better understand why reading comprehension likely was higher for the experimental group, we focus in on a more fine-grained analysis of particular AOIs. Due to the limited paper length, we just look at a subset of gaze annotation on the same page of the read paper from one faculty participant (see Figure 2). AOI48, AOI50 and AOI54 had salient annotations, such as light gray shadings and thick borders. They indicate that the faculty member read slowly and re-read these AOIs, and also switched gaze between AOI48 and AOI50, and AOI50 and AOI54.

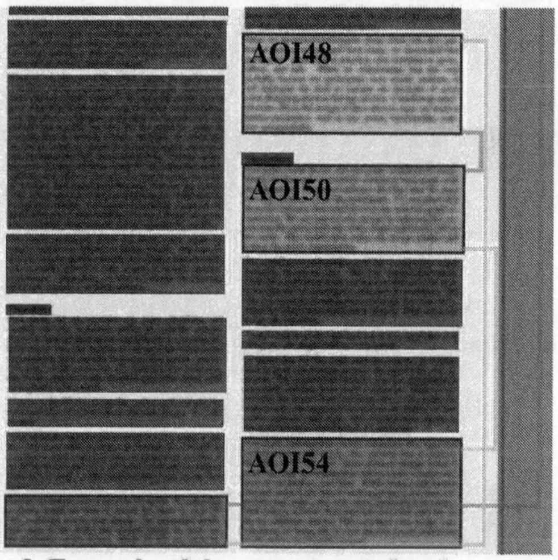

Figure 2. Example of the gaze annotation for some AOIs.

We considered 4 metrics to explore participants' gaze patterns for each AOI: average fixation duration (ms), average saccade length (px), re-reading frequency and switching frequency. We conducted a statistical analysis with Mann-Whitney U tests: (1) For AOI48, there was a significant difference in average fixation duration for the control (M=102.5, SD=77.8) and experimental groups (M=156.8, SD=49.4); U=53.5, $p<0.05$. (2) For AOI50, there was a significant difference in average saccade length for the control (M=62.7, SD=41.3) and experimental groups (M=91.6, SD=30.4); U=58.0, $p<0.05$. (3) For AOI54, there was a significant difference in re-reading frequency for the control (M=0.7, SD=0.5) and experimental groups (M=1.0, SD=0.4); U=77.5, $p<0.05$. There was also a significant difference in switching frequency between AOI54 and AOI50 for the control (M=1.3, SD=1.0) and experimental groups (M=2.0, SD=0.8); U=77.5, $p<0.05$. Accordingly, the metrics of the faculty member were: average fixation duration in AOI48 was 171.4; average saccade length in AOI50 was 110.8; re-reading and switching frequency for AOI54 (to/from AOI50) was 1 and 2, respectively. We also found that gaze patterns of the experimental group in these AOIs were similar to (and likely influenced by) the faculty members, but different from the control group.

Participants find gaze annotations are helpful

From the questionnaire, participants in the experimental group (15 participants) rated (5-point scale, 1= not helpful at all, 2=slightly not helpful, 3=neutral, 4=very helpful, 5=extremely helpful) each type of visualization: gray shading (1, 4, 5, 2, 3 participants rated 1-5 respectively), border (1, 6, 4, 3, 1 participants rated 1-5 respectively) and transition line (3, 3, 4, 3, 2 participants rated 1-5 respectively). 8 participants rated the gray shading (reading speed) to be the most helpful for reading comprehension. 9 participants rated the gaze annotations as being "very helpful" for improving the quality of their summary.

After the questionnaire, we interviewed the experimental group participants. When speaking about the gray shading , some of them said, "*the reading speed visualization is the most visually salient*", "*gray shading distinguishes importance of paragraphs*", and "*professor's reading speed is a good proxy for what is/isn't important, fast reading means content s/he disregards, and slow reading means content s/he deems important*". When speaking about the summary writing using the gaze annotations, some said, "*[gaze annotation] shows you the paper's focal points*", and "*If I and my professor agree that a paragraph is important, then I will know to include it in a summary*".

DISCUSSION

Our approach for visualizing expert readers' gaze data can help non-experts to achieve improved reading comprehension. Here we discuss future modifications to our approach that we will explore. One participant said: "*Do people re-read a paragraph because it is important, or it is poorly written? Also, some people can read an important paragraph quickly because they are familiar with the content*". To address this ambiguity, we will integrate our approach with semantic analysis of documents. This analysis can determine which passages may be difficult to understand *(e.g.,* have professional terms or equations) or are important (*e.g.*, include key words of the paper).

Reading behavior differences between expert and novice readers may reduce the usefulness of our approach. As a participant said: "*Professors have expertise, so they may skip sections. This sometimes makes their visualizations less helpful for students*". We will explore the sharing *other students'* gaze annotations with student readers as well.

When faculty members evaluating the students' summaries for reading comprehension quality, they judged the quality based on their own criteria and experience. Hence, there may be some subjective judging. For example, if one student captured the main point of the paper, but this point was not valued by the faculty member, the student may have low ratings for the reading performance. We will refine our reading comprehension measure. Finally, in our study, the reading styles of two faculty members were similar to each other, so we merged two sets of gaze data before showing the annotations to students. We will continue to explore how to merge multiple annotations when experts' reading styles are different, or visualize these differences for students.

CONCLUSION

We record users' gaze data during their reading process, and then visualize them using reading-related features. We share the gaze-based annotations from faculty reading a paper with students who were asked to read the paper. We found that the gaze-based annotations resulted in greater reading comprehension and increased the similarity between the reading process for the students and faculty.

ACKNOWLEDGMENTS

This work was supported by NSF grant SES-0968566 and NSFC grant 61272308.

REFERENCES

1. Biedert, R., Buscher, G., Schwarz, S., *et al.* Text 2.0. *Ext. Abstracts CHI 2010*, 4003-8.
2. Biedert, R., Dengel, A., Elshamy, M.,*et al.* Towards robust gaze-based objective quality measures for text. *ETRA 2012*, 201-204.
3. Buscher G., Dengel A., Elst, L., *et al.* Generating and using gaze-based document annotations. *Ext. Abstracts CHI 2008*, 3045-3050.
4. Chircop, L., Radhakrishnan, J., Selener, L.,*et al.* Markitup: crowdsourced collaborative reading. *Ext. Abstracts CHI 2013*, 2567-2572.
5. Connor, C. E., Egeth, H. E., and Yantis, S. Visual attention: bottom-up versus top-down. *Current Biology 14*, 19 (2004), 850-852.
6. Kunze, K., Iwamura, M., Kise, K., *et al.* Activity recognition for the mind: toward a cognitive "quantified self". *Computer 46*, 10 (2013), 105-108.
7. Kunze, K., Utsumi, Y., Shiga Y. Kise K.,*et al.* I know what you are reading: recognition of document types using mobile eye tracking. *ISWC 2013*, 113-116.
8. Lenzner, T., Kaczmirek, L., and Galesic, M. Seeing through the eyes of the respondent: an eye-tracking study on survey question comprehension. *Int'l Journal of Public Opinion Research 23*, 3 (2011), 361–373.
9. Tashman, C. and Edwards, W. Active reading and its discontents: the situations, problems and ideas of readers. *CHI 2011*, 2927-2936.
10. Vo, T., Mendis, B. and Gedeon, T. Gaze pattern and reading comprehension. *ICONIP2010*, 124-131.

Long-Term Use of Motion-Based Video Games in Care Home Settings

Kathrin M. Gerling
University of Lincoln
Brayford Pool
Lincoln, LN6 7TS, UK
kgerling@lincoln.ac.uk

Regan L. Mandryk
University of Saskatchewan
110 Science Place
Saskatoon, SK, Canada
regan@cs.usask.ca

Conor Linehan
University of Lincoln
Brayford Pool
Lincoln, LN6 7TS, UK
clinehan@lincoln.ac.uk

ABSTRACT
Recent research suggests that motion-based video games have the potential to provide both mental and physical stimulation for older adults in residential care. However, little research has explored the practical challenges and opportunities that arise from integrating these games within existing schedules of activities in these contexts. In our work, we report on a qualitative enquiry that was conducted over a three month period at two long-term care facilities. Findings suggest that older adults enjoyed playing video games, and that games can be a valuable means of re-introducing challenge in late life, but that the impact of age-related changes and impairment can influence people's ability to engage with games in a group setting. We outline core challenges in the design for care context and discuss implications of our work regarding the suitability of games as a self-directed leisure activity.

INTRODUCTION
Many older adults in Western societies depend on the care of others (e.g., family caregivers, or care facilities). Despite consistent findings that mental and physical activity are crucial for well-being [23], providing stimulating and accessible leisure activities for older adults in residential care can be difficult, due to the impact of age-related changes and impairments. Researchers have explored the potential of video games – particularly motion-based video games requiring some physical effort to play [18] – as an activity appropriate for this audience. Previous work has demonstrated positive effects of such games on the cognitive [2], physical [3] and emotional [13] well-being of older adults in long-term care. In this context, games are frequently cited as a means of fostering social interaction between older adults [26], and one that can be carried out without extensive support [20]. However, this topic has only begun to be explored [12], and the existing research is relatively disjointed. For example, human-computer interaction (HCI) researchers have focused on questions of accessibility and player experience, using research methodologies derived from lab-based usability studies [10]. Researchers from other disciplines have focused primarily on health outcomes [2, 3]. An aspect that has not been explored extensively is the interaction of challenges and opportunities that arise, on a practical basis, from the deployment of games in a group setting in long-term care.

In this paper, we present a qualitative enquiry into the experiences that arose from the deployment of motion-based video games at two care facilities. Weekly gaming sessions were organized for three months at two locations that differed in terms of both the level of care offered and the cognitive and physical ability of participants. Data was analyzed using Thematic Analysis [6] and revealed three main themes of interest: 1) the game experience of older adults; 2) implications of playing games in a social setting; and 3) levels of support required to engage with games. First, our findings suggest that video game playing can be a challenging and appealing activity that allows older adults to experience competence. However, the extent to which people experience the benefit of gaming is determined largely by their specific experience of age-related changes and impairments, as demonstrated by the very different experiences observed in our two study locations. Second, our results show that learning to play new games in a social (i.e., public) context may be uncomfortable for people experiencing vulnerability over their age-related changes and impairments. Third, our results show that some older adults require extensive support, both to gain access to gaming sessions and throughout play, suggesting that the value of games as self-directed activity may be limited for some groups of players.

Our work makes three contributions: (1) we provide an enquiry into the deployment of video games at two fundamentally different long-term care facilities, a senior residence that offers assisted living for older adults, and a care home that accommodates older adults with cognitive and physical impairment; (2) we discuss elements of shared video game play that may increase the vulnerability of older adults, and we address the value of shared play for community building; and (3) we identify challenges in the deployment of games in care facilities, and outline

CHI 2015, April 18 – 23, 2015, Seoul, Republic of Korea.

http://dx.doi.org/10.1145/2702123.2702125

strategies to support designers wishing to create engaging games for older adults in long-term care.

If games are to benefit older adults in long-term care, it is crucial to examine the gaming experiences of older adults, and to develop a more detailed understanding of the potential benefits and risks of video gaming in the caregiving context to ensure that games provide positive and empowering experiences for older adults regardless of age-related changes and impairments.

RELATED WORK

In this section, we summarize existing research efforts addressing the deployment of technologies in residential care and game development for older adults.

Technology to Facilitate Caregiving and Assisted Living

Technologies to facilitate caregiving and to support assisted living are an important and active area of research. Much work in the field of human-computer interaction has focused on improving the caregiving process [7], e.g., by deploying information technology to monitor older adults and thereby support caregivers [15], or the development of systems in the field of ambient-assisted living that aim to help older adults maintain independence, e.g., applications to facilitate medication routines [14].

Technology to Connect and Entertain

Other researchers have focused on the deployment of technology to improve the quality of life of older adults in residential care by fostering mental, physical and social activity. Blythe et al. [4] report on the deployment of four interactive interventions in a care home in the UK, which were designed to stimulate older adults by enhancing their awareness of their surroundings. They showed that playful applications can foster socialization between older adults and across generations by providing tickets to talk. Work by Müller et al. [19], exploring the deployment of a large-screen display in a German care home, suggests that technology can help older adults connect with each other and staff members. Finally, Lindley et al. [16] present a literature review that suggests that technology can be applied to help older adults maintain relationships with family members and friends, and outline play as one of the main areas of interest in HCI for older adults.

Video Games for Older Adults

In this context, the design of video games has been approached from two perspectives, (1) looking at how older adults interact with commercially available games, and (2) the design of video games addressing the needs of older adults from the perspective of human-computer interaction.

Deploying Commercially Available Games

Researchers have explored potential benefits of video game play on the emotional well-being of institutionalized older adults. A six-week study by Jung et al. [13] showed that video game play had a significantly higher positive impact on participants' overall well-being than traditional board games. Marston et al. [17] present a review of long-term studies that deploy commercially-available video games in residential care. Their summary shows that such games have the potential of fostering social interaction and improving the emotional well-being of older adults in residential care; however, many studies follow a quantitative approach (e.g., [13]) instead of exploring the value of games in the context of day-to-day routines of care, and do not examine the effects of play on older adults with a wide range of cognitive and physical abilities. In this context, results of an uncontrolled longitudinal quantitative study by Ulbrecht et al. [27] suggest that cognitive functioning has a profound impact on institutionalized older adults' engagement with motion-based video games. In our work, we follow up on these findings through a qualitative enquiry that investigates how the context of play and individual abilities influence older adults' engagement.

Designing Games for Older Adults

Research has addressed game design for older adults from different perspectives, exploring the value of games to entertain, to connect players, and as a tool to support therapy and rehabilitation. For example, Rice et al. [24] explore how motion-based games can foster inter-generational play between younger and older adults, showing that games have the potential to connect different generations. Uzor and Baille [28], as well as Alankus et al. [1], demonstrate that motion-based games can successfully be applied to motivate participation in physical therapy and rehabilitation in the home. Specifically investigating the use of gaming technology in group settings, Pedell et al. [21] explore the value of mobile gaming applications to connect older adults. Their results show that games may bring older adults together, but also note that "some older adults are shy in groups". Gerling et al. [10, 11] investigate the design of motion-based game interfaces for older adults in residential care, focusing on the individual player experience of institutionalized older adults, as well as general considerations regarding game accessibility.

On a general level, while work on games for therapy and rehabilitation has previously addressed aspects related to the long-term engagement of older adults with games in their own home [1, 28] and in long-term care [27], little is known about social and contextual dynamics that develop when older adults in residential care are invited to engage with games. A first enquiry into this area is provided by Harley et al. [12] who explore how older adults in long-term care engage with Nintendo Wii Sports Bowling. In our work, we build on their findings and further explore how older adults in residential care approach games, and how individual cognitive and physical abilities as well as the social setting influence their experience.

EXPLORING GAMES FOR OLDER ADULTS IN RESIDENTIAL CARE

In our case study, we provide a qualitative enquiry into the experiences of older adults living at two long-term care facilities who were invited to engage with video games in the context of three months of weekly gaming sessions.

The Care Facilities

We worked with two care facilities to study how different groups of older adults experience video game play; Brightwater Senior Living – referred to as 'the senior residence' – is a senior residence offering independent and assisted living apartments, and Sherbrooke Community Centre – referred to as 'the care home' – is a nursing home that provides extensive care for its residents.

Brightwater Senior Living is a newly opened, privately run senior residence in Saskatoon, SK, Canada. The residence offers independent and assisted living apartments for older adults. Most residents are independent or only experience mild age-related changes and impairments that do not have a severe impact on their ability of attending to personal needs. At the time of the study, the oldest resident was 96 years old, and the youngest resident was aged 59. The routines at the home are roughly structured by three optional meals served in a restaurant-style area (residents also have a kitchenette in their apartment), as well as morning and afternoon activities. Activities are usually facilitated by staff and include physical exercise, cultural activities (e.g., museum visits) and creative expression (e.g., writing and painting), as well as movie showings and excursions to local leisure facilities (e.g., bowling). Staff is available throughout the day to support residents based on individual needs. While most residents require light assistance (e.g., cleaning services), others experience higher levels of age-related changes that result in a need for support in personal areas (e.g., running errands).

Sherbrooke Community Centre is a government-funded care facility in Saskatoon, SK, Canada, that specializes in providing care for individuals with special needs, including older adults who experience high levels of age-related impairments, e.g., persons with dementia or complex mobility disabilities. The facility follows the Eden Alternative[1] approach to care, which emphasizes the importance of meaningful activities and community living in caregiving for older adults. It also offers palliative care and a day program. At the time of the study, the oldest resident was more than 100 years old. The day is broken up by three meals during which some residents require assistance, as well as optional morning and afternoon activities. Leisure activities offered at Sherbrooke range from physical activity, movie afternoons, and bingo sessions to music and entertainment (e.g., pizza nights). They generally take place at the care facility and are supported by several members of staff. Most residents require extensive assistance when attending to personal needs (e.g., getting dressed, bathing, or being taken to the toilet), and medical routines; this support mostly takes place in the early morning or replaces participation in optional leisure activities. Additionally, many residents also rely on assistance getting around the care facility, e.g., help to attend meals and social events.

Figure 1-4. Screenshots of the four games applied in this study (top to bottom): Prairie Hunter, Candy Kids, Harvest Time, and Cooking Challenge.

Games

Keeping in mind the different groups of older adults at the two care facilities, we developed custom-designed games to ensure that participants would be able to gain access to video game play regardless of age-related changes and prior knowledge on how to play games. Additionally, we included commercially available video games to offer examples of more complex video game play.

Custom-Designed Games

We created four games based on design recommendations for games for older adults [10, 29]. All games can be played in single-player or competitive multiplayer mode. In *Candy Kids*, players have to feed a child different types of candy: items move across the upper area of the screen and can be fed to the child by moving the player avatar (represented by a virtual hand hand) over the food at the same time. *Prairie Hunter* invites players to set out on a virtual animal hunt. In order to increase their score, they have to hunt as many animals as possible. This is achieved by moving the crosshairs over the animal. Both Candy Kids and Prairie Hunter use *pointing input*, where the player's hand controls an avatar within the game. In *Cooking Challenge*, players have to prepare a salad. Ingredients are presented in the central area of the screen and have to be cut into pieces by imitating chopping movements and then pushed into the bowl by extending one's hand to the front. Once all ingredients are added, they have to be mixed which can be achieved by the imitation of a mixing gesture. *Harvest Time* invites players to cut down an apple tree using the same chopping gesture as in the previous game, and then shake the tree by moving one's hand left and right until an apple drops, and handing the apple to a girl who appears on screen by extending one's arm to the front. Cooking Challenge and Harvest Time implement gesture-based input that tries to mimic the real-world actions associated with the content of the games.

All games were implemented in C# using Microsoft XNA Game Studio 4.0, and are played using the Microsoft

[1] http://www.edenalt.org/about-the-eden-alternative/

Kinect. Our implementation invites players to use their strong hand to perform gestures and pointing actions to control the avatar.

Commercially Available Games

We included two commercially available games in our study. Both games are played on the Microsoft Xbox 360 and use the Kinect sensor as input device. Games were selected to represent casual Kinect gaming, and because input paradigms were likely to be accessible to older adults.

Kinect Sports. Kinect Sports offers a range of mini games that are based off traditional sports. In our study, we included Kinect Sports Bowling, a bowling simulation that is controlled by imitating real-world motions associated with bowling, e.g., swinging one's arm back and to the front to throw the ball. The game supports up to four players and allows for quick turn-taking similar to the actual sport. Additionally, games that were offered to residents included track and field (controlled through foot-based input), and boxing (imitation of boxing movements with one's arms), in which two players directly compete against each other.

Kinect Adventures. Kinect Adventures is a full-body motion-based video game that consists of a number of mini-games in which players are invited to apply their whole body to overcome in-game challenges in outdoor and fantasy settings. In our study, we included the following three games: In River Rush, the player stands on a raft and has to navigate down a river by jumping, ducking, and stepping to the sides. Space Pop is a game in which players need to flap their arms and move back and forth to float in a box that simulates a gravity-free environment to collect bubbles. In Rally Ball, players use a ball to hit targets displayed at the end of a box-sized playing area; after each strike, the ball bounces back to the player and he or she can use their body (i.e., arms and legs) to attempt another strike.

Games can be played in single player mode or with a partner; gameplay usually lasts for a couple of minutes. Both games use the Microsoft Kinect sensor as input device, if games are controlled with hand gestures, users are invited to use their strong hand.

Procedure

At each of the facilities, we offered a weekly supervised gaming session over the course of three months. In total, residents had the opportunity of participating in twelve supervised sessions. In addition, we invited residents to engage with the games outside the gaming sessions to understand whether games could serve as self-directed leisure activity. At the senior residence, supervised gaming sessions were paused for a month after the first two months to understand whether older adults would still engage in weekly play regardless of the availability of a facilitator. During this time, a member of staff was available to set up the gaming system, but did not facilitate play. We had planned to follow the same scheme at the care home, but were unable to do so because of the level of support required by participants. Players at the care home were unable to gain access to the set of commercially available games due to the complexity and nature of input (e.g., sequential actions necessary to play both Kinect and Wii Bowling, or participants with complex needs who would not be able to hold the Wii Remote – the home in fact owns a Wii, but residents do not use it due to accessibility barriers), and only interacted with the custom-designed games. Participants at the senior residence played the custom-designed games during the first month of the activity, and gradually transitioned to playing commercially available Kinect games. At the senior residence, gaming sessions were hosted in a community room. Games were displayed on a 40" TV screen. At the care home, gaming sessions were hosted in a media room on the floor that most residents lived on. Games were displayed on a 46" TV screen. Player input was tracked using the Kinect sensor.

This study was approved by the University of Saskatchewan behavioural ethics board, and was granted operational approval by Saskatoon Health Region. Additionally, it was approved by the internal review board at Sherbrooke Community Centre. Regarding consent procedures, we obtained informed written consent from participants at Brightwater Senior Living, and we obtained oral assent from participants at Sherbrooke Community Centre, which was witnessed and signed by a guardian acting on the behalf of the participant.

Method

We made observations and kept notes during each supervised gaming session, and at the end of each month, older adults participated in a focus group interview to reflect upon their gaming experience. Questions were designed to investigate the perceptions of video games among older adults (e.g., "What are your thoughts on the games that you played during the past month? Was there anything that you did not like?"). Additionally, we collected demographic information to gain insights into the personal background of participants, and examined their cognitive fitness using Folstein's Mini Mental State Exam (MMSE) [9] prior to their first gaming session. It was decided not to video or audio record gaming sessions to minimise the intrusiveness of our research upon this sensitive environment as much as possible.

Participants

Sixteen older adults (care home: six participants, one female, senior residence: ten participants, seven female) participated over the course of the study. Participants were recruited with the help of staff (social director and volunteer coordinator). At the care home, the average participant age was 73.5 (SD=4.18). All participants required walking assistance and were using wheelchairs. Mean scores for the Mini-Mental State Exam (MMSE) were at 13.3 points (SD=1.86), suggesting that all participants experience significant cognitive impairments.

Only two participants had prior video game experience, mainly focusing on casual games. At the senior residence, average participant age was 79.2 (SD=4.80). Four participants used walkers, however, all of them were able to play the games without assistance. One participant used a wheelchair. Mean MMSE scores of 27 (SD=2.33) showed that none of the participants experienced significant cognitive impairments. Two participants had prior experience playing casual games on the computer or iPad.

Data Analysis

We report both quantitative and qualitative results and then provide explanations of our findings. Qualitative data were analyzed using inductive Thematic Analysis [6]. Interview results and observations were transcribed by the main investigator, analysis was carried out in line with the six phases of Thematic Analysis as proposed by Braun and Clarke [6]. We identified three main themes and nine subthemes. Table 1 shows an overview of the coding structure and relative frequencies at each facility.

Results

We organize our results around themes that were identified during analysis of qualitative data, and we contrast observations that we made at the two care facilities.

Exploring The Game Experience of Older Adults

The main theme that emerged during our analysis was the game experience of older adults, and we identified three subthemes: *player experience and engagement* is focused on the participants' perceptions of the games, *competition and challenge* explores how older adults perceive these core elements of games, and *ownership of the gaming sessions* summarizes participants' input that shaped the activity.

Player experience and engagement. Data on session attendance (Figure 5) show that seven of the ten participants at the senior residence and three out of six participants at the care home participated in at least half of the gaming sessions. The drop in attendance at the care home was caused by lack of support staff to help older adults attend gaming sessions, see theme "Support Before and After Play". Analysis of focus group interviews shows that older adults who continued to participate in our study generally consider motion-based games an enjoyable activity, pointing out that "*it's fun to do something physical*" (P2, senior residence); many participants at the senior residence explained that they enjoyed playing video games that simulated real-world activities they can no longer participate in. When asked about differences between custom-designed mini games and commercially available games, players at the senior residence pointed out that the mini games were appropriate to get more familiar with video games, but that the long-term appeal of more complex commercially available applications was bigger, which is also reflected by their choice of games throughout the gaming sessions where participants increasingly requested to play Kinect Sports Bowling. Participants at the

Table 1. Structure and relative code distribution within each theme at the care home (CH) and senior residence (SR).

Theme	Subtheme	%CH	%SR
Game Experi-ence	Enjoyment & Engagement	39	33
	Challenge & Competition	44	49
	Ownership	17	18
Social Setting	Player Inhibition	55	18
	Disruptive Interactions	45	23
	Community Value	0	59
Support	Group Support	0	47
	Facilitator Support	50	47
	Staff Support	50	6

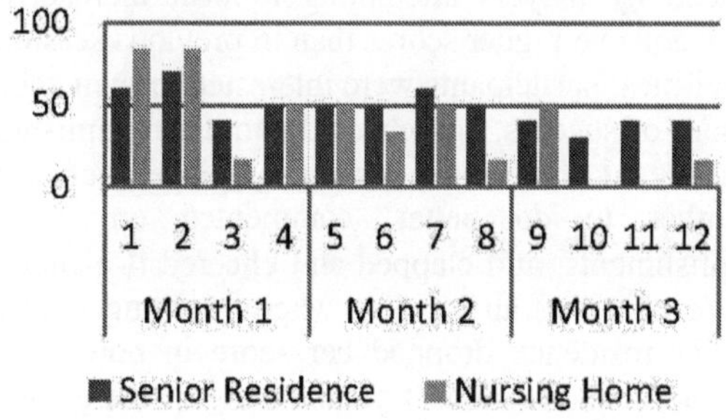

Figure 5. Attendance rates of supervised gaming sessions (in percent per week) at the senior residence and nursing home.

care home preferred playing the hunting game due to the appeal of the theme and simplicity of game input; participants at both facilities reported physical fatigue as a result of motion-based play.

To better understand the game experience of older adults, we followed up with participants who decided to quit the activity. Many participants who permanently dropped out of the gaming sessions pointed out that they simply lost interest in playing video games. One participant stated she found out "*it simply wasn't my cup of tea*" (P5, care home), another one outlined she felt she could "*do better things with my time*" (P7, senior residence), outlining the need for further research to explore suitable game concepts for older adults. Some players commented on being bored during the course of the session, particularly if games did not support quick turn-taking (e.g., Kinect Adventures), or if changing between players took too much time (particularly at the care home due to prevalence of age-related impairments), with one participant falling asleep during the gaming session while waiting his turn. Finally, health issues were a barrier to continued participation for participants at both facilities. While some participants only experienced minor health problems (e.g., feeling tired or seasonal illness) that caused them to miss single sessions and allowed them to join up with the group after their recovery, three participants who showed great interest in the initial gaming sessions (one at the care home, two at the senior residence) permanently dropped out due to major health problems (e.g., long-term hospitalization).

Game challenge and competition. Observations made during our study revealed that challenge and competition play an important role in the gaming experience of the participants at both facilities, suggesting that overcoming challenge – a core aspect of video games – can be a strong source of enjoyment, but also induce frustration and discouragement. Many participants pointed out that they enjoy a feeling of accomplishment when successfully overcoming in-game challenges. At the senior residence, accomplishment mostly stemmed from competition with other players, but also from some individual achievement (e.g., throwing a strike in bowling). At the care home, accomplishment was associated with successfully being able to engage with the games; challenge was sometimes introduced by players attempting to beat themselves by trying to achieve higher scores than in previous sessions. At both facilities, participants were interested in their scores as a measure of success, and cheered about accomplishments. Particularly at the senior residence, players encouraged each other to do better, commented on individual accomplishments, and clapped and cheered if a player did well. We observed an incident where a stronger player at the senior residence dropped her score in bowling when another participant couldn't get the hang of the game. This reduced the negative experience for other player and allowed her to ease back into play.

Our analysis also revealed negative aspects of the competitive nature of play. Participants at both facilities showed frustration and disappointment when not performing as well as expected. This is particularly difficult in the context of social play. For example, one player at the care home brought along a friend to a gaming session, and got visibly angry when he could not keep up with her. Likewise, participants at the senior residence became frustrated about a particularly strong player when engaging with the custom-designed mini games and refused to compete against her in future sessions. We also observed potentially harmful forms of discouragement as a result of competition. Comments of weaker players at the senior residence revealed signs of self-consciousness after watching stronger players, and some were discouraged by large score gaps. Two female participants in particular were very hard on themselves, reflecting upon their own skills and the impact of age-related changes, with one of them commenting that "*I can hardly walk, how can I bowl?*"

Ownership of gaming experience. At both facilities, participants took ownership of their gaming experience. While players at the care home mostly expressed preferences in some mini games over others, players at the senior residence did not only choose preferred games from the pool offered in the context of the activity, but also inquired about other commercially available games that might be suitable for them. In particular, two participants had a personal interest in winter sports and considered the purchase of Kinect Winter Stars after it had been identified as a suitable candidate. Furthermore, players at the senior residence gradually extended the duration of the gaming sessions beyond the facilitated time, and considered the introduction of a second session later in the week.

Implications of Playing Games in a Social Setting

Our analysis revealed that playing games together with a group of others in the context of a programmed activity had a profound impact on the experience of the participants. In our data, we identified three recurring subthemes: The *inhibition of player engagement* as a result of the group setting, and *disruptive interactions* between players that negatively influenced the experience of individuals, but also the large *potential that games have to build community* between players.

Inhibition of player engagement. Participants at both facilities felt that playing video games in front of their peers was intimidating. Players at the senior residence were mostly concerned about the process of learning how to play and needed encouragement during the first gaming sessions. During the focus group interview, one participant noted that she would have been more comfortable during this stage without the presence of others, stating she felt as if "*everybody was watching, you know they are there*" (P3, senior residence). Another participant had a discouraging experience when first playing Kinect Adventures. One of the mini games required him to lift both arms; however, he was unable to reach high enough, exposing his age-related impairment in front of other group members. Likewise, the group setting caused major problems for participants at the care home. Observations revealed that players found it extremely difficult to learn how to interact with the games in front of a group and were self-conscious about their ability to play games, which is backed up by interview results where one participant was pointing out that you "*gotta work your way into the games, then it's okay [to play with others]*". Two participants specifically suggested that they would prefer individual gaming sessions, and one participant who continued to participate in these individual sessions outlined that he enjoyed playing on his own, because he could play at his own pace and "*not worry about what others are doing*" (P2, care home).

Disruptive interactions. The group setting occasionally caused friction among participants at both facilities. We observed disruptive interactions between individual participants, within the group, and as a result of the general setting. Participants at the care home mostly experienced basic communication problems due to the impact of age-related changes. For example, at one point, a participant with a hearing impairment tried to communicate with another participant who had a speech impairment, both growing increasingly frustrated about the inability of the other person to understand what they were trying to express. Disruptive interactions between individuals at the senior residence mostly took place on a higher level, e.g., one participant attending one of the gaming sessions with bare feet, offending another participant who felt the attire was inadequate for the group event. A quick conversation revealed that the barefoot participant was unwilling to put on shoes, which caused the other person to leave the session in disagreement. Finally, participants at the senior residence became openly frustrated about other players who did not understand the turn-taking process and therefore acted out of turn (e.g., when playing Kinect Sports Bowling) on multiple occasions. During one session, this led to the early departure of one participant. However, emerging conflict was usually resolved through group intervention.

Community value. In contrast to the often-difficult experiences of social play at the care home, gaming sessions at the senior residence revealed great potential to build community over the course of the programmed activity. As the residence was a newly established facility, participants of the gaming sessions did not know each other prior to participation in the activity, and we observed that shared play served as a catalyst for community building. We observed how participants gradually became more familiar with each other over the weeks (e.g., learning each other's names), and communication throughout the sessions evolved beyond play and moved on to topics not directly related to the games. Within the first month, a core group of four participants emerged that would continuously engage in the sessions. We observed that this group grew closer every week (e.g., sharing personal stories, and making arrangements to have lunch together at the end of the session), but at the same time remained welcoming and supportive of new members, actively encouraging the participation of other residents in the gaming sessions. Additionally, other residents, staff, and guests frequently dropped into gaming sessions to spectate, suggesting that the activity may also provide value for persons not actively participating in play. Feedback collected during focus groups at the senior residence supports the appeal of gaming sessions as social activity. Participants highlighted that they enjoyed the opportunity to meet other residents, pointing out that "*it's being involved that feels good*" (P8, senior residence) and that "*it's good fun to be together and participate*" (P3, senior residence).

Forms of Support Before and During Play

Another theme that emerged during analysis is focused around support that older adults require to participate in gaming sessions. We identified three subthemes – staff support and facilitator support, which are both external sources initially required at both care facilities, and group support, which focuses on participant efforts of taking ownership of the gaming sessions at the senior residence.

Staff support. At each of the care facilities, different levels of staff support were necessary to support the gaming sessions. At the senior residence, staff activity was limited to the recruitment of participants by announcing the activity to residents, and the support of an additional month of play by setting up the gaming system, but then withdrawing from the sessions and leaving them to the participants. In contrast, staff was required before all gaming sessions at the care home. Due to the prevalence of age-related impairments, participants depended on the support of staff to be able to attend the gaming sessions: many older adults at the care home needed help when navigating their environment (e.g., to attend meals). If staff was unavailable due to other tasks (e.g., supervising community outings), residents could not be helped to transfer into their wheelchairs, and moved to the media room and could therefore not participate in gaming sessions, which is reflected by low attendance rates of gaming sessions during month three, where the social coordinator who had previously supported residents was on leave, and no other support staff was available (Figure 5).

Facilitator support. Facilitator support was offered for all of the gaming sessions. At both facilities, participants received an introduction to the games, and the facilitator was available to set up the gaming system and guide participants through gaming sessions similar to support available during other activities (e.g., a fitness instructor during physical activity sessions). While participants at the senior residence mostly needed support when switching between games (e.g., help navigating complicated menu structures of Kinect games) and some support organizing the session (e.g., assistance to organize turn-taking through verbal cues when feedback of the game is unclear, especially when playing Kinect Sports Bowling), participants at the care home heavily relied on the facilitator over the entire session, needing assistance when swapping players (e.g., pushing wheelchairs), but also continuous help while engaging with the games (e.g., reminders on how to interact, the goal of the game, etc.).

Group support. At the senior residence, facilitator support throughout the gaming sessions was gradually replaced by group support. This is another example of how participants took ownership of gaming sessions, actively explaining how to play the games to persons that decided to participate in the activity after the initial introduction. Throughout the sessions, the group also played a role in supporting weaker players, e.g., by reminding them of interaction paradigms: one participant with early onset dementia repeatedly forgot part of the interaction sequence necessary to play Kinect Sports Bowling, and the group patiently reminded her of the necessary steps. Additionally, stronger players also shared strategies for improvement with the group; particularly when playing Kinect Sports Bowling and Boxing, ways for improvement were frequently debated. Finally, the group also took over staff support that would have been necessary to remind participants of the activity prior to session start by making their rounds through the residence and informing others about the activity.

CORE CHALLENGES IN THE DEPLOYMENT OF GAMES IN LONG-TERM CARE

This section provides insights into the core challenges related to the development and deployment of video games in residential care that stem from the three main themes identified in our work. We particularly focus on differences that we observed between participants at the care home and senior residence that emerged as a result of different levels of age-related changes in cognitive and physical abilities.

(1) Considering the Ambiguity of Social Play
Our results suggest that playing games in a social setting introduces challenges and opportunities for older adults and their peers. While the opportunity to socialize with other residents represented one of the biggest pulls to participate at the senior residence, having to play games in a group created additional barriers for players at the nursing home. It is therefore important that game designers understand the ambiguity of social play. On the one hand, it is an opportunity for older adults to come together as a group, allowing older adults to enjoy the company of others while watching them play. On the other hand, social play and the presence of others can be a barrier for persons who experience higher levels of age-related changes and impairments, have little confidence in their ability of playing games, or are not comfortable being observed when learning how to play. While a lot of research highlights the potential benefits of social play, particularly in the context of games for older adults [21], it is important that designers understand the risk of games exposing the vulnerability of institutionalized older adults by revealing individual age-related changes, which is particularly challenging when working with persons with cognitive or physical impairments. In this context, game developers need to re-think traditional design principles: challenging players and pushing limits in multiplayer settings may be appealing for active older adults, but can turn into a major barrier for players who are challenged to adapt to cognitive and physical changes later in life.

(2) Providing Adequate Levels of Challenge
Previous work has identified game challenge as one of the core motivations for active older adults to engage with games [8]. Our work suggests that challenge can indeed function as a source of long-term player motivation. Regardless of cognitive and physical abilities, participants at both facilities enjoyed and sought out the feeling of accomplishment experienced after successfully overcoming challenging in-game tasks. However, differences in player abilities and their impact on play also underline the importance of offering adequate levels of challenge. Game challenge also functioned as a source of frustration and discouragement when players were unable to meet the goals specified in the game, or unable to match the scores of their co-players. This highlights a risk for the emotional well-being of players if failure is perceived as a consequence of age-related changes rather than weak game balancing. However, frustration at failure is a natural consequence of participating in challenging activities, so game designers cannot design to avoid these types of experiences entirely. Therefore, designers must be creative in designing challenges that do not repeatedly present frustrating and discouraging experiences while accommodating a wide range of cognitive and physical abilities among players.

(3) Embedding Games in the Context of Long-Term Care
Our study shows that the long-term deployment of games in residential care facilities requires considerations that take into account aspects of daily life in residential care facilities, particularly the availability of staff or volunteers to support residents in attending and setting up gaming sessions, and the ability of residents of taking ownership of gaming sessions. Previous studies [10, 17] have discussed the role of staff members in the basic upkeep and setup of games. Our study shows that depending on the nature of care facility, more specialized help is often necessary. While participants at the senior residence took the lead in facilitating gaming sessions beyond system setup, participants at the care home who experienced age-related cognitive and physical impairments required additional assistance to be able to participate in play. Specifically, if older adults require the support of staff to be able to attend gaming sessions as observed at the care home, care facilities must provide higher levels of assistance in order for gaming sessions to function as accessible and successful activities for their residents. However, games could be designed to better accommodate group support (i.e., independent older adults leading sessions) by offering accessible setup routines, increasing group ownership and reducing the need of staff support.

DISCUSSION
This paper presents a qualitative enquiry into the long-term deployment of motion-based video games for older adults in residential care. Our results suggest that playing video games in the context of a weekly activity is enjoyable and empowering for independent older adults, but difficult when persons experience complex age-related changes and impairments. These changes impact a person's ability to engage with games for reasons beyond simple game accessibility, for example, influencing how older adults view the context of play and how much assistance they require. In this section, we discuss the implications of our findings. We summarize key considerations in designing video games to be deployed in residential care, and we discuss the role of games in the lives of older adults.

Designing for Older Adults in Residential Care
Previous studies suggest that accessible games for institutionalized older adults can be created by accounting for age-related changes [10, 11]; while these considerations remain valid in the context of our work, results suggest that this is only a first step toward the successful deployment of games in long-term care, and that a more comprehensive approach to development is necessary. Age-related changes and impairments do not only influence whether basic gameplay is accessible, but how older adults see themselves in the gaming context, how they perceive the participation of others, and how they respond to in-game challenge. These aspects need to be reflected by game concepts; the range of skills and abilities among older adults in

residential care is wide; to be successful, games need to engage players of all abilities, meaning that games may have to be tailored towards specific groups.

Understanding the Role of Games in Residential Care

Our study provides new insights into the role of games for older adults in residential care. In the following sections, we discuss the value of games as a self-directed leisure activity, and we explore whether games could serve as a means of re-introducing challenge in the lives of older adults in long-term care.

Games as a Self-Directed Leisure Activity

Previous research has suggested that video game playing can function as a valuable self-directed leisure activity for older adults in residential care. The findings of our study suggest a more nuanced understanding is needed of the audience targeted by a game in order to ensure that those benefits are experienced. Specifically, for people with more advanced age-related changes and impairments, the deployment of games becomes increasingly challenging and requires extensive support of nursing staff both prior to play and during gaming sessions. For these participants, games cannot be considered an independent activity to participate in without the support of others. This must be considered carefully when evaluating the benefits of games compared to other supervised leisure activities in care facilities.

Games as a Source of Challenge in Late Life

For many people, overcoming challenges and accomplishing goals are important contributors to their self-efficacy and self-esteem [22]. In late life, we can no longer accomplish many of the tasks from which we once drew a sense of achievement. Research suggests that older adults who adapt and find new sources of challenge and self-esteem have better mental health [5]. However, residential care environments rarely present challenging activities, to older adults. Our work shows that games may be a means of re-introducing challenge in the lives of older adults in long-term care: if games provide appropriate levels of challenge, they are a means of enabling older adults to experience accomplishment, can foster competition, and allow older adults to experience competence within their peer group.

Satisfying Needs through Games

Ryan et al. [25] have demonstrated that video games can be a means of needs satisfaction because they allow players to experience competence, autonomy, and relatedness in combination with an experience of immersion and intuitive control. Examining our work through the lens of needs satisfaction sheds an interesting light on our findings. In residential care, games offer an opportunity to experience competence; however, in situations where games highlight age-related changes, they may actually reduce perceived competence. Games offer players the opportunity to socialize and satisfy their need for relatedness; however, the embarrassment of not keeping up with peers might prevent the satisfaction of this need. Finally, giving players in residential care the opportunity to choose participate in play can help satisfy their need for autonomy; however, presenting games as a leisure option where people feel like they are not participating under their own volition can reduce this experience. Therefore, to allow older adults in long-term care to leverage games to satisfy their core needs for overall well-being, the unique effects of age-related changes and challenges associated with the context of long-term care must be considered.

LIMITATIONS AND FUTURE WORK

There are limitations to the work discussed in this paper; our study is of an exploratory nature and only includes a small number of participants at both care facilities; our findings presented in this paper should be viewed in this light. In this context, our study provides several opportunities for future work. First, studying the long-term gaming behaviour of older adults in a quantitative context would be valuable to expand on the findings of our qualitative enquiry. Addressing the question of how games could be designed to facilitate the involvement of staff, and how care facilities could best be supported in the deployment of games is an important step towards supporting care facilities wishing to turn video games into a valuable leisure activity for their residents. Additionally, conducting research with a detailed focus on social aspects of play among older adults – for instance, the role of competition among players – could provide further insights into how games can successfully be applied to strengthen social relationships among care home residents.

CONCLUSION

Understanding how older adults in residential care experience video game play in the context of a programmed activity is important to arrive at a better understanding of how games can be applied to benefit this audience. Our results suggest that playing games in a social setting can be an empowering and appealing experience for independent older adults, but may expose the vulnerability of those who experience age-related impairments. Generally, our work shows that games offer an opportunity of diversifying leisure activities in long-term care, and may be leveraged to promote positive self-views among older adults. However, to offer these benefits, the research community needs to be aware of the risks of play for vulnerable older adults, and carefully design games to meet their needs. This is particularly important when evaluating the value of games for improving the quality of life of older adults, and when creating games with a purpose beyond entertainment, such as therapy and rehabilitation.

ACKNOWLEDGMENTS

We would like to thank Sherbrooke Community Centre and Brightwater Senior Living and all study participants for supporting our research.

REFERENCES

1. Alankus, G., Lazar, A., May, M., and Kelleher, C. Towards Customizable Games for Stroke Rehabilitation. In: *Proc. of CHI 2010*, ACM Press (2010), 2113-2122.

2. Anderson-Hanley, C., Arciero, P.J., Brickman, A.M., Nimon, J.P., Okuma, N., Westen, S.C., Merz, M.E., Pence, B.D., Woods, J.A., Kramer, A.F., and Zimmerman, E.A. Exergaming and Older Adult Cognition: A Cluster Randomized Clinical Trial. *Am J Prev Med* 42, 2 (2012), 109-119.
3. Bateni, H. Changes in balance in older adults based on use of physical therapy vs the Wii Fit gaming system: a preliminary study. *Physiotherapy* (2011).
4. Blythe, M., Wright, P., Bowers, J., Boucher, A., Jarvis, N., Reynolds, P., and Gaver, B. Age and Experience: Ludic engagement in a residential care setting. In: *Proc. of DIS 2010*, ACM Press (2010), 161-170.
5. Brandstädter, J., and Greve, W. The Aging Self: Stabilizing and Protective Processes. *Developmental Review*, 42 (1994), 52-80.
6. Braun, V., and Clarke, V. Using Thematic Analysis in Psychology. *Qualitative Research in Psychology 3*, 2 (2006), 77-101.
7. Chen, Y., Ngo, V., and Park, S.Y. Caring for Caregivers: Designing for Integrality. In: *Proc. of CSCW 2012*, ACM (2012), 91-102.
8. De Schutter, B. Never Too Old to Play: The Appeal of Digital Games to an Older Audience. *Games and Culture 6*, 2 (2011), 155-170.
9. Folstein, M.F., Folstein, S.E., and McHugh, P.R. "Mini-Mental State" – A Practical Method for Grading the Cognitive State of Patiens for the Clinician. *J Psychiat Res* 12, (1975), 189-198.
10. Gerling, K.M., Livingston, I.J., Nacke, L.E., and Mandryk, R.L. Full-Body Motion-Based Game Interaction for Older Adults. In: *Proc. of CHI 2012*, ACM Press (2012).
11. Gerling, K.M., Mandryk, R.L., and Kalyn, M.R. Wheelchair-Based Game Design for Older Adults. In: *Proc. of ASSETS 2013*, ACM Press (2013).
12. Harley, D., Fitzpatrick, G., Axelrod, L., White, G., and McAllister, G. Making the Wii at home: game play by older people in sheltered housing. *HCI in Work and Learning*, Life and Leisure, Springer (2010), 156-176.
13. Jung, Y., Li, J.K., Janissa, N.S., Gladys, W.L.C., and Lee, K.M. Games for a better life: effects of playing Wii games on the well-being of seniors in a long-term care facility. In: *Proc. of IE '09*, ACM Press (2009).
14. Khan, D.U., Siek, K.A., Meyers, J., Haverhals, L.M., Cali, S., and Ross, S.E. Designing a Personal Health Application for Older Adults to Manage Medication. In: *Proc. of IHI '10*, ACM (2010).
15. Kientz, J.A., Patel, S.N., Jones, B., Price, E.D., Mynatt, E.D., & Abowd, G.D. The Georgia Tech Aware Home. In: *EA of CHI 2008*, ACM Press (2008), 3675-3680.
16. Lindley, S.E., Harper, R., and Sellen, A. Designing for Elders: Exploring the Complexity of Relationships in Later Life. In: *Proc. of HCI 2008*, ACM (2008), 77-86.
17. Marston, H.R., Greenlay, S., and van Hoof, J. Understanding the Nintendo Wii and Microsoft Kinect consoles in long-term care facilities. *Technology and Disability* 25, 2 (2013), 77-85.
18. Mueller, F., Edge, D., Vetere, F., Gibbs, M.R., Agamanolis, S., Bongers, B., and Sheridan, J.G. Designing Sports: A Framework for Exertion Games. In: *Proc. of CHI 2011*, ACM (2011), 2651-2660.
19. Müller, C., Neufeldt, C., Randall, D., and Wulf, V. ICT-Development in Residential Care Settings: Sensitizing Design to the Life Circumstances of the Residents of a Care Home. In: *Proc. of CHI 2012*, ACM Press (2012).
20. Nap, H.H., de Kort, Y.A.W., and IJsselteijn, W.A. Senior gamers: Preferences, motivations and needs. *Gerontechnology* 8, 4 (2009), 247-262.
21. Pedell, S., Beh, J., Mozuna, K., and Duong, S. Engaging Older Adults in Activity Group Settings Playing Games on Touch Tablets. In: *Proc. of OzCHI'13*, ACM (2013), 477-480.
22. Pelham, B.W., and Swann, W.B. From Self-Conceptions to Self-Worth: On the Sources and Structure of Global Self-Esteem. *Journal of Personality and Social Psychology 57*, 4 (1989), 672-680.
23. Penedo, F.J., and Dahn, J.R. Exercise and well-being: a review of mental and physical health benefits associated with physical activity. *Curr Opin Psychiatry*, 18 (2005).
24. Rice, M., Tan, W.P., Ong, J., Yau, L.J., Wan, M., and Ng, J. The Dynamics of Younger and Older Adult's Paired Behaviour When Playing an Interactive Silhouette Game. In: *Proc. of CHI 2013*, ACM (2013), 1081-1090.
25. Ryan, R., Rigby, C., and Przybylski, A. Motivational pull of video games: A self-determination theory approach. *Motivation and Emotion*, 30 (2006), 347-365.
26. Theng, Y.-L., Chua, P.-H., and Pham, T.P. Wii as Entertainment and Socialisation Aid for the Mental and Social Health of the Elderly. In: *EA of CHI 2012*, ACM (2012), 691-702.
27. Ulbrecht, G., Wagner, D., and Gräßel, E. Exergames and Their Acceptance Among Nursing Home Residents. *Activities, Adaptation & Aging 36*, 2 (2012), 93-106.
28. Uzor, S., and Baille, L. Investigating the Long-Term Use of Exergames in the Home With Elderly Fallers. In: *Proc. of CHI 2014*, ACM (2014), 2813-2822
29. Vanden Abeele, V. and De Schutter, B. Meaningful Play in Elderly Life. In: *Proc. of ICA* 2008, (2008).

CoFaçade: A Customizable Assistive Approach for Elders and Their Helpers

Jason Chen Zhao[1], Richard C. Davis[2], Pin Sym Foong[1], and Shengdong Zhao[1]

[1]NUS-HCI Lab, National University of Singapore
13 Computing Drive, Singapore 117417
zhaoch21@gmail.com, {pinsym, zhaosd}@comp.nus.edu.sg

[2]SIS, Singapore Management University
80 Stamford Road, Singapore 178902
rcdavis@smu.edu.sg

ABSTRACT
We present *CoFaçade,* a novel approach to helping elders reach their goals with IT products by working collaboratively with helpers. In this approach, the elder uses an interface with a small number of *triggers,* where each trigger is a single button (or card) that can execute a *procedure*. The helper uses a *customization interface* to link triggers to procedures that accomplish frequently-recurring high-level goals with IT products. Customization can be done either locally or remotely. We conducted an experiment to compare the CoFaçade approach with a baseline approach where helpers taught elders to perform IT tasks. Our results showed that CoFaçade can reduce helpers' time and effort, reduce elders' frustration, and improve elders' success rate in completing IT tasks.

Author Keywords
Silver Computing, Accessibility design, CoFaçade, Collaboration

ACM Classification Keywords
H.5.m. Information interfaces and presentation (e.g., HCI): Miscellaneous

INTRODUCTION
Silver computing, which provides technological solutions to help senior citizens better utilize information technology (IT), has become increasingly important in today's aging society. Though recent studies indicate increasing IT usage among elders, many find computerized technologies too challenging to use [13]. Elders often have difficulty facing the complexity of modern technology and need simpler solutions. For example, many elders are still challenged by procedures like starting Skype conversations with their children or finding a TV station among dozens of options.

We see four approaches to making IT products accessible to elders. One approach is to design products especially for them [14]. This can be helpful, but elders' needs are varied and changing over time, making it unlikely to find a universal design that fits all elders' needs [16]. Another approach is to make systems that can adapt to the needs of individual elders [29], but few products have been designed with such adaptation in mind. A third approach is to support customization of existing products (e.g., [10], [11], [19]) but the customization process itself can be too complex for elders. Since even simple procedures can be complex for some elders, we advocate a fourth approach where a third party works with an elder to help them accomplish their goals with IT products.

CHI 2015, April 18 - 23, 2015, Seoul, Republic of Korea
Copyright 2015 ACM 978-1-4503-3145-6/15/04...$15.00
http://dx.doi.org/10.1145/2702123.2702588

Consider situations like the following. Chye is 78 and lives alone. He has a domestic helper Kim, who visits twice a week. Chye is a fan of music from the 50's, but there is no FM station near him that plays this music. When Kim is around, she will tune into 50's music using Spotify on the computer Chye's children gave him. Also, Chye's son gave him an AppleTV so he can watch his favorite shows. He loves shows from the History Channel and the Discovery Channel. However, Chye has trouble finding them from AppleTV's on-screen menu and often asks Kim for help. Both Chye and Kim wish that Chye could enjoy his favorite music and shows even when Kim is not around. Kim spends lots of time teaching Chye how to do these things by himself, but Chye is often unable to do so.

Using *CoFaçade,* elders can accomplish frequently-recurring, high-level goals through a few customizable triggers on a simple interface, such as the physical remote control shown in Figure 1. Helpers use a familiar

Figure 1. Elders' trigger interface in our *CoFaçade* prototype, with five programmable button triggers on top and a reader for RFID card triggers on the bottom. Implemented with Arduino for less than US$ 50.

customization interface to map triggers to procedures, which perform a sequence of subtasks on both software applications and consumer electronics. This customization can be done either locally or remotely.

The contributions of this paper are three-fold.

- We present the *CoFaçade* approach and the background research that led to it.
- We describe a prototype artifact we developed that implements this approach.
- We present an empirical evaluation that shows how the *CoFaçade* approach reduces helpers' workload while empowering elders to achieve their goals through IT products.

RELATED WORK

In this section, we discuss existing strategies for making IT products more accessible to elders.

Design for elders

"Universal Usability" has the goal of making interfaces usable by all people [25], and this has led to design guidelines for various groups. In "Designing for Older Adults," Fisk et al. provided a list of guidelines for elders [13]. These guidelines emphasize interface changes that respond to age-related changes in perception and cognition: larger displays, fonts, buttons, accessibility improvements in specific contexts (navigation [13], web [20], email [10], etc.), and fewer options. While these guidelines are very useful, adopting them requires dedicated effort in the design and implementation phases, thus excluding many currently existing applications. In addition, it is difficult to come up with a universal solution that caters to needs of elders, as their needs can differ among individuals and change over time [16].

Adapt to elders

To cater to elders' varied and changing needs, researchers have considered adaptive solutions. Wobbrock et al. define this shift as an ability-based design, in which "we move away from assisting human users to conform to inflexible computer systems, and instead consider how systems can be made to fit the abilities of whoever uses them" [29]. Adaptive interfaces can be configured according to individual user profiles [26], with some work done in making these profiles portable [4]. Since determining a user's profile can be difficult, systems may adapt based on automatically collected health information, and this poses a serious privacy risk [1]. Also, adaptive solutions require dedicated efforts to include them before releasing a product, while the majority of today's products or applications have not included such solutions.

Third-party customization tools

To make existing applications accessible to individual needs, researchers have proposed approaches that enable third-parties to modify the interface or behavior of existing applications. These customization tools could be used to make applications more accessible to elders. These approaches typically operate either on the surface-level of the interface, intercepting input events and/or manipulating views before they are delivered to the application (e.g., Prefab [11], CoScripter [15], Chickenfoot [6]) or via a toolkit, which integrates the system with the toolkit to gain access to the internal program structures (e.g., Scotty [12], OldGen [21], WADE [19]). However, using these solutions to create elderly-friendly interfaces can still be tedious and complex, making it difficult for elders to use.

In summary, while designing for and adapting to elders are effective strategies, these strategies need to be incorporated during design time, and may not work with many existing IT products. Third-party customization tools can make existing products accessible to elders, but the customization process can be too complex and tedious for elders to handle. On the positive side, elders are not alone. They often have technologically capable social contacts who are willing to offer assistance, which offers an opportunity for a fourth approach which considers both stakeholders together, alleviating some of the design constraints.

Assisting elders

Researchers have investigated making IT products more accessible to elders through collaboration with helpers. Some of these researchers have studied the nature of such help and how to do it effectively.

For example, training takes significantly more time for elders compared to younger learners, and elders commit more errors in post-training evaluations [5] [8]. This highlights the need to design instruction to compensate for elders' slower cognitive performance, limited processing resources, lack of inhibition, and sensory deficits. Fisk et al. provided detailed guidelines on how to design training and instructional programs to teach the elders more effectively in Chapter 7 of their book [13].

In addition to teaching elders, another common form of assistance is to perform tasks for elders. Research has found that significant help comes from both household members as well as external social circles, such as volunteers [2] [23], [24]. Within the household, Grinter et al. [17] found that one person typically becomes a guru, routinely helping other household members who are less technically inclined. Outside the house, non-profit organizations often send volunteers to elders' homes to help them with various tasks, including computer tasks[1].

Since some elders have cognitive impairments, we also mention research that investigates helpers creating reminders for people with cognitive disabilities. Carmien, for example, proposes the use of a dual-interfaces approach for caregivers to create memory-aid scripts for people with cognitive disabilities [7]. Legion:AR collected crowd-sourced labels for images of a disabled person's

[1] www.newyorkcares.org; www.sgcares.org

environment to keep them on track while performing daily activities [28].

While we are investigating situations where a helper works together with an elder, our approach differs from all the previously mentioned approaches. We envision situations where the helper seeks neither to teach an elder how to accomplish a task, nor does it for them, nor reminds them how to do it. Rather we enable helpers to create customized procedures that help elders to accomplish tasks and link these procedures to simple triggers.

EXPLORATORY INTERVIEWS

To better understand how elders interact with IT products, we conducted three sets of interviews. The first were in-depth, semi-structured interviews[2] with 8 elders to help identify a productive design strategy. Since we saw many elders getting help from others, we conducted a second set of interviews with 40 adults below 50 years old who help elders. We later realized that elders' difficulties with IT products are not limited to computer applications. We therefore conducted a final round of interviews with 10 elders to know more about their experiences with consumer electronics.

Elders using Computer Applications

For our initial interviews, we found participants through a social worker at a community center for elders in Singapore. We asked to meet people over 50 years old with some computer experience and were introduced to 5 men and 2 women, ranging in age from 51 to 76. Another woman (Chinese residing in Canada, age 68) was later recruited through an author's social connection. Four participants had tertiary education, and six were retired. Participants reported using email, Skype, watching videos, and playing games on their computers. Some also used various work-related applications such as customer relationship management software or word processors.

Interview questions aimed to elicit elders' experience with computer usage, in particular focusing on difficulties encountered in usage. If difficulties were reported, there were follow-up questions on the nature of the difficulty and how the elders attempted to resolve the issue. In addition, interviewees were asked to demonstrate their usage of applications that they reported using. Their behavior was observed and noted. Interviews were transcribed and analyzed against the background information of the older users experience with computers.

Overall, our participants all demonstrated difficulties with eye and neck strain after using computers, some despite verbally claiming they have no difficulties. Some coped by enlarging the text on the screen, others by taking more breaks or working for shorter periods of time.

[2] Link to detailed list of questions: http://www.nus-hci.org/?attachment_id=1357

Participants with lower educational attainment tended to report difficulties with English and with 'learning'. One participant (P8) attributed his difficulty with dialog boxes to an "education issue".

Interviewees seemed to prefer interfaces that did not change. This theme occurred regardless of educational attainment or usage of computers at work. P7, despite claiming he has no difficulties with computers, indicated that he would like to be informed of web interface updates, stating that "Older people are more resistant to changes". He would like more time to "learn" new interfaces as they are updated. P6 described it as "old people like to use old thing (sic)". As indicated by [18], constantly updating interfaces can be a challenge to older users because of the ongoing learning needed. Even P5, who reported over forty years of computer usage, said she "did not like too much change" when discussing changing interfaces.

All participants reported difficulties with computers. One participant (P1) reported difficulty with troubleshooting her computer network. Six participants reported difficulties with memory or vision. These difficulties were particularly obvious when participants were asked to demonstrate their usage of applications.

When asked how they deal with difficulties, two said they went to family members, four went to people in their social circle, one went to both family and friends, and one said he did not ask anyone for help. P5 and P8 said that they were reluctant to ask their children for help, because they were "impatient" or "too busy" to teach. It should be noted here that, since our participants were drawn from a socially active pool of elders in a volunteering group, the number calling friends for help (instead of family) may be inflated.

Helpers Working with Elders

As turning to people for help was prevalent in our first interview study, we then surveyed adults about their experiences when offering help to elders. We used snowball sampling (starting from the authors' social connections) to collect 43 responses from people aged from 25 to 49 (M=32). Most participants were from Southeast Asia, ten were from China, one was from Australia, and one was from Germany. There were 23 men and 18 women. Ten were students, and the remainder were working adults.

Participants were asked to relate an instance of offering IT help, specifying who was helped and the nature of that help. The majority of help instances (n=35) were with parents or grandparents, while the remainder (n=8) were with non-related elders or friends. Help instances fell into four (non-exclusive) categories: offering help from a remote location (n=15), repeated tutoring (n=13), helping only with setup (n=5) and helping by sourcing or preparing entertainment content such as videos or music (n=4).

More than half of the participants expressed some form of frustration with the helping process. Six participants specifically labeled the help instance as "difficult" or "bothersome." For example, one participant complained about repeatedly needing to teach an elder how to perform a seemingly simple task: "I just feel frustrated to teach them to use web browser when the same problems happens again and again".

Distance was an important factor for many participants. For example, one participant reported, "I only have the opportunity to help my mother use Skype only when I went back to my country". Another participant shared: "I cannot guide my parents on computer troubleshooting through the mobile phone when I am working".

Some of our participants found creative workarounds to difficulties they encountered. For example, one participant gave her mother a video recording that showed how to perform a computer task. Another participant created a written tutorial: *"I write all the steps how to start the TV and change to my father's favorite channel on a paper."* Other participants try to setup elders' devices in a simple way that avoids confusion. One said, *"I bought an iPhone for my mom, and only install three applications on that. I told her 'If you want to call me, click the first application, if you have emergency, click the second [...].'* Another said, *"I bought a computer for my father and put the most commonly used applications on the desktop."*

Elders using Consumer Electronics

After conducting these interviews, we realized that we had not explored elders' use of consumer electronics. Since these can also be a source difficulty for some elders, we conducted a final round of interviews with 10 elders that focused specifically on consumer electronics. Again, participants were recruited through snowball sampling. Six were from Southeast Asia, three were from China, and one was from the United States. There were four men and six women, ranging in age from 55 to 87. Four had tertiary degrees, four had secondary degrees, and two had completed diploma programs. Participants varied in their comfort level and experience with computers much as our earlier interview participants did.

Regarding consumer electronics, participants felt comfortable with most electronics devices, but 7 of 10 participants complained about major difficulties when using TVs or DVD players. Problems ranged from navigating complex digital TV interfaces to switching channels on a conventional TV. Many experienced problems with remote controls. P3 reported difficulty turning on subtitles. P7 reported that her universal remote control would not turn on her TV properly. She then added, "...it does 50,000 things that are supposed to be so nifty. It's too complicated."

When participants experienced problems with electronics, all reported calling a friend or relative for help as our original interview participants did. If they could not find someone to help, they would simply give up using the device.

Discussion

In summary, while some elders we interviewed are quite technologically advanced, most encounter recurring difficulties with some IT products, and a few find all IT products complex and intimidating. We found no evidence that the level of difficulty encountered was tied to participants' education level or even experience with technology. Rather, elders find that keeping up with the rapid pace of change in modern IT products is simply too tiring.

Many elders turn to friends or relatives when they need help. When this happens, new technologies are often hard to avoid, because helpers often bring technologies that they are more familiar with. Therefore, when the current difficulty has passed, the elder may encounter new difficulties. But the helper often has limited time and is not always present when needed. Also, many helpers grow impatient when training elders to use new products. Some helpers customize elders' products to make them easier to use, but this is not always possible.

COFAÇADE APPROACH

Our exploratory interviews shed light on the nature of elders' problems with IT products, the role played by helpers, and the challenges encountered by helpers. Considering all of these insights together leads to a new approach to helping elders reach their goals with IT products, which we call CoFaçade. In software engineering, the term "façade" refers to a design pattern that provides a simplified interface to complex program procedures [3]. This name highlights the fact that the helper creates a simple trigger interface collaboratively with an elder.

In CoFaçade, the *elder* is an older adult who has goals they wish to accomplish with IT products but has recurring difficulties and may even find technology intimidating. The *helper* is more comfortable with a technology that can help the elder realize their goals. Note that the helper may not be a technology expert.

Systems built with the CoFaçade approach have separate interfaces for elders and helpers. The elder uses an interface with a small number of *triggers*, where each trigger is a single button (or card) that can execute a *procedure*. The helper uses a *customization interface* to define procedures and map them to triggers.

The trigger interface should be embedded in a familiar artifact. Such artifacts are stable, comfortable, and part of the elder's everyday life. A physical remote control is an example of a familiar artifact, but a trigger interface could also be embedded into any other artifact ranging from a smartphone to a coffee cup, as long as the elder is familiar with it. Also, since our exploratory interviews showed that most elders wish to accomplish a fairly small number of frequently-recurring tasks, a small number of triggers is often sufficient.

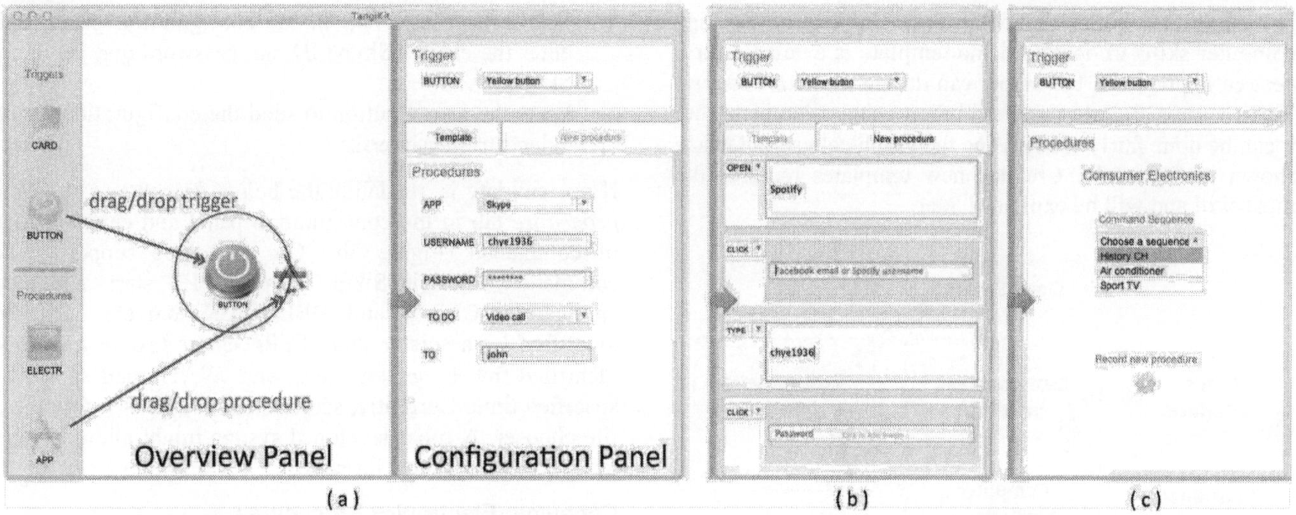

Figure 3. Helper's customization interface (a) Button trigger, Skype app template. (b) Configuration panel for button trigger, new computer application procedure (Spotify). (c) Configuration panel for button trigger, new consumer electronics procedure.

The customization interface is for defining procedures that accomplish frequently-recurring high-level goals with IT products. The procedure definition process needs to be fast and easy, because helpers often have limited time. Since there is a wide variety of products and new products are constantly begin created, the customization interface needs to work with any existing IT product. Also, the helper should be able to customize triggers and procedures either in the elder's presence or at a remote location.

The approach we have described has four key elements; all are necessary to address the problems revealed in our exploratory interviews:

1. Distinct roles for elders and helpers
2. Elders have a simple interface with small number of triggers embedded in a familiar artifact.
3. Triggers are mapped to procedures that accomplish high-level goals with any IT product.
4. Helpers have a simple interface for defining and modifying procedures either locally or remotely.

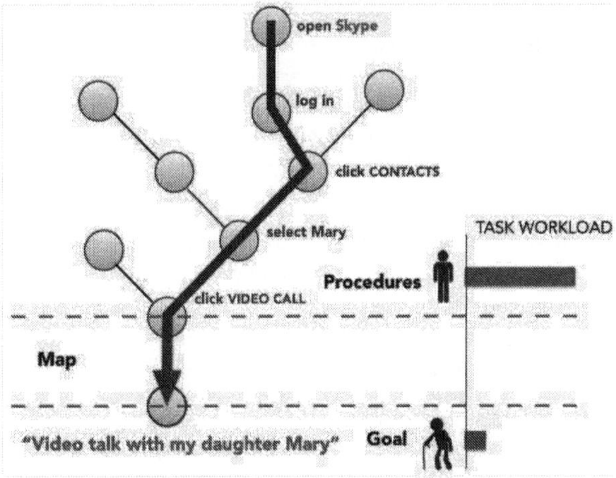

Figure 2. The CoFaçade approach: distinct roles for elders (goal) and helpers (sub-goals composition).

We define the user interface containing sets of triggers which can accomplish different high-level goals as *goal-oritiented interface*. In summary, CoFaçade enables elders to achieve frequently-recurring IT tasks with a simple goal-oriented interface and enables helpers to create related procedures seperately. Figure 2 illustrates the goal-tree structure of CoFaçade approach, where the decision-making path for creating procedures can be made by helpers with their preferred methods through composing each sub-goals. Therefore, we envision CoFaçade approach has three advantages: 1) Helpers have the freedom to choose their familiar methods to create procedures (e.g., use Skype rather than Google Hangouts for video calling task). 2) Elders can express their needs in a high-level (e.g., video talk to my daughter Mary). 3) Benefit both parties by seperating the task into goal and procedures, with respect to their distinct roles in this collaborative approach and thereby increasing the overall efficiency.

PROTOTYPE DESIGN AND IMPLEMENTATION

To help us evaluate the CoFaçade approach, we implemented a prototype system. Our trigger interface prototype is the remote control shown in Figure 1. To keep this interface as simple as possible, we included only five button triggers with different shapes and colors. The number of triggers can be expanded through RFID-tagged cards, which we describe later. This remote control also includes a Bluetooth network connection and infrared (IR) sensors and emitters for recording and playing back procedures that control consumer electronics.

The helper uses the customization interface shown in Figure 3 to define procedures that control the elder's computer applications and consumer electronics. This interface can be used in three ways requiring increasing levels of computer expertise. Using <u>*templates*</u> requires the least expertise, and we expect this to be the most common case. Templates give helpers simple customization interfaces with pre-defined procedures for common applications and require average computer skills to operate. If no template is available for a desired application, the helper can define a *new procedure.* This requires slightly more skill than using a template, but it can be done fairly easily using the graphical user interface shown in Figure 3b. Creating new templates requires the most skill and will be explained later.

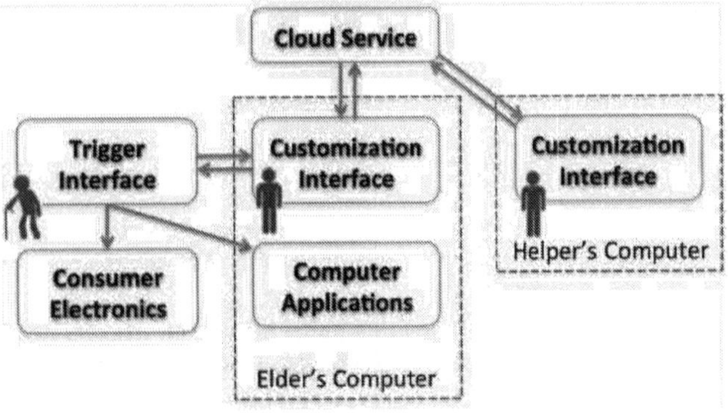

Figure 4. Overview of our CoFaçade prototype.

Figure 4 shows how the components of our prototype are connected. Triggers and procedures are loaded into the elder's trigger interface via the customization interface on the elders' computer. The elder can then use the trigger interface to control their computer applications or consumer electronics. The customization interface can also store triggers and procedures in a cloud service, giving the helper access to the customization interface even when they are not physically present.

Currently, our prototype supports two types of triggers: buttons and cards. We first explain how helpers can configure buttons to control two types of procedures: computer applications and consumer electronics. We then explain how to create new templates and explain why and how to use card triggers.

Computer Application Procedures

Our prototype uses Sikuli Script [30] to control applications on the elder's computer. This allows helpers to make procedures for any application on the elder's computer by capturing a series of screen shots. Since this can be cumbersome, however, we also provide templates that give helpers high-level control of commonly used applications. Currently, we have one fully functional template for placing calls with Skype.

Imagine that a helper wished to configure an elder's trigger interface to make the yellow button place a call to the elder's son. To do this, the helper would take these steps in the configuration interface (see Figure 3a):

1. Drag the *BUTTON* icon from the trigger palette to the overview panel.
2. Select *Yellow button* in the configuration panel.
3. Drag the *APP* icon from the procedure palette to the ring around the button in the overview panel.
4. Select the *Skype* app in the configuration panel, and enter the elder's Skype ID and password and the son's Skype ID.
5. Press the arrow button to send the configuration to the elder's trigger interface.

If no template is available, the helper can choose the *New procedure* tab in the configuration panel and enter a series of commands (Figure 3b). Our prototype supports five commands found in Sikuli Script. OPEN starts a named application. CLICK and DBLCLICK activate a button identified by a screen shot. TYPE enters text in a control identified by a screen shot, and WAIT pauses for a specified time. Currently, screen shots are chosen through a file chooser. A fully developed system might allow helpers to capture screenshots directly.

Consumer Electronics Procedures

Our current prototype does not provide templates for consumer electronics, but helpers can define new procedures for consumer electronics devices. To define a new procedure, a helper would begin with the same steps 1 and 2 used for a computer application procedure. The remaining steps are as follows (see Figure 3c and Figure 5).

3. Drag the *ELECTR* icon from the procedure palette to the ring around the button in the overview panel.
4. In the configuration panel, press Record new procedure. A pop-up window appears (see Figure 5).
5. Enter a name for the new command sequence and press the *Record* button (on the right).
6. Point the device vendor's remote control at the IR sensor at the top of the elder's trigger interface and press the desired sequence of buttons.
7. Press *Stop* (on the right) and close the pop-up window.
8. In the configuration panel, select the newly entered name from the command sequence menu.
9. Press the arrow button to send the configuration to the elder's trigger interface.

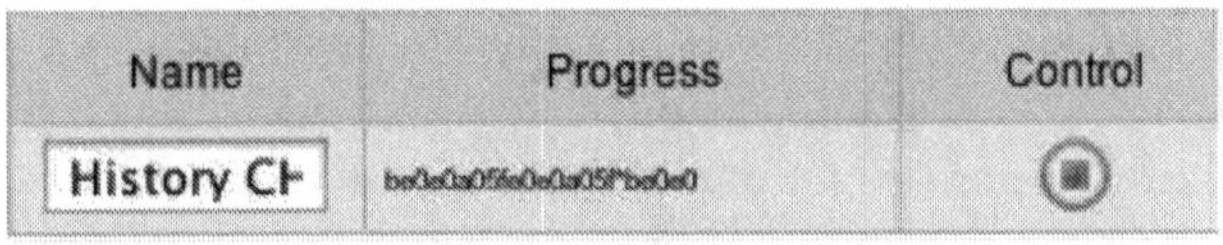

Figure 5. Recording a new command sequence. Point the device's remote at the trigger interface and press the desired buttons. *Progress* shows numbers as buttons are pressed.

Note that the helper may need to be physically present with the elder to capture a new sequence of commands from a device vendor's remote control. Once a sequence has been captured, however, the helper can configure the trigger interface from a remote location.

Creating New Templates

As stated earlier, we expect using templates to be the common case for helpers. Since devices and applications change frequently, our prototype makes it easy for people with basic programming skill to define new templates. We expect that templates will be created and updated fairly quickly either by companies or by highly skilled helpers.

To make a computer application template, a creator begins by using a graphical user interface like the one shown in Figure 3b to define Sikuli scripts for typical use cases. These scripts continue to work if interface elements move, but need to be revised if elements change appearance. (Note that some apps allow control through web services or other programming interfaces that change less frequently than the visual interface. Highly skilled template creators can use these interfaces instead of Sikuli to create templates that will last longer.) After defining use case scripts, the creator then identifies steps that require user configuration (e.g. user name, password) and links these parameters to text fields or list boxes using a markup language.

This process requires only basic programming skill, allowing numerous programmers to create templates and share them through a common repository or marketplace. Also note that, while we currently support only computer application templates, our approach could be extended easily to support consumer electronics templates.

RFID Card Triggers

When elders require more than five triggers, our prototype allows helpers to create new triggers using numbered cards with RFID tags. We chose to expand the number of tasks through RFID cards, because physical cards are more familiar and easier to handle by people with no computer skill. Previous research [31] has shown that at least 25 cards can be organized effectively in a photo album by people with little computer expertise, and our exploratory interviews suggest that this is sufficient for most elders.

Elders can write descriptive labels on cards to help them remember which card accomplishes which goal. Helpers can then map cards to procedures in the customization interface by (1) dragging the card icon from the trigger palette into the overview panel and (2) choosing the card number in the configuration panel (see Figure 6). This simple method makes it easy to keep track of a large number of procedures, and it avoids overwhelming elders with a large array of buttons.

Figure 6. Choosing a card number in the trigger config. panel.

Our prototype captures the core ideas in the CoFaçade approach. Elders have a simple interface with small number of triggers that accomplish high-level goals with any computer application and any consumer electronics device with an IR remote control. Helpers have a simple interface for configuring procedures, and they can do this either locally or remotely.

EVALUATION

We are interested in whether the CoFaçade approach *improves helpers' experience* and *lowers barriers to elders using IT products*. To answer this question, we evaluated the CoFaçade approach in the context of helpers assisting elders with setting up Skype calls. Skype call is a task faced by many elders [27] and it has similar complexity to many other common tasks elders often want to perform, such as checking an email inbox or choosing a TV channel from dozens of options.

We evaluate the improvement in helpers' experience by measuring the time taken in the helping process. We evaluate the reduction of barriers to using IT products by elders by measuring: 1) the frustration level by the elders to learn to perform the task, and 2) their success rate in completing the task.

Our hypotheses are that the CoFaçade approach can reduce the time and effort involved in the helping process and improve the success rate for elders in completing the IT task and reduce their frustration.

Participants

A total of 18 elder-helper pairs (36 participants) were recruited. The 18 elders were recruited from a local organization (13 female; age range from 55 to 80; M = 64.83, SD= 7.20). All elders had taken part in local senior computer classes and had basic computer skills and Internet experience. The 18 helpers were young adults recruited from the university community. They are students majoring in a variety of disciplines including design, chemical engineering, business, and computer science. All of them reported at least 5 years of using computers and were comfortable with technology. The matching between the

Simple task (6 steps)	Intermediate task (9 steps)
Start a video call to a designate person from three candidates.	Start a new group call to two designate people from three candidates and adjust to the suitable volume.
1) Click the Skype icon from desktop; *2) Input username and password;* *3) Click "login";* *4) Click "contact list";* *5) Choose the designated person from a list of three candidates;* 6) *Click "video call".*	*1) Click the Skype icon from desktop;* *2) Input username and password;* *3) Click "login";* *4) Click "file";* *5) Click "new conversation";* *6) Click the "add" button;* *7) Find two designated people in a list;* *8) Click "video call";* *9) Adjust volumes.*

Table 1: Task description

elder and helper was based on their availability for the experiment schedule. Task and Stimuli

As previously mentioned, we choose Skype as our testing environment as we believe it represents a typical task an elder would like to perform and want to seek help with. For the task design, we wanted to simulate realistic scenarios. The baseline condition simulates the common situation in which a helpers teaches an elder to use an IT product so that the elder can use it on their own when the helper is not available. The baseline is compared with the CoFaçade condition in which the helper first configures the elder's trigger interface, and then the elder completes the task independently using the trigger interface. We designed two level of complexity for both methods: one simple task and one intermediate task (Table 1).

Apparatus

Participants in both conditions used a MacBook Pro laptop computer with 2.5GHz dual-core i5 processor, 4GB RAM, and 13' display, running OS X Mountain Lion. The software in the laptop included both our prototype's customization interface for the helper and Skype 6.4 for OS X. In the baseline condition, helpers also used the Skype tutorial available at support.skype.com to teach the elders. In the CoFaçade condition, elders also used the physical trigger interface described earlier in the Prototype Design and Implementation section.

Experimental Design

We used a within subjects experimental design with two independent variables, each with two levels: approach (baseline vs. CoFaçade) and task complexity (simple vs. intermediate). Approach was counterbalanced among participant pairs while task complexity was presented in a sequential order from simple to intermediate. This is because we were not interested in comparing the performance between levels of difficulties.

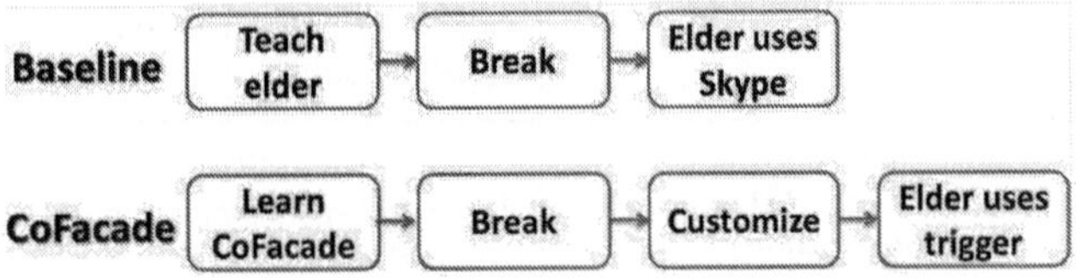

Figure 7. The workflow of the experiment

The workflow of the experiments is described in Figure 7. At the beginning of the experiment, the helper was introduced to the elder and both were given 10 minutes to acquaint themselves with each other.

Then, in the baseline condition, the helpers taught the elders how to achieve the task goal by using a standard printed tutorial from the official Skype website and also by offering guidance until the elders informed the helper that they felt well-prepared. Following a three minute break, the elder performed the task with no help apart from the availability of the printed tutorial. If the elders failed to accomplish the task, they were asked to try again with the aid of the helper.

In the CoFaçade condition, the experimenters taught the helper how to use the CoFaçade customization interface. Following a three minute break, the helper used the customization interface to define procedures for the elder's trigger interface. Next, the helper was asked to introduce the trigger interface to elder and let them use it to complete the task.

All participants (both elders and helpers) ended the experiment by filling in a questionnaire and going through a post experimental interview. In summary, we had 18 pairs of participants x 2 approaches (baseline vs CoFaçade) x 2 task difficulties (simple vs. intermediate) = 72 collaborative help/teaching tasks total.

Results and Discussion

The main quantitative measures for the study were the overall time to complete each task and elders' frustration rate when performing the task. Overall time included all aspects of the task, as shown in the following formulas:

$$T_{baseline} = t_{teach\_elder} + t_{elder\_uses\_Skype}$$

$$T_{CoFaçade} = t_{learn\_CoFaçade} + t_{customize} + t_{elder\_uses\_trigger}$$

To measure frustration rate, we computed the ratio of elders' self-reported perceived time to the actual time they spent performing tasks. This is an established method for measuring frustration implicitly [22]. Research has shown that more frustration tends to be overestimated (ratio>1) while less frustration is underestimated (ratio<1) [9].

		Baseline		CoFaçade	
		M	*SD*	*M*	*SD*
Overall Time					
	Simple	8.33	5.11	3.02	0.69
	Intermediate	10.07	6.10	3.36	0.77
Frustration Rate					
	Simple	1.46	0.82	0.49	0.64
	Intermediate	0.90	0.48	0.63	0.60

Table 2: Results of overall time spent on the collaborative task (in minutes), and elder's frustration rate.

Detailed results for both overall time and frustration rate are shown in Table 2. We conducted a two-way repeated-measures ANOVA and found a significant main effect of approach on overall time ($F_{1,17} = 25.25$, $p < 0.001$), but no significant main effect of complexity on overall time. Averaging across complexities, overall time was 9.20 minutes in the baseline condition and 3.19 minutes in the

CoFaçade condition, which shows that the CoFaçade saves considerable time when compared to the baseline approach. In the baseline condition, elders spent 70% of the overall time learning and 30% performing tasks. In the CoFaçade condition, helpers spent 56% of the overall time learning to use our prototype and 27% customizing the elder's trigger interface, while elders spent the remaining 17% of the time using the trigger interface. Note that since the intermediate task was always performed after the simple task, it is likely that participants spent more time learning in the simple task. This may explain why the overall time for the intermediate task was not much longer than the simple task.

On frustration rate, we found significant main effects from both approach ($F_{1,17} = 7.73$, $p < 0.05$) and complexity ($F_{1,17} = 15.4$, $p < 0.05$). Pairwise t-tests with bonferroni correction showed that frustration rate decreased significantly in the CoFaçade condition for both complexity levels when compared to the baseline condition ($p < .05$ for both complexity levels).

We also found a significant approach and complexity interaction effect on frustration rate ($F_{1,17} = 15.57$, $p < 0.01$). Pairwise t-tests with bonferroni correction showed that the difference in frustration rate between complexity conditions is significant for the baseline condition ($p < .05$), but not significant for the CoFaçade condition. In the baseline condition, the decrease in elder's frustration from the simple task (M=1.46) to the intermediate task (M=0.9) is largely due to learning effects. The intermediate task shared several common steps with the simple task, and it was always performed second in this study. Under more realistic conditions, there would be more time between tasks, and elders would be much more likely to forget what the helper taught them. This is supported by our exploratory interviews, where many helpers reported teaching elders the same procedure repeatedly.

In addition to improvements in overall time and frustration rate, we also noticed that elders' task completion rate improved when using the CoFaçade approach. All elders were able to complete both tasks in their first attempt when using our prototype's physical trigger interface. In the baseline condition, 4 of 18 elders failed their first attempt to complete the simple task, and 2 other elders failed their first attempt to complete the intermediate task.

We also discovered that several helpers were concerned about the need to see elders' passwords. P20 and P27 suggested adding features to capture elders' passwords without making them visible to helpers. Elders were less concerned about privacy, especially when giving passwords to family members. As P3 said, "*My son helps me set up all these computer things, I cannot remember these accounts.*"

Finally, we note that using university students as helpers is a limitation of our study. Many of the university students we recruited came from fields like design and business and fit into the criteria we expect for a typical helper: comfortable with technology, but not necessarily experts. Most elders we interviewed had at least one person in their social circle with this level of comfort with technology. However, some of our helpers had more experience with technology. The usability of CoFaçade could be further evaluated with helpers outside a university setting, and we leave this for future work.

In conclusion, the significant reduction in frustration rate and the improved task completion rate for first attempts indicates that the CoFaçade approach is both easier and more effective for elders. This is shown in P11's comments, for example: "*I am very happy to let them help me in this way. This method is much easier for me to use computer [sic].*" Furthermore, the significant reduction in overall time shows that the CoFaçade approach reduces helpers' burden when working with elders. As P33 explained, "*I would prefer this method rather than guiding them time and time again.*"

Figure 8. A virtual trigger interface for elders.

Our current implementation supports buttons and RFID card triggers. However, other types of triggers are possible. For example, Figure 8 shows a software interface we developed for elders. Elders can trigger computer tasks by clicking the corresponding buttons on their computers.

CONCLUSION AND FUTURE WORK

This paper introduces the *CoFaçade* approach to helping elders realize their goals using IT products. To demonstrate the effectiveness of this approach, we implemented a prototype using a handheld physical trigger interface and a desktop customization interface for defining procedures for both computer applications and consumer electronics.

We conducted an evaluation where 18 helpers either taught elders to perform a computer task or customized the trigger interface to perform that task. Our experimental results showed that the CoFaçade approach reduces helpers' workload, reduces elders' frustration, and improves elders' task completion rates. Another main advantage of CoFaçade is that it can provide elders a stable interface, even as user interfaces rapidly evolve.

Further research should investigate uses in the household setting as well as the feasibility of additional types of input such as voice input, gesture input, etc. These should be intuitive and provide convenience for elders.

ACKNOWLEDGMENTS

We thank Arne Wessels for helping with formatting. We also thank the support from the National University of Singapore and Singapore Management University.

REFERENCES

[1] Abascal, J. and Nicolle, C. Moving towards inclusive design guidelines for socially and ethically aware HCI. *Interacting with Computers 17*, 5 (2005), 484–505.

[2] Ackerman, M.S. and Palen, L. The Zephyr Help Instance. In *Proc. CHI '96*, 268–275.

[3] Alves, V. and Paulo, B. Distributed adapters pattern: a design pattern for object-oriented distributed applications. In *First Latin American Conference on Pattern Languages of Programming* (2001).

[4] Ayotte, D., Vass, J., Mitchell, J. and Trevarinus, J. Universal Access in Human-Computer Interaction. *Design and Development Methods for Universal Access Lecture Notes in Computer Science* 8513 (2014), 191-202

[5] Brett, D, J. and Ute, J, Bayenb. Teaching older adults to use computers: recommendations based on cognitive aging research. Educational Gerontology.

[6] Bolin, M., M. Webber, P. Rha, T. Wilson, and R. C. Miller. Automation and customization of rendered web pages. In *Proc. UIST '05*, 163-172.

[7] Carmien, S, P. Socio-Technical Environments Supporting Distributed Cognition for Persons with Cognitive Disabilities. *Ph.D. dissertation*, University of Colorado, 2006.

[8] Catherine, L,K and Neil C. Issues in training older adults to use computers. *Behaviour & Information Technology* 14, 2 (1995), 107-120.

[9] Czerwinski, M., Horvitz, E., and Cutrell, E. Subjective Duration Assessment : An Implicit Probe for Software Usability. In *Proc. of IHMHCI '01*, 167–170.

[10] Dickinson, A., Newell, A., Smith, M.J., and Hill, R.L. Introducing the internet to the over-60's: Developing an email system for older novice computer users. *Interacting with Computers 17*, 6 (2005), 621–642.

[11] Dixon, M. and Fogarty, J. Prefab : Implementing Advanced Behaviors Using Pixel-Based Reverse Engineering of Interface Structure. In *Proc. CHI '10*, 1525–1534.

[12] Eagan, J.R., Beaudouin-Lafon, M., and Mackay, W.E. Cracking the cocoa nut. In *Proc. UIST '11*, 225–234.

[13] Fisk, A.D., Rogers, W.A., Charness, N., Czaja, S.J., and Sharit, J. *Designing for Older Adults: Principles and creative human factors approaches*. 2009.

[14] Fisk, A.D., Rogers, W.A. Toward a psychological science of advanced technology design for elders. J Gerontol B Psychol Sci Soc Sci. 2010;65(6):645–653.

[15] Gilly, L., Eben M. H., Tara M., and Tessa L. CoScripter: automating & sharing how-to knowledge in the enterprise. In *Proc. CHI '08*, 1719-1728.

[16] Gregor, P., Newell, A.F., and Zajicek, M. Designing for dynamic diversity: interfaces for older adults. In *Proc. Assets '02*, 151.

[17] Grinter, R.E., Edwards, W.K., Newman, M.W., and Ducheneaut, N. The Work to Make a Home Network Work. *ECSCW 2005*, Springer (2005), 469–488.

[18] Hanson, V.L. Technology skill and age: what will be the same 20 years from now? *Universal Access in the Information Society 10*, 4 (2011), 443–452.

[19] Meng, X. Zhao, S. Huang, Y. Zhang, Z. Eagan, J. Subramanian, R. WADE: Simplified GUI Add-on Development for Third-party Software. In *Proc. CHI '14, 2221-2230.*

[20] Milne, S., Dickinson, a., Carmichael, a., Sloan, D., Eisma, R., and Gregor, P. Are guidelines enough? An introduction to designing Web sites accessible to older adults. *IBM Systems Journal 44*, 3 (2005), 557–571.

[21] Olwal, A., Lachanas, D., and Zacharouli, E. OldGen: Mobile phone personalization for elders. In *Proc. CHI' 11*, 3393–3396.

[22] Picard, R.W., Street, A., and Daily, S.B. Evaluating affective interactions : Alternatives to asking what users feel. *Sciences. New York 1*, (2004), 1–4.

[23] Poole, E.S., Chetty, M., Grinter, R.E., and Edwards, W.K. More than meets the eye: transforming the user experience of home network management. In *Proc. DIS '08*, 455–464.

[24] Poole, E.S., Chetty, M., Morgan, T., Grinter, R.E., and Edwards, W.K. Computer Help at Home : Methods and Motivations for Informal Technical Support. *Methods 34*, 3 (2009), 739–748.

[25] Shneiderman, B. Universal usability. *Communications of the ACM 43*, 5 (2000), 84–91.

[26] Sloan, D., Atkinson, M.T., Machin, C., and Li, Y. The potential of adaptive interfaces as an accessibility aid for older web users. In *Proc. W4A 10*, (2010), 1.

[27] Sue, S. When Elderly Loved Ones Live Far Away: The Challenge of Long-Distance Care. *Wall Street Journal*, 2004.

[28] Walter S. Lasecki, Young Chol Song, Henry A. Kautz, Jeffrey P. Bigham: Real-time crowd labeling for deployable activity recognition. In *Proc. CSCW '13*, 1203-1212.

[29] Wobbrock, J.O., Kane, S.K., Gajos, K.Z., Harada, S., and Froehlich, J. Ability-Based Design: Concept, Principles and Examples. *ACM ToCHI '11:3*, 3, 1–36.

[30] Yeh, T., Chang, T. H., & Miller, R. C. Sikuli: using GUI screenshots for search and automation. In *Proc. UIST '09*, 183-192.

[31] S. Zhao, K. Nakamura, K. Ishii, and T. Igarashi. Magic cards: a paper tag interface for implicit robot control. In *Proc. CHI '09*, 173-182.

"My Hand Doesn't Listen to Me!": Adoption and Evaluation of a Communication Technology for the 'Oldest Old'

Barbara Barbosa Neves[1] Rachel L. Franz[1] Cosmin Munteanu[2,1] Ronald Baecker[1] Mags Ngo[1]
[1]Technologies for Aging Gracefully Lab, Department of Computer Science, University of Toronto
[2]Insitute for Communication, Culture, Information, and Technology, University of Toronto Mississauga
[barbara, rachel, ron, cosmin, mags]@taglab.ca

ABSTRACT
Adoption and use of novel technology by the institutionalized 'oldest old' (80+) is understudied. This population is the fastest growing demographic group in developed countries, providing design opportunities and challenges for HCI. Since the recruitment of oldest old people is challenging, research tends to focus on older adults (65+) and their use of and attitudes towards existing communication technologies, or on their caregivers and social ties. Our study deployed a novel communication appliance among five frail oldest old people living in a long-term care facility, which included field observations and usability and accessibility tests. Our findings suggest factors that facilitate and hinder the adoption of communication technologies, such as social, attitudinal, digital literacy, physical, and usability. We also discuss issues that arise in studying technology adoption by the oldest old, including usability and accessibility testing, and suggest solutions that may be helpful to HCI researchers working with this population.

ACM CLASSIFICATION KEYWORDS
H.5.2 [User Interfaces]: Evaluation/Methodology, User-centered design. K.4.2 [Social Issues]: Handicapped persons/special needs.

AUTHOR KEYWORDS
Oldest old; communication technologies; adoption; evaluation; usability; accessibility; methodology.

INTRODUCTION
The 'oldest old', people over 80 years of age, are the fastest growing demographic group in developed countries [35, 1]. According to recent demographic projections, this age group will account for 19% of the global population in 2050: i.e., approximately 400 million people [36]. This demographic trend presents both design opportunities and challenges for human-computer interaction. For instance, the interest in communication technologies to enable social interaction and connectedness among older adults (aged 65+) is increasing in the HCI community [2]. However, the oldest old are still an understudied population in the field, particularly those living in institutional settings, such as long-term care facilities (nursing homes).

Living in long-term care facilities is one of the top factors that may put older adults at risk of social isolation and loneliness, because of reduced interaction with social networks [6]. Thus, communication technologies can help older adults overcome the physical barriers of interacting with their social networks [10]. In addition, recent literature suggests that communication technologies can enhance active aging and sense of independence in older adults [29]. Therefore, designing communication technologies for institutionalized oldest old is critical because this group is at high risk of social isolation, loneliness, and lack of independence. Oldest old people that experience social isolation and loneliness are more likely to suffer from depression, stress, cognitive decline, morbidity, and mortality [3].

In this context, we developed a digital communication appliance for older adults living in environments associated with social isolation and loneliness. Our appliance, InTouch, is an accessible software application (currently running on Android-based tablets) that has a non-language specific interface (based on icons) and supports asynchronous communication (see Figures 1 and 2). No typing is required, only tapping or swiping, since it was developed for older adults with dexterity problems resulting from motor impairments. It allows older adults to send "waves" (pre-set "I'm thinking of you" messages) to family

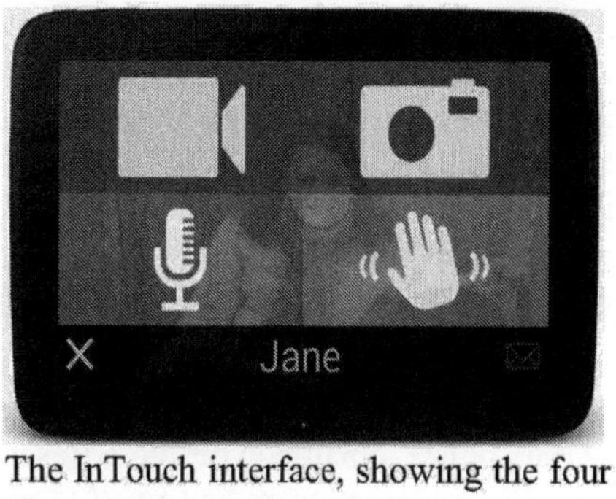

Figure 1: The InTouch interface, showing the four message options: video, picture, audio and 'wave'.

CHI 2015, April 18 - 23 2015, Seoul, Republic of Korea

ACM 978-1-4503-3145-6/15/04...$15.00
http://dx.doi.org/10.1145/2702123.2702430

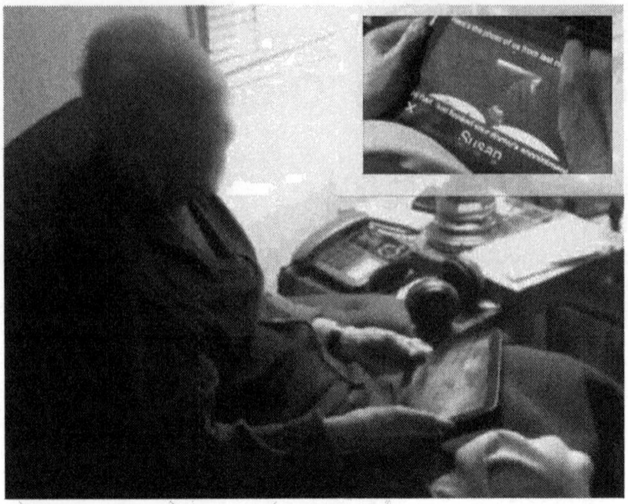
Figure 2: A participant using InTouch.

members and friends, and also photo, voice, and video messages. They can also receive photos, text, voice, and video messages sent by family members and friends. It follows the design of "communication appliances for intimate social networks" [25] and several iterations of field studies and prototype design and deployment [3].

This study examines factors for adoption and use of this communication technology among five oldest old living in a long-term care facility. Since our appliance is icon-based, we tested it with a Canadian-based cultural group whose first language is Chinese. Our findings show factors that facilitate and hinder adoption and use. We also discuss technology evaluation with this population (e.g., recruitment, training, and usability and accessibility testing), suggesting solutions for some of the problems we encountered.

RELATED WORK

How and why people adopt new technologies is a key issue for researchers and designers. Several models of technology adoption exist in the literature [15, 11, 20, 39], but most consider adoption in the workplace. Nonetheless, the 'Technology Acceptance Model' (TAM) developed by Davis (1985) has been applied outside of workplace studies and has become a common model for predicting system use [4, 8]. TAM contains three main indicators: 'Perceived Usefulness', 'Perceived Ease-of-Use', and 'Attitude Toward Using/Behavioral Intention' [11, 8]. Despite some criticisms on accounts of weak theoretical frameworks and simplistic deterministic relationships, it continues to be used as a baseline model [4, 8, 20]. TAM has also been used in the study of older adults and their adoption of communication technologies [29].

Although several studies focus on the adoption of communication technology among older adults, most investigate their use of and attitudes towards existing technology (i.e., phone, email, Skype, etc.). Research shows that weighing the perceived costs and benefits is one of the main factors for adoption: for instance, many non-computer users perceive the costs to be too great to compensate for the benefits of using newer communication technology [9, 26, 32]. But older adults who adopted email perceived the greatest benefit as being able to keep in touch with family, supplementing visits and phone calls [9, 14, 26, 32]. The ability of email to bridge time zones and distance was also an important perceived benefit [14, 23, 26]. Another major factor for the adoption of current technology is the desire to be included in family interaction, which leads many older users to adapt to the communication methods of their close ties [9, 23, 30]. For example, many participants in [32, 30] used Skype to keep in touch with young grandchildren. Yet, these findings apply to older adults (65+) in general and do not specifically address the oldest old.

The study of adoption of novel technologies among the oldest old is lacking in the literature. A few studies, however, explored the perceptions of older adults towards novel communication technology. These studies have mainly focused on the design phase, since participatory design with older adults has great potential for facilitating their adoption [24, 37, 40, 41]. In addition, much of the literature targets caregivers and family members: for example, reports on devices that enable monitoring older adults' well-being have explored acceptance by the social unit in general rather than the older adult [5, 10, 22, 28, 42]. In one notable exception, Lindley investigated older adults attitudes and use of a novel technology, concluding that convenience, asynchronicity, the informal conversational aspect of the technology, direct contact with grandchildren, and their ability to be creative were factors for adoption. Nonetheless, other factors such as the usability of the device were not investigated [22]. Usability factors seem to be relevant for adoption, because research shows that the 'fear' or 'anxiety' expressed by older adults does not result from technophobia but from lack of digital literacy [9, 29].

RESEARCH QUESTIONS

We contribute to the aforementioned literature by examining how an understudied population (oldest old people living in an institutionalized setting) adopts and uses a novel communication technology. This study expands upon prior work [3], which included interviews about general communication patterns of older adults living in a variety of sites, two probes introducing early prototype communication appliances, and the use of a first version of InTouch by a female older adult living in a retirement residence.

In this paper, we report on our new deployment of InTouch with five oldest old individuals living in a long-term care facility. This study is guided by the following research questions:

RQ1 What facilitates the adoption of a communication appliance among institutionalized oldest old people?

RQ2 What hinders the adoption of a communication appliance among institutionalized oldest old people?

The unique characteristics of our user group (frail and low-digital literacy oldest old living in institutionalized settings) presented significant challenges in selecting appropriate evaluation methods. Therefore, this paper also contributes to the literature on human-computer interaction by discussing those challenges, ranging from recruitment and training to usability and accessibility testing with this population. For example, although Dickinson et al. [13] suggest ways of adapting usability tests to older adults, the suggestions were not sufficient to overcome the challenges we encountered when selecting and conducting an appropriate usability and accessibility testing technique. Thus, we describe our challenges and advance possible solutions in order to answer:

RQ3 How to conduct technology evaluation with the oldest old?

Our study sheds light on a specific group of users (their perceptions, meanings, and contexts) and provides insight into research and design opportunities that helps refine our understanding of design implications for seniors, complementing our previous work [3]. This is reflected in a set of extended and refined considerations for the design of elder-centric technologies (numbered as **Di** throughout the paper) and for the evaluation of such technologies (numbered as **Ei**).

METHODS

To explore factors that facilitate and hinder the adoption of communication technology amongst this understudied population, we conducted a two-month deployment of InTouch with five residents of a long-term care facility in Toronto, Canada. Following a mixed methods approach (i.e., a combination of qualitative and quantitative research techniques), the deployment included field observations and usability and accessibility tests. Each participant was taught individually by the researchers to use the device in one training session at the beginning of the study. Then InTouch was given to each participant to use as they saw fit. At least one family member had to be part of the study and participate in this training session to understand how InTouch works. These family members were encouraged to use their own devices to send messages to their participating seniors, but were not followed-up during the study to prevent bias related to 'topic involvement' (e.g., obligation to increase communication with loved ones due to the study).

The training sessions were staggered, so that only one participant was introduced to the study per week. These staggered starts were required by the long-term care facility, due to staff support and logistics (the facility only had one conference room and participants lived in shared rooms). The researchers followed-up with each participant weekly for approximately 20-25 minutes. Data from these weekly visits (informal conversations and observations) were written as field notes both in situ (if possible) and retrospectively.

The usability and accessibility tests were conducted four weeks after the training session, and were audio and video recorded. The participants, if interested, were able to keep InTouch at the end of the study. Our university Office of Research Ethics approved this study.

Participants

Staff of the long-term care facility, i.e., geriatric professionals, recruited our five participants. We asked staff members to distribute recruitment materials, namely a flyer about the study, a brochure about our lab, and a study description document, during meal times and social activities. Staff members then approached both interested and potential participants according to age and cognitive criteria. The selection criteria excluded residents with advanced levels of dementia, who would not be able to understand informed consent. Staff has access to residents' health records (for ethical reasons not shared with us), so they made the final selection. Recruitment among this population of oldest old is particularly challenging due to health and ethical issues. For instance, we were working with one long-term care facility and one independent living community and expected to have 8 participants in each institution. Some of the challenges we faced included health decline (cognitive and functional) and death within the initial pool of participants, which considerably affected the sample size. This sample size suits, nonetheless, our research strategy of an in-depth study of oldest old. Of these five participants (see Table 1), only four were able to fully participate in the study. Due to health problems, Ms.

Pseudonym	*Age*	*Gender*	*Previous occupation*	*Marital Status*	*Impairments*
Ms. A.	90	F.	-	Widowed	Stroke survivor; Wheelchair user
Ms. B.	81	F.	Factory worker	Widowed	Parkinson's disease
Mr. C.	88	M.	Businessman	Married	Stroke survivor; Wheelchair user; Use of one hand
Mr. D.	84	M.	Teacher	Widowed	Stroke survivor; Reduced hearing; Wheelchair user; Use of one hand
Ms. E.	93	F.	Farmer and factory worker	Widowed	N/A

Table 1. Socio-demographics of the participants

A., is still in an early stage of introduction to the device (even though she was the first to be enrolled in the study).

Because we wanted to test our icon-based appliance in a cross-cultural context, the participants of our study were Chinese Canadian and spoke primarily Chinese: four spoke Cantonese and one spoke Mandarin. In the opinion of the researchers, they had a basic functional level of English. However, one of the researchers was fluent in Cantonese and the conversational data was mainly collected in the participants' native language with staff support. The age of the participants ranged from 81 to 93 ($M = 87.2$, $SD = 4.8$). Three were women and two were men. Additional socio-demographic information can be found in Table 1.

Data Procedures & Analysis

A Chinese-speaking researcher conducted the fieldwork accompanied by a Chinese-speaking staff member at the long-term care facility and by an English-speaking researcher. The Chinese-speaking researcher and staff member translated the conversations in situ for the English-speaking researcher, who took notes. Before the coding process, the data was translated to English by the Chinese-speaking researcher and complemented by the field notes of the non-Chinese speaking researcher. We made provisions to independently validate translations by using a second Chinese-speaking researcher, when necessary.

The data were analyzed with individual profiling and thematic analysis: first, we crafted profiles of each participant, which "allows us to present the participant in context, to clarify his or her intentions, and to convey a sense of process and time, all central components of qualitative analysis" [33]. Second, we examined categories, patterns, and connections, trying to find a balance between within-case and cross-case analysis [31]. The thematic analysis mostly involved an inductive approach, i.e., themes emerged from and were grounded in the data. However, due to its centrality in the literature on technology adoption and older adults, TAM's indicators were also considered as a priori themes in the coding process (deductively). Yet, the inductive work provides an in-depth coding that overcomes the limitations of a deductive approach based on a single model such as TAM.

We used the following procedures: Firstly, the main, second, and fifth author coded independently to identify categories and themes. Secondly, the first and second authors coded together, using a label-coding scheme, and tested for convergence. Thirdly, the coded categories were conceptualized into broader themes. Finally, the fifth author examined the data to determine coding reliability: the inter-rater reliability for coding was 95%, calculated by counting discrepancies in category assignment between the codes and themes of the three authors, and by dividing them by the total category assignments.

RESULTS AND DISCUSSION

Critical Factors for Adoption

In this section, we consider factors that facilitated and hindered the adoption of a communication technology among our group of institutionalized oldest old. Of the five participants, only four fully adopted and used the device. Frequency of use varies across the four participants: on average, Ms. B. uses it four days per week, Mr. C. uses it twice every two weeks, Mr. D. uses it three days per week, and Ms. E. uses it three days per week.

From our field observations and usability and accessibility tests, we uncovered a set of factors, which included social, attitudinal, digital literacy, physical, and usability. These factors are not meant to be mutually exclusive categories; most are interconnected.

Social Factors

Social support, i.e., having family members deeply engaged in the adoption and use of our appliance, was a determinant factor for two of our participants. Even though Ms. B. and Ms. E. were digitally illiterate, the support provided by their family members enabled them to become functional users. The family of Ms. B. (daughter and granddaughter) would visit her often and would help her learn to use it; the daughter of Ms. E. would visit her daily and they would use it together. Within the four weeks between the start of the study and the testing phase, Ms. B. became the most frequent user of our participants. She also had the most social ties in her app contacts, which allowed her to communicate with a large social network and gain experience with the tool. Ms. E. did not use the appliance by herself frequently, but she seemed confident about the options that she used the most.

By contrast, Mr. C. only had one family member, his son, involved with the project. His son was not very engaged, did not visit often, and was his only app contact. In the four weeks of the study, there was very little communication between Mr. C. and his son on the appliance. During the usability and accessibility test, Mr. C. was unable to recall how to use the device and had to be prompted to perform tasks such as sending a picture message.

Besides reduced social support, other social factors that may act as demotivators for the adoption of a communication technology are related to contexts and cultural issues. With regards to contexts, adoption and usage may be reduced if participants are living in a setting that for security reasons requires devices to be locked and attached to their beds as in our study. As such, we recommend that designers

> **Factor security into the design of the interaction**, e.g., use of device while secured by a cable lock. (Recommendation *D1*)

Cultural idiosyncrasies can also affect the adoption of a device: for example, one of the icons (the wave) was not perceived by the participants as a greeting sign but as a cancel sign, because this gesture means 'no' in Chinese culture. In our previous research with participants whose first language was English, the wave was considered the most basic function and, therefore, frequently used as the preferred option for novice users [3]. However, as our Chinese Canadian participants did not understand the cultural meaning of the wave, it was seldom used. For this, we suggest that designers

> **Consider (and evaluate early) cultural issues in the design of icons, particularly given users' age and strong attachment to a specific culture.** (*D2*)

Attitudinal Factors

The attitudinal factors entailed perceived usefulness, positive attitudes towards learning, and sense of ownership. Perceived usefulness is a category drawn from TAM, being primarily defined as "the degree to which a person believes that using a particular system would enhance his or her job performance" [12]. Although expressed in an organizational context, this category refers broadly to the ability of a system to be used advantageously. In our case, perceived usefulness included users seeing value in our appliance for communication with family members. It also included the ability to choose different message types, for instance, three of the participants, Ms. B., Mr. C., and Mr. D., preferred to send audio messages to their family members and to receive text messages. According to these participants the audio option was more convenient, which seems to tap into their familiarity with the telephone as a communication medium. As Mr. D. puts it:

"They can listen to my voice and it's more personal, there is more communication in it".

The preference for the reception of text messages shows the importance of text or "paper-based" communication [18].

Usefulness was also connected to the fact that our technology allowed for different types of use: active vs. passive. Some participants reported preferring a more passive usage, including Ms. E. and Ms. B., which meant receiving messages instead of sending out messages (lurking), whereas others preferred a more active approach, such as Mr. D. For example, Mrs. E. was very assertive about her preference for using the device to receive messages, particularly pictures, as she was illiterate. As such, we encourage designers to:

> **Design a communication system that allows for different types of use (passive vs. active) and different types of messages (audio, text, etc.) that suit the large diversity of uses and users.** (*D3*)

Other aspects that confirm the perceived value of our appliance were 1) the message history, and 2) its advantage over existing communication technologies, especially when communicating with family members living abroad. For instance, Mr. D. explains:

"The telephone is hard to hear, so this is better because I receive a text message in Chinese and can reply with an audio message...Email is hard because the keyboard of computers are in English...With this I can send audio messages in Chinese and my son can respond with text in Chinese."

We found that four participants, with the exception of Ms. A., were active learners, displaying positive attitudes towards learning. During the researchers' weekly visits as well as participants' family visits, participants would ask questions about how to use the device. Ms. B. and Ms. E.'s family were especially instrumental in the learning process, reminding them how to do things on the appliance when they forgot. Mr. D. reported referring to the paper-based manual when using the device. All participants expressed the need to practice to become proficient users, indicating their desire to master InTouch. In Mr. D.'s words:

"I don't say it's very easy [to learn the tool], because then you won't have a good attitude to learn more about it"

Ms. B., Mr. C., and Mr. D. had a sense of ownership or property of the tool, which seemed to facilitate its adoption. For example, Mr. D. changed the language settings of the tablet to Chinese. He also frequently used the tablet to browse Chinese news sites. Both Mr. D. and Ms. B. had a clear sense of preferences for message types.

To address learning challenges, we suggest that researchers

> **Provide a variety of assists (e.g., frequent face-to-face training, a printed user manual) because this population appreciates additional support.** (*D4*)

Digital Literacy

Mr. D. had experience with a desktop computer, so he was also very comfortable with the idea of using InTouch. He understood the purpose of our appliance because he uses email to communicate with family. In fact, he was familiar enough with technology to be able to brainstorm some additional features for our appliance, such as a voice-to-text and translation feature. He suggested that this would enhance inter-generational communication for this cultural group since younger family members mainly speak English.

The other four participants (Ms. A., Ms. B., Mr. C., and Ms. E.) were digitally illiterate, which means that compared to Mr. D. they showed an overall lack of understanding of tablets and applications; in other words, they did not know much about what could and could not be done with the device. However, the strong social support of two of our participants, Ms. B. and Ms. E. compensated for their lack of digital literacy. These observations reinforce the recommendation we made in [3] to:

Design a communication technology more as an appliance and less as a computing device. *(D5)*

Physical Factors

All of our participants were frail, which at times hindered their use of the device. Motor and dexterity issues were the main demotivators, as Ms. B. puts it:

"My hand does not listen to me! Sometimes my hand does not listen to me…"

Mr. D also adds:

"I have fat fingers…"

All participants complained about the heaviness of the tablet (10"), and reported that it made it difficult to use some of the app features such as the camera and video camera. Although we provided a tablet cover that converted to a stand, this was not sufficient to use the tablet comfortably. Even though participants viewed the weight of the tablet as a significant barrier to its use, they found ways to overcome it including resting the tablet in their arm and having other people help them lift the device. As such, we suggest that designers

Address physical factors, such as the weight of the device and dexterity issues of this population, and account for limitations in the mobility of the appliance, e.g. users may not be able to use the appliance while walking. *(D6)*

Usability Factors

We found that perceived ease of use was a major facilitator of adoption. Perceived ease of use is a category drawn from TAM that refers to the "degree to which a person believes that using a particular system would be free of effort" [12]. But we observed that even though many of our participants had difficulty completing some tasks, they reported that the task was not difficult per se. Therefore, we had to separate this category into conceptual ease of use and practical ease of use.

1. Conceptual Ease of Use

Often users were not able to remember the steps to complete a goal, such as sending a video message to a contact. However, once the researchers reminded the participant how to complete the task, the participant would rate the task as not difficult. The researchers observed that once the participant got the hang of using the device in the usability test, they became noticeably comfortable with the device. Another interesting finding was that two of our participants (Mr. C. and Mr. D.) mentioned repeatedly that if they had more practice, they would know how to better use InTouch. They also felt that it was easy to use, but they were not completely familiar with it after the four weeks of having the device. This suggests that at a conceptual level, they perceived it as not difficult to use even though it was not easy for them to perform some tasks at that moment.

2. Practical Ease of Use

Our participants reported that some functions were easy to execute and we could see them comfortably executing them. For instance, Ms. B., Mr. C., and Ms. E., remembered how to access the message history and scroll through and view old messages. They rated these tasks as easy to complete, and they were very relaxed with these features during the usability tests. The same happened to Ms. B., Mr. D., and Ms. E. in terms of getting to and swiping through their contacts.

Our data also shows that they were able to infer, guess, and recall how to perform certain functions easily. For example, Mr. C. was able to send a video message during the usability test even though he had struggled before with sending a picture message. These examples demonstrate the level of learnability of our appliance.

3. Ambiguous Affordances

One of the aspects worth reporting about this particular group of older users was their literal understanding of the icons and functionality. For example, when asked to send a wave message, Mr. D. wanted to record a video message of himself waving. Ms. B. thought that the camera icon indicated the ability to send both picture and video messages. Mr. C. and Mr. D. interpreted the arrow icons as a description of the required gesture. The icon for switching front and back cameras was a circular arrow, and the icon for going back was a curvilinear arrow icon – we observed both participants tracing the icons with their fingers when interacting with them.

None of the participants were familiar with touchscreen gestures, so they did not know when to use swiping vs. tapping. It seemed that they would choose one over the other at random whenever appropriate feedback from the appliance was not provided. Although we did not ask for their preference of swiping over tapping, we noticed that swiping seemed to give them a sense of control. In fact, Mr. C. explains:

"Sometimes when I poke at it doesn't go anywhere, but swiping gives a response."

Because ambiguous affordances can hinder adoption and create frustration among users, we recommend to

Avoid the use of ambiguous affordances, and test/redesign the interface early on with the target users to detect any unexpected meanings attached to the interface elements. *(D7)*

And, given this population's lack of understanding for gestures and non-familiarity with conventions surrounding mobile interface affordances, we suggest that:

Explicit affordances are provided and the icons indicate how to gesture (e.g. arrows for swiping), **even if this means sacrificing aesthetics.** *(D8)*

Recursive Approach to Technology Adoption

Our data shows that even though most models of technology adoption consider different factors [19], the adoption of a communication technology by the oldest old is the result of a complex interaction of social, individual (physical and attitudinal), and usability factors. Some of these factors were encountered in prior research with older adults [22, 24, 29, 41], and even in other user groups, for instance, in low-literacy adults [27]. However, the specific context of institutionalized frail oldest old demonstrates that these factors cannot be evaluated individually. Our findings indicate that some factors seem to compensate for others, e.g., strong social support compensated for digital illiteracy.

In this sense, TAM is limited as a theoretical model since it neglects the interplay of social context, human agency (individual choices), and inherent properties of technology. As such, a recursive approach is more adequate to frame the critical factors for technology adoption found in this study. A recursive approach assumes that contexts and technologies are not distinct dimensions but mutually related, so researchers should study "technologies-in-use" and the relationship between structure (social context) and human agency over time [17]. Our in-depth study over a two-month period allowed us to explore those relationships. Within this recursive approach, Strong Structuration Theory (SST) offers a quadripartite framework to study those relationships that includes: 1) external structures (conditions/dispositions of action), 2) internal structures (knowledge of external structures), 3) active agency (actions/practices), and 4) outcomes [34]. Adapted to the study of technology [17], SST helps to illustrate that our social, attitudinal, physical, and usability factors are intertwined in a dynamic network of structural (e.g., living settings, social support, literacy), agentic (e.g., attitudinal), and technological (e.g., InTouch's characteristics) dimensions. In other words, all these factors interact to provide a particular context of adoption of a novel technology among the oldest old. Context is not only the cause but also the outcome.

Therefore, researchers interested in this population should:

> **Account not only for technological and non-technological factors but also for the interplay between them during technology adoption and evaluation.** *(E1)*

Technology Evaluation with the Oldest Old: Challenges and Suggested Solutions

During our study of oldest old and their adoption of a novel technology, we encountered several challenges concerning not only the selection and implementation of evaluation methods but also the recruitment and training of participants. Some of these methodological issues were mentioned in a few studies with older adults [13, 24, 37, 40, 41], but not yet addressed in a systematic or sufficient way. This section answers RQ3 by describing our challenges and advancing possible solutions, which aims to improve the research on adoption of technology by this population.

Recruitment of Participants

The recruitment of institutionalized oldest old poses a significant challenge for research, due to their different levels of frailty, ability to consent to the process, and low digital literacy. A crucial part of the recruitment process was getting meaningful buy-in from the staff. In a previous attempt to conduct the study in a different setting we found that the lack of engagement by the staff was a major impediment to recruitment and ultimately to the study. By contrast, the staff member at the location of our study was extremely engaged in the process. But the lack of involvement of other staff members put pressure on scheduling sessions with participants. In addition, we did not have direct contact with participants' family members outside of the facility, having to rely solely on staff to communicate with them. This added to scheduling issues and lack of follow-ups. Another challenge was that the cognitive decline of one of the participants was not promptly reported to us, which limited the participation and interaction with her and raised ethical concerns.

To address the above challenges, we suggest that researchers:

> **Ensure proxies (staff, caregivers) are engaged since the inception of the study, in its design, recruitment, and evaluation.** *(E2)*

This would ensure an ongoing relationship between staff and researchers, facilitating access to important information about family interactions and possible changes in participants' health (which could affect consent and participation). If staff is engaged, they will be more willing to give access to the participants' family members. Staff engagement could be accomplished by info sessions tailored to staff members, where the project, researchers, and goals are presented and discussed in an informal and interactive meeting. To increase the trust of the staff and to alleviate their burden, researchers should also be involved in the recruitment of participants. For example, researchers can organize open info sessions for residents and family members, since existing literature on recruitment of older adults shows the importance of face-to-face activities [2].

Introduction to the Technology

Our deployment included an initial training session with the participants. In these training sessions we encountered five main challenges: first, we did not account for the level of security of the institution before starting the study, which meant that the tablet had to be secured by the staff before the participant was able to start using it alone. Additionally, adding a security lock to the tablet after the training session introduced an unfamiliar element to the appliance. Second, we prepared an interactive scenario between the two researchers conducting the training session to demonstrate the use of the technology and put it into context, but during the training sessions we had to change our approach because the participants were eager to interact with the appliance. Third, another challenge we encountered was the lack of digital literacy of one of our participant's family members. During the training sessions, family members were supposed to interact with participants using their own devices (computers or smartphones) as a part of the demo. Even though one of the participants' family members had an android phone, she did not know how to send or receive emails. Therefore, the demo with the participant was not interactive since one of the researchers had to teach the family member to use email on her smartphone. Fourth, although we introduced touch screen gestures (tapping and swiping) during the training session, we did not teach them outside of the context of the appliance. In our usability and accessibility tests, we observed that the participants were still not comfortable with touchscreen gestures. This observation highlights the need to teach gestures in isolation from the outset. Fifth, we observed that due to the frailty of the participants and the deviation from their established routine, 50-70 minutes sessions were overwhelming and did not allow them to fully absorb the information.

We put forward some suggestions to overcome the limitations described above. First, ask staff if participants will be able to keep their devices with them in a secure place. If not, add a locking system before the introduction. This would prevent the addition of a possibly negative element to the device. To address the second, third, fourth, and fifth challenges, we suggest that researchers

> **Conduct training sessions that are frequent, flexible, brief, and inclusive of family members.** (*E3*)

In particular, we recommend a **less structured approach** to the training session allowing for customization. Researchers should guide participants through the demo facilitating their interaction with the device. If participants' family members are not sufficiently tech-savvy to be able to communicate with the participant through their own device, arrange a training session **with the family member prior to the introduction session** to teach them. Finally, training sessions should be **shorter** (40 minutes or less) and **more frequent** to accommodate for the participants' pace and mental endurance – especially since practice and repetition are crucial to enhancing learning and usage [7, 30]. This is supported by recent research that shows that fluid intelligence, which declines with age and affects working memory, can be improved by training [19]. And all participants indicated the need to practice more as to improve their digital literacy.

Usability and Accessibility testing

Our study followed a user-based testing approach to improve upon the interface and user experience. The usability and accessibility tests included an ordered task list and a set of questions and scales [21]. Although we applied the standard procedures for usability and accessibility testing, we found that some aspects were difficult to follow due to the characteristics of our sample. Firstly, the **Think Aloud technique** [38] **did not work** with our participants since they were too frail to perform tasks and explain them at the same time. Secondly, they **could not quantify their answers in terms of the 5-point Likert scales** that we used to measure their perception of the difficulty of the task or in some cases the appearance of the interface. For instance, Ms. B. reported that some tasks were:

"Sometimes easy, sometimes hard..."

In most other cases, quantifying the difficulty of a task seemed to be too abstract for them to rate. Thirdly, self-presentation and impression management [16] (the need to make a good impression on the researcher) were obvious during the testing sessions: two participants (that only had the use of one hand, Mr. C. and Mr. D.) reported that the device was easy to lift, but when asked to perform it they acknowledged that it was actually not that easy. In another example, all participants expressed that they did not find anything wrong or difficult with our appliance but then we saw them struggling with some tasks. The feeling of being tested or evaluated, even though we set it up as an informal activity, could have contributed to their impression management efforts.

Because of these problems, we encountered two limitations with the usability and accessibility testing: we could not fully understand their strategies and perceptions or grasp their mental model of the system. For example, we did not know if they recalled the steps to perform a task, if they were able to infer them or if they were simply using trial and error. Furthermore, as the participants were unfamiliar with touchscreen gestures, they had no notion of gesture conventions (i.e., swipe to scroll). Therefore, we did not understand why at some times they would choose to swipe over tap and vice versa. With regards to their mental model of the system, we did not know if they understood that the interface was consistent across icons and actions on different screens. Sometimes it seemed like they had a notion that they could perform the same sequence of steps in a different context, but other times it seemed that they were pressing the most salient icons at the time.

To address some of these issues, we advise researchers to

> **Ensure the evaluation techniques are appropriate to the ability and level of literacy of the participants.** (*E4*)

In order to take the burden off the participants and possibly reduce impression management efforts (the perceived need of participants to make a good impression on the researcher), we recommend:

Asking about how other older adults they know or that live in the same residence would perceive or assess that communication technology. (*E5*).

Finally, we suggest that researchers

Aim to shed light on users' mental model of the system and their strategies to perform tasks (*E6*)

While evaluating InTouch in situ with oldest old users, several approaches emerged for implementing the above recommendation (*E6*). For example, researchers may ask participants to **explain the meaning of icons and features**. This can provide insight into their level of understanding of what they know they can do with a communication technology. Additionally, by having participants use a mock-up designed specifically for testing purposes that has same icons and similar steps might help to test for inference and their understanding of consistency across different screens. To explore their strategy for accomplishing a task, ask if they guessed or remembered how to do it **from their previous experience** with the original communication technology. This can also reduce anxiety and impression management, since they will not be expected to know how to do everything in the new context.

Another way to shed light on their mental model of the system is to **ask users to explain to a friend** what the communication technology does. This will reveal their overall understanding of the tool, and whether they are missing some important concepts. Users' perceptions towards the use of the tool can be revealed by **asking comparative questions**, such as their preference for swiping vs. tapping. Having the participant **perform the task before answering** the researcher's question will likely produce a more accurate response (i.e., lifting the device before reporting how difficult it is to lift it). Finally, we found it useful to **remind participants** how to do the next step in the sequence to get them back on track, as they often could not remember how to achieve the overall tasks even though they were able to recall some of the steps.

CONCLUSION

This article explored factors that facilitate and hinder adoption of a novel communication technology by institutionalized oldest old (80+). Our findings show that a complex interplay of factors – social, attitudinal, physical, digital literacy, and usability – influence the adoption of communication technologies. Researchers and designers should not consider these factors in isolation, but as inter-related: for example, strong social support compensated, in some cases, for the lack of digital literacy. Despite the fact that this age group is often considered homogeneous because of their overall frailty, we also found that even within our sample there was significant diversity between individuals. In addition, our study reveals a set of challenges in the technology evaluation process. These challenges relate to recruitment, training, and usability and accessibility testing. Based on our experiences, we suggest a set of possible solutions to overcome some of these challenges.

Since we aimed to gain an in-depth understanding of a group of institutionalized oldest old, this research is limited by a small and non-representative sample and by possible cultural idiosyncrasies of Chinese Canadians. Yet, our work adds to the existing but scant literature on the field and contributes further with a reflection on research and design difficulties and recommendations. Future research should compare technology adoption across different cultural groups, consider longitudinal studies of adoption and use, and also test and expand upon our proposed solutions. In light of the lessons learned, we are now designing a new deployment study in a multi-site strategy (including residents of long-term or complex care facilities and home-care recipients) to deepen our recursive approach to technology adoption and to test our evaluation solutions.

ACKNOWLEDGEMENTS

We are grateful for financial support to Revera Inc., the GRAND NCE, OCE, Connect Canada, and NSERC Canada. We are also grateful to all TAGlab members who have contributed to this project.

REFERENCES

[1] Andersen-Ranberg, K., et al. Who are the oldest old? In: A. Börsch-Supan et al. Health, Ageing and Retirement in Europe, MEA, Mannheim, Germany (2005)

[2] Auster, J., Janda, M. Recruiting older adults to health research studies: A systematic review. Australasian journal on ageing 28, 3 (2009).

[3] Baecker, R., Sellen, K., Boscart, V., Crosskey, S., Neves, B.B. Technology to reduce social isolation and loneliness. In Proc. ACM ASSETS 2014

[4] Bagozzi, R.P. The legacy of the technology acceptance model and a proposal for a paradigm shift. Journal for the Association for Information Systems 8, 4 (2007)

[5] Blythe, M., Wright, P. Bowers, J., Boucher, A., Jarvis N., Reynolds, P., Gaver, B. Age and experience: Ludic engagement in a residential care setting. In Proc. ACM DIS 2010

[6] British Columbia Ministry of Health. Social isolation among seniors: An emerging issue. www.health.gov.bc.ca/library/publications/year/2004/Social_Isolation_Among_Seniors.pdf

[7] Chaffin, A. J., & Harlow, S. D. Cognitive learning applied to older adult learners and technology. Educational Gerontology 31, 4 (2005)

[8] Chuttur, M.Y. Overview of the technology acceptance model: Origin, developments and future directions. Working Papers on Information Systems 9, 37 (2009).

[9] Coleman, G.W., Gibson, L., Hanson, V.L., Bobrowicz, A., McKay, A. Engaging the disengaged: How do we design technology for digitally excluded older adults? In Proc. UAHCI 2009, Springer-Verlag

[10] Dadlani, P., Sinistyn, A., Fontijn, W., Markopoulos, P. Aurama: caregiver awareness for living independently with an augmented picture frame display. AI & Society 25, 2 (2010)

[11] Davis, F.D. A technology acceptance model for empirically testing new end-user information systems: Theory and results. Doctoral Dissertation, MIT, 1985.

[12] Davis, F. Perceived Usefulness, Perceived Ease of Use and User Acceptance of Information Technology. MIS Quarterly 13, 3 (1989)

[13] Dickinson, A., Arnott, J., Prior, S. Methods for human-computer interaction research with older people. Behaviour & Information Technology: Designing Computer Systems for and with Older Users, 4 (2007)

[14] Dickinson, A., Hill, R.L. Keeping in touch: Talking to older people about computers and communication. Educational Gerontology 33, 8 (2007)

[15] 15. Dourish, P. The appropriation of Interactive Technologies: Some lessons from placeless documents. Computer Supported Cooperative Work 12, 4 (2003)

[16] Goffman, E. The presentation of self in everyday life. Penguin, London, UK, 1959.

[17] Greenhalgh, T., Stones, R. (2010). Theorising big IT programmes in healthcare: strong structuration theory meets actor-network theory. Social science & medicine, 70(9)

[18] Hope, A., Schwaba, T., Piper, A. Understanding the digital and material social communications for older adults. In Proc. CHI 2014. ACM Press (2014)

[19] Jaeggi, S. M., Buschkuehl, M., Jonides, J., & Perrig, W. J. Improving fluid intelligence with training on working memory. In Proc. PNAS 2008

[20] Lampe, C., Vitak, J., & Ellison, N. Users and nonusers: Interactions between levels of adoption and social capital. In Proc. ACM CSCW 2013

[21] Lazar, J., Feng, J.H., Hochheiser, H. Research methods in human-computer interaction. John Wiley Sons, 2010

[22] Lindley, S.E. Shades of lightweight: Supporting cross-generational messaging through home messaging. Universal Access in the Information Society, 1 (2012)

[23] Lindley, S.E., Harper, R., Sellen, A. Desiring to be in touch in a changing communications landscape: Attitudes of older adults. In Proc. ACM CHI 2009

[24] Lindsay, S., Jackson, D., Schofield, G., Olivier, P. Engaging Older People using Participatory Design. In Proc. ACM CHI 2012

[25] McKay, W., Riche, Y., LaBrune, J.B. Communication Appliances: Shared awareness for intimate social networks. In Proc. ACM CHI 2005

[26] Melenhorst, A.S., Rogers, W. A., Caylor, E.C. The use of communication technologies by older adults: Exploring the benefits from the user's perspective. In Proc. HFES Annual Meeting 2001

[27] Munteanu, C., et al. Tale of two studies: challenges in field research with low-literacy adult learners in a developed country. In ACM CHI 2012

[28] Mynatt, E.D., et al. Digital family portraits: Supporting peace of mind for extended family members. In Proc. ACM CHI 2001

[29] Neves, B.B., Amaro, F., Fonseca, J.R. Coming of (old) age in the digital age: ICT usage and non-usage among older adults. Sociological Research Online 18, 2 (2013)

[30] Neves, B.B., Amaro, F. Too old for technology? How the elderly of Lisbon perceive and use ICT. The Journal of Community Informatics 8, 1 (2012).

[31] Patton, M.Q. Qualitative research and evaluation methods. Sage, 1990.

[32] Sayago, S., Sloan, D., Blat, J. Everyday use of computer-mediated communication tools and its evolution over time: An ethnographical study with older people. Interacting with Computers 23, 5 (2011)

[33] Siedman, I. Interviewing as Qualitative Research. Teachers College Press, 2006.

[34] Stones, R. Structuration theory. Basingstoke: (2005).

[35] Suzman, R. M., Willis, D. P., & Manton, K. G. (Eds.). The oldest old. Oxford University Press, 1995

[36] United Nations, World Population Aging. United Nations, New York, NY, 2013

[37] Uzor, S., Baillie, L., Skelton, D.A. Senior Designers: empowering seniors to design enjoyable falls rehabilitation tools. In Proc. ACM CHI 2012

[38] van Someren, M.W., Barnard, Y.F., Sandberg, J.A.C. The think aloud method: A practical guide to modeling cognitive processes. Academic Press, 1994

[39] Venkatesh, V., Morris, M.G., Davis, G.B., Davis, F.D. User acceptance of communication technology: Toward a unified view. MIS quarterly, (2003)

[40] Vines, J., et al. Questionable Concepts: Critique as a resource for designing with eighty somethings. In Proc. ACM CHI 2012

[41] Vines, J., et al. Cheque Mates: Participatory Design of Digital Payments with Eighty Somethings. In Proc. ACM CHI 2012

[42] Waycott, J., et al. Captioned photographs in psychological aged care: Relationship building and boundary work. In Proc. ACM CHI 2014

Working with Machines: The Impact of Algorithmic and Data-Driven Management on Human Workers

Min Kyung Lee[1], Daniel Kusbit[1], Evan Metsky[1], Laura Dabbish[1, 2]
[1]Human-Computer Interaction Institute, [2]Heinz College
Carnegie Mellon University
{mklee, dkusbit, emetsky, dabbish}@cmu.edu

ABSTRACT
Software algorithms are changing how people work in an ever-growing number of fields, managing distributed human workers at a large scale. In these work settings, human jobs are assigned, optimized, and evaluated through algorithms and tracked data. We explored the impact of this algorithmic, data-driven management on human workers and work practices in the context of Uber and Lyft, new ridesharing services. Our findings from a qualitative study describe how drivers responded when algorithms assigned work, provided informational support, and evaluated their performance, and how drivers used online forums to socially make sense of the algorithm features. Implications and future work are discussed.

Author Keywords
Algorithm; algorithmic management; human-centered algorithms; intelligent systems; CSCW; on-demand work; sharing economies; data-driven metrics; work assignment; performance evaluation; dynamic pricing; sensemaking.

ACM Classification Keywords
H.5.m. Information interfaces and presentation (e.g., HCI): Miscellaneous.

INTRODUCTION
Increasingly, software algorithms allocate, optimize, and evaluate work of diverse populations ranging from traditional workers such as subway engineers [16], warehouse workers [28], Starbucks baristas [19], and UPS deliverymen [7] to new crowd-sourced workers in platforms like Uber, TaskRabbit, and Amazon mTurk [13]. How do human workers respond to these algorithms taking roles that human managers used to play?

We call software algorithms that assume managerial functions and surrounding institutional devices that support algorithms in practice *algorithmic management*. Algorithmic management allows companies to oversee myriads of workers in an optimized manner at a large scale, but its impact on human workers and work practices has been largely unexplored. In recent years, the press and many scholars have brought attention to the importance of studying the sociotechnical aspects of algorithms [2, 10, 37], yet to our knowledge, there has been little empirical work in this area.

We explored the impact of algorithmic management in the context of new ridesharing services Uber and Lyft. Algorithmic management is one of the core innovations that enables these services. Independent, distributed drivers with their own cars are algorithmically matched with passengers within seconds or minutes, and the fare dynamically changes based on where passenger demand surges, all through the app on their mobile phones. Drivers' performance is evaluated by passengers' rating of their service quality and drivers' level of cooperation with algorithmic assignment. Algorithmic management allows a few human managers in each city to oversee hundreds and thousands of drivers on a global scale. Drivers have little direct contact with company representatives, but can interact with each other through online forums to gain social knowledge of the rideshare systems. This setting allowed us to explore the practices that emerged when algorithms assigned work, optimized work behavior through information processing and evaluated job performance. Do human workers cooperate with algorithmically-assigned work? How much are people motivated or demotivated by algorithmic optimization? How effective is algorithmic, data-driven evaluation and how do workers feel about it?

As a first step toward answering these questions, we interviewed 21 drivers with Uber and Lyft and triangulated their experiences by interviewing 12 passengers and conducting archival analysis of online driver forums and official company communication materials. The findings highlight opportunities and challenges in designing human-centered algorithmic work assignment, information, and evaluation as well as the importance of supporting social sensemaking around algorithmic systems. We use the findings to discuss how algorithms and data-driven management should be designed to create a better workplace with intelligent machines, offering implications for future work.

Our study makes the following two contributions to human-computer interaction (HCI): 1) we describe the upside and

[redacted]

downside of algorithmic and data-driven management, its impact on human workers, and sensemaking strategies that workers developed; 2) our results highlight new areas of research for HCI, computer-supported cooperative work (CSCW) and intelligent systems.

IMPACT OF MACHINES ON WORK

Two threads of research are closely relevant to the topic of this paper: research on the impact of technology in the workplace and interaction with intelligent machines.

The impact of technology in the workplace

A long and rich stream of research in HCI and CSCW has investigated the impact of technology in the workplace: email [15], instant messaging [18], organizational information repositories [1], groupware [31], video conferencing [9], awareness technologies [12], desktop office software [8, 39], GPS for taxies [11], and robots in hospitals [30]. Collectively, this research shows how psychological, social, and organizational factors shape the adoption of new technologies and how new work practices and norms emerge in the workplace. To our knowledge, very little empirical research has investigated the impact of algorithmic management in the workplace, with the exception of emerging studies of new work-monitoring devices such as GPS for bus drivers [34].

Interaction with intelligent machines

Much research has investigated how people respond to intelligent machines such as automated manufacturing technologies [23, 36, 44], recommender systems [6], context-aware systems [3, 43], agents [35], and robots [30]. As intelligent machines are only recently being integrated into workplaces outside of factories, there is relatively little work that examines intelligent machines in work contexts with exceptions being systems in hospitals [30] and offices [22]. To our knowledge, our paper is one of the first studies that investigates how people respond when intelligent machines take on managerial roles in a workplace. Research on intelligent systems with different roles in other contexts such as home, entertainment, or education has identified important theoretical concepts and design principles for successful human interaction with automated and intelligent machines: establishing trust and cooperation [33], creating accurate mental models [21, 35], providing transparency and explanations [3, 6, 20, 24], and designing shared control between humans and intelligent machines [23, 36]. Our study significantly extends this work by probing the consequences of these design dimensions of intelligent systems in a new context, and by identifying new problems and implications arising from novel managerial roles of intelligent systems.

METHOD

We conducted a qualitative study on algorithmic management in Uber and Lyft. To understand drivers' experiences and perspectives, we interviewed 21 drivers and triangulated our findings by interviewing 12 passengers and analyzing 128 posts by drivers on online forums and 132 official blog posts and communication materials from both of the ridesharing companies.

Research context: Uber & Lyft ridesharing services

Uber and Lyft are currently the largest peer-to-peer ridesharing companies. Founded in 2009 and 2012 respectively, Uber and Lyft operate in over 100 cities in 37 countries. Lyft attempts to create a social culture among customers by encouraging passengers to sit in the front seat and greet the driver with a friendly "fistbump." Uber creates a more professional chauffeur environment where social experience with the driver is not stressed. Anyone over 21 years of age with a valid drivers license and a personal vehicle in good condition can apply to be a driver. Companies screen applicants with a background check, and new drivers go through brief video-based online orientations. Once accepted, new drivers become "independent contractors," not employees, and are in complete control over where, when, and how often to drive.

Algorithmic management in the ridesharing platforms

Three algorithmic features of Uber and Lyft – passenger-driver assignment, the dynamic display of surge-priced areas, and the data-driven evaluation that uses acceptance rates and ratings – respectively correspond to decisional, informational, and evaluation roles of human managers in organizations [29].

Work assignment: Driver-passenger assignment algorithms. Drivers need to turn on their ridesharing app to be able to receive and execute their work. According to Uber, after a rider requests a ride through the mobile application, "the closest driver to that rider automatically receives the trip request with a 15 second window to accept it [42]." (Uber and Lyft will not reveal details of proximity-based assignment algorithm, but in our study, we learned that other things could be factored into the algorithm.) The request includes information about the passenger's location, rating, picture, and name. If the driver accepts the request, the passenger is notified, and the driver drives to the passenger location to start the ride. With both Uber and Lyft, drivers cannot choose or set preferences for specific passengers or rides they wish to receive on their app. Lyft, however, does allow drivers to block assignments from passengers that do not pay the full suggested donation in areas where pricing is still donation based. Uber and Lyft allow only passive rejection of assigned passengers in that, if the driver does not wish to accept the request, they must wait out the allotted 15-second window. After this, the app goes into stand-by mode until there is a new request.

Informational support: Dynamic in-app display of surge-priced areas. Pricing is determined by a standard fare and fluctuates according to a dynamic pricing algorithm. The companies explain this feature to drivers and the public in broad terms. For example, "when demand outstrips supply, dynamic pricing algorithms increase prices to help the market reach equilibrium [41]." In this paper we will refer to this as "surge pricing," adopting the term that Uber uses

(Lyft uses the term "Prime Time"). Surge pricing can play a major role in shaping driver income, as their eighty percent commission remains constant through these periods of peak pricing. As of September 2014, both companies show surge-priced areas in-app with map areas shaded in different colors based on the price in real time. This is designed to motivate drivers to move to areas where demand (and price) is surging, in order to meet passenger demand and maximize the total number of transactions.

Performance evaluation: Rating systems and acceptance rates that track driver performance. After the ride both the passengers and drivers evaluate each other through a 5-star rating system. Lyft instructs that when rating a driver, passengers should "consider whether your driver was friendly, safe, a good navigator, and made you want to use Lyft again [25]." Drivers also have an acceptance rate that is calculated by the number of accepted rides divided by the total number of requests sent to the driver. Drivers are encouraged to keep a high ride acceptance rate through occasional promotions that offer a guaranteed hourly pay if the driver's acceptance rate is above a certain threshold.

Drivers with a low average passenger rating and acceptance rate may be subject to review or even immediate deactivation on the ridesharing platform. Likewise passengers who fall below a rating threshold risk rejection by drivers, as drivers have the ability to ignore incoming requests from passengers with ratings below their liking. Long-standing drivers who maintain a high passenger rating and acceptance rate are occasionally promoted to become mentors or recruiters. In addition to driving for the service, mentors and recruiters recruit new drivers and oversee the application process, while earning extra income for these activities.

Interviews

We conducted semi-structured interviews with drivers to understand their experience with algorithmic management. We also interviewed passengers to confirm drivers' opinions and perceptions about passenger behaviors expressed in their interviews.

Participant recruitment

Online postings and paper flyers were used to solicit current or former Uber or Lyft drivers and passengers. We posted ads on Facebook driver groups, volunteer sections of Craigslist, and relevant Reddit webpages. Paper flyers were posted in three major cities in the US. A $10 gift card was offered for participating in a 30-45 minute interview.

Driver interviews

We interviewed 21 drivers for ridesharing platforms who operated in 13 cities across the United States (15 Males; average age of 35 (SD=8.86)). Of the drivers interviewed, 5 drove for Uber only, 5 drove for Lyft only and 11 drove for both Uber and Lyft. The drivers worked an average of 23.5 hours (SD=21.4) per week and had a range of experience driving for a ridesharing platform (3 weeks to a year) with an average tenure of 149 days (SD=107). 19 of the drivers drove part time and 2 drove full time. Four of the 21 drivers were also working for, or had previous experience with similar driving services including taxis, trucks, and personal chauffeurs, and car services. We conducted additional 30-45 minute long interviews with these drivers to compare their experience with more traditional driving jobs to Uber and/or Lyft.

Interviews were done through video chat, phone, or in person, depending on the interviewee's location. The interviewer began with questions about the driver's last ride, best or worst assignment and ride experiences. Follow-up questions probed drivers' understanding of three algorithmic features and how their understanding influenced their work strategies. For the ridesharing drivers who also worked as taxi drivers, personal car service drivers, or chauffeurs, we asked them to compare work assignment and evaluation models in two driving jobs.

Passenger interviews

We interviewed 12 passengers who had used or currently use Uber and/or Lyft in 4 cities across US (8 Females, average age 24.2 years (SD=7.1)). On average, the passengers had used the services 2-3 times per month for about 5 months (SD=4.46). 8 of the passengers had used both Uber and Lyft, 3 only used Lyft, and 1 only used Uber. Interview questions focused on confirming or disconfirming drivers' perceptions of passengers' use of services, in particular, how they rate drivers and their attitudes toward and behaviors around surge pricing.

Archival data: online driver forums & company websites

Online driver forums. We analyzed postings on online driver forums as all drivers in our interviews mentioned that the forums were primary knowledge sources and places for socialization. We looked at two categories of online forums: groups unmoderated by Uber and Lyft, including various Facebook groups and Reddit pages, and official company Facebook "lounges." One author signed up to become a Lyft driver, and was given access to a "new driver" Facebook forum, hosted by Lyft, in which information was disseminated with direct relation to the company. We accessed other unmoderated private driver forums on Facebook by requesting to join as researchers, to avoid deceptively posing as drivers, and maintained an observation-only status. Following the approach used in [27], we sampled 128 online forum posts and comments mentioning the algorithmic features selected out of thousands made in a five-month period.

Company websites. We also looked at how companies officially educate and communicate with drivers in order to understand how much information they share about the underlying mechanisms of the platforms' algorithmic features. We analyzed information on the Uber and Lyft company websites and 132 official blog posts posted between 2012 and 2014.

Analysis

We triangulated our findings from interviews and archival data. We qualitatively analyzed [32, 38] interview transcripts, excerpts of online forum postings and comments, and company communication materials using Dedoose, a qualitative data coding software. We used three algorithmic features of the ridesharing services to divide the data set, and then open-coded the data about each feature at the sentence or paragraph level. We analyzed the rest of the data to identify important themes including social sensemaking and socialization. This resulted in a total of 372 concepts. We then categorized the concepts into 18 themes explaining emerging phenomena. In addition to the ones reported in the paper, themes such as employee (de)identification with company culture emerged but were excluded in further analysis. We focused on 8 categories relevant to our research questions around algorithmic management, and used modeling techniques and affinity diagrams in order to explain the relationship between the categories. The final coding scheme had good reliability across two coders when tested with 10% of the transcripts (Kappa=.71). Conflicts between coders were resolved through discussion.

FINDINGS

We describe how drivers responded when algorithms assigned work, provided informational support, and evaluated job performance, as well as how drivers used online forums to socially make sense of the algorithmic features of the system.

Background: driver motivation

According to drivers, one main advantage of working for a rideshare platform was the flexibility that the system affords in terms of where and when to work, and the low level of commitment that is required by signing up. Some individuals drove full-time, but many also drove for fun, out of curiosity, or on a part-time basis. Many drivers used the ridesharing app in collaboration with their own daily routine to earn extra income, turning the driver app on for the daily commute for example, or doing chores around the house while waiting for a ride request to come in. In addition to the added financial flexibility that rideshare work affords, many drivers we interviewed mentioned social motivations for rideshare driving. Several drivers, for example, weighed the fun of meeting and having conversations with new people and the desire to help out the community as greater than or equal to their motivation to earn extra income.

Algorithmic work assignment: proximity-based driver-passenger assignment

Our findings highlight how transparency of algorithmic assignment influences worker cooperation, work strategy and workaround creation, and describe the potential impacts of automating choices that workers used to have in similar work settings.

Accepting and cooperating with algorithmic assignments

Previous research suggests that people may cooperate less with work assignments made by machines rather than people [33]. In Uber and Lyft, the way that assignments were presented to drivers on their app and the regulation of acceptance rate cut-off influenced drivers to accept as many assignments made by the assignment algorithms as possible. *"I mean you can always decline to pick up a passenger if you can make that decision within 12 seconds. (Uber/Lyft) make it sort of difficult to say no for a couple of reasons. [...] when they show the spot on the map where you're going to pick someone up its very zoomed in so if you're not immediately familiar with the area you probably wouldn't be able to discern within 12 seconds if its somewhere you want to go or not. They just tell you how far away it is in driving time (P4)."*

Interestingly, one factor that influenced driver cooperation was whether the assignment made sense to them. While the assignment was generally based on proximity, there were other factors that influenced assignment such as passenger-driver mutual rating and driver login time. This sometimes caused drivers to receive requests from distant passengers to which they were not the closest driver. When this happened, many drivers reported rejecting the unfavorable ride assignment given that they would have to drive a great distance (such as 15 minutes) to the pick-up location. For example, P23 stated: *"I'm one that keeps a close watch of where [other drivers] are when I'm not with a passenger. So if I'll see three [other drivers] over on the [area A] and I get a request from [area B] to the [area A] knowing that there should have been three [drivers] sitting right there ready to go, tells me one of two things happened. Either all three of them passed on the ride which is highly unlikely that they're sitting here and they pass on a ride that's right in front of them. Or the system didn't coordinate the GPS correctly and sent it to me over ten minutes away instead of somebody that was 30 seconds away."* In this quote, it is unclear whether the assignment was due to errors in the system, or for other legitimate reasons, because no explanation was given about how the assignment was decided on the drivers' app. P23 assumed that the assignment was made by mistake and rejected the assignment. On the other hand, even with distant and inconvenient requests, drivers accepted rides when the assignment made sense to them. For example, P13 stated: *"Distance wise, sometimes I've gone like 17 miles, but that's not really the [passenger's] fault; that's because there's just not that many drivers out right now and I just really am the closest."* This suggests that an explanation of why certain assignments were made might be an important, but currently missing feature.

Creating work strategies and workarounds for algorithmic assignments

Drivers used their understanding that assignments are based on proximity to create their work and workaround strategies that helped them maintain control that the automated assignment did not support as part of the existing system functionality.

Drivers strategically controlled when and where to work and when to turn on the driver mode of the app to get the types of requests and clienteles that they preferred: limiting the area that they worked in by turning off the driver mode when returning from a long-ride, avoiding bad neighborhoods to avoid dangerous situations, going downtown for successive short-rides during the lunch time, not going to bar areas to avoid drunk passengers, and instead, staying in residential areas to drive people to bars. Drivers attracted repeat passengers by arranging rides via phone, asking passengers to request a ride once they were in the driver's car to get matched. Drivers used online forums to post about bad passengers so that other drivers could avoid them, similar to self-regulation strategies of mTurkers [17].

Drivers also distanced themselves from one another by checking other drivers' locations on the map so that they did not compete with each other for passenger requests. When drivers desired a break but did not want to turn off their driver applications to benefit from an hourly payment promotion, they parked in between the other ridesharing cars in order not to get any requests.

The companies communicated only general rules of assignment, e.g., "the closest drivers get assigned," and this general understanding helped drivers create their work strategies. The lack of details of the assignment algorithm, however, seemed to foster drivers' ambivalent, sometimes negative feelings toward the companies: *"Uber is very close lipped about what actually happens right I mean they say 'oh we route it to the closest driver' or whatever but who really knows what's going on behind the scene it's up to whoever engineers their iPhone app (P4)."*

More knowledge more advantage

Our findings suggest drivers benefited from deeper knowledge of the assignment algorithm. Drivers with more knowledge created workarounds to avoid undesirable assignments, whereas those with less knowledge rejected undesirable assignments, lowering their acceptance rating, or unwillingly fulfilled the uneconomical rides. For example, P2 had knowledge that Lyft's assignment algorithms take into consideration how long drivers have been online and that a driver's radius for pickups will increase as they wait for passenger assignments. He used his knowledge to periodically turn on and off his driver application while at traffic signals, so that he did not get distant requests. However, this information was not publicly made available to all drivers, and in our interviews, Lyft drivers who did not have this knowledge attributed the distant assignment to the error of the assignment system, or drivers with higher ratings getting priority. These drivers could not create workaround strategies to avoid distant requests.

Getting assigned versus choosing whom to pick up

Drivers were generally satisfied with their level of control over assignment algorithms, except for a few drivers who desired to have control over the radius that the assignment algorithm searches to assign the passenger. Interestingly, one driver P17 who was also a Yellow Cab driver preferred his Taxi dispatching system where he could see all the incoming requests and choose freely from among them. He explained that he could strategically choose the location of ride requests in the taxi system, and he had developed knowledge of how to best use them: *"At certain times of certain days, you know that they're usually a lot of really good trips happening in those areas. Like, Thursdays around four o'clock in, like, [area names] you know that there's gonna be a lot of airport trips, for instance. So you can focus on those. Another thing that's good about it is [...] if it's [...] a busy Friday night. You're just growing tired of mining a certain area. You can totally shift. And a good way to do that is to take something that's not in a close area that you think maybe going from far, but then coming back in. [...] It gives us the option for a change of pace."* Uber and Lyft's automated assignment got rid of this fine level of control and predictability. He said that while he could try to be in those locations in Uber and Lyft's system, it did not guarantee that he would get requests in the area. Often, he would get requests outside of the area, and he did not want to drive to these areas just for a change of pace.

Algorithmic information support: dynamic in-app display of surge priced areas

Surge-pricing algorithms are used to optimize pricing in online, airline, and hotel markets, among others. Our findings show breakdowns when these algorithms are used to influence human behavior.

Algorithmic information not accommodating human abilities, emotion, and motivation

Some drivers in cities where surge pricing was applied citywide, instead of being neighborhood-based, reported that they would go out to drive when they received surge-pricing notifications. Other drivers reported that the times when they were available to drive were already in line with surge-priced timing.

More than half of interviewed drivers, however, were not influenced by surge pricing information as the supply-demand control algorithms failed to accommodate their abilities, emotion, and motivation. Surge pricing changed too rapidly and unexpectedly to utilize the information in a strategic way to boost their incomes. Surge areas were on and off, sometimes by the second, and being in the surge area did not guarantee requests from within the surge area. Drivers reported getting no requests or requests from outside of the surge area (which do not qualify for surge pricing), or the surge price disappearing when they arrived to the surge area.

The economic and rational assumptions of the supply-demand control algorithm did not always motivate drivers' behaviors, as it does not account for feelings of unfairness about dynamic surge pricing [14]. Most passengers reported that surge pricing was unfair, and they tried to avoid it if they could. Some drivers, in particular ones that used the ridesharing services as passengers, expressed that they thought that surge pricing was unfair and they did not try to chase surge-priced areas. The appeal of increased incomes in surge priced areas did not motivate some drivers who also drove primarily for social, rather than financial reasons.

Trusting their own knowledge more than algorithmic data

A couple of drivers had more trust in their own knowledge and experience driving in the city than in the unpredictable surge pricing algorithms. In part, the drivers did not have knowledge to evaluate how accurate surge-priced areas were. For example, P19 stated: *"They probably do have some kind of algorithm over people who open up the app to request the ride, and they might have noticed, but they don't tell us how those [surge-priced areas] work. I ignore them for the most part, because I'm from here. [...] I've lived here 35 years."*

Algorithmic, data-driven evaluation: performance evaluation through acceptance rate and driver rating

The regulation of the acceptance rate threshold and the driver-passenger rating system offered many benefits to overall service functioning. However, these numeric systems that made drivers accountable for all interactions were sometimes seen as unfair and ineffective and created negative psychological feelings in drivers.

Unfairness in treating all assignment rejections equally

The regulation of the acceptance rate threshold encouraged drivers to accept most requests, enabling more passengers to get rides. Keeping the assignment acceptance rate high was important, placing pressure on drivers. For example, P13 stated in response to why he accepted a particular request: *"Because my acceptance rating has to be really high, and there's lots of pressure to do that. [...] I had no reason not to accept it, so [...] I did. Because if, you know, you miss those pings, it kind of really affects that rating and Lyft doesn't like that."*

Assignment algorithms penalized equally all drivers' rejections of passenger requests, which lowered the drivers' acceptance rates. Sometimes drivers, however, had legitimate reasons and circumstances for rejecting passengers. For example, female drivers did not accept male passengers without pictures at night because of safety concerns. Drivers often rejected passengers "blacklisted" for their misbehavior on online driver forums. Sometimes technical glitches in the app showed the request with only a few seconds left to accept. When they felt that they had legitimate reasons for rejecting the requests, drivers would sometimes send emails to company representatives, hoping that they would not get penalized for the legitimate assignment rejects, but often times they did not hear back from the companies.

Inaccuracy in using only numeric metrics of service quality

Our findings suggest the passenger-driver rating system established basic trust and service attitudes in the ridesharing systems, however they fell short when used for driver performance metrics.

Drivers used passenger ratings to decide whether to accept the request or not, trusting 5-star passengers and being cautious with 3-star passengers. While not paying equal attention to driver ratings, passengers reported that the existence of a rating system gave them a sense of security. The rating system also promoted a service mindset in all drivers. For example, P16 said: *"[...] I want to get all five's. So I try to be friendly and engaging with the passengers. And give them options when they get in, like, you know, 'Do you want A/C? Do you want the windows down? What kind of music do you want to listen to?' I even have a candy tray, gum, stuff like that."*

Drivers took their ratings seriously. High ratings such as 4.98 became a source of pride whereas a rating below 4.7 became a source of disappointment, frustration, and fear of losing their jobs. Being tracked, evaluated, and judged by each passenger seemed to have a negative psychological impact on drivers who did not have scores near 5. P11 said: *"[the rating system] makes you cautious that what you're doing is being judged and rated and if you're rated poorly enough over a period time then eventually the platform could ask you to stop driving for them."*

Many drivers felt that the average of the passengers' ratings of the drivers was not reflective of their driving performance and services, as P22 stated: *"It's like in baseball a stat line doesn't always tell the particulars of a player. A player could hit 35 homeruns and knock in 100 runs but if they're hitting .240 and strike out 150 times, that doesn't mean they were such a productive player."* Many reported that various physical and psychological states of passengers such as being in a hurry and late for a flight or being drunk, could influence them to give a lower rating after the ride. Additionally, drivers noticed that passengers misattributed system faults and negative experiences that drivers could not control to drivers themselves, which in turn resulted in lower ratings (e.g., surge pricing, traffic jams, GPS errors etc.). Drivers also often attributed their low rating to passengers reviewing them using inappropriate review rubrics. For example, drivers often perceived that passengers rated them as if it were a 5-star rating system for products, movies, or restaurants, where perfect ratings are rare. This led many drivers to conclude that passengers needed education for the rating system in ridesharing services. On the other hand, most passengers we interviewed reported that they are more lenient and positive when rating drivers, while they are more critical in their online reviews of other goods.

Because of their perception that there are many uncontrollable factors influencing driver ratings, drivers seemed to develop a detached, indifferent attitude once their scores were above a certain threshold of deactivation risk. The rating averages scores from one hundred or more rides. With this average, the impact of each ride is reduced. For example, P8 stated: "*Well I used to micromanage my rating so to speak. I used to sweat and be oh my gosh my rating is now going down - it's a 4.85 that kind of thing. Now I don't worry about it. I see there's a lot of error that can take place in the rating.*"

Online social sensemaking

As drivers worked independently in distributed locations, online driver forums became a primary avenue for the driver socialization and system sensemaking. Drivers discussed the workings of the ridesharing systems' algorithmic management. One of the successful online sensemaking examples was about improving and maintaining driver performance in ratings and acceptance rate. When novice drivers asked for tips to improve their ratings, other drivers shared strategies and lessons that they learned over time. For example, one driver posted questions about how to improve her rating (4.63) after giving 38 rides in three weeks. About 50 comments were made within two hours of her posting, empathizing with her feelings, disclosing common experiences of going through the initial hurdle, and sharing specific strategies that they developed – creating their own service information brochure for the backseat, going to downtown during the day for many short rides, etc. The experienced drivers also explained that the rating would stabilize over time, and advised that she should not stress about it too much. Often times, original question askers followed up on the posting, making comments that the strategies had worked.

On the other hand, sensemaking activities around assignment algorithms and surge pricing seemed less successful in terms of informational usefulness. Common posts were questions of how assignment algorithms and surge-pricing work, how to interpret dynamic visualization of surge pricing areas, and real-time questions of frustrating events—from getting no requests in surge priced areas or getting distant requests that required long driving.

When answers to drivers' questions went beyond the information that the company officially communicated, the social discussion on the online forums focused on providing social and emotional support, rather than informational support. For example, one driver posted frustration in real time that he just got an assignment from across the city from east to west even when he saw other drivers around the requesting passenger that were closer. Many comments were made to the posting that provided emotional support. For instance, another driver from the west chimed in to say "I should have logged in to save you (from driving from east to west)," and other drivers said "it sucks when it happens." But none of the comments provided an explanation as to why such an assignment was made. Postings that made jokes on the surge pricing areas that seemed wrong according to common sense (e.g. a surge area extending into a lake), or ones that humorously interpreted shapes of surge-priced areas as "Surgemon," also reflect an attempt to have control over the unknown through humor and emotional processes instead of rational, cognitive ones [40]. On rare occasions, company representatives came to the forums and answered drivers' questions, but their answers were usually washed away in the influx of other forum postings and comments.

DISCUSSION

We discuss how to use our findings to improve the design of algorithmic and data-driven management.

Designing algorithmic work assignment

Algorithmic passenger assignment in Uber and Lyft automatically distributes myriad ride requests to drivers in a matter of seconds. Drivers' quick and frequent acceptance of the assignments ensures the efficiency of the service, maximizing the number of passengers able to get a prompt ride. Our findings suggest that in algorithmic work assignment, not only the source of the assignment (i.e., human versus algorithm), but also how the assignment was presented and regulated, influences worker cooperation with the assignment. Choices of which information to present on screen, a short time limit to accept the ride, and the acceptance rate collectively reinforced drivers' cooperation with the assignments in our study.

Our findings also suggest that transparency of assignment process could elicit greater cooperation with assignments, especially undesirable ones. While the company explained that their assignments are based on proximity, there were various additional factors that the algorithm took into account in addition to passenger-driver distance. This sometimes resulted in assignments where passengers were not assigned to the closest driver. Providing explanations for [6], or allowing workers to ask questions about [20, 24] each assignment could reduce drivers rejection of distant assignments by reducing their attribution of such assignments to technical errors. Transparency may also improve some drivers' ambivalent feelings toward the companies. This finding is consistent with previous research on recommender systems where transparency improved people's trust and acceptance of recommendations [6]. Moreover, the study highlights new implications of transparency, which have received relatively little attention in previous research on intelligent systems: how transparency in algorithmic assignment helps people create better work strategies and workarounds. Drivers with more detailed knowledge about the assignment algorithm could create workarounds to avoid less economical rides whereas people only with a general understanding of proximity-based assignment could not.

The stakeholders involved with work platform apps (companies and workers) complicate providing transparency. In previous work on transparency of intelligent systems, explaining a user model usually sufficed [3, 6, 20, 24]. Algorithmic work assignment offers new challenges in design transparency where fully disclosing the algorithm may not be a viable solution. Companies may be unwilling or unable to share the underlying mechanisms of their assignment algorithms, as they might be patented or proprietary assets. Companies may also desire a degree of user ignorance to prevent the system from being gamed.

We were surprised that ridesharing drivers desired little (or did not feel entitled to) direct control over the assignment algorithm, for example, specifying pick-up locations or being able to see and choose from all requests. We believe the organizational context of being independent contractors played an important role: the flexibility and choices that the ridesharing drivers have in work compensate for the lack of control in assignment algorithms. Another explanation for why drivers did not desire control could be the lack of experience with other systems. For example P17, who worked as both a taxi and rideshare driver, preferred the taxi assignment process where he could directly access and choose passenger requests. P17 did not like the ridesharing assignment systems because algorithms made decisions that he used to make himself, making him feel he lost agency regarding strategies that he had developed to maximize his income. This could be interpreted as resistance to change, but also raises open-ended, ethical questions about the trend in new technology that sacrifices individual control for the sake of overall system efficiency, and its implications for learning and development on the job.

Designing algorithmic information support

Supply-demand control algorithms were originally designed to solve mathematical optimization problems that involve non-human entities. In Uber and Lyft, however, they are used to motivate and control human behaviors. This causes problems, as the supply-demand control algorithm does not consider the pace at which drivers work. Consistent with previous research on a smart agent that tried to encourage sustainable behaviors [5], the algorithm failed to account for feelings of inequity people had toward surge pricing, and ignored the social and altruistic motivations of drivers. This highlights the importance of making algorithmic management accommodate: a) the speed and the way humans work, b) diverse types of motivations rather than only economic ones, and c) emotions that people feel about the decisions that algorithms make. In addition, some drivers did not trust the surge-priced areas as they trusted in their experiences more. Transparency in how the surge-priced area was computed in real-time could improve workers' trust toward the algorithmic information.

Designing algorithmic, data-driven performance evaluation

Using driver ratings and acceptance rate, companies are able to evaluate drivers at a large scale. Driver ratings in particular may seem to be a legitimate evaluation metric because customer satisfaction is an important metric of service success and human service provider quality. Using only the tracked performance data in evaluating workers, however, revealed many complications that can occur when one relies too heavily on quantified metrics without deeper consideration of their meanings and nuances. Consistent with previous research on letter-grading systems or numeric evaluation of teaching skills [4], many random factors that are out of drivers' control influence the way passengers rate drivers. The efficacy and accuracy of averaged collective evaluation, rather than an in-depth holistic evaluation done by a human manager or peer, is also in question. As P18 put it, *"you are at the mercy of random people, in [his other work], you are evaluated by people that you know."* Our study also shows drawbacks of adopting the 5-star rating system shared with online products, content, or business reviews to review human workers. Drivers felt that passengers rated conservatively as they do in online reviews; yet interviews with passengers suggest that they are being more lenient and positive than drivers think. This misconception suggests that a 5-star rating metaphor and rubric may have brought up inappropriate associations. Finally, the long-term motivational effect of the rating is also in question. As the drivers' ratings were averaged over multiple rides, the impact of one positive or negative ride was minimized, and drivers in our study became less sensitive to the changes in their ratings once they were above a minimum threshold.

Successful management provides work protocols and allows improvisation in response to changes and exceptions [29]. On the other hand, assignment algorithms penalized equally all driver rejections of assignments even when certain drivers had legitimate reasons and circumstances for doing so. While we did not observe serious problems from this lack of flexibility in algorithmic assignment in our study, it brings up an open challenge in creating flexibility in algorithmic management.

In most online rating systems, review is optional, and many even skip the process. In the ridesharing services, all passengers were encouraged to rate their service encounter, and most of them did. Being held accountable for every interaction, drivers were very aware of the existence of this external evaluation. Trying to deliver good services for all service interactions could pose psychological stress to workers. Additionally, as extensive research on the impact of extrinsic rewards on intrinsic motivation suggests, the external device could weaken the intrinsic motivation that drivers might have and change the meaning that they attribute to their behaviors. From the passengers' point of view, the ambiguities in providers' motivation for friendliness and good services risks rendering provider-client interaction more superficial and perfunctory.

Supporting social sensemaking online

Our study showed that online forums became a main place where drivers socialized, asked questions of each other, and exchanged knowledge and strategies. In most research on sensemaking and mental models of intelligent systems, the focus has been on individual sensemaking [20, 21, 24, 35, 43]. Our study shows that social sensemaking is another important activity that needs to be better understood and supported for intelligent systems to be successfully adopted. Social sensemaking activities on the driver forums followed the form of "fragmented social sensemaking [26]" where there were many active contributors but no central authority figure to synthesize different ideas and narratives into a coherent story. This type of sensemaking was effective for discussing rating improvement strategies where there were no right or wrong answers, and workers' experiences and learned and improvised strategies played critical roles. On the other hand, fragmented social sensemaking fell short on subject matters where only an authority figure had the right information. This highlights opportunities to design structured online social sensemaking of algorithmic features where individuals can build on each other's knowledge.

LIMITATIONS

Like any study, this work has some limitations. Our results are from interviews with a small sample of drivers, passengers and archival data analysis. We could not interview developers or official representatives of the companies as it was against company policy. Our findings should be complemented by future research that uses different research methods such as ethnography, surveys or experiments. Our study was done in the specific context of ridesharing (on-demand, independent contractor work) thus further work needs to be done in different organizational contexts such as with full-time or co-located employees.

IMPLICATIONS

HCI and CSCW have a long history of research on computational systems that support individual work and collaboration. Our work suggests that algorithmic management in the workplace is a new and fruitful ground for research, where the same effort can be made to establish theories and design principles for algorithmic management. The research presented in this paper also offers implications for research on intelligent systems. Much of the previous work on intelligent systems was done in the context of individual user and non-work settings. Our work suggests that important concepts and theories in the field of intelligent systems such as transparency and control of systems, user mental models, and sensemaking need to be updated to accommodate social and organizational contexts that involve multiple stakeholders and new roles of intelligent systems in workflows. Finally, this research raises the need for new methodological research in HCI and interaction design on designing human-centered algorithmic management. HCI and interaction design have established systematic processes and methods for designing human-centered interfaces and interactions. Compared to designing and building traditional user interfaces, designing algorithmic management will require different ways of specifying and evaluating requirements, states, and interactivity.

CONCLUSION

Increasingly, software algorithms allocate, optimize, and evaluate work. In this paper, we explored the impact of this algorithmic, data-driven management in the context of new ride sharing services, Uber and Lyft. Our findings from a qualitative study highlight opportunities and challenges in designing human-centered algorithmic work assignment, information, and evaluation and the importance of supporting social sensemaking around the algorithmic system. The implications for HCI, CSCW, and research on intelligent systems are discussed. We hope this research inspires future work, so that we support human workers to work with intelligent machines not only in an effective, but also a satisfying and meaningful way.

ACKNOWLEDGEMENT

This research was supported by NSF grants CNS-1205539 and ACI-1322278. We thank Su Baykal for helping us collect and analyze data, and the anonymous reviewers for their feedback that improved the paper.

REFERENCES

1. Ackerman, M. S. (1998). Augmenting organizational memory: a field study of answer garden. *TOIS, 16*(3), 203-224.
2. Barocas, S., Hood, S., & Ziewitz, M. (2013). Governing algorithms: A provocation piece. *SSRN.*
3. Bellotti, V., & Edwards, K. (2001). Intelligibility and accountability: human considerations in context-aware systems. *HCI, 16*(2-4), 193-212.
4. Braga, M., Paccagnella, M., & Pellizzari, M. (2014). Evaluating students' evaluations of professors. *Economics of Education Review, 41*, 71-88.
5. Costanza, E., Fischer, J. E., Colley, J. A., ...& Jennings, N. R. (2014). Doing the laundry with agents: a field trial of a future smart energy system in the home. In *Proc. of CHI*, 813-822.
6. Cramer, H., Evers, V., Ramlal, S., ... & Wielinga, B. (2008). The effects of transparency on trust in and acceptance of a content-based art recommender. *UMUAI*, 18(5), 455-496.
7. Davidson, A. & Kestenbaum D. (2014). The Future of Work Looks Like a UPS Truck. *NPR.*
8. Dourish, P. (2003). The appropriation of interactive technologies: Some lessons from placeless documents. *CSCW* 12(4), 465-490.
9. Egido, C. (1988). Video conferencing as a technology to support group work: a review of its failures. In *Proc. of CSCW*, 13-24.
10. Gillespie, T. (2014). The Relevance of Algorithms. *Media Technologies: Essays on Communication, Materiality, and Society*, 167-193.

11. Girardin, F., & Blat, J. (2010). The co-evolution of taxi drivers and their in-car navigation systems. *PMC*, 6(4), 424-434.

12. Grudin, J. (1988). Why CSCW applications fail: problems in the design and evaluation of organizational interfaces. In *Proc. of CSCW*, 85-93.

13. Hassan, U., O'Riain, S., & Curry, E. (2013). Effects of expertise assessment on the quality of task routing in human computation. In *Proc. of Workshop on Social Media for Crowdsourcing and Human Computation.*

14. Haws, K. L., & Bearden, W. O. (2006). Dynamic pricing and consumer fairness perceptions. *Journal of Consumer Research, 33*(3), 304-311.

15. Hinds, P., & Kiesler, S. (1995). Communication across boundaries: work, structure, and use of communication technologies in a large organization. *Org. Sci.*, 6(4), 373-393.

16. Hodson, H (2014). The AI Boss that Deploys Hong Kong's Subway Engineers. *New Scientist*

17. Irani, L., & Silberman, M. (2013). Turkopticon: Interrupting Worker Invisibility in Amazon Mechanical Turk. In *Proc. of CHI*, 611-620.

18. Isaacs, E., Walendowski, A., Whittaker, S., ...& Kamm, C. (2002). The character, functions, and styles of instant messaging in the workplace. In *Proc. of CSCW*, 11-20.

19. Kantor, J. (2014). Working Anything But 9 to 5. *NYT*

20. Kay, J. & Kummerfeld, B. (2012). Creating personalized systems that people can scrutinize and control: Drivers, principles and experience. *TiiS*, 24-42.

21. Kulesza, T., Stumpf, S., Burnett, M., & Kwan, I. (2012). Tell me more: the effects of mental model soundness on personalizing an intelligent agent. In *Proc. of CHI*, 1-10.

22. Lee, M. K., Kiesler, S., Forlizzi, J., & Rybski, P. (2012). Ripple effects of an embedded social agent: a field study of a social robot in the workplace. In *Proc. of CHI*, 695-704.

23. Lee, J., & Moray, N. (1992). Trust, control strategies and allocation of function in human-machine systems. *Ergonomics, 35*(10), 1243-1270.

24. Lim, B. Y., Dey, A. K., & Avrahami, D. (2009). Why and why not explanations improve the intelligibility of context-aware intelligent systems. In *Proc. of CHI*, 2119-2128.

25. Lyft (2014) Rating Your Driver. Retrieved from https://www.lyft.com/help/article/1453135

26. Maitlis, S. (2005). The social processes of organizational sensemaking. *Academy of Management Journal, 48*(1), 21-49.

27. Martin, D., Hanrahan, B. V., O'Neill, J., & Gupta, N. (2014). Being a turker. In *Proc. of CSCW*, 224-235.

28. McClelland, M. (2012). I Was a Warehouse Wage Slave. *Mothers Jones.*

29. Mintzberg, H. (1973). *The Nature of Managerial Work.* Harpercollins College Div.

30. Mutlu, B. & Forlizzi, J. (2008). Robots in organizations: the role of workflow, social, and environmental factors in human-robot interaction. In *Proc. of HRI*, 287-294.

31. Orlikowski, W. J. (1992). Learning from notes: Organizational issues in groupware implementation. In *Proc. of CSCW*, 362-369.

32. Patton, M. Q. (1990). *Qualitative evaluation and research methods.* SAGE Publications, inc.

33. Parise, S., Kiesler, S., Sproull, L., & Waters, K. (1999). Cooperating with life-like interface agents. *Computers in Human Behavior, 15*(2), 123-142.

34. Pritchard, G., Vines, J., Briggs, P., ... & Olivier, P. (2014). Digitally driven: how location based services impact the work practices of London bus drivers. In *Proc. of CHI*, 3617-3626.

35. Rodden, T. A., Fischer, J. E., Pantidi, N., ... & Moran, S. (2013). At home with agents: exploring attitudes towards future smart energy infrastructures. In *Proc. of CHI*, 1173-1182.

36. Sheridan, T. B., & Parasuraman, R. (2005). Human-automation interaction. *Reviews of human factors and ergonomics, 1*(1), 89-129.

37. Steiner, C., & Dixon, W. (2012). *Automate this: How algorithms came to rule our world.* New York.

38. Strauss, A., & Corbin, J. M. (1990). *Basics of qualitative research: grounded theory procedures and techniques.*

39. Suchman, L. A. (1983). Office procedure as practical action: models of work and system design. *TOIS*, 1(4), 320-328.

40. Tracy, S., Myers, K., Scott, C., (2007). Cracking jokes and crafting selves: Sensemaking and identity management among human service workers. *Communication Monographs,* 283-308.

41. Uber (2014). a Deeper Look at Uber's Dynamic Pricing Model. http://blog.uber.com/dynamicpricing

42. Uber (2014). How the Uber System Works [Video file] https://www.youtube.com/watch?v=makYbqd7mGA

43. Yang, R., & Newman, M. W. (2013). Learning from a learning thermostat: lessons for intelligent systems for the home. In *Proc. of PUC*, 93-102.

44. Walker, C. R. (1958). Life in the automatic factory. *Harvard Business Review,36*(1), 111-119.

TurkBench: Rendering the Market for Turkers

Benjamin V. Hanrahan, Jutta K. Willamowski, Saiganesh Swaminathan, David B. Martin
Xerox Research Centre Europe
6 chemin de Maupertuis 38240 Meylan, France
Contact: ben.hanrahan@xerox.com

ABSTRACT
Crowdsourcing is a relatively new model of labor where both the workers and work providers are experiencing its growing pains. A dominant platform that implements this model of labor is Amazon Mechanical Turk (AMT). While AMT has evolved over the years, the changes have focused mainly on work providers and have not addressed the problems workers face (e.g. dealing with market volatility and unpaid time searching for work). In this paper we present *TurkBench*, a tool meant to provide workers with personalized market visualization and session management. We discuss the design philosophy of the tool, briefly discuss four Turkers' reaction to a demo, and outline future work.

Author Keywords
Crowdsourcing; Amazon Mechanical Turk

ACM Classification Keywords
H.5.2 User Interfaces

INTRODUCTION
Crowdsourcing is a relatively new model of labor where both the workers and work providers are experiencing its growing pains. Amazon Mechanical Turk (AMT) is one of the first and most dominant platforms for this model of labor. AMT has experienced a number of difficulties, for which Amazon has implemented several features to mitigate. However, Amazon has primarily focused on the problems of requesters (work providers), e.g. improving the Human Intelligence Task (HIT) creation interface and providing an Application Programming Interface (API) for posting and managing HITs. While, in our assessment, many of the issues experienced by the Turkers (workers) have not been addressed.

In fact, AMT provides a salient example of what can happen when the developers of a platform are also one of its users, especially when there is a power differential between this role and that of the other users. In the case of AMT, Amazon is both the platform developer and a major requester. Perhaps unsurprisingly they seem to have developed functionality primarily for requesters, the role they most easily identify with. Whether intentionally or not, this cements inequalities in the system. The effect runs deep and is even seen in the available API calls, where there is no support for Turkers.

This phenomenon has several direct consequences for Turkers, many of which are rooted in the way the market is *rendered* to the Turkers. AMT does not display or prioritize HITs in a way that reflects the needs or wants of Turkers. This results in a large amount of unpaid work in finding HITs; difficulty in maintaining awareness in the face of market volatility; and a difficult on-boarding process [10]. This means that Turkers have to make compromises, e.g. choosing to do low-paying HITs instead of spending and potentially wasting time trying to locate higher paying ones.

These interface issues lead to larger consequences for AMT as a 'free market'[1] of labor, as the worker does not have sufficient information to make reasonably informed decisions. Lack of functionality and information also make many decisions more difficult, such as which employers are trustworthy, which jobs pay a reasonable wage, or which skills would be more profitable to acquire. Furthermore, Turkers do not have the means to declare these choices within the AMT platform, where requesters are provided mechanisms like blocking specific Turkers (for which there are broader consequences for Turkers). Turkers are put at a disadvantage (especially in comparison with requesters) through the structuring of information and functionality. When trying to frame AMT as a 'free market' of labor, one must remember that this labor market is in fact influenced a great deal by the functionality and information made available (or not) to the different roles. Not to mention the rules, procedures, and policies that surround a system like AMT.

In order to mitigate problems encountered by Turkers we built *TurkBench*. The goal of *TurkBench* is to reduce the difficulty in navigating the market by locating the most lucrative HITs, requesters, and qualifications available in the market. *TurkBench* also seeks to eliminate much of the unpaid search time by guiding users through an adaptive schedule. *TurkBench* provides several novel capabilities around adaptive scheduling and discovering new opportunities. We describe the related work and design of *TurkBench* in more detail in the following sections.

CHI 2015, April 18 - 23 2015, Seoul, Republic of Korea
Copyright 2015 ACM 978-1-4503-3145-6/15/04$15.00
http://dx.doi.org/10.1145/2702123.2702279

[1]We mean 'free market' in the mundane sense, where prices for labor and tasks are set by supply and demand.

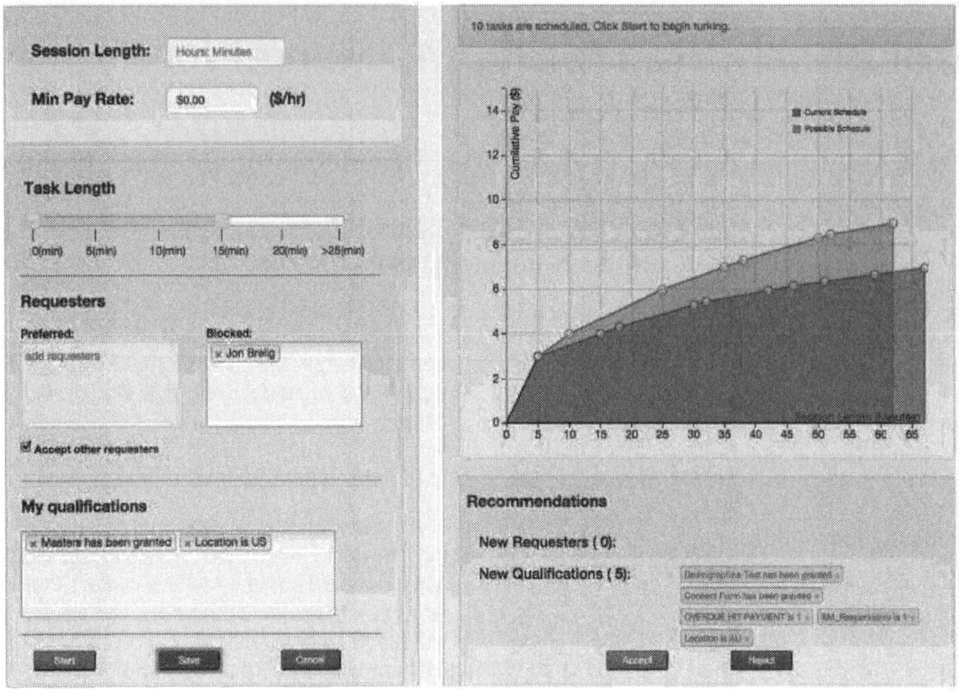

Figure 1. Overview of Personalized Market Visualization interface.

RELATED WORK

Several tools have been developed to address the difficulties that requesters experience on crowdsourcing platforms. For example, *CrowdWeaver* [7] helps requesters create workflows to manage complex work. Similarly, Kulkarni et al. [9] devised *Turkomatic* to recruit workers in order to help requesters plan and solve complex jobs.

In contrast, there are only a few tools available to Turkers. The AMT platform itself suffers from usability problems and provides poor support for finding tasks [6]. As a result there is evidence that requesters take advantage of this and manipulate the search results to get HITs completed quickly [3].

There have been several studies that point to the imbalances in available information, power, and systems of redress [10, 11, 1, 13]. Researchers have also created a workers bill of rights[2] and posed the question, *"Can we foresee a future crowd workplace in which we would want our children to participate?"* [8]. Others have simply asked that tools frame their workers as more than just faceless computation [11, 12].

Of the tools that have been developed for Turkers, *TurkOpticon* is foremost. *Turkopticon* [5] helps workers identify "fair" requesters through collaborative ratings. Ipeirotis [4] has also done extensive work in defining the AMT market, and produced a site that Turkers use to gauge aspects of AMT[3]. Along the lines of *TurkBench*, Callison-Burch created *Crowd-Workers* in order to provide more transparency to the hourly wage of HITs [2]. In addition to the tools developed by researchers, Turkers have created several scripts and plugins to make turking easier. For example, *MTurkList*[4], which helps Turkers sort tasks based on pay; and *TurkAlert*[5] which notifies its users when certain HITs become available. In fact, the creating of scripts and plugins is a feature of the Turker culture, with entire sites dedicated to sharing them[6].

Similar to these tools and scripts, our goal is to facilitate turking. Also like these tools we must operate within the constraints of the AMT infrastructure, which provides limited support for Turkers. Tools have dealt with this problem in a variety of ways, *Turkopticon* collects user ratings in order to communicate requester reliability, adding the information directly to HITs. While, *Crowd-Workers* tracks the hourly rate of HITs by instrumenting the browser to record how long HITs take. Still others (e.g. *MTurkList* and *TurkAlert*) crawl the available HITs to provide ongoing information about the status of the market. We combine several of these methods in that we crawl AMT, record usage statistics, and augment the AMT interface. The various compromises that these tools must make due to the limitations of the AMT infrastructure, have an impact on their potential effectiveness and accuracy.

TURKBENCH DESIGN

TurkBench provides Turkers with a personalized *rendering* of AMT (e.g. available HITs, requesters, and qualifications), aiming to minimize unpaid work and increase earnings. More concretely, *TurkBench* is designed to eliminate search time between HITs, reduce the impact of market volatility, create an on-boarding path, and locate the highest paying HITs. While there are certainly more aspects to fulfilling work (e.g.

[2]`http://turkwork.differenceengines.com`
[3]`http://mturk-tracker.com/`
[4]`http://www.mturklist.com/`
[5]`http://www.turkalert.com/`
[6]`http://mturkscripts.com/`

Figure 2. An example session displayed in the Session Manager.

education, entertainment, acquiring desirable skills), we feel that the two largest problems Turkers experience in AMT are the very low wages and the large amount of unpaid, invisible work involved. It is our hope that through using our tool, or similar ones, Turkers will gain the ability to find reasonably paying HITs and avoid exploitative requesters.

TurkBench is comprised of three primary components: the *Personalized Market Visualization*, where Turkers specify their settings and view the current state of the market; the *Session Manager*, which guides Turkers through automatically constructed work sessions; and the *Scheduler*, which crawls and constructs adaptive schedules for Turkers, based both on the volatile market of HITs and Turkers' settings.

Personalized Market Visualization

The *Personalized Market Visualization* (Figure 1) makes it easier to maintain awareness of AMT's volatile market and also provides support for on-boarding. It is implemented as a standalone webpage separate from the AMT interface.

The personalized *rendering* of AMT is done by collecting several settings from the Turker and displaying two possible schedules. Settings are located on the left of the interface and include the desired session length, minimum acceptable pay rate, preferred task length, preferred/blocked requesters, and any qualifications that the Turker has. Once these are specified, *TurkBench* constructs and displays the Turker's projected schedule (shown in grey) and an optimal schedule regardless of settings (shown in orange). This visualization helps the Turker to determine whether Turking is 'worth it' right now by displaying their projected pay rate and its relation to the optimum. If the optimum pay rate is higher than the projected pay rate, then *TurkBench* makes recommendations of 'missed' requesters and/or qualifications under the graph, which also helps to create an on-boarding path. The graph is interactive, in that Turkers are able to get specific information about each HIT by hovering over its respective data point. The combination of these features also enables Turkers to explore how their settings impact their pay. For example, Turkers are able to perform *what-if* analyses to gauge the value of different qualifications (or any of their settings). This assists the Turker to personalize the *rendering* of the AMT market based on their own priorities. Once the Turker is satisfied with their projected schedule, they can begin turking by clicking *Start*, which constructs their actual schedule and brings them to the *Session Manager*.

In regards to how we are calculating pay rate, we estimate it with increasing accuracy as Turkers use the system. In the worst case we use the *Time Allotted* as an estimate for the time required, however, once Turkers complete tasks with the *Session Manager* plugin installed, we are able to improve this estimate. We do this in two ways: 1) if the Turker *has not* completed any of the specific HITs then we use the global average of all Turkers; 2) however, if the Turker *has* completed at least one of the specific HITs then we use their individual average. We acknowledge that this will result in some false negatives, in that some HITs that have lots of *Time Allotted* will be unfairly rated as low paying tasks. However, in our experience our tool constructs realistic schedules that locate relatively high paying HITs. If we find that too many HITs are being unfairly rated we will introduce an estimation mechanism that Turkers can participate in.

Session Manager

The *Session Manager* (Figure 2) guides Turkers through their schedule of HITs, thereby eliminating unpaid search time between HITs. The personalized schedule is adaptive, in that it adjusts to market fluctuations in terms of available HITs. This feature relieves the effect of market volatility while working.

The *Session Manager* displays a timeline[7] which contains one cell for each scheduled HIT. The timeline indicates the current time with a red line, giving Turkers an idea at how they are performing in regards to the estimates. Turkers can advance to the next scheduled HIT by either clicking *Next HIT* to mark the current HIT as completed, or *Dismiss HIT* to remove it from the schedule. If a Turker likes or dislikes the current HIT, they can either save or block the corresponding requester for future scheduling. At any point in time the Turker can quit the session, freeing up any HITs that have not been completed for other Turkers. The top of the toolbar contains aspects of the current session, i.e. earnings, number of HITs completed, and time elapsed/remaining.

The *Session Manager* also keeps track of the amount of time that each HIT takes to complete. This is done by tracking the time between when the Turker accepts the HIT and marks the HIT as complete. This length is what is used by our system to calculate the aforementioned pay rate of each HIT.

Task Scheduler

The engine behind the *Personalized Market Visualization* and *Session Manager* is our *Task Scheduler*. The *Task Scheduler* crawls all of the HITs on AMT periodically and ranks them according to their estimated pay rate. When constructing schedules it selects the earliest available Turker and then walks through the sorted list of HITS, testing whether each HIT satisfies the Turker's settings. As HITs fail to satisfy the settings, the reasons for failure are logged. This log is the basis for any recommendations given to the Turker, which aids in discovering new opportunities. The scheduler runs every few minutes and continually prunes or updates Turkers'

[7]https://github.com/almende/vis

schedules as tasks appear, are completed, or expire. This continually optimizes each Turking session, eliminating the need to maintain awareness of market volatility.

TURKER REACTION

Before deploying *TurkBench* we conducted four 30 minute demos with individual Turkers to get a first impression of the tool. We used their settings, preferences, and resulting schedules to achieve a realistic condition for the demo.

The most enthusiastic reactions came from Turkers 1 and 3. Turker 1 was a female that had been turking on and off for a year and Turker 3 was a male who had been turking for 3-4 months. Neither Turker used many customizations and turking was not their primary income. Both Turkers reported difficulty finding HITs and they were the only participants who abandoned turking sessions because they could not find HITs. Both Turkers spent a great deal of time searching for HITs and were excited to see the session manager walking through a schedule. During the demo *TurkBench* found a pay rate of $6 an hour for Turker 3 (his typical rate was $2-3 an hour) and he intended to work after our interview.

Turker 4 was a male who had been turking for 1 year, used a modest amount of scripts, and drew his primary income from turking. He set a target of $20 per day and did not always meet it. He was not as enthusiastic as the previous two Turkers since he had no trouble knowing which HITs to find. However, he did have trouble with the mechanics of quickly locating HITs and thought he would use *TurkBench* to help him gauge the difficultly and speed of hitting his quota, as well as help him quickly execute a series of HITs.

Turker 2 was a male who had been turking for 1 year, used extensive customizations, and did not draw a primary income from turking. Turker 2 was the most experienced of the Turkers. He maintained relationships with requesters that directly recruited him through email so that he would complete specific upcoming tasks. His target was to earn $20 a day, which he said he could normally do within 2-3 hours without much trouble. Turker 2 said that he would probably not use the session manager since he completed longer tasks outside of the AMT platform, but would use the market visualization to explore which qualifications would help him earn more.

Taking the impressions from our demo into consideration, we believe that the use of *TurkBench* will provide a better understanding of the market and result in higher pay for Turkers by reducing search time, especially for less experienced Turkers.

DISCUSSION

The goals of *TurkBench* are to eliminate unpaid work, make it easier to maintain awareness of market volatility, and support on-boarding/discovery. These goals are shaped by our analysis of Turkers' position within AMT. Through the design and argumentation that we have presented in this paper, we hope to shine further light on the impact of the design decisions made by the platform developer, particularly in regards to the balance of features across roles. We acknowledge the extreme difficulty in foreseeing the challenges of each user role when developing an interface for a system like AMT. However, when the user community signals that they have problems with their level of agency, we draw attention to the fact that the platform developer clearly has the fullest ability to grant more agency to each of the user roles.

Our near term goal is to deploy *TurkBench* to Turkers. Through this deployment we hope to answer several questions around the efficacy and resulting impact of our tool. The easier of these questions relate to individual effects, such as whether *TurkBench* decreases unpaid work activity. The more difficult questions are around broader impacts on the market. For example, will the more powerful, personalized *rendering* of the market reduce the number of low paying tasks?

REFERENCES

1. Bederson, B. B., and Quinn, A. J. Web workers unite! addressing challenges of online laborers. In *CHI 2011 EA*, ACM (2011), 97–106.
2. Callison-Burch, C. Crowd-workers: Aggregating information across turkers to help them find higher paying work. In *HCOMP-2014* (November 2014).
3. Chilton, L. B., Horton, J. J., Miller, R. C., and Azenkot, S. Task search in a human computation market. In *ACM SIGKDD Workshop on Human Computation*, ACM (2010), 1–9.
4. Ipeirotis, P. G. Analyzing the amazon mechanical turk marketplace. *XRDS: Crossroads 17*, 2 (2010), 16–21.
5. Irani, L. C., and Silberman, M. Turkopticon: Interrupting worker invisibility in amazon mechanical turk. In *CHI 2013*, ACM (2013), 611–620.
6. Khanna, S., Ratan, A., Davis, J., and Thies, W. Evaluating and improving the usability of mechanical turk for low-income workers in india. In *DEV '10*, ACM (2010).
7. Kittur, A., Khamkar, S., André, P., and Kraut, R. Crowdweaver: Visually managing complex crowd work. In *CSCW 2012*, ACM (2012), 1033–1036.
8. Kittur, A., Nickerson, J. V., Bernstein, M., Gerber, E., Shaw, A., Zimmerman, J., Lease, M., and Horton, J. The future of crowd work. In *CSCW 2013*, ACM (2013), 1301–1318.
9. Kulkarni, A., Can, M., and Hartmann, B. Collaboratively crowdsourcing workflows with turkomatic. In *CSCW 2012*, ACM (2012), 1003–1012.
10. Martin, D., Hanrahan, B. V., O'Neill, J., and Gupta, N. Being a turker. In *CSCW 2014*, ACM (2014), 224–235.
11. ONeill, J., and Martin, D. Relationship-based business process crowdsourcing. In *INTERACT '13*. Springer Berlin Heidelberg, 2013, 429–446.
12. Quinn, A. J., and Bederson, B. B. Human computation: a survey and taxonomy of a growing field. In *CHI 2011*, ACM (2011), 1403–1412.
13. Silberman, M., Ross, J., Irani, L., and Tomlinson, B. Sellers' problems in human computation markets. In *SIGKDD Workshop on Human Computation*, ACM (2010), 18–21.

Exploring the Role of Activity Trace Design on Evaluations of Online Worker Quality

Jennifer Marlow[1,2]
[1]FX Palo Alto Laboratory, Inc.
3174 Porter Drive
marlow@fxpal.com

Laura A. Dabbish[2,3], Jodi L. Forlizzi[2]
[2]Human-Computer Interaction Institute, [3]Heinz College
Carnegie Mellon University
{dabbish, forlizzi}@cs.cmu.edu

ABSTRACT

Websites can record individual users' activities and display them in a variety of ways. There is a tradeoff between detail and abstraction in visualization, especially when the amount of content increases and becomes more difficult to process. We conducted an experiment on Mechanical Turk varying the quality, detail, and visual presentation of information about an individual's past work to see how these design features affected perceptions of the worker. We found that providing detail in the display through text increased processing time and led to less positive evaluations. Visually abstract displays required less processing time but decreased confidence in evaluation. This suggests that different design parameters may engender differing psychological processes that influence reactions towards an unknown person.

Author Keywords

Activity traces; Impression formation; Information presentation; Crowdsourcing

ACM Classification Keywords

H.5.m. Information interfaces and presentation (e.g., HCI): Miscellaneous.

INTRODUCTION

From social media sites to online work environments, technological platforms are increasingly recording and displaying individuals' activity histories. This is characteristic of a general trend in online social settings, where we are starting to see activity streams as a widely used form of information about other Internet users [5]. In the context of online peer production, access to individuals' past behavior and history can benefit collaborations and jump-start interactions by indicating who knows what or who has done what [7]. Visualizing this information can also influence how we feel about other people [8]. However, a variety of activity history design decisions could influence the positivity of and confidence in initial impressions formed. Activity traces can be designed with varying levels of *abstraction* (the degree to which they use text versus visual abstractions) and *granularity* (the degree to which they provide detail versus aggregation).

CHI 2015, April 18 - 23 2015, Seoul, Republic of Korea.

ACM 978-1-4503-3145-6/15/04…$15.00.
http://dx.doi.org/10.1145/2702123.2702195

One main challenge in presenting activity histories is managing information overload [4], and the choice between making information more accessible and easy to interpret (in the form of visual vs. textual presentation) is a primary consideration when displaying a large amount of information [12]. The amount of detail or granularity provided in an activity history has implications for the amount of mental effort required to process the information. A tradeoff exists between the level of detail of available information about a person's past behavior and the amount of time and cognitive effort required to fully interpret that information [11]. Careful information processing may come at the expense of efficiency [6].

To investigate these tradeoffs in activity history design, we conducted an experiment using an online peer review work task. We compared abstracted visual displays with detailed text displays of a participant's past work in an online crowdsourcing platform. We wanted to understand how the visual display of activity history affects the positivity of and confidence in evaluations of a worker in a lightweight peer production context.

The contribution of this work is insight into how the design parameters of granularity and aggregation influence psychological reactions to and perceptions of individuals. Our results inform the design of systems that record and display individual work traces.

RELATED WORK AND HYPOTHESES

Here we discuss how different visualizations of work history may affect psychological reactions to the worker.

Detailed textual displays

Text-based lists of activity information are detailed but require effort to interpret. A visual summary of the same information might be easier to process quickly but be less informative overall, as is the case with the London Underground map [1].

Assuming the content of activity is neutral (neither positive nor negative,) providing additional detailed information about past activities could help to reduce uncertainty about a person, which has been associated with increased liking [3]. Prior work has also indicated that when people have a more detailed and concrete mental image of what a person is like, they feel more familiar and behave more pro-socially towards that person [11].

H1a: More granular activity traces will lead to more positive subsequent evaluations of the person through providing more concrete details about a person's past behaviors.

However, if expending mental processing effort leads to negative reactions [13], then an easy to process visual summary may induce positive impressions:

H1b: Less granular activity traces will be easier to process and increase positivity of impressions.

Processing fluency and abstracted visual displays
In addition to granularity (or amount of detail in the information), displays may be more or less abstract, which could affect effort of interpretation. Processing fluency can be defined as the subjective experience of ease with which people process information (or how effortful it is for them to do so) [2]. Fluency, or reduced processing effort, has been linked to positive interpersonal evaluations such as liking and perceived intelligence [2]. Therefore, it is possible that making things easier to process through presenting them in an abstract summary format will lead to more positive evaluations.

H1c: More abstract activity traces will lead to more positive evaluations of the person than less abstract traces by providing information in a way that is easier to interpret.

Impression confidence
Prior research suggests that people's behavior is influenced not just by what they think but by how confident they are in their likes and beliefs [13]. We were therefore interested not only in the evaluations made by people but by the degree to which they were confident in their attitudes.

Prior research on confidence of impressions suggests that increasing the amount of information available about a person increases confidence in in impressions of that person [13]. In addition, more details (even uninformative ones) increase the clarity of a perceiver's mental picture and in turn increase confidence [13]. Thus we expect:

H2a: More granular and detailed textual displays will lead to more confidence.

However, processing fluency can also increase confidence in evaluations [2]. This means detail may reduce confidence as a function of processing effort, and abstraction should enhance it.

H2b: More visually abstract representations of activity traces will lead to more confidence.

Hypothesized interaction effects
Finally, we might also expect that the effects of abstraction versus detail could depend on whether the work history being generated is generally positive or generally negative. For example, minimizing evidence of bad work through abstraction could improve positivity of impressions of the worker by de-emphasizing mistakes.

H3: Visual abstraction will affect positivity of impressions for bad quality work but will not affect impressions for good quality work.

METHOD
In order to investigate the effects of level of detail versus visual aggregation, we designed three types of history visualizations. The designs (see Figure 1) were inspired by common formats of activity trace presentation on sites that use multiple formats to showcase individual work history in the context of software production, including GitHub, Stack Overflow and Masterbranch (see, e.g.[10])

	High abstraction (aggregate view, visual cues [color])	Low abstraction (no aggregation or visual summary)
High granularity (contain text)	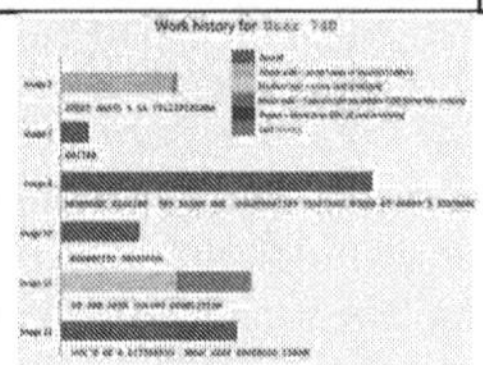	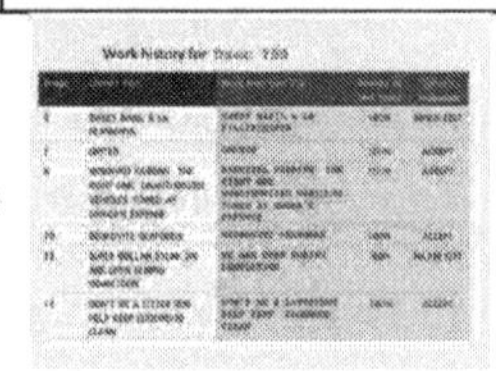
Low granularity (minimal text)	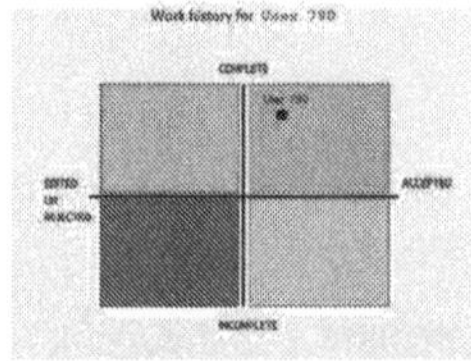	N/A

Figure 1. History visualizations (top row: graph (L), table (R); bottom row: quadrant). Examples shown here depict good work.

To separate the effects of granularity and abstraction, the visualizations varied from each other in the following ways: The *table* condition was high in granularity (with detailed text) and a low degree of abstraction. The table condition showed a grid filled with the text the participant had typed, the correct answer, the rating by the editor, and the percent of the work that had been completed. It showed a worker's work actions for six pieces of work.

The *graph* condition also had a high degree of granularity (textual information) but also featured some other visual abstraction cues in the form of color codes pertaining to the quality of the work. It contained the same information as the table, except the percent of the work completed and the rating by the editor were displayed in a visual format (through colored bar graphs.) It also showed work actions for six pieces of work. Finally, the *quadrant* condition was the most abstract, contained minimal text and plotted the participant on a grid showing the average completeness of their six pieces of work and the average evaluation of their work.

Work history quality

Finally, to test H3 we manipulated work history quality. For each of the conditions, there was a "good" quality history and a "bad" quality history. The information seeding the work activity history was taken from real performance on the task by Mechanical Turk workers. Overall, the good performance was on average 92% correct, while the bad performance was on average 50% correct.

Experimental setup

The experiment was set up as a crowdsourced task (HIT) in Amazon's Mechanical Turk. Participants were paid 20 cents to participate in a task billed as "Transcription Worker Evaluation." The description of the task was: "You will be shown some image transcription work done by another Turker and asked to evaluate its quality." Upon accepting the task, participants were shown an example of the task and told what they would be doing. The task involved transcribing the text found on images of various signs. Participants were shown examples of these signs.

At this point, participants were randomly assigned to one of the possible history visualization conditions. After viewing the history, they were asked to evaluate the person and the activity history display on the following criteria:

- Work quality ("How would you rate the overall quality of this person's work? Consider both the amount of text typed and the editor's evaluations.") This was on a sliding-point scale from 0 (poor) to 100 (excellent).
- Confidence in assessment of worker ("How confident are you in your response to the previous question?") (7 point Likert scale, 7=very confident)

RESULTS

184 participants completed the task, and they were roughly evenly distributed across the table, graph, and quadrant (good and bad) conditions. Table 1 shows the mean values for work quality rating, confidence, and time (in seconds) spent viewing the work history across the conditions.

	Granularity (Low=quadrant, High = graph + table)			**Abstraction** (Low= table, High=graph + quadrant)		
	Rating*	Conf.	Time*	Rating	Conf.*	Time*
Low	65.46[a]	5.63[a]	35.87[a]	59.75[a]	6.04[a]	50.4[a]
High	57.04[b]	5.72[a]	47.9[b]	60.08[a]	5.50[b]	40.04[b]

Table 1. Mean values for rating, confidence, and viewing time (in seconds) across conditions. Values not connected by same letter are significantly different at p <.05 (Wilcoxon test)

Manipulation checks

There was a significant main effect of history quality on impression positivity. That is, participants who saw the "good" history rated the work as significantly higher in quality (M=74.79) than participants who saw the "bad" history (M=44.98) (t[179]=37.01, p<.001). This confirmed that people were able to accurately interpret the quality of information portrayed in the visualizations, overall.

Additionally, to test the assumptions that detailed textual displays would require more mental effort to interpret than displays without text, we recorded the amount of time in seconds spent viewing the visualization page and compared that across the low and high granularity conditions. Because combining conditions led to uneven numbers in categories, we used a Wilcoxon non-parametric test to compare values across low and high-granularity visualizations and low and high-abstraction visualizations. As Table 1 shows, participants spent significantly more time viewing displays that were high in granularity. The same occurred for abstraction: Low abstraction involved more time spent on the display than high abstraction.

Effects on positivity of impressions

Hypothesis 1a predicted that a more granular visualization would lead to more positive impressions. Conversely, Hypothesis 1b predicted that a less granular, or aggregated visualization would lead to more positive impressions of worker quality. There was a significant main effect of granularity on rating quality (Z=2.09, p=.03), with the no-text (quadrant) condition providing more positive ratings than the granular, text-containing (graph and table) conditions. This supported Hypothesis 1b, and the notion that "less can be more" when learning about others [9]. The quadrant condition was also more accurate in their ratings of worker quality than the graph and table.

Hypothesis 1c, which posited that the more abstract visualization would lead to more positive impressions because it was easier to interpret, was not supported; abstraction did not have a significant effect on positivity of rating.

Effects on confidence

Hypothesis 2a predicted that more detailed textual displays would lead to greater confidence than less detailed ones, while Hypothesis 2b predicted that more abstracted visual displays would lead to greater confidence than less abstracted displays. There was no significant main effect of granularity on confidence but there was a significant main effect of abstraction on confidence (Z=3.79, *p*<.001). However, the opposite of Hypothesis 2b occurred: participants viewing the low abstraction format (table) were significantly more confident (M=6.04) than those who viewed the high abstraction graph or quadrant (M=5.50).

Interactions between work quality and visualization

We also were interested in further exploring the significant results to see if different visualizations had differing effects for good and bad quality. For example, minimizing details of bad work might lead to higher impressions than presenting bad work in a detailed format.

We conducted a 2x2 ANOVA comparing bad vs. good work and detailed vs. not-detailed presentations on positivity. We used planned contrasts to compare the effect of exposure to bad work (detailed) and bad work (not detailed) as well as good work (detailed) and good work (not detailed). While the details did not affect positivity of impressions for good work, they did for bad work. Bad work presented in a textually detailed format (M=40.42) led to less positive ratings of quality than bad work presented in a format without text (M=53.67). This supported H3.

We conducted a similar 2x2 ANOVA comparing bad vs. good work and abstract vs. non-abstracted displays. In this case, abstraction did not affect confidence when the work was bad. However, when the work was good, lack of abstraction made people more confident (M=6.16) than when the work was presented in a visual abstraction (M=5.49).

DISCUSSION

In this work we saw how presenting activity history in a detailed, text-based versus visually abstract summary display had differing effects on various attitudinal outcomes such as positivity and confidence. Displays high in text-based detail fostered positivity in ratings of a worker but not confidence. On the other hand, displays that featured information in a visually abstracted format employing features such as color and aggregation decreased confidence in rating but did not influence positivity.

This could have implications for how people interact with one another or assess others' competence and ability in a peer production and peer review type setting (where typically little to no information about others' past work is provided). Increasing confidence in impressions may be detrimental if the initial impressions that people form are inaccurate. It could be that making activity history more detailed would increase confidence but discourage accuracy of processing by making observers less likely to consider all information [6]. A promising direction for future work will be to examine the effects of initial impressions (including positivity and confidence) on behavioral outcomes as well to see what the downstream implications of initial impressions are for a work product.

Our work contributes to research on impression formation online, especially by providing insight into how the presentation style and the quality of information interact. Designers of systems that employ activity traces should consider how display decisions can lead to confidence or positivity and adapt presentations accordingly to achieve desired goals. For example, if a system is able to automatically detect that a worker is performing poorly, it might display that information in a summary display in order to reduce negative opinions of that person (in accordance with findings supporting H3). However, if the goal of the system is to have workers improve each other's work, then providing bad work history in a detailed format could induce a negative impression that might make editors more sensitive to finding mistakes in the work.

ACKNOWLEDGMENTS

This work was supported by NSF grants IIS-1111750, SMA-1064209, OCI-0943168, ACI-1322278, and the Center for the Future of Work, Carnegie Mellon University.

REFERENCES

1. Ainsworth, S. The functions of multiple representations. *Computers & Education* 33, 2–3 (1999), 131–152.
2. Alter, A.L. and Oppenheimer, D.M. Uniting the tribes of fluency to form a metacognitive nation. *Personality and Social Psychology Review* 13, 3 (2009), 219–235.
3. Berger, C.R. and Calabrese, R.J. Some explorations in initial interaction and beyond: Toward a developmental theory of interpersonal communication. *Human Communication Research* 1, 2 (1975), 99–112.
4. Bontcheva, K. and Rout, D. Making sense of social media streams through semantics: a survey. *Semantic Web Journal*, (2012), 373-403.
5. Counts, S. and Fisher, K. Taking it all in? Visual attention in microblog consumption. In *Proc. ICWSM* (2011), 97-104.
6. Hullman, J., Adar, E., and Shah, P. Benefitting infovis with visual difficulties. *IEEE Visualization and Computer Graphics* 17, 12 (2011), 2213–2222.
7. Kim, D. and Shipman, F.M., III. Visualizing History to Improve Users' Location and Comprehension of Collaborative Work. In *Proc. GROUP*, (2012), 11–20.
8. Liao, Q.V. and Fu, W.-T. Expert voices in echo chambers: effects of source expertise indicators on exposure to diverse opinions. In *Proc. CHI*, (2014), 2745–2754.
9. Norton, M.I., Frost, J.H., and Ariely, D. Less is more: the lure of ambiguity, or why familiarity breeds contempt. *Journal of Personality and Social Psychology* 92, 1 (2007), 97-105.
10. Singer, L., Figueira Filho, F., Cleary, B., Treude, C., Storey, M.-A., & Schneider, K. (2013). Mutual assessment in the social programmer ecosystem: An empirical investigation of developer profile aggregators. In *Proc. CSCW*, (2013), 103–116.
11. Stephan, E., Liberman, N., and Trope, Y. The effects of time perspective and level of construal on social distance. *Journal of Experimental Social Psychology* 47(2), (2011), 397–402.
12. Thompson, R.S., Rantanen, E.M., Yurcik, W., and Bailey, B.P. Command line or pretty lines? Comparing textual and visual interfaces for intrusion detection. In *Proc. CHI*, (2007), 1205-1214.
13. Tsai, C.I. and McGill, A.L. No pain, no gain? How fluency and construal level affect consumer confidence. *Journal of Consumer Research* 37, 5 (2011), 807–821.

We Are Dynamo: Overcoming Stalling and Friction in Collective Action for Crowd Workers

Niloufar Salehi[1], Lilly C. Irani[2], Michael S. Bernstein[1],
Ali Alkhatib[1], Eva Ogbe[1], Kristy Milland[3, 4], Clickhappier[4, 5]
[1]Stanford University, [2]UC San Diego, [3]Ryerson University, [4]We Are Dynamo, [5]MTurkGrind
niloufar@cs.stanford.edu, lirani@ucsd.edu, {msb, ali.alkhatib, eoogbe}@cs.stanford.edu,
kmilland@ryerson.ca, clickhappier@wearedynamo.org

ABSTRACT
By lowering the costs of communication, the web promises to enable distributed collectives to act around shared issues. However, many collective action efforts never succeed: while the web's affordances make it easy to gather, these same decentralizing characteristics impede any focus towards action. In this paper, we study challenges to collective action efforts through the lens of online labor by engaging with Amazon Mechanical Turk workers. Through a year of ethnographic fieldwork, we sought to understand online workers' unique barriers to collective action. We then created Dynamo, a platform to support the Mechanical Turk community in forming publics around issues and then mobilizing. We found that collective action publics tread a precariously narrow path between the twin perils of stalling and friction, balancing with each step between losing momentum and flaring into acrimony. However, specially structured labor to maintain efforts' forward motion can help such publics take action.

Author Keywords
Activism; infrastructure; human computation; Amazon Mechanical Turk; design; collective action.

ACM Classification Keywords
H.5.m. Information interfaces and presentation (e.g., HCI): Miscellaneous.

INTRODUCTION
In this paper, we examine the challenges that online collectives face when they gather not just to talk, but to take action. Collective action is inherently related to the work of human-computer interaction in a networked world. It marks the field's aspirations for the power of digitally mediated collectives to generate change, whether that take the form of pixels, profit, or progress.

CHI 2015, April 18 - 23, 2015, Seoul, Republic of Korea

http://dx.doi.org/10.1145/2702123.2702508

An overarching research narrative celebrates the web's affordances for galvanizing coordinated actions (e.g., [3, 4, 5]). However, many collective action efforts never succeed. The Internet's sword is double-edged: the same affordances that seem to make it an ideal setting to gather also seem to debilitate actual action. It is much easier to derail an effort than to push one onward to success [21]. People may talk past each other [24], and even when they do engage, more discussion can mean lower-quality outcomes [22]. Unfortunately, across many domains, the majority of collective efforts fail [17, 32]. Online coordination is even more challenged when political and social stakes are high or when action may expose participants to harm [4].

Amazon Mechanical Turk (AMT), a crowd work platform, embodies many of these promises and perils. To some, crowds bear the potential of mass action and people power. Yet as Irani and Silberman have argued [19], AMT's design directs this collective power into reliable, steadily humming computational infrastructure. This infrastructure is designed to keep questions of ethical labor relations out of sight.

Outside the infrastructures that AMT provides, Turkers have formed collectives such as TurkerNation, MTurkGrind, and Reddit's /r/HITsWorthTurkingFor. On these platforms they share well-paying work, discuss employers, educate newcomers, and consult with employers who are willing to communicate [30]. Turkers in these communities engage in some short-term or small-scale collective action (e.g., to raise funds for a colleague), but efforts that require sustained effort and critical mass are less likely to succeed. Workers told us that collective action is difficult because of divided loyalties, time pressures to earn money, and risks that agitation poses to their reputations and to the availability of crowdwork more generally.

We spent over a year engaged in crowd worker forums, discussing collective action with Turkers individually, and speculating on how collective actions could work with Turkers. We strengthened relationships between the design team and Turkers interested in collective action and, on the basis of those relationships, designed, adapted, and analyzed Dynamo, a platform for Turker collective action.

Dynamo is a community platform designed to gather ideas, energy, and support directed towards collective action. Workers can assemble, whatever their differences, to communicate pseudonymously through Dynamo. They nominate issues for change and make concrete steps to act on them. Over the course of design and development, we used the system with workers and continuously reconfigured [39] relationships, labor, and communication technology to support issues workers encountered in organizing around action. Workers first collectively authored a set of ethical guidelines to rein in problematic academic research practices. To date, 171 workers and 45 requesters have signed the guidelines. Dynamo has since been used by another group to develop an open letter campaign to humanize Turkers in the public imagination — a campaign that has since attracted coverage from major news outlets. Dynamo plays host to a still larger set of ideas for tactical interventions and alternative futures.

In order to act, workers needed to navigate between twin perils: *stalling* and *friction*. Efforts *stalled* — lost momentum — when consensus-building or the next concrete steps became too labor-intensive to sustain worker engagement. Efforts faced *friction* when an action — often one taken to avoid stalling — provoked divisive disagreement amongst workers, or when fly-by criticisms diminished motivation. Friction seemed inevitable when a proposed future affected people in different ways and evoked anxieties of worst-case outcomes. Stalling and friction are linked: efforts stalled when friction accumulated or when the fear of criticism led to no activity. Likewise, avoiding stalling by making a decision could result in friction when others disagreed. The work of organizing was time-consuming and exhausting.

When facing stalling and friction, we found that structured labor by a trusted actor could move the effort forward and prevent failure. We developed four strategies to transform friction into progress towards action. First, if the collective effort was stagnating, we proposed deadlines on the current goal. Second, we pursued an act-and-undo strategy, proposing actions that could be done experimentally without consensus but could easily be undone in the face of objections or negative outcomes. Third, we worked with organizers to portray an image of success to produce hope among participants. Fourth, if the effort was in conflict, we repeated posts using more neutral language or removed topics of unnecessary tension from consideration.

This paper details and reflects on our social and technical engagement with collective action among Amazon Mechanical Turk workers. We introduce Dynamo as a meeting space for publics that form to act on issues. We illustrate the challenges of friction and stalling with three vignettes drawn from two cases of collective action undertaken through Dynamo. We also explain our own involvement in moving efforts forward. We argue for recognition of design as well as structured emotional, cognitive labor as crucial in enabling online collectives.

THEORY AND RELATED WORK

The web enables dispersed groups to gather and act [3, 11]. Some celebrated examples include groups discussing democratic reforms [26], solving difficult math and science problems [5], and protesting unfair actions [10].

Collective Action

Research on online collective action largely explores the social dynamics involved when groups of people aggregate their efforts using the web to push a cause forward. In some cases, online crowds take roles to support an ongoing social movement [8]. Online crowds can also curate, filter, and recommend important information, doing work researchers have recognized as "functional, if not necessarily central" to social movements [38]. In this paper we focus on efforts that originate and function entirely online [4].

Social movements can succeed online when organizers have ready access to large audiences that are buttressed by anonymity [10]. Organizers can directly and cheaply communicate with like-minded individuals rather than leverage personal social networks. Earl et al. term this phenomenon "organizers without organizations," arguing that the complexities of coordination among social movement organizers is no longer necessary online [11].

In these success cases, participants have the possibilities of loyalty and exit (e.g., petitions, boycotts), but not voice (see [18]). In other words, they may choose to sign a petition or to leave if they don't agree. But, there is little place for discourse when the problem, its source, and its solution are not clear. Further, exit is an insufficient option when a project might still affect those who dissent. For example, research on Wikipedia identifies fights surrounding controversial edits, "gate-keeping" behavior around articles, and the chilling effects these phenomena have on content creation [21, 22]. This suggests that online collectives face particular challenges establishing complex strategies in the face of high political and social stakes.

The stakes are precipitously high for workers on Mechanical Turk, who fear the prospect of losing access to work. Actions taken by some could affect all members of the workforce. Goals are open-ended, actions bear consequences, and those repercussions are shared. The collective needs to work together to develop its goals and execute them. In the next section we further examine this challenge by relating it to the formation of *publics*.

Forming Publics

Designing for collectives to act requires deep theoretical understanding of the social dynamics of these groups: What brings them together? How can they use language to articulate issues? Further, how can they reach agreement and define shared goals? Groups that gather around shared issues echo Le Dantec's and DiSalvo's Deweyan formulation of publics [9, 27]. Publics emerge when "those indirectly and seriously affected for good or for evil form a group distinctive enough to require recognition and a name." These publics come together through their shared conditions and develop formulations and analyses of the issues they face. Habermas likewise views publics[1] as groups of people who gather to discuss issues of mutual interest and reach common judgment when possible. [16]

Much of the work on publics thus far has focused on the conditions of discourse and assembly [9, 27]. We build on such work, but take up the conditions by which these publics can successfully *act* together on shared issues. When shifting from deliberation to action, we argue that the challenges of *stalling* and *friction* threaten a public's success. We will expand on our experience to describe specific kinds of organizing infrastructures and communicative labors that can help such publics.

OUR METHOD AND POSITION

We undertake this project not as outside observers, but as people with stakes in the ecology of human computation. We have been requesters and workers on Amazon Mechanical Turk, and we have investments in Computer Science, a field that produces and legitimizes human computation. We produced Dynamo through a process of collaboration with interested workers not only to build something for them out there but also to call into question our own design practices and assumptions [41]. We approached this not through "detached intimacy" but by working towards "located accountabilities" [40] that recognized the perspectives and power relations between workers and our team. We drew from anthropologically informed design traditions, including ethnography for systems design and participatory design (see [31]), to address the politics of work [2, 12] in the face of an absence of institutions to represent worker interests. We also drew on anthropological methodology that examines how collaboration can generate insight about disciplinary methodology [33].

Our process was highly interactive, but structured only in hindsight. We began by looking for existing forms of collective action by reading publicly visible forums and posting surveys to AMT itself. We also found a few workers early on who were interested in the possibilities of collective action and engaged with us more directly. Slowly, as our design process progressed, we attracted engagement from larger numbers of workers, discussing Turking and the project with over 100 individuals in total. We talked with workers, proposed scenarios to check our understanding and imaginations, and we responded to their critiques, feedback, and suggestions as built and maintained Dynamo. Turkers are busy and distributed, so much of this talk happened through email threads, forum posts, Internet Relay Chat (IRC) conversations, and forum private messages. One member of our team was at times in communication with Turkers online for several weeks. This period of ethnographic research spanned more than a year.

Our observations helped us understand both the complexity of workers' existing social organizations, and the challenges of acting. Observing and asking yielded more than an understanding of workers' social categories. We also established an ongoing relationship of trust by showing ourselves to be accountable to worker critiques. The extent of our engagement mattered when our design work led to missteps, as we discuss later. Our first lesson was the extent of collective action already existing among Turkers.

AMT AND THE COLLECTIVES THAT MAKE IT WORK

Amazon Mechanical Turk is an online labor market where requesters publish microtasks, and crowd workers can perform those tasks for monetary compensation [30]. AMT describes this service as enabling users to incorporate labor directly into computer systems. Researchers have argued that human computation in its current form renders workers invisible, thus eliminating the moral impetus to consider worker conditions or needs [19].

In the backend, researchers describe large numbers of highly educated workers who work full-time to make ends meet. These workers are faced with a little-regulated labor marketplace, variable and often low wages, and unbalanced power relations favoring employers [20, 23]. For instance, employers can choose whether or not to pay for completed work; workers lack legal support in pursuing wage theft or minimum wages [19].

Workers already use social media and operate several forums where they share leads on good work, discuss their experiences, and support one another. Turkers have also created userscripts to add their own enhancements to the AMT interface, and maintain shared information repositories. These interactions constitute strong online communities [30]. The forums are an important way in which people learn to manage their work to meet their needs. As one worker explained to us:

> *"The community helped to introduce me to the rules, norms, and averages [...] how to choose the right HITs, which plugins or add-ons that would be helpful, and what to do in case of a rejection."*

Workers also act collectively in more eventful ways, such as supporting a particular member during a time of personal need. We found these cases to be very specific forms of collective action where group consensus was not crucial to success. For example, a worker told us about fundraising for a family who faced hardship close to Christmas: "*My forum put together something like 200$ all together in order to give the little girl a Christmas. I chipped in five bucks for it. We didn't make a list of contributors or anything, it was just something nice to do.*" We observed

[1] For Habermas, publics are part of a normative theory of democracy that must have a relationship with the sovereign state [14]. Future work will examine over a longer duree the relationship of Dynamo activism to the state itself.

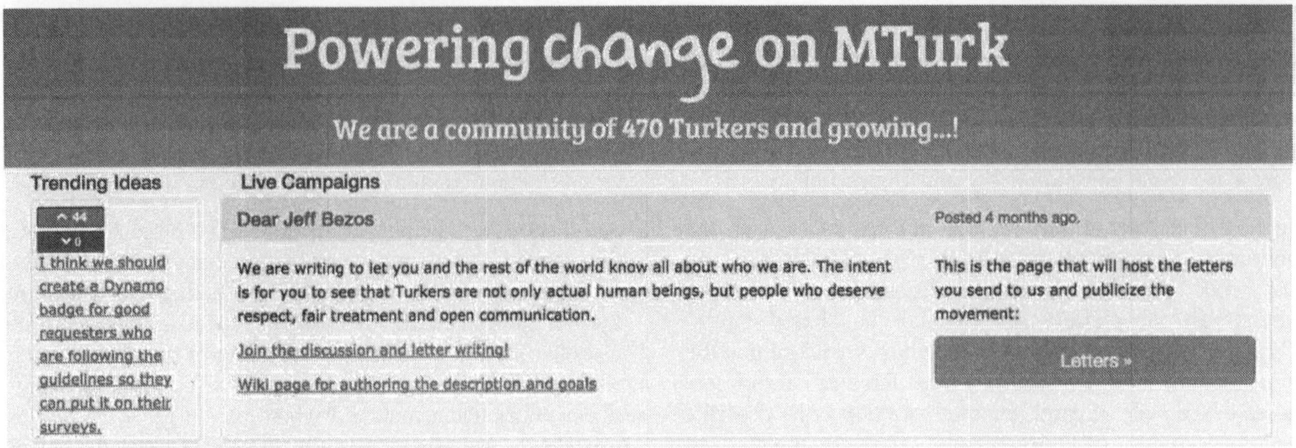

Figure 1. Dynamo is a collective action platform for Amazon Mechanical Turk workers. It has been used to author guidelines for ethical requester behavior, a letter campaign to Amazon CEO Jeff Bezos, and twenty other efforts.

that when individual actions had effect (e.g. emailing requesters), and when nobody would object to the effort, forums proved effective at coordinating. They struggled more when consensus to share a burden or discussion was required.

Trust grows fragile as the communities take on more members. All workers we spoke with interact exclusively online. Disagreements might erupt, or members may begin to suspect the motives of a particular member. We heard of disputes over members who were suspected of operating multiple accounts, colluding with employers behind the scenes, or even just making a statement taken as insult. The forums archive these interactions and reconciliation can be difficult online. Researchers have found that members of online-only communities may struggle to achieve trust [6].

These problems were compounded in interactions between workers of different online forums that maintained different norms of what it meant to be a good AMT worker. Disagreements among these workers were sometimes cast as fundamental rifts between entire communities. Workers call the most explosive of these exchanges "mega-drama."

Though the AMT workforce is host to many kinds of collective life, most of the Turkers we spoke with considered unions – the iconic form of worker collectivity – as inherently impractical in this environment. A number of dynamics made a unified voice and representation difficult to imagine. New workers join daily and some stay only for days or weeks. "Work contracts" between workers and employers last for minutes. Further, many workers were attracted to AMT because of the personal independence it afforded. Many worried that the unified voice could not account for their particular needs and ethics.

Turkers must weigh collective action against personal risk to their worker account, work environment, or reputation as online workers. For many, AMT serves as a crucial source of income; therefore they actively prevent any action that may put that source at risk. Some workers felt that if wages went up, they might lose sources of employment. Another worried about taking actions that attracted legal attention to crowd work. Still others worried about being singled out as agitators and getting blacklisted by Amazon or employers.

While some of these issues are shared with traditional labor organizing movements (e.g. [34]), many are exacerbated issues of organizing for online work. For example, the labor force on AMT has a very high turnover: hiring and firing employees is as simple as registering on a website and deleting a row in a database. Further, Turkers have (almost) no opportunity for face-to-face interactions, no way to communicate with all other Turkers, and no organizational body to make or enforce decisions.

We interpreted these social affordances and vulnerabilities as constraining the kinds of collective action that communities could undertake. With this understanding of existing collective action, we sought to build a system that mitigated these risks, promoted discovery of shared issues, and allowed for collaboration towards action goals.

DYNAMO

Based on our initial engagements, we worked with Turkers to design Dynamo (Figure 1), a platform to support collective action in the AMT ecology. We framed Dynamo around creating publics that are just large enough to take action — unities without unions.

Based on our interactions with workers, we focused Dynamo's design on three affordances: *trust and privacy*, *assembling a public*, and *mobilizing*. We describe the system design and each of these in detail below.

Trust and Privacy

For any kind of collective action, Turkers desired safety from external retribution. They anticipated retaliatory action from Amazon and requesters, expecting that Dynamo would become a target:

> *"are they asking for our worker id and why? to make easy fro [sic] Amazon to serve them with a subpoena so they know who to suspend*" –A Turker

Account suspension is excommunication from Mechanical Turk. Placing individual members' accounts at risk could seriously threaten a Turker's career and livelihood. Turkers needed to be able to gather in a venue where their words could not be tied to their professional reputation.

Dynamo's legitimacy relies on each user trusting that all other users are fellow Turkers. Participant safety, privacy, and the deferral of "mega-drama" led us to give workers the option of new identities in Dynamo. We achieved this in two ways. First, we require that workers complete a Dynamo HIT on Amazon Mechanical Turk. That HIT has a qualification requirement of more than 100 approved HITs. Workers who accept the HIT receive a unique, one-time registration code for their account. No record relates any worker IDs to any particular account. Second, workers used randomly generated screen names to disconnect their identity on Dynamo from previous forum identities. These names followed the pattern *adjective_animal* (e.g. light_dragonfly, excited_iguana). During registration, workers could generate new names at random until they found one they liked.

We were concerned that this approach risked losing the power of existing social ties. During deployment, however, we learned that Turkers were aware of their own community's activity on Dynamo through backstage conversations. But the screen names enabled more positive discussions with those from other communities, if only because they implied an onstage debate where the identities remained new and unknown.

Assembling a public

For actions to be successful they needed support and participants to share the labor. We designed Dynamo to allow for workers pressed for time to lend support or interject critique at different levels of involvement. Dynamo focuses on short idea pitches. Ideas act as polls that enable publics to form around them. Pitching a new idea requires a 140-character description, such as "I think we should create a Dynamo badge for good requesters who are following the guidelines so they can put it on their surveys."

Workers can vote the idea up or down, and the idea graduates to become a campaign once it acquires 25 upvotes and has more upvotes than downvotes. Once a user submits an idea, Dynamo automatically generates a new forum thread to host discussion and debate on the idea.

Mobilizing

Once an idea graduates to become an active campaign, Dynamo provides affordances that allow users to discuss, take action, and track progress.

Dynamo supports discussion through a web forum where each active campaign has at least one dedicated thread. The system automatically subscribes those who had previously upvoted the relevant idea or who later post a reply. It also engages users by notifying them when others "thank" them.

Campaigns need general software support. Dynamo hosts a MediaWiki installation for users to author content through their pseudonyms. It also allows workers to place buttons on the Dynamo site to capture calls-to-action, such as a button click to sign a declaration.

Dynamo shares a list of users who have performed an action to provide visibility into its popularity (e.g., "light_dragonfly and 170 others have signed the document"). The Dynamo team writes periodic update emails summarizing important campaign developments as necessary. The emails act as a megaphone, attracting attention to the task at hand and calling out to others to join.

DEPLOYMENT

In the six months since Dynamo's deployment on the web, 470 unique Turkers have registered. The site has had over 5,800 unique visitors and over 32,000 views. Among these are Turkers that post vigorously on other forums and are active participants of Turker communities. Our goal is not to motivate every single Turker to join; instead, we sought to attract small groups of motivated people, including those who could bridge communities.

Ideas for Action

So far, Turkers have gathered on Dynamo to discuss twenty-two ideas for action, and two have transformed into active campaigns. Turkers can execute some of these ideas on their own; others would require Amazon's support.

The system has hosted a range of ideas, including: creating a worker-operated alternative to Amazon's opaque Masters worker certification; software to store and publicly share messages that Turkers exchange with requesters; wiki-writing a history of AMT; getting rid of CAPTCHAs between HITs for workers who have completed more than 10,000 HITs; and creating a worker-run platform like AMT.

Two ideas on Dynamo have launched as campaigns. The "Guidelines for Academic Requesters" generated worker-generated guidelines for ethical research on AMT. A "Letter Writing Campaign" aims to create a positive image of Turkers in the public eye.

Guidelines For Academic Requesters

Somewhat surprisingly to us given our position, Turkers used Dynamo first to curb poor academic research practices on Mechanical Turk. In the weeks prior to Dynamo's launch, an academic researcher began experimenting on Turkopticon, an independent Turker rating system. This experiment included the injection of fabricated data into Turkopticon, causing disarray among Turkers who rely on the accuracy of this information for their work. After several days of investigation, the Turkopticon community identified the researcher who fabricated the data. This incident took up much time and energy and caused much frustration, prompting questions about the ethics of research on AMT. While the research in question was approved by an IRB, Turkers agreed that IRB committees lacked adequate exposure to the vulnerabilities that they faced.

A group of Turkopticon maintainers and users responded by suggesting the community draft publicly available ethics guidelines to guide IRBs and requesters towards better behavior. Like in many social movements, emotionally charged incidents became a trigger for collective action [15]. This became Dynamo's largest and most active campaign. Using the Dynamo Wiki, members collaboratively generated a comprehensive online guide covering matters such as fair pay, how to respect Turker privacy, and how to respect Turker communities online. The guidelines are also available as a 23-page document.

Once Turkers had authored the main content, the organizing team set a one week period for soliciting comments and edits before freezing and launching the document. This was a laborious period of listening for feedback, responding to critiques, and building consensus across multiple communities. After several days, Turkers began soliciting endorsement from others within their communities and later from researchers involved in crowd work. The drafting and initial push for signatories spanned just over one month. In total, 216 participants have signed the guidelines: 45 researchers and 171 Turkers. Members of one Turker forum have started to invite their peers by changing their forum signatures to: "Have you signed the Dynamo Guidelines to support fair treatment of MTurk workers?" We have also observed requesters referencing the guidelines in their HITs: *"Wow, [academic requester] survey's debrief page has recommendations from Dynamo. Nice one Turk community." – A Turker*

Letter Writing Campaign to Jeff Bezos

Another campaign on Dynamo calls for a collective effort to show the world who Turkers are, written from their own viewpoints. It is a reaction to media portrayals of Turkers as downtrodden, disempowered cogs in a machine. It instead aims to humanize perceptions of Turkers:

> *"This is a writing campaign for Turkers to let Jeff Bezos, head of Amazon and brainchild behind mTurk, and the rest of the world know all about who we are. The intent is to get Bezos to see that Turkers are not only actual human beings, but people who deserve respect, fair treatment and open communication."*

This idea reached 50 upvotes and launched as an active campaign early October 2014. However, the movement wasn't limited to Dynamo. Individual Turkers publicized the movement within their own communities by posting to daily threads and creating website banners. Campaign organizers also raised $60 to reach out to a larger group of Turkers through AMT. They posted a HIT that was a three-minute paid vacation inviting people to learn about Dynamo and participate in the letter writing campaign.

A page on Dynamo hosts the letters that Turkers have chosen to share publicly (wearedynamo.org/dearjeffbezos), 21 Turkers have posted their letters to this page but we anticipate that more people have participated by emailing Jeff Bezos directly. The letters focus mainly on Turkers' personal lives, their work on AMT, and the difficulties they face. The campaign has received attention from many media outlets including The Guardian, The Daily Beast, and two European radio stations. Hence, Turkers' have been successful in reaching their goal of positive publicity.

Historically, labor movements have made similar efforts to gain public recognition for workers and the difficulties of their work, as a stepping-stone for further achievements [34]. For online workers – hidden behind their monitors – this is even more challenging, since gaining visibility and recognition as "human beings with rights" is a task in itself.

PUBLICS THAT ACT AND THEIR PROBLEMS

The previous section detailed Dynamo's successes. In this section, we focus on its constant brushes with failure.

The loose groups that form around ideas and discuss them on Dynamo share the characteristics of Dewey's *publics* [7], in that it is a group rallying around an issue that affects the people therein. However, unlike most conceptualizations of publics, Dynamo's publics did not stop at identifying, articulating, and debating issues. They also needed to transform interest into concrete action. This meant significant effort: deciding (or arguing) between alternatives, and facing failure.

We argue that these are not only publics; they are *publics that act.* These publics are often entangled with discursive publics, but also require (as we will show) distinct kinds of labor, structuring, and organizing. Importantly, people had to make significant efforts to prevent the actions on Dynamo from failing due to one of these causes.

In Dynamo, these publics constantly threatened to disband. They navigated between twin failures we term *stalling* and *friction.* In this section, we detail these challenges of publics that act, and how they are intrinsic to the process of forming collective action in online environments.

Stalling

Due to the upvoting process, Dynamo's publics began with an air of excitement. When members believed that the effort would succeed, they were more likely to contribute, creating forward momentum that seemed self-perpetuating. However, the reverse was also true: when effort slowed, everyone was aware of the inactivity, and members became more averse to risks and less willing to spend time on these efforts. If this slowdown was not addressed, the gathering public quietly dissipated. We call this process *stalling.*

For example, emotions ran hot during the Turkopticon "mega-drama" event when a researcher injected false information. Several Turkers volunteered to lead the effort. However, weeks later when the requester wiki lay only half-finished with glaring TODOs throughout, contributions on Dynamo slowed to a trickle. The requester wiki only succeeded because one Turker decided to sprint and dedicate twenty hours to finish the first draft.

Like the lack of progress that becalmed the guideline draft, *stalling occurred when participants perceived that an effort was losing momentum.* The challenge was most directly characterized by a decline in activity. Often, it occurred when the next steps were difficult to identify or required too much effort for a single person to accomplish. Once stalled, it became difficult for the public to regain momentum.

The letter writing campaign also stalled. After weeks of discussion, 6 Turkers had written and submitted their letters. The campaign organizer contacted us:

> *"So, it seems no one is interested [...]. [A Turker] just says we're doing it wrong, but won't say how to do it right, and no one else has input."*

The movement had lost momentum. We discussed options with other invested Turkers. As active researchers, some of us knew journalists interested in microwork and got the group's go-ahead to get advice on publicity strategies. The journalist's enthusiasm and concrete advice reinvigorated the process by creating a new source of hope. All users who had shown interest (i.e. upvoted the campaign when it was an idea) were subscribed and received regular email updates on recent activity. This focused email barrage recaptured the attention of participants who had previously lost interest. We then set a deadline by which point all letters had to be finalized for a journalist. Another burst of activity came after an article was published in *The Guardian*.

Stalling may also stem from the inherent struggle to imagine practicable ideas, contrasted with the relative ease with which one can critique (perhaps hoping to refine) existing ideas. The creative and political challenge of identifying meaningful first steps toward a larger campaign can prove daunting to otherwise willing participants.

Friction

Debilitating as it was, stalling was in some ways preferable to *friction: active criticism and negative emotion targeted at a public's progress.* Friction occurred when someone in the community raised issues with the current direction.

Often friction came in the form of a new member or one who had been quiet so far. That person would arrive, realize that they didn't agree with the direction of the effort, and express general disappointment or criticism. Some even threatened to remove their endorsement from the effort unless a specific change was made, and tell their forum members to do so too. This would have broken the cross-forum coalition necessary to make this group's action take on the character of a broader public voice for workers.

While making progress on the academic guidelines, for instance, a Turker who had been previously engaged joined and expressed significant disappointment that the document was not in compliance with Amazon's Terms of Service. The document had provided guidance to requesters who want workers to download software (e.g., screen recording), a practice Amazon forbids. This worker critiqued this and then levied some more general critiques:

> *"I'm sorry to see the core document get excessively mired in technical detail in what purports to be a high-level document on ethics. I certainly hope this document sees fewer revisions than it will if it ties any of its own legs directly to the five-year-old 'beta test' which Amazon calls 'policy.'"*

This message caused a flurry of responses. Here, we worked to separate the worker's general unhappiness from a specific concern, and removed that concern from the public's scope to the member's satisfaction.

Understanding the high stakes involved in these actions for Turkers also sheds light on the reasons why Turkers might strive to stop an action from continuing on its current path. For example, one Turker expressed concerns that the letter writing campaign may attract legislative attention to crowdsourcing, thus threatening the whole system:

> *"As much as I am behind taking steps to better the plight of all crowdsource workers, might we not want to think through very carefully how loudly we start to shout, lest we end up attracting some attention that we might otherwise wish we would not have attracted."*

We addressed this concern by inviting this Turker to join in editing the goals of the campaign and to write his own letter to express his concerns.

Friction was typified by general criticism of an action without constructive suggestions to move forward, often causing negative emotions among participants. One Turker called this process a "circular firing squad of infighting." Kraut [24] suggests that these conflicts stem from a number of design characteristics inherent to the Internet. For example asynchronous communication tends to exacerbate conflicts and, resulting in flaming conversations [6].

From Stalling to Friction and Back Again

Stalling and friction are linked: addressing one can cause the other. We argue that these twin pitfalls are inherent challenges facing publics that act. Friction begets stalling. On Dynamo, movements would stall if participants faced or even feared having to face friction. Beyer [4] argues that the fear of drawing criticism and harming one's reputation is a deterrent to taking action in interpersonal settings. Taking action to avoid stalling will then beget friction. Sometimes a decision for the sake of forward progress would generate new sources of tension. For example, in an effort to move past one stalling debate, we suggested removing the whole section that was causing tension. This resulted in disagreement from the author of that content, which then had to be addressed.

An effort thus faces two likely causes of failure: either it loses its energy and stops; or it has energy and activity, but the activity is not pushing it in a constructive path. In the next section we will further expand on our experience dealing with these difficulties and describe the kinds of structured labor that went into supporting publics that act.

The Labor of Action: Overcoming Stalling and Friction

When actions on Dynamo faced stalling or friction, we stretched beyond code design and maintenance to perform the kinds of labor needed to preserve the kinetic energy of the movement. We call this *the labor of action*, and in this section we detail the lessons we learned from our involvement. We believe that these mechanisms can be replicated to catalyze action in other online communities. As we will argue, achieving *trust as actors* is necessary for any member who takes on these roles. We describe each mechanism in turn.

Debates with deadlines: *set deadlines for discussions so participants know when to gear towards consensus.*

One case of friction involved two Turkers disagreeing about the paragraph in the guidelines about whether requesters could ask workers to download software. Their disagreement quickly derailed the discussion about the guidelines and turned into a heated debate that evoked strong, negative emotions. We worked with these Turkers to set a deadline to reach consensus over the issue.

> *"We've spent so much time and energy on this, we need a last effort to reach consensus [...] We need your help for that to happen. Do you think setting a deadline would help?" – [Dynamo team]*

> *"I do agree we should wrap things up soon, if possible without unnecessary sacrifices." – A Turker*

Our role in situations such as this one was to suggest a deadline, giving debates a reason to find common ground. Members of the community could debate the date. However, people agreed that debates should respect the deadline. This prompted participants to aim at convergence and come up with concrete suggestions for moving forward.

Act and undo: *Take action, but leave space for objections and undo if necessary.*

When actions on Dynamo threatened to stall, we personally created forward movement. This effort variously involved creating early drafts of necessary content or simply making a decision. These actions restored a sense of forward momentum and of an active campaign. We accompanied these offers with invitations to ask us to undo.

For example, as we approached the deadline for writing the academic guidelines, one section, "What to do in case of violations", was left untouched. Our team took action by drafting three emails that Turkers could use as templates to contact requesters in order to: notify them of the guidelines and how they are violating them, notify them of next steps, and finally contact IRBs if the problem persisted. Our action started a heated debate. Some Turkers were angry that our framing of this section was restricting, one Turker who led the authoring of the guidelines noted: *"the purpose of Dynamo is/should be to add to the rights/recourse of Turkers, not to limit/replace them."* However, this action got the effort moving: we backed off on claims that caused friction to (as one participant described it) give *"the 'power' back to the original actor."*

Stating that we were open to undoing our work proved very important. In one case a member of the team made edits to the guidelines. Wiki software has perceived affordances that make it easy to revert changes, so she did not announce the fact that she was open to reverting the changes. A Turker expressed dissatisfaction, but was hesitant to make edits to the Wiki, out of fear of "stepping on toes":

> *"I find the revision unsatisfactory in several ways, but since I have no idea why she did it and don't want to step on toes, I am hesitant to re-revise..."*

Once the editor re-established the availability of undo, the effort made progress again.

Produce Hope: *Portray a tangible and achievable image of success.*

Researchers consider achieving a *perception of success* among social movement participants to be crucial to their active participation [15]. We similarly found actions on Dynamo stalling often because too few people believed in the possibility of success. In these cases, we worked with organizers to portray an image of success that was both valuable and achievable. For example, we made arrangements for the guidelines for academic requesters to be published in a major academic blog. This became an image that Turkers felt was worthy to work towards.

Achieving smaller steps of a larger goal is another way to portray success. For example, a Turker expressed doubts about whether the letter writing campaign would receive attention. An organizer of the campaign responded: *"Two of us have already emailed and received personal replies, I even got action on what I asked for. It works."* This created a more tangible image of success for the whole campaign.

Reflect and Propose: *When friction happens, reflect arguments and make concrete proposals to address them.*

On Dynamo, when members created friction, we aimed to diffuse the negative impact on community motivation. We first reflected back to users our best effort at understanding their criticism. We then proposed courses of action that might address the concerns expressed. In some cases, Turkers accepted our proposals. In others, they dismissed our suggestions as inadequate; nevertheless, they were galvanized to find other concrete solutions that they preferred.

In these cases, we reflected the discourse and also offered proposed distillations of the debate that could be addressed with a simple yes or no. In other words, by focusing and simplifying the discussion we prompted participants to step back and reflect on their arguments while articulating their stance. In our experience, this kept discussions productive and encouraged participants to think about the future they would like to see, as well as concrete steps to achieve it.

Accomplishing Trust as Actors

In order for each of our aforementioned actions to be effective, Turkers had to trust that we would act neutrally, fairly, and predictably, and we had to maintain that trust. We worked towards this by attending to people's responses and addressing critique. For example, Turkers grew to trust the first author as the Dynamo Wiki's system admin. She spent significant time talking with Turkers, exchanging ideas, and admitting error. With this trust built, she became the only user who could make changes to "locked" pages. We in turn made the circumstances for edits completely transparent. We also announced edits beforehand, leaving enough time for objections, and paralleling the previously discussed point of being able to "act and undo".

DISCUSSION: TACTICAL PUBLICS AND THE LABOR THAT MAKES THEM WORK

This paper attends to the challenges of *publics that act*, revealing the emotional and sense-making labor of facilitating these collectives – ones we name *tactical publics*. Like the publics articulated by DiSalvo's and Le Dantec's works [9, 27], Turkers discussed and analyzed the issues affecting them, from the socio-technical to the policy level. But converting public deliberation into tactical actions proved far more difficult, particularly online.

We name these collective forms *tactical publics* and have shown the labor and software that supported their formation. Tactical publics congregate around collectively pursued *actions*. These publics are often entangled with discursive publics, but also require distinct kinds of labor, structuring, and organizing. Through our research, we have identified stalling and friction as two of the major challenges that tactical publics face. However, much more work is needed to better understand these publics, their challenges, and tactics to support them.

On Dynamo, the labor we performed — debates with deadlines, act and undo, the production of hope, reflect and propose — could not have been written into software. They required contextual knowledge of the members of the public and their goals, as well as familiarity with their environment and its limitations. We used structured scripts to avoid stalling and friction, and we instantiated those scripts as each situation dictated. We inserted ourselves into their world and took actions that could have potentially harmed them. For this to be possible, those publics had to identify us as trustworthy and accountable actors.

This is an extension of the role that moderators play in conversational online forums. Moderators maintain norms to produce cohesion through acts like organizing threads or maintaining access levels. While Dynamo required some similar organization, its work also required cultivating inclusive, future-oriented propositions. This required particular kinds of emotional, cognitive labor. When critique was lodged, we undertook emotional labor of remedying friction, the critical labor of reflecting back, and the blame bearing labor of acting with an invitation to undo.

The structured labor of making tactical publics work online is not unique to our project, but this paper seeks to amplify and name it. We see hints of it elsewhere in social computing research and existing, real-world systems. Kriplean et al.'s integration of librarian factcheckers into a deliberation system offers a second intriguing data point [25]. Luther and Bruckman also identify leadership opportunities and challenges in creative collaborations online [29]. These forms of labor give lie to the idea that social software itself can produce the conditions for change. As a research community, we can begin to recognize the labors that combine with software to bring about change and ask how we can better support those labors.

A focus on the "human infrastructure" [28] that made Dynamo work troubles the passion for scalability we see in much computing research, including the push for scalable human labor that propels systems like Amazon Mechanical Turk (see [20:7-9]). In a field that seeks scalable, sometimes massive social change, we also suggest that some labors, by necessity, do not scale. With Dynamo, we tried to create the conditions by which Turkers could assert their own visions for "The Future of Crowd Work" [23]. If one views Mechanical Turk, requesters, HCI, and mainstream media portrayals of AMT collectively as a dominant public, then Dynamo, Turkopticon, and worker forums would represent counterpublics formed to articulate alternatives to wider public discourses [1]. This effort cannot itself be crowdsourced. Counterpublics require shields and temporary suspension of mainstream norms of discourse (e.g. [13]) to form.

CONCLUSION

Human-computer interaction envisions how design and technology can affect positive change in the world. To this end, one of its goals must be to support groups who come together to act via computer-supported collective action [36]. We focus on one such group, distributed workers on the Amazon Mechanical Turk marketplace. Over the course of a year, we talked, listened, and reconsidered the relationships Turkers have with each other, with us, and with collective action. The result was Dynamo, a platform for the creation of Turker publics that aim for action and change. We identified stalling and friction as twin failures that plague publics that act. We detail a set of structured behaviors that helped keep these tactical publics from dissipating, and look ahead to opportunities to better support such collectives.

ACKNOWLEDGEMENTS

Special thanks to Turkers who participated in, and helped shape this project. This work was supported by a National Science Foundation award IIS-1351131, an Open Society Foundation grant, and a Stanford Graduate Fellowship.

REFERENCES

1. Asen. "Seeking the 'Counter' in Counterpublics." *Communication Theory*, 2000

2. Beck, E. P for political: Participation is not enough. *Scandinavian Journal of Information Systems, 14*(1), 1, 2002.
3. Benkler, Y. The wealth of networks: How social production transforms markets and freedom. *Yale University Press, 2006.*
4. Beyer, J. L. Expect Us: Online Communities and Political Mobilization. *Oxford University Press, 2014.*
5. Cranshaw, J., and Kittur, A. The polymath project: lessons from a successful online collaboration in mathematics. *In Proc. CHI 2011.*
6. Dahlberg, L. Computer mediated communication and the public sphere: A critical analysis. *Journal of Computer Mediated Communication, 2001.*
7. Dewey, J. The public and its problems: An essay in political inquiry. *Penn State Press, 2012.*
8. Dimond, J. P., Dye, M., Larose, D., and Bruckman, A. S. Hollaback!: the role of storytelling online in a social movement organization. *In Proc. CSCW 2013.*
9. DiSalvo, C. Design and the Construction of Publics. Design Issues, 2009, 25(1), 48-63.
10. Earl, J. Pursuing Social Change Online The Use of Four Protest Tactics on the Internet. Social Science Computer Review, 2006, 24(3), 362-377.
11. Earl, J., and Kimport, K. Digitally enabled social change: Activism in the internet age. Mit Press, 2011.
12. Ehn, Pelle. Work-oriented design of computer artifacts. Vol. 78. Stockholm: Arbetslivscentrum, 1988.
13. Foucault. Two lectures. In Gordon (Ed.), Power / knowledge: Selected interviews and other writings, 1980
14. Fraser, N., and Kate, N. *Transnationalizing the public sphere.* Polity, 2013
15. Goodwin, J., and Jasper, J. M. (Eds.). The social movements reader: cases and concepts (Vol. 12). John Wiley & Sons, 2009.
16. Habermas, Jürgen. *The structural transformation of the public sphere: An inquiry into a category of bourgeois society.* MIT press, 1991.
17. Hill, B. M. Almost Wikipedia: What Eight Collaborative Encyclopedia Projects Reveal About Mechanisms of Collective Action. Berkman Center for Internet and Society, 2011.
18. Hirschman, A. O. Exit, voice, and loyalty: Responses to decline in firms, organizations, and states (Vol. 25). Harvard university press, 1970.
19. Irani, L. C., and Silberman, M. Turkopticon: Interrupting worker invisibility in amazon mechanical turk. *In Proc. CHI 2013*
20. Irani, L. The cultural work of microwork. New Media & Society, 2013, 1461444813511926.
21. Keegan, B., and Gergle, D. Egalitarians at the gate: One-sided gatekeeping practices in social media. *In Proc. CSCW 2010*
22. Kittur, A., and Kraut, R. E. Beyond Wikipedia: coordination and conflict in online production groups. *In Proc. CSCW 2010*
23. Kittur, A., et al. The future of crowd work. *In Proc. of CSCW 2013*
24. Kraut, R. E., et al. Building successful online communities. MIT, 2012.
25. Kriplean, T., et al. Integrating on-demand fact-checking with public dialogue. *In Proc. CSCW 2014.*
26. Kriplean, T., Morgan, J., et al. Supporting reflective public thought with ConsiderIt. *In Proc. CSCW 2012.*
27. Le Dantec, C. A., and DiSalvo, C. Infrastructuring and the formation of publics in participatory design. Social Studies of Science, 2013 43(2), 241-264.
28. Lee, C. et al. "The Human infrastructure of cyberinfrastructure." *In Proc. CSCW 2006.*
29. Luther, K., and Bruckman, A. Leadership in online creative collaboration. In *Proc. CSCW 2008*
30. Martin, D., Hanrahan, B. V., O'Neill, J., and Gupta, N. Being a turker. *In Proc. CSCW 2014*
31. Muller, M. Participatory design: the third space in HCI. *Human-computer interaction: Development process*, 2003, 165-185.
32. Open-Source, E. O., Healy, K., and Schussman, A. The ecology of open-source software development. In Department of Sociology. University of Arizona, 2003.
33. Riles, A. From Comparison to Collaboration: Experiments with a New Scholarly and Political Form. *Law and Contemporary Problems* 77 2014
34. Rudy, P. "Justice for janitors" not "compensation for custodians".Rebuilding labor: Organizing and organizers in the new union movement, 2004.
35. Schmidt, K., and Bannon, L. Taking CSCW seriously. *In Proc. CSCW 1992*
36. Shaw, A., et al. Computer supported collective action. *interactions* 21.2, 2014, 74-77.
37. Star, S. L., and Strauss, A. Layers of silence, arenas of voice: The ecology of visible and invisible work. *In Proc. CSCW 1999*
38. Starbird, K., & Palen, L. (How) will the revolution be retweeted? *In Proc. CSCW 2012*
39. Suchman, L. Human-Machine Reconfigurations: Plans and Situated Actions. Oxford Press, 2006
40. Suchman, L. Practice-based design of information systems: Notes from the hyperdeveloped world. The information society, 2002, 18(2), 139-144.
41. Taylor, A. "Out there." *In Proc. of CHI 2011*

Understanding Malicious Behavior in Crowdsourcing Platforms: The Case of Online Surveys

Ujwal Gadiraju, Ricardo Kawase, Stefan Dietze
L3S Research Center
Leibniz Universität Hannover, Germany
{gadiraju, kawase, dietze}@L3S.de

Gianluca Demartini
Information School,
University of Sheffield, United Kingdom
g.demartini@sheffield.ac.uk

ABSTRACT
Crowdsourcing is increasingly being used as a means to tackle problems requiring human intelligence. With the ever-growing worker base that aims to complete microtasks on crowdsourcing platforms in exchange for financial gains, there is a need for stringent mechanisms to prevent exploitation of deployed tasks. Quality control mechanisms need to accommodate a diverse pool of workers, exhibiting a wide range of behavior. A pivotal step towards fraud-proof task design is understanding the behavioral patterns of microtask workers. In this paper, we analyze the prevalent malicious activity on crowdsourcing platforms and study the behavior exhibited by trustworthy and untrustworthy workers, particularly on crowdsourced surveys. Based on our analysis of the typical malicious activity, we define and identify different types of workers in the crowd, propose a method to measure malicious activity, and finally present guidelines for the efficient design of crowdsourced surveys.

Author Keywords
Crowdsourcing; Microtasks; Online Surveys; User Behavior; Malicious Intent

ACM Classification Keywords
H.1.2 User/ Machine Systems: Human factors

INTRODUCTION
Over the last decade, crowdsourcing has gained rapid popularity, because of the data-intensive nature of emerging tasks, requiring validation, evaluation and annotation of large volumes of data. While developing a sound definition of crowdsourcing, Estelles and Guevara [11] suggest that microtasks are of variable complexity and modularity, and entail mutual benefit to the *worker*[1] and the *requester*[2]. Accumulating small contributions through such microtasks facilitates the accomplishment of work that is not easily automatable, through rather minor contributions of each individual worker.

With the ubiquity of the internet, it became possible to distribute tasks at global scales, leading to the recent success of crowdsourcing, being later defined as an 'online, distributed problem-solving and production model [3].'

In the recent past, there has been a considerable amount of work towards developing appropriate platforms and suggesting frameworks for efficient crowdsourcing. Amazon's Mechanical Turk[3], and CrowdFlower[4] are good examples of such platforms. An increasing number of research communities benefit from using crowdsourcing platforms in order to either gather distributed and unbiased data [23], to validate results, evaluate aspects, or to build ground truths [18].

While the demand for using crowdsourcing to solve several problems is on an upward climb, there are some obstacles that hinder requesters from attaining reliable, transparent, and non-skewed results. Herein, a primary nuisance is introduced through *malicious workers*, understood by [15, 9, 13] as workers with ulterior motives, who either simply sabotage a task or try to quickly attain task completion for monetary gains.

Gold-standards are the typically adopted solution to improve task performance [24]. In general practice, gold-standards are questions where answers are known apriori to the task administrators. Thus, if a worker fails to provide the correct answer for a particular question, he is automatically flagged as an *untrustworthy worker*[5]. However, with the flourishing crowdsourcing market, we believe that malicious activities and adversarial approaches will also become more advanced and popular, overcoming common gold standards. Quality control mechanisms should thereby account for a diverse pool of workers that exhibit a wide range of behavioral patterns. Methods have been designed and used in order to tackle poor worker performance in the past [6, 8]. However, there is a need to understand the behavior of these workers and the kinds of malicious activity they bring about in crowdsourcing platforms. In this paper, we present our work towards analyzing the behavior of malicious microtask workers, and reflect on guidelines to overcome such workers in the context of online surveys. An *online survey* is a questionnaire that can be completed over the Internet by a target audience.

We deployed a survey to 1000 workers in the crowd, and present evidence that a large number of workers are un-

[1]A user that performs tasks in exchange of monetary rewards on a crowdsourcing platform.

[2]A user that deploys tasks to be completed on a crowdsourcing platform, also called a *task administrator*.

[3]https://www.mturk.com/mturk/

[4]http://www.crowdflower.com/

[5]Note that being an untrustworthy worker does not necessarily imply being a malicious worker.

CHI 2015, April 18 - 23 2015, Seoul, Republic of Korea.
Copyright 2015 ACM 978-1-4503-3145-6/15/04$15.00
http://dx.doi.org/10.1145/2702123.2702443

trustworthy. This evidence shows that simple gold-standards might not be enough to provide reliable data or results. Then we conducted an analysis of both trustworthy and untrustworthy workers; we classified the behavior of the workers based on the different types of activity exhibited. To gain further insights into the prevalence of different kinds of malicious workers in the crowd, experts manually and exhaustively annotated the workers into established classes.

The main contributions of our work are listed below.

- Resulting from our analysis of workers, we present different types of malicious behavior exhibited in the crowd. This understanding of the prevalent kinds of malicious activity will be an aid in future task design.
- We suggest a novel method to measure the *maliciousness* of a worker based on the acceptability of her responses.
- We present a detailed analysis of the flow of malicious behavior of workers throughout the task, and define a *tipping point* which marks the starting point of a workers' malicious tendency.
- Finally, we propose a set of guidelines for the efficient, fraud-proof task design of *surveys*.

RELATED LITERATURE

Quality and Reliability of Workers

Behrend et al. showed the suitability of crowdsourcing as an alternative data source for organizational psychology research [2]. Kittur et al. promoted the suitability of crowdsourcing user studies, while cautioning that special attention should be given to the task formulation [19]. Although these works outline shortcomings of using crowdsourcing, they do not consider the impact of malicious activity that can emerge in differing ways. In our work, we show that varying types of malicious activity is prevalent in crowdsourced surveys, and propose measures to curtail such behavior.

Marshall et al. profiled Turkers who take surveys, and examined the characteristics of surveys that may determine the data reliability [21]. Similar to their work, we adopt the approach of collecting data through crowdsourced surveys in order to draw meaningful insights. Our analysis quantitatively and qualitatively extends their work, and additionally provides a sustainable classification of malicious workers that sets precedents for an extension to different categories of microtasks.

Through their work, Ipeirotis et al. motivated the need for techniques that can accurately estimate the quality of workers, allowing for the rejection or blocking of low-performing workers and spammers [15]. The authors presented algorithms that improve the existing techniques to enable the separation of bias and error rate of the worker. Baba et al. reported on their study of methods to automatically detect improper tasks on crowdsourcing platforms [1]. The authors reflected on the importance of controlling the quality of tasks in crowdsourcing marketplaces. Complementing these existing works, our work propels the consideration of both aspects (task design as well as worker behavior), for effective crowdsourcing.

Dow et al. presented a feedback system for improving the quality of work in the crowd [7]. Oleson et al. present a method to achieve quality control for crowdsourcing, by providing training feedback to workers while relying on programmatic creation of gold data [24]. However, for gold-based quality assurance, task administrators need to understand the behavior of malicious workers and anticipate the likely types of worker errors with respect to different types of tasks. Understanding the behavior of workers, is therefore an important objective of this paper.

In the realm of studying the reliability and performance of crowd workers with respect to the incentives offered, Mason et al. investigated the relationship between financial incentives and the performance of the workers [22]. They found that higher monetary incentives increase the quantity of workers but not the quality of work. A large part of their results align with our findings presented in the following sections.

Worker Traits, Tasks Design and Metrics

Researchers in the field have acknowledged the importance and need for techniques to deal with inattentive workers, scammers, incompetent and malicious workers.

Ross et al. studied the demographics and usage behaviors characterizing workers on Amazon's Mechanical Turk [25]. Kazai et al. defined types of workers in the crowd by type-casting workers as either *sloppy*, *spammer*, *incompetent*, *competent*, or *diligent* [17]. By doing so, the authors expect their insights to help in designing tasks and attracting the best workers to a task. While the authors use worker-performance in order to define these types, we delve into the behavioral patterns of workers.

Wang et al. presented a detailed study of *crowdturfing systems*, which are dedicated to organizing workers to perform malicious tasks [26]. While the authors of this paper investigated systems solely dedicated to malicious activities, in our work, we explore and analyze the prevalence of malicious workers and activities on regular crowdsourcing platforms. In their work, Eickhoff et al. aimed to identify measures that one can take in order to make crowdsourced tasks resilient to fraudulent attempts [9]. The authors concluded that understanding worker behavior better is pivotal for reliability metrics. Understanding malicious workers, is in fact the main goal of this paper.

Difallah et al. reviewed existing techniques used to detect malicious workers and spammers and described the limitations of these techniques [6]. Buchholz and Latorre proposed metrics for the post-hoc exclusion of workers from results [4]. In another relevant work by Eickhoff et al., the authors proposed to design and formulate microtasks such that they are less attractive for cheaters [10]. In order to do so, the authors evaluated factors such as the type of microtask, the interface used, the composition of the crowd, and the size of the microtask. While our work presented in this paper complements the prior work done by Eickhoff et al. it is significantly different, in that we investigate the behavioral patterns of trustworthy and untrustworthy workers, and suggest remedies to detect and inhibit their prominence based on the specific type of behavior.

Notably, we introduce novel metrics such as *maliciousness* of a worker, to quantify the behavioral patterns thus observed.

Yuen et al. present a literature survey on different aspects of crowdsourcing [27]. In addition to a taxonomy of crowdsourcing research, the authors present a humble example list of application scenarios. Their short list represents the first steps towards task modeling. However, without proper organization regarding types, goals and work-flows, it is hard to reuse such information to devise strategies for task design. As a step forward, in earlier work Gadiraju et al. proposed a comprehensive and exhaustive taxonomy for the different types of microtasks [12]. By studying the various kinds of behavior exhibited by trustworthy and untrustworthy workers in the crowd, in this work, we present a closer and detailed understanding of workers that will aid in developing anti-adversarial techniques.

BACKGROUND

We build on the previous work done by Gadiraju et al. [12], where the authors analyzed the nature of crowdsourced tasks. Firstly, the rationale behind the choice of workers to complete a job and the nature of the jobs themselves were studied. *Monetary reward* was found to be the most crucial factor that motivates workers across different task types, in their choice to complete a task. Additionally, *ease of completion* of a task is a driving force in the task selection process of a worker. An interesting topic, a high reward, a less time consuming task also play a role in the choice of task of a worker in the crowd, albeit to a less prominent extent.

Secondly, a generic umbrella classification of microtasks, which is conceptualized based on the final goal of the tasks was proposed. This goal-oriented taxonomy splits the tasks into six high-level categories:

- *Information Finding*: tasks that require workers to simply find pieces of information by following instructions.
- *Verification and Validation*: tasks that require workers to verify certain aspects as per the given instructions.
- *Interpretation and Analysis*: tasks that require workers to provide information that is subject to their individual interpretation.
- *Content Creation*: tasks that require workers to generate new content.
- *Surveys*: tasks that require workers to answer several questions based on their opinion and background.
- *Content Access*: tasks that require workers to simply access some online content.

This top classification encompasses different kinds of microtasks that vary according to specific goals, however, at this level the classification is considered to be exhaustive. From the analysis of Gadiraju et al. [12], we learnt that microtask workers are dictated by their top priorities; to maximize monetary gain and minimize effort. In particular, the indifference of workers towards their reputation leads to many microtask workers becoming malicious. It is clear that many workers attempt to exert a minimum amount of effort to receive their reward. Unfortunately, in many cases the minimum effort is not enough for a task administrator to accumulate good or even acceptable results. What is equally clear, is that a task administrator must therefore try to prevent alternatives that allow workers to receive their rewards without providing valid results, i.e. prevent *cheating*.

Based on this prior knowledge of the workers' preferences, and the taxonomy of microtasks, in this paper we analyze the malicious behavior of workers in a specific class of microtasks: *Surveys*. We specifically choose to study this category, since surveys present the most difficult challenges with respect to ensuring accurate responses from workers. This is due to the inherently subjective nature of most surveys. Thus, *gold standards* cannot be applied easily. For example, in an '*Information Finding*' task, the task administrator might typically be able to ensure the validity of workers' responses by employing questions for which the answers are priorly known (gold standard). Thus, verifying the character of the worker. On the other hand, in a simple demographic survey, which is subject to receive multiple valid responses for a single question from the target audience, such practice is infeasible.

In this work, we aim to address research questions (RQs) by using the following definitions.

Definition 1. *Malicious workers* are workers deemed to have ulterior motives that deviate from the instructions and expectations as defined a priori by the microtask administrator.
Definition 2. *Untrustworthy workers* are workers who provide wrong answers in response to one or more simple and straightforward attention-check or gold standard questions.

RQ #1: Do untrustworthy workers adopt different methods to complete tasks, and exhibit different kinds of behavior?
RQ #2: How can task administrators benefit from the prior knowledge of plausible worker behavior?
RQ #3: Can behavioral patterns of malicious workers in the crowd be identified and quantified?

DATA COLLECTION

We obtained response-based data from workers, that is representative of the usual occurrence in the crowd, by deploying a survey using the CrowdFlower platform. We gather information about typically crowdsourced jobs, and worker preferences through their responses.

Since we aim to study the behavior of malicious workers, we do not use all the existing quality control mechanisms provided by CrowdFlower[6]. By doing so, we do not inhibit the general behavioral patterns of malicious workers.

Survey Design

To begin with, the survey consisted of questions regarding the demographics, educational and general background of the workers. Next, questions related to previous tasks that were successfully completed by the workers, are introduced. In total the survey contained 34 questions, spanning a mixture of open-ended, multiple-choice, and Likert-type questions designed to capture the interest of the workers; we collected the responses from 1000 workers.

[6]`http://www.crowdflower.com/overview`

We asked the crowd workers open-ended questions, about two of their most recent successfully completed tasks, as shown in Figure 1.

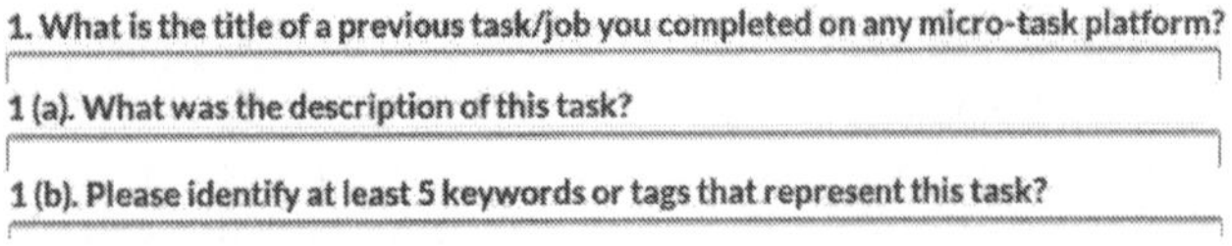

Figure 1. Open-ended questions to workers about their previous tasks.

We rely on open-ended questions in order to assess the malicious behavior depicted by untrustworthy workers. In addition, state-of-the-art qualitative research methods [5], have indicated that relying on recent incidents is highly effective, since respondents answer such questions with more details and instinctive candor. We pay all the contributors from the crowd 0.2 $ per unit, irrespective of whether or not we discard their data for further analysis.

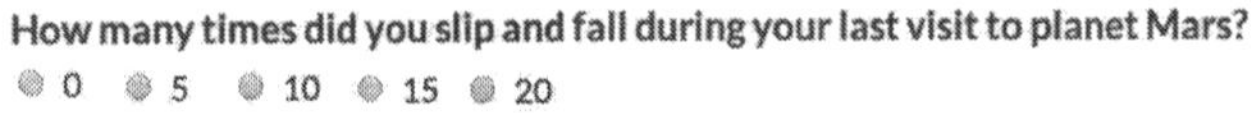

Figure 2. Engaging workers and checking their alertness by using *attention check* questions.

We used *attention check* questions, such as the one in Figure 2. The humor-evoking attention check questions interspersed with the regular questions, are known to keep the participants engaged, as indicated by Marshall et al. in previous work [21]. At the same time, these questions are also used to identify untrustworthy workers. We thereby follow the design recommendation given my Kittur et al. [19], where the authors suggest the importance of having explicitly verifiable questions. The authors also express the usefulness of having questions that require users to process the content, such as generating keywords or tags (see Figure1).

An important aspect to consider during the design of this survey, was to avoid influencing the workers into providing bad responses due to a poorly designed task. We took special care in order to ensure that the instructions and questions in the task were adequately clear. We gave workers unlimited time to complete the task. In addition, based on the optional feedback about the survey, received from 686 workers using the inbuilt facility on CrowdFlower, we observe that the workers were satisfied with the instructions ($4.1/5$), ease of the job ($3.8/5$), and the payments they received ($3.8/5$) with an overall job satisfaction of ($4/5$). Thus, we ensure that the workers behavior is not adversely effected by either a lack of time to complete the task, or the task design in general.

While in many crowdsourced tasks, the use of gold standards is widely applied to filter out malicious workers [24], this is not always applicable. For example, in crowdsourced tasks such as *Surveys* where none of the answers are known to the task administrators apriori, and in many cases, there is neither a correct nor a wrong answer. Note that we do not use other sophisticated means to curtail regular crowd worker behavior, in order to capture a realistic composition of workers (both trustworthy and otherwise).

DATA ANALYSIS

In this section, we first plot general results of the crowdsourced task. Later, we classify the behavior of trustworthy and untrustworthy workers in the crowd. We identify 432 untrustworthy workers by using test questions similar to the one depicted in Figure 2, who fail to pass at least one of two simple questions. These untrustworthy workers are then studied further in comparison to trustworthy workers, to determine plausible malicious traits.

Where are the workers from?

The Crowdflower platform forwards tasks to several different third-party crowdsourcing platforms, called *'channels'*[7]. In order to achieve coverage and results that are representative of the general crowdsourcing market, we do not impose any restrictions with respect to the channels. 50% of the workers who participated in the task used the 'Neodev' channel, while almost 25% of the workers used 'Clixsense'.

Since our survey was deployed in English, the first restriction we enforce via the platform is the language of the worker. However, it is difficult to accurately tell whether a worker is proficient in a given language. A simple workaround provided by the platforms exploits the location of the workers. Although imperfect, it is a reasonable assumption that a person located in an English speaking country, e.g. United States or Australia, is proficient in English (at least to an extent to understand and respond correctly to the questions in the task). Figure 3 shows the country distribution of the workers who participated in our task. We can observe that India leads by a large margin, followed by the USA, and Pakistan.

These numbers are anticipated since crowdsourcing is renown for widely employing workers from developing countries. In Figure 3, we divide the workers into two groups, trustworthy and untrustworthy, solely based on their responses to the attention check questions. In terms of percentage, we see that Pakistan, Sri Lanka, USA, and India lead in the number of workers who did not pass the attention checks.

Several hypotheses could be raised from these results. However further analysis of the influence of demographics, political, and economic factors are out of the scope of this paper. We are interested in analyzing and uncovering the universal user behavior that leads us to a coherent understanding of malicious activities. This can therefore provide us the required competence to restrict such malicious activity.

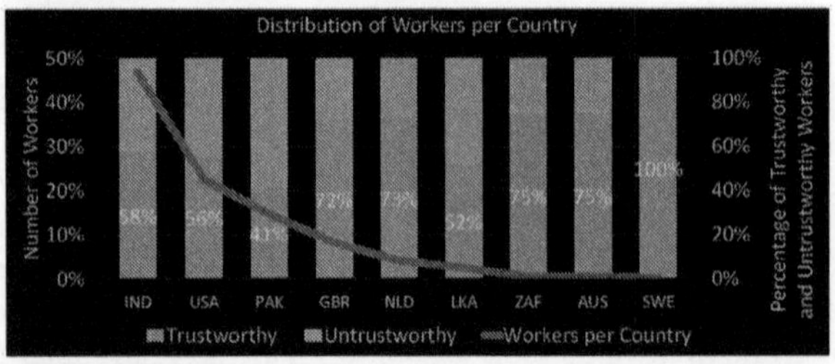

Figure 3. Distribution of the workers per country (left axis), and the distribution of trustworthy and untrustworthy workers (right axis).

[7] `http://www.crowdflower.com/labor-channels`

Analyzing Malicious behavior in the Crowd

Prior research has shown that by devising typologies, we can provide a better structure to organize knowledge and study the relationships between disorderly concepts [14]. We analyze the implicit behavioral patterns of malicious workers by the means of their responses. Based on aspects such as (i) the eligibility of a worker to participate in a task, (ii) whether responses from a worker conform to the pre-set rules, or (iii) whether responses fully satisfy the requirements expected by the administrator, we determine the following types of behavioral patterns.

- **Ineligible Workers** (*IE*). Every microtask that is deployed on crowdsourcing platforms presents the workers in the crowd with a task description and a set of instructions that the workers must follow, for successful task completion. Those workers who do not conform to the priorly stated pre-requisites, belong to this category. Such workers may or may not provide valid responses, but their responses cannot be used by the task administrator since they do not satisfy the pre-requisites. For example, consider a pre-requisite in our survey, '*Please attempt this microtask ONLY IF you have successfully completed 5 microtasks previously*'. We observed that some workers responded to questions regarding their previous tasks with, '*this is my first task*', clearly violating the pre-requisite.
- **Fast Deceivers** (*FD*). Malicious workers tend to exhibit a behavior that is strongly indicative of the intention to earn easy and quick money, by exploiting microtasks. In their attempt to maximize their benefits in minimum time, such workers supply ill-fitting responses that may take advantage of a lack of response-validators. These workers belong to the class of *fast deceivers*. For example, workers who copy-paste the same response for different questions. In our survey, some workers copy-pasted the title of our survey, '*What's your task?*', in response to several unrelated open-ended questions. Some others simply entered gibberish such as '*adasd*', '*fygv fxc xdgj*', and so forth.
- **Rule Breakers** (*RB*). Another kind of behavior prevalent among malicious workers is their lack of conformation to clear instructions with respect to each response. Data collected as a result of such behavior has little value. For instance, consider the question from our survey, '*Please identify at least 5 keywords that represent this task*'. In response, some workers provided fewer keywords. In such cases, the resulting response may not be useful to the extent intended by the task administrator.
- **Smart Deceivers** (*SD*). Some eligible workers that are malicious, try to deceive the task administrators by carefully conforming to the given rules. Such workers mask their real objective by simply not violating or triggering implicit validators. For example, consider the instruction, '*Transcribe the words in the corresponding image and separate the words with commas*'. Here, workers that intentionally enter unrelated words, but conform to the instructions by separating the words with commas, may neutralize possible validators and achieve successful task completion. While this type of workers behave to an extent like *fast deceivers*, the striking difference lies in the additional attempt of *smart deceivers* to hide their real goal and bypass any automatic validating mechanisms in place. In our survey, some workers provided irrelevant keywords such as '*yes, no, please*', '*one, two, three*', and so forth to represent their preferred task-types. Some of these workers take special care to avoid triggering attention-check or gold standard type questions.
- **Gold Standard Preys** (*GSP*). Some workers who abide by the instructions and provide valid responses, surprisingly fail to surpass the gold standard questions. They exhibit non-malicious behavior, only to be tripped by one or more of the gold standard test questions. This may be attributed to the inattentiveness of such workers.

568 workers passed the gold standard questions (*trustworthy*) and 432 workers failed to pass at least one of the two test questions (*untrustworthy*). On analyzing each response from the workers, we found that only 335 of the trustworthy workers gave perfect responses (*elite workers*). A panel of 5 experts were presented the responses of each worker from the remaining 665 non-elite workers (233 trustworthy and 432 untrustworthy workers), and they manually classified the workers into the different classes, according to the class behavioral patterns described earlier. The inter-rater agreement between the experts during the classification of workers as per Krippendorffs Alpha is 0.94.

Based on majority voting and the agreement between the experts, we finalize the worker classification without discrepancies. 73 untrustworthy workers and 93 trustworthy workers were classified into 2 different classes, while the rest were classified into unique classes. Note that a worker can depict different kinds of behavior and thereby belong to multiple classes. Figure 4 presents the experts' classification of these workers as per the different types of behavioral patterns.

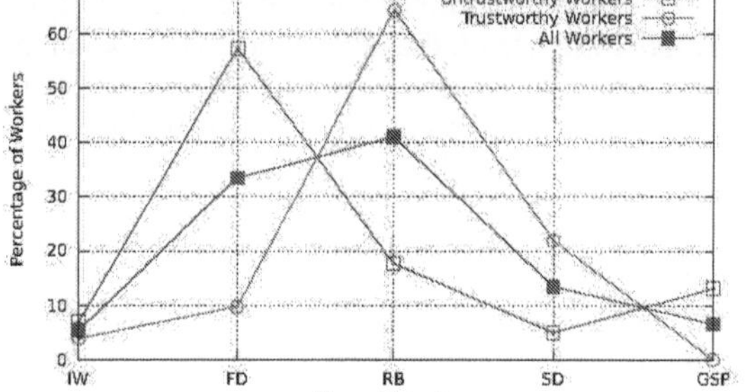

Figure 4. Distribution of non-elite workers as per their behavior.

More than 70% of all 665 workers classified are either *rule breakers* or *fast deceivers*. Nearly 60% of untrustworthy workers are *fast deceivers*, who intend to bypass response validators in order to earn monetary rewards easily. This is consistent with the findings of Kaufmann et al., wherein the authors establish that the number of workers who are mainly attracted by monetary rewards represent a significant share of the crowd [16]. About 65% of all non-elite trustworthy workers are *rule breakers*, who do not conform to the instructions laid out by the task administrators and thereby provide partially correct or limitedly useful responses.

The third most prevalent kind of untrustworthy workers are *smart deceivers*. Around 13% of all the classified workers take cautious steps in order to deceive task administrators and achieve task completion. These are malicious workers that tend to slip through most of the existing automated standards to prevent malicious activity, since they take special care to deceive the task administrators and receive the rewards at stake. This is made evident by the fact that over 20% of the non-elite trustworthy workers are *smart deceivers*, who give poor responses despite passing the gold standard questions.

Over 6% of all workers, seem to have failed the gold standard due to a lack of alertness (*gold standard preys*). This implies that a portion of workers' responses can be useful although the workers are deemed to be untrustworthy. Therefore, methods to identify and detect gold standard preys can benefit in maximizing the value of responses. This can be achieved either in a post-processing manner, or on the fly, at a relatively small additional cost.

Around 2.5% of workers attempt and complete tasks despite being clearly ineligible to take part (*ineligible workers*), as dictated by the pre-requisites. In our survey, such workers responded in languages other than in English, or in some cases claimed to have not completed any tasks before, thereby violating clearly stated pre-requisites.

Measuring Maliciousness of Workers

Next, we aim to measure the *maliciousness* of workers, as indicated by the acceptability of their individual responses.

Definition 3. The *acceptability* of a response can be assessed based on the extent to which a response meets the priorly stated expectations.

For example, consider the question, '*Enter the names of any 5 colors (separated by commas).*' A fully acceptable response to this question would be one which contains the names of 5 colors separated by commas (awarded a score of '1'). An *unacceptable* response on the other hand, is one which does not meet the requirements at all (awarded a score of '0'). So, in case of the same example, a response which does not contain names of colors would be completely unacceptable.

An important aspect to consider when measuring the maliciousness of a worker is interpreting the responses of the worker accurately. This means that we cannot reliably include subjective responses from the workers in such an analysis. For instance, consider a question with multiple checkbox options; any combination of responses to such a question may be acceptable. This means that in order to perform a reliable analysis, we have to consider only those responses with unambiguous corresponding acceptability. Therefore, we measure the maliciousness of workers by exploiting the acceptability of their responses to open-ended questions.

Experts manually annotated the responses from each worker for every open-ended question as either *acceptable* or *unacceptable*. The agreement between the experts was found to be 0.89 as per Krippendorf's Alpha. Figure 5 presents the average acceptability of workers' responses with respect to

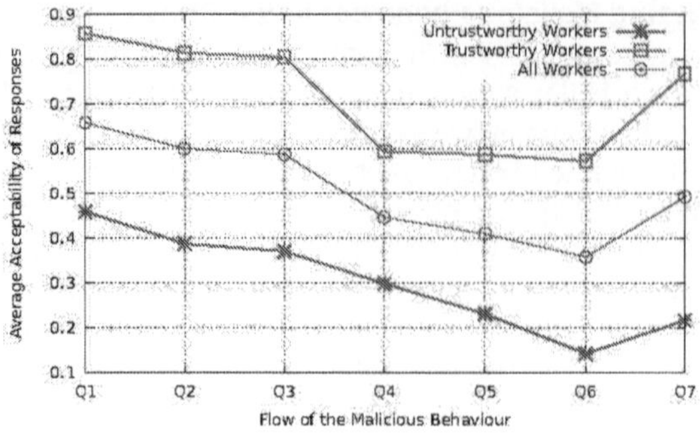

Figure 5. Average acceptability of responses from workers for each open-ended question *Q*.

each open-ended question. Note that the questions *Q1*, and *Q4* ask workers to share the titles of their previously completed tasks on crowdsourcing platforms. *Q2* and *Q5* correspond to the description of these tasks, while *Q3* and *Q6* correspond to keywords representing these tasks. In the last open-ended question (*Q7*), the workers are asked to provide keywords pertaining to tasks that they prefer.

Since we do not randomize the order of the questions for the different workers, we do not draw insights about the trend in acceptability through the course of the survey. However, we clearly observe that the acceptability of responses of the malicious workers reduces with the increase in required input from the workers (studied in literature as *task effort* [12]). It is easier for the workers to pass off a *title* as acceptable, than doing the same with either the *description* or *keywords* describing the task. On the whole, our findings indicate that the acceptability of individual responses of malicious workers decreases with an increase in the effort required to provide suitable responses.

Based on the acceptability of each response from a worker, we can compute the *average acceptability* (**A**) of a given worker pertaining to a task. In order to do so, we score each *acceptable response* with 1, and each *unacceptable response* with 0. Finally, we compute the *maliciousness* (**M**) of a worker using the following formula.

$$M_{worker} = 1 - (1/n \sum_{i=1}^{n} A_{r_i})$$

where,

n is the number of responses from the worker which are assessed, and A_{r_i} is the acceptability of response r_i.

$M_{worker} = 0$ indicates a completely non-malicious worker, while a worker is said to exhibit complete maliciousness if $M_{worker} = 1$. Figure 6 presents our findings regarding the distribution of workers with respect to the degree of their maliciousness, segmented by trustworthiness. In addition, the figure also depicts the corresponding average task completion time of the workers.

We can see that 50% of the untrustworthy workers exhibit a very strong maliciousness degree (greater than 0.8) while most of trustworthy workers (56%) have very low maliciousness. Nearly 20% of the untrustworthy workers exhibit a ma-

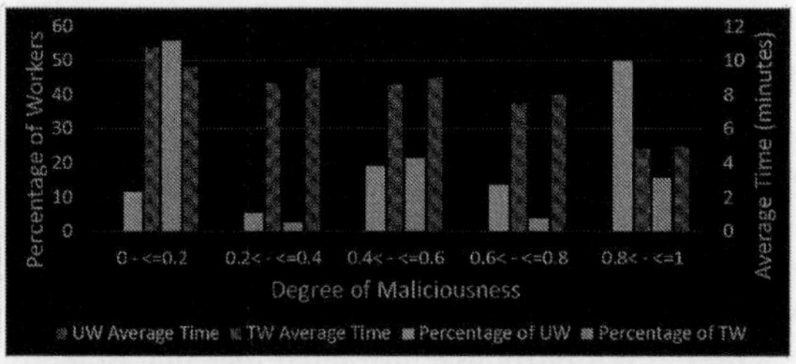

Figure 6. Degree of maliciousness of trustworthy (TW) and untrustworthy workers (UW) and their average task completion time.

liciousness degree between 0.4 and 0.6, while almost 15% indicate a high degree of maliciousness between 0.6 and 0.8. In addition, we observe that the average task completion time of untrustworthy workers decreases with the increasing maliciousness. The same is observed for the trustworthy workers, where the group with highest maliciousness has the lowest average times. We find that for untrustworthy workers, the maliciousness and average task completion time show a high correlation of 0.51, as measured using Pearson Correlation. For trustworthy workers this correlation is moderate at 0.37.

The Tipping Point

In our study of the trustworthy and untrustworthy workers, we find that several workers provide acceptable responses to begin with, before depicting malicious behavior. We thereby investigate this tendency of workers to trail off into malicious behavior, and present our findings here.

Definition 4. We define the first point at which a worker begins to exhibit malicious behavior after having provided an acceptable response, as the *tipping point*.
The tipping point can be determined in terms of the number of responses at which the worker exhibits the first sign of malicious activity. In our analysis, we consider the open-ended questions. Note that we do not consider the workers who begin with providing unacceptable responses (we find 233 such untrustworthy workers, and 81 such trustworthy workers).

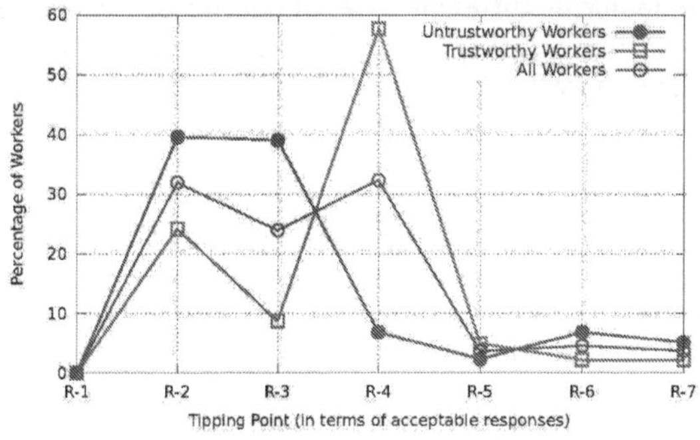

Figure 7. Distribution of Tipping Point of trustworthy and untrustworthy workers.

Figure 7 presents our findings. We can see that over 30% of all workers have a tipping point at their second response (R-2). This is largely due to the finding that almost 40% of all untrustworthy workers have a tipping point at R-2. Another 30% of all workers have a tipping point at their fourth response (R-4). Trustworthy workers largely contribute to this case. Nearly 60% of the non-elite trustworthy workers have a tipping point at R-4. On further analysis, we observe that these workers are mostly *rule breakers* who provide poor responses after the first set of questions about the previous tasks. Just below 25% workers depict tipping points at R-3, while under 5% of workers have a tipping point at R-5, R-6, and R-7. This shows that a significant number of malicious workers (especially untrustworthy workers) exhibit early signs of malicious activity, while a smaller percentage depict signs of malicious activity at a later stage.

Worker Maliciousness vs Tipping Point

We investigate the relationship between the maliciousness *(M)* of untrustworthy workers *(UW)*, trustworthy workers *(TW)* and their corresponding tipping points. We hypothesize that a worker with a greater maliciousness would have an earlier tipping point. Based on the analysis, we present our findings in Table 1.

Table 1. Relationship between the Maliciousness and Tipping Point of untrustworthy and trustworthy workers (percentage of workers having tipping point @R).

Maliciousness	UW	TW
$0 < M \leq 0.2$	40.9% @ R-7	28.5% @ R-7
	31.8% @ R-6	28.5% @ R-5
$0.2 < M \leq 0.4$	43.47% @ R-3	30% @ R-5
	21.73% @ R-6	30% @ R-3
$0.4 < M \leq 0.6$	66.19% @ R-3	88% @ R-4
	25.35% @ R-2	5.1% @ R-3
$0.6 < M \leq 0.8$	71.05% @ R-2	60% @ R-3
	28.95% @ R-3	40% @ R-2
$0.8 < M \leq 1$	100% @ R-2	100% @ R-2

We find that a majority of untrustworthy workers (40.9%) and trustworthy workers (28.5%) having a $M \leq 0.2$, have a tipping point at R-7. In case of the untrustworthy workers having $0.2 > M \leq 0.4$, 43.47% of workers have a tipping point at R-3, while 21.73% have a tipping point at R-6. In all the cases where $M > 0.4$, a great majority of workers have a tipping point at either R-3 or R-2. We observe a clear trend, which implies that the greater the maliciousness of a worker, the earlier is the 'tip' towards unacceptability. From this we learn that, a worker who provides poor responses in the beginning should be dealt with stricter measures, since there is a greater probability that the worker is malicious.

Worker behavior Beyond the Tipping Point

We analyzed the behavior of workers beyond their tipping points in order to verify whether the tipping point is a true indicator of further malicious activity from workers. Table 2 presents the amount of workers who depict malicious activity after their corresponding tipping points. We observe that over 95% of trustworthy and untrustworthy workers that have a tipping point at R-2, go on to provide at least one more unacceptable response.

All trustworthy workers having a tipping point at R-4 and all untrustworthy workers having a tipping point at R-3, go on to provide at least one more unacceptable response. From

Table 2. Percentage of workers that depict malicious activity after their corresponding Tipping Points.

Workers (in %)	R-2	R-3	R-4	R-5	R-6
Trustworthy	95.45	93.75	100	55.56	25
Untrustworthy	98.55	100	69.23	75	41.67

Table 2, we learn that the tipping point is a good indicator of forthcoming malicious activity within the task.

Task Completion Time vs Worker Maliciousness

We also investigate the time that workers take in order to complete the task. In order to draw a comparison across the different types of behavior exhibited by workers, with respect to the time that they take for task completion, we use the average task completion time for each type of worker behavior. Apart from this, we also compare the maliciousness exhibited by each group of workers constituting the different types of behavior. We find that the *average task completion time* and the *average maliciousness* of untrustworthy workers show a high Pearson Correlation of 0.514.

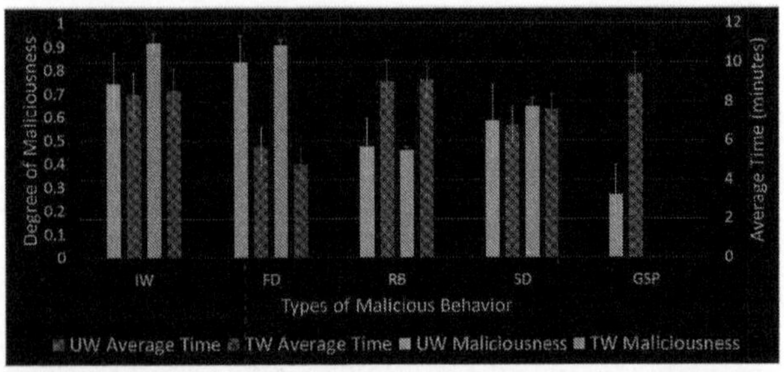

Figure 8. Comparison of Worker Maliciousness and Average Response Time of the different classes of malicious workers.

Figure 8 presents our findings with respect to the analysis described here. We observe that *fast deceivers* exhibit the most amount of maliciousness on average. Interestingly, they also take the least amount of time to complete the task. This is coherent with the type of behavior they exhibit, which is providing bad responses and achieve quick task completion (usually by copy-pasting same responses for multiple questions, or entering gibberish responses). On the other hand, we observe that *smart deceivers* also exhibit high malicious content, but they take more time to complete the task. We reason that this is due to the fact that *smart deceivers* take more precautions in order to bypass possible validators. *Gold standard preys* depict the least amount of maliciousness amongst all the types of untrustworthy workers. They also depict the highest average task completion time, indicative of a lower maliciousness. The *rule breakers* depict a high average task completion time, and a moderate maliciousness. This is attributed to their behavioral pattern; wherein the workers do not provide responses that meet the priorly stated requirements. *Ineligible workers* who complete the task, also depict a high maliciousness.

Caveats and Validity Threats

It is important to note that in this work, when we refer to 'maliciousness', we infer this based on the responses provided by a worker. There is no way to learn about the real intentions of a worker behind each response, based merely on the response itself.

While studying the major challenges that stand in the way of efficient crowdsourcing paradigms, Kittur et al. say that workers who are new and have relatively low expertise, as well as task administrators who do not provide clear instructions contribute to poor responses [20]. In order to ensure that we did not introduce unwanted bias due to the inexperience of workers (that could result in spiking the number of malicious workers), we ensured that all the questions in the crowdsourced survey were straightforward and easy to answer, even if a worker has little experience. Moreover, clear and thorough instructions were provided in the survey to aid the workers in completing the task.

We acknowledge that trustworthy workers may provide poor responses due to fatigue or boredom, as discussed in previous works. However, by varying the format of questions (open-ended, multiple choice check-boxes, Likert-type), limiting questions of the same type (two sets of 3 open-ended questions about previous tasks), and engaging the crowd with humor evoking attention-check questions, we attempt to curtail such bias.

The degree of *acceptability* corresponding to a worker's response is a metric that can be used at the discretion of the task administrator. In our case, we have computed the *acceptability* of a worker by awarding scores of '1' or '0' to each response, depending on whether a response is acceptable or unacceptable respectively. However, if a clear distinction with respect to the extent of usefulness of a response can be made, then a task administrator can use a continuous value between the closed interval of [0,1] in order to represent the acceptability of a response.

Since we do not randomize the order in which questions are answered by workers, we do not venture into analyzing the relationship between the type of question and the *tipping point*. We aim to extend this work with such an analysis in future. By doing so, we can empirically propose ideal lengths of tasks featuring different types of questions. Finally, more trials on different platforms, using varying design types would be ideal to further reinforce our findings.

DISCUSSION

Our experimental setup and findings are based on the task type, '*survey*'. A survey-type task inherently begets a general population of the crowd, without restricting participation due to the open design. Thus, the various kinds of trustworthy and untrustworthy workers presented in our work are representative of the general crowd. Having said that, the distribution of different kinds of untrustworthy workers depends on the type of task. This is due to the fact that a particular type of task may or may not be breached by some kinds of malicious workers, depending on the nature of the task and the gold standards being used.

Our experimental results showed that there was no significant correlation between the channels that the workers used for task completion and the behavioral patterns observed.

In our study of workers, we detect different types of worker behavior as described earlier. A key observation is that gold standard test questions alone remain insufficient to curtail malicious activity. We find that trustworthy workers who pass test questions can still provide ill-fitting responses (as in case of *rule breakers*), or deceive the task administrators (as in case of *smart deceivers*). By understanding the various kinds of behavior prevalent in the crowd, administrators can design tasks much more effectively. Being aware of the different ways in which malicious workers attempt to cheat their way towards task completion, can help in developing mechanisms to counter such activity. For instance, we find that tasks of the 'survey' type are most prone to activity of the kind exhibited by *fast deceivers* and *rule breakers*. This urges the need for stringent response validation especially for open-ended questions, to curtail possible attempts to cheat by *fast deceivers*, and *rule breakers* who provide sub-optimal responses.

The responses from *Gold Standard Preys* are valid and acceptable, though they are tripped by the gold standard questions, owing to a possible lack of attentiveness. By detecting such workers and consuming their responses instead of discarding them, task administrators can enhance the value of responses received from the pool of workers in a task. This essentially means that, by detecting gold standard preys the value of responses can be maximized without increasing the costs for task completion.

The measurement of *maliciousness (M)* of the workers, as presented earlier can be extended to different types of tasks, since the method relies on determining the acceptability of the individual responses from a worker in the context of the task. Depending on his needs, a task administrator can choose to discard responses from workers based on their maliciousness, thus using *M* as a sliding window for filtering responses.

Task Design Guidelines

We propose the following guidelines in order to design tasks of the *'survey'* type efficiently. By adhering to these key guidelines, we claim that the malicious activity prevalent in tasks of this type can be curtailed to a significant extent.

- The *tipping point* can be used to identify workers who 'tip early in the job. By excluding such workers, the quality of the produced results can be improved.
- In order to restrict the participation of *ineligible workers*, task administrators could employ a commonly used pre-screening method.
- Stringent validators should be used in order to ensure that workers cannot bypass open-ended questions by copy-pasting identical or irrelevant material as responses. This is an important guideline to enforce for survey-type tasks, since open-ended questions are popular in surveys and the majority of malicious workers are *fast deceivers*.
- *Rule breakers* can be curtailed by ensuring that basic response-validators are employed, so that workers cannot pass off inaccurate responses, or nearly fair responses. Even trustworthy workers tend to tip through the course of a task, providing poor or partially accurate responses. This demands for methods to monitor the progress of workers. Such validators can enforce workers to meet the exact requirements of the task and prevent ill-fitting responses.
- Additional methods and careful steps are required to prevent malicious activity by *smart deceivers*. Since such workers take care to avoid being flagged, they present the most difficulties in detecting and containing. Only a small number of workers make the additional effort to deceive task administrators in surveys. Yet, these workers can be restricted by using psychometric approaches such as repeating or rephrasing the same question(s) periodically and cross-checking whether the respondent provides the same response.
- Surveys garner a fair number of *gold standard preys*. Therefore, a post-processing step should be accommodated in order to identify such workers and consider their acceptable responses if needed.

CONCLUSIONS AND FUTURE WORK

The ubiquity of the internet, allows to distribute *crowdsourcing* tasks that require human intelligence at an increasingly large scale. This field has been gaining rapid popularity, not least because of the data-intensive nature of emerging tasks, requiring validation, evaluation and annotation of large volumes of data. While certain tasks require human intelligence, humans can exhibit maliciousness that can disrupt accurate and efficient utilization of crowdsourcing platforms. In our work, we aim to understand this phenomenon.

We have studied the behavior of malicious workers in the crowd by showcasing the task type of *Surveys*. Based on our analysis, we have identified different types of malicious behavior (**RQ #1**), which go beyond existing works and are better-justified through our data. An understanding of these aspects helps us to efficiently design tasks that can counter malicious activity, thereby benefiting task administrators as well as ensuring adequate utilization of the crowdsourcing platforms (**RQ #2**). By conducting an extensive analysis, we introduce the novel concepts of measuring 'maliciousness' of workers in order to quantify their behavioral traits, and 'tipping point' to further understand worker behavior (**RQ #3**). Our contributions also include a set of guidelines for requesters to efficiently design crowdsourced surveys by limiting malicious activity.

As part of our future work, we will develop machine learning methods to identify workers according to their behavior and classify them into the different types established in this work. Next, we intend to present an extensive set of methodologies and guidelines for effective task design and deployment on crowdsourcing platforms. In order to do so, we will delve into understanding malicious behavior for each type of task in the taxonomy introduced by Gadiraju et al. [12], namely, *information finding*, *verification and validation*, *interpretation and analysis*, and *content creation*.

REFERENCES

1. Baba, Y., Kashima, H., Kinoshita, K., Yamaguchi, G., and Akiyoshi, Y. Leveraging crowdsourcing to detect improper tasks in crowdsourcing marketplaces. In *Twenty-Fifth IAAI Conference* (2013).

2. Behrend, T. S., Sharek, D. J., Meade, A. W., and Wiebe, E. N. The viability of crowdsourcing for survey research. *Behavior research methods 43*, 3 (2011), 800–813.

3. Brabham, D. C. Crowdsourcing as a Model for Problem Solving. *Convergence: The International Journal of Research into New Media Technologies 14*, 1 (Feb. 2008), 75–90.

4. Buchholz, S., and Latorre, J. Crowdsourcing preference tests, and how to detect cheating. In *INTERSPEECH* (2011), 3053–3056.

5. Corbin, J., and Strauss, A. *Basics of qualitative research: Techniques and procedures for developing grounded theory*. Sage, 2008.

6. Difallah, D. E., Demartini, G., and Cudré-Mauroux, P. Mechanical cheat: Spamming schemes and adversarial techniques on crowdsourcing platforms. In *CrowdSearch* (2012), 26–30.

7. Dow, S., Kulkarni, A., Bunge, B., Nguyen, T., Klemmer, S., and Hartmann, B. Shepherding the crowd: managing and providing feedback to crowd workers. In *CHI'11 Extended Abstracts on Human Factors in Computing Systems*, ACM (2011), 1669–1674.

8. Dow, S., Kulkarni, A., Klemmer, S., and Hartmann, B. Shepherding the crowd yields better work. In *Proceedings of the ACM 2012 conference on Computer Supported Cooperative Work*, ACM (2012), 1013–1022.

9. Eickhoff, C., and de Vries, A. How crowdsourcable is your task. In *Proceedings of the workshop on crowdsourcing for search and data mining (CSDM) at the fourth ACM international conference on web search and data mining (WSDM)* (2011), 11–14.

10. Eickhoff, C., and de Vries, A. P. Increasing cheat robustness of crowdsourcing tasks. *Information retrieval 16*, 2 (2013), 121–137.

11. Estellés-Arolas, E., and González-Ladrón-de Guevara, F. Towards an integrated crowdsourcing definition. *Journal of Information science 38*, 2 (2012), 189–200.

12. Gadiraju, U., Kawase, R., and Dietze, S. A taxonomy of microtasks on the web. In *Proceedings of the 25th ACM conference on Hypertext and social media*, ACM (2014), 218–223.

13. Gennaro, R., Gentry, C., and Parno, B. Non-interactive verifiable computing: Outsourcing computation to untrusted workers. In *Advances in Cryptology–CRYPTO 2010*. Springer, 2010, 465–482.

14. Glass, R. L., and Vessey, I. Contemporary application-domain taxonomies. *IEEE Software 12*, 4 (1995), 63–76.

15. Ipeirotis, P. G., Provost, F., and Wang, J. Quality management on amazon mechanical turk. In *Proceedings of the ACM SIGKDD workshop on human computation*, ACM (2010), 64–67.

16. Kaufmann, N., Schulze, T., and Veit, D. More than fun and money. worker motivation in crowdsourcing - a study on mechanical turk. In *AMCIS* (2011).

17. Kazai, G., Kamps, J., and Milic-Frayling, N. Worker types and personality traits in crowdsourcing relevance labels. In *Proceedings of the 20th ACM international conference on Information and knowledge management*, ACM (2011), 1941–1944.

18. Kazai, G., Kamps, J., and Milic-Frayling, N. An analysis of human factors and label accuracy in crowdsourcing relevance judgments. *Inf. Retr. 16*, 2 (2013), 138–178.

19. Kittur, A., Chi, E. H., and Suh, B. Crowdsourcing user studies with mechanical turk. In *Proceedings of the SIGCHI conference on human factors in computing systems*, ACM (2008), 453–456.

20. Kittur, A., Nickerson, J. V., Bernstein, M., Gerber, E., Shaw, A., Zimmerman, J., Lease, M., and Horton, J. The future of crowd work. In *Proceedings of the 2013 conference on Computer supported cooperative work*, ACM (2013), 1301–1318.

21. Marshall, C. C., and Shipman, F. M. Experiences surveying the crowd: Reflections on methods, participation, and reliability. In *Proceedings of the 5th Annual ACM Web Science Conference*, WebSci '13, ACM (New York, NY, USA, 2013), 234–243.

22. Mason, W., and Watts, D. J. Financial incentives and the performance of crowds. *ACM SigKDD Explorations Newsletter 11*, 2 (2010), 100–108.

23. Ntalianis, K., Tsapatsoulis, N., Doulamis, A., and Matsatsinis, N. Automatic annotation of image databases based on implicit crowdsourcing, visual concept modeling and evolution. *Multimedia Tools and Applications 69*, 2 (2014), 397–421.

24. Oleson, D., Sorokin, A., Laughlin, G. P., Hester, V., Le, J., and Biewald, L. Programmatic gold: Targeted and scalable quality assurance in crowdsourcing. *Human computation 11* (2011), 11.

25. Ross, J., Irani, L., Silberman, M., Zaldivar, A., and Tomlinson, B. Who are the crowdworkers?: shifting demographics in mechanical turk. In *CHI'10 Extended Abstracts on Human Factors in Computing Systems*, ACM (2010), 2863–2872.

26. Wang, G., Wilson, C., Zhao, X., Zhu, Y., Mohanlal, M., Zheng, H., and Zhao, B. Y. Serf and turf: crowdturfing for fun and profit. In *Proceedings of the 21st international conference on World Wide Web*, ACM (2012), 679–688.

27. Yuen, M.-C., King, I., and Leung, K.-S. A survey of crowdsourcing systems. In *Privacy, security, risk and trust (passat), 2011 ieee third international conference on and 2011 ieee third international conference on social computing (socialcom)*, IEEE (2011), 766–773.

"I Saw Images I Didn't Even Know I Had"

Understanding User Perceptions of Cloud Storage Privacy

Jason W. Clark[†] jclarks@masonlive.edu
Peter Snyder[*] psnyde2@uic.edu
Damon McCoy[†] mccoy@cs.gmu.edu
Chris Kanich[*] ckanich@uic.edu

[†]Department of Computer Science
George Mason University

[*]Department of Computer Science
University of Illinois at Chicago

Abstract

More than a billion people use cloud-based storage for personal files. While many are likely aware of the extent to which they store information in the cloud, it is unclear whether users are fully aware of what they are storing online. We recruited 30 research subjects from Craigslist to investigate how users interact with and understand the privacy issues of cloud storage. We studied this phenomenon through surveys, an interview, and custom software which lets users see and delete their photos stored in the cloud. We found that a majority of users stored private photos in the cloud that they did not intend to upload, and a large portion also chose to permanently delete some of the offending images. We believe our study highlights a mismatch between user expectation and reality. As cloud storage is plentiful and ubiquitous, effective tools for enabling risk self-assessment are necessary to protect users' privacy.

Author Keywords

Cloud; Privacy; Security; Threat Modeling

ACM Classification Keywords

H.5.m. Information Interfaces and Presentation (e.g. HCI): Miscellaneous

INTRODUCTION

Cloud storage is immensely popular. The ubiquity of Internet connectivity, the low price of high density storage, and the efficiency of modern datacenters enables companies like Google, Apple, and Dropbox to provide multiple gigabytes of resilient, high speed, globally accessible storage without charging the user for the privilege.

The cloud has revolutionized services like email, web hosting, and file backup. While copious free cloud storage has no doubt greatly improved overall user experience, the risks of having multiple copies of files stored under different user agreements with different security safeguards introduces the possibility of greatly increased risks for the user.

Automatic storage greatly compounds the risk of exposure - a compromise at any one storage provider, or on the device itself, can leak private photos to unauthorized users. It is also possible that users are not even aware that their images are being saved to cloud services. The composition of multiple apps and services makes the situation even more insidious, as it creates a mismatch between a user's intent and the result. For instance, if a user takes a compromising photo, emails it to a friend, and then later deletes it from his camera, it is possible that even if the recipient deletes the email and the sender deletes the image, the image could still persist in automatic cloud-based photo backup services (e.g. Dropbox or iCloud), the "Sent Messages" folder of the sender, and even the local device memory of the recipient (and thus, transitively, the recipient's own cloud-based photo backup services).

Under normal circumstances, these solutions add a layer of convenience and resiliency for the user. However, when stored in the cloud, private files are often visible to anyone with the proper credentials or the ability to reset the account's password. The Apple iCloud breach of August 2014 which exposed several celebrities' private images is one high profile example of this risk. While these victims were high profile celebrities, phenomena like revenge porn and sextortion bring this risk to many other individuals. Being able to control the existence and proliferation of private images is an absolute necessity in our hyper-connected world.

As handheld, Internet-connected cameras with automatic cloud backup are ubiquitous, it is imperative that users understand how to fully control all copies of the images that they create, share, and save. The first step to empowering users is to understand their mental models and expectations related to cloud storage.

This paper reports the results of an exploratory study that evaluates participants' security postures toward and mental models of cloud based storage. Through the use of custom built software, we are also able to report on participants' expectations related to specific photographs stored within their cloud storage accounts. We find that 16 out of 30 participants' were unaware of private images that were stored in their cloud storage based webmail accounts. The results show that their understanding of threats of how images might become public are realistic. However, they largely perceive the consequences of their private images becoming public to be embarrassment and are less aware and concerned of extortion. Once they used our automated image audit software on their webmail accounts, 11 out of 30 participants chose to delete stored private images to protect themselves from these images becoming public.

CHI 2015, April 18–23, 2015, Seoul, Republic of Korea.
Copyright © 2015 ACM 978-1-4503-3145-6/15/04 ...$15.00.
http://dx.doi.org/10.1145/2702123.2702535

METHODOLOGY

Between the two surveys, participants used our 'Sensitive Image Audit' tool (or SIA tool), which we designed and implemented, to visualize and explore the images stored in their e-mail account.

SIA tool

The SIA tool works by searching users' gmail account for all images attached to messages. It then saves those images to the local disk. The user is then prompted to delete any images they wish to remove from their local disk. The SIA tool then finds which images have been deleted from the disk, and modifies the related messages on the gmail server to remove those attachments. This leaves the original version of the message in the users Gmail account with the attachment gone.

Participants

We recruited 30 participants from Craigslist to get a more diverse sample compared to posting fliers around campus. Each participant was offered $60.00 USD in compensation for their time and effort. The participants needed to be at least 18 years old and regular Google Mail users. The subjects' average age was 28, 50% were African American, 20% of Asian descent, 20% Caucasian, 7% Hispanic, and 3% other. 90% had at least some college and 50% had completed at least a 4 year degree.

Participants were heavy Internet users spending an average of 7.6 hours online. All of the participants accessed their email from home and most from work. Our pool of participants were also younger and more educated than the overall population demographics of the United States.

Surveys

All of the surveys were given through SurveyMonkey. We developed two surveys that were presented to the participants at different stages during the experiment. The initial survey (S1) consisted of 55 questions related to demographics, Internet use, and privacy strategies. The second survey (S2) asked 23 questions after the participant's use of the SIA tool as well as specific image related questions. While questions were asked about a broad range of subjects, questions relevant to this paper include: S2-2: Are there images saved in your email that you did not realize was there and that you would not want made public? S2-10: Are there images you deleted? S2-17: Why did you want to delete the image? What threat did it pose?.

Approach

The study was approved by our Institutional Review Board. Each of the 30 participants were provided with a private and secured office room. They were given access to a laptop running a virtual machine with the aforementioned software installed and the links to the surveys pre-loaded. After each participant completed their tasks we reset the virtual machine to ensure that no information from the previous participant was left on the laptop.

The participants' first task was to complete the preliminary demographics based survey. Upon completing this survey, the participants ran the SIA tool. At this point, the participants were given the option to deleted images if they so desired. Next, the participants completed a second survey associated with how they protect and share their images. Lastly, the participants completed a brief exit interview where we discussed the results of the SIA tool and asked more open ended questions that were not found on any of the surveys. These interviews were recorded with the consent of the participants and transcribed.

Bias and Limitations

One limitation is that our study only considered participants with Google Mail accounts, which might represent a biased group of users. Another potential source of bias are priming effects due to the order in which our survey questions were asked. We attempted to limit such bias in our survey design, but found afterward that some issues were missed. For example, question S2-8: What threat (source) did you see, that caused you to not to want the image made public? and S2-9: What consequences do you see if your image was made public? These questions were asked after priming questions such as S1-49 through S1-53, which all ask for a self evaluation of the user's concern with respect to several different Internet threats. For this reason, we focus on factual responses as well as relative popularity of answers where the bias is likely constant across all possible answers.

The full list of questions asked during this study can be found in the online appendix in the ACM digital library.

RESULTS

In this section, we describe three main themes regarding our research subjects' use of cloud storage: subjects' understanding and concerns regarding potential security breaches, subjects' understanding and concerns regarding actions that can increase risk of adverse consequences, and subjects' behavior and willingness to take action to mitigate or defend against these threats. We combine results from the software based security audits, individual subjects' quotes, and aggregate response metrics to support describe each theme.

For brevity's sake, we make the distinction between *threats*, which we define as the perpetrators and the potential harmful outcomes like stolen data or financial fraud, and *risks*, which we define as user behaviors which make harmful outcomes more likely or more damaging.

Understanding Threats

Security breaches are potential threats to users' well being. Here we describe both users conceptualization of who or what these threats are with respect to cloud storage, and what aspects of these threats are most important or concerning to the users.

Possible adversaries

While priming effects invalidate these questions' utility for judging how concerned users are about adversaries, the relative popularity of different adversaries is interesting: unintentional sharing by oneself was the most common threat (19/30) compared to cybercriminals (18/30) or acquaintances (15/30), perhaps indicating an apprehension regarding their own understanding of technological functionalities like automatic cloud uploads.

Furthermore, when asked what their primary threat of account break-in was during the exit interview, 23 respondents mentioned strangers (e.g. cyber hackers,"people out of foreign countries," "person who just wants to use my credit card"), while only three mentioned acquaintances in some capacity. This result indicates the subjects' mental models are focused mainly on global rather than local threats like inadvertent sharing by oneself or break-ins by acquaintances.

Possible Ramifications of a breach

The main ramification people are concerned with regarding stolen photos is embarrassment - 25/30 respondents mentioned embarrassment as a consequence, while only 8/30 mentioned being concerned regarding extortion and a different (but not distinct) 8/30 were concerned with stolen photos incriminating them.

Understanding Risks

Task-oriented users rarely stop to think about the security implications of their actions. However, characterizing how users conceptualize the risks involved with how they use cloud storage is an important aspect of understanding how they interact with these services.

Private Content

The main focus of our study is private photos - 16/30 respondents said that they have images saved in their email that they did not realize were there and that they would not want made public. To gauge how well users understand the risk of online account compromise, our survey asked subjects about their password hygiene habits. 14/30 respondents admitted to sharing their passwords with other people, and 9/30 admitted to saving passwords in their email. This latter action can lead to privilege escalation for attackers who gain access to an email account and then can gain access to other more sensitive accounts like brokerage or banking accounts.

Passive Storage

Several actions taken by software on behalf of users are automatic, passive, and/or opt-out. For instance, applications like Dropbox, Google Drive, and iCloud all encourage users to back up all photos taken on a mobile device automatically. Another example is the "Sent Mail" folder in a gmail account: even though some users' mental models understand email as a communication medium rather than a storage medium [6], a copy of every mail ever sent is stored in the web-based cloud storage of several different kinds of email accounts. This is often not immediately apparent to the end user. When this feature is combined with the use of mobile phone cameras to take private photos, a very dangerous interaction happens: users do not realize they are saving these private photos to the cloud, and even if they specifically intend to delete a photo, it might still exist on their device or in the cloud. This sentiment was expressed best by participant 5: "I saw images I didn't even know I had."

Understanding Countermeasures

Users exhibit a wide range of behaviors intended to limit the possibility of harmful outcomes. Here we characterize both the ways that users mitigate the potential for harm currently, as well as with the assistance of our privacy audit tools.

Current Strategies for Privacy Protection

The easiest and most effective defense against becoming a victim of photo theft is simply to not take or save private photos. We asked two questions of users regarding their photo protection strategies: one in the initial interview regarding how they share photos online, and one in reference to individual photos after the users had used our redaction tool.

With respect to possessing and sharing photos, several users exhibit thoughtful strategies for minimizing their risk of unwanted exposure. For photos that they are not willing to upload to the cloud, most subjects store the photos locally, on a hard drive or removable media (18/30), and several (11/30) choose not to store the photos at all and delete them instead. For photos that they do wish to share with others, subjects largely rely on service-provided privacy settings (22/30) and password protection (17/30) to limit photos' audiences.

Tool-assisted Strategies

The primary component of our user study was to instruct research subjects on the use of SIA tool and record their discoveries and reactions. After using the tool, 16/30 subjects reported finding pictures that they both did not realize were there and would not want to be made public. While we do not claim to have a representative sample, this initial finding suggests that users' expectations regarding cloud storage of personal photos, perhaps the most intimate medium available, are strongly at odds with reality either due to passive storage, information overload, or other factors. Participant 5 summed up the sentiment that removing these images has become increasingly difficult: "Now you've got to look at probably 15 different places if you want to get rid of that photo."

Not only were several subjects surprised to find unwanted photos stored in their accounts; 11/30 subjects chose to permanently delete those photos during their use of our tool. Most users were concerned both regarding pictures of one's self (9/11) and of friends (7/11). This finding echoes that of Klasnja et al.'s study of security concerns when on Wi-Fi, where subjects showed a strong concern for the security and privacy of their communication partners, sometimes even more than themselves [5].

Subjects indicated that they rely heavily on social bonds for defense; 22 of the 30 subjects said they ask others not to share private photos as a means of defending their privacy. When asked whether they would use this tool again if it were available, 23/30 answered in the affirmative. While the proximity to the revelation of private images in the account and the overall goal of the study likely biases this survey question, 4/30 subjects independently inquired during the exit interview about the availability of this software for further use.

RELATED WORK

While our study focuses on the specific domain of image security, several other research efforts have explored users' understanding of cloud computing based security and privacy.

Wang et al. [8] explored private content exposure concerns for users and their Facebook posts (including images) which they made but then regretted. Garg et al. [2] explore the reason for privacy failures and discover that privacy behaviors can be explained by risk perception, control usability, or privacy preferences, sometimes even by the same actor.

Ion et al. [3] investigate privacy concerns for users in the space of consumer cloud storage, and find that users prefer local storage for sensitive documents, which was not the case in our results where a large percentage of users had unintentionally stored sensitive images online. Odom et al. [6] studied how young people value and form attachments to virtual possessions with the goal of comparing them to their physical counterparts. They found that an increasing portion of users' possessions are digital, and that many used email as a way of moving "digital assets" between accounts.

The work of Klasnja et al. [5] presented an exploratory study of how users understand Wi-Fi and the associated privacy risks. They show that while users are aware of "expert hackers," they are less aware of the immediate risk of eavesdropping on unencrypted communications. The authors posit that end-user awareness tools and infrastructural improvements are necessary to address privacy and security problems with Wi-Fi use.

Multiple tools exist to improve users' cloud security. Egelman [1] performed a laboratory experiment to study the privacy tradeoff offered by Facebook Connect: they observed that most users understood the privacy convenience tradeoff and thus consciously chose to forfeit privacy for convenience. Kelley et al. [4] used the concept of a nutrition label as their inspiration for implementing a similar label for privacy. Synder and Kanich [7], designed a system called "Cloudsweeper" which gives users the opportunity to encrypt or redact sensitive, unexpected, and rarely used information to mitigate the risks of cloud storage accounts without sacrificing the benefits of clouds storage or computation.

FUTURE WORK & CONCLUSIONS

Our initial prototype SIA tool was well received and many of the participants expressed interest in using this tool again. This suggests that users want to know when they have unintended images stored and that providing them with tools could be an effective strategy for enabling them to remove images that were unintentionally stored. To address this gap, we are working on a powerful and flexible image auditing tool that can interoperate with most cloud storage providers, including backup, online social networking and webmail. The goal of this tool is to mitigate the problem of unintended image storage by allowing users to audit their images and make changes to a single cloud storage account or global delete and update images across all accounts in one place.

We have explored how our participants perceive the existence of sensitive images in their cloud email accounts and the privacy threats associated with storing these images in cloud storage. By allowing users to audit their stored images, we were able to discover that there is both a lack of awareness of this storage and a lack of desire to maintain copies of these images in this way. Furthermore, several participants deleted these images as soon as they were revealed by our tool. Clearly, more is being done on users' behalf than they necessarily desire. Cloud based storage providers must find a way to balance automatic features with the possibility that those features are potentially harmful to their users.

ACKNOWLEDGMENTS

We thank our study participants and the anonymous reviewers for their insightful comments. This work was made possible by National Science Foundation grant CNS 1351058 and a gift from Google.

REFERENCES

1. Egelman, S. My profile is my password, verify me!: the privacy/convenience tradeoff of facebook connect. In *Proceedings of the SIGCHI Conference on Human Factors in Computing Systems*, ACM (2013), 2369–2378.
2. Garg, V., Benton, K., and Camp, L. J. The privacy paradox: A facebook case study (2014).
3. Ion, I., Sachdeva, N., Kumaraguru, P., and Čapkun, S. Home is safer than the cloud!: privacy concerns for consumer cloud storage. In *Proceedings of the Seventh Symposium on Usable Privacy and Security*, ACM (2011), 13.
4. Kelley, P. G., Bresee, J., Cranor, L. F., and Reeder, R. W. A nutrition label for privacy. In *Proceedings of the 5th Symposium on Usable Privacy and Security*, ACM (2009), 4.
5. Klasnja, P., Consolvo, S., Jung, J., Greenstein, B. M., LeGrand, L., Powledge, P., and Wetherall, D. When i am on wi-fi, i am fearless: privacy concerns & practices in eeryday wi-fi use. In *Proceedings of the SIGCHI Conference on Human Factors in Computing Systems*, ACM (2009), 1993–2002.
6. Odom, W., Zimmerman, J., and Forlizzi, J. Teenagers and their virtual possessions: design opportunities and issues. In *Proceedings of the SIGCHI conference on Human Factors in computing systems*, ACM (2011), 1491–1500.
7. Snyder, P., and Kanich, C. Cloudsweeper: enabling data-centric document management for secure cloud archives. In *Proceedings of the 2013 ACM workshop on Cloud computing security workshop*, ACM (2013), 47–54.
8. Wang, Y., Norcie, G., Komanduri, S., Acquisti, A., Leon, P. G., and Cranor, L. F. I regretted the minute i pressed share: A qualitative study of regrets on facebook. In *Proceedings of the Seventh Symposium on Usable Privacy and Security*, ACM (2011), 10.

Sensitive Lifelogs: A Privacy Analysis of Photos from Wearable Cameras

Roberto Hoyle† Robert Templeman† Denise Anthony‡ David Crandall† Apu Kapadia†
†School of Informatics and Computing ‡Department of Sociology
Indiana University Bloomington Dartmouth College
Bloomington, IN, USA Hanover, NH, USA
{rjhoyle, retemple, djcran, kapadia}@indiana.edu, Denise.L.Anthony@dartmouth.edu

ABSTRACT
While media reports about wearable cameras have focused on the privacy concerns of bystanders, the perspectives of the 'lifeloggers' themselves have not been adequately studied. We report on additional analysis of our previous in-situ lifelogging study in which 36 participants wore a camera for a week and then reviewed the images to specify privacy and sharing preferences. In this Note, we analyze the photos themselves, seeking to understand what makes a photo private, what participants said about their images, and what we can learn about privacy in this new and very different context where photos are captured *automatically* by one's wearable camera. We find that these devices record many moments that may not be captured by traditional (deliberate) photography, with camera owners concerned about impression management and protecting private information of both themselves and bystanders.

Author Keywords
Lifelogging; wearable cameras; privacy

ACM Classification Keywords
K.4.2. Social Issues; K.4.1. Public Policy Issues: Privacy

INTRODUCTION
With several wearable cameras recently hitting the market, including the Narrative Clip,[1] Autographer,[2] and Google Glass[3] (Figure 1), the concept of 'lifelogging' has started to gain mainstream traction. Lifelogging cameras can automatically capture images throughout the day from a first-person view, easily collecting hundreds of images per hour. Lifelogging presents a new form of photography with different challenges: whereas the role of traditional photographers is to choose which moments to photograph and then to deliberately compose and take each picture, lifeloggers generate a deluge of automatically-taken photos, many of which are poorly composed, blurry, or have no useful content, and must curate them to decide which are worth keeping or sharing.

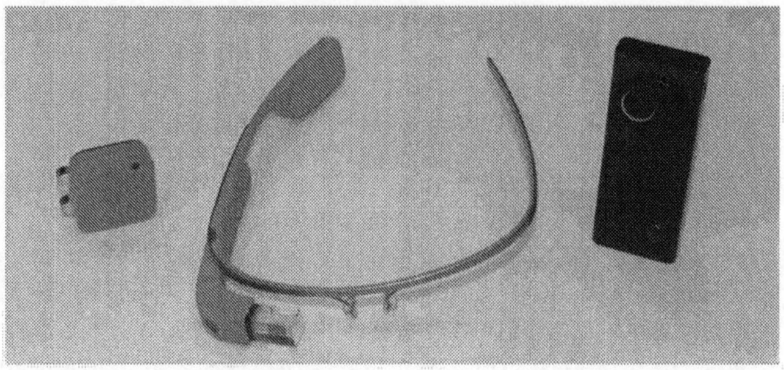

Figure 1. Lifelogging and wearable cameras, from left: Narrative Clip, Google Glass, and Autographer.

Lifelogging devices also raise important privacy concerns for both their wearers and the bystanders that are captured in the images. They may take photos in private, intimate settings that most people would not choose to photograph (e.g., in a bathroom or bedroom, or of a computer monitor). Bystanders are also typically unaware that they are being photographed by these discreet cameras. After images are captured, lifeloggers may upload them to a photo-management service on the cloud and/or share them with others. The very large number of images captured makes it difficult to ensure that photos are curated properly and this can lead to privacy leaks (e.g., by accidentally sharing a bathroom photo among a batch of vacation images, or a photo that captured part of a private document hidden in a corner of the image).

To better understand sharing behaviors and preferences of people with lifelogging cameras, we previously conducted a user study (N=36) where participants wore lifelogging cameras for a week and answered survey questions on a subset of images about how and why they would or would not share their photos [3]. We collected 14,477 images and obtained detailed sharing reasons for 1,015 images. We found that people exerted a high degree of physical discipline in private situations by stowing away the camera, pausing the collection, or immediately deleting private photos on the device rather than trying to delete them afterwards. We analyzed their survey responses, finding that many factors (like location, certain ob-

[1] `http://www.getnarrative.com`
[2] `http://www.autographer.com`
[3] `http://www.google.com/glass/start`

CHI 2015, April 18 - 23, 2015, Seoul, Republic of Korea
Copyright 2015 ACM 978-1-4503-3145-6/15/04... $15.00
http://dx.doi.org/10.1145/2702123.2702183

jects, and a sense of propriety for the privacy of bystanders) affect sharing decisions.

While the previous analysis provided a quantitative assessment of sharing behaviors, it did not analyze the contents of the images themselves, and thus could not connect image content with privacy concerns. In this Note, we fill this gap by annotating and analyzing the same rich dataset. Beyond the stated sharing preferences of the participants, we seek to understand 1) what makes a lifelogging photo sensitive; 2) what participants say about what makes an image private; and 3) what we can learn about privacy by looking at the images and the participants' reasons. To answer these questions, we had five researchers independently code images for a) the reasons participants gave for sharing or not sharing photos (combined with information gleaned from the actual image) and b) the subject matter within the images. The coders then met to resolve all differences and discuss the findings.

Our results show that a large number of lifelogging photos capture parts of people's lives that are *not normally documented by regular photography*. These include a variety of private information, including credit and ATM cards, emails on computer screens, answer sheets for exams, academic transcripts, and so on. We also observed that participants were concerned with their 'impression management' [2], avoiding capturing photos of "bad habits" like picking their nails or using nicotine. Our findings thus highlight the need for mechanisms to manage and curate images captured by lifelogging devices, and shed light on the important privacy challenges created by this new form of photography.

METHODOLOGY

We analyzed the image data from our previous study [3], which considered 36 participants' use of lifelogging devices over the course of a week but did not analyze image content as we do here. Each participant wore a smartphone on a lanyard around the neck that took a photograph every five minutes between 8am and 10pm. Participants were given *in-situ* controls to pause the study for up to an hour, or to retroactively undo recording by erasing up to the last hour of data. At the end of each day, they reviewed and deleted any images that they wanted to remove from the study (e.g., those with nudity), then marked images that had no recognizable content and explained any use of the *in-situ* controls. Participants were then asked to describe sharing preferences for each photo, choosing among: Close Friends and Family; Other Friends and Family; Coworkers, Classmates, and Acquaintances; and/or Everybody Else. They were asked to give reasons why they chose to share or not share for a subset of images.

Dataset

The lifelogging dataset consists of 14,477 images from 36 participants, out of which 8,590 were labeled as "unusable" (having no recognizable content) by participants and were not analyzed further. Of the remaining images, 1,015 include freeform text explaining the reason behind the sharing decision. We identified images having some sensitive content by taking those that were not shared with at least one group. We further split these into two sets: a "private" set of images that were not shared with anyone (N=75), and a "semi-private" set which were shared with at least one group (N=186).

Reasons given for	Semi-private Photos Sharing		Semi-private Photos Not sharing		Private Photos Not sharing	
No good reason	140	(76%)	44	(24%)	49	(65%)
Image quality	37	(20%)	3	(2%)	6	(8%)
Person in the photo	30	(16%)	66	(36%)	13	(17%)
Person in photo's appearance	22	(12%)	0	(0%)	2	(3%)
Interest/Concern about self	14	(8%)	53	(29%)	17	(23%)
Interest/Concern about others	21	(11%)	9	(5%)	2	(3%)
Presentation management	13	(7%)	16	(9%)	9	(12%)
Screens or monitors visible	0	(0%)	18	(10%)	3	(4%)
Objects in image	1	(0.5%)	49	(27%)	20	(27%)
(written) Information visible	0	(0%)	15	(8%)	4	(5%)
Activity shown	3	(2%)	10	(5%)	7	(9%)
Location of image	1	(0.5%)	49	(27%)	12	(16%)
TOTAL # of Images	185 (100%)				75 (100%)	

Table 1. Reasons given by participants for sharing or not sharing photos, by whether photos were semi-private (shared with some but not all groups) or completely private (shared with no groups). More than one answer is possible, so columns add to more than 100%.

Coding of the Images

These 261 images were coded along two dimensions: (1) their visual content, and (2) the reasons provided by the user for sharing or not sharing them. Using an initial set of approximately 35 codes, five coders independently coded a random sample of 10 images from among the set of 261 images. We then discussed discrepancies until we developed a clearly defined set of 16 content and 15 reason codes. We then proceeded to code all 261 images, with at least three coders independently coding each one. We achieved initial 94.5% agreement on the image codes. Discrepancies were then discussed until consensus was reached on all codes for each image.

Ethical considerations

Our analysis was approved by our IRB. Privacy concerns prohibit publishing images, so we only describe them here.

FINDINGS

The results of our coding are summarized in Tables 1 and 2. A large number of images were simply shared by default ("for no good reason"), highlighting the need for effective mechanisms to manage images, since otherwise images with subtle privacy violations may be shared accidentally. Our analysis found private information, impression management, and respect for others' privacy were key reasons that participants kept images private, and we now discuss each of these here.

Private Information

Our analysis shows that private information in images was a key reason that users chose not to share, and a major specific concern was computer and smartphone screens. For 10% of semi-private and 4% of private photos, participants explicitly mentioned screens, and private photos were also significantly more likely to have screens than semi-private ones (private=0.55, semi-private=0.38, ANOVA F-test = 5.9 (df=1), $p < 0.02$), indicating that their presence is sensitive. Beyond screens, users indicated that 27% of photos were not shared because of "objects within the photo." We suspect that a large number of these concerns are related to text content; according to our coding, 62.3% of these photos had monitors, 37.7% had documents, and 59.0% had text clearly visible.

Content of photos	Semi-private		Private	
Image quality (in focus)	122	(66%)	42	(56%)
# People in the photo = none	97	(53%)	56	(77%)
= 1	55	(30%)	15	(22%)
= 2	20	(11%)	1	(1.4%)
= 3-5	1	1 (6%)	0	(0%)
Faces visible in photo	51	(28%)	9	(12%)
Screens/Monitors visible	71	(38%)	41	(55%)
Any written text visible	86	(47%)	33	(44%)
Bottles/cups/alcohol visible	35	(19%)	3	(4%)
Location				
Indoor	154	(83%)	63	(84%)
Bedroom	9	(6%)	19	(30%)
Bathroom	8	(5%)	2	(3%)
Outdoor	15	(8%)	3	(4%)
Sidewalk/street	8	(53%)	1	(33%)
Other/not clear	7	(47%)	2	(66%)
In-Transit	14	(8%)	8	(11%)
Car	3	(21%)	3	(38%)
Public bus	10	(71%)	4	(50%)
TOTAL # of Images	185	(100%)	75	(100%)

Table 2. Content of images by whether photos were semi-private (shared with some but not all groups) or private (shared with no groups). More than one answer is possible, so columns add to more than 100%.

We highlight several examples to show the diversity of private content in images. In one, P36[4] is seen writing a course evaluation for a class, with answers clearly visible. In another, P50 is seen writing a note, and chose not to share because *"the page in the picture is actually part of a surprise for a close friend, so I wouldn't want her seeing it. I also wouldn't necessarily want certain people seeing it because it contains something that could be deemed 'unsanctioned' "* (which, we believe, refers to a reference to alcohol). One participant's camera captured an image of their ATM card, and they chose not to share it for fear of the card number being stolen. P37 decided not to share an image because it depicted a friend's apartment number.

In contrast, others seemed unconcerned about photos that we would have considered private. One user captured many images at work that included numerous clearly legible academic transcripts, and marked them to be publicly shared. [5] This participant did restrict sharing of other images, so he or she was aware of other privacy issues.

Impression Management

Many users chose to share or not share based on 'impression management,' in order to portray traits that they want to present to the world. As described by Goffman, *"...control is achieved largely by influencing the definition of the situation which the others come to formulate, and he can influence this definition by expressing himself in such a way as to give them the kind of impression that will lead them to act voluntarily in accordance with his own plan"* [2]. Impression management could involve sharing an image to show a positive trait, or suppressing an image that shows a negative one.

[4]Participant IDs ranged from 32 – 68 in the dataset.

[5]These images were shared publicly, so were not included in the pictures that we coded earlier. We highlight them here as it shows an interesting user behavior. As all sharing in the study was hypothetical, no transcripts were leaked, and we removed these images from our dataset after discovering them.

In our dataset, we identified impression management as the reason why 7% of semi-private images were shared, and why 9% of semi-private and 12% of private photos were not shared. P53, for example, chose not to share an image of watching a movie, explaining that they were *"not studying when I should be."* P50 did not share a photo of their bedroom with coworkers, because *"I would just feel weird if employers or coworkers saw a picture of my bedroom."* P40 avoided sharing a picture of an electronic cigarette because *"I don't want my family to know that I have a nicotine addiction,"* but shared it with coworkers, classmates, and acquaintances. P55 did not share one of nail picking , because *"I am performing a bad habit and would not want people I know to see."*

On the other hand, several participants specifically chose to share photos in order to promote a positive impression. For instance, P45 shared several images depicting computer work because it showed "studying." Another participant captured a photo of a coffee mug with a crude slogan on it; they chose not to share the photo with the public, but did share it with friends because *"they would understand my sense of humor."*

Other reasons for sharing that commonly co-occurred with impression management were "Someone in Photo" (22.2%), "Physical Appearance" (18.5%), and "Image Quality" (14.8%). Images shared because of impression management often had text visible (59.3% of the images), computer screens (66.7%), and documents (40.7%). Reasons not to share that were related to impression management included "Object in the image" (45.7%), "Activity in the image" (45.7%), and "Someone in Photo" (34.3%), and often had computer screens (75%), text (25%), or documents (12.5%). It thus appears that participants tried to prevent association with certain objects and activities, and to associate themselves with high-quality photos and nice physical appearance.

Privacy of Bystanders

We found that lifeloggers based sharing decisions not only out of concern for their own privacy, but also out of concern for others. In particular, 36% of semi-private photos and 17% of private photos were not shared because of "someone in the photo." In some of these cases, the participant was referring to themselves, because of a photo in the bathroom mirror. However, our content coding showed that 68% and 31% of these photos contained someone other than the participant, and specifically mentioned the privacy of another person for 12% and 8% respectively. Thus participants avoided sharing a large number of photos because of bystanders in the image.

Privacy seems to be somewhat related to the presence and number of people within a photo. Private photos were less likely to have any people in them, as only 23.3% of private photos had any people compared to 47% of semi-private photos, (χ^2-stat $= 12.2, df = 1, p < 0.001$). Similarly, they had significantly fewer people than photos shared semi-privately (based on analysis of number of people in a photo regressed on sharing status of private vs. semi-private, accounting for clustering of observations within users: β coeff.. $= -0.429$, robust std. err. $= 0.100, p < 0.001$). These results hold if analysis is restricted to only photos with any people in them.

A wide range of images attracted concern about other people's privacy. P60 captured one of a woman they were chatting with and chose not to share it because *"my friend should have a right to her privacy."* P42 chose not to share a photo of a woman sitting in a chair at home, saying *"my mother would be embarrassed by the photo taken without her knowing."* P55 captured a woman in the background of a photo but said *"I do not know this person and am unwilling to share their face publicly."* Finally, for a photo of a dorm room showing a bunk bed and some wall decorations, P38 indicated *"this picture is of someone else's bedroom. It is private, and should not be shared without their permission."*

DISCUSSION AND LIMITATIONS

Our long-term goal is to develop automated mechanisms that will help curate a user's lifelogging pictures, scanning for private content based on user-supplied privacy policies. Jana *et al.* [4] and Thomaz *et al.* [9] preserve the privacy of the lifelogger by extracting non-visual semantic information from images, but do not help users find which photos to share, which is a major goal of lifelogging. Rawassizadeh [7] postulated that lifelogging data would be shared and studied how to model sharing patterns. O'Hara and Tuffield [6] propose that the primary use of lifelogging data is for sharing and public consumption, and that privacy concerns that had been the focus of lifelogging research were not targeted appropriately. In their view lifeloggers collect images for sharing, making privacy-preserving transformations counterproductive.

Our study finds that lifeloggers are interested in suppressing private information, typically corresponding to specific objects (especially computer displays and physical documents) and activities. They are also interested in sharing because of presentation management, as well as protecting the privacy of bystanders appearing in a photo. The large number of images that were shared for no good reason, though, suggests that users may be overwhelmed by the number of collected images. Fortunately, most images are banal, without sensitive content, partially since users tended to use *in-situ* physical control over devices in sensitive situations [3]. However, the constant presence of such devices in intimate settings leaves the possibility that sensitive images may leak, underscoring the need for automated techniques to manage privacy. These sharing decisions are likely to be context-dependent and highly subjective based on an individual, suggesting that automatic privacy-preserving mechanisms need to be able to analyze images to detect people and certain objects, places, and activities. Initial work has examined detecting sensitive places and objects in lifelogging streams [8, 5].

The images analyzed in this study were collected over only a week and from participants who are not regular lifeloggers. The consequences of widespread long-term lifelogging are unclear, and are an interesting area for research. Allen [1] postulated that the effects of unforgettable memories could be detrimental. The chore of curating lifelogging images may prove so overwhelming that people give up and stop lifelogging, or perhaps privacy attitudes will change so that people compromise their expectations of privacy.

CONCLUSION

Our analysis of a large-scale lifelogging dataset showed traits that had only been hypothesized before. Not only were lifeloggers concerned about protecting their own private information and managing their own image, but they also considered the privacy of bystanders. We reported on the content of sensitive images with the hope that this may help to develop image analysis programs to gauge the sensitivity of images automatically, in order to help users curate the large amount of data that lifelogging devices collect.

ACKNOWLEDGMENTS

This material is based upon work supported by the National Science Foundation under grants CNS-1408730, CNS-1407788, CNS-1016603, CNS-1252697, and IIS-1253549. This work was also partially funded by a Google Research Award and by the Office of the Vice Provost for Research at Indiana University Bloomington through the Faculty Research Support Program.

REFERENCES

1. Allen, A. Dredging up the past: Lifelogging, memory, and surveillance. *University of Chicago Law Review* (2008).
2. Goffman, E. *The presentation of self in everyday life*. Doubleday, Garden City, NY, 1959.
3. Hoyle, R., Templeman, R., Armes, S., Anthony, D., Crandall, D., and Kapadia, A. Privacy behaviors of lifeloggers using wearable cameras. In *ACM Int'l Joint Conference on Pervasive and Ubiquitous Computing* (2014), 571–582.
4. Jana, S., Narayanan, A., and Shmatikov, V. A Scanner Darkly: Protecting User Privacy from Perceptual Applications. *IEEE Symposium on Security and Privacy* (2013), 349–363.
5. Korayem, M., Templeman, R., Chen, D., Crandall, D., and Kapadia, A. Screenavoider: Protecting computer screens from ubiquitous cameras. In *CoRR arXiv Technical Report arXiv:1412.0008* (2014).
6. O'Hara, K., Tuffield, M. M., and Shadbolt, N. Lifelogging: Privacy and empowerment with memories for life. *Identity in the Information Society 1*, 1 (Dec. 2008), 155–172.
7. Rawassizadeh, R. Towards sharing life-log information with society. *Behaviour & Information Technology 31*, 11 (Nov. 2012), 1057–1067.
8. Templeman, R., Korayem, M., Crandall, D., and Kapadia, A. PlaceAvoider: Steering First-Person Cameras away from Sensitive Spaces. In *21st Annual Network and Distributed System Security Symposium (NDSS)* (2014).
9. Thomaz, E., Parnami, A., Bidwell, J., Essa, I., and Abowd, G. Technological approaches for addressing privacy concerns when recognizing eating behaviors with wearable cameras. In *ACM Int'l Joint Conference on Pervasive and Ubiquitous Computing* (2013).

Somebody's Watching Me?

Assessing the Effectiveness of Webcam Indicator Lights

Rebecca S. Portnoff[1], Linda N. Lee[1], Serge Egelman[1,2], Pratyush Mishra[1], Derek Leung[1], and David Wagner[1]

[1]University of California, Berkeley, CA
{rsportnoff,lnl,egelman}@cs.berkeley.edu, {pratyushmishra,derek.leung}@berkeley.edu
[2]International Computer Science Institute, Berkeley, CA, egelman@icsi.berkeley.edu

ABSTRACT

Most laptops and personal computers have webcams with LED indicators to notify users when they are recording. Because hackers use surreptitiously captured webcam recordings to extort users, we explored the effectiveness of these indicators under varying circumstances and how they could be improved. We observed that, on average, fewer than half of our participants (45%) noticed the existing indicator during computer-based tasks. When seated in front of the computer performing a paper-based task, only 5% noticed the indicator. We performed a followup experiment to evaluate a new indicator and observed that adding onscreen glyphs had a significant impact on both computer-based and non-computer-based tasks (93% and 59% noticed the new indicator, respectively). We discuss how our results can be integrated into current systems, as well as future ubiquitous computing systems.

Author Keywords

Privacy Indicators; Ubiquitous Computing; Usable Security

ACM Classification Keywords

K.6.5. Management of Computing and Information Systems: Security and protection; H.5.2. Information Interfaces and Presentation (e.g. HCI): User Interfaces

INTRODUCTION

As we enter the age of wearable and ubiquitous computing, more and more consumer computing devices will accept continuous input via audio and/or video sensors. These devices allow applications to perform a wide range of actions, from recognizing objects in the user's environment to parsing voice commands. Similar to smartphone platforms [26], ubiquitous computing platforms will need permission mechanisms to allow users to regulate *how* specific applications access sensitive data, and privacy indicators to communicate *when* that data is accessed. In order for us to understand the design space of these privacy indicators, we examined the effectiveness of similar privacy indicators that are already sufficiently pervasive: webcam recording indicators.

For several years now, laptop sales have surpassed desktop sales [21], and with few exceptions, it is standard for a new laptop to come equipped with a built-in webcam. These webcams face the user and have indicator LEDs to communicate when the webcam is recording. Ideally, the user will notice the indicator, understand that a recording is being made, and take defensive actions in the event that the webcam is recording without the user's consent. Anecdotal evidence suggests that these assumptions are incorrect [13].

Remote Administration Tools (RATs) allow hackers to control an unsuspecting user's computer remotely, allowing them to execute programs, send taunting messages, or eavesdrop via the webcam and microphone [4]. In some cases, hackers have used videos of victims in various states of undress as part of "sextortion" plots: the perpetrator threatens to publicly post the captured videos and/or photos unless the victim pays a ransom [3]. The most famous case of this involved a high school classmate of Miss Teen USA who surreptitiously captured photos of her naked in her bedroom [19]. Unauthorized access to laptop webcams is not just limited to extortionists, however. In 2010, the Lower Merion School District in Pennsylvania paid a settlement to victims after it was reported that school administrators were spying on students in their homes using school-provided laptops [30].

While users can buy stickers to cover up the webcams to prevent unauthorized video capture [25], we wanted to explore the effectiveness of current webcam LED indicators and examine ways in which they could be improved, so that our findings can be applied to future technologies. We performed a series of experiments to quantify how often users are likely to take notice when their webcams unexpectedly turn on. First, we turned on the webcam unexpectedly while participants were using the computer, to see how often they noticed and whether this was affected by their activities. Next, we studied the effectiveness of a new indicator. In this work, we contribute the following:

- We show that in our laboratory environment, a minority of participants (45%) noticed an illuminated webcam LED indicator when performing a computer-based task, regard-

CHI 2015, April 18 - 23 2015, Seoul, Republic of Korea.

ACM 978-1-4503-3145-6/15/04...$15.00.
http://dx.doi.org/10.1145/2702123.2702164

less of what that task specifically was. When performing tasks not on the computer, but in its proximity, only 5% of participants noticed the webcam LED.
- We show that the use of full-screen glyphs significantly increases the likelihood that participants notice the webcam indicator: both when performing computer-based tasks (93%) and non-computer-based tasks (59%).

RELATED WORK

In this section, we present related work on webcam indicator attacks, privacy/security indicator design and evaluation, and privacy considerations for ubiquitous computing.

Attacks on Webcam LEDs

In order for users to notice and comprehend privacy indicators, they must be reliably present. Although our work assumes that webcam LEDs will reliably illuminate when a recording is being made, recent studies demonstrate that this assumption is not always correct. Most webcam LEDs are wired in the same logical connection as the webcam, so that the LED will turn on with the webcam. This varies from device to device, however, with some indicators controlled by software [34]. Nevertheless, because of this, many people incorrectly believe that it is not possible to disable the indicator without attacking the hardware.

Recent research, however, shows that an attacker can exploit software vulnerabilities to cause some of these indicators to malfunction. Broker *et al.* demonstrated an attack on webcam firmware that enables video capture without turning on the webcam LED on older versions of Mac laptops [9]. While these attacks are troubling, we assume that devices will eventually be designed so that indicators cannot be disabled; research on understanding whether the indicators are effective at communicating risk to users is still necessary.

Indicators and Warnings

Cranor discusses various evaluation criteria for indicators and warnings [16], such as how an indicator interacts with other indicators, and whether users notice, understand, and follow its recommendations, both after first exposure and then repeated exposures. Other considerations include how warnings are displayed [23], when they are displayed [24], and how they make use of icons and signal words [2].

Poorly designed indicators not only fail to communicate the appropriate message to users, but can have other unintended negative consequences, such as desensitization, habituation, or annoyance [39]. They can also create a false sense of security [10]. For example, when people notice the HTTPS lock icon (and they tend not to [40]) they often incorrectly assume that it indicates a secure website, rather than a secure connection [29]. Users also do not change their behavior when this indicator is absent [38]. When designing privacy and security indicators, it is important to examine these potential pitfalls.

Privacy Concerns for Ubiquitous Sensing

Wearable devices and ubiquitous sensing platforms are moving towards automated capture and access [1]. More and more often, people will interact with sensors while carrying out daily activities, from a myriad of sources and for a variety of reasons: "lifelogging" devices to record their daily lives [31, 18], memory augmentation devices [14, 17, 32], smart homes that optimize living conditions [12, 11, 22], devices that create augmented reality environments [7, 6], and even devices integrated into clothing [5].

The ubiquitous capture and storage of information naturally raises concerns about the preservation of privacy [35]. Privacy in the field of ubiquitous computing relies on principles including notice, choice, and consent [33]. Certain privacy problems stem from poor feedback mechanisms [8, 20]: indicators failing to reliably inform people *when* they are being captured and *what* information is being saved.

Clearly, there is a critical need for effective privacy indicators that users will notice and understand. Research has suggested that notifications in a user's peripheral field of vision may be acceptable for certain cases [15]. It is not clear, however, whether this is an effective strategy for every or even most privacy and security notifications.

Although significant work has been done to explore privacy/security indicator designs, researchers have not yet focused specific attention on the ubiquitous webcam LED.

AWARENESS AND PERCEPTIONS

To quantify the problem of "webcam spying," we first conducted an online survey. Our goal was to better understand whether people are likely to be at risk, their awareness of the danger, and how many claim to have already been victimized.

Methodology

We recruited 500 participants on December 9th, 2013 via Amazon's Mechanical Turk. We restricted participants to those over 18 years old residing in the U.S. All participants stated that they owned a laptop or desktop computer with either an external or internal webcam. We asked questions about participants' webcam use and their understanding of the indicator LED. The questions fell into three categories:

1. *Behavior*: The types of participants' webcams and whether they obscure them when not in use.
2. *Risk Awareness*: Whether participants believe that webcam spying is possible.
3. *Victimization*: Whether participants have noticed the webcam LED previously come on against their wishes.

The entire survey took approximately 7 minutes to complete, upon which we compensated them $1.

Results

After removing 8 incomplete responses, our sample consisted of 492 participants (64% male and a median age range of 26-30). Two researchers independently coded 1,476 open-ended responses (94.3% agreement), discussed any disagreements, and resolved them to reflect unanimous agreement.

Behavior

We asked laptop-owning participants whether they "always," "sometimes," or "never" close their laptop lids when not using it. We found that 45% reported "always" doing so, whereas another 36% reported doing so "sometimes." We also asked whether participants were comfortable doing any of the following in front of an open laptop:

- Going to the restroom
- Eating meals
- Changing clothes
- Talking to friends
- Taking a shower

We found that 28% were comfortable using the restroom, 85% were comfortable eating meals, 41% were comfortable changing clothes, 80% were comfortable talking to a friend, and 18% were comfortable taking a shower. Because we previously subjected participants to questions regarding webcams before answering this question, these numbers are likely under-reported and therefore represent lower bounds. While we are not aware of any peer-reviewed literature on the matter, an industry-commissioned survey reports that 44% of respondents use their laptops in the bedroom and 8% in the bathroom [37]. Our data suggests that large groups of users practice behavior that puts them at risk of webcam spying.

Risk Awareness

We asked participants whether they thought it would be possible for a hacker to spy on them through their webcam, and to indicate why or why not. We found that 13% did not think it would be possible, and 19% were unsure. The open-ended responses ranged in technical fluency, ranging from distrust of the notion of foolproof technologies to discussing how root access could allow an attacker to control a device.

Victimization

Nineteen participants reported that their webcam LED turned on when they were not using it. Almost all of them (18 of 19) believed this was normal behavior or just due to human error, while one participant was the victim of ransomware, stating:

> *"I had contracted a virus on my laptop the FBI classifies as 'ransomware.' It tells you you cannot access your computer unless you wire money to an account, and it turns on the webcam to frighten people. I was surprised and very anxious, and I responded by covering my webcam with black electrical tape."* (P30)

Our survey showed that many people practice habits that increase their risk and that they are unaware of the danger. In the following section, we describe our empirical evaluation of the common webcam LED, in terms of the proportion of users who are likely to notice it when it unexpectedly illuminates, and whether this varies based on the task being performed.

LABORATORY EXPERIMENT

We conducted a laboratory experiment to examine the extent to which people notice and understand current webcam LEDs, as well as the extent to which their activities impact the likelihood of noticing the LEDs. We explored this because an attacker with remote access to a victim's webcam would also be able to see what the victim is doing, and potentially use this information to increase attack effectiveness. In this section, we provide details of our methodology and results.

Methodology

We conducted an experiment with 98 participants. All participants used Toshiba Tecra R850 laptops, which use a blue LED next to the webcam lens to indicate when the webcam is recording. We examined whether participants noticed the webcam LED turning on when performing a computer-based task, as well as a non-computer-based task within close proximity of the webcam (i.e., answering a written questionnaire).

Procedure

We conducted each session in a laboratory space at our university that consisted of 36 laptops, in 6 rows, with cubicle walls separating each laptop. No more than 15 participants attended each session. We distanced each participant from every other participant by at least one desk, by only using every other laptop in each staggered row. Our goal was to prevent participants from viewing each other's laptops.

Upon arriving, participants sat down at laptops of their choosing, where consent forms were present. Once participants read and signed the consent forms, the researcher outlined participants' tasks and explained that the purpose of the study was to see how people perform various tasks on a computer. Again, the true purpose of the study was not revealed. Each session proceeded as follows:

1. Participants answered the 30-item Barratt Impulsiveness Scale [36], which was used as a distraction to make them comfortable with the environment.
2. Participants performed one of four randomly-assigned computer-based tasks lasting 10-15 minutes. At some random point after 5 minutes, the webcam made a 10 second recording. Participants were prevented from advancing to the next task until at least 10 minutes had elapsed. There were four different types of computer-based tasks:
    - **Reading**: Participants read a provided passage [27]. We told them that they would be asked questions about the reading, so they should read it thoroughly.
    - **Essay**: Participants saw a previous year's SAT writing prompt. We told them to write an essay based on the prompt as part of a college or job application.
    - **Game**: Participants played the 2048 game.[1] We instructed them to try to get as high a score as possible in 10-15 minutes.
    - **Video**: Participants watched a TED talk,[2] which we told them they would be asked questions about.
3. Each participant took the Cognitive Reflection Test on a printed sheet of paper on the desk in front of the laptop [28]. At some random point after 60 seconds into the task, the webcam made a 10 second recording. Participants were prevented from advancing to the exit survey until at least 2 minutes had elapsed.
4. Each participant filled out an exit survey on the computer.
5. Upon completing the exit survey, we debriefed participants. We gave each participant a re-consent form, which would allow us to use the webcam video in our analysis, and paid them with $35 debit cards.

[1] http://gabrielecirulli.github.io/2048/

[2] https://www.youtube.com/embed/xMj_P_6H69g

	Noticed light	
Computer Task	27.6%	n = 98
Reading	46.4%	n = 28
Essay	25.0%	n = 28
Game	25.0%	n = 20
Video	9.0%	n = 22
Written Task	0%	n = 98

Table 1. Unprompted responses: the number of participants who described noticing the webcam LED turn on during each task.

Recruitment

We placed an online recruitment advertisement on Craigslist in June of 2014, under the "writing/editing" jobs section for our city and surrounding cities. The advertisement stated that the study was about how people perform various tasks on a laptop. Those interested in participating filled out an online screening survey in which they provided information about their age, gender, laptop make and model, amount of time using their laptop, various ways they have used their laptop (social networking, video recording, playing games, making video calls, making online purchases), contact information, and availability. We screened out those who were under 18 years of age or who had a laptop that did not have a webcam.

We recruited 98 participants who showed up for sessions lasting 30-60 minutes. Of our 98 participants, 55 were female (56%), and ages ranged from 18 to 72 ($\mu = 37.9$, $\sigma = 15.4$).

Results

Our primary goal was to assess the effectiveness of the webcam LED. We found that the majority of participants did not notice it turn on during either task, and many did not understand what it indicated, even when they did notice it. In this section, we provide details for whether participants noticed the webcam LED, our efforts to corroborate the self-reports using the captured videos, whether any of the computer-based task conditions influenced the participants to notice the webcam LED more or less, and participants' understanding of the purpose of the webcam LED.

Noticing the Indicator

We determined whether participants noticed the webcam LED through multiple exit survey questions. First, we asked them if anything unexpected had occurred as they completed the computer-based task and the written task. We used open-ended formats so as to not prime them (i.e., we made no mention of the webcam). We accepted responses that reported the webcam or the LED turning on as evidence that they noticed it. Only 27.6% (27 of 98) of participants reported noticing it during the computer-based task (Table 1). No participants reported noticing the webcam LED during the written task.

On the next page of the exit survey, we asked participants which (if any) of the following occurred during the computer-based task, and then during the written task. For each participant, we randomized the order of the following options:

- The webcam began recording
- A light above the screen turned on
- The desktop background changed
- An unexpected sound played
- The screen flickered
- The computer rebooted
- None of the above

	Light turned on	Recording	
Computer Task	44.9%	33.7%	n = 98
Reading	53.6%	32.1%	n = 28
Essay	35.7%	32.1%	n = 28
Game	45.0%	30.0%	n = 20
Video	45.5%	40.9%	n = 22
Written Task	5.1%	5.1%	n = 98

Table 2. Prompted responses: the number of participants who selected either that the webcam LED turned on or the webcam began recording.

	Made Eye Contact	
Computer Task	48.9%	n = 94
Reading	63.0%	n = 27
Essay	40.7%	n = 27
Game	55.6%	n = 18
Video	36.4%	n = 22
Written Task	4.26%	n = 94

Table 3. Participants observed making eye contact with the webcam.

Once prompted, the rate at which participants reported noticing the light increased. During the computer-based task it increased to 44.9% (44 of 98), whereas during the written task, it increased from 0% to 5.1% (5 of 98).

To corroborate our exit survey data, we examined the webcam recordings. Four of our 98 participants declined to give us permission to use their recordings. Three researchers independently coded all 188 recordings (two per participant) to judge whether each participant made eye contact with the camera (i.e., an indication that they were looking at it), and if so, at what point in time during the 10 second recording. The researchers then resolved any disagreements, so that final codings were unanimous. Prior to achieving consensus, they disagreed on 26 instances (86.2% agreement).

Based on the recordings, 48.9% (46 of 94) of participants noticed the webcam LED during the computer-based task, and 4.26% (4 of 94) noticed it during the written task (Table 3). During the computer-based task, of the 46 participants who we observed making eye contact with the webcam, all of them did so within the first four seconds; 71.7% (33 of 46) noticed it immediately (Figure 1). During the written task, all four of them noticed within the first seven seconds.

Using our three different metrics (unprompted responses, prompted responses, and recordings), we concluded that 27%-49% of participants noticed the webcam LED during the computer-based task, whereas $\leq 5\%$ noticed it during the written task. Since the recordings and prompted responses were similar, we did not consider the recordings further.

Task Influence

We examined the effects of participants' tasks on noticing the webcam LED. We analyzed differences between computer-based tasks and the written task (within-subjects), as well as between specific computer-based tasks (between-subjects).

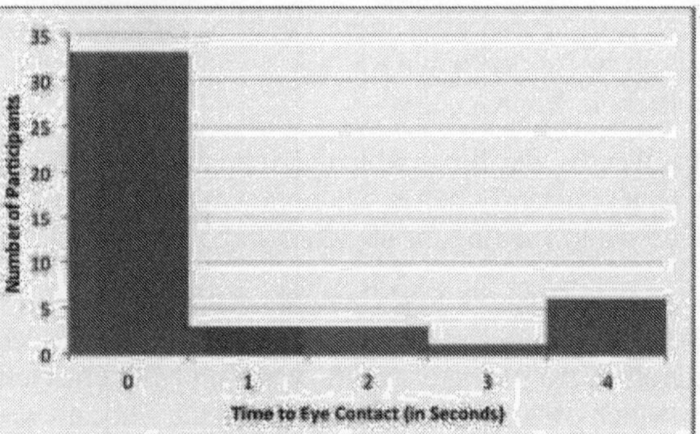

Figure 1. Time into recording at which participants made eye contact.

We determined using McNemar's test that participants were significantly more likely to notice the indicators when performing the computer-based task, based on both the unprompted ($p < 0.0001$; $\chi^2 = 25.037$) and prompted ($p < 0.0001$; $\chi^2 = 33.5814$) responses. Using either measure, we observed relatively large effect sizes ($\phi_{unprompted} = 0.505$, $\phi_{prompted} = 0.585$), which indicates that participants were more likely to notice the webcam LED while performing a task on the computer, rather than merely in its proximity.

When it came to differences between specific computer-based tasks, we did not observe statistically significant results when examining both unprompted ($\chi^2(3) = 5.917$, $p < 0.116$) and prompted ($\chi^2(3) = 1.000$, $p < 0.8013$) responses. Thus, we conclude that the specific computer-based tasks that we evaluated had no observable effect on whether participants noticed the indicator.

Understanding the Webcam LED

We examined whether participants understood that the blue webcam LED indicated that the webcam was recording by observing their responses to the multiple-choice prompting question. For the computer-based task, we found that 45.5% (20 of 44) of the participants who reported noticing a light above the screen *only* reported the light, and not also that the webcam recorded them. For the written task, this rate was 40.0%. While it is impossible to conclude with certainty without directly asking the question, these results may suggest a comprehension problem with the webcam LED: even when the participants did notice the webcam LED turning on, up to 45.5% of them may not have understood what it meant. Alternately, it is possible that they did not know that they could select multiple options (despite the question instructions allowing them to do so), and therefore selected the first one that applied, without reading the other possibilities.

The results of our experiment demonstrate that the webcam LED needs to be more noticeable, and potentially more understandable. In the following section, we describe a follow-up experiment to test a possible alternative indicator: a full-screen flashing translucent camera glyph.

MITIGATION

We created a new mitigation whereby every time the webcam turned on, a full-screen red translucent camera glyph appeared in the center of the screen and blinked three times

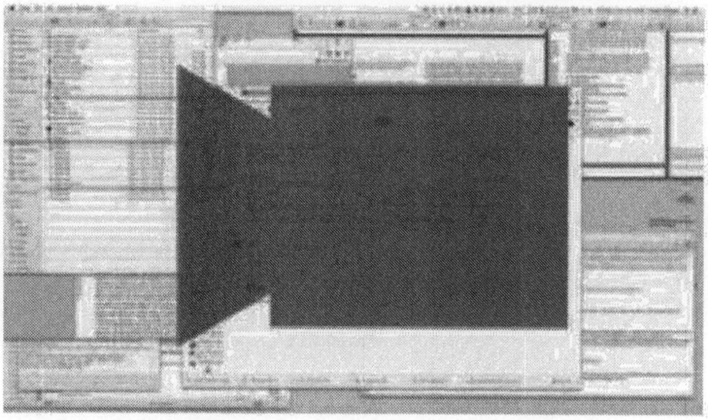

Figure 2. Full screen image of the red camera glyph.

(Figure 2). The glyph then shrunk into the upper right hand corner where it continued blinking once per second. In total, the red translucent camera glyph blinked for 10 seconds (3 seconds full screen, and 7 seconds in the upper right hand corner). We intentionally made the glyph translucent so that it would not occlude other items on the screen (to account for the case when the user is expecting the webcam to be on).

Methodology

We randomly assigned participants to one of two between-subjects conditions, which varied based on the webcam indicator shown: *control* group participants viewed the blue webcam LED, whereas *experimental* group participants additionally viewed the red camera glyph described at the beginning of this section (Figure 2).

Our followup experiment followed the same protocol as our initial laboratory experiment, with a few exceptions. Given the lack of noticeable effect of different computer-based tasks on participants noticing the webcam LED, we focused on just the video task. Additionally, given that self-reported noticing of the webcam LED was found to be reliable, we chose not to save webcam recordings of participants.

We recruited 81 participants in the exact same manner as our first experiment. In total, 46 were female, and ages ranged from 18 to 65 ($\mu = 33.7$, $\sigma = 13.1$). Of the 81 participants, 37 were randomly assigned to the control group. We observed no statistically significant demographic differences between participants in the control and experimental groups.

Results

We found that using the red camera glyph substantially increased the rate at which participants reported noticing the indicator. We also found that their understanding of what the warning indicated diminished, but not by a statistically significant amount. In this section, we compare the rates at which test group and control group participants noticed and understood the meanings of their respective indicators.

Noticing the Red Camera Glyph

We asked participants whether anything unexpected had occurred during the computer-based task or the written task. We accepted any statement that reported the webcam turning on or the red camera glyph appearing as evidence that

	Noticed	
Computer Task		
Experimental	65.9%	n = 44
Control	16.2%	n = 37
Written Task		
Experimental	40.9%	n = 44
Control	2.7%	n = 37

Table 4. Unprompted responses: the number of participants who described noticing the indicator appear/turn on.

	Indicator	Recording	
Computer Task			
Experimental	93.2%	25.0%	n = 44
Control	40.5%	37.8%	n = 37
Written Task			
Experimental	59.1%	18.2%	n = 44
Control	5.41%	5.41%	n = 37

Table 5. Prompted responses: number of participants who selected either that the indicator appeared or that the webcam began recording.

they noticed the red camera glyph. We observed that 65.9% (29 of 44) of participants in the experimental group reported noticing the camera glyph appear (Table 4). In contrast, only 16.2% (6 of 37) of control group participants reported noticing the webcam LED. This difference is statistically significant ($p < 0.0001$; two-tailed Fisher's exact test), with a very large effect size ($\phi = 0.500$).

When asked the same question for the written task, over 40% of the experimental group participants reported noticing the red camera glyph, whereas only one participant in the control group reported noticing the webcam LED turn on (see Table 4). This difference was also statistically significant ($p < 0.0001$; two-tailed Fisher's exact test), with a very large effect size ($\phi = 0.449$).

When prompted, participants saw the same seven options as in the first laboratory experiment, but with an added option: "a red camera image appeared on the screen." When prompted, 93.2% (41 of 44) of experimental group participants reported noticing the red camera glyph during the computer-based task (Table 5). For the control group, fewer than half reported noticing the webcam LED. This difference was statistically significant ($p < 0.0001$; two-tailed Fisher's exact test), with a very large effect size ($\phi = 0.568$).

When asked the same question for the written task, over half of our participants in the experimental group reported noticing the red camera glyph, whereas only two control group participants reported noticing the webcam LED turn on (Table 5). This difference was statistically significant ($p < 0.0001$; two-tailed Fisher's exact test), with a very large effect size ($\phi = 0.562$).

We used McNemar's test to determine that participants were significantly more likely to notice the red camera glyph when performing the computer-based task than the written task, based on both the unprompted ($p = 0.0003$; $\chi^2 = 13.067$) and prompted ($p = 0.0026$; $\chi^2 = 9.091$) responses. Using either measure, we observed relatively large effect sizes ($\phi_{unprompted} = 0.402$, $\phi_{prompted} = 0.335$), which indicates that participants were more likely to notice the red camera glyph while performing a task on the computer, rather than merely in its proximity.

In all cases, the rate at which participants noticed the indicator was significantly better when viewing the red camera glyph than when viewing the standard webcam LED.

Understanding the Red Camera Glyph

We were curious to see whether or not using the red camera glyph as the indicator vs. the webcam LED changed the rate at which participants understood that the webcam was recording. When looking at the unprompted responses for the test group, of the participants who noticed the glyph, but did not explicitly state it was a camera, most reported seeing some combination of red blocks, shapes and symbols:

> *"[I saw] a few red arrows or shapes flashed on the screen."* (P2)

> *"[I saw] flashes of a faint red arrow across the screen."* (P3)

> *"...a couple red flashing symbols appeared on the screen."* (P19)

We found that 25.0% (11 of 44) of experimental group participants reported that the webcam began recording during the computer-based task, compared to 37.8% (14 of 37) of participants in the control group (Table 5). For the written task, the corresponding rates were 18.2% (8 of 44) and 5.41% (2 of 37), respectively.

In both cases, the difference was not statistically significant: ($p = 0.236$, two-tailed Fisher's exact test) and ($p = 0.101$, two-tailed Fisher's exact test) for the computer-based task and written task, respectively. These results seem to indicate that the number of participants who understood our warning mechanism was essentially the same as the number that understood the standard webcam LED.

The results of our experiment demonstrate that our red camera glyph indicator significantly outperformed the standard webcam LED in terms of participants' rate of noticing the indicator, with similar comprehension rates. In the next section, we analyze the results of our exit survey to see whether any correlations can be found between participants' previous experiences noticing their personal webcam turning on unexpectedly, and noticing the indicator in our experiments.

EXIT SURVEY

In this section, we examine participants' previous experiences with having their personal webcams turn on unexpectedly, their security and privacy concerns, and their security behavior regarding their webcams, as gathered from our exit survey.

Experienced Webcam Turning on Unexpectedly

Of the 179 participants from our two lab experiments, 13.4% (24 of 179) had experienced a webcam turn on unexpectedly some time in the past (i.e., prior to this study), 79.9% (143 of 179) had not, and the remaining 6.70% (12 of 179) were unsure if this had ever happened.

We compared participants' prior experiences with their behaviors in the laboratory, excluding those who were unsure whether their webcams had ever turned on unexpectedly. Of the 24 who claimed to have experienced it in the past, when prompted, 20.8% (5 of 24) reported noticing the indicator during the computer-based task; of the 143 who had not experienced it, 56.6% (81 of 143) reported the same. This difference was statistically significant ($p < 0.0025$; two-tailed Fisher's exact test) with a medium effect size ($\phi = 0.251$). For the written task, 8.33% (2 of 24) reported noticing the indicator; of the 143, 16.8% (24 of 143) reported the same. However, this difference was not statistically significant.

In other words, for the computer-based task, it seems that those who had prior experiences with webcams turning on unexpectedly were *less* likely to notice it happen in the laboratory, which seems counterintuitive. It seems likely that some other confounding factor is in effect here. It could be the case that previous victims have become accustomed to the protection their personal security measures provide, and as a result do not pay as much attention to the webcam indicator. We found that 29.2% (7 of 24) of participants who have previously noticed their webcams turn on unexpectedly claim to now cover the camera lens of their home computer/laptop when not in use, as compared to 9.79% (14 of 143) of those who have not. The difference was statistically significant ($p = 0.0157$, two-tailed Fisher's exact test) with a medium effect size ($\phi = 0.2050$), though this effect may not be statistically significant upon correcting for multiple testing (e.g., using the Bonferroni correction).

Security/Privacy Concerns

When asked to state any and all possible consequences if the webcam on their home computer/laptop unexpectedly recorded them and the video became public, most participants offered multiple responses. The most frequent response was "violation of privacy." As one participant poignantly stated:

> *"I would look foolish, I'm sure. People would see me at my best and at my worst. They would see my daughter and husband when they weren't expecting it. They would see us in our most intimate moments. I would be devastated that our privacy was violated so completely. It would be like someone broke into our home and stole our secrets."* (P90)

Many participants stated concern over intimate moments being made public:

> *"There would be a sex video online somewhere, I would be seen completely naked from changing out of the shower, or I would be sleeping in my bed."* (P127)

> *"I'd feel really violated, I mean sometimes I'm sitting in front of my computer naked, or smoking weed, and I'd be really uncomfortable with video like that becoming public."* (P150)

> *"The camera might... record me masturbating."* (P156)

> *"I live in a studio with my boyfriend, so the video might end up on a porn site."* (P188)

A smaller subset of participants were more worried about what other data/information a hacker might be able to gain access to while spying on them:

> *"Not sure. Possibly home burglary because they can see what's in the house."* (P10)

> *"...identity theft or loss of money."* (P34)

> *"I'm more concerned about this being a warning sign that someone has access to all the information on my computer..."* (P51)

Security Behavior

When asked to state what participants would do if the webcam on their home computer/laptop began recording unexpectedly, the most frequent response was "cover the camera lens," followed closely by "seek outside help." Almost every participant stated that they would try some way to "fix" the problem, even if they could not state exactly what steps they would take:

> *"I would try to determine the cause of the unexpected recording and then take measures to prevent it from happening in the future."* (P21)

> *"I would investigate and see if I could stop [it]..."* (P78)

> *"I would try to figure out how to stop it from doing it and try to figure out how to not let that happen again."* (P188)

Some participants stated they would resort to more extreme measures:

> *"Scan, and if necessary, bomb the harddrive."* (P17)

> *"Disconnect it when not in use, possibly destroy it."* (P44)

> *"Throw it out the window..."* (P63)

It is clear to see from these responses that participants value their security and privacy, and are troubled by the thought of someone watching them without their permission.

LIMITATIONS

After completing our experiments, we realized that by not randomizing the order in which the computer task versus the written task was performed, we could not guarantee that there was no learning or habituation effect. Although this was an unfortunate oversight, we found that for everything but the mitigation experimental group, it had no observable effect on our results. We performed Phi correlations between the rates of noticing the indicators between the two tasks and found no statistically significant correlations for the first laboratory experiment ($p < 0.49$, $\phi = 0.07$) or for the followup mitigation experiment in the control group ($p < 0.083$, and $\phi = 0.29$). For the experimental group (i.e., the red camera glyph), we found a potentially significant correlation ($p < 0.029$, $\phi = 0.33$), though upon correcting for multiple testing, it is unlikely to remain statistically significant. Given these results, there is no evidence to suggest that this oversight impacted our conclusion regarding the utility of the webcam LED as a warning mechanism, or the improvement gained by the red glyph.

DISCUSSION

In this section, we discuss the space of future mitigation research as we see it, as well as more sophisticated attacks.

Mitigations

While we found the red camera glyph, taken as a whole, to be significantly more effective than the status quo, it is by no means the only solution (or necessarily the best). More work is needed to show how each change contributed individually, as the red camera glyph differed in size, color, and movement, as compared to the existing webcam LED. More broadly speaking, more work is needed to explore other potential design improvements. We see two main categories of study which remain to be explored in regard to webcam indicators, as well as privacy indicators in general:

1. Designing indicators that users will notice
2. Improving user understanding of the indicators

Noticeable Indicators

We see two main classes of potential indicators for the webcam, namely hardware-based and software-based indicators. Hardware-based solutions are preferable, as they prevent a hacker who has used a root exploit to gain control of the machine from accessing the webcam without triggering the indicator. Existing webcam LED indicators are typically implemented in hardware. For our experiments, we implemented the red camera glyph in software, which means that an attacker with root access could disable it. Any real-life implementation of the red camera glyph as an indicator would need to be implemented in hardware, like the standard webcam LED currently is.

One natural way to expand on the current webcam LED is to have it flash/blink, rather than hold steady. The most basic set up would be to have the webcam LED blinking constantly throughout the duration of the recording, though this might be distracting or irritating for users. Alternatively, the LED could blink when the webcam is first turned on, in order to draw the user's attention to it immediately, and after some amount of time, it could return to a steady light. The LED could also blink intermittently throughout the recording; this might be useful in drawing the user's attention to the LED even when the user did not initially notice it.

In a pilot experiment, we explored whether simply blinking the webcam LED would be sufficient. While blinking the LED did not yield significantly improved results over the control condition, that may have been because the frequency of blinking was only 0.5 Hz. We were not able to increase this speed due to hardware limitations. It seems possible that with a faster blinking speed, more users might notice the LED.

Exploring a larger variety of computer-based tasks could also be worthwhile. Determining whether users are more likely to notice the webcam indicator when performing tasks that are menial and/or automatic vs. active and require conscious attention could allow researchers to design indicators that have a varying signal size based on task. For example, if the webcam turned on while the user was performing a menial or automatic task, the indicator signal would be smaller; if it turned on while the user was performing a task requiring conscious attention and focus, the signal would be larger.

Another challenge is to to help users notice the indicator when they are not using their computers, but are in the same room as their computers. This challenge is especially important because it includes the scenario of when a person is in a compromising or intimate situation. A brighter webcam LED might help in this circumstance (e.g., a flash LED). Using an audio signal could also be helpful in this scenario, although not for people who regularly leave their headphones plugged in, mute their computer, or have hearing problems.

Improving Understanding

It is critically important for people to comprehend what the warning signal means: without understanding, the indicator is useless. One possibility for improving comprehension would be to display a one-time-only explanation of the warning that appears the first time a person uses the webcam, and never again. This solution would not be dependent on a user's prior knowledge. However, it is unclear whether or not users would actually pay attention to the explanation. Given that current users are not used to a message appearing when they turn their webcams on, it is possible that users may automatically close it without paying attention, or even believe the message indicates the presence of malware on their machine.

Over time, people may come to learn the meaning of a new indicator such as our red camera glyph, simply because it always appears each time the webcam is in use. However, even time and experience are not a perfect solution: people have used the presence of a light as an indicator that video is recording for ages, and yet people still have confusion as to what exactly the webcam LED indicates. One possible alternative is to change the form of the webcam LED light; rather than having a small circle of light, the LED could be designed to emit light in the shape of a video camera. It is possible that the combination of the traditional LED light and the video camera shape could fix what time and experience have not.

Sophisticated Attacks

There are a number of ways in which attackers could attempt to spy on users through their webcams without the users realizing. One natural method would be to distract users from looking in the direction of the webcam LED when the webcam turns on, possibly by drawing their eye to somewhere else on the screen with a pop-up or some other distraction. Other techniques could use social engineering: an attacker could implement a false webcam driver update message that appears whenever he turns on the victim's webcam. The intention of the message would be to lull the user into a false sense of security, so even if she notices that the webcam is on and recording, she believes it is part of the update process.

Attackers could also use other features to infer when users are away from their computers, and are less likely to notice the webcam LED turning on. In the most trivial scenario, an attacker could wait until there is no activity on the computer to turn the webcam on. This could get more complex: a clever attacker could learn his victim's schedule and habits of computer usage to learn the optimal time to turn the webcam on.

An attacker could potentially pick up this kind of information by remotely turning on the microphone. This sensor currently has absolutely no indicator for when it is turned on. This is a very serious concern, given the security and privacy implications of a malicious attacker listening in on a user's daily life and activities.

CONCLUSION

We demonstrated that the current webcam LED is not effective as an indicator to communicate when the webcam is recording. We created our own indicator which significantly improved the rate at which participants noticed it, both during computer-based tasks and for non-computer-based tasks, without significantly decreasing their understanding. We analyzed our participants' previous experience with the webcam on their personal computer/laptop turning on unexpectedly, finding that this previous experience inversely correlated to noticing the webcam LED in our experiments. Based on our experimental results, we offer an initial step towards designing better webcam indicators for user. Finally, we outline the space of future mitigation research as we see it, to make sure users both notice and understand future privacy indicators.

ACKNOWLEDGEMENTS

This work was supported by the Intel Science and Technology Center for Secure Computing (ISTC-SC), NSF under award CNS-1318680, and AFOSR under MURI award FA9550-12-1-0040. We would like to thank Vitaly Dubnovitsky for assistance implementing the webcam glyph.

REFERENCES

1. Abowd, G. D., and Mynatt, E. D. Charting past, present, and future research in ubiquitous computing. *ACM Transactions on Computer-Human Interaction (TOCHI) 7*, 1 (2000), 29–58.

2. Amer, T., and Maris, J.-M. B. Signal Words and Signal Icons in Application Control and Information Technology Exception Messages-Hazard Matching and Habituation Effects. *Journal of Information Systems 21*, 2 (2007), 1–25.

3. Anderson, N. How an Omniscient Internet "Sextortionist" Ruined the Lives of Teen girls. `http://arstechnica.com/tech-policy/2011/09/how-an-omniscient-internet-sextortionist-ruined-lives/`, September 7 2011. Accessed: September 6, 2014.

4. Anderson, N. Meet the Men Who Spy on Women through Their Webcams. `http://arstechnica.com/tech-policy/2013/03/rat-breeders-meet-the-men-who-spy-on-women-through-their-webcams/`, March 10 2013. Accessed: September 5, 2014.

5. Anliker, U., Lukowicz, P., Troester, G., Schwartz, S. J., and DeVaul, R. W. The WearARM: Modular, High Performance, Low Power Computing Platform Designed for Integration into Everyday Clothing. In *Wearable Computers, 2001. Proceedings. Fifth International Symposium on*, IEEE (2001), 167–168.

6. Azuma, R., Baillot, Y., Behringer, R., Feiner, S., Julier, S., and MacIntyre, B. Recent Advances in Augmented Reality. *Computer Graphics and Applications, IEEE 21*, 6 (2001), 34–47.

7. Azuma, R. T., et al. A Survey of Augmented Reality. *Presence 6*, 4 (1997), 355–385.

8. Bellotti, V., and Sellen, A. Design for Privacy in Ubiquitous Computing Environments. In *Proceedings of the Third European Conference on Computer-Supported Cooperative Work 13–17 September 1993, Milan, Italy ECSCW'93*, Springer (1993), 77–92.

9. Brocker, M., and Checkoway, S. iSeeYou: Disabling the MacBook Webcam Indicator LED. In *Proceedings of the 23rd USENIX Security Symposium*, USENIX Association (2014).

10. Cannella, S., Polivy, D. J., Shin, M., Straub, C., and Tamassia, R. Secure Visualization of Authentication Information: A Case Study. In *Visual Languages and Human Centric Computing, 2004 IEEE Symposium on*, IEEE (2004), 35–37.

11. Chan, M., Campo, E., Estève, D., and Fourniols, J.-Y. Smart Homes—Current Features and Future Perspectives. *Maturitas 64*, 2 (2009), 90–97.

12. Chan, M., Estève, D., Escriba, C., and Campo, E. A Review of Smart Homes—Present State and Future Challenges. *Computer methods and programs in biomedicine 91*, 1 (2008), 55–81.

13. Check Point Software Technologies Ltd. Are You Being Watched Through Your Webcam? `http://www.zonealarm.com/blog/2013/10/are-you-being-watched-through-your-webcam/`, October 2 2013. Accessed: September 6, 2014.

14. Chen, Y., and Jones, G. J. Augmenting Human Memory Using Personal Lifelogs. In *Proceedings of the 1st Augmented Human International Conference*, ACM (2010), 24.

15. Costanza, E., Inverso, S. A., Pavlov, E., Allen, R., and Maes, P. Eye-q: Eyeglass Peripheral Display for Subtle Intimate Notifications. In *Proceedings of the 8th conference on Human-computer interaction with mobile devices and services*, ACM (2006), 211–218.

16. Cranor, L. F. What Do They Indicate?: Evaluating Security and Privacy Indicators. *Interactions 13*, 3 (2006), 45–47.

17. DeVaul, R. W., Corey, V. R., et al. The Memory Glasses: Subliminal vs. Overt Memory Support with Imperfect Information. In *2012 16th International Symposium on Wearable Computers*, IEEE Computer Society (2003), 146–146.

18. Dickie, C., Vertegaal, R., Fono, D., Sohn, C., Chen, D., Cheng, D., Shell, J. S., and Aoudeh, O. Augmenting and Sharing Memory with eyeBlog. In *Proceedings of the the 1st ACM workshop on Continuous archival and retrieval of personal experiences*, ACM (2004), 105–109.

19. Dobuzinskis, A. California Man Agrees to Plead Guilty to Extortion of Miss Teen USA. `http://www.reuters.com/article/2013/10/31/us-usa-missteen-extortion-idUSBRE99U1G520131031`, October 31 2013. Accessed: September 5, 2014.

20. Dourish, P., Grinter, R. E., De La Flor, J. D., and Joseph, M. Security in the Wild: User Strategies for Managing Security as an Everyday, Practical Problem. *Personal and Ubiquitous Computing 8*, 6 (2004), 391–401.

21. Eddy, N. Notebook sales outpace desktop sales. `http://www.eweek.com/c/a/Midmarket/Notebook-Sales-Outpace-Desktop-Sales/`, December 24 2008. Accessed: September 9, 2014.

22. Edwards, W. K., and Grinter, R. E. At Home with Ubiquitous Computing: Seven Challenges. In *Ubicomp 2001: Ubiquitous Computing*, Springer (2001), 256–272.

23. Egelman, S., Cranor, L. F., and Hong, J. You've been warned: an empirical study of the effectiveness of web browser phishing warnings. In *Proceedings of the SIGCHI Conference on Human Factors in Computing Systems*, ACM (2008), 1065–1074.

24. Egelman, S., Tsai, J., Cranor, L. F., and Acquisti, A. Timing is Everything?: The Effects of Timing and Placement of Online Privacy Indicators. In *Proceedings of the SIGCHI Conference on Human Factors in Computing Systems*, ACM (2009), 319–328.

25. Electronic Frontier Foundation. Laptop Camera Cover Set. `https://supporters.eff.org/shop/laptop-camera-cover-set`. Accessed: September 6, 2014.

26. Felt, A. P., Chin, E., Hanna, S., Song, D., and Wagner, D. Android permissions demystified. In *Proceedings of the 18th ACM Conference on Computer and Communications Security*, CCS '11, ACM (New York, NY, USA, 2011), 627–638.

27. Filkins, D. What we left behind. *The New Yorker* (April 28 2014).

28. Frederick, S. Cognitive reflection and decision making. *Journal of Economic perspectives* (2005), 25–42.

29. Friedman, B., Hurley, D., Howe, D. C., Felten, E., and Nissenbaum, H. Users' conceptions of web security: A comparative study. In *CHI '02 Extended Abstracts on Human Factors in Computing Systems*, CHI EA '02, ACM (New York, NY, USA, 2002), 746–747.

30. Hill, K. Lower Merion School District and Blake Robbins Reach a Settlement in Spycamgate. `http://www.forbes.com/sites/kashmirhill/2010/10/11/lower-merion-school-district-and-blake-robbins-reach-a-settlement-in-spycamgate/`, October 11 2010. Accessed: September 9, 2014.

31. Hoyle, R., Templeman, R., Armes, S., Anthony, D., Crandall, D., and Kapadia, A. Privacy Behaviors of Lifeloggers Using Wearable Cameras. In *Ubicomp 2014: Ubiquitous Computing* (2014).

32. Kalnikaite, V., Sellen, A., Whittaker, S., and Kirk, D. Now Let Me See Where I Was: Understanding How Lifelogs Mediate Memory. In *Proceedings of the SIGCHI Conference on Human Factors in Computing Systems*, ACM (2010), 2045–2054.

33. Langheinrich, M. Privacy by Design—Principles of Privacy-Aware Ubiquitous Systems. In *Ubicomp 2001: Ubiquitous Computing*, Springer (2001), 273–291.

34. Logitech Forum: Can I Turn off the Red LED? `http://forums.logitech.com/t5/Webcams/Can-I-turn-off-red-LED/m-p/277305#M52816`. Accessed: 2014-09-06.

35. Palen, L., and Dourish, P. Unpacking Privacy for a Networked World. In *Proceedings of the SIGCHI conference on Human factors in computing systems*, ACM (2003), 129–136.

36. Patton, J. H., Stanford, M. S., et al. Factor structure of the barratt impulsiveness scale. *Journal of clinical psychology 51*, 6 (1995), 768–774.

37. Rouse, R. A. Is someone watching you through your webcam? `http://campatch.com/wp-content/uploads/2012/05/CamPatch-Academy-Study-on-Webcam-Hacking-Awareness-May2012.pdf`, May 2012.

38. Schechter, S. E., Dhamija, R., Ozment, A., and Fischer, I. The Emperor's New Security Indicators. In *IEEE Symposium on Security and Privacy* (2007), 51–65.

39. Stewart, D. W., and Martin, I. M. Intended and Unintended consequences of Warning Messages: A Review and Synthesis of Empirical Research. *Journal of Public Policy & Marketing* (1994), 1–19.

40. Whalen, T., and Inkpen, K. M. Gathering Evidence: Use of Visual Security Cues in Web Browsers. In *Proceedings of Graphics Interface 2005*, Canadian Human-Computer Communications Society (2005), 137–144.

From Third to Surveilled Place: The Mobile in Irish Pubs

Norman Makoto Su and Lulu Wang
School of Informatics and Computing
Indiana University Bloomington
normsu@indiana.edu, luluwang@indiana.edu

ABSTRACT
A home away from home, the pub is synonymous with good conversation. Yet, the art of conversation in pubs is changing with the ubiquity of mobile phones. We present a qualitative study spanning over three years describing experiences and rhetoric surrounding the relationship that mobiles have and should have with our conversation in the pub. We found that mobile phones are able to enhance conversation but can also cause a disruption to the informal and adhoc nature of pubs. The use of Facebook on mobile phones has also changed pubs from what Oldenburg terms a third space to a space that is potentially being surveilled. We suggest future designs should not necessarily discourage or encourage mobile use in pubs, but rather provoke us into reflecting on how intertwined modern conversation is with mobile technology in the context of the pub space.

Author Keywords
Mobile phone; cell phone; pub; bar; third place; conversation

ACM Classification Keywords
H.5.m. Information Interfaces and Presentation (e.g. HCI): Miscellaneous

INTRODUCTION
Oldenburg, in his landmark work, *The Great Good Place*, describes the English pub as an exemplar of a *third place* [27][p.123–144]—a home away from home, a site for jest, a business devoid of architectural extravagance, a spot where "regulars" visit, and a "local" that accommodates people from all walks of life. Most importantly, pubs are where the art of conversation is actively practiced and preserved. In a third place, "conversation is not just the main attraction but the sine qua non of the third place" [27][p.28]. These attributes set pubs apart from other social settings like family gatherings that are private and exclusive in character.

In this paper, we describe an analysis of pub goers' experiences with conversation in Irish pubs. Globally, Ireland's identity is closely associated with the public house; *The Lonely Planet Ireland* simply lists "The Pub" as one of Ireland's top destinations and "still the best place to discover what makes the country tick" [13][p.12]. Stereotypically known for their gift of the gab [25][p.97], the Irish have their own terms for describing good conversation—something that involves fun, having the "crack" [17], and "slagging" [34], having good-natured banter. In Ireland, conventions of good conversation such as egalitarianism, inclusiveness, and playfulness are vigorously enforced [34].

CHI 2015, April 18–23, 2015, Seoul, Republic of Korea.

ACM 978-1-4503-3145-6/15/04 ...$15.00.
http://dx.doi.org/10.1145/2702123.2702574

Smoking bans, drunk-driving laws, and increasing costs of alcoholic beverages have all threatened to topple the institution of pubs in Ireland [11]. The number of pubs has declined dramatically since 1908 when there was nearly one pub for every 35 people in some regions of Ireland [17]. Yet, despite these threats, the pub remains an integral part of Irish culture and society. For example, rural pubs are so important for isolated locals to remain engaged with their communities that so-called "booze buses" [5] and publican-owned taxi services [11][p.113,139] are available to transport individuals from their homes to their neighboring water hole.

By altering the prime activity of a third place, modern technology presents another challenge for the livelihood of pubs. From the 1940s, jukeboxes were decried for destroying conversation [27][p.141]. Beer gardens, large screen televisions, built-in restaurants, dance spaces, and blaring music may all signify the inevitable technologization of pubs, but perhaps no artifact has so insidiously technologized pubs as the *mobile phone* (we use the term "mobile" and "cell" phone interchangeably in this paper). Much research has examined the transformative nature of mobiles phones on our society. Infamously, mobiles are known to force people to isolate themselves rather than engage with their immediate surroundings ("present but absent") [15, 18].

Drawing from three years worth of fieldwork in Ireland, we argue that the intersection of mobile phones and conversation has shifted third places into what we call *surveilled places*. Despite the negative connotation of surveillance, this is not meant to be an entirely negative assessment of the relation of mobiles to conversation. Rather, the notion of surveilled places help examine what people value in their conversations and situate the changing and sometimes reflective practices that meld technology with group interactions.

We will make three key contributions that examine at a macro and micro-level how mobiles are having a transformative effect on conversation in pubs.

1. We detail how and to what degree conversation in Irish pubs has been colored by mobile phones. In doing so, we also describe how patrons construct notions of "proper" talk in pubs. Our findings reveal that the art of conversation has become one of balancing the degree to which digital truth from mobile phones play a role in banter.
2. We note how mobiles have visibly become part of the pub landscape. The mobile itself and its apps (the technology) become a topic of conversation in pubs, yet also serves to deflect the adhoc nature of conversations usually afforded by pubs.
3. Finally, we describe how Facebook specifically has transformed pubs from a third place—a home away from home—into a space that, while providing rich content for illustrative purposes in conversation, is potentially surveilled by friends and others.

DATA COLLECTION AND METHODOLOGY

Fieldwork of Irish pubs and mobile phones was conducted over a three year period in Ireland (2011-2013). As part of their degree requirement, students in a masters of information and library science program at a university in Dublin were supervised by the first author to carry out semi-structured interviews and observations on the relationship of technology with Irish pubs. Interviews were audio recorded and transcribed. Interviews were 45 minutes to an hour long, and observations were an hour long. The study was approved by the university's ethical review board. Consent forms clearly specified that interviews were part of a research study.

Data collection was iteratively supervised over three phases:

Phase I 2011–2012 (144 interviews): Interviews with pub goers (those who visit a pub at least once a week) focused broadly on technology's place in Irish pubs. Observations and interviews examined at least two pubs—one where informants recently went to and a different pub with a contrasting environment (e.g., urban vs rural).

Phase II 2012 (15 interviews): A select team of master students were supervised to conduct grounded theory analysis of the Phase I interviews. The topic of conversation and mobile phones in Irish pubs was found to be a prevalent theme in the data. A new interview protocol focused on conversation and mobile phones in pubs was created. Using this new protocol, 15 new interviews were conducted.

Phase III 2013 (64 interviews): Students utilized the new interview protocol from Phase II to conduct 64 new interviews. As in Phase I, observations were conducted in pubs, and interviews were done with pub goers in Ireland.

Our total dataset had 54% (121) males and 46% (102) females. All interviewees were at least 18 years old, but we were unfortunately unable to collect detailed age information on our informants. Based on our interview content and the typical age range of the master students, we can surmise that most of our informants would be classified as young professionals. Informants from Phase I discussed pubs both in and away from Dublin (e.g., informants often discussed pubs in their hometown). Latter interviews were biased towards pubs in Dublin. Overall, a wide variety of pubs were discussed (e.g., traditional, sport, dance, trendy, etc.), irrespective of location. In Dublin, for example, it is easy to find an assortment of dissimilar pubs within walking distance of each other.

Guided by a grounded theory approach, a team of researchers carried out open coding on the student collected data to identify and iterate general themes of cell phones and conversation in pubs. Generated codes were then refined through axial coding and written into the findings of this paper. Interviews from each year and phase were analyzed until knowledge saturation was reached. Findings were also triangulated with the first author's extensive fieldwork in Irish pubs from a separate ethnographic study focusing on the use of technology by traditional musicians [38]. Our analysis drew from a discourse analysis viewpoint [31] where we take the informants' interviews not simply as empirical reports of activities and thoughts but as texts whose rhetoric construct what makes proper conversation in the space of pubs. 129 interviews (41 from Phase I 2011, 45 from Phase I 2012, 15 from Phase II 2012, and 28 from Phase III 2013) in total were analyzed by the researchers.

RELATED WORK

The public use of mobiles subjects them to scrutiny from others and exerts influence on others. There is a large body of work centering on the consensus that mobiles are a double-edged sword: they engender newly efficient forms of coordination and social contact while creating new challenges for users who must cope with this pervasive overlap between public and private spheres of life.

In urban landscapes, mobile phones have been noted to encourage a new frenetic and adhoc style of coordination and communication. A study of mobile users in Norway found that cell phones provide a bridge between transportation and coordination in the everyday life of cities. Called "micro-coordination," this behavior allows meeting times and places to be continuously negotiated amongst local and remote actors [24]. Going beyond micro-coordination, a study [33] of Tokyo youths observed what they call "hyper-connectivity": the continual real-time cultivation of virtual companionship via text messages and emails. Another study [41], this time with Taiwanese college students, found that this cultivation strengthens and creates new bonds with professional contacts, friends, and family. Mobile phones have served to create a "personal community society" [7] where person-to-person contact is now independent of place, and, in fact, the public space is appropriated for private use.

With near instantaneous access to "different social relationships, groupings, organizations or institutions" [16] the management of boundaries between these actors becomes difficult. For example, mobiles were found to create distressing spillovers between boundaries of work and family [8, 36] and an expectation of constant availability [16] in our social worlds. This collision of spaces [30] is especially problematic when trying to discern proper behavior in interacting simultaneously with one's virtual participants and those locally around in public places.

Indeed, the freedom gained through unprecedented connectivity comes at the cost of unwanted encroachment of personal interactions into public spaces. As Daslgaard and Hansen [12] might frame it, mobiles are a public performance of a visibly private interaction. Simply put, mobile users steal away public space and force bystanders to become eavesdroppers: "the mobile telephone disturbs...a whole complex of interactions used to manage our navigation through a conversation and more generally through everyday situations such as bus rides and the like" [23]. In public spaces such as restaurants, cafes, theatres, and public transport, proximate spectators feel that etiquette has been irritatingly breeched by mobile users [40, 3]. Yet, researchers have noted that the ephemeral nature of mobile conversations combined with a growing acclimation to mobiles in everyday public spaces has led to constant redefinition of mobile phone etiquette [14].

There are a number of works noting the phenomena of "absent presence" [15], "telecocooning" [18], "fragmentation of attention in mobile interaction" [29], and being "oblivious to their surroundings" [2]. All these concepts touch upon the observation that one's mobile interactions can often conflict with our proximate interactions. As a result, the quality of real interactions suffer when one is forced to overhear strangers' mobile conversations [39, 26], friends interrupt their companions with their mobiles [22], and spontaneous encounters with strangers are rebuffed with publicly visible mobile use [14]. The level of disruption is dependent on the implicit rules imbued with a particular public place [14].

Another related topic studied has been on mobile search behavior in social settings. The current location, time, activity, and people involved have been found to be valuable contexts in shaping a mobile search query [35]. A series of excellent studies by Church et al. [10, 9] utilizing diary study and experience sampling methods over a 2-week period examined the information seeking behaviors of cell phone and smartphone users. A large percentage of mobile searches were found to be fact-checking/trivia and general informational type searches [10]; moreover, nearly 65% of searches take place in the presence of other people. Perhaps most relevant to this paper is a later study scrutinizing mobile search in social settings [9]. Church et al. showed that location and a need to assist an activity was a important factor for initiating a social mobile search; the leading—over a third of diary study entries—information need was trivia and pop culture. Like our own study, they note that mobile search can enhance conversation but also artificially remove users from a conversation, end conversations prematurely, and can label the searcher as a "know-it-all." Without minimizing Church et al.'s contributions, our own work employs a broader ethnographic angle (not just mobile search) that seeks to go beyond categorizing mobile use and its motivations by unpacking the coupling of technology and people with place.

Some studies have focused on specific loci. Ling [22] notes that restaurants have both public and private spaces as well as a strong set of norms and rituals. Cafeterias on the other hand are noisy environments where the invasion of personal space with mobiles is more lax. Campbell [6] carried out a cross-cultural comparison of perceptions of mobile phones in public settings such as movie theaters, restaurants, buses, grocery stores, classrooms, and sidewalks. Participants reported less tolerance for mobile phone use in settings involving collective action—settings like classrooms and restaurants where participants are engaged in activities. Ames's [2] enlightening study of iPhones amongst "digital-natives" focuses on a locale, Stanford University, whose members represent the extreme side of technological savviness and privilege. Such users embraced email rather than texting and found voice to require undue attention and intimacy. Some of the results confirm other studies such as the increased pressure to be constantly contactable, behaviors reflecting differences in the "proper" etiquette to balance virtual networks with immediate surroundings, and complaints about telecocooning. Perhaps most relevant to our study are her findings that iPhones can contribute to conversation or the creation of new collaborative activities through the showing off of novel apps, music, videos, or information found online. Lastly, Benford et al. [4] reflect upon the use of technology in the context of Irish traditional music. Benford et al. examined the accomplishment of sequencing tunes in folk music sessions and suggests designing for "situated discretion." Since cell phones are a common, accepted sight in pubs, they are ideal platforms for designing technologies that facilitate traditional music making.

Our research builds upon past work by providing a holistic perspective into the socio-technical practices in a third place. That is, we describe how the third "place" [20], as we recognizably understand it, is a constant blend of both long-held and evolving practices of conversation. In this paper, mobiles as a technological foci allow us to extrapolate what people *value* in their pub conversations, how technology itself becomes a subject of conversation, how new innovations reconfigure what it means to be a third place, and how patrons endeavor to make sense of this reconfiguration. Our novelty perhaps does not lie on any single piece of our findings, but rather in attempting to bring these pieces together in a rich narrative about the mobile's ubiquity in the third place.

MOBILE AS TRUTH: CONVERSING WITH MOBILES

What makes a great conversation? Our pub goers thought good conversation entailed a variety of topics, had good flow, and was inclusive. Good conversation is emotive and evokes banter. However, as Oldenburg and Brissett [28] note, "even exceptionally witty persons, and even when they are in 'rare form,' will not dominate conversation for long, for people are there...not to enjoy monologues." Mobile phones serve to both enhance and stunt back-and-forth conversation by providing instant, truthful statements. All quotes below are labeled with a unique identifier representing the informant.

Winning the Debate

Heated debates are a key form of play in a pub. As a place for friendly banter and slagging, pub goers enjoyed being able to show each other up. Echoing work by Church et al. [9], nearly all of the informants remarked on how phones allow them to find information to settle debates. Google, Wikipedia, Facebook, IMDB (a movie database app), Shazam (an app to recognize music), sports apps (e.g., Sky Sports), dictionary/thesaurus apps, and news apps (e.g., thejournal.ie) were commonly mentioned as information sources during debates. These data sources transform the mobile into a definitive symbol for truth against which no one can argue. Common topics of debate were current events, historical facts (e.g., has anyone died from a hockey injury?), scientific trivia (e.g., does this drug contain caffeine?), pop culture—movie and TV trivia was especially prominent, and sports (e.g., how many goals did a soccer player score?).

Satisfaction was gained when something unknown or unclear was resolved: "You're thinking 'Aw I know that' and it's on the tip of your tongue, but then with the phone in your hand it's, you have all the information there and you can look it up and [laughs], you can make yourself feel better when you find out the answer (P303)." Conversations that struggle from "group amnesia (P308)" need to be cured. P301 describes the frustration of stagnant, struggling conversations: "You can be milling about the same thing in circles, going round...and round it, and I suppose that [mobile] pulls you out of that...little circle, and moves you on to something fresh...So it can move the conversation along that bit quicker, and get you on to a new topic." One informant particularly relishes being the "first" to find a fact (P239): "I would probably go to the phone first of all because I always like to be first with the answer on things or kind of know all the facts to have the right answer. So I would tend to be a bit impetuous and kind of go straight away."

Not only can it end topics quicker, mobiles help transition topics. Here, a pub goer remembers a conversation about the movie *Jaws* and how looking up facts on the movie eventually led to a new topic about an actor in the movie:

> We talked about the end scene in Jaws and talking about how shit a movie it is, and how amazing it is at the same time, and one of our other friends looked it up, and said "Aw, it's Quint," and then he said, "I can't remember even who the actor is now" But, then we started talking about one of the actors and he said "Aw he was in this movie as well," and then we completely turned the conversation away from Jaws. Just, it about-turned straight away just from somebody looking up one piece of information on the Internet.

In this case, information seeking on the mobile kept the flow of conversation going in a positive manner.

Facebook also featured prominently in debates. Because it serves as a historical backdrop to past events, patrons were able to bolster their arguments by providing *evidence*—citing past posts, comments, or photos. One informant related a debate between two of her girlfriends:

> One of the other girls was saying, "Oh, you know, I'm stronger than you,"...as a joke, but Lara was like "What are you talking about? Like, I'm stronger than you" or...I play sports I'm stronger, and Alice was saying "No, I'm pretty sure that you told me, one day when you were drunk or not, that *I* am strong," and then this went back and forth... and then they were convinced that it had been put online, on Facebook somewhere, one day after a night out, so they then went and...basically searched through comments...trying to find the one time that someone might have said something, about being stronger than the other.

Debates have a competitive spirit to them that might threaten a third space's democratic spirit. One informant mentioned how the routine use of phones for information seeking has made debates more fair and less susceptible to bullying: "I think people are less likely to...jam an opinion in a factual manner—in a pseudo-factual manner—down someone's throat just because they can be more aggressive or more domineering in the conversation, and that's how they win it (P246)." Another informant called this "bullshit detection" (P308). More commonly, pub patrons told us that phones were able to help point out statements that they *knew* were true or false. For example, during a discussion regarding the 2013 meat adulteration scandal (Irish ground beef was found to contain horse meat), an informant was able to support what he knew to be patently false—that horse-meat is more expensive than beef. Here, social mobile search not only enabled "personal empowerment" [9], but a form of *evidentiary empowerment* that prevented them from being marginalized in the pub's competitive environment.

With the mobile playing a key role in conversational debate, the definition of being skilled in the art of conversation shifts. Now, the "authoritative person," rather than being knowledgeable, is someone skilled at looking for information on mobile phones. Such a person has an upper-hand in settling debates, winning bets, and gaining access to the truth.

Losing Authentic Banter

While mobiles allow a satisfactory conclusion to a debate or struggling conversation, they also threaten to remove the characteristic back-and-forth banter that debates encourage. Church et al. [9] noted that mobile search can end an interesting discussion. More specifically, our informants believed talk *about* facts (rather than talk containing real facts) was important. P252 noted in a debate discussing actor Daniel Day-Lewis's Oscar winnings that before mobiles there would be a spirited discussion of truth: "you'd generate this...healthy debate about who knew more or what was right and...it was...using this skill of debating things out that would go on for a while, and might cause some tension or some heat or might just be friendly banter."

Mobiles aid in finding the truth but at the loss of "authentic fact finding," or using your "own brain to think" (P304). P401 describes the eureka moment achieved as a group as immensely satisfying but lost now: "you can't have the sort of discussion where somebody can't remember a fact anymore, and it kind of eats away at everyone for the evening until someone finally remembers what they were trying to remember." P303 called the experience of remembering "it for yourself instead of...looking it up online...really, really satisfying." In contrast, by immediately settling a debate, the conversation is "diluted" (P252). It may be "better not knowing...being uncertain (P242)". One group of friends had an "informal ban on using the smart phone" (P354) to ensure that conversations remain authentic—that they kept going before reaching a foregone conclusion with smartphone usage. This authentic way towards fact finding is a form of challenge [9].

The awkward pause instigated by looking up facts affects the rhythm of conversation. P308 eloquently describes an ideal conversation as one that has a particular *rhythm* to it:

> A conversation will ebb and flow, and especially with people that know each other really well and can unconsciously get into this kind of rhythm where just the conversation kind of passes around, and if you're talking about pure trivia, about what actor appeared in what film back in the 70's or something, and you say "Well we could look it up?" I'd say, "Well don't bother, I don't want to break the rhythm of the conversation, the conversation's flowing quite nicely. I'm enjoying it, and if we stop and everyone goes and checks...what some unimportant fact is, it might come back and the conversation, the rhythm is broken."

When people bring out mobiles to look up information, it creates an unnatural chasm in the conversation. Conversation doesn't "flow...when you have a phone there to access information: you...have to pause, check it up, and then give the answer. (P308)" A fragmented conversation [29, 22] does not possess the seamless flow desired in the pub. Spotty wifi or mobile network access serve to exacerbate the situation. In a group, the mobile phone also demarcates the haves and have-nots, creating a different kind of marginalization: "I'm especially conscious when...say if there's six of us out and three of us have phones where you can look stuff up and the other three don't, because I think that's really boring for the other three. (P408)"

By poisoning the third place's conversation with instant truth, participants become reluctant to debate on shaky grounds: "So the debate doesn't continue onto, em, 'I bet you 7 pints, that I'm right'...[B]ecause nobody is going to risk it anymore with that. (P395)" The need for banter untouched by hard facts reflects the belief of the pub as an informal space. Conversations situated in informal spaces need not be factual. Some informants questioned whether knowing the truth mattered in a pub: "[Someone saying,] 'No, you're wrong, look at this on Wikipedia. You're wrong.'...would...kill the conversation and at the end of the day what difference does it really make? I mean, if it's only a conversation—a light hearted conversation in the pub? (P314)"

As a result, some informants choose to either not search (and let the other party think he or she is right) or to defer searching for the sake of conversation. Others worried about being perceived as a "know-it-all" [9] or "bully." By always being the devil's advocate, one pub patron opined, "I'd go so far as to say it can damage a friendship, or can ruin your evening (P241)." One person (P260) described how she looked up data "diplomatically": "I might subtly check it...when the person isn't looking and...I may even keep the information to myself if I was right and they were wrong."

Last, our informants mentioned that effect that mobiles had on table quizzes. Obviously, informants are able to cheat by looking up answers on their phone. Quizzes sometimes have policies to reduce cheating like requiring everyone to place their phone face down in the front of them or put all the phones in a bucket. Perhaps more surprising, however, is that cheating is generally tolerated—turning the table quiz into a test of one's information seeking skills. Here P401 notes that cheating and accusations of cheating are par for the course: "There were definitely allegations going around of people cheating as far as phones go but...it was the sort of thing that people, in the usual banter of a table quiz, [do]." While a minority of our informants who took table quizzes seriously admonished the rampant cheating going on, many of our table quiz participants readily confessed to being the "worst cheaters (P431)." Thus, even table quizzes are not to be taken too seriously, and the banter gained from cheating with mobiles may make it worthwhile.

Having discussed how mobiles augment conversation, we now turn to how mobiles themselves become the topic or focus of conversation.

THE VISIBLE MOBILE: MOBILES WITH CONVERSING

Without doubt, the mobile phone is ubiquitous in pubs. Informants assumed their friends had mobile phones with them. They overwhelmingly acknowledged that mobiles, used tactfully, was not a breach of etiquette [14]: "in reality you just...get used to people texting and...people checking their Internet and...as long as it's not for the whole night you don't mind. (P422)" Many pubs now have free wifi—"it's like they expect their patrons to have...their phones" (P428). In congruence with past works [2], nearly all our informants acknowledged being attached to their phone. Informants remarked that their phone was "glued" to their hand (P238) and that whenever they forgot to bring their phone at the pub, they felt "half naked" (329).

In some cases, mobile attachment itself became a topic of conversation in pubs. P252 gave a synposis of the "iPhone tower" game she played with her friends:

> There was a game called the iPhone tower when you go to the pub everyone has to put their smart phones in a tower in the middle of the table, upside down and...the first person to pick up their phone...[you'd]...make them buy a round of drinks just to give out to them for not being able to sit down with their phone for ten minutes.

P252 played this game to hold her friends accountable, shaming those that become a "present but absent" [15] friend into buying drinks. Informants acknowledged that though they understood the detrimental effect of prolonged phone usage on conversation, their own behaviors labeled them as hypocrites. This observed attachment of mobiles by others became a source of light hearted slagging: "if ever any of our friends have their phone out for ages so that they haven't been contributing much to the conversation, we'll kinda jokingly say to them...'Put your phone away there! (P303)' "

Many informants *did* feel that a particular behavior of phone *non-usage* was disrespectful and encouraged people to become removed from conversation: putting the phone visibly on the table in a pub. On the surface this may seem like a way to balance being alert of people trying to contact you and participating in conversation. However, informants like P401 despair of this practice: "Everyone...puts their phone on the table in a little pool in the middle. And I think that's a kind of strange thing to do because it's almost as if people are not happy with the company they're in—that they're waiting to see...is somebody else going to contact them or is something exciting going to [happen]?"

By making a concerted *effort* to meet together in the pub, informants expected their colleagues to engage in the third place's primary activity: face-to-face conversation: "I don't really like when we're in...conversation and suddenly it's like you have to stop talking because they're texting somebody ten miles away...I feel that I've made the effort to come out so...I want some attention...I feel unloved [laughter] (P300)." One respondent told us that these heavy users of the phone at the pub might as well be talking to them online because they aren't contributing. Anything that detracts from "the whole point of going to the pub, to talk and to catch up" is unauthentic.

Pub patrons acknowledged that the degree of technologization of a pub influences the acceptability of phones. In so-called "old man pubs," informants were less likely to bring out their phones. One patron described how the ambience of the pub shapes the visibility of her phone (P252): "So there's O'Neills on Suffolk Street where you go in and get a good dinner but it's still a kind of old fashioned pub, they don't have TVs everywhere, they have kind of snug booths where you're forced to converse with each other and I find you're looking at kind of older men at the bar reading papers and doing crosswords....You're a lot less likely to take your phone out for something because you're kind of in that environment." Just as tolerance with mobiles in spaces like restaurants may be limited [22, 6], certain types of pub seem to implicitly prioritize conversation over technology.

Social Camouflage and Meeting Strangers

Pubs not only offer the chance to converse with friends but to converse with strangers. In a pub, chatting with unfamiliar people is not unusual. P395 makes a distinction between the public nature of a pub and a street: "If you were in the pub and you seen somebody sitting there, you can walk up to somebody randomly, and it [the pub] kinda removes all of the...faux-pas. You can go and talk to somebody that you wouldn't if you seen somebody standing on the side of the road." Our informant further remarks that the nature of pubs to encourage such interactions is *weakened* once people use phones in dead time: "If you're looking at a screen...you're not going to be able to initiate any interaction because somebody looking at the side of your head means nothing [unless] you make eye contact with somebody."

As *social camouflage*, mobile phones allows patrons to perform an act (e.g., texting) that is perceived as being socially engaged, thus signaling that he or she is busy or "unapproachable" (P323). Remarkably, informants described this act guiltily, as a sort of nervous twitch they have acquired. Whether arriving early to a pub or waiting for friends in the bathroom, the phone was a comforting things to turn to. The phone becomes a "security blanket"; one informant described how his "busy work" was not even real:

> You take it [mobile] out just to kinda remove yourself from being...exposed to everybody else...[chuckle]. You're pretending to text even if you're not doing so. Or you're reading old texts, text messages or maybe cleaning up your phone. Carrying out a ridiculous task that you wouldn't do in any other occasion. So I suppose we use technology to shield ourselves from possible interaction with other people.

Another informant called her phone her "new cigarette": "You're trying to avoid looking like a loner, and the kind of sympathetic glances that you might get because you're sitting on your own, and how do you...pass the time? But it's like the new cigarette for me, because...when you used to be able to smoke, it was kind of a comfort thing, to kind of have something to do (P239)." This security blanket has similarities to telecocooning [18] but, when situated in pubs, has the added effect of limiting spontaneous conversations with strangers, a key characteristic of third places.

The Phone as Entertainment

P321 succinctly told us that "since the smartphone came in...your phone is now a source of entertainment rather than just a contact tool." In some sense, the phone can now serve as a replacement for traditional pub games (e.g., drinking games, darts, pinball machines, and slot machines).

Novel, weird, and quirky apps can catalyze new conversations. In this excerpt, a pub goer talks of using an app to check your eyesight for entertainment, passing the phone around:

> There's an App to check your eyesight, it's a Vision Express App...but clearly it's just to make you go to Vision Express to buy a pair of glasses, but, we were all passing it around, there was a good maybe, 10 or 15 of us. The phone actually tells you that you've [got] astigmatism, which is a bit bizarre that a phone can tell you that...we just ended up talking around that kind of thing.

Other unusual cases involve setting the language on a phone to Chinese, texting a friend in the pub in Chinese, and translating Chinese text to English. Several users had "weird fact" apps that generate random trivia they would read out loud to friends—essentially, a conversation generator.

With video and music, the smartphone becomes a literal entertainment system. Several informants described using their phones in this manner: "I mean even when you're predrinking with a friend...a random song comes into your head, you...whip out your iPhone. Somehow, you can go onto YouTube...and you can just type in that song and all of a sudden you're like [informant dances]. (P317)"

As a device capable of video, the mobile has the ability to create a more impactful, funny story than words alone could accomplish. Here, an informant describes showing his friends in a pub a clip of President Obama singing (P318): " I showed clips of President Obama singing...friends of mine said no way, ya didn't see it, there he is lots of oohing and aahing, that's really cool, it was cool to have the ability to show it on the Internet, rather than just describe it."

The use of apps to, as P317 put it, "spark" a conversation is good, but not when it *leads* the conversation. The use of apps can inadvertently lead to a "domino effect." Just as people can get distracted by multitasking applications on a desktop, pub goers's conversations can get sidetracked by their apps/websites. This can give the conversation a desired flow but can dominate the direction of the conversation, wresting control away from the participants:

> Cause if you look one thing up, and then go "Oh what's this?", and then you're there reading your phone at the table with your friends all around you. There's not much point in going out and being in a pub and being social if you're gonna have your head stuck in a phone the whole time, you know.

Another informant thought this back-and-forth with videos on the phone essentially "dries up a conversation (P240)."

We next discuss the ubiquity of Facebook in Irish pubs and how it functions to illustrate and enhance conversations with factual statements about events and people but possibly at the cost of privacy.

FACEBOOK: SURVEILLED CONVERSATION

Facebook is immensely popular in Ireland; in 2013 there were 2.2 million Facebook users in Ireland and 57% of users over 15 years old have a Facebook page [1]. Dublin has the highest penetration of Facebook users of any county in Ireland: 3 out of every 4 Dubliners has a Facebook profile [1]. As a result, the Facebook app occupied such a significant portion of our informants' experiences in the pub that we believe it merits dedicated discussion. Church et al. [9] briefly mention that photo mobile search results are often shared in a group. We will go into detail how Facebook creates a new role for the phone as an *illustrator* of events and the implications of capturing and publicly displaying such events.

The Phone as an Illustrator

Pub regulars used their phones as an illustrative tool to enhance their conversations. Facebook photos were an extremely popular way to illustrate new (e.g., a new bandanna for a dog), funny/racy (e.g., someone they had "scored" last weekend), or significant events in a person's life. For example, P240 talks about a conversation in the pub with her coworkers: "Someone had just got engaged, so she was showing us pictures of her fiancé and of their engagement party."

Interestingly, phones were used to illustrate events or facts that pertained to *absent* members of the conversation such as mutual friends abroad: "You know how Kate is getting on? Oh well, she was over in Newcastle there and...these are the photos from the weekend (P245)." One informant (P239) joked, "It's talking about them behind their back and you literally have access to all their information instantly in your hand." Facebook expands one's proximate circle of friends to include absent peers.

Phones were also used in pubs to illustrate with the group about shared past experiences such as vacations or past recordings in the pub. An informant (P302) talks about his trip to Spain with his friends: "We were bullfighting in Bilbao and somebody got video footage of it so it'd be a funny thing to show around...you know [laughs] a bunch of Irish boys bull fighting in Spain!"

Interestingly, the pub itself was seen as a place to immediately illustrate events to several co-located groups around them in a pub. P238 here talks of a Christmas dinner party held at a pub:

> So there's 10 tables of 10 people...and if you [do] something silly at one table, well 9 other people have cameraphones and smartphones. So 9 other people will probably take it out of their pocket and video it and at least 2 of them, if not more, I would say guaranteed two or more, will post it up on Facebook. Pretty much straight away. So that the people on the other side of the room, if they're friends, have now just seen [it].

Lastly, the phone's capacity to illustrate allows it to explain connections better than words could. Here, P305 jogs another's memory: "I was telling the girls that I'm in college with that my sister was starting college next year and one of them she tried to think if she knew who my sister was, and I just showed her on Facebook and she was able to then say, 'Oh yeah, I've seen her before.' " In effect, the mobile serves to richly include one's network of friends and acquaintances into the conversation.

Surveilling the Third Place

With all the advantages afforded by phones and their apps, a constant fear permeated most of the interviews: the apparent paradox of the pub being a place to relax and the increasing rate at which activities in a pub are captured and publicly displayed. For the illustrative functionality in the previous section to be possible, activities in pubs must be captured by someone. What the mobile captures is seen as a true representation of transpired events. P413 puts it well: "In terms of social media sites, it's there in black and white. It's recorded digitally. So it means that there's a history that these will be accessible to a lot of people." Thus, photos and videos are "evidence" (P413) on Facebook for others to peruse.

As pubs are locales for drinking and entertainment, the most obvious concern for informants was that phones would capture them in embarrassing situations. With the younger crowd, "coming towards like the middle of the night or the end of the night people are not so much aware and it's not until the next day that you see photos that...I can't remember...being taken (P420)." As people get drunk one will inevitably "take some stupid photographs of myself with my friends, and I'll send it to everyone together (P241)."

Most informants agreed that the phone was valuable in capturing special events in a pub such as a going-away or birthday party. In that sense, it was *expected* that there would be active recording of activities in the pub. Naturally, pub participants would want to reminisce about these significant events (as mentioned in the previous section).

However, one informant disclosed a story regarding his coworker at a work event in a pub. His coworker was caught singing; however, the singing, while embarrassing, was not the main issue:

> There was an email sent around work the following day and I know everyone had a bit of a chuckle with it. One of the fellas I worked with made an interesting point to me...[H]e wasn't best pleased he was videoed singing and didn't want everyone to know. He made a point if he was standing beside the person who was videotaping not realizing he was being videotaped he could have been talking about anybody from work. He could have been saying something about the boss or a co-worker...that would have been caught on tape and if that was sent around...that could cause all sorts of ructions.

The coworker realized his own conversations were being (probably innocuously) monitored. Though a pub is seen as a place where you can let your guard down and relax, the possibility of capture completely changes the nature of pubs.

One informant (P317) vehemently felt that Facebook was destroying his freedom in pubs:

> I feel sorry for people. I'd know some younger people—I'd be friends with them on Facebook, and they'd go out on a night out, just on an innocuous night to the pub, and it would be documented with about sixty photos taken on a phone, put on Facebook, checked in, all commenting on it, checked out, 3 o'clock—is now in bed...I don't think...they realise...how much they're putting their civil liberties in jeopardy by just giving this information away so freely...I don't partake in this stuff because I want to...try keep whatever freedoms I can.

For this patron, pubs should be a place where you can just slip off the map and enjoy a pint with your closest friends. Facebook friends would not necessarily be his closest friends and most informants agreed that many of their Facebook "friends" would not be people they would feel comfortable sharing any sort of photo with.

MAKING/LIMITING THE SURVEILLED SPACE

Some pub owners have taken radical approaches to keep "modernisation" out of their premises by banning all "disruptive electrical contraptions on their premises." One such publican is Eugene Kavanagh of the Gravedigger pub: "We've no TV, no noise box, no phone, and people really talk to one another." Similarly, publican Tommy Smith kept his pub, Grogan's, free from all radio and television devices, which is why, Kearns [21] believes, it is "Dublin's last genuine literary pub." Previously, it was largely agreed that a non-technological artifact has had the most effect on conversation in pubs—the 2009 smoking ban in Ireland [11]. The smoking ban created a proliferation of beer gardens and other areas where smokers could smoke and converse in peace. In fact, it is not uncommon to find many non-smokers in the smoking area conversing with their fellow smoking friends. Pubs, while sharing the goal of fostering conversation, are nonetheless a contested place where everyone's own conception of conversation (and technology's role in it) must deal with each other's.

We do not suggest that phone bans are a "solution" for preserving pub conversation. Indeed, our main contribution is to unpack the interplay between mobiles and, ostensibly, the pub's main activity—conversation. However, we believe there is utility in provoking users to confront what effects their mobile uses may have on the pub space as well as others. In other words, by surveilling our own surveillance, we can better reflect and judge what sort of conversation we may be missing or want to happen. Robles et al. [32] suggest that systems that transparently reveal who is being monitored are more accepted by users. Thus, instead of creating technologies that fit the mold of situated discretion [4], we can develop technologies that are conspicuous—announcing one's practices. We outline two possible venues for reflecting on mobile use in pubs through design ideations.

Making Mobile Use Conspicuous: Our findings show that people are often unaware of the effects their mobile have in pubs. Yet, many acknowledge that use can transform the nature of conversations. The below exploratory designs make mobile use obvious to allow participants to reexamine the space and group dynamics in pubs:

The Fact Finder Jukebox: When pub goers wish to look up facts on the smartphone, they must now physically go to a visible machine, "a jukebox of facts," to find and retrieve them. The jukebox forces one to physically get up and remove themselves from the conversation. This act mimics the act of being present but absent due to mobile use.
The Phone Timer/Tower app: Pub goers use this app to keep track amongst their friends how long/often they have been on their phones. This allows users to be accountable for being part of the conversation; users will avoid being "that person" who is always on the phone. The tower app is similar to the phone timer but forces the first person to use their phone to buy everyone a drink.
The Fake Post Projector: This is a projector in the pub that pretends to post, in real-time, the Facebook posts or SMS texts happening within the pub. This may be provocative but will allow pub goers to consider how capture and display of events in the pub may violate the privacy of those around them.

Reconfiguring the Pub Space: The pub itself is a socially constructed place. Our study has emphasized how actors seek to maintain the pub as a third place—a place whose primary activity is conversation. We suggest ways in which apps may empower patrons to more easily reconfigure the pub space to reflect their own balance between the phone's intrusion and benefits.

Making Facts Ambiguous: Pub goers may look up trivia for conversation, but the answers are deliberately ambiguous to foster further discussion. Thus, the phone can continue to encourage new topics for conversation.
Mobile Areas: Just like smoking areas, pubs can adopt areas that allow mobiles or are free of mobiles. Just as traditional pubs often have private and public areas, a mobile area gives users the freedom to choose to what degree conversation should include mobiles.
Smartphone Limiter: The pub as a whole has a limit on mo-

bile usage. Users become aware (e.g., no more drinks served) if that limit is collectively reached. Users then must consider how much disruption phones can have on the entire pub.

App Limiter: People use an app beforehand to enforce what apps are allowed during conversation. This again forces people to reflect upon their reliance on apps when conversing.

Making Capture Ambiguous: Here, social media apps reduce, or make more hazy, the factual, evidence-based capture of photos and videos. For example, photos may automatically redact who you are with or a Facebook check-in into a pub will only vaguely state "some pub in Dublin." Redacted data may be uncensored when used for brief, face-to-face illustrative purposes. This will protect the privacy of pub goers while allowing the use of the phone to improve conversation.

CONCLUSION AND FUTURE WORK

Surveilled places can simultaneously reinforce and threaten the ideals of third places. In such a place, technologies provide quick, instant access to the truth. For pubs, this allows one to settle debates, win competitions, richly illustrate stories, end struggling conversations, and transition to new uncharted topics of conversation. Mobiles provide new and fluid forms of entertainment to the group as well as the opportunity to incorporate other networks of acquaintances into the conversation. In a surveilled place, however, technologies threaten conversation by creating the present-but-absent, anti-social, and app-addicted patron. Facebook and similar apps may transform the third space into a policed space ripe for recording and broadcasting in the pub.

Our informants are fully aware of the rhetoric to maintain the authenticity of the pub as a space for banter, slagging, and good conversation while leveraging the benefits afforded by mobile phones. This dual-edged sword of mobile phones has been remarked upon by other researchers. Harmon & Mazmanian [19] describe an ongoing discourse between the benefits and detriments in choosing to increase technological integration or "dis-integrate" the smart phone from daily life. Ames [2] observed that college students had to reconcile their own definition of what an authentic, natural relationship to others was with the authenticity forced upon them by the technological behaviors afforded by the mobile phone (e.g., constant connectivity and non face-to-face interactions). Each mobile user has his or her own conception of an "authentic" conversation (which may change depending on the context).

For patrons, there is no single notion of proper conversation in a third place. For example, some are more willing to jump to the mobile for fact finding than others, whereas others use the phone as a last resort in a struggling debate. Similarly, each pub space has its own conception of authentic conversation. For example, some pubs may offer or refuse access to free wifi. Our work dealt in broad strokes of modern and old man pubs. Future work may focus on the edges cases—pubs that have taken deliberate attempts (e.g., phone bans) to prevent any move to a surveilled place.

The scope of our paper does not allow us to address other important aspects of Irish pubs. Our study did not touch on pubs as gendered spaces. For instance, our informants sometimes had stereotyped notions of how men and women use mobiles with conversation (e.g., females prefer to post photos on Facebook, while males prefer to use sport apps). There is also a need to systematically understand shifting viewpoints on conversation in pubs. Different generations or life phases (e.g., birth of first child), may influence one's practices and rhetoric regarding third places. Lastly, future work may contrast third places, which are characteristically *public* locales, with the particular practices and rhetoric regarding mobile use elicited in *private* social settings such as family gatherings and private parties [37].

ACKNOWLEDGMENTS

We wish to acknowledge Aoife Cassidy, Kristen Coulas, James Flannery, Evelyn Gallagher, and Sarah Reidy for assistance with data collection, related work, and refinement of the interview protocol. We thank Steven Voyk for coding some of the interviews and conducting a literature search. Amanda Lazar and Leslie S. Liu provided invaluable last minute assistance with our paper edits. Lastly, our anonymous reviewers have all helped to improve this paper.

REFERENCES

1. Abbott, L. News on Digital Advertising, Online Marketing, Social Media & Trends from EigthyTwenty » Facebook Users in Ireland by County, Dec. 2013. http://www.eightytwenty.ie/blog/facebook-users-in-ireland-by-county/
2. Ames, M. G. Managing Mobile Multitasking: The Culture of iPhones on Stanford Campus. In *Proc. of CSCW'13*, ACM (New York, 2013), 1487–1498.
3. Banjo, O., Hu, Y., and Sundar, S. Cell Phone Usage and Social Interaction with Proximate Others: Ringing in a Theoretical Model. *Open Communication Journal 2* (2008), 127–135.
4. Benford, S., Tolmie, P., Ahmed, A. Y., Crabtree, A., and Rodden, T. Supporting Traditional Music-Making: Designing for Situated Discretion. In *Proc. of CSCW'12*, ACM (New York, 2012), 127–136.
5. Bowcott, O. 'Boozer Bus' to Save Irish Pubs. *The Guardian* (Jan. 2007).
6. Campbell, S. W. Perceptions of Mobile Phone use in Public Settings: A Cross-Cultural Comparison. *International Journal of Communication 1*, 1 (Nov. 2007), 20.
7. Campbell, S. W., and Park, Y. J. Social Implications of Mobile Telephony: The Rise of Personal Communication Society. *Sociology Compass 2*, 2 (Mar. 2008), 371–387.
8. Chesley, N. Blurring Boundaries? Linking Technology use, Spillover, Individual Distress, and Family Satisfaction. *Journal of Marriage and Family 67*, 5 (Dec. 2005), 1237–1248.
9. Church, K., Cousin, A., and Oliver, N. I Wanted to Settle a Bet!: Understanding Why and How People Use Mobile Search in Social Settings. In *Proc. of MobileHCI'12*, ACM (New York, 2012), 393–402.

10. Church, K., and Oliver, N. Understanding Mobile Web and Mobile Search Use in Today's Dynamic Mobile Landscape. In *Proc. of MobileHCI '11*, ACM (New York, 2011), 67–76.
11. Connolly, R. E. *The Rise and Fall of the Irish Pub*. The Liffey Press, Dublin, Nov. 2010.
12. Dalsgaard, P., and Hansen, L. K. Performing Perception—Staging Aesthetics of Interaction. *ACM TOCHI 15*, 3 (2008), 1–33.
13. Davenport, F., Nevez, C. L., Quintero, J., Berkmoes, R. V., and Wilson, N. *Lonely Planet Ireland*, 11th ed. Lonely Planet, Melbourne, Australia, Apr. 2014.
14. Fortunati, L. The mobile phone: Towards new categories and social relations. *Information, Communication & Society 5*, 4 (2002), 513–528.
15. Geser, H. Towards a sociological theory of the mobile phone. In *E-Merging Media: Communication and the Media Economy of the Future*, A. Zerdick, A. Picot, K. Schrape, J.-C. Burgelman, and R. Silverstone, Eds. Springer-Verlag, Berlin, 2005, 235–260.
16. Geser, H. Is the Cell Phone Undermining the Social Order?: Understanding mobile technology from a sociological perspective. *Knowledge, Technology & Policy 19*, 1 (2006), 8–18.
17. Grantham, B. Craic in a box: Commodifying and exporting the Irish pub. *Continuum: Journal of Media & Cultural Studies 23*, 2 (Apr. 2009), 257–267.
18. Habuchi, I. Accelerating Reflexivity. In *Personal, Portable, Pedestrian: Mobile Phones in Japanese Life*, M. Ito, D. Okabe, and M. Matsuda, Eds. MIT Press, Cambridge, MA, 2005, 165–182.
19. Harmon, E., and Mazmanian, M. Stories of the Smartphone in Everyday Discourse: Conflict, Tension & Instability. In *Proc. of CHI'13*, ACM (New York, 2013), 1051–1060.
20. Harrison, S., and Dourish, P. Re-Place-ing Space: The Roles of Place and Space in Collaborative Systems. In *Proc. of CSCW'96*, ACM (New York, 1996), 67–76.
21. Kearns, Kevin C. *Dublin Pub Life and Lore: An Oral History*. Gill and Macmillan, Dublin, 1996.
22. Ling, R. *" One Can Talk about Common Manners!": The Use of Mobile Telephones in Inappropriate Situations*. Telenor, 1996.
23. Ling, R. The social juxtaposition of mobile telephone conversations and public spaces. In *Conference on the Social Consequence of Mobile Telephones* (Chunchon, Korea, July 2002).
24. Ling, R., and Yttri, B. Hyper-coordination via mobile phones in Norway. In *Perpetual Contact: Mobile Communication, Private Talk, Public Performance*, J. E. Katz and M. Aakhus, Eds. Cambridge University Press, Cambridge, UK, 2002, 139–169.
25. McGovern, M. 'The Cracked Pint Glass of the Servant': The Irish Pub, Irish Identity and the Tourist Eye. In *Irish Tourism: Image, Culture and Identity*, M. Cronin, B. O'Connor, and M. Robinson, Eds., no. 1 in Tourism and Cultural Change. Channel View Publications, Clevedon, UK, 2003, 83–103.
26. Monk, A., Carroll, J., Parker, S., and Blythe, M. Why are mobile phones annoying? *Behaviour & Information Technology 23*, 1 (2004), 33–41.
27. Oldenburg, R. *The Great Good Place: Cafes, Coffee Shops, Bookstores, Bars, Hair Salons, and Other Hangouts at the Heart of a Community*, 3rd ed. Marlowe & Company, New York, Aug. 1999.
28. Oldenburg, R., and Brissett, D. The Third Place. *Qualitative Sociology 5*, 4 (Dec. 1982), 265–284.
29. Oulasvirta, A., Tamminen, S., Roto, V., and Kuorelahti, J. Interaction in 4-Second Bursts: The Fragmented Nature of Attentional Resources in Mobile HCI. In *Proc. of CHI'05*, ACM (New York, 2005), 919–928.
30. Palen, L., Salzman, M., and Youngs, E. Going Wireless: Behavior & Practice of New Mobile Phone Users. In *Proc. of CSCW'00*, ACM (New York, 2000), 201–210.
31. Phillips, N., and Hardy, C. *Discourse Analysis: Investigating Processes of Social Construction*, 2nd ed. Sage Publications, Thousand Oaks, CA, 2002.
32. Robles, E., Sukumaran, A., Rickertsen, K., and Nass, C. Being Watched or Being Special: How I Learned to Stop Worrying and Love Being Monitored, Surveilled, and Assessed. In *Proc. of CHI'06*, ACM (New York, 2006), 831–839.
33. Schiano, D., Elliott, A., and Bellotti, V. A Look at Tokyo Youth at Leisure: Towards the Design of New Media to Support Leisure Outings. *CSCW 16*, 1 (Apr. 2007), 45–73.
34. Share, P. A Genuine 'Third Place'? Towards an Understanding of the Pub in Contemporary Irish society. In *Proc. of the SAI Annual Conference*. (2003).
35. Sohn, T., Li, K. A., Griswold, W. G., and Hollan, J. D. A Diary Study of Mobile Information Needs. In *Proc. of CHI'08*, ACM (New York, 2008), 433–442.
36. Srivastava, L. Mobile phones and the evolution of social behaviour. *Behaviour & Information Technology 24*, 2 (2005), 111–129.
37. Stelmaszewska, H., Fields, B., and Blandford, A. The Roles of Time, Place, Value and Relationships in Collocated Photo Sharing with Camera Phones. In *Proc. of BCS-HCI'08*, British Computer Society (Swinton, UK, 2008), 141–150.
38. Su, N. M. The Social Life of Tunes: Representing the Aesthetics of Reception. In *Proc. of ECSCW'13*, Springer (London, 2013), 207–228.
39. Sutter, N., and Holtgraves, T. Perceptions of public mobile phone conversations and conversationalists. *Telematics and Informatics 30*, 2 (May 2013), 158–164.
40. Wei, R., and Leung, L. Blurring public and private behaviors in public space: policy challenges in the use and improper use of the cell phone. *Telematics and Informatics 16*, 1–2 (Feb. 1999), 11–26.
41. Wei, R., and Lo, V.-H. Staying connected while on the move: Cell phone use and social connectedness. *New Media & Society 8*, 1 (Feb. 2006), 53–72.

Is This Thing On?
Crowdsourcing Privacy Indicators for Ubiquitous Sensing Platforms

Serge Egelman[1,2], Raghudeep Kannavara[3], Richard Chow[4]
[1]University of California, Berkeley, CA, egelman@cs.berkeley.edu
[2]International Computer Science Institute, Berkeley, CA, egelman@icsi.berkeley.edu
[3]Intel, Hillsboro, OR, raghudeep.kannavara@intel.com
[4]Intel, Santa Clara, CA, richard.chow@intel.com

ABSTRACT
We are approaching an environment where ubiquitous computing devices will constantly accept input via audio and video channels: kiosks that determine demographic information of passersby, gesture controlled home entertainment systems and audio controlled wearable devices are just a few examples. To enforce the principle of least privilege, recent proposals have suggested technical approaches to limit third-party applications to receiving only the data they need, rather than entire audio or video streams. For users to make informed privacy decisions, applications will still need to communicate what data they are accessing and indicators will be needed to communicate this information. We performed several crowdsourcing experiments to examine how potential users might conceptualize and understand privacy indicators on ubiquitous sensing platforms.

Author Keywords
Crowdsourcing; Ubiquitous Computing; Privacy

ACM Classification Keywords
H.5.2. Information Interfaces and Presentation (e.g. HCI): User Interfaces; D.4.6. Operating Systems: Security and Protection

INTRODUCTION
Within a week of its release, eight thousand beta testers signed up to pay $1,500 each for Google Glass [33], while countless others were added to a waiting list. We have also seen a recent demand for "smart watches," devices worn on the wrist and paired with a smartphone, allowing the user to take calls, view messages, and run third-party applications. One such device, the Pebble, raised over $10 million from 85,000 individuals using a crowd funding campaign [28], clearly illustrating public demand for these devices. Microsoft's Xbox One features voice and gesture control, as well as camera-based user recognition [26]. Intel has also announced that by mid-2014, many laptops will be equipped with their "RealSense" camera, which can be used to recognize gestures and voice commands [16]. All of these platforms allow third-party application developers to design applications that take advantage of new interaction modalities.

These devices all have the ability to perform ubiquitous sensing, which means that they require microphones and cameras to continuously monitor the user's environment for input. The sudden demand for these devices suggests that they will soon become a part of everyday life, which will create new security and privacy challenges [18]. Research on smartphone privacy and security has shown that granting third-party applications access to sensor data can create rich user experiences, but it can also be used for things other than application functionality (e.g., advertising and analytics), which users find concerning and surprising [25]. Thus, ubiquitous sensing platforms should employ privacy indicators so that users can better understand and control how data inferred from audio and video channels may be used by applications.

Research on smartphone privacy has shown us that care needs to be taken with the design of these privacy indicators. For instance, the Android operating system attempts to make this privacy information available to users, but as Felt *et al.* showed, most users do not notice or understand these notifications [11]. Thus, it is important to thoroughly evaluate privacy indicators prior to their widespread deployment. At the same time, privacy indicators for ubiquitous sensing systems pose an interesting challenge because researchers cannot fully predict all the ways that data from audio and video sensors might be used in the future.

We document the creation and evaluation of a set of privacy indicators for ubiquitous sensing platforms. Because these technologies are not yet widely deployed, we examined how potential users would conceptualize these privacy indicators and what pitfalls we might be able to identify prior to these privacy issues becoming too entrenched. These indicators are meant to be as universally understood as possible, so we adopted an approach based on crowdsourcing. We collected 238 sketches from participants based on 14 ubiquitous sensing concepts. We performed thematic analyses and used the uncovered themes as templates for new privacy indicator designs. We then performed comprehension evaluations with

CHI 2015, April 18 - 23 2015, Seoul, Republic of Korea.

ACM 978-1-4503-3145-6/15/04...$15.00.
http://dx.doi.org/10.1145/2702123.2702251

over 1,500 participants. We discuss how some privacy concepts were well-understood and are therefore not necessarily endemic to specific technologies, whereas other concepts may require the technologies to be in widespread use before they can be adequately communicated to end-users. Besides identifying future focus areas for risk communication surrounding ubiquitous sensing technologies, we present a new method for privacy indicator design based on crowdsourcing.

BACKGROUND

While research pertaining to privacy in ubiquitous computing systems has been performed for over two decades, there are still many open questions about how to integrate usable privacy controls into specific systems, because it is impossible to know the full functionality of future systems. At the same time, researchers have shown that the "crowd" is a useful resource for many different research areas, including usable security and design [19, 17], and can be used to rapidly evaluate new systems and designs using sample sizes that were previously unheard of. In this section, we discuss some of the related work as it pertains to privacy for ubiquitous computing systems and crowdsourcing-based evaluations.

Ubiquitous Sensing

In 1991, Marc Weiser predicted the rise of ubiquitous computing and warned that "hundreds of computers in every room, all capable of sensing people near them and linked by high-speed networks, have the potential to make totalitarianism up to now seem like sheerest anarchy" [36]. He observed that many of these concerns could be mitigated by integrating privacy mechanisms into the earliest stages of system designs.

Over the past two decades, in recognition of the growing ubiquitous computing trend, many researchers have offered suggestions for how these systems should be designed (e.g., [2, 9, 20, 24, 1]), including methods for addressing privacy concerns (e.g., [29, 13, 15, 30]). For instance, Bellotti and Sellen introduced a set of eleven criteria for the evaluation of privacy in ubiquitous computing environments that focus on giving users control over information capture [3]. Langheinrich recommended a set of six principles for system design based on privacy guidelines from the Organization for Economic Cooperation and Development (OECD) [23]. However, most of this research has focused on general design principles, rather than specific implementations.

To help users understand how applications access sensitive data, most smartphone platforms employ some sort of permission system. Felt *et al.* examined the Android permission system, which uses install-time dialogs to list the abilities that an application will have, and found that most users do not notice or understand these permission requests [11]. Enck *et al.* developed the TaintDroid system to allow users to examine how applications may be using personal data in realtime [10]. Others have designed system to limit the amount of data received by applications (e.g., [4, 14, 12]). However, most of this research has been conducted after the platforms were already in wide deployment, making it difficult for developers to radically alter their systems to support the researchers' recommendations. Thus, our work is motivated by the fact that ubiquitous sensing platforms are beginning to receive public demand, so there is a unique opportunity to solve privacy and security problems before they become entrenched.

Roesner *et al.* looked at privacy and security issues related to the types of ubiquitous sensing platforms that our research is aimed at benefitting [31]. D'Antoni *et al.* suggested ways in which platforms can be designed to mitigate some of these problems [7]. Specifically, they advocated supporting the principle of least privilege: applications should only be given access to the data that they need to function, and nothing more [32]. Thus, if an application needs to recognize a voice command, the operating system should parse the raw audio and pass the command to the application without granting access to the entire raw audio stream, as this information is personally identifiable and could be used for other purposes. For systems to be trustworthy, they need to communicate how and when applications are accessing potentially sensitive data.

Crowdsourcing

Crowdsourcing, the process of leveraging large groups of people to perform short tasks, has attracted a lot of attention as a research tool [21]. Researchers have explored crowdsourcing as a tool for gathering subjective judgments about various online media. Most famously, von Ahn *et al.* created the ESP game to get Internet users to agree on image labels [35]. Kumar *et al.* used crowdsourcing to classify varying website layouts [22]. Bernstein *et al.* created a word processor that uses crowdsourcing for on-demand editing [5].

Dow *et al.* showed how crowdsourcing can benefit the design process. In their study, they used crowdsourcing to get feedback about different types of banner advertisements [8]. We build on this work by using crowdsourcing as an evaluation mechanism for the design of various privacy indicators.

Perceptual Computing

The privacy indicators that we designed for this project were directly inspired by Intel's RealSense SDK [16]. The SDK implements the recommendations of D'Antoni *et al.* [7]: application developers are provided with a set of API methods for extracting information from audio and video sensors so that those applications can request only the data needed to function, rather than requesting raw audio or video. This has the benefit of limiting privacy-sensitive information, while also making it easier for applications to make use of rich sensor data (i.e., the platform does most of the processing and feature extraction so that developers do not need to). In essence, the platform enforces a permissions model and the role of the indicators is to communicate what type of data the application is accessing. Note that in this paper we do *not* examine participants' privacy sensitivities surrounding the data. Instead, we concentrate on the issue of whether users understand what data is being requested by applications, a prerequisite for making informed privacy decisions.

INITIAL COMPREHENSION RATES

When we began this project in August of 2013, Intel was in the process of internally developing a set of privacy indicators. These initial indicators were designed *ad hoc* by an Intel

Video Recording	Audio Recording	Age Detection

96.5% of 57	94.4% of 89	8.7% of 46
Camera-Based Emotion Detection	Voice-Based Emotion Detection	Gender Detection
	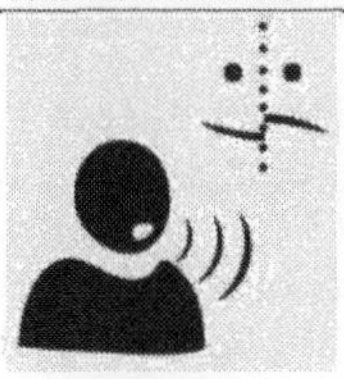	
21.8% of 78	11.7% of 94	50.0% of 40
Face Detection	Face Recognition	Voice Command & Control

0.0% of 21	11.9% of 59	3.6% of 195
Language Detection	Heart Rate Detection	

16.9% of 77	14.7% of 190	

Table 1: Comprehension rates for the initial icons (the icon with the highest comprehension rate per concept is depicted).

UI designer. Our initial goal was to examine whether potential users would be able to understand the meaning of these icons, and if not, which ones needed to be improved to better convey their intended concepts. We received a total of 26 indicators representing 11 different concepts:

1. Video Recording (3 icons)
2. Audio Recording (2 icons)
3. Age Detection (4 icons)
4. Camera-Based Emotion Detection (3 icons)
5. Voice-Based Emotion Detection (2 icons)
6. Gender Detection (4 icons)
7. Face Detection (2 icon)
8. Face Recognition (3 icons)
9. Voice Command & Control (1 icon)
10. Language Detection (1 icon)
11. Heart Rate Detection (1 icon)

Open-Ended Survey

We recruited participants from Amazon's Mechanical Turk to participate in a survey on "camera icons." At the start of the task, we gave participants the following instructions:

> *Imagine in the future all computers (e.g., laptops, desktops, public displays/kiosks, etc.) will have cameras and microphones attached to them, which are always on so that applications can be controlled through gestures or spoken commands. Symbols or icons will be needed to indicate when a camera/microphone is recording, and whether an application has access to raw data (i.e., audio or video of the user) that can be used for any purpose, or if it can only access less-sensitive data that can only be used for limited purposes (e.g., determining the user's gender, a spoken command, the user's approximate age, etc.). In this survey, we will show you various icons that might be used for this purpose (i.e., these icons would appear in the designated area of the camera/microphone in the picture above). Your job is to describe what you think the camera/microphone is doing based on the icons that you are shown.*

Each page of the survey featured one of the icons followed by a text box asking, "based on this icon, what do you believe is being captured?" Each participant only viewed one random icon per concept, and we randomized the order of the concepts. We compensated participants $1.00 per survey submission and collected 208 responses in this manner. Our sample consisted of 56.7% females, an average age of 34 ($\sigma = 11.6$, range of 18-74), and 50.5% held a bachelor's degree or higher (23 held graduate degrees, including 4 doctorates).

Three researchers independently scored each response based on whether it matched the intended meaning for each icon. To measure inter-rater reliability, we calculated Fleiss' kappa ($\kappa = 0.757$). In total, we received descriptions for 2,181 icons, but for the remainder of our analysis, we only focus on the 1,853 (85%) for which all three raters were in agreement.

We were surprised at how similar the comprehension levels were for different icons depicting the same concepts. Of the 11 concepts that we examined, eight had multiple candidate icons. Thus, we performed Fisher's exact test to measure the comprehension rates between the highest and lowest ranked icons for each of these concepts. We performed eight tests in this manner and therefore applied the Bonferroni correction ($\alpha = 0.006$). Only in one case, recording video, was one icon significantly more intuitive than another for the same concept ($p < 0.004$). Regardless, for the remainder of our analysis we selected the icon with the highest comprehension rate in order to pair each concept with a single icon (Table 1).

Common Misunderstandings

By and large, video and audio icons were understood by almost everyone (97% and 94%, respectively). Therefore, we focused on the incorrect responses for the remaining nine icons to see if any patterns emerged, and whether these misconceptions could further guide the design process. Three independent coders performed a thematic analysis on the incorrect responses to the open-ended survey. They each identified the most common themes among the incorrect responses for each of these nine icons. We enumerated these themes and calculated the Intraclass Correlation Coefficient (ICC) to be approximately 0.94, indicating almost perfect agreement.

Age Detection
Of the 42 incorrect responses for the age detection icon, a majority of participants stated that the icon meant that a group of people were being captured on video: "multiple people in front of it," "it looks like a group of people are on the camera," and "the camera is capturing a group shot of people." These responses also mentioned families or video conferences. Averaging across all three coders, this theme accounted for 67% of the incorrect responses. Common among this theme was the misconception that the icon was meant to indicate multiple people, rather than multiple phases in an individual's life. Based on this, we believe that this icon could be improved by focusing on extreme differences in age, rather than simply using similar figures that only vary based on size.

Camera-Based Emotion Detection
Of the 61 incorrect responses to the camera-based emotion detection icon, a plurality of participants stated that they believed the icon indicated that a theatrical event was being captured (41%): "the camera is recording theatrical events or using a theater app," "this could signal making videos to put online for display," and "I think that a creative movie is being captured." We suspect that one reason for this confusion was that the drama masks used for the icon are a common theatrical symbol, and that this could potentially be corrected by focusing on the facial expressions and not using recognizable symbols with broader meanings.

Voice-Based Emotion Detection
Of the 83 incorrect responses to the voice-based emotion detection icon, a majority (63%) said that the icon indicated voice capture: "audio being captured" and "a person singing on camera." This suggests that participants focused on the figure speaking and overlooked (or were confused by) the emotion icon in the corner. We reasoned that applications employing emotion detection will receive the same data regardless of whether detection is performed with a camera or microphone, and therefore this distinction may be unnecessary, especially if it leads to confusion about what data an application is ultimately receiving.

Gender Detection
Of the 20 incorrect gender icon descriptions, most of them (85%) said that they believed that the icon was indicating *both* a male and female were present. An argument could be made that this is correct: if the device can infer that both genders are present, then the user understands that gender is being detected. This suggests that the gender aspect of the icon was clear, and that participants were confused by the silhouettes of two individuals next to each other. We felt the design could be improved by only showing one individual or using symbols.

Face Detection
None of our participants were able to correctly identify any of the face detection icons. The problem stems from distinguishing face *detection* with *recognition*; the former refers to determining whether an individual is present, whereas the letter refers to the identity of that individual. Of the 21 participants who viewed this icon, eighteen said it had to do with a picture being taken (86%), ten specifically mentioned that the box indicated the focus area: "this icon means the camera is capturing a visual, zooming in or focusing" and "the camera is determining where to focus." While it is technically correct to say that the camera is focusing on this area, this icon was supposed to indicate that only the user's presence would be shared with applications, and not her identity.

Face Recognition
Similar to the face detection icon, the face recognition icon had a very low rate of comprehension. Of the 52 incorrect responses, a plurality (37%) focused on concepts surrounding detection *errors*: "cannot tell who the person is...facial recognition did not work," "I believe my image is being recorded but the camera is having a hard time recognizing my face," and "the camera cannot discern who the person is." This suggests that much of the confusion was due to the question mark over the face; participants believed that this meant that the detection had failed, rather than that it was in progress.

Voice Command & Control
While the voice command icon also received a very low rate of correct responses in the open-ended survey, the incorrect responses were extremely similar: of the 188 incorrect responses, 83% said that the icon meant that either all audio or the user's voice was being captured. These responses were all incorrect, because the intent for the icon was to convey that only the name of a command would be accessible, rather than the user's voice, which is personally identifiable. This suggests that an improved icon might better demonstrate the command aspect, and downplay the speaking element.

Language Detection
We received a total of 64 incorrect responses for the language detection icon. A plurality of these (48%) had to do with the incorrect belief that voices and/or raw audio was being captured: "the microphone is capturing the user's voice," "the microphone is picking up sounds," and "the icon looks like your voice is being recorded." These errors were very similar to the errors seen with the voice command icon and therefore suggest that less emphasis should be placed on the speaker.

Heart Rate Detection
Finally, we received a total of 162 incorrect responses to the heart rate detection icon. Of these, a plurality (37%) had confused the icon with emotion detection. Specifically, they interpreted this icon to mean that the user is in love or is otherwise emotionally attached to someone or something: "this icon looks like this person really enjoys something," "this looks like romance," and "this seems to be indicating strong emotion, love in particular." One way of disambiguating the love aspect of the heart may be to indicate that it is beating, such as by superimposing an electrocardiogram (EKG).

Broadly speaking, the types of errors that we observed fell into four categories. First, many participants were confused by common symbols that they may have recognized in other contexts. For instance, in the heart rate detection icon, they

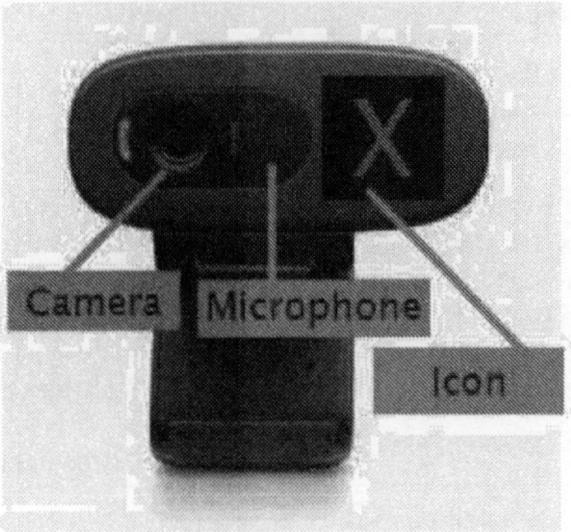

Figure 1: The picture used in our instructions so that participants could understand how the icons would be used.

assumed that the heart had to do with "love" or "emotions;" in the face recognition icon, they assumed that the question mark indicated that the computer was indicating an error; and in the emotion detection icon, they assumed that the drama masks had to do with drama or the theater. Second, many participants were confused when we attempted to describe both *what* and *how* data was being captured (e.g., camera-based emotion detection vs. voice-based emotion detection). Next, many participants found the depiction of multiple individuals in the gender and age icons to be misleading. Finally, several of the concepts were too similar to other concepts, for instance audio recording vs. voice command & control, or face detection vs. face recognition.

CROWDSOURCING THEMES

Our first experiment yielded insights into how our initial set of privacy indicators could be improved, however, it is possible that the comprehension rates were so low for some of the concepts because these indicators were the work of a single designer. We examined how potential users might choose to depict each of these concepts. We performed a second crowdsourcing experiment in which we described various ubiquitous sensing concepts and asked participants to draw their own icons to convey them. In this manner, we built a corpus of icons on which we performed thematic analysis to examine the common themes that each concept evoked.

Methodology

We posted a Mechanical Turk task with the following prompt:

> *Imagine in the future every computer has a camera and microphone that can be used to capture user input (e.g., spoken commands or hand gestures). This might include desktops, laptops, entertainment systems (TVs), and even public displays.*
>
> *To protect privacy, these devices will need to communicate when they are on and recording, and how this data will be used.*
>
> *In this task, we will describe a scenario and then you must design an icon to communicate how the recorded audio and/or video will be used. These icons will be displayed on the devices whenever an application is requesting data for a particular purpose.*

We then showed participants a picture of such a device (Figure 1) so that they could get a better idea of this icon's function. After reading these instructions, we presented participants with one of fourteen concepts,[1] drawn at random:

1. **Video Recording**: The video camera will record video of whoever is in front of it (i.e., applications will have access to all recorded video/images).
2. **Audio Recording**: The microphone will record audio of whoever is nearby (i.e., applications will have access to all recorded audio).
3. **Face-Based Age Detection**: The camera will only be used to determine the user's approximate age, and then will allow various applications to learn the user's age. However, no applications will have access to pictures or video of the user.
4. **Face-Based Emotion Detection**: The camera will take pictures to determine the user's approximate emotional state, and then allow various applications to learn the user's emotional state. However, no applications will have access to raw camera data (i.e., pictures or video of the user).
5. **Face-Based Gender Detection**: The camera will take pictures to determine the user's gender, and then allow various applications to learn the user's gender. However, no applications will have access to raw camera data (i.e., pictures or video of the user).
6. **Face Detection**: The camera will monitor whether a human being is in front of the computer and then notify applications when a user is present. However, applications will not have access to pictures or video of the user, nor will they learn the user's identity.
7. **Face Recognition**: The camera will take pictures to determine the identity of the individual in front of the camera, and then allow various applications to learn the identity of this user. However, no applications will have access to raw camera data (i.e., pictures or video of the user).
8. **Voice Command & Control**: The microphone will be used to recognize spoken commands, and then will share those commands with applications. However, no applications will have direct access to audio.
9. **Speech to Text**: The microphone will capture audio and convert it to text, and then allow various applications to access this text. However, no applications will have access to raw microphone data (i.e., audio from the user).
10. **Language Detection**: The microphone will be used to determine the language being spoken, and then will notify various applications of the user's language. However, no applications will have direct access to audio.
11. **Gesture Recognition**: The camera will take pictures to recognize gesture-based commands, and then allow various applications to access these commands. However, no applications will have access to raw camera data (i.e., pictures or video of the user).
12. **Voice-Based Emotion Detection**: The microphone will capture audio to determine the user's approximate emo-

[1] We included 3 new concepts supported by the latest RealSense platform that were not included with the previously-evaluated designer-created icons: speech to text, gesture detection, and eye tracking.

tional state, and then allow various applications to learn the user's approximate emotional state. However, no applications will have access to raw microphone data (i.e., audio from the user).

13. **Eye Tracking**: The camera will determine approximately where the user is looking on the screen, and then will share the coordinates with various applications. However, no applications will have access to raw camera data (i.e., pictures or video of the user).
14. **Heart Rate Monitor**: The camera and microphone will capture audio and video to determine the user's approximate heart rate, and then allow various applications to learn the user's heart rate. However, no applications will have access to raw camera or microphone data (i.e., video/images or audio of the user).

We included a use case for each concept to better convey why an application may want access to that data (and why it might be beneficial to the user). Alongside the concept description and use case, we provided participants with a sketching applet, as well as a box to explain how their drawing illustrates the given concept. We restricted our task to participants 18 years of age or older, but did not restrict it to a particular geographic area, in hopes of receiving submissions from a wide variety of individuals. We paid each participant $0.25.

Results

We received a total of 274 different sketches across all 14 concepts (an average of 17 sketches per concept). We discarded 36 (13%) sketches because the textual descriptions either contained gibberish or had nothing to do with the concepts, indicating that these participants did not take the task seriously. With the remaining 238 sketches, we performed a thematic analysis. Three of us independently made lists of themes that appeared across multiple sketches of the same concept. We then created a codebook based on these themes and two of us enumerated how many sketches embodied each of the coded themes. Based on our independent calculations of how frequently each theme occurred, we calculated the ICC to be 0.86, indicating almost perfect agreement. Our next step was to establish how many themes for each concept we would focus on in future experiments. After observing that for most concepts the top two themes were found in a majority of sketches, we focused on only the top two most prevalent themes in each concept. Table 2 depicts these themes and Figure 2 depicts some of participants' drawings.

Based on these themes, we made several observations. First, we were surprised that at least one of the themes for each concept appeared in our set of designer-provided icons:

- The video and audio icons embodied the camera and microphone, respectively.
- The age detection icon depicted child and adult.
- The emotion detection icon featured a happy and sad face.
- The gender detection icon featured male/female symbols.
- The face detection icon featured a framed face.
- The face recognition icon featured a face.
- The voice command icon featured a person speaking.

Concept	Top Themes
Video Recording (19)	• camera (10) • recording light (7)
Audio Recording (25)	• microphone (16) • sound waves (14)
Face-Based Age Detection (16)	• child or adult (6) • child and adult (4)
Face-Based Emotion Detection (13)	• smiley face (9) • happy and sad face (6)
Face-Based Gender Detection (14)	• male/female symbols (7) • male/female figures (5)
Face Detection (16)	• face (15) • camera frame or crosshairs (5)
Face Recognition (16)	• face (14) • camera frame or crosshairs (7)
Voice Command & Control (13)	• person speaking (6) • sound waves (6)
Speech to Text (15)	• letters or text (11) • sound waves (7)
Language Detection (21)	• foreign characters/words (9) • mouth (5)
Gesture Recognition (11)	• hand (10) • waving motion (6)
Voice-Based Emotion Detection (14)	• happy or sad face (14) • sound waves (7)
Eye Tracking (25)	• eyes (24) • arrow or directional lines (8)
Heart Rate Monitor (20)	• heart (14) • EKG (11)

Table 2: The two most prevalent themes for each of the 14 concepts for which participants submitted sketches. The number after each concept reflects the total number of sketches, whereas the numbers after the themes reflect how many sketches reflected each theme (not mutually-exclusive).

- The language detection icon featured a mouth with foreign characters.
- The voice-based emotion detection icon featured both sound waves and a happy and sad face.
- The heart rate monitor icon featured a heart.

We also observed that the exact same themes emerged for both the face detection and face recognition icons, which also occurred in our initial comprehension survey. This suggests that users may have a very difficult time differentiating these two concepts. This is especially concerning since they represent very different privacy concerns: an individual's identity vs. that *an* individual is present. Because we believe that the latter represents a much lower risk, we decided to eliminate the face detection concept from future evaluations.

Finally, we previously observed that between camera-based emotion detection and voice-based emotion detection, the same data would be accessed—the user's emotional state. Therefore, because it does not matter how that emotional state is determined, we merged these two concepts into a single indicator. This resulted in a set of 12 final concepts for which we made new privacy icons based on the themes in Table 2.

EVALUATION

Using the themes that we uncovered from participants' sketches, we created icons for each of the 12 concepts. For each concept, we created an average of six icons that em-

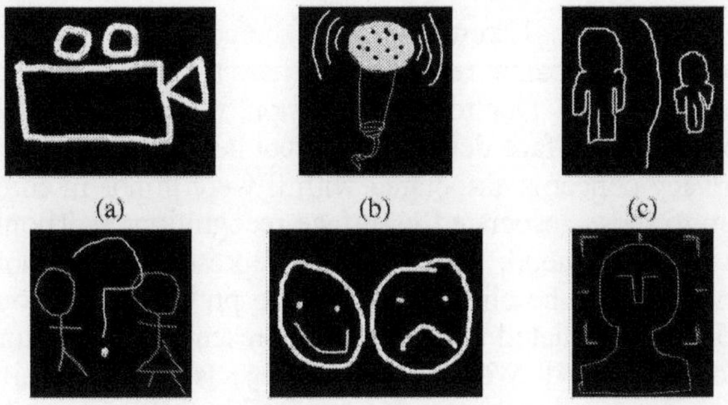

Figure 2: Crowdsourced drawings for six concepts: video recording (a), audio recording (b), age detection (c), gender detection (d), emotion detection (e), and face recognition (f).

bodied the themes in different ways. We based our icons on concrete concepts, following the findings of Curry *et al.* that concrete icons are initially much more understandable than abstract icons (e.g., line art) [6].

We iteratively deployed a survey 5 times, wherein participants defined an icon by choosing from a set of concepts. With each iteration, consisting of roughly 250 participants, we reduced the set of candidates until we were left with 1-2 icons per concept. Ultimately, we tested 71 different icons on 1,234 participants. We then performed a final evaluation to compare the designer-supplied icons (control condition) with our final set of crowdsourcing-inspired icons (experimental condition). In this section, we describe this final evaluation.

We presented participants with the following instructions:

> *Imagine in the future all computers (e.g., laptops, desktops, public displays/kiosks, etc.) will have cameras and microphones attached to them, which are always on so that applications can be controlled through gestures or spoken commands, as well as to learn things about their users. Symbols or icons will be needed to indicate what data is being collected about the user.*
>
> *In this survey, we will show you various icons that might be used for this purpose (i.e., these icons would appear in the designated area of the camera/microphone in the picture above). Your job is to describe what data you believe is being collected based on the icons that you are shown.*

On each of the 12 pages of the survey (one page per concept), we randomly displayed either a control condition icon or an experimental condition icon[2] and asked them, *based on this icon, what data do you believe is being collected?* We provided them with the following options, in random order:

- The language spoken
- A hand gesture
- Text of anything spoken (speech to text)
- Your approximate age

[2]In the final evaluation, we examined two different experimental icons for the gender detection and face recognition concepts, and three icons for the voice command icon.

Video Recording	Audio Recording	Age Detection

E: 84.7% of 138 C: 85.8% of 141 $p < 0.872$	E: 68.8% of 144 C: 79.4% of 160 $p < 0.036$	E: 86.3% of 160 C: 27.1% of 144 $p < 0.001$
Emotion Detection	**Gender Detection**	**Face Recognition**

E: 91.2% of 148 C: 83.3% of 156 $p < 0.058$	E: 96.2% of 104 C: 97.1% of 105 $p < 0.721$	E: 74.0% of 104 C: 85.3% of 95 $p < 0.055$
Voice Command & Control	**Language Detection**	**Heart Rate Detection**
		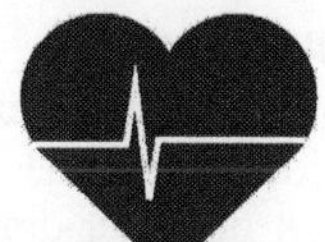
E: 44.1% of 59 C: 42.6% of 54 $p < 1.000$	E: 90.5% of 158 C: 67.6% of 145 $p < 0.001$	E: 98.8% of 160 C: 90.9% of 143 $p < 0.002$
Speech to Text	**Gesture Recognition**	**Eye Tracking**

E: 73.0% of 141	E: 98.6% of 147	E: 98.5% of 134

Table 3: Results of the final evaluation survey with the experimental icons displayed. The comprehension rates are listed below each icon for both the experimental (E) and control (C) conditions. Comprehension rates in the experimental condition were significantly higher for three concepts ($\alpha = 0.006$): age detection, language detection, and heart rate detection.

- Eye tracking data (where you are looking)
- Video of you
- A command (voice control)
- Your gender
- Your emotional state (mood)
- Audio of you
- Your face or identity (face recognition)
- Your heart rate

For each concept, we performed Fisher's exact test on the comprehension rates between the control icon and the experimental icon with the highest comprehension rate. To account for multiple testing (nine of the twelve concepts featured designer-supplied control icons), we applied the Bonferroni correction ($\alpha = 0.006$). Our sample ($n = 304$) was 52.2% male (158 of 304), the average age was 33 years old ($\sigma = 11.3$, range of 18 to 68), and 43.1% held a bachelors degree or higher (23 participants held graduate degrees, including two doctorates). Thus, we believe our sample is representative of the U.S. online population.

Overall, we were surprised at how similar comprehension rates were between the two icon sets (Table 3): none of the control condition icons had significantly higher comprehension rates than the corresponding experimental condition icons. This indicates that the crowdsourced icons were no worse than the original set. More importantly, three experimental condition icons exhibited significantly higher rates of comprehensions than their control condition counterparts. Thus, for a third of the concepts—age detection ($p < 0.001$), language detection ($p < 0.001$), and heart rate detection ($p < 0.002$)—the icons that we created from crowdsourced themes were more intuitive than the initial icons.

DISCUSSION

In our initial experiment, we asked participants to provide open-ended explanations for what they believed various designer-drawn privacy indicators represented. In our last evaluation, we asked participants to perform a similar task, but instead selecting their responses from a multiple-choice list of possible explanations. As one might expect, the latter evaluation resulted in higher comprehension rates.[3] We believe that taken together, these two different ways of evaluating comprehension—open-ended vs. multiple-choice responses—represent lower and upper bounds, respectively.

As Moyes *et al.* observe, "if an icon is not guessable it is not necessarily an unsuccessful icon" [27]. They hypothesize that learnability through repeated exposure may bridge this gap. Because the technologies that we hope to influence are not yet widely available, it is unlikely that many subjects were familiar with their capabilities, which is likely to result in lower rates of comprehension—guessability—in response to the open-ended questions (than if subjects had familiarity with the devices). This may be why subjects exhibited much higher rates of comprehension for the video and audio recording indicators: technologies that perform these actions are already in widespread use, and therefore concrete representations of these concepts were recognizable.

Along these lines, we believe that one of the biggest as-yet-unsolved challenges that we faced with this work was distinguishing face recognition from face detection. The former is used to identify an individual user, whereas the latter is used to determine whether someone is present (without identifying them). In our initial experiments, the designer-created icons were unable to disambiguate these concepts. We observed that during the sketching task, the themes that we extracted from the drawings representing each concept were identical. Likewise, during the comprehension experiments, participants' responses to these two concepts were interchangeable. Due to this confusion, we ultimately decided to remove the face detection concept because we felt that the privacy concerns associated with it were minor in comparison to those associated with face recognition; as Thompson *et al.* recommend, indicators that represent very minor risk levels should be eliminated so as to prevent users from becoming habituated to indicators representing much more serious risks [34]. We suspect that subjects' lack of familiarity with these concepts may be responsible for their inability to distinguish them. Additionally, it is possible that these concepts are just so similar, that the only way to communicate the concepts will be through learned association. That is, this problem may only be solved by simply assigning an icon to each concept and then expecting subjects to learn each icon's meaning through repeated exposure.

Limitations

This study was not without its limitations. Specifically, we have several questions about the generalizability of our results. First, with the exception of the drawing task, all of the evaluations were performed on participants based in the U.S. Obviously, the systems that we hope to benefit through this research will be deployed globally. Therefore, more work needs to be done to examine whether these indicators are effective at communicating the concepts to an international audience. This may pose a challenge, as the evaluations need to be conducted in a language that is understood by all participants, which could potentially mean hundreds of variants of a single experiment in order to ensure that an indicator is universally recognized.

Another limitation of this study is that we only examined a single set of control icons. Our control icons were developed internally at Intel by a professional designer and they provided a good baseline for us to compare our crowdsourcing-inspired icons against. However, they represent but a single designer's work and therefore are not representative of the entire profession. It is possible that icons from a different designer would yield substantially different results.

Finally, the concepts that we examined consist of use cases for ubiquitous sensing platforms that are likely to be supported in the near term. Because these technologies are still under development and we cannot possibly know what the "killer applications" are going to be ten years from now, it is possible—indeed likely—that many more privacy-sensitive use cases are likely to be identified in the coming years. While our findings are likely to be relevant as these platforms continue to be developed, they are by no means complete. More work needs to be performed to thoroughly understand the range of privacy risks associated with these technologies, how users perceive those risks, and how the relevant information can best be communicated to users.

Conclusion and Future Work

We present a crowdsourced approach to the design of privacy icons for a ubiquitous sensing platform. These icons are meant to communicate specific data collection scenarios to

[3] We cannot perform a direct statistical comparison because different indicators were examined, at different times, on different subjects.

users, for instance, video recording or gender detection. We experimented with a three-stage process where (1) Mechanical Turkers would design icons, (2) synthesis of new icons from the Mechanical Turk icons, and (3) Mechanical Turk evaluation of the synthesized icons. We compare our process with a set of designer-drawn icons, and for each of our scenarios the crowdsourcing approach performed no worse and sometimes significantly better.

In the future, one can imagine a multitude of sensors that are constantly being used to make inferences about and detect objects in the users' environment; some sensors may be used for redundancy or improved accuracy, for instance, simultaneously using both audio and video to identify a user. For access control purposes, all of these sensors will need to be managed by the platform and abstracted away so that applications need only access the resulting data. In this case, the role of a privacy indicator is to convey what information is being accessed by the application, not what sensors were used by the platform to extract that information. We observed that when we examined indicators that included additional information about how the data was extracted (i.e., what sensors were used), it was a distraction that resulted in lower comprehension rates. Participants focused on this information instead of the more important elements—what data was being accessed. Thus, our results suggest that these types of privacy indicators should be designed to convey *what* information will be used by applications, not *how* it will be collected. However, additional studies are needed to examine whether users really care about this distinction.

Another interesting area is the difficulty in disambiguating the face detection and face recognition concepts. Future work needs to be conducted to examine potential users' risk concerns surrounding these data collection concepts.

ACKNOWLEDGEMENTS

We would like to thank Jacob Carter for creating the initial icon set and the Intel Software and Services Group (SSG) for their assistance. This work was supported by the Intel Science and Technology Center for Secure Computing (ISTC-SC).

REFERENCES

1. G. D. Abowd, G. R. Hayes, G. Iachello, J. A. Kientz, S. N. Patel, M. M. Stevens, and K. N. Truong. Prototypes and paratypes: Designing mobile and ubiquitous computing applications. *IEEE Pervasive Computing*, 4(4):67–73, Oct. 2005.
2. G. D. Abowd and E. D. Mynatt. Charting past, present, and future research in ubiquitous computing. *ACM Trans. Comput.-Hum. Interact.*, 7(1):29–58, Mar. 2000.
3. V. Bellotti and A. Sellen. Design for privacy in ubiquitous computing environments. In *Proceedings of the third conference on European Conference on Computer-Supported Cooperative Work*, pages 77–92, Norwell, MA, USA, 1993. Kluwer Academic Publishers.
4. A. R. Beresford, A. Rice, N. Skehin, and R. Sohan. Mockdroid: Trading privacy for application functionality on smartphones. In *Proceedings of the 12th Workshop on Mobile Computing Systems and Applications*, HotMobile '11, pages 49–54, New York, NY, USA, 2011. ACM.
5. M. S. Bernstein, G. Little, R. C. Miller, B. Hartmann, M. S. Ackerman, D. R. Karger, D. Crowell, and K. Panovich. Soylent: A word processor with a crowd inside. In *Proceedings of the 23Nd Annual ACM Symposium on User Interface Software and Technology*, UIST '10, pages 313–322, New York, NY, USA, 2010. ACM.
6. M. B. Curry, S. J. McDougall, and O. de Bruijn. The effects of the visual metaphor in determining icon efficacy. In *Proceedings of the Human Factors and Ergonomics Society Annual Meeting*, volume 42, pages 1590–1594. SAGE Publications, 1998.
7. L. D'Antoni, A. Dunn, S. Jana, T. Kohno, B. Livshits, D. Molnar, A. Moshchuk, E. Ofek, F. Roesner, S. Saponas, M. Veanes, and H. J. Wang. Operating system support for augmented reality applications. In *Proceedings of the 14th USENIX Conference on Hot Topics in Operating Systems*, HotOS'13, pages 21–21, Berkeley, CA, USA, 2013. USENIX Association.
8. S. P. Dow, A. Glassco, J. Kass, M. Schwarz, D. L. Schwartz, and S. R. Klemmer. Parallel prototyping leads to better design results, more divergence, and increased self-efficacy. *ACM Trans. Comput.-Hum. Interact.*, 17(4):18:1–18:24, Dec. 2010.
9. W. K. Edwards and R. E. Grinter. At home with ubiquitous computing: Seven challenges. In *Proceedings of the 3rd International Conference on Ubiquitous Computing*, UbiComp '01, pages 256–272, London, UK, UK, 2001. Springer-Verlag.
10. W. Enck, P. Gilbert, B.-G. Chun, L. P. Cox, J. Jung, P. McDaniel, and A. N. Sheth. Taintdroid: an information-flow tracking system for realtime privacy monitoring on smartphones. In *Proceedings of the 9th USENIX conference on Operating systems design and implementation*, OSDI'10, pages 1–6, Berkeley, CA, USA, 2010. USENIX Association.
11. A. P. Felt, E. Ha, S. Egelman, A. Haney, E. Chin, and D. Wagner. Android permissions: user attention, comprehension, and behavior. In *Proceedings of the Eighth Symposium on Usable Privacy and Security*, SOUPS '12, New York, NY, USA, 2012. ACM.
12. S. Guha, M. Jain, and V. N. Padmanabhan. Koi: A location-privacy platform for smartphone apps. In *Proceedings of the 9th USENIX Conference on Networked Systems Design and Implementation*, NSDI'12, pages 14–14, Berkeley, CA, USA, 2012. USENIX Association.
13. J. I. Hong, J. D. Ng, S. Lederer, and J. A. Landay. Privacy risk models for designing privacy-sensitive ubiquitous computing systems. In *Proceedings of the 5th Conference on Designing Interactive Systems: Processes, Practices, Methods, and Techniques*, DIS '04, pages 91–100, New York, NY, USA, 2004. ACM.

14. P. Hornyack, S. Han, J. Jung, S. Schechter, and D. Wetherall. These aren't the droids you're looking for: retrofitting android to protect data from imperious applications. In *Proceedings of the 18th ACM conference on Computer and communications security*, CCS '11, pages 639–652, New York, NY, USA, 2011. ACM.

15. G. Iachello and G. D. Abowd. Privacy and proportionality: Adapting legal evaluation techniques to inform design in ubiquitous computing. In *Proceedings of the SIGCHI Conference on Human Factors in Computing Systems*, CHI '05, pages 91–100, New York, NY, USA, 2005. ACM.

16. Intel Corporation. Intel RealSense Technology, 2014. http://www.intel.com/content/www/us/en/architecture-and-technology/realsense-overview.html.

17. R. Kang, S. Brown, L. Dabbish, and S. Kiesler. Privacy Attitudes of Mechanical Turk Workers and the U.S. Public. pages 37–49. USENIX Association, Submitted.

18. R. Kannavara and K. Shippy. Topics in Biometric Human-Machine Interaction Security. *Potentials, IEEE*, 32(6):18–25, 2013.

19. P. G. Kelley. Conducting Usable Privacy & Security Studies with Amazon's Mechanical Turk. In *Proceedings of the 6th Symposium on Usable Privacy and Security (SOUPS)*, SOUPS 2010. USENIX Association, 2010.

20. T. Kindberg and A. Fox. System software for ubiquitous computing. *IEEE Pervasive Computing*, 1(1):70–81, Jan. 2002.

21. A. Kittur, E. H. Chi, and B. Suh. Crowdsourcing User Studies with Mechanical Turk. In *CHI '08: Proceeding of The Twenty-Sixth Annual SIGCHI Conference on Human Factors in Computing Systems*, pages 453–456, New York, NY, USA, 2008. ACM.

22. R. Kumar, J. O. Talton, S. Ahmad, and S. R. Klemmer. Bricolage: Example-based retargeting for web design. In *Proceedings of the SIGCHI Conference on Human Factors in Computing Systems*, CHI '11, pages 2197–2206, New York, NY, USA, 2011. ACM.

23. M. Langheinrich. Privacy by design - principles of privacy-aware ubiquitous systems. In *Proceedings of the 3rd international conference on Ubiquitous Computing*, UbiComp '01, pages 273–291, London, UK, UK, 2001. Springer-Verlag.

24. S. Lederer, J. I. Hong, A. K. Dey, and J. A. Landay. Personal privacy through understanding and action: Five pitfalls for designers. *Personal Ubiquitous Comput.*, 8(6):440–454, Nov. 2004.

25. J. Lin, N. Sadeh, S. Amini, J. Lindqvist, J. I. Hong, and J. Zhang. Expectation and purpose: understanding users' mental models of mobile app privacy through crowdsourcing. In *Proceedings of the 2012 ACM Conference on Ubiquitous Computing*, UbiComp '12, pages 501–510, New York, NY, USA, 2012. ACM.

26. Microsoft Corporation. Xbox One, 2014. http://www.xbox.com/en-US/xbox-one/innovation.

27. J. Moyes and P. W. Jordan. Icon design and its effect on guessability, learnability, and experienced user performance. *People and computers*, (8):49–60, 1993.

28. J. Newman. Pebble smartwatch pre-orders are sold out, $10+ million pledged. Time, May 10 2012. http://techland.time.com/2012/05/10/pebble-smartwatch-pre-orders-sold-out/.

29. L. Palen and P. Dourish. Unpacking "privacy" for a networked world. In *CHI '03: Proceedings of the SIGCHI conference on Human factors in computing systems*. ACM New York, NY, USA, April 5-10 2003.

30. A. Raij, A. Ghosh, S. Kumar, and M. Srivastava. Privacy risks emerging from the adoption of innocuous wearable sensors in the mobile environment. In *Proceedings of the SIGCHI Conference on Human Factors in Computing Systems*, CHI '11, pages 11–20, New York, NY, USA, 2011. ACM.

31. F. Roesner, T. Kohno, and D. Molnar. Security and privacy for augmented reality systems. *Communications of The ACM*, 2014. http://www.franziroesner.com/pdf/arsec-cacm2014-preprint.pdf.

32. J. H. Saltzer and M. D. Schroeder. The protection of information in computer systems. *Proceedings of the IEEE*, 63(9):1278–1308, 1975.

33. J. Stern. Google glass explorer edition to ship this month. ABC News, April 10 2013. http://abcnews.go.com/blogs/technology/2013/04/google-glass-explorer-edition-to-ship-this-month/.

34. C. Thompson, M. Johnson, S. Egelman, D. Wagner, and J. King. When it's better to ask forgiveness than get permission: Designing usable audit mechanisms for mobile permissions. In *Proceedings of the 2013 Symposium on Usable Privacy and Security (SOUPS)*, 2013.

35. L. von Ahn and L. Dabbish. Labeling images with a computer game. In *Proceedings of the SIGCHI Conference on Human Factors in Computing Systems*, CHI '04, pages 319–326, New York, NY, USA, 2004. ACM.

36. M. Weiser. The computer for the 21st century. *Scientific American*, pages 94–104, 1991.

Blood Pressure Beyond the Clinic: Rethinking a Health Metric for Everyone

Logan Kendall[1,2], Dan Morris[1], Desney Tan[1]
[1]Microsoft Research
{dan; desney}@microsoft.com
[2]Biomedical and Health Informatics
University of Washington
kendall5@uw.edu

ABSTRACT
Blood pressure (BP) is typically captured at irregular intervals, mostly in clinic environments. This approach treats BP as a static snapshot for health classification and largely ignores its value as a continuously fluctuating measure. Recognizing that consumers are increasingly capturing health metrics through wearable devices, we explored BP measurement in relation to everyday living through a two-week field study with 34 adults. Based on questionnaires, measurement logs, and interviews, we examined participants' perceptions and attitudes towards BP variability and their associations of BP with aspects of their lives. We found that participants modified their use of BP devices in response to BP variability, made associations with stress, food, and daily routines, and revealed challenges with the design of current BP devices for personal use. We present design recommendations for BP use in everyday contexts and describe strategies for re-framing BP capture and reporting.

Author Keywords
Personal informatics; blood pressure; self-monitoring.

ACM Classification Keywords
J.3. Life and medical sciences: Health.

INTRODUCTION
Blood pressure (BP) is an important and widely used indicator for assessing cardiovascular health. One in five hypertensive individuals are not even aware they have high BP and overall public understanding of BP is poor [3,11]. Young adults in particular are less likely to be aware of their blood pressure. However, recent longitudinal studies have shown that capturing blood pressure at an earlier age and evaluating it over a lifetime provides valuable data for understanding and predicting cardiovascular risk [1].

Limited awareness and understanding of blood pressure is due in part to the fact that BP measurement is typically situated in the clinic. However, metrics typically captured in this context or through cumbersome devices are becoming more accessible to consumers through noninvasive, wearable sensors designed to support personal monitoring. The success of consumer devices like the Fitbit demonstrates deep interest in leveraging sensor data to learn about, reflect upon, and inform lifestyle choices. In particular, the ubiquitous nature of these sensors creates a shift from ad hoc measurement towards continuous capture within the context of normal daily activities. For a health indicator like blood pressure, continued advancement of tools such as wrist-worn, cuffless, continuous BP monitors [22] suggest a future in which cardiovascular metrics are captured as easily as the activity data dominating the current wearable technology market.

For this study, we explore the concept of ubiquitous health sensing in relation to BP monitoring by evaluating how people use and relate to their BP measurements outside of a typical medical context. To explore this potential future state for personal health sensing, we first describe related work on home BP measurement, its relationship to personal health informatics, and challenges with communicating measurement uncertainty. Second, we describe our study design and descriptive findings. Third, we outline the themes elicited from questionnaires, participants' BP logs, and semi-structured interviews conducted with each study participant. We conclude with a discussion of design opportunities to enhance the experience of BP measurement for personal health and well-being.

Based on participants' experiences, we provide three main contributions in this paper: (1) we improve understanding of a healthy population's attitudes and motivations toward BP variability and monitoring, (2) we identify aspects of everyday living that people associate with their BP measurement, and (3) we recommend design strategies to make this metric intelligible and relevant for personal monitoring.

CHI 2015, April 18 23, 2015, Seoul, Republic of Korea.

ACM 978-1-4503-3145-6/15/04...$15.00.
http://dx.doi.org/10.1145/2702123.2702576

BACKGROUND AND RELATED WORK

Fundamentals of BP and BP variability
A BP measurement is a snapshot of the force of blood pressing on the arteries as the pressure rises and falls with each heartbeat. BP is measured in units of millimeters of mercury (mmHg), typically using an inflatable cuff that exerts pressure on the outside of a part of the body to obtain the arterial pressure. Optimal BP is clinically defined as less

than 120/80 mmHg, where the upper value is systolic pressure (SBP) and the lower value is diastolic pressure (DBP).

BP is frequently discussed as a static snapshot of SBP and DBP, however it is a dynamic process with natural fluctuations over the course of days, weeks, and months. People usually experience changes throughout the day such as a nighttime dip in pressure in accordance with one's circadian rhythm [14]. Systolic BP typically varies by approximately 10-15 mmHg during the daytime and 5-10 mmHg at night [27]. BP can also fluctuate dramatically due to short-term influences that affect cardiac output and vascular resistance. Caffeine significantly increases SBP by 5-10 mmHg and psychological stress and physical exertion can cause an increase of 20-60 mmHg [16,21,27]. Sleeping, eating, and a variety of other activities are also correlated with dynamic changes in BP yet occur sporadically, making the changes difficult to identify without continuous monitoring [27].

Value of BP measurement outside the clinic

These short-term fluctuations in BP are important because significant variation may cause subtle arterial damage that raises average BP over long periods [20]. However, clinic-based measurement, considered the standard for BP classification, is how most people assess their BP. The clinic setting may not be optimal due to limitations in its capacity to accurately measure BP in certain contexts [26] and the fact that 15% of adults do not visit their providers annually [23]. Instead, studies show that BP monitoring at home is better at predicting cardiovascular risk than measurements in the clinic [19,24]. Though automated ambulatory monitoring is becoming more widespread, it is cost-prohibitive, requires clinical guidance, and necessitates wearing a cuff that auto-inflates every 30-60 minutes for at least 24 hours.

As a result, home BP devices have become a preferred alternative for BP assessment. Yet home devices are still designed based on clinical needs and not with personal use in mind. In a study focused on elderly adults, researchers described usability challenges with patients reliably measuring their BP, interpreting the results, and integrating measurement into daily routines [12]. Despite these challenges, home monitoring has the potential to positively influence quality of life and empower individuals when it is integrated successfully into everyday living [5].

Growth of personal health monitoring

Challenges with user-device interaction for health monitoring are not limited to elderly or at-risk populations despite the research emphasis on these groups. Increasingly cheap sensors have encouraged rapid growth in the personal health sensing market in the US [9]. Tracking health metrics enables people to learn more about their specific context and motivate lifestyle changes. Li et al. described how collecting behavioral information along with physiological metrics helps foster insight and promote positive behavior [17]. Choe and colleagues build on this work, noting a strong interest in health metrics among self-trackers, but highlighting breakdowns that may inhibit tracking behavior [4]. Other research highlights how perceptions of personal monitoring devices for general living, wellness, or illness affect how people use them in the home [13]. Epstein et al. identified how various data representations supported users to make discoveries about their behavior and identify opportunities for change [8]. These conclusions align with the observations of Bentley et al. regarding the importance of promoting self-reflection and linking multiple streams of data to promote meaningful personal monitoring [2]. As BP becomes easier to capture, it can serve as a key metric supporting lifestyle monitoring and personal health.

Measurement uncertainty with BP devices

BP measurement also introduces variability due to signal noise and lenient validation protocols. Devices that meet current validation criteria may still be inaccurate by more than 5 mmHg in a given measurement for more than half of users [10]. This level of error introduces challenges to interpreting singular snapshots of BP and can lead someone to classify their blood pressure and health risk incorrectly.

How users understand and accept this type of variability reflects a common challenge with sensing tools that must provide reliable feedback despite measurement uncertainty. Lim and Dey introduce the concept of intelligibility to describe how well context-aware systems communicate reasoning or uncertainty [18]. In the health domain, Kay et al. explored the intelligibility of scales in communicating weight fluctuations. Importantly, Kay et al. found that a person's understanding of weight fluctuation was associated with their trust in the scales' capabilities [15]. Similar to scales, displaying BP as a static snapshot without communicating measurement uncertainty may impact user perception of BP devices over time.

Based on this related work, we assert there is an opportunity to reframe BP for a broader audience, motivated by personal monitoring outside of the clinic. Brief, infrequent clinic visits limit the ability of providers to assess short-term changes in BP or to account for in-clinic measurement variation. Individual use of BP devices outside the clinic more accurately encapsulates BP as dynamic variable, however, the way users respond to this variability is poorly understood. Moreover, BP's sensitivity to environmental variables shows promise as a metric for self-tracking and linking with aspects of daily living. Our study illuminates the value and challenges of BP capture for personal informatics use among a population not familiar with BP monitoring.

STUDY OVERVIEW

Participants

Since monitoring has been studied extensively in populations with high BP, we excluded persons who were actively taking BP medication or had been diagnosed with hypertension or other cardiovascular diseases. This increased the likelihood that our participants had limited experience with

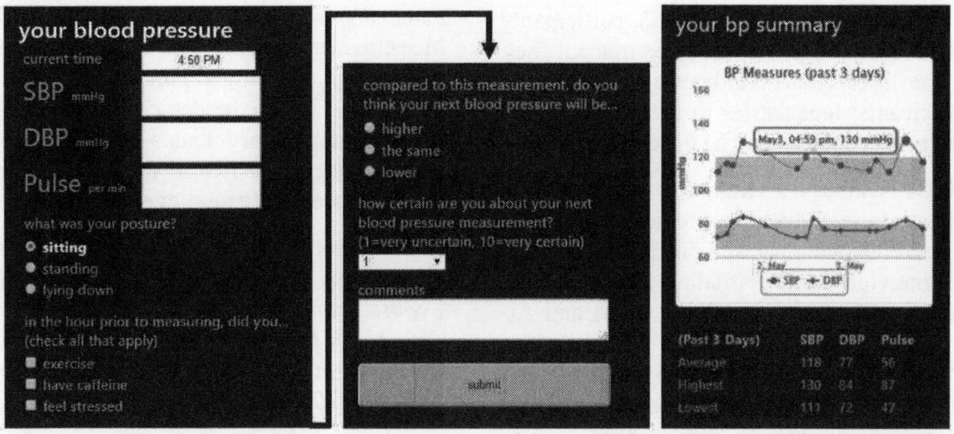

Figure 1. Screenshot of a mobile web app used by participants to collect each blood pressure measurement. For the second week of the study period, participants could see a 72 hour visual summary of their BP data.

monitoring their BP. We also required that participants own a smartphone or tablet so that they could use our web-based logging tool (Figure 1) regardless of their location.

Using purposeful sampling based on age and gender to ensure representation from an adult population, we recruited participants from a large volunteer database. Thirty-four (17 female) persons, aged 23 to 53 (mean=36.6, SD=7.8), participated in the study. All participants had some college-level education, with 27 holding a college degree or higher. Participants indicated a high level of physical activity, with 79% reporting exercising outside of work on a daily basis. Also, 68% of participants stated that they had previously measured their BP outside of a clinic, such as at a pharmacy kiosk or at home with a personal BP device.

Study protocol and analysis

At the beginning and end of the study, participants completed a questionnaire covering demographic details and knowledge, beliefs, and attitudes about BP. For evaluations of changes in responses pre- and post-study, we used paired Wilcoxon Signed-Rank tests. We also collected and summarized a brief follow-up survey distributed 60 days after the end of the study. Each participant received a gratuity and kept their BP cuff after finishing the study. To encourage adherence to our protocol, participants who averaged at least four recordings daily received an extra gratuity.

At baseline, participants received a MicroLife BP3MC1-PC portable upper-arm BP monitoring cuff that has been validated for clinic and home use [7]. The investigators also reviewed standard protocol for BP measurement with each person and had them take their baseline BP reading. Participants then measured their BP daily at five points spread throughout the day for 14 days. This served as an experimental surrogate for a future of more continuous, cuffless measurement for which technology is already emerging. Our study design differs from clinic-defined home protocols to give participants the opportunity to see their BP as a continuously fluctuating variable and not just a means for diagnosis and monitoring. All participants opted in to receive text and/or email reminders sent periodically during the day to support adherence. After each measurement, participants completed a mini-questionnaire delivered through a web-based app that assessed contextual data known to influence BP—caffeine intake, stress, or exercise—based on activities in the hour preceding the BP recording (Figure 1). The questionnaire also provided space for participants to comment on each measurement. For the final week, participants were given access to a 72-hour visual summary of their BP trends and a table summary of their average, highest, and lowest values for SBP, DBP, and pulse.

n=2,181	Mean	Median	Min	Max	SD
SBP	127	126	90	170	13.1
DBP	81	80	42	145	10.2
Pulse	74	72	28	145	15.5

Table 1. Descriptive summary of BP measurements recorded by participants during the 14 day study period.

Summarized in Table 1, over the course of the study period, participants recorded 2,181 BP measurements (mean 4.6 per day per participant) and entered brief structured information about each measurement. Figure 2 shows the distribution of measurements by time of day with peaks at 8am, 12pm, and 9pm. Across the BP recordings, 84% were measured while sitting, 11% standing, and 5% while lying

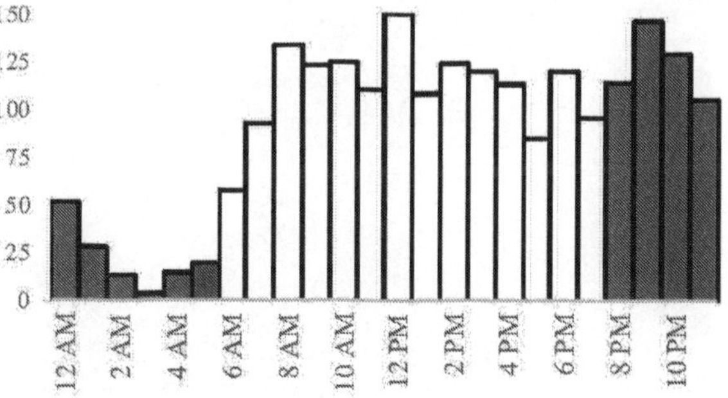

Figure 2. Overview of the number participant recordings by time of day. Evening hours are shaded in gray.

down. For more than half of the entries (56%), participants made brief, open-ended notes about the measurement they had just taken. The three authors independently coded a subset of the participants' logs entries to identify common themes that were then used to code all of the entries.

At days 7 and 14, we conducted a semi-structured interview with each participant during which we provided them with a summary of their BP log and reviewed the data with them. We conducted 68 interview sessions totaling 45 hours. Each session averaged 40 minutes (range: 26 61 min) and focused on the participant's recent experiences with using the BP device. All interviews were transcribed and reviewed for preliminary themes. The authors organized the emerging concepts into an affinity diagram to help identify higher-level concepts and relationships among terms. They iterated on codes through several rounds in order to focus in on the core themes used for this article. One author used these themes to analyze each interview using Atlas.ti 7. Finally, the remaining authors each coded a subset of the interviews to validate the themes and ensure reliability.

RESULTS

Based on interviews, BP logs, and questionnaires, we review participants' attitudes toward their use of BP devices in terms of accuracy, relevance to daily living, and impact on their sense of well-being. We also highlight challenges this cohort associated with using a BP device every day.

Participant response to BP variability

Prior research has established measure-to-measure variation at clinics between 10 and 20 mmHg [27]. Our analysis of participant recordings that were measured while sitting showed within-person variation of ±5 to ±15 SBP during the study (Figure 3). We found that participants were very sensitive to the variation that they experienced over the study period and demonstrated a variety of behaviors and strategies when they noticed deviations from their usual BP.

Evaluating measurement accuracy and consistency

Measurement variability, whether from the device or a natural change, challenged participants' level of trust in a given measure. When the device reported a value outside of an expected range, participants would take extra steps such as taking repeat measures to evaluate its accuracy. If the results appeared consistent over time, they seemed reassured:

> *"I wouldn't bet on those numbers with my life, but I would say that they are within a range that works, because I can literally sit down and sometimes I do just take my blood pressure three times in a row just to see how accurate it is. And the numbers will fluctuate plus or minus 5 to 10 on the blood pressure [device]." (P18)*

Recognizing consistency in the measurements was an important consideration for many of the participants. They mentioned challenging settings such as being on a boat or in a car where they questioned the numbers because, *"taking it in places with me in different variables and environments and stuff, I feel like you have to kind of baby it or it's going to give you some crazy reading" (P27)*. However, finding a comfortable location and the appropriate amount of time to sit down and take the measurement was often a challenge.

Comparing to other sources

In the interviews, participants often compared the study-provided BP device with other sources of BP measurement. They visited their primary care clinic to compare with their doctor, went to pharmacy kiosk machines, and also tested their device relative to other BP devices that family members or friends owned. One person (P14) seemed satisfied with the device used in the study, *"because one of the days I actually went to the doctor and it was only like the number is only like one or two different."*

Within the questionnaire, participants indicated what sources of BP measurement they trusted the most. Methods that involved multiple measurements were ranked highest. Although the overall order of rankings across participants did not change over the study period, more participants

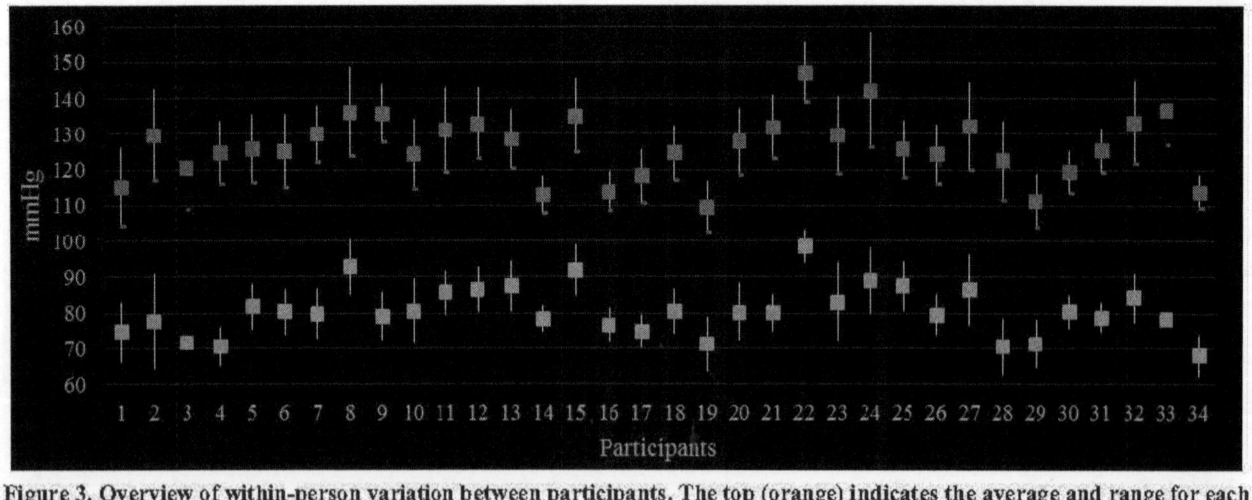

Figure 3. Overview of within-person variation between participants. The top (orange) indicates the average and range for each participant's SBP, the bottom (blue) for each person's DBP. Overall within-person variation ranged from ±5 to ±15 SBP.

gave a lower ranking to single-point measurements at the end of the study (one-tail, $p<0.025$ after Bonferroni correction). This suggests that our study cohort placed greater value on having multiple measurement points to assess BP versus casual, ad hoc approaches (Table 2).

Using heart rate to gauge validity

In the interviews, participants commented that they paid attention to specific values within a given BP reading, especially heart rate, as a way of deciding if the measurement seemed reasonable or not. When this relationship broke down, participants expressed greater doubt in the measurement. P34 had a normal BP reading but was skeptical because of what seemed like an inaccurate hear rate. *"I don't know why my heart rate was so elevated. I wasn't doing anything, I felt fine but that's what I read on the machine. I don't know. Maybe it's accurate, maybe it wasn't" (P34).*

Understanding counter-intuitive fluctuations in BP

The variability that participants experienced occasionally ran counter to their expectations in relation to level of activity during the day. Participants expected their BP to be lower in the mornings as, *"that's going to probably be my most relaxed part of the day" (P16)*. In contrast, the afternoons are when, *"you would expect it to be a little higher because that's the more 'active" portion of the day" (P30)*. Participants intuitively expected their BP to be low at times when they felt relaxed or when they had not recently been active, such as after sleeping. Similarly, they believed that the greater amount of activity during the day or immediately after exercising would lead to higher measurement values.

In the questionnaire, 47% of participants both pre- and post-study selected the afternoon (defined as 2-5pm) as the highest BP point of the day. Moreover, there was an increase from 18% to 38% of participants that selected the morning as the lowest BP point of the day. Their intuition seemed to influence their expectations for BP despite a lack of evidence in the recordings or in the literature supporting this. Within a typical sleep-wake cycle there are natural oscillations in BP levels—a rise in BP that begins before waking, peak BP in the late morning, and a drop in the early afternoon [14]. P08 was also surprised by this trend at first, but then she recalled an article about women who have heart attacks in the morning because *"it has something to do with something rising in their bodies."* She was able to adjust her expectations with greater understanding of BP variability.

Adjusting behavior to achieve desired BP

Participants also described how they learned over the course of the study factors that might influence their BP level and then altered their behavior to achieve a desired BP target. P09 explained, *"I would know that from what I had been looking at, that my pressure would be jacked up at certain times,"* so he avoided caffeine and took his BP at times when he thought it would be lowest, *"because I want to see my overall average go down"*. P09 framed his BP monitoring as a competition that he wanted to win. Other participants used their observations of BP variability and avoided stressful settings that they linked to elevated pressure, reduced their caffeine intake, and made other changes to their behavior to affect measurements.

Measure	Rank
Measured continuously by a cannula (small tube) that is inserted into an artery in the body.	1
Average of measurements automatically recorded every hour for 24 hours by an auto-inflating device.	2
Average of self-measurements taken at home 3 times a day for 3 days using an automated BP cuff.	3
Measured once by a doctor using a manually inflated cuff with a stethoscope.	4
Measured once by a nurse using an automated blood pressure cuff.	5
Self-measured once at home using an automated blood pressure cuff.	6
Measured once at a kiosk machine with auto-inflating cuff commonly found in drug stores.	7

Table 2. Participant ranking of the most trustworthy sources for measuring blood pressure at baseline. Order did not change when re-evaluated at the end of the study.

Correlating BP with daily living

Using structured fields in the web application, we asked participants to mark if they exercised, felt stressed, or drank caffeine in the hour prior to each measurement. At least 1 out of 8 recordings was linked to one of these three variables (Table 3). In the free-text log notes, participants made connections with other aspects of their lives including emotion, food intake, and physical state. These same themes appeared throughout the interviews as well, suggesting a desire to relate daily activities with their BP levels.

	Descriptor	Count	%
Structured from web app Total log entries=2,181	Caffeine	353	16
	Stress	291	13
	Exercise	279	13
Author coded from participant comments in web app Total comments=1,225	Context: activities	549	45
	Context: part of day	340	28
	Context: location	99	8
	Intake (food, drink)	209	17
	Commentary on BP	180	15
	Emotional State	106	9
	Physical State	72	6

Table 3. Participant descriptors for BP measurements. Caffeine, Stress, and Exercise were structured options; other themes were coded from comments in log entries, where there were multiple descriptors possible for a given entry.

BP's relationship to patterns of everyday living

The most common annotation (45% of all comments) from participants was to provide context about a recent or upcoming activity, the part of the day (e.g. bedtime), and their location when they captured their BP. Participants reported taking measurements in a wide variety of settings outside the home including in vehicles and in public spaces. However, having a routine setting, "*was probably the most relevant to me because it was the most controlled environment. Same time of the day, I'm doing the same type of work. I'm interacting with the same type of people... It's so more relevant to me to see during that time because I think more factors are controlled" (P07)*. Participants described work and home as stable places through which to capture a meaningful set of measurements. Participants also explained how a change in pattern, "*shows that our weekends are totally different than the weekdays. I guess keeping that in mind, I'm not too surprised but it is surprising that the blood pressure is so sensitive to I guess routine versus whatever ad hoc thing we're doing" (P01)*. Throughout the logs and interviews, participants stated that their BP data heavily reflected their recent activities and routines.

BP's relationship to food and drink

Food and meals were an important contextual factor that participants associated with BP, despite the fact that there is no clear evidence supporting this type of acute effect. Beyond having caffeine, 17% of the notes included comments about other forms of consumption, including recent meals, alcohol, and cigarettes. Further reflecting this belief, participants responded in the questionnaire about whether different scenarios would lead to an acute increase, decrease, or no change in an average person's BP. More than 75% of participants at baseline and 85% post-study believed a high-sodium meal would increase BP. Though popular discussion about the link between sodium and heart disease is a possible reason for participants' focus on meals, they felt it added relevance and meaning to highlight instances where they either consumed food or drink or had missed a meal.

BP's relationship to emotional and physical states

In the interviews, participants rationalized a given BP reading based on whether they were feeling stressed, anxious, or unwell at the time. P13 mentioned how, *"Stress is a big thing and I know that that definitely raises blood pressure because when I feel stressed and I take it, it's up."* Participants marked 13% of their entries as feeling stressed. In addition, noting physical states, such as feeling tired or unwell, was another way for participants to give more context to BP readings. Ultimately, our study cohort expressed how a given BP value helped them realize how their emotional or physical state was affecting them. Seeing their BP measurement brought attention to, *"my surroundings, my intake, my stress intake and wanting to know more about that and what the triggers are, and how to stop those" (P27)*. Monitoring provided a reflection of their current state and validated periods where they felt stress or excitement.

Hypotheses and experiments to understand BP

The process of incorporating more contextual data alongside the BP measurements helped participants to triangulate possible causes for the fluctuations. Fifteen percent of the log entries included comments about participants' reactions to a particular reading where they often provided explanations for why they recorded a particular BP value. After getting an unusual reading, P33 explained, *"I am wondering if it was the shirt fabric I had on. I will experiment with that tomorrow."* In response to confusion or questions about a given reading, participants began to hypothesize and test out how their BP behaved in relation to a certain activity or aspect of their lives. P27, for example, expressed a desire to set up an experiment where, *"One day for lunch, I would eat a whole bunch of pizza and take it and the next I would eat salad, and see if that was different, and it would make you feel good if you could see a big change in it."* Participants would take their BP before and after climbing stairs, after coming out of a meeting, or in other contexts to see how the activities affected their BP.

Impact on Perceptions of Well-being

BP is a widely used health indicator for clinic diagnosis and treatment. Accordingly, participants framed their experience of measuring BP in relation to health and well-being.

Classifying blood pressure risk

Although participants had heard of hypertension, pre-hypertension, and normal BP prior to this study, most were not able to correctly identify the corresponding numerical thresholds of these categories when asked in the questionnaire. At baseline, 35% and 26% of participants selected the correct thresholds of hypertension and normal BP respectively. We observed an increase to 44% correctly answered for hypertension ($p=0.366$) and 53% correctly answered for normal BP ($p=0.020$) by the end of the study.

We also asked participants to self-describe their BP as normal, pre-hypertensive, or hypertensive (Figure 4). Prior to the study almost all participants (91%) self-identified as having normal BP and only one participant stated they were pre-hypertensive. However, after the study, 24% and 6% classified themselves as pre-hypertensive and hypertensive, respectively ($p=0.003$). This change is corroborated by the calculated average of all sitting measurements that participants recorded in their BP logs. Using clinic-based thresholds for classification, 62% had normal BP and 38% were

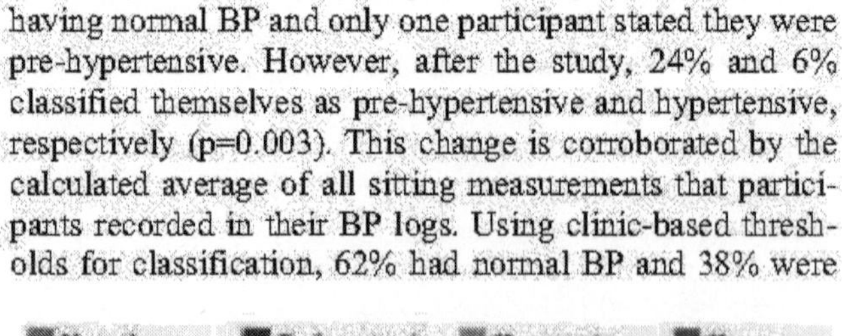

Figure 4. Participants' self-reported classification as either normal, pre-hypertensive, or hypertensive (pre/post), and calculated classification of measurements taken while sitting.

pre-hypertensive or hypertensive. The reason for this change pre- to post-study is unclear, but factors such as enhanced knowledge of BP definitions, greater awareness of their typical BP, or possibly increased anxiety from the readings could have affected participants' classification.

Defining BP beyond "clinical" normal

The change in how participants perceived their BP-related risk reflects a larger interest among participants in understanding how their BP compared to others. During the interviews, participants made comparisons to friends, family, or other groups. They expressed a desire to know, *"is what I'm seeing typical from other people? That was what I'm just trying to figure out" (P30).* How participants defined normal varied. Some simply wanted to know whether they were "healthy". However, many wanted to compare their measurements to individuals that were in a similar age group, the same gender, and a similar lifestyle in terms of physical activity, smoking, and diet. This discussion also led several of the participants to hypothesize that comparisons to others that are younger or healthier might be an effective way to stay motivated around health goals:

> *"So I would like to see not only for my age group because I think the medical community tends to have lower expectations as we age...I want to compare to younger people not—it's the whole thing why people think, 'Oh, we're older so it's okay to have 25 lbs. on.' No it's not." (P08)*

Challenges to BP use in everyday contexts

Prior work has revealed measurement and interpretation challenges with using BP devices [12,13], however, participants in this study also discussed the emotional impact of measurement, concerns about the stigma of using a BP device, and their interest in continuing to measure their BP.

Emotional impact and reactions to BP readings

When the participants measured their BP, the health implications associated with blood pressure would create strong positive and negative emotional reactions. As P27 explains, *"I think subconsciously even looking at it, I would get a little stressed or kind of little anxious because I would be scared it would be really high again."* P10 commented how the process of the cuff inflating was "anxiety-inducing" as it cut off circulation in his arm. Feelings of apprehension about future measurements or the discomfort of using the device put off some participants. Others that had an atypical measurement described feeling panicked and obsessed, taking repeated measurements well beyond the 5 requested per day in order to make sure the readings were correct.

Conversely, participants had positive reactions to their data when they focused less on individual readings. For example, after seeing a graphic visual of his data, P10 explained that, *"Once I thought I was in the norm I was like, 'Yeah, I'm good, nothing to worry about,' and then I just go on with my life."* Another participant actually felt more secure over time while taking measurements at home because, *"You get like an emotional attachment to the thing... it's a little buddy because it's with you and so it feels like it's protecting you, that might sound so funny" (P09).* Participants' framing and association with the BP data and devices influenced their emotional experience.

Associations of BP with illness

Framing is important, as participants described challenges with using the device in an open setting. They felt uncomfortable with how others would perceive them and were concerned about how the device attracted attention and was disruptive to others. Participants described instances where co-workers, friends, or family expressed concern or asked if they were unwell because they were capturing their BP.

> *"This isn't exactly a device that you go for and buy it—you relate this to sickness. So you try to avoid those devices...The design, it does not attract me and it's an aisle that I just try to avoid. It's something with health issues...You never relate this design to I just want to be healthy and I want to keep it there. Versus the [fitness] watch, when I keep it there, I want to be healthy and I want to track it. The design helps to inspire you." (P26)*

P26's experience reflects a current challenge with existing perceptions of BP. The stigma of its association with having a disease or being unwell was a concern across participants.

Continued use of BP device

During the interviews, participants commented on their motivation to continue using the device after the study ended. Regularly monitoring BP helped some to *"understand the readings better. That it does fluctuate. And one reading at the doctor once a year is not going to tell the whole story. Which I thought it did. I really thought that's all you needed" (P31).* Not everyone identified immediate value from using the BP device, however. P10 expressed a desire for additional context to add value or significance to the BP results. He preferred that, *"if the program could be designed that was like—you just had this amount of calories or this kind of food and you'll see this bump in your blood pressure. Yeah, maybe I would be more intrigued to keep up with that kind of data and learn."*

At the study end, seventeen participants stated that they would continue to measure their BP at least once per day. Another thirteen mentioned an interest in capturing their BP periodically, such as, *"one to two times a month just to see. That's about it. And I think that would be sufficient just to kind of—and I would do my three [measurements]—get my average because I think that that's important" (P34).* Four mentioned they were unlikely to continue measuring it regularly, *"because I know I'm more or less in the healthy range—I mean yes I do go into the 120's, but whatever—so I wasn't as concerned about it" (P30).*

We also followed up with participants 60 days after the study to assess their continued use. Twenty-six (76%) of the participants responded. Even though several people continued to measure their BP at least once a week, most respondents reported less frequent measurement than during their final interview (Table 4).

DISCUSSION

Based on the experiences of our participants, there is an opportunity for redesigning future BP devices for a general audience that addresses issues of stigma, measurement variability, and the lack of meaningful, actionable, feedback with current devices. The themes discussed in the previous section are especially relevant as we shift from ad hoc BP measurements in the clinic to more frequent measurement at home by consumers seeking to track and understand general well-being based on their data. Our participant experiences demonstrated that a BP value means little in isolation.

For our participants with limited knowledge of BP, the variation that they experienced influenced their attitudes and understanding of blood pressure. In some cases their intuition of BP during the mornings or after exercise broke down. In other cases, participants associated BP with moments of stress or factors related to their environment. Increased interaction with their BP led many participants to alter their behavior, experiment with how their BP responded to stimuli, and reflected a desire for greater knowledge of how BP links with different aspects of their lives.

Importantly, measuring BP and experiencing variation had an emotional impact on many participants. Observing unusual values caused confusion, frustration, and anxiety that influenced their interest in using the BP device. They discussed their use in terms of normative social influences that aligns with the findings in the autoethnography reported by O'Kane et al. [25]. Participants expressed a desire to situate their BP relative to others—to motivate change or establish a sense of what is normal BP and normal variation. However, some participants started to measure their BP well beyond the study requirements after becoming concerned with a particular elevated reading. This contributed to feelings of stress and may have led to even more elevated readings. Because measuring BP has such strong connotations with illness, devices designed for personal use should consider how this metric will be accepted and interpreted—both positively and negatively—as it becomes more pervasive.

Envisioning future BP devices for personal use

Many participants expressed an interest in regular measurements to ascertain their BP and gain an intuitive understanding of BP variability through introspection. Others wanted to explicitly test the acute impact of certain activities on their BP. To support this need, we envision an unobtrusive, wearable BP device that can capture BP as a dynamic variable throughout the day. This type of device should link with other data such as stress measures and food logs that many of the participants highlighted as relevant to their BP variation. We also know that the relationship between BP and risk of cardiovascular disease is continuous and short-term changes can be meaningful indicators of health risk. Capturing these changes in real-time can provide immediate feedback to users regarding trends and help them to reflect, review, and engage with their BP data.

Post-Study Use	Count	%
More than once/week	4	12
Once/week	4	12
Once/month	9	26
Haven't used device	9	26
No response	8	24

Table 4. Follow-up survey of average self-reported measurement frequency 60 days after the end of the study.

Other participants described the value of BP measurement in terms of a periodic check-up, such as monitoring for preeclampsia for a short duration of time. As an alternative to a device built for continuous monitoring, we envision a system that reimagines the pharmacy BP kiosk. However, unlike a kiosk, our participants did not want a snapshot of their BP at a single point in time, but preferred a way to temporarily capture their BP for a period of time—such as monitoring several days to capture an average and evaluate longitudinal trends. They also did not want to manage or find a place for a cumbersome, infrequently used device in the home, nor have to go to a fixed location like a pharmacy. The users of this new system do not need to monitor their BP every day, but are interested in a momentary, repeated measure assessment that reports their health status and how they compare to others. They prefer measuring their BP in an environment that is convenient and comfortable using a system that is either disposable or can be integrated unobtrusively into their home environment.

Design recommendations

Even though our participants strongly desired to track their BP at home, they were dissatisfied with the capabilities of typical home devices. Here, we consider the implications of short-term fluctuations and an audience new to BP monitoring. We suggest several design considerations that can improve the relevance, actionable value, emotional impact, and intelligibility of BP data captured for generalized use.

Making BP data relevant and context-sensitive

The importance of situating BP in context is evident with the variety of environmental and situational variables that participants highlighted in the study. Participants did not discuss their BP values independently, but often connected readings with their workplace, stress, food and drink, exercise, or other activities. Bentley and other researchers have argued that for longer-term personal monitoring, a multifaceted, holistic outlook on what to track can enable more nuanced and personalized feedback from sensor data [2]. BP devices should have greater integration with sensors that detect location, movement, stress, and other physical metrics to help individuals understand changes in blood pressure in relation to relevant aspects of their lives.

Participants also described adding context to BP data by comparing their numbers to other groups to get a sense of what is "normal". This desire for having a certain BP status is a clear opportunity to leverage crowd-sourcing to provide an individual with an understanding of their data relative to others with similar age, gender, or lifestyle. Participants also wanted to compare to others' BP in order to set goals for self-improvement. Based on data from younger or healthier users, devices could even infer and recommend activities and lifestyle changes that would help users attain health goals. Having a personalized history of BP changes in combination with other persons' data can provide users with valuable trajectories for predicting health risks [1] and help motivate behavior changes in a person's life.

Making BP data meaningful and actionable
The manner in which BP data is presented seemed to have a large impact on participants' interpretations and perceived value. The typical device's display of a snapshot of SBP, DBP, and pulse values provides little sense of the form or shape of their blood pressure over time. In cases of strong variation this may have hindered pattern recognition, and participants' prior experience influenced their assumptions and expectations. For example, many participants expected their lowest BP reading in the morning and were often confused by the rise and fall of BP throughout the day. The participants also cited the order that the numbers are presented and their relative magnitude as why they focused on SBP or DBP. Recognizing these situations where expectations break down or when the data display directs user attention provides an opportunity to focus design to educate users about meaningful BP variability and trends.

Blood pressure devices can also move beyond supporting reflection toward providing actionable information. Systems should flexibly handle diverse representations of BP data such as binary (healthy or not), categorical (health risk), ordinal (population comparisons), or continuous (trends, correlations with everyday living) to not only answer user queries but support active decision-making aligned with personal goals. A continuous monitoring tool that can recognize patterns, learn baselines, and identify meaningful trends can support real-time decisions through contextually aware feedback. Instead of placing a burden on the user or a third party to analyze a large, complex dataset, the device can produce an appropriate data representation that helps evaluate actions relative to changes in BP.

Making BP data desirable
Even though participants expressed interest in evaluating correlations between their current mental state and their BP, atypical BP readings among some participants increased their anxiety in a manner similar to the white coat effect observed in clinics. The way that individuals perceive BP devices and how BP results are communicated to them can affect this type of emotional response. We suggest that future designs frame BP data in terms of averages and ranges to reflect measurement uncertainty and mitigate the psychological impact of a single high reading. Framing measurements this way also offers an opportunity to incorporate better visual displays that emphasize patterns, trends, and deviations from the mean rather than single-point measures.

Making BP data trustworthy and intelligible
Most home BP devices, including the one used in this study, will provide a clinical stratification of BP based on a single measurement. Yet within person variation, environmental stimuli, and device inaccuracy create significant measurement variability [10]. Even clinical guidelines recommend incorporating additional factors such as comorbidities and lifestyle behaviors in order to classify cardiovascular risk [19]. A single reading provides a misleading understanding of an individual's BP. In a home setting, participants have the ability to capture regular measurements of their BP. Therefore, classification of a person's health status may be more relevant and representative as an average or visualization of BP trends. Devices could begin with typical variance as ascertained from other users or based on existing literature and slowly personalize this to the individual, emphasizing their BP as a range. The devices can also improve their intelligibility by providing an indication of confidence in a given reading depending on factors such as deviation from an average BP or awareness of the possible influence of environmental variables.

Limitations
Because our study was primarily qualitative, and because our participant sample skewed slightly towards a physically active and educated demographic, we caution against overgeneralizing our findings. Moreover, although participants were exposed to their BP repeatedly during the study period, a two-week interval might be inadequate to fully reflect and understand their blood pressure. However, we believe the open log entries and the multiple interviews provide insight into how non-hypertensive individuals begin to understand and relate to BP as a personal health metric. This type of real-time in situ data capture is a well-recognized approach to understanding ubiquitous technologies [6].

CONCLUSION
BP is a valuable metric to incorporate as part of personal informatics systems for health. We identified self-tracking needs including responding to BP variability through repeated or continuous measures and supporting personal discovery of BP fluctuations linked to everyday living. Reframing BP devices away from disease management toward well-being can help reduce the stigma and emotional anxiety associated with BP and stimulate greater adoption and use of these devices. Future designs should consider more casual use contexts in addition to health maintenance.

Through our analysis of participant experiences with tracking their BP, we illuminate how individuals collecting more frequent at-home BP measurements perceive BP variability and make associations with activities and aspects of daily living. We also demonstrate the impact and relevance that measurement of BP had on a young, healthy population. Finally, we discuss opportunities to improve the design of BP devices through better support of individual reflection, diverse data representations, transparency around BP variability, and integration with other sensor data. Many BP devices currently on the market are still designed for clinical needs and uses. The shift towards sensor-based personal health monitoring provides an opportunity to innovate on this metric and make blood pressure measurement more accessible and relevant to a broader audience.

REFERENCES

1. Allen, N.B., Siddique, J., Wilkins, J.T., et al. Blood pressure trajectories in early adulthood and subclinical atherosclerosis in middle age. JAMA 311, 5 (2014), 490–7.
2. Bentley, F., Tollmar, K., Stephenson, P., et al. Health Mashups: Presenting Statistical Patterns between Wellbeing Data and Context in Natural Language to Promote Behavior Change. ACM TOCHI 20, 5 (2013), 1–27.
3. Cheng, S., Lichtman, J.H., Amatruda, J.M., et al. Knowledge of blood pressure levels and targets in patients with coronary artery disease in the USA. Journal of human hypertension 19, 10 (2005), 769–74.
4. Choe, E.K., Lee, N.B., Lee, B., Pratt, W., Kientz, J.A. Understanding quantified-selfers' practices in collecting and exploring personal data. Proc CHI 2014, ACM Press (2014), 1143–1152.
5. Clemensen, J., Craggs, M., Marcussen, C., et al. Chronically Ill Citizens and Home Monitoring: "Nothing to talk about"!. eTELEMED 2013, (2013), 47–52.
6. Consolvo, S., Harrison, B., Smith, I., et al. Conducting In Situ Evaluations for and With Ubiquitous Computing Technologies. International Journal of Human-Computer Interaction 22, 1-2 (2007), 103–118.
7. Cuckson, A.C., Reinders, A., Shabeeh, H., Shennan, A.H. Validation of the Microlife BP 3BTO-A oscillometric blood pressure monitoring device according to a modified British Hypertension Society protocol. Blood pressure monitoring 7, 6 (2002), 319–24.
8. Epstein, D., Cordeiro, F., Bales, E., Fogarty, J., Munson, S. Taming data complexity in lifelogs. Proc DIS 2014, ACM Press (2014), 667–676.
9. Fox, S., Duggan, M. Tracking for Health. Pew Internet & American Life Project, Washington, DC, 2013.
10. Gerin, W., Schwartz, A.R., Schwartz, J.E., et al. Limitations of current validation protocols for home blood pressure monitors for individual patients. Blood pressure monitoring 7, 6 (2002), 313–8.
11. Go, A.S., Mozaffarian, D., Roger, V.L., et al. Heart disease and stroke statistics-2013 update: a report from the American Heart Association. Circulation 127, 1 (2013), e6–e245.
12. Grönvall, E., Verdezoto, N. Understanding challenges and opportunities of preventive blood pressure self-monitoring at home. Proc ECCE 2013, ACM Press (2013), 1.
13. Grönvall, E., Verdezoto, N. Beyond self-monitoring. Proc UbiComp 2013, ACM Press (2013), 587.
14. Hermida, R.C., Ayala, D.E., Portaluppi, F. Circadian variation of blood pressure: the basis for the chronotherapy of hypertension. Advanced drug delivery reviews 59, 9-10 (2007), 904–22.
15. Kay, M., Morris, D., Schraefel, M., Kientz, J.A. There's no such thing as gaining a pound. Proc Ubicomp 2013, ACM Press (2013), 401.
16. Le, V.-V., Mitiku, T., Sungar, G., Myers, J., Froelicher, V. The blood pressure response to dynamic exercise testing: a systematic review. Progress in cardiovascular diseases 51, 2 (2008), 135–60.
17. Li, I., Dey, A.K., Forlizzi, J. Understanding my data, myself. Proc Ubicomp 2011, ACM Press (2011), 405.
18. Lim, B.Y., Dey, A.K. Investigating intelligibility for uncertain context-aware applications. Proc Ubicomp 2011, ACM Press (2011), 415.
19. Mancia, G., Fagard, R., Narkiewicz, K., et al. 2013 ESH/ESC Guidelines for the management of arterial hypertension. European heart jrnl 34, 28 (2013), 2159–219.
20. Mancia, G. Short- and long-term blood pressure variability: present and future. Hypertension 60, 2 (2012), 512–7.
21. Mort, J.R., Kruse, H.R. Timing of blood pressure measurement related to caffeine consumption. Annals Pharmacotherapy 42, 1 (2008), 105–10.
22. Nair, D., Tan, S.-Y., Gan, H.-W., et al. The use of ambulatory tonometric radial arterial wave capture to measure ambulatory blood pressure: the validation of a novel wrist-bound device in adults. Journal of human hypertension 22, 3 (2008), 220–2.
23. National Center for Health Statistics. Percent Distribution of Number of Visits to Health Care Professionals by Selected Characteristics: 2000 and 2009. Statistical Abstract of the U.S.: 2010, 2010.
24. Niiranen, T.J., Hänninen, M.-R., Johansson, J., et al. Home-measured blood pressure is a stronger predictor of cardiovascular risk than office blood pressure: the Finn-Home study. Hypertension 55, 6 (2010), 1346–51.
25. O'Kane, A.A., Rogers, Y., Blandford, A.E. Gaining empathy for non-routine mobile device use through autoethnography. Proc ACM CHI '14, ACM Press (2014), 987–990.
26. Pickering, T.G., White, W.B., Giles, T.D., et al. When and how to use self (home) and ambulatory blood pressure monitoring. J Am Soc Hypertens 4, 2 (2010), 56–61.
27. Rothwell, P.M. Limitations of the usual blood-pressure hypothesis and importance of variability, instability, and episodic hypertension. Lancet 375, 9718 (2010), 938–48.

Concealing or Revealing Mobile Medical Devices? Designing for Onstage and Offstage Presentation

Aisling Ann O'Kane
UCL Interaction Centre
University College London
London, United Kingdom
a.okane@cs.ucl.ac.uk

Yvonne Rogers
UCL Interaction Centre
University College London
London, United Kingdom
y.rogers@ucl.ac.uk

Ann E. Blandford
UCL Interaction Centre
University College London
London, United Kingdom
a.blandford@ucl.ac.uk

ABSTRACT

Adults with Type 1 Diabetes have choices regarding the technology they use to self-manage their chronic condition. They can use glucose meters, insulin pumps, smartphone apps, and other technologies to support their everyday care. However, little is known about how their social lives might influence what they adopt or how they use technologies. A multi-method study was conducted to examine contextual factors that influence their technology use. While individual differences play a large role in everyday use, social factors were also found to influence use. For example, people can hide their devices in uncertain social situations or show them off to achieve a purpose. We frame these social behaviours using Goffman's theatre metaphor of onstage and offstage behaviour, and discuss how this kind of analysis can inform the design of future mobile medical devices for self-management of chronic conditions.

INTRODUCTION

Type 1 Diabetes (T1D) is a serious chronic condition that can involve the use of various mobile medical devices to support everyday self-care, and people's adoption and use of diabetes technologies can differ significantly as devices become individually appropriated [36]. The range of T1D technologies includes glucose meters, continuous glucose meters, insulin pumps, and mobile phone applications. As T1D devices are mobile and need to be used in various contexts, it is important to understand how user experience might influence how devices are used in practice.

T1D is an auto-immune chronic condition that is often associated with childhood onset [27], but people of all ages can be diagnosed with it. It involves the pancreas producing insufficient quantities of insulin, a hormone required for the regulation of blood glucose (BG), but the condition can be managed [21]. For T1D, careful self-management practices are encouraged by medical practitioners: low BG levels (hypoglycemia, or 'hypos') can lead to immediate health concerns, including feeling physically ill or even falling unconscious, while excess levels of BG (hyperglycemia or 'hypers') can eventually culminate in complications, such as eye, foot, kidney, and heart disease. Personal management practices include calculating medication doses to inject based on factors such as personal situation (e.g. digested sugars and carbohydrates, exercise, sickness, and stress), temperature/weather, their current BG level, and past experience. Balancing BG levels with ingested glucose and injected insulin can control the condition, significantly reducing the impact on a person's life.

Most diabetes care involves some form of self-management. This means people with diabetes are *"more than passive recipients of medical expertise"* [10]. Lutfey and Wishner [22] suggest that the term 'compliance' should not be used in efforts to improve self-management practices. Instead, they propose using 'adherence', which suggests appropriate autonomy in defining and following self-management plans for diabetes. However, people's plans are not necessarily the same as the actions they take: actions are contingent on the unfolding context [39], which is relational, dynamic, occasioned, and arising from the on-going activity [9]. This is of particular relevance when looking at the self-management plans of people with T1D, where self-management occurs on a *"daily basis within the context of the other goals, priorities, health issues, family demands, and other personal concerns that make up their lives"* [10]. Self-management practices vary [37] but there is little research on how mobile T1D technologies are chosen to be used for everyday self-management and how everyday social life might influence practice.

To address this gap, we conducted three user studies that examined how T1D devices are adopted, carried, and used. We used contextual interviews, a diary study, and observation of a T1D group meet-up. In the data analysis reported here, we used Goffman's theatre metaphor of how people present themselves to others. This conceptual framing provides insight into the nuanced ways adults with TID conceal or reveal the use of mobile self-management devices in social situations, which could benefit the design of future mobile self-management devices for chronic conditions.

CHI 2015, April 18–23, 2015, Seoul, Republic of Korea.

ACM 978-1-4503-3145-6/15/04...$15.00.
http://dx.doi.org/10.1145/2702123.2702453

SOCIAL FACTORS AND SELF-MANAGEMENT

A person's sociocultural context has an impact on how they cope and prioritize care when self-managing a chronic condition [18, 19, 24, 31, 38]. It has been found that chronic conditions can lead to disruptions in relationships, and that how people adapt self-care is influenced by social factors [5]. Healthcare is personal, so privacy can be important to people with diabetes (e.g. [29]). They can perceive stigma from their communities and their workplaces [26]. Perceived stigma can also cause self-consciousness around glucose meter testing and insulin pump use [30, 33], and people often go to great lengths to hide their condition [18]. Beyond stigma, concerns about discretion around family and friends can interfere in diabetes self-care practices [26], and strangers can ask awkward questions [30].

On the other hand, showing off medical devices has become a popular trend in social media. For example, recently, a model posted bikini pictures showing the colostomy bag that she requires for self-managing Crohn's disease. These pictures were intended to spread awareness of the condition. They went viral, with over nine million people viewing them [41]. Similarly, Miss Idaho 2014 showed off her insulin pump during the bikini competition, causing #showmeyourpump to trend on Twitter leading to more people posting photos of their devices [7].

The social act of broadcasting versus hiding devices presents a dilemma for designers. Should they design future ones to be hidden from view or make them more visible, even fashionable? To help address this question we propose using Goffman's theoretical framing of the ways that people present themselves in their daily lives [13]. Goffman uses the metaphor of theatre to explain face-to-face interactions where people attempt to control the impression they give: *"Sometimes the individual will act in a thoroughly calculating manner, expressing himself in a given way solely in order to give the kind of impression to others that is likely to evoke from them a specific response he is concerned to obtain"* [13]. People perform in front of others as if they were actors, choosing the props, and costume they present *onstage* to their audience. In their *offstage* life, while still in a social context, they can set aside the performance and interact with others without performing, yet still managing the impression they give. *Backstage* is when people can put down their 'front' and be themselves, for example when they are alone. In social settings, people present themselves to others either offstage or onstage, which is the focus of this paper.

Goffman's concept of performance has been used previously in HCI to discuss 'stages' in social media [42] or collaborative tablet use [14]. In the healthcare domain, Benjamin and colleagues found that seniors with chronic pain went to great lengths to manage the impressions they gave others [2]. It was found that people participated in revealing as well as concealing their chronic pain to different audiences, depending on factors such as how supportive the social context was. For the presentation aspect of Goffman's metaphor, the setting and the appearance of the act are influenced by the props the player is using or, in the case of diabetes, the technologies used. Although there have been attempts to mitigate the influences of social factors on self-care through educating people with T1D about potential social challenges [11], less is known about how the design of mobile medical devices might impact the presentation of self for people with T1D in the context of their everyday social lives.

CONTEXT AND MEDICAL DEVICES

Stressing the importance of understanding context, the usability engineering standard for medical devices, including T1D technologies, provides methods, processes, and considerations that suggest observation of real world use. As *"context of use can have a significant impact on usability of the medical device user interface"* [1], practitioners are urged to understand spatial, social, technological, hygienic, physical, and activity contextual factors. Given a defined clinical workplace such as a hospital, this is difficult with regards to ethics, access, privacy, etc. [12], but for pervasive healthcare technology used beyond the walls of an institution, observation becomes notably more complex.

Studying technology use 'in the wild' is inherently difficult and there is uncertainty in the outcomes [15]. It can be challenging as *"the researcher has to make sense of data in the wild, where there are many factors and inter-dependencies at play that might be causing the observed effect"* [34]. These inter-dependencies have led to a broadening of concerns, and the incorporation of perspectives such as Technology as Experience [25], which according to Rogers [33] promotes expanding the realm of focus to not only include usability or utility, but also the felt experience of technology use as these *"interlinked facets and concerns are what most of us engage with in our everyday actions and interactions with others"* [34].

DIABETES TECHNOLOGIES IN EVERYDAY LIFE

Isomursu, Kuutti, and Väinäm point out that *"mobile applications are designed to be used in a mobile context, so they should also be evaluated in a mobile context"* [16]. However, this can be hard to achieve with T1D technologies, so retrospective measures of experience have typically been used such as self-report and clinical outcomes, as well as contextual probes [24]. In building a mobile phone application, Owen and colleagues [30] interviewed people about their use of glucose meters focusing on their need for contextual information to interpret results, particularly during non-routine times. Also for the purpose of building technology to aid reflection on how lifestyle might impact self-care practices [23], Mamykina et al. [24] conducted interviews, attended support groups, and used cultural probes to investigate self-management practices, highlighting how participants generate hypotheses during self-care.

Storni used an ethnomethodological approach and also attended support groups, shadowed participants, and conducted in-depth interviews to understand technology use [36, 37]. His work focused on the different ways technology is appropriated individually and how people's lay expertise informs management, ultimately arguing for an approach to design that is less technologically deterministic and focused on non-compliance, as there are large individual differences between users.

User studies conducted in the healthcare technology domain have adopted a variety of methods to understand the context of use (e.g. [35]), but there is very little research on how people use a range of mobile T1D technologies during their everyday self-management in social settings. Here we use a pragmatic multi-method situated approach in conjunction with Goffman's analytic framing to reveal the nuanced contextual factors that influence mobile device use, with a focus on how they are used in social settings during people's everyday lives.

METHODOLOGY

Technologies Investigated

As noted above, a range of devices can be used in T1D self management care, and it is necessary to understand their use and functions, at least superficially, to 'make sense' of the studies reported here. Glucose meters (Figure 1, left) are most frequently used to measure BG levels for the everyday calculation of medication doses as well as for identifying hypos and hypers [8]. The meter is used in conjunction with a finger-pricking device so that a small droplet of blood is put on a testing strip, and the meter reports BG levels via an interface. Continuous glucose monitors (CGM) are not as commonly used, but still part of some people's everyday T1D care routines (Figure 2, right). They give a BG reading every few minutes [17]. A sensor is attached to a person's torso or arm with a small needle to test the level. This is communicated through a small wearable transmitter or cord to a receiving device with an interface showing the levels.

A self-administered shot (e.g. in the arm, abdomen, or thigh) or an insulin pump is used to inject the required amount of insulin. Insulin pumps come in various form factors, including being attached to the back of a user's arm or in a pager-sized device attached by a tube to a removable patch with a needle on the abdomen (Figure 1, right). The user adds insulin to the device and they can use an interface to control the injection.

People with diabetes can track their own health data and get suggestions for insulin doses using apps that they have downloaded on their mobile phones or other devices. There are many diabetes apps currently available (over 900 in Apple App store and 1500 in Google Play at the time of writing).

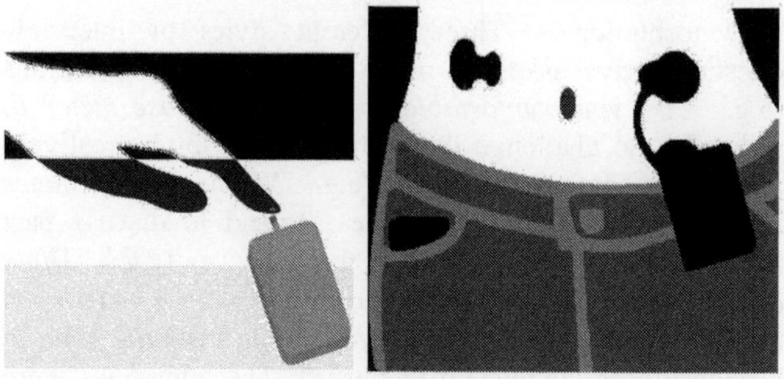

Figure 1: A glucose meter on the left and a continuous glucose monitor with remote and an insulin pump on the right

Although adults with Type 1 Diabetes can choose to use a variety of these mobile technologies, the majority have typically used at least one, a glucose meter, for many years. We were interested in how people carry their technologies throughout the day and the ways they use them in a variety of everyday contexts.

Methods

A multi-method approach was used to explore the use and adoption of T1D technologies, including contextual interviews, a diary study, and observation of a T1D tech meet-up, all conducted by the first author.

Contextual Interviews (CI)	7 (5 female) in Los Angeles aged 23-53 6 (2 female) in London aged 26-65 7 (5 female) in Toronto aged 23-31
Diary Study (DS)	9 (9 female) in London aged 24-39
Tech Meet-Up (TM)	12 (10 female) in London aged 20-60
TOTAL	**41 participants aged 23-65**

Table 1. Participants' location, ages, and gender

All participants (Table 1) were over the age of 18, had been diagnosed with T1D at least six months prior to the study, were responsible for their own self-management, and used at least a glucose meter in their daily self-care. Because of difficulties with recruitment [28], a variety of recruitment methods were used: posters at grocery stores, flyers given out in pharmacies, online recruitment notices on public forums such as Reddit and Craigslist, diabetes email lists, T1D charity social media, and through snowball sampling. All participants were compensated for their time and gave informed consent as stipulated by UCL ethics clearance and human protection policies for international fieldwork research.

Contextual Interview Study

Interviews in the context of use can give a richer account than other types of interviews [3]. We conducted our interviews with participants in a public social situation. The first author met participants (n=20) in cafes or restaurants of their choosing and discussed their use and adoption of

T1D technologies. Three different styles of interview questions were asked to probe a range of use situations (e.g., *"Are you comfortable using your glucose meter in public?"*), to challenge the participants to think creatively about their T1D technologies (e.g., *"If my glucose meter had a personality, it would be..."*), and to discuss past issues that they have had with their devices (e.g., *"Think about the last time you did not use your glucose meter even though it might have been useful. What were the general circumstances leading up to this?"*). The interviews were semi-structured and the interviewer probed any issues with adoption or use of the devices. Each interview concluded when the interviewer felt a clear picture of the participant's everyday use of the devices had been gained. They were then asked to demonstrate their use of the glucose meter and were free to add any further thoughts in an open conversation format. All interviews lasted at least one hour and were audio recorded for transcription.

Diary Study

Diary studies are a non-invasive way of gaining information from users' natural settings [32]. We asked participants (n=9) to capture the moment after they had used their glucose meter and a diabetes application used to track blood glucose levels [6]. An entry interview using the same interview questions as above was conducted at UCL, where the diabetes app was set up on their iPhone and an observation took place with their first use of it. The participants then made diary entries (a range of photos, wide angle lens photos, and text entries) for four weeks when they used their glucose meter. An exit interview was then held using an open conversation format where the entries were reviewed. The entry interviews were at least one hour long, there were 5-minute weekly phone check-in conversations, and the exit interviews were at least 90 minutes long; all were audio or video recorded for transcription.

Observation of a Group Meet-Up

Participant observation can capture the situated use of technologies [3]. The first author attended a diabetes tech meet-up that happens every four months in London, where people gather at a hotel restaurant to casually drink, eat, and chat about T1D technologies, which also allowed for insights from friendly group discussions. She was introduced to the group through their email list and then attended the meet-up where she introduced herself to people (n=12) arriving at different times. She wore her university ID and did not attempt to participate in the conversations, other than to answer questions about her research interests. Audio recording was determined to be inappropriate for the setting, so she took detailed handwritten notes for the duration of the meeting. These were based on the conversations between attendees and observations of their diabetes tech use as they ate and drank over the course of the evening. The meet-up lasted five hours.

Data Analysis

Thematic analysis was used to analyse what the participants said, did, and revealed in the three different studies [4] and AtlasTi was employed together with discussions among the authors about the themes. The first set of themes focused on the misuse, inappropriate use, appropriate use, and unintended use of the technology discussed by the participants. Issues included not bringing the technology with them, not adopting the technology at all, not using the technology when they should, or using it in a way that it was not designed for; instances of appropriate use were compared against those of misuse. The second phase examined what circumstances led to these instances, including looking at contradictions within an individual's data set or inconsistencies between participants. The third phase of analysis involved identifying commonalities and contradictions across the data set. The emergent themes were each considered in relation to Goffman's conceptual metaphor for presentation of self.

FINDINGS

As it is a condition that requires management throughout a person's day (and particularly around mealtimes), the use of T1D devices sometimes happens in situations that involve other people. A number of specific issues with adoption of devices, carrying devices, and use of devices were identified, and these often occurred in social situations. They included encounters with family, friends, colleagues, romantic partners, people in different countries while travelling, and strangers. Everyday normal routine involved a broad range of self-care practices in front of familiar people and social situations (offstage), but non-routine times led to uncharacteristic hiding in uncertain social situations and showing off in social situations where there was something to be gained (onstage).

There is a Wide Variation in "Normal Use"

Participants showed a wide range of individual differences in how they handled their devices in their everyday offstage routines, which involve familiar public situations, routine work lives, and their personal lives.

Public Use

Some participants do not care about strangers noticing if they are using their devices or that they have T1D. Many described how they were blind to the general public (*"Honestly, honestly I don't care. Everybody's got something."* – CI6). Others explained that they did not care if strangers were squeamish about blood: *"They've got a problem with it, they've got to deal with it."* – DS6.

Many participants described how their normal routine would involve consistent use of their devices on public transport. One participant described herself as *"always late for something"* and said that she would wait until she got on public transport to use the devices as she considered it *"dead time"*, and did not bother to try to hide her glucose meter or insulin pump: *"People usually stare at me on the tube if there's anyone around when I pull that out but, again, I think I'm so used to it sort of, it's like, I don't know no one's... [It doesn't matter someone will see?] Yes."* – DS8.

Other participants tended to be more private with their device use and self-care in public, often trying to conceal their devices. One participant described it as *"secrecy in a way"* and she did not want attention of strangers: *"I won't want to do anything too out in the public that might create, sort of, someone looking at me or something."* – DS2.

Another participant said that although she doesn't care if strangers know she has a medical condition, sometimes she just didn't want to risk having to bother answering any questions about it if someone noticed and was curious: *"Sometimes that's fine and sometimes I'm, like, kind of a bugger to explain, whereas if you're obviously trying to do it discreetly, they're less likely to ask a question."* – DS9.

Work Life Use

Although a few participants were currently unemployed or were students, most had full-time jobs. As going to work was part of their weekly routine, they developed habits for dealing with self-care in front of colleagues. Some people were quite protective and secretive about their diabetes when with colleagues. One participant discussed how she had to tell her boss when she started for health and safety reasons, but avoided conducting self-care activities when co-workers were around: *"There's no one that walks past me, you know. And maybe I just pick it when it's quiet. Although people over the other side of the desk won't see me."* – DS4.

Others were far more open with their self-care activities and use of their devices. One participant travelled to different construction sites as part of her job, as well as having a desk in an open office. She routinely tested herself at her desk and *"on site"* with no concerns about being seen by her co-workers: *"I would have told most people [...]. And then, because you're doing blood tests and doing injections, people will just figure it out or they'll ask you or whatever."* – DS9.

Use Around Family, Friends and Partners

Participants' everyday lives involved regular contact with family, friends, and romantic partners. This regular contact allowed for self-care regimes to become routine, but how open people were in front of close family and friends differed quite significantly.

Some people were very comfortable with their romantic partners and did not hide their self-care from their view. One participant (DS5) described an inside joke among insulin pump users that their *"partner knows when they're going to get lucky because, you know, you're snuggling in bed and then you're, like, "let me just disconnect my pump.""* She was very comfortable showing her devices in these intimate situations: *"We've got to disconnect the insulin pump because we don't want to get the tubing wrapped up in any awkward places. And sometimes... well, not sometimes, it's, kind of, like, clockwork there will be some buzz or some vibration from the table while we're... you know."* – DS5.

CI7 was also very open with her self-care regime in front of her live-in partner so he was familiar with the devices and how she used them. She was so comfortable with him being involved in her self-care, that if she fell asleep when drunk, he would use her glucose meter to test her BG levels and then would inject her if necessary.

Some participants were very open with their use of the devices around close friends who also had T1D or who worked in diabetes care. For example, DS5 described a glucose meter drinking game they made up called *"blood glucose bingo."* CI6 described borrowing insulin saying *"he owed me one"* and DS1 described testing together as well: *"If she's testing and then I'm like, I may as well and then try and see who gets the best reading"* – DS1.

In other cases, participants concealed their routines from their friends and families, incorporating knowledge from prior experience about how people react to their self-management practices. One participant knew that her sister was quite squeamish about blood, and chose to hide her use of the glucose meter from her: *"It's a weirder, sort of, social thing to do, and then others might be a little bit squeamish, a little bit... because testing of blood in front of someone, some people... my sister, she's just like, "ooh!""* – DS7.

CI18 was very private about her self-management in front of her parents, who she lived with. She knew that her diagnosis from three years ago was very upsetting for her mother and that she still got upset when reminded of it, so she tended to go to her bedroom where she could keep her self-care and devices away from her mother's eyes, including before every family meal.

Summary of 'Normal Use'

The findings highlight individual differences between the participants in how they practice self-care in their day-to-day lives, leading to varied use of the mobile medical technology. People ranged from open use to slightly hidden use to going into different rooms to conceal device use. Routine social situations influenced how people use their devices, dependent on their preferences, past experiences, and the social situations they regularly encounter. Although they were accustomed to the social situations, they were still aware of the way they presented themselves to others when using their T1D devices, despite their familiarity (offstage).

Uncertainty in Social Situations can Lead to Hiding

Familiarity with a social situation enabled some participants to adopt consistent management strategies, while unfamiliar settings led to a sense of uncertainty among participants, which influenced their use of the devices. Several participants described situations where they felt uncomfortable using their devices out in the open. For example, DS2 described the link between uncertainty and the personal aspect of the condition: *"When you take it out you feel like you're exposing something about yourself for people to, sort of, either, sort of, judge that it's good or bad, in a way, and then I more, sort of, fear someone's reaction"* – DS2.

Practices of hiding the devices in times of uncertainty, such as in new romantic situations, starting a new job, and meeting unfamiliar people, are examples of Goffman's *"protective practices"* [13].

Uncertainty in Romance and Attraction

When asked about times they may have benefited from using their devices, but chose not to, people described instances related to their romantic lives. Even chance encounters in public could lead to hiding devices: *"It sounds really silly, but if you see someone, like, attractive or on the bus or something, you don't really want to do something potentially, like, weird, and they'd be like, "ugh""* – DS2.

The first author met CI20 in a cafe where he ordered a sandwich and proceeded to test and inject visibly in front of a busy line of people at the counter. He was very relaxed in describing his self-management habits, but looked uncomfortable when asked if there were times when he should have used his glucose meter and didn't. He went on to describe a time he did not use his glucose meter for an entire day. He was on a first date and they spent the day at the beach. As there were no washrooms or places to hide his use of the glucose meter, he decided not to use it at all, leaving it in his backpack. He did not want his date to see his medical device kit, nor want her to know about his condition that early in their courting.

A first date can be a nerve-racking experience where you might not want to reveal everything about yourself. The beginning of a relationship is a time when people can be quite uncertain, as they do not know where the relationship will lead, and do not want to mess it up. Although one participant did not personally agree, she said many friends concealed their conditions and devices: *"I have lots of friends that go out with guys, and they don't even tell them they're diabetic for, like, months. I don't even know how they hide it"* – DS1. Another participant said that she did not want to make it an issue too early: *"I try to keep it secret but not secret as in I don't ever want them to know; it's just whether it comes up or not because I don't want to make it a big deal."* – DS2.

Even when relationships are established, there can be uncertainty over time with regards to attraction. Attraction can change with life changes, including the addition of a new mobile medical device. A lot of participants avoided adopting an insulin pump, as they said they did not want to feel physically attached to something and mentioned it looked unattractive to be physically hooked up to a device. An older married participant (TM1) initially said she was interested in getting an insulin pump, but revealed to the group at the meet-up that she was concerned that *"it is not very sexy"* to use during intimate situations and also that she was concerned about *"what it will be like to use it in the summer with tighter and more revealing clothing."*

Furthering Jobs and Careers

Some first dates can feel like job interviews and both involve what Goffman calls *"impression management"* [13]. Uncertainty in jobs or careers was also found to influence participants in hiding their medical devices. DS8 was very open about her glucose meter use and wore an insulin pump quite openly. She was quite adamant that there were no times where she would hide or not use them. However, in one of her diary entries, there was a photo of what looked like a trade show and the first author probed further on how she used her devices at this time. She said she hid them when there were potential clients around. She went on to explain that even when in the office, if she had a face-to-face meeting with a client *"I normally schedule it around a time where I don't necessarily have to take my blood sugar."* This was because she felt a certain level of vulnerability with regards to her career, saying that only *"if I were very senior in my position I'd feel comfortable doing it."*

In the case of changing jobs or trying to get a new one, there was even more uncertainty about the situation. A participant in the diary study had changed jobs recently, so was more private at work. Another participant was unemployed at the time of the study and was going for job interviews. As Goffman describes: *"the interviewee will pay much attention to his appearance and manner, not merely to create a favourable impression but also to be on the safe side and forestall any unfavourable impression that might be unwittingly conveyed"* [13]. In one case, the participant did not want to risk being seen with her medical devices, so she used her glucose meter in the building beside where her interview was to take place: *"Something like that could possibly sway them to take someone else rather than me. Because yes, as much as people say the discrimination doesn't happen, it does happen."* – DS2.

In other situations, the reason for participants hiding their devices was not based on conjecture, but on past experiences. A participant who was a substitute teacher described a situation where she was at a new school and went to the staff room to test and inject. The principal at the school saw her and told her that it was a health and safety concern, which she believed led to her losing that job. Even after leaving that place of employment, the experience had a lasting effect preventing her from again openly using her devices or injecting in front of people at work: *"I'm more careful about injecting when I'm in a new school, like, in the staff room and stuff. I don't really just, like, flash all the syringes around. I just do it really quickly, you know."* – DS3.

Unfamiliar People

Some social situations involved uncertainty with people at arm's length. For example, DS9 referred to a *"group of people who I know but I don't really know"* influencing her self-care practices. Many participants discussed how they were either comfortable or uncomfortable using their devices among the public, friends, and family at meals as part of their more regular routines, but sometimes meals involved engaging with new people, such as meeting friends of friends for dinner. This kind of new encounter also influenced participants to hide their devices: *"The under the desk or under the table or whatever scenario. It's people who I'm just acquainted with rather than friends with or don't know at all."* – DS9.

There were also cases where the general public became a lot more uncertain. For example, one participant used a diabetes app to track her BG levels in an area of London where she would not normally show off her iPhone (DS1). There were other unfamiliar situations people found themselves in, such as taking public transport when on holiday. One participant, who had earlier described herself as not caring about strangers, found herself hiding behind her boyfriend as she was uncertain of the social situation: *"Maybe in Morocco, I might be more particular about... I'd maybe get my boyfriend to just stand there and I'll do this, you know."* – DS9.

Summary: Hiding Devices

Most of the participants discussed times where they hide or might not use their medical devices even though it would be useful for them to do so. Many of these situations were linked to the nature of the social situation that they were in. Specifically, that they felt uncomfortable using the devices because of the presence of other people they were not familiar with. Such situations made them feel uncertain, leading them to actively hide their self-care and their mobile medical devices rather than show them off, not knowing what might happen. Being uncertain about their audience means they participate in *"protective practices"* [13] onstage to manage the impression that they give off.

Showing Off to People can Achieve a Purpose

There were situations described by participants where they actively showed off their devices to other people. These situations were not as common as instances where they felt they needed to hide their devices, but there were numerous instances where participants used their devices to achieve a purpose, performing onstage to a specific audience.

Making it Normal

There were several instances where participants went out of their way to show off their self-care activities in order to make it seem normal. This included trying to educate children about T1D: *"There was another kid there, I'd kind of talk them through it. I'd say, "oh, I'm going to do a blood test. This is how I, you know, manage..." you know, to make it so I'm not sick"* – DS9.

In another case, a participant who was normally quite private with her self-care went out of her way to show a newly diagnosed child that it was normal: *"At a friend's house today. Her 16 month olds just been diagnosed weirdly with type1 so we tested together!"* – DS2 (diary entry).

Getting Perks

There were also cases where the purpose of showing off the device was not as noble as educating people about T1D self-care practices: where the devices were shown off in order to get personal benefit. For example, during the tech meet-up, participants talked about instances akin to Goffman's notion of *"misrepresentation"* [13].

One participant described how she used the condition, including her mobile medical devices, to get a disability pass at a large amusement park. She was even able to get her brother a caregiver pass so they could skip lines for popular rollercoasters: *[Sheepishly] "I get the Alton Towers Priority line. Me and my brother for years never lined up. Not even a sob story needed: given right away."* – TM5.

This instance steered the conversation at the table towards times where they used their condition for gaining benefits in other ways. This included a participant proudly telling the table that she had been bumped up twice to first class. TM1 had *"made a fuss about it"*, including showing off her mobile medical devices to the airline staff in order to benefit from a better seat on the plane. When asked by TM6 *"word for word, what did you do?"* TM1 suggested *"lay it on thicker next time!"*

Controlling a Social Situation

There were times when a participant wanted to have more control over the social situation, and used their devices to achieve this. In these cases, their mobile medical devices became props in these outward displays. This was the case for one participant who perceived that a woman was being disdainful of her and her mother on a train. In order to elicit a reaction from the woman, the participant, who is normally quite private about her condition, actively used her glucose meter when she didn't need to. She made sure that the woman saw what she was doing in order to 'wind her up': *"A snooty woman that was sitting opposite us and she didn't like the fact that we were sitting opposite her, and so I, like, got it out of my bag, and was, like, "really, why not? Bet she's not going to like this.""* – DS2.

There were also situations where participants wanted to make a certain impression on new people, which sometimes involved showing devices off. TM10 was discussing that she had been Internet dating and *"tried to get out of one"*. She wanted to deter the unsuitable suitor, so she made a big deal about her medical condition. She warned how she got crazy when hypo and tried to make her self-management activities seem overwhelming: *"It didn't turn him off, but it didn't turn him on!"* – TM10.

New romantic situations that were going well also meant that some of the participants were showing off their devices, however to achieve a different purpose. DS1 described first dates where she was using the glucose meter more often than usual to test a potential partner: *"I, kind of, almost do it more, [...] like, the first date; just get it out of the way, and if they can't deal with it then too bad."* – DS1.

Summary of Showing Off for a Purpose

There were fewer cases mentioned of onstage showing off than of onstage hiding, but some participants described times when they used their mobile medical devices as props in social situations. The reasons behind this included showing that T1D self-management is normal, getting perks because of the condition, and controlling social situations. In these cases, the medical devices weren't being used as per adherence plans and the medical aesthetic of the device was important for the social situation. These outward displays with their devices being used as props meant that the participants were performing onstage to an audience to achieve a particular purpose, noble or otherwise.

DISCUSSION

The three studies have revealed how instrumental the social setting is in influencing how people with T1D use their mobile medical devices: feeling comfortable or uncomfortable to reveal their devices in their normal routines, hiding or retreating to private places in uncertain situations, and showing off for good effect. However, our study has also shown that use of a device is socially situated and a device that might be appropriate for someone in one situation might not be appropriate in others they encounter. A participant who is quite private and would normally hide their devices from friends and family (offstage), wanted to show off their devices in order to make it normal for a child who was just diagnosed (onstage). A person who wears their medical device visibly outside their clothing on their routine train commute (offstage), wanted to actively hide it from a potential external client (onstage). Goffman's notion of presentation of self shows how these behaviours are not consistent across individuals: there isn't one practice. People have multiple 'fronts' depending on the social situation they encounter.

So what are the implications for designers? The divergent everyday uses of mobile medical devices point to a need for both impressing and concealing designs. For adults who prefer to hide their devices during their everyday routines, a device designed to be inconspicuous would be best. For others who are more open about their everyday device use, a design should be more eye-catching. For instance, an insulin pump that can be worn outside the clothing with different covers might be appropriate for some people with T1D who consistently use their devices in an outward way. On the other hand, an insulin pump that was designed to look like an inconspicuous mobile phone might suit those who prefer to carry their devices in a pocket and are discreet about their self-care activities. But could they be designed to accommodate both attributes? Some might want a device that looks fashionable but also one that is small and subtle for when they want to try to hide their use.

In other situations, some might want it to look clearly like a medical device so that they are treated preferentially: for example, in situations that were not everyday occurrences, such as trying to get upgraded to first class on a plane. In this case, neither a fashionable nor a subtle device would suit the person who is trying to 'misrepresent' their condition to get a perk, as it would benefit them most if it looked 'medical'. But this raises ethical issues for the designer to contend with. Should they be condoning this kind of behavior, when the person does not really need to be upgraded?

Medical devices can be designed to be smaller and compact. However, this might not suit the social needs of users. Such a move to miniaturization might reduce the participant's onstage efforts to make the condition normal for a newly diagnosed child and would make it harder to present the condition to control a social situation. Moreover, it might cause self-care to fade into the background where it becomes invisible, increasing the potential for feelings of stigmatization [18]. This might lead people to feel they need to perform self-care privately, such as not using a device all day during a first date.

There is also a push towards making devices that are embedded into existing consumer products or making medical devices look like them, such as mobile phones and smart-watches. This of course brings with it all the onstage issues of adoption, use and carrying associated with consumer devices, such as not wanting to show off expensive looking technology on holiday nor wanting to use a diabetes app on their iPhone in rough areas of London. Furthermore, neither of these trends to make devices smaller or more like mobile phones take into account the times when people are onstage showing off the device to achieve a purpose, such as preferring a medical aesthetic when trying to get a disability pass.

It is clear that a one-size-fits-all solution is not appropriate, but this idea is further complicated by the discovery that even one device does not fit all social situations. Adults with chronic conditions have a variety of values, preferences, and past experiences, as well as different health concerns. Furthermore, they vary their onstage or offstage strategy depending on the social context. The failure of a device to fit into a person's everyday life and also non-routine occurrences means that devices may not be adopted, carried, or used for self-care in all circumstances when they might be needed. Adults choose to carry and use mobile medical devices as part of everyday self-management. As such, they are both medical devices and consumer technology, and consumer needs have to be accommodated if they are to be adopted, carried, and used for self-management.

This has implications for the design and evaluation of current and future mobile medical devices used for self-management of chronic conditions. Like using design probes with children [40], using cognitive probes with people with T1D and T2D [24], and conducting participatory design and running a living lab with families [19, 20], *user-driven design* might provide another way forward for self-management tools. This could involve using rapid prototyping and open source hardware and software in creating bespoke mobile medical technology. Empowering people with T1D could help designers understand more how to develop devices that can serve multiple purposes in people's everyday and non-routine social lives.

CONCLUSION

Our study has revealed how the vagaries of the real world use of T1D technologies can affect how open people feel when using them in different social situations. Using Goffman's conceptual framing, we have explored the motives people have for hiding or showing off their technologies in their everyday social lives, hiding them when they are in uncertain social situations, and how people show off technologies to achieve a purpose. We have discussed this form of adaptation in terms of its implications for designing future technologies. While customisation might seem the obvious route, it needs to be flexible enough to switch from being a prop that is shown off to being small and inconspicuous. Hence, although there are design trends towards making devices smaller or more like other consumer technology, our study has shown how changing social contexts influence the way adults choose to use and adopt mobile medical technology, both onstage and offstage, in their everyday social lives.

ACKNOWLEDGEMENTS

This research has been funded by the UK Engineering and Physical Sciences Research Council CHI+MED project [EP/G059063/1] and European Commission Marie Curie IRSES Program UBI-Health project.

REFERENCES

1. ANSI. Medical devices - Application of usability engineering to medical devices. ANSI/AAMI/IEC 62366:2007, 2007.
2. Benjamin, A., Birnholtz, J., Baecker, R., Gromala, D., and Furlan, A. Impression Management Work: How Seniors with Chronic Pain Address Disruptions in Their Interactions. In *Proc. CSCW 2012*, ACM Press (2012), 799–808.
3. Beyer, H. and Holtzblatt, K. Contextual Design: Defining Customer-Centered Systems. Elsevier, San Diego, 1997.
4. Braun, V. and Clarke, V. Using thematic analysis in psychology. *Qualitative Research in Psychology*, 3(2), 77–101.
5. Bury, M. Chronic illness as biographical disruption. *Sociology of Health and Illness 4*, 2 (1982), 167–182.
6. Cafazzo, J.A., Casselman, M., Hamming, N., Katzman, D.K., and Palmert, M.R. Design of an mHealth app for the self-management of adolescent type 1 diabetes: a pilot study. *JMIR 14*, 3 (2012), e70.
7. Diabetes UK. Diabetes UK gets behind #showmeyourpump movement. *Diabetes UK*. 2014. http://www.diabetes.org.uk/About_us/News/Diabetes-UK-gets-behind-showmeyourpump-movement/.
8. Diabetes UK. Testing - Diabetes UK. *Diabetes UK*. 2013. http://www.diabetes.org.uk/Guide-todiabetes/Monitoring/Testing/.
9. Dourish, P. What we talk about when we talk about context. *Personal Ubiquitous Comput. 8*, 1 (2004), 19–30.
10. Funnell, M. and RM, A. The problem with compliance in diabetes. *JAMA 284*, 13 (2000), 1709.
11. Funnell, M.M., Brown, T.L., Childs, B.P., et al. National Standards for Diabetes Self-Management Education. *The Diabetes Educator 33*, 4 (2007), 599–614.
12. Furniss, D., O'Kane, A.A., Randell, R., Taneva, S., Mentis, H., and Blandford, A. Fieldwork for Healthcare: Case Studies Investigating Human Factors in Computing Systems. *Synthesis Lectures on Assistive, Rehabilitative, and Health-Preserving Technologies 3*, 1 (2014), 1–129.
13. Goffman, E. *The Presentation of Self in Everyday Life*. Penguin Books Ltd., London, 1959.
14. Harry, D., Gordon, E., and Schmandt, C. Setting the Stage for Interaction: A Tablet Application to Augment Group Discussion in a Seminar Class. In *Proc. CSCW 2012*, ACM Press (2012), 1071–1080.
15. Hutchins, E. Cognition in the Wild . MIT Press, Cambridge, MA, 1995.
16. Isomursu, M., Kuutti, K., and Väinämö, S. Experience Clip: Method for User Participation and Evaluation of Mobile Concepts. In *Proc. PD 2004*, ACM Press (2004), 83–92.
17. JDRF. Continuous Glucose Monitors. *JDRF*. 2013. http://www.jdrf.org.uk/life-with-type-1-diabetes/managing-type-1/treatments/cgms.

18. Kanstrup, A.M. Design concepts for digital diabetes practice: Design to explore, share, and camouflage chronic illness. *Int. J. of Design 8*, 3 (2014), 49–60.

19. Kanstrup, A.M., Bertelsen, P., Glasemann, M. and Boye, N. Design for More: An Ambient Perspective on Diabetes. In *Proc. PD 2008,* ACM Press (2008), 118–127.

20. Kanstrup, A.M., Bjerge, K. and Kristensen, J.E. A Living Laboratory Exploring Mobile Support for Everyday Life with Diabetes. *Wirel. Pers. Commun.* 53, 3 (2010), 395–408.

21. Linekin, P.L. Diabetes Pattern Management: The Key to Diabetes Self-Management and Glycemic Control. *Home Healthcare Nurse 20*, 3 (2002), 168–177.

22. Lutfey, K.E. and Wishner, W.J. Beyond "compliance" is "adherence". Improving the prospect of diabetes care. Diabetes Care 22 , 4 (1999), 635–639.

23. Mamykina, L., Mynatt, E., Davidson, P., and Greenblatt, D. MAHI. In *Proc. CHI 2008,* ACM Press (2008), 477.

24. Mamykina, L., Mynatt, E.D., and Kaufman, D.R. Investigating Health Management Practices of Individuals with Diabetes. In *Proc. CHI 2006*, ACM Press (2006), 927–936.

25. McCarthy, J. and Wright, P. *Technology as Experience.* The MIT Press, 2004.

26. McMahon, B.T., West, S.L., Mansouri, M., and Belongia, L. Workplace discrimination and diabetes: the EEOC Americans with Disabilities Act research project. *Work: A Journal of Prevention, Assessment and Rehabilitation 25*, 1 (2005), 9–18.

27. NHS Choices. Diabetes, type 1 - NHS Choices. *NHS Choices.* http://www.nhs.uk/Conditions/Diabetes-type1

28. O'Kane, A.A. and Blandford, A. 2013. Recruiting Diabetes Patients: a Success and a Failure. In *CHI 2013 Workshop HCI fieldwork in healthcare: Creating a Graduate Handbook Workshop*. 2013. http://www.chi-med.ac.uk/publicdocs/WP179.pdf

29. O'Kane, A.A., Mentis, H.M. and Thereska, E. 2013. Non-static nature of patient consent: shifting privacy perspectives in health information sharing. In *Proc. CSCW 2013,* ACM Press (2013), 553–562.

30. Owen, T., Buchanan, G., and Thimbleby, H. Understanding user requirements in take-home diabetes management technologies. In *Proc. BCS HCI*, British Computer Society (2012), 268–273.

31. Piette, J.D. The Impact of Comorbid Chronic Conditions on Diabetes Care. *Diabetes Care 29*, 3 (2006), 725–731.

32. Rieman, J. The diary study: a workplace-oriented research tool to guide laboratory efforts. In Proc. INTERACT 1993 and CHI 1993 , (1993), 321–326.

33. Ritholz, M.D., Smaldone, A., Lee, J., Castillo, A., Wolpert, H., and Weinger, K. Perceptions of psychosocial factors and the insulin pump. Diabetes Care 30, 3 (2007), 549–54.

34. Rogers, Y. Interaction design gone wild: striving for wild theory. Interactions 18 , 4 (2011), 58.

35. Sharples, S., Martin, J., Lang, A., Craven, M., O'Neill, S., and Barnett, J. Medical device design in context: A model of user–device interaction and consequences. Displays 33 , 4–5 (2012), 221–232.

36. Storni, C. Multiple forms of appropriation in self-monitoring technology: Reflections on the role of evaluation in future self-care. IJHCI 26 , 5 (2010), 537–561.

37. Storni, C. Patients' lay expertise in chronic self-care: a case study in type 1 diabetes. Health Expectations, (2013).

38. Strauss, A.L., Corbin, J., Fagerhaugh, S., Glaser, B.G., Maines, D., Suczek, B. and Wiener, C.L. *Chronic illness and the quality of life*. Mosby, St. Louis, USA, 1984.

39. Suchman, L. *Plans and Situated Actions: The Problem of Human-Machine Communication*. Cambridge University Press, Cambridge, UK, 1987.

40. Tsvyatkova, D. and Storni, C. Adapting Design Probes to Explore Health Management Practices in Pediatric Type 1 Diabetes. In *Proc. IDC,* ACM Press (2014), 277–280.

41. Writtle, J. Colostomy bag bikini photograph seen by nine million people. *BBC News*, 2014. http://www.bbc.co.uk/news/uk-england-herefordworcester-28138485.

42. Zhao, X., Salehi, N., Naranjit, S., Alwaalan, S., Voida, S., and Cosley, D. The Many Faces of Facebook: Experiencing Social Media As Performance, Exhibition, and Personal Archive. In *Proc. CHI 2013*, ACM Press (2013), 1–10.

Understanding Individual Differences for Tailored Smoking Cessation Apps

Jeni Paay, Jesper Kjeldskov, Mikael B. Skov, Lars Lichon and Stephan Rasmussen
Department of Computer Science / Research Centre for Socio+Interactive Design
Aalborg University, Aalborg East, Denmark
{jeni, jesper, dubois}@cs.aau.dk

ABSTRACT
Finding ways to help people quit smoking is a high priority in health behavior change research. Recent HCI studies involving technologies using specific quitting techniques such as social support and SMS messaging to help people quit have reported some success. Early studies using computer generated print material report significant success of tailored versus non-tailored material, however, there is limited understanding on what aspects of digitally delivered quitting assistance should be tailored and how. To address this, we have conducted an empirical investigation with smokers to identify perceived importance of different types of help when quitting and the potential role of technology in providing such help. We found that people are highly individual in their approach to quitting and the kind of help they regard as relevant to their situation. Our contribution is a collection of empirically derived themes for tailoring smoking cessation apps to individual quitting needs.

Author Keywords
Smoking cessation; tailoring; individual differences; health behavior change; qualitative research.

ACM Classification Keywords
H.5.m. Information interfaces and presentation (e.g., HCI): Miscellaneous.

INTRODUCTION
Our health is important to us. Over recent years, there has been an increased focus in media, in government policy and in research on preventing the serious risks caused by the effects of behavior choices leading to obesity, smoking, alcoholism, medication abuse and diabetes. In Denmark 25% of annual deaths are caused by smoking. The habit of smoking can cause serious health issues such as cancer, heart disease, chronic obstructive pulmonary disease, and poor blood circulation. Smoking also has an economical impact on society; the latest numbers showing a yearly cost in Denmark of 7.5 billion DKK. Therefore, health organizations are working to reduce the number of smokers; both by preventing people from starting in the first place, and helping those who smoke to reduce and/or quit. By informing the design of more effective smoking cessation apps we aim to support people's transition from smokers to non-smokers, and help them to stay quit.

While hundreds of apps are available for use on various smart phone platforms, HCI research studies on smoking cessation are very few. This means that there is an opportunity to do more research within this domain, of value for both people trying to quit smoking, and developing of smoking cessation apps. The convenience and flexibility of smart phones offer great potentials for creating tailored smoking cessation apps. But in order to provide tailored advice, it is essential to learn about individual habits. Understanding the gains that people express about their smoking habit allows us to design applications that can offer suitable compensations. If personal gains are based on enjoyment, relaxation, pleasure, personal image, rather than nicotine addiction, then what is enough of a substitute for them? A nicotine patch may help some, but might not work for others. From this perspective it makes little sense to aim for "one fits all" solutions.

In this study we specifically look at individual differences in relation to facilitating smoking cessation. To do this we have taken a participatory approach to explore why smokers continue to smoke, in order to remain mindful not only of serious health implications of smoking, but also of the serious challenges that quitting poses to smokers. From this our contribution is a collection of empirically derived themes for tailoring smoking cessation apps to individual quitting needs. Our participants found it very difficult to quit smoking even though they expressed a desire to quit and were aware of the negative health implications if they didn't. We acknowledged their struggles to stay quit and explored with them their ideas on how technology might help them achieve this. Through focus groups and design workshops we discovered 12 themes that should inform the design of smoking cessation apps – making them individualized, monitoring actual smoking behavior, and appropriately compensating and supporting smokers on the personal needs, and the individual cravings, that they each struggle with while trying to quit.

CHI 2015, April 18 - 23 2015, Seoul, Republic of Korea
Copyright 2015 ACM 978-1-4503-3145-6/15/04...$15.00
http://dx.doi.org/10.1145/2702123.2702321

RELATED WORK

Smoking addiction and cessation are the focus of an extensive body of research in the health behavior change and psychology fields. Research on addictive behaviors that can inform our understanding of why people smoke, what can motivate them to change this behavior and how to prevent relapse can be found in [6, 19, 20, 21, 22, 26, 36, 42, 43]. West and Brown [42] provide a theory of addiction explaining that it is a reflective choice and that the concepts of impulse and self-control play an important role in curbing addictive behavior. Their PRIME theory of motivation to quit is based on a combination of having the capability to do it, the physical and social opportunity to do it, and the motivation to engage in it at that time. This same model is at the centre of Mitchie et al.'s [22] behavior change wheel, which provides a method for characterizing and designing behavior change interventions. It focuses on sources of behavior, interventions functions and policy categories that could enable those interventions. Mitchie and West [20] present the PRIME theory of motivation and the Behaviour Change Wheel as frameworks to government to influence future behavior change interventions and policies. In terms of individual support for smoking cessation, West et al. [43] provide smokers with The SmokeFree Formula to help people to stop smoking. In this book they facilitate smokers taking an individual approach to quitting, acknowledging that there is no one way of quitting that works for everyone. Mitchie at al. [21] acknowledge that little is known about the "active ingredients" of smoking addiction, and amongst other support mechanisms suggest motivation to quit through provision of rewards for abstinence.

The use of technology to support behavior change is increasingly of interest to researchers in both CHI and behavioral science, for health and sustainability, but the work is "siloed" within the two communities. To help bridge this theoretical gap, Heckler et al. [17] provide guidance for interpreting, using and contributing to behavioral theories. They highlight that much more work is needed in this area before HCI researchers can both utilize and contribute to these theories. In terms of creating working prototypes, Klasnja et al. [18] propose that in evaluating them we need to focus on efficacy evaluations of specific interventions and studies that gain a deeper understanding of people's experiences with the technology.

In looking at specific HCI research on smoking cessation we note that previous studies have indicated a need to investigate the gap between research and practice, as many available smoking cessation apps have not been evaluated for efficacy [1, 2, 7]. In fact, we could not find studies that involved actual smokers in the design process, to better understand their needs within this context. In our review of 92 HCI and health behavior change papers we found that there were very few studies designing technology to support smoking cessation, i.e. [4, 16, 25, 28, 29, 30, 34, 35, 41]. Within these, we did not find any designs created through participatory practices, such as focus groups and design workshops. This inspired us to see if we could find new insights to inform design of smoking cessation technology by involving users in the understanding and envisionment phases of interaction design. In this way, real smokers and their goals and challenges would be behind design considerations and features of the smoking cessation applications, making them more directly relevant to the people who are actually struggling to quit smoking.

In a recent study, we designed and evaluated a smoking cessation application, Quitty. This app offered three different types of content (tips, stories and motivators), which were recommended by either an expert or by fellow smokers in their community [25]. Our findings showed that in order to make an application useful, it should consider users' needs by tailoring content to their situation. This includes consideration of both their quitting stage and demographics. We found that using mobile technology was important so that people could access the app at the times and places that they needed support to stop smoking. Daily SMS messages about new content delivered to the system proved to be both useful and a positive reminder of what they were trying to achieve. Participants were also interested in contributing to and improving the application, based on their own experiences with the app and their own struggle to quit smoking. However, we discovered widely differing wishes in respect to including additional services, such as social media, tracking and games.

In 2009, Abroms et al. [1] reviewed available smoking cessation apps on the iTunes store (47 apps in total) and found little correlation between established guidelines within smoking cessation and the apps available. They recommended that current apps be revised and future apps developed based on evidence-based practices. In 2012, a follow up study by Abroms et al. [2] on popular smart phone apps for smoking cessation (400 apps in total) concluded that these could be improved by better integration with the Clinical Practice Guidelines and other evidence-based practices. Other HCI research studies have created apps with a variety of focuses, in order to support people in quitting smoking, but mostly as targeted materials. Ploderer et al. [28, 29, 30] focused their research on understanding social support amongst peers to inform the design of a "Distract Me" app for mobile phones. Valdivieso-López et al. [41] focused on providing "healthy games" in a mobile app for teenagers. Murnane and Counts [24] analyzed posts on Twitter to discover how people succeed in quitting using social media, and Zhang and Yang [44] studied Facebook posts to discover patterns of behavior that aligned with smokers' quitting stages. A review by Strecher [39] of printed quit smoking materials found that in the majority of the cases, tailored quit smoking material had a statistically significant impact compared to non-tailored materials. While not specifically about smoking cessation, the idea of people crafting their own personal health technologies by Ananthanarayan et al.

[5] aligns well with our approach of responding to individual differences in health technology design.

Backinger et al. [7] claim that emerging technologies, such as smart phones, have the possibility to offer resourceful means to help within a smoking cessation context. Our interest in the smart phone platform is not only the flexibility and functionality that they provide to make advanced tailoring of content possible, but also the fact that they are likely to be with the smoker at the time and place when they are tempted to have a cigarette, and therefore can provide timely intervention.

EMPIRICAL STUDY

We conducted an empirical study of smokers' and ex-smokers' attitudes towards quitting, and their ideas about how interactive technology might be used to help them quit. The study involved focus groups and design workshops to explore effective tailoring of smoking cessation in a participatory way.

Recruitment and Participants

We recruited participants over a two-month period through a dedicated web site, which was advertised through social media (Facebook, Twitter and forums), Google AdWords, physical posters and business cards. The website described the project and provided a link to join the study. The national Health and Medicines Authority also helped us recruit by placing an advertisement on their smoking cessation website, and the local Municipality helped recruit participants through their weekly smoking cessation courses. Participants had to be current or previous smokers and own a smart phone (to be able to reflect on the use of this technology in respect to trying to quit).

When agreeing to join the study, each participant completed an online survey with questions about basic demographics (age, occupation, city of residence, etc.) and their smoking habits including stage of quitting based on the TransTheoretical Model of health behavior change (TTM) [32]. This information was used to determine their nicotine dependence using a shortened version of the Fagerströms test [40]. We also collected data on their reasons for smoking, when they usually smoke, if they had ever tried to quit, and their motivations to quit. Lastly, we asked the participants what method (if anything) they had previously used to try and become smoke-free.

We recruited a total of 18 participants from North Jutland, Denmark: 11 males and 7 females. Their ages ranged from 20 to 61, with an average age of 31. They had been smoking for between 1 and 40 years, the average for the group being 11.7 years. Out of our participants, 13 had previously tried to quit. In terms of quitting stages, 5 were considering quitting, 5 trying to remain quit, 4 considered themselves as being quit, and 4 were not interested in quitting. For the smokers, their nicotine dependency, based on the Fagerströms test, was: 2 had a score of 0 (no dependence), 6 had a score of 1-2 (very low dependence) and 6 had a score of 3 (low to moderate dependence).

Procedure

The study was conducted during the spring of 2014, and included 4 focus groups and 2 participant design workshops. The 6 sessions lasted approximately 1.5 hours each, and involved different activities and discussion points.

We chose focus groups to reveal determinants and experiences related to their social smoking behaviors. We were building on the work of Ploderer et al. [28] where interviews were used to gain understanding. We encouraged open discussion on what participants liked about having a cigarette and why they began smoking in the first instance. We then focused on participants' smoking habits including: reasons for smoking, situations and places where they do and do not want to smoke, where they keep their cigarette packets, and what they consider the positives and negatives of smoking. In questions of a personal nature we allowed participants time to write down their response first and then share them with the group in an open forum if they wished to. We were also interested in learning if they had tried to quit before, what they learned from the attempt, what their reasons were for trying, their strategies, the difficulties they faced, and where they would get help, if at all. We also investigated their use of smart phones, choice of general apps and whether they had tried using a smoking cessation app before. We were interested in knowing if social networks could be used in the context of quitting and if/how participants used social media to help them stop smoking. Finally, we showed an example commercial app, "QuitNow - My Quitbuddy" (http://www.quitnow.gov.au) to get their impression of it. This app was chosen because it uses a variety of techniques to help people to stay quit. At the end of the session, participants were presented with two quit smoking messages: a gain-framed one and a loss-framed one. We did this to get their immediate impression of these messages, and see how they responded to positive statements about the benefits of quitting versus negative facts about smoking.

The design workshops involved 9 of the same participants, a mixture of smokers and smokers who had quit. The goal was to gain a better understanding of how the findings from the focus groups could inform the design of smoking cessation apps. We did this by first presenting the findings from the focus group, with examples and explanations to participants. We asked participants to validate the themes as representing important issues of quitting and to add to them if necessary. We then encouraged them to use the final themes as inspirations for sketching designs of possible smoking cessation technologies. Participants were encouraged to discuss and collaborate in creating ideas and sketches and to use technology in their solutions. We asked them to share their ideas with the group explain what inspired their particular design idea. The group then worked together to refine their most promising designs.

Data Analysis

For the purpose of analysis, we recorded each session on audio and/or video to be reviewed and transcribed. In the analysis we used open coding [38] to identify distinct concepts and categories. We then iteratively recoded these, looking for relationships amongst the codes. Each session was analyzed separately by two researchers then merged, to achieve concordance, to get different perspectives and ensure that all concepts of importance were included. We found 40 different themes from our merged coding effort. These were further synthesized using affinity diagramming to establish 12 overarching themes. These themes emerged from issues raised about what was perceived as important when quitting smoking and the possible role of technology.

FINDINGS

Our findings are a collection of empirically derived themes for informing the tailoring of smoking cessation apps to individual quitting needs. In this section we describe these themes, relate them to previous work where relevant, and include design implications where appropriate. We then present ideas from our design workshops as exemplars on how the themes might be used in design. In our findings, we bring new insights on acknowledging and accommodating individual differences in the design of tailored smoking cessation technologies.

Focus Group Findings

The themes of importance when quitting smoking found in our study are: 1) quitting stage, 2) immediate impact, 3) smoking habits, 4) personalization, 5) flexibility, 6) reminders, 7) self-monitoring, 8) novelty, 9) meaningful rewards, 10) social support, 11) solo struggle, and 12) competition. While some of these are well known (e.g. 1, 3, 4, 9, 12), others have not yet been addressed in the context of designing for smoking cessation (e.g. 2, 5, 8, 11).

1 – Quitting Stage

Quitting stage describes whether you are thinking of quitting, trying to stay quit, or still want to smoke. Our participants were at different quitting stages, in respect to the six-stage model TTM [32], with 4 of the 6 stages represented. We found a correlation between quitting stage, finding the motivation to quit smoking and the kind of support needed during this stage. Many participants expressed a mismatch between generic quitting information or health risk information and their own quitting needs or stage, and so they ignored it.

This confirms findings from other studies using TTM. Aveyard et al. [6] proved that TTM-based interventions were more successful than interventions not considering the different quitting stages of smokers. The TTM model has been used in several research studies to increase success rates [3, 14, 15, 25, 35, 39]. To achieve the highest efficacy in a smoking cessation app it is important to provide interventions that are tailored to a smokers' quitting stage.

2 – Immediate Impact

When discussing motivation to quit smoking, and to stay quit, we found that participants faced with an "immediate impact" said they were more likely to accept the advice given. An immediate impact message is one that presents the person with an implication of their current behavior that affects them *now*. This could be related to health or money, both seen as the main motivators. For example, student participants saw their personal economic state as directly impacting their smoking habits. When they smoked they could see they had less money to spend on other things, having an immediate effect on their lifestyle. One participant said: *"the economical aspect is something you can feel right now"*. Older participants with full-time work were not so concerned by this, as they usually had enough money to comfortably cover their habit. The important immediate impact in their case was generally health-related. They were aware that many years of smoking, coupled with advancing age, placed them at a higher risk of smoking-related problems.

This finding confirms Morris's [23] guideline: *Show people what they could lose.* Showing people what they will lose in the short and long-term if they don't change behavior motivates them to change. What constitutes an "immediate impact" differs from person to person, so it is important that tailoring takes this aspect into account.

3 – Smoking Habits

Smoking can be habit driven. Choosing to have a cigarette can be the result of multiple external factors. Participants had very different smoking habits: some smoked out of enjoyment, others smoked when stressed, some smoked as soon as they walked outside. Participants discussed which cigarette during the day was the most important and whether or not they should smoke in front of children. We found that people's smoking habits and attitudes to smoking were very individual. For example, by knowing a person's smoking pattern, a system could intervene with relevant information/advice/distraction at the time when it is most needed. Being able to judge an individual's critical smoking moment - by time, place or situation - makes it possible to intervene "just-in-time".

West and Brown [42] support the impact of habit on smoking cessation, saying that relapse can be caused by habits that are both unthinking, e.g. lighting up without thinking, and learned behaviors, e.g. rewarding ourselves. Chung et al. mapped the smoking landscape of South Korea in terms of demographics and smoking behavior [9]. They concluded that in knowing peoples smoking habits, appropriate anti-smoking measures could be set, greatly reducing cigarette consumption. Scholl et al. [34] gathered personal smoking habits using sensing technology to prompt smokers to reflect on their own smoking habits with the goal to improve their health. We suggest the same sensing technology could be used to determine people's individual smoking habits and provide smoking cessation advice to individuals at the most effective times.

4 – Personalization

Smoking advice needs to be personalized - the smoker needs to relate to the content as if it was created directly for and about them. Many participants did not feel motivated to quit as they regarded the many health issues associated with smoking as never becoming a problem for them - they felt that it happens to somebody else. One participant said she did not feel motivated when she saw pictures of tar-filled lungs: *"... It just doesn't have any effect when those black lungs come up on the screen, because we all think 'Well that isn't my lungs, so how can you say that?"* This indicates a need for content to be personalized and as directly relevant to the user and their situation as possible.

Information can be personalized on many different aspects of the smoker's life, such as quitting stage, age, family situation, socio-economic situation, etc. Strecher [39] found that tailored materials seemed to have the greatest impact on pre-contemplators (defined as people thinking about quitting). West et al. [43] provide a printed personalizable quitting program to help people stop smoking. Using an app on an person's smart phone makes it possible to know about their individual needs and to deliver content that matches their situation and quitting stage, just as face-to-face counseling can [39].

5 – Flexibility

Smokers have very different needs and approaches when it comes to quitting. They need different tools, information and compensations at different times in the process and at different times in the day to deal with the difficult and important activity of giving up cigarettes. All of our 18 participants had different approaches to quitting, no matter what quitting stage they were at. Some preferred going "cold turkey", while others wanted to reduce their cigarette intake gradually. When participants were shown the QuitBuddy app during the focus session, and it's built in "distraction" game, one said, *"... I would need to be able to say 'I want WordFeud instead' and then just easily via a few steps be able to have WordFeud there."* So a distraction needs to interesting to the individual and easy to access if it is going to distract them from smoking. Any smoking cessation app hoping to facilitate peoples' quitting approaches needs to be flexible enough to adapt to the user's current needs.

6 – Reminders

SMS messages have been successfully used to remind people to use their smoking cessation app. However, we found that reminders also bring the idea of smoking cigarettes to the front of people's thoughts - and in the worst case, actually prompt them to smoke. As one participant said, *"It must not remind people of having a smoke. Enough is doing that already. If I had an app that kept giving me messages, I would just think 'I could really use a cigarette right now'"*. In discussing phone usage with participants it became apparent that engaging with their mobile phones was often dependent on their context and happened mostly when they were out. Reminders to use a smoking app needs to be sent out when and where a smoker tends to crave cigarettes to avoid making them think about smoking when they otherwise wouldn't, and to help them resist.

Fogg and Allen [12] found the use of texting to persuade health behavior change effective, using SMS messages to remind and notify people in regard to specific health topics. Roubroeks et al. [32] studied the forms that such notifications should take in order to achieve maximum efficacy. Both studies confirm the effectiveness of reminders. In our recent study [25] we found that some participants responded positively to messages that were sent at different times of the day, surprising them and making it difficult for them to plan to avoid the message. It was important that these messages were sent by a person, rather than computer generated.

7 – Self-Monitoring

Self-Monitoring is a well-known technique in persuading people to change their health behavior [11]. By self-monitoring we mean both data input by the user and data about that user measured by the system. When shown the QuitBuddy app the participants all liked the idea of the self-monitoring elements. Based on daily estimates input by users, QuitBuddy provides a smoke-free timer, the total amount of money the user has saved, and the amount of tar avoided. One participant said: *"I think that the timer is good, but it is because I see the timer like somewhat a high score and as soon as you are having a cigarette, the number hits zero and you have to start all-over again."* "Seeing" a representation of how much they smoked had a motivating effect toward not smoking. The money saved by participants was an "eye-opener" for them, which they also said would be a strong motivator to reduce their smoking.

"Quantified Selfers" [8] have shown that being aware of various aspects of their self, by counting things such as steps taken during a day using devices such as pedometers, helps them reflect on their own health and well being. Self-monitoring could therefore be used to help people understand their own smoking habits and create strategies to cope with cravings [36]. Self-monitoring was used by Ali et al. [4] to automatically detect when people were smoking using a device measuring respiration. Scholl et al. [34] created a lighter that registers when the user is lighting a cigarette to count the number of cigarettes smoked in a day. These technologies for measuring different aspects of a person's activity could be used to feed individual data into a smoking cessation app, which would then be tailored to respond appropriately. The forms that this response could take, such as visualizations of smoking behaviors, calculated compensations in the form of financial or health gains, or stories and tips tailored to a persons behaviors, are all design possibilities and based on actual behaviors.

8 – Novelty

Presenting people with new and surprising information attracts attention and sparks interest. Our participants said it would be better if smoking cessation information was delivered in more creative ways in terms of content, technology and interaction. All agreed that information that is already known to them is easily ignored. For example, smoking cessation campaigns often target negative health impacts of smoking, but this is information that smokers are well aware of and tired of hearing about, *"It is fine that we have some smoking cessation campaigns, but it is not something you should apply in the application that smokers should use, because they already know it."* Smokers feel bombarded and underwhelmed by general health warnings and scare tactics. They said that knowing these impacts has not yet stopped them from smoking - they need something else, something they don't already know.

Designers and developers of smoking cessation apps need to provide novelty in the way that they distract, compensate and motivate smokers. We discovered in our study that the needs of smokers quitting are both more complex and subtler than those represented in the literature reviewed, and that this is strongly influenced by the different needs of individuals in terms of what they already know and what has an impact on them personally.

9 – Meaningful Rewards

People quitting smoking need suitable compensations to successfully counteract the personal gains that they get from smoking. These "rewards" for not smoking are highly individual. It needs to be something that holds value and meaning for that person. Participants saw meaningful rewards as a huge motivator, both in terms of reducing current intake of cigarettes, and staying quit. Examples of suitable rewards discussed included money "earned" from not smoking, items that could be bought with that money, specific health improvements, and personal achievements. One participant said, *"It was just so nice to be able to go to the bike store and say 'I am going to get a proper bike' which is what I have now."* Another participant stressed that it is important that the reward is greater than the satisfaction gained from smoking, *"My reward should be bigger than how delicious I think it is to smoke."* Rewards need to be defined by the smoker, so that they are meaningful and significant enough for that person to compensate for smoking a cigarette.

Mitchie et al. [21] propose reward as an important part of individual behavior support for smoking cessation. Other studies have shown that financial rewards can be highly motivational. A study conducted with pregnant women who were given monetary incentives to stay off cigarettes showed that one-third had completely abstained from smoking by the twelfth week of the study [37]. Snuggs et al. [36] discovered that stimulation obtained from rewards increased within a week of stopping smoking and after 4 weeks had increased even more.

10 – Social Support

Social support for smoking cessation using online forums and social networking sites presents an interesting alternative to stand-alone apps in terms people getting support and stories from others in a similar situation. Participants' views on the usefulness of social support while quitting differed widely. Most said they would not use Facebook for social support, as they regarded the content on social networking sites as generally banal, while quitting smoking was perceived as a very important and personal quest, which they did not want to share openly. They generally felt that adding a social aspect would make them become dishonest about their struggle to avoid the embarrassment of failing. They also felt that telling their friends and family about their quitting attempt added unnecessary pressure and became a stressing factor, which in a worst-case scenario would make them start smoking again. Participants agreed that social support works best when shared with strangers.

Studies of different online smoking cessation groups give understanding of the patterns of posting and responses between people trying to quit [24, 29, 42, 44]. Ploderer et al. [27] found that some individuals who participate in Facebook groups take on leadership roles to support others, depending on their own quitting stage. Our study found that any social support in the app should allow for anonymity.

11 – Solo Struggle

Quitting smoking is a very personal challenge, and our participants felt that at some point in time you just have to *"do it alone"*. Rather than adding a social aspect to the struggle, some felt they would much rather take on the challenge by themselves, as one person clarified, *"because others cannot fight for you"*. Another participant explained, *"There is nothing they can say that influences me. It is only my own expectations that influence me"*. In fact, making it a personal struggle would motivate smokers to stay abstinent, *"Okay now I have been smoke-free for 4 days by myself"*. Being able to do it alone becomes a reward in itself.

It was very important to our participants that any app gave them the flexibility to tailor their own quitting attempt in respect to doing it by themselves, and what they needed to achieve this.

12 – Competition

Competition was a subject of discussion in all focus groups. Participants felt that it was highly motivational to be involved in competition, either against others or against themselves. One participant explained, *"But when you think that you want to have a cigarette and when you think 'no I will take a look at my score, making sure that I do not break it'. It is like a game, where you always gain new levels, and when you take a cigarette you lose levels. Then it is like 'Ah crap'... I want to win this competition against others and for how long can I keep off the smokes compared to others?"* indicating that competition can give smokers an incentive to stay quit.

In a study by Cummings et al. [10] smokers were placed in a worksite Stop-Smoking Contest in which cash prizes were awarded for quitting smoking. The study showed that one-third of participants managed to stay abstinent after 3 months, indicating that competition and/or monetary gain are strong motivators to stop smoking.

Design Workshop Sketches

In our two design workshops we presented the 12 quit smoking themes to 9 participants from the focus groups. We did this to provide inspiration for generating technology design ideas to support quitting. The outcomes from these workshops were 15 different sketched designs. These designs were highly diverse, addressing different opportunities, challenges and requirements for people at different quitting stages. Most involved the use of mobile phones, either as the main tool or in collaboration with other technologies. This was due to the easy accessibility of their smart phones as a physical prop at the design session. As an illustration of the diversity of ideas, and to demonstrate how our quit smoking themes can inform design ideas we briefly describe three design ideas from the workshops: Show The Losses and Gains for Me; Automated Self-Monitoring and Personalized Interactive Cigarette Package.

Show Losses and Gains for Me

The *Show Losses and Gains for Me* design idea displays timelines showing the health and economic consequences of the user's smoking choices. The system is primed by entering personal interests, goals, cigarette brand and number of cigarettes smoked per day in order to give individualized feedback. The number of cigarettes is used to calculate their current position on the timeline in respect to projected losses or gains from increasing, maintaining or reducing their cigarette intake. If they reduce their smoking, they move along a "Rewards" timeline toward a bigger reward (e.g. a holiday). If they continue smoking, they move along a "Health Consequences" timeline towards declining health (e.g. cancer). This makes the user aware of things to be lost or gained depending on their smoking habits. As one participant said, *"I want the system to say that you could have had all this now, making me think about my habits."*

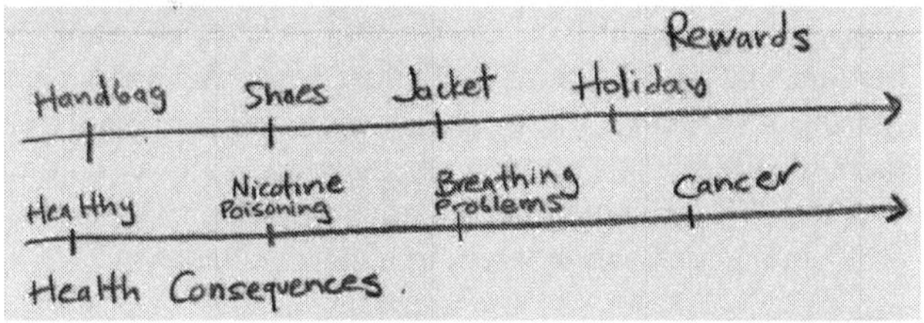

Figure 1. Sketch showing examples of losses and gains from smoking on a personal timeline

In this sketch there are two timelines. There is an economic rewards timeline showing personally chosen compensations for not smoking. The other timeline shows health consequences important to this person. Included in the design is the idea that the rewards could be shown as images of the actual items. By having data and representations based on personal habits, health concerns, and chosen rewards, it becomes more pertinent to the user and provides stronger motivation to *not* smoke that next cigarette.

Automated Self-Monitoring

In the *Automated Self-Monitoring* design, the user wears a wristband measuring their pulse rate as an indicator of when they are smoking. Smoking causes an acute elevation of blood pressure [31], although alcohol intake, body mass, age and gender can all affect the blood pressure-smoking relationship. It is also difficult to measure a single cigarette against several smoked in one session. So, given that it is a complex interrelationship, this design is based on the ability to accurately register individual cigarettes using temporary blood pressure elevation. This was done to avoid the unreliability of people retrospectively remembering the number of cigarettes smoked during the day. The wristband is wirelessly connected to the user's smart phone, to display their data. The user can then compare their current smoking patterns with past patterns, encouraging them to reflect on their actual smoking habits.

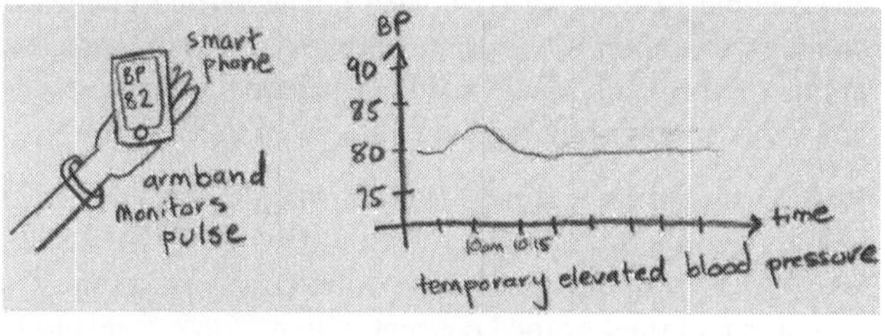

Figure 2. Sketch of the Automated Self-Monitoring Wristband

Personalized Interactive Cigarette Package

The *Personalized Interactive Cigarette Package* was very popular with design workshop participants; they found it novel and surprising. The cigarette pack with an interactive screen on the front would showing information about the number of cigarettes left in the pack, illustrating the implications of smoking this number of cigarettes as a health consequence.

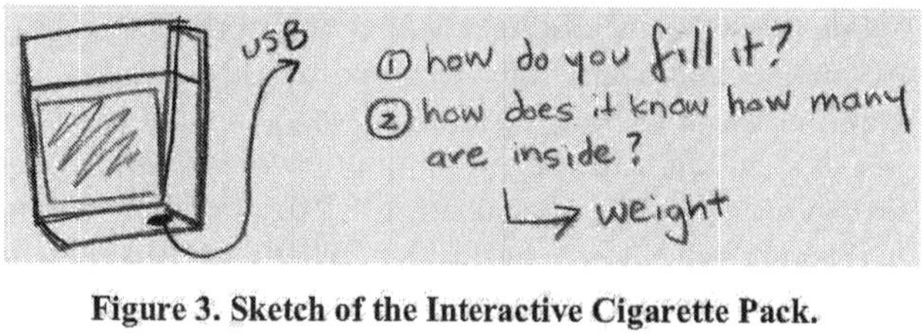

Figure 3. Sketch of the Interactive Cigarette Pack.

This idea was partly inspired by the kind of anti-smoking information that can already be seen on many cigarette packages showing the health risks of smoking. Design workshop participants stressed the importance of being able to personalize the messages and images on the screen to make them more motivational.

DISCUSSION

Tailored smoking cessation apps present a unique challenge for design. While there are successful health behavior change apps that encourage people to *do* something healthy (e.g. exercise), a different approach is needed when wanting to encourage people *not to do* something.

It is important to understand that *quitting* smoking is not as straightforward as just *stopping* smoking. Many people "stop smoking" several times during their attempt to quit, but find themselves starting again. In these cases the quitting process then starts all over again. During a quitting attempt, smokers can transition and iterate through the different quitting stages at different rates, in order to become smoke free on a long-term basis. We need to acknowledge that for some, just reducing the number of daily cigarettes in a maintainable way is a victory - and a step in the right direction. Reducing the number of cigarettes per day is also important in achieving improved health and reducing the risks of cancer [15, 39].

Designing for Individual Differences

By presenting insight into the character and importance of individual differences in smoking cessation, we aim to influence the design of future smoking cessation apps. As an example of this, we have used our identified themes of smoking cessation to envision smoking cessation apps that are tailored to individuals and their personal quitting needs, and hence more useful during all stages of quitting.

Related studies have shown that tailoring information when helping people quit smoking is important [3, 5, 14, 15, 25, 34, 35, 39]. In our study we found that tailoring is a complex and fine-grained concept with multiple facets to be considered in concert including the twelve themes presented: a persons quitting stage; implications that have the most immediate impact on a person; their individual smoking habits, including time, place and triggers; personalized advice they can relate to; flexible choice of quitting tools; reminders that come at the most appropriate time for a person; self-monitoring data about their own behavior; advice or facts that are new to a person; rewards and compensations that hold meaning for a person; and the option of social support or doing it solo at different times. While these themes can be related to the work and findings of others, and some of them are already known, our contribution is in bringing them forward as a collection of insights on the challenges of quitting smoking and the design of technology to support this. Together, they outline a design space for considering individual changes in tailored smoking cessation apps.

Monitoring Actual Smoking Behavior

From the presented themes we found that, in particular, self-monitoring using technology is an interesting approach, and one that is being used in different behavior change research projects, e.g. [4, 8, 34, 36]. During focus group and design workshop discussions, smokers expressed the necessity of having an automated system to monitor their smoking behavior. They claimed that it was difficult to manually enter data, given that smoking often happens in social situations such as parties, where it would not only be awkward to enter that data, but embarrassing. Relying on the memory of such events and entering the data retrospectively was perceived to be a completely unreliable method of counting cigarettes smoked. They felt this made the monitoring and reflecting on habits exercise invalid, as it would not represent true data about their behavior.

An interesting challenge that came out of our study, is that the very use of a quit smoking app tends to bring smoking to the front of a smokers mind, making them think about cigarettes and even increasing their desire to have one. Apps that run on a their smart phone, sending reminding SMS messages to smokers to use the app or reflect on their smoking habits run the risk of actually prompting the very cravings that they are trying to avoid. This raises an interesting issue, when designing technology for this context: How can we create a technology to help people quit, without reminding them about cigarettes?

Providing Appropriate Compensation

Another issue is related to the idea of rewards for not smoking that are significant enough to compensate for the cigarette they are replacing. If people are smoking for pleasure, we found that they had no trouble listing things and experiences that they would find a suitable substitute for a cigarette, ranging from a new hat to making love with their partner. However, if people are using smoking as a form of self-medication against stress or social awkwardness, a suitable compensation is much more difficult to define. Even more difficult is finding a role for technology to play in this situation. Turning to your smart phone may simply waste time that you are already feeling pressured about, and it certainly does not help the social confidence of a person already feeling awkward.

Methodological Concerns

In reflecting on our methodological approach, we found that the topic of people's smoking habits was very sensitive, making it difficult to investigate and gain the trust of our participants. One participant approached us at the end of a focus group session and told us that answering one of the questions during the session was very painful for her. In retrospect, it would have been useful to add an empirical method that creates more individual space for participants sharing sensitive or taboo topics or to capture data from them while in their context of smoking, such as cultural probes [13], giving participants the opportunity to express their smoking cessation issues in a more private way.

Limitations

We acknowledge that our findings are based on a qualitative study with fewer participants than would be involved in a quantitative clinical study. As the study aims to understand the phenomenon of individual differences in smoking cessation, rather than test the effectiveness of a particular treatment or app, we have deliberately chosen a qualitative approach. As per the qualitative research method paradigm, this has allowed us work very closely with our study participants, and to gain richer insights into their thoughts and motivations in relation to quitting smoking.

CONCLUSIONS

We have conducted an empirical investigation with smokers to identify and understand what types of assistance are perceived and experienced as important when trying to quit, and explore the role that technology can potentially play in providing such assistance. To do this we have taken a participatory approach of working closely with a group of smokers and ex-smokers through focus groups and design workshops. Our study showed that people are highly individual in their approach to quitting and in the kind of help they regard as relevant to their situation. To design effective smoking cessation applications, these individual differences should be at the core of our designs. In tailoring smoking cessation apps it is important to consider: 1) quitting stage, 2) immediate impact, 3) smoking habits, 4) personalization, 5) flexibility, 6) reminders, 7) self-monitoring, 8) novelty, 9) meaningful rewards, 10) social support, 11) solo struggle, and 12) competition. Our contribution is in bringing these themes forward as a collection is that jointly outline a design space for considering individual differences in tailored smoking cessation apps. As an illustration of the use of the identified themes in technology design, we have presented and discussed three different design ideas for tailored smoking cessation apps produced by our participants.

Our findings present new insights, and confirm findings from previous related research on supporting health behavior change. We have put previous findings into the context of tailored smoking cessation apps, have contributed with a deeper understanding of important factors when trying to quit smoking and elaborated on how to cater for individual differences when providing tailored quitting assistance.

ACKNOWLEDGMENTS

We thank all study participants for taking time to provide insights into the life of being a smoker and trying to quit. We also thank the Danish National Health and Medicines Authority and the Municipality of Aalborg for their help in recruiting participants for the study.

REFERENCES

1. Abroms, L., Padmanabhan, N., Thaweethai, L. and Phillips, T. iPhone Apps for Smoking Cessation: A Content Analysis. *Am. J. of Preventive Medicine, 40,* 3 (2011), 279-285.
2. Abroms, L., Westmaas, L., Bontemps-Jones, J., Ramani, R. and Mellerson, J. A Content Analysis of Popular Smartphone Apps for Smoking Cessation. *Am. J. of Preventive Medicine, 45,* 6 (2013), 732-736.
3. Ahijevych, K. and Wewers, M. Processes of Change Across Five Stages of Smoking Cessation. *Addictive Behaviors, 17* (1992), 17-25.
4. Ali, A., Hossain, S., Hovsepian, K., Rahman, M., Plarre, K. and Kumar, S. mPuff: Automated Detection of Cigarette Smoking Puffs from Respiration Measurements. In *Proc. IPSN '12*, ACM Press (2012), 269-280.
5. Ananthanarayan, S., Lapinski, N., Siek, K. and Eisenberg, M. Towards the Crafting of Personal Health Technologies. In *Proc. DIS '14,* ACM Press (2014), 587-596.
6. Aveyard, P., Massey, L., Parsons, A., Manaseki, S. and Griffin, C. The effect of Transtheoretical Model based interventions on smoking cessation. *Social Science and Medicine, 68* (2009), 397-403.
7. Backinger, C. and Auguston, E. Where There's an App There's a Way? *Am. J. of Preventive Medicine, 40,* 3 (2011), 390-391.
8. Choe, E., Lee, N., Lee, B., Pratt, W. and Kientz, J. Understanding Quantified-Selfers' Practice in Collecting and Exploring Personal Data. In *Proc. CHI '14*, ACM Press (2014), 1143-1152.
9. Chung, W., Kim, H., Lim, S., Lee, S. and Cho, K. Factors influencing cigarette smoking and quantified implications for anti-smoking policy: evidence from South Korea. *Int. Journal of Public Health, 54*, 6 (2009), 409-419.
10. Cummings, K., Hellmann, R. and Emon, S. Correlates of Participation in a Worksite Stop-Smoking Contest. *Journal of Behavioral Medicine, 11,* 3 (1988), 267-277.
11. Fogg, B. *Persuasive Technology*. Morgan Kaufmann, 2003.
12. Fogg, B. and Allen, E. 10 Uses of Texting to Improve Health. *In Proc. Persuasive '09*, ACM Press (2009), Article 38.
13. Gaver, B., Dunne, T. and Pacenti, E. Design: Cultural probes. *Interactions, 6,*1 (1999).
14. Girma, E., Assefa, T. and Deribew, A. Cigarette smokers' intention to quit smoking in Dire Dawa town Ethiopia: an assessment using the Transtheoretical Model. *BMC Public Health, 10* (2010).
15. Godtfredsen, N. and Prescott, E. Effect of Smoking Reduction on Lung Cancer Risk. *J. of the Am. Medical Association, 294,* 12 (2005), 1505-1510
16. Graham, C., Benda, P., Howard, S., Balmford, J., Bishop, N. and Borland, R. *"heh – keeps me off the smokes..."*: Probing Technology Support for Personal Change. In *Proc. OzCHI'06*, ACM Press (2006), 221-228.
17. Heckler, E., Klasnja, P., Froehlich, J. and Buman, M. Mind the theoretical gap: interpreting, using, and

developing behavioral theory in HCI research. In *Proc. CHI'13*, ACM Press (2013), 3307-3316.

18. Klasnja, P., Consolvo, S. and Pratt, W. How to evaluate technologies for health behavior change in HCI research. In *Proc. CHI'11*, ACM Press (2011), 3063-3072.

19. Marlatt, G. and Donovan, D. *Relapse Prevention.* Guilford Press, 2005.

20. Michie, S. and West, R. Behaviour change theory and evidence: a presentation to Government. *Health Psych Review,* 7, 1 (2013), 1-22.

21. Michie, S. Hyder, N., Walia, A. and West, R. Development of a taxonomy of behaviour change techniques used in individual behavioural support for smoking cessation. *Addictive Behaviors, 36* (2011), 315-319.

22. Michie, S., van Stralen, M. and West, R. The behaviour change wheel: A new method for characterising and designing behaviour change interventions. *Implementation Science, 6* (2011), 42.

23. Morris, M. Motivating Change with Mobile: Seven Guidelines. *Interactions, 19,* 3 (2012), 26-31.

24. Murnane, E. and Counts, S. Unraveling Abstinence and Relapse: Smoking Cessation Reflected in Social Media. In *Proc. CH I'14*, ACM Press (2014), 1345-1354.

25. Paay, J., Kjeldskov, J., Brinthaparan, U., Lichon, L., Rasmussen, S., Srikandaraja, N., Smith, W., Wadley, G., Ploderer, B. Quitty: Using Technology to Persuade Smokers to Quit. In *Proc. NordiCHI'14*, ACM Press (2014).

26. Park, E., DePue, J., Goldstein, M., Niaura, R., Harlow, L., Willey, C., Rakowski, W. and Prokhorov, A. Assessing the Transtheoretical Model of Change Constructs for Physicians Counseling Smokers. *Annals of Behavioral Medicine, 25,* 2 (2003), 120-126.

27. Ploderer, B., Smith, W., Howard, S. Pearce, J. and Borland, R. Patterns of Support in an Online Community for Smoking Cessation. In *Proc. C&T'13*, ACM Press (2013), 26-35.

28. Ploderer, B., Smith, W., Howard, S. Pearce, J. and Borland, R. Things You Don't Want to Know About Yourself: Ambivalence About Tracking and Sharing Personal Information for Behavior Change. In *Proc. OzCHI'12*, ACM Press (2012), 489-492.

29. Ploderer, B., Smith, W., Howard, S. Pearce, J. and Borland, R. Introducing the Ambivalent Socialiser. In *Proc. CHI'12*, ACM Press (2012), 1511-1514.

30. Ploderer, B., Smith, W., Pearce, J. and Borland, R. A Mobile App Offering Distractions and Tips to Cope With Cigarette Craving: A Qualitative Study. *JMIR mHealth uHealth 2,* 2 (2014), e23.

31. Primatesta, P., Falaschetti, E., Gupta, S., Marmot, M. and Poulter, N. Association Between Smoking and Blood Pressure. *Hypertension, 37* (2001), 187-193.

32. Prochaska, J. and Velicer, W. The Transtheoretical Model of Health Behavior Change. *Am. J. of Health Promotion, 12,* 1 (1997), 38-48.

33. Roubroeks, M., Ham, J. and Midden, C. When Artificial Social Agents Try to Persuade People: The Role of Social Agency on the Occurrence of Psychological Reactance. *Int. J. of Social Robotics, 3,* 2 (2011), 155-165.

34. Scholl, P., Kücükyildiz, N. and Laerhoven, K. Demo: When Do You Light a Fire? Capturing Tobacco Use with Situated Wearable Sensors. In *Proc. UbiComp'13*, ACM Press (2013), 1309-1310.

35. Shimoda, T. and Stapel, L. Increasing Relevance of Smoking Cessation Messages in an Online Software Agent Environment. *In Proc. HICSS'06, Vol. 5*, IEEE (2006), 89a.

36. Snuggs, S. and Hajek, P. Responsiveness to reward following cessation of smoking. *Psychopharmacology, 225,* 4 (2013), 869-873.

37. Springer Healthcare News. Financial reward stubs out smoking habit. *Published online*, Springer Healthcare (2012).

38. Strauss, A. and Corbin, J. *Basics of Qualitative Research: Techniques and Procedures for Developing Grounded Theory.* Sage Publications, 1998.

39. Strecher, V. Computer-tailored smoking cessation materials: A review and discussion. *Patient Education and Counseling, 26,* 2 (1999), 107-117.

40. The Fagerströms Test. http://www.health.wa.gov.au/smokefree/docs/Fgerstrom_Test.pdf. Government of Western Australia Department of Health.

41. Valdivieso-López, E., Flores-Mateo, G., Molina-Gómez, J., Rey-Reñones, C., Uriarte, M.B., Duch, J. and Valverde, A. Efficacy of a mobile application for smoking cessation in young people: study protocol for a clustered randomized trial. *BMC Public Health 2013, 13* (2013).

42. West, R. and Brown, J. *Theory of Addiction.* Wiley Blackwell, 2013.

43. West, R. with Smyth, C., West, J. *The SmokeFree Formula.* Orian, 2013.

44. Zhang M. and Yang, C. The Effectiveness of Smoking Cessation Intervention on Facebook: A Preliminary Study of Posts and Users. In *Proc. ICSH'13,* Springer (2013), 7-17.

FeedFinder: A Location-Mapping Mobile Application for Breastfeeding Women

Madeline Balaam, Rob Comber, Ed Jenkins, Selina Sutton and Andrew Garbett
Culture Lab
School of Computing Science
University of Newcastle, UK
{madeline.balaam, rob.comber, edward.jenkins, selina.sutton, a.garbett}@ncl.ac.uk

ABSTRACT
Breastfeeding is positively encouraged across many countries as a public health endeavour. The World Health Organisation recommends breastfeeding exclusively for the first six months of an infant's life. However, women can struggle to breastfeed, and to persist with breastfeeding, for a number of reasons from technique to social acceptance. This paper reports on four phases of a design and research project, from sensitising user-engagement and user-centred design, to the development and in-the-wild deployment of a mobile phone application called FeedFinder. FeedFinder has been developed with breastfeeding women to support them in finding, reviewing and sharing public breastfeeding places with other breastfeeding women. We discuss how mobile technologies can be designed to support public health endeavours, and suggest that public health technologies are better aimed at communities and societies rather than individual.

Author Keywords
breastfeeding; mobile; user-centred design; public health; preventative health

ACM Classification Keywords
H.5.m. Information interfaces and presentation (e.g., HCI): Miscellaneous.

INTRODUCTION
Breastfeeding is viewed as a positive health behaviour that has lasting health benefits for the breastfeeding mother and her child. In the UK women are recommended to breastfeed for the first six months exclusively and to supplement additional food for at least a year [19]. Research has suggested that infants who are not breastfed are more likely to contract short-term infections (including respiratory and ear) and in particular infections that require a period of hospitalization. Longer-term implications can include a greater likelihood to become obese in later life, to develop type 2 diabetes, as well as slightly higher levels of blood pressure and blood cholesterol. For breastfeeding women, evidence suggests that benefits include a reduction in the risk of breast and ovarian cancer [24].

CHI 2015, April 18–23, 2015, Seoul, Republic of Korea.

http://dx.doi.org/10.1145/2702123.2702328.

According to the 2010 Infant Feeding Study [19] 81% of women in the UK initiate breastfeeding within the first 48 hours, with 69% of women continuing to breastfeed their infant at 1 week. By the six to eight week medical check-up 55% of women are continuing to breastfeed their infant. By six months just over a third of women (34%) are continuing to breastfeed their infant, well below the target of exclusive breastfeeding up to six months. Those women that are most likely to breastfeed are older, with 87% of women aged over 30 choosing to breastfeed their infant, compared to 58% of women aged under 20 choosing to breastfeed. In addition, women who undertook managerial and professional occupations were more likely to breastfeed (90%), than women who have never worked (71%).

There is much perceived pressure among women to breastfeed [25], from midwifery care through to public health messaging, where the choice to breastfeed is framed in moralistic terms. Choosing to breastfeed therefore becomes strongly linked with being a "good mother", while choosing not to breastfeed is viewed as morally and socially deviant [22]. And, while breastfeeding is often described as the natural and trouble-free feeding method [42], many women experience practical difficulties and concerns in breastfeeding during the first few weeks of a baby's life. Breastfeeding requires learning on behalf of both the mother and baby, which requires support from local health services, practice, perseverance and persistence [8]. Less than optimal techniques can result in an extremely painful breastfeeding experience. And as the quantity of breast milk a baby consumes through breastfeeding is not known, women can have concerns about insufficient milk supply and milk consumption, which undermine confidence in their ability to breastfeed and their bodies ability to ensure their baby thrives [6]. Finally, social, cultural and public values, familial history, class and regional influences all play a part in a woman's choice to breastfeed or not [33].

The Public Construction of Breastfeeding

Women's feeding choices are influenced not only by their own opinions, but also by the socio-cultural context in which those decisions take place. A woman's family, partner and the community in which she lives and works all play a part in the decision she makes as to whether she will breastfeed and continue to breastfeed up to and past six months [32, 33]. Previous research has identified that support for breastfeeding outside of the home is limited within the UK [33]. The act of breastfeeding is considered intimate and personal and therefore not appropriate for public consumption [9]. This lack of perceived public, practical and moral support for breastfeeding can be extremely problematic for breastfeeding women, as this sense of disapproval is viewed as a negative judgment of them as a person [32]. In response women arrange their day such that they remain close to home or to designated lactation rooms, in order that they never have to feed in public [39]. The work of keeping breastfeeding invisible clearly increases the labour associated with breastfeeding [41]. This paucity of day-to-day contact with breastfeeding is also evident in media production and consumption. For example, content analysis of British TV showed that bottle-feeding was shown often in televised programmes, but breastfeeding only appeared once [21]. Photos of women breastfeeding have, until very recently, been banned from social networking sites [31]. In addition, news stories in print media regularly report on instances where women have been asked not to breastfeed in a public place. This contrives to achieve a context where it is rare to see a woman breastfeeding an infant in public [9], and, where public breastfeeding is a necessity, there is a social expectation it will be discreet [36]. As less women are seen breastfeeding in public, breastfeeding is seen as a less available infant feeding option, especially for those from socio-economic groups where breastfeeding is less common [28, 39].

Lactivism and Community Support

It has been suggested that the transition to motherhood can be a motivational force for women to engage in political activism [38]. And, since breastfeeding in public is not a neutral activity [33], but rather a political performance where the caring practice associated with, in particular, very young babies is made visible to the public [9, 40], there has been an increasing amount of activism in relation to breastfeeding in public in recent years. Nurse-ins are perhaps the pinnacle of this kind of 'lactivisim', where breastfeeding women congregate to breastfeed en-mass, typically in restaurants, cafes and shops where a women has previously been told that they can't breastfeed. Breastfeeding picnics similarly focus on bringing women together en-mass to breastfeed, but usually take place in family friendly places such as parks. Boyer et al [9] make the distinction between these two forms of lactivisim, stating that nurse-ins focus on breastfeeding mothers rights as consumers (to breastfeed in cafes, airplanes, etc.), whereas breastfeeding picnics focus on breastfeeding mothers rights as citizens (to breastfeed in parks, on benches). However, she also highlights how these forms of lactivism can further alienate some women who simply see themselves as trying their best to cater to their infant's needs when breastfeeding publically.

HCI, the New Mother, Gendered Spaces and Feminism

HCI has turned to new mother- and parent-hood as a transitional time in life which digital technologies may be well placed to support [3]. There exists a diverse range of design studies and devices from pregnancy suits to enable the non-pregnant partner to better empathise with the experiences of the pregnant women [23] through to devices to support pregnant women manage and share their healthcare records [17]. Research has investigated how new mothers use social networking technologies to find confidence in their new role, as well as maintain their identity beyond that of 'mother' [18]. Recently a small body of work has responded to needs around breastfeeding specifically, with for example the development of a relational agent that is able to engage in an empathetic dialogue with a mother to deliver information about breastfeeding [16]. Other projects have explored how a mobile application can aid people in correctly pasteurising breastmilk donated to human milk banks in developing countries [10]. Contributing to this work, this paper provides a case study of a user-centred design process undertaken with new mothers in the design, development and evaluation of a mobile application which enables women to find, review and share public places for breastfeeding. We report on methods used for engaging new mothers in a design process.

Recent discourse within HCI has identified that sites and spaces of gender and domesticity are actively produced by individuals and communities [4, 5], and that (ubiquitous) technologies may both play a role reinforcing gender stereotypes within spaces, or alternatively transform the beliefs, rituals and power dynamics associated with a space. Here, we reflect on the role that mobile technologies can play in delivering public health by focusing on change in the community, rather than change in the individual, arguably offering a concrete example of how a ubiquitous technology can transform perceptions of public space.

BREASTFEEDING IN THE NORTH EAST UK

The North East UK has low rates of breastfeeding initiation and continuation when compared with the national average. Around 54.5% of new mothers initiate breastfeeding within the first 48 hours, below the national average of 72.5%. While breastfeeding initiation in the area has improved slightly since 2006, continuation of breastfeeding beyond the first six to eight weeks is the lowest in the country, with only 31.9% of infants receiving some breast milk at six to eight weeks. Recent research notes that despite good maternity units and innovative interventions to support breastfeeding, breastfeeding is rarely seen in public [33], with participants stating that adequate and comfortable places were rarely provided.

DESIGNING FEEDFINDER

We followed an iterative user-centred design cycle in the design of FeedFinder, initially seeking to develop a sensitising account of women's experiences of breastfeeding locally. Generative design ideation around these accounts led to the concept of a breastfeeding mapping application to allow women to find, review and share places for breastfeeding. Further inquiry took the form of a series of design workshops that explored what values contribute to good and bad breastfeeding experiences. Finally, a medium fidelity prototype was evaluated using cooperative evaluation to identify any usability issues.

Sensitising Interviews with Breastfeeding Mothers

At the outset of the project we conducted four one-to-one 30-minute interviews with new mothers in a local café, 12 to 16 weeks after the birth of their first baby. Each mother had reported prior to giving birth that it was their intention to breastfeed their baby. At the point of interview three women were breastfeeding their babies exclusively and one woman was formula feeding her baby exclusively. These interviews focused primarily on initial experiences of breastfeeding, but also touched on wider experiences of early motherhood. Each interview was audio recorded, transcribed and analysed using an inductive thematic analysis. We report on two reoccurring themes related to breastfeeding pressures and the act of public breastfeeding.

Pressures on Unfamiliar Ground

For each of the women the choice to breastfeed had initially been entangled with social, professional and familial identities and relationships. Two women had chosen to breastfeed as a result of their professions (a nutritionist and a support worker at a charity supporting early years education and health). *"I felt pretty pressured [to breastfeed] in the first place cause I work for Sure Start, so there we encourage Mums to breastfeed and it's best thing obviously, I know it is anyway"* (Sandra). Cara on the other hand stated that she had never really questioned whether she would breastfeed. As a nutritionist she considered it to be the best start for her child and "*... was determined to try and try and try even if it doesn't work.*" Sarah similarly reported the sense that breastfeeding was the best thing for her baby and although she "*... wasn't overly enthusiastic about it*" she felt that breastfeeding was a familiar option since her mother had breastfed her and her siblings.

While each woman might have made the decision to at least try breastfeeding for their own reasons, their choices were made antenatally. And for each of the women the experience is something quite different from their original perception. Cara explained: *"I knew it would be tiring – but I didn't realize how tiring it was going to be. I've got a couple of friends who have already given up because they found it too tiring. Some days you have more time between feeds, but most of the time it's sort of every hour, hour and a half.*" And, while Cara was able to overcome some of the uncertainty associated with breastfeeding a baby (for example, knowing when to feed and knowing whether the baby has had enough), Sandra found herself unable to: *"I'm not breastfeeding anymore. I started mix feeding. It's just too, too hard, too tiring. She was too greedy, but she's in a lot better routine now, I wish I hadn't given up, but... I didn't realise how difficult it was going to be ... I had no idea when she was going to need feeding.*"

The choice to continue or not with breastfeeding has to be both the best choice for the baby and the mother. So while Sandra might wish she hadn't given up breastfeeding, she is now better able to sleep as she can share the care of her baby with her partner more fully, and feels *"much happier now I have stopped."* However, having made this choice Sandra had to fight to legitimise it. She considers that she continued to breastfeed *"more for other people than for me, like the midwives and things. They ask you if you are still breastfeeding and if you have any concerns they push you to do a couple more days... I was terrified about telling my midwife I didn't want to breastfeed anymore so I avoided her.*"

Exposing a New Self

In the early weeks of motherhood the women we interviewed attempted to confine breastfeeding to the home. Cara would *"try and time feeds so I could feed him at home, get out and then be back at home for the next one or somewhere where I could hide away"*. But the attempt to provide this care for their babies in private hindered the extent to which they could continue managing other aspects of their lives. Sandra tells us how '*I couldn't even nip to the shops*', '*I didn't come into town in case she did wanted to be fed*'. Yet, for most breastfeeding women there comes a time when one must breastfeed in public. In doing so, they are confronted with the public perception of breastfeeding. For instance, Sarah was aware *"from my antenatal classes that breastfeeding is really low in the north east*". As a result when the women made the decision to breastfeed in a public place they seemed to anticipate that it would be perceived by others as a controversial activity. Sarah told us with surprise *"I haven't had any problems – no one has said anything to me or anything like that.*" while Sandra armed herself with legal knowledge when breastfeeding outside of the home: *"because of the job I do I would know I was well within my rights to be doing it."*

Having *"jumped in at the deep end*" and fed in public, Cara seemed to positively embrace a sense of freedom: *"I don't care where I do it. I fed him on the Quayside market sitting on a step the other day! I've turned into one of those mothers who will just get their boobs out everywhere. I just don't care anymore.*" While Sarah is also *"not that bothered about breastfeeding in public"*, she took a much more deliberated approach to breastfeeding in a public place: "*...I've spoken to a few people at church just to like gage what other people's opinion* [of breastfeeding in public] *is, like am I too confident, should I be more like reserved? But I don't think I* *have been. Like, I only do it when I'm sitting out of the way or in a café I'd sort of sit in a corner, like I try and sit somewhere more discreet..."* This concern with whether there is a proper way to feed in public is felt by Cara not through her own concerns, but through the concerns of others she is close to: "*My friends who don't have babies, they would be like, this woman just got her boob out in McDonalds, and I would tell them well I hope you know I'm going to be doing that don't you. And they were like well you will have to be discreet won't you and I was like well I'll try.*" And, while both Sarah and Cara use a feeding scarf in order to be discreet in public if and when necessary, Sarah attempts to be discreet also through planning and choosing where she can breastfeed when out and about: "*I think it's useful in bigger department stores knowing there's somewhere you can go which I hadn't known existed beforehand... but I'm quite happy to sit in a coffee shop if I need to.*" Similarly although Cara will breastfeed anywhere she has at times sought to find places where breastfeeding is welcome, but has found online resources to be lacking: "*...the resources are old, they aren't kept up to date. Like it said there was a good one* [breastfeeding room] *in Boots and I went in and they don't have one anymore. It didn't matter in my case but that could panic people who don't like to feed in public at all.*"

While drawing attention to a range of issues related to early experiences of motherhood, the interview data highlights some challenges experienced by new mothers who choose to breastfeed. In line with [39], we see how breastfeeding a young baby can be unpredictable, such that women do not feel confident to leave the house in case they have to breastfeed outside of their home. Similarly to [32], we find that breastfeeding outside of the home is considered a challenge not only because of the fact that intimate parts of one's body may be exposed, bodily fluids might be leaked, but also because women are unsure how their breastfeeding might be perceived by the public, and how they might cope with public hostility.

Design Workshops

Following analysis and ideation our design response took the form of a mobile phone application that allows women to find, review and share places for public breastfeeding. The application could serve the very practical benefit of allowing women to know where other women have had positive experiences of breastfeeding in public places, while also potentially highlighting the variety and breadth of places where women do have positive experiences of breastfeeding in public. To explore the design as well as understand the specificities of how such an application we conducted a series of design workshops.

Within the UK context local community breastfeeding support groups are available to offer informal places for women (often with new babies) to gather and breastfeed. On the whole, these groups offer a much needed space for women to meet other women who have recently become mums, as well as a place where women can come to solicit support and advice on breastfeeding. We were invited to run our design sessions within four of these community support groups around the city and its suburbs, and through this engaged with a further 21 mothers. Our design sessions were structured around two lightweight and flexible activities, the first focused on mapping women's experiences of breastfeeding locally (*mapping past experiences*) and the second focused on drawing out the experiential qualities that make a place good for breastfeeding (*prioritising location qualities*). Each activity was designed to be relatively quick to complete, require minimum hands-on activity from the women (since they could be breastfeeding) and could be conducted either with individual women, or with groups of women. Each workshop was audio recorded, transcribed and analysed using an deductive thematic analysis.

Mapping Past Experiences

Using an annotated map of the area surrounding each breastfeeding community group we asked the women to map places where they had breastfed publically and to describe some of their (positive and negative) experiences of breastfeeding locally.

The data further suggested that women experience anxiety in relation to breastfeeding in public. And while this anxiety and feeling of embarrassment fades over time and with experience ("*I don't find it embarrassing because I think you get over that really quickly, within the first of weeks...*") it was considered to exacerbate stress relating to early breastfeeding experiences ("*What am I going to do, where am I going to go and that's another anxiety you've got to get over and not only have you got to make sure they latch on properly and you're doing all the other things, you're trying to go through a mental checklist and the problem of finding somewhere and then thinking are they going to let me, is it going to be alright?*")

In discussing public breastfeeding with our participants we heard a handful of negative stories. Nancy told us of her experience breastfeeding in a high-end pizza chain: "... *They were absolutely awful in there... When they saw me getting [my baby] ready to feed they were like 'oh don't come and sit over here. Oh no no, go and sit over here in this corner...' I'm like no what's wrong with me sitting here because I was quite near the window and they were like 'oh no, we'd rather you go and sit there' and then I had people walking out of there because I was feeding...*"

However, overall the women's experiences were positive when they did breastfeed in public, with one participant reporting that a stranger in cafe had congratulated her for breastfeeding. In our group discussions women often shared with one another good places to breastfeed around the city, as well as discussing certain problems that had to be overcome when looking for somewhere to breastfeed. The pragmatics of navigating a busy café with a buggy ("*...there's nothing worse than banging into every table and chair going...*"), to knowing that a member of staff would carry a hot drink to the table (*"because you can't manage a buggy, a baby, a toddler if you've got one and whatever drink"*), or that free drinking water was available. Common strategies for juggling these practical concerns was to only visit places which had baby changing facilities as the women considered that this indicated some level of baby friendliness.

Prioritising Place Qualities

The second activity aimed to understand what qualities of a place were important to a positive public breastfeeding experience. We explored this through a card sorting activity. 14 cards were designed, each representing a feature or quality used to describe a place: clean, open, bustling, stylish, convenient, baby facilities, friendly, comfy, familiar, privacy, spacious, affordable, entertaining, calm. To complete the activity an individual or group of women were asked to provide a description of the quality in question and then place it on a target; the nearer the centre the more important, the nearer the perimeter the less important. Blank cards were also available for women to include additional qualities of places that they considered important to a positive breastfeeding experience.

Through this activity we discovered that the qualities central to a positive experience of public breastfeeding were in part changeable dependent upon the age of the women's baby and thereby their experience in breastfeeding. For example, for those new to breastfeeding, women tended to prefer to feed their babies somewhere private so as to concentrate on getting the baby to latch on properly. Alternatively, women with older babies tended to prefer somewhere quiet so as to reduce possible distractions (*"Especially now as he's got older I need somewhere quiet rather than somewhere that there's loads going on because literally he'll be on and off and on and off to see what's going on."*) Similarly, while women got used to breastfeeding and in particular different ways of holding and supporting their baby while feeding, they tended to seek out places to breastfeed with supportive soft seating. However, as women became more experienced and in tandem their baby developed better head control and strength, women found they could feed on hard seats, or the ground if necessary.

Cooperative Evaluation

The final element of our user-centred design cycle saw the cooperative evaluation [30] of a wireframe, medium-fidelity prototype of FeedFinder. We brought the wireframe, which illustrated interactions required to find a review, add a review and add a place, to one of the breastfeeding community groups who had participated in the original design workshops. We asked six women to walkthrough the wireframe, completing three activities: finding and viewing the reviews for a place, adding a review for a place, and adding a new breastfeeding place to the map. As the women completed each task, we asked the women to 'think-aloud' there actions and discuss with any problems that they were encountering. Notes were made throughout each evaluation and any usability issues and potential remedies were discussed with the user.

FEEDFINDER

FeedFinder is a mobile application, available for free on both iOS and Android that enables women (and other interested parties, such as breastfeeding community workers, midwives, partners, business owners) to explore and contribute to a map which describes how supportive the local community and services are toward women who breastfeed. Women can use FeedFinder to search for and view places on the map where other women have previously breastfed, along with those women's reviews and ratings along five categories: Comfy(ness), Clean(liness), Privacy, Baby Facilities and Average Spend. Women can also add new places to the map where they have breastfed and leave reviews for that place.

We added a brief survey to FeedFinder to collect an overview of women's experiences of using the application. The short survey asks users to rate how happy they are with the application, whether they would recommend the application to a friend and whether the application has helped them to find a place to breastfeed in the last week. The survey has an open text box for any additional comments. The survey is made available to women four weeks after the application was first downloaded.

Imagining FeedFinder in Use

Sally had her first baby four weeks ago. She hasn't left the house for weeks and she hasn't wanted to. It's been enough to try and get on top of nappy changes, feed her new baby as well as try to make sure she looks presentable for all the many visitors to her home since Ian was born. Today, Sally has decided to head into town to meet a friend for coffee. She's excited to show Ian off, but worried about where she's going to breastfeed Ian and whether people will stare at her if Ian cries or if she can't get him latched on quickly. A friend recommended FeedFinder to her which she's downloaded to her smart phone. She looked at the FeedFinder map before organising a place to meet her friend to find somewhere that would be breastfeeding friendly. She was surprised to see there were lots of places positively reviewed by women, and feels comforted that she's not the only person trying to breastfeed a baby in Newcastle. She's looked at a few of the reviews for places she used to visit before having a baby and found one of her favourite cafés is well rated by breastfeeding women, but those women have noted that there aren't baby change facilities or much chance of privacy. Sally doesn't want other people to get an eyeful while she's feeding Ian, so she decided on a different café where she understands there's a sofa at the back of the café which is quite quiet and private, and which other women have said is clean with good changing facilities.

After her trip into the city Sally is feeling very pleased with herself. She's managed to change Ian's nappy in a café, dealt with a possetting incident and breastfeed Ian in public for the first time. As Ian sleeps in his buggy on the metro ride home, Sally opens FeedFinder, finds the café she visited earlier and adds her own review of the facilities and experience for other breastfeeding women to use. Sally keeps using FeedFinder throughout the first four months of Ian's life. As she gains confidence and Ian becomes more competent at feeding she doesn't need to use FeedFinder as often to find places to breastfeed, instead deciding to give back to the community by adding more places and reviews to the map in order to support other women.

RELEASING FEEDFINDER

The release of FeedFinder was planned to coincide with the birth of Prince George (July 2013) in order to maximise on possible interest within both regional and national press. The project was featured in television, radio and print media, including Sky News, BBC News as well as local press venues such as 'the Journal', the Metro radio and LBC radio.

We wanted the women who downloaded the application when it was first released to feel there was content there for them to interact with before hopefully moving onto adding reviews and new places to breastfeed based on their own experiences. As such, we invited a number of local breastfeeding women (recruited primarily through the university and informal networks) to use an early version of the application to add reviews for places where they had experience of breastfeeding. In addition, we added reviews to the map within the local area based on data collected in our design workshops, and particularly in relation to the 'Mapping Past Experiences'.

EVAULATING FEEDFINDER

FeedFinder has now been running for over 12 months and has seen an uptake of just under 3,000 members. FeedFinder has been used primarily in the UK however a smaller, but growing, number of venues and reviews have been added in the USA, Western Europe and Australia. At present, FeedFinder has over 3000 women who have used or currently use FeedFinder, 1900 places added and a total of 1810 reviews.

Members on average used FeedFinder on 2.6 separate occasions over a period of 25 days. However those that interacted with the application on more than a single day, around 48% (1366 users), used the application almost twice that, with an average of 4.16 sessions over an average period of 53 days. The average session use time was 164.14 seconds (~3 minutes), which is more than twice the average amount of time spent interacting with a mobile application (71.56 seconds) reported by Böhmer et al [7]. However, the FeedFinder average session time is similar to the average amount of time that users were found to interact with health focussed applications specifically (an average of 153.80 seconds) [7].

During each session members performed on average 7.37 actions, viewing 1.45 venues and performed 5.2 map searches, with members searching 1.17 miles from their starting location. In addition, we found that 16% (475) of FeedFinder members have added at least one venue. A similar figure 14% (399) of members have contributed at least one review. This level of participation is similar to that reported by Van Mierlo in [29], who found that between 17 – 24% of members of online health communities made at least one post during their membership.

Members used the application throughout the day, but there were peaks in use three points during the day: 9am, 4pm and then 9pm. The application usage in the morning may reflect women searching to find places to breastfeed for later in the day. The 4pm peak in map searching may correspond with members attempting to find places to breastfeed while out and about. At 9pm the majority of reviews are submitted and places added suggesting that members find it easier to contribute to FeedFinder when in the evening, perhaps once the baby is in bed.

As FeedFinder made use of the Foursquare API it was possible to categorise places added to FeedFinder. The four place types added most commonly were Coffee Shops (108), Cafés (95), Pubs (82) and Department Stores (74). The most reviewed venue categories were Department Stores (119), Coffee Shops (95), Cafés (87) and Pubs (60).

Survey Data, Feedback and Member Correspondence

So far, a total of 109 unique comments have been received in the "additional comments" section of the survey. These comments provided insight on the need for more places (49), specific faults (43), potential new features (15), motivations for use (33), and miscellaneous items (1).

Not Many Local Places Yet!

Most prominent was the identified need for more places, which was linked to the need for more users (15), for pre-populated data (6), and for more promotion and advertising (5). In some cases, despite its usefulness, members recognised the need for further content: "*Easy to use app and has helped me to locate breastfeeding friendly locations. Would benefit from further reviews and more locations however I understand this requires user feedback.*" Members were also keen to either be directly involved in this member feedback, or in recruiting or promoting feedback from others. One member wanted to integrated FeedFinder with Facebook to promote other member to provide reviews. "*great concept. will improve with more recommendations. anyway of linking it to check ins with eg Facebook to remind people to add venues?*"

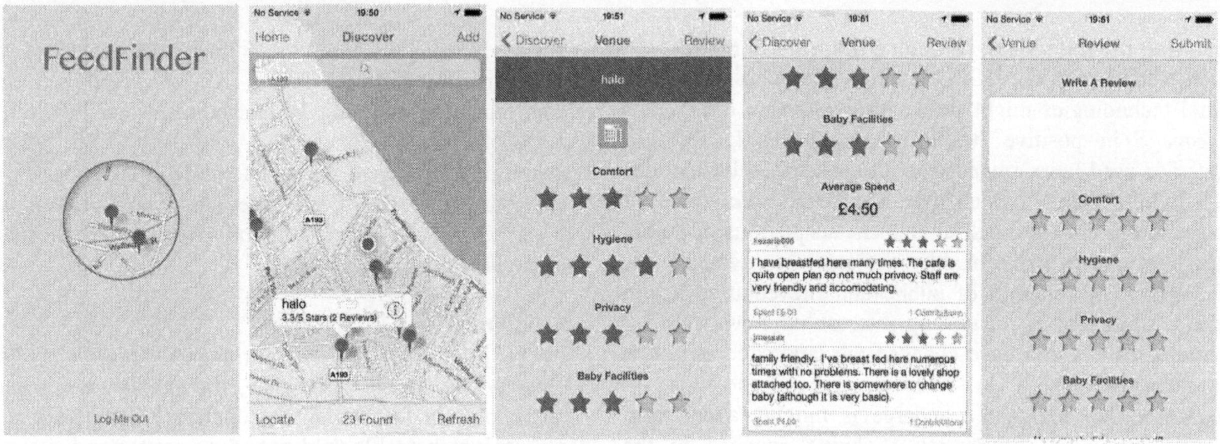

Figure 1: FeedFinder on iOS, the home screen, a mapped breastfeeding place, a review for a place, and the add a review screen

Yet, feedback also pointed to a need to prepopulate the app with 'obvious' locations, and contradicts the above suggestions of member feedback. As one comment suggests: "*I love the idea but there's no places listed! Would have been much better if you'd done some research and pre-populated it with a few of the obvious places in advance. Mothercare, Mamas and Papas, John Lewis etc. You shouldn't just rely on user submissions as people won't use an app with no content. Hopefully it'll have more content soon though.*" These comments point to a conflict in the expectations for authoritative data and the design of FeedFinder to promote community generated data.

Consumers and Citizens

Motivation for use appears to come from both its current usefulness (9) and expected usefulness for expecting mothers (7). Four commenters were active promoters of the application, while eight others identified their use as 'helping others', often despite their own comfort in public breastfeeding and reduced need for the app (4). Promoters of the app were particularly interested in demonstrating the ease of public breastfeeding to nervous mothers. This was both for professional support workers: "*As a breastfeeding worker, I use this app to show new mums how easy it is to find a decent place to feed, especially if they are worried about public feeding. It's a great local app*!" And for mothers: "*I am happy to bf* [breastfeed] *my 22 month anywhere but will review places to aid new bf mothers or mothers that are more nervous to feed in public*." The use FeedFinder as a tool to promote breastfeeding more formally was also confirmed in email correspondence with three NHS trusts and two local councils. In all five cases FeedFinder is being used as part of campaigns to support and increase breastfeeding.

There was also a change in how these members approached FeedFinder as they grew in confidence. "*I used the app more when my baby was new born, now my baby is 4-5 month I am more confident and feed where ever I want! I think it's great for more nervous mothers so will still review places for them.*" One of these commenters disagreed with the notion of only certain places being breastfeeding friendly: "*If someone was nervous about feeding in public and found confidence in others feeding at a location without issue then that's where this would be handy. For this reason only I've added some locations. But I hate the idea of acceptable places to feed, if your baby wants feeding then it's fine to feed them, wherever, whenever. Focus on baby and be proud of what you're doing.*" This perspective was also evident in e-mail correspondence received by the authors, where, following the UK's Equality Act, all locations across the country should be 'relatively breastfeeding friendly'. Although FeedFinder aims to expand on the 'relative' element to this, some users (and non-users) reject this for an absolute model of breastfeeding friendly places.

Beyond using the application to support other breastfeeding mothers in finding places to breastfeed, we know some women used FeedFinder to attempt to influence local service provision. In email correspondence with a FeedFinder member and local lactivist, Violet, discusses how she used FeedFinder to show the customer service manager of a large department store how reviews for his store compared with a local competitor, and where his store might improve its facilities to improve women's breastfeeding experience.

DISCUSSION

Feeling comfortable breastfeeding in public is, as suggested by much of our interview and design data, a time sensitive issue. For many, it is a case of doing it once or twice before feeling at ease with the act. FeedFinder appears to have been helpful in giving women the confidence to go out and breastfeed, with a large number of women (and breastfeeding supporters) downloading and using the application over a short period of time. Some women then go onto to continue adding places and reviews to support a community of women after them who are entering into public breastfeeding. Other women simply leave the community, their needs hopefully fulfilled. Here we frame FeedFinder as a *supportive health technology*. We highlight how FeedFinder as an everyday mundane design and service that enables women to engage in matters of the everyday also has the potential to facilitate publics to form to *engage with matters of concern*.

Changing the Individual, Changing the Environment

Much work within the HCI community has focused on how digital technologies might persuade or motivate individuals to engage in positive health behaviour [1, 2, 13, 27]. Strategies used have ranged from those inspired by theories of individual behaviour change, and lived experiences of motivation [2, 14], through to ambient adaptations of public space that aim to make healthy choices more available [1, 37]. Within the domain of public and preventative health there is similarly an increasing interest on how web 2.0 technologies can and have changed the landscape of health communication [11]. In such discussion, there is an acceptance that the public at large is moving away from simply consuming information to being engaged in the production of information for themselves and others. And examples exist of public health web 2.0 interactions that enable individuals to share healthcare experiences [20] or supporting the personalization of healthcare messages to specific communities.

Key to public health messaging and many persuasive health interventions is the notion of a "right" health behaviour regardless of culture and context. Accordingly, the core tenant of criticism in relation to public health 2.0 approaches therefore is that these channels allow for patients to share their own healthcare advice and views, which will not necessarily agree with official, and rigorously evaluated (i.e. "right") advice, and in fact may even be classified by experts as bad advice. When a critical lens from within the field of HCI is applied to technologies which seek to persuade or motivate healthy behaviour [12, 26, 34, 35], concerns are raised such that technologies have the potential to produce a context where healthy behaviour is forced and where negative comparisons with others are rife (in turn leading to neurosis).

The choice over whether to breastfeed or not is often constructed as a moral one, where breastfeeding is a value and cornerstone of "good" mothering [22, 25]. We cannot argue that FeedFinder is an example of a valueless technology, since its core focus is providing support to mothers who have chosen to breastfeed, and not those who haven't. But, FeedFinder was not designed to persuade mothers to breastfeed. Instead, FeedFinder was designed from the position of offering a *supportive health technology* for women who have chosen to breastfeed, or for women who might chose to breastfeed should the socio-cultural context prove accepting. As such, we consider that FeedFinder contributes to a vision for public health services where the focus is not on whether particular (healthy) choices are actually made in practice, but instead on whether individuals within a society have the opportunities to make a particular (healthy) choice where it suits them [22]. FeedFinder has the potential to help women find out for themselves (from the comfort of their own home) how their local community and services respond to breastfeeding women, provide feedback to their local services about how they might improve their services in relation to breastfeeding women, as well as, with time, increase the number of women seen breastfeeding in public. All of which can help to contribute to providing breastfeeding as an infant feeding option for those women who want to try. So, rather than attempting to change the individual [2, 14], or design a new environment [1, 37], FeedFinder attempts to provide women with the tools to understand and affect change in their own environment for themselves.

FeedFinder as a Public Thing

In [15] DiSalvo et al. introduces Latour's notion of "Dingpolitik" to HCI, discussing the role that design and HCI might play in facilitating contemporary democracy through objects which enable publics to form around and engage with matters of concern i.e. groups committed to addressing a specific issue. Through this lens, we can identify FeedFinder as a tool that facilitates the collection of data about the lived experience of breastfeeding in public locally, regionally and nationally. FeedFinder thus enables individuals, groups and communities to compare the lived experience of breastfeeding against the presumed rationality (that the public is not supportive of public breastfeeding). By facilitating the collection of this lived and affective experience, FeedFinder offers a platform through which the qualities that categorise political conditions can become better known, and acted upon by publics. We have evidence that a minority of women used FeedFinder to actively fight for the rights of women in their local community to receive good breastfeeding support, highlighting the capability for publics to form around FeedFinder. For example, Violet used FeedFinder to show a local business how it could better support breastfeeding women by making improvement to its parents' room.

Departing from [15] we argue that there are gains to be made through both designing to engage and capture something of the lived experience of a social condition, while in conjunction providing solutions to a perceived problem. FeedFinder can be and is viewed by many as a convenient service and solution to the problem of not knowing where to breastfeed in public. This characterisation of FeedFinder is demonstrated through its large and growing user population, and the fact that most users used FeedFinder to search for and find places to breastfeed. But, FeedFinder as a service (as well as a design that engages with a matter of concern) only works if those using it decide not only to use FeedFinder to consume information, but also to contribute information. Based on our analysis of community participation, as well as existing quantitative analysis of social networks [29], we know that relatively few users will actually contribute elements of their lived experiences to online communities. However, we also know that the focus of FeedFinder as a service that provides support to breastfeeding women acted to motivate some women to contribute content about their lived experiences of breastfeeding in public. They did this often not as a political act of being engaged with a matter of concern, but as an act of supporting other women engaged in the everyday act of caring for their baby in a manner that suits them. As such, we consider that the success of design seeking to make known the qualities of contemporary social conditions through active user participation may very well be contingent upon an ecosystem of different types of members and users, with a large pool of (happy) consumers central to the emergence of publics.

Designing with Mothers with Babies

The involvement of breastfeeding women within our iterative user centred-design process was essential in identifying and confirming the design space, as well as understanding how breastfeeding experiences might be rated and reviewed. When working with women with young children we quickly learned that design tasks needed to be incredibly flexible, quick and undemanding. Young babies crave to be held, even when they're not being fed, which means that individuals participating in a design tasks will likely only ever have one hand free, ruling out many creative tasks. In addition, because the needs of a young baby can be particularly demanding and unpredictable it is important to develop design methods that can be easily paused and re-started, as well as not requiring a large amount of time to complete (we found ten minutes to be about right). Finally, since a participant's attention will be split consider developing methods that are easy to respond to. We found tasks which were already part completed, or required ordering were sufficient for supporting useful design dialogue while being respectful of the amount and time and energy a woman would have for participating in the project.

CONCLUSION

Breastfeeding in public causes many women anxiety and can make the early weeks of motherhood a lonely and isolating time. In response we have designed, developed and deployed a mobile application which supports women in finding, reviewing and sharing places for public breastfeeding. Through so doing, we have identified one vision for the design of technologies to support public health, which moves the focus away from the individual and instead holds a lens to communities and societies and asks whether these contexts provide opportunities within which healthy choices can be made.

REFERENCES

1. Arroyo, E., Bonanni, L. And Valkanova, N. 2012. Embedded Interaction In A Water Fountain For Motivating Behavior Change In Public Space. *In Proc. CHI 2012* Pp. 685–688.
2. Balaam, M., Rennick Egglestone, S., Fitzpatrick, G., Rodden, T., Hughes, A.M., Wilkinson, A., Nind, T., Axelrod, L., Harris, E., Ricketts, I. And Others 2011. Motivating Mobility: Designing For Lived Motivation In Stroke Rehabilitation. *In Proc. CHI 2011*, Pp. 3073–3082.
3. Balaam, M., Robertson, J., Fitzpatrick, G., Say, R., Hayes, G., Mazmanian, M. And Parmar, B. 2013. Motherhood And HCI. *In Proc CHI EA '13*, Pp. 3215 – 3218.
4. Bardzell, S. 2010. Feminist HCI: Taking Stock And Outlining An Agenda For Design. (2010), *In Proc. CHI 2010*, Pp. 1301–1310.
5. Bell, G. And Dourish, P. 2006. Back To The Shed: Gendered Visions Of Technology And Domesticity. *Personal And Ubiquitous Computing*. 11, 5 (Oct. 2006), 373–381.
6. Berridge, K., Mcfadden, K., Abayomi, J. And Topping, J. 2005. Views Of Breastfeeding Difficulties Among Drop-In-Clinic Attendees. *Maternal & Child Nutrition*. 1, 4, 250–62.
7. Bohmer, M., B, H., Schoning, J., Kruger, A. And Bauer 2011. Falling Asleep With Angry Birds , Facebook And Kindle – A Large Scale Study On Mobile Application Usage. *In Proc. Mobilehci* (2011), 47 – 56.
8. Bottorff, J.L. 1990. Persistence In Breastfeeding: A Phenomenological Investigation. *Journal Ofadvanced Nursing*. 15, 2, 201–9.
9. Boyer, K. 2011. "The Way To Break The Taboo Is To Do The Taboo Thing" Breastfeeding In Public And Citizen-Activism In The UK. *Health & Place*. 17, 2, 430–7.
10. Chaudhri, R., Vlachos, D., Borriello, G., Israel-Ballard, K., Coutsoudis, A., Reimers, P. And Perin, N. 2013. Decentralized Human Milk Banking With ODK Sensors. *In Proc. Computing For Development* (New York, NY, USA, 2013).
11. Chou, W.S., Prestin, A., Lyons, C. And Wen, K. 2013. Web 2.0 For Health Promotion: Reviewing The Current Evidence. *American Journal Of Public Health*. 103, 1, E9–18.
12. Comber, R., Hoonhout, J., Van Halteren, A., Moynihan, P. And Olivier, P. 2013. Food Practices As Situated Action : Exploring And Designing For Everyday Food Practices With Households. *In Proc. CHI '13* (2013), pp. 2457–2466.
13. Comber, R. And Thieme, A. 2012. Designing Beyond Habit: Opening Space For Improved Recycling And Food Waste Behaviors Through Processes Of Persuasion, Social Influence And Aversive Affect. *Personal And Ubiquitous Computing*. 17, 6, pp. 1197–1210.
14. Consolvo, S., Mcdonald, D.W., Toscos, T., Chen, M.Y., Froehlich, J., Harrison, B., Klasnja, P., Lamarca, A., Legrand, L., Libby, R., Smith, I. And Landay, J.A. 2008. Activity Sensing In The Wild : A Field Trial Of Ubifit Garden. *In Proc. CHI '08* (2008), pp. 1797–1806.
15. Disalvo, C., Lodato, T., Jenkins, T., Lukens, J. And Kim, T. 2014. Making Public Things: How HCI Design Can Express Matters Of Concern. *In Proc. CHI '14* (2014), 2397–2406.

16. Edwards, R. A, Bickmore, T., Jenkins, L., Foley, M. And Manjourides, J. 2013. Use Of An Interactive Computer Agent To Support Breastfeeding. *Maternal And Child Health Journal*. (Jan. 2013).
17. Enquist, H. And Tollmar, K. 2008. The Memory Stone – A Personal ICT Device In Health Care. *In Proc. NordiCHI '08*, pp. 103–112.
18. Gibson, L. And Hanson, V. 2013. Digital Motherhood: How Does Technology Help New Mothers? *In Proc. CHI '13*, pp. 313–322.
19. Health and Social Care Information Centre (2012). *Infant Feeding Survey*.
20. Healthtalkonline.Org: *Http://Healthtalkonline.Org/*. Accessed: 2014-09-18.
21. Henderson, L., Kitzinger, J. And Green, J. 2000. Representing Infant Feeding: Content Analysis Of British Media Portrayals Of Bottle Feeding And Breast Feeding. *BMJ*. 321, 7270, 1196–8.
22. Knaak, S.J. 2010. Contextualising Risk, Constructing Choice: Breastfeeding And Good Mothering In Risk Society. *Health, Risk & Society*. 12, 4, 345–355.
23. Kosaka, T., Misumi, H., Iwamoto, T., Songer, R. And Akita, J. 2011. "Mommy Tummy" A Pregnancy Experience System Simulating Fetal Movement. *SIGGRAPH 2011*, Article 10.
24. Lawrence, R. A 2000. Breastfeeding: Benefits, Risks And Alternatives. *Current Opinion In Obstetrics & Gynecology*. 12, 6, 519–24.
25. Lee, E. 2007. Health, Morality, And Infant Feeding: British Mothers' Experiences Of Formula Milk Use In The Early Weeks. *Sociology Of Health & Illness*. 29, 7, 1075–90.
26. Maitland, J. 2011. Towards Negotiation As A Framework For Health Promoting Technology. *ACM SIGHIT Record*. 1, 1, 10.
27. Maitland, J., Chalmers, M. And Siek, K.A. Persuasion Not Required Improving Our Understanding Of The Sociotechnical Context Of Dietary Behavioural Change. *In Proc. PervasiveHealth '09*, pp. 1-8.
28. Mclntyre, E., Hiller, J.E. And Turnbull, D. 1999. Determinants Of Infant Feeding Practices In A Low Socio-Economic Area: Identifying Environmental Barriers To Breastfeeding. *Australian and New Zealand Journal of Public Health*. 23, 2 (1999), 207–209.
29. Van Mierlo, T. 2014. The 1% Rule In Four Digital Health Social Networks: An Observational Study. *J. Of Medical Internet Research*. 16, 2 (2014), E33.
30. Monk, A., Wright, P., Haber, J. And Davenport, L. 1993. *Improving Your Human- Computer Interface : A Practical Technique*. Prentice Hall.
31. Mums Furious As Facebook Removes Breastfeeding Photos: 2008. *http://eww.theguardian.com/media/2008/dec/30/facebook-breastfeeding-ban*. Accessed: 2014-09-17.
32. Nelson, A.M. 2006. A Metasynthesis Of Qualitative Breastfeeding Studies. *Journal Of Midwifery & Women's Health*. 51, 2 (2006), E13–20.
33. Pain, R., Bailey, C. And Mowl, G. 2001. Infant Feeding In North East England: Contested Spaces Of Reproduction. *Area*. 33, 3 (Sep. 2001), 261–272.
34. Parker, A., Kantroo, V., Lee, H., Osornio, M., Sharma, M. And Grinter, R.E. 2012. Health Promotion As Activism: Building Community Capacity To Effect Social Change. *In Proc. CHI '12*, pp. 99–108.
35. Purpura, S., Schwanda, V., Williams, K., Stubler, W. And Sengers, P. 2011. Fit4Life : The Design Of A Persuasive Technology Promoting Healthy Behavior And Ideal Weight. (2011), 423–432.
36. Renfrew, M. 2011. Infant Feeding Survey 2010 : Early Results. (2011).
37. Rogers, Y., Hazlewood, W.R., Marshall, P., Dalton, N. And Hertrich, S. 2010. Ambient Influence : Can Twinkly Lights Lure And Abstract Representations Trigger Behavioral Change? *In Proc. UbiComp '10*, pp. 261-270.
38. Ruddick, S. 1989. *Maternal Thinking: Towards A Politics Of Peace*. Beacon Press.
39. Scott, J. A. And Mostyn, T. 2003. Women's Experiences Of Breastfeeding In A Bottle-Feeding Culture. *J. Of Human Lactation*. 19, 3, 270–277.
40. Smyth, L. 2008. Gendered Spaces And Intimate Citizenship: The Case Of Breastfeeding. *European Journal Of Women's Studies*. 15, 2 (May 2008), 83–99.
41. Stearns, C. 1999. Breastfeeding And The Good Maternal Body. *Gender and Society* 13, 3, pp. 308–325.
42. Williamson, I., Leeming, D., Lyttle, S. And Johnson, S. 2012. "It Should Be The Most Natural Thing In The World": Exploring First-Time Mothers' Breastfeeding Difficulties In The UK Using Audio-Diaries And Interviews. *Maternal & Child Nutrition*. 8, 4, pp. 434–447.

Using an Interactive Animated Avatar's Facial Expressiveness to Increase Persuasiveness and Socialness

Jennifer Hyde, Elizabeth J. Carter, Sara Kiesler, Jessica K. Hodgins
Carnegie Mellon University
5000 Forbes Avenue
Pittsburgh, PA 15213
{jdtam, ejcarter, kiesler, jkh}@cs.cmu.edu

ABSTRACT
Research indicates that the facial expressions of animated characters and agents can influence people's perceptions and interactions with these entities. We designed an experiment to examine how an interactive animated avatar's facial expressiveness influences dyadic conversations between adults and the avatar. We animated the avatar in realtime using the tracked facial motion of a confederate. To adjust facial expressiveness, we damped and exaggerated the avatar's facial motion. We found that ratings of the avatar's extroversion were positively related to its expressiveness. However, impressions of the avatar's realism and naturalness worsened with increased expressiveness. We also found that the confederate was more influential when she appeared as the damped or exaggerated avatar. Adjusting the expressiveness of interactive animated avatars may be a simple way to influence people's social judgments and willingness to collaborate with animated avatars. These results have implications for using avatar facial expressiveness to improve the effectiveness of avatars in various contexts. Adjusting the expressiveness of interactive animated avatars may be a simple way to influence people's social judgments and willingness to collaborate with animated avatars.

Author Keywords
Animated characters; avatars; facial motion; conversation; persuasiveness; computer-mediated communication.

ACM Classification Keywords
H.5.1 Information Interfaces and Presentation (e.g. HCI): Multimedia Information Systems

INTRODUCTION
Animated characters have the ability to influence how people behave [2] and think [3]. These characters include animated agents controlled by computer algorithms and avatars controlled by people. Researchers have found that agents and avatars are useful because they can improve learning and administer effective therapy (e.g., [3, 24]). When agents and avatars exhibit humanlike behaviors (e.g., facial expressions [4]), people usually respond well to them. These attributes make animated characters attractive as stand-ins for people in educational and therapeutic applications.

Avatars are especially useful in these applications because they enable people to craft new personas, maintain anonymity, and create a sense of social presence remotely. For example, virtual therapy with avatars allows people with social disorders to experience realistic social situations that are difficult to recreate otherwise. Clients and therapists can use avatars to practice various social situations and to act out different roles [24].

For agents and avatars to be effective educators and therapists, these characters may need to exhibit the traits of successful people in these roles. Students and clients prefer human educators and therapists who are warm and respectful [1, 41], and characters with typical cartoon appearances may not convey those qualities well. People may view cartoon characters animated using traditional practices [39], including exaggerated movements and facial expressions, as incompetent and silly. Exaggerating characters with a realistic appearance may result in even worse outcomes, such as unnerving and uncanny movements [19]. To gain people's respect and trust, agents and avatars may need to be somewhat realistic looking. They also may need to exhibit realistic movements and subdued and calm social behaviors. Because people make social judgments based on nonverbal facial cues, it may be beneficial to mimic human facial motion accurately or even with reduced movement.

In a prior experiment using cartoon and comparatively realistic animated characters [20], we measured viewers' perceptions of the characters' social traits, such as extroversion, warmth, and competence. The characters exhibited damped, normal, or exaggerated facial motion while delivering a monologue regarding a personal experience. Facial motion magnitude did not affect participants' ratings of realistic characters' warmth and competence. However, exaggerating the facial motion of cartoon characters resulted in lower ratings of competence. Additionally, facial motion magnitude was positively correlated with ratings of extroversion for both types of characters.

CHI 2015, April 18–23 2015, Seoul, Republic of Korea

ACM 978-1-4503-3145-6/15/04$15.00
http://dx.doi.org/10.1145/2702123.2702465

If facial motion magnitude influences perceptions of the personalities of interactive animated avatars, then animators could customize interactive avatars to suit different situations or user preferences. Customization could be useful for adapting interactive characters to different domains in which it is important for clients and providers to have relationships involving collaboration and trust, including education and therapy. Adjusting people's perceptions of personality by damping or exaggerating an avatar's facial movement could make it easier for therapists to act out different roles. However, it is unknown whether the perceptual effects of facial motion magnitude that exist for animated characters will apply to interactive animated avatars. When people interact and become acquainted with one another, their social judgments of each other are more accurate than when they passively observe one another (e.g., [9]). While interacting, people can create situations that cause other people to exhibit additional personality cues [27]. During collaborative tasks, people's perceptions may also be more accurate because they may care more about determining the credibility of others' information and the best ways to promote compromise.

In this paper, we examine whether the perceptual effects found in our prior work [20] are applicable when people actively interact with an animated avatar rather than passively observe a character. Although we predict that the facial motion magnitude of an interactive animated avatar will influence participants' judgments, other research suggests that other personality cues may override the effect of facial motion magnitude. We expect that participants' perceptions of the interactive animated avatar's extroversion will be positively related to its facial motion magnitude, and perceptions of the interactive avatar's warmth and competence will be negatively related to its facial motion magnitude.

PERSONALITY EFFECTS ON INTERACTION

To understand how avatar personality can be manipulated to influence human-avatar collaboration, we reference the literature in psychology and human-agent interaction. Researchers have found that people's personalities affect how well they collaborate with one another (e.g., [16]). For example, because extroversion is related to dominance, extroverts tend to be more influential and less persuasible than introverts (e.g., [33]). Researchers have also found that open individuals are more willing than closed individuals to consider new ideas and perspectives, making them more persuasible [33].

To improve people's interactions with computer agents, researchers have experimented with adjusting agent behavior and appearance, and these adjustments have influenced people's attitudes, willingness to collaborate, and persuasibility (for a review, see [14]). Nass and colleagues [32] examined participants while they interacted with a computer agent that used a dominant or submissive style of speech while collaborating with the participant using text only. The authors found that when the agents and participants had similar personalities, the agents were more persuasive than when the personalities of the two were complementary. Nass and Lee [31] reported further evidence supporting this similarity-causes-attraction phenomenon when they evaluated participants' attitudes towards extroverted and introverted agents represented by computer-synthesized speech and text. In that experiment, they found that participants preferred the agents with similar levels of extroversion to their own. Additionally, the authors found that participants found similarly extroverted agents more credible and convincing than dissimilar agents.

Studies with embodied agents have also investigated how similarity between agents and users can affect interaction. Researchers have evaluated how agents and users that vary in similarity on characteristics, such as physical resemblance, race, and gender (e.g., [30, 40]) affect collaboration and learning, but few studies have used embodied agents to investigate the effect of agent and user personality on collaboration. Isbister and Nass [23] used an embodied agent to investigate how the consistency of agent personality cues would influence agent-user collaboration. They also analyzed the interactions of users whose personalities were similar and dissimilar to the agents. Their agents exhibited dominant and submissive personalities through their speech and body posture cues. The authors found that agents using speech and posture cues that were consistent with the personality styles of the participants influenced the participants more than agents using inconsistent cues. In contrast with their own prior work, Isbister and Nass [23] found that participants preferred agents with complementary personalities to their own. The authors attributed this difference to the fact that their agents were more interactive and humanlike than the agents used in previous experiments [32, 31]. They reasoned that in prior psychology experiments, participants presented with textual descriptions of others exhibited similarity-attraction, but participants who interacted with others exhibited complementarity effects. The complementarity principle [37, 26] posits that people prefer and seek others who have complementary interaction styles as this will result in a balance of power and less tension. It is unclear from these studies whether people will prefer or interact better with animated avatars that exhibit similar or complementary personalities. In this study, we explore the possibility of an interaction between participants' personalities and the perceived personality of an interactive animated avatar on the participant-avatar interaction.

INFORMATION PROCESSING MODELS

In our experiment, participants discussed a variety of items with a confederate-controlled avatar. The confederate attempted to persuade participants to change their opinions about the items. Research on information processing suggests that the way in which people process information can predict their persuasibility. The heuristic-systematic model [7] and the elaboration likelihood model [34] describe two ways in which people process persuasive information. Systematic or central route processing occurs when people focus on the actual information presented in a persuasive argument, whereas heuristic or peripheral route processing occurs when people use cues like source credibility and attitude judgments to form opinions. People tend to use systematic processing for important decisions that require more attention, and they tend to use heuristic processing for non-essential tasks or when they have time constraints. Researchers have shown that when people use heuristic processing, they may ignore the actual information presented and instead rely on cues like source credibility, people's opinions, and length of the argument (for a review, see [12]). Because people rely on social judgments when they use heuristic processing, the facial motion magnitude of interactive animated avatars may affect their persuasiveness. For example, an avatar that has exaggerated motion and appears dominant may be more influential than an avatar with damped motion that appears submissive.

AN EXPERIMENT ON THE IMPACT OF AVATAR FACIAL MOVEMENT ON CONVERSATION

We present a study in which participants collaborated with a confederate-controlled avatar that exhibited damped, unaltered, or exaggerated facial motion. We measured the participants' personalities, their perceptions of the confederate and avatar, their conversational behaviors, and the confederate's influence. Participants completed the Desert Survival Problem [25], which has been used in prior work on interaction with agents (e.g., [23, 31]). Participants independently ranked a list of items in order of importance for survival. They then discussed their rankings with the confederate-controlled avatar, who argued for a permutation of the participants' initial rankings. After the discussion, participants re-ranked their items, allowing for measurement of the confederate's influence on participants' rankings. If a participant changed his or her rankings to align better with the confederate's rankings, then the confederate was considered to have influenced the participant. We compare how participants changed their rankings across the different avatar facial motion conditions to analyze the effect of facial motion magnitude on confederate influence.

HYPOTHESES

We expected facial motion magnitude to affect perceptions of the interactive animated avatar in much the same way as it did the perceptions of the non-interactive animated characters [20].

(H1) Facial motion magnitude will positively influence ratings of confederate extroversion and negatively influence ratings of confederate warmth and competence.

In an experiment using a non-interactive animated character to investigate perceptions of emotional expression [21], we found a negative relationship between facial motion magnitude and ratings of naturalness. For this study, we investigate whether this relationship exists with an interactive avatar. We examine naturalness using measures of humanness and eeriness.

(H2) Ratings of humanness will decrease and ratings of eeriness will increase as facial motion magnitude increases.

In addition to generalizing the perceptual results found in prior work [20, 21] to an interactive avatar, we also examined how to customize avatars to improve confederate persuasion. Based on the psychology literature, the confederate's influence should increase with perceptions of increased extroversion. Moreover, Burgoon and colleagues [6] found that

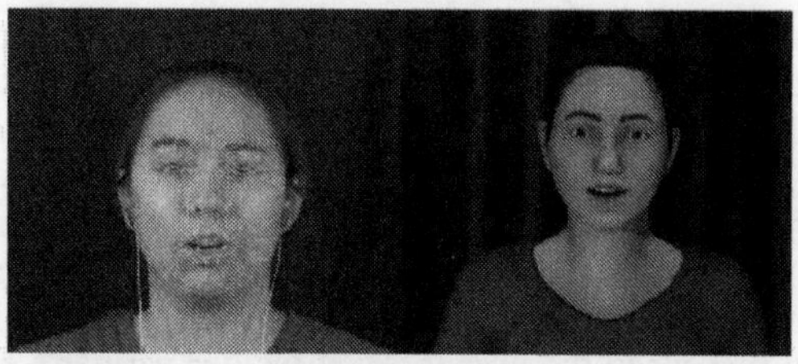

Figure 1. Example of the AAM tracking a confederate and retargeting her motion to the corresponding character.

greater facial expressiveness was related to increased persuasiveness. Therefore, we expect that increasing the avatar's facial motion will increase the confederate's persuasiveness.

(H3) The confederate's persuasiveness will be positively related to avatar facial motion magnitude.

METHOD

We designed a between-subjects study in which each participant spoke with a confederate-controlled avatar that exhibited one of three different motion levels (damped, unaltered, exaggerated). The avatar exhibited perceptually equivalent damped (80%) and exaggerated (125%) motion, based on prior work [20]. The avatar was animated in realtime by tracking the face of a female confederate and retargeting her motion to the avatar. Participants communicated with the confederate's avatar using a custom audiovisual telecommunications system.

Realtime Tracking and Animation

To create an interactive animated avatar with realistic facial expressions, we used active appearance models [10, 11, 28], a computer vision algorithm, to track a confederate's facial motion as she spoke and used this motion to animate an avatar. Active appearance models (AAMs) can create mappings between the faces of people and characters. With AAMs, a person and character's face shape and appearance are modeled. Once the model of the person is learned, the AAM tracks his or her face in realtime and moves corresponding points in the character model (Figure 1).

We followed the procedure from Boker, Theobald, and colleagues [5, 38] to exaggerate and damp the facial motion of our avatar. We measured the distance that each AAM vertex moved from a neutral position. The confederate's neutral position consisted of a relaxed face with closed eyes and closed mouth. By selecting the specified neutral pose, the avatar always closed her eyes and mouth when the confederate did so. Given that each AAM vertex changes position during movement, we multiplied those changes in position by scale factors to exaggerate and damp the spatial movements across all features of the face. We exaggerated motion by multiplying the face shape variation by values greater than 1, and we damped motion by multiplying the face shape variation by values less than 1.

Audiovisual Telecommunications System

To facilitate interactive conversations between participants and the confederate, we built a custom-designed desktop audiovisual telecommunications system (Figure 2). The system allows two people to converse with one another using natural audiovisual cues. Users see each other life-size from the shoulders up. Unlike traditional desktop conferencing systems, this system enables users to make eye contact with one another. The system uses a beam splitter, which acts as a one-way mirror, to hide a camera directly in front of users. The video of a user's partner is reflected off of the beam splitter so that when the user looks at his/her partner's eyes, the user is actually looking directly into the camera. When the confederate uses the system, we can use AAMs to track her motion, map the motion to her avatar, and send the animation to the participant so that it matches with the confederate's voice. Because the AAMs allow us to adjust facial motion, we can spatially exaggerate and damp the characters during conversation.

By using realtime tracking and animation, the participants could have conversations with an avatar that responded with humanlike mannerisms (e.g., blinking, smiling, mirroring, nonverbal feedback). Artists modeled the avatar after the confederate. During the experiment, participants saw the avatar animated with the confederate's facial motion while hearing the confederate's voice.

Task

Participants completed a modified version of the Desert Survival Problem (DSP) [25]. In the DSP, participants are given a survival scenario and must rank a list of items in order of their importance for survival. We modified the original DSP because prior research (e.g., [35]) and our own pilot testing indicated that the original task included outdated items and lasted more than 30 minutes. Following Rae and colleagues [35], we modified the task by exchanging obscure items for more familiar items, and we shortened the item list from twelve to nine (flashlight, pocketknife, raincoat, compass, first aid kit, water, book, vodka, mirror). We also shortened the scenario and emphasized that participants were supposed to match an expert ranking. Shortening the task was necessary because the confederate had to mentally keep track of what she was saying about each item while maintaining contingent discourse. On average, the conversations between participants and the confederate lasted 9.5 minutes.

An experimenter presented the scenario to participants and informed them that they would be discussing the items with a partner. Participants were also told that their partner would appear as an animated cartoon character while they appeared as themselves via video. We provide an excerpt of the scenario below:

> *"... You have just crash-landed in an unfamiliar desert. The helicopter you were in has completely burned... you and the other passenger have escaped uninjured, but you were unable to contact anyone before the crash. ...Before everything caught fire, you managed to salvage nine items."*

After reading the scenario, participants ranked the items, conversed with the confederate, and then reranked their items. The confederate's rankings differed from the participants' rankings to ensure that the discussion involved why specific items should be ranked higher or lower. As in other research studies (e.g., [35]), the confederate in this study argued for ranking the items in an order that was a consistent permutation of the participants' initial rankings. We used the same permutation as Rae and colleagues [35] did throughout the study so that the confederate would always follow the same argument structure. We allowed the confederate to respond to participant comments to maintain the impression of the confederate as another participant, but all conversation and commenting was structured: the confederate provided two reasons for why each item should be ranked differently, and she only stated these reasons once in each conversation. For example, the two reasons for ranking the flashlight higher were that the flashlight could be used as a nighttime signaling device and that its parts could be used to start a fire. The confederate practiced her role with 26 participants during a pilot phase and prepared responses to common questions and comments. More importantly, the confederate was blind to avatar motion level so that her conversation would not be biased by this knowledge. After the discussion, participants reranked their items. We measured the confederate's persuasiveness by comparing participants' rankings before and after conversing with the confederate.

Materials

Participants completed all surveys, rankings, and questionnaires using a MacBookPro running OSX 10.6. We presented materials on a Dell UltraSharp 2408WFP monitor (22-in.$\times$15.6-in.), and participants used an external keyboard and mouse to complete the digital forms. When participants submitted their initial rankings, the form would automatically print a list of the participants' and confederate's ranks. The experimenter gave this list to the participants and confederate to reference during their conversation. When participants entered their final rankings, the form displayed their initial rankings and the confederate's initial ranking.

Participants

We recruited sixty-four native English-speaking adults (age range: 18-64 years, median age: 23 years, 36 females) using a university experiment scheduling website. We eliminated the data from five participants because the confederate could not maintain the conversation structure, or the participants were too familiar with the DSP. In total, we analyzed the data from 59 participants. The experiment lasted 20 to 40 minutes. We compensated participants for their time. The university's institutional review board approved this study.

Measures

The main independent variable was avatar facial motion magnitude. Participants saw the confederate with either damped, unaltered, or exaggerated facial motion. We also included participant characteristics as control variables. Participants completed a set of questionnaires that measured their age, gender, personality, and computer usage. The personality measure included scores for extroversion, agreeableness, conscientiousness, emotional stability, and openness. We calculated personality scores from participants' responses to the

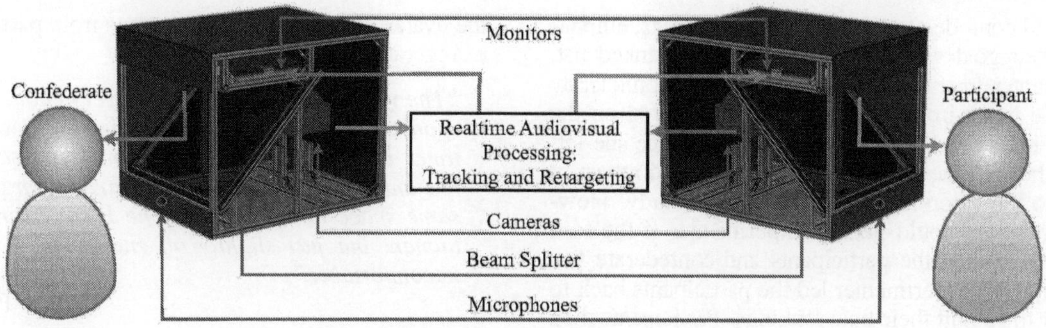

Figure 2. Diagram of telecommunications system.

Ten Item Personality Inventory (TIPI) [17], an experimentally validated measure of the Big-Five personality dimensions (for a review, see [29]). We categorized participants into low and high groups for each of the personality dimensions using Gosling and colleagues' [17] average scores for a sample of 1,813 participants. We used a modified version of Schroeders and Wilhelm's questionnaire [36] to measure participants' computer usage. We replaced their questions on chatting with four questions that asked about chatting with text, voice, video, and avatars. Participants answered how often they engaged in various computer activities. The majority of participants had never chatted with avatars. Because there were not enough participants with this experience to analyze, we did not include participants' experience with avatar chatting in the analysis. The participants had more varied experiences with videoconferencing, but their familiarity with videoconferencing did not affect the results; therefore, we did not include it in the analysis.

We recorded participants as they spoke with the confederate. Annotators labeled the videos with the conversation start and end times and the times when participants looked at the screen. We used these annotations to measure conversation length, percent of gaze (on-screen), and average length of gaze (on-screen). A primary annotator completed gaze annotations for all of the conversations, and a secondary annotator completed one third of each conversation so that we could calculate interrater reliability using Cohen's Kappa (κ). Because the annotators were determining the start and end times of the annotations in addition to labelling the annotations, we first calculated the percentage of aligned annotations. Aligned annotations overlapped by at least 50%. Alignment was 89%, and the annotators agreed on the labels for the aligned annotations with perfect reliability (Cohen's $\kappa = 1$).

To measure confederate influence, we calculated the correlation between the confederate's initial rankings and the participants' final rankings. We used a Spearman's rank correlation coefficient (ρ) to quantify the amount that participants changed their rankings to match the rankings of the confederate. Values closer to 1 indicate that participants changed their rankings to align more with the confederate's rankings. This measure has been used in previous studies to compare rankings from the Desert Survival Problem (e.g., [35]).

Measure	Items	Cronbach's α
Warmth	warm, good-natured, sincere, friendly, well-intentioned, trustworthy	.88
Competence	competent, skillful, capable, efficient, confident, intelligent	.88
Extroversion	extroverted, sociable, dramatic, inhibited	.84
Humanness	artificial – natural, synthetic – real, inanimate – living	.82
Eeriness	reassuring – eerie, numbing – freaky, ordinary – supernatural	.61

Table 1. Self-report measures.

Participants rated the confederate on scales of warmth, competence, and extroversion, and they rated the avatar on scales of humanness and eeriness (Table 1). We asked participants to rate, *"How ___ was your partner?"* on the warmth, competence, and extroversion items using five-point rating scales (i.e., *1=Not at all, 2=Slightly, 3=Moderately, 4=Very, 5=Extremely*). We used items from a questionnaire developed by Fiske and colleagues [13] to measure warmth and competence. To measure confederate extroversion, we used items from a previous study [20], but we removed items from the extroversion measure to improve reliability. We used semantic differential scales from the humanness and eeriness indices developed by Ho and MacDorman [18]. After rating the confederate and avatar, the participants could submit additional comments, which we used in a qualitative analysis.

Procedure

An experimenter told participants that they would be evaluating a new animation technique by conversing with another participant (the confederate), who would appear as an animated avatar. The experimenter also explained that participants would appear as themselves to the other participant. Participants completed an initial survey (see Measures), listened to the experimenter read the DSP scenario, and then ranked the items using a computer form. Afterwards, the experimenter gave each participant a paper copy with both the participant's and confederate's rankings. The experimenter then directed the participant to sit in front of the audiovisual telecommunications system and introduced the confederate to the participant. Next, the experimenter instructed the participant and confederate to discuss their rankings, emphasizing that their goal was to match an expertly ranked list. The experimenter instructed the participant and confederate to discuss the items in the order that they appeared on the participant's list and to begin the conversation once she left the room. She told the participant that she would return in 15 minutes to transition to the next part of the study. However, the participant could get the experimenter if the task took less time. When the participants and confederate finished speaking, the experimenter led the participants back to the computer to submit their final rankings. Participants then completed more surveys to measure their perceptions of the confederate and avatar. The experimented ended when the experimenter thanked, debriefed, and paid the participants.

RESULTS

We conducted analyses of variance (ANOVAs) and post-hoc contrasts using joint F-tests to examine the effects of facial motion magnitude on participants' perceptions and behaviors. We included participants' personality traits and gender as control variables. We also conducted a qualitative analysis on the voluntary comments that 24 (41%) participants submitted.

Effects on Perceptions

We expected facial motion magnitude to influence participants' perceptions of the interactive avatar in ways similar to how facial motion magnitude influenced perceptions of non-interactive animated characters (H1 and H2). In our previous study [20], facial motion magnitude influenced ratings of extroversion, warmth, and competence. We replicated the previous effect of facial motion magnitude on extroversion in this study, $F(2,48) = 3.28$, $p = .05$ (Figure 3(a)). The effect size ($\eta^2 = .10$) was medium to large according to Cohen's [8] conventions. Participants rated the confederate as less extroverted when she used the damped avatar compared to when she used the unaltered or exaggerated avatars, $F(1,48) = 5.11$, $p = .03$, $\eta^2 = .08$ and $F(1,48) = 4.42$, $p = .04$, $\eta^2 = .07$, respectively. Avatar facial motion magnitude did not affect perceptions of confederate warmth (Figure 3(b)) or competence (Figure 3(c)), $F(2,48) = 1.45$, $p = .25$ and $F(2,48) = 0.28$, $p = .75$, respectively. The effect sizes ($\eta^2 = .05$ and $\eta^2 = .01$, respectively) were small. These results partially support hypothesis H1: avatar facial motion magnitude related positively to perceptions of extroversion but had no influence on perceptions of warmth and competence.

We also hypothesized (H2) that participants would perceive exaggerated avatars as less human and more eerie than damped avatars. We found no effect of facial motion magnitude on participants' ratings of the avatar's humanness and eeriness, $F(2,48) = 1.52$, $p = .23$ and $F(2,48) = 0.30$, $p = .74$, respectively. The effect sizes ($\eta^2 = .05$ and $\eta^2 = .01$, respectively) were small. Although the humanness and eeriness ratings were not different across facial motion levels, eleven participants in the exaggerated condition made comments, and ten of these referred to discomfort with the avatar. Below are two comments from participants in the exaggerated condition:

> *"The voice of the character was very good, and her responses were natural and well-timed. It was weird at times because it was so well-timed and casual, while her animation still lacked. The animation exists in the same space in my head as The Polar Express — very human, but just slightly off enough to make me feel uncomfortable."*
>
> \- Participant 7

> *"Felt a bit taken back at first impressions, but got used to the picture after sometime [sic]."*
>
> \- Participant 35

Five participants in the damped condition made comments, four of which referred to the avatar's lifelikeness and realism. The fifth participant commented on the confederate's helpfulness. Here are two comments that indicate that participants found the avatar to be natural in the damped motion condition:

> *"Wow! The ability to capture the various extents of the smile was really impressive and really did convey a good sense of realism to the 'other person' I was speaking to."*
>
> \- Participant 15

> *"I was surprised by the detail of the animation on my partner Rachel's face. I could see every little facial movement as she spoke, and it gave her a very life-like quality. It didn't seem like I was talking to an animated image, but a real person."*
>
> \- Participant 46

From this partial qualitative analysis, we conclude that the avatar may have appeared less natural in the exaggerated condition than in the damped condition, mimicking the result from our previous study with non-interactive characters [21].

Effects on Behavior

We hypothesized that the confederate would be more persuasive when she appeared as the exaggerated avatar than when she appeared as the damped avatar (H3). We found a significant main effect with large effect size ($\eta^2 = .18$) of facial motion magnitude on confederate influence, $F(2,48) = 7.61$, $p < .01$. Participants changed their rankings following the confederate's recommendations more when the confederate appeared as the damped and exaggerated avatars compared to when she appeared as the unaltered avatar, $F(1,48) = 13.84$, $p < .001$ and $F(1,48) = 10.29$, $p < .01$, respectively (Figure 3(d)). These effect sizes were large ($\eta^2 = .16$) and medium to large ($\eta^2 = .12$), respectively. This result partially supports the hypothesis (H3) because the exaggerated avatar more than the unaltered avatar persuaded participants to change their rankings. However, the damped avatar also was more successful than the unaltered avatar at persuading participants to change their rankings. We found no effect of facial motion magnitude on conversation length, average length of gaze, or percent of gaze on-screen (Figures 3(e)-3(g)).

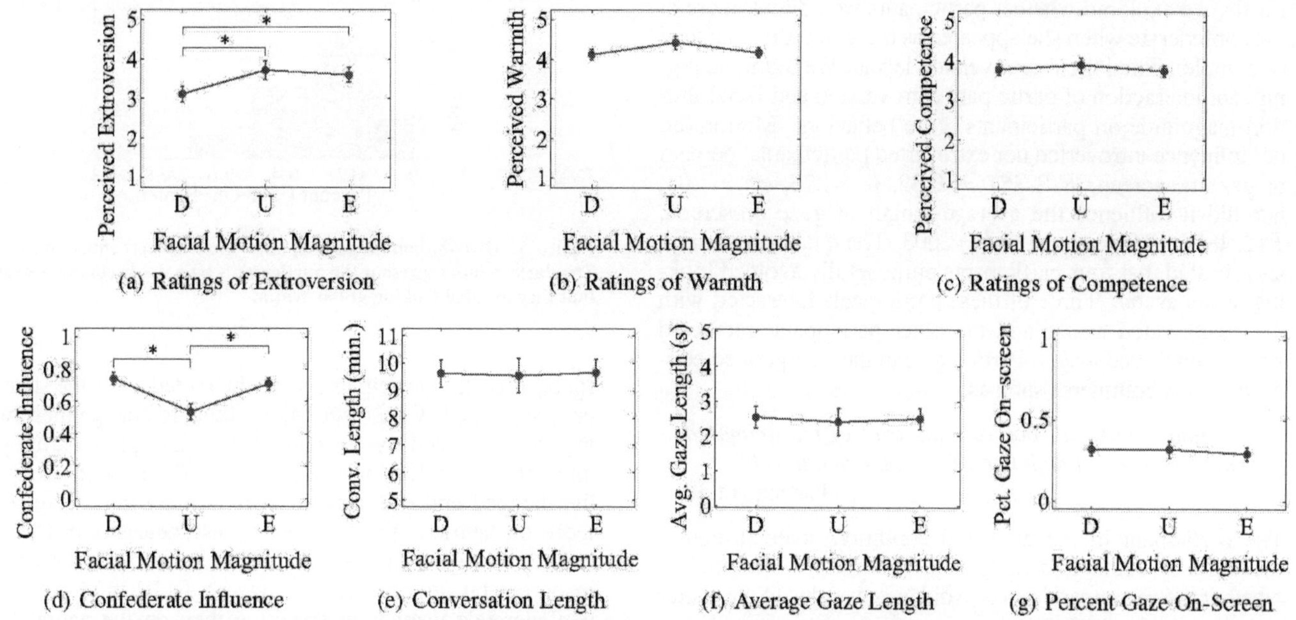

(a) Ratings of Extroversion (b) Ratings of Warmth (c) Ratings of Competence

(d) Confederate Influence (e) Conversation Length (f) Average Gaze Length (g) Percent Gaze On-Screen

Figure 3. The graphs illustrate the influence of avatar facial motion magnitude (D=damped, U=unaltered, E=exaggerated) on participants' ratings and behavior. The asterisk indicates significance at $\alpha = .05$ or less.

Other Results

We explored the possibility that participants' personalities might moderate the effect of avatar facial motion magnitude on the confederate's influence. There are two competing theories regarding whether people with similar or complementary personalities work better together (see the Personality Effects on Interaction section). Therefore, we considered both of these theories in our exploratory analysis.

The statistical analysis, although not significant at the $\alpha =$ .05 level, indicates a possible interaction of avatar facial motion and participant extroversion on confederate influence with medium effect size, $F(2, 48) = 2.93, p = .06, \eta^2 = .07$ (Figure 4(a)). The confederate influenced extroverted participants more than introverted participants across avatar motion levels. This result was supported by a significant main effect with large effect size of participant extroversion level on confederate influence, $F(1, 48) = 15.49$, $p < .001$, $\eta^2 =$ .18. Extroverted participants may have been more persuasible because they also were more open to new experiences, $r(59) = 0.39$, $p < .01$. Researchers have found that open people are more persuasible than closed people [15, 33], and the data from this study aligns with this idea. We found a significant main effect with medium to large effect size of participants' openness on confederate influence, $F(1, 48) = 9.36$, $p < .01$, $\eta^2 = .11$. The participants' extroversion and openness may have trumped any similarity or complementary personality effects on confederate influence.

In contrast, introverted participants accounted for most of the variation in confederate influence. When the confederate appeared as the damped and exaggerated avatars, she persuaded introverted participants more than when she appeared as the unaltered avatar, $F(1, 48) = 14.74$, $p < .001$ and $F(1, 48) = 8.77, p < .01$, respectively. The effect sizes were large ($\eta^2 = .17$) and medium to large ($\eta^2 = .10$), respectively. The data suggest that introverts may have interacted better with the confederate when her extroversion level appeared as both similar and complementary to the participants' extroversion level. An alternative explanation for why introverted participants agreed more with the confederate when she appeared extroverted is that the exaggerated avatar may have intimidated participants. Both of these situations could induce similar changes in rankings.

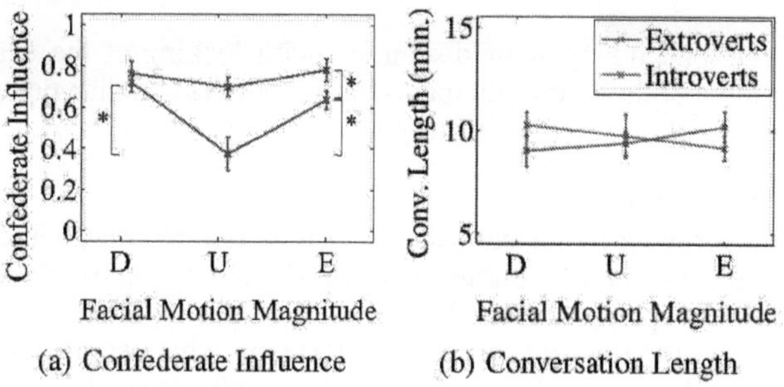

(a) Confederate Influence (b) Conversation Length

Figure 4. Graphs illustrating the interaction of participants' extroversion and avatar facial motion magnitude on (a) confederate influence and (b) conversation length. The asterisk indicates significance at $\alpha = .05$ or less.

We also examined how long participants conversed with the avatar that matched or complemented their extroversion levels. The interaction of participant extroversion and avatar facial motion magnitude was not significant, $F(2, 48) = 1.55$, $p = .22$, $\eta^2 = .04$. Figure 4(b) illustrates a slight similarity-causes-attraction phenomenon. If participants had more extreme levels of extroversion, then their interactions with the avatars may have differed more.

Lastly, we explored whether participants would look more at the confederate when she appeared as the avatar that matched or complemented their extroversion levels. We found no significant interaction of participant extroversion and facial motion magnitude on participants' gaze behaviors. Motion did not influence introverted nor extroverted participants' percent of gaze on-screen, $F(2,48) = 0.32$, $p = .73$, $\eta^2 = .01$, nor did it influence the average length of gaze on-screen, $F(2,48) = 0.08$, $p = .92, \eta^2 = .003$. The qualitative analysis revealed that four participants purposefully avoided looking at the avatar. Three of these participants interacted with the exaggerated avatar and the other participant interacted with an unaltered avatar. Participants in the exaggerated condition made comments such as,

> *"I found it hard to look into the eyes of the animated character, even though her voice sounded natural."*
> - Participant 38

The participant in the unaltered condition noted difficulty making eye contact in daily life. Therefore it is unclear whether the participant's gaze avoidance was due to the avatar or to its social presence.

> *"It was hard for me to keep looking at it. Though, I have trouble keeping eye contact normally."*
> - Participant 39

Despite noting their discomfort with looking at the avatar, three of the four participants had higher than median percentages of on-screen gaze (Figure 5).

DISCUSSION

Prior work indicated that the facial motion of non-interactive characters could influence viewers' perceptions of the characters' personalities. However, interactivity provides more opportunities and sources of information that people can use to judge personality. It was unclear whether the perceptual effects of facial motion found using non-interactive characters would apply to interactive avatars. We examined the perceptions and behaviors of participants who spoke with an interactive animated avatar that was controlled in realtime by a confederate. The avatar's facial motion was exaggerated and damped to investigate the influence of avatar facial motion magnitude during conversation. Our results indicate that even with other strong personality cues, facial expression magnitude influences perceptions of an animated avatar. Avatar facial motion affected participants' perceptions of the confederate's extroversion, warmth, and competence. Participants found the confederate less extroverted when she appeared as the damped avatar compared to when she appeared as the unaltered or exaggerated avatars. Our qualitative analysis also indicated that participants may have found the damped avatar more realistic and lifelike than the exaggerated avatar. Several participants commented on feeling uncomfortable while interacting with the exaggerated avatar. These comments match our previous findings regarding participants' perceptions of non-interactive characters' naturalness [21].

In this study, we also examined the confederate's influence on participants by comparing the participants' rankings before and after their conversations with the confederate. We found that the participants who interacted with the damped or exaggerated avatars were more likely to change their rankings as suggested by the confederate than participants who interacted with the unaltered avatar. When participants saw the damped and exaggerated avatars, they may have relied more on heuristic processing. To use heuristic processing, participants would have spent more attention and cognitive resources on interpreting the avatar's facial motion and the confederate's manner of speaking than on the actual arguments.

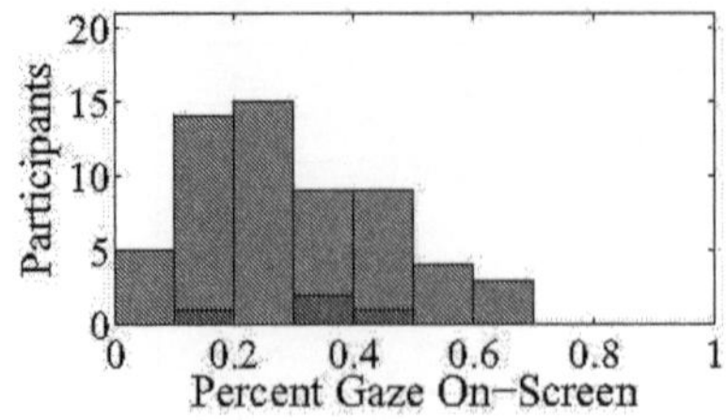

Figure 5. Distribution of participants' gaze by percentage on-screen. The darker bars represent the participants who wrote comments saying that they avoided looking at the avatar.

In our exploratory analysis, we found that the behavior of the introverted participants was responsible for most of the variation in confederate influence. We suspect that the introverted participants responded well to the damped avatar because its extroversion level was more similar to their own, supporting the idea of similarity-causes-attraction. Alternatively, the exaggerated avatar may have intimidated introverted participants due to its perceived increase in extroversion level and dominance. It is unclear from these results which of the changed perceptions also changed the confederate's influence. Exaggerated and damped facial motion may have increased attention to the avatar, resulting in more confederate influence, or the combination of participants' personalities and avatar facial motion may have been responsible. Future work using participants with more extreme levels of extroversion would help answer this question. Differences in behavior may be more extreme between highly extroverted and introverted participants. Participants with extreme levels of extroversion also may behave more consistently than participants with mid-levels of extroversion.

From the quantitative analysis, we found that participants spent on average 30% of their conversation time looking at the avatar, and we saw no differences in participants' gaze behavior across facial motion conditions. Some participants noted their aversion to looking at the avatar, but these participants' behavior indicated that they looked at the avatar more than average. These participants may have consciously forced themselves to look at the avatar because they were aware of their discomfort. We did not include a video condition, so it is unclear whether participants looked less at the avatar than they would a person.

Our goal is to design interactive characters for therapy and education when video may not be appropriate. We found that some participants responded well to the avatar even though the experience may have been unsettling at first.

"It was only errie [sic] due to the life like emotions depicted by the Interface, other than that I want one :-)"
- Participant 10

"Great experience. I thought if more humans were like it I might interact socially more."
-Participant 48

It would be interesting to examine participants over time to see if they become more accustomed and receptive to interactive avatars. We did not measure participants' social anxiety, but it is also possible that the participants who responded well to the avatars have difficulty interacting with people. Future research should investigate the use of interactive avatars with people who have social and communicative difficulties.

Our method for changing the facial expressiveness of the avatar may have created an emotive mismatch between the avatar's facial and vocal expressions. We examined this type of emotive mismatch in a prior study [21], in which animations combined characters with different levels of facial expression with emotional speech of varying intensity. The mismatch affected naturalness ratings of the characters, but only if the characters were extremely emotional. We believe that the conversations between participants and the confederate in this study were less emotional than the animations in the prior work. Therefore, we do not believe that a mismatch in facial expression and speech occurred.

Additionally, our experiment used a single confederate and avatar, therefore we cannot generalize our findings to other confederates, face shapes, or genders. However, in our prior work using multiple confederates and actors [20, 22], we found that confederate characteristics did not interact with avatar facial expressiveness to influence perceptions.

Finally, there are limitations associated with the tracking and animation method that we used. Although the avatar displayed the facial motion of the confederate, the confederate's body motion was not tracked. The torsos of the animated characters moved rigidly with respect to a pivot located at the characters' mouths. Additionally, the characters always faced forward as they were created from 2D data, and they were unable to nod or shake their heads. It is possible that the lack of head nods and shakes may have influenced the participants' acceptance of our human-like avatar. One participant commented on the avatar body's rigid movement and lifelike face. The juxtaposition of realistic and unrealistic behaviors may have affected participants' feelings of discomfort, especially for the exaggerated character. It is unclear whether participants would be more comfortable with a less realistic looking character that exhibited similar behaviors. In the future, a similar interactive experiment comparing people's responses to cartoon and realistic characters would help answer this question. A comparison of different tracking and animation techniques would also be useful.

CONCLUSION

We determined that avatar facial motion magnitude positively affected participants' ratings of the confederate's extroversion. Facial motion also affected people's comfort with the avatar and their persuasibility. Participants changed their beliefs to align more with the confederate when she was represented by a damped or exaggerated avatar compared with an unaltered avatar. These results suggest that interactive avatars could be used to improve collaboration in education and therapy. Additionally, although some participants found it difficult to maintain eye contact with the avatar, others felt that conversing with the avatar was easier than conversing with other people. Our results suggest that interactive avatars may be suitable in therapy and counseling for adults with social and communicative difficulties.

ACKNOWLEDGMENTS

We thank our participants and collaborators, R. Browne, C. Evans, R. Backstrom, K. Miller, T. Simon Kreuz, P. Carr, I. Matthews, M. Mahler, C. Heiner, and M. Danver. This work was funded by Disney Research and award R03HD068816 from the Eunice Kennedy Shriver Institute of Child Health and Human Development of the National Institutes of Health.

REFERENCES

1. Ackerman, S. J., and Hilsenroth, M. J. A review of therapist characteristics and techniques positively impacting the therapeutic alliance. *Clin Psychol Rev 23*, 1 (2003), 1–33.

2. Andrist, S., Mutlu, B., and Gleicher, M. Conversational gaze aversion for virtual agents. In *Proc. IVA 2013*, Springer (2013), 249–262.

3. Bailenson, J. N., Yee, N., Blascovich, J., Beall, A. C., Lundblad, N., and Jin, M. The use of immersive virtual reality in the learning sciences: Digital transformations of teachers, students, and social context. *J Learn Sci 17*, 1 (2008), 102–141.

4. Bates, J. The role of emotion in believable agents. *Commun ACM 37*, 7 (1994), 122–125.

5. Boker, S. M., Cohn, J. F., Theobald, B.-J., Matthews, I., Brick, T. R., and Spies, J. R. Effects of damping head movement and facial expression in dyadic conversation using real-time facial expression tracking and synthesized avatars. *Phil Trans R Soc B 364*, 1535 (2009), 3485–3495.

6. Burgoon, J. K., Birk, T., and Pfau, M. Nonverbal behaviors, persuasion, and credibility. *Hum Commun Res 17*, 1 (1990), 140–169.

7. Chaiken, S. Heuristic versus systematic information processing and the use of source versus message cues in persuasion. *J Pers Soc Psychol 39*, 5 (1980), 752.

8. Cohen, J. *Statistical Power Analysis for the Behavioral Sciences*. Routledge, 1988.

9. Colvin, C. R., and Funder, D. C. Predicting personality and behavior: A boundary on the acquaintanceship effect. *J Pers Soc Psychol 60*, 6 (1991), 884–894.

10. Cootes, T. F., Edwards, G. J., and Taylor, C. J. Active appearance models. *IEEE TPAMI 23*, 6 (2001), 681–685.

11. Cootes, T. F., Wheeler, G. V., Walker, K. N., and Taylor, C. J. View-based active appearance models. *Image Vision Comput 20*, 9 (2002), 657–664.
12. Eagly, A. H., and Chaiken, S. *The Psychology of Attitudes*. Harcourt Brace Jovanovich College Publishers, 1993.
13. Fiske, S. T., Cuddy, A. J., Glick, P., and Xu, J. A model of (often mixed) stereotype content: Competence and warmth respectively follow from perceived status and competition. *J Pers Soc Psychol 82*, 6 (2002), 878–902.
14. Fogg, B. J. Computers as persuasive social actors. In *Persuasive Technology: Using Computers to Change What We Think and Do*, J. Grudin, J. Nielsen, and S. Card, Eds. Science & Technology Books, 2002, ch. 5, 89–120.
15. Gerber, A. S., Huber, G. A., Doherty, D., Dowling, C. M., and Panagopoulos, C. Big Five personality traits and responses to persuasive appeals: Results from voter turnout experiments. *Polit Behav 35*, 4 (2013), 687–728.
16. Gorla, N., and Lam, Y. W. Who should work with whom? Building effective software project teams. *Commun ACM 47*, 6 (2004), 79–82.
17. Gosling, S., Rentfrow, P., and Swann, W. A very brief measure of the Big-Five personality domains. *J Res Pers 37*, 6 (2003), 504–528.
18. Ho, C.-C., and MacDorman, K. F. Revisiting the uncanny valley theory: Developing and validating an alternative to the Godspeed indices. *Comput Hum Behav 26*, 6 (2010), 1508–1518.
19. Hodgkinson, G. The seduction of realism. In *Proc. SIGGRAPH ASIA 2009 Educators Program*, no. 4, ACM Press (2009), 1–4.
20. Hyde, J., Carter, E. J., Kiesler, S., and Hodgins, J. K. Perceptual effects of damped and exaggerated facial motion in animated characters. In *Proc. FG 2013*, IEEE Press (2013), 1–6.
21. Hyde, J., Carter, E. J., Kiesler, S., and Hodgins, J. K. Assessing naturalness and emotional intensity: A perceptual study of animated facial motion. In *Proc. SAP 2014*, ACM Press (2014), 15–22.
22. Hyde, J., Kiesler, S., Hodgins, J. K., and Carter, E. J. Conversing with children: Cartoon and video people elicit similar conversational behaviors. In *Proc. CHI 2014*, ACM Press (2014), 1787–1796.
23. Isbister, K., and Nass, C. Consistency of personality in interactive characters: verbal cues, non-verbal cues, and user characteristics. *Int J Hum-Comput St 53*, 2 (2000), 251–267.
24. Kandalaft, M. R., Didehbani, N., Krawczyk, D. C., Allen, T. T., and Chapman, S. B. Virtual reality social cognition training for young adults with high-functioning autism. *J Autism Dev Disord 43*, 1 (2013), 34–44.
25. Lafferty, J. C., and Eady, P. M. *The Desert Survival Problem*. Human Synergistics, Plymouth, Michigan, 1974.
26. Leary, T. *Interpersonal Diagnosis of Personality*. Ronald Press, 1957.
27. Letzring, T. D. The good judge of personality: Characteristics, behaviors, and observer accuracy. *J Res Pers 42*, 4 (2008), 914–932.
28. Matthews, I., and Baker, S. Active appearance models revisited. *Int J Comput Vision 60*, 2 (2004), 135–164.
29. McCrae, R. R., and Costa Jr, P. T. A Five-Factor theory of personality. In *Handbook of Personality: Theory and Research*, L. A. Pervin and O. P. John, Eds., 2 ed. Guilford Press, New York, NY, USA, 1999, ch. 5, 139–153.
30. Moreno, R., and Flowerday, T. Students' choice of animated pedagogical agents in science learning: A test of the similarity-attraction hypothesis on gender and ethnicity. *Contemp Educ Psychol 31*, 2 (2006), 186–207.
31. Nass, C., and Lee, K. M. Does computer-synthesized speech manifest personality? Experimental tests of recognition, similarity-attraction, and consistency-attraction. *J Exp Psychol-Appl 7*, 3 (2001), 171–181.
32. Nass, C., Moon, Y., Fogg, B., Reeves, B., and Dryer, D. C. Can computer personalities be human personalities? *Int J Hum-Comput St 43*, 2 (1995), 223–239.
33. Oreg, S., and Sverdlik, N. Source personality and persuasiveness: Big Five predispositions to being persuasive and the role of message involvement. *J Pers 82*, 3 (2014), 250–264.
34. Petty, R. E., and Cacioppo, J. T. *Attitudes and Persuasion: Classic and Contemporary Approaches*. Brown, Dubuque, IA, 1981.
35. Rae, I., Takayama, L., and Mutlu, B. One of the gang: Supporting in-group behavior for embodied mediated communication. In *Proc. CHI 2012*, ACM Press (2012), 3091–3100.
36. Schroeders, U., and Wilhelm, O. Computer usage questionnaire: Structure, correlates, and gender differences. *Comput Hum Behav 27*, 2 (2011), 899–904.
37. Sullivan, H. S. *The Interpersonal Theory of Psychiatry*. WW Norton & Co, 1953.
38. Theobald, B.-J., Matthews, I., Mangini, M., Spies, J. R., Brick, T. R., Cohn, J. F., and Boker, S. M. Mapping and manipulating facial expression. *Lang Speech 52*, 2/3 (2009), 369–386.
39. Thomas, F., and Johnston, O. *Disney Animation: The Illusion of Life*. Abbeville Press New York, 1981.
40. Vugt, H. C. V., Bailenson, J. N., Hoorn, J. F., and Konijn, E. A. Effects of facial similarity on user responses to embodied agents. *ACM TOCHI 17*, 2 (2008), 7:1–7:27.
41. Young, S., and Shaw, D. G. Profiles of effective college and university teachers. *J High Educ 70*, 6 (1999), 670–686.

Study on Gaze Direction Perception of Face Image Displayed on Rotatable Flat Display

Ikkaku Kawaguchi
University of Tsukuba
Tsukuba, Ibaraki, Japan
s1430196@u.tsukuba.ac.jp

Hideaki Kuzuoka
University of Tsukuba
Tsukuba, Ibaraki, Japan
kuzuoka@iit.tsukuba.ac.jp

Yusuke Suzuki
OKI Electric Industry Co., Ltd.
Corporate Research and Development Center
Warabi, Saitama, Japan
suzuki543@oki.com

ABSTRACT

A long-standing challenge of video-mediated communication systems is to correctly represent remote participant gaze direction in local environments. A telepresence robot with a movable display that shows the face of a remote participant is a promising approach for solving this issue. Researchers generally consider that display orientation is effective for local participants to properly estimate the gaze direction of remote participants. We investigate how subjects estimate gaze direction of a remote participant ("Looker") when his/her face is displayed on a rotatable flat display. Our experiment reveals that both the Looker's head-eye rotation in the display and display rotation affect subject estimation, but the effect of the display rotation is relatively small. Furthermore, we reveal that subjects tend to overestimate Looker gaze direction. Based on our results, we propose a design implication for a telepresence robot to reduce overestimation and properly represent the remote participant gaze direction.

Author Keywords

Telepresence robot; perception of gaze direction; head-eye coordination ratio.

ACM Classification Keywords

H.5.3. Information interfaces and presentation (e.g., HCI): Group and Organization Interface-Computer-supported cooperative work.

INTRODUCTION

Gaze is one of the most important factors in human communication. For example, the importance of eye contact [10], mutual gaze [19], and gaze awareness [14] has been discussed in several studies. However, when people communicate through a video communication system, the gaze direction of remote participants cannot be represented properly on a display, which undermines certain collaborative tasks between participants [13]. For example, eye contact plays an important role in controlling the floor in face-to-face communication. However, when an ordinary video conferencing system is used for a multi-party meeting, it is impossible for a participant to direct attention toward a specific remote person, thus inhibiting a smooth group turn-taking process [15, 28]. Not only is eye contact important, but also the assessment of the focus of attention from other individuals toward a physical object, especially for collaborative physical tasks. However, ordinary video conferencing systems do not allow local participants to properly assess a remote participant's attention toward an object in a local environment, thus making joint attention difficult to achieve [7]. Consequently, allowing local participants to correctly read a remote participant's gaze direction [14] is one of the important issues of telecommunication systems.

One of the solutions to this problem is a telepresence robot, which acts as a surrogate for a remote participant [1, 16, 23, 29]. A telepresence robot is especially effective when a remote participant requires mobility in the local environment to enhance his/her visual freedom and physical presence. Such a robot tends to have a display that shows the remote participant's face (hereafter, "face display"). When a camera is built into the face display unit [1, 29], its orientation indicates the direction in which the remote person is gazing. By rotating the face display unit, a remote participant can look around the local environment. In terms of this feature, researchers seem to consider that the orientation of the face

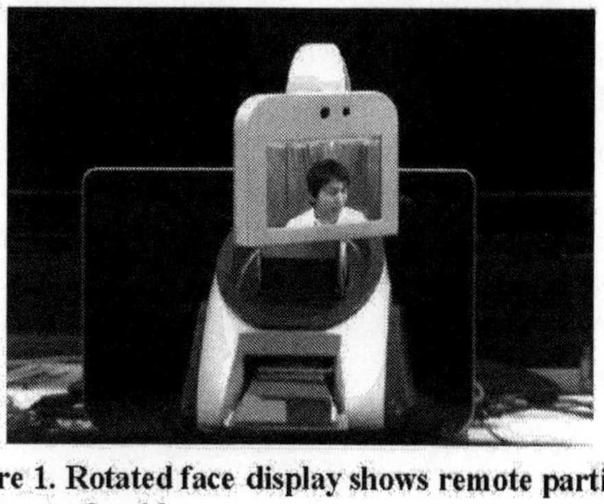

Figure 1. Rotated face display shows remote participant looking to the side.

CHI 2015, April 18–23, 2015, Seoul, Republic of Korea.

http://dx.doi.org/10.1145/2702123.2702369

display and/or the remote participant's face image is effective in representing his/her gaze direction [1, 16, 23, 29].

This assumption might be true if the face display is aiming directly at a local participant. However, the rotation of the face display leads to the local participant seeing it from an oblique angle, thus making it difficult to read the remote person's gaze direction properly [4]. This problem is partially attributed to the Mona Lisa effect, a phenomenon that causes the eyes in a portrait to appear to follow observers as they move. In fact, this situation is quite common for telepresence robots because the remote participant inevitably controls the face display camera unit to look around the local environment. In addition to this effect, if the face image in the display is looking to the side (Figure 1), this issue could become more complicated [2]. Because we want to allow the local participant to correctly estimate the remote participant's gaze direction, it is important to understand the inherent problems of existing telepresence robots.

Consequently, the aim of our study is to investigate how the combination of display orientation and face-eye orientation affects viewer perception of a remote participant's gaze direction. Because our goal is to develop a telepresence robot, we focus specifically on a relatively small display (approximately 10 in.) that can be mounted on a mobile platform. We believe that the findings from this study will provide researchers with insight for designing a telepresence robot: how the robot's face display should be controlled, how the face image should be displayed, and how we should design the remote person's user interface.

Note that our main interest in this study is for meeting participants to use "video-as-data, in which video images of the workspace and work objects are the focus of interest" [20] (p. 327). In other words, rather than with assisting eye contact, we are interested in assisting with joint attention towards an artifact that exists in one of the participant's local environment. In the initial stage of this study, we assume one-to-one communication, thus aiming to contribute to the design of telepresence robots in order to support accurate joint attention between one remote participant and one local participant. Therefore, our findings might not be directly applicable to the design of a telepresence robot for assisting smooth turn-taking during remote multi-party meetings [25, 26]. However, we believe that our findings can be part of a fundamental knowledge to understand various gaze-related phenomena that can be observed during such meetings.

In this paper, we first discuss prior research and focus our research questions. Then, based on our experiment, we discuss the inherent problems that existing telepresence robots might have. Finally, we propose a design implication to improve gaze direction estimation by local participants.

RELATED WORK

Telepresence Robot with Face Display

It is quite common for telepresence robots to use LCDs as face displays. For example, Porta-Person [29] is a telepresence device that consists of a face display, video camera, microphone, speaker, and servo motor attached to a rotating platform. MeBot [1] has a three-degrees of freedom (3DOF) movable display (head) and two 3DOF arms. The system detects the remote participant's face orientation and synchronizes MeBot head orientation. In either case, the researchers expected the face displays to have the ability to provide gaze awareness. However, they did not conduct a detailed investigation of how the orientation of the LCD itself and the face image on the LCD affect estimation of the remote participant's gaze direction.

Sirkin et al. aimed at supporting "hub-and-satellite meetings, where most participants are collocated, except for one participant at a satellite location" [26] (p. 163). For that purpose, they developed a kinetic videoconferencing proxy with a swiveling face display to indicate the direction in which the remote participant is looking. Sirkin et al. compared their system with a typical stationary video display, and revealed that the motion of the face display led to smoother turn-taking and higher engagement in conversation. Our study is similar to theirs in that both studies are interested in how viewers perceive the remote participant's gaze direction. However, although their work focuses mainly on the effect of the swiveling face display on conversation effectiveness, our work focuses on how three factors of a telepresence robot, mainly face display rotation, the remote participant's head rotation in the display, and his/her eye rotation, affect a viewer's perception of the remote participant's gaze direction. Thus, our study investigates what can be considered a lower level of communication (i.e., at the perception level). Therefore, we believe that our findings can be useful for designing an experiment for investigating higher communication layers and understanding its results.

Existing Solutions to Mona Lisa Effect

To solve the problem of the Mona Lisa effect, some new technologies have been proposed. Divorra et al. and Nguyen et al. developed flat displays that can provide the correct perspective of remote participants to each local viewer by selecting the appropriate camera from multiple cameras in a remote site [5, 21]. Based on the experiments, Nguyen et al. showed that their system was effective in alleviating the Mona Lisa effect. Pan et al. used technologies similar to those of Nguyen et al., but proposed the use of a cylindrical display instead of a flat display, and proved that their system can improve the accuracy of distinguishing a remote participant gaze direction [22]. Although these technologies are effective in assisting multi-party meetings, they require relatively large-scale equipment, and force local participants to sit at predetermined positions. Thus, their systems are applicable to dedicated conference rooms only.

Misawa et al. developed LiveMask [18], a face-shaped screen with a 3DOF motion platform, and displayed a remote person's live face image on the screen. The results from their experiment showed that LiveMask is effective in representing the remote person's gaze direction accurately. However, a limitation with the system is its lack of general versatility. The screen needs to be made individually to match the remote person's face. In our study, we focus on a normal LCD because it is commonly used for face displays in the majority of existing telepresence robots.

Perception of Human Gaze Direction

Anstis et al. conducted experiments to examine how a subject determines the gaze direction of a "Looker," either face-to-face or video-mediated [2]. In both scenarios, the Looker focused on nine target points that spanned from −20° to +20° on a horizontal scale placed symmetrically and perpendicular to the subject's line of sight. Furthermore, these targets were combined with the Looker's horizontal head rotation of −30°, 0°, or +30°. Anstis et al. compared the two scenarios. In face-to-face communication, the subject looked directly at the Looker's face. In video-mediated circumstances, the subject viewed the Looker's face displayed on a TV (CRT) screen. In this case, the Looker's fixation and head rotation were further combined with horizontal rotation of the TV screen from −30° to +30°.

Their experiments identified three factors that affect the perception of gaze direction: TV-screen-turn effect, head-turn effect, and overestimation effect. The TV-screen-turn effect is an apparent displacement of the perceived direction of the Looker's gaze in the same direction as the rotation of the TV screen. Anstis et al. hypothetically attributed this effect to the curvature of the TV screen. The head-turn effect is an apparent displacement of the perceived direction of the Looker's gaze in the opposite direction to the Looker's head turn. Cine [3] and Gibson et al. [9] reported a similar phenomenon. The overestimation effect is the overestimation of the deviation of the Looker's gaze. For example, when the Looker focuses on a target at +20°, the subject might overestimate the direction as +30°.

Although our study is similar to the study [2], there are three major differences. First, because they attributed the TV-screen-turn effect to the curvature of the CRT, we might observe a difference because we use a flat LCD as the face display. Second, Anstis et al. managed head rotation and eye rotation separately. In reality, however, it is well known that head and eyes move coordinately when a human focuses on a displaced target [11], i.e., both head rotation and eye rotation contribute to the focus in a specific ratio. We believe we need to investigate how a subject determines the gaze direction of a remote participant in a face display when the Looker displays natural head-eye coordination. Third, considering the different ways of implementing the user interface for the remote participant and the telepresence robot, we can consider several combinations of the face display orientation and the head-eye orientation in the face display to represent the Looker's head-eye coordination.

To the best of our knowledge, our study is the first to consider these three factors together: 1) use of a flat LCD, 2) consideration of natural head-eye coordination for focus, and 3) as experimental conditions, comparison of the different ways of combining face display rotation and head-eye rotation in the display.

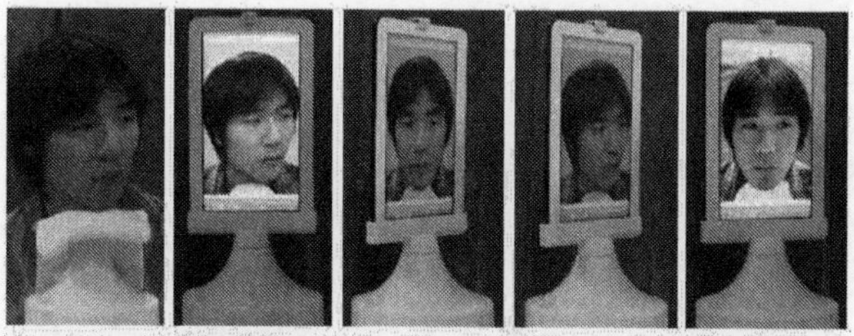

Figure 2. Experimental conditions. Condition 1: Face-to-face. Condition 2: Rotating face and fixed display. Condition 3: Fixed face and rotating display. Condition 4: Rotating face and rotating display (full). Condition 5: Rotating eyes and rotating display (half).

Research Questions

Drawing upon related work, our research questions are as follows. When a remote participant focuses with natural head-eye coordination,

- what is the effect of head rotation and eye rotation in the display on the local participant's estimation of gaze direction?
- what is the effect of the face display rotation on the local participant's estimation of gaze direction?

We conducted an experiment to investigate these questions.

EXPERIMENT

We conducted an experiment to investigate how a local participant (subject) perceives the gaze direction of a remote participant (Looker) in a face display. In particular, we are interested in the case in which the Looker's natural head-eye coordination is combined with the face display's rotation.

Experiment Design

In this study, the subject's task was to observe the Looker's face and estimate the direction in which the Looker was gazing. We compared five conditions (Figure 2):

Condition 1 (Face-to-face): the subject sat facing the Looker at a distance of 83 cm. Both individuals used chin rests. We placed an arc-like scale with center set to the Looker's chin-rest in front of the Looker. The Looker focused on designated targets with natural head-eye coordination. The targets were arranged only on the right side of the subject, and they were placed at 0°, 5°, 10°, 15°, 30°, 45°, and 60°. These targets were invisible to the subject. This is the baseline condition for comparison with other conditions. The remaining conditions had the same settings, but the Looker was replaced with a 10.8-in. display that showed a pre-recording of the Looker's face.

Condition 2 (Rotating head and eyes, and fixed display): the subject looked at the Looker's face displayed on the 10.8-in. screen. The display showed pre-recorded still images of the

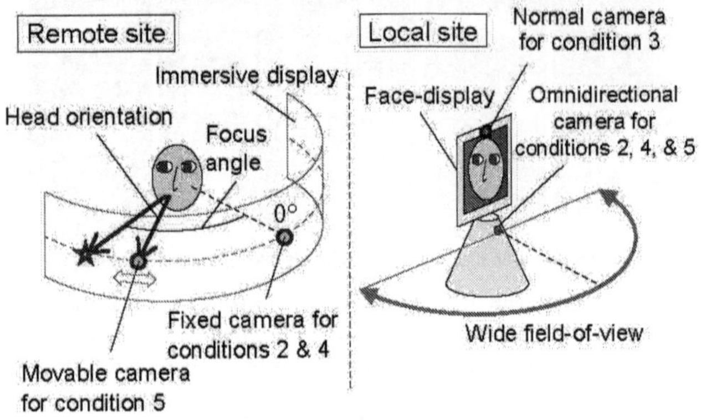

Figure 3. Assumed telepresence robot setup for conditions 2, 4, and 5.

Looker focusing on designated targets with natural head-eye coordination. The target placement was the same as in condition 1. Although the Looker used natural head-eye coordination, the display itself did not rotate and faced the subject directly. This condition assumes that the telepresence robot has an omnidirectional camera, and its image is displayed on the remote participant's immersive display [27]. The remote participant looks around the displayed image with natural head-eye coordination, and a camera set at 0° captures his/her face image (Figure 3). The face display does not rotate in this condition.

Condition 3 (Fixed head and eyes, and rotating display): the subject looked at the Looker's face displayed on a 10.8-in. screen. The display showed pre-recorded still images of the Looker looking in a straight line. In this condition, the Looker's head and eyes did not rotate, but the display was rotated at 0°, 5°, 10°, 15°, 30°, 45°, and 60°. This condition assumes that the remote participant looks at a relatively small display and uses a mouse or keyboard to control the orientation of the display-camera unit of the telepresence robot [6, 24], which means that the remote person continually looks in a straight line in the display. A camera on the remote participant's display device captures his/her face.

Condition 4 (Rotating face and rotating display [full]): the subject looked at the Looker's face displayed on a 10.8-in. screen. The display showed the same images as in condition 2. In this condition, the display was rotated to the same angle as the Looker's target angle. This condition assumes that the remote participant is in an immersive display and a camera for the telepresence robot is an omnidirectional camera independent from the face display [16, 17]. The remote participant's face is captured by a camera set at 0° (Figure 3). An eye tracker detects his/her focus angle and rotates the face display to the equivalent angle [26].

Condition 5 (Rotating eyes and rotating display [half]): the subject looked at the Looker's face displayed on a 10.8-in. screen. The display showed pre-recorded still images of the Looker. In this condition, the Looker's head was stationary, looking out from the display, and only the eyes were rotated. Eye rotation was combined with a corresponding display rotation. The basic concept used to determine the rotation angles of the eyes and the display was head-eye coordination. Our experiment, to be described later, revealed that when the gaze was directed at 0°, 5°, 10°, 15°, 30°, 45°, and 60°, the combinations of head-eye rotation were (0°, 0°), (2°, 3°), (4°, 6°), (7°, 8°), (14°, 16°), (23°, 22°), and (32°, 28°), respectively, on average. Therefore, in this condition, the eye rotation angles were 0°, 3°, 6°, 8°, 16°, 22°, and 28°, and the accompanying display rotation angles were 0°, 2°, 4°, 7°, 14°, 23°, and 32°, respectively. This condition assumes a system similar to condition 4. In this condition, however, a movable camera moves along the screen so that the camera always captures the remote participant's face from the front. Although this setup is somewhat artificial, we included this condition mainly because we wanted to investigate the effect of the Looker's eye rotation on the perception of the focus angle.

This experiment used a within-subject design, i.e., all subjects experienced all five different conditions. The order of the conditions was randomized to minimize the learning effect.

Apparatus

Figure 4 shows an overview of the experiment environment, and Figure 5 shows a schematic overview of the same. For conditions 2 to 5, the apparatus consisted of a 10.8-in. face display on a rotating platform, an arc-like scale, and a marker. We used a Dell Venue 11 Pro as the face display, which employs IPS-LCD with 178° viewing angle. Although different display sizes can produce different results, we chose this size because similar sizes are widely used for commercially available telepresence robots [6, 24]. During the experiment, the face display showed only one male Looker. We captured some still images of the Looker's face focusing on designated targets.

We placed the arc-like scale with center set to the rotation center of the rotating platform around the face display. The arc radius was set to 41.5 cm. The marker was a rod placed slightly higher than the scale, and we covered its top with a small red cap. We allowed the rod to orbit around the rotation platform, thus allowing the subject to move the marker easily along the scale in order to indicate the point on which he/she estimated the Looker to be focusing. The distance between display and subject was 83 cm, which is a typical distance for one-to-one communication [12].

For condition 1, we replaced the face display with the actual Looker. During the experiment, he focused on the target points on the scale, which were only visible to the Looker.

During the experiment, the height of the subject's eyes was adjusted to match the height of the Looker's eyes. The height of the scale was set to 1 cm lower than the height of the subject's eyes so that the scale did not interfere with observing the Looker's eyes.

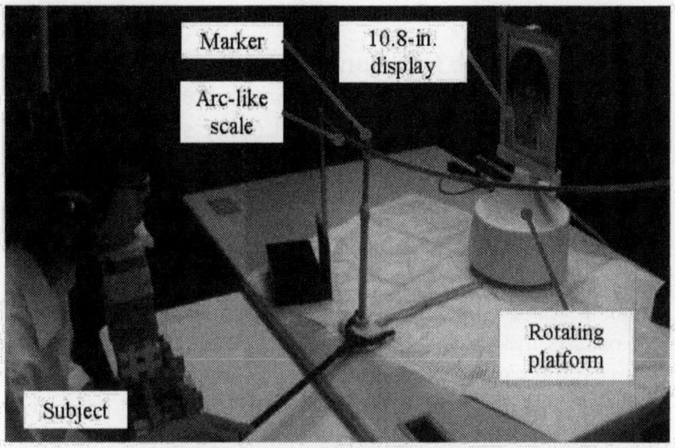

Figure 4. Overview of experiment environment. In this photo, Looker acts as subject for demonstration only. His data is not included.

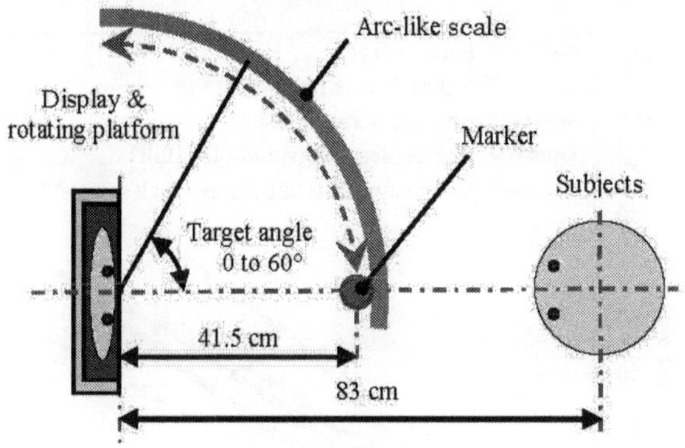

Figure 5. Top-down schematic overview of experiment environment.

Head-Eye Coordination Ratio Measurement

It is known that the head and eyes move coordinately when people focus on a displaced target [11]. For our main experiment, we wanted the Looker to show typical head-eye coordination. To find the appropriate Looker, we recruited four subjects and measured their head-eye coordination ratio ($head\ angle/target\ angle$) (Figure 6). To measure this ratio, we used the apparatus for condition 1. First, the subject put his/her head on the chin-rest, looked in a straight line (head at 0°), and maintained his/her position for 10 s. Then, he/she slightly moved his/her head up to free him/herself from the chin rest, focused on the designated target, held the position for 10 s with natural head-eye coordination, and returned to 0°. We asked the subjects to repeat this procedure for six targets in ascending order, i.e., 0°, 5°, 10°, 15°, 30°, 45°, and 60°. We also asked them to repeat the sequence three times. We measured the subjects' head rotation using a motion capture system (CyVerse Stereo Labeling Camera).

The result (Figure 7) shows that the average head-eye coordination ratio linearly increased from 40% to more than 50% as the target angles increased from 5° to 60°. Then, we chose one subject whose head-eye coordination ratio was closest to the average and used him as the Looker for the following experiment.

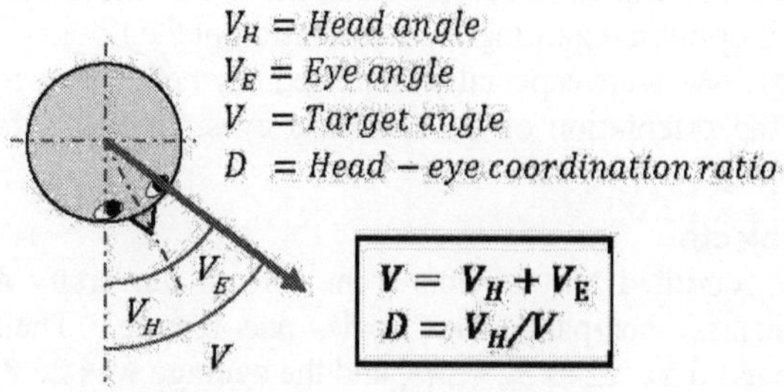

Figure 6. Head–eye coordination ratio.

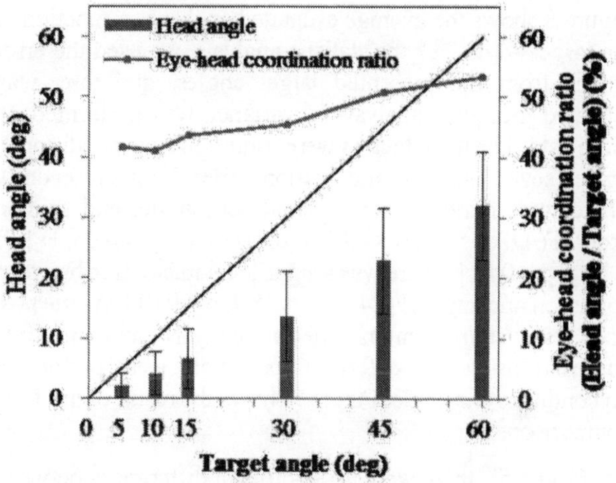

Figure 7. Relationship between target angle to head angle (blue bar) and target angle to head-eye coordination ratio (red line).

Procedure

First, the researcher asked the subject to sit on a chair and set his/her head on the chin rest. Then, the researcher showed the subject the stimuli (either the actual Looker's face or his face shown in the display) one by one. The subject was instructed to close his/her eyes before looking at the stimuli. After the researcher set the stimuli, he gave a sign to start estimation. Then, the subject opened his/her eyes, looked at the stimuli, moved the pointer to the estimated focus angle, and closed his/her eyes again. In this way, we eliminated the display motion factor, which might affect the subject's estimation.

First, as a practice session, the researcher showed the subject four stimuli. Then, the researcher started the actual experiment. One session consisted of seven randomly ordered targets, and each subject participated in two sessions per condition. Consequently, during one condition, the subject estimated the Looker's focus angle twice for each target. To minimize the learning effect, we used the Latin square design to properly randomize the order of five conditions for each subject. In total, we presented each subject with 70 stimuli (**7 stimuli × 2 sets × 5 conditions**) ; the entire experiment required approximately 50 min. per subject.

After the experiment, the researcher asked the subjects for their opinion regarding their estimation of the Looker's focus angle. We were especially interested in whether they referred to the orientation of the Looker's eyes, Looker's face, or display.

Subjects

We recruited ten subjects from a local university and an industrial company (nine male, one female). Their ages ranged from 22 to 37 years, and the average was 26.8 years. All had normal or corrected vision.

RESULTS

Figure 8 shows the average estimated angles as a function of the target angle. For the statistic analysis, we used the error values from the presented target angles, and three-way repeated measures analysis of variance was performed on these data. The three factors were condition (five conditions), angle (seven angles), and session order (first or second). There were main effects on condition, angle, and session order [$F(4,6) = 59.8$, $p < 0.01$; $F(6,4) = 7.15$, $p < 0.05$; $F(1,9) = 13.6$, $p < 0.01$]. There was a significant interaction between condition and angle [$F(24,216) = 35.7$, $p < 0.01$]. As the post hoc test, simple main effects analysis and multiple comparisons (with Bonferroni correction) were performed on condition and angle. Figure 9 shows the result of multiple comparisons.

For 0° and 5°, there were no significant differences between conditions. For 10° and 15°, there were significant differences between condition 3 and conditions 1, 2, and 4, and between condition 5 and conditions 1, 2, and 4. For 30°, 45°, and 60°, there were significant differences between condition 3 and all other conditions, and between condition 4 and all other conditions.

DISCUSSION

Effect of Head-Eye Rotation and Display Rotation

In condition 1 (face-to-face), in line with previous studies [2], the subject overestimated the Looker's focus angles, especially when they were greater than 10°. In this paper, we use this result as a baseline to compare with other conditions.

In condition 2 (Rotating face and fixed display), the result is quite similar to the face-to-face condition. Although the result is somewhat predictable from the previous literature [8], ours is the first study (to the best of our knowledge) to examine the case in which the Looker presents natural head-eye coordination. Given that the display was not rotated in this condition, this result shows that head-eye rotation in the display has a strong effect on the subject in estimating the Looker's focus angle. Because the result is quite similar to

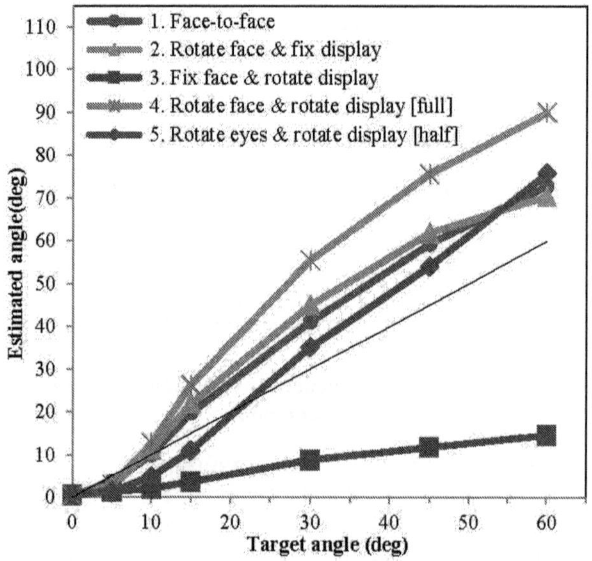

Figure 8. Experiment results for each condition.

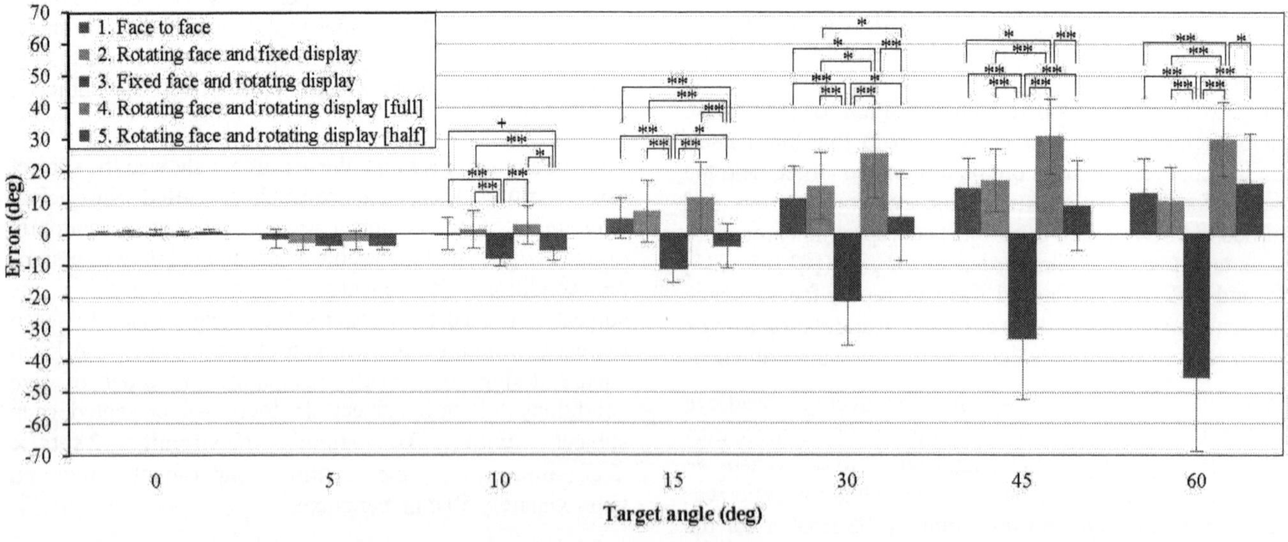

Figure 9. Results from multiple comparisons between the conditions for each angle. (: p < 0.01, *: p < 0.05, +: p < 0.1)**

the face-to-face situation (condition 1), this result is a seemingly favorable solution for a telepresence robot. However, for the corresponding telepresence system, the requirement for uncommon equipment, such as immersive display, is slightly prohibitive.

Condition 3 (Fixed face and rotating display) showed a strong Mona Lisa effect throughout the display rotation angles of 0° to 60°. Interestingly, in interviews with the subjects, at least six answered that they referred to both the Looker's eyes and the rotation angle of the display frame to estimate the Looker's focus angles. In fact, however, seven of the subject estimations were almost constantly 0° across the focus angles of 0° to 60°, two of the estimations were almost the same as the display rotation angles, and one of the estimations was between the two groups. This result indicates that the orientation of the Looker's face has a stronger effect on estimation compared to the orientation of the display frame. Furthermore, this result predicts a problem with a system that employs a small display for the remote participant to monitor the local environment, in which case the system will not yield the remote participant's head rotation. In such a case, no matter how the display rotates, the local participant might have difficulties estimating the remote participant's focus angle.

In condition 4 (Rotating face and rotating display [full]), the subject's overestimation of the Looker's fixation angles were significantly greater than most of the other conditions when the focus angle was 10° or larger. In particular, a comparison of the results between condition 4 and condition 2 indicates that the rotation of the display has the effect of shifting the subject's estimation in the same direction as the rotation of the display. Although Anstis et al. attributed a similar effect to the curvature of the TV screen they used, our result shows that a flat screen has the same effect. We call this effect the "*flat-display turn effect.*" A comparison between conditions 4 and 3 indicates a strong effect of the head-eye turn on increasing the estimation of the Looker's focus angle (hereafter, "head-eye turn effect").

In summary, the results of condition 4 indicate a weak flat-display turn effect and a strong head-eye turn effect. Because this condition shows the strongest overestimation, a system that combines the Looker's head-eye movement with display rotation might not be preferable.

The result of condition 5 is interesting. Compared with condition 3, the rotation angle of the display was approximately halved and only the rotation of the Looker's eyes was added. As a result, notwithstanding the decreased rotation angle of the display, the addition of the eye rotation significantly increased the subject's estimation, bringing accuracy close to that seen in condition 2. From this result, we can assume that through an appropriate combination of the rotation of the Looker's head, eyes, and the flat display, it is possible to enable the local person to estimate the correct focus angle.

Based on these results, it is clear that head-eye and display turns affect estimation of the Looker's focus angle, but the effect of the head-eye turn seems to be stronger.

Design Implications

Interestingly, our experiment revealed that, although the Looker showed natural head-eye coordination, the subject tended to overestimate the Looker's focus angle in most conditions, including face-to-face. In the case of face-to-face communication, people can use cues such as finger pointing to fix such overestimation, whereas in the case of telecommunication, the communications cues that are available are quite limited. Thus, it is preferable for a telepresence robot to minimize the local participant's overestimation as much as possible.

One way to do this is to make the Looker's head-eye and display rotation angles smaller. We can easily make the display rotation angle smaller simply by multiplying the original rotation angle by an appropriate coefficient. Reducing the head-eye rotation angle is also simple. In the case of conditions 4 and 5, for example, we can simply use a smaller display for the remote participant instead of the full immersive display.

Let us discuss this solution by considering condition 4 in more detail (Figure 10). For simplicity, let us assume that we maintain the display rotation angle the same as the original condition 4. By calculating the difference between conditions 4 and 2 for each target angle, we can deduce the relationship between the target angle and the flat-display turn effect (Figure 10 blue broken line). Here, let us assume that the contribution of the head-eye rotation is the difference between the flat-display turn effect and condition 4. For example, when the target angle is 60°, the contribution of the head-eye rotation is 90.0° – 19.5° = 70.5°. Assuming that this

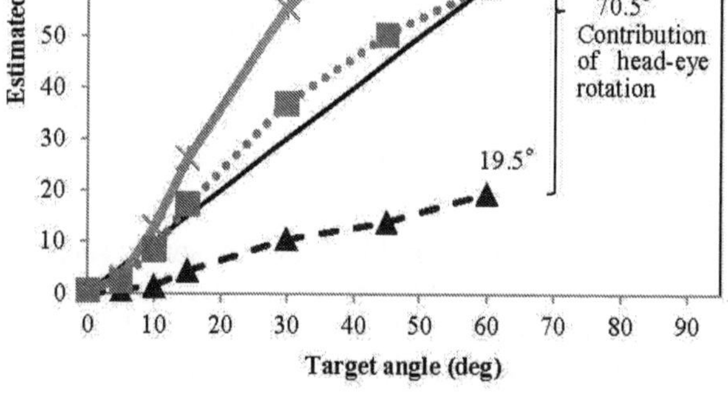

Figure 10. Overview of correction method.

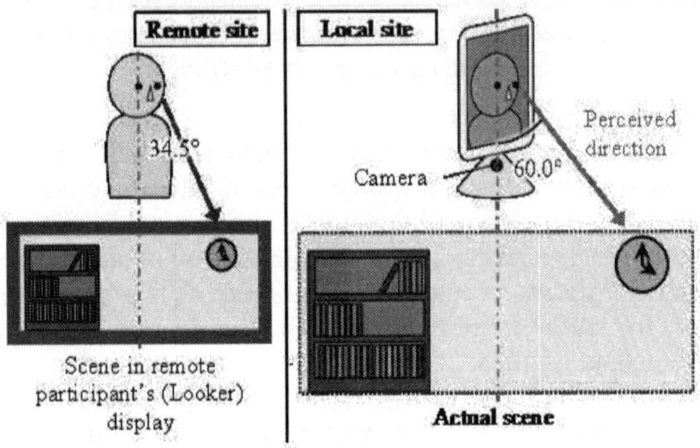

Figure 11. Alleviating overestimation using a small display.

contribution is proportional to the target angle, we can calculate the transformed target angle by 60.0° × (60.0° – 19.5 °)/70.5° = 34.5°. Consequently, if we use a small display so that it transforms the target angle from 60.0° to 34.5°, the Looker's head and eye rotation is reduced and an observer can estimate the Looker's gaze angle as 60.0° (Figure 11). By using this small display, we can expect the relationship between the target and estimated gaze angles to be corrected as shown by the green dotted line in Figure 10. If we assume that the distance between the display and user is 50 cm, a 32-in. display mostly supports this viewing angle. Naturally, these assumptions are quite crude and a more careful design is still necessary. However, we believe that we can decrease the display size for the remote participant by taking advantage of the flat-display turn effect.

Generalizability to Multi-party Meeting

Many studies on telepresence robots are focused on assisting multi-party meetings [22, 25, 26]. In this study, however, we are mainly interested in the joint attention between one remote and one local participant. We have not examined cases where viewers observe the face display from multiple positions. Therefore, our results might not be directly applicable to solving the problems of multi-party meetings. However, the findings of this study with Anstis et al. [2] suggest that it is almost impossible to support accurate eye contact between a telepresence robot (particularly with a flat-face display) and multiple participants. Therefore, as Sirkin et al. mentioned in their paper [26], an additional direction indicator, such as a physical robot head or a pointer similar to a weathervane, might be necessary to alleviate this problem.

Limitations

Following are the limitations of our research that require further investigation.

The number of subjects for this study is relatively small and not gender balanced. For more accurate results, more rigorous experiments that include more subjects and considers gender, age, eyesight, and so on are required.

We focused only on horizontal rotation. We do not know the effect of vertical rotation on the estimation of the Looker's focus along the vertical axis.

In this paper, we assumed that the local person is looking at the telepresence robot situated directly in front. In reality, however, local participants do not necessarily sit directly across from the telepresence robot, but may walk around in the environment and look at it from an oblique angle. It may even be possible for the local person to view the robot from behind, precluding him/her from seeing the remote person's face and affording him/her a view of only the robot's posture. In such cases, and to the best of our knowledge, it is not known how the local person might estimate the remote person's gaze direction.

Finally, in this study, the subject observed the display only when it was not moving. It has not been clarified how motion of the face display could affect the local person's estimation of the remote person's gaze direction.

CONCLUSION

The main purpose of this study was to design a telepresence robot that allows a local person to correctly estimate a remote person's gaze direction. As the first step, this study aimed to acquire basic knowledge regarding how the local person estimates the remote person's gaze direction when the remote person's face is shown in various ways. In particular, we conducted an experiment to investigate the effect of the face display orientation and the remote person's head-eye orientation in the display on the local person's estimation of the remote person's focus angle. Unlike previous studies, we were especially interested in the situation where the remote person focuses on a target with natural head-eye coordination.

The results revealed that the local person could not correctly estimate the remote person's gaze direction from most of the existing telepresence robots. The major factors were that 1) the local person overestimated the remote person's gaze direction, 2) the display rotation had the effect of increasing the estimation, and 3) the Mona Lisa effect was greater than the flat-display turn effect. To alleviate the problem of incorrect estimation, we suggested a method for adjusting the display rotation and the remote person's head-eye rotation.

We expect this paper to benefit researchers who design telepresence robot systems and user interfaces for remote persons. Our future work will include the investigation of other factors of gaze estimation and the development of a new telepresence robot that reflects the results of our experiment.

REFERENCES

1. Adalgeirsson, S. O., and Breazeal, C. Mebot: a robotic platform for socially embodied presence. In *Proc. HRI 2010*, IEEE Press (2010), 15-22.
2. Anstis, S. M., Mayhew, J. W., and Morley, T. The perception of where a face or television 'portrait' is looking. *The American journal of psychology* (1969), 474-489.

3. Cline, M. G. The perception of where a person is looking. *The American journal of psychology* (1967), 41-50.
4. Delaunay, F., de Greeff, J., and Belpaeme, T. A study of a retro-projected robotic face and its effectiveness for gaze reading by humans. In *Proc. HRI 2010*, IEEE Press (2010), 39-44.
5. Divorra, O., Civit, J., Zuo, F., Belt, H., Feldmann, I., Chreer, O., and Braspenning, R. Towards 3Daware telepresence: Working on technologies behind the scene. In *Proc. CSCW 2010*, ACM Press (2010), 6-10.
6. Double Robotics - Telepresence Robot for Telecommuters. http://www.doublerobotics.com
7. Fussell, S., Setlock, L., and Kraut, R.: Effects of Head-Mounted and Scene-Oriented Video Systems on Remote Collaboration on Physical Tasks, In *Proc. CHI 2003*, ACM Press (2003), 513-520.
8. Gale, C., and Monk, A. F.: Where am I looking? The accuracy of video-mediated gaze awareness. *Perception & psychophysics 62*, 3 (2000), 586-595.
9. Gibson, J. J., and Pick, A. D. Perception of another person's looking behavior. *The American journal of psychology 76*, 3 (1963), 386-394.
10. Goodwin, C. Professional vision. *American anthropologist 96*, 3 (1994), 606-633.
11. Gresty, M. A. Coordination of head and eye movements to fixate continuous and intermittent targets. *Vision Research 14*, 6 (1974), 395-403.
12. Hall, E. T. *The Hidden Dimension.* Doubleday&Company (1966).
13. Heath, C., and Luff, P.: Disembodied conduct: communication through video in a multi-media office environment. In *Proc. CHI 1991*, ACM Press (1991), 99-103.
14. Ishii, H., Kobayashi, M., and Grudin, J.Integration of interpersonal space and shared workspace: ClearBoard design and experiments. *ACM Transactions on Information Systems (TOIS) 11*, 4 (1993), 349-375.
15. Issac, E. and Tang, C., What video can and can't do for collaboration: a case study, In *Proc. ACM Multimedia* (1993), ACM Press (1993), 199-206.
16. Kawanobe, H., Aosaki, Y., Kuzuoka, H., and Suzuki, Y. iRIS: a remote surrogate for mutual reference. In *Proc. HRI 2013*, IEEE Press (2013), 403-404.
17. Kuzuoka, H., Kosaka, J., Yamazaki, K., Suga, Y., Suga, Y., Yamazaki, A., Luff, P. and Heath, C. Mediating dual ecologies. In *Proc. CSCW 2004*, ACM Press (2004), 477-486.
18. Misawa, K., Ishiguro, Y., and Rekimoto, J. Livemask: A telepresence surrogate system with a face-shaped screen for supporting nonverbal communication. In *Proc. AVI 2012*, ACM Press (2012), 394-397.
19. Moore,C., and Dunham,P.J. *Joint Attention: Its origins and Role in Development.* Lawrence Erlbaum (1995).
20. Nardi, B., Schwarz, H., Kuchinsky, A., and Leichner, R. Turning Away from Talking Heads: The Use of Video-as-Data in Neurosurgery, In *Proc. INTERCHI 1993*, ACM Press (1993), 327-334.
21. Nguyen, D., and Canny, J. MultiView: spatially faithful group video conferencing. In *Proc. CHI 2005*, ACM Press (2005), 799-808.
22. Pan, Y. and Steed, A. A Gaze-preserving Situated Multiview Telepresence System, In *Proc. CHI 2014*, ACM Press (2014), 2173-2176.
23. Paulos, E., and Canny, J. PRoP: personal roving presence. In *Proc. CHI 1998*, ACM Press (1998), 296-303.
24. Revolve Robotics - Kubi. https://revolverobotics.com
25. Sellen, A., Buxton, B., and Arnott, J. Using spatial cues to improve videoconferencing. In *Proc. CHI 1992.* ACM Press (1992), 651-652.
26. Sirkin, D., Venolia, G., Tang, J., Robertson, G., Kim, T., Inkpen, K., and Sinclair, M. Motion and attention in a kinetic videoconferencing proxy. In *Human-Computer Interaction–INTERACT 2011*, Springer (2011), 162-180.
27. Tanaka, K., Hayashi, J., Inami, M., and Tachi, S. Twister: An immersive autostereoscopic display. In *IEEE Virtual Reality Conference*, IEEE Press (2004), 59-66.
28. Vertegaal, R., Weevers, I., Sohn, C., and Cheung, C. GAZE-2: Conveying Eye Contact in Group Video Conferencing Using Eye-Controlled Camera Direction, In *Proc. CHI 2003*, ACM Press (2003), 521-528.
29. Yankelovich, N., Simpson, N., Kaplan, J. and Provino, J. Porta-person: telepresence for the connected conference room. *CHI'07 extended abstracts on human factors in computing systems*, ACM Press (2007), 2789-2794.

DynamicDuo: Co-presenting with Virtual Agents

Ha Trinh, Lazlo Ring, Timothy Bickmore
College of Computer and Information Science
Northeastern University
Boston, MA, USA
{hatrinh, lring, bickmore}@ccs.neu.edu

ABSTRACT
The quality of most professional oral presentations is often poor, owing to a number of factors, including public speaking anxiety. We present DynamicDuo, a system that uses an automated, life-sized, animated agent to help inexperienced speakers deliver their presentations in front of an audience. The design of the system was informed by an analysis of TED talks given by two human presenters to identify the most common dual-presentation formats and transition behaviors used. In a within-subjects study (N=12) comparing co-presenting with DynamicDuo against solo-presenting with conventional presentation software, we demonstrated that our system led to significant improvements in public speaking anxiety and speaking confidence for non-native English speakers. Judges who viewed videotapes of these presentations rated those with DynamicDuo significantly higher on speech quality and overall presentation quality for all presenters.

Author Keywords
Co-presentation; Virtual Agent; Slideware; PowerPoint; Embodied Conversational Agent

ACM Classification Keywords
H.5.2. Information interfaces and presentation: User Interfaces.

INTRODUCTION
Despite the ubiquity and importance of oral presentations, many presentations have very low quality, resulting in their failing to engage, inform, and persuade the audience, and even damaging the credibility and social standing of the speaker. There are many reasons for these failures, including: deficiencies in language, speech, and presentation skills; lack of content mastery; time and resource constraints; lack of preparation and rehearsal; and public speaking anxiety. Prior research has demonstrated that these problems are very prevalent. An extensive survey of 2,501 professionals [9] revealed that 35% of respondents rarely or never rehearse for their presentations, and because of this and many other problems, respondents gave an average grade of "C-" (2.9 on a 1-to-5 scale) for presentations they had attended. Other research has reported that public speaking anxiety affects at least 35% of the population [4].

Imagine if all speakers could give their presentations in the company of a polished, flawless, co-presenter – one who not only shared the cognitive burden of presentation preparation and delivery, but whose presence and delivery was engaging enough to keep the audience spellbound. The mere presence of a talented co-presenter should also be comforting to those who experience speech anxiety. Social impact theory predicts that the presence of a co-presenter reduces performance anxiety, and this effect has been demonstrated in empirical studies [11]. A co-presenter also enables dialogical presentation formats that are impossible in single speaker talks, in which the speakers perform a rehearsed conversation to dramatically illustrate a point. Finally, a polished co-presenter could function as a real-time role model, providing both a helpful demonstration of presentation skills and an increase in self-confidence that comes from being part of a talented team.

We have designed and developed an automated co-presenter that can perform many of these roles and functions, as an aide to less experienced presenters. The co-presenter is an embodied conversational agent that appears in the form of a life-sized human character that can seamlessly present part of a talk given with conventional presentation software (Figure 1). The co-presenter agent uses appropriate verbal and nonverbal behavior for content delivery, highlighting and emphasis, speaker hand-offs (turn-taking), and attentive listening when the human presenter is speaking. We also developed an authoring tool to allow human presenters to easily control the verbal and nonverbal behavior of the agent. We call the overall presentation technology system "DynamicDuo".

Our contributions include:

1. Identification of common presentation formats used by "gold standard" human co-presenters, and description of the verbal and nonverbal behavior used during introductions and turn transitions.
2. Development of the DynamicDuo authoring system, which allows non-technical users to easily define agent behavior as part of presentation authoring in a widely-used, commercially-available presentation support application.

CHI 2015, April 18 - 23 2015, Seoul, Republic of Korea

ACM 978-1-4503-3145-6/15/04…$15.00
http://dx.doi.org/10.1145/2702123.2702584

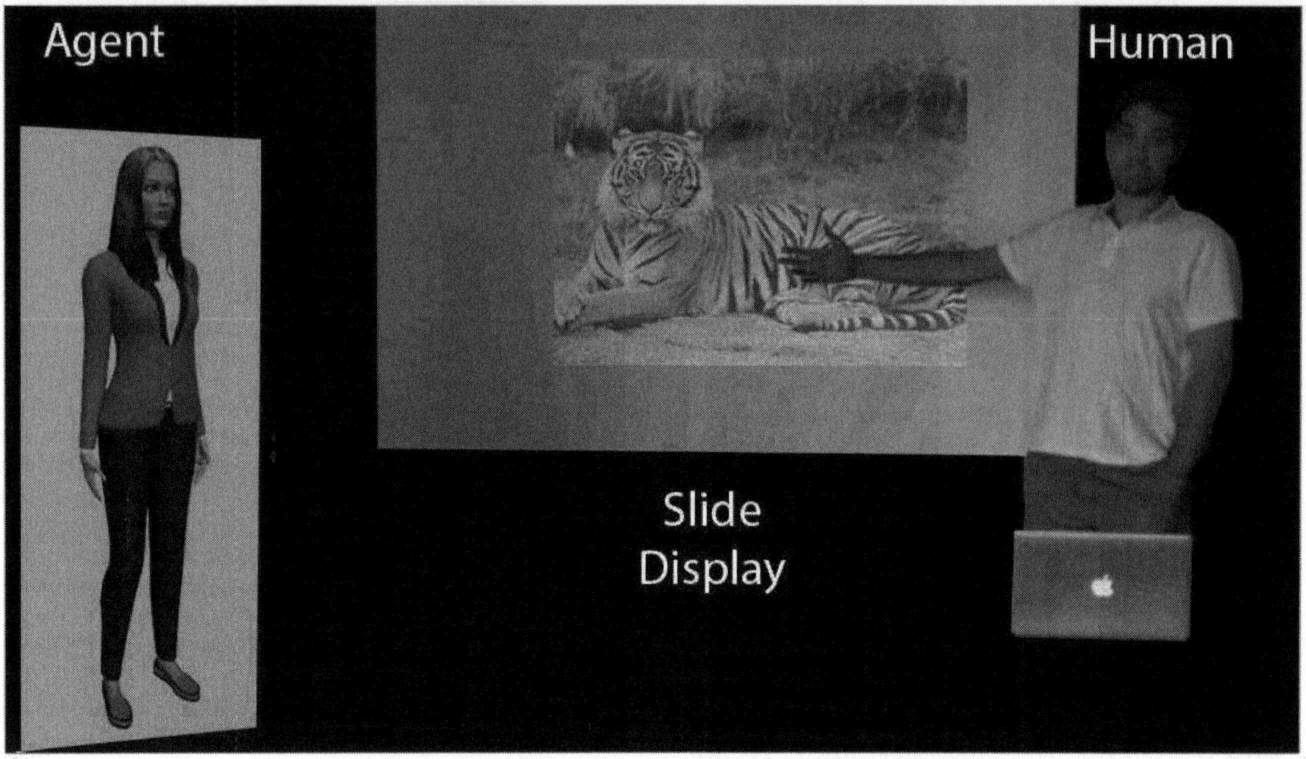

Figure 1. Collaborative presentation environment with slideshow display and Angela appearing on a standing display

3. Development of the DynamicDuo runtime system, to support co-presented oral presentations in front of an audience.
4. Validation of DynamicDuo in a comparative study that demonstrates its potential to improve the overall experience of both presenters and audiences.

RELATED WORK

In this section we explore the causes of public speaking anxiety in light of social impact theory, followed by a review of related presentation technologies and existing virtual presenter systems.

Public Speaking Anxiety

Public speaking is often regarded as one the most anxiety provoking situations. In a survey of 803 American college students, over 35% of respondents expressed the need for assistance with public speaking anxiety (PSA) [4]. Characterized by an increase in physiological arousal (e.g. increased heart rate) and an intense fear of what other people are thinking (e.g. I'm appearing incompetent) [6], PSA can lead to ineffective speech preparation [7], degraded performance quality [16] and increased speech disturbances [13]. Often categorized as either a trait or a state, PSA has been linked to environmental factors such as the size of the audience as well as the number of co-presenters present [11].

One of the seminal works into this phenomenon was Jackson and Latané's research on the impact of co-performing on stage fright [11]. In their study, 60 participants were recruited to imagine themselves in one of 72 different performance scenarios. In each of these scenarios, participants were shown images of the co-presenters and audience they should imagine themselves performing in front of. These images depicted different possible audiences and co-presenters varied in both size and social status. Their results showed that as the size of the audience increased, the participants' imagined tension grew. However, as the number of co-presenters increased, the imagined tension decreased logarithmically. To further explore this finding, a second experiment was conducted in which 48 student performers were asked to fill out a questionnaire prior to giving a live performance. Results of this experiment matched the previous findings, in which presenters performing with as few as one co-presenter experienced an exponential decrease in reported nervousness.

The main explanation behind this finding was social impact theory [14], which explains phenomena such as public speaking anxiety through the concept of social force fields. By imagining a force field projected from an individual, one's social impact can be measured based on the importance, immediacy, and number of people in presence. In addition to specifying the influence of the audience, the theory also accounts the dispersion of social impact felt when other people are co-performing, thus explaining why negative evaluation or embarrassment feels divided up if more than one person is performing at a time. This concept acts as one of the fundamental motivations behind our work, since it suggests that a co-presenter agent may help diffuse the social impact felt by a human presenter.

Presentation Technologies

There have been several commercial products designed to improve oral presentations, with the most ubiquitous being Microsoft's PowerPoint [17] and Apple's Keynote [2]. A number of research projects have also proposed methods to support various presentation activities, from authoring [8] to rehearsal [24] and delivery [22]. A recent example of these is the PitchPerfect system [24], which provided an integrated rehearsal environment for structured presentation preparation. The system enables presenters to break down speaking notes into a series of note segments corresponding to specific visual elements on slides. It also includes a special note segment called transition note, which encourages presenter to prepare for verbal linkage between slides. Although not specifically designed for co-presenter note authoring, this structured note approach could potentially be adopted for distribution of speaking notes among co-presenters and preparing for transitions between presenters.

Virtual Agents and Presentations

Virtual Agents as Presenters

Over the last 20 years there have been a number of attempts to use virtual agents in presentation technology. One of the earliest attempts is the WebPersona system [1], which presented information automatically generated from the World Wide Web to a user via an animated cartoon character. In a user study with 30 participants, the virtual presenter was found to be easier to understand and more entertaining than the same information presented without the presenter. However, users were limited in the way they could interact with the character, since the only interaction option was to navigate to other generated scripts by clicking on embedded hyperlinks in the agent's response.

In addition to fully automated presentation systems, there has been a number of studies on the use of virtual agents to present manually authored speech text on behalf of a human presenter. One such example is Noma et al.'s 3D virtual presenter system [19]. The system enables users to annotate the presenter's speech text with various gesture commands, which could be performed by a 3D animated computer character capable of non-verbal behaviors and synthesized speech. Additional interaction options could also be programmed into the system using a menu-based scripting template. The interface to the system was, however, highly technical and was not evaluated in a user study.

Following from this research, Nijholt et al. explored the creation of an embodied virtual presenter agent for use in a virtual meeting room [18]. Similar to Noma's work, a virtual presenter system was developed to parse manually annotated presentations into animation scripts for a 3D character. Unlike the previous work however, this system was designed for real-time use in a virtual meeting environment. The system could capture audience motions via cameras placed in a meeting room, thereby allowing for a more realistic simulation of audience members and the person controlling the virtual presenter. However, similar to Noma's study, there was no reported user evaluation of the system.

Although all of these systems acted as virtual presenters, their main goal was to replace the human presenters instead of augmenting their performance through human-agent collaboration. Additionally, the interfaces of these systems were highly technical in nature, requiring users to be familiar with the scripting languages or programming toolkits specifically developed for the systems.

Virtual Agents as Audiences

Besides giving presentations for people or acting as their virtual avatar, virtual agents have also been used as virtual audiences to support public speaking training [12, 21]. Pertaub et al. conducted a study investigating the effects of virtual audiences on public speaking anxiety [21]. 40 students were recruited to give two talks in front of a virtual audience of eight male agents. Participants were randomly assigned to one of three groups in which they presented to either a neutral, positive or negative audience. Their results showed that the negative audience significantly decreased the users' confidence after their presentation, suggesting that the system could be used as a virtual environmental therapy tool for those experiencing fear of public speaking.

Virtual Agents as Coaches

Virtual presenters have also been used to coach people on other communication skills, such as job interviewing. A recent example of this is the MACH system [10], a highly realistic virtual interview coach that provides real-time visual feedback on various verbal and non-verbal behaviors of human interviewees, including speech, prosody and facial expressions. The design of the virtual coach was informed by an exploratory study that recorded interactions between a professional career counselor and students. The system was evaluated with 90 undergraduates, who were asked to practice their interviews by either interacting with MACH or watching an educational video. Students who interacted with MACH showed a significant improvement in interview performance compared to those in the control group, as rated by human experts.

UNDERSTANDING CO-PRESENTATION MODELS

To motivate and inform the design of our co-presenter agent, we analyzed ideal examples of talks given by two presenters. Our aim was to identify common collaboration models between co-presenters, as well as their verbal and non-verbal behaviors exhibited during the co-presentation process. We focused on TED talks (www.ted.com) since they are widely considered to be exemplary oral presentations, are freely available, and short in duration. Of the 1,732 talks available online (accessed 9/1/14), only 34 (1.9%) were given by two presenters. Of these, we selected 15 for detailed analysis.

From our analysis we identified the following interaction formats:

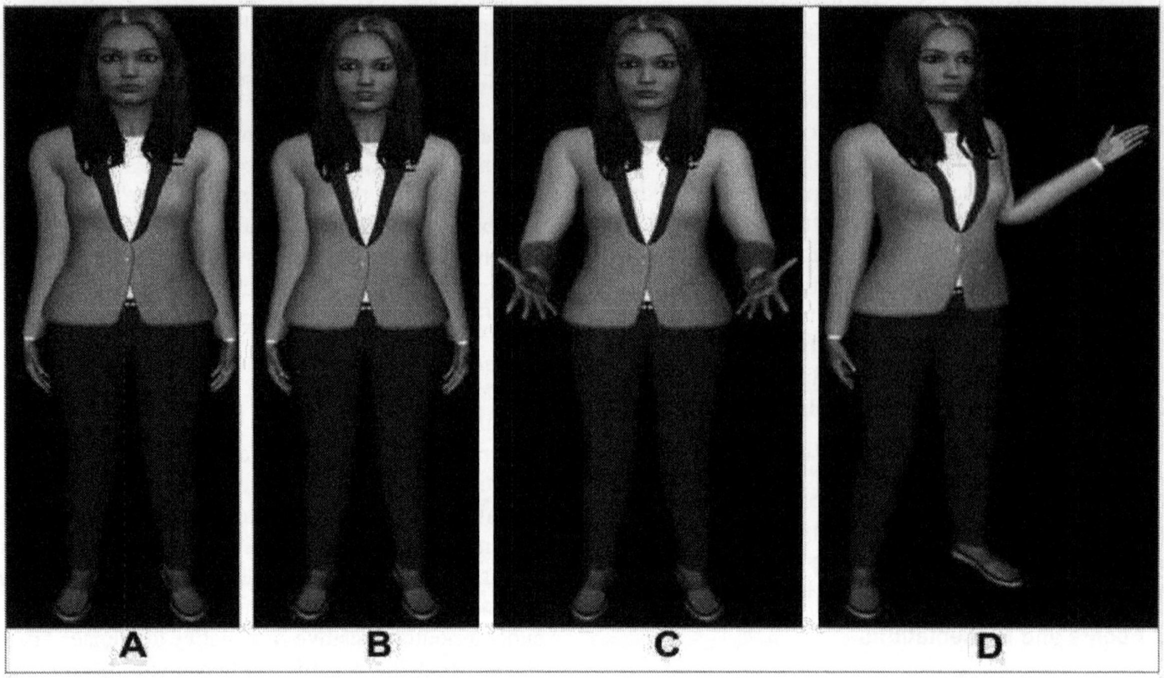

Figure 2. Virtual presenter: (A) relaxing posture; (B) smile; (C) contrast gesture; (D) pointing to slides

Iterative turn-taking. This was the most common format observed (47%), in which presenters take turns giving parts of the presentation. Transitions normally occur at presentation slide boundaries. Occasionally (in 57% of these talks), an embedded dialogue is used, for example, in which one speaker asks a question of the other. However, speaker transitions mostly occur by one speaker simply stopping and the other starting. The average speaking turn lasted 43.7 seconds (SD 27.8), although there was significant variability between dyads (18.9 seconds to 171.6 seconds).

Single turn. The second most common format observed (27%) was one in which each presenter spoke exactly once, sometimes after a brief introduction, with each sharing the floor approximately half of the time.

Dialogue. Although several talks in the iterative turn-taking format had brief embedded dialogues, one of the presentations we analyzed featured a staged dialogue for the entire talk. Turn length was considerably shorter than in iterative turn-taking, averaging 11.0 seconds (SD 8.5).

Interview. One of the talks followed an interview format, in which an interviewer asked each of the co-presenters a question as a prompt for the next part of their talk.

Debate. One of the presentations followed a debate format, in which a moderator introduced the co-presenters, gave them each a fixed time to make an argument, then opened the floor for interaction.

We also analyzed the verbal and non-verbal behavior used by co-presenters, particularly in the iterative turn-taking and single turn formats. Introductions of any kind at the start of talks were rare, occurring in only 20% of our dyads. The majority of talks began with one speaker simply taking their first turn. Explicit verbal turn transitions (e.g., "Sean's going to tell you…") were also rare, occurring in only 30% of talks, and only once or twice in each of these. Nonverbal behavior was obscured in 29% of the turn transitions (with the video showing a presentation slide). Of the visible transitions, the current presenter gazed at the next speaker when it was their turn to speak 36% of the time, and gestured at them 6% of the time. Gaze transitions appeared to most frequently represent listener behavior – in which the current speaker is passively attending to the next speaker once they start – and only rarely represent proactive signals to the next speaker that it was their turn.

DEVELOPMENT OF DYNAMICDUO

Informed by the findings of our presentation corpus analysis, we designed the DynamicDuo system, which supports dual presentations between human and virtual presenters. Implemented as an add-in in PowerPoint 2013 [17], our system consists of three primary components: (1) a *life-size co-presenter agent* that exhibits a range of verbal and non-verbal behaviors; (2) a *collaborative note authoring* tool that enables human-agent note scripting at slide level; (3) a *collaborative presentation environment* that is integrated into the PowerPoint's slideshow delivery mode. Unlike other virtual presenter systems, DynamicDuo enables presenters to incorporate different interaction formats into a dual presentation using a simple interface seamlessly integrated into PowerPoint, without the need for any markup scripting commands. This eliminates any cognitive overhead associated with learning complex scripting languages.

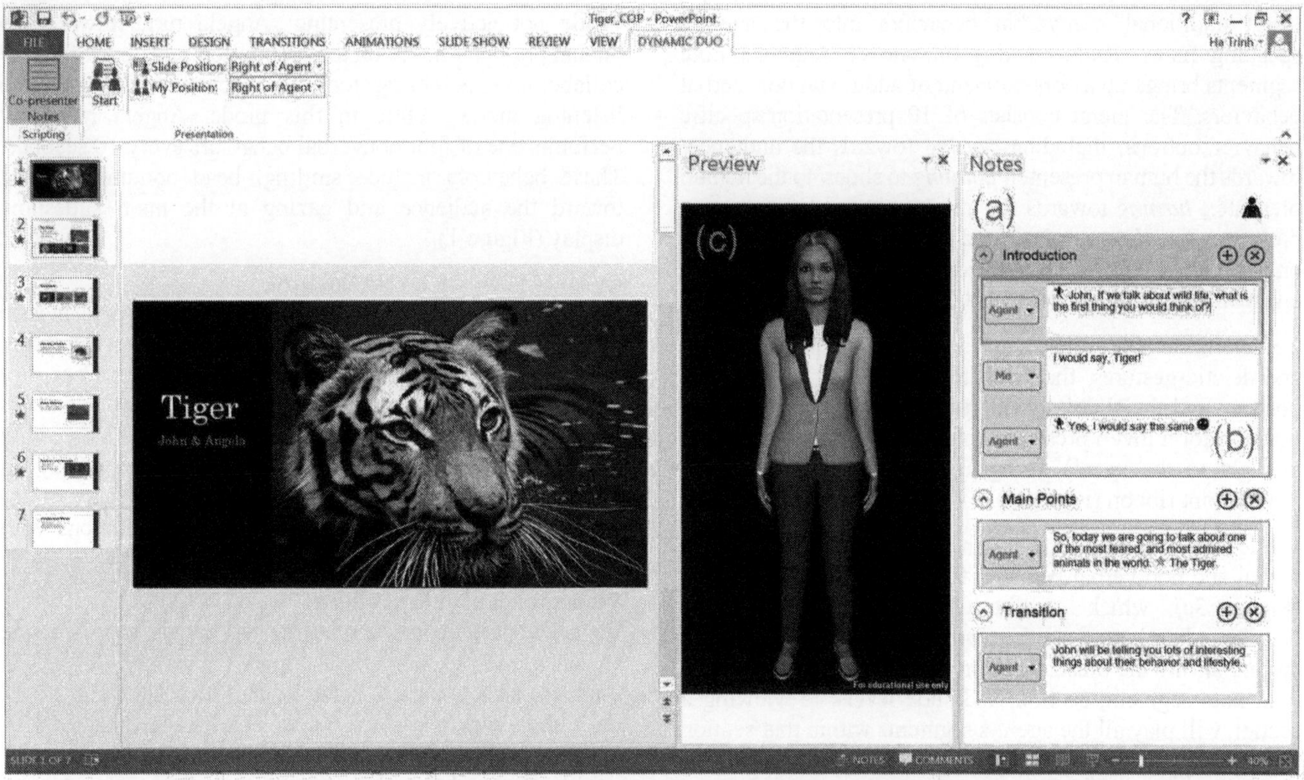

Figure 3. Collaborative note authoring interface with: (a) human-agent note segments; (b) icons representing manually added non-verbal behaviors; (c) agent speaking preview.

Co-presenter Agent: Angela

Our virtual presenter, Angela, is an animated human-like character developed using the Unity game engine (Figure 2). In terms of visual appearance, Angela was designed with a highly realistic look and appears to be multicultural in ethnicity. Synthesized speech is used to generate Angela's speech in real-time using CereProc's Speech Synthesis Engine [3]. Using viseme callbacks from the text to speech engine, Angela lip-syncs the synthesized speech using blend shape animations.

Angela is also capable of displaying a variety of non-verbal behaviors, including facial expressions of affect (smile, neutral, concern), eyebrow movement, directional gazes, head nods, posture shifts, and contrastive, beat (emphasis), and deictic gestures (e.g. pointing to a slide). A number of these behaviors are parameterized to allow for variable degrees of expression. Figure 2 illustrates four of Angela's non-verbal behaviors.

The majority of the agent's non-verbal behaviors are automatically generated using BEAT (Behavior Expression Animation Toolkit) [5]. Given the agent's speaking text, BEAT performs linguistic and contextual analysis of the text and automatically inserts five types of nonverbal behavior: *beats* (formless hand waves for emphasis, that account for approximately 50% of naturally occurring gestures), *eyebrow raises* (for emphasis), *gaze toward/away from* the conversational partner (for turn-taking), *contrastive hand gestures* (marking two items being contrasted, such as "Is it good or bad?"), and *posture shifts* to mark topic boundaries (based on analysis of discourse markers such as "anyways").

Collaborative Note Authoring

DynamicDuo enables the human presenter to enter human-agent speaking notes using the *Co-presenter Notes* side pane built in PowerPoint (Figure 3), which can be activated by clicking the corresponding control on the PowerPoint ribbon. As the presenter selects a slide, the system automatically creates placeholders for three note sections: *Introduction*, *Main Points*, and *Transition* (Figure 3a). These structured notes provide enhanced support for speech organization, while encouraging presenters to prepare for transitions, which are particularly important for smooth human-agent interaction.

Each note section is further divided into a series of note segments, each of which can be assigned to either the co-presenter agent or the human presenter (Figure 3a). The presenter can insert or remove selected note segments by clicking appropriate buttons on the side pane. Our note authoring interface provides a simple, yet flexible mechanism to incorporate different dyadic interaction formats identified in our presentation corpus analysis. For instance, Figure 3a shows an example slide note that contains an embedded dialogue in the introduction section, followed by main points and transition sections assigned to the agent.

In addition to BEAT's automatically generated non-verbal behaviors, our system also enables the presenter to manually insert additional non-verbal behaviors into the agent's speaking notes. Right-clicking on one of Angela's note segments brings up a context menu of additional non-verbal behaviors. The menu consists of 10 presentation-specific behavior options, including: *gazing* towards the audience/ towards the human presenter, *pointing* to slides/ to the human presenter, *turning* towards the audience/towards the human presenter, *facial expressions*, and *playing selected animation* on the current slide. Each inserted behavior is represented by a visual icon in the note segment (Figure 3b).

To determine appropriate directions of gazes, posture shifts and deictic gestures, the presenter can specify their spatial position and the slide's position in reference to the agent's position for a given presentation room (i.e. either at the left or right to the agent), using appropriate controls on the PowerPoint ribbon (Figure 3).

While authoring agent's notes, the presenter can preview her verbal and non-verbal behavior from the *Preview* side pane (Figure 3c), which can be displayed by clicking the corresponding button on the *Co-presenter Notes* pane. Our system allows the presenter to preview the agent's speech at both note segment, section, and slide levels. Previewing a section will play all the agent's segments within that section sequentially, while previewing at slide level will play all the agent's segments in the current slide.

Collaborative Presentation Environment

To present with the co-presenter agent, the presenter enters our *collaborative presentation environment* by clicking the Start button on the PowerPoint ribbon (Figure 3). Once started, PowerPoint projects its standard slideshow view to the first external display and optionally displays the standard presenter view (with timing and speaking notes) onto to presenter's computer screen (Figure 1). The speaking notes are arranged into human-agent's note segments clearly labeled and separated by blank lines. The co-presenter agent is projected onto a second external standing display, allowing Angela to appear life-size, as shown in Figure 1.

In the presentation mode, the presenter advances the slides and cues the co-presenter agent's speech using an IR remote control from Turning Technologies [25] with four buttons: Next Slide, Previous Slide, Speak, and Stop. The Next and Previous Slide buttons advance the PowerPoint slides as usual, while the Speak button cues Angela to present the next available agent segments on the current slide. Once cued to speak, Angela presents her segments while automatically advancing the slides and playing pre-specified animations, and stopping when she reaches the next note segment of the human presenter. Angela performs a posture shift to turn and gaze toward the human presenter as an indicator of turn-giving. At any point during the presentation, the human presenter can pause the agent's speech using the Stop button. This allows the presenter to spontaneously elaborate on the agent's speech, or navigate to different slides in response to feedback and questions from the audience. The presenter can also resume the agent's speech using the Speak button.

While not actively presenting, Angela turns toward the human presenter based on the orientation selected within the collaborative authoring tool, and goes into an attentive listening mode. While in this mode, Angela randomly performs one of four nonverbal behaviors every 10 seconds. These behaviors include smiling, head nodding, turning toward the audience and gazing at the main slideshow display (Figure 1).

EVALUATION OF DYNAMICDUO

To examine the effectiveness of our co-presentation approach in improving the experience of both presenters and audiences, we conducted two user studies. Our *Presenter* study evaluated the presenter experience of preparing and co-presenting with Angela against solo-presenting with conventional presentation software (PowerPoint 2013). In our follow-up *Judge* study, we compared the quality of co-presentations with Angela against sole presentations with standard PowerPoint, as perceived by an audience.

Presenter Study: Procedure

We asked participants to rehearse and deliver two 7-minute presentations on comparable topics (Lions and Tigers) in English using prepared PowerPoint slide decks and notes. Each slide deck contained 6 slides and approximately 850-word supporting notes, covering 16 key points, in addition to introduction and transition notes. One of the presentations was co-presented with Angela, while the other was a sole presentation with the standard version of PowerPoint 2013. This study scenario is well-grounded since delivering pre-scripted and rehearsed presentations with minor or no variance is common, as evidenced in our analysis of TED talks and previous research on presentation rehearsal [24].

The study was a within-subject, counterbalanced design across two sessions. Each session lasted between 60-90 minutes, with 1 to 6 days between sessions. The ordering of the conditions (Human-Agent vs. Human-only) and the slide decks were randomly assigned and counterbalanced. Each presentation was videotaped for later evaluation.

Human-Agent Session: We asked participants to rehearse and deliver a presentation with Angela using the DynamicDuo system. We added the notes into the *Co-presenter Notes* side pane in advance. We distributed the slides and notes between the human presenter and Angela as follows: In slide 1, Angela and the human presenter engaged in a scripted dialogue in the introduction, followed by the human presenter's parts. At the end of slide 1, the human presenter transitioned to Angela, who presented slides 2 and 3 before transitioning back to the human presenter. Slides 4 and 5 were presented by the human presenter, and Angela took turn again to present slide 6.

At the beginning of the session, we introduced participants to the scenario of presenting a pre-made slide deck, and gave them brief instructions on presenting with Angela using DynamicDuo. We then gave the participants 30 minutes to rehearse their presentation, before delivering their videotaped presentation. We conducted a semi-structured interview at the end of the session eliciting their attitudes towards presentation preparation and delivery with Angela.

Human-only Session: In this session, we asked participants to rehearse and deliver their presentation without Angela, using the standard version of PowerPoint. Notes were pre-loaded into the PowerPoint notes section, in which introduction, main points, and transitions were clearly separated using blank lines.

We gave participants brief instructions on the notes and Slide Show mode of PowerPoint, then gave them 30 minutes to prepare before delivering their videotaped presentation. We concluded the session with a semi-structured interview.

Presenter Study: Measures

Presenters were assessed using the following self-report measures:

Communication Competence: Assessed at intake using the Self-Perceived Communication Competence Scale [15].

State Anxiety: Assessed prior to each presentation using the State Anxiety questionnaire [23].

Speaker Confidence: Assessed at intake and after each presentation using the Personal Report of Confidence as a Speaker questionnaire [20].

Virtual Co-presenter Rating: Assessed after the human-agent presentation using a 6-question, 7-point scale measure.

Presenter Study: Participants

We recruited 13 students and professionals (4 male, 9 female, ages 23-62, mean 39) via an online advertisement. Of these 13 participants, 8 were native English speakers and 5 were non-native English speakers. The inclusion of both native and non-native English speakers allowed us to examine the effect of speech and language abilities on the presenter's presentation experience. Our participants had varying presentation experience and occupational backgrounds, ranging from law, medicine to administration. Participants were compensated for their participation.

Presenter Study: Quantitative Results

12 presenters successfully completed the study resulting in 24 total interactions, 12 with Angela and 12 without. Participant P1 (a female native English speaker) had to be dropped from the study due to technical issues.

Of the 12 remaining participants, 4 were categorized as high competence public speakers, 2 were categorized as low competence public speakers, and 6 had moderate competence according to the Self-Perceived Communication Competence Scale.

Our data was normal according to results of Shapiro-Wilk tests, thus we performed parametric tests (repeated-measure ANOVAs and t-tests) to examine the effects of our DynamicDuo system on the presenters' state anxiety and speaker confidence.

State Anxiety

There was a significant interaction effect of *Condition* (human-agent vs. human-only) and *Native Language* (native vs. non-native English speakers) on state anxiety, ($F_{1,10}$=8.909, p=.014, partial η^2=.471) (Figure 4). The virtual presenter significantly decreased state anxiety for non-native English speakers (t(4)=3.492, p=.025, d=1.562). There were no significant effects of condition on state anxiety for native English speakers.

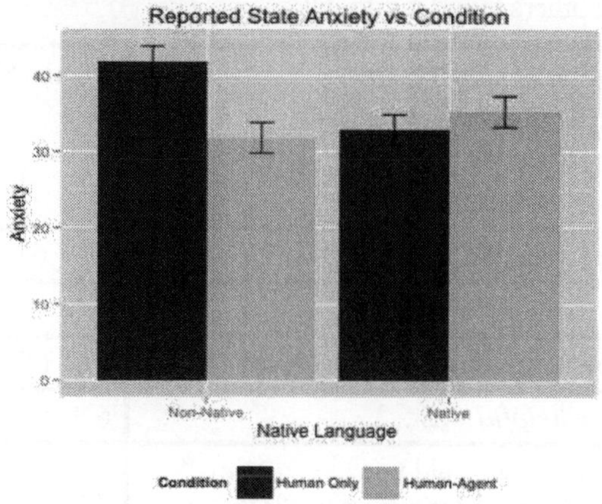

Figure 4. Self-reported state anxiety for human-only and human-agent conditions from non-native and native participants.

Speaker Confidence

There was a significant interaction effect of *Condition*Native Language* on speaker confidence ($F_{1,10}$=11.934, p=.006, partial η^2=.544) (Figure 5). The co-presenter agent significantly increased confidence for non-native speakers (t(4)=4.083, p=.015, d=1.826), while there were no significant differences for native speakers.

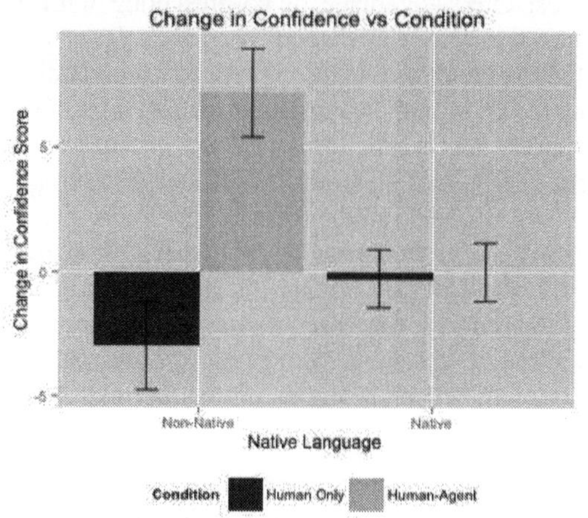

Figure 5. Self-reported speaker confidence for human-only and human-agent conditions from non-native and native participants.

Virtual Co-presenter Ratings

The ratings for the co-presenter agent were highly positive across all participants (Table 1). The virtual presenter was rated to be satisfying to work with (M = 6.5, SD = .67), likeable (M = 5.83, SD = 1.27), trustworthy (M = 6.58, SD = .9), helpful (M = 6.3, SD = 1.15) and participants expressed that they desired to use the system in their future presentations (M = 6.3, SD = 1). The one rating for which we received mixed results was ease of use (M = 4.25, SD = 2.56), since some participants found the system easy to use while others found it difficult.

Rating of Co-Presenter: *(Scale Measures from 1-7)* *1 – Not at All* *7 – Very Much*	**Mean (SD)**
How ***satisfied*** are you with...?	6.5 (.67)
How much do you ***like***...?	5.83 (1.27)
How much do you feel you ***trust***...?	6.58 (.9)
How ***helpful*** was...?	6.3 (1.15)
How much would you like to ***give future presentations*** with...?	6.3 (1)
How **easy** was it to use...?	4.25 (2.56)

Table 1. Average ratings of the virtual co-presenter.

Presenter Study: Qualitative Findings

We conducted semi-structured interviews at the end of each session, eliciting the presenter's experience of preparing and delivering a presentation with the agent and suggestions for improvement. We performed high-level coding on our transcribed interviews and derived three main themes related to workload, stage pressure and feelings of assurance.

Reducing Workload through Division of Labor

The most cited advantage of co-presenting with a virtual presenter was that it *"relieved you from a lot of workload"* [P13] during both presentation preparation and delivery. By sharing the cognitive *"burden of absorbing a lot of material"* [P3] under strict time pressure, our co-presenter agent reduced the human's memorization load, allowing them to focus and polish other aspects of their presentation, alleviating the nervousness of *"forgetting so many things"* [P9] and consequently helping them *"feel more confident"* [P6]. This reduced workload was especially appreciated by our non-native speakers, who often operate under a heavy cognitive load when presenting in their second language.

While reducing workload through shared content and responsibility, co-presenting with the agent imposed an extra coordination load as the presenters had to *"memorize the proper time to interact with the agent"* [P6]. During delivery, it required the presenters to *"multi-task, remember facts, deliver facts to the audience, try to interact with the audience and at the same time remember which button to push"* [P5]. For some participants, this added *"mental gymnastics"* [P12] caused additional stress during delivery. However, many participants expressed the confidence to *"master pretty quickly"* [P5] with practice. These findings suggest the need for further research to minimize the amount of coordination required to use the system, with possible integration of a natural user interface, such as speech or gesture recognition.

Reducing Stage Pressure through Shared Attention

In line with social impact theory and previous research, many participants stated that Angela helped with sharing *"the audience attention, and drew a little bit of the heat away"* [P5], which was particularly helpful for highly anxious presenters. It also allowed the human presenters more time to *"figure out what to say next"* [P8] while the agent was speaking, to *"observe the audience for their reaction"* [P6], enabling them to mentally review and rehearse their notes, leading to reduced note reliance and boosted confidence in their delivery.

Increasing Assurance with a Reliable Assistant

The dependability was also cited as being a key characteristic of our co-presenter agent. Comparing to a human co-presenter, the agent provided a high level of reliability, assuring the participants that *"there are going to be no curveballs"* [P5] and that *"she is not going to mess up the presentation"* [P2].

While being highly reliable and consistent, our agent still lacked the ability to provide spontaneous support, e.g. providing prompts when her co-presenters forget their lines. Thus, a future improvement could be to provide a monitoring and backup mechanism to track the presentation progress and automatically provide timely, appropriate cues for the human presenter.

To summarize, our qualitative findings demonstrated that our co-presenter agent helped improve the presentation experience for the majority of our participants, particularly for novice and non-native speakers. One of our participants emphasized: *"this was one of the greatest experience of my presenting"* [P9], while P2 stated: *"It helped me as much as someone could help me"*.

Judge Study: Procedure

In this study, we aimed to evaluate the relative quality of the 12 pairs of videotaped presentations (Human-Agent vs. Human-only), which were delivered by the 12 participants in our Presenter study.

We ask each judge participant to watch two pairs of videotaped presentations. After watching each pair, judges compared each presentation pair on six criteria adopted from [24], including: organization, content coverage, note reliance, speech, timing and pacing, and overall quality. Each criterion was judged on a 4-point ordinal scale of "no difference", "slight difference", "moderate difference", and "substantial difference", with an indication of the superior presentation, if any. The ordering of the presentations were randomly assigned and counterbalanced across the judge participants. In addition, after watching each presentation of a pair, judges were also asked to evaluate the *human presenters* using a 7-item, 7-point scale questionnaire assessing competency, engagingness, nervousness, understandability, excitement, entertainingness and satisfaction. Each session lasted approximately 60 minutes.

Judge Study: Participants

12 judges were recruited for the study (4 male, 8 female, ages 24-58, mean 39, J1-J12) via an online advertisement. Our judges had varying presentation experience and occupational backgrounds, with four of them reported as expert presenters (researchers and lecturers in the field of communication). Our participants were compensated for their participation.

Judge Study: Quantitative Results

12 judges successfully completed the study resulting in 24 comparisons. We performed non-parametric tests (Wilcoxon signed-rank tests) to examine the effects of our co-presenter agent on the judges' ratings of presentation quality and human presenters.

Presentation Rating

There were significant differences on the judges' ratings of *note reliance* ($p<.05$), *speech* ($p<.01$) and *overall presentation quality* ($p<.05$), in favor of the Human-Agent condition. No significant differences were found for organization, timing and pacing, and content coverage.

The inter-rater reliability of the judges was moderate (Kappa = 0.439), which could be explained by the highly subjective nature of the rating task, the varying degrees of presentation experience across the judges, and the limited training given on the task.

Audience Perception of Human Presenters

There were no significant differences between the conditions on the judges' ratings of the human presenters for any of the seven measures. These results indicate that employing the support of the virtual co-presenter did not result in significant lower ratings of the human presenters, while significantly improving the overall presentation quality.

Judge Study: Qualitative Findings

We conducted a semi-structured interview at the end of each judging session, prompting for the judges' impressions of the overall presentation quality as well as their evaluation of the human presenters and the co-presenter agent. We performed high-level coding on our transcribed interviews and categorized the feedback into three themes.

Improving Content Understandability

Our judges consistently reported the role of the co-presenter agent in elevating the understandability of the presentations with her clear speech delivery that was timely synchronized with slide visuals: *"The character was able to deliver a lot of information without any uhm or ah, and clearly knew what was going on, and there was synchrony with the presentation aid"* [J7]. When presenting with inexperienced human speakers, *"who are not as strong, who are less confident with the material and less confident with their overall public speaking"* [J2], the professional and clear speech delivered by the agent provided a *"nice balance"* [J2], helping the audience *"take your mind off of the human's mistakes"* [J6]. Clearly planned transitions between human-agent sections also resulted in a *"more structured"* [J4] presentation with *"better previews"* [J4], further aiding the presentation understandability.

Injecting Variety into Presentations

As *"it can get monotonous listening to one voice the whole time"* [J8], having co-presenters on stage helped to *"break up the monotony of a PowerPoint lecture"* [J4], thereby maintaining the audience engagement. The variety of interaction formats, such as rehearsed dialogue and iterative turn-taking, also created a *"good interplay"* [J2] between the two presenters when the interactions were well-coordinated. Switching between the different presenters with different voices using different interaction models, however, could impose an extra cognitive load on the audience. Therefore, in the design of dual presentations, it is important to maintain a balance in the amount and the formats of interactions.

Additionally, many of the judges reported the lack of inflection and emotion in Angela's voice, a common problem of synthesized voices. Further research is warrant to add emotional variance to our agent's speech.

Increasing Audience Engagement

Most judges reported the novelty effects of a virtual co-presenter in attracting the audience's attention: *"People that may automatically yawn at a human may sit up and like 'oh what is it about' when they see an animated character. So it can spice it up a little"* [J1]. Judges were generally attracted to the agent's highly realistic appearance and human-like behaviors, as well as her charisma: *"She had more charisma, she seemed much more posh, much more prepared [...]. I liked her mannerism, I liked the way she turned around and looked at the screen but made eye contact with the audience" [J4].*

This novelty effect from the audience's initial exposure to the agent could, however, divert the audience attention from the presented content: *"it makes the listeners more engaged in the newness of her rather than what you are actually presenting about"* [J8]. Longitudinal studies are required to understand the effectiveness of the co-presenter agent on the audience engagement when they are exposed to the agent over a longer-term period.

Assessment of Classroom Acceptance

In addition to controlled studies, we have also further assessed our system in classroom settings. One of our co-authors gave a 90-minute lecture to 20 undergraduates with the virtual co-presenter. Students commented on the engaging nature of the co-presenter agent: *"It was a fresh approach to class"*, *"It forced me to pay attention a little more"*, and *"The change in presenter changed things up nicely and led to better attention"*. This positive feedback further confirmed the acceptability and practicality of our system.

LIMITATIONS AND FUTURE WORK

Results of our user studies provided a strong support for the acceptability and potential of a virtual co-presenter to improve the overall experience of both audiences and presenters, especially for novice and non-native speakers. However, with the small sample size and the presence of confounding factors such as novelty effects, it is difficult to generalize these findings without further studies. As future work, we aim to evaluate our system in longitudinal studies within more naturalistic settings, using larger and more diverse user groups who have varying speech, language and public speaking skills.

Our current co-presenter system was relatively simplistic and only provided limited support for extemporaneous presentations. We plan to improve the usability of our system through the incorporation of more natural human-agent interaction modalities, potentially using speech and gesture recognition. We also aim to employ sensing technologies for real-time monitoring of presentation progress, human presenter's performance and audience interaction. This would allow our system to offer timely support for the human presenter and dynamically adapt to changes in the presentation context. Finally, we wish to explore the applicability of virtual agents to various presentation formats, from presenting in front of an audience to remote presentations in virtual environments and online lectures.

ACKNOWLEGEMENTS

We thank Elizabeth Bates and Karlyle Pilones for their help on our user studies, and Zach Berwaldt for his support on the design of our virtual presenter.

REFERENCES

1. André, E., Rist, T., & Müller, J. (1998). WebPersona: a lifelike presentation agent for the World-Wide Web. Knowledge-Based Systems, 11(1), 25-36.
2. Apple Keynote. http://www.apple.com/iwork/keynote.
3. Aylett, M. P., & Pidcock, C. J. (2007). The CereVoice characterful speech synthesiser SDK. Lecture Notes in Computer Science, 4722, 413.
4. Bishop, J. B., Bauer, K.W., & Becker, E.T. (1998). A survey of counseling needs of male and female college students. Journal of College Student Development, 39, 205-210.
5. Cassell, J., Vilhjálmsson, H. H., & Bickmore, T. (2004). BEAT: The behavior expression animation toolkit. Life-Like Characters, 163-185. Springer Berlin Heidelberg.
6. Daly, J. A., McCroskey, J. C., Ayres, J., Hopf, T., & Ayres, D. M. (1997). Avoiding communication: shyness, reticence, & communication apprehension (2nd ed.). Hampton Press.
7. Daly, J. A., Vangelisti, A. L., & Weber, D. J. (1995). Speech anxiety affects how people prepare speeches: A protocol analysis of the preparation processes of speakers. Communication Monographs, 62, 383 -397.
8. Edge, D., Savage, J., Yatani, K. (2013). HyperSlides: dynamic presentation prototyping. CHI'13, 671-680.
9. Goodman, A. (2006). Why bad presentations happen to good causes. Andy Goodman & Cause Communication.
10. Hoque, M. E., Courgeon, M., Martin, J. C., Mutlu, B., & Picard, R. W. (2013). MACH: my automated conversation coach. UBICOMP'13, 697-706.
11. Jackson, J. M., & Latané, B. (1981). All alone in front of all those people: Stage fright as a function of number and type of co-performers and audience. Journal of Personality and Social Psychology, 40(1), 73.
12. Kang, N., Brinkman, W. P., van Riemsdijk, M. B., & Neerincx, M. A. (2013). An expressive virtual audience with flexible behavioral styles. IEEE Transactions on Affective Computing, 4(4), 326-340.
13. Kasl, S. V., & Mahl, G. F. (1965). The relationship of disturbances and hesitations in spontaneous speech to anxiety. Journal of Applied Behavioral Analysis, 1, 425-433.
14. Latané, B., & Nida, S. (1980). Social impact theory and group influence: A social engineering perspective. Psychology of Group Influence.
15. McCroskey, J. C., & McCroskey, L. L. (1988). Self-report as an approach to measuring communication competence. Communication Research Reports, 5, 108-113.
16. Menzel, K. E., & Carrell, L. J. (1994). The relationship between preparation and performance in public speaking. Communication Education, 43, 17 - 26.
17. Microsoft PowerPoint. http://office.microsoft.com/en-us/powerpoint.
18. Nijholt, A., van Welbergen, H., & Zwiers, J. (2005). Introducing an embodied virtual presenter agent in a virtual meeting room. Artificial Intelligence and Applications, 579-584.
19. Noma, T., Badler, N. I., & Zhao, L. (2000). Design of a virtual human presenter. Center for Human Modeling and Simulation, 75.
20. Paul G. L. (1966). Insight and desensitization in psychotherapy: An experiment in anxiety reduction. Stanford University Press.
21. Pertaub, D. P., Slater, M., & Barker, C. (2002). An experiment on public speaking anxiety in response to three different types of virtual audience. Presence: Teleoperators and Virtual Environments, 11(1), 68-78.
22. Saket, B., Yang, S., Tan, H., Yatani, K., & Edge, D. (2014). TalkZones: section-based time support for presentations. MobileHCI'14, 263-272.
23. Spielberger, C. D. (1989). State-trait anxiety inventory: bibliography (2nd ed.). Consulting Psychologists Press.
24. Trinh, H., Yatani, K., & Edge, D. (2014). PitchPerfect: integrated rehearsal environment for structured presentation preparation. CHI'14, 1571-1580.
25. Turning Technologies. http://www.turningtechnologies.com/response-solutions/responsecard-ir.

From User-Centered to Adoption-Centered Design: A Case Study of an HCI Research Innovation Becoming a Product

Parmit K. Chilana[1], Andrew J. Ko[2] and Jacob O. Wobbrock[2]

[1]Management Sciences
University of Waterloo
Waterloo, ON Canada N2L 3G1
pchilana@uwaterloo.ca

[2]The Information School | DUB Group
University of Washington
Seattle, WA 98195 USA
{ajko, wobbrock}@uw.edu

ABSTRACT
As we increasingly strive for scientific rigor and generalizability in HCI research, should we entertain any hope that by doing good science, our discoveries will eventually be more transferrable to industry? We present an in-depth case study of how an HCI research innovation goes through the process of transitioning from a university project to a revenue-generating startup financed by venture capital. The innovation is a novel contextual help system for the Web, and we reflect on the different methods used to evaluate it and how research insights endure attempted dissemination as a commercial product. Although the extent to which any innovation succeeds commercially depends on a number of factors like market forces, we found that our HCI innovation with user-centered origins was in a unique position to gain traction with customers and garner buy-in from investors. However, since end users were not the buyers of our product, a strong user-centered focus obfuscated other critical needs of the startup and pushed out perspectives of non-user-centered stakeholders. To make the research-to-product transition, we had to focus on *adoption-centered design*, the process of understanding and designing for adopters and stakeholders of the product. Our case study raises questions about how we evaluate the novelty and research contributions of HCI innovations with respect to their potential for commercial impact.

Keywords
Commercialization; productization; dissemination; research impact; technology transfer; adoption-centered design.

ACM Classification Keywords
H.5.2. Information interfaces and presentation (*e.g.*, HCI): User Interfaces—*evaluation / methodology*.

INTRODUCTION
What constitutes success for a system innovation emerging from human-computer interaction (HCI) research? One way to address this question might be to look at how well the design is validated in the target context and to what extent its findings are generalizable. Yet there are numerous debates and disagreements within HCI about what constitutes an adequate systems evaluation [8,22]. Some scholars have even claimed that the bar for evaluation at UIST, CHI, and other HCI publication venues is increasingly unrealistic for systems papers [1,14] by insisting on having results from controlled studies or large cohorts of representative users.

Since HCI is still an evolving field that is striving to bridge multiple disciplines, debates and disagreements about adequate system evaluation and what makes a system successful are necessary. Part of doing "good science" is ensuring that our work has rigor and that we are able to match our claimed contributions with actual findings. But as we strive for scientific rigor and generalizability in research, should we entertain any hope that by doing good science, our discoveries will eventually be more transferrable to users or customers? Or are such concerns beyond the scope of applied technology researchers in HCI? In short, must we care?

Despite decades of HCI research, these are not easy questions to answer and indeed, they have rarely been tackled head-on (with a few noteworthy exceptions [7,9,11]). There has been repeated concern that even though we are accumulating great innovations in the HCI field, we rarely see HCI innovations develop into commercial products [11]. Given that researchers usually lack the knowledge, resources, connections, experience, interest, or time to pursue commercialization [26], perhaps the lack of products emerging from HCI research is not surprising. But could another hindrance to HCI technology transfer be that we often look at our innovations "too narrowly" by focusing on generalizability only from end users' perspectives [9]? What if end users are not the paying customers so vital for getting a product to market?

For any commercial product to successfully emerge, there are multiple stakeholders beyond end users, such as business customers, target buyers, approvers, administrators, regulators, financers, reporters, analysts, and more [5]. Although we have seen the development of methods in HCI and usability practice that allow researchers and practitioners to understand stakeholder needs [23], we rarely see these methods employed in system evaluations for the sake of beyond-the-user market adoption. Could these additional perspectives give HCI innovations better chances at being adopted? Or would employing such methods distract from delivering high-quality, innovative research?

CHI 2015, April 18-23, 2015, Seoul, Republic of Korea

http://dx.doi.org/10.1145/2702123.2702412

In this paper, we investigate how one HCI innovation is transitioning from a research project to a commercial product and startup business, and how well the research foundation for the innovation generalizes along this path. Specifically, we present an in-depth case study of several evaluation methods applied to *LemonAid* [4] (Figure 1) over the last five years, from its inception as a university research project to commercialization through a venture capital financed startup called *AnswerDash*.[1] We trace the motivations for adopting different HCI methods at different stages during the evolution of the research, product, and startup business and the tradeoffs made between user-centered design and what we call *adoption-centered design*—understanding and designing for product adopters and stakeholders beyond just end users.

The main contribution of this paper is providing insight into how an HCI innovation can evolve from an academic endeavor to a commercial product when the end user is not the main adopter or customer of the system. In our discussion, we tackle the question of whether HCI technology researchers should develop and employ methods for concerning themselves with beyond-the-user stakeholder concerns—stakeholders that lie along the "adoption path" that must be trod for innovations to gain market traction and become widespread.

RELATED WORK

To contextualize our case study, we focused our literature review on three areas: (1) perspectives on evaluation and generalizability of HCI innovations; (2) experiences of technology transfer from research in related areas, such as software engineering; and (3) the challenges inherent in the process of commercializing disruptive innovations.

Generalizability and System Evaluation in HCI Research

The concept of generalizability in research refers to the extent to which we can use research results based on specific cases to form abstractions about the general case, or the degree to which empirical results can be generalized to an entire population [16,17]. In the context of HCI, an important form of generalization is the extent to which the design of a system is applicable to a broader set of target users [18]. In the design stage, we strive for generalizability by moving from individual user data (*i.e.*, through formative studies) to general requirements for the system being designed. In the evaluation stage, generalization becomes the process of determining the extent to which study results achieved with a particular population doing specific tasks with a system can apply to the target user population [18].

The extent to which we can demonstrate generalizability varies based on the research domain and type of method used [16]. In technical HCI research, the debate has often been about showing the generalizability of interaction techniques versus whole interactive systems. For example, unlike novel interaction techniques that can be validated through controlled experimentation, novel systems can be

[1] http://www.answerdash.com

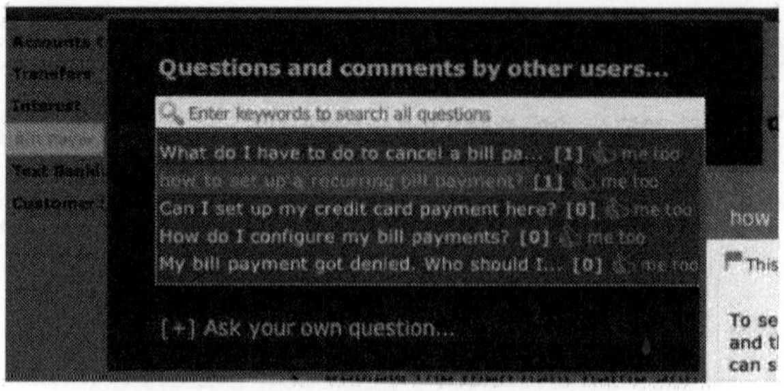

Figure 1. The LemonAid retrieval interface.

difficult to evaluate as they often introduce new platforms or capabilities that do not have obvious benchmark systems for comparison [8,22]. Systems in emerging areas such as social computing face additional intractable challenges—for example, evaluations may be penalized for snowball sampling or for not demonstrating exponential growth [1].

Increasingly, evaluations of systems in HCI stress external validity and ecological validity for increased generalizability [18]. Citing the potential perils of limited usability tests, questions have risen about prematurely validating an innovation before "a culture" is formed around it [8]. Similarly, emphasis is being placed on the need for evaluations to consider more realistic situations, tasks, and users [22].

At what point do we know that our evaluation is sufficient to demonstrate success, at least in research? What if end users are not the eventual customers, adopters, or buyers of our HCI innovations? Does the soundness of our user-centered methods matter to transferability? Although ideas about the applicability and generalizability of HCI research systems have been previously raised, to our knowledge, no work has directly investigated the link between the soundness of HCI technology research conducted and the likelihood that a system will eventually see widespread adoption and market traction. Our case study adds another dimension to this debate: if we care about adoption, and if adoption depends on more than end users, are user-centered evaluation criteria enough to maximize our chances for success?

Perspectives on Tech-Transfer in Software Engineering

While HCI is a relatively young field, technology transfer has a long history in more established domains, such as software engineering. Experiences of software engineering researchers going through technology transfer offer a wide range of perspectives—from internal transfer at NASA [27] and IBM [6], to formation of a startup from a research lab [19], to several other examples of tech-transfer successes and failures in software engineering research [15,26]. One of the main themes reflected in these perspectives is that successful tech-transfer is not only about an idea or its implementation—it is about knowing the audience for the technology and establishing relationships with customers to understand market needs.

Our experience shows that compared to less user-centered computing innovations, HCI innovations can perhaps get a "head start" on adoption because they inherently consider end users as the audience. However, similar to questions that have already been raised about HCI technology transfer [7,9,11], we also ask if the strong focus on end users is necessary for having impact through commercialization if software ventures clearly have different goals.

Disruptive Innovations in the Marketplace

While our case study raises some questions about the limits of user-centered evaluation methods for achieving commercialization, we realize that it is also important to understand perspectives on market forces that are not unique to HCI, but bound to affect *any* innovation [21].

For example, Christenson [5] coined the term, *disruptive innovation* to describe a technology that shakes up an existing market because of the radical change it brings, but may, in fact, be "too radical." Wary of solutions ahead of their time, market leaders are often inclined to support *sustaining innovations*, which are well-matched to well-understood customer needs. Although disruptive innovations can be successful if enough early adopters are convinced and an appropriate market strategy can be created, commercialization of such innovations is a challenge [24].

Our case study shows that even though our novel contextual help tool succeeded in several user-centered research evaluations, it faced challenges while entering the mainstream market through early adopters. Such challenges were not anticipated during the research phase where the focus was on end user perceptions and usage.

BACKGROUND OF THE INNOVATION

The case study presented here is based on LemonAid, a novel selection-based crowdsourced contextual help tool and its transition to AnswerDash, a startup company based on LemonAid. We first give an overview of the original HCI research and its key features. For detailed information on LemonAid, readers are directed to our previous papers [3,4].

Motivation for LemonAid

Our initial motivation for inventing LemonAid was to help end users find answers to their questions that arise while using websites. Web-based technical support such as discussion forums, knowledge bases, FAQ pages, and social networking sites have been successful at ensuring that most technical support questions eventually receive helpful answers. Unfortunately, *finding* these answers is still difficult, since the queries that end users submit to search engines are often incomplete, imprecise, or use different vocabularies to describe the same problem. LemonAid improved the retrieval of relevant help by introducing a selection-based contextual help approach that embedded end users' questions and answers directly in the user interface (UI).

LemonAid User Interface and System Design

Instead of searching the web or scouring web forums, lists of frequently asked questions, or other knowledge bases, LemonAid allowed users to retrieve help by selecting a label, widget, image, or other UI element on any page of a website. The user's selection of a UI element triggered the retrieval of questions related to the selection (Figure 1) by matching the selection's contextual data against all the questions in the repository. The contextual data consisted of the underlying Document-Object Model (DOM) element's text, tag type, and location within the UI (described in detail in [3]). The retrieval algorithm used a relevance ranking approach, sorting questions based on the highest-scoring matches. In addition to viewing answers, users could also search for another question, submit their own question, or vote on the helpfulness of answers.

LemonAid worked with standard HTML pages, without making any assumptions about the implementation of the underlying website and did not require developers to use any specific UI toolkits. LemonAid presented contextual Q&A in a separate visual layer atop an application's UI that did not interfere with the underlying site's functionality. To add LemonAid to a site, developers had to extract text labels appearing in the UI from a web application's code and include the LemonAid framework in their client-side deployment with one line of JavaScript. The vision was that this small amount of technical work would significantly lower the barrier to adoption.

TOWARDS A GENERALIZABLE USER-CENTERED DESIGN: EVOLUTION OF THE RESEARCH PROTOTYPE

Consistent with expectations for an academic HCI research project, we focused on addressing user-centered concerns and showing the validity of our innovation from the end user's perspective. We first carried out a formative evaluation to inform the system and algorithm design, followed by an evaluation of the system's feasibility using crowdsourcing, and finally, a longitudinal field study to assess the innovation's ecological validity. As we progressed through each of these stages, our goal was to explicitly increase the scope of our innovation's generalizability (Figure 2). However, these activities were not conducted with commercialization in view; they were strictly knowledge-generating research activities. In later sections of this paper, we describe our commercialization efforts and how we had to make the transition to focus more on adopter and stakeholder perspectives rather than end users.

How do we solve the general problem? Informing the system design with a user study

The core problem that we first tackled was designing a way for end users to retrieve relevant questions asked by other end users on the website. The goal was to find a design so-

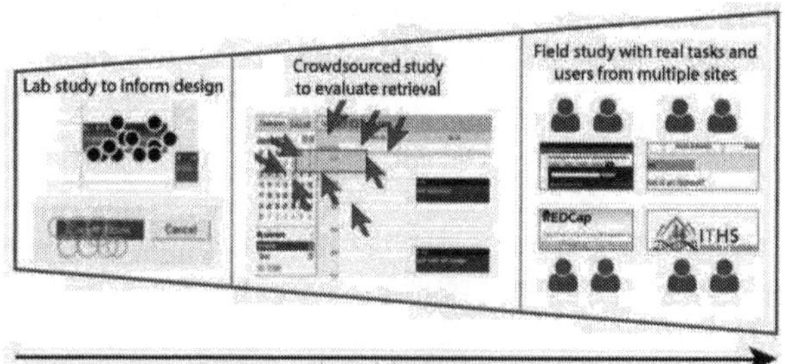

Figure 2. Increasing scope of evaluation at different stages to inform and evaluate design.

lution that would generalize across different sites and help scenarios and not be tied to the underlying implementation of the website or web application.

In exploring the design space of this concept, there were different types of contextual data that LemonAid could gather from the website to associate with relevant Q&A. Since building and testing all of these possible solutions would be time-intensive and costly, we decided to first use a low-fidelity paper-based approach to discern which aspects of the interface might be useful in discriminating between different help problems in the application.

We designed a paper-based *Wizard-of-Oz* study that reflected 12 different help-seeking scenarios from the help forums of Facebook, Google, and Wikipedia. The paper showed participants a printed screenshot and a brief paraphrased description of a help need. We provided physical stickers and asked participants to pretend that they had a "magic wand" to point anywhere in the interface to get help, indicated by placing the sticker somewhere on the screenshot.

This low-fidelity approach provided us with the key insight for designing a generalizable version of our selection-based retrieval interaction and algorithm: participants tended to select similar application-specific UI elements for similar help needs and different UI elements for different help needs, making UI elements useful discriminators. These findings suggested that LemonAid could determine similarity between selections largely based on the text on UI elements and leverage additional attributes of the selected DOM object such as its layout position and appearance.

Over the last five years, this key insight about how users can retrieve relevant Q&A by making UI element selections has been validated repeatedly. However, at the time, our paper-based study could only inform the novel interaction design, not provide evidence about the effectiveness of the retrieval approach for real-world sites and applications.

Does the system behave as intended? Assessing system feasibility using simulated data

In our second evaluation, our focus shifted to investigating the technical feasibility and effectiveness of our selection-based contextual retrieval interaction and algorithm. In particular, we focused on answering the following research question: *across a corpus of help-problem scenarios, how effective is LemonAid at retrieving relevant Q&A asked by other users based only on the current user's selection*?

To address this question, we used the Mechanical Turk (mTurk) platform to get access to a large number of users and their help selections. Alternatives, such as simulating the selections or running a lab study, were not feasible as we wanted our corpus to reflect crowdsourced selections.

Similar to the protocol in our formative study, we generated detailed help scenarios created from a random sample of 50 questions in *Google Calendar's* forums and instrumented different interactive screens of this calendar application to collect users' selections. Over 500 users on mTurk read one or more of 50 help scenarios and performed a help request by selecting a UI element relevant to those help scenarios.

We ran our retrieval algorithm against the 2,748 selections generated by the mTurk study. Since LemonAid used a ranked retrieval approach, we assessed our algorithm's performance based on the rank of the first relevant question among all of the retrieved questions matching an end user's selection. LemonAid's performance was promising, retrieving 1 or more results for 90.3% of the selections with a median rank of 2 across the whole corpus, meaning the relevant result was in the top 2 results most of the time.

In addition to the overall performance of the retrieval algorithm, it was important for us to understand its performance over time, as users were likely to ask more questions. In an initial test of the effect of corpus size, we found that the median rank of the results degraded as the number of selections increased, but that this was a slow degradation. Still, determining whether LemonAid's algorithm would scale to any live application and a growing database of Q&A was not considered within the scope of our evaluation. Our focus was primarily on the acceptability to users from an interactive perspective and the quality of the Q&A retrieval.

How does the system behave in the "real world?" Assessing ecological validity with field deployments

Although our retrieval evaluation was promising, its promise was based on pre-defined tasks and a simulated community of users through mTurk, which did not reflect how users may actually use Q&A sites for troubleshooting. Thus, we did not know whether the retrieval approach we developed was ecologically valid or actually helpful for users' real tasks in real applications. To investigate these questions, we worked on deploying LemonAid "in the wild" [2].

Since LemonAid was not designed to be a tool that end users could download on their own, we had to first find website owners who would be willing to add LemonAid to their site. We began by contacting a number of web teams at our university who offered web applications to support teaching and research. From the start, we had to "sell" our solution and its benefits to would-be adopters. Over the course of several weeks, we had many meetings with over a dozen software developers and site owners across campus. We showed them demos of what LemonAid would look like on their site, clarified that they did not need to modify their site, and assured them that they would only have to commit minimal time to seeding the initial Q&A database and answer new questions. After each meeting, we iterated on our design and implemented additional features to facilitate adoption—for example, we built features for monitoring and flagging user content, allowing teams to receive notifications when new questions were asked, and building basic analytics to show the evolution of Q&A during the deployment period. Since some of these university-based sites had thousands or more visitors a day, we had to spend additional weeks engineering our prototype to be robust across our field sites.

The four sites that adopted LemonAid included the university library's main homepage, our academic department's site, a clinical data capture application, and a personnel and grant management site at the university's medical school. The deployments across the four sites lasted between 6-15 weeks. A common adoption motivation among the host teams was to move away from one-on-one assistance, which was difficult for them to maintain with small teams. They were intrigued by the idea of answering a question once and making its retrieval easier for future end users.

The teams that were reluctant to try LemonAid were mainly concerned about the time it might take from their already constrained schedules and the quality of the content that end users might contribute. They also hesitated to change the look and feel of their website, even for a few days during the deployment study. (As we will discuss in our next section, uncovering more of these adoption concerns would have been helpful for our later commercialization efforts, but during our research, we were only focused on showing the validity of our design from the end user's perspective.)

Our main research questions were assessing whether the LemonAid Q&A retrieval approach would be helpful, usable, and desirable for reuse from the perspective of end users. Using data triangulation [12], we assessed these variables from over 1200 usage logs, 168 exit survey responses, and 36 follow-up interviews. Overall, we found that end users responded positively to LemonAid across all of our deployments. Our analysis showed that they selected "helpful" on answers over 73 % of the time across the four sites and this finding corroborated with the helpfulness responses on the survey. Further analysis showed that new or infrequent site users found LemonAid to be more helpful than frequent users, particularly for learning about unfamiliar features. In addition, the survey responses across all deployments indicated that over 72% of end users agreed that LemonAid was intuitive and that they would use this help feature again.

These results on end users' perspectives provided a strong contrast to literature on help systems that show users often fear clicking on help after their initial exposure to a help system [20]. Our findings suggested there was high potential in helping users retrieve relevant help using our approach on different kinds of websites and applications.

After our deployments, we again probed into the software team perspective and interviewed team members who had integrated LemonAid onto their site. In particular, the teams were intrigued by LemonAid's basic analytics dashboard that aggregated frequently accessed questions and their locations of occurrence. The team members agreed that they were not able to obtain such analytics data from anywhere else and that it could be a useful way to augment their existing usage-based analytics services, like Google Analytics.

Although our field study showed that LemonAid was successful in helping end users locate relevant Q&A, it also shed light on other technical and organizational issues that would have to be addressed for users to actually benefit from this tool. For example, whether LemonAid would actually be available for end users would require a website owner to adopt it effectively. However, since such concerns were not directly relevant to assessing the novelty or the generalizability of our approach for end users, we did not investigate them in depth.

Summary of Research Evaluations

After these three evaluations, we had learned many things. First, we had reasonable confidence that our interaction design was usable and the underlying algorithm could effectively retrieve relevant Q&A. We also had heard feature requests and concerns that software teams had in adopting our solution and made improvements accordingly. Overall, the use of multiple evaluations of formative, technical, and ecological forms helped us to capture the end users' perspectives at different points in the design process.

Second, it became clear that there was a lot we did not know. Because our evaluations made inevitable tradeoffs between generalizability, precision, and realism [17], primarily in the size of our samples, it was difficult to say with confidence how our findings would fare beyond a university setting. In fact, while we were publishing our findings, we were also beginning conversations with investors, who naturally wondered whether our initial studies were enough evidence of success for financing, let alone whether paying customers would see business reasons to adopt something for which we had mainly demonstrated end user value.

In reflecting on our experience as researchers, there was little incentive for us to invest more time and resources during our field deployments in understanding adopters and other stakeholder issues. Such research may not strengthen the research contribution of our innovation; neither would it lead to more publications. Moreover, releasing our innovation online as an open source project would not likely lead to significant uptake. However, given the importance of these issues for commercialization, our field evaluations raised crucial questions about whether "potential for adoption" is something that can be assessed effectively when evaluating HCI research systems during peer review.

BEYOND END USERS: TRANSITIONING FROM A RESEARCH PROJECT TO A COMMERCIAL PRODUCT

With the benefits to end users arising from our field deployments, the rapid growth of e-commerce websites and web applications in the past decade, and the simplicity of implementing our contextual help solution, we felt there could be widespread value created by commercializing LemonAid. In this section, we highlight our transition from user-centered to adoption-centered design and the key questions we tackled in translating LemonAid into a commercially viable product now known as AnswerDash (Figure 3).

Startup Fundraising and Team Building

Using demos from our research prototype and findings from our field deployments, we were able to raise $50,000 from our university commercialization gap fund. The second and third authors used this funding in 2012-2013 to attract pilot

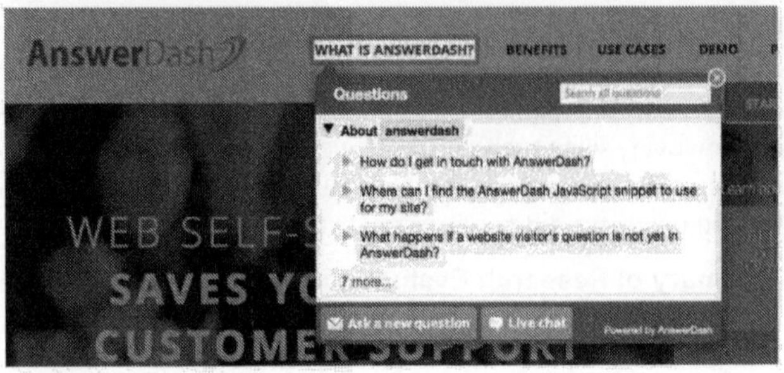

Figure 3: The AnswerDash end user interface showing questions retrieved on a UI element, in this case a link label.

customers, develop a beta product, secure the help of entrepreneurs-in-residence, and attract investors.

Our fundraising efforts revealed a number of concerns well outside the scope of our HCI research efforts. Investors rarely asked about our technology *per se*. Instead, they probed our understanding of the customers we were selling to, which type of customers saw the greatest benefit from the technology, how many companies might be viable customers, our strategies for acquiring customers through sales and marketing, and how we would build a top-notch go-to-market team. Although our HCI research taught us little about these concerns, our initial success at selling our solution to customers provided enough confidence to investors that we were able to raise a round of venture capital to launch a business. The purpose of the investment was for building the v1.0 product, developing a top-notch team, identifying a target market, and securing the initial 50+ customers within that market.

Now with funds, we began to hire. We began with engineers, as they would have to build the v1.0 product for us to sell. We then focused on marketing and sales to attract and convert trial customers to paying customers. Within a year, the team was 11 employees, half of whom were engineers.

What Exactly Is the Product?

As with any startup, the first major question we had to tackle was: *what would have to be added to LemonAid, as a research prototype, for it to become a salable product*? In business terms, a product is anything that satisfies a particular need or desire in a market and is sold for profit [26]. Some products are consumer-based and can be directly purchased or used by end users (described as *business-to-consumer*, or *B2C*). For example, a subscription to an online music-playing service or a mobile photo-capture application are both examples of B2C products. Other products are *business-to-business*, or *B2B*, where the buyer is another business. For example, enterprise software is a type of B2B product.

Since our help retrieval tool was designed for integration with existing websites and web applications, our product required a B2B model. We realized that it would be difficult to market our B2B product if its *only* benefit was for end users: it would have to provide some other clear value to the business integrating our tool on their site. The question was: *how can our product create value for customers who will pay us to adopt our contextual help approach?*

All of this paper's authors were co-founders of AnswerDash. The second and third authors also served full-time as CTO and CEO, respectively. They shared the responsibility of defining the *minimum viable product*, or *MVP*—the smallest set of features that would produce paying customers. As we would soon learn, our background in HCI was very relevant for identifying customer needs, translating them into feature ideas, and designing those features for engineers to build. Nearly all of our requirements emerged from conversations with customers both before and after they were paying us.

Many requirements came from the need to optimize the rate at which sales pitches and marketing efforts led to new customer signups. This included many *marketable* features that brought little end user value. For example, the ability to add video to answers was hugely popular in demos to customers, even though in practice, none of AnswerDash's current customers have yet added videos to answers. Similarly, we had to provide a mobile version of the product for customers to view AnswerDash as a "whole product," even though many businesses today still have little mobile traffic.

Other requirements emerged from needing to support existing customer support processes within our customers' businesses. We had to think carefully about how to integrate with customers' existing tools and customer support workflows, which required integrations with other services, such as Zendesk and desk.com, which many customers used for managing support requests via email.

Although LemonAid had basic content moderation and analytics during its research field deployments, AnswerDash customers immediately wanted more advanced features for managing their AnswerDash integrations. Before customers could seamlessly adopt, we had to perfect tools for styling and configuration, content moderation, answer authoring, installation and setup, and testing and analytics. Moreover, every usability issue with these features was a measurable risk to customers successfully deploying and paying for AnswerDash, and so we invested heavily in ensuring setup was fast, usable, and simple. All of our efforts, however, took time away from further focusing on end-user benefits as the original HCI research had done.

We also had to further evolve AnswerDash along many software quality dimensions. Our implementation had to be: (1) secure, so as not to risk information about our customers or their customers; (2) robust, so as to support rapidly evolving our product's features and scaling our customers; (3) reliable, so that the AnswerDash service would rarely be offline; and (4) small and fast, so as to have no discernable impact on our customers' site's loading speeds.

Overall, making the transition from our HCI innovation to a salable B2B product was more about understanding and designing a solution for which there was a *business* need and much less about solving the end user interaction problem.

Consequently, nearly 80% of the source code in the product supported customer needs, rather than end user needs. This required the founders to shift their thinking from classic HCI end-user concerns to business and adoption concerns.

Who Will Adopt the Product? Who Is the Target Buyer?

A related challenge to defining and building the product was determining which businesses would be AnswerDash's target customers, who within those businesses would purchase AnswerDash, and *why*. In our research deployments, we primarily interacted with employees who had authority over both the content of a site and its design. These team members typically included interaction designers, software engineers, content analysts, and project managers. But university-based teams may be different than industry teams.

As we explored the commercial scope of our innovation, we learned about many other types of stakeholders who were critical to adoption. The key decision-makers were directors of customer support, customer experience, customer success, marketing, and e-commerce. People in these roles, however, were not the ones using our product, but rather the target buyers paying for it. Our business-side end users included customer support staff, junior marketers, product designers, and data scientists (Figure 4). We had to keep these roles in mind, optimizing for those most often buying our product.

The stakeholders in a company varied depending on whether the website was a startup, a large corporation, or a government site. For example, at e-commerce companies, the adopters were usually directors of marketing, who were focused on increasing revenue. If they would not believe AnswerDash could impact revenue, AnswerDash would not be considered. We therefore presented revenue lifts directly from multiple successful A/B tests on customer sites. Even when we showed dramatic increases in revenue, there were sometimes other initial concerns: "we don't want another service to manage," "will it work for *us*?", and "not our pixels." Sometimes visual designers would raise concerns over visual appeal, requiring us to increase the range of style customizations available. The more stakeholders there were, the higher the chance of encountering an adoption barrier that would have to be removed through improvements to our product, marketing, and sales.

In companies that offered online applications (software-as-a-service, or "SaaS" companies), the primary adopter was usually a director of customer support. Directors of customer support viewed their job as keeping expenses down, reducing the time to resolve an email-based support request, and increasing customer satisfaction, which was usually measured by tracking "was this helpful" links in support emails and on knowledge base articles. To sell to these customers, we needed to show them how AnswerDash positively affects customer satisfaction and enables a customer support team to remain effective even as its business grows. In contrast, directors of customer success were more concerned with usability, user experience, and whether customers were successful with their website, even if it sometimes led to more support requests. Unfortunately, evaluating these metrics was often highly subjective. Directors of customer success were much less common than directors of customer support; in fact, at the time of this writing, many companies aspire to convert their reactive support organizations into proactive success organizations, and are only beginning to learn how.

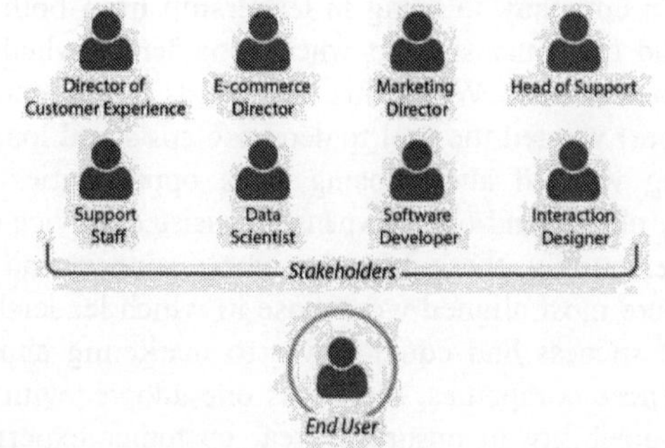

Figure 4. Typical stakeholders for AnswerDash.

In contrast to e-commerce customers, government customers were often driven by idiosyncratic, non-commercial motives. For example, some were interested in AnswerDash because it represented a way to give their constituency a voice. Others were concerned with improving the perceived quality of government information technology projects. Others still had *no* support staff, and viewed AnswerDash as a way to provide assistance with a very small impact on personnel and budget. Unfortunately, we found many government customers required support for very old web browsers, which we could not offer without unwise strain on our engineering resources.

As we worked with companies, we often encountered stakeholders with conflicting needs. For example, many customers disliked our original LemonAid modal design, especially the visual "shade" overlay, because they felt like we were "taking over their site." (Our best interpretation of this concern is that they worried that the experience felt more focused on AnswerDash than on moving their customers closer to purchasing.) However, as we found in our research studies, end users benefited from this usable modal interaction when using the product. We eventually removed the mode, causing a small amount of harm to end users' ability to find answers, but assuaging the concerns of many digital marketers and e-commerce directors, none of whom seemed to evaluate the product interactively, just visually.

Another example was in the actual content of the Q&A: end users benefit most from honest answers that transparently answer their questions, but customers often needed to write answers that avoided exposing undesirable or unhelpful truths about their products or services. We never observed any customers publishing lies, but positive spin was common in the answers our customers wrote for end users.

Other tradeoffs occurred among stakeholders *inside* AnswerDash's business customers. For example, it was common for a company to bring in leadership from both marketing and customer support when considering whether to adopt AnswerDash. When this happened, it was common that support wanted the tool to decrease costs and load, but marketing worried about losing sales opportunities from live chat, phone, and other expensive assisted service channels. Interestingly, the companies where support and marketing were most aligned were those in which leadership in customer success had equal power to marketing and support. In these companies, there was one adopter with a direct responsibility to ensure a great customer experience, regardless of what other impact it might have.

Providing Business Value through the Product

Understanding the needs of potential adopters and stakeholders was an ongoing challenge. Another challenge was developing a product that would actually provide quantifiable business value [13] to all adopters and stakeholders, beyond just providing value to the end users.

To reveal opportunities for creating business value, we had to first understand what business value meant to different stakeholders and how it could be measured. For AnswerDash, we believed our system had three potential value propositions: (1) the ability to increase sales on transactional websites, (2) the ability to decrease customer support costs, and (3) the ability to give insights into user behavior and needs, by surfacing frequent questions, along with where and when those questions were asked. All of these value propositions were plausible but untested by our HCI research on LemonAid.

After working with over 50 companies in a span of two years, it quickly became clear that end user benefit alone was not of premiere value to companies. "Improve your user (or customer) experience" was not a message that resonated with most companies, despite much hype to the contrary. On the other hand, customer support teams saw great value in saving time and doing more with less. Marketing teams responded well to messages about increased sales, and often had larger budgets. And executives were concerned with scaling their customer support team's efforts for their growing businesses without making additional investments in customer support headcount. All of these value propositions resonated, conveying business value.

In delivering this value, we had to build many new features that made our value measurable and visible. For example, we built an extensive A/B testing tool that enabled a simple comparison of the number of sales with and without our service on a site. Fortunately, over 90% of the sites on which we measured changes in sales and signups saw increases of 15-80%. In a few rare cases, sales and signups remained flat because companies published answers revealing shortcomings of their own products (*e.g.*, compatibility limitations). Such answers helped end users determine they did not want the products, but revealing this information was not always beneficial to companies, even if it was beneficial to their end users.

Other strategies we used to encourage adoption included: deploying AnswerDash on small portions of customers' sites initially, regularly communicating value through automated and manual emails, email marketing campaigns, and offering an extensive analytics dashboard that showed measurable value at login. It became clear that for trials to be successful, we needed customers to define what "value" meant to them prior to a trial. Many suggested measures they had adopted from industry best practices, but without a deep understanding of those measures' limitations. It was our responsibility to ensure measures and desired value aligned.

When confronted with AnswerDash's value, most customers adopted. But for those that did not, the prime reasons for resistance usually concerned *internal process change*. Even a small amount of additional work for employees, especially the target buyer and her team, was sometimes enough to outweigh clear evidence of increased revenues, cost savings, and time savings that customers saw had occurred. For example, one customer said that their team loved the product, the insights, the cost savings, and the benefits to their end users, but they did not want to write AnswerDash answers in addition to lengthier knowledge base articles (which were hardly ever used by comparison). It did not matter that this company was only writing one three-sentence answer per day. The *perception* of an internal process change was enough to create concerns. (It was due to such comments that AnswerDash created integrations with popular existing customer support tools, which alleviated these issues.)

Ultimately, whether a customer adopted AnswerDash only partially concerned quantifiable evidence. Despite a number of successful A/B tests, the biggest question for every customer was, "But will it work for *me*?" and "How much work will it be?" Showing customers that it would work well for them with little effort was important for success.

It is fair to say that our original research goal of providing end users with better online help has been validated across dozens of customer sites via AnswerDash, but this value to end users was never enough to drive B2B adoption. Rather, successful adoption depended on showing how target buyers would be more successful at their jobs because of AnswerDash, and in turn, produce value for their businesses in measurable bottom-line terms.

DISCUSSION

Although the extent to which any innovation becomes a widely adopted product depends on markets, customers, teams, and timing (among other factors), our experience shows that a user-centered research innovation can be the invaluable foundation of a B2B software company. In particular, our user-centered system design and evaluations that maximized realism and ecological validity helped us acquire early customers, facilitated fundraising, and provided a research prototype that directly informed the AnswerDash product roadmap. Paradoxically, however, our initial user-centered focus typical of HCI research also occluded B2B adoption issues by not revealing important insights about the real-world customer support ecosystem and stakeholder dependencies. AnswerDash has therefore spent most of its existence engaged in adoption-centered design, uncovering knowledge specific to our business and product to fuel customer acquisition and inform product priorities.

While our case study has clear limitations and there are many ways to respond to our report, here we focus on three key questions about the future of HCI technology research and adoption: (1) Is there merit in including "potential for adoption" as a criteria for evaluating research systems and their contributions? (2) How can we augment systems research evaluations with stakeholder perspectives? (3) Given the inherent lag in the successful adoption of innovations, does a research focus on adoption even make sense? Should researchers even bother?

Investigating Adoption-Centered Concerns in Research

Many researchers argue that commercialization is *not* the only, or even the best, way to have impact and that researchers should not be bothered with adoption. In fact, many researchers believe in making research contributions for the sake of advancing knowledge alone, leaving the job of commercialization to startups, open source projects, large companies, and industrial research and development (R&D) efforts.

At the same time, today's exploratory industry research labs and universities increasingly face pressure to demonstrate research impact and many encourage (or even require) tech-transfer. For example, universities are investing in setting up startup incubators, spin-offs, license agreements, and other strategies for greater research commercialization. Such endeavors inevitably require a shift to adoption-centered design, as seen in our case study. Even if commercialization is not the eventual goal, a focus on adoption might still be helpful for reflecting on design choices and research questions [26].

This raises a key question for HCI research: should some aspect of the "success" criteria for an HCI technology innovation be knowledge about its adoption barriers? In the current paradigm of HCI technology research, we are not required (or encouraged) to consider adoption as part of the system's validation. Our contributions are usually assessed on novelty, feasibility, claim-delivery, and the possibility of the system or technique generalizing to a specific user population [8]. But given the importance of adoption for potential impact, might we consider (and value) adoption and stakeholder perspectives in HCI technology research? Is there a role for research that focuses on adoption of HCI research innovations *exclusively*, assuming novelty and feasibility have already been established? Or is that not the role of HCI research? Would the HCI research community even recognize it as research?

Methods for Incorporating Adoption-Centered Concerns

If we agree that adoption and stakeholder perspectives are important, how can we adapt our evaluation methods to incorporate such perspectives? One possibility is to learn from practitioners, who may already engage in adoption-centered research. For example, interaction designers and user researchers often study target adopters, buyers, and stakeholders to inform the design of new products. These practitioners have evolved several methods to uncover stakeholder needs (*e.g.*, participatory design [23], product design walkthroughs [25], *etc.*) and methods that help align user needs with business needs (*e.g.*, [10]). Such methods orient practitioners to stakeholder needs, helping them think about the whole product ecosystem rather than optimizing a design based only on end user needs.

Adapting practitioner methods to research would require new notions of rigor, generalizability, and possibly new research communities for dissemination. These methods are also often used by practitioners on products for which there already is a market. Researchers, by contrast, often spur the creation of new markets. Also, as we discovered in our B2B sales efforts, adopters and stakeholders can actually be a moving target—uncovering such perspectives during research can be an intractable challenge. This raises critical questions about the feasibility and longevity of the knowledge these methods produce.

Adoption-Centered Concerns vs. Visionary Innovations

Even if we were to develop adoption-centered approaches in HCI technology research, some might question whether they would even apply to most HCI discoveries. After all, disruptive innovations [5] can take a long time to become successful and often initially underperform established products in mainstream markets. Why should we focus on the adoption of HCI research innovations if markets are not yet ready to accept them?

While some HCI innovations may truly be decades ahead of their time, many contributions at conferences such as CHI and UIST have a much shorter lifespan and relevance, due in part to many inventions coming from industry labs with an incentive to serve product needs or identify new product categories. It is therefore possible that a more explicit adoption-centered approach to research might increase the chances that an investor, entrepreneur, or prospective employee would see business opportunities in HCI research. Combined with other systemic changes, such as more extensive and rapid publicity of research innovations for the public and greater awareness of university intellectual property policy, an adoption-centered focus in HCI research might lead to a discipline of HCI technology transfer. There is certainly ample precedent. For example, fields such as health sciences and public health have applied a "bench-to-bedside" philosophy to the creation of the Translational Medicine discipline, which helps bridge the gap between basic and applied research and practice.

CONCLUSION

Our case study raises key questions about the link between HCI technology research and widespread adoption. Should we even be concerned about such a link? Is it sufficient to argue that we simply should not have to be bothered with such things? Would such an attitude risk making our work less relevant? Although this case study is one of the first to provide in-depth insights into the commercialization of an HCI research innovation, we have only presented one technology, one business, one university project and one perspective. A larger collection of case studies from other researcher-entrepreneurs, particularly ones reflecting on B2C businesses, would be valuable for informing efforts to transform HCI technology research from a source of ideas to a source of commercially disseminated solutions that create widespread value. We hope that our case study will be a starting point for these important discussions.

REFERENCES

[1] Bernstein, M.S., Ackerman, M.S., Chi, E.H. & Miller, R.C. 2011. The trouble with social computing systems research. *ACM CHI-Extended Abstracts*, 389–398.

[2] Brown, B., Reeves, S. & Sherwood, S. 2011. Into the wild: challenges and opportunities for field trial methods. *ACM CHI*, 1657–1666.

[3] Chilana, P.K., Ko, A.J., Wobbrock, J.O. & Grossman, T. 2013. A multi-site field study of crowdsourced contextual help: usage and perspectives of end users and software teams. *ACM CHI*, 217–226.

[4] Chilana, P., Ko, A.J. & Wobbrock, J.O. 2012. LemonAid: selection-based crowdsourced contextual help for web applications. *ACM CHI*, 1549–1558.

[5] Christensen, C. 2013. *The innovator's dilemma: when new technologies cause great firms to fail*. Harvard Business Review Press.

[6] Colyer, A.M. 2000. From research to reward: challenges in technology transfer. *ICSE*, 569–576.

[7] Foley, J. 1996. Technology transfer from university to industry. *Comm. ACM*. 39, 9, 30–31.

[8] Greenberg, S. & Buxton, B. 2008. Usability evaluation considered harmful (some of the time). *ACM CHI*, 111-120.

[9] Henderson, A. 2005. The innovation pipeline: design collaborations between research and development. *interactions*, 12, 1, 24–29.

[10] Hornbæk, K. & Frøkjær, E. 2008. Making use of business goals in usability evaluation: an experiment with novice evaluators. *ACM CHI*, 903–912.

[11] Isaacs, E.A., Tang, J.C., Foley, J., Johnson, J., Kuchinsky, A., Scholtz, J. & Bennett, J. 1996. Technology transfer: so much research, so few good products. *ACM CHI Companion*, 155–156.

[12] Jick, T.D. 1979. Mixing qualitative and quantitative methods: Triangulation in action. *Administrative science quarterly*, 24, 4, 602–611.

[13] Kolko, J. 2014. Running an entrepreneurial pilot to identify value. *interactions*, 21, 4, 22–23.

[14] Landay, J. 2009. I give up on CHI/UIST. *DUB for the Future blog*. Retrieved Jan 1, 2015: http://dubfuture. blogspot. com/2009/11/i-give-up-on-chiuist.html.

[15] Larsson, M., Wall, A., Norström, C. & Crnkovic, I. 2006. Technology transfer: why some succeed and some don't. *Software Tech Transfer in Soft. Engr.*, 23–28.

[16] Lee, A.S. & Baskerville, R.L. 2003. Generalizing generalizability in information systems research. *Information systems research*, 14, 3, 221–243.

[17] McGrath, J.E. 1995. Methodology matters: doing research in the behavioral and social sciences. *Human-computer interaction*. R.M. Baecker, J. Grudin, W.A.S. Buxton, & S. Greenberg (eds.) Morgan Kaufmann Publishers, 152–169.

[18] Mcgrenere, J., Bunt, A., Findlater, L. & Moffatt, K. 2010. Generalization in Human–Computer Interaction Research. *Generalization of Knowledge: Multidisciplinary Perspectives*. M. Banich and D. Caccamise, eds. Psychology Press, 277–295.

[19] Pfleeger, S.L. 1999. Understanding and improving technology transfer in software engineering. *J. of Systems and Software*, 47, 2, 111–124.

[20] Rettig, M. 1991. Nobody reads documentation. *Comm. ACM*, 34, 7, 19–24.

[21] Rogers, E.M. 2010. *Diffusion of innovations*. Simon and Schuster.

[22] Olsen, D. 2007. Evaluating user interface systems research. *Proc ACM UIST*, 251-258.

[23] Schuler, D. & Namioka, A. 1993. *Participatory Design: Principles and Practices*. Lawrence Erlbaum Associates, Inc. Mahwah, NJ, USA.

[24] Slater, S.F. & Mohr, J.J. 2006. Successful development and commercialization of technological innovation: insights based on strategy type. *J. Product Innovation Management*, 23, 1, 26–33.

[25] Szuc, Daniel. 2007. Walking through your product design with stakeholders. *UX Matters*. Retrieved Jan 1, 2015 from *http://www.uxmatters.com/mt/archives/2007/06/walking-through-your-product-design-with-stakeholders.php*.

[26] Winkler, D., Mordinyi, R. & Biffl, S. 2013. Research Prototypes versus Products: Lessons Learned from Software Development Processes in Research Projects. *Systems, Software and Services Process Improvement*. Springer, 48–59.

[27] Zelkowitz, M.V. 1996. Software engineering technology infusion within NASA. *IEEE Engineering Management*, 43, 3, 250–261.

Creating Sustainable Cyberinfrastructures

David P. Randall
The Information School
University of Washington
Seattle, WA, USA
dpr47@uw.edu

E. Ilana Diamant
Human Centered Design
& Engineering
University of Washington
Seattle, WA, USA
ilanadm@gmail.com

Charlotte P. Lee
Human Centered Design
& Engineering
University of Washington
Seattle, WA, USA
cplee@uw.edu

ABSTRACT

In this paper we report the results of a qualitative research study of the GENI cyberinfrastructure: a program of four federated cyberinfrastructures. Drawing on theories of stakeholder positioning, we examine how different GENI stakeholders attempt to enlist new participants in the cyberinfrastructures of GENI, and leverage existing relationships to create sustainable infrastructure. This study contributes to our understanding of how cyberinfrastructures emerge over time through processes of stakeholder alignment, enrollment, and through synergies among stakeholder groups. We explore these issues to better understand how cyberinfrastructures can be designed to sustain over time.

Author Keywords

Actor-Network Theory; Enrollment; Synergizing; Cyberinfrastructures

ACM Classification Keywords

H.5.3. Group and Organization Interfaces.

INTRODUCTION

The use of large-scale distributed scientific collaborations, powered by advanced computational and networking technologies has increased rapidly in recent years [21]. These endeavors, known largely as *cyberinfrastructures*, have wide potential to dramatically alter the way science is performed. Through utilizing such organizations, scientists can examine very large datasets from a wide variety of sources across geographic and interdisciplinary boundaries with relative ease, greatly increasing opportunities for effective scientific collaboration [36]. Despite this potential, and much prior research into the issues surrounding the design of such infrastructures in both the CHI and CSCW fields [5,6,12,28,30,46], creating effective and enduring cyberinfrastructure remains a complex challenge.

CHI 2015, April 18–23, 2015, Seoul, Republic of Korea.

ACM 978-1-4503-3145-6/15/04…$15.00.
http://dx.doi.org/10.1145/2702123.2702216

Despite the challenges involved in designing robust and sustainable cyberinfrastructures, and understanding how they can be maintained over time, many funding agencies and governments continue to enthusiastically support and fund such infrastructure projects. However, the lack of understanding results in cyberinfrastructures breaking down, as the tensions between the various stakeholders lead to collapse. When cyberinfrastructures fail, science is impeded and so it is critical that we attain a fuller understanding of how we can better design cyberinfrastructures that will endure.

Cyberinfrastructures are huge, complex and multifaceted organizations, often embedded in and across many differing social, organizational and technological entities [5]. As a result of this complexity "nobody is really in charge of infrastructure" [38] meaning that their maintenance and longevity is the result of a great deal of negotiation between the various stakeholders. Many early cyberinfrastructure development projects were funded with little consideration about how the resources would be maintained at their conclusion [31]. Recent research has turned to investigating how sustaining cyberinfrastructure entails "continually realigning the relationships among people, technologies, and organizations." [6] However, despite this research, we still know far too little about how people, groups, and larger organizations work to continually reposition their relationships with themselves and with relevant technologies in order to sustain these virtual organizations. Through understanding these relationships, and how stakeholders reposition themselves, we can better identify how cyberinfrastructures can be designed to accommodate such repositioning from their inception.

In this qualitative study we use a grounded theory approach to draw on the frameworks of *Actor-Network Theory* and *Synergizing* in order to better understand stakeholder positioning practices in the development of a program of four interrelated cyberinfrastructures, known as Global Environment for Network Innovations (GENI). These positioning practices are undertaken to cultivate the relationships necessary to create and maintain a functional cyberinfrastructure. We examine how the different GENI stakeholders attempt to enlist new users to the four cyberinfrastructures that comprise GENI, and also how they use leveraging to realign already existing relationships. We focus explicitly on stakeholder positioning for two main reasons. Firstly because it presents a critical challenge for the sustainability and long-term maintenance of cyberinfrastructures and for the creation of scientific artifacts (data, software, algorithms, and research products) that cyberinfrastructures are designed to support. And secondly because there is still relatively little understanding of how the concept of synergizing works 'on the ground', especially in the context of cyberinfrastructure design. We then relate the implications of these results to the design on future cyberinfrastructures.

To this end, we focus on the following research question:

RQ: How do existing stakeholders use positioning practices to develop and sustain cyberinfrastructures?

LITERATURE REVIEW

Cyberinfrastructures represent a new front in both science and technology. They are comprised of cutting-edge information technologies with the explicit goal of supporting large-scale, collaborative, inter-disciplinary research.

The term cyberinfrastructure (CI) was first used by the National Science Foundation (NSF) in 2003 [1], in reference to so-called 'collaboratories', which utilized emerging high speed networks in order to support distributed science [39,14,17,28]. The NSF, along with many other US government agencies, has placed a high priority on CIs as part of their strategy for developing tools to promote scientific research and discovery, in both the natural and social sciences. Even though collaboratories and CIs were initially considered technological artifacts, more recent research has conceptualized them as virtual organizations that include both technical and social aspects [11]. The social and relational aspects comprise the "human infrastructure" [21] of cyberinfrastructure which is the complex aggregation of social forms and interactions.

Research on technology adoption [10,41], innovation [32], user participation [2], and information systems development [9,24] has tended to conceptualize users as a predictable group of entities, operating within the physical or cultural boundaries of an organization or a community with a common value system (e.g., open-source community). CI systems differ in that their users and stakeholders are not always homogenous, specified or known ahead of time [21,37]. However, research has shown CIs to be highly emergent—changing and evolving over time[37]

Star et al. [37] have shown that infrastructures are fundamentally relational, in the sense of being embedded in multiple organizations, communities of practices and also in multiple technologies. They describe embeddedness, as the way an infrastructure "is 'sunk' into, or inside of, other structures, social arrangements, and technologies." More specifically, when we describe an infrastructure as embedded we mean that it is "situated within a network, the web, or other arrangement of relationships to other systems" [5]. The infrastructure's relationships thus both enable it to provide valuable services, but also constrain the processes which supply those services. In addition an infrastructure may be embedded in multiple structures simultaneously, such as technological, social, or organizational networks. That relational aspect creates social and technical challenges, not only for the long-term maintenance and sustainability of CIs, but also for their design [6].

While many large scale systems have traditionally been the focus of a purely technical design strategy [35] [30], the unique intricacies of CIs require their design to be approached from a more socio-technical perspective. Temporal aspects also need to be considered, as such large-scale collaborative endeavors may be impeded by failure to plan for the alignment of the multiple temporalities involved in such infrastructure projects, and so it is critical to coordinate the discordant rhythms and events emanating from such organizations that could negatively affect sustainability [39]. In focusing cyberinfrastructure design around the interactions and relationships between both the technological components and the human infrastructure [21] involved, designers are in a position to better secure longevity and sustainability in these systems.

Studies of IT development outside the field of cyberinfrastructures have shown that user involvement is a critical element for the success of IT-development projects and for the long-term adoption and use of IT systems. However, the specific mechanisms through which user involvement can best benefit IT projects is unclear [2,3,25,29]. Similarly, studies of large-scale IT systems have discussed the need to identify actions of "user advocacy" whereby stakeholders of a system's user groups promote the new system to other stakeholders and potential new users [4,23].

Below we discuss in more detail the stakeholder positioning theories in the field of cyberinfrastructure development we will be using in this study.

Theories of Stakeholder Positioning in Cyberinfrastructure Development

The design and development of large cyberinfrastructures involves complex decisions and tasks that require the input of experts with different backgrounds such as engineering, information technology and systems design. Past research has noted the challenge and need for positioning of the divergent goals, values and cultures of CI's stakeholders [41, 31, 35, 36, 28]. More specifically, stakeholders need to be positioned in ways that promote both effective development and long-term use and sustainability of the CI resources. However, achieving such a positioning of diverse stakeholders across organizational and disciplinary boundaries is a challenge. Funding and sponsoring organizations (e.g., NSF) play a role by promoting workshops and other activities that bring together key actors, and by working closely with project leaders throughout the development and maintenance of the cyberinfrastructure.

Positioning diverse stakeholders is not only a challenge for the systems-development effort but also presents challenges for the CI's sustainability and long-term maintenance. Making a CI sustainable means making it last for long (or even indefinite) time periods, beyond the scope of a single event, site or research project. However, as Ribes & Finholt [30] note, the sustainability of CIs is characterized by tensions such as the "development vs. maintenance" tension which arises from the necessity of doing ongoing maintenance work even though developing new tools and software tends to be more rewarded. More recent research by Bietz et al. [6] has discussed the sustainability of CIs in terms of two specific goals: creating sustainable institutional resources and the preservation of scientific products. Creating sustainable institutional resources includes challenges of funding, long-term planning and resource allocation [15,48]. Whereas creating sustainable scientific products includes challenges of designing reusable technologies, "big data" models and artifacts that cross disciplines, and scientific software that can be used by newcomers and future scientists beyond the immediate research questions they were designed to address [6,22,30,33,40]. Below we discuss two theories that can help us understand how infrastructural sustainability and stakeholder positioning were achieved in the case of the GENI infrastructures.

Actor-Network Theory

Actor-network theory (ANT) originated in the 1980s through the work of the science and technology studies theorists Michel Callon [7] and Bruno Latour [18,19], as well as sociologist John Law [20]. Originally constructed as a concept for explaining how theories, techniques and ideas in science become accepted and adopted, ANT has since been refined and applied by many disciplines. In information systems it is often utilized as a sociotechnical perspective through which to view technology adoption [42]. Understanding how interests are positioned in a heterogeneous network is key to understanding how CIs are developed and sustained.

Actor-networks may comprise any number of human and non-human actants [19], these can be anything that has an impact upon what is being investigated. This can include people, organizations, tools and artifacts. Actants are recruited to actor-networks through a process of translation, whereby the values and interests of the outside actants are brought into line with those of actants inside the network; in order to create the actor-network [34]. Callon [7] lays out this process into four distinct stages known as: *problematization, interessement, enrollment,* and *mobilization.*

Through these translation actions and activities, actants join or form networks. The process starts with identifying the actant, engaging those actants by supporting them with their interests/perspectives, and making them part of the network by negotiating roles for them. At the completion of the process enrolled actors can be thought of as allied actors.

In that sense, translation can be seen in the formation of networks and their dynamics. Callon discusses the *enrollment* stage specifically as "the device by which a set of interrelated roles is defined and attributed to actants who accept them. To describe enrollment is thus to describe the group of multilateral negotiations, trials of strength, and tricks that […] enable them to succeed." [7]. Enrollment involves negotiation of roles and relationships. Thus enrollment is the process of translating the interests of a large body of allies onto an actant so as to bring into line their interests with those of the other actants. This is done in order to create a heterogeneous network of aligned interests who are "willing to participate in particular ways of thinking and acting which maintain the network." [42]

Synergizing

Observing the need to investigate how organizational sustainability and change is accomplished, Bietz et al [5] introduced the concept of *Synergizing.* Synergizing recognizes that infrastructures, rather than being stand-alone systems, are embedded into pre-existing sociotechnical structures, and other social arrangements and technologies [5]. Synergizing is not just a point in time, but rather, it denotes a process of creating interactions that generate a greater combined effect by successfully utilizing an expansive array of technological, human and organizational entities. As a theoretical concept, synergizing allows us to consider the relational structures of a cyberinfrastructure and how they affect the cyberinfrastructure's sustainability over time [6]. It includes two sub-processes:

Aligning – the work done by developers to bring entities together in such a way as to create a relationship that will "produce, and function within, the nascent cyberinfrastructure."[5].

Leveraging – the process of utilizing an existent relationship with an organization, actor or artifact so as to reinforce that relationship, or to create a productive relationship with some other organization, actor or artifact.

In this paper we report the results of a qualitative research study of the GENI cyberinfrastructure program, which is an innovative program that funded not just one, but four interrelated cyberinfrastructure systems for computer networking science. We draw on the concepts of *Actor-Network Theory* [18,19] and *Synergizing* [5] to aid in our understanding of how GENI stakeholders encourage others to use their technologies, how they enroll new stakeholders, and how they leverage the existing ties between stakeholders to reposition relationships and create stronger and more stable connections within the infrastructure; especially in the context of cyberinfrastructure design. These two theories are closely related - synergizing's concept of alignment is similar to ANTs translation process at a high level – and the actions they explain were evident from the grounded theory analysis of the data.

RESEARCH SITE

The Global Environment for Network Innovations (GENI) is a program of four interrelated cyberinfrastructure systems ("technology clusters") that exist within a federation. GENI is funded by the National Science Foundation (NSF) and administered by an independent organization known as the GENI Project Office (GPO), who provide project management expertise, administer grants to project teams, organize regular conferences for GENI stakeholders and provide oversight and support for workgroups within GENI [47].

Each infrastructure within GENI is developed by a different team of computer scientists and houses different groups or communities of experimenters. GENI was created as "a virtual laboratory" for "exploring future internets at scale". That involves experimenting with alternative network architectures to the Internet's current TCP/IP design.

Experimenters and developers may choose any of the four infrastructures, and research projects are assigned to (or join) one of those four technology "clusters". GENI was selected for this study because it is comprised of multiple experimental cyberinfrastructures (PlanetLab, ProtoGeni, ORCA and ORBIT), with a common management and funding agency. In that sense, it is structured as a federated socio-technical organization of cyberinfrastructure systems.

METHODS

We conducted a series of semi-structured interviews with 49 GENI stakeholders including researchers, lead scientists and/or engineers (known as Principal Investigators or PIs), designers, experimenters, GENI managers, instructors and students using GENI for research or coursework. Table 1 shows a breakdown of interviewees by role (note that some interviewees held more than one role). In order to conduct these interviews the researchers attended a number of GENI Engineering Conferences (GECs) during a period of 18 months starting in March 2013. The GECs occur 4 times a year and are used as a forum for participants involved in the various GENI projects to share details of their work. The interviews lasted around one hour on average, the audio was recorded and then transcribed. Participants were selected for the study from across the four GENI infrastructures using a purposive sampling technique based upon their role within GENI (ranging from masters students to senior researchers, developers, and managers). The advantage of purposive sampling is that it allows researchers to focus on particular characteristics of the sample that might not be typical of the population [27,44].

Interviews were supplemented with participant observations of demos, presentations and group meetings that took place at the GECs. That allowed for triangulation of the data, [13,16]. Interview data was coded using Atlas.ti software and analyzed using a grounded theory approach [8], we then drew on this data to identify actor-network theory and synergizing as frameworks from which to view the activities of the GENI stakeholders. The names of all participants and their projects discussed in this paper are pseudonyms.

Role	Interviewees
Experimenter	11
GPO Manager	4
Developer	12
PI (experimenters & developers)	9
NSF	2
Student	15

Table 1. Breakdown of interviewees

FINDINGS

Our findings revolve around three aspects of stakeholder participation in the GENI infrastructures. First we identify the major stakeholder groups and their role in the four GENI infrastructures. Then we describe the methods various stakeholders use to enroll other individuals in the GENI infrastructures or projects that they are a member of. Finally we describe how stakeholders leverage existing relationships to increase stakeholder participation and solidify the ties between them.

Major GENI Stakeholder Groups

There are a large number of stakeholders involved in the development and administration of GENI, these can be broken down into a number of sub-groups, with some individuals having roles that span one or more of these groups.

Funding Agency & GENI Managers

Stakeholders in this group administer the GENI infrastructures. The funding agency stakeholders are the NSF directors and employees that are overseeing the GENI projects. Those individuals have responsibilities for funding, allocating resources, and high-level design decisions. So far there have been two program directors at NSF working on GENI since its inception in 2005. This stakeholder group also includes the GENI managers, who are members of the GPO. The GPO and its managers are responsible for planning, coordinating and making design and architectural decisions for the GENI infrastructures.

Developers

This group consists of the GENI developers and architects, who are computer scientists/engineers responsible for building the four infrastructures. Developers are primarily affiliated with one of the four infrastructures, but they may be involved technology projects which span across multiple infrastructures. Also included here are users and developers of the PlanetLab GENI infrastructure, which are *outside GENI*: these are individuals who are not currently attending or participating in the GENI conferences but who have contributed to the development of Planetlab in the past.

Experimenters
Stakeholders in this group are mostly using technologies developed in a single infrastructure. They include computer scientists/engineers whose work is primarily focused on an experimental research study of GENI, funded by the NSF. The work of these experimenters also involves development and design of software, protocols, hardware and other technologies that are part of GENI.

Students and Instructors
Yet another stakeholder group consists of students who contribute to the development of GENI technologies or are developing a technology based on a particular infrastructure as part of their research/dissertation project. This group also includes Computer Science instructors/educators in universities and colleges who are primarily interested in developing/implementing/using a specific GENI technology in the classroom in undergraduate or graduate courses focusing on networking science (e.g., with the goal of demonstrating principles of networking science).

Enrollment and Aligning Practices

Our analysis reveals the various GENI stakeholders engage in five different positioning practices: collaborating with domain scientists, conducting outreach programs for experimenters, improving communications between experimenters and developers, technology integration, and tool creation. These practices demonstrate how stakeholders are actively involved in the enrollment practices of actor-network theory, as well as the alignment and leveraging practices of synergizing, as they reposition existing relationships and form new ones in processes which help to maintain the cyberinfrastructures.

Collaboration with Domain Scientists
Developers from GENI's ORCA infrastructure, using the ExoGENI test bed, conduct experiments in collaboration with a number of domain scientists from bioinformatics, earth science and astronomy. Through these experiments the developers build new relationships with domain scientists, adding new experimenters to GENI, who in turn help to expand the GENI infrastructure and its related technologies, bolstering its capabilities and further expanding its potential user-base.

Through these collaborations on experiments, developers move to enroll scientists from disciplines outside of computer science. One of the ORCA/ExoGENI PIs described these experiments as benchmarking tests of computational applications that are being developed specifically for the domain-science users. They also discussed the involvement of domain experts in another project in which developers have teamed up with the scientists from Information Sciences Institute-West (ISI) who brought in both other domain scientists as well as their own software for managing complex computational workflows. Existing collaborators sometimes bring in new experts:

"[The ISI scientists] *brought in their software that manages complex computational workflows, but they also brought in some domain scientists in astronomy and earth science"* (Issac, ORCA/ExoGENI)

In such cases, new users might be enrolled into an infrastructure initially as testers, and start collaborating with the development teams, and through that collaboration they can adapt/adjust the infrastructure to the specific needs of the domain scientists.

Much like the ISI developers brought in domain scientists from their institution, the ORCA/ExoGENI team similarly enlisted the help of local experts from computational biology and chemistry that collaborated with the developers to configure the infrastructure to the needs of domain scientists. The ORCA team views CI applications as needing to be dynamically adapted, based upon domain scientists needs.

"*Basically the idea is to learn about the behavior of these complex applications that heretofore are run on grid systems and static resources. We look at their behavior as a more dynamic environment that can be scaled and configured to their [domain scientists'] needs*" (Issac, ORCA/ExoGENI)

Through their collaboration with domain scientists, the GENI stakeholders are engaging in the translation processes of actor-network theory. Enrolling the domain scientists into GENI where they may in turn enroll new experimenters, or in ANTs parlance, actants.

Conducting Outreach Activities
Studies of large-scale IT systems have discussed the need to identify actions of "user advocacy" whereby stakeholders of a system's user groups promote the new system to other stakeholders and potential new users [4,23]. However, some of the enrollment activities we see go beyond mere advocacy towards user outreach.

GENI managers are actively involved in outreach activities. Originally they tried to attract new experimenters though a series of town hall meetings held throughout the U.S. Currently they use direct outreach activities that advertise new uses of the infrastructure's components at conferences and workshops.

"*We are really encouraging people who want to organize workshops, run summer schools, all that kind of stuff to put in proposals and we will fund them, but then they're in charge.*" (GENI Manager)

The managers also use more indirect practices, such as funding current experimenters and developers to train new users and to demo/present their work, as well as funding travel grants to get new people to attend the GENI conferences. That includes putting the developers and existing users in charge of workshops and GENI-wide user meetings, such as trouble-shooting sessions and roundtable design-discussions about new components of the infrastructure.

The ORCA/ExoGENI team mentioned previously do not have a pre-existing plan or strategy for attracting new users, rather the PI for the project stated that instead they are actively involved in "user outreach". This means that they try to adapt the technology/infrastructure to the existing user groups while at the same time participating in the experiments themselves to understand how the system works from the users' perspective. This way they are adding new users in the form of themselves, as well as expanding the technology to work with new user groups, widening the potential user-base.

In using this approach the ORCA/ExoGENI team are utilizing already existing relationships to expand to new users, creating new relationships between the infrastructure and themselves, as well as expending to a new user-base and forming additional ties to other domain experts outside of GENI's immediate focus of computer science experiments. Through these actions the ORCA/ExoGENI team are engaging in the leveraging practices of the synergizing framework, by working to solidify already existing ties between stakeholders, and then utilizing these ties to create new relationships with others; in this case domain scientists.

In addition to bringing in new users, stakeholders are also solidifying the already existing relationships between the participants of the GENI infrastructures, or using those relationships to create new connections with other stakeholders.

User-Support

Most interviewees (developers and experimenters) mentioned that they receive or provide some type of technical support. Through this user-support stakeholders leverage their existing relationships with the respective other parties involved. For example when experimenters take grievances to developers and see changes in applications or procedures, the relationships are solidified.

"You know, we have [...] dialogue with users [...] at, like, this GEC and at previous GECs as to what they want". (Jack, ProtoGENI)

One experimenter talked about how experimentation is a function of academic training that is lacking in their field. Supporting experimenters is matter of providing training in how to run scientific experiments, a more complicated issue than technical user-support.

"It's not like physics or chemistry, any of those really established scientific disciplines where there's a clear process for experimentation. There is not such a thing in networking. We're still learning how to do this" (Jessica, GENI Experimenter)

Other developers talked about trying to make their technologies and frameworks usable by providing user support through listservs, being accessible and responsive to users through email and in person during the GECs, and sometimes by trying to support multiple user groups such as experts and students. For example, Julia, the main GUSH developer, noted that the goal of GUSH was to support both advanced and novice users.

In some cases experimenters have been involved in the development of GENI since its early stages. One interviewee described their team's process of adapting ProtoGENI for experimental purposes. It involved understanding the underlying platform/architecture of the infrastructure and its dependencies, and then discussing their coding with the ProtoGENI developers to find solutions and improve access.

"[user-support is an issue of] *basically understanding the platform, understanding the system dependencies that they have and what we wanna do and if we have issues. Then we sort of discuss with them for workarounds and sort of the network connecting issues of getting people to access our software through ProtoGENI."*(Peter, ProtoGENI)

They further mentioned that their team had many early-stage interactions with experimenters and that because of their team's long involvement with GENI they can provide expert level peer-support to other experimenters that are new to GENI.

In the PlanetLab infrastructure, developers, and also sometimes Principal Investigators, often help experimenters with their requirements-definition process during the development of experimental technologies, even without going so far as to collaborate on the same research project. For example, one of the main developers of PlanetLab, mentioned that they have not done any experimentation outside of development, but had collaborated with experimenters in determining system requirements.

"I've certainly in PlanetLab interacted with a lot of experimenters. Something that we believe in pretty strongly in PlanetLab, and I think this is part of the reason why PlanetLab is successful is really engaging experimenters to figure out what are their requirements if they need new capabilities of the platform, trying to help build and deploy that. Actually the best case is if we can get the experimenters to actually help us build the new things and test it. We've had pretty good success there." (Alex, PlanetLab)

PlanetLab developers encourage experimenters to be involved in development by working together to determine system requirements for PlanetLab, or ways in which PlanetLab can be adapted to support experimentation. In doing so the PlanetLab developers work to leverage and solidify their existing relationships with experimenters while also forging new ties with them as they take on a small developer role. These efforts are intended to make experimentation across the GENI infrastructures consistent. Not only does this act to reduce overhead for experimenters, but it also encourages synergizing's alignment sub-process, where-by experimenters seamlessly switch between infrastructures, forging new relationships with those infrastructures which works to encourage user retention.

Common Tools

Another practice of positioning stakeholders and new users is by leveraging GENI's existing systems, which includes modifying existing technologies and applications to produce new common systems that are more widely usable, or that can be re-used to build and expand new systems.

When GENI started, PlanetLab, along with several other projects, was sought after to join the GENI community. Originally there were four clusters involved in GENI, over time it became clear that a common API was needed to talk between them. As a result GENI moved towards creating a common user interface for experimenters that spanned across the various clusters and their underlying frameworks – allowing experimenters and developers to access different project resources with ease.

This project was called the GENI User Shell (GUSH) and it was designed - by both PlanetLab and GENI stakeholders - to allow users access to common GENI resources, with minimal effort (usually requiring just a small XML header change to switch frameworks). GUSH was heavily based off the pre-existing PlanetLab User Shell (PLUSH) utilizing around half of its original code. In addition to the utilization of the PLUSH code, a number of projects that were once part of PlanetLab were rolled into GENI's GUSH.

In particular, the developers worked on improving the interoperability among the infrastructure's components. This is a process whereby a tool is created to allow individuals to utilize resources across several platforms seamlessly, for example GENICloud, which allows experimenters to easily deploy and configure slices that span PlanetLab and Eucalyptus (an ORCA project). Traditionally in infrastructure development, the job of creating such tools has been the developers' responsibility. Those trying to work with multiple incompatible components of the larger infrastructure would devote some part of their work to integrating those components, before being able to use them in their research projects. Occasionally the GENI Project Office (GPO) has taken charge of that task as well:

"The GPO has gone so far as to write software to make things interoperable, so we've occasionally gone to that length." (GENI Manager)

Technology Integration

In an effort to attract more PlanetLab experimenters to GENI there has recently been a push to further integrate PlanetLab resources into the GENI infrastructure, and leverage the existing relationships, by placing PlanetLab nodes into InstaGENI racks.

"So this model of using InstaGENI we hope will be attractive to PlanetLab community. They're already familiar with PlanetLab tools going to the PlanetLab website, setting things up, and so we're hoping to steer some PlanetLab users into GENI in this way"(PlanetLab Manager)

Despite the existence of a shared GENI API and a drive for further GENI integration, PlanetLab still maintains its own API, allowing PlanetLab machines to run as part of GENI, or independently as PlanetLab.

Integration Issues in PlanetLab

As suggested in the previous sections there have been a number of issues with the integration of PlanetLab into GENI. Despite the push to further assimilate the GENI infrastructure with PlanetLab there is still some question of where PlanetLab sits within GENI today.

Much of these issues stem from PlanetLab's initial involvement with GENI, unlike many other projects that were incorporated into GENI, PlanetLab never fully integrated itself, instead maintaining its own API, user-base and applications to run alongside GENIs. Essentially PlanetLab was never fully enrolled in GENI and the resulting relationship is one of uncertainty and instability.

One interviewee even mentioned that they were unsure if PlanetLab would continue to support the GENI API (in some form), although they expressed a wish for such support to continue. It would also seem that even PlanetLab is unsure of its future direction, or if that will continue to include GENI, as one PlanetLab interviewee stated that:

"PlanetLab isn't just about GENI. We have our own vision, which overlaps a lot with GENI, but it's maybe not exactly the same, so on the PlanetLab side we're exploring our own kind of agenda with trying to reach out to the SDN community and try to figure out."

Despite the effort by various GENI stakeholders over the years to better integrate PlanetLab, the future of PlanetLab within GENI still looks uncertain. Continued efforts to integrate PlanetLab nodes and ProtoGENI racks, and the support of the GENI API by PlanetLab indicate a continuation of PlanetLab's incorporation into GENI, at least for the short term. However, it is apparent that PlanetLab has its own goals and there is a possibility that such goals could involve leaving GENI behind.

There was some initial success with GENI enrolling PlanetLab, after PlanetLab joined the GENI effort and contributed its resources to the development of GUSH, but over time efforts to further attract the PlanetLab community seem to stall, not only because of technical differences, but also because of slight differences in vision, and agendas. Leaving PlanetLab and GENI's combined future ambiguous.

Much of this ambiguity stems from the short-term vision of both PlanetLab and GENI during their original integration. From an actor-network perspective, the process of translation was never truly completed. Although GENI has a vision for what it wanted from PlanetLab, PlanetLab never completely accepted this, as evidenced by their decisions to keep much of their own applications and technologies active alongside GENI's. Both GENI and PlanetLab had their own initial goals when they came together, but neither truly had an idea for what the long term relationship between the two projects would be. The result has therefore been a continued ineffectiveness in attempts to reposition and leverage the existing relationships between PlanetLab and GENI and an uncertain future for the ties between the two.

DISCUSSION

Positioning stakeholders within a cyberinfrastructure involves complex and interrelated sociotechnical processes. We know from past research that cyberinfrastructures can be considered as "systems of systems" in the sense of including multiple inter-dependent technologies, software, networks and databases. This is certainly the case with GENI as it is a system of interrelated infrastructures, networks, and other smaller technical components.

Our findings present a number of implications for the design of future cyberinfrastructures. We can see from the example of PlanetLab's ineffective integration with GENI that not designing for the long term has negative consequences. In other GENI infrastructures the positioning practices they engaged in demonstrated how stakeholders are actively involved in the enrollment practices of actor-network theory, as well as the alignment and leveraging practices of synergizing. These infrastructures engaged in designed, conscious and forceful efforts to reposition existing relationships and form new ones in processes which helped to maintain and sustain the cyberinfrastructure. Whereas in the PlanetLab integration there was no design for these. Without such considerations for designing for synergizing and enrollment, the attempts to leverage existing relationships or further align/enroll new users from PlanetLab were continually ineffective; to the point where today the future of PlanetLab in GENI is extremely uncertain. This shows the critical importance of designing cyberinfrastructures throughout their lifecycles for the long-term, with particular emphasis on designing for the continual repositioning and realignment processes of actor-network theory and synergizing.

In GENI, stakeholders are constantly involved in a process of recruiting new users to their projects, be this through active recruitment or through indirect practices such as "demoing" their work. In bringing these new users on board, stakeholders engage in the translation processes of actor-network theory. This starts when new individuals (or actants) are identified by existing stakeholders - or display an interest themselves independently - the interests and needs of these new potential stakeholders are then teased out, and current stakeholders outline how GENI can be a solution to their problems; this is the *problematization* stage. A negotiation then takes place where changes are made and roles defined depending on an actants needs, once this negotiation is complete the actants become full stakeholders, free to bring new stakeholders into the project as they wish.

The enrollment of new experts and individual experimenters makes a difference for the long-term sustainability of GENI's infrastructures. By bringing in new stakeholders in this way GENI combats user-attrition and allows itself to become increasingly diverse, giving it a robust and sustainable user-base. Such enrollment also aided groups in gaining additional funding, and expanding their infrastructure by enrolling not only experimenters but also scientists from other disciplines such as computational biology.

Once stakeholders have been enrolled and brought into GENI there is still the risk of long-term user attrition as the needs of the enrolled user-base changes over time. In GENI however we see stakeholders engaging in activities whereby they utilize established relationships in order to adapt infrastructure to meet the changing needs of their users. This in turn allows them to solidify their already existing ties and open up new relationships as the changes attract new users to the projects. These actions are examples of the leveraging processes of the synergizing framework and not only is this occurring among a diverse group of individual stakeholders (or potential individual stakeholders) but it is also occurring at the higher levels of whole infrastructures. Stakeholder positioning in GENI also takes on the flavor of co-enrollment or of mutual alignment. Stakeholders try to align with other stakeholders, or potential stakeholders, incrementally and part-way by changing technologies or holding workshops. Potential stakeholders incrementally align with stakeholders by engaging in dialog about the potential of creating new system requirements or a common user "shell" to access resources. Common types of positioning practice entail promoting usability efforts requiring iteration between developers and experimenters who subsequently enroll still more experimenters.

Through these practices we can see how GENI stakeholders engage readily in the processes of synergizing. This enables us to show synergizing as a framework in action and also shows how actor-network theory and synergizing are complimentary and powerful theories involved in the design of successful and sustainable cyberinfrastructures. This is perhaps best demonstrated not by the success of the many GENI infrastructures but in the ineffectiveness of the

PlanetLab infrastructure's incorporation into GENI. Throughout the entire process of PlanetLab's participation in GENI it was unable to effectively leverage existing relationships or to sufficiently align its resources and practices with the rest of the GENI infrastructures. As a result, PlanetLab's position within GENI remains uncertain as it continues in a stagnant maintenance state, underutilized and with a shrinking user-base.

CONCLUSION

The design of cyberinfrastructures emerge over time through processes of stakeholder alignment, enrollment, and through synergies among developers and other stakeholder groups. This study examined how GENI stakeholders enroll new actors (individuals, groups, and technologies) into the cyberinfrastructures they are developing or working with, and how they leverage their existing relationships with other stakeholders to create sustainable infrastructure. GENI stakeholders (developers, experimenters, and managers) promote the development and use of the GENI infrastructures through various means and thus promote the enrollment of new stakeholders and technologies into their respective projects within GENI.

Further research is needed to build a more nuanced understanding of the sociotechnical processes underlying the development, adoption and use of cyberinfrastructures, particularly in complex scientific research domains such as GENI's "infrastructure of infrastructures". Consideration of the social and technical aspects of enrollment and leveraging practices can enrich explanations of how cyberinfrastructures can be sustained over the long term. We can then use this understanding to aid in the design of more sustainable cyberinfrastructures.

ACKNOWLEDGMENTS

This research was supported by NSF Award OCI-1220269. Thanks to our participants and to our anonymous reviewers for their feedback.

REFERENCES

1. Atkins, D. *Revolutionizing Science and Engineering Through Cyberinfrastructure: Report of the National Science Foundation Blue-Ribbon Advisory Panel on Cyberinfrastructure.* 2003.
2. Barki, H. and Hartwick, J. Rethinking the Concept of User Involvement. *MIS Quarterly 13*, 1 (1989), 53.
3. Baroudi, J.J., Olson, M.H., and Ives, B. An empirical study of the impact of user involvement on system usage and information satisfaction. *Communications of the ACM 29*, 3 (1986), 232–238.
4. Bettencourt, L.A., Ostrom, A.L., Brown, S.W., and Roundtree, R.I. Client Co-Production in Knowledge-Intensive Business Services. *California Management Review 44*, 4 (2002).
5. Bietz, M.J., Baumer, E.P.S., and Lee, C.P. Synergizing in Cyberinfrastructure Development. *Computer Supported Cooperative Work (CSCW) 19*, 3-4 (2010), 245–281.
6. Bietz, M.J., Ferro, T., and Lee, C.P. Sustaining the development of cyberinfrastructure. *Proceedings of the ACM 2012 conference on Computer Supported Cooperative Work - CSCW '12*, ACM Press (2012), 901.
7. Callon, M. Some elements of a sociology of translation: domestication of the scallops and the fishermen of St Brieuc Bay. In J. Law, ed., *Power, action and belief: a new sociology of knowledge?*. Routledge, London, 1986, 196–223.
8. Charmaz, K. *Constructing Grounded Theory: A Practical Guide Through Qualitative Analysis.* Pine Forge Press, 2006.
9. Cockburn, A. *Agile Software Development.* Addison-Wesley, Reading, MA, 2001.
10. Davis, F. Perceived usefulness, perceived ease of use, and user acceptance of information technology. *MIS Quarterly 13*, 3 (1989), 319 – 340.
11. Edwards, P.N., Jackson, S.J., Bowker, G.C., and Knobel, C.P. *Understanding infrastructure: Dynamics, tensions. and design.* 2007.
12. Edwards, W.K., Newman, M.W., and Poole, E.S. The infrastructure problem in HCI. *Proceedings of the 28th international conference on Human factors in computing systems - CHI '10*, ACM Press (2010), 423.
13. Eisenhardt, K.M. Building Theories from Case Study Research. *Academy of Management Review 14*, 4 (1989), 532–550.
14. Finholt, T.A. Collaboratories as a new form of scientific organization. *Economics of Innovation and New Technology 12*, 1 (2003), 5–25.
15. Galison, P. *Big Science: The Growth of Large-scale Research.* Stanford University Press, 1992.
16. Gallivan, M.. Value in triangulation: a comparison of two approaches for combining qualitative and quantitative methods. In A.. Lee, J. Liebenau and J. DeGross, eds., *Information Systems and Qualitative Research.* Chapman & Hall, London, 1997, 417–443.
17. Hey, T. and Trefethen, A. e-Science and its implications. *Philosophical transactions. Series A, Mathematical, physical, and engineering sciences 361*, 1809 (2003), 1809–25.
18. Latour, B. *Science in Action: How to Follow Scientists and Engineers Through Society.* Harvard University Press, 1987.
19. Latour, B. Reassembling the Social - An Introduction to Actor-Network-Theory. *Reassembling the Social - An Introduction to Actor-Network-Theory, by Bruno Latour, pp. 316. Foreword by Bruno Latour. Oxford University Press, Sep 2005. ISBN-10: 0199256047. ISBN-13: 9780199256044 -1*, (2005).

20. Law, J. Notes on the theory of the actor-network: Ordering, strategy, and heterogeneity. *Systems Practice 5*, 4 (1992), 379–393.
21. Lee, C.P., Dourish, P., and Mark, G. The human infrastructure of cyberinfrastructure. *Proceedings of the 2006 20th anniversary conference on Computer supported cooperative work - CSCW '06*, ACM Press (2006), 483.
22. Lee, J.W., Zhang, J., Zimmerman, A.S., and Lucia, A. DataNet: An emerging cyberinfrastructure for sharing, reusing and preserving digital data for scientific discovery and learning. *AIChE Journal 55*, 11 (2009), 2757–2764.
23. Mambrey, P., Mark, G., and Pankoke-Babatz, U. User Advocacy in Participatory Design: Designers' Experiences with a New Communication Channel. *Computer Supported Cooperative Work (CSCW) 7*, 3-4 (1998), 291–313.
24. Miranda, S.M. and Kavan, C.B. Moments of governance in IS outsourcing: conceptualizing effects of contracts on value capture and creation. *Journal of Information Technology 20*, 3 (2005), 152–169.
25. Mirel, B. *Interaction Design for Complex Problem Solving: Developing Useful and Usable Software.* Morgan Kaufmann, 2004.
26. Olson, G.M., Zimmerman, A., and Bos, N. Scientific Collaboration on the Internet. (2008).
27. Palys. *Research Decisions: Quantitative and Qualitative Perspectives.* Thompson, Toronto, 2008.
28. Procter, R., Borgman, C., Bowker, G., et al. Usability research challenges for cyberinfrastructure and tools. *CHI '06 extended abstracts on Human factors in computing systems - CHI EA '06*, ACM Press (2006), 1675.
29. Redish, J. Expanding Usability Testing to Evaluate Complex Systems. *Journal of Usability Studies 2*, 3 (2007), 102–111.
30. Ribes, D. and Finholt, T. The Long Now of Technology Infrastructure: Articulating Tensions in Development. *Journal of the Association for Information Systems. May2009 10*, 5 (2009).
31. Ribes, D. and Lee, C.P. Sociotechnical Studies of Cyberinfrastructure and e-Research: Current Themes and Future Trajectories. *Computer Supported Cooperative Work (CSCW) 19*, 3-4 (2010), 231–244.
32. Rogers, E.M. *Diffusion of Innovations, 4th Edition.* Simon and Schuster, 2010.
33. Schopf, J.M. Sustainability and the Office of CyberInfrastructure. *2009 Eighth IEEE International Symposium on Network Computing and Applications*, IEEE (2009), 1–3.
34. Şeker, Ş.E. Possible Social Impacts of E-Government: A Case Study of Turkey. 2004.
35. Shin, D.-H. A socio-technical framework for cyber-infrastructure design. *Technological Forecasting and Social Change 77*, 5 (2010), 783–795.
36. Sonnenwald, D.H. Scientific collaboration. *Annual Review of Information Science and Technology 41*, 1 (2007), 643–681.
37. Star, S.L. and Ruhleder, K. Steps Toward an Ecology of Infrastructure: Design and Access for Large Information Spaces. *Information Systems Research 7*, 1 (1996), 111–134.
38. Star, S.L. The Ethnography of Infrastructure. *American Behavioral Scientist 43*, 3 (1999), 377–391.
39. Steinhardt, S. and Jackson, S. Reconciling rhythms: plans and temporal alignment in collaborative scientific work. *Proceedings of the 17th ACM conference on Computer supported cooperative work & social computing*, (2014), 134–145.
40. Stewart, C.A., Almes, G.T., and Wheeler, B.C. (eds. . Cyberinfrastructure Software Sustainability and Reusability: Report from an NSF-funded workshop. (2010).
41. Venkatesh, V., Morris, M.G., Davis, G.B., and Davis, F.D. User acceptance of information technology: toward a unified view. *MIS Quarterly 27*, 3 (2003), 425–478.
42. Walsham, G. Actor-network theory and IS research: current status and future prospects. In A.S. Lee, J. Liebenau and J.I. DeGross, eds., *Information Systems and Qualitative Research.* Springer US, Boston, MA, 1997, 466–480.
43. Wulf, W. The collaboratory opportunity. *Science 261*, 5123 (1993), 854–855.
44. Yin, R.K. *Case Study Research: Design and Methods.* SAGE, 2009.
45. Zimmerman, A. and Finholt, T.A. Growing an infrastructure. *Proceedings of the 2007 international ACM conference on Conference on supporting group work - GROUP '07*, ACM Press (2007), 239.
46. Zimmerman, A. and Nardi, B.A. Whither or whether HCI. *CHI '06 extended abstracts on Human factors in computing systems - CHI EA '06*, ACM Press (2006), 1601.
47. GENI » Meet the GENI Project Office (GPO). http://www.geni.net/?page_id=26.
48. National Research Council. Committee on Metagenomics: Challenges and Functional Applications New science of metagenomics: Revealing the secrets of our microbial planet0. 2007.

Standards and/as Innovation: Protocols, Creativity, and Interactive Systems Development in Ecology

Steven J. Jackson
Cornell University
208 Gates Hall, Ithaca NY
sjj54@cornell.edu

Sarah Barbrow
Wellesley College
106 Central St, Wellesley MA
sbarbrow@wellesley.edu

ABSTRACT
Standards and protocols play important but under-theorized roles in HCI research and design efforts, including those dedicated to the development of new collaborative infrastructures in the sciences. Building on several years of ethnographic fieldwork, this paper examines standardization efforts attached to new forms of design and computational development in American ecology. We explore the role that standards play in large-scale research networks; how standards are enacted and enforced in complex interactive systems like science; how standards struggle and fail (and what happens when they do); and how actors work across the gaps that standards leave to produce more effective forms of practice and design. We also argue for the potentially *creative* role of standards, including contexts in which they function as fulcrums for change and innovation. We conclude with reflections on how HCI researchers might rethink the nature and possibilities of standards and standardization in their own work.

Author Keywords
Standards; standardization; infrastructure; science; ecology; collaboration; ethnography.

ACM Classification Keywords
H.m. [Information systems]: Miscellaneous.

INTRODUCTION
Standards have long been central to human-computer interaction in complex real-world settings. Standards order and constrain the sprawl of worldly activity, producing stable contexts of action and expectation into which new artifacts and systems can enter. Standards support the exchange of knowledge, experience and objects across scale and context, making practices that are simultaneously distributed and collective possible. And by holding parts of complex systems constant while others change, standards establish the possibility of growth from old to new, allowing complex interactive systems to learn, grow, and change over time. In all these ways, standards help to gather, organize, and stabilize the worlds around us, making the environments we study and design for more stable, coherent, and predictable places. To repurpose Woodrow Wilson's old point on democracy, standards help produce a "world made safe for design" [37].

Topically, this paper joins a growing body of HCI research [16,18,21,24,29] that explores the nature and challenge of collaborative work and computational development in the sciences – a site of research and practice that sometimes flies under the name of 'cyberinfrastructure' or 'e-science'. This work represents a large and growing area of HCI insight and opportunity. It also poses an ongoing challenge to HCI researchers to rethink their work both 'outwards' and 'upwards': towards wider and more varied fields of human-computer encounter; and towards scales of technical and social practice larger than discrete artifacts, systems, and users [22,28].

This paper addresses the tensions and ambivalences of standards and infrastructure development at two separate scales and moments of collaborative ecological practice: the traditional PI-led research group, which continues to characterize and define the social and practical organization of much ecological research today; and newer forms of big data and continental-scale research associated with the development of new computational tools and infrastructures (above all with the National Ecological Observatory Network, described more fully below).

Building on scholarship in HCI and the social sciences, and long-term ethnographic fieldwork in ecology, we seek empirically grounded answers to four basic questions. What role do standards play in coordinating collaborative work and new systems development in ecological research today? How are standards enacted, realized and enforced across complex distributed activities? How can standards struggle or fail, and what consequence might this have for the forms of practice and discovery they are meant to support? And how do individuals, groups, and organizations work across the holes and gaps that real-world standards inevitably leave, to produce more effective forms of design and collective action in the world? We conclude with reflections on the potentially *creative* role of standards, and argue for

CHI 2015, April 18 - 23 2015, Seoul, Republic of Korea

ACM 978-1-4503-3145-6/15/04...$15.00
http://dx.doi.org/10.1145/2702123.2702564

new approaches that move standards more to the center of HCI thinking and practice.

BACKGROUND AND LITERATURE REVIEW

In their immediately technical form, standards drive and constrain the design and operation of interactive systems across a wide variety of application areas. In the field of software engineering, for example, standards and protocols can play an important role in managing or overcoming the severe coordination challenges that often attend distributed software development efforts [7,14,15]. Standards pervade spaces ranging from home networking [12,23], to sustainability [8,9,27], to the development of first responder systems [26,31], supporting (or trying to) the forms of interoperability needed to produce coherent, stable, and extensible technical systems at the margins of complex and variable human environments. Standards also establish points of connection between parts of systems actively designed by HCI researchers and those received from wider worlds of computing, including those structured, for better or for worse, at 'lower' or 'deeper' levels of operation [13].

The centrality of technical standards in HCI work is matched by findings in other fields. Work in information policy from both academic and industrial sources has pointed to problems of technical standardization as an issue both poorly understood and badly practiced among technology players in industry, academia, and government [6,36]. And work in science policy and the social studies of science has pinpointed technical standards as key and widely misrecognized features of robust, sustainable, and scalable communities of knowledge [11,17,22].

These problems only intensify when we expand our definition beyond the technical frame to include *all* forms of standardization that go into distributed collective practices of all sorts. Standardized interfaces establish the baselines and connection points to wider technological systems to which our own design efforts can attach (such that we can build applications around, for example, mobile health or environmental sustainability without navigating the insides of Android or iOS). Standards structure the forms of data we pull from the web into our applications and programs, making large bodies of numeric, textual and visual data tractable and actionable through analysis. Other standards – for example, around privacy or accessibility – make sure that our work gets out into the world in its most general and inclusive form. Standards also structure the way we take the world in: for example, through user studies that sort unruly masses of individuals into more and less stable categories of 'users' (see for example [25]). At the most general level, standards channel and regularize the conduct and behavior of actors of all sorts, making practices and systems of exchange or interaction possible: while we can imagine a market without laws for example, it's harder to imagine one without standards.

Such insights are backed by a growing but still nascent body of HCI research that seeks to restore standards and standards work from a background element of technical development and social practice to an active and sometimes contested feature of collaborative life. Within the broader HCI field, this work has shown up most forcefully in the Computer Supported Cooperative Work (CSCW) literature to date. Classic work from the early years of CSCW on problems of collaboration and joint work identified standards as one among a suite of "coordination mechanisms" by which distributed and technically supported work is accomplished [30]. Separate work by Star and Griesemer [33] and Star and Strauss [35] identify standards as integrally connected to the sorts of "boundary objects" and "articulation work" that support collaboration across complex and heterogeneous landscapes.

Standards make a more direct appearance, however, in an influential line of work on infrastructure beginning from Star and Ruhleder [34] and Bowker [3] and extending up through more recent work in HCI, CSCW, and the social sciences [10,11,16,22,29]. In this definition, infrastructure provides the framework or scaffolding for social and technical activities of all sorts, and exemplifies a number of key features or properties: its embedding in other structures; its frequent transparency (or invisibility) in use; its reach or scope beyond single sites of practice; its connections to conventions and communities of practice; its embodiment in standards; its dependence on an installed base of practices and material; and its tendency to 'reappear' (or return to conscious reflection) upon breakdown [4,34].

Within this list, standards take on special scope and importance, embodying and extending many of the other features in Star and Ruhleder's list. Standards for example perform a special role in linking infrastructure to established communities of practice (think of the frequency with which professional groups issue standardized credentials, guidelines, or professional codes of conduct, for example). Standards account in part for the inertia and stability of the installed base named in Star and Ruhleder's description: once grooved and certified through standards, local departures from global or more general practices can become costly or impossible. And per design discussions above, standards are a key mechanism by which problems and questions at the margins of systems can be made to disappear, helping infrastructure sink into the obscurity it 'seeks'.

More recent work by Lampland and Star [20] has called out this connection more explicitly, devoting additional attention to the nature of standards as an integral aspect or component of infrastructure. In this work, they argue that standards are: 1. nested inside one another; 2. distributed unevenly across the sociotechnical landscape; 3. relative to communities of practice; 4. linked and integrated (to each other and to organizations, nations, and technical systems); and 5. codify or embody ethics or values. The relationship between this list and the earlier infrastructure list is striking, calling out the deep and arguably inseparable connections linking the two concepts: to a large extent, infrastructure works through standards, and vice versa.

While much of the emphasis above is on the stability of infrastructure and the consequences of being excluded from it (as in Star's later discussions of 'infrastructural orphans' [32]), it's also important to note the potentially *dynamic* character of a world structured through standards. Imagine for example the challenge of changing the world one system, practice, or user at a time across a truly non-standardized landscape (a situation echoed in parts of the empirical section that follows). Now imagine the task of changing those practices by switching or flipping a standard that exists. The latter case is hard (maybe impossible, depending on circumstance) but in principle and with the right alignment of forces doable. That's because standards provide a fulcrum or pivot point around which change can unfold, reconciling innovation in parts of systems with 'global' demands for stability and coherence.

In all these ways, standards and protocols maintain the practices and expectations of users and designers against the messy churn of the worlds around them. Standards shape the space available to system developers, ensuring that innovation meets the world in workable fashion. From a traditional design perspective, this is a rich story of artifacts, tools, and the complexities associated with bringing features of the built world around us into better and more sustainable alignment through design. But it's also a story of everything that design touches: practices, organizations, values, and expectations – all of which may be implicated and shaped by the work of standards development. We design to, from, and with standards. If there weren't standards, we'd have to design *everything*, and be a lot smarter than we in fact are.

The sections that follow develop these claims by reference to an ongoing program of work around the development of new computational infrastructures in American ecology. We explore the role that standards play in the large-scale research networks increasingly (yet perhaps erroneously) viewed as the future of ecology and other fields; how standards in complex interactive environments can struggle and fail (and what happens when they do); and how actors work across the gaps that standards leave to produce more effective forms of design and interaction in the world.

STANDARDS & INTERACTIVE SYSTEMS IN ECOLOGY

In this section, we report on data from a long-term ethnographic field study around patterns of computational development, governance, and collaboration in American ecology. Since 2010, we have interviewed over 150 ecologists and conducted participant observations across more than a dozen centers of ecological research, including both the individual lab and large-scale research network described in greater detail below. Interviews ran from one to three hours, and several participants were interviewed more than once in the course of the research. Wherever possible, interviews included observation and sometimes direct participation in research work practices. Interviews were transcribed by members of the project team or hired transcriptionists, producing more than 2000 pages of transcript data. These were then coded using grounded theory concepts and the NVivo software application. The code set developed for this paper focused heavily on issues of standards development, practices, training, difficulties, and challenges, and the wider tasks of coordination and interoperability these activities were meant to support.

The empirical accounts that follow focus on practices and problems of standards in two immediate contexts: an individual research program ('the Lab') operating out of a Midwestern university whose primary field work occurs in a remote northern site; and the National Ecological Observatory Network, a continental-scale observatory for ecological work and collaboration that is currently under construction and headquartered in Boulder, Colorado. This structure is designed to pull out similarities and differences in problems of standardization and design in interactive systems development at scales both local and global in nature.

LOCAL STANDARDS

Our first empirical case concerns an ecological research lab ("the Lab") based at a large Midwestern research university. Its fieldwork is primarily located at "Northern Station," a remote and mostly seasonal research site that is part of the larger Long-Term Ecological Research Network (LTER), a grouping of 26 diverse field sites dedicated to building long-term ecological knowledge critical to understanding ecological processes ranging from invasive species and nutrient cycling to food chain dynamics and climate change. While the Lab is invested in routine, long-term monitoring at Northern Station, it runs additional grant funded projects at the site as well. It also works collaboratively with other labs operating onsite, sharing infrastructure, expertise, and occasionally data.

At first glance, the Lab would seem to represent a relatively straightforward case of standardization. The Lab is small (fewer than 10 people in a given field season), its research is mostly restricted to a single field site, the PI has worked at the site for over two decades, and the Lab's responsibilities to coordinate with outside research programs are fairly light. If there is a simple case for standards in collaborative ecological work, this should be it. That standards and standardization are *not* simple in such a setting tells us much about the function and complexity of standards work in complex interactive environments.

At the heart of the Lab's standardization efforts lies its protocol book, a 375+ page manual that contains methods and protocols for each and every action performed by the research team, whether in the field or back in the lab at their home institution. The manual includes sections covering preparations for the field season, starting up and shutting down field operations, sampling methods and equipment usage, laboratory and analysis procedures, data processing and storage, methods for fieldwork in other sites and projects, software and key statistical analysis packages, and a series of short-form descriptions called "wallocols" described in greater detail below. The protocol book is constantly updated (it is currently in its 29th edition) and supports standardization in all things the lab does. A lab manager explained to us that he consults the protocol book "anytime [he's] starting anything new," and cited several instances of using the protocol book to successfully execute unfamiliar tests and procedures. New graduate students and summer research assistants are given relevant entries from the protocol book to read upon joining the lab, more experienced technicians periodically consult it, the protocol book is regularly checked and updated to reflect new equipment and minute changes in practice, and the entire research team reviews and amends the protocols at the end of the active research season. These changes are themselves meticulously documented, so that the entire document ends up containing a history of its own development. If the fictional cartographers of the Borges story, *A Universal History of Iniquity* [2] ('the map that covers the territory'), ever wrote a protocol book, this would be it.

While the protocol book serves as the master reference, its formal prescriptions of action are carried into the world through an intermediate set of documents. As the protocol book has grown into a dense and unwieldy artifact, the lab has created shortened versions of key techniques called "wallocols." These wallocols function as "a reminder note of the major steps" and convey the essentials of a particular protocol boiled down to one page and literally taped to a wall in their lab at the site. These range from reminders of what to pack before heading out for a day of fieldwork to an abbreviated list of critical steps for particular field or lab procedures. One lab manager has gone on to create versions that are shorter still and printed in field notebooks to map out key and notably tricky field operations (e.g. measuring stream discharge rates under varying local terrains). The field notebooks themselves have become standardized over time: twenty years ago they were blank "Rite in the Rain" notebooks, but have since evolved to include pre-printed form-like pages that guide the field worker on what data to record (time, date, weather, temperature, etc.) at a particular site. These intermediate forms and artifacts are important parts of the Lab's efforts to coordinate data collection and interpretation across time and space, and are crucial to the standardizing ambitions of the Lab's research efforts.

The scale of these efforts is best understood when mapped against the difficulties that standards are meant to address. As the Lab's Principal Investigator (PI) explains to us,

> Just about everything that we do, either in the field or in the lab can have an impact on the final numbers that we produce. So there is a direct link from each step all the way through to saying, "This is the number. The number is 5 plus or minus 1." We feel that either shows there's an impact of climate change or doesn't. And because each and every step is linked to the other and can have an impact on the final numbers that we generate, we have to be extremely explicit about how to do each step.

Standards protect the integrity of this chain, and provide infrastructure crucial to the integrity and ultimately credibility of the work.

Despite the care and intensity of this work, efforts at formal standardization as represented by the protocol book face challenges grounded in the material, placed-based, and human dimensions of ecological work. Ecology is a messy field and heterogeneity in environments and organisms makes data collection, use, and interpretation challenging. At the same time, while some routine activities performed by the Lab lend themselves to formal and abstract description, others rely on elements of 'feel' or 'touch' that are much harder to codify in this way. One lab member for example offered the following description of difficulties in formalizing protocols for the measure of permafrost:

> Is this a rock or ice? So you stick a metal probe into the ground and the steel probe penetrates it, it's just a big T handle. You stick it down; you put your hands across the top on the T and push it down into the ground until it won't go any further. And then you put your hand down at this little surface and wrap your fingers around the thaw probe, pull it out, and then it's graduated. You measure where your fingers are, "Oh that's 10 centimeters, that's 20 centimeters, and that's 32 centimeters." And that's the depth. So one of the things you can read about in the protocol, it says, "Make sure that you're hitting ice, that you're hitting frozen soil and not a rock because a rock will stop you just like the ice will stop you." And you could read that all day and never know the difference between a rock and the ice. You wouldn't know that in the field unless you actually had a feel for it and someone was there telling you: *Dink!* "Hear that sound?" "Yeah, I haven't heard that before." "Yeah, that's a rock. Now move it a little bit over and do it in the permafrost, that is the ice. Do you see the difference?" "Yes." "Do you feel the difference?" "Yes." "Done."

Other difficulties stem from over reliance on formally expressed protocols, to the neglect of contingencies and mitigating factors necessitating workarounds, improvisation, and discretionary judgment. All manner of occasions arise where a person must make creative decisions that mediate between the protocol in its formal dimensions and the details of a non-compliant reality. Have voles chewed through some wires? Is a thunderstorm on the horizon likely to shorten available field time? Has a bear eaten or disrupted the collection equipment? Even apparently simple processes like measuring the water discharge rate of a stream by sticking a rod in the water and reading a number off an attached box may provoke exceptions:

> Let's say there's a big rock in the middle of the stream and you stick the probe right behind it and it measures zero discharge because all the water's flowing around it, right? And someone did that because that's what the protocol says, just step two steps across the stream every meter. Or if there's vegetation, or if you can tell like, oh wait a minute, you can see there's an eddy here pooling the water so it's actually flowing like, negative discharge or something, which can happen.

Adding an additional layer of complexity, small labs depend on teams of research assistants, graduate students, and post-doctoral workers whose composition can change from season to season, affecting the apprenticeship styles of learning that shape the deployment of protocols in lab and field, and may cause shifts or breaks in practice. Even where teams remain the same, memory or habits can fail, introducing subtle variations in technique that may affect the data, suggesting patterns where none exist and obscuring others that are real. These problems can be traced to minute and usually innocent changes in practice that can produce collective forms of protocol "drift" over the course of time – an example of 'bad' creativity that PIs at Northern Station often worry about and frequently encounter. The Lab PI described one such seasonal example:

> There has to be constant checking, because protocols evolve extremely rapidly and constantly. So, I'll leave at the start of the summer, and I'll come back at the end. They say, "No, this is the way we always done it," and I'm looking and they're doing it completely different. "What do you mean this is the way you've always... ?! I told you how to do this in June, what happened?" [laughs]. So, constant vigil on that is required.

To meet these challenges, standards processes, even highly ambitious and formalized ones like those represented in the Lab's protocol book (or the more computational forms described under NEON below), will frequently return to the trust and judgment of human agents. For this reason, a great deal of the standards action at Northern Station resides in training and apprenticeship: periods of collaboration, teaching, and practice in the field through which procedures are taught and corrected, discretionary skill and judgment is built, and basic understandings of standards and the broader objectives behind them are shared. Operating in this mode, standards take on a clear authoritative or "disciplinary" role vis-à-vis the human and object worlds around them, enforcing fealty and conformance to worlds of established practice and expectation. To stray from this path is to court disaster, and turn data, sometimes literally, into dirt. It is also to leave the community of science (and if you're a field tech or undergraduate research assistant making too many such departures, to earn an early one-way ticket home).

But the same processes also build creative and discretionary skills that can in fact rescue and renovate standardized programs when things go wrong or new opportunities arise. Humans can be flexible, contextually aware, and creative, applying discretionary judgment in appropriate and science-saving ways when breakdowns and unexpected situations arise. Skilled field workers with deep knowledge of the science (rather than rote or mechanical understanding of the protocol) can adjust in subtle and consequential ways when the need and opportunity arises – *changes which can then be incorporated into the living body of the standard.* It is this history of change and emergence that accounts for the length and ongoing elaboration of the protocol book (now in its 29th edition), and provides the counterbalance to the purely constraining or 'disciplinary' view above. The story of standards as practiced at Northern Station is not solely about freezing practice, or locking it into variants established in unchanging form at the moment of launch or origination. Rather, standards retain important and necessary dimensions of discretion and creativity (though these capacities may be jealously guarded and differentially distributed). If standards constrain change, they also enable it, and are in fact central to ongoing processes of innovation by which ecological knowledge and technique learns and grows [5]. The protocols of Northern Station are written in solid and well-pressed pencil, but it's not indelible ink.

GLOBAL STANDARDS

Our second empirical case involves the National Ecological Observatory Network (NEON), a $434 million observatory system funded by the U.S. National Science Foundation. NEON plans to gather ecological data across a diverse suite of ecosystems throughout North America for 30 years to better understand and predict continental-scale ecological questions of climate change, land use change, and invasive species. Having successfully navigated its design and planning phases, NEON is now in a five-year construction process that will culminate in full operational status by 2017 (though parts of the observatory are already collecting live data). NEON intends to use existing data from satellites, site-based remote sensing data, and a standardized field collection program to describe ecosystem changes across space and over the next three decades. Data collected at over 100 sites will reflect information about climate, atmosphere, soils, streams, and other water bodies, and a range of organisms. This data will in turn be repackaged into high-level data products, calibrated and curated for open use through the network website.

Within this world, standards take on complex and important roles. Some of the standards issues faced by NEON parallel those experienced by the Lab above, though often magnified and made more complex by the greater collaborative and ecological range of the work in question. Others represent problems specific to scale, or that attach in particular to organizations and research endeavors in their moments of start-up and formation. In either case, through a good part of its planning and current construction phase, a disproportionate amount of the efforts of NEON staff have been dedicated to crafting, building, anticipating, and working around the difficulties that standards pose. This work begins with the efforts of the science team, and proceeds through most or all members of the NEON engineering, computing, education, civil construction, data products, project management and field operations staff.

NEON's standards challenges stem from a single daunting fact: namely, that through most of its history and across many of its disciplinary and methodological sub-communities, ecology has remained radically non-standardized (or rather, has resolved its standards issues at the scale and through mechanisms as outlined in the case of the Lab above). NEON's organizational scale and its ambition to function as a single 'instrument,' collecting and distributing comparable data across the vast array of sites and ecological diversity represented under the network's sampling footprint make this solution untenable. But it also produces sometimes severe and perplexing challenges for those seeking to build effective standards to support NEON's growing program of work.

Some of these challenges attach to the extreme range and heterogeneity that standardized tools and protocols in NEON are required to address. From rivers that freeze for large portions of the year to those that dry up in the summer, scientists in the NEON field program – the side of the organization most closely aligned with the types of activities described earlier at Northern Station – are required to arrive at sets of standards sufficient to preserve the integrity and comparability of data, while remaining workable in the varied sites in which they'll be practiced. Within this range, some things are harder to standardize than others, reflecting differences in sampling methods but also the prior organization of the underlying scientific communities. As one staff scientist described:

> Because of the breadth of those sampling activities, plants, insects, mammals, aquatic environments and so on, you're sourcing information from a variety of different communities. And even within each of those communities, there are no standard methods of practice. One PI and another PI will differ quite strenuously about the right way to do it, and so there is no standard within the community of practice.

While some of these differences connect to personal choice and history (and the desire to have the new network produce data consistent with extant field programs), others stem from legitimate differences in site-specific needs at individual sites and the difficulties of one-size-fits-all protocols in meeting these. Another staff scientist for example described the challenges of insect collection, and how emergent NEON protocols for mosquito sampling were bad at capturing the specific species responsible for carrying dengue fever in NEON's more southerly sites (even though insect-borne diseases were one of the stated targets of the network). Working across such differences, and making the inevitable trade-offs and compromises that result, can involve NEON protocol developers (many of them junior and early-stage researchers) in complicated and sometimes contentious disciplinary negotiations.

Even after a network-wide standard is achieved, the difficulties don't go away. If the Lab faced challenges coordinating standards across the turnover of graduate and seasonal workers, NEON faces the daunting task of practicing and enforcing its standards across a still larger and more distributed team of field workers, themselves coming out of specific trainings but required, under the organization of the NEON field teams, to perform field operations that in fact span several disciplinary and methodological traditions. As with the Lab, some of these procedures involve elements of feel or judgment that do not reduce well to formal description. Still others concern matters of skill and routinized action whose appropriate level of description – when is the protocol detail insufficient, and when is it too much? – is a subject of ongoing debate and experiment between members of the science and field operations staff. (One of the more interesting versions of this work involves the process of 'cold-testing' protocols, in which non-domain experts are handed draft protocols and asked to reproduce the procedures described, to wildly different outcomes).

Under such conditions, risks of error and protocol drift become acute: in an ecological variant of the 'broken telephone' game, there is a real and frequently expressed worry that even if the field teams *start* doing things in a standardized way, they may very soon not be. At the same time, risks of mindless or too-literal adherence to the protocol (especially among field workers with little background in the technique or science behind it) may grow, raising the prospect that NEON data will be rendered useless by failing to exercise the discretionary adjustments and accommodations needed to preserve the spirit as sometimes against the letter of the protocol. The geographic distribution of NEON makes these issues all the more acute, as individual technicians and field managers in some of the farther flung domains cannot easily 'drop by' NEON headquarters in Colorado to check such issues.

To counter this, members of the science and field operations team we spoke to described a number of ideas and strategies, some of which indeed pushed the organization further in the direction of standardization. One of these predictably involves training, and in particular a strategy by which field managers routinely travel to Boulder to 'recertify' on core NEON methods operative in their domain. Another involves quality assurance through periodic and randomized tests and spot-checks, checking the local application of NEON protocols as these develop in specific domains over time. Yet another concerns the ultimate authority of staff scientists in Boulder for checking and certifying any domain-specific departures from protocol, and the evolution of the protocol as a whole over time. As one field manager argued,

> The local workaround is exactly what we want to try to avoid. I think it's just going to be not only talking to my fellow people, but I really view the scientists in Boulder as kind of that point of contact for any potential challenges and making sure that they're the holder of the keys that says, "Oh, it's okay to adjust your process because of where you are," versus, "No. You need to do it the same way"... I am a trained scientist. I can figure this stuff out, but it's really not my call, and it shouldn't be my call, and it shouldn't be my technicians' call. It's really the folks in Boulder—the ones that wrote that protocol, came up with that design.

If standards challenges in the NEON field program show up in particularly acute and immediate ways, subtle but no less consequential issues confront other operational groups at NEON. Members of the remote sensing team described to us the difficulties of deriving common and reliable forest cover and vegetation density readings on the basis of satellite and airborne measure, and the practices of calibration dependent on overflying well-characterized sites. Cyberinfrastructure team members spoke about the challenges of standardized file names and structures, and NEON's efforts to leave the one-off spreadsheet world behind. Members of the sensor team talked about the challenges of ensuring reliable and comparable sensors, and their work with manufacturers to ensure equipment would meet the quality assurance and error tolerance standards set by NEON. And project management and systems engineering staff described to us the challenges of making the organization cohere as a whole, holding the various project teams and sub-units to standardized schedules and project interfaces. While few of these match the scale and complexity of standards challenges facing the field team, standards issues are fully absent for none.

The NEON case sketched here extends and amplifies many of the practices and challenges experienced by the Lab above. Like the Lab (but more so), NEON faces challenges of coherence and coordination rooted in the natural variability of the landscapes it covers. It also faces issues owing to the collaborative and distributed character of ecological work, and the multiplicity of human agents involved in carrying it out. Some of its challenges are rooted in the character of the work itself, including forms of skill work and discretionary judgment that fit uneasily within the world of formally codified standards. Others are rooted in the nature and organization of NEON itself, and the work required to make such an entity cohere. Given these challenges, many of NEON's efforts in the standards space are oriented to limiting, constraining, and otherwise managing the sprawl of the human, technical and natural environments they face.

But not all of NEON's efforts and conversations point in this direction. Scientists in our interview set also spoke to us about NEON's need to grow and evolve, and the danger that rigid standards and protocols, narrowly and statically applied, might compromise the network's capacity to respond to new techniques, opportunities, and new scientific and social interests in the phenomena under study. This concern accounts in part for the network's choice to retain mobile and relocatable sites and units that can be shifted and redeployed in strategic and opportunistic ways. It has also prompted internal discussions around the appropriate conditions and procedures under which the standards they are working so hard and painfully to produce might be changed, relaxed, or abandoned.

DISCUSSION

As the above analysis makes clear, problems of standards and standardization constitute central and ubiquitous elements in programs of computational development and collaborative work in the sciences. These came to the fore with particular clarity in the context of NEON, both because standards there are still being established, and because the effort to connect ecological work and infrastructure across previously unconnected sites and practices raises deep challenges of coordination to which standards are a natural, if by no means simple, response. But standards and protocols were no less present or challenging in the context of our lab-level study, despite the much smaller scale of sites and personnel involved. While we saw how the Lab manages unevenness and variability in the natural, material, and human environments around it through elaborate exercises in standardization built around the protocol book, we also saw how hard and necessarily incomplete such efforts were, and the constant work needed to update, maintain, and work around the problems and gaps that standards, as practiced in this domain, inevitably leave.

These cases demonstrate the range of forms that standards may take. While the examples foreground immediate problems of artifact, practice and environment, the worlds of standardization encountered in our work were more varied and complicated than that, and included many instances where scientific efforts met standards processes and problems in other domains. Members of the environmental safety and permitting team at NEON, for example, described the challenges of navigating the legal and institutional procedures emanating from a maze of municipal, county, state, and federal institutions, each with their own requirements and procedures. Standards questions also arose around the evaluation and long-term career trajectories of NEON employees, many of whom operate in modes and roles relatively new to ecology, and that sit uneasily within the standardized metrics of performance and reward (publication, research productivity, teaching, etc.) that have typically structured the field.

Our cases also point to just how hard standards work is, whether measured by time devoted to activities, incidents of breakdown, or the sheer frustration that standards and their failure can occasion. Despite the Lab's best efforts, the practices of seasonal and even veteran field workers can drift over the course of one or several summers. This is exacerbated when new or inexperienced field workers miss key contextual clues that necessitate flexible and appropriate tweaks to standard practices. Scientists, engineers, and systems developers at NEON face the same problems of consistency and coordination in radically expanded form, exacerbated by organizational scale and the ecological diversity their procedures are required to cover.

Finally, our cases point to the varied ways such effects play out across the range of activities, practices and entities that go into the production and maintenance of a collaborative research program (and other complex distributed practices). Some practices and entities reduce to standards more easily than others. Some build on past histories of standardization, or occur in forms that lend themselves to clear and uncontested descriptions that *can* be effectively captured, codified, and reproduced. Others don't codify so neatly, and are marked by forms of contingency and emergence that resist easy simplification: 'square' or irregular pegs in the 'round' holes that systems of standardization inevitably require and produce. Some things are 'hard' to standardize, and others are 'easy' (which often simply means that the work has happened in the past, or that entities left outside of the standard lack the power or position to contest it). Any complex interactive system (science, for example!) is likely to contain a mix of such elements, leading to complex internal dynamics and accommodations. Such differences can become a source of frustration and misunderstanding, including in the development of new computational systems designed to bridge and coordinate such heterogeneity.

So: standards are everywhere and come in many varieties, some of them surprising. They're also hard, and hard *differentially*, affecting different parts of complex interactive systems in different ways. These difficulties may increase with scale, as practices move towards higher levels of aggregation. They also grow with heterogeneity, as systems seek to bring increasingly diverse worlds – people, artifacts, and environments – into alignment.

But standards are also intimately connected to much of what HCI researchers seek to accomplish in the world. Whether it's new forms of environmental monitoring and awareness [8,9,27], new infrastructures for crisis management and response [31], or new collaborative infrastructures in the sciences [16,17,22], standards are at the heart of what we do. A great deal of HCI work relies on standards produced elsewhere [13], whether those constraining the tools and objects we build with, those shaping practices of use amongst our target populations, or those sustaining the conditions of action and knowability in our target domains (try to imagine the field of sustainable HCI, for example, without the standards of environmental measure and accounting it depends on). At the same time, HCI researchers may be important *producers* of standards, establishing protocols for action and design with long-standing weight, durability, and 'stickiness' across the systems and fields we engage.

For all of these reasons, building more thoughtful and productive relationships with standards constitutes an HCI research and design priority of the highest order. The following rules of thumb are some practical starting points:

Build from extant standards: We have seen how efforts at new infrastructure development in the sciences must account for the uneven landscape of inherited standards, formal and informal, and how such initiatives may struggle when such standards are sidelined. But this principle holds true across many (perhaps all!) spheres of HCI engagement. New and perhaps especially integrative design efforts must negotiate with what may be very old standards that structure work and interaction in the settings they cover and in part construct. Viewed positively, extant standards provide crucial shortcuts to action, bounding and limiting the design space in frequently useful ways: we design further by standing on the shoulders of standards. More problematically, contradictory, divergent or unaccounted for standards may undermine or torpedo our best efforts, producing frictions, breakdowns, or simple non-adoptions that limit the scope and impact of HCI work.

Work creatively across scale: We have seen how much of the value (and challenge!) of standards arises at the transit points between 'bigger' and 'smaller' (or simply *different*) systems. Standards are often most needed and most formalized when moving to larger or more distributed levels of aggregation. This is true of the challenges faced by NEON in moving ecology from its history of small and locally controlled field operations towards its vision of robust interoperability at a global scale. But it's also true of demands placed on standards as HCI design efforts move towards higher levels of aggregation: the move to global, distributed (as opposed to in-house) software development efforts; the movement from experimental to production-grade systems in environmental monitoring and sustainable HCI; the incorporation of a growing range of regional and national organizations in crisis response settings; etc. In Ribes [28] terms, standards constitute crucial "scalar devices," building bridges between design and action at a local level, and possibilities of growth, extension, and interoperability at higher or wider levels of operation. This makes them integral to the ambitions of scale and impact that inform much of HCI research and design.

Accommodate contingency, change, and growth: Finally, we have seen how the actors in our study responded to the simultaneous threat and opportunity of change around the standards that guide their work. This speaks to a potentially *dynamic* character of standards, and the need to balance a too-assiduous fealty to them with opportunities for change and growth emerging in the environment. While periods of stasis are crucial to anchoring or coordinating role of standards, so too are moments and opportunities for change.

This too holds true across other fields of HCI practice and engagement. If we build from standards, we also build *to* them. Reflective consideration of the numerous tweaks, breakdowns, and departures from standards (including in the systems we build) may support a more thoughtful, creative, and resilient engagement with standards over time.

In sum, we should learn to engage proactively with standards, working *with* rather than *against* the 'grain' of the world that standards, in part, supply. This may involve new forms of listening to fields we encounter, seeking new insights into the forces that structure value and action in the worlds we engage – a form of accommodation and humility that may sit uneasily with more heroic notions of design. But we may also need to find *creative* and *improvisational* potentials in and around the settled worlds of standards around us. An outside example of this may be found in the significantly different relationship between standards and innovation to be found in the interactive system of jazz. As described in Paul Berliner's masterful *Thinking In Jazz: The Infinite Art of Improvisation* [1], standards have long played a special role in this world. Standard tunes passed down through generations provide historical continuity, connecting early masters to present practitioners. They establish the basis of 'interoperability,' such that previously unacquainted practitioners (who may share no other background or referent) can 'spontaneously' interact. They also fix the rules and gradations of practice that constitute key markers of belonging and hierarchy in the field: to be a good jazz musician is above all to play the standards well. They are also, however, *the field's key site of novelty and invention.* Some of these emerge as elements of voice and style: for example, where new jazz stylists turn to standards to demonstrate the novelty and value of a 'new sound.' Some emerge from breakdowns not entirely dissimilar to those described in ecology: arranging to available instruments when star performers depart or fall ill, or the novel trains of action that can be set in motion by a single wrong note (as in Klemp et. al.'s [19] analysis of the consequences of a wrong note during a Thelonious Monk recording of "In Walked Bud.") Such thoughtful and sometimes contingent appropriation of standards has anchored forms of improvisation grounding and renewing jazz from generation to generation, preserving its continuity and liveness as a musical form. HCI and other fields of information science could learn much from this example.

CONCLUSION

Our findings hold important lessons for HCI research around new tool and system development in the sciences, whether we're talking about the maintenance and operation of existing systems or the design of new field-specific tools, middleware, or infrastructures. These findings are timely and salient in light of the significant transformations in scale, practice and value currently being attempted across ecology and other fields of science – transformations in which HCI research has had an important role to play.

But our findings also hold implications for wider bodies of HCI knowledge and practice. Standards shape and constrain the worlds of design and practice that HCI researchers inherit and engage. They organize practice, producing forms of stability, routinization, and predictability around which subsequent design can build. They guide local action and expectation towards systemic or collective demands, allowing for the exchange of objects, labor, and knowledge through which larger interactive systems may be constituted. These features become additionally important as HCI scholarship enters into increasingly complex relations with wider and more varied fields of practice. When they're on our side, standards are our friends, adding force and strength to our efforts to make the world flow in the directions we seek, and supporting whatever broader goals – sustainability, innovation, justice, participation – we might assign to our work. When they're against us, no amount of smart and creative design is likely to prevail.

ACKNOWLEDGMENTS

We thank our interviewees for their time and insights. This research is supported under U.S. National Science Foundation Grant #0847175.

REFERENCES

1. Berliner, P. *Thinking in jazz: the infinite art of improvisation.* University of Chicago Press, Chicago, 1994.
2. Borges, J.L. *A universal history of iniquity.* Penguin, London, 2001.
3. Bowker, G.C. *Science on the run: information management and industrial geophysics at Schlumberger, 1920-1940.* MIT Press, Cambridge, MA, 1994.
4. Bowker, G.C. and Star, S.L. *Sorting things out: classification and its consequences.* MIT Press, Cambridge, MA, 1999.
5. Burton, M. and Jackson, S.J. Constancy and Change in Scientific Collaboration: Coherence and Integrity in Long-Term Ecological Data Production. *HICSS 2012*, (2012), 353–362.
6. Cargill, C.F. Eating Our Seed Corn: A Standards Parable for our Time. 2005. http://blogs.adobe.com/standards/files/2012/04/Eating-Our-Seed-Corn-revised-April-2012.pdf.
7. Cataldo, M. and Herbsleb, J.D. Coordination Breakdowns and Their Impact on Development Productivity and Software Failures. *IEEE Transactions on Software Engineering 39*, 3 (2013), 343–360.
8. DiSalvo, C., Sengers, P., and Brynjarsdóttir, H. Mapping the Landscape of Sustainable HCI. *Proc. CHI 2010*, ACM Press (2010), 1975–1984.
9. Dourish, P. HCI and environmental sustainability. *Proc. DIS 2010*, ACM Press (2010), 1–10.

10. Edwards, P.N., Jackson, S.J., Bowker, G.C., and Knobel, C.P. *Understanding Infrastructure: Dynamics, Tensions, and Design.* Ann Arbor, MI, 2007.

11. Edwards, P.N., Jackson, S.J., Chalmers, M.K., et al. *Knowledge Infrastructures: Intellectual Frameworks and Research Challenges.* Ann Arbor, MI, 2013.

12. Edwards, W.K. and Grinter, R.E. At Home with Ubiquitous Computing: Seven Challenges. *Ubicomp 2001*, Springer Berlin Heidelberg (2001), 256–272.

13. Edwards, W.K., Newman, M.W., and Poole, E.S. The infrastructure problem in HCI. *Proc. CHI 2010*, ACM Press (2010), 423–432.

14. Grinter, R.E. Doing Software Development: Occasions for Automation and Formalisation. *Proc. Euro CSCW 1997*, Springer Netherlands (1997), 173–188.

15. Howison, J. and Herbsleb, J.D. Scientific software production: incentives and collaboration. *Proc. CSCW 2011*, ACM Press (2011), 513–522.

16. Jackson, S.J. and Barbrow, S.K. Infrastructure and vocation: field, calling and computation in ecology. *Proc. CHI 2013*, ACM Press (2013), 2873–2882.

17. Jackson, S.J., Edwards, P.N., Bowker, G.C., and Knobel, C.P. Understanding infrastructure: History, heuristics and cyberinfrastructure policy. *First Monday 12*, 6 (2007).

18. Jackson, S.J., Steinhardt, S.B., and Buyuktur, A. Why CSCW needs science policy (and vice versa). *Proc. CSCW 2013*, ACM (2013), 1113–1124.

19. Klemp, N., McDermott, R., Raley, J., Thibeault, M., Powell, K., and Levitin, D.J. Plans, Takes, and Mistakes. *Critical Social Studies 1*, (2008), 4–21.

20. Lampland, M. and Star, S.L. *Standards and their stories: how quantifying, classifying, and formalizing practices shape everyday life.* Cornell University Press, Ithaca, NY, 2009.

21. Lee, C.P., Dourish, P., and Mark, G. The human infrastructure of cyberinfrastructure. *Proc. CSCW 2006*, ACM Press (2006), 483–492.

22. Monteiro, E., Pollock, N., Hanseth, O., and Williams, R. From Artefacts to Infrastructures. *Computer Supported Cooperative Work (CSCW) 22*, 4-6 (2013), 575–607.

23. Newman, M.W., Elliott, A., and Smith, T.F. Providing an Integrated User Experience of Networked Media, Devices, and Services through End-User Composition. In J. Indulska, D.J. Patterson, T. Rodden and M. Ott, eds., *Pervasive Computing*. Springer Berlin Heidelberg, 2008, 213–227.

24. Olson, G.M., Zimmerman, A., and Bos, N. *Scientific collaboration on the Internet.* MIT Press, Cambridge, MA, 2008.

25. Oudshoorn, N. and Pinch, T.J., eds. *How users matter: the co-construction of users and technologies.* MIT Press, Cambridge, MA, 2003.

26. Palen, L., Vieweg, S., and Anderson, K.M. Supporting "Everyday Analysts" in Safety- and Time-Critical Situations. *The Information Society Journal 27*, 1 (2010), 52–62.

27. Pierce, J., Fan, C., Lomas, D., Marcu, G., and Paulos, E. Some consideration on the (in)effectiveness of residential energy feedback systems. *Proc. DIS 2010*, ACM Press (2010), 244–247.

28. Ribes, D. Ethnography of Scaling, or, How to a Fit a National Research Infrastructure in the Room. *Proc. CSCW 2014*, ACM Press (2014), 158–170.

29. Ribes, D. and Lee, C.P. Sociotechnical Studies of Cyberinfrastructure and e-Research: Current Themes and Future Trajectories. *Computer Supported Cooperative Work (CSCW) 19*, 3-4 (2010), 231–244.

30. Schmidt, K. and Bannon, L. Taking CSCW seriously. *Computer Supported Cooperative Work (CSCW) 1*, 1-2 (1992), 7–40.

31. Starbird, K. and Palen, L. Working and sustaining the virtual "Disaster Desk." *Proc. CSCW 2013*, ACM Press (2013), 491–502.

32. Star, S.L. Orphans of Infrastructure: A New Point of Departure. Presentation given at Newnham College, Cambridge UK. 2007. http://events.stanford.edu/events/97/9744/.

33. Star, S.L. and Griesemer, J.R. Institutional Ecology, `Translations' and Boundary Objects: Amateurs and Professionals in Berkeley's Museum of Vertebrate Zoology, 1907-39. *Social Studies of Science 19*, 3 (1989), 387–420.

34. Star, S.L. and Ruhleder, K. Steps Toward an Ecology of Infrastructure: Design and Access for Large Information Spaces. *Information Systems Research 7*, 1 (1996), 111–134.

35. Star, S.L. and Strauss, A. Layers of Silence, Arenas of Voice: The Ecology of Visible and Invisible Work. *Computer Supported Cooperative Work (CSCW) 8*, 1-2 (1999), 9–30.

36. Updegrove, A. ICT Standard setting today: A system under stress. *First Monday 12*, 6 (2007).

37. Wilson, W. Request for Declaration of War. 1917

Tactum: A Skin-Centric Approach to Digital Design and Fabrication

Madeline Gannon
Carnegie Mellon University
mgannon@andrew.cmu.edu

Tovi Grossman
Autodesk Research
tovi.grossman@autodesk.com

George Fitzmaurice
Autodesk Research
george.fitzmaurice@autodesk.com

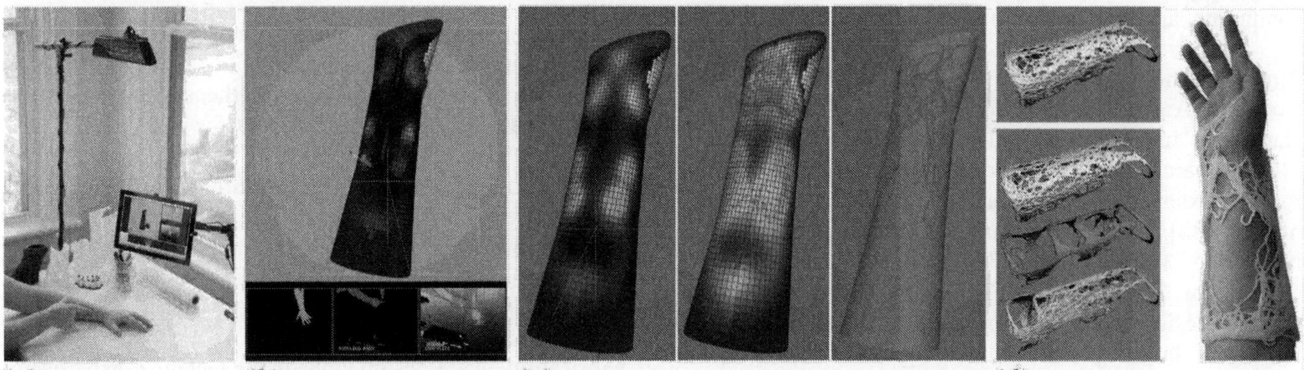

(a) (b) (c) (d)

Figure 1. Our fabrication-aware design system captures a user's skin-centric gestures for 3D modeling directly on the body. (a) the system captures skin input on a user's forearm and (b) translates it to a digital 3D modeling environment model. (c) skin-centric gestures enable the user to create a 3D printable design, (d) which inherently fits the complex geometry of their forearm.

ABSTRACT
Skin-based input has become an increasingly viable interaction model for user interfaces, however it has yet to be explored outside the domain of mobile computing. In this paper, we examine *skin* as an interactive input surface for gestural 3D modeling-to-fabrication systems. When used as both the input surface and base canvas for digital design, skin-input can enable non-experts users to intuitively create precise forms around highly complex physical contexts: our own bodies. In this paper, we outline design considerations when creating interfaces for such systems. We then discuss interaction techniques for three different modes of skin-centric modeling: *direct*, *parametric*, and *generative*. We also present *Tactum*, a new fabrication-aware design system that captures a user's skin-centric gestures for 3D modeling directly on the body. Lastly, we show sample artifacts generated with our system, and share a set of observations from design professionals.

INTRODUCTION
Skin-based input has become an increasingly viable interaction model for user interfaces. This large, always-available surface enables intuitive, tactile interactions [30, 43] and can even be reliably accessed without visual feedback [30, 23, 43]. However, skin-based input has yet to be explored outside the domain of mobile computing. In this paper, we examine *skin* as an interactive input surface for gestural 3D modeling-to-fabrication systems.

CHI 2015, April 18 - 23, 2015, Seoul, Republic of Korea.
Copyright 2015 ACM 978-1-4503-3145-6/15/04…$15.00
http://dx.doi.org/10.1145/2702123.2702581

Gesture-based interfaces for 3D modeling offer a number of unique affordances that can empower non-expert users to participate in digital design. They facilitate the expressive creation of digital geometry, while requiring little prerequisite skill for most interactions [8, 36]. However, their intuitive use comes at a cost: it is difficult for these systems to enable both high precision control *and* expressive form generation. As a result, the digital geometry generated is often limited to abstract or sculptural forms [20, 25, 34, 35, 49]. *Skin*, as both the input surface and base canvas for digital design, can enable non-experts users to intuitively create precise forms around highly complex physical contexts: our own bodies.

Further, as new forms of 3D printing and digital fabrication are reaching wider, non-technical audiences, there is a potential for users to design and fabricate personalized products [7]. In some cases, such personalization may relate to a user's own body – such as jewelry, braces, and other wearable devices. As such, we explore both design *and* fabrication workflows that utilize skin as an input platform.

In this paper, we make four contributions along these lines. First, we outline design considerations when creating interfaces that use skin-based input for gestural 3D modeling-to-fabrication. Second, we discuss interaction techniques for three different modes of skin-centric modeling: *direct, parametric,* and *generative*. Third, we present *Tactum*, a new fabrication-aware design system that captures a user's skin-centric gestures for 3D modeling directly on the body (Figure 1). Last, we show sample artifacts generated with our system, and share a set of observations from design professionals.

RELATED WORK

Our research builds upon existing work in digital garment design, gestural 3D modeling, skin-based mobile computing, and fabrication-aware design.

Digital Garment Design

Computer-Aided Design (CAD) for the body brings unique challenges in simulation, interaction, and manufacturing [24]. Research for screen-based garment CAD systems has focused extensively on simulating the drape or movement of cloth [38], generalizing models of human anatomy [40], interactive 3D modeling [37], and deconstructing 3D designs for 2D fabrication [26]. Tangible interfaces for garment design and fabrication have attempted to augment traditional tailoring tools with computer vision [44] or embedded intelligence [47].

However, none of these systems attempt to use skin as an interactive input surface for a gestural 3D modeling-to-fabrication system. In addition, these systems only focus on cloth-based garment design, and do not incorporate CAD for rigid or semi-rigid 3D printed materials.

Gesture-Based Modeling

Interfaces for gesture-based 3D modeling primarily capture input as mid-air interactions [8, 9, 34, 41, 49] or through tangible props [25, 35, 36]. One problem with both means of capture is the lack of precision and control, when compared to more conventional, mouse-based 3D modeling software. In addition, arm fatigue is prevalent in gestural interfaces using mid-air interactions [14]. Content creation in these gesture based modeling systems is often limited to sculptural or abstract modeling [8, 25, 34, 35, 49] or simple 3D navigation [20, 41]. One approach to bypass these limitations is by capturing mid-air gestures to search databases of pre-existing, detailed 3D models [17]. This, however, does not enable users to create new geometry.

More recently, researchers have begun incorporating physical contexts into the digital modeling environment [5, 6, 21, 22]. Bridging analog and virtual contexts helps novices of fabrication-based 3D modeling understand a sense of scale in what would otherwise be a scale-less virtual environment. *MixFab,* for example, incorporates physical props with gesture-based geometry creation for 3D printing [42]. This system is limited to basic 3D Euclidean modeling operations, which aren't sufficient when digitally designing for geometrically complex physical contexts, such as the human body.

Skin-Based Mobile Computing

The unique affordances of skin—its tactility, availability, and elasticity—have enabled a vast array of interaction scenarios to push beyond traditional, screen-based input surfaces. Solutions for sensing interactions with one's skin have been explored in devices worn on the body [2, 3, 13, 19, 23, 28, 30, 48], embedded in body [16], and embedded in the environment [10, 11, 29]. Combining these sensors with projectors enables skin to act as both an input and display surface [10, 12, 29].

Visual feedback is not entirely necessary to effectively interact with skin-based interfaces [12, 17, 31]. The body can act as a persistent anchor for the spatial and tactile memory of users, which is important for spatial input [15]. Recently, the social, physical, and psychological implications of skin-input have emerged as important design criteria for skin-based mobile interfaces [12, 31, 43, 44]. However, this prior research has not explored skin as an input surface for gestural 3D modeling.

Fabrication Aware Design

Fabrication-aware design embeds the technical expertise of an experienced fabricator into the workflow of a digital design environment. This method is traditionally used for large-scale engineering projects, where multiple material assemblies must join together to create complex geometries [32]. However, the rise of affordable CNC machines (*e.g.*, 3D printers, laser cutters, routers), has made fabrication-aware design an invaluable technique for opening advanced modeling and fabrication to non-expert users. Researchers are looking for new interfaces that engage this wider, non-technical audience. *Sketch-to-fabrication* systems, for example, link sketch-based 2D geometry to additive or subtractive processes in fabrication [4, 18, 26, 33]. Alternatively, *Interactive fabrication* systems enable a user to digitally design and fabricate directly on a material using intelligent hardware [27, 45, 50]. These systems, however, use neither skin nor the body as the design interface for a fabrication process.

In summary, our literature review reveals significant work in both skin input and gesture-based design. However, these two areas have yet to be explored in combination. They are particularly compatible because skin has the potential to provide persistent spatial and tactile references for gesture based design tools. Thus, the intersection of skin input and gesture-based design tools is an area ripe for exploration.

DESIGN CONSIDERATIONS

In this section we present a number of design considerations for the appropriate *content, configuration,* and *input and output* of skin-centric gestural modeling-to-fabrication systems.

Possible Content

Skin is an appropriate input surface for design tools intended for on-body artifacts. The non-Euclidean nature of our anatomy can make the design of wearable objects unintuitive in conventional CAD environments. However, appropriating skin as a starting canvas could help embed ergonomic principles into the foundations of a design. We therefore see three domain spaces that could specifically benefit from skin-centric interfaces for digital design.

First, fashion items, like garments, shoes, accessories, and jewelry can be adapted to skin-based input and 3D printing. Second, wearable computing devices, such as watches, smart eyewear, and fitness trackers, can also be customized or personalized using skin-centric design and fabrication tools. Third, medical devices – such as braces, splints, or casts – can be designed, customized, personalized, and fabricated through these systems for at-home rehabilitation.

Possible System Configurations

Three important aspects of a skin-centric design tool's system configuration are the user's point-of-view, the location of the canvas area, and the number of users interacting with the system.

Point-of-View

Figure 2 illustrates three possible point-of-view configurations. In *first-person* systems, the point-of-view of the modeler is directed at their own body [13]. This method is appropriate when there is a clean line of sight between the user and the canvas area. The forearms, hands, and upper thighs are likely locations for this system (Figure 2a). *Second-person* systems have parts of the desired canvas area occluded from the user's line of sight. As a result, these systems should provide representations of the body through an auxiliary display [49]. The face, neck, bust, back, or full body are likely locations for second-person systems (Figure 2b). *Third-person* systems have the canvas area located on a person other than the modeler [29]. This method is appropriate when multiple users collaborate on a single design (Figure 2c).

Single versus Multi-User Systems

Recent research has surveyed the propriety of touch for different locations of body-based interfaces [11, 30, 43]. While the social acceptance of touch may not be applicable to first- or second-person systems, it becomes an important factor when designing multi-user interfaces. Skin is useful as a collaborative modeling platform in scenarios where professionals work with non-experts. This scenario could occur with a doctor working directly on a patient [29], a fashion designer working directly on a model, or an engineer working with a consumer. It is important to give each party agency in the design process, although one user may have more influence over the final design than another. Moreover, additional instrumentation, such as touching with a stylus instead of the hand, can be introduced in locations where touch is necessary, but socially inappropriate or awkward.

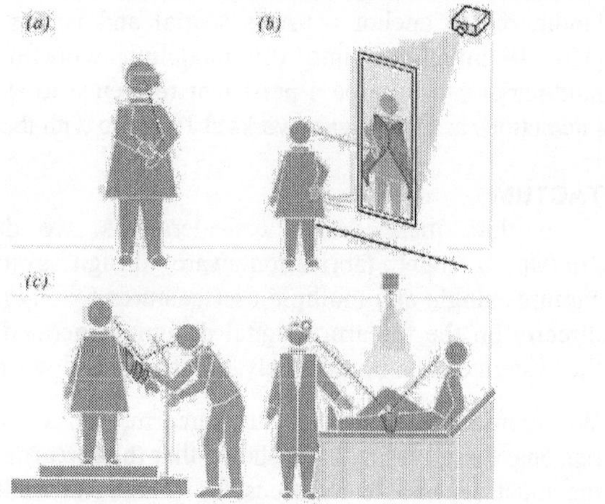

Figure 2. The point-of-view of the user or users determine the physical configuration of a skin-centric design tool. (a) first-person systems have a direct line of sight to the user's canvas area, (b) second-person systems have partially occluded canvas areas, and (c) third-person systems enable multiple users to participate in design.

Input

Hardware options for detecting touch input on the body have increased in recent years, however not all techniques are applicable skin-centric 3D modeling interfaces. Skin-based input for gestural 3D modeling must be able to detect both tactile input from *on-body* interactions and spatial input from *near-body* interactions. Moreover, sensor readings must be translatable to local and global Cartesian coordinate systems. Therefore many of the hardware solutions that infer touch based solely on disruptions in electric or acoustic signal may provide insufficient information for 3D modeling purposes [*e.g.*, 2, 3, 13, 23, 28]. However, pairing these devices with optical sensors, such as RGB, IR, or depth cameras, can provide robust information for 3D modeling with skin-based gestures.

Output

Visual output for skin-centric design tools can exist both *on* and *off* the user's body. As mentioned previously, one valuable affordance of skin as an input surface is that it facilitates the user's tactile and spatial memory of the body. Therefore, conventional off-body displays can effectively aid a user's bodily interactions. However, there are also a number of output devices that can provide direct visual overlays. Mobile or embedded projectors (Figure 2c) can provide robust visual feedback, especially when mapping two-dimensional forms onto parts of the body [10, 12]. For depth-rich three-dimensional designs, augmented reality devices, such as translucent screens (Figure 2c) or head-mounted displays (Figure 2a), may be better suited to overlay 3D visuals on the body. However, these devices are still limited by the canvas areas a user can directly see.

Spatial Landmarks

In addition to touch input, individual variations of skin, such as freckles, veins, and tattoos, can provide spatial landmarks to anchor a user's spatial and tactile memory [10]. If integrated into the modeling workflow, these landmarks can provide a persistent reference to skin-based interactions as the designer works at 1:1 scale with their body.

TACTUM

To explore these design considerations, we developed *Tactum*, a new fabrication-aware design system that captures single and multiple user gestures for 3D modeling directly on the forearm. Digital designs generated through the system can be immediately 3D printed and worn.

We focus specifically on the forearm, for a number of reasons. First, research has shown that the forearm is one of the most acceptable locations for single and multi-person touch [12, 31, 39, 44]. Second, a wide range of applicable artifacts, from jewelry to medical devices, can be designed for the forearm. Third, fatigue is a major challenge for gesture-based interfaces [14]. Limiting interactions to the forearm allows both the modeling hand and canvas arm to use a tabletop surface for continuous support.

Our system uses four core design principles to link meaning between skin-centric gesture and purposeful 3D modeling: (1) favor natural over symbolic gesture, (2) make digital geometry dynamically react to user input, (3) balance high precision control with expressive gesture, and (4) embed fabrication constraints into the design of a digital model.

Implementation

Hardware Configuration

The workstation is comprised of a first generation Kinect mounted ~800mm above the work area and a Microsoft Surface Pro 3 mounted on a desk. The desk is also used as a base surface to place the arms (Figure 3). The effective tracking region is 90cm x 65cm, with an approximate 3-5mm working resolution. The system was implemented using the Java programming language at 12-15 FPS, and uses following the open-source libraries: processing for graphics, opencv image processing, and toxiclibs for physics simulation.

Arm Tracking

The depth camera detects a user's forearm as they sit at the workstation. The contours of the arm are then processed to define anatomical regions (e.g., the elbow, wrist, hand, fingers). With these regions defined, we simplify the forearm's point cloud into two 3D planes. These 3D planes dynamically segment the depth image into a *modeling hand* and *canvas arm* mask. Everything above these planes becomes a part of the modeling hand mask, and everything between the planes and a given maximum distance becomes the canvas arm mask (Figure 4a).

Touch and Gesture Detection

To reliably detect skin-centric interactions between the modeling hand and canvas arm, we adapt the image processing techniques in [46] to the three-dimensional geometry of the forearm: the dynamic 3D planes used to segment the *modeling hand* and *canvas arm* masks are offset by a minimal distance (~20mm in our implementation). When a finger of the modeling hand enters the space between the offset and original planes, we know a touch has occurred (Figure 4b). This enables skin-centric gestures that will be described later.

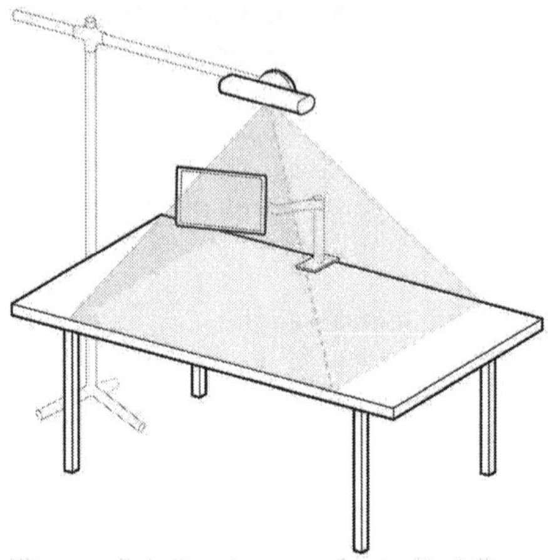

Figure 3. The workstation is comprised of a Microsoft Kinect mounted above the work area for input, and a Microsoft Surface tablet mounted within the work area for output.

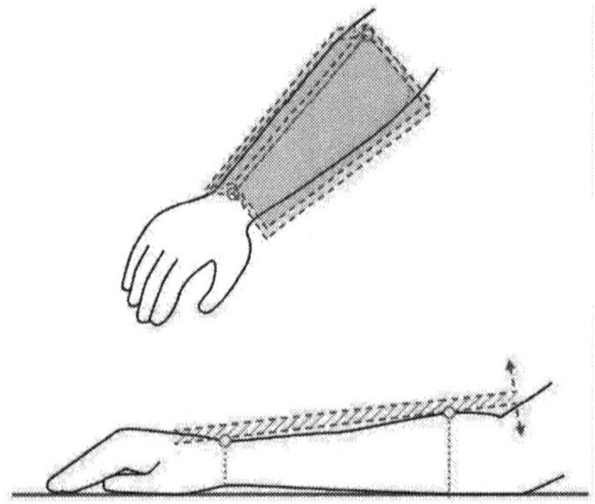

Figure 4. Image segmentation and touch detection are generated from the anatomy of the forearm. (a) The axes from elbow to wrist and from middle-of-arm to side-of arm create the 3D plane for segmentation. (b) an offset from the 3D plane defines the 3D touch region of the forearm.

Real-Time Display

The flat panel display above the work area is used to provide users with real-time visual output of the arm and finger tracking, within the context of a 3D modeling environment (Figure 5).

Once the canvas arm is detect and processed, the 3D modeling environment is generated on the auxiliary display. While the system's depth camera can continuously 3D scan the user's forearm, this data was found to be too noisy and incomplete to provide a useful virtual reference in the modeling environment. Instead, we built an accurate representation of the forearm using a simulated spring system in the modeling environment. Live scan data from the depth camera then updates select particles in the spring system with a small number of 3D points from the elbow, wrist, and hand (Figure 6a). The spring system both dampens depth noise from the streaming points and facilitates smooth motion for the virtual forearm.

Figure 5. Real-time visual output shows the 3D modeling environment, and a computer vision panel with the raw depth image, modeling hand segmentation, canvas arm segmentation, and hand and gesture tracking.

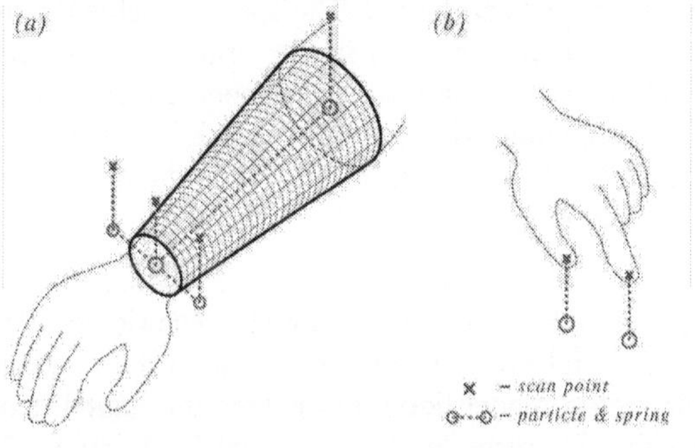

Figure 6. Virtual geometry is updated by live scan data from the depth camera. (a) elbow, wrist, and wrist axis points update the canvas arm, and (b) index and thumb points update the modeling hand.

A similar strategy is used to visualize the modeling hand in the virtual environment: a 3D scan point from each finger is rigged to a heavier particle with a spring (Figure 6b). This dampened particle is visualized as the user's virtual finger.

Skin-Centric Gestures for Design

Our system implements both natural and symbolic gestures based on the tracking of the modeling hand and canvas arm. Figure 7 summarizes the gesture set of our system. Gestures performed with one or two fingers of the modeling hand are used for design operations. These include *touch*, *poke*, *grab*, *rub*, *drag*, and *pinch*. Additional gestures performed with canvas arm are used for 3D navigation. These include *flip*, *orientation of arm*, and *rotation of wrist*.

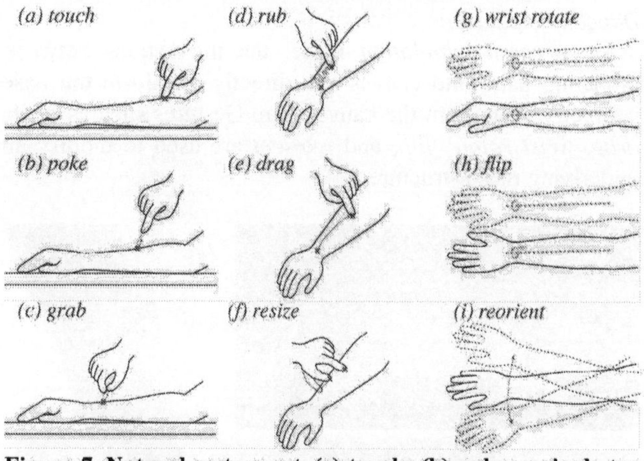

Figure 7. Natural gesture set. (a) touch; (b) poke: a single tap on forearm; (c) grab: pinch thumb and index, and touch forearm; (d) rub: touch and drag repeatedly; (e) drag: touch and move; (f) resize: touch and move thumb and index; (g) wrist rotate: rotating hand about the wrist; (h) flip: flipping the forearm; (i) reorient: moving the forearm.

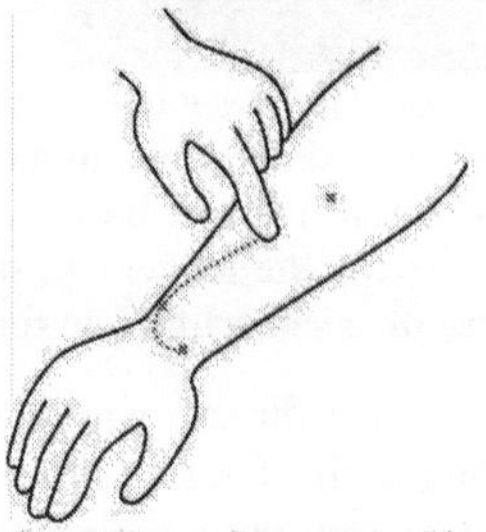

Figure 8. Skin-centric gestures incorporating landmarks are generated through an initial calibration step: a user selects landmarks by touching desired points on the forearm, then records a gesture by drawing a path to each point.

The system also includes skin-centric symbolic gestures by incorporating landmarks on a user's forearm. For example, a user can touch their middle knuckle to export a design for fabrication, or they can touch a set of freckles in a particular order to run an application-specific command. An initial calibration step generates landmark gestures: the user first selects landmarks by touching the desired points of their forearm, then records a gesture by dragging their finger to each landmark (Figure 8).

Modeling Modes and Workflow

Tactum illustrates how skin-centric input can be used as a gestural 3D modeling-to-fabrication system through three distinct modeling modes—*direct*, *parametric*, and *generative*. These modes are adapted from the primary 3D modeling techniques of conventional CAD environments. Although bodily interactions and geometric manipulations may vary, the goal of each mode is the same: balance high precision control with expressive gestures, and to ensure fabricated digital designs have an ergonomic fit to the geometry of the forearm.

Direct Manipulation

With *direct manipulation* mode, the interactions between modeling hand and canvas arm directly transform the base geometry built from the canvas arm. Gestures such as *grab, drag, wrist rotate, flip,* and *reorient* are used to modify an underlying mesh structure.

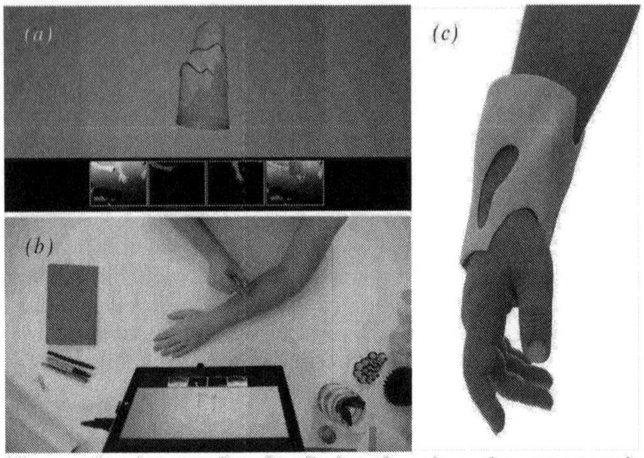

Figure 9. An armlet is designed using the parametric manipulation mode. (a) skin input updates the arm's base geometry, and simulated rubber bands can be pulled and deformed by the user; (b) the model can be customized to the user; (c) the resulting physical artifact on the user.

In our prototype, we use direct manipulation to design and fabricate an armlet for the forearm (Figure 9). When the user's forearm is detected, the system generates a malleable digital surface from four control edges built from the virtual forearm (Figure 9a). These control edges are digitally simulated rubber bands that are manipulated by the user's touch (Figure 9b). Using a *grab* gesture, the user touches a corresponding spot on their physical arm and pulls the virtual point off of their body. An elasticity threshold built into the control edge releases the deformed edge once breached, thereby updating the underlying surface.

This lower level manipulation of geometry is most similar to conventional gestural modeling systems, and it therefore brings similar limitations: while it allows high formal variation, it is difficult for users to have precise control over the final form. To compensate for this lack of control, we ensure the digital design will have an ergonomic fit to the body by subtracting the volume of the virtual forearm from the final manipulated surface. The geometry can then be exported for fabrication, and the 3D printed artifact can be placed back on the body of the user (Figure 9c).

Parametric Manipulation

Within *parametric* mode, the user's gestures interact with open parameters of a pre-designed digital form. This mode allows a base design generated by an expert to be manipulated by a non-expert. Gestures such as *touch, poke, resize, flip,* and *reorient* are used to manipulate and stimulate an interactive parametric model.

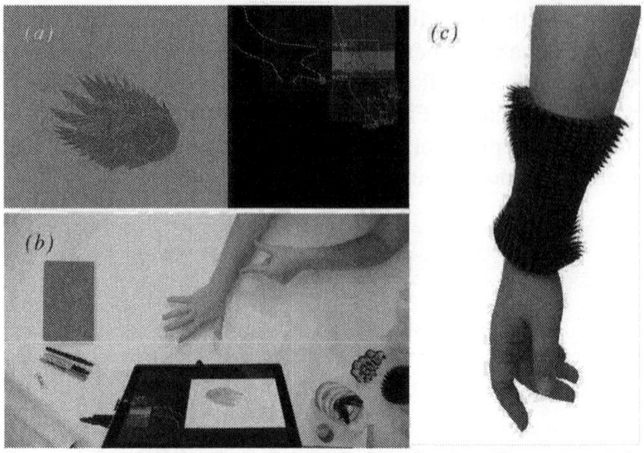

Figure 10. A piece of jewelry is designed using the parametric manipulation mode. (a) skin-centric gestures manipulate a pre-designed 3D model, and the animated digital geometry responds to the users movements; (b) the model is customized by the user; (c) the resulting physical artifact on the user.

In our prototype, we use parametric manipulation to customize the design of a piece of 3D printed jewelry (Figure 10). When the user's forearm is detected, the system generates a base 3D surface between the wrist and the elbow, and then subdivides it into planes. Next, a pre-designed, interactive module is placed on each plane of the subdivided surface. In our implementation, each surface module was programmed as a pyramid, with springs along each edge and a repelling particle at the top. The springs enable the module to sway as it is manipulated in the virtual environment, and the repelling particle prevents each module from intersecting with its neighbors (Figure 10a). Each surface model is connected to its neighbor at its base, thereby creating a closed, ready-to-fabricate mesh.

Once the parametric model is generated, the user can interact with the virtual environment using skin-centric gestures, like *touch*, *rub*, and *poke*. The spring-based surface modules of the parametric model definition enable the digital geometry to dynamically react to the user's gestural input. In our model definition, for example, the *touch* gesture the forearm attracts each module to the user's finger, the *rub* gesture repels each module from the finger, and *poke* gesture agitates the modules. Moreover, the user can shake their forearm to disrupt the entire field of animate modules (Figure 10b) or close their fist to *freeze* the physics simulation. A *resize* gesture is also used to allow the user to scale and position the design along the forearm. The final design was printed from a rubber-like material, and a magnet closure was added (Figure 10c).

While designs generated through parametric manipulation may have limited variation in form, they facilitate both expressive gesture from the user and a high level of quality control through the pre-designed module. In the current implementation this module must be pre-programmed, however future development could create an interface for user-defined parametric modules. This mode may be particularly useful for personalizing consumer products where high tolerance precision is required.

Generative Manipulation

With *generative manipulation*, a user's gestures manipulate the underlying abstractions that guide the behavioral properties of an expert defined design. Gestures such as *touch, rub,* and *drag* are used so a user can guide how a design is regenerated on the forearm.

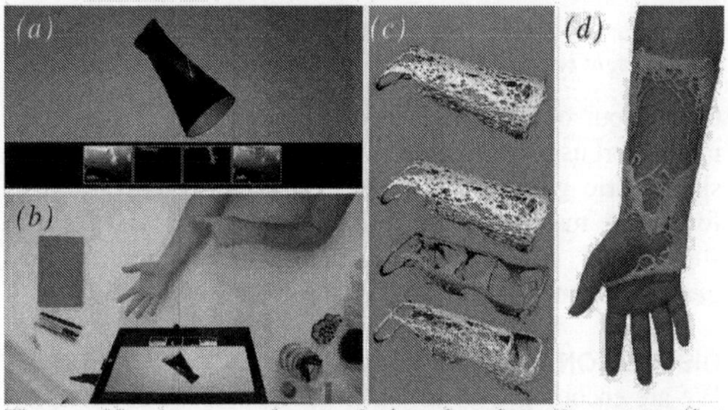

Figure 11. An arm brace designed using the generative manipulation mode. (a) skin input updates a touch heatmap of the user's forearm; (b) a design is generated using virtual agents; (c) resulting geometry is processed for fabrication; (d) the resulting physical artifact on the user.

Our prototype enables a user to personalize the structure and support of an arm brace (Figure 11). When the user's forearm is detected, the system generates a touch heatmap around the forearm, wrist, and hand of the user. Areas where the user *rubs* become brighter to indicate repetitive touch along the heatmap (Figure 11a). Once the user achieves a desired pattern for the heatmap, they use a landmark gesture to generate a digital design, and the system then deploys a pre-designed generative algorithm that processes the touch heatmap. In our implementation we programmed hundreds of Braitenberg vehicles [1] to seek out bright areas and avoid dark areas of the user-defined heatmap. As they move across the three-dimensional surface, the trails left behind each vehicle are used as the digital geometry. So in effect, areas where the user touches more add extra support for the arm brace, and areas where the user touches less receive less support. Once the simulation has finished, the geometry is exported and post-processed for 3D printing (Figure 11c).

For this example, we have also implemented a multi-user mode, where a *client* and *professional* user design a brace together. In this scenario, touch interactions from the *client* are given less weight than the *professional*: *client* touches appear in red, whereas *professional* touches appear in white on the touch heatmap (Figure 12). The *client* can therefore indicate where they would like brace supports to be generated, but the *professional* controls the actual location and density of the generated design.

Generative manipulation strikes a balance between the formal variation of *direct manipulation* and the precision and control of *parametric manipulation*. It enables the user to directly influence highly complex geometry, but can also ensure quality control over design and fabrication parameters. This mode may be particularly useful in scenarios where a high amount of user agency is desired in the design process of a complex artifact, such as in personalized medical devices or prosthetics.

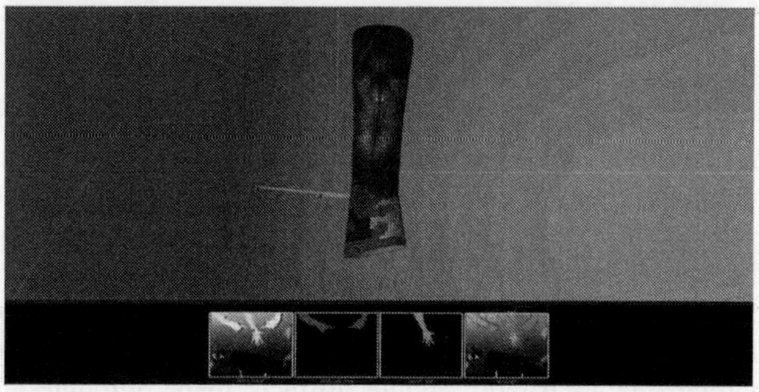

Figure 12. In multi-user mode, users can have a different level of impact over the design. Here, one user adds suggestions (red), and the other user implement the design (white).

Fabrication-Aware Design

To 3D print a 3D model, digital geometry must satisfy three conditions: it must have a minimum thickness, it must be made of closed-meshes, and these meshes cannot have self-intersecting faces. Rather than fix invalid geometry to meet these conditions, our strategy is to only allow properly formatted geometry to be created. In the *direct* and *parametric* manipulation examples, we achieve this by basing the user-manipulated geometry on spring-mass models simulated in a virtual physics environment. Digital geometry is first initialized as a closed mesh with a minimum thickness. This minimum thickness is maintained, and self-intersecting faces are prevented, by inflating the spring-mass model with repelling particles. In the *generative* manipulation example, we build these conditions into the geometry processing: the trails of the virtual vehicles are first converted from lines to closed-mesh pipes, and then exported as one closed-mesh. Building expert knowledge directly into the modeling environment lessens technical overhead for users, thereby enabling them to focus on their interactions while designing with *Tactum*.

The fidelity of printed geometry created through *Tactum* was tested by printing artifacts on 3 kinds of 3D printers, using a variety of materials: artifacts from the *direct manipulation* example were printed with ABS and PLA plastic on a Fuse-Deposition Modeling (FDM) printer; the *parametric manipulation* example was printed from resin on a SLA printer; and the *generative manipulation* example was printed with nylon and rubber on an SLS printer.

INITIAL USER OBSERVATIONS AND DISCUSSION

Although our system is still in the research prototype stage, it is important to get early feedback from potential users. Since the system is intended for both expert and non-expert users, we invited 10 participants to participate in an observation and feedback session. Participants had varied backgrounds and experience levels in 3D modeling and 3D printing. Three participants were design professionals, two were professional artists, two were design students with engineering backgrounds, and three were design students with architecture backgrounds. The 3D modeling and fabrication experience of each participant varied from complete novice to seasoned expert.

Procedure

In each session we first explained the setup and sensing of our system, and went through the different skin-centric interactions for gestural 3D modeling. We then demonstrated each of the three modeling modes, and highlighted the differences between each mode. After each demonstration, participants were able to try the system, and were guided them through the gestural modeling process. We also allowed participants to try on sample artifacts made through our system. Below we summarize the key observations and comments collected from these sessions.

Participant Feedback

In general, participants gave positive feedback about our system. They were all able to create or manipulate digital models with the three modeling modes, although most participants took longer to create a satisfactory design with *direct* modeling than with *parametric* or *generative*. When prompted for their thoughts on skin as an input surface for 3D modeling participants were enthusiastic about integrating touch and tactility into the digital design processes. One participant made a comparison to a haptic mouse:

"I've used a Phantom [haptic mouse] before for 3D modeling, and it's kind of cool, but it still feels like poking something with a stick instead of actually touching it." (p5)

They also appreciated how a digital design would inherently be scaled to fit. One novice to 3D modeling noted:

"It makes sense that if you're designing something to wear on your body, you should be able to literally design it on your body." (p1)

However, we received mixed reactions on the usefulness of landmark gestures. Most participants liked the novelty of it, but didn't see a significant improvement over clicking or pressing a button with a mouse or keyboard:

"I guess it's really only useful when you have to keep both arms highly engaged in modeling." (p4)

"It's neat, but I could also just press a key to export my file." (p2)

In general, participants with little experience in 3D modeling appreciated the *direct* and *parametric* modeling modes most, and found them "engaging" and "empowering". Those with experience in 3D modeling and printing tended to favor the *parametric* and *generative* modes. When discussing the generative mode, one experienced modeler noted:

"I have no idea how I would recreate that in the 3D modeling software I'm used to." (p3)

However, the experienced modelers showed concern with *how* the model definitions would be created. One participant suggested:

"I don't really want to have to learn another parametric modeling software [...] it would be great if you could just import the parameters from Grasshopper or Maya or something." (p9)

All the participants with some experience in 3D printing liked that they didn't have to think about formatting the digital geometry for fabrication. One beginner noted,

"It's great that it takes care of that for you [...] I always get nervous about it right before I go to print something I modeled." (p6)

Overall our observation sessions show that both expert and non-expert users were able to design wearable artifacts using skin-centric gestures. They were also eager for additional forms to manipulate in *parametric* mode, and offered suggestions for other algorithms to incorporate into *generative* mode.

DISCUSSION AND FUTURE WORK

We are encouraged by initial results and observations of our system. Despite the preliminary nature of these evaluations, our observational study provides insights into the feasibility of skin input for fabrication-aware design. However, our work only begins to explore what could be a wide design space around skin-centric input for design. As our system develops further, more thorough evaluations will be necessary to fully understand issues around ease-of-use and ergonomic fit for printed designs. This section reflects on lessons gathered from our implementations and observation sessions, in addition to topics for future work.

Both expert and non-expert participants showed enthusiasm for what can be produced through our system, however experts were concerned with how parametric and generative content could be created. For our research prototype to engage design professionals, back-end content creation would need a friendlier, non-programing interface. This back-end interface could be designed as a stand-alone, modular design system, or it could integrate workflow pipelines from existing design-to-fabrication software.

In our implementation, we wanted to push the envelope by relying solely on skin-based input for all interactions. However, as noted by some participants, traditional desktop input devices could also be used in combination with the skin-based gestures we developed. Integrating voice commands could be an effective means for hands-free communication with the gestural modeling system.

With regards to our implementation, we relied on a single depth camera to sense skin-input on the forearm. While this one sensor did allow for many gestures to be recognized, issues of image resolution and occlusion were inherent limitations that we had to negotiate. To reconcile the low-resolution and noisy data of the kinect with the high resolution and fidelity of the user-manipulated 3D geometry, we chose to visualize the forearm and hands in the modeling environment as simplified representations. However, directly visualizing the skin and hand in the virtual modeling environment may help strengthen the connection between a user's on-body interactions and the manipulation of digital geometry. Using additional cameras or sensors to capture and map a user's actual skin texture and hand details onto user-manipulated geometry could help bridge bodily interactions and geometry manipulation.

Relying a single sensor also limited the fidelity of our arm tracking. While our system allowed a user's free arm movement to manipulate digital geometry, only canvas arm gestures (*e.g., flip, rotate, reorient*) directly manipulate geometry through free movement. In two-handed interactions, our tracking and recognition strategy requires the canvas arm be stationary to adequately detect gestures from the modeling hand. Integrating additional modes of sensing into skin-centric gestural modeling system could allow for more dynamic interaction between both arms. It could also enable better detection of skin-specific gestures.

There are several output modalities that are appropriate for skin-centric design systems. In our implementation we elected to use an auxiliary display, as it provides consistent visual representation without suffering any possible occlusions. However, direct visual overlay onto the user's forearm (through head-mounted displays, projection mapping, or see-through displays) could also provide a strong connection between bodily interactions and geometry manipulation. Projection in particular could be a useful means of visual overlay. Future work could investigate how projection could also display three-dimensional volumetric geometry that comes off the forearm, such as the geometry created in our direct and parametric manipulation examples.

Although our system implements basic multi-user interactions, there are more ways for skin to be a collaborative input surface for design. For example, we show how two users can collaborate on one forearm. But an alternative scenario would be for two users to remotely work on one design on their own forearms. This scenario can increase in complication when design teams work on a single design.

Finally, our system focuses only on gestural modeling on the forearm. However there are other parts of the body that are appropriate for skin-centric design tools: the face and head can become an interactive canvas for designing eye-wear, masks, or apparel; the shoulders and neck can be used to design jewelry or medical braces; full body systems can be used to design costumes or garments; legs and feet can be used for shoes, medical braces, or casts. Moreover, skin-centric tools for deformable body parts, such as the joints of the neck, back, elbow, knee, or ankle, could combine complex mechanical design with intuitive customization.

CONCLUSION

We have shown how skin as an input surface for gestural 3D modeling-to-fabrication systems can enable non-expert users to create highly complex and expressive designs for the body. Moreover, our observation session with design professionals and students indicates a potential for skin-centric gestural modeling to be a collaborative platform for experts and non-experts. We have also outlined design considerations for future skin-centric systems, and discussed three separate manipulation techniques for balancing geometric precision and expressive control in such systems. While advances in hardware have increased *accessibility* to 3D printing, software interfaces have yet to provide increased *agency* in who can use this technology. We believe that *skin* can act as the interface that bridges digital and physical contexts, and can better enable experts and non-experts alike to participate with this technology.

REFERENCES

1. Braitenberg, V. *Vehicles: Experiments in synthetic psychology*. Cambridge, MA: MIT Press. 1984.
2. Chan, L., Liang, R-H., Tsai M-C., Cheng K-Y., Su, C-H., Chen, M.Y., Cheng, W-H., and Chen, B-Y. FingerPad: private and subtle interaction using fingertips. UIST '13. 255-260.
3. Chen, K., Lyons, K., White, S., Patel, S. uTrack: 3D input using two magnetic sensors. UIST'13. 237-244.
4. Coros, S,. Thomaszewski, B., Noris, G., Sueda, S., Forberg, M., Sumner, R., Matusik, W., and Bickel, B. Computational design of mechanical characters. ACM Trans. Graph. 32, 4 (July), 83:1–83:12.
5. Follmer, S., Carr, D., Lovell, E., and Ishii, H. CopyCAD: remixing physical objects with copy and paste from the real world. UIST '10, 381–382.
6. Follmer, S., and Ishii, H. KidCAD: digitally remixing toys through tangible tools. CHI '12, 2401–2410.
7. Gershenfeld, N. *Fab: The Coming of Revolution on Your Desktop–from Personal Computers to Personal Fabrication. Basic Books, New York, 2005.*
8. Gross, M., and Kemp, A. Gesture Modeling: Using Video to Capture Freehand Modeling Commands. CAAD Futures '01, 33-46.
9. Grossman, T., Wigdor, D., and Balakrishnan, R. Multi-finger gestural interaction with 3d volumetric displays. UIST '04, 61-70.
10. Gustafson, S., Holz, C., and Baudisch, P. Imaginary phone. UIST '11, 283-292.
11. Harrison, C., Benko, H., and Wilson, A.D. OmniTouch: wearable multitouch interaction everywhere. UIST '11, 441-450.
12. Harrison, C., Ramamurthy, S., Hudson, S.E. Onbody interaction: armed and dangerous. TEI'12, 69-76.
13. Harrison, C., Tan, D., Morris, D. Skinput: appropriating the body as an input surface. CHI'10. 453-462.
14. Hincapie-Ramos, J-D,. Guo, X., Moghadasian, P. and Irani, P. 2014. Consumed Endurance: a metric to quantify arm fatigue of mid-air interactions. CHI'14, 1063-1072.
15. Hinckley, K., Pausch, R., Goble, J. C., and Kassell, N. F. A survey of design issues in spatial input. UIST '94, 213-222.

16. Holz, C., Grossman, T., Fitzmaurice, G., and Agur, A. Implanted user interfaces. CHI '12, 503-512.
17. Holz, C., Wilson, A.D. Data Miming: inferring spatial object descriptions from human gesture. CHI '11, 811–820.
18. Johnson, G., Gross, M., Do, E. Y.-L., and Hong, J. 2012. Sketch it, make it: sketching precise drawings for laser cutting. CHI'12, 1079-1082.
19. Kim, D., Hilliges, O., Izadi, S., et al. Digits: freehand 3D interactions anywhere using a wrist-worn gloveless sensor. In UIST '12 , ACM Press (2012), 167-176.
20. Kim, H., Albuquerque, G., Havemann, S., and Fellner, D. W. Tangible 3D: hand gesture interaction for immersive 3D modeling. EGVE '05, 191–199.
21. Lau, M., Hirose, M., Ohgawara, A., Mitani, J., and Igarashi, T. Situated modeling: a shape-stamping interface with tangible primitives. TEI '12, 275–282.
22. Leithinger, D., Lakatos, D., DeVincenzi, A., Blackshaw, M., Ishii, H. 2011. Direct and gestural interaction with relief: a 2.5D shape display. UIST '11, 541-548.
23. Lin, S.-Y., Su, C.-H., Cheng, K.-Y., Liang, R.-H., Kuo, T.-H., and Chen, B.-Y. Pub - point upon body: exploring eyes-free interaction and methods on an arm. UIST '11, ACM Press (2011), 481-488.
24. Liu, Y-J., Zhang, D-L., Yuen, M-F. *A survey on CAD methods in 3D garment design*. Computers in Industry, 61:6, August 2010, 576-593.
25. Llamas, I., Kim, B., Gargus, J., Rossignac, J., and Shaw, C. D. Twister: a space-warp operator for the two-handed editing of 3D shapes. ACM Trans. Graph 22 (3), 2003. 663-668.
26. Mori, Y., and Igarashi, T. Plushie: an interactive design system for plush toys. In ACM SIGGRAPH (2007).
27. Mueller, S., Lopes, P., and Baudisch, P. Interactive construction: interactive fabrication of functional mechanical devices. UIST (2012), 599–606.
28. Mujibiya, A., Cao, X., Tan, D.S., Morris, D., Patel, S.N., and Rekimoto, J. The sound of touch: on-body touch and gesture sensing based on transdermal ultrasound propagation. ITS '13 , 189–198.
29. Ni, T., Karlson, A.K., and Wigdor, D. AnatOnMe: facilitating doctor-patient communication using a projection-based handheld device. CHI '11, 3333-3342.
30. Ogata, M., Sugiura, Y., Makino, Y., Inami, M., and Imai, M. SenSkin: Adapting Skin as a Soft Interface. UIST'13, ACM Press (2013), 539-544.
31. Olberding, S., Yeo, K.P., Nanayakkara, S., and Steimle, J. AugmentedForearm: exploring the design space of a display-enhanced forearm. AH '13, 9-12.
32. Pottmann, H. *Architectural Geometry and Fabrication-Aware Design*. Nexus Network Journal, 15:2, August 2013, Springer, Basel. 195-208.
33. Saul, G., Lau, M., Mitani, J., and Igarashi, T. Sketchchair: an all-in-one chair design system for end users. TEI (2011), 73–80.
34. Schkolne, S., Pruett, M., and Schröder, P. Surface drawing: creating organic 3D shapes with the hand and tangible tools. Proc. CHI '01, 261-268.
35. Sheng, J., Balakrishnan, R., and Singh, K. An interface for virtual 3d sculpting via physical proxy. GRAPHITE (2006), 213–220.
36. Smith, R.T., Thomas, B.H., and Piekarski, W. Digital foam interaction techniques for 3D modeling. VRST '08, 61-68.
37. Umetani N., Danny M., Igarashi T., and Grinspun E. Sensitive couture for interactive garment modeling and editing. ACM Trans. Graph., 30:90:1–90:12, 2011.
38. Volino, P., Cordier, F., and Magnenat-Thalmann, N. *From early virtual garment simulation to interactive fashion design*. Computer-Aided Design, 37:6, May 2005, 593-608.
39. Wagner, J., Nancel, M., Gustafson, S.G., Huot, S., and Mackay, W.E. Body-centric design space for multisurface interaction. CHI'13, 1299-1308.
40. Wang, J., Lu, G., Li, W., Chen, L., and Sakaguti, Y. *Interactive 3D garment design with constrained contour curves and style curves*. Computer-Aided Design, 41:9, September 2009, 614-625.
41. Wang, R., Paris, S., and Popovíc, J. 6D hands: markerless hand-tracking for computer aided design. UIST'11, 549–558.
42. Weichel, C., Lau, M., Kim, D., Villar, N., and Gellersen, H.W. MixFab: a mixed-reality environment for personal fabrication. CHI '14, 3855-3864.
43. Weigel, M., Mehta, V., Steimle, J. More Than Touch: Understanding How People Use Skin as an Input Surface for Mobile Computing CHI '14.
44. Wibowo, A., Sakamoto, D., Mitani, J., and Igarashi, T. DressUp: a 3D interface for clothing design with a physical mannequin. Proc. TEI '12, 99-102.
45. Willis, K.D.D., Xu, C., Wu, J.K., Levin, G., and Gross, M.D. Interactive fabrication: new interfaces for digital fabrication. TEI '11, 69-72.
46. Wilson, A. D. Using a depth camera as a touch sensor. ITS (2010), 69–72.
47. Yamashita, M. M., Yamaoka, J., and Kakehi, Y. Enchanted Scissors: a scissor interface for support in cutting and interactive fabrication. In *ACM SIGGRAPH 2013 Posters*. SIGGRAPH '13.
48. Yang, X.-D., Grossman, T., Wigdor, D., and Fitzmaurice, G. Magic finger: always-available input through finger instrumentation. ACM UIST'12, 147–156.
49. Zhang. Y., Han, T., Ren, Z., Umetani, N., Tong, X., Liu, Y., Shiratori, T., and Cao, X. BodyAvatar: creating freeform 3D avatars using first-person body gestures. UIST'13, 387-396.
50. Zoran, A., Shilkrot, R., and Paradiso, J. (2013) Human-computer interaction for hybrid carving. *UIST '13*, 433-440.

A Layered Fabric 3D Printer for Soft Interactive Objects

Huaishu Peng[*†] hp356@cornell.edu
Jen Mankoff[‡] jmankoff@cs.cmu.edu
Scott E. Hudson[*‡] scott.hudson@cs.cmu.edu
James McCann[*] jmccann@disneyresearch.com

[*]Disney Research Pittsburgh [†]Cornell University [‡]Carnegie Mellon University

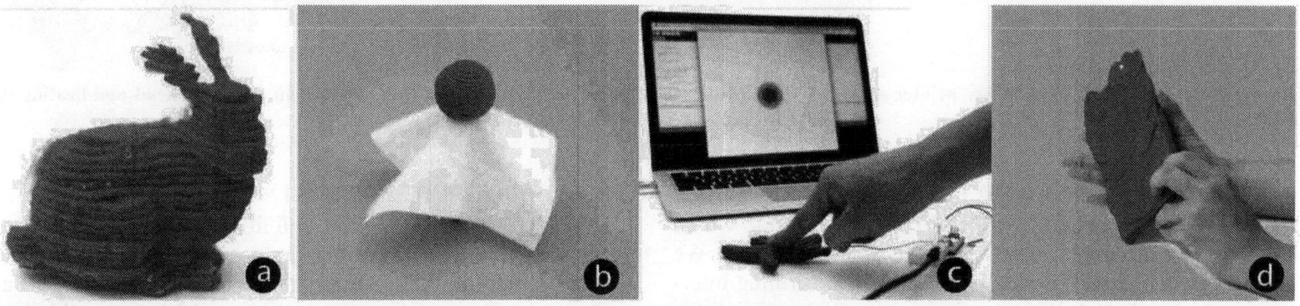

Figure 1. 3D printed objects from our layered fabric 3D printer: (a) printed fabric Stanford bunny, (b) printed Japanese sunny doll with two materials, (c) printed touch sensor, (d) printed cellphone case with an embedded conductive fabric coil for wireless power reception.

ABSTRACT
We present a new type of 3D printer that can form precise, but soft and deformable 3D objects from layers of off-the-shelf fabric. Our printer employs an approach where a sheet of fabric forms each layer of a 3D object. The printer cuts this sheet along the 2D contour of the layer using a laser cutter and then bonds it to previously printed layers using a heat sensitive adhesive. Surrounding fabric in each layer is temporarily retained to provide a removable support structure for layers printed above it. This process is repeated to build up a 3D object layer by layer. Our printer is capable of automatically feeding two separate fabric types into a single print. This allows specially cut layers of conductive fabric to be embedded in our soft prints. Using this capability we demonstrate 3D models with touch sensing capability built into a soft print in one complete printing process, and a simple LED display making use of a conductive fabric coil for wireless power reception.

Author Keywords
3D printing; laser cutting; soft materials; computational crafts; rapid prototyping; interactive devices

ACM Classification Keywords
H.5.m. Information Interfaces and Presentation (e.g. HCI): Miscellaneous

CHI 2015, April 18 - 23 2015, Seoul, Republic of Korea.

ACM 978-1-4503-3145-6/15/04 ...$15.00.
http://dx.doi.org/10.1145/2702123.2702327

INTRODUCTION
We are witnessing a boom in the arena of custom manufacturing technologies, from custom jeans (*e.g.*, `www.makeyourownjeans.com`) to websites that will print and mail a 3D model on demand (*e.g.*, `www.shapeways.com`).

At the same time, consumers increasingly prefer high quality and beautiful bespoke objects, as evidenced by the success of websites such as Etsy (`www.etsy.com`). However, these websites typically require individual craftspeople to produce such objects by hand. New additive manufacturing technologies (more commonly known as *3D printing*) provide an opportunity to manufacture highly custom objects on demand. However, the materials widely available for 3D printing and the range of functions supported by automated techniques are generally limited to plastic and metal. (Notable exceptions being printers using materials similar to silicon rubber such as [29], and the printer described in [10] which deposits layers of needle felted yarn).

Simultaneously, the use of electronics to create interactive physical objects from materials of daily life is becoming not only a research area (*e.g.*, [2, 3, 9, 20]) but also a commercial success (*e.g.*, `www.makeymakey.com`). Advances in toolkits for the construction of physical interfaces have made it easier to add circuitry, sensors, and actuators to physical objects (*e.g.*, [7, 8, 11, 13, 19, 25]). However, in these tools, the actual task of construction still may require special skills like sewing and soldering. In addition, as with bespoke objects, each new physical interactive system must be hand crafted.

Bringing these two threads together, our contribution is a printer that fabricates *soft objects* and provides *support for interactivity* including touch sensing and wireless power. Our printer can create objects with complex 3D geometry (Figure 1a), unique effects such as draping (Figure 1b), variable

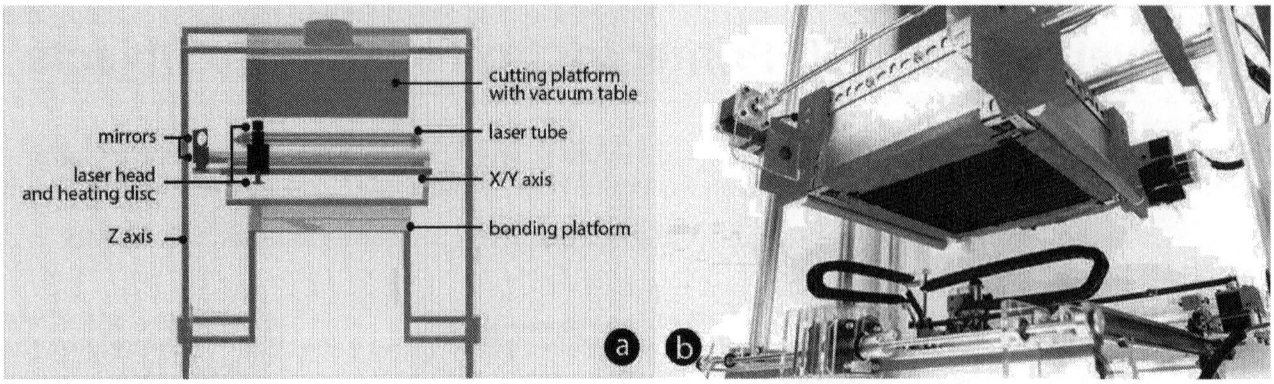

Figure 2. Layered fabric 3D printer: printer structure with cutting platform on top, bonding platform on bottom and laser head and heating disc moving in the XY plane.

flexibility (Figure 10), support for capacitive touch sensing (Figure 1c), and even coils made of conductive fabric which can be used for wireless power transmission (Figure 1d). We believe our printer opens new opportunities in forming interactive and functional 3D printed objects which are flexible and soft to the touch. This in turn adds a new tool to the HCI toolbox which expands our capacity to build interactive objects that reach the user in new (and more familiar) ways.

Our approach is conceptually related to other layered printing technologies involving paper [15] and metal [5]. Our printer cuts the contour for each layer from a roll of fabric and bonds it to layers of a 3D object already formed below it. Our printer cuts this 2D contour from a flat section of fabric using a high-powered laser and bonds it to the previous layer using a fusible heat sensitive adhesive sheet of a type already widely used in consumer sewing.

Mechanically, our printer is structured similarly to other 3D printers in which the print head can easily be moved within a Cartesian system (along the X, and Y axes of the print area). Unlike past printers, ours uses two separate working platforms, one for cutting, and one for bonding. The bonding platform, on which the 3D form is fabricated, is at the bottom (and moves along the Z axis). The cutting platform is located upside down above this, directly below a vacuum table which secures the fabric in place while it is being cut (Figure 2).

Our device supports printing with two separate types of off-the-shelf cloth (such as felt and conductive fabric) within an object. By manipulating fabric types and/or interior geometry we are able to add functionality to 3D printed cloth objects.

We next describe our primary contribution, the design of a novel soft object printer. Following that, we demonstrate the basic application of the printer to printing soft objects, manipulating the deformability of those objects, and printing in multiple materials. Having introduced the basic construction and functionality of our 3D printer, we go on to show how it can be used to construct interactive objects that can sense and react to the user through the use of conductive fabric. We end with a discussion of limitations of our current printer and possible future improvements.

3D FABRIC PRINTER DESIGN

Fabric is a material that by definition is manufactured from raw materials into sheets that are normally intended to be cut and bonded into new forms (most typically by sewing). Fabric is usually sold in rolls, and is available in a wide variety of colors, patterns, textures and thicknesses. Fabric can therefore potentially be used to form 3D objects with unique features and rich tactile qualities.

However, fabric is not suitable for traditional additive 3D printing technologies like fused deposition modelling (FDM), stereo lithography (SLA), or selective laser sintering (SLS); which use homogeneous materials (plastic filament, liquid, and powder, respectively) that can be deposited only at selected locations within a print.

An alternative more suited to fabric is layered fabrication [6, 32], which builds objects from sheets of material, cutting each sheet to shape and bonding it to the print in progress. While layered fabrication printers exist for paper [15] and metal [5], fabric presents a unique set of handling and cutting challenges that we address in our design.

Specifically, tool-based cutting (used in metal and paper printers) is likely to snag and deform fabric layers, and laser-based cutting – while snag-free – requires layers to be cut on a separate bed and moved to the print in progress, potentially requiring a complex transfer system. Our design (Figure 2) solves this problem by using an inverted cutting bed, which allows our printer to laser cut fabric while avoiding complex fabric handling schemes.

The rest of the printer design (Figure 2) follows from this notion of an inverted cutting bed. The cutting bed is fixed in place at the top of the printer. Fabric is fed to the bottom face of the bed by rollers mounted to the sides, and held in place by a vacuum during cutting. Cutting is performed by a laser directed through a print head which can move freely in X and Y below the cutting bed. The print head also carries a downward-facing heated metal disc, which is used to bond layers together. The final print is assembled on a bonding platform, which generally remains below the print head, but can raise and lower in Z in order to facilitate cutting and bonding operations.

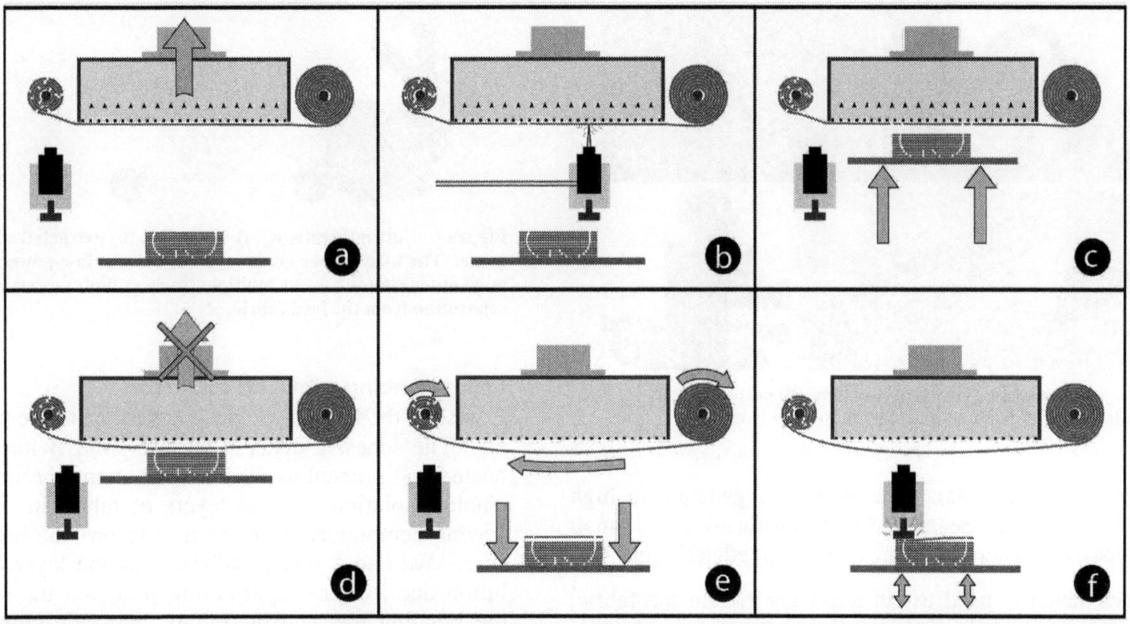

Figure 3. Adding a layer to a print. (a) the vacuum holds the fabric to the cutting table; (b) the layer shape and bounding box are laser cut; (c) the bonding platform is raised; (d) the vacuum is turned off and the freshly cut layer remains on the stack; (e) the bonding platform is lowered and the fabric is advanced; (f) the new layer is bonded to the existing layers with the heating disc.

Before describing these systems in detail, we first discuss the printing process. Before printing, fabric prepared with fusible adhesive (Figure 5a) is rolled and loaded onto the machine, the bonding platform is covered in a layer of fabric, and the heating disc is brought up to temperature. Then the print process proceeds as follows (illustrated in Figure 3):

	Printing Routine
a	Turn on vacuum to hold fabric to cutting table
b	Cut 2D layer shape(s) and bounding box in fabric
c	Raise bonding platform to touch cut fabric
d	Release cut fabric by turning vacuum off
e	Lower bonding platform and advance fabric
f	Heat bond new layer to print

Once the 3D model is fully printed, the result is a rectangular prism made up of layers of fabric. The outside support material must be manually peeled off if the inside model has a complex shape, or simply cut off with scissors if the inside model is straightforward. This post process step is analogous to the remove of support material in a traditional 3D printing process.

The build volume for our current prototype is 10 x 10 x 10 inches ($254mm^3$). However, printers of larger sizes could be easily constructed using this same design. The primary physical structure of the printer is constructed with off-the-shelf aluminum extrusion. Following the design of a number of current consumer 3D printers, motion is actuated with stepper motors and timing belts for the X and Y axes, and with a paired set of stepper motors and lead screws for the Z axis.

The printed object slowly stacks up on the bonding platform during this process. However, the cutting platform for our printer is located at the top of the printer. To hold the fabric flat, the printer makes use of a 12 x 12 ($305mm^2$) inch vacuum table, visible on the right side of Figure 2, largely enough to cover the build volume, and to hold the fabric at the top of the printer. The vacuum table consists of a thin metal grid and a small closed chamber with a 2 inch (50mm) air pipe on top. The vacuum is provided by a conventional shop vacuum and hose which also serves to remove smoke and fumes during laser cutting.

The fabric is stored on rollers mounted at the four sides of the printer (supply and take-up rolls for each type of fabric that is loaded). Stepper motors move the fabric, rolling up the section that was just cut on the take-up side and unrolling fresh fabric off the supply side so that a flat section of fabric is located in the cutting area (just below and suctioned to the vacuum table). Note that we pre-process our rolls of fabric by cutting them into 10" wide strips and attaching a heat sensitive adhesive sheeting to the bottom surface of the fabric.

The most complex parts of the print algorithm are layer cutting and layer bonding. Cutting is performed with a laser. For a single layer the profile shape(s) forming the layer are cut, and then a surrounding rectangle, which forms support material for possibly overhanging layers later is cut around this. Bonding is performed with the heating disc. After each layer is bonded, the roller supplying fabric to be used in the next cut moves a new segment of fabric into place for cutting. Both cutting and bonding are described in more depth in the next two subsections.

Layer Cutting with a Laser

To cut 2D shapes for each layer out of a segment of fabric, we employ a laser beam generated from a water cooled 40 Watt CO_2 laser tube of the type commonly used in commercial

Figure 4. Layer cutting. (a) laser in action, (b) cutting fabric, (c) laser beam path, (d) laser head containing mirror and lens.

laser cutters (Figure 4a). The laser tube generates a high power infrared laser beam which, when focused to a small spot, vaporizes material leaving a clean cut edge (Figure 4b).

The laser beam is used to cut a 2D layer from the fabric, which is located on the fixed cutting platform vacuum table at the top plane of the printer. Thus, the laser beam needs to be capable of cutting at any (X, Y) position, but does not need to be adjusted in the Z axis. To facilitate this, the laser tube is arranged at the back right of the 3D printer along the bottom plane. As shown in Figure 4c, the beam travels along the back of the printer in the X direction by a fixed amount. A moveable mirror then controls the distance it travels first in the Y direction (along the left side of the printer) and next in the X direction (inwards into the printing area). Finally the beam travels through the laser head (shown in Figure 4d), which contains another mirror and a focusing lens, and finally up by a fixed amount in the Z direction to the fabric. Direction changes in the beam are accomplished using silicon coated gold reflective mirrors (two of which are visible as small squares in Figure 4c).

Note that the second mirror and the laser head are attached to a movable gantry which moves in the Y direction. In addition the laser head can move in the X direction. Together, these movements can cover the entire XY cutting plane. Laser intensity is relatively unaffected when the laser head moves, ensuring a continuous cutting beam without the need to move the large laser tube.

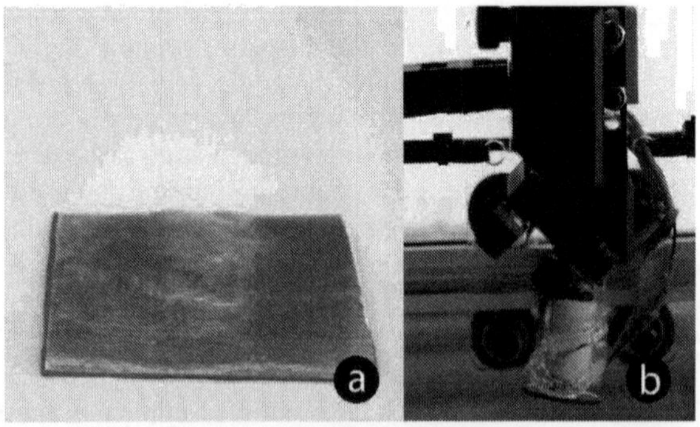

Figure 5. Bonding. (a) fabric with fusible adhesive, (b) heating disc with heating cartridge and temperature sensor.

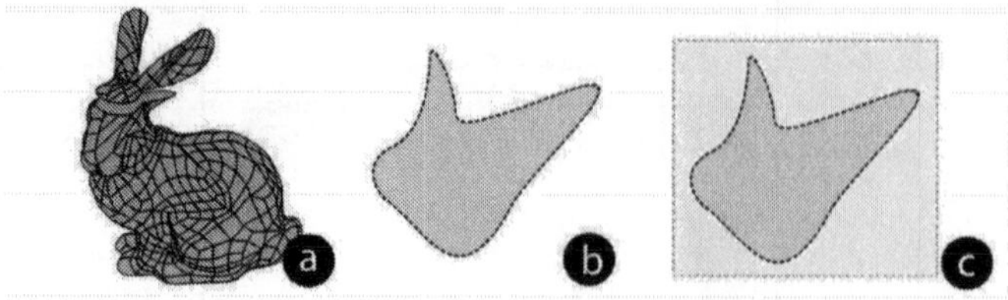

Figure 6. Cutting strategy. (a) 3D model, (b) extracted slice, (c) cutting route. The black inner contour is cut once at low power, while the orange outer contour is cut multiple times at high power to ensure clean separation from the feed fabric.

Layer Bonding with a Movable Iron

Once cut, the fabric for a layer is bonded to the previous layers. The adhesive material we use bonds with fabric when heated and pressed together. It is commonly used as a non-stitched solution to bond layers of fabric in the handcraft sewing community using an iron to provide heat and pressure. We chose fusible adhesive as the layer bonding solution due its very rapid curing time and the simplicity of the bonding mechanism (Figure 5a). We currently attach the adhesive to the fabric feed stock in a manual process before printing starts, but this could be automated in future devices. The fusible adhesive we chose is Heat-n-Bond™ (`www.thermowebonline.com`) for its convenient paper backed configuration, but we also tried several other fusible adhesives and obtained similar results.

To apply bonding heat and (slight) pressure our printer makes use of a 20mm *heating disc* (Figure 5b). This heating disc was constructed from an off-the-shelf soldering disc (`www.masterappliance.com/content/35404-tip-disc-round`. This is the smallest soldering disc we could find at the time) with a small heating cartridge (`www.makergeeks.com/cecahefor3dp.html`) and temperature sensor (thermistor) inserted. The disc is heated to 200°C and held there using a PID temperature controller. Once one layer is printed and placed on the previous layer stack, the heating disc is moved in and pressed onto the cut out pieces to bond the two layers. In our tests with 2mm acrylic felt, we found that 7 seconds ensures a strong bond.

Cutting and Bonding Algorithms

The previous two sections introduced the hardware structure of our printer. This section provides details on the software side of fabric printing. The basic approach used in our printer software involves slicing a 3D model as with conventional 3D printers. The model is sliced into 2D contours with a height corresponding to the height of the fabric being used. To ensure that contours stay in the correct position no matter how small, and to enable overhang geometry, our printing uses the fabric that is not part of the final model as support. A rectangle of support just larger than the bounding box of the object being printed is cut from the fabric at each layer (Figure 6).

To further ensure the stability of potentially small blobs that are part of the 2D contour, we set the laser to cut almost but not entirely through the fabric during the contour cut. This leaves a few points with weak connection to the support rectangle, ensures that even if the 2D contour shape is smaller

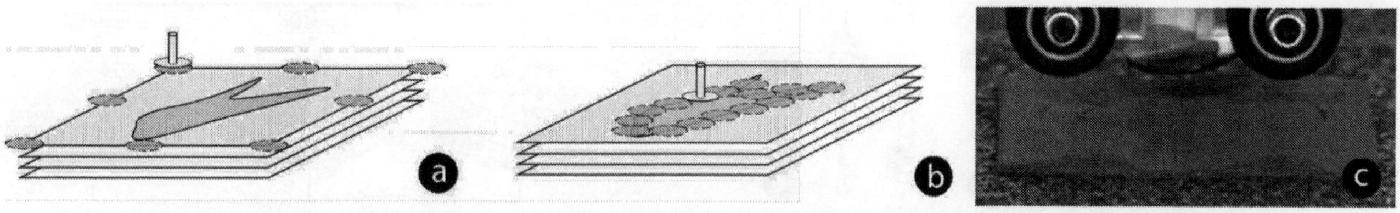

Figure 7. Bonding strategy. (a) bonding at side and corners, (b) bonding along the contour, (c) bonding in action.

than the grid size of the vacuum table it will not fall prematurely or be sucked into the vacuum table before the bonding platform arrives. These cuts are easy to 'finish' during the manual support removal process simply by tearing away the support material.

The bounding rectangle is cut with high power at least two times to ensure that it completely separates from the original fabric sheet and is easily released onto the bonding platform when it arrives.

Once the bonding platform has retrieved the new layer and lowered back to its base position, bonding can begin. The heating disc is typically not big enough to iron the entire rectangle at once. Thus, we designed a stamping route plan for bonding (Figure 7). Each 'stamp' in the route is performed by moving the print head to the given location, raising the bonding platform so that the top layer of the print is firmly in contact with the heating disc, waiting a set amount of time, and then lowering the bonding platform again.

The stamping route begins with the the four corners and four center points of each side of the cutout support rectangle. This ensures a stable bond at the outer edges. Only eight points are stamped so that support removal will be easier (Figure 7a). Next, the heating disc stamps along the contour path with the diameter of the disc as the step distance. This ensures that the whole contour will be fully stamped and bonded to the previous layer (Figure 7b). If the entire contour area is smaller than the disc area, it is stamped only once. Figure 6c shows the bonding head in action.

The shallow dent in Figure 7c is caused by the heating disc pressing into the material. We found that the dent did not deform the overall shape of the printed object, although it might be visible in a model with a very large, flat top layer. In the future, such dents could be reduced with a higher temperature heating disc, with shorter stamping time, or with a steaming iron that can transmit heat to the fusible adhesive more efficiently.

The control software used is Repetier-Host v0.95 (`www.repetier.com`) with no modification and the 3D model slicer is Slic3r v1.1.7 (`www.slic3r.org`, also unmodified). The printer is controlled with an Arduino Mega 2560 microcontroller driving a RAMPS1.4 printer control board (`www.reprap.org/wiki/RAMPS_1.4`) with Repetier firmware (`www.repetier.com`). The only modification we made to the firmware is to support generation of a pulse width modulated (PWM) signal for laser beam intensity control. GCode generated from the unmodified Slic3r program is processed by a custom GCode rewriting script to generate cutting path, vacuum machine control, stamping and bonding platform moving code. This modified GCode is then sent to the printer using the Repetier-Host program.

PRINTING SOFT OBJECTS

In this section we showcase the basic printing capabilities of our 3D fabric printer in forming soft objects, including complex soft geometries with sharp edges and overhang structures, soft objects with different stiffness in different areas, and soft objects with a draping effect printed with two different types of fabric.

The Stanford bunny model (Figure 8a) is printed with standard printing routine introduced above. It consists of 32 layers of acrylic felt fabric resulting in a 64mm high final product. Despite the relatively thick 2mm felt used in the print, it preserved most of the details in the underlying 3D digital model like the nose and ears. Also notice the relatively complex overhanging shape in the ears of the bunny. Because of the cutting strategy we used, fabric from the bounding box area of the previous layer serves as support for overhangs, including very small and sharply overhung features such as these. Figure 8b shows the completed printed object enclosed within its support. The very top layer of the fabric is not flat because of the stamping of the heating disc, but the finished result is not influenced by the uneven surface. Figure 8c shows the support partially removed and the bunny emerging from the printed cube. The printed object is true to the under-

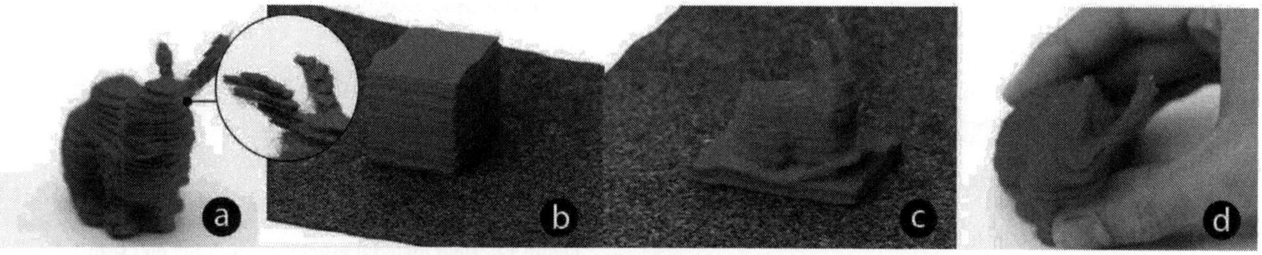

Figure 8. Printed soft Stanford bunny. (a) Stanford bunny, (b) finished cube, (c) removing support, (d) deforming the model.

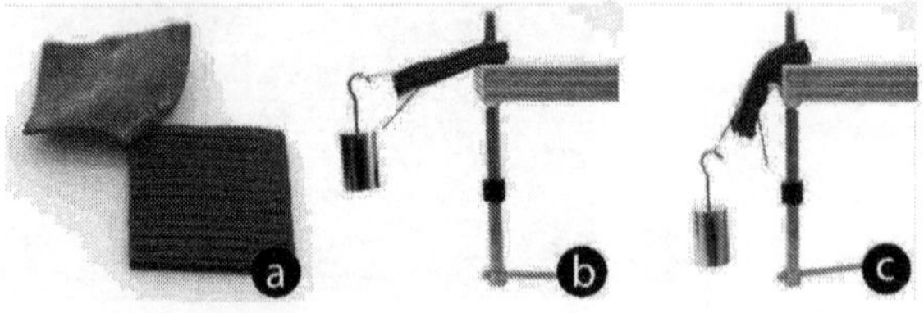

Figure 9. Deformation manipulation. This square has many parallel cuts in its internal layers (a). It is stiff when bent perpendicular to the cuts (b), and quite flexible when bent parallel to them (c).

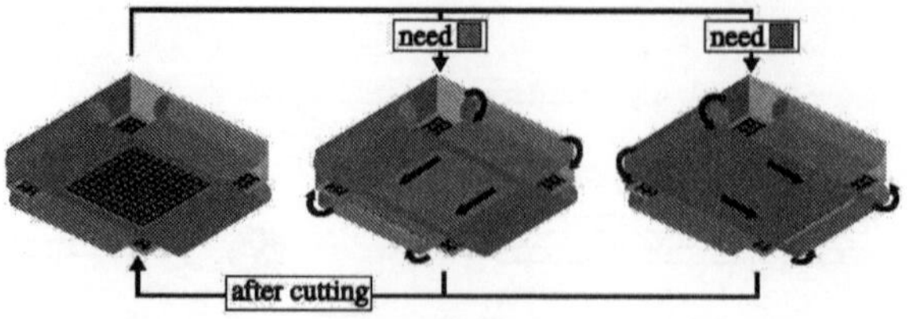

Figure 11. Dual material printing. (View of the cutting bed from below). Only the material for the next layer is advanced, leaving a 'window' in the unused material.

lying model, yet soft and deformable as is shown in Figure 8d.

Note that because of the bonding method we employed, as well as the relatively thick and compressible fabric used in our examples, the area being pressed can become slightly condensed and in some cases slightly stiffer than the untouched areas. This could be avoided by using an improved bonding mechanism, an area of future work we cover in the discussion section.

Resolution along the Z axis (*layer height*) is limited by the material thickness. In our examples the layers are apparent because the layer thickness to overall height ratio is high. This, however, does not imply our printer has a low precision design. In fact, our printer shares similar positioning mechanisms as other consumer grade 3D printers and laser cutters. Although we did not run a full measurement on this, we expect that our printer can achieve resolutions in the range of 50 microns, similar to consumer 3D printers with similar motion platform design. Also, if a thinner material were used, the layers would become less noticeable. Printing time, however becomes longer when thinner layers are used.

The printing time for our Stanford bunny example is two and a half hours (operated with double cutting of outer support rectangles and a five second bonding stamp time). Printing time varies based on the model size, height and the length of the layer contours. By a rough estimation, our printer's bonding speed is 10 to 13 sec per 20mm, and the time for raising or lowering of the bonding platform is 62s per travel on average. Thus unlike conventional printers where printing and filling the model are the most time consuming parts, with our printer, movement of the bonding platform, along with the bonding steps take most of the time.

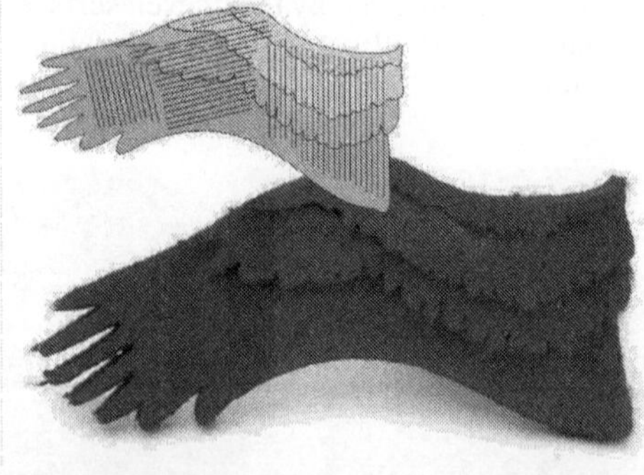

Figure 10. Deformation manipulation. This wing was printed with internal slots that change how it bends.

Deformation Manipulation

By embedding appropriate patterns of cuts inside a solid print we can manipulate the bending and deformation properties of different areas within one printed 3D soft object. To accomplish this, we can use very small cuts (removing gaps of material twice the narrow kerf width of the laser cut) placed inside an otherwise solid 3D print, but leaving the surface of the model intact. As is shown in Figure 9, a row of parallel cuts will substantially reduce the stiffness of that section of the print in one bend direction, but much less so in the orthogonal direction. With this approach we can manipulate bending direction and stiffness of different areas in one printed process without manual intervention. Figure 10 showcases a wing example where the apex and the root of the wing are easier to bend vertically while the middle part of the wing is more bendable horizontally by making use of inner cut patterns in different directions. This manipulation is hidden in the interior and does not affect the outside of the object.

Dual Material Printing

With the ability to feed two separate types of fabric into different layers of one print, we can produce 3D objects with additional variations. Here we will first introduce how the two layer printing works and follow this with a simple printed example.

Separate layers of material can be loaded onto the cutting bed from one roll feeding left-to-right and another feeding front-to-back (with slightly offset vertical positions so that they will not affect each other as they are being loaded but can both be pulled to the vacuum bed). Before printing, a 'window' the size of the support bounding box is cut in both materials. Then, during printing, only the material to be used in the next layer is advanced. When the layer moves to the stack, its bounding cut becomes a window in the material, and the process can be repeated. This process is illustrated in Figure 11.

In Figure 12 we show two objects created with dual fabric printing. The first is a toy clothes example printed with cotton fabric and fleece (different from the felt used in other

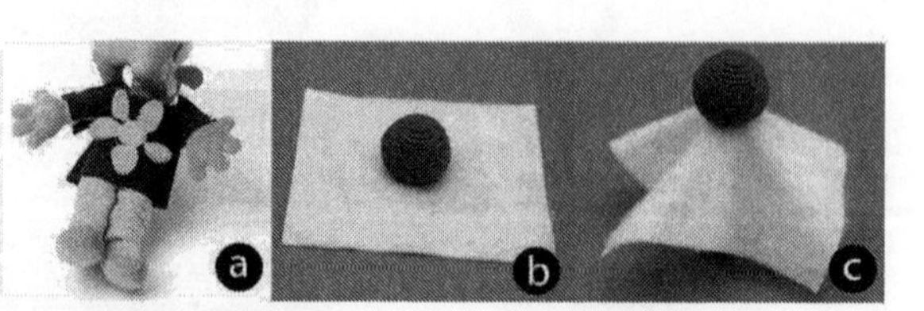

Figure 12. Dual material examples. (a) a toy doll t-shirt printed with cotton and fleece, (b & c) printed object with a draping effect.

examples). In this example only the center of the flower is bonded to the clothes, creating a decoration with an organic shape. The second example is a traditional Japanese sunny doll (named *teru teru bozu*) used to pray for good weather. The doll is usually made with paper or cloth with a round top as the head and draping cloth as the body. In this example we printed the head in red felt and the body in white felt. Though printed as a flat square, the white felt body drapes – like the cloth it is – to form a body. This would be hard to acheive for a printer that did not use cloth as its material.

PRINTING ELECTRICALLY FUNCTIONAL OBJECTS

As stated in the introduction, our goal in doing this research was not only to use novel materials to create 3D printed objects, but to enable manufacturing of the next generation of *interactive* devices using such materials. This requires the introduction of electrically conductive material and possibly electronic components into soft objects, in a fashion that preferably requires little manual intervention.

In this section we consider how such electrically functional, but still soft and flexible, objects can be created with our printer. The key to our method is to embed profiles cut from off-the-shelf conductive fabric sheets into printed objects as a functional layer. With one roll loaded with normal non-conductive fabric and the other loaded with conductive fabric, we can print electrically functional 3D objects with no or minimal human intervention.

Printing Touch Sensors

By utilizing a conductive fabric as one of our material feeds, we can make custom printed capacitive touch sensors as a part of a normal print. Figure 13a showcases a necklace pendent in the form of a soft starfish with an embedded capacitive touch sensor (connected to an external microcontroller such as an Arduino). Figure 13b is a printed capacitive sensor configured as a slider, connected to an off-the-shelf teensy microcontroller (`www.pjrc.com/store/teensy31.html`). After connecting it with only two wires, the soft printed pad is ready to serve as a physical slider for interaction. One can imagine a more complicated 3D printed soft toy with muliple touch sensitive areas.

Printing Circuit Paths and Vias

Since we can place arbitrarily cut shapes within a layer, we can also use conductive fabric to create the 'wiring' between

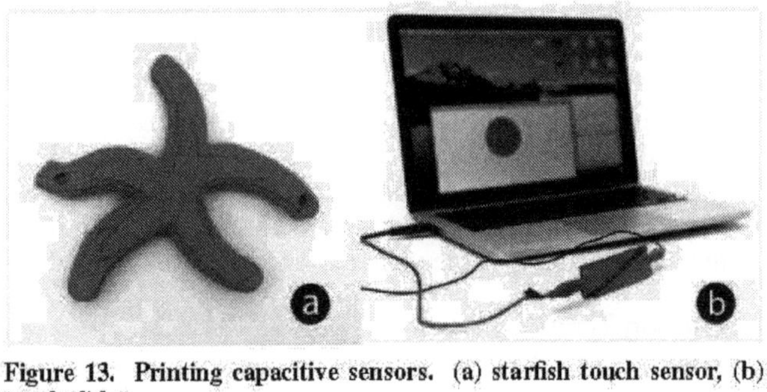

Figure 13. Printing capacitive sensors. (a) starfish touch sensor, (b) touch slider.

electronic components — the rough equivalent of printed circuit boards, but made entirely from, and embedded inside of, soft fabric. Because our printer leaves both the conductive material that makes up the paths and the conductive material outside them in place, we need to take care that this does not create shorts in the circuit. One approach to ensure this is to pause the print and manually remove segments of this extra conductive material.

It would also be possible to cut conductive traces in a purely automatic fashion without the need to pause the print. We can do this by increasing the kerf of the laser cut to create a sufficient gap between the intended conductive trace and the material around it. This approach is similar to what was done in the wing to remove inner material automatically so that it would bend more easily. Such small amounts of inner material can be removed by increasing laser power, slowing down movement of the cutting beam and/or cutting the path multiple times with a small offset. However, we feel that more testing is needed to determine how much gap is required in order to ensure robust long term functioning of traces constructed in this fashion, especially when objects are subjected to substantial bending or other deformations over time. For example, it may be that additional bonding time is needed along the gaps between traces to avoid short circuits from forming.

To allow 'circuit boards' whose traces cross, and to allow wiring to be routed throughout a 3D form, it is also important to be able to create connected circuit paths which go beyond a single horizontal layer. As in conventional printed circuit boards we can do this by connecting otherwise separate layers at a single point — a *via* connection between the layers

To construct a via connection we place a non-conductive fabric layer between two conductive fabric layers containing the circuit traces we wish to join. As illustrated in Figure 14a we place a hole in the insulation layer at the point of the via (which must be manually removed during the print). We then press our heating disc down slightly further than normal in order to bond the top and bottom conductive layers through that hole. In experimenting with this technique we found that the adhesive we used for other parts of the printing was not suitable for via bonding because it formed an insulating layer between the conductive sheets it was bonding. We were however, able to use a different fusable *mesh* adhesive (`www.dritz.com/quilting-sewing-supplies/sewing/glues-bonding-stabilizers/stitch-witchery-fusible-bonding-web/`). This form of adhesive, while still heat activated, is porous and allows fabric from the top and bottom conductive layers to be pressed into contact through those pores while still bonding the layers firmly together. Another important limitation of this technique for constructing printed vias is that the via hole must be comparatively large — large enough to allow the heating disc to push material through it and reliably bond on the other side. In all our examples, we used a via hole slightly larger than the 20mm diameter of the heating disc. Smaller vias could be accommodated in future printers by providing an alternate, much smaller, heating element for bonding vias.

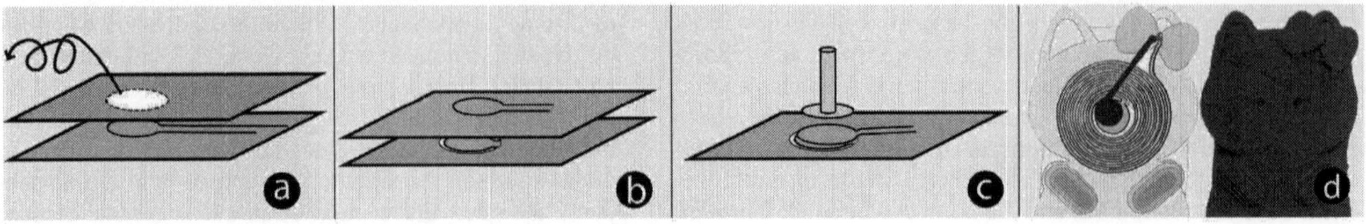

Figure 14. Printing a multi-layer circuit. (a) via hole on insulation layer, (b) top conductive layer, (c) press to bond top and bottom conductive layer, (d) conductive coil embedded in cellphone case design.

Figures 14d and 1d showcase an embedded circuit example with a printed via. Here we designed a smartphone case with an LED that can be wirelessly powered with energy harvested from the near-field communication (*NFC*) hardware built into the phone. To achieve this, two layers of circuit are embedded in the phone case. The bottom layer consists of eight loops of conductive fabric coil serving as an inductor to receive energy from the coils of the NFC hardware in the phone. The second conductive layer is a circuit trace from the center of the coil to the top right corner of the phone case to complete the circuit loop. The two layers of circuit are connected in the center using the via approach introduced above. A set of fabric through hole pads the size of an LED is designed into the model so that after the phone case is printed, one just needs to plug in an LED through the holes to complete the circuit.

RELATED WORK

The work introduced here builds on personal fabrication and soft material printing. Personal fabrication is a recently emerging research area. Different approaches have been explored in printing functional actuators and sensors (including interactive light pipes and speakers) with commercial 3D printers [33, 12]. Researchers have also fabricated mechanical functional objects such as 3D printed balancing and spinning objects [1, 22]. Interactive fabrication has also been examined with pen annotations in 3D [28], interactive laser cutting [17], and interactive handheld cutting and spray painting [35, 26].

Research has also examined the design process associated with 3D printing. Because printing can be very slow, significant effort has been put into supporting iterative design through rapid prototyping. Recent work in this domain has including printing objects that can be quickly assembled from a mix of Lego® and 3D printed parts [18] and printing 3D objects using a wireframe structure instead of a solid structure [16].

With respect to printing materials, soft objects have been printed with needle felted yarn [10]. In contrast to our approach, [10] only supports a single material and produces less physically robust results. There are also printers which produce soft prints using materials such as a UV cured silicone rubber-like material [29], and specially formulated thermoplastic elastomer filaments [4, 14]. These materials all lack the variety of textures of fabric and thus cannot be as easily customized to the preferences of users.

We have also seen a wide increase in the range of objects being enhanced with sensors and actuators including for example plush toys [30], fabric [9], knitting [23], and objects such as a candy dispensers and picture frames [31]. Most objects that we wear or otherwise hold close are best made from soft materials such as cloth, and thus we are particularly interested in work being done to advance the interactivity of soft materials. Much of this work comes from advances in soft robotics [21], which has driven the development of flexible soft sensors [34, 27]. Other advances have involved the use of conductive fibers (*e.g.*, [20, 3]) and soft circuits (*e.g.*, [2]).

While advances in what can be constructed are critical, widespread use of these technologies requires efforts that make construction easier for end users, support repeat manufacture of the same device and so on. For example, Phidgets [8] lowered the floor for end users to make use of sensors and actuators, while tools like Midas [25] and Sauron [24] provide support for the design and fabrication of touch sensors which can be applied to 3D objects (but not for soft materials). While many toolkits that support the construction of physical interfaces in various ways have been created [8, 11, 7, 13, 19, 25], they do not remove the need for special skills like sewing and soldering. In addition, as with bespoke objects, in most cases each new physical object must be hand crafted. Our work builds on this past work by supporting the automatic creation of 3D objects with embedded interactivity.

DISCUSSION

We now discuss lessons learned when designing our printer including limitations and possibilities for future improvements.

Bonding Method

The bonding method for our current printer design is to use heat sensitive adhesive with a heating disc. To ensure a solid bond, each press of the heating disc lasts several seconds. This leaves a shallow dent at the pressed area and makes a printed surface with slightly heterogeneous stiffness. One way to improve this is to implement a steaming head in combination with the heating disc. Steam delivers heat more easily through fabric and may, therefore, reduce pressing time and press strength. Another improvement that could be made is to upgrade the heating disc to a small heating roller so that instead of stamping at discrete points, the roller head might press and heat the contour in a more continuous manner along its path. This may further eliminate uneven surfaces and make the edge stiffness of the object more evenly distributed.

Printing Time

Printing time in our current printer design is relatively slow and is limited first by our bonding method, which currently requires each bonding location to be pressed for several seconds, and next by the movement of the bonding platform up and down, which takes roughly one minute per one-way travel. Bonding time might be improved using one or more of the techniques described above, or by using a large area heating element to bond the entire layer at once. However, for this second approach it is likely that modifications to surrounding support material may be required in order to both make it removable and ensure that it does not firmly bond where it is not desired. In addition, it should be possible to substantially increase the vertical speed of the bonding platform using larger motors and a drive train that is geared more aggressively.

CONCLUSION

In this paper we have presented a new type of layer-based 3D fabric printer that can form precise, yet soft and deformable 3D objects from rolls of off-the-shelf fabric. Our printer cuts fabric in the profile of layer slices with a high powered laser and bonds those shapes to previously cut layers using a heat activated fusible adhesive. In this way, objects are built up layer after layer to form whatever 3D geometry has been specified. Material outside layer profiles is temporarily left in place to provide support for overhang features in the layers above it (but removed at the end of the print to reveal the printed object). Our printer supports the use of two different fabric types in one print. This allows a number of additional features to be included in prints. For example, objects with printed 'wiring' can be constructed using conductive fabric. This 'wiring' is completely flexible since it is formed with, and entirely embedded inside of, fabric sheets. We have used this capability in several proof-of-concept demonstration objects including a soft cell phone case which contains a printed fabric coil capable of harvesting power from the NFC hardware of an off-the-shelf cell phone.

REFERENCES

1. Bächer, M., Whiting, E., Bickel, B., and Sorkine-Hornung, O. Spin-it: Optimizing moment of inertia for spinnable objects. *ACM Transactions on Graphics 33*, 4 (July 2014), 96:1–96:10.
2. Buechley, L., Eisenberg, M., Catchen, J., and Crockett, A. The lilypad arduino: Using computational textiles to investigate engagement, aesthetics, and diversity in computer science education. In *CHI '08*, ACM (2008), 423–432.
3. Cherenack, K., Zysset, C., Kinkeldei, T., Münzenrieder, N., and Tröster, G. Wearable electronics: Woven electronic fibers with sensing and display functions for smart textiles. *Advanced Materials 22*, 45 (2010), 5071.
4. Drives, F. NinjaFlex. `http://www.fennerdrives.com/ninjaflex3dprinting/_/3d/`.
5. Fabrisonic. Soniclayer 4000. `http://fabrisonic.com`.
6. Feygin, M., Shkolnik, A., Diamond, M. N., and Dvorskiy, E. Laminated object manufacturing system, 1998. US Patent 5,730,817.
7. Gellersen, H., Kortuem, G., and Schmidt, A. Physical prototypnig with smart-its. *Pervasive Computing 04* (2004), 1536–1268.
8. Greenberg, S., and Fitchett, C. Phidgets: Easy development of physical interfaces through physical widgets. In *UIST '01*, ACM (2001), 209–218.
9. Holleis, P., Schmidt, A., Paasovaara, S., Puikkonen, A., and Häkkilä, J. Evaluating capacitive touch input on clothes. In *MobileHCI '08*, ACM (2008), 81–90.
10. Hudson, S. E. Printing teddy bears: A technique for 3D printing of soft interactive objects. In *CHI '14*, ACM (2014), 459–468.
11. Hudson, S. E., and Mankoff, J. Rapid construction of functioning physical interfaces from cardboard, thumbtacks, tin foil and masking tape. In *UIST '06*, ACM (2006), 289–298.
12. Ishiguro, Y., and Poupyrev, I. 3D printed interactive speakers. In *CHI '14*, ACM (2014), 1733–1742.
13. Lee, J. C., Avrahami, D., Hudson, S. E., Forlizzi, J., Dietz, P. H., and Leigh, D. The calder toolkit: Wired and wireless components for rapidly prototyping interactive devices. In *DIS '04*, ACM (2004), 167–175.
14. MakerBot. Flexible filament. `https://store.makerbot.com/flexible-filament`.
15. Mcor Technonlogies. Mcor IRIS. `http://mcortechnologies.com/3d-printers/iris/`.
16. Mueller, S., Im, S., Gurevich, S., Teibrich, A., Pfisterer, L., Guimbretire, F., and Baudisch, P. WirePrint: Fast 3D printed previews. In *UIST'14* (2014).
17. Mueller, S., Lopes, P., and Baudisch, P. Interactive construction: Interactive fabrication of functional mechanical devices. In *UIST '12*, ACM (2012), 599–606.
18. Mueller, S., Mohr, T., Guenther, K., Frohnhofen, J., and Baudisch, P. fabrickation: Fast 3d printing of functional objects by integrating construction kit building blocks. In *CHI '14*, ACM (2014), 3827–3834.
19. Ngai, G., Chan, S. C., Cheung, J. C., and Lau, W. W. The teeboard: An education-friendly construction platform for e-textiles and wearable computing. In *CHI '09*, ACM (2009), 249–258.
20. Perner-Wilson, H., and Buechley, L. Making textile sensors from scratch. In *TEI '10*, ACM (2010), 349–352.
21. Pfeifer, R., Lungarella, M., and Iida, F. The challenges ahead for bio-inspired 'soft' robotics. *Communications of the ACM 55*, 11 (Nov. 2012), 76–87.
22. Prévost, R., Whiting, E., Lefebvre, S., and Sorkine-Hornung, O. Make it stand: Balancing shapes for 3D fabrication. *ACM Trans. Graph. 32*, 4 (July 2013), 81:1–81:10.
23. Rosner, D., and Ryokai, K. Weaving memories into handcrafted artifacts with spyn. In *CHI EA '08*, ACM (2008), 2331–2336.

24. Savage, V., Chang, C., and Hartmann, B. Sauron: embedded single-camera sensing of printed physical user interfaces. In *The 26th Annual ACM Symposium on User Interface Software and Technology, UIST'13, St. Andrews, United Kingdom, October 8-11, 2013* (2013), 447–456.
25. Savage, V., Zhang, X., and Hartmann, B. Midas: Fabricating custom capacitive touch sensors to prototype interactive objects. In *UIST '12*, ACM (2012), 579–588.
26. Shilkrot, R., Maes, P., and Zoran, A. Physical rendering with a digital airbrush. In *ACM SIGGRAPH 2014 Emerging Technologies*, SIGGRAPH '14, ACM (New York, NY, USA, 2014), 19:1–19:1.
27. Slyper, R., Poupyrev, I., and Hodgins, J. Sensing through structure: Designing soft silicone sensors. In *Proceedings of the Fifth International Conference on Tangible, Embedded, and Embodied Interaction*, ACM (2011), 213–220.
28. Song, H., Guimbretière, F., Hu, C., and Lipson, H. Modelcraft: Capturing freehand annotations and edits on physical 3d models. In *Proceedings of the 19th Annual ACM Symposium on User Interface Software and Technology*, UIST '06, ACM (2006), 13–22.
29. Stratasys. Objet connex multi-material printer. `http://www.stratasys.com/3d-printers/design-series/objet-connex500`.
30. Sugiura, Y., Lee, C., Ogata, M., Withana, A., Makino, Y., Sakamoto, D., Inami, M., and Igarashi, T. Pinoky: A ring that animates your plush toys. In *CHI '12*, ACM (2012), 725–734.
31. Truong, K. N., Richter, H., Hayes, G. R., and Abowd, G. D. Devices for sharing thoughts and affection at a distance. In *CHI EA '04*, ACM (2004), 1203–1206.
32. White, D. Ultrasonic object consolidation, 2003. US Patent 6,519,500.
33. Willis, K., Brockmeyer, E., Hudson, S., and Poupyrev, I. Printed optics: 3D printing of embedded optical elements for interactive devices. In *UIST '12*, ACM (2012), 589–598.
34. Yoshikai, T., Fukushima, H., Hayashi, M., and Inaba, M. Development of soft stretchable knit sensor for humanoids' whole-body tactile sensibility (2009). 624–631.
35. Zoran, A., Shilkrot, R., and Paradiso, J. Human-computer interaction for hybrid carving. In *Proceedings of the 26th Annual ACM Symposium on User Interface Software and Technology*, UIST '13, ACM (New York, NY, USA, 2013), 433–440.

Platener: Low-Fidelity Fabrication of 3D Objects by Substituting 3D Print with Laser-Cut Plates

Dustin Beyer, Serafima Gurevich, Stefanie Mueller, Hsiang-Ting Chen, Patrick Baudisch
Hasso Plattner Institute, Potsdam, Germany
{firstname.lastname}@hpi.uni-potsdam.de

ABSTRACT

This paper presents Platener, a system that allows quickly fabricating intermediate design iterations of 3D models, a process also known as low-fidelity fabrication. Platener achieves its speed-up by extracting straight and curved plates from the 3D model and substituting them with laser cut parts of the same size and thickness. Only the regions that are of relevance to the current design iteration are executed as full-detail 3D prints. Platener connects the parts it has created by automatically inserting joints. To help fast assembly it engraves instructions. Platener allows users to customize substitution results by (1) specifying fidelity-speed tradeoffs, (2) choosing whether or not to convert curved surfaces to plates bent using heat, and (3) specifying the conversion of individual plates and joints interactively.

Platener is designed to best preserve the fidelity of *functional* objects, such as casings and mechanical tools, all of which contain a large percentage of straight/rectilinear elements. Compared to other low-fab systems, such as faBrickator and WirePrint, Platener better preserves the stability and functionality of such objects: the resulting assemblies have fewer parts and the parts have the same size and thickness as in the 3D model.

To validate our system, we converted 2,250 3D models downloaded from a 3D model site (*Thingiverse*). Platener achieves a speed-up of 10x or more for 39.9% of all objects.

Author Keywords: rapid prototyping; 3D printing; building blocks; physical prototyping.

ACM Classification Keywords: H5.2 [Information interfaces and presentation]: User Interfaces.

General Terms: Design; Human Factors.

INTRODUCTION

Personal fabrication tools, such as laser cutters and 3D printers [5], allow users to prototype one-off objects and to iterate over designs. While there is a range of fabrication machines, 3D printers are the most versatile in that they

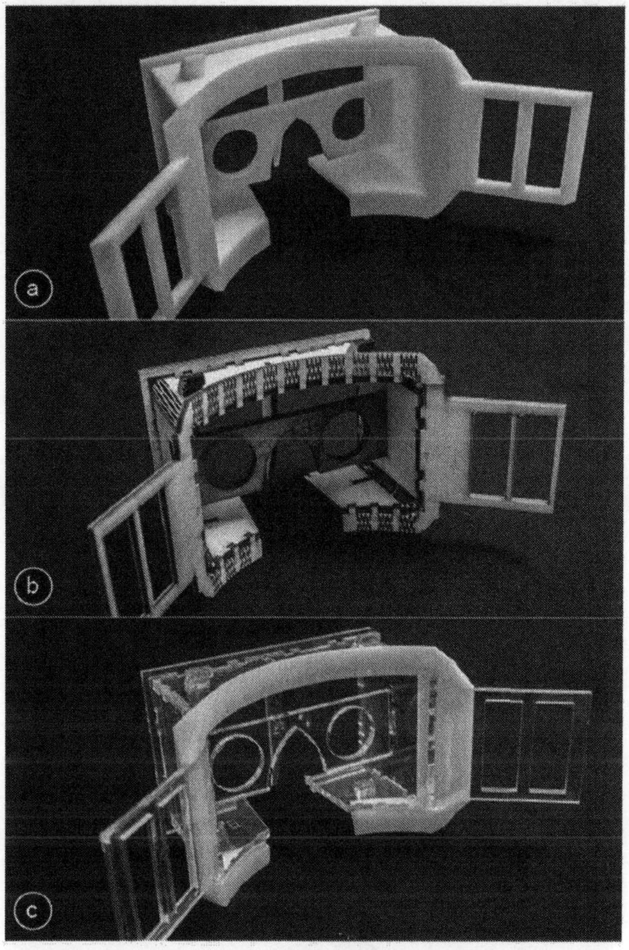

Figure 1: Platener speeds up the fabrication process by substituting parts of 3D models with straight and curved plates that can be fabricated quickly on a laser cutter. Here Platener optimizes (a) the 3D model of a head mounted display body for (b) quickly testing the ergonomic fit of the forehead piece, and (c) for evaluating the industrial design of the forehead piece.

allow creating arbitrary 3D shapes. Because of this benefit, thousands of 3D models for 3D printing are available on sharing sites, such as *Thingiverse*.

While for some types of objects, such as 3D scans of people, the full expressiveness of a 3D printer is crucial, this is less the case for types of objects that are defined by their technical function, such as casings and mechanical tools. At the same time, these types of objects often require extensive iteration, as they have to match exact specifications

CHI 2015, April 18 - 23 2015, Seoul, Republic of Korea
Copyright 2015 ACM 978-1-4503-3145-6/15/04...$15.00
http://dx.doi.org/10.1145/2702123.2702225

and constraints. A case, for example, has to fit its contents, and a gearbox has to be sturdy enough to bear a load.

3D printers tend to be too slow for fast design iteration. Many objects print over night, limiting users to a single design iteration per day. Researchers therefore proposed speeding up the early stages of design by fabricating *simplified* representations for intermediate versions. Only the regions that are of interest in the current design iteration are fabricated in full detail. This concept is referred to as *low-fidelity fabrication* or *low-fab* [15]. FaBrickator, for example, substitutes 3D print material with Lego bricks [17], while WirePrint prints 3D models as wireframes [15].

Unfortunately, faBrickator and WirePrint produce only very coarse approximations as both of them convert 3D models into a coarse grid of Lego bricks or wireframe meshes. For functional objects this is often not sufficient. Approaches from computer graphics that preserve surface contours, e.g., by folding paper strips [14] represent the shape of an object better, but since they are generally hollow inside do not preserve the technical function of an object either.

In this paper, we present a low-fab method designed specifically for functional objects. By replacing parts of the 3D model with laser-cut plates of the same dimensions and thickness and by keeping the number of parts low, Platener preserves many of the aspects relevant to functional objects.

PLATENER

Platener speeds up fabrication by converting a model designed for 3D printing entirely or in part to a 2D representation that can be fabricated using a laser cutter. Figure 1b illustrates this at the example of a head-mounted display body. Platener created this version by extracting straight and curved plates from the 3D model and substituting them with laser cut parts of the same size and thickness. This approximates the stability of a 3D print of the same model well and largely preserves its function (see Figure 2).

Figure 2: The head-mounted display created using Platener, ready to be worn.

However, the Platener model can be produced using a laser cutter, allowing for much faster fabrication. Platener allows producing this head-worn display in 20 min (15 min cutting plus 5min manual assembly), which is 44 times faster than the 3D print (14:30h) the model was designed for.

Platener returns the 3D model in the form of one or more 3D printable .stl files and laser cuttable .svg files, which can be sent directly to the 3D printer and laser cutter. Figure 3 illustrates this at the example of the head-mounted display body from Figure 1c.

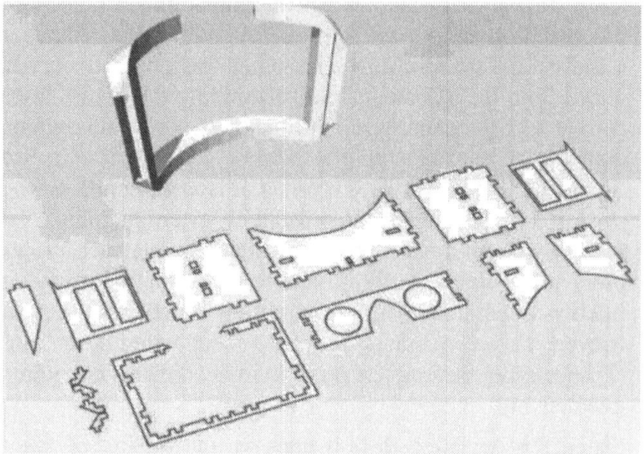

Figure 3: Platener exports 3D printable parts and laser-cut parts as .stl and .svg files, here the model from Figure 1c.

Adapting the conversion to the current design phase

To best suit the needs of the current design phase, Platener allows users to convert 3D models under different settings. For an early design phase, for example, users may convert their models with speed in mind; in later phases they may gradually shift the emphasis to fidelity. Note that here fidelity refers not only to shape but also to other physical property such as appearance, structure, and material.

As an example, Figure 1 shows three different versions of the head-mounted display. They were generated from the same 3D model, but with different fidelity-speed settings. Platener allows users to specify these trade-off settings using a global slider.

Speed-fidelity: Setting this slider all the way to "fidelity" (Figure 4a) produces an object that is all 3D printed, which trivially preserves fidelity, but obviously at the expense of having no speed-up. Moving the slider towards "speed" causes Platener to initially replace very large regions with individual laser-cut plates (Figure 4b); then more and more regions get replaced, resulting in increasingly higher speed-ups (Figure 4c). Platener performs this in interactive speed, i.e., as the user is dragging the slider, Platener continuously updates the model. This allows users to see the changes right away and thus to quickly find the conversion that best suits their needs.

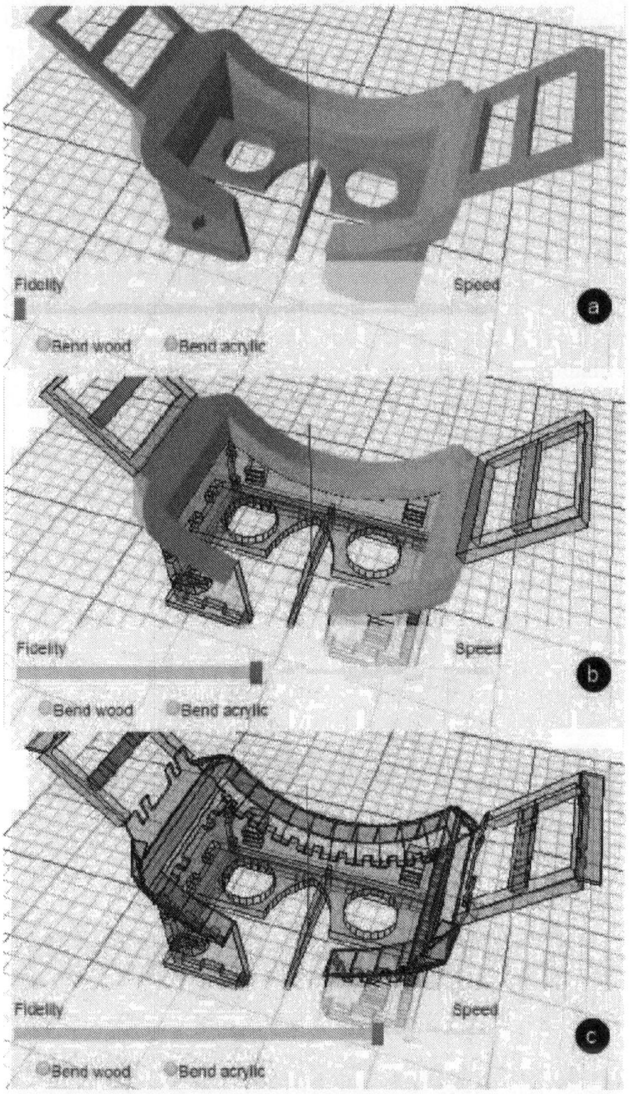

Figure 4: Platener's user interface provides users with a global slider to define the fidelity-speed trade-off.

Curved surfaces: Platener also provides options for handling curved plates. When the curved plate option is deactivated, Platener approximates curved plates using individual plates connected by finger joints (Figure 4c). Activating the curved plate option causes Platener to convert cylindrically curved regions in the 3D model to one plate that can be laser-cut and bent.

Curved plates come in two styles: The first option *bend acrylic* fabricates a flattened version of the respective surface using the laser cutter that can then be bent using a heat gun. As illustrated by Figure 5, users (a) cut the pieces, (b) heat them up using a heat gun or strip heater [3], (c) pre-shape them along the dashed instruction lines Platener provided, and (d) press them into the corresponding positions in the model, which gives them the desired shape.

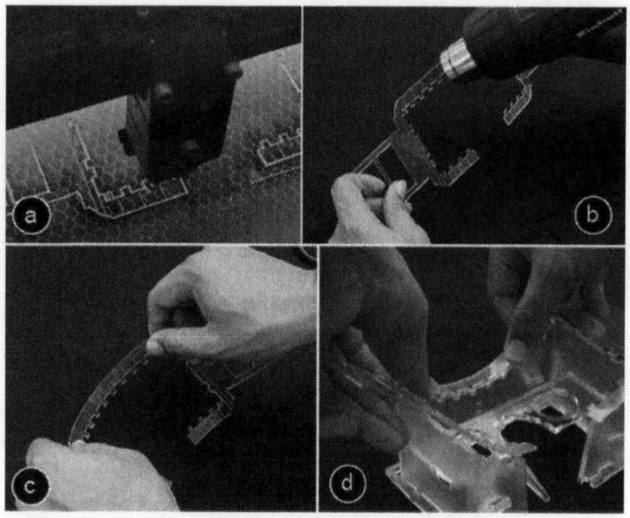

Figure 5: Creating a curved plate from acrylic: (a) cut plate, (b) heat it using a heat gun, (c) pre-curve it, and (d) press it into position to give it the right shape.

The second curved plate option uses a wooden living hinge. As illustrated by Figure 6, for this to work, Platener cuts a dense pattern of living hinges into the plate. This results in a plate that is flexible along the intended dimension [10]. In this case, users only have to (a) cut the curved plate and then (b) mount it using the provided finger joints.

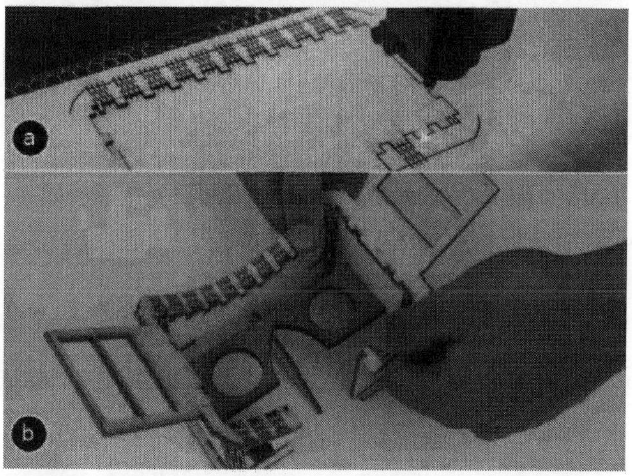

Figure 6: Creating a curved plate from wood. (a) Cut the object on the laser cutter, (b) mount it into position.

As shown in Figure 7, Platener helps users assemble parts by embedding matching pairs of labels.

Figure 7: Platener 3D prints/engraves instructions.

Specifying the *focus* of the current design iteration

On top of these global settings, different design iterations tend to put the focus on different parts [17]. Platener allows users to define such a focus by assigning a specific fabrication technique using *brushes*. For the head mounted display, the global threshold defines that the forehead piece should be 3D printed. Within this context, the user can now choose the focus of the current design iteration:

Case 1: The current design iteration is about some other part, such as the optical path. The forehead piece thus does not matter. In this case, the user can use the *do not print* brush on the forehead piece and the device will be fabricated without this part (Figure 8).

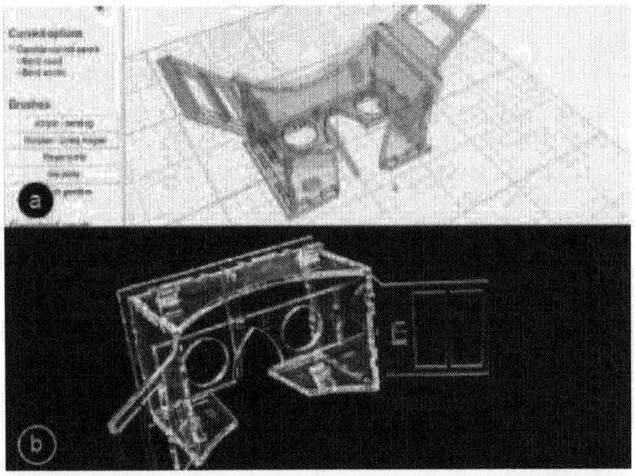

Figure 8: The design iteration does not require the head piece. The user thus uses the *do not print* brush.

Case 2: The current design iteration is about the ergonomics of the forehead piece, thus the contact area of the forehead piece matters. The user has a heat gun and decides to use the *curve acrylic* brush on the forehead piece (Figure 9).

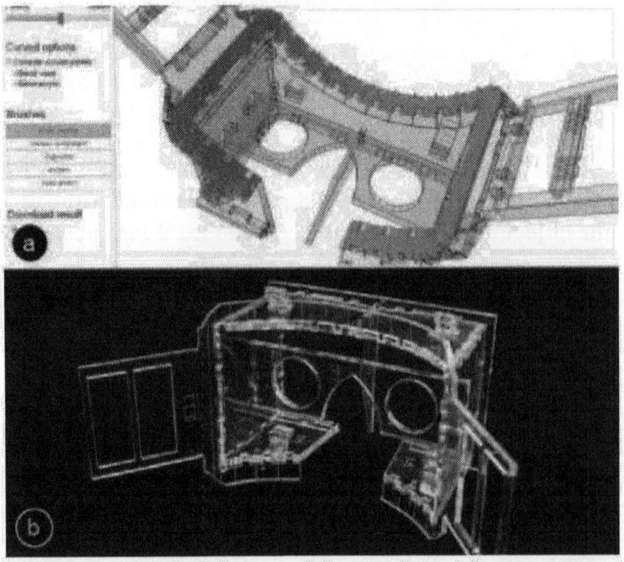

Figure 9: Overwriting the default with the *curve acrylic* brush to obtain a curved version for ergonomic testing.

Case 3: In this round of design, not just the ergonomics, but also the entire industrial design of the forehead piece is in focus. The user thus overwrites the setting of the forehead piece in the last iteration by using the *3D print* brush, resulting in the hybrid object shown in Figure 1c.

Case 4: In yet another round of design, the mechanics and the stability of the object are in focus. Per default, Platener has chosen to represent the four vertical edges of the casing as finger joints. These are easy to assemble, but brittle and thus not a good approximation for the stability of a 3D print. The user handles this by customizing these edges/connectors, similar to how one customized plates. As shown in Figure 10a, the user uses the *bend acrylic* brush and brushes across the connectors. This causes Platener to merge the four wall segments into a single long strip (Figure 10b). The assembled result is shown in Figure 10c—a version of the head mounted display that is sturdier than any of the converted versions we showed earlier, as its main body consists of only three pieces.

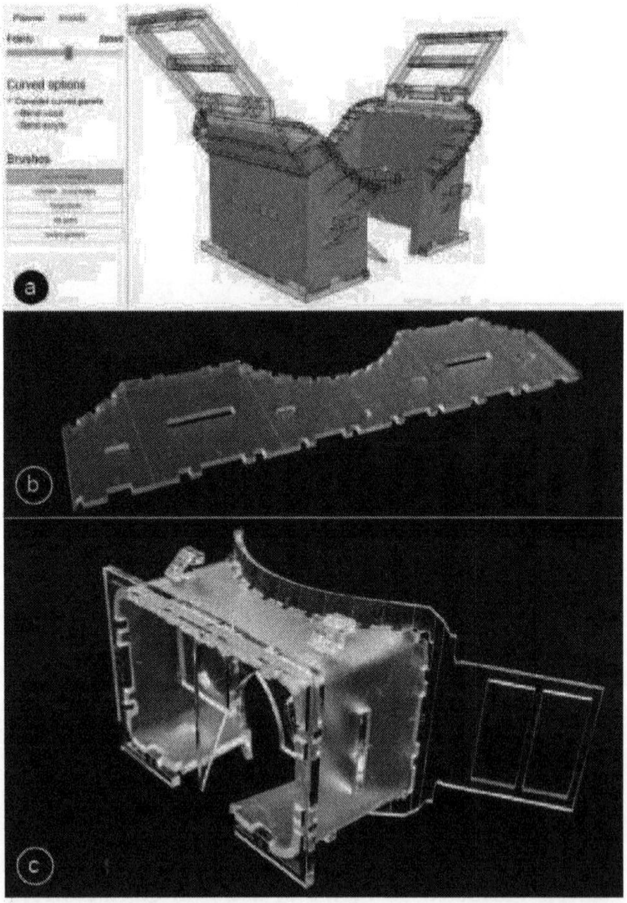

Figure 10: Using the *bend acrylic* brush, the user defines the casing as being made from one piece, which makes it sturdier.

BENEFITS AND CONTRIBUTION

Compared to low-fab techniques from the related work [15,17], Platener generally better preserves a model's geometry. We illustrate this at the example of the three objects used in the faBrickator paper [17], i.e., the penny ballista (Figure 11), the soap dispenser (Figure 12), and the head mounted display (Figure 13). Platener objects are generally sturdier as they are made from fewer pieces than when using building blocks (penny ballista: 17 plates vs 99 Lego, soap dispenser: 21 plates vs 53 Lego, head mounted display: 9 plates vs 160 Lego). The curved surface, despite requiring more manual effort, results in particularly sturdy results.

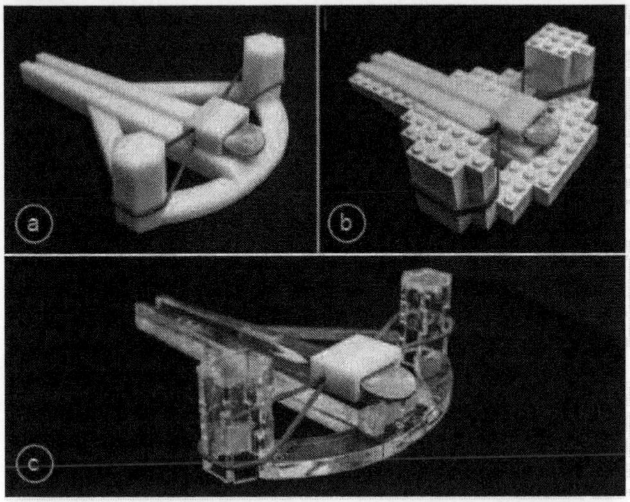

Figure 11: Penny ballista: (a) original 3D model, (b) faBrickator, (c) Platener.

Platener is intended to be a low-fab technique, i.e., users are supposed to use it for intermediate test prints while still iterating, and to only 3D print *the final* version. That said, some objects produced by Platener are of sufficient fidelity that users may choose to use the Platener conversion to fabricate also the final output.

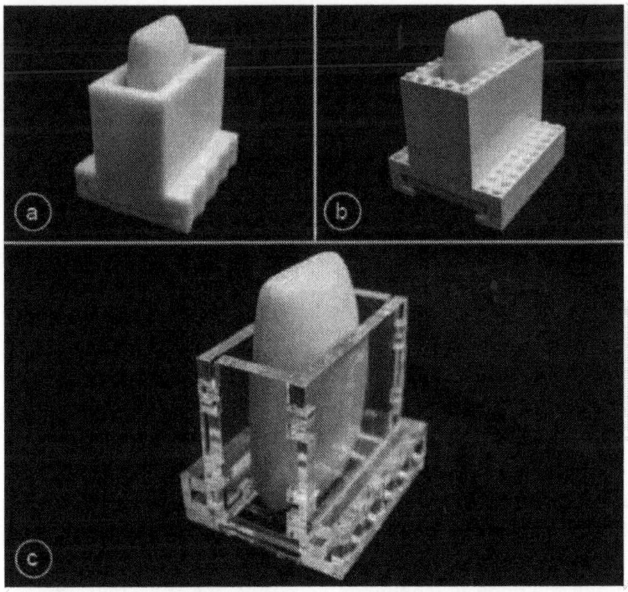

Figure 12: Soap dispenser: (a) original 3D model, (b) faBrickator, (c) Platener.

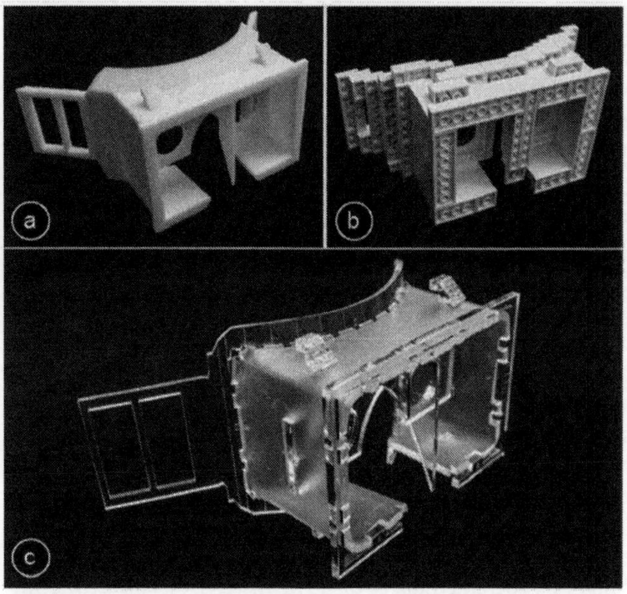

Figure 13: Head mounted display: (a) original 3D model, (b) faBrickator, (c) Platener.

On the flipside, Platener is subject to the following limitations: The thickness of the extracted plates is limited to the capabilities of the laser cutter (e.g., 10 mm maximum plate thickness on our ULS PLS6.150D laser cutter). While Platener speeds up design iteration of functional objects, it is less suitable for objects that are solely defined by their shape, such as 3D scans of people.

RELATED WORK

The work presented in this paper builds on personal fabrication, low-fidelity fabrication, and shape approximation.

Personal Fabrication and Laser Cutting

Laser-cutters are used for a wide variety of objects in personal fabrication as they allow users to quickly fabricate objects that fulfill a technical function: Coros et al. [2] show how to fabricate animated mechanical toys using laser cutters, *SketchChair* [19] shows how to build functional furniture, and *Pteromys* [21] shows how to laser cut functional model airplanes.

Low-fidelity fabrication

Platener shares the same goal as previous low-fidelity fabrication system, which aim at reducing fabrication time by replacing the original 3D representation with an alternative one: faBrickator replaces sub-volumes of a 3D model with Lego bricks [17]. LaserOrigami [16] approximates 3D shape by bending laser-cut 2D using a defocused laser. WirePrint replaces the surface of a 3D model with a wireframe structure [15].

Converting 3D models into stackable 2D plates

The most common approach to represent a 3D model using laser-cuttable parts is to convert it to a stack of 2D plates. This stack is generated by rasterizing/slicing the model along its vertical axis at a fixed interval. This functionality is included in many commercial products, such as the 3D editor *123D Make* [1]. Hildebrand et al. [7] take this approach one step further by slicing parts of the model in different orientations to better approximate the overall shape. While stackable plates ensure that the volume of a 3D object is well approximated, they are a less accurate surface representation.

Converting 3D models into intersecting 2D pieces

A different representation of a 3D model can be achieved using intersecting planar pieces. The resulting objects require less material and consist of fewer parts and thus are easier to assemble. *SketchChair* [19], for instance, provides a user interface for creating chairs based on intersecting pieces. McCrae et al. [6] and Schwartzburg et al. [20] provide algorithms that guarantee the constructability of designs based on intersecting pieces. *Slices* [12], finally, minimizes the number of pieces based on a study of human perception of shape. For some classes of objects, such as many types of furniture, a representation based on intersecting pieces equals the original shape (e.g., *Furniture Factory* [18] and Lau et al. [9]). Instead of converting an existing 3D model to intersecting pieces, *FlatFitFab* [13] allows users to create 3D models directly from laser-cuttable parts.

Converting 3D models to foldable 2D sheets

To better represent the shape of a 3D model, several systems have been developed to convert 3D models into planar sheets that can be folded into the desired 3D shape. Mitani et al. [14] propose an algorithm that unfolds a 3D model into a set of strips that can be cut out of paper. Besides using hard creases to fold material into 3D shapes, *Curved Folding* [8] proposes to integrate smooth curves in the bending pattern. *Soft folding* [22] combines both approaches and allows users to include creases and soft folds into a flat sheet. While foldable sheets result in an accurate surface representation, they have no infill and are thus not sturdy enough to perform mechanical functions.

Combining different fabrication techniques

In the context of architecture, Martens et al. [11] manually segment a 3D model into both laser-cut and 3D printing parts to make use of the benefits of both tools. Platener facilitates combining different fabrication techniques by automating the substitution.

IMPLEMENTATION

This section describes Platener's core data structure and the implementation of the processing pipeline.

#1 Mesh Segmentation

The mesh segmentation algorithm takes a 3D printable manifold mesh as input and outputs laser-cuttable plates and 3D printable parts. Platener then generates the *plate graph* of the 3D model according to the adjacency relationship of these segments.

The segmentation algorithm first extracts all flat planes from the 3D mesh then identifies *plates* by iteratively grouping plane pairs that are parallel, have an opposite normal, and are within distance *d*. The variable *d* represents the thickness of the *plate* and users manually configure it according to the laser cutting material. Each *plate* consists of two planes. The size and shape of the plate are determined by projecting both planes into 2D and intersecting them. We repeat the algorithm with all planes that remain after intersection until no more planes can be converted to *plates*. After extracting all *plates*, the algorithm labels the remaining parts of the 3D mesh as to *3D print*.

#2 Plate Graph Generation

After the mesh segmentation, Platener constructs a *plate graph* that records the fabrication method for each segment and joints between them. As illustrated by Figure 14, each node in the plate graph represents one part of the 3D model and each edge represents a connector between two plates. Each node has one of the three states: *3D print*, *laser-cut*, or *ignore*. Each edge, i.e., connector, has one of the five states: *no connector*, *bending connector*, *finger joint*, *interlocking joint*, *bending connector*, or *glue connector*.

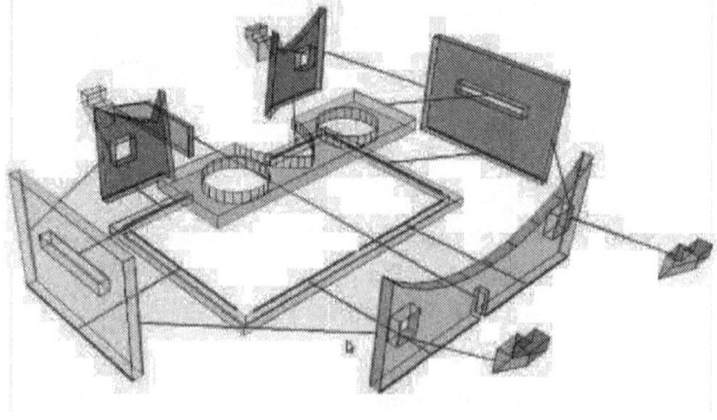

Figure 14: The plate graph represents the 3D model as a graph of nodes (plates) with edges (connectors).

Initially, Platener labels all nodes as *3D print* and all edges as *no connector*. As users move the fidelity-speed slider towards *speed*, Platener gradually labels the largest laser-cuttable segments as *laser-cut* and their adjacent edges as *finger joints*. Similarly, as users manually specify a fabrication method for each part, Platener interactively updates the corresponding labels in the graph.

#3 Mesh Processing

At the end of the process pipeline, Platener processes the mesh segments according to the *plate graph*.

Unfolding Curved Parts

When the curved plate option is activated, Platener gradually unfolds the curved segment onto a 2D plane. Platener also adds the bending lines or the living hinge pattern perpendicular to the unfolding direction. If the 3D segment cannot be unfolded without overlapping itself [4], Platener converts it to 3D printing as a fall back method.

Joint Generation

According to the labels on the edges, Platener places joints between segments or merges segments into a single piece. When the edge is labeled as *no connector*, e.g., both nodes are 3D printed, or *bending connector*, e.g., users applied the *bend acrylic* brush on the joints, Platener merges them into one single 3D mesh or *plate*. When using *finger joints*, Platener extends the boundaries of the segments and generates finger joints on the overlapping volume. The *interlocking joint* label is used when there is a cross-section between two segments. In such cases, Platener creates a slit on the laser-cut piece, allowing another plate to slide into and interlock with. Finally, in case the overlapping volume is too small, Platener switches to the *glue connector*, i.e., creates flat surfaces on both segments that afford gluing.

TECHNICAL EVALUATION

We evaluated the effectiveness of Platener by analyzing the speed-up after conversion for a range of different models. Given that Platener was designed for functional objects, such as casing and mechanical tools, we focused on 3D models that their creators described in such terms.

3D Meshes from Thingiverse

In order to obtain an objective sample, we downloaded 3D models from the online 3D model repository *Thingiverse*. At the day of the download, *Thingiverse* contained more than a hundred thousand 3D models in total.

We collected the 3D models by searching the website using the site's built-in search box and downloaded the top 200 results. In order to obtain an objective sample, we did not perform any further selection or removal of mislabeled objects at this stage, so our sample represents the "noise" level currently contained in these sites. Also note that many 3D models on *Thingiverse* consist of multiple 3D meshes. We processed them separately without merging them into one single 3D model.

The 10 search terms we used were *box*, *camera*, *controller*, *gadget*, *gear*, *household*, *mechanical*, *phone*, *speaker*, *tool*. We obtained an overall number of 2,250 3D meshes.

Measurements

We evaluated the effectiveness of Platener based on two measurements: (1) *Fabrication Time* before and after conversion, and (2) *Number of pieces* as a metric indicating the manual assembly effort required.

Results

Platener processed all 3D models and generated 3D printable stl files and laser-cuttable svg files. We estimated the 3D printing time with the *slic3r* (http://slic3r.org) g-code simulator, the laser-cut time by the length of the path contained in the svg files, and we approximated the assembly time via the simple formula of number of pieces multiplied by 15 seconds.

Figure 15 shows the time savings achieved by Platener. It shows that 39.9% of the downloaded 3D models achieve a speed up of more than 10x, which is faster than any of the systems in the related work. Another 13.4% achieve a speed up of 3-10x. 22.8% of models result in *no* speed up.

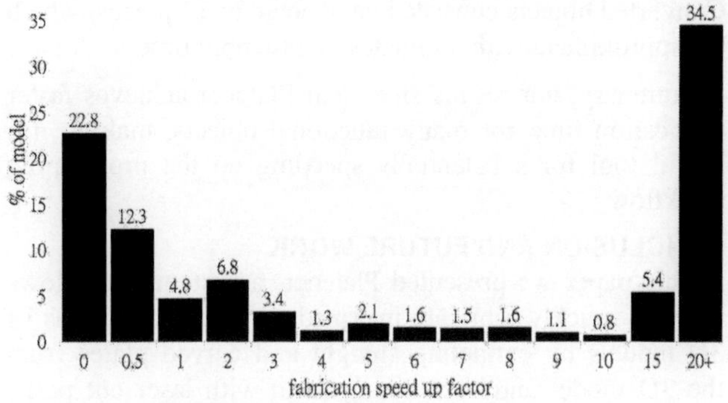

Figure 15: Fabrication time speed up.

Figure 16 shows some example objects that resulted in high speed ups (>10x). These objects consist mainly of flat pieces and contain few parts that cannot be laser cut.

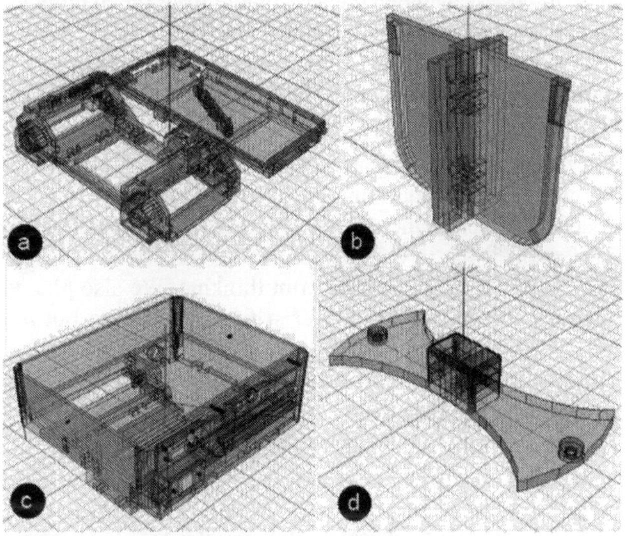

Figure 16: Some of the models that Platener fabricated 10x+ faster: (a) camera body, (b) hardware divider, (c) raspberry pi casing, (d) mount.

In contrast, Figure 17 shows two examples for which Platener was unable to produce any time savings. As expected, these objects are characterized by spherical curvature—shapes that lie outside of what Platener was designed to handle.

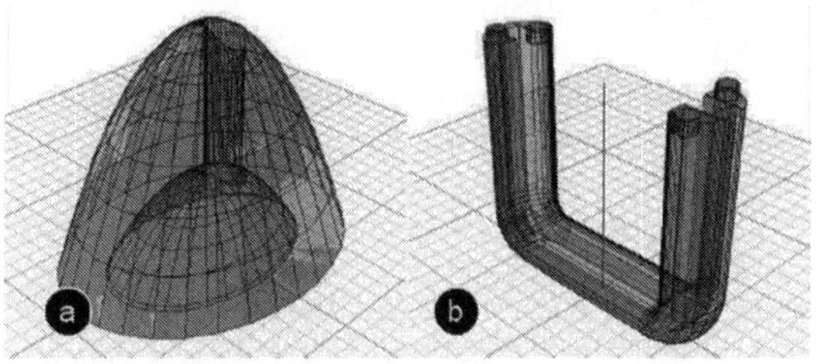

Figure 17: We would not use Platener for these objects as conversion results in no time-savings: (a) cone shaped mini heater part, (b) Kindle Fire comfort grip.

Converted objects consisted on average of 12 pieces, which we approximate with 3 minutes of assembly time.

In summary, our results show that Platener achieves faster fabrication time for many functional objects, making it a useful tool for substantially speeding up the prototyping workflow.

CONCLUSION AND FUTURE WORK

In this paper we presented Platener, a system that allows users to quickly fabricate intermediate design iterations of 3D models by extracting straight and curved plates from the 3D model and substituting them with laser cut parts. We showed that Platener preserves the technical function of an object better than existing low-fab techniques, such as faBrickator: objects converted with Platener have (1) fewer parts and thus are more sturdy, and (2) have a better approximated shape since Platener uses plates that have the same thickness as the extracted volume from the 3D model. Finally, our evaluation shows that for 39.9% of 2,250 objects downloaded from Thingiverse, Platener achieves a speed up of 10x or more, while on average requiring an estimated 3 minutes of assembly time.

For future work, we plan to conduct a formal evaluation that will help us understand how Platener and other low-fab systems influence the design process, i.e., if speeding up fabrication leads to a more trial-and-error oriented design process rather than extended prior thinking. We also plan to integrate materials that only exist for laser cutting but not for 3D printing (e.g., fluorescent acrylic). Integrating LaserOrigami would also make an interesting addition.

ACKNOWLEDGEMENTS

We would like to thank Lifeng Zhu for sharing his knowledge on developable surfaces, Tobias Mohr for manually building a first example object, Arthur Silber for helping us with the final touches on the laser cut prototypes, and Saiganesh Swaminathan for his help with the video.

REFERENCES

1. Autodesk 123D Make. http://www.123dapp.com/make
2. Coros, S., Thomaszewski, B., Noris, G., Sueda, S., Forberg, M., Sumner, R. W., Matusik, W., and Bickel, B. Computational design of mechanical characters. *ACM Trans. Graph.* 32, 4, Article 83, '13.
3. CRClarke. 2014. Strip Heater. http://www.crclarke.co.uk/products/LB/LB.html
4. Do Carmo, M. Differential Geometry of Curves and Surfaces. *Prentice-Hall,* '76.
5. Gershenfeld, N. *Fab: The Coming Revolution on Your Desktop--From Personal Computers to Personal Fabrication.* Basic Books, '07.
6. Hildebrand, K., Bickel, B. and Alexa, M. crdbrd: Shape Fabrication by Sliding Planar Slices. *Comp. Graph. Forum* 31, 2.3., 583-592, '12.
7. Hildebrand, K., Bickel, B., Alexa, M. Orthogonal slicing for additive manufacturing. *Computers & Graphics* 37, Article 6, 669-675.
8. Kilian, M., Flöry, S., Chen, Z., Mitra, N.J., Sheffer, A., Pottmann, H. Curved Folding. *ACM Trans. Graph.* 27, 3, Article 75, '08.
9. Lau, M., Ohgawara, A., Mitani, J., Igarashi, T. Converting 3D Furniture Models to Fabricatable Parts and Connectors. *ACM Trans. Graph.* 30, 4, Article 85, '11.
10. Living Wooden Hinge, https://www.snijlab.nl/en/p/30/products
11. Martens, B. and Stellingwerff, M. Creating Physical Models Using Virtual Reconstructions: Mixed CAM-techniques for a Viennese Synagogue Scale-model. *SIGraDi'05*, 108-113.
12. McCrae, J., Singh, K. and Mitra, N. Slices: a shape-proxy based on planar sections. *ACM Trans. Graph.* 30, 6, Article 168, '11.
13. McCrae, J., Umetani, N., Singh, K. FlatFitFab: Interactive Modeling with Planar Sections. *Proc. UIST'14*, 13-22.
14. Mitani, J. and Suzuki, H. Making papercraft toys from meshes using strip-based approximate unfolding. *ACM Trans. Graph.* 23, 3 259-263, '04.
15. Mueller, S., Im, S., Gurevich, S., Teibrich, A., Pfisterer, L., Guimbretière, F. and Baudisch, P. WirePrint. *Proc. UIST'14*, 273-280.
16. Mueller, S., Kruck, B. and Baudisch, P. LaserOrigami: Laser-Cutting 3D Objects. *Proc. CHI'13*, 2585-2592.
17. Mueller, S., Mohr, T., Guenther, K., Frohnhofen, J. and Baudisch, P. faBrickation: fast 3D printing of functional objects by integrating construction kit building blocks. *Proc. CHI'14*, 3827-3834.
18. Oh, Y., Johnson, G., Gross, M., Do, E.Y. The Designosaur and the Furniture Factory. *Proc. Design Computing and Cognition'06,* 123–140.
19. Saul, G., Lau, M., Mitani, J., Igarashi, T. SketchChair: an all-in-one chair design system for end users. *Proc. TEI '11*, 73-80.
20. Schwartzburg, Y., Pauly, M. Fabrication-aware Design with Intersecting Planar Pieces. *Proc. Eurographics'13,* 32, Article 2, 317-326, '13.
21. Umetani, N., Koyama, Y., Schmidt, R. and Igarashi, T. Pteromys: interactive design and optimization of free-formed free-flight model airplanes. *ACM Trans. Graph.* 33, 4, Article 65, '14.
22. Zhu, L., Igarashi, T. and Mitani, J. Soft Folding. *Computer Graphics Forum*, 32: 167–176, '13.

D-Coil: A Hands-on Approach to Digital 3D Models Design

Huaishu Peng
Cornell University
Information Science
hp356@cornell.edu

Amit Zoran
The Hebrew University of
Jerusalem (HUJI)
zoran@cs.huji.ac.il

François Guimbretière
Cornell University
Information Science
francois@cs.cornell.edu

ABSTRACT
We introduce D-Coil, a new digital 3D modeling approach using wax coiling to bring tangibility to the design of digital models. After defining a shape to extrude, the users follow the lead of a hand-held actuated extruder to instantiate the actual extrusion using wax. The tangibility of the wax extrusion sets the stage to create the next components until the digital model is completed. The digital model affords all digital attributes (ease of transformation, distribution, and 3D printing) while the wax artifact can be discarded or kept as a one-of-a-kind memento. We present a proof-of-concept implementation of D-Coil and showcase how this additive approach can also be extended to a subtractive process using a digitally actuated cutter. By adding a 6DOF mouse, users can also include scaling, rotation, and bending effects to create a wide variety of shapes often difficult for novices to produce in standard CAD software.

Author Keywords
Computer-Aided Design (CAD); Craft; Digital Fabrication; Extrusion.

ACM Classification Keywords
H.5.2 [Information interfaces and presentation]: User Interfaces.

INTRODUCTION
As predicted by Gershenfeld [5], we have seen a rapid advance towards the democratization of 3D printing in recent years. One can draw a parallel with the rise of desktop printing in the 1980's [1], with one significant difference: it is still difficult to create complex digital models ready for 3D printing. Though the interface of CAD systems has been greatly improved, the learning curve remains steep and creating complicated, smooth shapes requires the mastery of complex construction commands (such as lofting between multiple contours using guide rails). Further, the isolation of the design and fabrication process in digital CAD software makes it difficult for all but experts to anticipate how a digital model will look and feel once it is built. This stands in sharp contrast with traditional craft activities such as clay coiling in which design and construction can occur at the same time. As observed by Schön [15], the intimate interaction between the designer and the material at hand establishes a constant reflective "conversation" promoting a faster convergence towards a satisfactory design. Clay coiling also has the advantage of being easy to learn for beginners (low floor), but offering sufficient flexibility to enable experts to create highly complex models (high ceiling) [13].

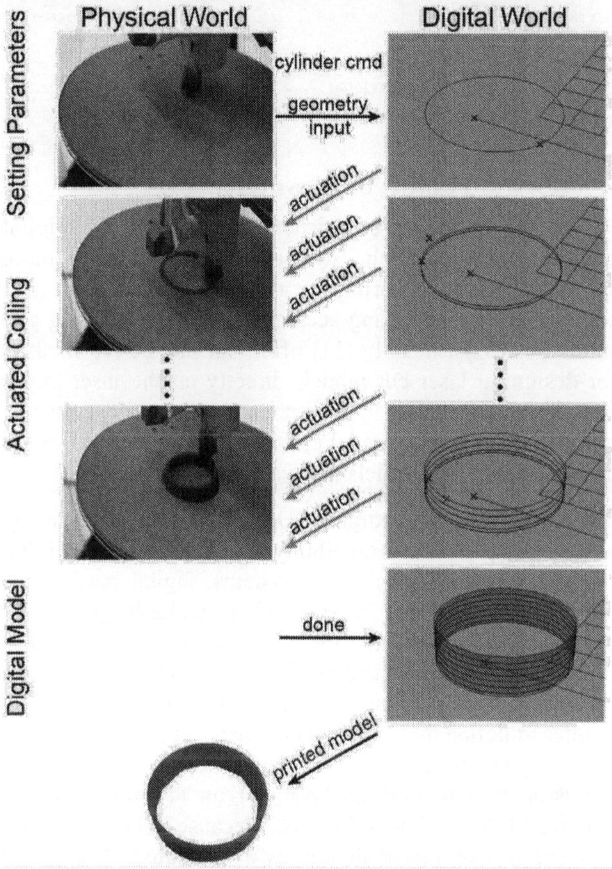

Figure 1: D-Coil concept: supporting 3D design using a wax proxy.

Several systems have proposed to bridge the gap between digital and hands-on building methods. Rivers et al.'s [14] proposed a hand-held, computer controlled 2D router to cut accurate shapes. FreeD V2 [25-27] offers a personalized rendering of an existing 3D model. Yet, none of these

CHI 2015, April 18 - 23, 2015, Seoul, Republic of Korea

http://dx.doi.org/10.1145/2702123.2702381

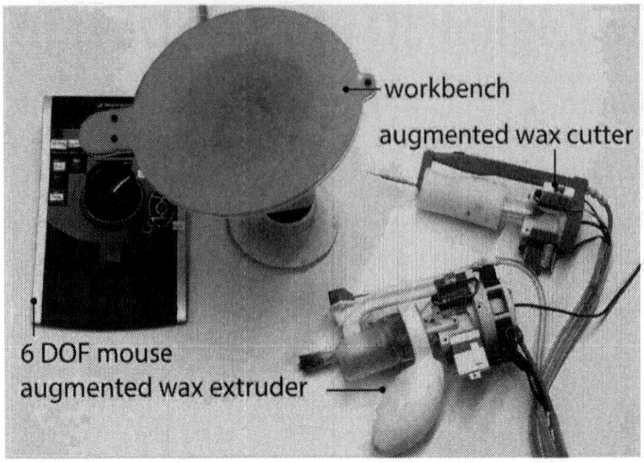

Figure 2: D-Coil system setting.

provides a hands-on experience for building 3D digital models from scratch. Others have focused more specifically on supporting model design. dePENd [21] supports users in creating accurate 2D drawings using pen actuation. Constructable [11] offers an interactive method for designing laser cut models directly on the laser cutter bed. Finally Cutter [19] instruments a hot wire cutter as input method for 3D model constructions. Both are limited in the scope of the models they can build.

We present D-Coil, a digital 3D modeling approach using wax coiling to bring tangibility to the design of digital models. As in standard CAD systems, digital models are designed by creating a succession of basic geometric primitives, but with D-Coil, additive construction takes place in the real physical world. For example, to build a cylinder (Figure 1), one would use the D-Coil tool as a pointer to define the center and diameter of a circle to serve as the cylinder base, then follow the lead of the actuated extrusion tool to coil up layers of an accurate physical version of the cylinder in wax. Because each geometric element is instantiated in wax as it is created, design and construction happen at the same time, providing explicit support for the reflective approach advocated by Schön [15]. This interaction greatly simplifies the conceptual model to be mastered for modeling because the wax model creates a natural reference for new additions to the digital model. Yet, the final output of the D-Coil design is *the digital model,* which affords all the benefits of the digital world such as ease of modification, distribution and replication (e.g., through 3D printing). The wax model meanwhile can be discarded, recycled, or kept as a memento of the design process.

We present a proof-of-concept implementation of D-Coil and illustrate how this basic creation cycle can accommodate subtractive operations using a computer actuated cutting tool. We also show how the basic extrusion method could be extended to create complex geometric shapes. To do so, we let users scale, translate, rotate, or change the orientation of the 2D profile from one layer to the next using a 6DOF mouse operated by the non-dominant hand (Figure 2). Finally we illustrate how segmenting single contour 2D profiles into independent sub-contours further enhances the expressiveness of our approach. These capabilities make the system attractive for both novices and experts, providing both with a more reflective approach to their design process.

We conclude by presenting the limitations of the current system and discuss possible extensions including tools to repair broken objects or create complex additions to existing artifacts in situ.

PREVIOUS WORK

The common 3D printing work cycle (designing the 3D model on a computer, printing, iterating) requires a high level of skill for all but the simplest models and is hampered by the isolation between the design and the slow production process. This is a long-standing problem and several solutions have been proposed to address it. One is to improve the interface of 3D modeling tools as exemplified by Teddy [7], Sketch [24], Sketch-Up [6], and more recently I♥Sketch [3] among others. Another is to create a more tangible interface for the construction process. For instance, Anderson et al.'s system [2] uses digital Lego blocks to support model construction. It offers a low floor but the use of rectangular blocks limits its expressiveness. Shen et al.'s system [16] uses the deformation of a foam proxy to drive construction, but still creates a high barrier between the creation process and the instantiation of an artifact. It is also possible to support 3D sketching in the real world through an augmented reality interface as suggested by Yee et al. [22] and Yuebo et al. [23]. D-Coil goes one step further by creating a tangible artifact reflecting the 3D model being built.

Digitally Supported Fabrication

Several previous projects explore digitally supported fabrication. Some improve the hands-on tooling experience with computer aided precision. For examples, Rivers et al.'s propose a digitally controlled 2D router [14] to improve cutting precision. FreeD V2 [25-27] use a hand-held computer controlled milling tool to encourage users to create a personal rendering of a digital model. Others have focused on additive processes: Haptic Intelligentsia [8] provides real-time haptic feedback when creating the outline of an object with hot gun glue; Mataerial [9] uses a robotic arm to create 3D curves in free space with additive fabrication. However, none of these approaches empower users to create an accurate digital model from scratch.

3Doodler [20], a handheld additive fabrication tool, is also related to our work because it brings 3D construction into the real world. Unlike D-Coil, 3Doodler does not focus on creating a digital model and it requires skill to create accurate geometries. By actuating the extrusion mechanism, D-Coil can help users create accurate shapes with little or no experience (similar to what the dePENd system [21] offered in 2 dimensions). Like Constructable [11], D-Coil is promoting a more direct relationship between digital and physical construction. While Constructable focuses on models suitable for laser cutting, D-Coil extends the concept to a more general 3D modeler with a hands-on interface. To some extent, D-Coil represents a generalization of the Cutter system proposed by Willis et al. [19] but to a much wider range of designs.

ModelCraft [17], finally, allows users to modify 3D models by combining annotations with a set of pen-based commands, but the modifications are virtual until a new 3D print is executed.

D-COIL DESIGN

The main design goal of D-Coil is to add a hands-on building experience to 3D digital model design. Coiling is well-suited to this aim as it is easy to learn yet very expressive. However, creating accurate shapes while coiling requires practice. It would be counterproductive to simply sample the movement of the extruding tool as this would lead to poor digital models. To address this problem, our system is designed around a dialog between the user and an actuated tool. As shown in Figure 1, to design 3D geometry, the user first defines the digital base shape using the tool as a 3D pointer. In turn, this information is used by the system to create a digital model and control the actuated extrusion mechanism to create the same shape in wax. As the user creates more layers in wax, the height of the digital model is adjusted accordingly. Once the extrusion reaches the appropriate height, the user simply stops extruding and enters the parameters for the next primitive to be created. The same principle applies to substantive operations using a heated blade. At each step, the instantiation of the digital model in wax makes it easier for users to specify the geometric context necessary to proceed with the design. Yet, the main output of the process is a digital model that is easy to scale or otherwise modify, distribute, and replicate using a 3D printer. The one-off wax model is only a memento of the design process. In the rest of this section, we present our implementation of a proof-of-concept prototype of the D-Coil system. We then describe advanced construction methods in the next section.

Wax Extruder

We used the FreeD V2 hardware design [26] as a starting point for our wax extruder, but replaced the milling tool with a customized wax extrusion mechanism described in more detail in the implementation section. As in FreeD V2, a 6D magnetic tracker which is attached to the backbone of the extruder is used to capture the location and orientation of the extruder head. This is used to capture user actions during the input phase and provides feedback to the actuation mechanism during extrusion.

We extended the capability of the FreeD V2 design (which only controls the back and forth motion of a milling tip) by introducing a reverse-kinematic model, which precisely controls the deposit of the wax in a 3D working volume. This feature is important because it leads users' hand movements along the correct extrusion path. We illustrate in Figure 3 that our system enables user to follow an accurate path without visual feedback. We provide three extruding heads of various diameters (1.5mm, 2mm and 3mm) to adapt to different needs in terms of modeling resolution and extruding speed.

Workbench

During coiling, it is often useful to reorient the wax model - either for construction comfort or to limit the impact of gravity on the shape of the wax coil. To address this need, we designed a workbench with a swivel base (Figure 2). The workbench encapsulates the magnetic tracker source as a reference origin for tracking coordination. Note that the user does not need to understand the workings of this coordinate system to successfully use D-Coil.

Building a Simple Extrusion

We use the process of a simple tube extrusion as a running example to illustrate D-Coil's basic interaction cycle (Figure 1). As in CAD systems, the process starts with the user defining the design base plane by using the extrusion tool to input 3 points. The user then inputs the shape to be extruded. For example, to define a circle, two data points are assigned on both the center and the periphery. Each time a data point is provided, the system extrudes a small dot of wax as a visual reference to help users construct the very first layer. The system offers other geometric shapes such as rectangle, ellipse, polygon as well as free hand drawing using the extrusion tip.

With the base profile defined, the system is ready for extrusion. During this phase, the actuation mechanism helps the user creating an accurate extrusion in wax. Extrusion will start as soon as the extrusion head is within reach of the path. From there the tool will "lead" the user to move forward along the path. The user simply needs to follow the extruding head movement so it is always in the center of the actuation range. This approach alleviates the need for an auxiliary digital display that may cause distraction from design activity. Once a given layer is finished, the system will automatically guide the user to build the next layer by raising the extrusion plane up one

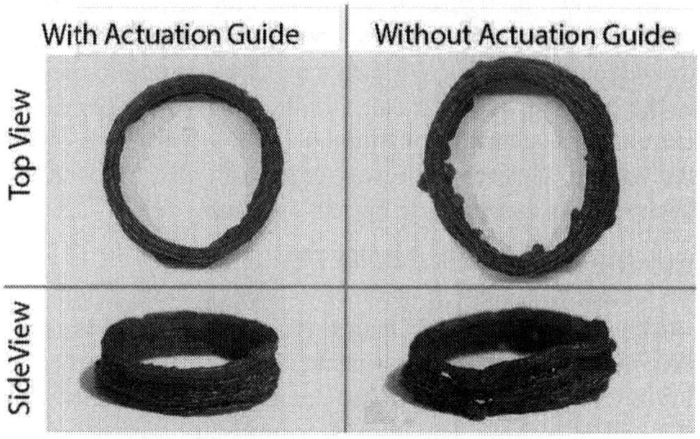

Figure 3: Left model is extruded with actuated mechanism, right model is extruded with pure hand movement.

Figure 4: (a) A candlestick with multiple 3D geometries, (b) A castle with gate and ramparts created using wax cutter.

layer height. The model is created one layer at a time until the user decides to stop extrusion by simply moving the extruder away. Once the first extrusion is completed, the user can choose to add a new part to the model by simply extruding on top of an existing part. Our workbench design makes it easy to reorient the piece for comfort. Figure 4a shows a candlestick as a compound model example.

Cutter, Cut, and Undo

D-Coil also includes an actuated wax cutting tool as the subtractive counterpart of the extruder (Figure 2). We first considered using FreeD V2 as our subtractive tool, but initial testing revealed that milling is not well-suited for wax. Instead, we opted for a heated blade system replacing the wax extruder. The wax cutter tip is heated up to melt the wax model where a cut is needed. Like the extruding tool, the cutting tool carries a 6D magnetic tracker and is very similar in use. For example, to create the gate in the model shown in Figure 4b, we defined the 2D cutting shape by pointing out two opposite corners of the gate rectangle directly on the model. We then moved the cutting tool close to the opening. With the same guiding mechanism as in the extruder, the cutting actuation guided the user to cut along the profile. Note that the wax cutter can also be used for simple undo operations to correct overextrusions.

BUILDING COMPLEX GEOMETRY

To create a complex geometry, we departed from the standard CAD tools' reliance on construction geometry (such as sweeping a contour along a path to create a tube or lofting successive contours to create complex shapes like the hull of a ship). The implicit, command-based nature of these features makes them ill-suited for a direct coiling approach. Instead, we revisited common clay coiling practice and observed that craftsmen achieve complex 3D shapes by layering different 2D profiles on top of each other. For example, piling up 2D profiles with increasing diameter can create a tapered 3D shape and rotating 2D profiles along the same axis will form a twisted object. This inspired us to explore a fully explicit local control method to construct complex 3D models.

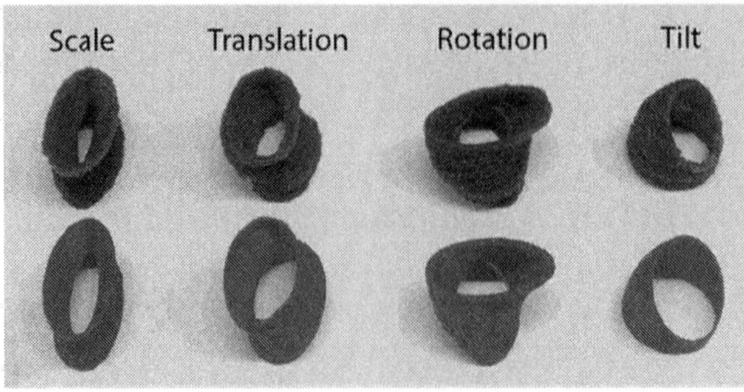

Figure 5: Transformation supported with 6DOF mouse.

Controlling Geometric Transformation of a Coil

We first consider operations that do not modify the basic shape of the 2D base profile, including translation, rotation, scaling, and changing orientation. As shown in Figure 5, these transformations can create a wide variety of shapes when used in isolation or combined. Although the tool tracking system can be used to command such a transformation, we found that, in practice, it is much easier to use the 6DOF mouse (Figure 2) operated by the non-dominant hand to specify the required transformation. We use a direct mapping between the puck movement and the intended transformation with scaling achieved by pulling or pushing the puck. We opted for stepwise inputs to achieve better control and precision for the transformation. More specifically, translations are specified by 0.5mm increments, rotations by 10deg increments, and scaling by enlarging or shrinking by 1/100 of the current size. The user can get a sense of current profile location by observing the tool tip movement while operating the mouse. The tip will move towards the new profile to outline the new location.

The geometric transformations are easily translated into a new tool path with the exception of rotations around the X and Y axis, which result in changes in the orientation of the top layer. Such rotations are achieved by modulating the rate of extrusion along the coil to create a wedge by thickening the coil in certain sections (Figure 5 far right).

Editing the Coil Shape

So far, we have considered operations for which the basic coil shape is invariant. Such operations implicitly assume that, if a new 3D shape is needed, the user will create it by drawing new base 2D shape. In practice, there are occasions when the newly designed shape needs to be similar to the previous one. It will then be difficult and tedious for the user to reproduce the shape by tracing the contour. To address this problem, D-Coil offers two

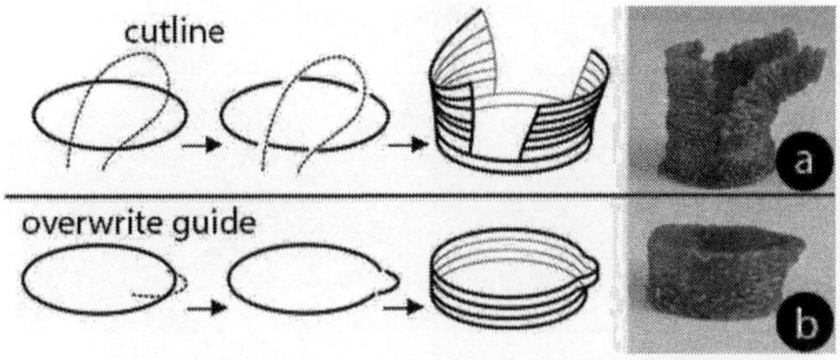

Figure 6: (a) Splitting a 2D profile and extruding each side. (b) Partially overriding a 2D profile.

primitives to transform the profile. The first is a split operation, which lets users split a coil into several independent segments. To split a 2D profile (Figure 6a), users press a split button with the non-dominant hand and draw a cutline with the extruder. The original 2D profile is replaced by several profiles, which can be operated on independently.

One can also override a profile (Figure 6b). Here, one selects the override command with the non-dominant hand and draws a path with the extruder. By default, the new profile will be integrated into the original profile, but it is also possible to have the system consider the addition as an independent profile. Figure 7 showcases the creation of a pitcher spout using this feature.

Copying and Pasting Geometry

One of the advantages of D-Coil compared to traditional craft techniques is that it enables fast replication of any part of a design using the digital 3D model as a template. This makes it possible to implement a copy-and-paste feature. To copy a part of a model, the user can hold down the copy button and move the extruder tip along the part of the model to be selected. All coils that are being crossed will be selected and placed on the clipboard. The model will be anchored at the selection point of the first coil being crossed. To paste the selected geometry, the user points the

Figure 7: Pitcher with spout. The spout is made using the overwrite function and the profile is considered independent from its original profile to achieve a taper shape separated from the main pitcher body.

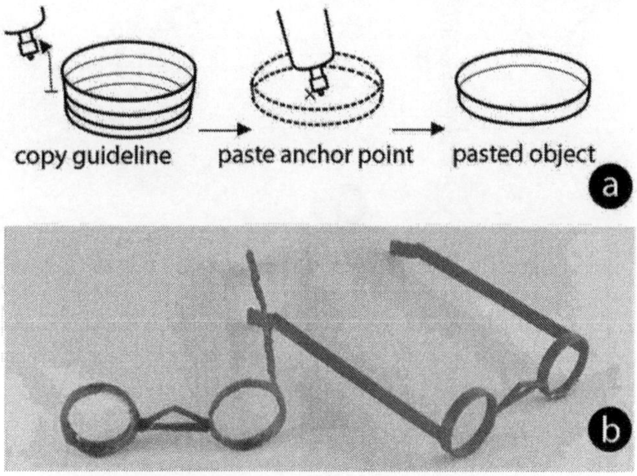

Figure 8: (a) Partially copy and paste of an extruded object. (b) Glasses made with the copy function. Both frames are made in the wax model, but the arm is pasted digitally without being instantiated. The printed model has both arms.

tool at the target location and presses the paste button. In our current implementation, the geometry will be replicated with the same orientation as the original model (Figure 8a). The user can then start to extrude the copied object. Note that our system does not require that all copies be instantiated physically. Figure 8b shows a pair of glasses where the replication function has been used to create two identical frames. In addition, one of the arms has been copied into the digital model without being instantiated in the wax model. Note that the printed glasses have both arms.

CREATING COMPLEX 3D MODELS

We now use a teapot example (Figure 9) to illustrate how we combine multiple functions introduced above for complex 3D modelling. We started by extruding a circle profile while scaling it to form the teapot body. We then used the cutting tool to cut a hole for the spout on the physical extrusion and added a spout combining scaling and bending operations. The handle was made via freehand drawing into the air. To compensate for gravity and

Figure 9: A completed teapot.

Figure 10: Various models created with the system: (a) Pen holder; (b) House with windows and doors; (c) Simple car.

sagging of the wax, we repositioned the workbench as needed during the construction. We show other examples in Figure 10.

Fitting a Model to an Existing Artifact

Using the free-hand drawing feature to start an extrusion, it is possible to create models that fit to complex surfaces. For example, one might want to add a crown or hat to a frog model (Figure 11a). To do so, one would use freeform drawing to create a path fit to the frog's head and extrude it following system guidance. If desired, one may flatten the top with another planar extrusion built up on the base shape with wax filling the small gap in between. Along with the wax model, a digital model featuring a good fit to the original frog is generated (Figure 11b). Note that such model fitting would be much more difficult in current CAD practice and would require scanning of the physical target surface, integrating this surface with the digital hat model, and printing to check fit and appearance. In the time it takes to design and print the crown once using the standard design cycle, a D-Coil user could explore several designs, getting immediate feedback on shape, location, and proportion.

IMPLEMENTATION

Our tools are partially based on the physical design of the FreeD V2 system [26]. We added a handle (Figure 2) to improve comfort and a new wax delivery system (Figure 12). The wax delivery was built using two rubber-geared continuous servos oriented against each other to increase the grasp of the wax wire. We did not use teeth gear as in common 3D printers because wax is too soft for this approach. The extruder tip is custom printed in brass covered with two 5Ω/10w film power SMD resistors (PFC10) as heating elements and NTC thermistors (EPCOS B57540) attached for temperature monitoring. The extruder tip can heat up to 78°C within 1 minute and maintain the temperature while extruding at different speeds. At this temperature the wax is malleable but not liquid, and solidifies quickly after extrusion. To further speed up the solidification process, compressed air is blown on the extruded waxed using 4 jets located at the corners of the extrusion head. The cutter tip is modified from an off-the-shelf wax cutter (SJK Digital Wax Carving Pencil) with the same temperature setting as for the extruder.

Tracking (Polhemus Patriot) and actuation (MKS 6125 servos) hardware is adapted from FreeD V2 with a tracking source mounted inside a customized workbench. The 6DOF mouse communicates with the main program via UDP.

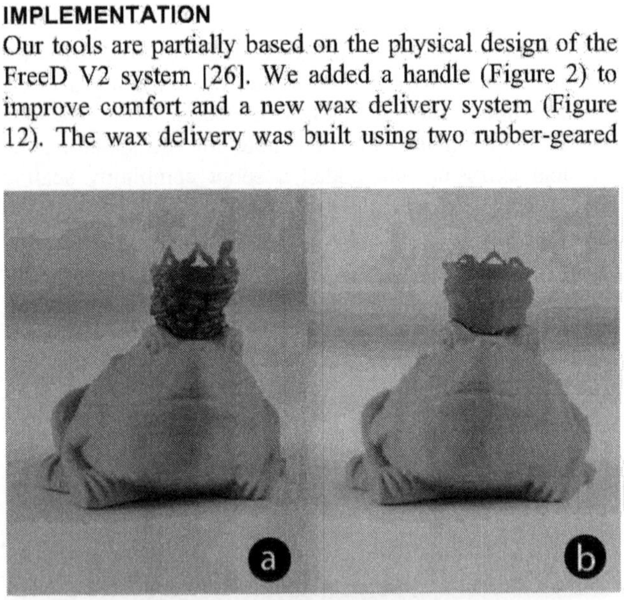

Figure 11: Fitting example. Frog prince wearing an add-on crown fitted to the head surface. The corresponding wax model is shown on the left, and the final design is shown on the right.

Software Implementation

The tool is based on a custom Grasshopper plug-in running inside Rhino CAD software (www.rhino3d.com). During the input phase of each interaction, the plug-in receives data from both the motion tracking system and the 6DOF mouse to update the model being created in Rhino. The digital model consists of a succession of 2D profiles, mapping the actual series of wax ribbons in the physical world (Figure 1). Digital models are updated automatically when the user starts a new layer. The current digital model is surface-based, a good match for our coiling system and

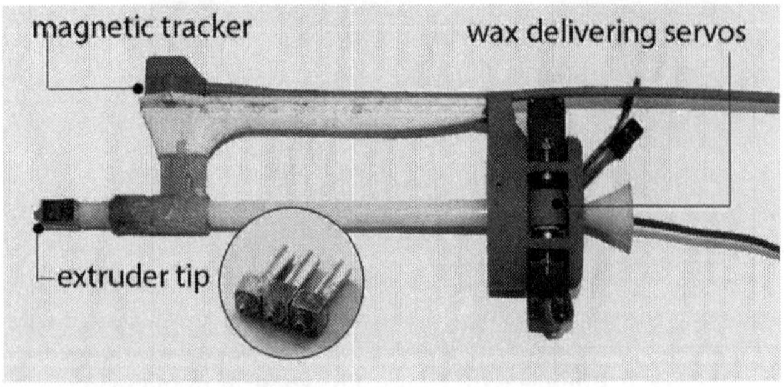

Figure 12: Extrusion system with wax delivery servos and printed brass extruder tips (several diameters shown). For clarity, the cooling system is not shown.

widely used in CAD software. However, our approach could easily be adapted to a volumetric modeler by applying shelling operations when needed.

During the extrusion phase, the extrusion and actuation is triggered when the tool head reaches the contour to be extruded. At this point, two things happen. First, the system initiates a feedback loop attempting to keep the position of the head fixed in space. This is done by sampling the position of the head at 30 Hz and using a reverse kinematic model to counterbalance any movement of the hand by adjusting the setting of each servo. This is not always successful because the user might move the tool too far away from the assigned position.

Second, we initiate active guiding along the contour. The system continually computes the position of a point on the path which is slightly (5% of the total length or the next path vertex) ahead of the current extruder position. The tip will physically lean towards the target point and thus lead the user to move along the path.

Our system also modulates the speed of the extrusion mechanism to reflect the actual speed of the user as well as any change in orientation required by user input. We also tabulate the completion level of each layer to decide when it is time to move to the next layer. A similar approach is used for the cutting tool.

DISCUSSION

We now discuss the lessons learned when designing the D-Coil prototype.

Coiling as Model Building Tool

The unique contribution of our system is to add tangible feedback and a reflective design experience to additive 3D digital modeling. We chose coiling as an interaction metaphor because it has a low conceptual barrier yet allows for the creation of fairly complex shapes. However, our approach also bears limitations and trade-offs like speed and expressiveness.

Design Speed

Though physical instantiation is not a fast process in general, our current prototype has attempted to solve this by introducing active guiding to "lead" the construction process and offering multi-size extruders to mass volume. We have anecdotal evidence that actuation itself could provide a 4-fold increase in speed when compared to an off-the-shelf wax extruder without augmented guidance (www.dumatt.com/Tools/tools.html). We believe that the speed could be further improved by refining the actuator design and the control loop of our system.

Yet, the reliance on bi-directional collaboration between user and computer introduces a fundamental upper speed limit. This is because the users must instantiate most elements of their design. This will become more noticeable when users become comfortable with implicit constructs familiar to expert CAD users. At that point, combining fast printing techniques such as WirePrint [12] with a CAD system might offer a better solution. We believe that both techniques are complementary because they are serving different points on the skill continuum. We plan to compare the strengths of both techniques in future research.

Wax as a Building Material

We started our design with a clay extrusion tool. However, during preliminary tests, we discovered that the clay ribbon broke too easily during extrusion. Clay also takes a long time (about two hours) to fully dry, and is difficult to modify with a subtractive tool. We also considered plastic wire (ABS or PLA), one of the most common materials for desktop 3D printing and also used in 3Doodler. PLA and ABS set very quickly once extruded, but they are fairly rigid which poses challenges for the cutting/subtraction tools. We eventually chose GEO wax wire [4] because of its low melting point, fast cooling, and ease of cutting.

However, wax material has its own limitations. During our use of the D-Coil prototype, we discovered that the newly extruded wax might stay malleable for too long, leading to small offset or gaps (see Figure 13). This is, however, more of a visual aesthetic concern than a usability concern. First, our construction process is very robust to gaps in one layer. Users can fill up the gaps or simply coil over them at the next layer. More importantly, the digital model, not the wax model is the final outcome of the construction process. The wax model only provides scaffolding to support a reflective design process. In that respect, our construction method is sufficiently accurate for the intended purpose.

Of course the flexibility of wax could be beneficial as well. Inspired by art work by Henrik Menné [10], we imagine one kind of decorative design tool using dripping effects to add unique textures to a physical model while keeping its overall shape intact.

Expressiveness

Our main goal with D-Coil was to explore the feasibility of an extensive 3D modeling tool supporting reflective design. By combining both additive and subtractive tooling with local modification functions, D-Coil has demonstrated great expressiveness. However, the current version of D-Coil does not include implicit/command-based constructs. This is mostly because we believe that a purely explicit/direct tangible model design will be most suitable for novices and intermediate users. Our system, however, could be extended to a mixed paradigm. To support

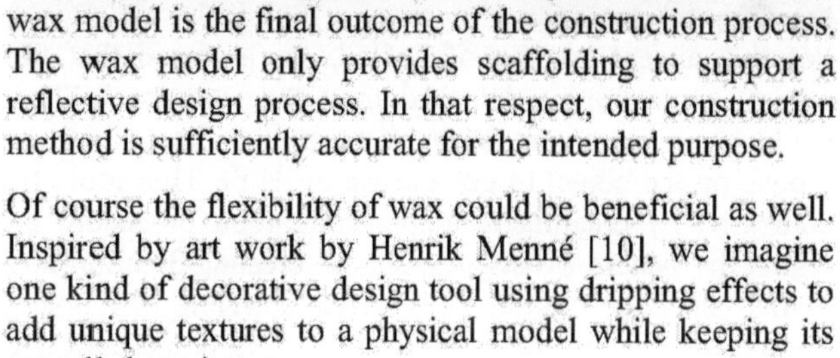

Figure 13: Imperfect extrusions. Left with a gap in one layer and right with wax offset.

implicit commands, we would need to provide a greater level of feedback in the context of the digital model so that users can place construction geometries (planes, virtual control points, etc.) and sketch accurately in the physical world. We would also need to provide visual feedback of the outcomes of implicit operations so that users can delay the start of the construction until they are satisfied with the outcome. Augmented reality glasses are one strategy to provide such feedback. Supporting implicit constructs would also require extending our extruding system to accept self-intersecting geometries which our current prototype does not support.

Model Accessibility

D-Coil adds tangibility to 3D digital modeling by creating a physical construction. However, tangibility will sometimes limit the accessibility of some parts of the model (inner structure), a problem that does not exist using a digital tool. In part, this could be addressed by careful planning, a common approach in constructing complex wax artifacts. Another approach is to simply destroy the parts of the model that are in the way since the wax model is just a proxy for the digital model. Empirical studies will be required to better understand how users react to this approach.

Incremental design

For the current version of D-Coil, we assumed that the model would not be detached from the workbench. This could be inconvenient when users would like to hold or reposition the object to get a sense of its fit. This could be addressed by creating a simple calibration procedure by which the system assists the users in creating 3 calibration marks using the cutting tools. After detaching the object and returning it to the platform, the users could calibrate the position and orientation of the new position by indicating the three reference points. This procedure could even be extended to situations in which the user already printed the object and would like to continue adding features on the 3D printout. The calibration feature would also allow for the creation of compound models from different parts.

FUTURE WORK

In this paper, we have focused on presenting the expressiveness of the D-Coil system. Next, we intend to implement a more robust version for broader deployment and evaluation with both novice and expert coilers. We would also like to explore whether the system can support more implicit constructs by extending it with various kinds of displays.

D-Coil as a Fixing Tool

We have shown in Figure 11 that the D-Coil system could be used to create models with a good fit to existing artifacts placed on the workbench platform. This feature could be extended to larger artifacts that may not fit to the platform by simply changing the tracking mechanism from a magnetic to an optical system (the simplest solution being binocular cameras). After setting up the tracking system, users would define the origin of the working volume and start working. This approach would make it possible to create quick add-ons to existing objects or missing parts for broken objects (akin to a digital version of sugru [18], a clay-like compound that hardens to hard plastic).

CONCLUSION

In this paper we presented D-Coil, a digital modeling system using wax coiling to bring tangibility to the design process. Combining an extrusion tool, a cutting tool, and a 6DOF controller to control the coiling process, users can create a wide range of digital models often difficult to create in classic 3D design tools. We presented an implementation prototype illustrating how our approach can help novices to get started with modeling and can provide experts with a more reflective creation approach. We described the design and operation of the system and provided several examples illustrating its expressiveness. Once deployed, this system could let a broader range of potential users take full advantage of 3D printing.

ACKNOWLEDGEMENTS

This work was supported in part by NSF Award ISS 1422106 and Microsoft Research. We thank Corinna Loeckenhoff for her comments on the paper.

REFERENCES

1. Anderson, C., *Makers : the new industrial revolution.* 2012, New York: Crown Business.
2. Anderson, D., J.S. Yedidia, J.L. Frankel, J. Marks, A. Agarwala, P. Beardsley, J.H.D. Leigh, K. Ryall, and E. Sullivan. Tangible interaction + graphical interpretation: a new approach to 3D modeling. *Proceedings of SigGraph'00*, pp. 393 - 402.
3. Bae, S.-H., R. Balakrishnan, and K. Singh. ILoveSketch: As-Natural-As-Possible Sketching System for Creating 3D Curve Models. *Proceedings of UIST' 08*, pp. 181-190.
4. Geo Wax Wire, http://www.renfert.com/24185/Preformedwaxes/GEO Waxwire/20836/catalog.aspx,
5. Gershenfeld, N., *FAB: the Coming Revolution on your Desktop - From Personal Computers to Personal Fabrication.* 2005, New York: Basic Books.
6. Google, SketchUp. 2006.
7. Igarashi, T., S. Matsuoka, and H. Tanaka. Teddy: a sketching interface for 3D freeform design. *Proceedings of SigGraph'99*, pp. 409 - 416.
8. Lee, J.H., Haptic Intelligentsia, http://studio-homunculus.com/, September 4th.
9. Mataerial, Mataerial, http://www.mataerial.com, September 4th.

10. Menné, H., http://www.tomchristoffersen.dk/artists/henrik_menne/henrik_menne.html, Accessed Jan 07 2015.
11. Mueller, S., P. Lopes, and P. Baudisch. Interactive construction: interactive fabrication of functional mechanical devices. *Proceedings of UIST'12*, pp. 599-606.
12. Mueller, S., S. Im, S. Gurevich, A. Teibrich, L. Pfisterer, F. Guimbretiere, and P. Baudisch. WirePrint: 3D printed previews for fast prototyping. *Proceedings of UIST'14*, pp. 273-280.
13. Myers, B., S.E. Hudson, and R. Pausch, Past, present, and future of user interface software tools. *ACM Trans. Comput.-Hum. Interact.*, 2000. 7(1): p. 3-28.
14. Rivers, A., I.E. Moyer, Fr, #233, and d. Durand, Position-correcting tools for 2D digital fabrication. *ACM Trans. Graph.*, 2012. 31(4): p. 1-7.
15. Schön, D.A., *The Reflective Practitioner: How Professionals Think In Action*. 1984: Basic Books.
16. Sheng, J., R. Balakrishnan, and K. Singh. An Interface for Virtual 3D Sculpting via Physical Proxy. *Proceedings of GRAPHITE 2006*, pp. 213 - 220.
17. Song, H., F. Guimbretiere, H. Lipson, and C. Hu, ModelCraft Framework: Capturing Freehand Annotations and Edits on Physical 3D Models. *ACM Trans. Comput.-Hum. Interaction*, 2009. 16(3): p. 1 - 33.
18. Sugru, Sugru, http://sugru.com/, 01/12/2014.
19. Willis, K.D.D., C. Xu, K.-J. Wu, G. Levin, and M.D. Gross. Interactive fabrication: new interfaces for digital fabrication. *Proceedings of TEI'11*, pp. 69-72.
20. WobbleWork, 3Doodler: The World's First 3D Printing Pen by WobbleWorks LLC, http://www.the3doodler.com/, September 4th.
21. Yamaoka, J. and Y. Kakehi. dePEDd: augmented handwriting system using ferromagnetism of a ballpoint pen. *Proceedings of UIST'13*, pp. 203-210.
22. Yee, B., Y. Ning, and H. Lipson. Augmented Reality In-Situ 3D Sketching of Physical Objects. *Proceedings of IUI'09*, pp.
23. Yuebo Shen, K.D., and Jiawei Gu. RoCuModel: an iterative tangible modeling system. *Proceedings of TEI '14*, pp. 73-76.
24. Zeleznik, R.C., K.P. Herndon, and K.P. Herndon. SKETCH: an interface for sketching 3D scenes. *Proceedings of SigGraph'96*, pp. 163 - 170.
25. Zoran, A. and J.A. Paradiso. FreeD: a freehand digital sculpting tool. *Proceedings of CHI'13*, pp. 2613-2616.
26. Zoran, A., R. Shilkrot, and J. Paradiso. Human-computer interaction for hybrid carving. *Proceedings of UIST'13*, pp. 433-440.
27. Zoran, A., R. Shilkrot, S. Nanyakkara, and J. Paradiso, The Hybrid Artisans: A Case Study in Smart Tools. *ACM Trans. Comput.-Hum. Interact.*, 2014. 21(3): p. 1-29.

Performance and Ergonomics of Touch Surfaces: A Comparative Study Using Biomechanical Simulation

Myroslav Bachynskyi*‡ Gregorio Palmas* Antti Oulasvirta‡ Jürgen Steimle*† Tino Weinkauf*
*Max Planck Institute for Informatics †Saarland University ‡Aalto University

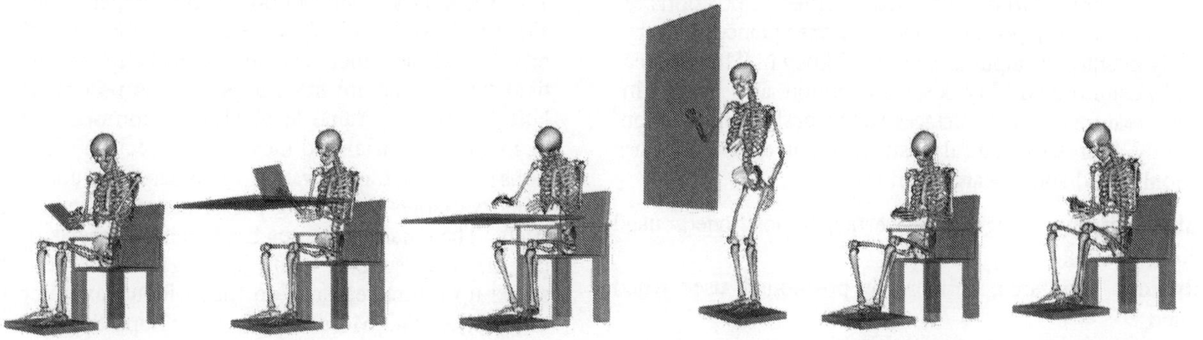

Figure 1. This paper presents performance and ergonomics indices for six typical touchscreen surfaces. Motion capture-based biomechanical simulation was used to understand differences in speed, accuracy, posture, energy expenditure, and muscle group differences. This figure shows the median postures recorded in the study.

ABSTRACT
Although different types of touch surfaces have gained extensive attention in HCI, this is the first work to directly compare them for two critical factors: performance and ergonomics. Our data come from a pointing task (N=40) carried out on five common touch surface types: public display (large, vertical, standing), tabletop (large, horizontal, seated), laptop (medium, adjustably tilted, seated), tablet (seated, in hand), and smartphone (single- and two-handed input). Ergonomics indices were calculated from biomechanical simulations of motion capture data combined with recordings of external forces. We provide an extensive dataset for researchers and report the first analyses of similarities and differences that are attributable to the different postures and movement ranges.

Author Keywords
Touchscreen surfaces; Biomechanical simulation; Fitts' law; Comparative study; Touch input; Pointing study.

ACM Classification Keywords
H.5.2. Information Interfaces and Presentation (e.g. HCI): User Interfaces

CHI 2015, April 18–23 2015, Seoul, Republic of Korea.

http://dx.doi.org/10.1145/2702123.2702607

INTRODUCTION
This paper addresses the fact that we are using a growing variety of touch devices in daily life. Smartphones and tablets have reached the status of a standard input device, and tabletops and public displays are receiving increasing attention.

We investigate the performance and ergonomics factors of common touch surfaces. While these have been studied in the past (e.g., [3, 20, 21, 9]), the studies have considered a *single* surface type at a time, such as tabletops [14], vertical displays [24], tilted displays [13], or handheld devices [20]. It has been impossible to form an overview of how the surface types differ in interaction. First, earlier studies did not compare surface types. Second, previous work has typically studied performance or ergonomics in isolation. Third, there are critical differences in experimental tasks, metrics, participants, devices, and so on, that prevent a direct comparison across studies.

This paper is the first in HCI to present results from a direct experimental comparison of common touch surface types in a target selection task. The within-subjects design sheds light on important differences and similarities among the surfaces. We see two benefits. First, the results illuminate the strengths and weaknesses of each surface as well as trade-offs among them. Our study permits looking at trade-offs in throughput, postures, and the expected fatigue in sustained interaction. Moreover, recommendations can be derived for better ergonomics and performance. In the past, poor ergonomics has often been identified anecdotally as a limiting factor for the prolonged use of surfaces. This is exemplified by the "touch thumb" and the "gorilla arm"—now popular metaphors of fatigue caused by touch interactions. The results of our study allow comparing such effects across surfaces.

Our point of departure is the assumption that differences among touch surfaces in performance and ergonomics can be attributed to biomechanical causes. Even though the input device is seemingly the same, touch surfaces can involve very different postures and movements. On the one hand, this increases tremendously the possibilities for using touch surfaces for input. On the other hand, different positions require different body postures, and the consequences of varying body posture on input are less well known. The implications of postural flexibility deserve attention, as it is a distinguishing feature of touch surfaces versus desktop interaction. Our study addresses natural postures for five surface types commonly used and researched in HCI:

1. **public display**: large area, vertically positioned, used while standing
2. **tabletop**: large area, horizontally positioned, used when seated
3. **laptop**: medium area, adjustable tilted position, used when seated
4. **tablet**: medium area, handheld
5. **smartphone**: small area, used with one or two hands

These align with the prototypical postures in previous HCI studies.

Our methodology builds on recent advances in unobtrusive data-driven ergonomics analysis. We use optical motion capture and biomechanical simulation to compute several indices of ergonomics. Biomechanical simulation describes motion capture data as velocities and angles of limbs, forces and moments at joints, and muscle activations. The use of biomechanical simulation not only provides a very rich description of biomechanical events in the body, it also overcomes challenges that the traditional ergonomics instruments have, such as goniometers and surface-EMG. Recently, the predictions of mocap-based biomechanical simulation were validated against EMG data [1]. The results were positive for all participants, highlighting that the correlation is higher for aimed motions involving larger muscles on male subjects closer to the population average in anatomical dimensions. We take this into account in study design and data analysis.

Unique to our study is that we allow users to freely choose their posture within each condition. We cluster these postures based on the recorded data to identify commonalities, e.g., leaning forward or backward. This allows us to analyze the amount of posture variation, and how different each posture type is in terms of performance and ergonomics. Full-body biomechanical simulation was not previously applied for analyses of interaction while sitting due to difficulties in measuring external forces. To allow users to change their posture while seated and record the main external forces acting on the human body, we constructed a chair instrumented with force sensors. The recorded forces are fed into our biomechanical analysis.

Our experimental task centers on the multidirectional version of Fitts' pointing task. This task allows the measurement of throughput (bits/s) by considering the accuracy and speed of aimed movements [25]. Moreover, it allows us to cover all movement directions on each surface. We selected pointing gestures as the subject of our study, because discrete aimed movements are the most widespread input across all surfaces, and encompass both capacitive and resistive techniques. Future work can extend this work to multitouch gestures following our methodology.

The secondary contribution of this paper is the dataset, TOUCHCORPUS, which we release for the research community. The dataset includes the raw data captured with the optical motion capture system as well as processed data, the latter on both a frame level (1.3 million observations) and aggregated per trial and movement direction (4280 observations). For each observation the dataset includes more than 1,000 variables describing performance and ergonomics aspects. The dataset captures fundamental aspects of touch input that may support many investigations. The corpus can speed up future research on touch input, avoiding repeated data collection. Moreover, it is our hope that a shared corpus will contribute to the replicability of studies and make it possible to compare findings from different publications.

RELATED WORK

We review previous work from two areas: physical ergonomics and performance, two areas which have rarely intersected in previous work.

Physical Ergonomics

Studies of physical ergonomics in touchscreen interaction have looked at comfort, user preferences, joint angles, postures and muscle use. Each study has focused on a particular type of surface.

Müller-Tomfelde et al. [16] collected user preferences for touch display workspace design. They found that the majority of participants preferred a tilted display at 45° or 30° angles to horizontal or vertical configurations. They explained this preference by better visibility and reachability of the display, improved comfort for the visual system and body posture. Barbé et al. [2] simulated postures for interaction with different touch displays in airplane cockpit. They validated the models using motion capture data and a simple biomechanical simulation CATIA/HUMAN. The location and orientation of the display had a strong influence on physical effort. In particular, it needs to be taken into account for prolonged tasks longer than 60 s. Davis et al. [5] analyzed data entry comparing touchscreens to physical keyboards. They found that a touchscreen is equal to or better than a keyboard in terms of kinematics, discomfort, usability, and error rates. A tilted orientation was preferable to a horizontal or vertical orientation, an effect that was influenced by both physical and visual ergonomics [23]. The authors conclude that the biomechanical analysis was limited, as a deeper analysis of physical loads *inside* the body could not be performed. Young et al. [31] assessed postures and muscle activity in shoulder and forearm during tablet interaction. They made several findings: the wrist is often operating in close-to-extreme angles, the forearm extensor muscles are highly activated in text entry, the trapezius muscles have higher activation when the tablet is on the table, and that the anterior deltoid has high variance when the tablet is heavier. Kim et al. [12] analyzed smartphone interaction and found that the body posture (sitting, standing, sitting at desk) affects the range of motion and the muscle activity of the thumb. They concluded that deeper analyses of ergonomics are necessary in future work.

Performance

Touch input has been found to be advantageous but also challenging when compared to mouse and keyboard [29, 3]. Touch lacks the haptic feedback of a physical button, and it suffers from occlusion and the fat finger problem. However, it performs relatively well in pointing tasks that involve medium-sized and big targets. Due to its directness it has additional advantages for novice users [29, 24].

Multiple studies have analyzed input performance with touch surfaces. However, as noted, most exclusively focused on a particular device [14, 24, 13, 20]. We are aware of only a single publication comparing different types of surfaces. However, it analyzes only reading comfort and performance [15].

Many previous studies look at accuracy. Beringer et al. [4] analyzed response times and accuracy on vertical touch displays, finding them to be non-uniform with respect to the target location and to the angle between line-of-sight and the screen. They also modeled input offsets between touch points and targets, which improved the accuracy of touch for a particular participant. Park et al. [20], similarly to Beringer et al., assessed the accuracy of single-thumb interaction with a smartphone. They found that distributions of touch points are Gaussian and distinct for each participant, button location, and size. Similarly, Parhi et al. [19] reported touch accuracy limits for PDAs, recommending minimum target sizes of at least 9.2 mm for single target tasks and 9.6 mm for multi-target tasks. Wang et al. [27] analyzed the touch area for all fingers on a tabletop and extracted touch area properties as shape, size, and orientation. Holz et al. [9] analyzed human errors while using touch and concluded that the origin of errors is not the fat finger problem, but the perceived input point, which they model based on roll, pitch and yaw. Their projected center model [10] performs significantly better than the standard method, decreasing input offsets to as low as 1.6 mm.

A large number of other studies investigate input performance in general, taking speed into account. Most of the analyses have used Fitts' law modeling [25]. Sears et al. [24] found that direct touch outperforms mouse input on vertical touchscreen when pointing to targets larger than single pixel. With additional stabilization the performance was the same and the error rate for 4 pixel and 1 pixel targets significantly decreased. Micire et al. [14] confirmed the suitability of Fitts' law models for horizontal tabletops. The study found that touch performes better than mouse input for all but 10mm targets; however, for 10mm and 20mm targets, the error rate was higher for touch input. Kin et al. [13] found that any

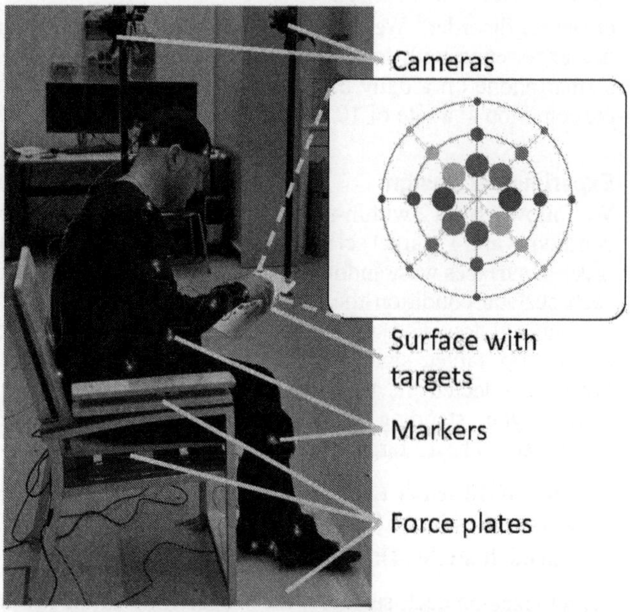

Figure 2. The experiment was carried out in a motion capture laboratory equipped with a special chair instrumented with force plates. Surfaces were emulated with cardboard. The targets were registered in 3D space and tracked during performance. Here a user is performing the task in the Tablet condition (seated). The inset shows an example of the multi-directional target setups used in the experiment.

touch-based method outperforms mouse input in a multitarget selection task, while the difference between multitouch and touch is very small. Sasangohar et al. [22] found that direct touch input on a tabletop provides significantly better performance for most targets in a tapping task, although it has the worst error rate for the smallest targets. Po et al. [21] compared pointing performance of mouse and direct touch input in the upper and lower visual field of a large vertical display. Oehl et al. [17] compared pointing with a stylus to the same target setup on touch displays of different screen sizes. Their surprising finding was that for difficult targets (small, distant) the participants performed better on bigger rather than smaller displays.

To sum up, previous work has mostly analyzed only a single surface type at a time, and focused either on ergonomics or performance. All surface types were treated the same way. In contrast, we consider the two factors together.

EXPERIMENTAL METHOD

This experiment compares six surface conditions in a multidimensional target selection task. All movements are recorded with a motion capture system. We built a chair with sensor plates to record external forces while seated. Figure 2 provides an overview of the setup.

Participants

40 participants (26 males and 14 females) were recruited at the local university campus. The age range is 19 to 39 years, with a mean of 24.9. The range of heights is 156-190 cm (mean 171.4 cm). The range of weights is 47-95 kg (mean 67.4 kg). The right hand was the dominant hand for 38 of the subjects. No participant had a known musculoskeletal

or neural disorder. We also collected their reports of previous experience with touch screens. Most participants used a smartphone on a daily basis. They were compensated for participation at a rate of 10 Euro/hour.

Experimental Design

We follow a 6 x 12 within-subject design with 6 surface type conditions and 12 target selection conditions (see below). The order of surfaces was randomized for each subject, and within each surface condition the target selection conditions were randomized, too. The surface types are: public display, tabletop, laptop, tablet, smartphone two hands, and single hand. We have selected the most widely used condition for each surface type: standing for the public display, and seated in other cases. The 12 target selection conditions consist of:

- **index of difficulty (3):** 2, 3.5 and 5 for small and medium surfaces; 2, 4 and 6 for large surfaces;
- **approach angle (4):** 0°, 45°, 90°, 135°

Target sizes on each surface were proportional to the screen size. They were 60, 28 and 10 mm for the public display; 50, 22 and 8 mm for the tabletop; 20, 14 and 7 mm for the laptop; 18, 10 and 7 mm for the tablet; and 7.5, 5 and 3.6 mm for the smartphone. Movement amplitudes on all surfaces matched screen size. In smartphone conditions amplitudes were shorter than marker error limits, limiting the applicability of the full-body simulation. Because biomechanical simulation has limited validity for small-scale movements [1], only 10 users participated in the two smartphone conditions in addition to the other ones. The remaining 30 participated in all other conditions except the smartphone conditions.

Task and Materials

We used a multidirectional Fitts pointing task [25] with circular targets, 3 index of difficulty (ID) and 4 directionality conditions: in total, 12 conditions for each type of surface (the target setup is visualized in Figure 2). In contrast to a typical multidirectional pointing task in which users perform pointing movements, changing the target direction after each one, in our experiment the participant performed around 50 repetitive aimed movements for each condition, without changing direction on the fly. The participant had to select the given target and then auditory feedback was given. Next he needed to select the opposite target.

To minimize the effect of surface friction, we used target setups printed on paper. They were printed on surface-size paper and affixed to a stand, a tabletop, and a tablet-shaped piece of plywood. The "tablet" is also tracked by the motion capture system through three rigidly attached markers. For the "smartphone" conditions we used a real device, as we needed higher tracking accuracy than our motion capture system could provide. We selected the Galaxy S3 for this condition as a representative device, because its screen size is close to the market average, and it offers a screen with high performance and resolution. The target setup on the device was represented statically, similarly to the printed setups.

Procedure

Each study began with the subject wearing the motion capture suit and standing in an upright static pose. This is necessary for musculoskeletal model scaling. Then the subject sought a comfortable posture for the surface we had selected randomly. The experimental task was then introduced and practiced. Next, the experimenter selected a random task condition and administered it with a custom-written software. The participant first performed a calibration for two given targets by touching their centers, and the system stored the end-effector positions. We used this to provide auditory feedback while the task was performed.

Next, the participant could practice the task before the experimenter started the recording. The participants were instructed to perform repetitive aimed movements between a given pair of targets "as fast as possible while keeping the accuracy at a specified level". The system counted 50 aimed movements and then gave the signal to stop the selections.

After the participant completed the task in all conditions of a surface type, a break was provided and the next device brought. Each session was split into 6 blocks corresponding to surface type, lasting approximately 15 minutes. The participants were allowed to take breaks when they wanted to rest. After the trials, we conducted an informal interview. We asked about participants' experience with touchscreens and their preferred experimental condition, and we measured the weight of the participants.

Apparatus

Motion capture system: The experiment was performed in a motion capture laboratory with no vocal or visual distractors during the tasks. Motions were tracked with a PhaseSpace Impulse optical motion capture system featuring 12 cameras. The system tracked 38 active markers attached to a skin-tight motion capture suit at defined anatomical points. We added extra markers to the end-effectors (relevant fingertips). The motion was tracked with a frame rate of 480 Hz and an accuracy of 1/2 mm.

Chair: External forces were recorded with a custom-built low-cost force chair and platform with two integrated Phidgets bridges and 8 load cells (2000N, 2x1000N, 5x500N; max error = 0.2%) (Figure 2). The chair sensed the most significant forces on the platform under the feet, under the seat, on the backrest and both arm rests and at two movable force platforms of 30cm x 40cm. The height of the seat was 50cm, width 45cm and depth 40cm; the height of the armrest was 70cm and width 8cm; and the backrest height was 95cm. The chair provided the force data at 125 frames per second. Figure 2 shows a user sitting on the chair in the Tablet condition.

Synchronization: Motion capture and force data were synchronized in real time using a custom-developed application on a high-end machine (Dell Precision M4800) to minimize latency (<5ms). For the smartphone conditions, we created an Android application for tracking touchscreen events. The touch screen tracking had non-uniform sampling with an average framerate close to 60Hz.

ANALYSES

We here describe the preprocessing and analysis of data for performance and ergonomics indices.

Preprocessing

Our preprocessing follows practices in motion capture based biomechanical simulation (see e.g. [1]). We clean marker data from occlusions, reflections, and other artifacts with a heuristic approach and Kalman smoothing. We then align mocap data with force data and touchscreen recordings, and segment trial-level data into individual aimed movements.

Performance modeling with Fitts' law

We follow recommendations from previous research [25] and use the Shannon formulation of the index of difficulty (ID):

$$ID = \log_2\left(\frac{D}{W}+1\right)$$

where D is the amplitude and W is the target width. The unit of ID is bits. We compute the *effective* target width $W_e = 4.133\sigma$ and amplitude $D_e = \sum_{i=1}^{N} D_i/N$ instead of D and W, where σ is the standard deviation of endpoint positions, D_i is the distance between start point and end point of a single movement and N is the number of aimed movements. We compute the coefficients a and b of Fitts' law using least squares fitting for a linear model:

$$MT = a + b \times ID_e$$

where MT is the average movement time. We assess goodness of the fit by computing R^2 for each model. Furthermore, we calculate throughput TP for each condition as:

$$TP = \frac{1}{y}\sum_{i=1}^{y}\left(\frac{1}{x}\sum_{j=1}^{x}\frac{ID_{e_{ij}}}{MT_{ij}}\right)$$

where y is the number of subjects and x is the number of trials performed in a particular condition.

Biomechanical Simulation

Although biomechanical computations have been known for decades [30], tools for motion capture based biomechanical simulation [6] and high-fidelity muskuloskeletal models[1] have reached maturity only recently. In HCI, the tools appeared in publications last year [1]. The simulation provides a great opportunity to "look inside the body" of users as they interact with computers, with no obtrusive instruments. It essentially reverse engineers observed motion to infer the relevant anatomical events. The variable transformations performed during biomechanical simulation are described below. Motion of markers in 3D space is first explained as rotations of joints given skeletal structure. Then, given the mass distribution of the body, required moments and forces at joints are estimated. Finally, given muscle anatomy, plausible muscle activations are estimated.

In our work we use the state-of-the-art, open-source biomechanical simulator OpenSim [6] and a high-fidelity musculoskeletal model from MusculoGraphics. The model is anatomically correct with respect to previous work.[1] It represents the full body of an average adult male with 63 bones (rigid segments), connected through 63 movable joints with a total of 109 degrees of freedom, and actuated by 236 Hill-type muscles which can exert active force along the muscle action path between the attachment points [11]. The simulator and the full-body model were recently validated against EMG data in full-arm movements in an HCI task [1].

The simulation consists of multiple steps, the latter of them yielding variables relevant for ergonomics assessment:

1. **Scaling** adjusts the generalized model size and weight to match the anthropometry of the participant based on the motion capture data recorded in the static pose and the participant's weight. Each bone is scaled according to the ratio between corresponding marker pairs in motion capture data and virtual markers attached to the model. The model's weight is scaled proportionally to the participant's weight, and then its distribution is adjusted according to segment scaling ratios.
2. **Inverse Kinematics** computes *angles at all joints* of the model which correspond to the cloud of points in 3D space recorded by the motion capture system. Intuitively, it transforms motions of points in 3D space to relative motions of skeletal segments. The angles are estimated for each frame by global minimization of the sum of squared errors between the markers recorded in the experiment and corresponding virtual markers attached to the bones of the model, while keeping the movement constraints of the joints.
3. **Inverse Dynamics** computes *moments at joints* and *forces inside the joints* occurring between the bones and joint capsule. They are calculated by directly applying Newton's motion laws to the kinematics data obtained in the previous step and the inertial and mass properties of the model assigned at the Scaling step.
4. **Static Optimization** resolves the moments at joints to *forces exerted by the muscles* acting at that joint and corresponding *muscle activations*. Muscle forces and activations are estimated by minimization of the sum of squared muscle activations for each frame, with each muscle represented by Hill's model. The static optimization assumes that humans recruit their muscles in an optimal way with respect to the sum of squared activations. This sum represents muscle stress and performs better than other criteria in load sharing problems [7]. In some situations this assumption can be false and human muscle usage can be non-optimal, for example when co-contracting opposite muscles; however, it has been shown to correlate well with EMG recordings for the aimed movements we analyze [1].

The simulation is resource-intensive: the average time to run Inverse Kinematics for a single trial is 4 hours. However, to make proper posture assessment and accommodate posture changes during a trial, we calculated Inverse Kinematics for the whole dataset. On the other hand, the subsequent steps of Inverse Dynamics and Static Optimization are computed only for "representative" movements. Even then, Static Optimization takes an average of 1.2 hours per movement. Follow-

[1] `http://www.musculographics.com/html/publications/publications.html`

ing prior work [1] we select one *representative* movement for every trial in each direction. We use the closest-to-average performance for this selection.

Posture Clustering

During the trials, users were free to take any posture they wanted. To make sense of this data, we use hierarchical clustering on the Inverse Kinematics data to identify the main types of postures for each surface type.

The Inverse Kinematics outputs serve as input for this step: the angles at joints calculated by Inverse Kinematics are applied to the musculoskeletal model of an average adult male, putting the model into the corresponding posture. In this posture we extract 3D locations of 22 keypoints at all joints of the human body and use them as input for the clustering algorithm. We have selected hierarchical clustering [8] because it is flexible and does not make assumptions about the data. We use Euclidean distance measure to treat all keypoints and dimensions equally. To acquire compact clusters with minimized variance we use Ward's linkage criteria.

To select the correct number of clusters we examine computed dendrograms and use multiple goodness-of-clustering indices: Pearson gamma, Dunn index, average silhouette width, and within-to-between ratio. The computations are performed in R with *hclust* from the *stats* package and *cluster.stats* from the *fpc* package. Following this approach, we obtained 7 clusters for the tablet, 3 for the laptop, 2 for the tabletop, 2 for the large display, 3 for the 2-handed smartphone, and 4 for the 1-handed smartphone. We introduce these postures later on in the paper.

THE TOUCHCORPUS DATASET

The outcome of these analyses is a dataset that integrates all variables extracted at different processing steps in a synchronized way. As can be seen in Table 1, the dataset includes 1181 variables describing different aspects of performance, ergonomics and experiment metadata. While the performance variables have been studied for years in HCI, the ergonomics variables from biomechanical simulation are more recent and therefore described here in more detail:

- *Joint angles* are related to the discomfort during the interaction. Operation of a joint at close-to-extreme angles causes postural discomfort and poses high risk for future musculoskeletal disorder, for example repetitive strain injury or carpal tunnel syndrome. In the dataset we consider extreme values at all joints.
- Excessive *joint moments* cause high load on the joint tissues and can cause damage to the joint, in particular when high moments are sustained for a prolonged period of time. We consider peak moments as well as the values integrated over the whole movement.
- Large *muscle forces* stress the muscle and tendon and can cause damage to their tissue.
- *Muscle activations* take into account the muscle forces, but normalized by the muscle size. The activation value of each muscle ranges from 0 when muscle is at rest to 1 when the muscle is maximally recruited. We use the muscle activations integrated over a whole movement as an index of muscular energy expenditure and fatigue.

Variable	Count	Aspect
Subject ID	1	Exp metadata
Device ID	1	Exp metadata
Trial ID	1	Exp metadata
Index of difficulty condition ID	1	Exp metadata
Approach angle ID	1	Exp metadata
Target ID	1	Exp metadata
Location of targets	6	Exp setup
Location of endpoint centroids	6	Performance
Offset to target center	1	Performance
Mean offset to centroid	1	Performance
Movement time	1	Performance
Target amplitude	1	Performance
Centroid amplitude	1	Performance
Index of difficulty	1	Performance
Index of difficulty effective	1	Performance
Fitts model parameters	2	Performance
Fitts model parameters effective	2	Performance
R^2 of Fitts models	2	Performance
Throughput	2	Performance
Throughput effective	2	Performance
Total mean muscle activation	1	Ergonomics
Total integrated muscle activation	1	Ergonomics
Extrema (min/max) of joint angles	218	Ergonomics
Peak joint moments	109	Ergonomics
Integrated joint moments	109	Ergonomics
Peak muscle forces	236	Ergonomics
Mean muscle activations	236	Ergonomics
Integrated muscle activations	236	Ergonomics
Posture cluster	1	Ergonomics

Table 1. Dataset variables extracted by the different types of analyses.

Condition	Size	Support	Orientation	Color
Tablet	19 x 24.3 cm	Handheld	—	●
Laptop	31 x 23 cm	Supported	Tilted	●
Tabletop	110 x 70 cm	Supported	Horizontal	●
Public display	85 x 120 cm	Supported	Vertical	●
Smartphone 2-hands	6 x 10.6 cm	Handheld	—	●
Smartphone 1-hand	6 x 10.6 cm	Handheld	—	●

Table 2. The surface types studied in this paper. We introduce a color convention for the remaining analyses.

RESULTS

We used MATLAB, R and MovExp [18] for exploring the dataset. This section presents the main findings. We focus on basic indicators of performance (throughput) and ergonomics (muscle activation, muscle groups), and postures. For statistical testing, we use repeated measures ANOVA with an alpha-value of .05.

Performance

We here focus on throughput as an aggregate metric of performance. Full data on speed and accuracy is provided in TOUCHCORPUS.

Figure 3(a) provides an overview of throughput versus surface type. The effect of surface type on throughput was statistically significant ($F_{5,8} = 9.24$, $p < .0001$). It can be clearly seen in the figure that the tabletop has the highest throughput and 2-hand smartphone follows in second place. The public display showed a slightly lower performance, while the laptop and tablet conditions saw the worst user performance.

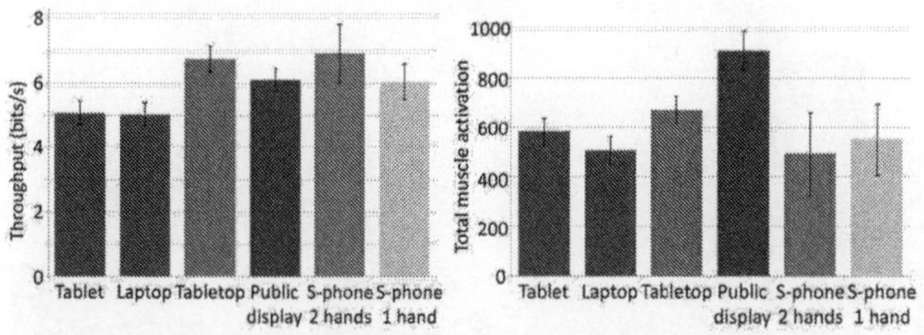

(a) Throughput (b) Total muscle activation

Figure 3. Throughput and total muscle activation per surface type. Vertical bars denote confidence intervals.

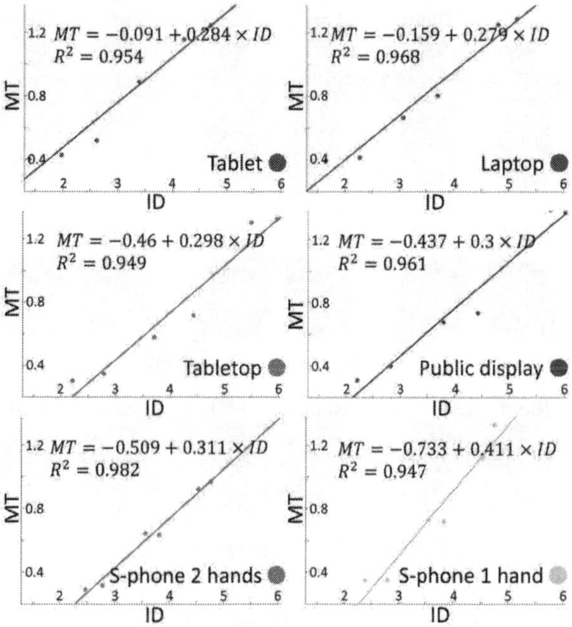

Figure 4. Fitts' law models for each surface type.

Average throughput was 6.55 bits/s. In the tabletop condition it was 20.5% higher than average. With the 2-hand smartphone it was 5.3% higher than average, and in the public display condition 5.2% higher. By contrast, with the 1-hand smartphone it was 8% lower than average, with the tablet 10.9% lower than average, and in the "laptop" condition 12.1% lower. Fitts' law models elaborate this view.

Figure 4 shows Fitts' law models for the six surface types. The plots show Movement Time (MT) against Index of Difficulty (ID). All Fitts' law models had high fit, with $R^2 > 0.95$ in most cases. However, there are some non-linear components visible for tablet, laptop, tabletop, and public display. Still, fitting a nonlinear model increased the fit by only 1-1.5%, and we therefore continued to use the linear model.

The Fitts' law models elaborate the overview by crossovers. For example, there is a crossover for the 2-hand smartphone condition versus the tabletop condition. The tabletop is worse in low ID conditions. The plots also show that the 1-hand smartphone is different from other surface types, because it provides high performance that is pronounced in the low ID conditions. However, performance degrades much faster than in other conditions when ID increases.

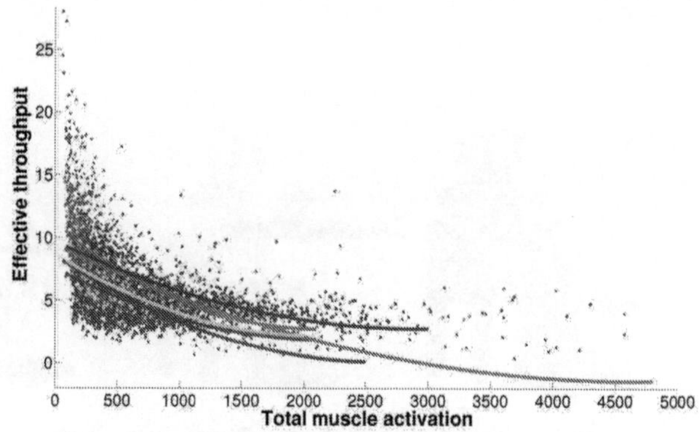

Figure 5. Total integrated muscle activation vs. effective throughput.

Total Muscle Activation

The effect of surface type on total muscle activation was statistically significant ($F_{5,8} = 10.59$, $p < .0001$). Figure 3(b) provides an overview.

We report standardized effect sizes for Total Muscle Activation, as its units are coupled with our musculoskeletal model. We learn that total muscle activation was lowest in the laptop and 2-hand smartphone conditions. In the tablet condition, it was slightly lower than average ("touchscreen in general"). It was the highest for the public display. The mean of total muscle activation was 608.1. For 2-hand smartphone use it was 19.2% better than average, for the laptop 18.6% better, for the 1-hand smartphone 9.6% better, and for the tablet 6.9% better than average. By contrast, the tabletop was 9.3% worse and the public display 45% worse than average.

Trade-offs: Muscle Activation vs. Performance

We found a non-trivial relationship between (effective) throughput and total muscle activation, as illustrated in Figure 5. The figure shows second order polynomials fitted to the original data. The most surprising pattern in the plot is that *low* throughput movements are associated with high muscle activations. The reason is that the lowest throughputs come from conditions with difficult-to-reach targets that require more careful control of muscles.

We also found that the approach angle influences throughput. However, it has no effect on total muscle activation. As stated before, average throughput is 8.5 bits/s. When considering the different movement directions, the highest throughput was found for horizontal movements (+9%) and the lowest for movements on a diagonal with 45° negative slope (-6%) and vertical movements (-5%). Movements on the diagonal with 45° positive slope have throughput close to the average.

Muscle Groups

Although input with all surfaces is carried out with the same arm, biomechanical simulation exposes large differences in which muscle groups are involved.

Interaction with tablet is characterized by high activations of side and back deltoids for interacting arm. For the arm that holds the surface, we see higher activation in frontal deltoid, triceps, and infraspinatus. Laptop use is characterized by high activations of the front and medial deltoids and infraspinatus.

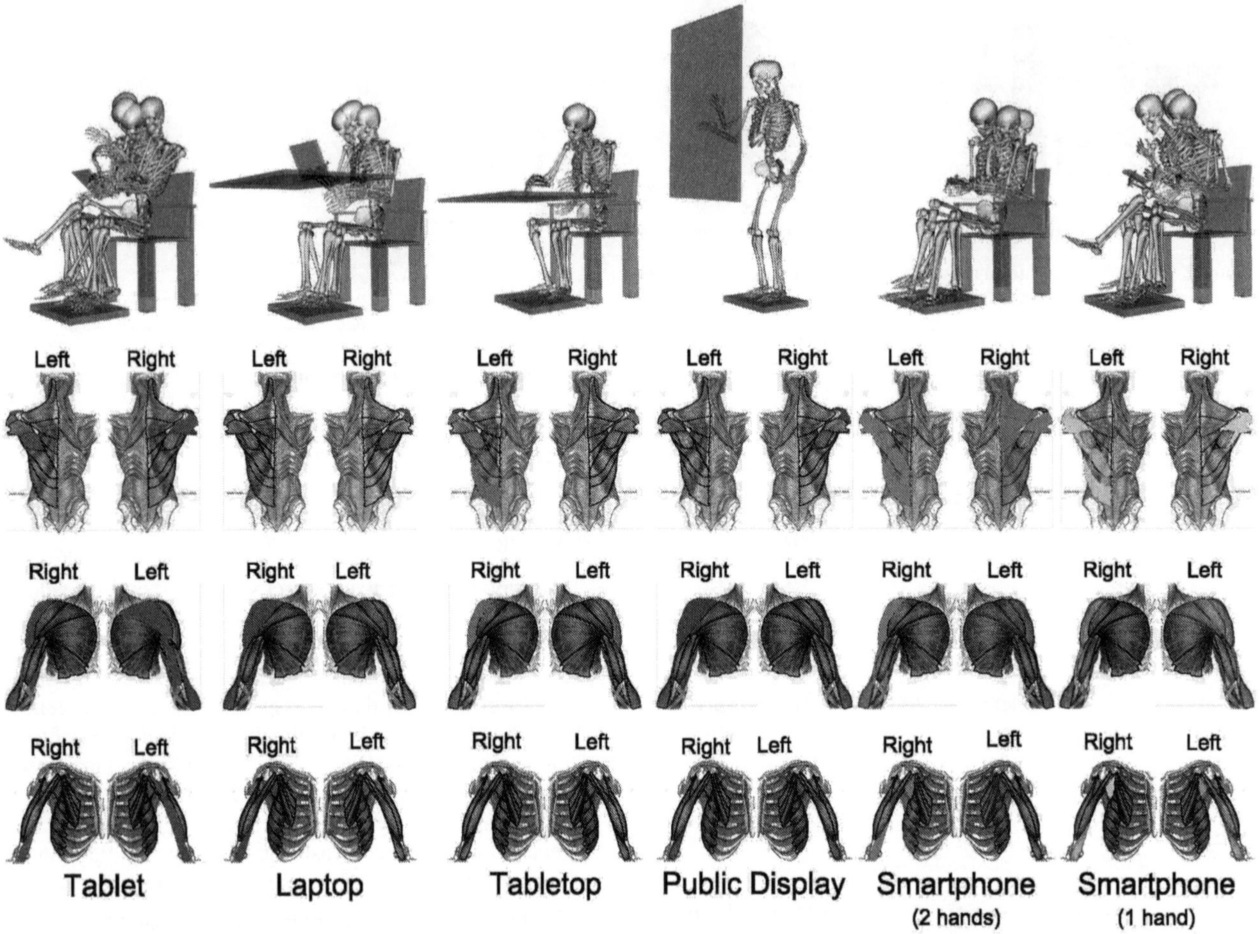

Figure 6. Posture clusters (top) per surface. Total activations of major muscles are shown below per surface type.

The tabletop recruits muscles of the lower back and the medial deltoid of the input arm. The public display, similarly to the laptop, recruits frontal and medial deltoid muscles of the input arm. Additionally, due to the standing posture, it shows higher total activation in all postural muscles. When interacting with the smartphone with two hands, the lower back muscles of the holding arm, as well as upper back, medial, and back deltoid muscles, are strongly activated. When interacting with one hand, upper back muscles are not that activated, but the medial and back deltoids of the interacting arm are more strongly activated.

Posture Analysis

Our posture clustering permits insight into differences within surfaces. Recall that users were allowed to take whatever postures they liked. We first report on the postures used by our participants. The clusters are visualized in Figure 6.

The following observations can be made.

- **Tablet**: These postures were grouped into six clusters. In the first five, the subjects hold the tablet in their hands in a low position close to their stomach. In the sixth cluster, they hold the surface closer to their face in a higher position. None of the subjects rest their back on the backrest of the chair, while four sit with his/her legs crossed.
- **Laptop**: These postures were grouped into three clusters. In all three, the subjects keep their left arms under the table and none of them rest their back on the backrest of the chair.
- **Tabletop**: Two clusters were found. In the first, the subjects mainly rest their left arm on the armrest while they perform their task. In the second, they have both arms on the table. Again, none of the subjects rest on the backrest of the chair.
- **Public display**: Two clusters were found. In both, subjects keep their left arm along their body. The main difference is that in the first cluster, the subjects have their trunk closer to the surface.
- **Smartphone, 2-handed**: Three clusters were found. In the first, the subjects rest on the backrest of the chair and place their elbows on the armrests, so that the trunk is oblique with respect to the seat. They keep the phone very close to their face. In the second, they sit instead in a straight position keeping the phone close to their knees. In the third, they sit back on the chair, resting their back. They keep the phone close to their face and their legs are outstretched.
- **Smartphone, 1-handed**: Four clusters were found. In the first, the subjects keep their right elbow on the right armrest

and they have their torso bent toward the front. In the other clusters, the subjects sit in an upright position. In the third, the subjects keep their legs crossed, and in the fourth they keep the phone close to their face.

Note that by using the clusters, we can improve the fit of Fitts' law models by 10%. The new goodness scores are shown in Table 3. This is in line with the idea that muscle groups affect Fitts' law model parameters. By decreasing heterogeneity in postures we can therefore also improve model fit. This effect is not achieved by arbitrary reclusterings, for example per user only.

DISCUSSION

The study was successful in exposing several novel findings about touch surfaces. The main thrust of the results is that even if surface interactions superficially appear similar, there are considerable differences in performance and fatiguability. In performance, we find large but not extreme differences among the surfaces. Performance-wise, even selection tasks with a high ID can be deployed on all surface types. By contrast, the differences we found in muscle activation and muscle groups are more pronounced. We summarize the observations as follows:

- The tablet has poor performance and is suitable for long-term use only after adjustment of the pose to avoid neck problems.
- The laptop has mediocre, almost poor performance, but it is suitable for long-term use.
- The tabletop has high performance but it is not suitable for long-term use, unless proper posture support is provided.
- The public display has high performance but it is not suitable for long-term use.
- The smartphone used with two hands has high performance but it is unsuitable for long-term use.
- The smartphone used with one hand has medium performance and is also unsuitable for long-term use.

While anyone can inspect the data for further comparisons, we highlight two surface types here: laptop vs. public display. They differ in interesting respects although both are used via movements of the arm. Laptop users' postures vary only slightly, with most users keeping neutral posture and avoiding excessive stresses. These postures activate mainly shoulder and arm muscles and are associated with low total muscle activation, which suggests that the surface is suitable for longer-term use. Contrary to expectations, the laptop provided the best physical ergonomics of interaction with the most neutral posture and low muscle activations, while providing acceptable throughput. While public display users' postures also vary very little, these postures are associated with high total muscle activation in the shoulder. The surface is not suitable for longer-term use although users' performance with this surface was very good. As expected, interaction with public displays is very demanding in terms of total muscle activation, not only because of the standing pose, but also due to longer movements in the vertical plane, in particular when reaching targets that are located higher on the display.

To contextualize our findings, we qualitatively compared them with previous studies. Similarly to Barbe et al. [2], our results confirmed significant differences among different postures. Although the conditions cannot be directly compared, the laptop in front of the user in our study demonstrated the lowest fatigue index among conditions, agreeing with Barbe et al.'s "tilted display." The recruitment of shoulder muscles in the tablet condition varied with respect to posture and the presence of support, and the upper trapezius on the dominant side was more activated than on the non-dominant side, as in the study of Young et al. [31]. Similarly to Oehl et al. [17], we observed an effect of display size on throughput for tilted and horizontal displays, but not for handheld and vertical display conditions. As in the study of Wagner et al. [26], we observed different grips during the experiment, including both novice and expert grips. However, in our case users were seated, and they often adjusted their posture and supported the tablet with their knee or leg.

In addition to decisions on which surfaces to use and how, these results could also be used to inform the design of *multi-surface setups*. These are becoming common in control rooms, aircraft, and currently also in desktop settings (e.g., [28]). The design problem here is how to allocate parts of the interface across many surfaces.

Finally, we note that the present paper has provided only the very first overview of this dataset. The TOUCHCORPUS allows researchers to continue empirically-founded analyses of touch input. By releasing it to the community, we wish to support further studies of this kind.

ACKNOWLEDGMENTS

We thank Mirella Scholtes for her help with the user study. This research was funded by the Cluster of Excellence for Multimodal Computing and Interaction at Saarland University, the Max Planck Centre for Visual Computing and Communication, the Academy of Finland and the ERC Starting Grant project COMPUTED (637991).

The dataset can be accessed under the following link:
`http://resources.mpi-inf.mpg.de/touchbiomechanics.`

REFERENCES

1. Bachynskyi, M., Oulasvirta, A., Palmas, G., and Weinkauf, T. Is motion capture-based biomechanical simulation valid for HCI studies?: Study and implications. In *Proc. CHI*, ACM (2014), 3215–3224.
2. Barbé, J., Chatrenet, N., Mollard, R., Wolff, M., and Bérard, P. Physical ergonomics approach for touch screen interaction in an aircraft cockpit. In *Proc. IHM*, ACM (2012), 9.
3. Benko, H., and Wigdor, D. Imprecision, inaccuracy, and frustration: The tale of touch input. In *Tabletops-Horizontal Interactive Displays*. Springer, 2010, 249–275.
4. Beringer, D. B., and Peterson, J. G. Underlying behavioral parameters of the operation of touch-input devices: Biases, models, and feedback. *Human Factors* 27, 4 (1985), 445–458.

Cluster / Variable	Tablet							Laptop			Tabletop		Pub disp		S-phone 2 hands			S-phone 1 hand			
	1	2	3	4	5	6	7	1	2	3	1	2	1	2	1	2	3	1	2	3	4
Fitts' a coefficient	-0.34	-0.15	-0.14	-0.15	-0.16	-0.37	-0.27	-0.15	-0.18	0.04	-0.52	-0.48	-0.47	-0.41	-0.57	-0.46	-0.42	-1.20	-0.58	-0.67	-0.45
Fitts' b coefficient	0.44	0.28	0.30	0.27	0.29	0.46	0.37	0.29	0.28	0.21	0.30	0.30	0.31	0.29	0.34	0.29	0.24	0.56	0.36	0.42	0.29
Fitts' R^2	0.85	0.97	0.95	0.78	0.84	0.62	0.54	0.97	0.97	0.82	0.97	0.94	0.96	0.94	0.96	0.89	0.98	0.91	0.96	0.93	0.95
Throughput($bits/s$)	4.39	5.79	5.20	5.40	4.99	4.67	4.45	5.08	5.39	4.67	7.41	6.84	6.24	6.27	6.42	7.42	8.54	5.72	6.09	4.92	6.83
Muscle activation	608	569	619	602	627	1561	522	597	549	600	710	686	1025	849	672	616	357	632	578	755	236

Table 3. Performance and ergonomics indices for posture clusters.

5. Davis, K., Hammer, M., Kotowski, S., and Bhattacharya, A. An ergonomic comparison of data entry work using a keyboard vs. touch screen input device while standing and sitting. *J Ergonomics S 4* (2014), 2.
6. Delp, S. L., Anderson, F. C., Arnold, A. S., Loan, P., Habib, A., et al. OpenSim: Open-source software to create and analyze dynamic simulations of movement. *IEEE Trans. Biomedical Engineering 54*, 11 (2007), 1940–1950.
7. Glitsch, U., and Baumann, W. The three-dimensional determination of internal loads in the lower extremity. *Journal of Biomechanics 30*, 1112 (1997), 1123 – 1131.
8. Hastie, T., Tibshirani, R., Friedman, J., Hastie, T., Friedman, J., and Tibshirani, R. *The elements of statistical learning*, vol. 2. Springer, 2009.
9. Holz, C., and Baudisch, P. The generalized perceived input point model and how to double touch accuracy by extracting fingerprints. In *Proc. CHI*, ACM (2010), 581–590.
10. Holz, C., and Baudisch, P. Understanding touch. In *Proc. CHI*, ACM (2011), 2501–2510.
11. Holzbaur, K. R. S., Murray, W. M., and Delp, S. L. A model of the upper extremity for simulating musculoskeletal surgery and analyzing neuromuscular control. *Ann. of Biomed. Eng. 33* (2005), 829–840.
12. Kim, D.-S., and Chae, W.-S. Biomechanical analysis of a smartphone task with different postures. *Korean Journal of Sport Biomechanics 22*, 2 (2012), 253–259.
13. Kin, K., Agrawala, M., and DeRose, T. Determining the benefits of direct-touch, bimanual, and multifinger input on a multitouch workstation. In *Proc. GI*, Canadian Information Processing Society (2009), 119–124.
14. Micire, M., Schedlbauer, M., and Yanco, H. Horizontal selection: An evaluation of a digital tabletop input device. *Proc. AMCIS* (2007), 164.
15. Morris, M. R., Brush, A. B., and Meyers, B. R. Reading revisited: Evaluating the usability of digital display surfaces for active reading tasks. In *Proc. Tabletop*, IEEE (2007), 79–86.
16. Muller-Tomfelde, C., Wessels, A., and Schremmer, C. Tilted tabletops: In between horizontal and vertical workspaces. In *Proc. Tabletop*, IEEE (2008), 49–56.
17. Oehl, M., Sutter, C., and Ziefle, M. Considerations on efficient touch interfaces–how display size influences the performance in an applied pointing task. In *Human interface and the management of information. Methods, techniques and tools in information design*. Springer, 2007, 136–143.
18. Palmas, G., Bachynskyi, M., Oulasvirta, A., Seidel, H.-P., and Weinkauf, T. MovExp: A versatile visualization tool for human-computer interaction studies with 3D performance and biomechanical data. *IEEE Trans. Vis. Comput. Graphics 20*, 12 (Dec 2014), 2359–2368.
19. Parhi, P., Karlson, A. K., and Bederson, B. B. Target size study for one-handed thumb use on small touchscreen devices. In *Proc. MobileHCI*, ACM (2006), 203–210.
20. Park, Y. S., and Han, S. H. One-handed thumb interaction of mobile devices from the input accuracy perspective. *IJIE 40*, 6 (2010), 746–756.
21. Po, B. A., Fisher, B. D., and Booth, K. S. Mouse and touchscreen selection in the upper and lower visual fields. In *Proc. CHI*, ACM (2004), 359–366.
22. Sasangohar, F., MacKenzie, I. S., and Scott, S. D. Evaluation of mouse and touch input for a tabletop display using Fitts' reciprocal tapping task. In *Proc. HFES*, vol. 53, SAGE Publications (2009), 839–843.
23. Schultz, K. L., Batten, D. M., and Sluchak, T. J. Optimal viewing angle for touch-screen displays: Is there such a thing? *IJIE* 22, 4 (1998), 343–350.
24. Sears, A., and Shneiderman, B. High precision touchscreens: Design strategies and comparisons with a mouse. *IJMMS 34*, 4 (1991), 593–613.
25. Soukoreff, R., and MacKenzie, I. Towards a standard for pointing device evaluation, perspectives on 27 years of Fitts' law research in HCI. *IJHCS 61*, 6 (2004), 751–789.
26. Wagner, J., Huot, S., and Mackay, W. BiTouch and BiPad: Designing bimanual interaction for hand-held tablets. In *Proc. CHI*, ACM (2012), 2317–2326.
27. Wang, F., and Ren, X. Empirical evaluation for finger input properties in multi-touch interaction. In *Proc. CHI*, ACM (2009), 1063–1072.
28. Weiss, M., Voelker, S., Sutter, C., and Borchers, J. BendDesk: Dragging across the curve. In *Proc. ITS*, ACM (2010), 1–10.
29. Whitefield, A. Human factors aspects of pointing as an input technique in interactive computer systems. *Applied Ergonomics 17*, 2 (1986), 97–104.
30. Winter, D. A. *Biomechanics and motor control of human movement*. Wiley, 2009.
31. Young, J. G., Trudeau, M. B., Odell, D., Marinelli, K., and Dennerlein, J. T. Wrist and shoulder posture and muscle activity during touch-screen tablet use: Effects of usage configuration, tablet type, and interacting hand. *Work: A Journal of Prevention, Assessment and Rehabilitation 45*, 1 (2013), 59–71.

How Much Faster is Fast Enough? User Perception of Latency & Latency Improvements in Direct and Indirect Touch

Jonathan Deber [1,2] Ricardo Jota [1,2] Clifton Forlines [1,2] Daniel Wigdor [1]
[1] Dept. of Computer Science, University of Toronto
Toronto, ON, Canada
{jdeber, jotacosta, daniel}@dgp.toronto.edu
[2] Tactual Labs
New York, NY, USA
cliff.forlines@tactuallabs.com

ABSTRACT
This paper reports on two experiments designed to further our understanding of users' perception of latency in touch-based systems. The first experiment extends previous efforts to measure latency perception by reporting on a unified study in which direct and indirect form-factors are compared for both tapping and dragging tasks. Our results show significant effects from both form-factor and task, and inform system designers as to what input latencies they should aim to achieve in a variety of system types. A follow-up experiment investigates peoples' ability to perceive small improvements to latency in direct and indirect form-factors for tapping and dragging tasks. Our results provide guidance to system designers of the relative value of making improvements in latency that reduce but do not fully eliminate lag from their systems.

INTRODUCTION
Interface latency – the time interval between a user's action and the system's response to that action – is inherent in any computer system; input sensors must be sampled, computations performed, graphics generated, and displays updated. Existing commercial touchscreen devices have latencies that range between 50 and 200 ms [19]. In an ideal world, system designers would keep this latency below the threshold that is detectable by the human visual system, making the experience indistinguishable from a truly latency-free system. However, despite vast increases in the performance of computer systems, latency remains an ever-present blemish on the user experience.

Latency has been the subject of a large body of research, as it has a fundamental impact on the feel of a system and on user performance in pointing tasks. Early work provided guidelines for both direct and indirect pointing tasks [16] in the 100–1000 ms range. Performance-based measurements on indirect input devices showed little improvement below 75 ms [14]. More recent work has focused on direct touch user interfaces, in which the touch surface and display are co-located [8,18,19]. As a whole, this body of work paints a conflicting picture, with results indicating that the minimal perceivable latency rests anywhere between 2 ms and 100 ms. We argue that this discrepancy is due in large part to the various form-factors used in the previous work (indirect vs. direct) as well as the different input tasks (tapping vs. dragging). One of the goals of the present work is to help clarify the picture by conducting an experiment in which the relationship between direct and indirect input for tapping and dragging tasks is explored. The results of this work shed light on the likely sources of discrepancy in the literature and inform system designers about the minimal perceived latency for different touch-enabled systems.

Another shortcoming of the previous research in this space is that it focuses exclusively on identifying the minimum perceivable latency for different input tasks. A system designer reading this research would know the ideal latency to reach in order to deliver a perceptually "latency-free" system; however, they are given no guidance as to the value of making improvements to the latency of their device that do not reach this ultimate goal. In this paper, we also present a second experiment in which we aim to investigate people's ability to perceive improvements to latencies that fall well above this zero lower bound. Our results outline the value of improving latency by varying amounts in modern-day direct and indirect touch-based systems.

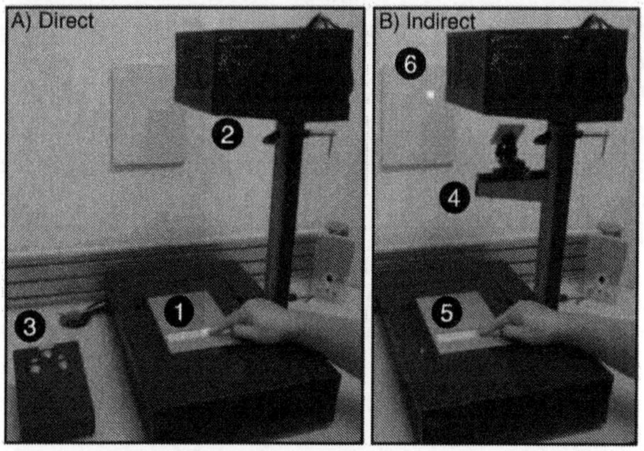

Figure 1. Experimental setup. A) In Direct mode, participants touch the surface (1) and output is produced by the downward-facing projector (2). After seeing a pair of latencies, participants indicate the faster of the two using the control box (3). B) In Indirect mode, the mirror assembly (4) redirects the projector's beam. The participant still touches the surface (5), but the output is displayed on the wall (6).

CHI 2015, April 18 – 23, 2015, Seoul, Republic of Korea

ACM 978-1-4503-3145-6/15/04...$15.00
http://dx.doi.org/10.1145/2702123.2702300

RELATED WORK

Latency, defined as the "delay between input action and the output response" [14], is an unavoidable part of any system, resulting from a variety of factors: reading the sensor(s) in an input device and transferring that data to the system, processing the input and performing application logic, rendering the updated UI, and waiting for the display to refresh its current image. The effects of latency on user interaction have been studied in previous works. Much of the prior work addresses *system latency*; they operate on the assumption of an existing baseline system latency and introduce additional latency as a factor. Techniques, such as those presented by Steed [25] and Kaaresoja et al. [9], can be used to measure baseline system latency. Researchers have also examined the point of subjective simultaneity (the separation at which two distinct stimuli are perceived as simultaneous) for haptic and visual stimuli [27], although most studies have not focused on touch input due to hardware limitations.

It is understood that latency affects how humans perceive virtual environments. Allison et al. studied the effect of latency in augmented reality, noting that latency degrades the illusion of stability – a major fault for an interactive system [1]. Nelson et al. reported that latencies of 50 and 100 ms impacted the ability to visually follow a virtual object with a head-mounted display [17]. Meehan et al. found that increased latencies of 50 and 90 ms reduced users' sense of presence in virtual environments [15].

We are particularly interested in the latency of input devices, and next examine work on indirect and direct systems.

Latency in Indirect Input Systems

Indirect systems separate input and output regions and require a pointing tool such as a mouse, touchpad, or stylus to provide information to the computer.

So et al. introduced latency (0, 55, 110, 220, and 440 ms) to indirect pointing, and found the effect was correlated with the width of a target and latency [24]. Pavlovych et al. tested mouse input for a targeting task with latencies above 20 ms and found that error rates increase significantly when latency rises above 110 ms [20,21,22]. Teather et al. observed that adding latency to a mouse and to a 3D tracker significantly impacted device performance; adding 40 ms to the system baseline latency affected performance by 15% [26]. Ware et al. studied the effect of latency for reaching tasks in 3D scenarios, and found that latency between 70 and 800 ms affects performance [28]. Ellis et al. found that latencies between 100 and 500 ms significantly degraded performance of path tracing tasks, and that users could distinguish latencies as low as 33 ms [5,6]. None of these studies examined touchpad-based interaction.

The disparity of the aforementioned results are likely due to the different devices being tested, supporting the suggestion that latency effects are task- and device-dependent.

Latency in Direct Input Systems

Unlike indirect input systems that separate the input device and the display surface, direct input devices (e.g., touchscreens) have no intermediary; the user inputs directly on the display surface. As with indirect systems, direct touch input devices also suffer from the effects of latency.

Anderson et al. conducted a qualitative study with users performing touchscreen tasks (e.g., web browsing and eBook reading) to determine the level of latency users find to be "acceptable" [2]. A delay above 580 ms was deemed unacceptable to the users, but it was noted that the experimental tasks were relatively brief (zooming, panning, and page-turning) suggesting that latency might be tolerable for longer tasks. Ng et al. studied the user perception of latency for touch input. For dragging actions, users were able to detect latency levels as low as 6 ms [19]. Jota et al. also studied touch input, and found that dragging task performance is affected if latency levels are above 25 ms, and that users are unable to perceive latency in response to tapping that is less than 24 ms [8]. Kaaresoja et al. looked at the visual perception of latency in physical buttons, and found the lower threshold of perception was 85 ms, but that the perceived quality of the button declined significantly for latencies above 100 ms [10].

Direct input systems that rely on a stylus, instead of touch, have also been studied. Ng et al. [18] focused on latency perception limits, and reported perception limits of 2 ms for a dragging task and 6 ms for a scribbling task. Using the same apparatus, Annett et al. studied writing and drawing tasks, and found that users could perceive latencies down to 50 ms [3]. The combined findings of Ng et al. and Annett et al. suggest that latency perception is dependent on the task, and can still be perceived well below the latencies of 55 to 200 ms provided by currently available digital pens.

These direct and indirect studies educate us on specific tasks or form-factors, but there are no single comparisons between direct and indirect systems. Furthermore indirect studies have not taken advantage of the recently available low latency prototypes [12,19], which might explain why the results of direct input studies that do take advantage of this hardware are significantly lower. We therefore set out to conduct a series of experiments that leveraged low latency hardware to directly compare the perception of latency on both direct and indirect form-factors.

Measuring Latency Perception: Just Noticeable Difference

A Just Noticeable Difference (JND) is the minimum difference in a pair of stimuli that is detectable by a person, and can be measured for any perceptual stimuli (e.g., light, pressure, sound). A trial in a JND experiment [13] presents a pair of different stimuli (*A* and *B*) to a participant and asks them to identify which is faster (or brighter, louder, etc.). One stimulus, the *reference*, is held constant throughout the experiment; the second stimulus, the *probe*, is varied in each trial. The probe begins far from the reference and is moved closer to the reference whenever a participant is able to correctly distinguish them, and further from the reference when they cannot. The series of probe values is termed a *staircase*, due to its series of up and down movements. A *reversal* in the direction of the staircase occurs when a correct answer is given after an incorrect response, or vice versa. After a series of trials, the probe will converge at the point where the participant is just able to distinguish it from the reference and will oscillate indefinitely above and below this point (given a sufficiently patient participant). This threshold is termed the *JND threshold*.

EXPERIMENT 1: PERCEPTION OF LATENCY IN DIRECT AND INDIRECT POINTING TASKS

In this first investigation, we aimed to clarify and extend previous efforts on measuring the minimal perceivable latency for common touch-based interactions. We conducted a pair of JND studies in which participants performed either tapping or dragging tasks in both direct and indirect form-factors. We selected dragging and tapping tasks because they represent the basic input primitives used in most user interfaces. Our goals with this experiment were two-fold. First, we aimed to gather data for finger-based indirect (i.e., touchpad) interaction, which had previously been unexplored. Second, we aimed to gather a unified set of data for both direct and indirect form-factors with an identical set of hardware and experimental conditions in order to enable an apples-to-apples comparison.

Hypotheses

Our hypotheses center on the belief that input task and form-factor play major roles in peoples' ability to perceive input latency and that these differences explain the variety of reported JNDs in the literature.

Dragging provides the most visible manifestation of latency, since an on-screen object will begin to trail behind a user's finger as the latency increases. We hypothesize that this physical distance between a finger and the graphical cursor is more easily perceived than the purely temporal difference between a tap and its graphical response.

H1: Users will perceive a lower JND threshold when dragging than when tapping.

With direct input, the finger and graphical response are co-located, allowing the user to perceive both through the visual channel. We hypothesize that the visual difference between input and response in the direct form-factor is more easily perceivable than the difference between the kinesthetic touch and visual response in indirect input.

H2: Users will perceive a lower JND threshold with direct input than with indirect input.

Apparatus

We used a high-speed Fast Multi-Touch (FMT) sensor and projector similar to that described in Leigh et al. [12] and illustrated in Figure 1.The system provides a 15 cm × 20 cm capacitive touch sensor, which would have provided too much freedom of movement for our participants; since we were interested in the JND thresholds for dragging and tapping input primitives, unconstrained movements over the entire touch sensor would have provided an unwanted confound. We therefore placed a cardboard mask on the touch surface to constrain the participant's movements to the appropriate input method, thereby ensuring a one-dimensional movement during a dragging trial and preventing any dragging movement during a tapping trial. Dragging trials used a 14 cm × 3 cm rectangular slot while tapping trials used a 2 cm square. A custom-built controller box with illuminated mechanical push buttons informed the participant whether stimulus *A* or *B* was currently visible and allowed the participant to provide input (e.g., switching between the two stimuli and entering their responses). The box was powered by an Arduino microcontroller and connected to the control laptop via USB. Simple audio feedback (e.g., beeps and tones) was provided to indicate the start of each trial, the end of each block, and whenever the user made an invalid selection on the control box.

In its normal configuration, the FMT hardware is a direct manipulation system; the touch surface is parallel to the desk, and the high-speed projector is mounted on a support arm above the surface, top-projecting an image onto the touch sensor. To convert the system to an indirect form-factor, we designed a removable bracket containing a front-surface mirror mounted on a 45° angle. When the mirror assembly was in place, the path of the projector's beam was redirected so that it appeared on a reflective screen mounted on the wall perpendicular to the touch surface, thereby simulating an indirect setup akin to a laptop touchpad and screen. The mirror assembly could be quickly inserted or removed, facilitating a rapid transition between form-factors. The positions of the mirror and screen were adjusted so that the images drawn by the projector were of the same apparent size, regardless of whether they were projected on the touch surface or on the wall. To maintain the same reflectivity and apparent brightness, the screen was covered in the same contact paper used in the top-most layer of the touch sensor. In both cases, the visual feedback provided after a touch was a solid white 2 cm square.

The FMT hardware is capable of running at latencies as low as 0.29 ms as well as at a wide range of higher latencies. However, it cannot run at any arbitrary latency; the possible latencies are discretely quantized based on two parameters: the sample interval and the queue length. The sample interval can be configured from 0.29 ms to 25.07 ms, in step sizes of 0.098 ms. The queue length is the number of samples buffered prior to processing, and ranges from 1 to 255. The overall latency of the system is the product of these two parameters. For example, a sampling interval of 0.98 ms and a queue length of 10 results in a latency of $0.98 \times 10 = 9.8$ ms. For this study, we held the sampling interval constant at 0.98 ms (the closest value to 1 ms) and varied the queue length to alter the latency; this yielded a possible range of latencies of 0.98 ms to 250.67 ms, with a step size of 0.98 ms. It should be noted that while these non-integer latency values do not impact the analysis of the data, they do result in atypical values for some of the experimental parameters (e.g., the staircase step size is 7.86 ms, a value which corresponds to a queue length of 8). At the start of each trial, parameters were sent to the FMT hardware by a MacBook Pro laptop running custom control software connected over a dedicated Ethernet connection. We empirically validated a variety of latencies using an oscilloscope triggered by vibration and photo sensors, as well as with a high-speed camera.

Procedure

After participants were briefed on the study, they completed a short warm-up session. Participants then began the main experiment consisting of four blocks of trials. For each trial, a participant was first presented with latency *A* and asked to tap or drag; all interactions in a single session used the same input technique. After trying latency *A*, the participant used the control box to switch to latency *B* and performed the interaction again. At this point, they could either switch back to see latency *A* a second time or indicate their decision as to which latency they thought was shorter[1]. If they elected to see latency *A* a second time, they were then required to make a decision and could not switch back to latency *B*. Each trial was a forced choice. When participants could not distinguish the two stimuli, they were instructed to make their best guess [23]. After they entered their decision, the system would beep and move to the next trial. Halfway through the session, after the first two blocks, the mirror assembly was inserted or removed to change the form-factor of the device and the final two blocks of trials were completed with the second form-factor. At the end of the session, participants were quickly debriefed about the latency detection techniques they had used.

For tapping tasks, participants were instructed to use their right index finger to press and release inside the target region. Participants could tap as many times as they wanted and could hold the tap for any length of time. However, extremely rapid tapping (i.e., oscillating the finger up and down as quickly as possible) was not permitted.

For dragging tasks, participants were instructed to use their right index finger to press down on the left side of the target, move their finger to the right side of the target, and then back to the left. They could drag as many times as they wanted and at any speed. The dragging cardboard mask was sized so that the drag would be a predominantly one-dimensional left/right movement on the x-axis, with little or no y-axis movement towards or away from the user.

Sessions were designed to be completed in 90 to 120 minutes. Participants were permitted breaks at any point in the experiment, either between blocks or within them.

Participants

A total of 24 sessions were run across both form-factors (12 drag and 12 tap). The sessions were performed by 14 right-handed participants (6 male) recruited from the broader university community, with a mean age of 28 (sd = 5.4). All had experience with consumer touchscreen devices. Participants were offered the opportunity to perform either one or two sessions (one of each form-factor), separated by at least two hours to account for learnability biases and fatigue effects. 10 participants chose to participate in both sessions. Participants were compensated $20 for each session they completed.

Design

Each session consisted entirely of either a tapping or dragging JND study. Participants were randomly assigned to one type of session; those that participated in two sessions were randomly assigned the first session, and were given the other input technique in their second session.

The latencies used in each trial were generated using an adaptive staircase algorithm. The reference was held constant at 0.98 ms (i.e., a FMT queue length of 1) throughout the experiment. The second latency, the probe, was varied according to Kaernbach's simple weighted up-down method [11]. A base step size of 7.86 ms (i.e., queue length of 8) was used, which was halved upon each of the first three reversals until it reached 0.98 ms. Decreases in the probe were reduced by the base step size while increases were increased by three times the base step size.

A total of eight staircases were run for each participant, arranged in four blocks that each contained a pair of interleaved staircases. Two blocks were run using one form-factor, followed by two blocks using the other form-factor. The ordering of the form-factors was counterbalanced. Within a block, trials from the two staircases were interleaved to prevent the participant from being able to (consciously or subconsciously) identify a pattern in the trials. For interleaved tapping staircases, one began at 117.96 ms and the other began at 58.98 ms; dragging staircases began at 98.30 ms and 39.32 ms. Within each trial, the order of presentation of the two latencies was randomized.

The length of each staircase was not fixed in advance; a block continued until both staircases reached 10 reversals, yielding a 75% confidence threshold for the JND threshold [13]. In most cases one staircase reached 10 reversals before the other one since the order of correct/incorrect responses in each staircase is extremely unlikely to be synchronized. When this occurred, trials from the completed staircase continued to be alternated with the unfinished staircase in order to maintain the interleaving. This meant that a block would usually yield more than 10 reversals for the staircases that finished first. When analyzing the staircases, we ignored reversals past the 10th.

[1] The term "shorter latency" was not used during the experiment since it was felt that it might be needlessly confusing to non-computer scientists. Instead, participants were instructed to choose the latency that was "faster", "more responsive", and "most closely following your finger".

The overall design of the experiment was:

12 sessions ×
2 input techniques (*tapping*/*dragging*) ×
2 form-factors (*direct*/*indirect*) ×
2 repetitions =
96 staircases

As indicated above, the number of trials in a staircase depended on the pattern of responses. The average length across all staircases was 89.1, with a total of 8,556 comparisons of latency pairs in the raw dataset.

Results

To analyze our results, we performed a repeated-measures ANOVA using *Input Task* and *Form-Factor* as between-participant independent variables. Our dependent variable was *JND*, which was the average of the thresholds found from the two staircases in a block. To justify the use of a between-participants analysis, we first checked for asymmetrical transfer effects by performing a within-participant analysis to look for effects from *Form-Factor* ordering (direct-then-indirect vs. indirect-then-direct) or *Repetition*. Finding none, we were able to proceed with the between-participant design.

Our results confirmed both hypotheses. We found a significant main effect from *Input Task* ($F_{1,22} = 55.79$, $p < 0.001$, $\eta^2 = 1.00$), with mean latency *JND*s of 33 ms and 82 ms for *Dragging* and *Tapping* tasks respectively. There was also a significant main effect from *Form-Factor* ($F_{1,22} = 48.43$, $p < 0.001$, $\eta^2 = 1.00$), with mean latency *JND*s of 40 ms and 75 ms for *Direct* and *Indirect* input respectively. No other effects or interactions were detected.

To dig deeper into the results, we computed two additional ANOVAs for the *Tapping* and *Dragging* tasks independently. For *Dragging*, *Form-Factor* had a significant main effect on *JND* ($F_{1,11} = 77.11$, $p < 0.001$, $\eta^2 = 1.00$) with mean *JND*s of 11 ms and 55 ms for *Direct* and *Indirect* input. Equivalent results were also found for *Tapping*, where *Form-Factor* also had a significant main effect on *JND* ($F_{1,11} = 9.44$, $p = 0.011$, $\eta^2 = 0.80$), with mean *JND* values of 69 ms and 96 ms for *Direct* and *Indirect* input. Combined *JND*s (counting both tasks for a given form-factor) were 40 ms (*Direct*) and 75 ms (*Indirect*). The mean latency *JND*s are shown in Figure 2.

Discussion

Our results confirm our hypotheses surrounding the importance of form-factor and input task on the limits of latency perception. It is clear that people are much better overall at noticing latency with direct input touch devices than with indirect ones, suggesting that the threshold that system designers must reach in order to provide perceptually "latency-free" experiences is higher for touchpads than for touchscreens. Similarly, users perceive latency at a much finer level when dragging than when tapping. Indeed, with direct input, dragging provides the most visible manifestation of latency, since an on-screen object will

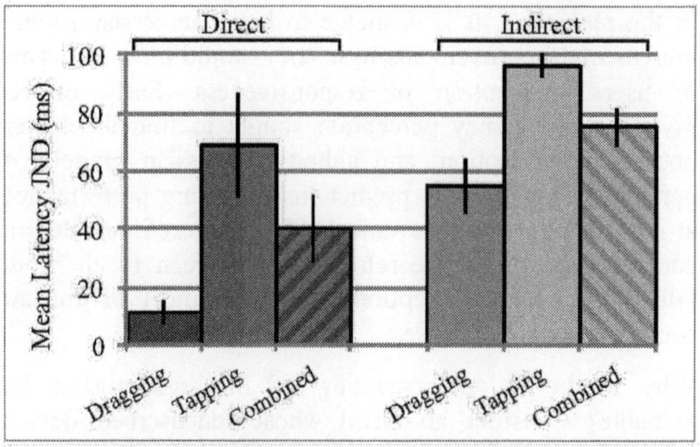

Figure 2. Mean latency JND thresholds for direct and indirect form-factors. Dragging, tapping, and combined (counting trials from both techniques) are shown in blues, greens, and striped bars. Error bars show 95% confidence intervals.

begin to trail behind a user's finger as the latency increases, creating a readily perceivable spatial distance between the two. This relationship between input task and latency perception was discussed by Jota et al. [8] in their own comparison to Ng et al. [19]; however, our results indicate that this relationship extends to indirect form-factors as well. Recent UI trends towards more fluid dragging actions are therefore likely to amplify the perceived latency in both form-factors and encourage system designers to further improve the latency of their devices.

As a whole, these results bring some clarity to a disagreement in the literature over latency JNDs since they suggest that form-factor and input task must be considered. Ng et al. [19], who report a JND of 6.04 ms, argue that the textbook threshold of 100 ms (a value based on Miller's work [16] and guidelines for audio in the telecommunications industry [4], among other sources) is incorrect and an artifact of the limited performance of input devices and measurement techniques available at the time of its origin. Our results suggest that both are correct, as Ng et al. report on a direct input dragging task and most others report on a variety of indirect input tapping tasks (menu selection, key typing, path drawing, etc.). Indeed our reported mean JNDs of 11 ms, 69 ms, and 96 ms for direct dragging, direct tapping, and indirect tapping correspond very closely to the reported JNDs of 6.04 ms (Ng et al., direct dragging), 64 ms (Jota et al. [8], direct tapping), and 100 ms (textbook guideline) – with all of these previously reported values falling well within the 95% confidence intervals of our estimated means.

EXPERIMENT 2: UNDERSTANDING INCREMENTAL IMPROVEMENTS ABOVE THE LOWER BOUND FOR DRAGGING AND TAPPING TASKS

The results from Experiment 1 inform system designers as to what latency targets they must meet in order to provide a perceptually "latency-free" UI. As stated in the introduction, the vast majority of commercial devices fall well above these limits of perception; thus, reaching this goal is likely to be a long and laborious process.

In the meantime, it is desirable to better understand what incremental improvements to latency would mean in terms of users' perception of responsiveness. Early efforts investigating latency perception sought to find the lower bounds of perception, and although Gaussian models of perception can provide predictions regarding performance at interim latency improvements [7], we were interested in concretely mapping the relationship between touch input latency and user perception at levels typical of current consumer-level hardware.

Why might an understanding of this relationship be valuable? Consider an OEM whose touchscreen device operates with 100 ms of latency. Would reducing this latency to 90 ms be noticeable by their users? How about a reduction to 80 ms? If that 20 ms improvement was applied to a device that operates at 50 ms, would that be noticed? Perhaps there would be no noticeable difference until a device passed some intermediate threshold. Similarly, an OEM wishing to produce a lower-cost device might consider components that would increase the latency, and may wish to know if and how much this increase would be perceived by their customers. When considering such questions, one understands the value of examining the perception of input latency improvements above the lower bound. Experiment 2 aims to begin this valuable investigation for both tapping and dragging. Not knowing what we would find, it was difficult to generate specific hypotheses; as such, we proceeded with an exploratory study to help enhance our understanding of the space.

Display Refresh Rate

One major contributor to system latency in current touch devices is display refresh rate. No matter how quickly new graphical information is ready, it cannot be displayed as soon as it is available as it must wait to appear until the display can redraw its image. At the time of this writing, 60 Hz displays are still the norm, meaning that a new frame is drawn every 1000 ms / 60 = 16.67 ms. This refresh rate has the perverse effect of quantizing and possibly masking improvements to latency that fall out of sync with this 16.67 ms heartbeat. As a concrete example, consider a 60 Hz system with a latency of 32 ms. Such a device will be able to update its UI within two frames. If this latency was reduced to 16 ms, then it would be able to update within one frame, resulting in a displayable difference. However, if the latency was reduced from 32 ms to 25 ms, the system would still require two frames before a UI update could occur, meaning that the reduction down to 25 ms will have had no visible impact. This observation governed many of the magnitude choices used in our experiment as we gravitated to base latencies and latency improvements that were multiples of a 60 Hz display.

Apparatus and Participants

We used the apparatus described in Experiment 1. For this experiment, we recruited 15 right-handed participants (7 male) from the broader university community, with a mean age of 25 (sd = 4.3). Nine of our participants took part in both the dragging and tapping sessions, for a total of 24 sessions (12 tapping and 12 dragging). Participants were compensated $20 per session.

Design and Procedure

As in Experiment 1, each session consisted of a series of blocks of A/B trials in which the participant was asked to identify the faster latency. Each session consisted entirely of either tapping or dragging, and contained a total of 8 blocks; the first 4 consisted of one form-factor, and the last 4 of the other. As with Experiment 1 the order of the form-factors was counterbalanced. Each pair of latencies consisted of a *baseline* latency, and that *baseline* minus a *difference*. All blocks contained the same set of latencies pairs; the order of the pairs was randomized, and the A/B position of the individual latencies within a pair were counter-balanced so that each latency appeared twice in the A (first) position and twice in the B (second) position.

To determine our set of baselines, we considered the common case of a 60 Hz display, which displays a new frame every 16.67 ms, as discussed above. We therefore selected baselines that corresponded to updates occurring every 1 to 10 frames: 16.7, 33.3, 50.0, 66.7, 83.3, 100.0, 116.7, 133.3, 150.0, and 167.7 ms. For completeness, we also added a baseline of 8.3 ms (0.5 frames), for a total of 11 baselines. We then selected differences that corresponded to 0.5, 1, 2, 3, 4, and 5 frames of improvement: 8.3, 16.7, 33.3, 50.0, 66.7, and 83.3 ms. Each difference was subtracted from each baseline. Pairs that resulted in a negative latency (e.g., 8.3 ms − 16.7 ms) were excluded, and differences that resulted in 0 ms (e.g., 8.3 ms − 8.3 ms) were rounded up to 1 ms, the minimum latency that the experimental configuration of the system could produce. This resulted in a total of 51 pairs, which constituted the contents of one block of the experiment. All latencies were then converted to the nearest latency that could be reproduced on the FMT hardware, as described in the Apparatus section of Experiment 1 (e.g., 100 ms was converted to 100.27 ms); this conversion resulted in differences of less than 0.5 ms (0.3%). The overall design of the experiment was:

12 sessions ×
2 input techniques (*tapping*/*dragging*) ×
2 form-factors (*direct*/*indirect*) ×
4 repetitions ×
51 valid comparisons/repetition =
9,792 trials.

Results

As in Experiment 1, we first checked for asymmetrical learning effects by looking for an ordering effect from *Form-Factor*. Finding none, we proceeded with the analysis presented in the following sections. While not included in the same statistical model, a comparison between *Dragging* and *Tapping* input reveals a large difference in latency perception. Overall, participants correctly identified improvements to latency 81.6% of the time when *Dragging*

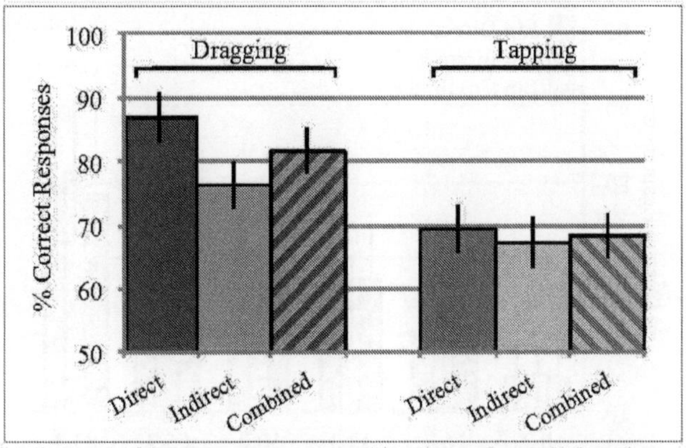

Figure 3. Mean percent correct for dragging and tapping. Direct, indirect, and combined (counting trials from both form-factors) are shown in darker, lighter, and striped bars. As a group, participants are better at recognizing improvements to latency when dragging than when tapping. Error bars show 95% confidence intervals.

and only 68.2% of the time when *Tapping*. The lower bound of the 95% confidence interval for both means fall well above the 50% chance value one would expect if users were guessing. Figure 3 shows the mean percentage of correct trials for each input technique for both direct and indirect form-factors as well as the overall percentage combining all trials of both form-factors.

Dragging Analysis

We conducted a repeated-measures ANOVA using *Form-Factor* (*Direct/Indirect*), *Latency Improvement*, and *Base Latency* as independent variables, and *Percent Correct* as a dependent variable.

As expected, *Form-Factor* had a significant main effect on *Percent Correct* ($F_{1,11} = 47.56$, $p < 0.001$, $\eta^2 = 1.00$) with participants correctly identifying differences in direct input latency 86.9% of the time, compared to 76.3% of the time with indirect input. As was the case for the direct dragging JND threshold, this combination of technique and form-factor provides the most visible manifestation of latency. In addition, *Latency Improvement* also had a significant main effect ($F_{1,11} = 118.31, p < 0.001, \eta^2 = 1.00$), with larger *Latency Improvements* being easier to notice. A post-hoc pairwise comparison shows a significant difference between most pairs of *Latency Improvements*. Figure 4 shows the mean *Percent Correct* for each *Latency Improvement*, broken down by form-factor.

Overall, there was no significant main effect on *Percent Correct* from *Base Latency* ($F_{10,110} = 0.85, p = 0.58$, $\eta^2 = 0.43$); however, there was a significant interaction between *Base Latency* and *Form-Factor* ($F_{10,110} = 3.76, p < 0.001, \eta^2 = 0.99$). In general, participants' ability to identify improvements in indirect latency is consistent across *Base Latencies*, but is more accurate in the lower *Base Latencies* when working in the *Direct Input Form-Factor*. This may be due to the inherent perceptual advantage associated with a large percentage difference between stimuli (i.e., an 8.3 ms decrease from 16.7 ms is a 50% decrease, while an 8.3 ms decrease from 166.7 ms is only 5%), and/or the fact that a decrease from a smaller baseline is more likely to result in a perceptually "zero latency" stimulus once the post-decrease value crosses the JND thresholds established in Experiment 1. In a trial where one of the two stimuli appears to be instantaneous, the task of discriminating the pair becomes easier, since the task is reduced to the simpler question of identifying the single stimulus that had any visible latency at all.

Figure 5 shows the mean *Percent Correct* for each *Base Latency / Form-Factor* combination. There were no other significant effects or interactions found in the *Dragging* activity.

While the effects of *Activity, Base Latency, Latency Improvement, Form-Factor* and their interactions are an interesting and useful topic for study, our primary motivation for this experiment was to work toward answering the question "Can people recognize improvements to latency *across the latency spectrum*?"

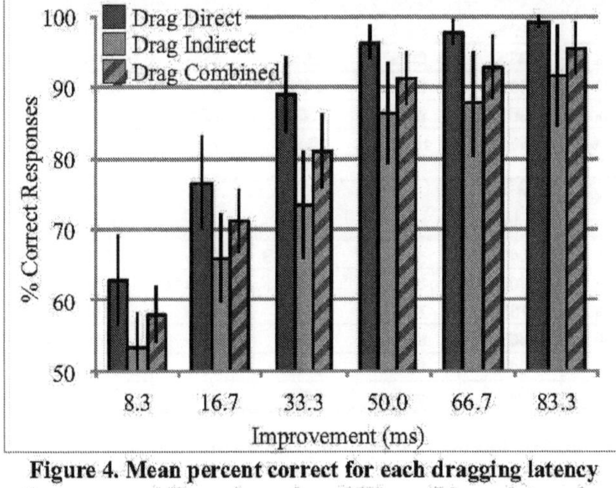

Figure 4. Mean percent correct for each dragging latency improvement. Error bars show 95% confidence intervals.

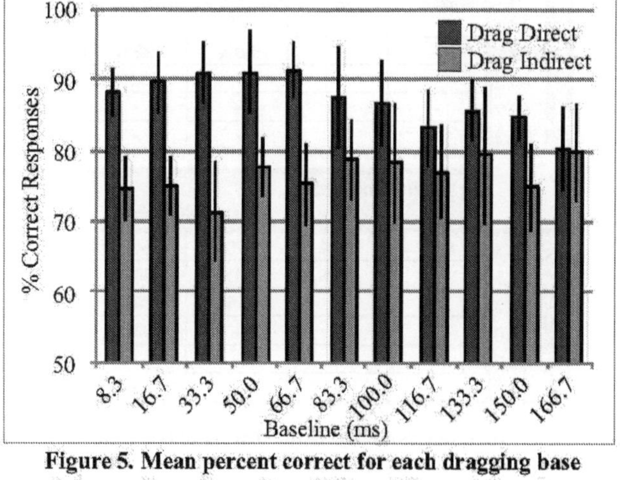

Figure 5. Mean percent correct for each dragging base latency. Error bars show 95% confidence intervals.

Previous efforts (in this paper and others) have investigated the limits of human perception in respect to near-zero latency, but we are equally interested in whether or not people can perceive improvements to latency away from this lower bound.

Table 1 shows the percentage of trials in which our participants (as a group) correctly identified the lower latency dragging interaction. These tables show each *Base Latency / Latency Improvement* combination. Cells marked with an asterisk have true means that are within a 95% confidence interval of the 50% chance threshold, and are therefore not statistically distinguishable from chance (i.e., combinations where the reduction in latency was not perceived), and are in the clear minority. Colored regions of the Tables are areas that are discussed in more detail below.

Dragging Discussion

Overall, the results from our exploration into the perception of latency improvements when dragging shows that there are not only clear effects from *Base Latency* and *Latency Improvement,* but also significant room for perceivable improvement to latency without eliminating it altogether. Considering Table 1, for the *Direct Dragging* condition, any improvement in latency of 1 frame/sec (fps) or more is easily observable by our participants as a whole (uncolored area). Furthermore, even a small improvement of 0.5 fps is observable by a significant fraction of our participants for base latencies at or under 3 fps (orange area). For systems with higher base latencies, this small improvement did not yield observable differences (blue area). For *Indirect Dragging* input, there are clearly observable improvements to be had for latency improvements of 2 or more fps (uncolored area), with less value for smaller improvements of 0.5 or 1 fps (yellow area). These trends seem relatively stable for base latencies across the tested spectrum.

Tapping Analysis

We ran another repeated-measures ANOVA using *Form-Factor* (*Direct/Indirect Input*), *Latency Improvement*, and *Base Latency* as independent variables, and *Percent Correct* as a dependent variable.

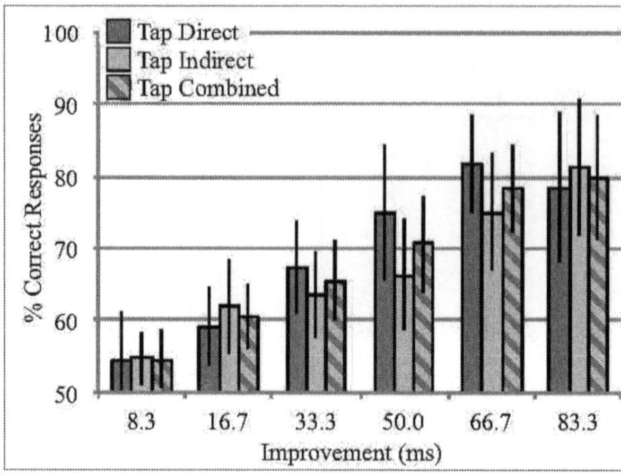

Figure 6. Mean percent correct for each tapping latency improvement. Error bars show 95% confidence intervals.

Unlike with *Dragging*, we did not find a significant main effect for *Form-Factor* on *Percent Correct* ($F_{1,11} = 2.18, p = 0.17, \eta^2 = 0.27$), with participants as a whole correctly identifying the lower latency in 69.3% and 67.1% of *Direct Input* and *Indirect Input* trials respectively.

Again, as expected, *Latency Improvement* also had a significant main effect ($F_{1,11} = 19.55, p = 0.001, \eta^2 = 0.98$), with larger *Latency Improvements* being easier to notice in the *Tapping* task. A post-hoc pairwise comparison between means shows a significant difference between all pairs of *Latency Improvement.* Figure 6 shows the mean *Percent Correct* for each *Latency Improvement.*

Base Latency had a significant main effect on *Percent Correct* ($F_{1,11} = 8.85$, $p = 0.01$, $\eta^2 = 0.77$), with improvements to higher *Base Latencies* being correctly identified more often than those to lower *Base Latencies.* Figure 7 shows the mean *Percent Correct* for each *Base Latency* in the *Tapping* task. There were no significant interactions found in the *Tapping* analysis.

Dragging Direct	Baseline Latency (ms)										
Improvement (ms)	8.3	16.7	33.3	50.0	66.7	83.3	100.0	116.7	133.3	150.0	166.7
8.3	60%	69%	69%	73%	67%	60% *	75%	54% *	60% *	54% *	50% *
16.7	-	77%	85%	79%	85%	75%	69%	63% *	75%	83%	73%
33.3	-	-	90%	92%	94%	94%	94%	90%	85%	81%	79%
50.0	-	-	-	100%	100%	96%	90%	94%	92%	98%	90%
66.7	-	-	-	-	100%	98%	96%	98%	100%	92%	92%
83.3	-	-	-	-	-	100%	96%	100%	100%	98%	98%

Dragging Indirect	Baseline Latency (ms)										
Improvement (ms)	8.3	16.7	33.3	50.0	66.7	83.3	100.0	116.7	133.3	150.0	166.7
8.3	54% *	56% *	42% *	54% *	50% *	56% *	54% *	48% *	54% *	65%	52% *
16.7	-	60% *	54% *	69%	75%	75%	69% *	69% *	67% *	54% *	73%
33.3	-	-	69%	79%	58% *	79%	73%	79%	81%	69%	81%
50.0	-	-	-	83%	88%	85%	88%	85%	92%	88%	90%
66.7	-	-	-	-	88%	83%	94%	90%	92%	81%	88%
83.3	-	-	-	-	-	92%	92%	90%	90%	92%	94%

Table 1. Mean percent correct for dragging trials for each combination of base latency / latency improvement. Cells marked with an asterisk are not significantly different from chance (50%). Colored regions are areas of interest that are discussed in the text. 95% confidence intervals range from 5% to 21%.

As with *Dragging* interactions, we are keenly interested in whether or not small improvements to latency are perceivable to participants across the latency spectrum. Table 2 shows the percentage of trials in which our participants (as a group) correctly identified the lower latency tapping interaction. These tables show each *Base Latency / Latency Improvement* combination; as with Table 1, cells marked with an asterisk are statistically indistinguishable from chance. While there are clear effects from *Base Latency* and *Latency Improvement*, these tables are included to suggest that there is a great deal of room for perceivable improvement to latency without eliminating latency entirely.

Tapping Discussion

Considering Table 2, it appears that for systems with base latencies at or below 33.3 ms there is little room for improvement in latency perception in either form-factor (red areas). When considering systems that have a higher base latency, improvements of 2 or more fps seem to have an observable difference (uncolored area) for all base latencies tested. Smaller improvements of 0.5 or 1 fps were generally not observable to our participants (purple area).

CONCLUSION

In this paper, we have examined user's perception of latency for both dragging and tapping tasks under both direct and indirect form-factors. A set of JND studies indicated that the detectable thresholds for dragging (direct: 11 ms, indirect: 55 ms) are lower than for tapping (direct: 69 ms, indirect: 96 ms), and that direct touch systems are more susceptible to noticeable latency than their indirect counterparts. A second set of studies demonstrated that improvements in latency as small as 8.3 ms are noticeable from a wide range of baseline latencies, particularly when dragging.

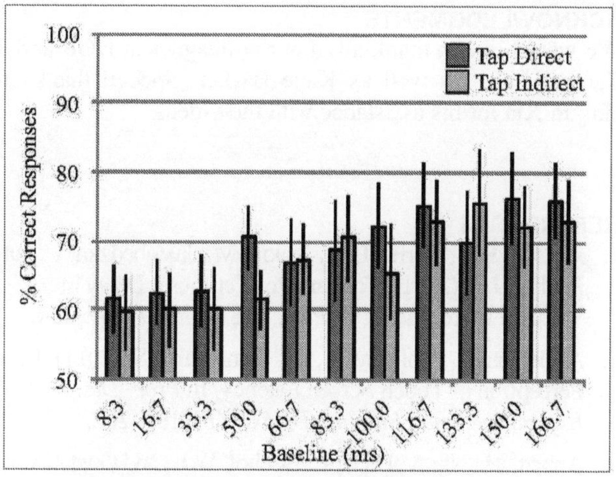

Figure 7. Mean percent correct for each tapping base latency. Error bars show 95% confidence intervals.

While the end goal of a zero-latency system will of course require a significant engineering effort, our results provide clear guidance to system designers that interim steps along that path are in fact worthwhile. The latency improvements that result from the removal of just a single 60 Hz frame (i.e., a decrease of 16.7 ms in latency) are perceptibly noticeable under many circumstances.

While we are happy to report some clarity on users' ability to *perceive* latency improvements (not only at the lower bound, but at higher levels as well), further effort is required. Next steps will include understanding the *desirability* of such improvements to a user, as well as any benefits to *performance* in common touch tasks, such as tapping, docking, crossing, and scrolling. We have begun investigating these follow-on efforts as we continue to strive to understand and provide zero-latency touch experiences.

Tapping Direct	Baseline Latency (ms)										
Improvement (ms)	8.3	16.7	33.3	50.0	66.7	83.3	100.0	116.7	133.3	150.0	166.7
8.3	46% *	52% *	56% *	56% *	48% *	52% *	50% *	73%	56% *	58% *	52% *
16.7	-	50% *	48% *	69%	58% *	60% *	65%	60% *	60% *	58% *	71%
33.3	-	-	52% *	77%	73%	71%	63% *	75%	69%	81%	77%
50.0	-	-	-	69%	71%	73%	79%	79%	77%	92%	79%
66.7	-	-	-	-	79%	83%	85%	77%	79%	88%	90%
83.3	-	-	-	-	-	73%	92%	88%	77%	81%	88%

Tapping Indirect	Baseline Latency (ms)										
Improvement (ms)	8.3	16.7	33.3	50.0	66.7	83.3	100.0	116.7	133.3	150.0	166.7
8.3	50% *	52% *	50% *	46% *	58% *	56% *	44% *	56% *	67%	60% *	63%
16.7	-	58% *	60% *	58% *	63% *	69%	54% *	69%	63% *	69%	60% *
33.3	-	-	48% *	63%	67%	69%	67%	77%	75%	69%	71%
50.0	-	-	-	56% *	71%	79%	69%	71%	73%	69%	73%
66.7	-	-	-	-	67%	71%	77%	90%	92%	79%	83%
83.3	-	-	-	-	-	79%	83%	75%	85%	88%	88%

Table 2. Mean percent correct for tapping trials for each combination of base latency and latency improvement. Cells marked with an asterisk are not significantly different from chance (50%). Colored regions are areas of interest that are discussed in the text. 95% confidence intervals range from 7% to 19%.

ACKNOWLEDGMENTS

We would like to thank all of our colleagues at DGP and at Tactual Labs, as well as Katie Barker. Special thanks to Haijun Xia for his assistance with the videos.

REFERENCES

1. Allison, R.S., Harris, L.R., Jenkin, M., Jasiobedzka, U., and Zacher, J.E. (2001). Tolerance of Temporal Delay in Virtual Environments. In *Proc. IEEE VR '01*, 247–254.
2. Anderson, G., Doherty, R., and Ganapathy, S. (2011). User Perception of Touch Screen Latency. In *Proc. Design, User Experience, and Usability (DUXU) '11*, 195–202.
3. Annett, M., Ng, A., Dietz, P., Bischof, W.F., and Gupta, A. (2014). How Low Should We Go? Understanding the Perception of Latency While Inking. In *Proc. GI '14*,167–174.
4. Cheshire, S. (1996). *Latency and the Quest for Interactivity.* White paper for the Synchronous Person-to-Person Interactive Computing Env Meeting, Nov. 1996.
5. Ellis, S.R., Bréant, F., Manges, B., Jacoby, R., and Adelstein, B.D. (1997). Factors Influencing Operator Interaction with Virtual Objects Viewed via Head-Mounted See-Through Displays: Viewing Conditions and Rendering Latency. In *Proc. IEEE VR '97*, 138–145.
6. Ellis, S.R., Young, M.J., Adelstein, B.D., and Ehrlich, S.M. (1999). Discrimination of Changes of Latency During Voluntary Hand Movements of Virtual Objects. In *Proc. Human Factors and Ergonomics Society '99*, 1182–1186.
7. Harris, L., Harrar, V., Jaekl, P., and Kopinska, A. (2010). Mechanisms of Simultaneity Constancy. In Nijhawan, R., and Khurana, B. (Eds.). *Space and Time in Perception and Action.* Cambridge: Cambridge University Press, 232–253.
8. Jota, R., Ng, A., Dietz, P., and Wigdor, D. (2013). How Fast is Fast Enough? A Study of the Effects of Latency in Direct-Touch Pointing Tasks. In *Proc. CHI '13*, 2291–2300.
9. Kaaresoja, T., and Brewster, S. (2010). Feedback is… Late: Measuring Multimodal Delays in Mobile Device Touchscreen Interaction. In *Proc. ICMI '10*, Article 2, 8 pages.
10. Kaaresoja, T., Brewster, S., and Lantz, V. (2014). Towards the Temporally Perfect Virtual Button: Touch-Feedback Simultaneity and Perceived Quality in Mobile Touchscreen Press Interactions. *ACM Trans. Appl. Percept.* 11, 2, Article 9 (Jun. 2014), 25 pages.
11. Kaernbach, C. (1991). Simple Adaptive Testing with the Weighted Up-Down Method. *Perception & Psychophysics* 49, 3 (Mar. 1991), 227–229.
12. Leigh, D., Forlines, C., Jota, R., Sanders, S., and Wigdor, D. (2014). High-Rate, Low-Latency Multi-Touch Sensing with Simultaneous Orthogonal Multiplexing. In *Proc. UIST '14*, 355–364.
13. Levitt, H. (1971). Transformed up-down methods in psychoacoustics. *J. Acoustical Soc. of Am.* 49, 2 (Feb. 1971), 467–477.
14. MacKenzie, I.S., and Ware, C. (1993). Lag as a Determinant of Human Performance in Interactive Systems. In *Proc. CHI '93*, 488–493.
15. Meehan, M., Razzaque, S., Whitton, M.C., and Brooks, F.P. (2003). Effect of Latency on Presence in Stressful Virtual Environments. In *Proc. IEEE VR '03*, 141–138.
16. Miller, R.B. (1968). Response Time in Man-Computer Conversational Transactions. In *Proc. AFIPS '68*, 267–277.
17. Nelson, W.T., Roe, M.M., Bolia, R.S., and Morley, R.M. (1998). Assessing Simulator Sickness in a See-Through HMD: Effects of Time Delay, Time on Task, and Task Complexity. In *Proc. IMAGE '00.*
18. Ng, A., Annett, M., Dietz, P., Gupta, A., and Bischof, W.F. (2014). In the Blink of an Eye: Investigating Latency Perception During Stylus Interaction. In *Proc. CHI '14*, 1103–1112.
19. Ng, A., Lepinski, J., Wigdor, D., Sanders, S., and Dietz, P. (2012). Designing for Low-Latency Direct-Touch Input. In *Proc. UIST '12*, 453–464.
20. Pavlovych, A., and Gutwin C. (2012). Assessing Target Acquisition and Tracking Performance for Moving Targets in the Presence of Latency and Jitter. In *Proc. GI '12*, 109–116.
21. Pavlovych, A., and Stürzlinger, W. (2011). Target Following Performance in the Presence of Latency, Jitter, and Signal Dropouts. In *Proc. GI '11*, 33–40.
22. Pavlovych, A., and Stürzlinger, W. (2009). The Tradeoff between Spatial Jitter and Latency in Pointing Tasks. In *Proc. ACM EICS '09*, 187–196.
23. Savage, W.C. (1970). *The Measurement of Sensation: A Critique of Perceptual Psychophysics*. Berkley: UC Press.
24. So, R.H.Y., and Chung, G.K.M. (2005). Sensory Motor Responses in Virtual Environments: Studying the Effects of Image Latencies for Target-directed Hand Movement. In *Proc. IEEE-EMBS '05*, 5006–5008.
25. Steed, A. (2008). A Simple Method for Estimating the Latency of Interactive, Real-Time Graphics Simulations. In *Proc. ACM VRST '08*, 123–129.
26. Teather, R., Pavlovych, A., Stürzlinger, W., and MacKenzie, I.S. (2009). Effects of Tracking Technology, Latency, and Spatial Jitter on Object Movement. In *Proc. 3DUI '09*, 43–50.
27. Vogels, I.M.L.C. (2004). Detection of Temporal Delays in Visual-Haptic Interfaces. *Hum. Fact.* 46, 1 (Spr. 2004), 118–134.
28. Ware, C., and Balakrishnan, R. (1994). Reaching for Objects in VR Displays: Lag and Frame Rate. *ACM Trans. Comput.-Hum. Interact.* 1, 4 (Dec. 1994), 331–356.

The Effect of Edge Targets on Touch Performance

Daniel Avrahami
FXPAL
daniel@fxpal.com

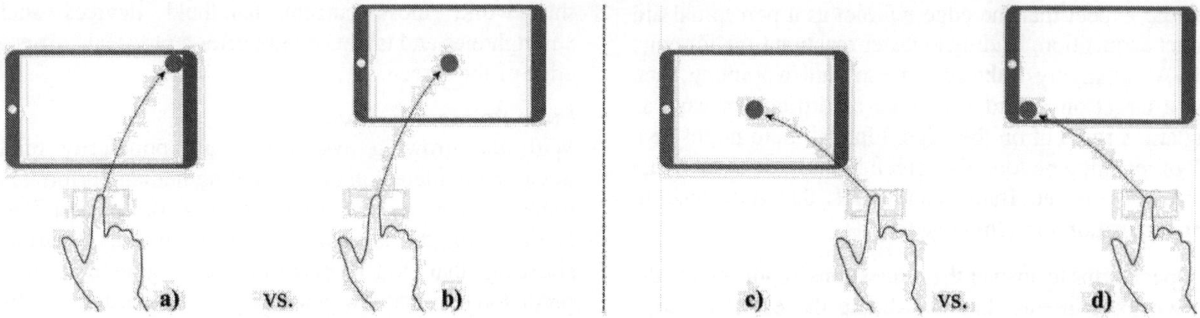

Figure 1. Edge-targets vs. Center targets on touch devices. Each pair shows a round target at a fixed distance from the user but at a different distance relative to the frame. In each pair, which target, if either, will have a faster reaction time?

ABSTRACT

Edge targets, such as buttons or menus along the edge of a screen, are known to afford fast acquisition performance in desktop mousing environments. As the popularity of touch-based devices continues to grow, understanding the affordances of edge targets on touchscreen is needed. This paper describes results from two controlled experiments that examine in detail the effect of edge targets on performance in touch devices. The results show that on touch devices, a target's proximity to the edge may have a significant negative effect on reaction time. We examine the effect in detail and explore mitigating factors. We discuss potential explanations for the effect and propose implications for the design of efficient interfaces for touch devices.

Author Keywords

Edge targets; target acquisition; human performance; touch

ACM Classification Keywords

H.5.2 [User Interface]: Input devices and strategies.

INTRODUCTION

Edge targets, such as buttons or menus along the edge of a screen, have long been used in desktop mousing environments to provide quick access to targets. Examples in commercial systems include menus along the top of the screen and the dock along the bottom of the screen in Mac OS, the taskbar and Start button along the bottom in the Windows operating system and buttons for closing and resizing windows at the top. However, with the growing shift to touch-based interaction, the advantage of edge targets must be revisited.

In mousing environments, the key attribute that makes edge targets advantageous is that the pointer stops when it reaches the edge of the screen. This allows the user to use a quick motion, without risk of over-shooting the target. In other words, since the pointer cannot advance beyond the edge of the screen (and thus the edge target), the effective size of edge targets can be considered as semi-infinite [3], along one or more dimensions (this attribute has been transferred and exploited also in the case of physical edges restricting the movement of a stylus [24]). Corner targets, for example, will have an infinite effective size along both horizontal and vertical dimensions, making them useful as quickly accessible targets (and the reason why they have been used as "hot spot" shortcuts in several operating systems).

Nowadays, finger touch is increasingly replacing traditional pointer interaction as the popularity of touch devices such as tablets and smartphones grows. The faceplate of most tablets and phones today is made of glass that spans to the edge of the bezel around the screen offering no physical break at the end of the screen (some touch devices even include bezel-less touchscreens).

This raises the question: Are edge targets on touch devices (that is, targets near the edge of the device screen) advantageous as they are in desktop environments? Are they harmful? Or does the proximity of a target to the edge of a touch device play no role in target acquisition performance?

CHI 2015, April 18 - 23, 2015, Seoul, Republic of Korea

ACM 978-1-4503-3145-6/15/04...$15.00
http://dx.doi.org/10.1145/2702123.2702439

Consider for a moment the target pairs shown in Figure 1. In each pair, the distance between the finger's starting position and the target is identical (the target is in the same global position in 2D space). However, in each pair, the targets have a different position relative to their frame; the target in one is an edge target, and in the other it is not. We ask:

Which target (1a vs. 1b, 1c vs. 1d) yield faster reaction time?

One could expect that the edge will act as a perceptual aid for target acquisition, leading to faster reaction time for edge targets. Alternatively, if the edge doesn't aid in pointing, then hitting a target on the edge may be as difficult or easy as hitting any target not on the edge. Finally, there might be a "fear" of touching beyond the screen bounds, or even visual interference between frame and target, that may lead to slower acquisition time for edge targets.

This paper begins to answer these questions, reporting results from two experiments that investigate the effect of edge targets on performance in touch devices. The first experiment shows that on touch devices, unlike edge targets in traditional desktop mousing environments, proximity to the edge can have a significant *negative* effect on reaction time. The second study examines the effect of edge targets on small and large targets, and explores whether small changes in a target's distance from the edge can affect reaction time.

We believe that the findings presented in this paper are important for growing our understanding of human performance with touchscreen interaction, and should be considered in the design of efficient touch interfaces.

RELATED WORK

Edge targets have been discussed extensively in the context of pointing with devices such as a mouse or trackpad. In [1] and [2], Accot & Zhai broadened our understanding of human performance of pointing and crossing tasks, extending Fitts' law [10] to account for the difficulty resulting from target size and distance independently. They show that targets that provide larger amplitude tolerance will be faster to point at than targets with larger directional tolerance. This is the case with edge targets, such as menus along the very edge of a desktop screen (as in the Mac OS).

Appert et al. [3] investigated in detail mouse-based pointing, comparing regular pointing and edge pointing, and proposed an extension of Accot and Zhai's definition of index of difficulty (ID) to account for the case of edge targets. In their studies, edge targets, with their "semi-infinite" size, were acquired up to 44% faster than regular targets at the same distance in the central screen area.

The Use of Physical Edges

The benefit of edge targets in pointing tasks can be attributed to their large amplitude tolerance; that is, since the pointer does not pass through an edge target rather stops at the edge of the screen, a gross motion can be used to acquire the target. Several systems have adapted this concept to stylus-based pointing, leveraging elevated physical edges, to support accessible interfaces. For example, *Edge Keyboard* and *EdgeWrite* are text entry techniques designed for a handheld device with a raised bezel around the input area [24, 25]. The raised edge physically prevents the stylus from moving past the edge of the screen, allowing target selection with coarse movement. Froehlich et al. extend this concept as a pointing technique called *Barrier Pointing* [11]. Unlike this work, most current handheld devices such as smartphones and tablets do not offer a physical barrier at the edge of the screen.

From Pointers to Touch

With the growing availability and popularity of touch devices, an interest in understanding human performance on touch devices has increased (*c.f.* [7, 21]). Lee and Zhai [15] studied finger tapping performance on smartphones, showing that touch performance degraded faster than predicted by Fitts' law when targets became smaller. In [13], Holz and Baudisch show that much of the negative effect attributed to the "fat finger problem" can be explained by offsets of touch location from the intended point, affected by the angles between the finger and the touch surface. In order to provide a general model of performance on touch devices, Bi et al. [6] proposed FFitts Law, an extension of Fitts' law for finger touch input. With FFitts Law, Bi et al. propose that the index of difficulty is a combination of the absolute precision of the motor system and the relative precision stemming from a speed-accuracy tradeoff.

Prior work also showed that the intended application of the interactor can have a significant effect on posture and grasp planning. Olafsdottir et al. demonstrated that the orientation of finger placement on a touch object was significantly affected by the position and orientation of the target [17]. In the special case of text entry on touch devices, [5] and [12] showed a consistent touch offset between the visual position of keys and user's touch.

Perry and Hourcade evaluated one-handed thumb-based target acquisition on a small handheld device [19]. They found that reaction to targets on the edges of the screen was slower, but more accurate (potentially because their device's touchscreen was surrounded by a raised bezel). Unfortunately, determining whether edge targets were slower because of dexterity or for other reasons is not possible because in one-handed operation, edge targets are physically harder to hit (*c.f.* [18]). The work presented here sheds further light on their findings.

While modern touch devices often don't have any physical affordances at the edge of the screen, the perimeter of the device (not the screen itself) has been shown as useful for quick, coarse, actions. These include edge gestures, common in many operating systems designed for touch, including iOS, Android, and Windows 8.1. [20] describes a rich set of interaction techniques called *Bezel Swipe* that support multiple selection, cut, copy, paste and other operations.

Figure 2. Apparatus for Experiment 1. An 18" touch-surface displays targets at known positions. A moveable 0.5mm 3D-printed frame simulates the boundaries of a 7.9" tablet.

This paper builds on this prior work, focusing on extending our understanding of the effects of targets' proximity to the edge of a screen on performance, when physical guides are not present.

EXPERIMENT 1

The first experiment was designed to test whether the time to acquire a target will be significantly affected by the target's proximity to an edge, while maintaining complete control over the target's distance to the user. This was achieved by physically decoupling the position of the target relative to an edge from the position of the target relative to the user: We used a large, 18" touch surface for displaying targets at known positions relative to the user, and used an extremely thin (less than 0.5mm) frame to simulate the bezel of a small tablet (see Figure 2). A light grey background around the frame, and near-black background inside, gave the illusion of a bounded device. In this experiment, we 3D-printed a frame such that it imitates the face of an Apple iPad Mini, which has a 7.9" screen. The frame is thin enough such that touch is sensed through it.

This unique setup allows displaying the same absolute target (in relation to the user), while placing the physical frame at different positions relative to that target. As illustrated in Figure 1, this allows, for example, a target to be a center target in one trial, and a corner target in another, while maintaining the same distance from the user.

Hypotheses

Our main hypothesis for Experiment 1 is that the time to acquire the same absolute target (in size and distance in relation to the user), will be significantly affected by the target's proximity to an edge. Put formally:

H_1: *Proximity to device edge will significantly affect touch-target acquisition time.*

Still, if H_1 is supported, would acquisition time of edge targets on touch devices be faster or slower? As mentioned earlier, different assumptions would suggest that acquisition time be affected in opposite directions. We thus pose two, contradicting, sub-hypotheses for H_1, expecting at least one to be rejected.

First we can hypothesize that the edge of the screen will act as an aid for target acquisition, leading to faster acquisition time for edge targets.

H_{1a}: *Independent of distance, proximity to device edge will result in faster reaction time.*

Conversely, reluctance to hit outside a border, or visual interference between frame and target, may lead to slower acquisition time for edge targets.

H_{1b}: *Independent of distance, proximity to device edge will result in slower reaction time.*

Method

Figure 3 illustrates the experimental setup. The experiment consisted of 3 blocks of target-acquisition trials. For each block, the frame was placed in one of three fixed positions (marked A, B, and C). For each trial, a round target, with a fixed diameter of 11mm, was selected from an 8x6 grid. The target and frame positions were designed such that a target in row 4 column 4 (from here on (4,4)) would appear in the center of the frame in position A, and in the corner of the frame in positions B and C. Likewise, targets (2,2) and (2,6) would appear in the center of the frame (in positions B and C, respectively) and in the top corners of the frame when in position A. As seen in Figure 3, each frame position contained 13 target positions. The area of overlap between frame positions contained 9 targets. So as to keep the overall number of trials small, but still collect as much data for targets in the area that overlaps between blocks, a non-uniform distribution was used, giving preference to targets in the overlap area. Targets belonged to one of four tiers, as labeled in Figure 3. Each tier-4 target (those targets without any overlap) would appear six times per block, each tier-3 target nine times per block, tier-2 18 times per block, and each tier-1 target (highlighted in Figure 3) 30 times per block, resulting in a total of 504 trials. As a result, 66% of

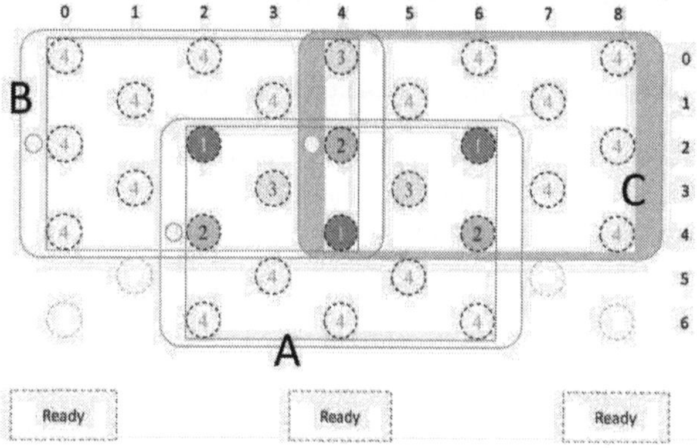

Figure 3. The experimental design: The frame was positioned in one of three locations (labeled A, B, C). Frame and target positions are such that a center target in one frame position is a corner target in another frame position. Targets within the overlap area are highlighted.

trials were of targets vital to the investigation. By including all possible target positions, however, participants still had to pay attention to the full area of the frame.

In order to have complete control over the point of origin for each target acquisition task, each trial started with the user pressing a button labeled "Ready" that appeared in one of three positions seen at the bottom of Figure 3 (In previous work (e.g. [6]), users were asked to start each trial with fingers rested comfortably off the screen.) Once pressed, the Ready button would disappear and a target (yellow on a near-black background) appeared. The time until the user tapped the screen and the location of the tap was measured. If the tap was outside the boundary of the target, time was recorded but the target's color was changed to red and the user would continue until successfully tapping within the target. This was done to encourage participants to be both fast and accurate. Upon successfully tapping the target, the target would disappear and a new Ready button would appear. Each target appeared an equal number of times with each Ready button.

Apparatus

The experiment was conducted on a Dell XPS 18 Portable All-In-One PC running Windows 8.1. The device was placed flat on a desk. Screen resolution was set to 1920 x 1080. The software for the experiment was written in C#. To avoid users accidentally touching the home button, the tablet was used upside-down, with the screen rotated 180 degrees.

Procedure

After completing a demographics form, each participant was given a short practice session. As part of the practice we asked the participant to miss one of the practice targets intentionally to highlight the need for accuracy. We also showed how tapping will work through the plastic frame so that they should not be worried about hitting it. Finally, we reminded participants that time is measured only between pressing a "Ready" button and hitting a target, so they can take a break if they need to when the Ready button is showing. Participants were instructed that after hitting a Ready button, they should acquire the target as quickly and accurately as possible.

Each participant then completed three blocks – one in each frame position. The order of blocks (ergo the position of the frame), and the order of trials within each block, was randomized. At the beginning of each block, the experimenter would move the frame to one of the three positions; invisible to participants, a thin layer of Play-Doh was used on the underside of the frame to create friction so that the frame wouldn't move during the block.

Measures

The following dependent and independent measures were determined for each trial:

- *Reaction Time*: The elapsed time (in milliseconds) between tapping the "Ready" button and tapping the screen again.
- *Touch-Point Offset*: Measured as the distance from the user's touch and the target's center.
- *Error*: A trial was marked an error if the distance from the user's touch to the target's center was greater than the target's radius.
- *Distance*: For each trial, we calculate the distance between the user's initial touch on the "Ready" button and the target's center. This measure is used in the analysis as a covariate to control for its known effect on performance. In keeping with Fitts' Law and related work, we apply a log2 transformation to this measure.
- *Ready-Button Position*: The starting position of each trial (Left, Center, and Right) was recorded and used as control.
- *Target Type*: Finally, this categorical measure describes the relationship between target and edge. Categories are: Corner, Horizontal Edge, Vertical Edge, Inner Target, and Center.

Participants

We recruited 12 participants (1 female), between the ages of 20 and 36 (M=27.6, SD=4.8), all were student interns in our lab and had experience using touch devices. 11 were right-handed and 7 wore glasses. Participants completed 504 trials each, taking 13:21 minutes, on average, to complete the experiment. This resulted in a total of 6,048 trials. However, one of the participants twice started the next block before the experimenter could move the frame to its new location, and so the first trials from these two blocks were discarded, leaving 6,046 trials. Upon completion, participants received a donut as a thank-you.

RESULTS (EXP 1)

In this section, we first describe the (lack of) effect of edges on error rate and touch point offset. We then describe a significant effect of edges on reaction time. Taking advantage of our experimental setup, we are able to examine how changing the position of the frame affected specific targets.

Removing outliers

In preparing the data for analysis, we first calculated T^2 Statistic for reaction time and distance from the target's center. We considered any trial with a T^2 greater than 2x the Upper Control Limit (UCL) as an outlier. This resulted in the exclusion of 86 trials (1.4% of the data), leaving 5,960 of the 6,046 trials for analysis.

Error Rate and Touch-Point Offset

Overall error rate was 6.2%. A Wilcoxon Signed Rank test showed no significant difference between error rates for edge targets (M=6%) and non-edge targets (M=6.4%; p=0.9).

We next looked at the effect of a target being an edge target on the Touch-Point Offset (the distance of touch from a target's center). We used a mixed model ANOVA with *Offset* as the dependent variable. Edge-Target (1 vs 0) as well as Trial Number, Reaction Time, and Distance were modeled as fixed effects, and Participant ID was modeled as a random effect. The analysis showed no significant effect for Edge-

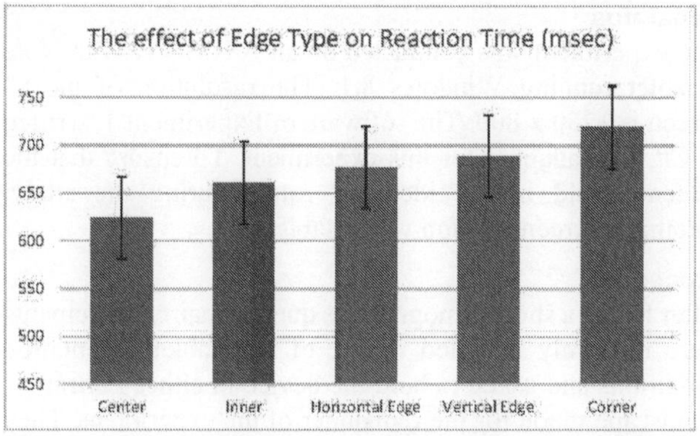

Figure 4. The significant effect of Target Type on Reaction Time, showing means and standard error. A Tukey-HSD pairwise comparison found a significant difference between each edge type.

Target on Offset (p=.56). Reaction Time had a significant effect (with faster reaction correlated with greater offset; F[1, 3887]=18.0; p<.001). Similarly, Distance had a significant effect (with longer distances correlated with greater offset; F[1, 3887]=18.0; p<.001).

Given no effect of edges on offset or error rate, in subsequent analyses we consider the first reaction time for all trials, including those coded as errors.

Reaction Time

Average reaction time in all trials was 651 milliseconds (SD=117). We first conducted a mixed-model ANOVA with *Reaction Time* as the dependent variable, and Trial Number, Distance, Touch-Point Offset, Ready-Button Position, Age, Handedness, and Corrected Vision (Yes/No) as fixed effects. Participant ID was modeled as a random effect.

As expected, Distance had a strong effect on reaction time (F[1,5943]=681.6; p<.001) with faster reaction to closer targets. Trial Number had a significant *negative* effect on reaction time, with reaction time getting faster over the course of the experiment (F[1,5943]=162.9; p<.001). Ready-Button position had a significant but small effect on reaction time (F[1,5943]=8.4; p<.001), with Tukey-HSD post-hoc comparison showing faster reaction time for trials beginning on the right (presumably because the vast majority of the participants were right-handed). Finally, Age showed a small significant effect (F[1,8]=6.1; p=.036) with higher age correlated with longer reaction time.

We were now ready to begin exploring hypothesis H_1.

Referring to Figure 3, we first compared reaction time to the trials of three targets: (2,2), (4,4), and (2,4). Each of these targets played the role of both Corner target and Center target, depending on the position of the frame. We created a second mixed-model ANOVA with *Reaction Time* as the dependent variable. In addition to the factors of our previous model, we also included *Target Type* (Center vs. Corner) and Target ID as fixed effects. Again, *Participant ID* was modeled as a random effect.

Our analysis found a large significant effect of Target Type on reaction time (F[1,2465]=1015.0; p<001), allowing us to **accept hypothesis H_1**. Our analysis shows that, independent of distance, reaction time to Corner targets was 14% *slower* than reaction to Center targets (M=723 msec vs. M=632 msec). This result allows us to accept hypothesis H_{1b} and reject H_{1a}, at least with regards to corner targets.

To further investigate H_{1b} and H_{1a}, and understand the relationship between target types (relative to the edge) on target acquisition performance, we repeated our model of the complete set of targets, including this time Target Type (Corner, Horizontal Edge, Vertical Edge, Inner Target, and Center) as a fixed effect, as well as the Frame Position (A, B, or C) for control.

The analysis showed a significant effect of Target Type on reaction time (F[4,5937]=313.6; p<.001). A post-hoc Tukey-HSD pairwise comparison, shown in Figure 4, revealed that the effect of proximity to the edge expands beyond corner targets. It shows a significant difference between each of the different target types, with corner targets resulting in the *slowest* reaction time, followed by targets along the vertical edge, targets along the horizontal edge, and finally inner then center targets. **This result allows us to fully accept hypothesis H_{1b} and reject H_{1a}.**

EXPERIMENT 2

The unique setup of Experiment 1, which allowed complete control over the absolute position of targets in 2D space in relation to the user, helped us uncover a significant negative effect of edge targets on performance, confirming hypotheses H_1 and H_{1b}, and rejecting hypothesis H_{1a}. However, several important questions remain: Would the effect persist when tested in a more natural setting on an actual handheld tablet? Would larger targets be susceptible to the same effect? And would varying the distance from the screen's edge, even slightly, mitigate the effect?

We designed Experiment 2 to try and answer these questions.

Hypotheses

In addition to re-testing hypothesis H_{1a}, Experiment 2 further tests several other hypotheses.

Since, according to models of target acquisition performance, larger targets are easier to acquire, we first hypothesize that increasing the size of targets will dampen the effect of the screen's edge.

H_2: Large targets will not be affected by proximity to the edge.

Furthermore, if the reason edge-targets are slower to acquire on touch devices is because they are harder to visually separate from the bezel, one would expect that introducing even a slight gap from the bezel should reduce or eliminate the effect. We thus hypothesize that:

H_3: The effect of proximity to the edge can be significantly reduced with even a slight gap between target and edge.

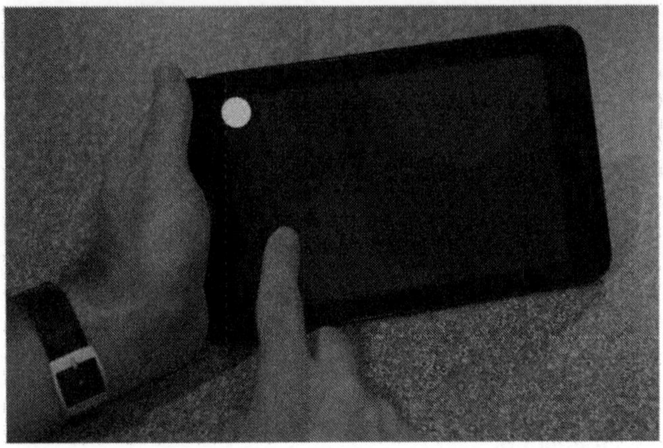

Figure 5. Apparatus for Experiment 2. An 8" tablet held in the user's non-dominant hand showing a corner target.

Method

Experiment 2 was conducted on an 8" tablet (see Figure 5), where both targets and Ready buttons were drawn. Since tablets are frequently used in either portrait or landscape modes, we introduced Tablet Orientation (Landscape vs. Portrait) as a between-subject condition. As in Experiment 1, each target acquisition trial started with the participant hitting a Ready button, and finished when the participant successfully hit the target. Targets appeared along the top and bottom edges of the tablet (e.g., top-left, top-middle, and top-right).

To test hypothesis H_2, we used targets of two sizes: 11 mm in diameter (similar to Experiment 1) and 22 mm. To test hypothesis H_3, the distance of targets from the edge of the device was manipulated for each trial. We used 4 edge offset values: 0 mm, 1.5 mm, 4 mm or 11 mm (an edge offset of 0mm means that the target is right along the screen's edge). Similar to Experiment 1, targets appeared as yellow circles.

Unlike in Experiment 1 where trials started at Ready buttons drawn outside the device's boundaries, in Experiment 2 trials started inside the tablet's bounds. Trials were performed in two blocks: In one block, the Ready button appears in one of two positions in the *bottom* part of the screen with targets at the top-left, top-middle, and top right. In the other block, the Ready button appears in one of two positions in the *top* part of the screen and targets were displayed at the bottom-left, bottom-center, and bottom-right. Figure 6 illustrates the positions of Ready buttons and targets in 4 trials. Figures 6a and 6b illustrate trials from the Landscape condition, with a small target and two edge gap values. Figures 6c and 6d illustrate trials from the Portrait condition with the large target size and two edge gap values. Using Figure 3 with frame position B as reference, possible positions for Ready buttons in Experiment 2 are (1,1), (1,3), (3,1), and (3,3). That is, the button's center is one column and one row inwards from the edge of the screen. In order to maintain control over the distance from Ready button to the target in each trial, the Ready button was offset the same amount and direction as the upcoming target (as can be seen in Figure 6).

Apparatus

The experiment was conducted on an ASUS VivoTab Note 8 tablet running Windows 8.1. The resolution of the 8" screen is 1280 x 800. The software of Experiment 1, written in C#, was adapted for this experiment. To ensure that the screen would not accidentally rotate during the study, automatic screen rotation was disabled.

Procedure

After filling a short demographics questionnaire, participants were randomly assigned to one of the Tablet Orientation conditions and asked to hold the device in either Portrait or Landscape mode for the remainder of the experiment. They performed tasks in a "hold-and-tap" posture [5]: holding the tablet using the non-dominant hand and acquiring the targets with the index finger of the dominant hand (see Figure 5).

Similar to Experiment 1, participants started with a short practice block of 6 trials. Participants were instructed that after hitting a Ready button, they should acquire the target as quickly and accurately as possible. Here, again, the result of missing a target was explained.

The number of trials completed by each participant was 384: 2 blocks (Up-Down vs. Down-Up) x 3 target positions x 2 target sizes x 4 offsets from the edge (0mm, 1.5mm, 4mm, 1mm) x 2 Ready button positions x 4 repetitions.

The order of blocks and of trials within each block was randomized.

Measures

The following measures were recorded for each trial:

- *Reaction Time*: The elapsed time (in milliseconds) between tapping the "Ready" button and tapping the screen again.

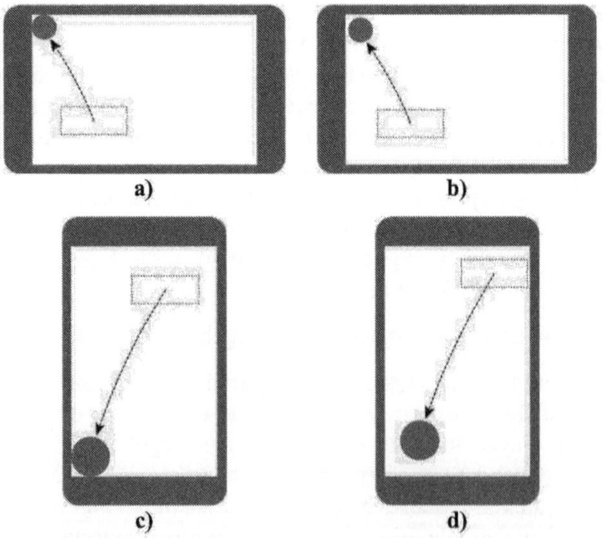

Figure 6. Examples of trials from Experiment 2 with Landscape and Portrait orientations. Trials vary by target size (11mm vs. 22mm) and the gap from the edge (0mm, 1.5mm, 4mm, or 11mm).

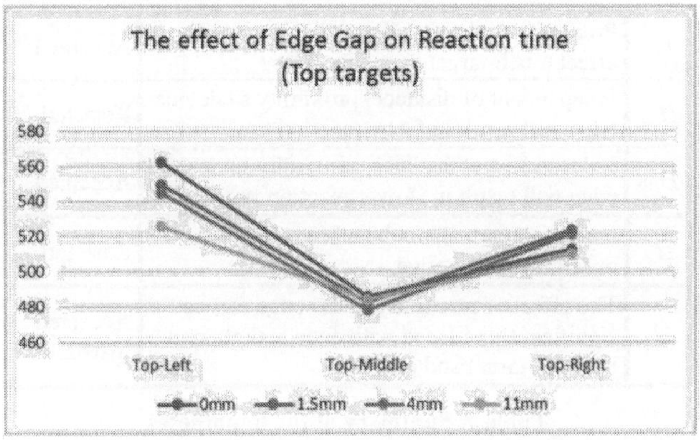

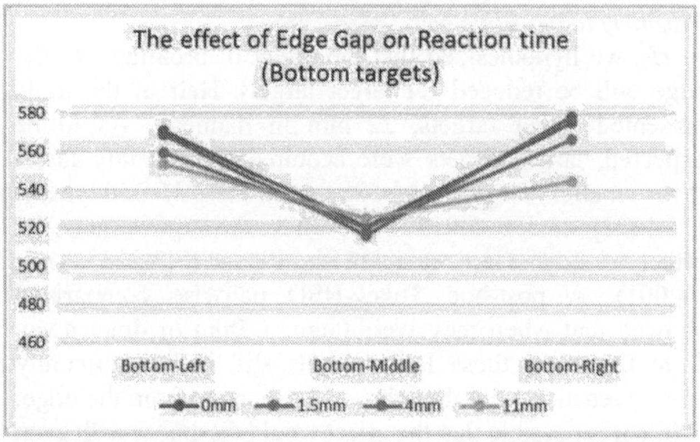

Figure 7. The effect of different gap sizes on reaction time, as a factor of the target's position on the screen. For readability, grouped by targets at the top and bottom of the screen.

- *Touch-Point Offset*: Measured as the distance from the user's touch and the target's center.
- *Error*: A trial was marked an error if the distance from the user's touch to the target's center was greater than the target's radius.
- *Distance*: For each trial, we calculate the distance (log2) between the user's initial touch on the "Ready" button and the target's center.
- *Target Position*: Targets were labeled Top-Left, Top-Middle, Top-Right, Bottom-Left, Bottom-Middle, or Bottom-Right.

Participants
We recruited 12 participants (5 women) at a local café. Participants' ages ranged from 15 to 42 (*M*=28.5, *SD*=8). All participants were right-handed and 3 wore glasses. Participants took 7:26 minutes, on average, to complete the study. Participants received a $10 gift card to the café where the study took place.

RESULTS (EXP 2)

Removing outliers
We collected a total of 4608 samples. As in Experiment 1, we excluded trials for which reaction time or offset from the target's center was greater than 2x the Upper Control Limit of the T^2 Statistic. This resulted in the exclusion of 65 trials (1.5% of the data) leaving 4,543 trials for analysis.

Error Rate and Touch-Point Offset
Overall error rate was 3%. A Wilcoxon Signed Rank test showed a significantly higher percent of error for the small target versus the larger targets (*M*=5.3% vs. *M*=0.7%; *p*=.001). However, the error rates for target at different distances from the edge of the screen were not different from one another.

We next tested whether a target's size and distance from the edge had an effect on the Touch-Point Offset (the distance of touch from a target's center). We used a mixed-model ANOVA with *Touch-Point Offset* as the dependent variable and Target Size (11mm vs. 22mm), Edge Gap (0,1.5,4, and 11), and the interaction between them as our main factors of interest. Trial Number, Reaction Time, and Distance were also modeled as fixed effects, and Participant ID was modeled as a random effect. The analysis showed no significant effect for Edge-Offset (p=.6), Target Size (p=.15) or the interaction (p=.36). Trial ID showed a small effect (F[1,4521]=4.0; *p*=.04) with touch accuracy dropping ever so slightly as the experiment progressed.

Given no effect of edges on touch-point offset or error rate, in subsequent analyses we consider the first reaction time for all trials, including those coded as errors.

Reaction Time
Average reaction time in all trials in Experiment 2 was 524 milliseconds (*SD*=117). To test the effect of the different factors on reaction time, we conducted a mixed-model ANOVA with *Reaction Time* as the dependent variable. Edge Gap, Device Orientation, Target Position, Target Size, and their 2-way interactions with Edge Gap were modeled as fixed effects. We also included Trial Number, Distance, Touch-Point Offset, Ready-Button Position, Age, and Corrected Vision (Yes/No) for control. Participant ID was modeled as a random effect.

Verifying Hypothesis H_{1b}
We started by testing whether the effect found in Experiment 1 holds in this setup. Our analysis found a significant main effect of Edge Gap on reaction time (F[3,4497]=13.1; *p*<.001), with significantly faster reaction time for targets farthest from the edge (Edge Gap = 11 mm). Recall that the distance between Ready Button and target remained the same, since both target and Ready button were shifted equally. **Accordingly, this result successfully reaffirms Hypothesis H_{1b}.**

While the difference in reaction time to targets at the very edge of the device and those 11mm away from the edge was smaller in comparison to the difference observed in Experiment 1 (only 3-7% slower), the presence of the effect is important, considering that non-edge targets in Experiment 1 were significantly farther from the edge than those present in Experiment 2.

Proximity to the Edge with Large Targets

In H_2, we hypothesized that the effect of proximity to the edge will be reduced for larger targets. Half of the trials presented larger targets, 22 mm in diameter. As to be expected, larger targets were acquired significantly faster than smaller targets (M=525 msec vs. M=550 msec; $F[1,4497]=48.3$; $p<.001$). Yet, even for the larger targets, the effect of Edge Gap remained significant ($F[3,2235]=7.7$; $p<.001$). A post-hoc Tukey-HSD pairwise comparison showed that when they were 0mm, 1.5mm or 4mm away from the edge, these large targets still had significantly *slower* reaction time than those 11mm away from the edge. While it is possible that the effect would disappear with even larger targets, the targets we used (22 mm) are already larger than a typical fingertip. **As a result, for the two sizes of targets we used, we *reject* hypothesis H_2.** Still, it is important to note that in our data, reaction time to a 22mm target with a 0mm gap was faster (M=524 msec) than to 11mm targets with an 11mm gap (M=538 msec).

The Effect of Gap Size in Detail

We next turn to examine whether introducing gaps of different sizes significantly changes reaction time to edge targets (to address H_3). While we already reported on the significantly faster reaction time of targets 11 mm away from the edge, we now examine whether introducing a 1.5 mm or a 4 mm gap would significantly affect reaction time.

In our study, moving targets 1.5 mm away from the edge did not produce a significant difference in reaction time ($F[1,2239]=.2$; $p=.7$). However, moving targets 4 mm away from the edge produced a small but significant difference in reaction time ($F[1,2234]=5.9$; $p=.02$). **We may thus only partially accept H_3.**

Looking again at all trials, our analysis shows a significant interaction between Edge Gap and Target Position on reaction time ($F[15,4497]=3.8$; $p<.001$). Figure 7 shows the effect of Edge Gap on reaction time for different target positions (for readability, we present reaction time to targets at the top and bottom of the screen separately). As is quickly evident from looking at Figure7, introducing gaps had an effect especially with targets at the Top-Left and Bottom-Right. On the other hand, non-corner targets (Top-Middle and Bottom-Middle) were faster, and different edge gaps had no effect on reaction time.

Proximity to the Edge and Device Orientation

Lastly, we examined whether the orientation of the device (Portrait or Landscape) would result in a different effect of edge targets on reaction time. However, Orientation did not show a significant effect on reaction time ($F[1,8]=.9$; $p=.4$), nor did the interaction between Orientation and Edge Gap ($F[3,4486]=.3$; $p=.8$). In fact, looking independently at the Portrait and Landscape conditions, both showed a significant effect of Edge Gap ($F[3,2246]=9.9$; $p<.001$ and $F[3,2223]=5.5$; $p<.001$, respectively).

H_1	Proximity to device edge will significantly affect touch-target acquisition time.	Accepted
H_{1a}	Independent of distance, proximity to device edge will result in faster reaction time.	Rejected
H_{1b}	Independent of distance, proximity to device edge will result in slower reaction time.	Accepted
H_2	Large targets will not be affected by proximity to the edge.	Rejected
H_3	The effect of proximity to the edge can be significantly reduced with even a slight gap between target and edge.	Accepted (partially)

Table 1. Summary of the hypotheses

DISCUSSION

In the two studies presented in this paper, we found a significant negative effect of a target's proximity to the edge of a tablet's screen on target acquisition performance. This slower reaction time to edge targets stands in stark contrast to the performance advantage that edge targets have in traditional desktop mousing environments. We also found that the negative effect persisted for larger targets, although, not surprisingly, the effect was lessened. Table 1 summarizes our hypotheses and whether our experiments allow us to accept or reject them.

Still, the effect found was not obvious and is, in some ways, surprising; while one may correctly argue that tablets' touchscreens don't offer physical affordances that could accelerate reaction to edge targets, we could then still expect that reaction to edge targets will be equally fast (or slow) as reaction to any target on the screen. In fact, for the most part, screen edges on current tablets are just barely distinguishable from the rest of the screen: the glass spans the screen and the bezel, and in many devices, the touch sensor itself extends into the bezel (albeit, with reduced accuracy). What could be the reason for the slower reaction time? While the experiments do not provide a definite answer, we will discuss several alternative explanations. Still, further investigations into these possible explanations is needed and is left for future work.

Visual Interference

A potential reasonable explanation for the slow reaction to edge targets may be that when a target is near the edge, the cognitive task of separating the edge and target into two distinct objects is more difficult. Extensive research exists in the field of cognitive psychology (for example, [4, 8, 14, 23]) that describes the cognitive processes involved in the perception of elements as objects (for a survey, see [22]).

Yet two points must be considered in relation to this potential explanation. First, our results show that reaction time to corner targets was consistently slower than reaction time to edge targets that are not edge targets (e.g., a target at the top-middle). Thus, if visual interference is indeed the culprit, it would mean that corner targets suffer from greater visual interference than an edge target (a reasonable expectation). However, in the second experiment, gaps of different values were added between target and edge. This allowed all targets except those with a 0mm gap to have some visual separation from the edge. Second, in the tablet used in Experiment 2, as with most tablets today, the visual difference between the edge of the screen and the bezel around it is subtle (see Figure 5): The screen is a very dark grey with backlight, but otherwise both are dark (when nothing is drawn on the screen) and covered by glass. Thus, the purely visual difference between edge targets and non-edge targets was minimal.

Global and Local Processing

Another potential and related cause for the slower reaction may be a two-level visual processing of a target's position. According to the theory proposed by [16], in a first stage, people will visually locate the large encompassing object and then, in a second stage, visually search for the smaller target within. Applying this theory to this case, the user would first visually locate the tablet, and then search within the tablet's bounds for the target.

This explanation properly accounts for the lack of statistical difference when targets were moved 1.5mm away from the edge (since the change to the second stage is minimal). However, if this explanation was sufficient, then no effect would be found in Experiment 2, since a user is already working within the boundaries of the tablet.

Preference for the center of the display

It is also possible that people "prefer" the inside area of a shape (in this case, a rectangular screen), and would be thus faster to react to targets in their preferred zone. However, in [9], Firestone and Scholl showed participants different shapes on a tablet (one shape at a time) and asked them to tap anywhere they wished. Their results show that in the aggregate, touches conformed to the medial-axis skeleton, and included many touches near corners.

Fear of going out of bounds

As mentioned above, the effect of edges persisted for large and small targets and even persisted when gaps were introduced around the targets. Since in the two experiments we fully control for distance and target size, we are allowed to assume that the cause for the effect is perceptual. Is it possible then that participants were, for some reason, reluctant to touch outside the edge of the screen? This, currently, seems like a most likely phenomenon behind the effect, but is insufficient to explain the cause of the phenomenon. To properly test this possibility, a setup would need to be created in which missing "outwards" is preferred to missing "inwards".

Implications for design

The findings presented in this paper may have immediate implications for the design of efficient interfaces for handheld touchscreens. Particularly, the findings highlight that edge targets, and in particular corner targets – often thought of as the prime position for quick interactions – may actually be slow in those touch devices. This is especially important with the growing popularity of interfaces that are used with touch and pointing devices interchangeably.

One recommendation that emerges from the results is that in order to mitigate the effect of proximity to the edge, when designing an interface for touch, edge targets should be made larger, particularly corner targets.

As mentioned above, the results of our second study hint that the reason for the slower reaction time is the visual appearance of the targets near the edge, and suggest that adding a gap as small as 4mm may partially improve reaction to corner targets (for our right-handed participants, these were the top-left and bottom-right corners).

For the design of underlying pointing acceleration and assistance techniques, it is interesting to note that edge targets did not result in significantly higher touch offset from the center of the target. This suggests that simply increasing the underlying effective area of a target, but not making it visually larger may not sufficiently improve reaction time. Still, an examination of the effect of edge targets with realistic interfaces is needed.

LIMITATIONS AND FUTURE WORK

One potential limitation of the findings is that in both experiments, only a single target was shown on the screen at any given time. Indeed, the case of a singleton target, common in abstract experiments of human performance, is quite rare in real-world interfaces. In future work, we plan to examine the effect of edge targets in the presence of competing targets. Whether edge targets suffer more or less from such distractors is an interesting question that would shed further light on the root cause of the effect described here, and allow for broader design recommendation.

Another limitation of this work is the focus on a single device category (8" tablets). While this represents a popular segment, investigating the effect of edge targets on performance on other form factors such as smartphones needs to be verified experimentally. One could expect that edge targets will have a smaller effect in smartphones, and potentially a greater effect in larger tablets geared at productivity applications. Testing the effect of edge targets with different size screens, more target sizes and additional edge gap values is necessary but left for future work.

Finally, the work presented here looked exclusively at tasks where a target's position was unknown in advance. Understanding the effect of edge-targets in cases where their position is fixed and known in advance is needed. In future work, we plan to investigate the effect of edge targets when the user plans, ahead of time, to hit them. This can be done, for example, by having participants tap targets (both edge and non-edge) in a pre-defined sequence.

CONCLUSIONS

Edge targets, such as buttons and menus organized along the edge of the screen, have long been used in desktop mousing environments to provide quick access to targets. This paper presented a surprising negative effect of edge targets on reaction time when using touch. The effect was found through two experiments: In the first experiment, we used a setup designed specifically to allow decoupling of the distance of targets from the user and the distance of targets from the frame around them. A second experiment confirmed the presence of the effect and explored potential mitigating solutions, including different sized targets, and the introduction of small gaps around the targets.

The findings presented in this paper grow our understanding of human performance with touchscreen interaction, and should be considered in the design of efficient interfaces for touch devices.

ACKNOWLEDGEMENTS

Thank you to Shumin Zhai and Darren Gergle for their suggestions and early comments on the results of the first experiment.

REFERENCES

1. Accot, J. and Zhai, S. More than dotting the i's: Foundations for crossing-based interfaces. In *Proc. CHI 2002*, ACM Press (2002), 73-80.
2. Accot, J. and Zhai, S. Refining Fitts' law models for bivariate pointing. In *Proc. CHI 2003*, ACM Press (2003), 193-200.
3. Appert, C., Chapuis, O. and Beaudouin-Lafon, M. Evaluation of pointing performance on screen edges. In *Proc. AVI* 2008, ACM Press (2008), 119-126.
4. Avrahami, J. Objects of attention, objects of perception. *Perception & Psychophysics, 61* (1999), 1604-1612.
5. Azenkot, S. and Zhai, S. Touch Behavior with Different Postures on Soft Smart Phone Keyboards. In *Proc. MobileHCI 2012*. (2012), 251-260.
6. Bi, X., Li, Y., and Zhai, S. FFitts law: modeling finger touch with fitts' law. In *Proc CHI* 2013, ACM Press (2013), 1363-1372.
7. Cockburn, A., Ahlström, D. and Gutwin, C. Understanding performance in touch selections: Tap, drag and radial pointing drag with finger, stylus and mouse. *Int. J. Human-Computer Studies, 70*, 3, (2012) 218-233.
8. Driver, J., & Baylis, G. Figure-ground segmentation and edge assignment in short-term visual matching. *Cognitive Psychology, 31*, (1996), 248-306.
9. Firestone, C., & Scholl, B. J. "Please Tap the Shape, Anywhere You Like" Shape Skeletons in Human Vision Revealed by an Exceedingly Simple Measure. *Psychological science, 25*, 2 (2014), 377-386.
10. Fitts, P.M. The information capacity of the human motor system in controlling the amplitude of movement. *J. Experimental Psychology, 47* (1954), 381-391.
11. Froehlich, J., Wobbrock, J. O. and Kane, S. K. Barrier Pointing: Using physical edges to assist target acquisition on mobile device touch screens. In *Proc. ASSETS 2007*. ACM Press (2007), 19-26.
12. Henze, N., Rukzio, E., and Boll, S. 100,000,000 taps: analysis and improvement of touch performance in the large. In *Proc. MobileHCI 2011*, (2011), 133-142.
13. Holz, C. and Baudisch, P. The Generalized Perceived Input Point Model and How to Double Touch Accuracy by Extracting Fingerprints. In *Proc. CHI 2010*. ACM Press (2010), 581-590.
14. Kramer, A., & Jacobson, A. Perceptual organization and focused attention: the role of objects and proximity in visual processing. *Perception & Psychophysics, 50* (1991), 267-284.
15. Lee, S., and Zhai, S. The performance of touch screen soft buttons. In *Proc. CHI 2009*. ACM Press (2009), 309-318.
16. Navon, D. Forest before trees: The precedence of global features in visual perception. *Cognitive psychology, 9*, 3 (1977), 353-383.
17. Olafsdottir, H. B., Tsandilas, T., & Appert, C. Prospective motor control on tabletops: planning grasp for multitouch interaction. In *Proc. CHI 2014*, ACM Press (2014), 2893-2902.
18. Park, Y. S., Han, S. H., Park, J., & Cho, Y. Touch key design for target selection on a mobile phone. In *Proc. MobileHCI 2008*, ACM Press (2008), 423-426.
19. Perry, K. B., & Hourcade, J. P. Evaluating one handed thumb tapping on mobile touchscreen devices. In *Proc. GI 2008*, Canadian Information Processing Society (2008), 57-64.
20. Roth, V. and Turner, T. Bezel Swipe: Conflict-free scrolling and multiple selection on mobile touch screen devices. In *Proc. CHI 2009*, ACM Press (2009), 1523-1526.
21. Sasangohar, F., MacKenzie, I.S., Scott, S. Evaluation of mouse and touch input for a tabletop display using Fitts' reciprocal tapping task. In *Proc. HFES 2009, 53*, 12 (2009), 839-843.
22. Scholl, B. J. Objects and attention: The state of the art. *Cognition, 80*, 1 (2001), 1-46.
23. Treisman, A. The perception of features and objects. In A. Baddeley, & L. Weiskrantz (Eds.), *Attention: selection, awareness, and control*, Oxford: Clarendon Press (1993), 5-35.
24. Wobbrock, J. O., Myers, B. A. and Hudson, S. E. Exploring edge-based input techniques for handheld text entry. In *Proc. IWSAWC 2003*, IEEE Computer Society (2003), 280-282.
25. Wobbrock, J. O., Myers, B. A. and Kembel, J. A. EdgeWrite: A stylus-based text entry method designed for high accuracy and stability of motion. In *Proc. UIST 2003*, ACM Press (2003), 61-70.

FlickBoard: Enabling Trackpad Interaction with Automatic Mode Switching on a Capacitive-sensing Keyboard

Ying-Chao Tung[1], Ta-Yang Cheng[1], Neng-Hao Yu[2], Chiuan Wang[1], Mike Y. Chen[1,3]
[1]National Taiwan University, [2]National Chengchi University, [3]Research Center for Information Technology Innovation, Academia Sinica
{tony61507, jimmyken793, jonesfish, timowang1991}@gmail.com, mikechen@csie.ntu.edu.tw

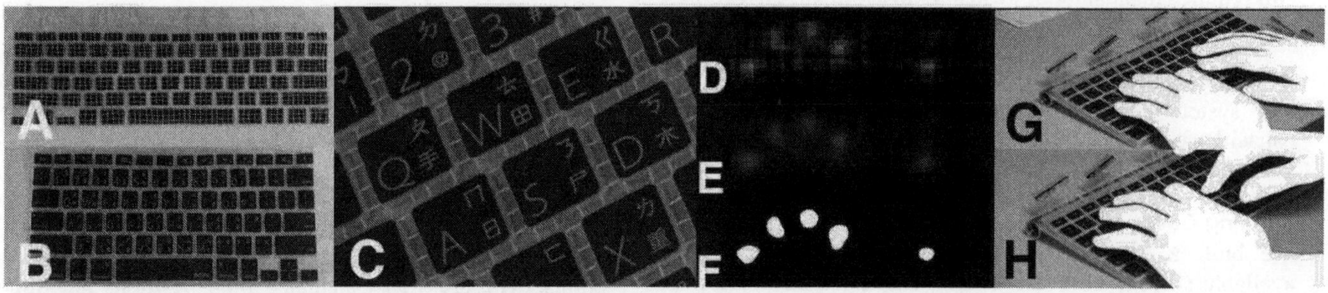

Figure 1. We present a keyboard cover with capacitive touch sensing capability which automatically disables itself while typing. Sensing wires are embedded into a typical keyboard cover (A), the modified cover is then put on an off-the-shelf keyboard (B). The sensing grid is all over the keyboard with 0.5cm grid size (C). This results in a low-resolution raw intensity image when hands are near the surface of the keyboard (D). The image is then processed to obtain touched areas (E+F). The raw image can also be used to robustly recognize whether user wants to type on the keyboard (G) or to control cursor with touchpad (H) using a machine learning-based classifier.

ABSTRACT

We present FlickBoard, which combines a touchpad and a keyboard into the same interaction area to reduce hand movement between a separate keyboard and touchpad. Our main contribution is automatic mode switching between typing and pointing, and the first system capable of combining a trackpad and a keyboard into a single interaction area without the need for external switches. We developed a prototype by embedding a 58x20 capacitive sensing grid into a soft keyboard cover, and used machine learning to distinguish between moving a cursor (touchpad mode) and entering text (keyboard mode). We conducted experimental studies that show automatic mode switching classification accuracies of 98% are achievable with our technology. Finally, our prototype has a thin profile and can be placed over existing keyboards.

Author Keywords

Keyboard; Touchpad; Co-located input devices;

ACM Classification Keywords

H.5.2. User Interfaces - Input devices and strategies: User Interfaces

CHI 2015, April 18–23, 2015, Seoul, Republic of Korea.

http://dx.doi.org/10.1145/2702123.2702582

INTRODUCTION

Operating a computer requires both pointing devices and text input devices. However, most of the commercially available computers present these as two separate devices, which require hand repositioning while switching between mouse and typing actions. Therefore, previous studies had explored how to co-locate touch sensing and regular typing. There are two main issues of the dual functional keyboard: 1) How to enable touch sensing capability on the keyboard? [1, 2, 5] provided different sensing approaches to combine gesture interaction and typing on the same area. 2) How to automatically switch between trackpad mode and typing mode? To our knowledge, this issue has not been resolved yet. We present FlickBoard, a keyboard cover with a smart capacitive touch sensing film with an automatic mode switching algorithm that recognises the user's intention based on the recorded usage data of 30 participants. In this work, we focus on automatic mode switching between typing and pointing, and the design of our sensing cover is based on the work, SmartSkin [3], which recognizes multiple hand positions and shapes by using capacitive sensing grids. Furthermore, we modified the software implementation provided by Type-hover-swipe in 96 bytes [5], which uses Motion Signature approach [5] to do gesture recognitions. We conducted experimental studies that show automatic mode switching classification accuracies of 98% are achievable with small amounts of training data per user.

RELATED WORK

Previous research has shown that co-locating two devices will improve user performance [1]. ThumbSense [4] helps users keep their fingers on the home row by using keyboard keys as mouse buttons when it detects a movement of the thumb on the touchpad. TypeHoverSwipe [5] implemented a modified keyboard with infra-red proximity sensors that recognizes in-air hand gestures and obtains coarse finger positions. The depth map generated by the infrared range finder is fast and stable, but the finger positions obtained by the system are too rough to control a mouse cursor because the sensors were interspersed between the key caps. DGTS [2] uses capacitive sensing technology, in contrast, to obtain a higher resolution image to control the cursor. However, the integrated device still requires manual mode switching to avoid false triggering of the pointing device.

SYSTEM OVERVIEW

Our system consists of four parts: 1) sensing film, 2) capacitance-to-digital converters and 3) automatic mode switching predictor.

Sensing Cover

We built a capacitive sensing grid on a commercially available silicone keyboard cover. The modified cover was placed over an Apple wireless keyboard. We connected the ground of the grid to the body of the Apple keyboard to stabilize the readings. The grid consists of 58 vertical and 20 horizontal 30 AWG copper wires. With mutual capacitance sensing techniques, each cross point of vertical and horizontal wires can be a single sensing point, so the film can capture a 58x20 frame. The sensing resolution could be higher if the conductive pattern would be printed directly on the cover with higher line density. With this modified keyboard cover, we can enable touch sensing capability on any keyboard by simply putting it over an unmodified keyboard.

Capacitance To Digital Converters(CDC)

We adopted the CDC design of SmartSkin [3] to measure the change of mutual capacitances at the sensor grid intersections. Here we briefly highlight our changes cover [3]. The main idea of this design is to measure the signal reduction of the square wave signal passed through the sensor film, which can be viewed as a very small capacitor. The square wave signal generated by a programmable clock generator is passed into sensor films through analog demultiplexers, so we can raster scan through all the 58 vertical wires by switching between the channels. 20 OP-Amps are connected to the horizontal wires of the sensor grid, amplifying the weakened signal by a factor of 5 for further processing. The CDC also has an analog subtractor for hardware-based background substraction. The CDC currently is capable of raster scanning through the sensor grid at 13 Hz. Calibration of the sensor is done by sampling through the sensor grid for 10 times. The data generated by the CDC can form a 58x20 pixels resolution. Each pixel has 10-bit intensity value ranging from 0 to 1023. The sensor grid only responds to conductive objects in a very short range(<0.2cm).

Signal Processing

The 58x20 10-bit intensity image is scaled up to 464x160 10-bit image with nearest-neighbor interpolation to provide a more accurate cursor positioning capability. (Figure 1.D) A Gaussian filter is then applied to the image for smoother blob images. Each row of the filtered image is subtracted with the mean of the row since we found that the sensor value will be interfered when there are some other touch points on the same horizontal sensing wire.(Figure 1.E) The image is binarized with a simple local adaptive thresholding algorithm. Finally, the system detects blobs in the binarized image as touched points. (Figure 1.F) Calculated blob positions are filtered with a Kalman filter to stabilize blob position and make cursor controlling possible.

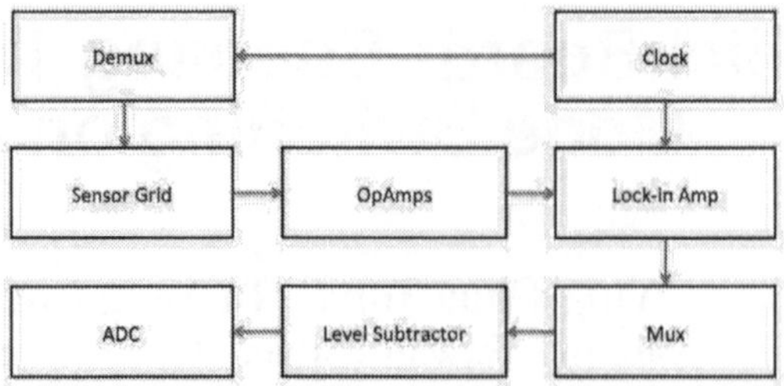

Figure 2. CDC circuit diagram. The switch and RC low-pass filter are the main components of the lock-in amplifier.

AUTOMATIC MODE SWITCHING PREDICTION

After co-locating the touch sensing and typing device, automatically switching between the touching and typing modes becomes an important issue. We classified the calculated MHIs with Random Decision Forests(RDF) into *keyboard mode* and *trackpad mode* to recognize which mode the user intends to use.

Task Design for collecting training data

We designed the tasks to meet the following criteria: 1) The tasks must be using both keyboard and touchpad alternately. Switching between two devices occurs frequently. 2) The task was extracted from the regular use of the keyboard and touchpad, and must be simple enough for the users to perform while they also need to operate an extra foot pedal to record their actual intention (see Figure 3.A). 3) The individual usage times of the keyboard and the touchpad should be as close as possible to each other. This would result in a more balanced dataset, which is better for building a classifier.

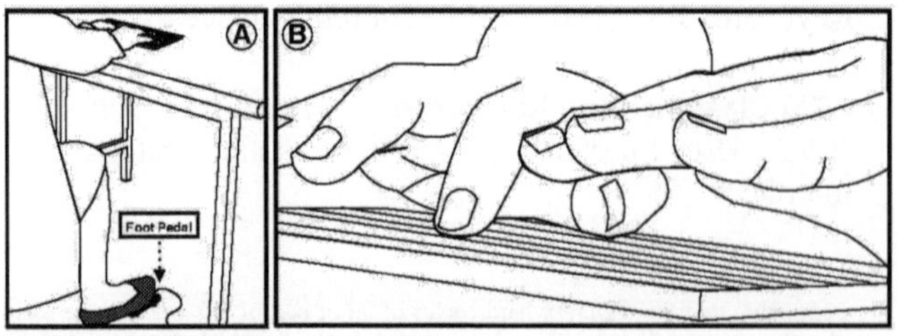

Figure 3. (A) Participants switched between typing and pointing by operating the foot pedal manually during the procedure of ground truth collection. Meanwhile, the system labeled each frame according to the current foot pedal's state. (B) A majority of the participants raised their left hand and used one finger of the right hand to perform cursor movements in the trackpad mode.

Procedure

We recruited 30 participants (15 females, 15 males, mean age 21) with an on-line form. All participants are right-handed. In the training session, participants were asked to fill in a questionnaire and learned how to use the foot pedal to switch modes. In the testing session, participants were asked to use FlickBoard to perform the following tasks: 1) Type a specified sentence in the text processing software. 2) Change the font size of the sentence by moving the mouse cursor to select a different size on the menu bar. 3) Continue typing another sentence and their own name. 4) Insert a picture in the document with the menu button, and resize the picture with the cursor. 5) Close the text processing software and open a web browser. 6) Type "www.facebook.com" in the location bar. 7) Browse the social network site, comment on one of the posts in the news feed. 8) Scroll back to the top of the page and upload a photo. 9) Add some comment on the uploaded photo. Participants were not allowed to use hot keys. They can only type and control the cursor or use a scrolling gesture(two finger swipe).

All of these tasks were very common tasks for a modern PC user, and should be performed without any difficulties. Videos of the hand postures and its interaction with the keyboard were recorded for further analysis. The total operating time of the recorded data is 187.36 minutes, average operating time is 6.24 minutes per user.

Labeling

The ground truth of whether the user is trying to use the keyboard or touchpad is collected with a foot pedal (see Figure 3.A) switch operated by the participant during the data collection session. Pedal down means pointing and pedal up means typing. We collected 150007 frames from the training data collection session, 25739 were *keyboard frames*, 61896 were *touchpad frames*. The remaining 62372 frames were frames without any touched blobs, we call them *blank frames*. Since those frames didn't contain any touched blobs. We could safely assume that no user operation was being executed at that moment, so we could classify it into neither keyboard nor touchpad frames. The blank frames were removed from training data while building a classifier, and directly skipped while running on a real-time interactive system, so there would not be any output from our system.

Classification Method

We also implemented Motion Signature [5] to recognize whether the user is trying to use the pointing device or not. Since our sensor's sampling rate of 13Hz is much lower than the sensor used in [5](325Hz), we only used 30 frames of raw signal to build MHIs. Also, we removed binary-MHI(bMHI) from the original MHI implementation because intensity-MHI already provides enough accuracy for recognizing user intention. We classify the calculated MHIs with Random Decision Forests(RDF), the same classifier used in TypeHoverSwipe [5]. With our hardware system, we can extract touch areas from the image collected with the capacitive sensor grid. Therefore, our system can recognize where the moving touch point is even if the second hand rests on the keyboard.

SYSTEM EVALUATION

We evaluated our system by running various cross-validation tests with usage data collected with 30 participants. In this section, we describe the details of the validation process and result.

Preprocessing Raw Data

After analyzing the raw data, we found all pointing operations are performed on the right side of every *touchpad frames*, because all of our participants are right-handed. This user behavior indicates we can build our classifier, which enables automatic mode switching, with right half of raw images. So we used a 29x20 10-bit image instead of a 58x20 10-bit image as input data for our RDF classifier to speed up the classification process.

Testing Parameters

The forest size improves the performance of RDF classifier at a linear cost of time, to build a real-time interactive system, we set the number of trees to 50 and the maximum depth per tree to 25 for more accurate recognition. While running the experiments, we found the number of frames referenced while building Motion Signature (N_f) can strongly affect the performance for recognizing user intention, so we need to find out a good parameter for the number of frames referenced. We run a 5-fold cross validation with 1-20 frames referenced. The results are shown in Figure 4. We can find that the recognition rate is very low when N_f is 1. Then gradually rising while N_f is increasing. The recognition rate stabilized around 98% when N_f = 30. This means we only need to remember 30 frames to achieve a good recognition rate, and we can recognize the user's intention with about 2.3 seconds of previous surface action. We found this parameter can have a great impact on the performance of the system, but previous work did not mention this. [5] According to the result, we set N_f = 30 in the following experiments.

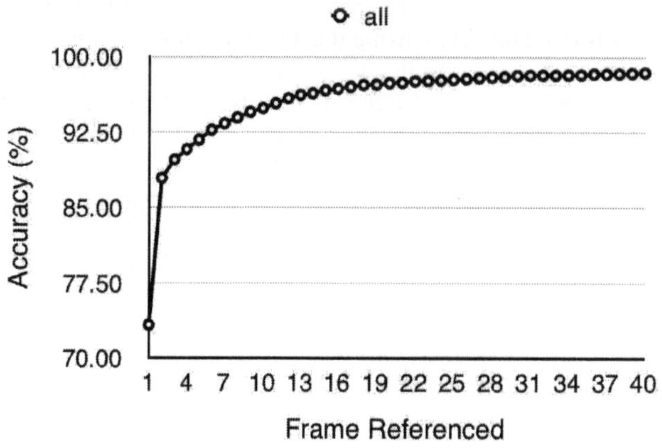

Figure 4. Classification accuracy of 5-fold cross validation for each user and leave-one-user-out cross validation. X axis is number of frame referenced while building Motion Signature (N_f)

Performance

We ran a 5-fold cross validation with each participant's own data with parameters shown above. The averaged overall

	Keyboard (Predicted)	Touchpad (Predicted)
Keyboard	98%	2%
Touchpad	2%	98%

	Keyboard (Predicted)	Touchpad (Predicted)
Keyboard	78%	22%
Touchpad	14%	86%

Table 1. Confusion matrix in a 5-fold cross validation(left) and leave-one-user-out cross validation(right)

recognition rate is 98.83%, with maximum 99.52% and minimum 96.91%. We also conducted a leave-one-user-out cross validation, the averaged overall recognition rate is 83.71%, with maximum 94.62% and minimum 49.53%. Accuracy of leave-one-user-out cross validation strongly depends on users' behavior. If a user's behavior is very similar to another one, his/her accuracy will be relatively higher. When we built a shared classifier with all participant's data, the performance was 98.42% recognition rate in a 5-fold cross validation. The confusion matrix of the shared classifier is shown at Table 1.

DISCUSSION

The performance evaluation of FlickBoard shows a satisfying result with usage data collected from a variety of participants. Because our implementation is based on RDF, it is very easy to adapt to new user behavior with a small amount of training data. In this section, we discuss user behavior, limitations and possible improvements of this prototype.

Observation of User Behavior

All of the participants used only one finger to move cursors without any instructions. Participants reported that they directly adapted their previous experience of using a traditional touchpad, so they used only one finger to touch on the surface of FlickBoard. While we expected most of the users would rest their fingers on the surface of the keyboard, we observed that a large part (19 out of 30) of the users lifted their left hand while using touchpad function(see Figure 3.B). None of the participants could explain the cause of this behavior. Our explanation is that users may treat the whole keyboard as a long touchpad so they remove all the obstacles before using it. Although one-third of the participants did not lift their non-dominant hands while using trackpad, the overall correctness of our classifier remain high (98%), so it is believed that the classifier can distinguish touch from typing whether users rest their non-dominant hands on the keyboard or not. In the meanwhile, most of the users tried to use the touchpad in a very small area, about 3x3 cm for shorter movement. 20 of 30 users operated the cursor on the center area of the keyboard, 9 users operated on the center of the right side, the other 1 user operated on the bottom of right side.

Uneven Touch Surface

Many users reported that the surface of FlickBoard is too uneven to perform smooth cursor pointing operations. The user's fingers may get stuck between the key caps, which make it harder to move his finger to the desired position. This drawback can be solved with some physical modification, such as adding a mechanical structure to lift the case of a Chiclet keyboard to the top of key caps, forming a flat and smooth platform for users to perform a surface operation.

Higher Frame Rate and Resolution

The frame rate of the current prototype may be too low for some time-critical interactions. There are two major bottlenecks of current implementations: sampling speed of the lock-in amplifier and the speed of MCU. Currently, sampling speed of the lock-in amplifier is bounded by two factors: the RC time constant of RC low-pass filter and sampling speed of ADC. Both of them can be improved by using better implementation options, which require modification of the hardware design. On the other hand, we can save more MCU computing power by dividing the raster scanning process into two stages. We can scan a lower resolution image first, calculate possible touch blobs position with it, and perform a higher resolution raster scanning around touched blobs. This modified process is faster in most of the cases (the number of touched blobs < 5), and does not sacrifice precision. As a result, the frame rate can be higher without modifying the hardware setup.

CONCLUSION

We built a prototype to combine a trackpad and a keyboard into a single interaction area and designed a system that can automatically switch between trackpad mode and typing mode with very high accuracy. Furthermore, our system can be adapted to a new user only with small amount of training data (about 6 minutes). Currently, we only enable pointing and 2-finger scrolling gestures in trackpad mode. In the future, we are planning to implement a gesture recognizing system to recognize more multi-touch gestures, such as, swipe, and pinch to enable more functions on our system.

ACKNOWLEDGEMENTS

We gratefully acknowledge helpful comments and suggestions from the Associate Chair, and the anonymous reviewers. This study was partially supported by the National Science Council, Taiwan, under grant NSC103-2218-E-004 -002.

REFERENCES

1. Fallot-Burghardt, W., Fjeld, M., Speirs, C., Ziegenspeck, S., Krueger, H., and Lubli, T. Touch&type: a novel pointing device for notebook computers. In *NordiCHI'06* (2006), 465–468.
2. Habib, I., Berggren, N., Rehn, E., Josefsson, G., Kunz, A., and Fjeld, M. Dgts: Integrated typing and pointing. INTERACT '09, Springer-Verlag (Berlin, Heidelberg, 2009), 232–235.
3. Rekimoto, J. Smartskin: An infrastructure for freehand manipulation on interactive surfaces. CHI '02, ACM (New York, NY, USA, 2002), 113–120.
4. Rekimoto, J. Thumbsense: Automatic input mode sensing for touchpad-based interactions. CHI EA '03, ACM (New York, NY, USA, 2003), 852–853.
5. Taylor, S., Keskin, C., Hilliges, O., Izadi, S., and Helmes, J. Type-hover-swipe in 96 bytes: A motion sensing mechanical keyboard. CHI '14, ACM (New York, NY, USA, 2014), 1695–1704.

ExtensionSticker: A Proposal for a Striped Pattern Sticker to Extend Touch Interfaces and its Assessment

Kunihiro Kato
Meiji University
Nakano, Tokyo, Japan
kunihiro162@gmail.com

Homei Miyashita
Meiji University
Nakano, Tokyo, Japan
homei@homei.com

ABSTRACT
In this paper, we propose a striped pattern sticker called ExtensionSticker that allows a touch input to be transferred from an external source by simply attaching the sticker to a touch panel. This allows the user to input touches or continuous scrolling actions by touching a sticker printed with stripes of conductive ink, without directly touching the touch panel. This method could be applied to the sides or back of a touch panel, or even the surface upon which a device is located as a touch interface, allowing us to freely construct interfaces in shapes matching the demands of the user. This paper also reports the results of evaluation experiments conducted to assess the recognition accuracy of scroll and tap actions using the proposed method.

Author Keywords
Striped pattern sticker; continuous touch input; conductive ink; capacitive touch panel.

ACM Classification Keywords
H.5.2. Information Interfaces and Presentation : User Interfaces Input Devices and Strategies.

INTRODUCTION
In recent years, devices equipped with touch panels, such as smartphones and tablets, have spread widely. These devices allow users to have more direct control over the devices themselves by allowing them to touch the screen with a finger or a touch pen. In addition, since these devices allow for creating interfaces with input buttons in arbitrary positions on the display, it is possible to adapt interfaces for use in different applications. Many studies are already being performed in relation to touch interfaces, such as methods for extending input interfaces and tangible interfaces to be used with touch panel terminals like smartphones outside the display [5, 3, 10]. However, the interfaces used in these studies require specialized objects and are for use in specific applications. An environment that allows a user to create an interface for himself has not yet been realized. Thus, it is impossible to extend an interface over a more accomplished application's interface.

CHI 2015, April 18 - 23 2015, Seoul, Republic of Korea

http://dx.doi.org/10.1145/2702123.2702500

Today, conductive inks are gaining attention as a method that can be used in prototyping [9]. Conductive inks are inks that have electrically conductive properties. By using this type of ink in a ballpoint pen or a home inkjet printer, we can easily create electrical circuits on paper.

In this paper, we propose the ExtensionSticker, a sticker that allows us to extend touch interfaces by simply attaching it to a capacitive touch panel (Figure 1). Using conductive ink to print a striped pattern and attaching it to a portion of a touch panel, we can transfer a touch input from the sticker to the touch panel. This allows us to use the sides and backs of a smartphone, as well as desktop surfaces, walls, and any other surface as a touch interface. This method is not limited to receiving a touch input at a specific position, but it can also receive continuous inputs such as scroll commands within the area of the attached sticker. Since the ExtensionSticker can be easily created with home-use inkjet printers, users can freely extend touch devices by creating the interfaces they need.

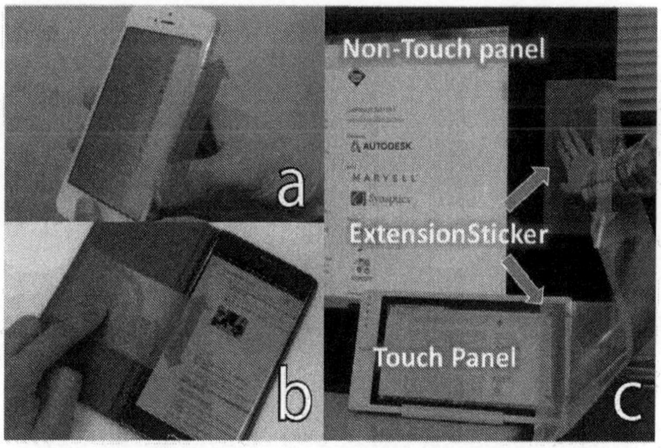

Figure 1. a) Smartphone side-input controls, b) rotation-scrolling control conversion, and c) touch controls for non-touch-panel displays.

RELATED WORK
Approaches to interfaces using capacitive touch panels include Rekimoto's SmartSkin [1]. Smartphones and tablets are also among the many interface studies that use capacitive touch panels [3, 7, 10]. Our proposed method can generate continuous touch inputs due to scrolling operations, for example, without moving interfaces that are arrayed with the conductive parts directly.

Studies employ a variety of approaches for extending smartphone input methods. With Clip-on Gadgets, clips with buttons or dials can be attached to the device and used as input interfaces [5]. In this system, a piece of conductive rubber is positioned on the clips attached to the device, making contact with the edge of the device's screen. When the user performs an action such as pressing a button, a touch input is recognized using changes in capacitance. It can also generate a continuous touch input by an outside attachment to the device. As compared with this study, our proposed method allows a user to create a variety of interfaces easily using an inkjet printer.

Midas proposes an environment that allows the user to create touch interfaces for applications that can be controlled by those interfaces [8]. The method for making touch interfaces using conductive ink is also proposed by [4, 6]. In this study, we propose a method for extending touch interfaces without any software interposition.

EXTENSIONSTICKER

Our method uses a sticker with a striped pattern printed using conductive ink and attached to a touch panel (Figure 2). The ExtensionSticker comprises three portions: the input portion, which the user touches directly; the output portion, which is attached to the area that generates touch events; and the connecting portion, which connects the other two portions. The user can transfer a touch input to the portion attached to the sticker (output portion) by touching part of the sticker (input portion). Multiple thin lines less than 1 mm thick each are tightly grouped. When a portion of these lines is touched with a finger simultaneously, it generates a change in capacitance sufficient for touch recognition.

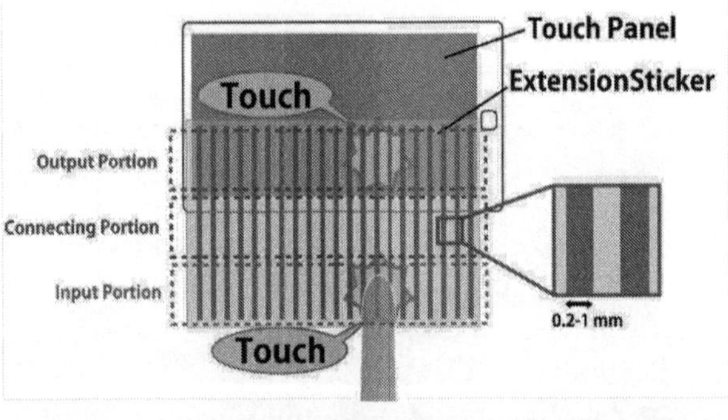

Figure 2. A Striped Pattern Printed Using a Conductive Ink.

The ExtensionSticker can be applied not only for receiving touch inputs at specific locations, but also at points that allow for continuous inputs, such as scroll operations. Then, the quality of the touch input can be controlled, so to obtain "finer accuracy through stripe pattern thickness or spacing", as the input to a capacitive touch panel is determined by the input position in the contact region.

Thus, when the finger is tilted while held down, the contact surface shifts and the touch input changes subtly. Figure 3 shows how this is being done, comparing the amount of movement on the x-axis as the finger moved left and right on the touch panel and sticker, so to generate a touch input.

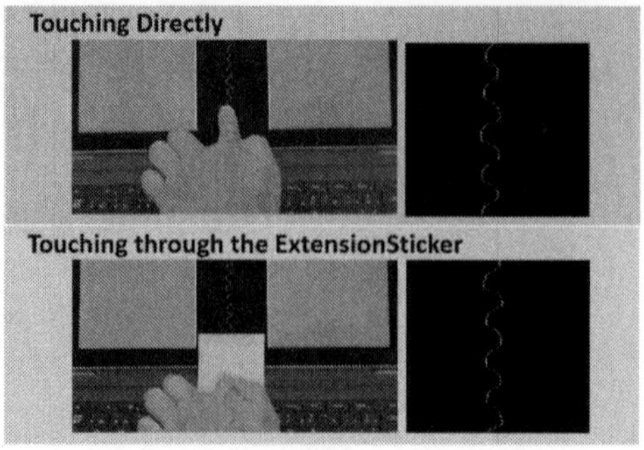

Figure 3. An example of tilting with a finger held down.

APPLICATIONS

Changing the form of the touch input area of the ExtensionSticker allows a user to create a variety of touch interfaces. Here, we describe three extension possibilities: touch input position extension, input operation extension, and input method extension. Figure 4 shows an overview of each method.

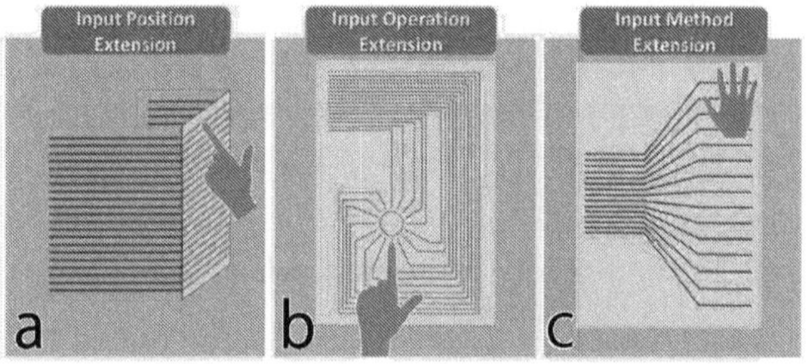

Figure 4. Extension methods for the input interface: a) input position extension, b) input operation extension, c) input method extension.

First, we attach the output portion of a sticker to a touch panel and then curve the sticker such that the input portion is on a side surface of the device (Figure 1 a). This allows us to use the side (or back) of a smartphone as a touch interface. Users can scroll through content on a web browser without blocking the screen with a finger. This method is also effective for a variety of other devices. For example, this could be applied to devices with small displays, such as smart watches, so to extend the input interface to the band portion.

Second, by changing the position of the input portion and connection portion of the printed sticker, we can extend the user's input operations (Figure 1 b). For example, as in the figure, the input area can be placed in a circular shape at a constant interval, and then connected to the output portion. As the user performs a circular operation by tracing the input portion with a finger, continuous up and down touch inputs can be generated.

Finally, by changing the printed spacing of the input portion and output portion of the sticker, we can extend the touch input method (Figure 1 c). Even if the conductors positioned on the input portion are separated, they can be combined into a single touch input on the output portion, meaning that if the user touches the necessary lines simultaneously, this action can generate a touch event. We can use this to transform a touch operation performed with the palm of the user's hand into a fingertip touch operation. For example, we can display the smartphone screen on a large display and connect the two displays with a sticker to transform large horizontal touches on the display to simulated scrolling. In the figure, an input is transferred from a sticker attached to a large non-touch panel display to a tablet device.

EVALUATION

It is necessary to ensure that each conductive line is thin enough to not generate a touch input through touching a stand-alone line, and the spacing between every two lines is tight enough to generate a touch input through touching multiple lines. So, we conducted an experiment to evaluate recognition accuracy of tap and scroll operations using the ExtensionSticker.

The experiment involved 10 participants, all of them were university undergraduate and graduate students with an experience in using smartphones. Assuming the size of a human finger, we attached the portion of a sticker that is 10.0 mm thick to the touch panel as the output portion. The experiment was conducted for stickers with striped patterns having different combinations of line thickness (0.2, 0.4, 0.6, 0.8, and 1.0 mm) and line spacing (0.5, 1.0, 1.5, and 2.0 mm). We limit the line thickness to 0.2 mm, because of the risk of disconnection when lines of conductive ink are printed with thickness of less than 0.1 mm; we limit the line length to 60.0 mm. The ExtensionStickers were printed on PET transparencies using silver nanoparticle ink (Mitsubishi Paper Mill, part number NBSIJ-MU01), and were attached to the display using a 10.0 mm wide double-sided tape.

In the tap operations, the participants tapped on specific locations on each sticker. Recognition mistakes are recognized as errors, and the recognition rate was recorded. Each participant performed the tap operations 20 times for each sticker. In all the experiments, line thickness and spacing patterns were given in random order (Figure 5 left).

In the scroll operations, a bar that moves at a constant speed from the left edge to the right edge of the display was demonstrated. The participants performed scroll operations on the sticker using the bar's location as a guide. Interruptions in a touch input task when the moving bar was between the start and end positions were recognized as errors, and the recognition rate was recorded. Scroll operations were performed 10 times for each sticker (Figure 5 right). Each experiment was performed using MS SurfacePro 3.

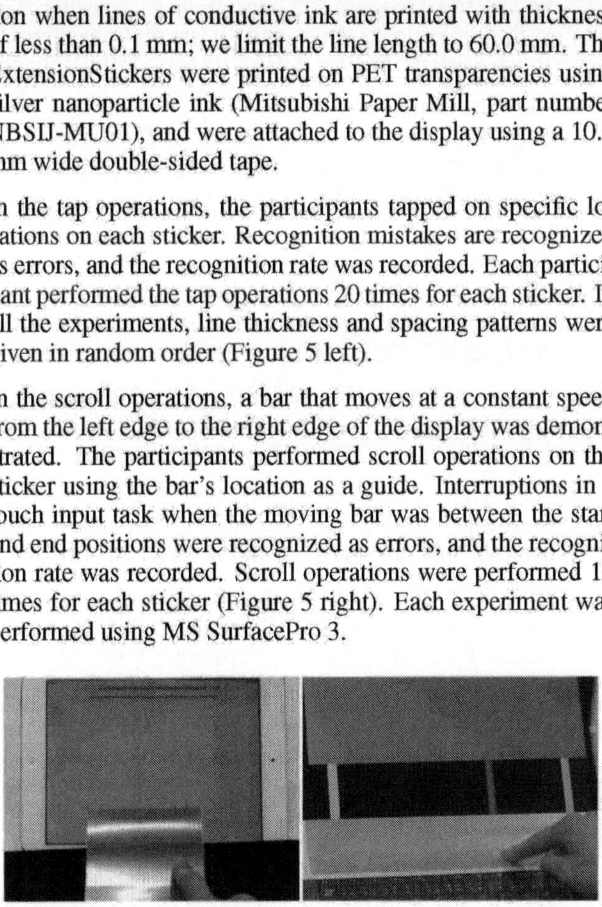

Figure 5. Experiments: tap operation experiment (left), scroll operation experiment (right).

Results

The results of the experiments are shown in Figure 6 (top). In the tap operations, the 0.5 mm spacing achieved over 97% accuracy for line thicknesses of 0.2, 0.6, and 1.0 mm. 1.0 mm line spacing also achieved recognition with accuracy above 90% for line thicknesses 0.4 and 0.6 mm, with significant variance in the results.

In the scroll operations, recognition was high for the 0.5 mm spacing (95%) and 1.0 mm spacing (90%) regardless of line thickness. Of these, all striped patterns with line thickness of 0.4-1.0 mm achieved high recognition accuracy of close to 99%.

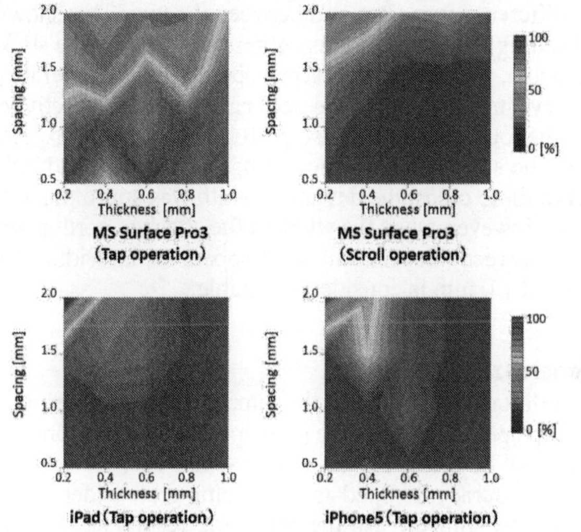

Figure 6. Results: tap operation experiment using MS SurfacePro 3 (upper left), scroll operation experiment using MS SurfacePro 3 (upper right), tap operation experiment using iPad mini & iPhone (bottom).

Discussion

In the tap operation experiment, our results show that the recognition accuracy dropped as the spacing grew wider for each device. Even of the combinations of spacing and thickness that resulted in high recognition in the scroll operation experiment, some patterns resulted in lower accuracy in the tap operation experiment, leading to wide variation in results. Since touching multiple thin lines generates a single touch input, we can assume that there is variation in touch recognition accuracy due to changes in the areas of the contact region caused by the finger of different finger sizes and at different tap locations.

When a touch input is performed on a capacitance touch panel through a conducting material such as a metallic foil, if the contacting surface is approximately the size of the finger, this may be recognized as a touch. However, as the contact surface becomes wider, the touch position is not constrained to a single point and therefore cannot be controlled. In the ExtensionSticker, we allowed the control of the touch position on the x-axis (the vertical direction of the striped pattern) by positioning the conducting material in a striped formation. However, we cannot currently control the y-axis of the striped pattern (the horizontal direction of the striped pattern), so the input position on the y-axis can change based on the width of the portion where the sticker is attached.

We then performed comparison of a scrolling operation using a sticker of 0.6 mm line thickness and 0.5mm spacing, which had the highest recognition rate, and performing it by touching the touch panel directly. The results show that the average movement on the y-axis per frame for the sticker was 0.35 px (approximately 0.04 mm), and the average of the largest deviations was 2.25 px (approximately 0.27 mm). When performing a scroll operation through touching the touch panel directly, the average movement on the y-axis per frame was 0.43 px (approximately 0.05 mm), and the average of the largest deviations was 3.11 px (approximately 0.37 mm). Little difference was observed between the two. This shows that by setting the width of the portion for attaching the sticker to 10.0 mm, we can perform scroll operations with operation accuracy similar to that of the performance when directly touching the touch panel. We also performed the scroll experiment with the same tasks for the settings of 0.4, 0.6, and 0.8 mm, but in these cases, the deviation width was approximately 1.0 mm. However, when the width of the attached portion was 0.4 mm, the recognition accuracy dropped, so the width between 0.6 and 1.0 mm is considered suitable.

Generalization

In addition, we conducted the same evaluation experiment for the tap operations with five participants using iPad and iPhone (Figure 6 bottom). The results show that each device's recognition accuracy dropped as the spacing grew wider and thickness grew thinner. As the following results show, the proposed method also allows the user to operate other devices in high recognition accuracy.

We tested the scroll operations on the ExtensionSticker attached to a variety of touch devices (iPad1 &2 &mini, iPhone5, Samsung Galaxy note edge & Gear Fit, ASUS Nexus7, Sony VAIO Pro11 &Type T, MS Surface1 &3) using some high recognition accuracy parameters. We attached the ExtensionSticker with the spacing of 0.5 and 1.0 mm, and thickness of 0.2-1.0 mm. While for all the parameters, ExtensionSticker allow us to control scrolling operations on all these devices, recognition accuracy occasionally dropped for certain thickness and spacing combinations. Thus, it is necessary to set the right condition parameters for each device. In this study, a successful touch input occurs on the ExtensionSticker even if there is a distance of several dozen centimeters between the input and the ExtensionSticker's output. However, the touch input is not transferred properly if the distance is longer. Furthermore, a touch input can occur unintentionally in the wiring area. This problem could be resolved by covering the exposed area with a relatively thick insulating material.

CONCLUSION

We gave a demonstration of the proposed application at UIST 2014, and in this study, we also presented results of recognition accuracy assessment in scrolling and tapping operations using a sticker. While we showed a number of application examples, this method can also be applied to a variety of other devices with capacitive touch panels [2].

This method could be used to freely create interactions for a variety of devices in our daily lives based on our needs. The ExtensionSticker reported in this paper used silver nanoparticle ink as the conductive ink for printing the striped pattern. This made it difficult to see the portion of the display attached with the striped pattern. However, this problem could be solved using transparent conductive inks. Furthermore, the printed surface degraded during use, necessitating the need for finding more suitable materials. Currently, this method only allows control of the touch input in one direction. Future improvements also include investigating how to control the touch input at arbitrary locations in an x-y plane.

REFERENCES

1. Jun Rekimoto: SmartSkin: An Infrastructure for Freehand Manipulation on Interactive Surfaces, In *Proc. CHI 2002*, pp.113-120, 2002.
2. Kunihiro Kato, Homei Miyashita: Extension Sticker: A Method for Transferring External Touch Input Using a Striped Pattern Sticker, In *Adjunct Proc. UIST 2014*, pp.59-60, 2014.
3. Liwei Chun, Stefanie Muller, Anne Roudaut, Patrick Baudisch: CapStones and ZebraWidgets: Sensing Stacks of Building Blocks, Dials and Sliders on Capacitive Touch Screens, In *Proc. CHI 2012*, pp.2189-2192, 2012.
4. Nan-Wei Gong, Amit Zoran, Joseph A. Paradiso: Inkjet-printed Conductive Patterns for Physical Manipulation of Audio Signals, In *Adjunct Proc. UIST 2013*, pp.13-14, 2013.
5. Neng-Hao Yu, Sung-Sheng Tsai, I-Chun Hsiao, Dian-Je Tsai, Meng-Han Lee, Mike Y. Chen, Yi-Ping Hung: Clip-on Gadgets: Expanding Multi-touch Interaction Area with Unpowered Tactile Controls, In *Proc. UIST 2011*, pp.367-372, 2011.
6. Simon Olberding, Nan-Wei Gong, John Tiab, Joseph A. Paradiso, Jürgen Steimle: A Cuttable Multi-touch Sensor, In *Proc. UIST 2013*, pp.245-254, 2013.
7. Sven Kratz, Tilo Westermann, Michael Rohs, Georg Essl: CapWidgets: tangile widgets versus multi-touch controls on mobile devices, In *Proc.CHI 2011*, pp.1351-1356, 2011.
8. Valkyrie Savage, Xiaohan Zhang, Bjorn Hartmann: Midas: Fabricating Custom Capacitive Touch Sensors to Prototype Interactive Objects, In *Proc. UIST 2012*, pp.579-588, 2012.
9. Yoshihiro Kawahara, Steve Hodges, Benjamin S. Cook, Cheng Zhang, and Gregory D. Abowd: Instant Inkjet Circuits: Lab-based Inkjet Printing to Support Rapid Prototyping of UbiComp Devices, In *Proc. UbiComp 2013*, pp.363-372, 2013.
10. Yvonne Jansen, Pierre Dragicevic, Jean-Daniel Fekete: Tangible Remote Controllers for Wall-Size Displays, In *Proc. CHI 2012*, pp.2865-2847, 2012.

MUBox: Multi-User Aware Personal Cloud Storage

Michael Nebeling, Matthias Geel, Oleksiy Syrotkin and Moira C. Norrie
Department of Computer Science, ETH Zurich
{nebeling,geel,norrie}@inf.ethz.ch

ABSTRACT
Personal cloud services such as Dropbox are used increasingly to support collaborative work, even though they typically have poor support for tracking files and users' activities and collaborators often rely on other communication channels to be notified of changes. We present a meta-cloud storage service, *MUBox*, that, independent of a particular cloud storage service, provides improved support for collaboration. First, users can switch to activity views that list user activities rather than files, which is an example of an increasingly available feature in popular cloud storage clients. Second, MUBox introduces multi-user aware folder views that embed information on the last changes performed by collaborators. These folder views are enhanced based on a new concept of shadow files which act as placeholders for files that have been moved or renamed. A user study (N=16) with realistic folder exploration tasks shows that activity views have a significant effect on the accuracy and confidence of users in workspace awareness tasks, while shadow files significantly improve the speed, accuracy and confidence of users in traceability tasks. We describe how existing services could implement these features as well as a new concept for *voting* on changes to shared folders that could improve asynchronous collaboration.

Author Keywords
personal cloud storage; collaborative work; workspace awareness; file traceability.

ACM Classification Keywords
H.5.2. User Interfaces: Interaction styles

INTRODUCTION
Personal cloud storage services were developed to enable users to synchronise their personal data across devices. However, they are nowadays often used for sharing files with friends and colleagues and even for collaborative work in professional settings. Many cloud services let a user share an entire folder with one or more other users. The folder becomes visible in the other users' workspaces, where they can add or modify files and subfolders. While there are some differences in how various cloud services treat the original owner of the file and the rest of the group, there is no explicit role management and any user can perform delete, rename or move actions. As the number of collaborators grows, it becomes more difficult to be aware of changes and track activities.

CHI 2015, April 18–23 2015, Seoul, Republic of Korea
Copyright 2015 ACM 978-1-4503-3145-6/15/04...$15.00.
http://dx.doi.org/10.1145/2702123.2702233

Based on our own experiences of using a shared Dropbox folder as the basis for collaboration in a European project, we identified a number of common problems. The project involves more than 25 people from 8 different organisations spread across Europe. The team decided to use a shared Dropbox folder as a repository for documentation, deliverables and various forms of media. Given the fairly large number of contributors, the level of activity in the shared folder is high, and it is difficult to track the actions of the other project members. Not everyone is able to closely follow the evolution of the shared folder and the more time that elapses since the last check, the more challenging it becomes to understand the changes. Specifically, we encountered five main problems:

1. **Lack of overview of specific collaborators' activities**: It is difficult to keep track of the activities of other users, especially when multiple users are responsible for changes.
2. **Tracking the origin of files**: When a new file or folder appears, it is not clear whether it has been uploaded (created), copied from another location, or just renamed. While some cloud storage providers list the user responsible for the last modification, the actual activity is often not clear.
3. **Tracking files that have disappeared**: Likewise, if a particular file or folder is not at its original location, it may have been deleted, moved or renamed.
4. **Hesitation to delete or otherwise modify a shared folder**: Even though everyone is entitled to make modifications, collaborators are often reluctant to do so and prefer to limit their activities to their own files. This problem can lead to an unwieldy folder structure over time [1, 14].
5. **Need for external communication channels**: Email is often used to alert users to activities.

In this paper, we present *MUBox*—a meta-cloud storage service that addresses these problems based on a small set of new features for asynchronous collaborative use. A key goal in designing MUBox was to alleviate Problem 1 by raising collaborators' workspace awareness which is integral and critical to successful collaborative work [5, 13]. We introduce multi-user aware folder views that embed information on the last changes of users. We specifically decided to focus on changes to file locations and filenames, rather than changes to file contents. We believe these constitute the most important activities that users need to become aware of in shared folders. As another way of supporting this, we introduce activity views that are activity-centric folder views showing a history of users' activities rather than the typical list of files.

We tackled Problems 2 and 3 by supporting the user's ability to establish a provenance relationship between files using backward and forward traceability mechanisms. We are primarily concerned with coarse-grained, file-level traceability where traces point to old or new locations of the files. Summarising the history of a file or identifying all provenance relationships based on different versions as done in [10] was deliberately left out of scope. In a shared folder, delete, rename and move activities are more disruptive to collaborative work than if a file was updated or copied. We develop the concept of shadow files to show relationships between files and users' activities that would otherwise not be clearly visible. Shadow files are placeholders for files that have been moved or renamed, so that no files appear missing to other users. Backward traces will point to previous locations of the files. Thus, tracking the origin of files should become easier.

We approached Problems 4 and 5 by introducing voting mechanisms with automatic notifications as a way of encouraging all users to modify shared folders. This can be done using two different strategies, inspired by common practices in version control systems. In the first strategy, a user can perform changes that may be reverted if other users reject them. In the second strategy, users may suggest changes, but no changes will be carried out unless approved by other users. In either case, no external communication is necessary as users will automatically be alerted via in-built notifications. In particular, users can delete files without fear that someone may still need the file or may not be aware of the deletion.

We begin by presenting the background to our work, followed by a detailed description of MUBox. Then we present the implementation and define a cloud service abstraction to make sure that our proposal is independent of current providers and make it easier for future developers to implement the concepts. Finally, we present an initial user study with 16 participants that evaluates activity views and shadow folders. The results show that activity-centric folder views significantly increase users' confidence and accuracy, but not efficiency, in understanding the actions of collaborators. On the other hand, shadow files significantly improve users' confidence, accuracy and speed in understanding file-to-file relationships

BACKGROUND

Insufficient visibility of the activities of collaborators is one of the major problems in information sharing [18]. A previous study [17] reports that the lack of notifications and lack of visibility are some of the biggest problems in file sharing systems. More recent work [16] investigates user experience with services such as Dropbox and Google Docs for multiple collaboration scenarios. The interviewed users complained about insufficient visibility of collaborators' activities and difficulties in being aware of the parts of the shared folder for which one is responsible. In [12], it was reported that users experience problems understanding the functionality of cloud providers because they have inaccurate conceptual models of the cloud. The authors propose design guidelines that cloud services should adhere to in order to become more accessible to users: notifying the user when a given file was last accessed; adding visual status indicators of syncing; phrasing user messages and labels accurately and unambiguously. The authors also argue that vendors need to work on a new conceptual model of cloud storage instead of trying to exploit a familiar paradigm, such as a file system or web-based collaboration application, in a new setting. Another study [14] investigating users' behaviour in group information repositories revealed that users almost exclusively touch files they have created themselves and are particularly reluctant to delete files that could be useful to someone else in the future. Such behaviour can result in clutter and frustrate users. One approach to overcome the particular problem of deletion was explored in GrayArea [1], which extends the folder view with a grey area at the bottom where users may drag unimportant files. GrayArea was shown to effectively reduce folder clutter, but requires major changes to common file system user interfaces and workflows.

Workspace awareness is known to be an important requirement for supporting productivity in collaborative work [5]. In the area of distributed software engineering many different ways of promoting awareness have been studied with the common aim of enhancing a person's understanding of the activities of collaborators, as well as increasing knowledge about tasks and artefacts [13]. Many of these are text-based: email, mailing lists, chats (instant messaging or group chats), RSS feeds and wikis. Collaborators frequently use version check-in logs in configuration management systems and commit logs in revision control systems to familiarise themselves with the actions of other users. Many proposed solutions use some form of tagging. For example, Jazz.net, CASS [9] and Augur [7] all use tags to help developers navigate the code and subscribe to notifications on topics of interest.

Others mainly focused on exploring the relations between software project entities and visualising them, e.g. Rational Team Concert [3]. Here, visualisations provide a view of the project that users can quickly grasp, thereby improving traceability of software components. The authors argue that this, in turn, helps to increase developers' awareness. Another approach is to track developers' interactions. For example, FASTDash [2] provides information about which class and method a given developer has currently checked out and is working on, signalling potential conflicts. Information about developer interactions and artefact relations can be combined. For example, Team Tracks [4] marks more frequently accessed parts of the code as more important. Further, in Mylyn [11], a notion of time was added so that more recently accessed artefacts are given an increased weighting.

In the domain of personal file sharing, providing information on file provenance, i.e. on the history of ownership and operations performed on the file [8, 15], is considered a key factor for improving awareness. Various systems that capture and manage provenance information have been developed, some of them application-specific. For example, Chimera [6] was developed for use with large scientific data repositories, storing data derivation procedures and derived

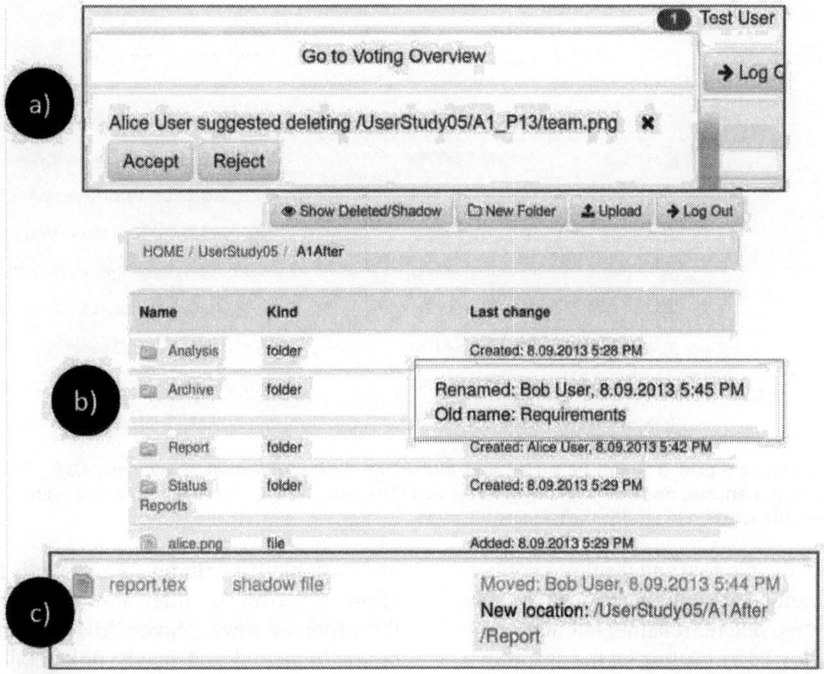

Figure 1. Main features of MUBox: a) notifications on changes *suggested* by other users, b) multi-user aware folder views highlighting last changes by others, e.g. Bob renamed Requirements to Archive, and c) shadow file with trace, e.g. Bob moved report.tex to the Report folder.

data and letting users query the data and provenance metadata using a domain-specific language. In contrast, FiPS [15] is an application-independent provenance system that could be added on top of any conventional file system and implemented as an operating system kernel module. It manages files as well as file provenance information by intercepting file system calls used to collect metadata that let it recreate the history of a file. Such provenance data was also used by Karlson et al. [10] who developed a copy-aware file system by hooking into the operating system and office applications to capture what they refer to as "copy events", e.g. Save As, Attach and Copy/Paste. Using this information, they constructed a new folder visualisation that included provenance relationships on different versions of files. Users found the new folder visualisation especially useful to make sense of unfamiliar data, e.g. their co-worker's folder.

Our first step was to review some of the most popular personal cloud services: Dropbox, Google Drive and OneDrive to identify typical shortcomings. As an example, in some services, when a user renames a file, it is regarded as newly created, and the file with the old name is displayed as deleted. Possible problems encountered by collaborators are, firstly, that the old file is marked as deleted, thus possibly confusing the rest of the team, and, secondly, that there is no apparent connection between the old and new filenames. Users would need to restore the old file first and compare it with the new file to see if they actually have the same content. Moreover, for files moved by another user to a different folder, other folders would have to be checked manually or a global search had to be performed.

In summary, cloud storage providers have only begun to add support for collaboration and different providers have opted for different techniques. Google Drive has presence indicators, chatting capabilities and an activity stream. Dropbox allows users to inform collaborators via email without leaving the web interface and also provides a list of events in all of the user's workspace or in a specific shared folder. Given the aforementioned shortcomings, we decided to experiment with new features to improve the folder sharing experience and make awareness of the other users' actions and file traceability easier to achieve.

MUBOX

MUBox (Figure 1) is a meta-cloud storage service with a web-based front-end through which users can access Dropbox and Google Drive accounts. While it resembles common interfaces, it is independent of a particular cloud storage solution and other providers could be easily integrated. MUBox is a lightweight, yet highly configurable, system allowing individual features to be turned on and off as required.

After a user logs in, they are presented with the folder view shown in Figure 1b). A grid with three columns displays the folder structure. The first column, *Name*, contains a list of folders and files ordered alphabetically. For each entry in the list, the second column specifies the *Kind* in terms of four categories: regular file, deleted file, shadow file and shared folder. The *Last change* column can display different information depending on the experimental settings. The minimum functionality is to display the username of the user who made the last change to the entry. If shadow folders and traces are enabled, the column also displays the last operation performed on the file and may also show a backward or forward trace. In the case that a user other than the current user was responsible for the change, that user will also be listed.

If the user clicks on a file row in the grid, the grid header displays a row of buttons signifying file operations. Alterna-

Action	Filename	Username	Date	Details
			From: To:	
move	Summary.docx	Bob User	08.09.2013 5:45 PM	Summary.docx: Moved from /Requirements: Bob User, 08.09.2013 5:45:00 PM
rename	Archive	Bob User	08.09.2013 5:45 PM	Archive: Renamed from Requirements: Bob User, 08.09.2013 5:45:00 PM
move	Presentation.pptx	Alice User	08.09.2013 5:44 PM	Presentation.pptx: Moved from /Presentation: Alice User, 08.09.2013 5:44:49 PM
rename	Final Presentation	Alice User	08.09.2013 5:44 PM	Final Presentation: Renamed from Presentation: Alice User, 08.09.2013 5:44:49 PM
move	report.tex	Bob User	08.09.2013 5:44 PM	report.tex: Moved from /: Bob User, 08.09.2013 5:44:29 PM
move	team.png	Alice User	08.09.2013 5:44 PM	team.png: Moved from /: Alice User, 08.09.2013 5:44:09 PM
copy	report.pdf	Bob User	08.09.2013 5:43 PM	report.pdf: Copied from /: Bob User, 08.09.2013 5:43:49 PM
copy	alice.png	Alice User	08.09.2013 5:43 PM	alice.png: Copied from /: Alice User, 08.09.2013 5:43:31 PM
upload	plot2.svg	Bob User	08.09.2013 5:43 PM	plot2.svg: Added: Bob User, 08.09.2013 5:43:08 PM

Figure 2. Activity views are shown as a grid that can be sorted and filtered by *Action*, *Filename*, *Username*, *Date*, *Details*. Possible actions are: `newfolder`, `upload`, `move`, `copy`, `rename`, `delete`. Details describe activities using verbs, "Created" (for new folder), "Added" (for file upload), "Moved", "Copied", "Renamed", "Deleted", along with the responsible users.

tively, a user may right-click the file row and display a context menu listing the same operations. Usual operations for a file are: download, show versions, delete, rename, cut and copy. Cutting or copying a file followed by pasting let the user move or copy the file to a different folder. For a folder, the operations are: share folder, delete, rename, cut and copy. Clicking a hyperlink displaying the filename starts a download of the file. Clicking a folder name opens that folder.

Below we describe the three main ideas implemented in MUBox to improve awareness, traceability and asynchronous collaboration: activity views, shadow files and voting. One key design goal was to maintain the simplicity. All the proposed collaboration features are either toggable (activity views/shadow files) or can be configured on a per-folder basis (voting). The design rationale is that the new awareness/traceability features should only be shown if the user has a concrete information need, but otherwise they should not increase the complexity of the system in place.

Activity-centric Folder Views

As a first step towards improving awareness, we introduced activity views (Figure 2) that list users' activities rather than files and folders. The user can switch to the corresponding activity view from each folder in order to access the following activity information: the name of the activity, the affected file or folder, the user who made the change, the time of the change, and any relevant details. In the case of a rename, move or copy, the details would include either the source or the destination file or folder. When the user hovers the mouse cursor over the filename, a tooltip displays the relative path to the file at the time the operation was completed. Our design of activity views differs from Dropbox's events or Google Drive's activity stream in two important ways.

First, it is essentially a different view of the folder rather than a log file based on journal-style text entries similar to `Bob renamed Paris.jpg to Eiffel Tower.jpg on 16.04.2014`. Activity-centric folder views are based on grids that show one operation per row and details of each operation in dedicated columns. The grid is both searchable and sortable by column. The search fields for each column allow the user to filter the rows, while sorting controls the order of rows. Since MUbox can distinguish between moved/renamed and newly uploaded files, a user may first filter by action, e.g. `upload`, and then by date to quickly get an overview of files that have been uploaded at a given time.

Second, we decided to present the activity information starting from a given folder and including all subfolders. We think this is a good trade-off as opposed to showing the activities for the entire workspace or limiting the view to only a single folder. The deeper in the folder hierarchy the user descends, the more specific the activity view becomes.

Shadow Files with Backward/Forward Traces

To keep track of deleted files (or folders), some providers such as Dropbox show a placeholder together with the information, "deleted file", at the previous location. We propose to extend this concept to track renamed or moved files and provide a link to the new location. Specifically, MUBox introduces the concepts of shadow files and forward and backward traces, allowing users to explore file provenance.

From the user's point of view, a shadow file is a placeholder used to indicate that a file has been renamed or moved to a different folder. In existing cloud storage services, such files are usually shown as deleted, which misrepresents the activities that resulted in the change and may therefore lead to confusion. Therefore, we explicitly distinguish shadow files from deleted files with the goal of making it clear to the user that a given file is in fact not deleted and exists under a different name or path in the shared folder. The *Show Deleted/Shadow* button shown in Figure 1 lets the user show or hide deleted and shadow files. MUBox lists all files in the same folder view, but visually separates regular files from deleted and shadow files by greying out the latter similar to how many operating systems show hidden files on demand.

Our notion of traces is closely related to shadow files. Figure 3 illustrates the two concepts. Forward traces are attributes of a shadow file that point to the new name or new location of

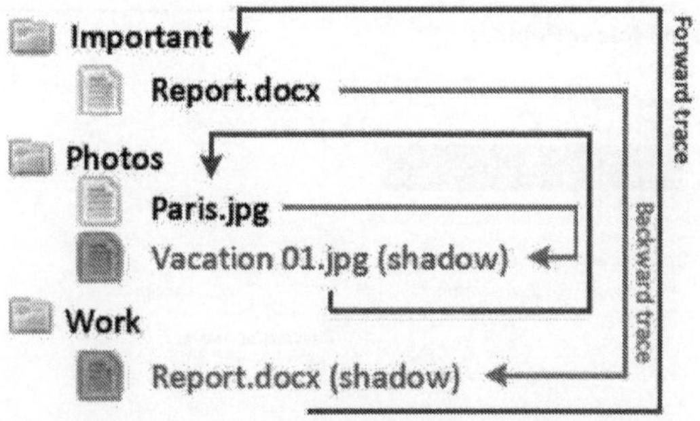

Figure 3. Shadow files are placeholder files shown in gray as part of the folder view. The concept above illustrates forward and backward traces. The file `Vacation 01.jpg` was renamed to `Paris.jpg`, and the forward trace of the corresponding shadow file `Vacation 01.jpg` points to `Paris.jpg`. The file `Report.docx` was moved to the folder `Important`, and a backward trace points back to `Work`.

(a) Forward trace

(b) Backward trace

Figure 4. After moving `report.tex` to a subfolder `Report`, a shadow file is shown at the original location with forward trace and the file at the new location shows a backward trace.

that file and occur after a rename or move operation. Backward traces are links from a current file to its source file. The source file may have been moved, renamed or copied. Thus, using our terminology, a backward trace is either a connection between a regular and a shadow file (in the case of moving or renaming) or between two regular files (in the case of copying). We decided for both a forward trace and a backward trace to provide the user with as complete information as possible. Entering a folder and glancing at the trace information should make it clear whether *new* files have originated from another location or are indeed newly uploaded files. Therefore, preserving both kinds of traces as opposed to only forward traces, makes navigation within the workspace more flexible. A trace is visualised simply as text and a hyperlink in the *Last change* column that tells the user the old or the new location of a file. Forward traces are displayed next to the shadow file to which they correspond (Figure 4(a)). Backward traces are displayed next to the file that was created as a result of a rename, move or copy operation (Figure 4(b)).

Shared Folders with Voting Strategies and Schemes

MUBox also aims to encourage more active asynchronous collaboration. To this end, we propose voting capabilities with an integrated notification system so that users can perform file operations without the fear of interfering with their collaborators' work. We differentiate between voting strategy (determines when a change is applied) and a voting scheme (determines how changes can be rejected/approved). Depending on the voting strategy, the change may be performed immediately, with the possibility of reverting it later, or performed later after approval. Additionally, whenever a user makes a disruptive change (i.e. delete, rename or move) to a file in a shared folder with voting enabled, the other users will receive a notification and may vote immediately or postpone their decision.

We believe that introducing such a voting system will not only increase the visibility of collaborators' activities, but also function as a safeguard and encourage team members to be more active in carrying out folder maintenance tasks, without waiting for the original owners to clean up their files and folders. We refer to the process when votes are collected and evaluated as the "voting process".

Since voting is a rather heavy process in contrast to lightweight aspects of cloud file sharing, it should only be implemented where necessary, for example, for folders that contain deliverables or business-critical files. As a consequence, it can be configured on a per-folder basis and is disabled by default. We decided against taking file and folder ownership into account in the voting process. First, a straightforward approach quickly breaks down when it comes to shared folders since an owner of a folder, i.e. the user that created it, may not necessarily be the one responsible for its content or the most active user of that folder. Second, popular services such as Dropbox have a very basic ownership model typically limited to top-level shared folders rather than subfolders and files, and explicit user actions are required to transfer ownership. For these reasons and based on our experiences with the EU project, we felt that an additional access control layer was not required and might actually work against facilitating easy collaboration, especially among equal project partners and with rapidly evolving folder structures.

Voting Strategies

A voting process is regulated by a voting strategy. We have developed the following two strategies: **1) perform a file operation subject to confirmation**, and **2) suggest a file operation subject to approval.** Strategy 1 performs an operation immediately, notifies other users and starts a voting process. Only if they vote against the operation, is it reverted. We have designed this strategy primarily for small teams with the intention of having minimal impact on existing workflows. Users can still work with their files as usual and the changes become instantly visible. However, notifications and voting in that case can help prevent major changes from going unnoticed and to correct mistakes. Strategy 2 allows any user to suggest an operation. The other users are then notified and the operation is only performed if approved. This strategy is well-suited to model more rigid workflows, for example weekly reviews of changes.

The difference between the two strategies is also reflected in the user interface. If a file is to be renamed with Strategy 1, the context menu option for files says "Rename (voting)". With Strategy 2, "Suggest rename" is displayed instead. Outside of voting-enabled folders, the menu item is simply "Rename". This ensures that users are aware of a) whether voting is enabled and b) if it is, which strategy is in effect. In the following, we will refer to the first strategy as *confirmation* strategy and to the second as *approval* strategy.

Scheme	Strategy	Default Action
Veto (*with* time constraint)	Either	Accept
Percentage (*with* time constraint)	Confirmation	Accept
	Approval	Reject
Percentage (*without* time constraint)	Either	None

Table 1. Voting scheme/strategy combinations ordered from least to most intrusive to optimistic workflows (accepting most voting processes).

Voting Schemes

Complementary to the voting strategies, we offer two distinct voting schemes. A voting scheme is a rule governing the decision on users' votes and when a voting process can be closed and the change either accepted or rejected. We derived the following schemes, which are inspired by well-known decision-making principles: **i) percentage with or without time constraint** and **ii) veto with time constraint**.

The percentage scheme is a variant of the majority vote that *accepts* a vote if the majority of a certain *percentage* of users vote in favour of the change. With that scheme, one can specify the percentage of users that need to participate in a majority vote before it is closed and evaluated. The core idea is to be able to lower the overhead which voting processes often carry with them. For example, a team-wide majority vote (100 % participation rate) might be unproductive in large teams because it can take a long time to collect all the votes. By contrast, having a lower percentage allows a few active users, e.g. core team members, to vote on changes quickly.

In contrast, the veto scheme *rejects* an action as soon as a single person with the power of veto votes against it. In our design of this scheme, any user has the veto power and can thus revert a change immediately. Veto power is particularly useful for teams with a designated leader who assumes the role of guardian or maintainer of a shared folder. If this is the case, the other team members may choose to simply mute the notifications by MUBox for that particular folder.

For both voting schemes, a configurable time constraint specifies a timeout after which a voting process is aborted with a default action. That default action depends on the particular combination of voting strategy/scheme chosen and is summarised in Table 1.

The percentage scheme combined with the confirmation strategy has the default action to accept, whereas the approval strategy defaults to reject if no consensus was reached within the given timeout. The implicit acceptance of changes in the former combination assumes an optimistic workflow and is most effective if most voting processes are likely to get accepted. In this case, a rejection may cause a major interruption to the workflow, which can be used intentionally to send a strong signal to collaborators that there is disagreement. With the veto scheme, the default action is always to accept a change, regardless of the current strategy. Due to its nature, the veto scheme works only in conjunction with a time constraint, whereas the percentage scheme can also be used without any timeout. In the latter case, a decision can only be reached after enough users have voted, making it the most rigid voting process available.

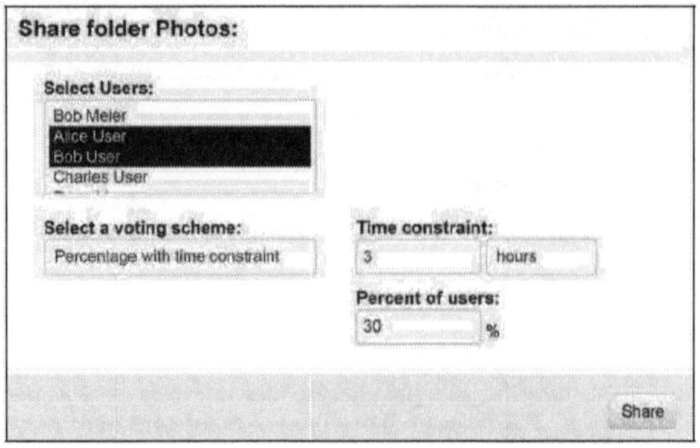

Figure 5. Voting scheme selection while sharing a folder

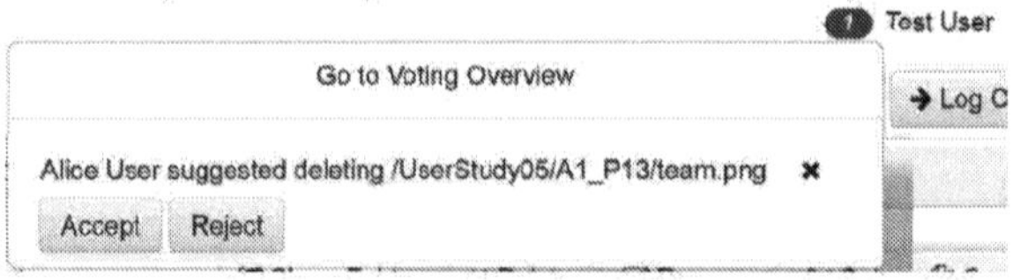

Figure 6. Notification badge and a voting alert dropdown

Sharing Folders and Ownership

MUBox allows any folder to be shared via a context menu. Figure 5 shows the modal dialogue presented to the user at the time of sharing the folder "Photos". The figure shows the selection of Alice and Bob as team members for this particular folder. The selected voting scheme is "Percentage with time constraint" and at least 30 % of the users have to vote on changes within 3 hours. The person who initially shared the folder (the owner) can later change the voting scheme and add or remove collaborators. The other collaborators do not have such privileges.

The choice of the "right" strategy/scheme is ultimately a social rather than a technical issue. Consequently, we do not impose or mandate one particular combination, but rather strive to provide the necessary configuration options to allow team leaders to model a wide range of organisational processes.

Notifications and Voting

After a user initiates a voting process by performing a disruptive operation, the user's vote is saved as a vote in favour of the change and notifications are sent to the collaborators. If they log into MUBox during the voting process, a red notification badge in the upper right corner of the screen informs them about ongoing votes. They can open the notification dropdown and choose to accept or reject the operation, as seen in Figure 6. After the change is accepted or rejected, a notification is sent to the vote initiator. MUBox can also show an overview of all pending voting processes in which the current user can cast a vote or exercise their right of veto.

IMPLEMENTATION

MUBox is implemented as a web application to facilitate deployment in distributed multi-user settings and provide a consistent user experience across different platforms. It com-

Method Name	Description
`getDeltaData(<delta cursor>)`	Retrieves a list of changes.
`createFolder(<path>)`	Creates a folder.
`shareFolder(<path>, <owner>, <user>)`	Shares a folder with another user.
`upload(<parent path>, <file name>)`	Uploads a file to folder.
`copyOrMove(<action>, <from path>, <to path>)`	Copies or moves a file/folder.
`rename(<old path>, <new path>)`	Renames a file/folder.
`delete(<path>)`	Deletes a file/folder.
`undelete(<file>)`	Restores a file/folder.

Table 2. Cloud abstraction methods

prises two components: 1) a service front-end on the client-side, and 2) a server-side web service that hosts the cloud abstraction layer and provides a persistence layer for the application. The service front-end is a client-side JavaScript application developed using AngularJS[1] and UI Bootstrap[2]. The client communicates with the server via HTTP calls to a REST-style interface using JSON for data exchange. The implementation of the web service is based on Spark[3]. Spark's primary abstraction is a route which maps HTTP methods (i.e. GET, POST, DELETE etc.) and URL patterns to callbacks that implement most of the business logic and calls to the cloud abstraction and persistence layer. To ease development, all layers have been implemented in Java and run within the same JVM as the web service. We will now explain each of the layers in more detail.

Cloud Abstraction Layer

To achieve a provider-independent solution, the *CloudStorage* interface provides a cloud storage abstraction for uniform access to vendor-specific protocols and API calls. This allows us to seamlessly switch between different cloud storage providers without having to adapt the web interface. The CloudStorage interface (without authorization) is summarised in Table 2. Each method additionally expects a user parameter which has been omitted for brevity. As proof of concept, we implemented the interface for Dropbox and Google Drive since both offer mature Java SDKs for their services and have gained widespread adoption.

Most interface methods are straightforward and can be easily mapped to existing cloud storage services. The *getDeltaData* method initialises the local copy of the cloud storage folder structure and keeps it synchronised with the underlying cloud storage provider. The first time this method is called, the implementation queries the cloud storage service for the entire folder structure of a user's account. The call also returns a token, i.e. delta cursor in Dropbox and change ID in Google Drive, that can be used in subsequent calls to get only the changes that have taken place since the last call.

A notable challenge arose when *shareFolder* had to be implemented. At the time of writing, Dropbox did not have a public API to share folders programmatically with other users. Even worse, folder metadata retrieved via the official Dropbox API neither indicated with whom this folder has been shared nor if the folder was shared at all. As a workaround, users have to share folders manually via the official Dropbox web interface and then specifically mark those folders as shared in MUBox. On the other hand, folder sharing is supported in Google Drive and the implementation therefore straightforward. Another limitation of the Dropbox API is the inability to restore an entire deleted folder. To restore a folder, one has to recursively restore the files originally stored in this folder and all its subfolders.

Another issues is the unification of file identifiers. In Dropbox, file paths are unique by design and used as identifiers. In Google Drive, however, paths are not unique and a global file id is used instead. We decided to adopt the Dropbox approach and access files and their metadata through our cloud abstraction layer using a combination of a unique path and user ID. To achieve interoperability with Google Drive, we internally maintain a mapping between paths and Drive's file ids, which are passed to Drive API calls when necessary.

As a consequence of adopting unique file paths, there cannot be more than one file with the same name in any given folder. Since this is the case in all major desktop file systems, such behaviour corresponds to the mental model that most end-users have of file structures and is an acceptable tradeoff.

Persistence Layer and Data Model

To realise the back-end of MUBox, we use MongoDB, a document-oriented NoSQL database. MongoDB stores data objects as JSON-like documents in binary format. Documents are grouped into collections which are mainly organisational, i.e. documents contained within them do not need to follow a specific schema. Having a flexible schema while experimenting with the data model allowed us to test our assumptions quickly. Moreover, data is exchanged as JSON, which facilitates integration with the MUBox web application because there is no need for serialisation.

For each user, we store a complete copy of the file hierarchy, i.e. metadata only, in the database. Each file node is stored as a single document in MongoDB. Whenever the folder structure is modified via the MUBox web interface, we update the metadata in the database and call the *CloudStorage* API to propagate the updates to the corresponding storage provider. We do not access the content of files in the cloud storage unless there is a user request to download a file.

To model hierarchical folder structures, the approach of materialised paths is used. For each filedata document, we store the complete path with / as separators including the filename. A single MongoDB query using a regular expression is suf-

[1]http://angularjs.org/
[2]http://getbootstrap.com/
[3]http://www.sparkjava.com/

ficient to select only the files in a given folder or all the descendants of a given folder. During normal interaction with a cloud storage client, users spend considerable time navigating the folder hierarchy. Therefore, looking up file metadata is one of the most frequent database queries. Using materialised paths not only makes querying easy and efficient, but also lets us use the same path in database queries as well as calls into the cloud storage APIs. If a folder is shared, the shared folder hierarchy is replicated for each user with whom the folder has been shared with. This approach made it easy to experiment with different views of the folder structure for each user if necessary.

EVALUATION

We conducted controlled experiments to evaluate users' efficiency, accuracy and confidence using activity views and shadow files with traces. For the voting system, we are planning a deployment of MUBox and a longitudinal study in the context of the EU research project mentioned earlier.

Method

We used a within-subjects design involving two experiments to evaluate 1) activity views and 2) shadow files and traces. Each experiment involved one task with the respective MUBox features turned on and one task with them turned off. We have refrained from direct comparison to existing personal cloud storage services and used MUBox in all tasks for better control. But the off conditions are similar to using Dropbox and hence provide a baseline. Also, we were only interested in comparing task performance within, not between, experiments. The off conditions used the same MUBox config but different tasks, and so results cannot be assumed to be equal.

Experiments and task order were rotated and counterbalanced to reduce carryover effects. Each task required participants to familiarise themselves with a shared folder structure different for each task. Before beginning the task, participants received a printout with a diagram of the folder structure. They were also shown an incomplete folder structure in the MUBox interface and asked to complete it so that it matched the structure on paper. In each task, completing the structure meant they had to create one empty folder and upload two files. The files to be uploaded were provided. The folder hierarchy completion was not part of the task per se, but it was our attempt to familiarise the users with the system and each of the shared folders. Then the actual study started. Assuming that the printout of the folder structure contained the initial hierarchy, the user was demonstrated what this folder structure looked like after two collaborators made changes to some files and folders. The collaborators were always two users with the names Alice and Bob. To save time, we pre-created the folder structure with the changes made. After participants saw the modified folder structure, they were given a questionnaire, and the timing started. Participants needed to use the available features in MUBox to fill in the questionnaire that tested their understanding of exactly what changes took place in the shared folder. When the users reported completion of the task, the timing stopped.

The goals of our experiments were to verify whether the features improved workspace awareness and file traceability. Our approach was to test the time it took to perform the task, the accuracy of the responses and the users' own estimates of their confidence, which they provided in post-task questionnaires. Because of the way the tasks were designed, we could argue that the time it takes to perform the task, as well as the user's confidence and accuracy while performing it, can be signs of whether the user is aware of the activities of the teammates and whether file history is traceable. Although we could obtain such indirect evidence, we cannot claim that the features actually improve awareness or traceability.

Evaluating Activity Views

We have argued that activity views may help users be more aware of others' activities and improve workspace awareness. We expected that the use of activity views would let participants do the task in less time, answer more questions correctly and be more confident in their answers. We developed an awareness questionnaire that contained the names of the collaborators, Alice and Bob, and asked participants to list the file operations each collaborator had performed. In both scenarios used for the tasks, each collaborator performed the following actions: creating a folder, uploading a file, renaming a folder with one file in it, copying a file and moving another file. Participants' answers were considered correct if they specified 5 correct operations per user, including the name of the operation (e.g., "copy") and the destination if applicable (for copying, moving, renaming). If the user listed other changes, they were ignored for the score. Participants received partial points if parts of the answers were correct. Shadow files were disabled for the duration of the two tasks. In the off condition without activity views, the user had to make educated guesses using the normal folder view. For example, if a file with a new name appeared in the shared folder and no other changes were apparent, one could assume that the file was uploaded. If a file with the same name appeared in a different folder, the best guess would be that the file was copied. In the on condition, participants could navigate to the folder's activity view and see the list of changes. All our participants chose to consult activity views for the task.

Evaluating Shadow Files and Traces

Our first goal was to test whether the use of shadow files with traces improves file traceability and lets the user understand a file's immediate history. If this was the case, enabling shadow files should reduce the time it takes to do the task, increase the number of correct answers the users give, and boost the users' confidence in their own correctness. The two test collaborators, Alice and Bob, each made the following changes: creating a folder, uploading a file, copying a file, moving a file, renaming a file and deleting a folder with two files in it. We developed a traceability questionnaire with 5 questions that concerned particular files and asked participants what happened to those files. The questions were about the two files that were renamed, two files that were moved, and the deleted folder. Participants had to select the operation performed on the file and write the name of the user who performed it. In the case of a move or a rename operation, they were also asked for the final name or location of the file. Participants

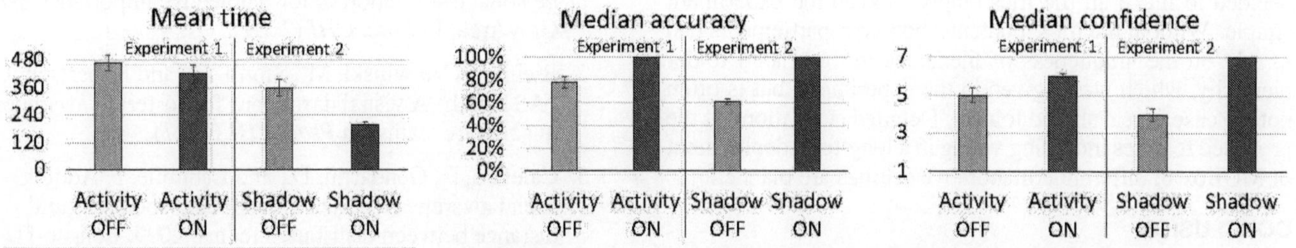

(a) **Mean task completion times** (in seconds) (b) **Median accuracy** (percentage of correct answers) (c) **Median confidence** (user's self-reported confidence, min=1, max=7)

Figure 7. Results of within-subjects experiments (N=16) with activity views and shadow files disabled/enabled (off/on). Error bars show standard error.

could get partial credit if parts of answers were correct. Activity views were disabled for the duration of the two tasks. In the off condition without traces, it was not possible to say conclusively who deleted a given file. Therefore, we accepted "it was deleted" without the username specified.

Results

We had 16 participants (5 female), aged between 23 and 31 (median age: 25.5), all with Dropbox experience, and 12 of them were also Google Drive users. First, Figure 7(a) shows mean completion times for both tasks per experiment. As can be seen, there is a larger difference in the average times for the tasks involving shadow files than the tasks evaluating activity views. Second, Figure 7(b) shows the median accuracy of the users. Using accuracy as a discrete measure, we refer to it as the number of points participants got for their answers. The maximum was 16 for the activity views tasks and 9 for the shadow files tasks. Finally, Figure 7(c) shows the median confidence of the users for all the tasks. In our experiments, confidence was a discrete value, from 1 (least confident) to 7 (most confident). In general, the differences between conditions look more pronounced for the shadow files than for the activity views tasks. In both experiments, the accuracy and confidence ratings were higher and showed much smaller variance in the on conditions.

For significance testing, we used built-in R functions to evaluate the results. The null hypothesis was that the measurements with the feature enabled and without it are not significantly different. The alternative hypothesis was that the measurements are significantly different. The independent variable was the presence of a particular feature. The dependent variables were the task completion time, the participant's accuracy, and the participant's own subjective estimate of their confidence. For ordinal quantities, such as accuracy and confidence, we ran the Friedman rank sum tests. If the p-value obtained in the test was less than 0.05 and therefore significant, we ran the Wilcoxon signed rank test to verify the significance of the result. Since the time it takes to do the task is a continuous measure, we ran the repeated measures ANOVA test as pairwise t-tests with the Holm correction. A p-value < 0.05 meant the result was significant.

For the activity view-related tasks, there was no significant effect on the time it took to do the tasks ($p > 0.22$). However, there were significant effects on confidence ($p < 0.003$) and accuracy ($p < 0.009$). Presence of shadow files and traces had a significant effect on the time ($p < 0.001$). In addition, the effects on confidence ($p < 0.007$) and accuracy ($p < 0.002$) were also significant. While not all results were significant, they are particularly encouraging since users showed more confidence in both tasks with MUBox's features on.

Based on the results, we can conclude that activity views appear to significantly increase people's accuracy and confidence. However, the use of activity views may not be significantly faster. On the other hand, shadow files with traces appear to increase participants' accuracy and confidence. Furthermore, the use of shadow files can be significantly faster.

Users generally agreed that the tasks were realistic (median scores of 6 on a 1-to-7 Likert scale for both activity views and shadow files tasks). This leads us to believe that the results of the study could also have an impact on real-life shared folder maintenance needs. We also asked the users for other subjective estimates in the post-task questionnaires. Here, the users tended to consider both activity views and shadow files effective features to help them do the tasks (median score of 6 for activity views and 6.5 for shadow files). These effectiveness estimates contrast with the ones in the off conditions (median of 4 for activity views and 2.5 for shadow files).

In post-study questionnaires, the users gave generally positive feedback. Specifically, they found that both activity views and shadow files were useful features (median scores of 7 for both). They also generally agreed that existing cloud storage providers should implement features similar to activity views and shadow files (median of 6.5 for both).

Limitations

We decided to do controlled experiments to demonstrate the potential of the proposed features. While users found the tasks to be realistic, there were two limitations.

First, the folder structures in the tasks were similar, but not identical. We especially strived to make them as similar as possible for the two tasks that pertained to the same feature. Each folder hierarchy had 14 files, but could have different numbers of folders (5 in the activity views and 6 in the shadow files tasks). The users were told to assume that filenames were unique within each task.

Second, opening a file that may have been moved or renamed to examine its contents can be one strategy to infer the operation performed on the file. When preparing the study, we decided to make all the files empty to keep the experiment simple. Without the files' contents, however, participants had to rely on the uniqueness of filenames in the shared folder hierarchy, which was a given in the experiment, but is often not the case in real shared folders. Detailed evaluations of the proposed features including voting in a long-term deployment of MUBox in different collaborative settings are planned.

CONCLUSION

There are powerful document management systems (e.g. Alfresco, Huddle, SharePoint) designed to support enterprise document management workflows. MUBox aims to be a lightweight extension of existing cloud storage solutions such as Dropbox–i.e. no version control and no heavyweight configuration in terms of file ownership and access control lists. We considered that the main reason for the vast adoption of Dropbox and the like is that they are simple and easy to use. MUBox adds important features for collaboration without adding unnecessary complexity. It was specifically designed to explore minimally invasive features to support collaborative work on top of existing solutions. We conducted controlled experiments to investigate the effects of two of the features implemented in MUBox and how they aid workspace awareness and file traceability. Our results are encouraging and could have an impact in that developers might be more confident in adopting such features in the future.

First, our study shows that the less invasive features, activity-centric folder views and shadow files with traces, already significantly improve awareness and traceability. Second, an important aspect of MUBox is that it can be tailored to different usage scenarios. That is, more advanced features such as voting and notifications can be turned on/off depending on requirements. Third, our initial user feedback and internal use of MUBox show that change voting schemes are easily understandable and useful. In particular, they align very well with how people work with shared files, but without the need for external communication such as email.

We think of MUBox as a platform for further research on extending personal cloud storage services to collaborative work rather than the final solution. We also note that it is not our intention to replace existing personal cloud storage services. Rather, the idea was to show how a system like MUBox could be designed to implement the proposed features for collaborative use on top of existing services. Therefore, the proposed cloud abstraction layer is an important contribution of this research. It is important in two different ways. First, the abstraction makes sure that MUBox is a vendor-independent solution so that collaborators can benefit from the same workspace awareness, file traceability and voting mechanisms across different providers—for now, this includes Dropbox and Google Drive. Second, the cloud abstraction is also meant to provide guidance to future developers of personal cloud storage services who may want to implement the proposed features.

REFERENCES

1. Bergman, O., Tucker, S., Beyth-Marom, R., Cutrell, E., and Whittaker, S. It's not that important: demoting personal information of low subjective importance using GrayArea. In *Proc. CHI* (2009).
2. Biehl, J., Czerwinski, M., Smith, G., and Robertson, G. FASTDash: A visual dashboard for fostering awareness in software teams. In *Proc. CHI* (2007).
3. Calefato, F., Gendarmi, D., and Lanubile, F. Adding social awareness to Jazz for reducing socio-cultural distance between distributed teams, 2009. Eclipse-IT.
4. DeLine, R., Czerwinski, M., and Robertson, G. Easing Program Comprehension by Sharing Navigation Data. In *Proc. VL/HCC* (2005).
5. Dourish, P., and Bellotti, V. Awareness and coordination in shared workspaces. In *Proc. CSCW* (1992).
6. Foster, I., Vöckler, J., Wilde, M., and Zhao, Y. Chimera: AVirtual Data System for Representing, Querying, and Automating Data Derivation. In *Proc. SSDBM* (2002).
7. Froehlich, J., and Dourish, P. Unifying artefacts and activities in a visual tool for distributed software engineering teams. In *Proc. ICSE* (2004).
8. Jensen, C., Lonsdale, H., Wynn, E., Cao, J., Slater, M., and Dietterich, T. G. The life and times of files and information: a study of desktop provenance. In *Proc. CHI* (2010).
9. Kantor, M., and Redmiles, D. Creating infrastructure for ubiquitous awareness. In *Proc. INTERACT* (2001).
10. Karlson, A. K., Smith, G., and Lee, B. Which version is this?: improving the desktop experience within a copy-aware computing ecosystem. In *Proc. CHI* (2011).
11. Kersten, M., and Murphy, G. C. Using task context to improve programmer productivity. In *Proc. SIGSOFT* (2006).
12. Marshall, C., and Tang, J. That syncing feeling: early user experiences with the cloud. In *Proc. DIS* (2012).
13. Omoronyia, I., Ferguson, J., Roper, M., and Wood, M. A review of awareness in distributed collaborative software engineering. *SPE* (2010).
14. Rader, E. Yours, mine and (not) ours: social influences on group information repositories. In *Proc. CHI* (2009).
15. Sultana, S., and Bertino, E. A file provenance system. In *Proc. CODASPY* (2013).
16. Voida, A., Olson, J. S., and Olson, G. M. Turbulence in the clouds: challenges of cloud-based information work. In *Proc. CHI* (2013).
17. Voida, S., Edwards, W. K., Newman, M. W., Griner, R. E., and Ducheneaut, N. Share and Share Alike: Exploring the User Interface Affordances of File Sharing. In *Proc. CHI* (2006).
18. Xu, J., Zhang, J., Harvey, T., and Young, J. A Survey of Asynchronous Collaboration Tools. *Information Technology Journal* (2008).

DocuViz: Visualizing Collaborative Writing

Dakuo Wang, Judith S. Olson, Jingwen Zhang, Trung Nguyen, Gary M. Olson
University of California Irvine
Irvine, CA USA
{dakuo.wang, jsolson, jingwz2, trungn3, gary.olson}@uci.edu

ABSTRACT
Collaborative writing is on the increase. In order to write well together, authors often need to be aware of who has done what recently. We offer a new tool, DocuViz, that displays the entire revision history of Google Docs, showing more than the one-step-at–a-time view now shown in revision history and tracking changes in Word. We introduce the tool and present cases in which the tool has the potential to be useful: To **authors** themselves to see recent "seismic activity," indicating where in particular a co-author might want to pay attention, to **instructors** to see who has contributed what and which changes were made to comments from them, and to **researchers** interested in the new patterns of collaboration made possible by simultaneous editing capabilities.

Author Keywords
Collaborative writing, co-authoring, groupware, Google Docs, revision histories, information visualizations, collaboration, concurrent editing.

ACM Classification Keywords
H.5.m. Information interfaces and presentation (e.g.; HCI); H.5.3 Group and organizational interfaces; computer-supported cooperative work; synchronous interaction.

INTRODUCTION
Collaborative writing is common and important in many professions [7, 19]. From collaboratively written academic papers to proposals and reports, authors collaborate more than ever before [32]. An earlier study showed that 85% of university writing and company reports are collaboratively written [7]. In software engineering, it is rare that there is only one contributor [4]. This behavior is predicated on the belief that the perceived quality of collaboratively written documents is higher [1], productivity increases [5, 17] and interpersonal relationships are enhanced [30].

CHI 2015, April 18 - 23 2015, Seoul, Republic of Korea
Copyright 2015 ACM 978-1-4503-3145-6/15/04...$15.00
http://dx.doi.org/10.1145/2702123.2702517

In educational settings, although students have mixed attitudes towards collaborative writing [31, 34], many researchers agree that collaborative writing helps with students' writing skills. A study found that when compared to the students who write individually, the students who work collaboratively produced shorter but better documents in terms of fluency, accuracy and complexity [34]. Collaborative writing could promote new ideas and encourage immediate feedback, which is useful for students to learn how to write [34]. It also helps students to learn critical thinking skills and to understand the audience perspective [14, 18]. Collaboration encourages co-authors to share responsibility and ownership; they are more willing to contribute to the entire writing process rather than only reviewing and editing each other's work [7, 20].

There is a long history of providing various views of the emerging document. In a flurry of work on collaborative writing in the 1990s, many explored ways to show the recent history [29], and today both Word [23] and Google Docs [12] offer views of recent changes. Word uses color to denote individuals' contributions, with additions in the text itself and deletions and comments in a side column. They stack together and remain in view until someone accepts them. Google Docs has a different underlying architecture in which changes are tracked and saved in revisions (depending on amount of activity and delays, usually about 30 seconds). These revisions then can be shown by selecting the "revision history" side panel and noting the color of the author who made the changes. In Google Docs, all changes are automatically made, although authors have the ability to revert to an earlier version if they disapprove of a change.

Co-authors may benefit from a richer view of activity over time to see who has been working in which part, how various parts relate, etc. A good visualization allows users to perceive information in context and according to their needs, shown to be more powerful than text-based commentary [11]. By seeing a bigger picture, authors can better infer each other's intentions, more easily reach common ground, and produce higher quality outcomes [3, 6, 22, 26, 35]. Instructors of writing also would likely benefit from a bigger picture of the student's writing process. And, finally, researchers have much to learn about collaborative writing especially now that modern word processors and other authoring tools allow simultaneous writing. Potential uses are described more fully in the closing sections.

There are a few earlier efforts to visualize text written by multiple authors. One that inspired our work is *HistoryFlow,* built to explore the massive co-authorship patterns in Wikipedia [35]. *HistoryFlow* is a tool to visualize how a Wikipedia page is created and edited over time. It uses columns to indicate revisions of a document and different sized sections to represent the size of the changed content and color to indicate authorship. In other words, it shows who did what, how much, and when. The authors suggested that the system could be useful in revealing collaboration patterns, identifying authorship and evaluating contribution evenness. However, *HistoryFlow* has its own limitations. The system is a proprietary IBM product and only worked with Wikipedia revision data. People outside of IBM cannot access it; researchers cannot build on it.

Another related visualization looks at differences between successive versions of a text document, displaying the history as a *revision map,* shown in Figure 1 [33]. The revision map is at the granularity of paragraphs. Color indicates the number of word changes in a paragraph. For example, in Figure 1, the document has two sections (Section A and B) indicated by the gray bars along the left side. Each cell represents a paragraph aligned with which section it is in. Green indicates that there are more additions than deletions in that revision, whereas red indicates more deletions than additions. The horizontal axis represents time going from left to the right. The authors are indicated with a code above the revision columns, which in turn are time stamped.

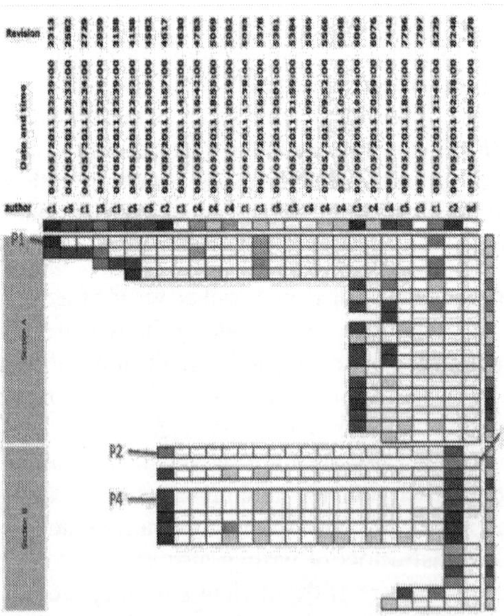

Figure 1. Revision Map visualization

A related set of visualizations has emerged in software engineering, in large part because most software systems are developed by many different programmers. The Seesoft system was the first to create visualizations of line-oriented software code data [8]. As shown in Figure 2, the visualization uses columns to represent files in a project and thin rows to represent lines of codes. The height of the column represents how large each file is, the color of the thin rows indicates the age of the code (e.g., red rows are the most recently changed lines of code, the blue ones are the oldest). These visualizations reveal programming details such as who wrote each line and when it was written with a mouse-hover over the line. The authors believe that this abstracted representation allows the users to gain insights into the whole system more easily and at a finer-grained level. Project managers and developers who used Seesoft confirmed its usefulness in balancing the team's workload, alerting developers to potential bugs and identifying existing errors [8].

Figure 2. Seesoft Visualization

Augur, shown in Figure 3, extends Seesoft's line-oriented visualization to show software development *activities* together with the code [11]. The line-oriented visualization has three columns: one thin column on the left represents different authors, the other represents activities (e.g., whether the entry is a comment or a method definitions, etc.) using various colors. The wide column shows the actual code, colored coded to show how recently it was written. The Augur system also provides concurrent access (the developers can see the visualization while in the development process), interoperability (it can support different source code repository systems) and it is online (any user with Internet access can use it).

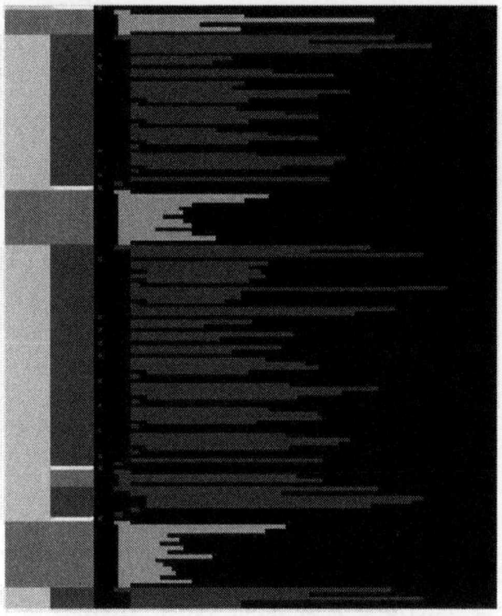

Figure 3. Augur Visualization

In response, CVSscan uses code repository data to visualize software code's evolution, shown in Figure 4 [35]. CVSscan shows either a line-oriented or file-based visualization. In the line-oriented view, CVSscan presents each revision of a single code file as a colored column and uses the horizontal axis to indicate time. The line-based mode clearly indicates the additions and deletions of each line of code. For example, the area in the yellow circle shows the *deletion* of one chunk of code in the middle, followed by another *deletion* of code earlier in the program, and then another chunk *added* in the middle. The system has been shown to be very useful in helping developers understand software repository histories and helping them maintain the software [35].

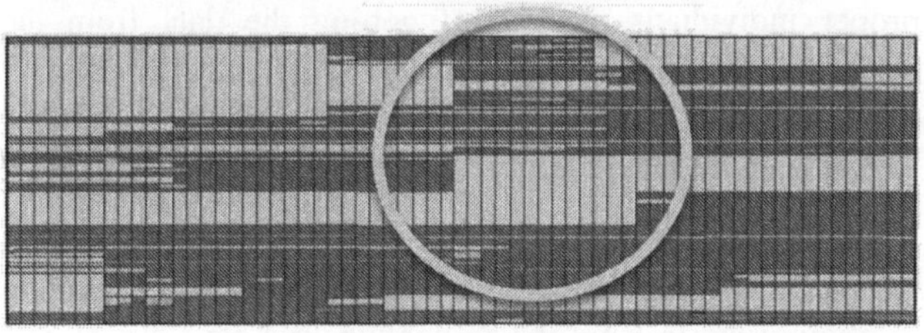

Figure 4. CVSscan

As we can see, all these systems have similarities. Most of them use one orientation (vertical or horizontal) to represent time and use the other one to represent the size of the file. Some of them use color to represent the authors, others use color to represent different activities or code structures. A few systems provide granularity at the class level or the file level, but most of the systems used the line-based approach. Some systems pay more attention to accessibility and interoperability issues, and try to explicitly address the collaboration awareness issues while designing the system.

None of the reviewed visualizations display simultaneous editing likely because the systems that people were collaborating through did not allow synchronous work. However, since the 1990s in research software [9, 21, 29] and now commercially (both in Google Docs and Word with the help of Microsoft OneDrive), authors can write simultaneously. During the synchronous work sessions, the co-authors can see where each other's insertion points are and the emerging text or changes, almost instantaneously. What are the new patterns of collaboration now made possible by these new systems?

These earlier visualizations inspired us to develop a new document visualization, DocuViz. In what follows, we first give an overview of DocuViz, and describe its architecture and the user interface, allowing the reader to imagine the sytem in use. We then present a number of implementation challenges and our solutions. We end with a number of cases illustrating potential uses, already realized, for authors, instructors and researchers.

SYSTEM OVERVIEW

DocuViz is a general-purpose, interactive visualization system for the revision histories of Google Docs, shown in Figure 5. Like *HistoryFlow,* DocuViz shows who did what when. Each column represents the document at that moment (called a *slice,* technically a piece of the revision history), with authorship of the segments of text noted in color. The height of the bar represents amount of text; successive columns represent time moving left to right. The sections between columns help the eye track the placement of text over time plus the additions and deletions. Additions are right facing openings; deletions are right facing contractions. Moves are blocks of identical text that have been repositioned. They are shown with a crossing bar between slices. The little bar at the top of the columns shows by color who was present in that slice of time, one of which is shown at **A**. We consider someone who is present but inactive to be collaborating at the moment. They could

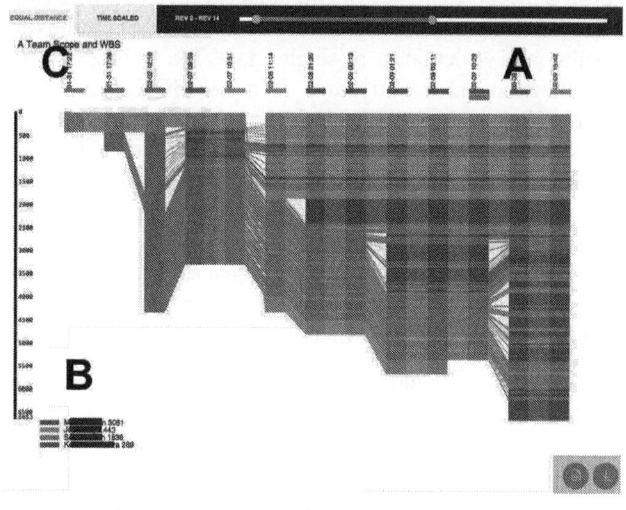

Figure 5. The User View of DocuViz results for an example text.

be reading to edit, conversing with other authors present, etc.

The colored bars at the bottom, **B**, show a compilation of the number of characters in the final document that were produced by each of the authors. The two tabs at **C** allow two views, one where the columns are equidistant, shown in Figure 5, and one where they are linear in time, shown in Figure 6. In Figure 6, one can better see the move of orange text and a burst of activity near the end. Hovering over the bars will show the text in that segment, a feature that turns out to be very helpful in analysis.

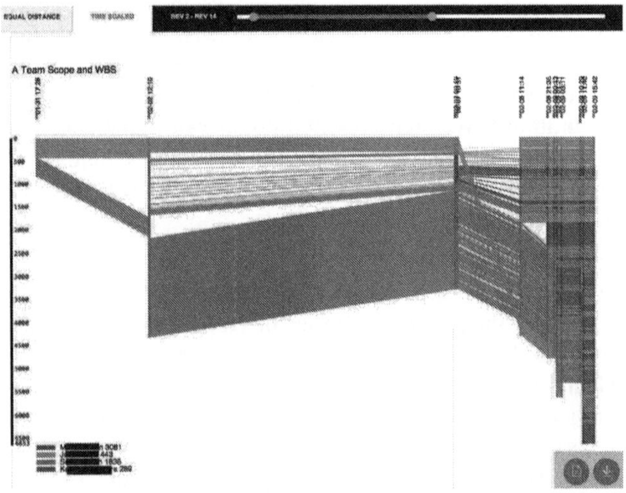

Figure 6. The same document as in Figure 5 but shown linear in time.

Architecture

The system's architecture is simple and straightforward, shown in Figure 7. After the user logs on and allows DocuViz to access their Google Docs, the system retrieves the user-selected document's revision history data from the Google Docs server using the Google Drive API [13]. The system then computes an intermediate differentiating (diff) result between each pair of two adjacent revisions using the Myers diff algorithm [25]. The system then takes all the diff results and calculates a single data file following the visualization rules and saves it as a JSON (JavaScript Object Notation) file [17]. A final visualization is rendered on the user's browser using the JSON data file. The system's user-end visualization and interacting functions are implemented in D3 [2] and JQuery [16] JavaScript libraries. Although the system now works only with Google Docs data, all sub-systems are packaged so that it can easily be upgraded to accommodate other document formats, such as MS Word files, as shown in the upper right of Fig. 7.

DocuViz is free and available to the public. It can be accessed at:

docuviz.ics.uci.edu

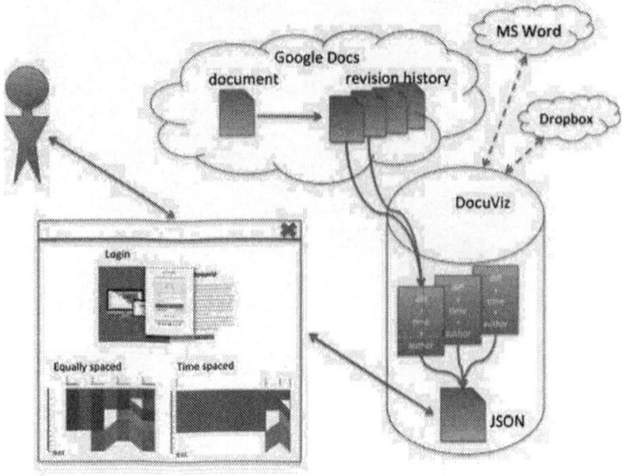

Figure 7. DocuViz Architecture

USER INTERFACE

The user interface is simple. After granting access to Google Docs and selecting one document to visualize, the rendering like that in Figure 5 is shown. Because one may not want to view and calculate participation on the entire history of the document, but rather on a smaller more focused period of time, the interface has a slider bar at the top to allow the user to select the range of possible slices to display. We used this, for example, to analyze student documents up to the moment they are turned in for a grade, even though in some cases, these documents were viewed and changed a number of times after that point.

IMPLEMENTATION CHALLENGES

Simultaneous work

The first challenge was that in the API, the activities in each slice are attributed to only one author (the last) even though the revision history indicates more than one active participant. If we want to attribute actual authorship to the proper individuals, instead of getting the data from the revision histories and their associated API we either have to re-architect our system to fit the data stream that actually creates the visual depiction of the revision history (not available in the current API) or we have to allow users to hand annotate those session. For the time being we chose the second alternative and designed an easy-to-use function to allow users to label the authorship. We have a technical solution that will allow us to implement the first option in DocuViz 2.0.

The second challenge is to define simultaneous work. In our analyses, some of which is reported below, we considered two authors to be working simultaneously if their activities were within 15 minutes of each other. We believe this is a reasonable window, given that people report having long conversations about what to include in the document and then periods of intense activity. If someone has the document open while they converse, they are considered part of the simultaneous work session.

Moves

The third major challenge we faced was to decide the difference between the deletion and addition of similar text (e.g. making subject-verb agreement by adding and subtracting "s") and an actual move. Two issues arise: How big is a change before it is considered a move, and do we give credit to the original author or to the one who moved it (for structural clarity, for example). Unfortunately, our data stream is only text based and we use diffs without the commands "cut" and "paste" indicated, which would have made this a lot easier.

Previous research in file comparison has produced promising algorithms to detect differences between two files and moves [15, 24, 25]. We chose the Myers algorithm for speed, but it does not automatically find identical pieces of text that might signal a move [25]. This is a tradeoff. The Myers algorithm is significantly more efficient (the algorithm complexity is $O(ND^1)$) and at a finer-grain level (characters) than the alternatives, but unfortunately lacks this capability. So based on a well-established program library of Myers algorithm [10], we implemented our own move-detection function that for every deletion of 20 or more characters, we look in the next slice for an addition of that size and exact content. If it matches, it is designated a move. If, however, the person who moves the text then edits it significantly, it is not considered a move.

What is not displayed

In the current API from Google Docs, comments are appended to the end of the text, without indication as to what text they were attached to or the structure of comment-reply-resolve. Furthermore, some of the changes co-authors make have to do with formatting and/or adding figures and graphics to the document. These do not appear in the API at all. In our analyses, these changes are noted when we examine the individual revision histories, not when we look at the visualizations. Future work will investigate whether these kinds of changes are noted in the data stream behind the API, and if so, we will architect DocuViz 2.0 with those indicated as well.

As mentioned above, we caution people against over-interpreting our calculation of participation. Ours is a simple count of how many of the document's final characters were entered by each author. We recognize that actual contributions may not be reflected in this character count. One contributor's key conceptualization, represented in only a few words, may be the most valuable part of the document. Another author may be conversing with the co-authors while one or more of them scribes the ideas.

Having reviewed the architecture, user interface, and challenges, we turn now to showing several cases in which DocuViz has been used in valuable ways.

---

[1] Where N is the sum of the lengths of the strings being compared and D is the length of the thing that was changed, the "difference."

WHAT CAN THIS TOOL BE USED FOR?

We can see DocuViz being useful for three kinds of people: Authors themselves, instructors or tutors who evaluate and help the work of others, and researchers.

Authors themselves

As noted in the introduction, co-authors need to be aware of what others are doing. We believe that the one-step view in MS Word Tracking Changes and Google Docs Revision Histories are helpful but impoverished. These display the latest changes made. This is often sufficient if the work is coordinated asynchronously, that there are clear handoffs with known responsibility of who is "in charge" now. But it is more difficult to track when there are rapid changes made in close succession or even simultaneous; in Word, the tracking changes stack up into a horrible mess and in Google Docs, it requires going back through a number of revision slices to know what changes are being made. Furthermore, there are patterns of interest that are not visible in the one-step view, like frequent changes in a section, contentious activity we might call "seismic."

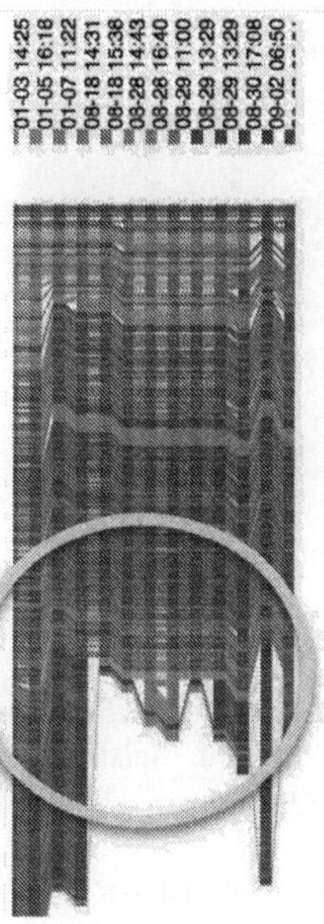

Figure 8. A particularly contentious collaborative episode.

In Figure 8, we show the DocuViz of a part of the co-authoring efforts of the Olsons in a chapter in *Working Together Apart* [27]. In this excerpt, beginning August 18, one author (orange) cut a very large section out of the second half of the chapter and began writing another take on it. Early afternoon on Aug 29, the original author (blue) deleted this new beginning and began anew. After a number of off-line conversations, the two authors agreed on what the deficiencies were in the deleted text and how to approach the section. The old section was then pasted back in and immediately shortened to reflect this conversation. Had DocuViz been available this change would have been recognized much sooner.

In some student team papers, we have seen portions with "seismic activity" as well, where all authors are editing the same area in a short period of time. This contrasts with pieces of text that remain stable over time, suggesting perhaps that people have read and agreed on those. Seeing where the "seismic" text is can be useful for people to go see "what the fuss is all about." We could imagine an extension that would alert in semi-real-time where seismic text was happening. In Figure 9, there appears to be some seismic activity in the sections in the yellow circle. Upon closer examination (by hovering over that section in the live DocuViz), this particular piece of text had to do with expectations of each other coming on time to meetings, and more importantly, what the punishments would entail.

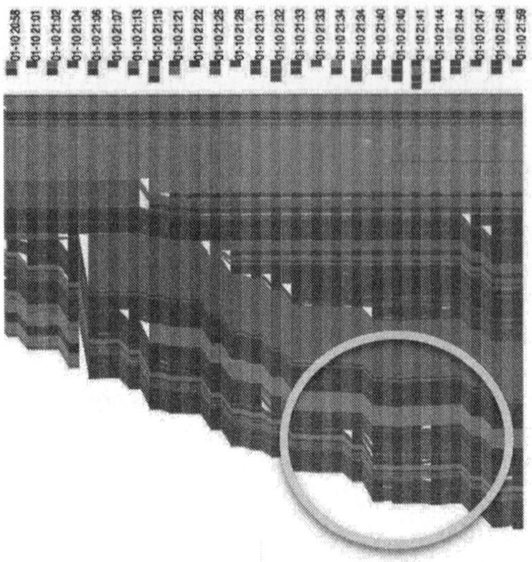

Figure 9. DocuViz that contrasts stable texts at the top with those more seismic near the end.

Figure 10. DocuViz of growing notes for a co-taught class in which the new material "pushes down" the old. Seismic activity is indicated in the yellow circle.

In another recent use of DocuViz, three instructors of writing at the City University of New York (CUNY) used the visualization to reflect on their own collaborations. In Figure 10, they visualized the growing set of course notes they kept on how to teach the courses they co-taught. They noted immediately that the new material was inserted at the top of the notes, with the older sections being pushed down to the bottom, out of sight without scrolling. One section was somewhat seismic, and the preface before the seismic sections enjoyed a lot of same-author editing. One author, blue in this case, was the major "owner" or leader in this document but the three instructors contribute key parts.

Instructors or tutors

The most immediate piece of information instructors might be interested is the simple calculation at the bottom of the visualization that shows how much of the final version was contributed by each author. Figure 11 shows an example.

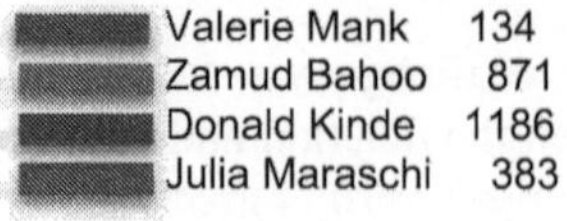

Figure 11. The report of how many characters each contributed to the final document. Names here are fictitious.

As mentioned above, two things might be missing from this count that could misinform the inference of how much each person contributed. The first is that people can be present and conversing, while others write what they say, a style called "scribe" [28]. The other is that people sometimes copy the work of others from another working document and paste it into the "final." This paste loses the attribution of original authorship and assigns it to the one who pastes.

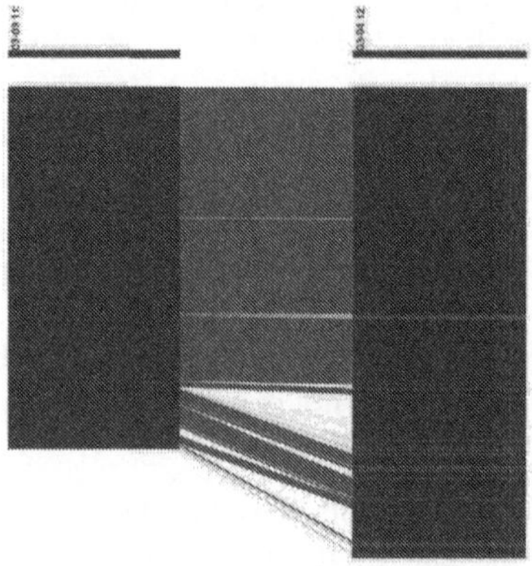

Figure 12. A simple edit of an essay by one student where the location of the edits were immediately visible, both in terms of quantity and by hovering, seeing the actual contents.

The three instructors whose own work is shown in Figure 10 also used DocuViz to see how a student responded to comments on a draft. Figure 12 shows the single authored document in its draft and final version. The instructor's comments (not shown) were telling the student author to include more references to the literature in the essay. On seeing the revision shown in DocuViz, the instructor could immediately see the quantity of the revision and where the additions and edits were. By hovering over the appropriate sections, the author could read the contents and assess whether the response was adequate.

Because these instructors found DocuViz useful, they introduced the system to their students and it turns out "… many [students] found the maps to give them useful information about how they wrote together - they made the invisible visible …".

Researchers

Our main goal in producing DocuViz was for research—to investigate the patterns of collaborative creation of documents and how they correlate with quality, using standard procedures for assessment [34]. For example, we are now examining a corpus of 99 documents produced by undergraduates in a Project Management class. Because students often used the capability of being able to work simultaneously, we are interested in, among other things, how often and how they work in this mode. We found, for example, that 96 of the 99 documents had some simultaneous work; in those few that had none, it was *all* hand-off. In contrast, in 7 of the 99 documents they *always* worked together, with no solo work. Most were a mix of both styles of work. The longest session with more than one person working was 155 min. In one case, the entire assignment was produced by all team members in 67 min, surprisingly *not* right before the deadline, but a full three days before it was due.

Other points of interest in our current work are the emergent patterns of contributions. So far, we have seen teams of students:

- Outline the assignment and then assign people to head different parts, either implied or directly through commenting.
- Paste in a full example (e.g. of a Business case) then maintain the structure but replace the example details with the specifics of their project.
- Each person on the team creates the *whole* assignment, pasting them all in the document and then choosing the best part from each.

As shown in Figure 13, the leader (the blue author) wrote a paragraph in the first revision. When we looked into the content of the first revision, it was the outline of the document. Then all co-authors including the blue, the orange, the red and the green wrote separate sections of the document. It is very clear that there is a boundary between each section of the document, as you can see that there is a tiny blue line between different sections. Most of co-authors did not edit others' writing except the orange author edited the blue's work at the last moment. This pattern was reported by the subjects interviewed by Posner and Baecker in 1992 [28], but this is the first time that someone has revealed it from actual data.

We are able to identify a new pattern of collaboration from students' class projects. As shown in Figure14, this visualization illustrates a collaboration pattern that students used very often in their assignments, which we called "example." For this assignment the students were required to write a business case for their project. It appears that the most intuitive way for students to write it is to find an example of a business case, paste it in and then modify it to fulfill their own case and the requirements of the class. That is why in this figure we can see the starting document very long which then gets smaller with sections replaced with their own text. This is opposite to the previous figure, in which the document was almost continuously increasing.

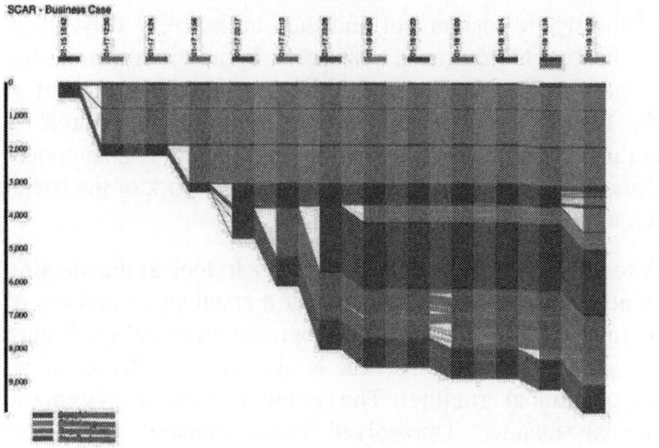

Figure 13. The *outline* pattern

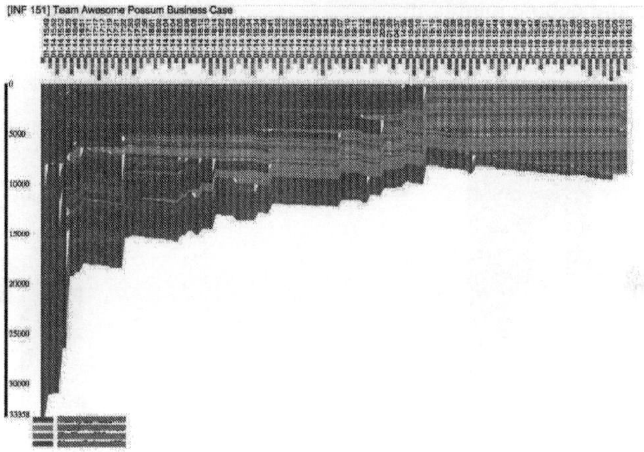

Figure 14. The *example* pattern

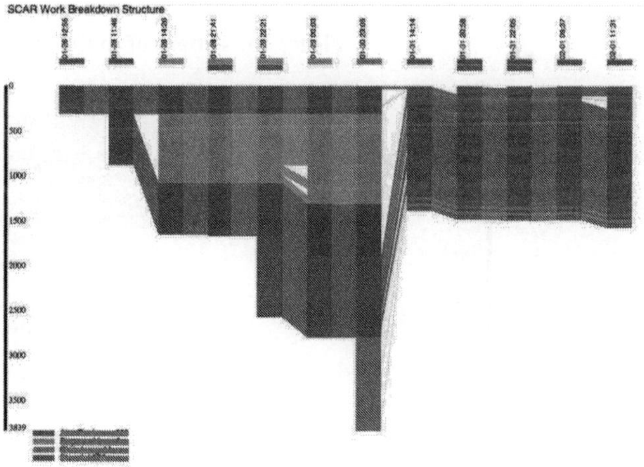

Figure 15. *The best out of all* pattern

In Figure 15, we found another interesting new pattern. We can see four different authors (blue, green, orange and red) contribute almost identical amounts of information at a certain time point (Jan 30, 23:05). The length of the document then decreased sharply in the next revision. After looking into the content of the document, we saw that the four authors agreed that each of them would write a version of the whole assignment and then collectively they chose the best parts from each. As shown in the visualization, the authors represented by blue and the red have a major part of the final draft, whereas most of the work contributed by authors represented by green and the orange is abandoned. This may be driven by the quality of their work or the social dynamics within the group.

A researcher colleague used DocuViz to look at the meeting minutes of a recurring meeting of a standing committee of an international standards development organization. Figure 16 shows the results. What is shown is evidence of an organizational routine: The minutes have a systematic regular manner. Unresolved issues remain; new ones emerge and are tacked on the end. Different people have a history of taking minutes, early on one or two, and later more people joining in.

In another real-world example, we ran DocuViz on the revision history of 8 researchers developing an NSF proposal. Figure 17 shows the remarkable story. In all, there were 139 sessions with only one author present (handoff) but a huge number (40) of sessions in which there were two or more authors. The whole document began with a "kickoff meeting" with 6 authors contributing in a session lasting one hour and 2 minutes.

We believe there is a lot of potential for DocuViz, both in practice and research. People are curious to see who did what, to reflect on their own social "dance" when they work collaboratively. And there is much to learn in research about how to capitalize on the new features to make *quality* work.

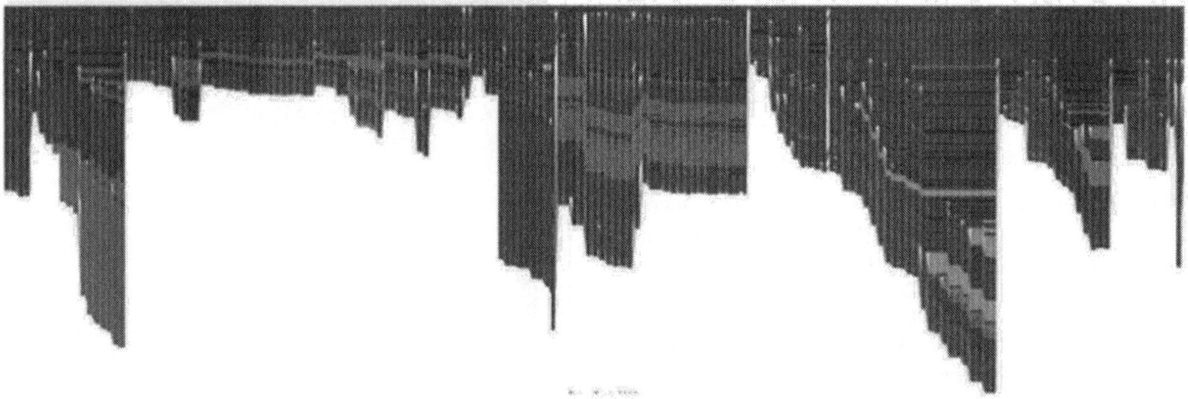

Figure 16. Pattern of contributions in a recurring meeting's note taking.

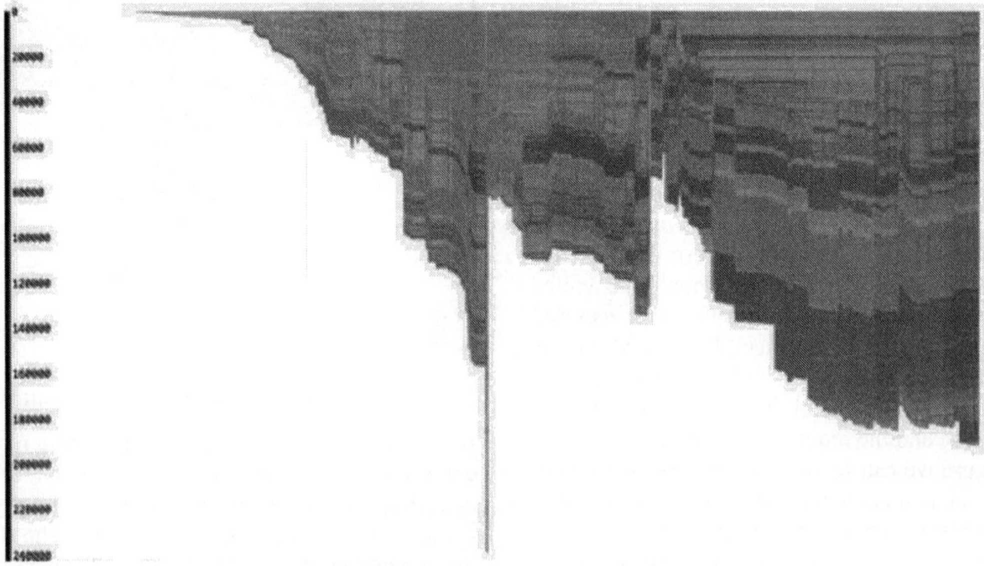

Figure 17. DocuViz of 8 authors developing an NSF proposal.

LIMITATIONS AND OPPORTUNITIES

As mentioned earlier, DocuViz is built using the Google Docs API. This limits our ability to visualize simultaneous work, the placement and "conversation" that appears in formal comments and the contributions of formatting and figures. These limitations are the result of the inconsistency between the data stream stored in Google's database and the data that they provide to the public developers through their API services. Because of this, we are building a DocuViz version 2.0 that is capable of bypassing the API, accessing the actual data stream. In this way, all the previous mentioned challenges will be addressed.

In sum, DocuViz is a tool that allows people to see a useful visualization of revision histories of Google Docs. The richer, longer-term view shows places of seismic activity where authors may want to have more focused discussion to come to agreement about a particular issue, to note large reorganizations of ideas and be sure to be in concordance, and explore others' novel approaches to creating documents. As of the date of writing, our web site has been accessed by more than 100 unique IP addresses, and DocuViz has been applied to 300 documents other than ours.

ACKNOWLEDGMENTS

This work is generously support by a Google Focused Faculty Research Award and a grant from the National Science Foundation (ACI-1322304). We are grateful to Andrew Lauden at Hunter College for sharing examples of his use of DocuViz, the authors of the meeting minutes that showed the organizational routine, and the authors of the NSF grant. We also acknowledge the thoughtful reviews of an earlier draft of this paper by the CHI paper review committee.

REFERENCES

1. Beck, E. E. (1993). A survey of experiences of collaborative writing. In E. E. Beck (Ed.) *Computer Supported Collaborative Writing* Springer London. 87-112.
2. Bostock, M., Ogievetsky, V., & Heer, J. (2011). D^3 data-driven documents. *Visualization and Computer Graphics, IEEE Transactions on, 17*(12), 2301-2309.
3. Cross, G. A. (1990). A Bakhtinian exploration of factors affecting the collaborative writing of an executive letter of an annual report. *Research in the Teaching of English*, 173-203.
4. Curtis, B., Krasner, H., & Iscoe, N. (1988). A field study of the software design process for large systems. *Communications of the ACM, 31*(11), 1268-1287.
5. Dabbish, L., Stuart, C., Tsay, J., & Herbsleb, J. (2012). Social coding in GitHub: transparency and collaboration in an open software repository. In *Proceedings of CSCW 2012*, 1277-1286.
6. Dourish, P., & Bellotti, V. (1992). Awareness and coordination in shared workspaces. In *Proceedings of the 1992 ACM conference on Computer-supported cooperative work*, 107-114
7. Ede, L. S., & Lunsford, A. A. (1990). *Singular texts/plural authors: Perspectives on collaborative writing*. SIU Press.
8. Eick, S. G., Steffen, J. L., & Sumner Jr, E. E. (1992). Seesoft-a tool for visualizing line oriented software statistics. *Software Engineering, IEEE Transactions on, 18*(11), 957-968.
9. Ellis, C. A., & Gibbs, S. J. (1989). Concurrency control in groupware systems. In *ACM SIGMOD Record* Vol. 18(2), 399-407.
10. Fraser, N. (2012). google-diff-match-patch Diff, Match and Patch libraries for Plain Text. https://code.google.com/p/google-diff-match-patch/
11. Froehlich, J., & Dourish, P. (2004). Unifying artifacts and activities in a visual tool for distributed software development teams. In *Proc. of the 26th International Conference on Software Engineering*, 387-396.
12. Google Docs. https://docs.google.com/
13. Google Drive API. https://developers.google.com/drive/
14. Higgins, L., Flower, L., & Petraglia, J. (1992). Planning text together: The role of critical reflection in student collaboration. *Written communication, 9*(1), 48-84.
15. Hunt, J. W., & Szymanski, T. G. (1977). A fast algorithm for computing longest common subsequences. *Communications of the ACM, 20*(5), 350-353.
16. JQuery. http://jquery.com/
17. JSON. http://json.org/
18. Keys, C. W. (1994). The development of scientific reasoning skills in conjunction with collaborative writing assignments: An interpretive study of six ninth-grade students. *Journal of Research in Science Teaching, 31*(9), 1003-1022.
19. Lowry, P. B., Curtis, A., & Lowry, M. R. (2004). Building a taxonomy and nomenclature of collaborative writing to improve interdisciplinary research and practice. *Journal of Business Communication, 41*(1), 66-99.
20. McCarthey, S. J., & McMahon, S. (1992). From convention to invention: Three approaches to peer interactions during writing. *Interaction in Cooperative Groups: The Theoretical Anatomy of Group Learning*, 17-35.
21. McGuffin, L. J., & Olson, G. M. (1992). *ShrEdit: A Shared Electronic Work Space*. CSMIL Technical Report #45, The University of Michigan.

22. Michailidis, A., & Rada, R. (1996). A review of collaborative authoring tools. *Groupware and authoring*. Academic Press, London, 9-43.
23. Microsoft Word. http://office.microsoft.com/
24. Miller, W., & Myers, E. W. (1985). A file comparison program. *Software: Practice and Experience, 15*(11), 1025-1040.
25. Myers, E. W. (1986). An O(ND) difference algorithm and its variations. *Algorithmica, 1*(1-4), 251-266.
26. Noël, S., & Robert, J. M. (2004). Empirical study on collaborative writing: What do co-authors do, use, and like? *Computer Supported Cooperative Work, (CSCW), 13*(1), 63-89.
27. Olson, J. S., & Olson, G. M. (2013). *Working Together Apart: Collaboration over the Internet.* Springer.
28. Posner, I. R., & Baecker, R. M. (1992) How people write together. In *Proceedings of the Twenty-Fifth Hawaii International Conference on System Sciences* Vol. 4, 127-138.
29. Rada, R. (1996). *Groupware and Authoring*. Academic Press.
30. Rice, R. P., & Huguley Jr, J. T. (1994). Describing collaborative forms: A profile of the team-writing process. *IEEE Transactions on Professional Communication, 37*(3), 163-170.
31. Roskams, T. (1999). Chinese EFL students' attitudes to peer feedback and peer assessment in an extended pairwork setting. *RELC Journal, 30*(1), 79-123.
32. Sharples, M., Goodlet, J. S., Beck, E. E., Wood, C. C., Easterbrook, S. M., & Plowman, L. (1993). *Research Issues in the Study of Computer Supported Collaborative Writing* (pp. 9-28). Springer London.
33. Southavilay, V., Yacef, K., Reimann, P., & Calvo, R. A. (2013). Analysis of collaborative writing processes using revision maps and probabilistic topic models. In *Proceedings of the Third International Conference on Learning Analytics and Knowledge*, 38-47.
34. Storch, N. (2005). Collaborative writing: Product, process, and students' reflections. *Journal of Second Language Writing, 14*(3), 153-173.
35. Viégas, F. B., Wattenberg, M., & Dave, K. (2004). Studying cooperation and conflict between authors with history flow visualizations. In *Proceedings of CHI 2004*, 575-582.
36. Voinea, L., Telea, A., & Van Wijk, J. J. (2005). CVSscan: visualization of code evolution. In *Proceedings of the 2005 ACM symposium on Software visualization*, 47-56.

Communication through Boundary Objects in Distributed Agile Teams

Johan Kaj Blomkvist
Linköping University
581 83 Linköping
johan.blomkvist@liu.se

Johan Persson
Linköping University
581 83 Linköping
johpe974@student.liu.se

Johan Åberg
Linköping University
581 83 Linköping
johan.aberg@liu.se

ABSTRACT
Personal communication between User-Centered Design (UCD) specialists and developers is important for communicating user needs and design solutions in agile development. In distributed projects where opportunities for personal communication are limited, the design documentation is an important surrogate. This study has investigated the perceived effectiveness of boundary objects in a distributed agile team, and their role in communicating target user needs. Six in-depth interviews with UCD specialists showed that the boundary objects rarely communicate underlying needs of the users but rather focus on interaction with the system that is being developed. The used boundary objects also do not work as stand-alone deliverables; they need to be explained and elaborated. Making the boundary objects comprehensive enough to be stand-alone is seen as too time consuming and not worth the effort. For agile projects with distributed teams, this creates hand-over and follow-up problems.

Author Keywords
User-Centered Design; Agile Development; Distributed Projects; Boundary Objects; Communication

ACM Classification Keywords
H.5.2 User interfaces; K.6.3 Software development

INTRODUCTION
Agile development methods are becoming increasingly popular in software engineering as the complexity of systems and their use of context continue to increase. However, it seems that agile development in itself does not provide the necessary insights or opportunities to realize the usability of a system [11]. The need therefore exists to integrate agile development with the perspective of usability and the methods included in User-Centered Design (UCD). This integration can however be problematic as there is no single unified agile development method. Rather, the term agile development refers to a set of principles for the creation of software. Furthermore, UCD is an umbrella term for a perspective on how usability is accomplished and several methods dedicated to this purpose. As possibilities and obstacles for a successful integration can vary due to differences in organization and project structure, it is necessary to examine and adapt the methods after each individual instance of integration.

The two methodologies also have different perspectives on how and where resources should be allocated [9,29], e.g. concerning the roles employed and how to approach the concept of usability (e.g. [8,12,28]). Furthermore, the two methodologies have different views on documentation. The agile methodology values working software and face-to-face interaction. Conversely, the UCD methodology aims to document the user and the use of the system in as much detail as necessary. This creates the question of what UCD techniques to use and how the result of these should be communicated [5].

The present study was performed in co-operation with a Swedish usability consulting company involved in a large project employing an agile development method. The project was developing an e-healthcare system with the agile method Scrum. The project consisted of several services that, in their own right, could be considered as individual projects. The complete project was on a national level with several organizations and consulting firms involved. This meant that the members of the agile teams were distributed on several locations across Sweden.

The aim of the study was to examine the difficulties, obstacles, and possible solutions in relation to a successful integration of UCD and agile development within the scope of the ongoing project. The focus was on the appropriateness of the used artifacts and deliverables for communicating the results of the UCD work with the software developers in the project, as perceived by the UCD specialists. Based on this, it should be possible to suggest improvements to the communication quality of design documentation. In the study, the artifacts and deliverables are viewed through the concept of *boundary objects*.

Research Questions
In a distributed agile software development project:

1. How do UCD specialists experience the communication with developers through boundary objects?

CHI 2015, April 18–23, 2015, Seoul, Republic of Korea.

http://dx.doi.org/10.1145/2702123.2702366

2. How is the UCD specialists' understanding of the target users communicated with developers through boundary objects?

BACKGROUND

User-Centered Design

UCD is a concept that covers both the methods and the underlying philosophy to create usable systems. UCD strives to create systems with high usability by focusing on the end-user. The term user-centered design is sometimes referred to as human-centered design to emphasize that there may be other stakeholders than users [13]. It has been defined as an *"approach to systems design and development that aims to make interactive systems more usable by focusing on the use of the system and applying human factors/ergonomics and usability knowledge and techniques"* [13]. Design methods such as Contextual design [2], Usability engineering [20] and Goal-directed design [6] have been developed for the purpose of achieving usability and the more general concept of user experience. A common trait for these methods is that they all contain three overarching phases; research (requirements gathering and analysis), iterative design, and evaluation. Representatives for the end-users of the product are involved to some extent in all these phases to secure the product's usability.

Agile Software Development

Most of the agile methods saw the light during the 1990s but were then called "lightweight" methods. These methods originate from early project methods in the 50s and 70s such as Iterative and Incremental design (IID) and Evolutionary project management (Evo) respectively [27]. There is no unified agile method but the different methods contain several common principles, such as iterative and incremental development, adaptive and flexible planning, and a focus on communication and people [15].

Scrum is an agile development method attempting to cope with the complexity of developing software [25] and does this by focusing on a variation of project management values [16]. By placing focus on project management, Scrum is considered suitable to be implemented with other, more programming-oriented agile methods (e.g. Extreme Programming) that provide more detailed work practices such as coding standards. Scrum uses an empirical process control instead of a defined process control to cope with the complexity of software development. The empirical process control consists of three cornerstones; 1) Visibility, 2) Inspection, and 3) Adaptation. Visibility means that the aspects of the process that affects the outcome must be visible for those who control the process. Inspection means that the various aspects of the process must be inspected so that unwanted variation can be discovered. Adaptation means that if the inspection results in finding unacceptable variations that can influence the product in a negative way, the process must be adapted to solve the variations. A basic element in Scrum is the iterative and incremental process which is called a *sprint*. A sprint normally lasts between 7-30 days. Every day during a sprint an inspection is held in the form of a team meeting. At the end of every sprint a functional increment of the system is delivered to the stakeholders who inspect the functionality and adapt the project as needed [25].

Developing software in distributed teams has recently become common place. Such distributed teams could belong to the same organization or make up a more complex configuration of different organizations. Similarly, the actual geographical distance could be in terms of meters (e.g. with teams in different office buildings in the same location), or on different continents with radically different time zones. Hence, the challenges that come with distributed teams vary from case to case. There is, however, a common denominator, and that is the lack of face-to-face communication. This makes coordination and communication more difficult, which in turn can affect project control and product quality [14]. In response to these challenges, a number of practices for distributed teams employing agile methods have been proposed, e.g. using shared and editable wiki pages to communicate progress, separate backlogs for regional customizations, as well as using IM to make communication easier [17].

Integration of UCD and Agile Methods

A recent systematic literature review uncovered five main challenges to the integration of UCD and agile methods [24]:

1. There is a lack of time for upfront design activities. As a result of the inherent flexibility and willingness to embrace change, agile methods oppose that extensive research and analysis precede development. This is in direct opposition to how UCD strives to create an understanding of the user by gathering requirements through upfront user research.

2. Modularizing design activities is difficult. Due to the incremental nature of agile methods and the preference for short sprints with working deliverables, design activities must be broken down into smaller modules to fit in. This may lead to a lack of holistic thinking which may affect the product's overall cohesiveness.

3. Managing the work dynamics between designers and developers. The agile development process requires continual active participation from designers. Hence, good communication between designers and developers is a key to a successful integration [18]. One limiting factor is that some developers are not interested in design and fail to see the value of design activities [1], which may e.g. lead to a reluctance to implement a design as specified [23].

4. Agile development poses challenges for usability testing. For example, scheduling test sessions is tricky since the rapid pace and frequent changes can make early test results invalid.

Table 1: Description of the interviewed participants

Participant	*Work experience*	*Time in the project*	*Typical work in the project*	*Additional information*
P1	5 years	June 2012 October 2013	Evaluation and prototyping a sub-service. Interviews, personas, scenarios, sketches, and a workshop. Also planning, contracts and procurement.	Worked 2-3 days with the scrum team each week.
P2	6 years	2009 September 2012	User research, prototypes, evaluations.	Occasional visits and telephone meetings with developers.
P3	6 years	From August 2013	Mainly lo-fi sketches and design specifications.	Has worked as both front-end developer and interaction designer.
P4	2 years	From April 2013	Interaction sketches, design specifications, evaluations and interviews.	Worked in the same place as the developers.
P5	6 years	From September 2013	Interaction sketches, user stories, business requirements.	Occasional visits to developers.
P6	5 years	From April 2013	Target group analysis, personas, scenarios, lo-fi prototypes, design specifications, user stories.	

Frequent testing throughout the development may be a way to overcome the difficulties, but is a costly solution.

5. The agile principle of minimal documentation leads to confusion when it comes to UCD deliverables. It has been pointed out that documenting design rationale is important for justifying earlier design decisions. Also, being able to trace the source of a requirement is important since it can affect changes made later on in the development.

Boundary Objects

The term boundary object was first coined by Star & Griesemer [26] and is used to describe a variety of objects that inhabit different worlds of knowledge. Boundary objects serve as a medium for actors from different cultural, social and scientific backgrounds. A boundary object is "*an analytic concept of [those] scientific objects which both inhabit several intersecting social worlds...*" [26, p. 393]. Furthermore, boundary objects are described as both flexible enough to adapt to individual actors and the constraints of several actors employing them. But they are also rigid enough to maintain a common identity across actors and backgrounds [26].

When it comes to communication and grounding of information in distributed agile teams, there are great difficulties due to the lack of grounding factors available to the teams [19]. Coordination of information depends on knowing what type of knowledge it is necessary to share [7]. It is thus vital to have awareness of team and task activities. This means that the importance of certain boundary objects, through which the team members can communicate, grows as they should also include a mediation of the underlying activities for the boundary objects. Furthermore these boundary objects become important as a reference for other communication in distributed agile teams as they allow actors from different communities to negotiate meaning and create a shared understanding [19].

METHOD

This study took the form of a case study, where the phenomenon under investigation is the communication through boundary objects as a part of the larger context of integration between UCD and agile methods. The context in which this phenomenon is being examined is the project where the consulting firm's UCD specialists were involved.

Project and participants

The usability consultancy got involved in the project in 2009, with the development of a platform for sharing digital health information. The project later transmuted into a larger project consisting of three sub-services in 2012. In each project, the developers followed a variant of scrum, using two week sprints which the UCD specialists were not part of regularly. The interviews were conducted in April 2014 with seven UCD specialists from the consultancy. One participant had not been communicating with the software developers and was excluded from the study. Four participants were currently working in the project, and all had been working as interaction designers at some point of the project. Development was carried out in different Swedish cities within the same time zone.

Procedure

The interviews were semi-structured and aimed at investigating the UCD specialists' experience of communication with developers through boundary objects. Four of the interviews were conducted face to face and two were conducted over a video call with the program Skype. The interviews were conducted in Swedish and audio was recorded for all the interviews. A template of questions was produced with the relevant previous research in mind to guide the interviews.

- What documents and deliverables do you produce for the developers?
- For every document/deliverable mentioned,
  - What is the communication purpose?
  - What is the content?
  - Is the communication effective?
- What pro's and con's do you experience with communicating through the mentioned documents and deliverables?
- If and when do you use the documents/deliverables as reference for other types of communication?
- If and how do you document your design decisions?
- How do you convey your understanding of the user in the documents/deliverables?

Each interview began with informing the participants and acquiring informed consent to participate in the study. The interviews were later transcribed in Swedish and subjected to content analysis [10] (excerpts have been translated from Swedish to English). Meaning units in the transcribed interview material were identified based on the research questions. For each question, the units were then condensed and interpreted. The analysis proceeded by identifying the common themes in the different interviews and comparing the answers. This step led to a further abstraction into emerging themes, which are presented in the result below.

RESULTS

How do UCD specialists experience the communication with developers through boundary objects?

The boundary objects discussed in this study were all dependent on verbal communication. For distributed agile projects, the limited communicative function of the boundary objects creates problems with both hand-over and follow-up. If the hand-overs are made without personal communication and the possibility for a discussion, much of the intent and solutions risk being overlooked or misunderstood. If the hand-over is final, i.e. there is no more time scheduled in the project for designers, then a lot of knowledge about the user and associated motivations for design suggestions will be unavailable to the team.

The results for this research question have been categorized according to seven different themes. The themes contain answers to what documents and deliverables are used and how, what their perceived purpose is, and what their experienced advantages and drawbacks are.

Potential Boundary Objects

To uncover the participants' experience with boundary objects they were asked what documents and deliverables they produced. The results were quite similar, with some differences due to variations of when they became involved in the design of a sub-service in the project. The different documents and deliverables they produced, and therefore the potential boundary objects, were; (1) Personas, (2) Scenarios, (3) Effect maps, (4) Sketches, (5) Design Specifications, (6) Prototypes, (7) Evaluation summaries, and (8) User stories. In addition to their own produced material (9) demo pages, created by developers also came up as a potential boundary object.

Different and Multiple Purposes

Some of the mentioned documents/deliverables have a single and clear purpose, others are used with multiple and different purposes. A few of the different types are viewed as work artifacts first and foremost and not communication material i.e. boundary objects. Personas and Scenarios were primarily viewed as working material for the initial design. The purpose of the personas was mainly seen as documentation for requirements gathering and the design process by identifying target users, prioritizing these and to convey an understanding of them. Scenarios were also primarily seen as documentation within the design phase and were used to represent possible future use situations based on personas and as a base for extracting interaction flows. Due to the focus on aiding the design process, personas and scenarios were seen as poor communication material to anyone not directly involved in the design process. The structure of the persona was created so that the creator, who also conducted the research, would later easily recall the most important elements.

This is shown by a statement from P1 "*(Personas) are hard to digest, even I experience this if someone else has created it. When I've made a persona I know exactly what parts I've created it from*" and "*personas are hard to extract information from in the text form when they are 2-3 A4 pages long. But at the same time you make them long so that you as a designer can use them later when designing, but then they might not work as well for communication purposes*".

Prototypes were also reported to have multiple purposes. In addition to communication artifacts (which will be discussed later) they were sometimes primarily used as evaluation tools. This reportedly affects the structure of the prototype as details in the prototype are held back to enable more responses from the participants in evaluation. By keeping the detail of the design at a lower level, participants can concentrate on the functions being evaluated and not be distracted by the details. Further it is reported that low fidelity gives the evaluating participants the feeling that the design is not carved in stone. It becomes apparent that as documents and deliverables like personas and prototypes are structured for the prioritized purpose, the suitability for other purposes diminishes.

TAGRI Principle

The TAGRI (They Ain't Gonna Read It) principle was indirectly or directly present in all interviews in relation to personas, scenarios, and effect maps. Though all of the documents and deliverables were submitted to the project database where everyone involved including developers had access, there was some uncertainty of what developers actually saw and used. P1 and P2 expressed the experience that none of the developers read material like personas and scenarios when sent out over email. P1 and P4 further expressed that there was an overflow of material in the project database that was difficult to filter through and that this rendered the database non-functional. Although accessible to developers, P3, P4 and P6 also reports that by their experiences neither of the personas, scenarios or effect maps was used by the developers. P1 and P2 also reported that they didn't see any use of the personas, scenarios or effect maps for the developers.

Due to the experiences that these artifacts and deliverables are not used by developers; personas, scenarios, effect maps, and evaluation summaries are *not* viewed as boundary objects between UCD specialists and developers.

Purpose as Boundary Objects

After excluding personas, scenarios, effect maps and evaluation summaries from analysis as boundary objects the remaining documents and deliverables are sketches, design specifications, prototypes, and user stories. The analysis of the interviews has identified the participants' view of the purposes of each of these. All of the participants reported using sketches as deliverables to the developers. The sketches were reported containing requirements from the scenarios and were used to visualize these. The main purpose of the sketches was to create an understanding of user flows, the interaction with the system and its functionality. It was also seen as a communication aid by grounding and structuring the verbal communication. Lastly its purpose was seen as providing instructions to the developers and to raise changes to the design.

A design specification was used by all participants except one. P5 reported using sketches instead because of arriving at a late stage in the sub-project and that there was no time to produce a design specification in its full extent. A design specification was reported by the other participants to contain sketches coupled with descriptive texts clarifying the interaction and system responses. One of the delimitations of the design specification was that it was not allowed to be interactive as it had to be printable. A design specification was also reported containing graphical design and the sketches used seemed to be hi-fi to convey the detailed design.

As P3 puts it "*We have created a design specification that basically describes every page of the service…with more or less finished windows in relation to design…*"

The purpose of the design specification was reportedly to communicate an understanding of the interaction and the system's response. It was used to eliminate and forgo questions but also to minimize misunderstandings. Further purposes were reported being to create quality and to produce criteria for verifying the implemented code.

P1, P2, P3, and P6 all reported using prototypes as a deliverable to the developers. The prototype was mostly seen as complementary to the design specification as its purpose also was to convey an understanding of the interaction and to minimize misunderstandings. But as an advantage P2 expresses the experience of prototypes as the strongest visualization tool. P3 reported a similar experience with prototypes as conveying a better overview and a stronger feeling for use than the design specification. Furthermore P6 reported that when using hi-fi prototypes they could almost replace the design specification.

P3, P5, and P6 reported using user stories as deliverables to the developers. P3 reported using them as a complement to the design specification and prototype with the purpose of describing possible interactions to each part of the service. P5 used them as complements for the sketches that replaced the design specification with the purpose of providing the developers with finished work packages. P6 reported translating the design specification to user stories with the same purpose of providing finished work packages to the developers.

Neither Comprehensive nor Stand-Alone

When the participants were asked how they experience the communication through documents and deliverables all of them pressed that the boundary objects were not comprehensive and therefore not able to stand alone as communication. As the boundary object's main purpose seem to be to communicate an understanding of interaction, underlying and explicit motivations were excluded. Further and as P6 reports, the process of arriving at a final design is iterative and ongoing throughout development, and the deliverables thus only as comprehensive as the design is final. P3 reports that since the deliverables can contain heavy texts it will always be ambiguous to some extent. As P4 points out, questions concerning the delivery will always arise. When trying to achieve the best possible result, the participants experienced that they always have to verbally communicate the intentions of the document/deliverable as well. P3 therefore experienced the need to deliver in person. P6 expresses a similar need with a face to face review of the deliverables. The notion of the boundary objects being neither comprehensive nor stand-alone is further evident as the different purposes of each boundary object is closely related to being a communication aid.

Time Consuming Boundary Objects

One of the emerging themes was that the boundary objects were experienced as very time consuming by all of the participants. This was reported in relation to the creation of the documentation/deliverables, maintaining them, and reviewing them when delivered. The participants experience that the deliverables could become very large and heavy. This made them difficult and time consuming to package for delivery. While wanting to explain in as much detail as possible to ensure the design, a balance has to be made between the comprehensiveness and the time spent on creating them. P6 describes this with "*it is a challenge to put together a material which is comprehensive enough but not too large*".

In relation to maintenance, P4 and P6 describe their experiences with updating sketches and design specifications as time consuming. Both further expressed that if they were given time initially to create a hi-fi prototype, time could later be saved on maintenance as master components can be used in prototypes. The experiences of the participants suggest that the more complex boundary objects become, the harder they are to interpret and get acquainted with. P6 points out that as a design specification grows the ability to convey an overview of the design as a whole diminishes.

Direct "Translation"

The participants had asked the developers what deliverables they needed and how they structured their tasks from the deliverables they received. The participants thus started to deliver user stories as complements to existing deliverables. This was reportedly done as it would otherwise require developers to have long meetings to turn deliverables like sketches, design specifications and prototypes into user stories as their usual structured tasks. In addition to lengthy meetings P5 also reports the experience with user stories having too much of a technical focus after these meetings and therefore saw the need for the UCD specialists to directly translate their work into user stories. This provided developers with finished work packages and allowed them to focus on the prioritization of the user stories in the product backlog instead of their creation. By creating user stories some of the participants could directly translate design issues, user research like interviews, and evaluations into easily interpretable deliverables for developers. It was also reported that due to time constraints in the project direct translation also occurred with sketches, as is shown by P1's statement: "*You don't put in a week's work on creating a nice presentation of evaluation results because it is more important to get the design going and update sketches.*"

Summarizing the results concerning how communication was experienced through boundary objects:

- Personas and scenarios could not be considered boundary objects but rather documentation of user research.
- Prototypes were used for multiple purposes, but mostly to test the design. Prototypes that were interactive could replace Sketches and Design specifications if they were hi-fi enough.
- Prototypes resulted in evaluation summaries, which were not read by developers.
- Effect maps were not read by developers.
- Sketches and Design specifications communicated requirements from user research, such as functionality, interaction, and flows.
- Personas, scenarios, effect maps and evaluation summaries could not be considered boundary objects. However they were important tools for the designers who felt that the value of these techniques lie in the process of creating them.
- User stories were used as boundary objects, sometimes as a way of clarifying Design specifications or Prototypes, or as a way of providing finished work packages

How is the UCD specialists' understanding of the target users communicated with developers through boundary objects?

The main finding concerning communication was that the objects in this study lacked motivations for what they communicate, and why the design looked like it did. This had to be communicated separately, which the participants did when developers requested more information. For instance, while personas and scenarios might be mentioned in verbal communication, it appears that the participants only used the existence of these to keep their backs clear if a design decision was questioned. Three themes emerged.

Problems Stronger than Solutions

The experiences reported by some of the participants were that usability problems seemed to stronger communicate an understanding of the user than suggested solutions would. P1 uses the example that a video recording of the user evaluation could much clearer show the frustration of the user and would therefore convey a much stronger understanding of the user. P1 continues with "*I believe that what would create more empathy is to involve the developers to a larger extent in the requirements gathering where they could meet the user...*" While P2 points out that personas and scenarios contain a lot of information about the understanding of the user, evaluation results were experienced to be the strongest means to communicate the understanding. P3 and P4 also report that interviews and evaluation results were the primary motivation for how user stories were created.

"Translation"

As previously stated, the documentation and deliverables created to convey an understanding of the user is primarily viewed as working material for the design process. This coupled with the time shortage experienced by participants meant that they felt the need to directly translate the understanding of the user to actual boundary objects such as sketches and user stories. P1 and P2 report on the view that it is not the developer's job to understand the user and therefore does not need to care. As described above, information concerning the understanding of the user acquired in interviews and evaluation was directly translated into user stories and sketches. Information about the understanding of the user which could be found in scenarios and personas was also translated into sketches and user stories respectively. In P5's sub-project, user research was missing due to time limitations and existing user stories had a technology focus. P5's response was to get involved with the creation of user stories. This was done to restore what P5 perceived to be the user flows, which would improve the understanding of the user.

On Demand

As it has been shown now, the documentation and deliverables directly containing information for the understanding of the user is not perceived by the participants to be received and read by the developers. Furthermore it has been reported that there are no explicated motivations for design decisions in the actual boundary objects to convey an understanding of the user and thereby the design. Instead the participants' experiences indicate that the understanding is translated into boundary objects as the information is not seen as relevant for the developers to do their job. However, the participants report that they later verbally communicate the understanding of the user if necessary i.e. on demand by developers. This verbal communication seems to be aided by the creation of personas and scenarios as participants report that they sometimes refer back to the existence of this documentation. What emerged in the interviews was that any connections between an understanding of the user (i.e. rationale) and the actual design is internalized in the participants and only externally verbalized when requested. As P2 and P6 states, this is done to cover their backs.

DISCUSSION

There are some possible implications of these results. The risk involved is that some design documentation is not useful. If the intention is that methods are used to communicate e.g. the end user's perspective (persona, scenarios), then those methods must be developed based on a realistic understanding of design work in various contexts, such as distributed development. Otherwise they will not be used, or worse, when they are used they simply take away time from more meaningful activities. When design tools are not used as intended it can lead to: the design is not being implemented in the intended way [25] and the voice of target users being lost during development. Both problems are associated with lower usability of the final product. This means, in some cases, that the role of design methods as boundary objects in development projects should be reconsidered.

It is possible that the reason why the objects are not used or read by developers is a lack of understanding or perceived usefulness of design work among developers. This affects the relationship between developers and designers, which is imperative for the willingness to implement design [23]. The relationship between designers and developers is important [18], especially if design methods are considered as aids that support interpersonal communication rather than stand-alone boundary objects.

There are two approaches possible in relation to the finding that the boundary objects are not stand-alone: 1) accept that boundary objects are communication aids rather than self-explanatory, or 2) try to change or develop new boundary objects for integration of UCD and agile development. We discuss the implications of each approach below.

Seeing boundary objects as communication aids

Accepting that boundary objects are complements to be used as support for coordination, collaboration and communication would mean that time have to be made for those activities in agile projects. This is in line with the sixth agile principle which states that the most efficient and effective way of conveying information to developers is through verbal communication. When verbally communicating their understanding of the users, the participants reported using boundary objects as communication aids but also referring back to the existence of personas and scenarios.

The finding in this case that there were too many documents, and that they were difficult to understand and overview, further supports the approach that the boundary objects should be seen as communication aids rather than stand-alone design documents. But when the agile team becomes distributed, communication and the grounding of information become more difficult. This puts a heavier load on boundary objects as references in other communication.

One obvious improvement for co-located teams is to involve both designers and developers in all activities [5], including user research. P1 expressed the need for developers to be more involved in the requirements gathering to get a better understanding of the user. This is further illustrated in [21] which reports on the use of a workshop with developers and stakeholders to perform user research and requirements analysis. It is claimed that this enabled a distribution of knowledge for the user throughout the team and that the resulting prototype could function as a communication aid later on [21].

This leads to the question of how e.g. personas and scenarios can be made relevant also for the developers. One of the projects in this study involved the whole team in creating user journeys (similar to personas and scenarios) as not doing so in the past had created problems. This however seems like a good idea in theory but that was less successful in practice, since so many projects fail to do so, and it is only feasible if the team is not distributed.

As [4] points out, for an integration to be successful, UCD does not only need to be integrated in the agile methods, agile methods should also be integrated in UCD. This should be done to allow a better integration of the underlying values. Not allowing enough time to adequately present the results of an evaluation could be seen as a failure to integrate the underlying values of UCD in agile development. The lack of a deeper integration on the abstract level also becomes apparent as P1 and P2 claim that it is not the developers' job or responsibility to care about and try to understand the target users. According to the agile principles the highest priority is to satisfy the customer. This should obviously include knowledge of whom the developers are actually building a system for.

Improving the design objects

The other approach is to interpret this research as showing opportunities to develop or tweak design documentation so that it can be more useful in agile development in general, but also more specifically for distributed teams. Such techniques must be both lightweight enough for designers to use them and comprehensive enough to satisfy developers.

Boundary objects in the project

Many potentially useful documents for communicating about users were created and used only by and for the UCD specialists. Naturally, objects that are created and used exclusively by designers do not improve collaboration and communication [5]. An alternative could be to train designers in customizing the objects for developers, rather than for themselves. If working in a distributed agile team, more time has to be spent on making the personas and scenarios easier to interpret. However, while it is important to integrate design work with the agile process [4], not all design work, including tools sketches and other documentation must be shared. Some tools are useful only for designers, just as other aspects of development do not necessarily concern designers.

Personas, scenarios and evaluation results

There seemed to be no physical use of personas and scenarios for aiding the communication with the developers (they are only verbally referred to). Pruitt and Adlin [22] described the persona lifecycle and pointed out that one of the most difficult tasks is the transition from creating a persona to using one in an organization. They stress the fact that personas have to be presented progressively in small and easily interpretable chunks. More importantly, the personas have to be structured after the intended receiver. This means that when creating a persona it must be clear how to access and retrieve information.

Translation also occurred from scenarios and evaluation results to sketches. As deliverables were seen to be neither comprehensive nor stand-alone, sketches could be presumed to be a preferable communication aid. This is in line with [3], where sketches are identified to be well adapted for focusing attention, grounding communication, recording design decisions and to explore relationships within design.

User stories

Some participants started using User stories as part of their communication. This shows the importance of the empirical process control which is a foundation in Scrum. Although not contingent on being co-located, the inspection of what developers needed to structure their work lead to an adaption of the deliverables to include user stories. The use of boundary objects such as user stories and sketches as communication aid is, as previously mentioned, supported by [3]. While sketches are suitable for visualizing and grounding the communication, user stories are well suited for making problems apparent and connecting designs to user groups. As stated in [19], the importance of boundary objects as communication aid grows as teams become distributed.

Sketches and User stories were actually part of a coping strategy that designer used in this study. The limited time for design work during a sprint meant that user research needed to be directly translated into some format that the developers would use. Hence, the participants started creating user stories to complement the other objects. User stories are already part of what the developers use, but focused on technical issues. This was an opportunity for the UCD specialists to make design more prioritized.

The advantages of having designers make User stories are that it complements the technical focus, and that it provides a way to directly translate UCD work into a format that is already used in agile development. However, they seem insufficient to fully communicate an understanding of the user.

According to [7], the understanding of what is critical to share increases as the team becomes co-located. From a boundary object perspective, user stories can be seen as standardized forms [26] as they are structured after user role and goal (e.g. *"as a [user role] I want to be able to [goal]"*). User stories thereby show an advantage of using the boundary object type standardized forms as communication means. User stories, created by UCD specialists, appear to provide the developers with a more direct translation of the UCD work than other deliverables like design specifications and prototypes as they already are an integrated part of the agile development. According to [2] user stories can be seen as relatively detailed definitions of system functions which are derived from user goals. In addition, user stories can connect the design to user categories and user goals [3]. Despite these previously reported benefits, none of the participants expressed that user stories communicated an understanding of the user.

Adding a motivation to the standardized forms might be a good way to provide the missing information about the users' motivation and needs: *"as a [user role] I want to be able to [goal] because [reason]"*.

Prototypes and design specifications

The experience of time consuming boundary objects related both to the creation and maintenance of them. In particular the design specification was reported to be time consuming in its creation because of heavy texts and in maintenance due to the need to update the sketches individually. P6 mentioned that sometimes, and if there was enough time, a hi-fi prototype could be created and function as a replacement for the design specification. What is represented in text in the design specification could possibly also be easier to represent in a hi-fi prototype. While the design specification with its static sketches allows the representation of specific flows within the design, coupling the prototype with user stories could just as easily convey this information.

As both the design specification and prototype was seen as neither comprehensive nor stand-alone, verbal communication was anyway needed to clarify the artifacts. The possible benefits of using a prototype for this purpose are that the prototype is reportedly easier to interpret and gives a clearer overview of the design. Furthermore, it was seen as a stronger communication material because of its interactive qualities. This finding emphasizes the usefulness of prototypes as boundary objects between designers and developers. Presently however, most prototypes also lack motivations for decisions and knowledge about users.

Design rationale

A design rationale as an additional boundary object could possibly be used for the purpose of bridging the design and the personas by externalizing the participants' internal connections. This would, hypothetically, not only relieve the UCD specialists of holding in the connections but also solve the access-related difficulties with the personas. The solution of a design rationale is not necessarily one created for the developers' ease of access (i.e. retrieval). A design rationale in the argumentative perspective could also be used to aid UCD specialists in the design process and therefore possibly help clarify what is essential to motivate. As suggested in [22], the persona should be adapted for the intended receivers. The persona could therefore be re-structured from the design rationale to possibly provide a better aid for communication with developers.

Boundary object repositories

From the interviews it was concluded that all documentation and deliverables were distributed through a project database or a product backlog. The project database and the backlog can through a boundary object perspective be seen as a boundary object type repository [26]. Distributed agile teams puts a heavy weight on the functionality of repositories and the need for easy access in them. The difference between the project database and the backlog seems to be that, while the functionality and easy access of the backlog is apparent as it is deeply integrated in the agile method, the project database failed, leaving some documents and deliverables unseen by developers.

LIMITATIONS AND FUTURE RESEARCH

This work covers one project in one company and the results cannot be generalized to other settings. The findings are limited to the UCD specialists' experiences because project management declined involvement of the developers. Additional studies should look at the developer perspective. Would developers have the same view on the effectiveness and limits of the boundary objects, or would they identify different boundary objects? Would there be any differences between front-end or back-end developers?

Since the project and its constituent sub-projects had such a clear distinction between requirements gathering tracks and development tracks, some of the involved UCD specialists in the projects had to be excluded from the study as they had not been communicating with developers through boundary objects. This meant that only six UCD specialists participated in the study. This rather low number may have affected the validity of the study. But this is to some extent compensated as the UCD specialists participating came from several sub-projects and still expressed somewhat similar experiences.

The data sources in the study were limited to interviews. It would have been interesting to directly study the use of boundary objects through observation or document analysis. This could also reveal other boundary objects that were not mentioned by the participants.

Communication problems can be associated with cultural differences. Further studies should look more carefully at the relation and empathy between designers and developers in agile development. This can influence the developers' willingness to implement designs [23] and use design objects.

CONCLUSIONS

This study has investigated UCD specialists' view on boundary objects for communication with developers in agile projects. The purpose of an actual boundary object was mainly seen as communicating an understanding of the interaction with the system and not necessarily an understanding of the user. The boundary objects created for this purpose were neither considered to be comprehensive nor stand-alone.

With respect to the boundary objects themselves, the study has shown the importance of well-functioning boundary object repositories with easy access. Without such repositories, the objects risk losing their boundary qualities. Although hi-fi prototypes are time consuming in their initial creation, they could save time on maintenance and updating as the design process continues throughout the development. The study also showed that UCD specialists tended to adapt their usual way of working to the special needs of agile development. For example, they translated their work into deliverables such as user stories with associated design sketches. The reason for doing this was to help developers structure their work and connect the user to the design and its elements.

Concerning the communication of UCD specialists' understanding of the user with developers, three themes were identified. Although identified problems were seen to strongly communicate an understanding of the user, any documents and deliverables containing these problems were not received by developers. For developers to truly understand the user, they would have to participate to some degree in the user research. The alternative, as participants reported, was to verbally communicate their understanding of the user to developers on demand. This makes the connections between the design and the user internalized within each individual participant. However, higher-level connections become externalized by coupling user stories with sketches and/or prototypes.

ACKNOWLEDGEMENTS

We express our sincere gratitude to the participating UCD specialists, our champions at the usability consulting company, and the anonymous reviewers.

REFERENCES

1. Aberg, J. Challenges with Teaching HCI Early to Computer Students. *Proc. ITiCSE'10*, ACM Press (2010), 3-7.
2. Bayer, H. and Holzblatt, K. *Contextual design: Defining customer centered systems*. Morgan Kaugmann, 1998.
3. Brown, J., Lindgaard, G. and Biddle, R. Stories, Sketches, and Lists: Developers and Interaction Designers Interacting Through Artifacts. *Proc. Agile'08*, IEEE (2008), 39-50.
4. Blomkvist, S. Towards a model for Bridging Agile Development and User-Centered Design. In *Human-Centered Software Engineering – Integrating Usability in The Development Process*, Springer (2005), 219–244.
5. Chamberlain, S., Sharp, H. and Maiden, N. Towards a Framework for Integrating Agile Development and User-Centered Design. In *Extreme Programming and Agile Processes in Software Engineering*, Springer (2006), 143-153.
6. Cooper, A. *The inmates are running the asylum*. Macmillan, USA, 1999.
7. Convertino G., Mentis H.M., Rosson M.B., Slavkovic A. and Carroll J.M. Supporting content and process common ground in computer-supported teamwork. *Proc. CHI'09*, ACM Press (2009), 2339-2348.
8. Ferreira, J., Noble, J. and Biddle, R. Agile development iterations and UI design. *Proc. Agile'07*, IEEE (2007), 50-58.
9. Fox, D., Sillito, L. and Maurer, F. Agile Methods and User Centered Design: How These Two Methodologies Are Being Successfully Integrated in Industry. *Proc. Agile'08*, IEEE (2008), 63-72.
10. Hsieh, H-F. and Shannon, S.E. Three approaches to Qualitative Content Analysis. *Qual Health Res 15*, 9 (2005), 1277-1288.
11. Hussain, Z, Slany, W. and Holzinger, A. Investigating Agile User-Centered Design in Practice: A Grounded Theory Perspective. In *HCI and Usability for e-inclusion*, Springer (2009a), 279–289.
12. Hussain, Z., Slany, W. and Holzinger, A. Current State of Agile User-Centered Design: A Survey. In *HCI and Usability for e-inclusion*, Springer (2009b), 416–427.
13. ISO 9241-210:2010 Ergonomics of human-system interaction — Part 210: Human-centered design for interactive systems.
14. Jiménez, M., Piattini, M. and Vizcaíno, A. Challenges and Improvements in Distributed Software Development: A Systematic Review. *Advances in Software Engineering 2009*, (2009).
15. Larman, C. and Basili V.R. (2003) Iterative and Incremental Development: A brief history. *Computer 36*, 6 (2003), 47-56.
16. Larman, C. *Agile and iterative development: A manager's guide*. Pearson, 2003.
17. Lee, S. and Yong, H-S. Distributed agile: project management in a global environment. *Empir Software Eng 15*, (2010), 204-217.
18. Miller, L. Case Study of Customer Input for a Successful Product. *Proc. Agile'05*, IEEE (2005), 225-234.
19. Modi, S., Abbott, P. and Counsell, S. Negotiating Common Ground in Distributed Agile Development: A Case Study Perspective. *Proc. Int. Conf. Global Software Engineering*, IEEE (2013), 80–89.
20. Nielsen, J. *Usability Engineering*. Morgan Kaufmann, 1993.
21. Patton, J. Hitting the Target: Adding Interaction Design to Agile Software Development. *Proc. OOPSLA'02*, ACM Press (2002), 1–7.
22. Pruitt, J. and Adlin, T. *The persona lifecycle: Keeping people in mind throughout product design*. Morgan Kaufmann, 2006.
23. Redish, J., Bias, R.G., Bailey, R., Molich, R., Dumas, J. and Spool, J.M. Usability in Practice: Formative Usability Evaluations – Evolution and Revolution. *Proc. CHI'02*, ACM Press (2002), 885-890.
24. Salah, D., Paige, R.F. and Cairns, P. A Systematic Literature Review for Agile Development Processes and User Centered Design Integration. *Proc. Int. Conf. Evaluation and Assessment in Software Engineering*, ACM Press (2014).
25. Schwaber, K. *Agile Project Management with Scrum*. Microsoft Press, 2004.
26. Star, S.L. and Griesemer, J.R. Institutional Ecology, `Translations' and Boundary Objects: Amateurs and Professionals in Berkeley's Museum of Vertebrate Zoology, 1907-39. *Social Studies of Science 19*, 3 (1989), 387–420.
27. Sliger, M. and Broderick, S. *The software project manager's bridge to agility*. Addison-Wesley, 2008.
28. Sy, D. Adapting Usability investigations for Agile User-Centered Design. *Journal of Usability Studies 2*, 3 (2007), 112–132.
29. Ungar, J. The design studio: Interface design for agile teams. *Proc. Agile'08*, IEEE (2008), 519–524.

How to Drive a London Bus: Measuring Performance in a Mobile and Remote Workplace

Gary W. Pritchard[1], Pam Briggs[2], John Vines[1], and Patrick Olivier[1]

[1]Culture Lab,
School of Computing Science,
Newcastle University, UK
{firstname.lastname}@ncl.ac.uk

[2]PaCT Lab,
Department of Psychology,
Northumbria University, UK
p.briggs@northumbria.ac.uk

ABSTRACT

This paper examines how London bus drivers have responded to performance monitoring via a telematics device called *Drivewell*. This device calculates a score based on various recordable driving-related events like abrupt braking or irregular turning actions. Our qualitative methodology incorporated semi-structured interviews and ethnographic fieldwork in order to explore drivers' attitudes towards the system and its effect on driving behaviour and working conditions. Our findings illustrate how bus operators simultaneously accommodate and resist the demands *Drivewell* places upon them. Our work also demonstrates how this digital intervention acts in conjunction with other driver-related technologies, creating a unique digital ecosystem on the modern London bus. Our research contributes to HCI understandings of digital surveillance and performance monitoring in the modern workplace.

Author Keywords

Public Transport; Ethnography; Telematics; Event Monitoring; Workplace Surveillance

ACM Classification Keywords

H.5.m. Information interfaces and presentation (e.g., HCI): Miscellaneous.

INTRODUCTION

Sensor technology is increasingly deployed as a part of intelligent vehicle infrastructures that give drivers the capacity to monitor traffic and navigation information, check vehicle status, improve driving quality and navigate adverse driving conditions [27]. Recent developments in Intelligent Transportation Systems (ITS) have also allowed interconnected vehicles to exchange information in order to operate a more efficient and passenger-friendly service [27], while minimizing cost and making the entire system more environmentally sound.

These developments have led to some drivers acquiring new responsibilities and being subject to new forms of performance monitoring. For instance, it is now relatively straightforward to install in-vehicle data recorders (IVDR) that monitor driving quality indicators like speed, braking and cornering. Individual drivers can benefit directly from this by registering to either a Pay As You Drive (PAYD) insurance system that charges for distance travelled, or one that rewards good driving by offering lower premiums to those who achieve target driving scores [23]. On an organizational scale, professional drivers may also be signed up to ‗fleet telematics' systems [18] that are used to monitor driving across an entire fleet. When integrated into driver appraisals these can become highly effective performance management infrastructures that reward good driving and penalize bad.

In 2010, Transport for London (TfL) integrated just such a system onto all of the city's buses. Before going into service and starting the engine, drivers are now required to place a key fob that identifies them as the operator onto a reader (Figure 1a). If they do not do this, an alarm will sound. This device—known as *Drivewell*—captures driver behaviour and provides feedback in two forms. The first offers immediate notification of undesirable driving or ‗events', communicated through a traffic-light module directly above the vehicle's windscreen (Figure 1b). The second provides a more detailed breakdown of performance that drivers can access via a computer terminal located in the capital's bus depots. Information provided includes date of journey, vehicle, duration, ‗achievement' (given as a percentage) and overall number of ‗events' (or incidences of poor driving). The driver can also assess their performance over time through a series of graphs or view on a map where ‗events' occurred (see Figure 1c). All of this data is also relayed to supervisors, who use it to monitor and assess performance. Some of the companies who manage bus routes offer prizes (e.g. a TV) for the best scores over a set period. If poor scores are consistently attained, the driver can be sanctioned formally or forced to undertake additional training.

CHI 2015, April 18 - 23 2015, Seoul, Republic of Korea.

ACM 978-1-4503-3145-6/15/04…$15.00
http://dx.doi.org/10.1145/2702123.2702137

Figure 1. From left to right: a) Placing the *Drivewell* key fob onto the reader; b) The *Drivewell* indicator in the driver's cabin (circled red); c) The *Drivewell* computer terminal; and d) close-up of computer terminal screen showing Drivewell scores.

The aim of this study was to explore the extent that *Drivewell* has been accepted by bus drivers and to understand its impact on their behaviour. In achieving this, we conducted ethnographic fieldwork, conducted over a period of 14 months, which consisted of continuous contact with research participants and formal interviews with 15 drivers. Through this, we sought to achieve a sophisticated understanding of the perceived costs and benefits of this kind of remote surveillance and the varying ways drivers incorporated *Drivewell* into their work practice. In this, we discuss both how some have accommodated to, whilst others have actively resisted, the technology; how it has transformed driving appraisals; and how it works interdependently with other surveillance technologies.

Our contribution to the field is three-fold. First, we advance HCI‘s knowledge on the ways that telematics influences driver behaviour, safety and wellbeing as well as large-scale transport informatics (a key issue for the Internet of Things). Second, the work also speaks to a highly controversial theoretical debate about the privileging of data-performance in the management of a workforce [5]. Finally, we assess the utility of *Drivewell* and consider new forms of resistance against modern forms of digital surveillance.

BACKGROUND

Telematics and Pay As You Drive (PAYD)

There have been numerous studies about the deployment of telematics technology in private vehicles, with considerable attention being paid to the relative costs and benefits of PAYD. Introduced in the late 1990s as an innovative method of determining insurance premiums, PAYD uses a GPS receiver and a small on-board computer to record data on location, speed, mileage and time of driving. A reduction in cost of this technology has facilitated the emergence of new business models that specifically target vulnerable drivers, like the young and inexperienced (who typically have to pay large insurance premiums) [12].

Studies in this field have illustrated how these initiatives can have a positive affect on driving behaviour. Bolderdijk et al [4] studied a group of young drivers who had signed up to a PAYD system that allowed them to save money on their insurance premium if they adhered to predefined speed limits. Speed was monitored over the period of a year with PAYD drivers showing significantly reduced speed when compared with non-PAYD drivers. Benefits extend beyond personal gain: economic and environmental impact studies have illustrated that PAYD schemes can be more effective for lowering fuel consumption than tax on gasoline [28].

Despite these benefits, a number of costs have been identified in the literature. Duri et al [14] for instance, identified the potential for data misuse, including the risk of it being sold to third parties without explicit consent. They also highlighted the danger of those with malicious intent accessing driver location. Subsequent studies by Iqbal et al [19; 20] have also outlined the privacy and security risks of leaked or hacked GPS data, in terms of the identification of home addresses and the unsolicited monitoring of driver behaviour and style.

There is also an argument that the telematic devices can over-complicate the task of driving. Lansdown et al [21], for instance, describe the problems associated with a range of new ‗additional-to-driving‘ activities, including both operations that are unrelated to driving (e.g. the use of mobile phones) and tasks that are driving-related, but make the activity more convoluted (e.g. navigation and route guidance systems). As such, there is reason to hypothesise that telematics systems—either because of in-car feedback or through a driver consciously changing their behaviour because of the awareness of being monitored—might adversely complicate driving and, thus, adversely affect it and increase the risk of accident.

Driver surveillance and appraisal

We see telematics in general and remote monitoring of driver performance in particular as sitting within the wider remit of surveillance. Sociological contributions in this field are often dystopian in theme (e.g. [16]), and concerned with the concepts of ‗power‘, ‗politics‘ and ‗employee meaning-making‘. This stands in contrast to psychological contributions where there is a greater concern for the efficacy of surveillance and those factors (including economic ones) that make it beneficial in the workplace [1]. The earliest published theories of management, dating back to 1916, understood control and monitoring as central to the supervisor‘s task [15]. Employee monitoring therefore is well established and related to long-standard practices such as clocking in and out, measuring output and payment by task completion. The development of information systems gave early large-scale organizations the ability to police their subordinates and gain an advantage over their commercial rivals [2]. It has also been shown surveillance can diminish employee wellbeing and the nature and intensity of it says much about how a company views its workers [1].

Surveillance and remote appraisal practices have steadily grown within vehicle fleet management, where issues such as speed, safety and timeliness are key to the successful running of a business. Historically, driver-appraisals were more subjective and made by a person. However, a number of key indicators can now be objectively measured via the various telematics platforms, which can identify and reward those who drive within established parameters. Simsek et al [33] identify a number of such objective indicators, including speed, the idle duration of vehicles, fuel costs—all indirect measurements of good driver performance. Additionally, where it is important to map the position of vehicles in the fleet in relation to each other, GPS based metrics such as headway (distance between vehicles) can also be used as a key performance indicator (e.g. [27]).

Bus drivers

Professional bus drivers face difficult and taxing daily tasks. They must negotiate a range of challenges in their physical environment, both outside and inside their vehicle, including traffic congestion, passenger demands and the maintenance of good operational control of the bus. Research spanning over fifty years has demonstrated that this is one of the most stressful jobs, leading to a range of negative physical, behavioural and psychological outcomes [35]. In the 1950s, a series of studies by Morris and colleagues (e.g. [24]) showed that bus drivers were twice as likely to die from coronary heart disease (CHD) than conductors working alongside them. In 1991 Rosengren et al [32] found CHD rates in bus drivers were three times the rate of 30 other sampled populations, once socio-economic factors had been taken into consideration. In a range of studies that assessed perceived stressors associated with such poor health outcomes, 69% of drivers cited traffic as the main problem [13] although fatigue associated with unusual or demanding shift patterns is also a known problem leading to poor driver health [8]. If we add to this the known psychological impact associated with difficult interactions with passengers [35]; the musculoskeletal disorders linked with poor cabin posture [35] and the gastrointestinal problems associated with meal hour irregularity and generally poor eating habits [35] then it is not surprising to find that bus drivers show unusually high levels of absenteeism [37] and high job turnover [25].

Recent years have seen further demands placed upon London's bus drivers, including the elimination of cash payments [29] and the introduction of ‗headway' system where drivers monitor the distance of the bus in front and behind via an LCD display [30]. In part, our work analyses a further technological demand placed upon this occupational group that further reduces their autonomy.

METHOD

The data presented here was collected over a period of 14 months as part of on-going research studying digital technologies and the work practices of London bus drivers. Our results are derived from qualitative data, collected primarily through ethnography and semi-structured, in-depth interviews with 15 bus drivers, 10 of whom were interviewed twice. On average, our interviews lasted 50 minutes and all were audio-recorded and transcribed verbatim.

Ethnography attempts to understand the ‗social meanings and ordinary activities' of a group, as they occur in ‗naturally occurring setting' [6, p.10]. This is achieved by researchers observing and participating in as many of the activities of a cultural group as possible. Although for practical reasons we were unable to participate in the activity of driving, we spent as much time as possible observing this activity. Our fieldwork consisted of ‗focused' bus riding around London for a total of five weeks (two at the beginning of fieldwork and three at the end). Here the researcher either shadowed a participant while they were driving or rode with one as a fellow passenger. During these rides, the driver would be asked to provide a commentary of the journey as it relates to *Drivewell* scores. One driver also wore a wearable camera that automatically takes pictures at 10-second intervals during two workdays. The images were later played back to the driver who was asked to reflect on *Drivewell* considerations for each part of his route. A detailed fieldwork diary was kept to record all of these interactions.

As the researchers already knew five participants, we were able to elicit perspectives in more sociable settings, either at bus garages during their breaks or in cafes and pubs after work. Employing the recruitment strategy of ‗snowball-sampling' [3], we asked these informants to identify other potential participants. A plethora of classic ethnographies have demonstrated how ‗key informants' like these work to smooth access (e.g. [36]). However this familiarity also meant that we had to pay acute attention to reflexivity, affording a genuine consideration of the partialities and bias we might bring into our work.

After fieldwork, we assembled all the raw data (interview transcripts and fieldwork diary) on a Microsoft word document to get an overview. We brought order to this by organizing sections under categories and then we drew out overarching themes. We then sorted the data further by breaking these themes into codes. This allowed us to group information together and assess related material.

FINDINGS

Four substantial themes were identified from this analysis: accommodating and accepting *Drivewell*; questioning the value of *Drivewell*; resisting and subverting *Drivewell* and managing multiple forms of performance monitoring. Each of these is discussed in the following sections.

Accommodating and accepting *Drivewell*

Interviews provided an initial opportunity to explore how our participants have incorporated *Drivewell* into their work routines. As will be noted throughout our findings, *Drivewell* is hugely divisive—while some drivers see it as a positive way of improving passenger service and gathering constructive feedback, others regard it as inherently flawed and counterproductive. However, it was clear that *Drivewell* had impacted on behaviour for some. Throughout bus journeys the lead author took with our participant drivers, it was observed how they would frequently glance at the *Drivewell* module located above their windscreen. Jimmy, who was one of the most enthusiastic drivers in regards to the system, was observed to check the indicator more than most:

> ***Interviewer:*** *Do you keep an eye on that a lot?*
>
> ***Jimmy:*** *Yes, yes, yes. Not to go red.*
>
> ***Interviewer:*** *And do you find it quite responsive, like if you brake?*
>
> ***Jimmy:*** *Yes, you have to go smoothly and nicely, so, otherwise they go red, it's not good.*

Jimmy's use of *Drivewell* is illustrative of its capacity to encourage a form of self-surveillance. Unlike most of the drivers we spoke to, Jimmy appears to have accepted *Drivewell* fully. When asked if he felt it had made him a safer driver, he noted: *Hundred percent. Hundred percent. If there's no monitors on the buses, some drivers, they don't care. They just drive whatever they like. Because of that [Drivewell], they are controlled.* Alan shared a similar sentiment: *"Well, it helps. It probably makes you try that little bit harder to get a better score, you know?"* As Alan alludes to here, one of the perceived values of *Drivewell* was the encouragement it would give drivers to achieve ―better" or ―good" scores. However, what was considered to be a good score or not differed widely across our participants. This was not helped by seemingly frequent changes from TfL and local bus garages in defining ―target" scores and how these related to the traffic light feedback system situated on the buses. Jimmy, for example, tried to achieve green all the time and a 100% target. Nobby was another driver that appreciated the system and the feedback it gave—however, he typically aimed for a much lower score: *"The thing is 80% is the guideline. As long as you stick to around that then you can go under the radar, as they say."* Alan explained how while he did check on his scores frequently, he was careful not to attain too high a score all the time:

> ***Alan:*** *I think I drive about the right speed and the right comfort, and I try and get the balance. If you try and get too much of a high score I think you're going to slow down a bit too much. I like to get a happy medium – get around reasonably quick but not too quick so it's too uncomfortable. Have the score sort of above average.*

It was notable how, while all of the drivers did check on their scores, it was only a small number who took it very seriously. For instance, Erik targeted *"between 86 and 94 percent"* but stated: *―I don't worry about it. [...] As long as I keep my score exactly the same every week, I like to be in the amber."* In a similar vein, Ray explained how he did check-in on his scores but he didn't feel this impacted on his driving behaviour: *―I drive the same way as I do day in day out. Like I say, I check my scores every now and again, and they seem fine to me."*

Bob was an example of a very cautious and careful bus driver, who prided himself in providing what he considered *"good service"* to passengers. He explained how: *―Service to me is comfortable drive and safe drive, and if passengers are happy, then you're happy and everybody is happy."* Bob had become weary in recent years of the ways various bus companies had developed systems to ―catch drivers out". He regularly checked his *Drivewell* score but admitted this was more out of curiosity rather than a genuine interest in receiving feedback on his driving.

> ***Bob:*** *I sometimes look to see; "They have invested so much money on it, let me see what they're up to," for that purpose, but it's not to see how well I was driving, because I know that I was driving well. I mean, I don't have customer complaints, so as long as they're thinking that I'm giving a good service.*

While the primary way in which drivers spoke about the feedback they got from *Drivewell* was their overall scores for certain periods of time or routes, it was also noted how the system provided a useful means for modifying driving in specific areas. As will be discussed in more detail in the next section, one of the attributes of the *Drivewell* system is that it registers changes in the quality of road surfaces and bus suspension. While this can lead to problems with the quality of data collected, this was also useful for some drivers in modifying how they drive certain routes. For example, Jack was initially very frustrated with *Drivewell* but has come to terms with it over time: *I hated it when it first came in, but as I now am regularly around 100% on it I don't mind."* Jack explained how he started to see the value of the system through the level of feedback it provides a driver about the locations of events. As highlighted in the introduction, drivers can also use a computer terminal at the garage to get more of a detailed breakdown of how *Drivewell* has measured their driving. He explained:

> ***Jack:*** *It will also tell you any number of incidents, which may be where you did break hard. You can then get out a map, it will produce a map on that, show you exactly where, and in a lot of cases you will go, "Oh, yes, I remember that. That car pulled out in front of me" and you had to hit the brakes.*

Through use of the *Drivewell* terminal, Jack explained how he eventually identified a specific location that always caused a negative event on his report. *"There was one pothole on my route. When I first started driving that route I hit it. From then on I noticed all the drivers on that route were just pulling out around there, because actually this pothole was so bad it broke a bus."* As a result, Jack explained how he had modified his driving down this stretch of road to avoid the pothole, and consequently saw an improvement in his *Drivewell* scores.

Some of our participants described how a competitive culture has emerged among some drivers; this was especially evident when a driver would log-on to the *Drivewell* terminal in the communal areas of the bus depot.

> ***Nobby:*** *When you put your Drivewell key in, which should be a personal thing, and it comes up, people start gathering, and they start looking at your score and what percentage you get. So yes, it can become a sort of competition*

As well as being seen as valuable as a source for reflecting upon and changing driving behavior, some drivers also felt that *Drivewell* contributed greater security and protection to drivers. Nobby explained how *―in many ways it's good, that if you have an accident it will hopefully in many ways help you, not hinder you. Because it can say that you weren't braking hard. You weren't driving stupid"*. This view was echoed by Jimmy: *―It's good because if you have accident, all covered. Because everything's recorded. Speed, how was the turns, everything recorded. So in that case we are covered, all the records are there."*

Questioning the value of *Drivewell*

While many of our drivers did see the value—or some of the value—in monitoring the quality of their driving, most also felt that *Drivewell* went beyond what was reasonable and necessary. A selection of our sample made explicit reference to ‗big brother' when asked about their general perceptions of the system: *"See, a lot of people when it first came out didn't like it, because it is like big brother is watching you"* (Nobby). Instead of judging it as a positive system that helps to improve their driving by giving them constructive feedback, *Drivewell* was regarded with some suspicion. Drivers believed the real motivation behind it was to increase the capacity to punish drivers: *"I don't think the people, who invented that, really thought about that [constructive feedback]. They thought about, "This is a way to catch drivers"* (Bob). Bob's comments illustrate how *Drivewell* has increased feelings of control and diminished feelings of trust between bus drivers and their employers.

Regardless of whether drivers had positive or negative feelings towards *Drivewell*, they were always framed by an overarching suspicion of the system's accuracy and efficacy. Employees felt that the system was somewhat simplistic as a measurement tool and too easily affected by a multitude of other factors that the driver had no control of. For instance many perceived that there were *"bad buses"*, typically older models with poor suspension (like the ‗DPS' Dennis Plaxton model) that, if driven, achieve a negative score:

> ***Jack:*** *They also give you the scores for the buses, so you can see that certain buses are not good. The other day I had a DPS, which are not exactly the easiest. These are older buses. Ordinarily on a DPS forget it. There's absolutely no point in worrying about it.*

Alan articulates a similar sentiment: *―Yes, the suspensions vary from bus to bus."* He goes on to explain that the management team were generally aware of this and sympathetic to how the varying nature of bus suspension affects drivers' scores. For this reason, scores had a duel purpose—to first monitor the driver and second, monitor the mechanics of the bus: *"If a bus is constantly getting low scores with every driver they [the management] try and do something about it"* (Alan).

As well as so-called ―bad" buses, drivers also argued that some routes were inherently ―bad" and if assigned to them, they would be disadvantaged in their assessment:

> ***Jack:*** *But then some routes are bad, and you will see that the drivers on those routes are constantly in the lower range. I don't think they take too much notice of those, because they know that there's nothing really they can do about it.*

Bob summarizes the reasons many of our participants feel that *Drivewell* is a poor measurement of driving quality: *"most of the time, the result is based on the road surface, and crappy buses."* The drivers also felt that there was a clear flaw and irrationality in this measurement as a poor score or a negative event might actually signal good driving. This would be the case if the driver had to brake suddenly to avoid a pedestrian who stumbles onto the road: *"You have reacted fast. To me, more than you have done worse, I think you have done well; that's the whole concept"* (Bob). Under these conditions, the reward structure doesn't provide the incentive to drive well for some drivers as through being given a ―bad bus" or a ―bad route" or even through safe driving they cannot fairly compete against their co-workers:

> ***Interviewer:*** *So those people would never have a chance of winning the TV?*
>
> ***Jack:*** *Not a hope.*

These findings are consistent with other research that has shown how sensor data can be fragile [11]. It is therefore important to attach narratives to such material and put it into context [31].

A further issue of contention was the ways that *Drivewell* generates reports that ‗flag' those employees who are potentially driving poorly so that managers can intervene. At this stage, drivers are interviewed by managers, following which a human form of surveillance—―the mystery passenger"—would be used to either confirm or contradict the findings of *Drivewell*. However, disagreement and anecdotal evidence about the inaccuracy of *Drivewell* as a tool to measure performance meant that many of our participants had crafted ready-made excuses in case they are called into the office for sanction. For example, Bob explained how he used to pay attention to *Drivewell* when driving but no longer did because he knew the system was flawed:

> ***Bob:*** *I know that if I get called in, for having a bad performance on that, I know how to back me up...I'd say, "Sort the bus out first, and sort the roads out, then I'll make*

> *sure that the performance will be 100%,". They can't catch me on that, definitely not. It doesn't tell me anything; it's just a waste of time and money.*

It was for these reasons that Bob felt that TfL should revert to the traditional method of human surveillance:

> ***Bob:*** *I would have more mystery shoppers [passengers], because that would give me a better result* [...] *remember, you could give a perfect service, but you could be having a bit of attitude to passengers; that, to me, is a bad service. That key thing [Drivewell] won't tell them that, but a human, at least if you're a mystery traveller, he could be able to tell you that.*

Bob here alludes to what was previously the primary means of assessing the driving quality. ―Mystery passengers" would rate aspects of the driving quality across a range of subjective measures, but also be assessing other aspects of their duties that are critical to providing passengers with a good service, such as politeness. Our work therefore contributes to recent literature that questions the privileging of data-performance in the management of a workforce [5]. However, the use of *Drivewell* to identify those drivers who should be assessed with a mystery passenger was seen as an inherent failing in this approach—an issue that was compounded further as most drivers were able to recognize these ―mystery" shoppers.

Resisting and subverting *Drivewell*

Despite all of the drivers accommodating *Drivewell* in some way into their work life, they simultaneously resisted and rejected its coercive potential. This type of resistance took a range of forms. Jack characterised his initial reaction to the system as illustrative of his *"natural anarchy"* and what appeared to a generally disobedient attitude to his relationship with management and performance monitoring: *―I went through a period of seeing how much red I could get"* (Jack). While Jack was initially dismissive of the system—and indeed other forms of management control—he did eventually see the value in the system. Other drivers displayed less overt resistances, instead preferring to modify their behaviour just enough so they wouldn't be liable for employer sanction. For instance, in a discussion with Erik and Justin, Erik started to explain how he would deliberately drive badly in order to reduce his overall score:

> ***Erik:*** *As long as you keep it between 70 and 90, they won't say nothing to you. Nothing at all. I keep mine – mine's literally the same every week. If I get into 100, when I'm running late, say I'm running from the garage to Peckham, all I keep doing is slamming the brakes on.*
>
> ***Justin:*** *Keep your score down.*
>
> ***Erik:*** *Yes.*
>
> ***Justin:*** *In case they expect you to get 100 every time?*
>
> ***Erik:*** *Yes, because if you stay in the 100s, then all of a sudden you drop down to the 80s, they'll want to know why. They'll start thinking, "Well, why's he doing that? Why has that gone like that?" So if you keep it the same all the way through, like mine is always between 86 and 94 per cent, and so I've got amber. Every time I look on it, it's amber all the way down. I won't be in your green.*

Erik regards *Drivewell* performance measurement as more complex than just managing to keep his scores in the green or amber zones on a given route. Instead, he looks at his scores over time and imagines the potential implications of him suddenly moving from very good to poorer (but not necessarily bad) scores. Through reflecting on this, he takes the decision to act by ensuring his scores are always *"good enough"* so as to avoid sanctions for consistently poor driving but also so as not to *"raise expectations"* that may not always be met. Furthermore, this tactic of purposefully driving bad on limited occasions affords Erik the luxury of not modifying his driving at other times.

We also observed ways that employees would resist *Drivewell* by attempting to discover ways to circumnavigate its use. As noted in the introduction, drivers are supplied with an individual key that they must plug into the *Drivewell* device every time they drive a bus. Two drivers admitted to neglecting to activate the machine if no passengers were on-board. This would typically happen when they were leaving the garage at the start of their shift. There was a general feeling that this was not a significantly disobedient practice as *Drivewell* is primarily explained to be a system for ensuring passenger comfort and satisfaction: *―It doesn't matter if you do give a rough ride, it's only yourself.* [...] *If you're the only one on the bus, what does it matter if you hit a few bumps or something? Like I say, if you take it off, it should make a noise after a while."* (Gordon). By not using the fob at the start of their shifts, the drivers are able to creatively carve themselves a ‗gap' in the apparatus of surveillance and resist the continuous extraction of performance information.

As well as removing their *Drivewell* keys at times when no passengers were on-board, a smaller number of drivers discussed how it was possible to circumnavigate it while the bus was in service. On one journey that the researcher accompanied a participant on, it was demonstrated how the key could be removed for a short period of time before the alarm started to become audible. This period of time—somewhere in the region of 10 to 15 seconds depending on the bus—was long enough to disable the system, restart it and stop the system from picking up on a potential event. Gordon explained how this was particularly useful: *―If you see a big pothole and you know you're going to hit it, you could take it off quickly."* However, Gordon was also at pains to explain how he would not do this regularly in practice himself: *"I don't think that's a good idea because you're not concentrating so much on your driving when you're doing things like that"* (Gordon).

Finally, a further instance of subversion was witnessed during fieldwork at a bus depot. As noted above, there were occasions where multiple drivers would gather around their colleagues as they were using the *Drivewell* kiosk to receive a detailed breakdown of their driving report. During one depot visit, drivers gathered around the terminal and listened intently to their colleague explain what was being displayed on the screen. The immediate response from the researcher was that this driver must have received some extraordinary *Drivewell* scores. However, upon further investigation it was revealed that this driver was showing his colleagues where his holiday home in Spain was: *"That machine is quite useful. One of the drivers, who bought a house in a village in Southern Spain, was able to get that up on the machine and show exactly where the house he bought was"* (Jack). This illustrates how drivers have, even in a small way, the ability to creatively reshape *Drivewell* and use it on their own terms.

Managing multiple forms of performance monitoring

Our final theme relates to the ways that *Drivewell* was considered an additional complication to our participants' already challenging job of bus driving. In some ways the *Drivewell* unit was considered a literal distraction in a driver's cabin. Pat spoke at length about the ways in which he found the system distracting, both within the cabin and as a way of focusing the driver too much on getting good scores:

> ***Pat:*** *In my eyes, the problem is it comes up on a traffic-light system above you. You can be distracted from driving because you're so concerned at getting a good score. [...] When it was first introduced, a lot of people were so concerned because, obviously, you're distracted. You're not looking at the road if you're looking up there.*

In many respects, *Drivewell* could be considered as a further addition to what is a complex job requiring great amounts of concentration. The complexity of the role was in many ways illustrated—yet also compounded—by the increasing modes of measuring driver performance. While our fieldwork was focused on the impact of the *Drivewell* system, very often participants talked about it in contrast, or alongside, these other ways their work is being monitored and judged. For instance, CCTV is used to add additional security to passengers but was also known to be a way of checking driver behaviour and action in the case of a complaint or road traffic incident. The iBus terminal—a GPS enabled system that visually displays distances between buses in front and behind on the same route (discussed in [30])—is a way of ensuring regular intervals between buses but is also a tool for real-time assessment of driver punctuality. In one joint interview with Nobby and Jack, there was a strong feeling that all aspects of their work life will soon be monitored: *"it knows your speed* [...] *they know everything"* (Jack); *"they know exactly"*; *"you've got cameras, what speed you're doing, if you accelerate too fast* [...] *You've got undercover, it's just endless"* (Nobby). The endlessness that Nobby here describes was demonstrated frequently to us as we accompanied drivers on journeys around London. After a limited amount of fieldwork we quickly noticed how many drivers are prone to glance at the iBus LCD and the *Drivewell* indicator almost as much as they check their wing mirrors.

We also observed the qualitative difference between *Drivewell* and other apparatus of surveillance present on London buses and the different ways drivers respond to them. Like iBus headway, *Drivewell* supplies immediate visual feedback. However, if headway performance is poor there are extra prods via text message and then a radio call, and so more importance is placed upon adhering to the demands of this apparatus of surveillance. The ―mystery passenger" as a type of surveillance is also experienced differently, as described in the following quote by Jack. It is less immediate and doesn't require a reflexive response, rather it adheres to Foucault's metaphorical use of *panopticon* when explaining modern forms of surveillance – a design that facilitates the discipline of subordinates because it is impossible for them to know when they are being watched [16]..

> ***Jack:*** *Oh, you get them regularly anyway. You will suddenly get a letter saying, "You were assessed the other day." They don't use our own staff very often, because-*
>
> ***Nobby:*** *We know them.*
>
> ***Jack:*** *You see somebody get on, and you see where they're going to sit, and from then on it's absolutely mirrors, mirrors.*
>
> ***Nobby:*** *Put away your sandwich. (Laughter)*
>
> ***Jack:*** *Yes. Wait until they all sit down.*

It was also apparent that it wasn't just the functional operation of duties in relation to these different forms of monitoring that was challenging, but also that sometimes trade-offs had to be made in prioritising certain measures over others. For example, Nobby explained how he was *"caught out"* one time when his score was adversely affected after he had to leave the bus garage late:

> ***Nobby:*** *Work informed me that I left late, and so obviously my driving was rather erratic. Basically I was driving it like a rally driver from Tottenham to – basically I left about 12 minutes late and given about 50 minutes to do it. So basically when I finished I realised, or when I put my score in, it was down to 60, and therefore I realised it was the way I was driving, because of obviously the braking and the acceleration. So I went from average 80 down to 60.*

On this occasion, Nobby acknowledged he had driven his bus *"like a rally driver"* in order to make up time and not be reprimanded for causing delays to services and not maintaining equal distances between services. However, he realised on reflection that in doing so he had significantly impacted on his *Drivewell* score. He acknowledged on reflection that he may think twice about trying to catch up to schedule like this in the future. In a similar example, Gordon explained how when it came to managing both *Drivewell* (monitoring of acceleration, speed and horizontal movement of the bus) and Headway (keeping a designated gap between the buses in front and behind on the same route) he aimed to keep both in balance with one-another: *"It's getting the happy medium, isn't it? Keep the bus on time, but give a reasonable ride. I try and get that balance about right. If it's too comfortable you might be going too slowly."* (Gordon). After being pressed further on this point, however, Gordon explained how maintaining headway would be prioritised over the quality of his driving:

Gordon: I don't like the bus in front to get too far away. If it gets a little bit ahead, especially if it's a fast bus driver, we can get further ahead. So you've got a wider headway, plus you can start and get later and later and later because you're picking up passengers who would have missed your bus had you been further down the road. I like to keep closer to the one in front. It makes it easy. You can't get too close because otherwise they will call you up. The controllers will call you up and say, "Hold back two minutes. Hold back three minutes" or whatever. I'd rather just have it so that I can just get away with it without any of them having to say anything to me.

Gordon reflects on the ways in which he has to negotiate the different forms of surveillance and the ways in which it may impact on his immediate work. He is aware that if he drives too close to the bus ahead of his then he will likely get some *"grief"* from the controller on his Headway system. This may mean being asked to wait for a short period to build the gap up further or receive further *"hassle"* from his controller and potential disciplinary action. The implication here, however, is that by slowing down the likelihood of picking up more passengers increases and thus the bus becomes delayed and becomes too close to one that may be following behind. This would mean having to increase the speed of the bus in order to maintain a distance to the one behind—which, of course, would likely mean more aggressive driving and acceleration, impacting on *Drivewell* scores. Therefore, by carefully managing his Headway all the time, Gordon considers himself better placed to keep his ideal *"middle ground"* between good Headway and *Drivewell* scores.

DISCUSSION AND IMPLICATIONS

Our fieldwork has highlighted the ways telematics systems like *Drivewell* can impact a remote and mobile workforce. The device undoubtedly has some positive impacts, seen most clearly in the way it affords real-time feedback and opportunities for reflection on driving practice. However, there are wider questions about the validity and accuracy of the data collected by *Drivewell*, which was indicative of broader concerns about digital surveillance. We discuss these issues below in three interrelated themes: first we explore the ways *Drivewell* carries assumptions about the nature of good driving and ask whether these assumptions reflect the drivers' own understanding of best practice; second, we consider *Drivewell* as one element in a complex technological ecosystem, asking how well the complexities of driving can best be captured by this integrated telematics platform and exploring the extent to which the systems set up competing demands for the driver; third, we ask whether driver surveillance techniques can be integrated into an effective driver appraisal and reward system that could ultimately improve performance.

What does it mean to drive well?

Drivewell is associated with a number of claims, with published benefits including improved passenger comfort and better fuel efficiency. However *Drivewell* does not directly measure these outcomes, but instead offers a simple proxy measure that can then become a target in its own right. We have seen that drivers can develop quite elaborate strategies to maintain their *Drivewell* score, but we should ask to what extent these strategies ultimately serve the company, the passengers and the drivers.

We have evidence that some drivers have used the system as a learning tool, using the scores to reflect on their driving and consider areas for improvement. These drivers maintain a more nuanced view of their role and responsibilities. They are likely to balance the demands of *Drivewell* with other work demands and in the process are likely to acquire new skills and knowledge that could genuinely lead to better driving. However, the score can become an end in itself—leading either to a race to the top, when drivers compete to get the best score, or a race to mediocrity, when drivers try to establish a readily achievable baseline score and stick to it. Under either circumstance, the score becomes the target and there is a real danger that genuinely good driving—like keeping a safe distance from the vehicle in front, gets lost along the way. This implication is consistent with other research that has highlighted the potential of sensor data to be insubstantial in the accurate measurement of an activity [11] and other work that has demonstrated the importance of attaching narratives to such data [31].

How to drive a London bus

The act of driving a London bus is quite unlike other forms of non-commercial driving, in large part because of a range of technological innovations that have been introduced in the last few years. *Drivewell* operates as part of a technological ecosystem where different devices monitor specific information in relation to driving style (*Drivewell*), location, speed and relationship to other buses (iBus), passenger behaviour (CCTV) and general conduct (mystery passenger). In short, the London Bus is now imbued with an intelligence and ability to communicate with other buses, with passengers and controllers in a way that anticipates the seamless communication of smart objects in the Internet of Things and the eventual roll out of driverless vehicles. There is one very important difference, however. In this system, the human driver is still in complete control of the bus. If the array of on-board devices will ultimately serve to reduce the autonomy of the driver, then two questions should be raised. First, do the different devices work collaborate to support the driver or do they compete for valuable attention and set up competing priorities? Second, do these systems lead to accurate and effective performance management?

In answer to the first question, we found that the different systems can compete in unhelpful ways. Driving well, being sensitive to local conditions and to the needs of passengers is not necessarily compatible with driving in a way that maintains headway between buses [30] or that keeps the bus on schedule. As we have already noted, on-board devices can place additional demands on the driver's attention, adding to the range of ‚multiple additional to driving' distractors that are becoming commonplace [21]. As such, if monitoring systems are to exist, they should be implemented in ways that do not immediately impact on bus drivers' attention and the way work is assessed.

In answer to the second question, we need to return to the organisational literature on performance monitoring and appraisal in order to ask whether telematics are likely to improve worker behaviour, organisational culture and management practice. We know that any surveillance or monitoring system should be designed to appropriately and accurately assess performance on a particular task. We also know that the best performance monitoring systems respect the psychological and emotional elements of a job—such that performance scores are not considered alone [34; 26; 10; 22; 7]. Given the various aforementioned stressors on those who choose bus driving as an occupation, there is a danger that *Drivewell* fails on both counts. As we have seen, drivers have challenged its accuracy, feel that they don't capture good driving in its fullest sense and fail to account for the quality of the vehicle being driven and the nature of the roads travelled. In terms of the integration of this system into the wider organisation we also encounter a perception that the technology is deployed to benefit the employer at the expense of employees. In short, we don't see much recognition of the known stressors already acting on the bus driver, nor much consideration of how new surveillance might add to those stressors.

Resistance in a mobile and remote workplace

Marx famously described the ways workplace surveillance is used as a tool to maintain managerial control on behalf of capital. The architecture of a factory renders workers highly visible and therefore controllable by their supervisors. Workers' resistances to coercion in these spaces consisted of literally throwing a spanner in the works to halt production lines and traditional forms of work solidarity like unionization. We see this in the modern workplace, where research on call centre workers has shown that intense surveillance generates acts of worker resistance, sabotage and non-compliance with managers [17; 9].

For decades, the driver workplace offered few points of comparison with the factory or call-centre context—they worked alone (or in pairs) in a remote and mobile context where performance monitoring was ad hoc and subjective. So what does the implementation of digital surveillance mean in terms of worker resistance? We have seen the various ways that drivers are able to discount the legitimacy of *Drivewell*—questioning its accuracy or appropriateness. We have also seen a number of resistances that include removing the fob for short periods in order to reduce recorded ‗events', purposefully performing poorly in order to reduce expectation and challenging managers' interpretation of scores by blaming vehicles and the road. In part, this would seem to be a reflection of the simplicity of the performance measure and it would be interesting to consider the ways the drivers themselves might be able to present their own ‗scores' as part of a more sophisticated package of evidence in support of skills. It is interesting, in this regard, that the drivers themselves have adopted the practice of using *Drivewell* in their own evidence-gathering efforts to illustrate problems with a particular bus or route and fostering this kind of agency might be a more acceptable way to go.

CONCLUSION

In this paper we have studied *Drivewell*, a telematics device installed by London's transport authority on their buses to measure and regulate driving. This is an example of an increasing range of driver-surveillance technologies on London's buses. Although drivers did see some value in these systems, they have also caused anxiety and there is deep suspicion about this technology's efficacy and accuracy. Our findings highlighted a range of resistances drivers have developed to compensate for and work-around the Drivewell system. We also saw how drivers have to negotiate between the demands of *Drivewell* and other monitoring systems, some of which are based on competing and contradictory forms of assessment. While these issues emphasise the deep challenges to accepting such monitoring technologies in remote and mobile workplaces, we suggest there are positive opportunities here to harness the learning potential around sensor data and to support the development of skills and self-advocacy in the workplace.

ACKNOWLEDGEMENTS

This work was supported by RCUK Digital Economy Program grant no. EP/G066019/1 SiDE.

REFERENCES

1. Ball, K. Workplace surveillance: an overview. *Labor History*, 51, 1 (2010): 87-106.
2. Beniger, J. *The Control Revolution: Technological and Economic Origins of the Information Society*. Cambridge, MA: Harvard University Press, 1986
3. Biernacki, P. and Waldorf, D. Snowball sampling: problems and techniques of chain referral sampling. *Sociological Methods & Research, 10*, 2 (1981), 141-163.
4. Bolderdijk, J., Knockaert, J., Steg, E. and Verhoef, E. Effects of Pay-As-You-Drive vehicle insurance on young drivers' speed choice: Results of a Dutch field experiment. *Accident Analysis & Prevention*, 43, 3 (2011), 1181-1186.
5. Bouskila-Yam, O. and Kluger, A. Strength-based performance appraisal and goal setting. *Human Resource Management Review*, 21, 2 (2011), 137-147.
6. Brewer, J. D. *Ethnography*. Philadelphia: Open University Press, 2000.
7. Brewer, N. and Ridgeway, T. Effects of supervisory monitoring on productivity and quality of performance. *Journal of Experimental Psychology: Applied*, 4 (1998): 211–27.
8. Brown, I. D. Driver fatigue. *Human Factors*, 36 (1994), 298–314.

9. Callaghan, G. and Thompson, P. We recruit attitude: the selection and shaping of routine call centre labour. *Journal of Management Studies*, 39, 2 (2002), 233–54.
10. Chalykoff, J. and Kochan, T. Computer-aided monitoring: its influence on employee job satisfaction and turnover. *Personnel Psychology*, 42 (1989), 807–29.
11. Choe, E., Lee, N., Lee, B., Pratt, W. and Kientz, J. 2014. Understanding quantified-selfers' practices in collecting and exploring personal data. In *Proc. CHI '14*, ACM, 1143-1152.
12. Desyllas, P., and Sako, M. (2013). Profiting from business model innovation: Evidence from Pay-As-You-Drive auto insurance. *Research Policy*, *42*(1), 101-116.
13. Duffy, C. and McGoldrick, A. Stress and the bus driver in the UK transport industry. *Work and Stress*, 4, (1990), 17-27.
14. Duri, S., Gruteser, M., Liu, X., Moskowitz, P. Perez, R., Singh, M. and Tang, J. Framework for security and privacy in automotive telematics. In *Proc. 2nd International Workshop on Mobile Commerce*, ACM Press (2002), 25-32.
15. Fayol, H. *General and Industrial Management*. London: Sir Issac Pitman, 1916.
16. Foucault, M. *Discipline and Punish: The Birth of the Prison*. New York: Vintage Books, 1995.
17. Frenkel, S., Tam, M., Korczynski, M. and Shire, K. Beyond bureaucracy? Work organization in call centres. *International Journal of Human Resource Management*, 9, 6 (1998), 957–79.
18. Goyal, M. Insurance telematics. *International Journal of Innovative Research and Development*, 3, 6 (2014), 72-76.
19. Iqbal, M. and Lim, S. A privacy preserving GPS-based Pay-as-You-Drive insurance scheme. In *Proc. Symposium on GPS/GNSS* (2006), 17-21.
20. Iqbal, M. and Lim, S. (2010). Privacy implications of automated GPS tracking and profiling. *Technology and Society Magazine, IEEE*, 29, 2 (2010), 39-46.
21. Lansdown, T., Stephens, A. and Walker, G. (2014). Multiple driver distractions: a systemic transport problem. *Accident Analysis & Prevention*, in press, available online, July 2014.
22. Larson, J. and Callahan, C. Performance monitoring: how it affects work productivity. *Journal of Applied Psychology*, 75 (1990), 530–38.
23. Litman, T., 2005. *Pay-As-You-Drive vehicle insurance: converting vehicle insurance premiums into use-based charges*. http://www.vtpi.org/tdm/tdm79.htm on the 23rd of June 2014.
24. Morris, J., Heady, J., Raffle, P., Roberts, A., and Parks, J. Coronary heart-disease and physical activity of work. *The Lancet*, 2 (1953), 1053–1057.
25. Mulders, H., Meijman, T., O'Hanlon, J. and Mulder, B. Differential psychophysiological reactivity of city bus drivers. *Ergonomics*, 25 (1982), 1003-1011.
26. Niehoff, B., and Moorman, R. Justice as a mediator of the relationship between methods of monitoring and organizational citizenship behaviour. *Academy of Management Journal*, 36 (1993), 527–56.
27. Papadimitratos, P., de La Fortelle, A., Evenssen, K., Brignolo, R. and Cosenza, S. (2009) Vehicular communication systems: enabling technologies, applications, and future outlook on intelligent transportation. *IEEE Communications Magazine*, November (2009), 84-95.
28. Parry, I. (2005) Is Pay-as-You-Drive insurance a better way to reduce gasoline than gasoline taxes?. *American Economic Review*, 288-293.
29. Pritchard, G., Vines, J. and Olivier, P. Your money's no good here: The elimination of cash payment on London buses. In *Proc. CHI '15*, ACM, to appear.
30. Pritchard, G., Vines, J., Briggs, P., Thomas, L. and Olivier, P. Digitally driven: how location based services impact on the work practices of London bus drivers. In *Proc. CHI '14*, ACM, 3617-3626.
31. Rooksby, J., Rost, M., Morrison, A. and Chalmers, M. Personal tracking as lived informatics. In *Proc. CHI '14*, ACM, 1162-1172.
32. Rosengren, A., Anderson, K., and Wilhelmsen, L. Risk of coronary heart disease in middle-aged male bus and tram drivers compared to men in other occupations: a prospective study. *International Journal of Epidemiology*, 20 (1991), 82–87.
33. Şimşek, B., Pakdil, F., Dengiz, B., and Testik, M. Driver performance appraisal using GPS terminal measurements: a conceptual framework. *Transportation Research Part C: Emerging Technologies*, *26* (2013), 49-60.
34. Stanton, J., and Barnes-Farrell, J. Effects of electronic performance monitoring on personal control, satisfaction and performance. *Journal of Applied Psychology*, 81 (1996), 738–45.
35. Tse, J., Flin, M. and Mearns, K. (2006) Bus driver well-being review: 50 years of research. *Transportation Research Part F*, 9 (2006), 89-114
36. Whyte, W. *Street Corner Society*. Chicago: University of Chicago Press, 1943.
37. Winkleby, M., Ragland, D., Fisher, J. and Syme, S. (1988) Excess risk of sickness and disease in bus drivers. *International Journal of Epidemiology*, 17, 255-262.

Managing Children's Online Identities: How Parents Decide what to Disclose about their Children Online

Tawfiq Ammari, Priya Kumar, Cliff Lampe, Sarita Schoenebeck
School of Information
University of Michigan
{tawfiqam,priyaku,cacl,yardi}@umich.edu

ABSTRACT

While extensive research has investigated the risks of children sharing their personal information online, little work has investigated the implications of parents sharing personal information about their children online. Drawing on 102 interviews with parents, we investigate how parents decide what to disclose about their children on social network sites (SNSs). We find that mothers take on the responsibility of sharing content about their children more than fathers do. Fathers are more restrictive about sharing to broad and professional audiences and are concerned about sharing content that could be perceived as sexually suggestive. Both mothers and fathers work to leverage affordances of SNSs to limit oversharing. Building on prior work, we introduce the concept of parental disclosure management, which describes how parents decide what to share about their children online. We also describe an emerging third shift of work that highlights the additional work parents take on to manage children's identities online. We conclude with theoretical and practical implications for designing SNSs to better support family life online.

Author Keywords

Parenting; Internet; social media; work; mothers; fathers.

ACM Classification Keywords

H.5.m. Information interfaces and presentation (e.g., HCI): Miscellaneous.

INTRODUCTION

Parents are anxious about raising their children in a technology-saturated world [24,31]. Parents are challenged to navigate increasingly complex choices about how to monitor, understand, and limit what kinds of content their children share online and with whom they share it [50]. Despite their concerns, parents themselves post extensively about their children online, often sharing personal content about children's behavior, development, and appearance [5,30,41]. While extensive research has investigated the risks and implications of children's use of SNSs (e.g., [25]), little work has investigated the responsibilities parents take on when they decide to post content about their children online. As a first step in this agenda, we investigate how parents share the responsibility of managing their young children's online identities. This is critical for understanding and preserving children's online identity, privacy, and digital footprints, as well as for promoting healthy relationships within the family. Doing so requires reconsidering theories that focus on identity and privacy from an individual perspective [4,36], and reframing them as shared concerns. We investigate three research questions:

RQ1: Who posts content about children to social network sites and what do they post?

RQ2: How do parents negotiate what is appropriate to post?

RQ3: In what ways do the affordances of social network sites affect how and what parents decide to post?

We draw on transcripts of 102 semi-structured interviews with parents. The interviews were conducted as part of our broader research agenda and were analyzed here with a focus on how parents interact with their partners and ex-partners about SNS use. We find that parents share the responsibility of managing a young child's identity and privacy when they post content about their children online. SNSs offer some affordances that support parents in this endeavor, but can also fail them in critical ways. We build on theories of information disclosure and boundary regulation to explore parental disclosure management, or how parents manage what information is shared about their children online. We also document an emerging third shift of parental responsibilities that highlights the additional work required to manage family life online on top of parents' existing work and home responsibilities. As online and offline family life becomes increasingly intertwined, understanding how parents negotiate roles is critical for the wellbeing of families and for designing the next generation of social platforms to support family life.

CHI 2015, April 18 - 23, 2015, Seoul, Republic of Korea

ACM 978-1-4503-3145-6/15/04...$15.00
http://dx.doi.org/10.1145/2702123.2702325

RELATED WORK

Disclosure and Privacy on Social Networking Sites

Affordances

Affordances refer to the relationships between the properties of an object and the agents that determine how a person could actually use the object [14]. Norman emphasizes the difference between real affordances, which are inherent to the technology, and *perceived affordances,* which are those that are visible or discoverable to the user [33,34]. Zhao et al. present four categories of perceived affordances based on how users adapt to SNSs over time: perceived physical affordances, perceived cognitive affordances, perceived affective affordances, and perceived control affordances [54]. Physical affordances refer to metaphors such as a "Home" icon on Facebook; cognitive affordances refer to users' understanding of an artifact such as Facebook's News Feed algorithm; affective affordances refer to emotional responses such as Facebook's "Like" option; and control affordances refer to users' ability to control their environment such as by limiting Facebook profile visibility to Friends Only.

Parents have always had to consider what is appropriate to share about their children with other people. Naturally, disclosure norms vary with parental philosophies, ranging from parents who freely share intimate details about their children's development (e.g., a daughter getting her period) to parents who consider such details to be intimate and private. We investigate how the affordances of SNSs interact with these disclosure choices, where the presence of unknown or imagined audiences [23] and loss of control over content [36] surfaces numerous questions about what should be shared online by whom, and to whom.

Disclosure

The way that SNS users disclose information follows normative values and varies based on SNS. Users engage in "profile work" to manage their online self-presentation and must balance the goal of showcasing their authentic self with the desire to abide by social norms of sharing [46]. These norms are in flux, and users employ various strategies to manage the risks of disclosure. Facebook users manage self-disclosure risks by regulating their Friend networks, targeting messages, or censoring themselves [48], but these strategies place considerable burden on users. Less burdensome would be for users to only post content that would be appropriate for any Facebook Friend to see [17], but this strategy could limit users' opportunities to experience self-disclosure benefits, such as building strong ties and increasing social capital [11,48].

SNS users recognize that their disclosure decisions affect other people, and vice versa. Individual users may adopt a variety of behavioral and mental strategies intended to either avoid unwanted outcomes from disclosure decisions (preventative strategies) or respond to disclosure decisions that resulted in negative outcomes (corrective strategies) [21]. However, SNSs lack tools that facilitate collaborative, preventative strategies for disclosure management [21]. Romantic partners, for example, have to regulate boundaries about how public they should be and how autonomous they should be [53]. Collaborative, preventive tools would allow users to take part in the decision process (and responsibility) when posting new material online. Online photo sharing in particular presents disclosure management challenges. Photos can convey significant amounts of personal information (e.g., identity, associates, location), and the rise of user tagging and automated facial recognition mean that third parties can glean even more information from photos [6]. Among Facebook users who have young children, 57% strongly dislike when other people post pictures of their children without first asking permission [43].

Privacy scholar, Sandra Petronio, has argued that when people take on the responsibility of guarding other people's private information, errors in judgment and deception arise [36]. Petronio describes this as boundary turbulence, which emerges when a person's intended privacy levels are inconsistent with how other people might treat that person's information. Within families, multiple boundaries exist. A whole family boundary encircles information that belongs to all family members, and additional boundaries bind individual family members to each other. These boundaries, as well as the rules that govern how information flows among them, are fluid and shift as the family changes and individual members mature [37].

Privacy

While identity and privacy have been explored extensively in the context of online SNSs, discussions have primarily revolved around how such sites can maintain and respect an individual's privacy preferences [26,36,49]. Studies of privacy needs of individuals who take on the responsibility of posting content about another person are less well developed. This is especially pertinent for families, where parents are entrusted with moral and legal rights to be their children's guardians, rights that also exist in the online world. Most parental and scholarly concerns to date have focused on the risks of children themselves (especially teenagers) sharing personal content on SNSs [25,50]. In this work, we explore how parents consider disclosure risks and benefits and how they imagine these decisions will affect their young children, who are often too young to decide for themselves what should be shared about them.

Parenting Roles and Responsibilities

Men and women take on a variety of new roles when they become parents. Historically, fathers worked out of the home in paid jobs while mothers stayed home to raise children and do housework. These imbalances have shifted extensively in the U.S. over the last century, and the roles that mothers and fathers carry out have begun to converge. Fathers now do more housework and childcare while more mothers work outside of the home [20]. Mothers and fathers report similar struggles with managing work-life balance: 56% of working mothers and 50% of working fathers say they find it somewhat or very difficult to balance work and home responsibilities [20]. Despite this convergence, roles are still imbalanced, with mothers doing about twice the number of hours of housework and childcare than fathers [20]. Mothers also still perform more overall hours of paid work, housework, and childcare combined than fathers. Hoschchild's seminal book "The Second Shift" articulates the extensive labor that parents—especially women—do at home, often in addition to paid labor completed out of the home [16]. Also known as a "double burden", this unpaid labor can have deleterious health and economic effects. Managing photos is a type of domestic labor, one that mothers have historically controlled [38]. While both fathers and mothers take snapshots, mothers have often been responsible for organizing them in family photo albums [40]. Labor economists and sociologists have extensively documented gender role differences in the home (e.g., [9,16]); here we investigate how these play out online.

Parents and Internet Use

HCI research has focused on developing new technologies to help families communicate, stay connected, and manage technology-related needs in the home (e.g., [8,32,51]). A line of HCI research has focused in particular on sharing behaviors among family members, including sharing photos, calendars, user accounts and passwords [8,10]. Parents share information, stories, and photographs about their children on a variety of social platforms. Parents share actively on Facebook, as well as on sites like Instagram [30]. A workshop on HCI and motherhood discussed ways that technology can support mothers [3]. Mothers turn to online sites to interact with other adults when they have young children [40]. Mothers also use anonymous sites to talk about children and husbands in ways that they would not necessarily be comfortable sharing face-to-face or on a site like Facebook [41]. Women may be more concerned about their privacy on Facebook than men [18] which they manage by setting higher privacy restrictions, culling their list of friends, and deleting unwanted contacts [26]. The literature on fathers online is scarcer but reports similar patterns of information seeking and social support. Fathers discuss challenges of fatherhood online and look to encourage and confirm one another [12]. They also rely on humor to offer social support to one another [13]. Both mothers and fathers share photos of their babies on Facebook, though mothers report doing this slightly more frequently than fathers do [5].

Studies of pre-Internet family photography show that parents take and share photos that depict an idealized family: happy, healthy, and having fun [35]. However, tensions may arise about how and when photos should be shared among friends and family when photos are shared online. For example, parents and teenagers may have different beliefs about what is appropriate to share [50], and these beliefs vary based on the audience, norms, and affordances of a site. Photo-sharing practices online have been studied extensively (e.g., [1,29,40]). We explore how families negotiate boundaries of what is appropriate to share online, especially in the context of young children.

METHODS

We conducted 102 interviews with parents between April 2013 and May 2014. The interviews were conducted as part of our team's broader research agenda focused on understanding the lives of parents online. Interviews were conducted with a variety of diverse demographics as part of three different research projects. In each of the three project interview protocols, we asked participants about what kinds of child-related content they shared on SNSs and how they and their partners or ex-partners negotiated what was appropriate to share. We recruited participants via online groups, support groups, parenting lists, craigslist, snowball sampling, and our Facebook and Twitter networks. We also distributed fliers in daycare centers, doctors' offices, and churches in a Midwestern city.

Because parenting studies have often oversampled mothers (e.g., [2,28,39,50]), we focused on recruiting fathers when possible in our research. As a result, overall participant demographics included 64 fathers and 38 mothers. Most identified as currently married, but 11 identified as separated or divorced, 2 as single parents, and 1 as widowed. All but two of the fathers in our sample identified as working fathers (n=62); the remaining two identified as stay-at-home fathers. Among the mothers, 15 out of 38 identified as working mothers and 17 identified as stay-at-home mothers. They had a total of 212 children, with a median of 2 children each. Ages ranged from newborn to over 18 and the median age was 7 (10 children's ages were missing from the interview data). Interviews were conducted in-person (n=25), over the telephone (n=34) or over Skype (n=43) by members of the research team. The length of interviews ranged from 20 minutes (due to technical difficulties) to 110 minutes (also due to technical difficulties) and the median length was 51 minutes.

We coded the 102 transcripts using an inductive open coding approach [45] that focused on negotiations with partners or ex-partners related to sharing about children online. Two of the authors conducted a first pass of the interviews, identifying themes relevant to our research questions and conducted peer debriefings and consistency checks [22]. One author conducted a second pass and exhaustively coded all transcripts based on themes that emerged from the first pass. Here, we report overarching themes that emerged across participants' stories. In addition to our inductive analysis, we also drew on a summative content analyses approach [19,52] to quantify how often mothers and fathers each reported sharing about their children relative to their partners across the 102 transcripts.

Summative content analyses involve counting and comparing content (or keywords) [19]. We used the software NVivo to assess how frequently themes appeared in the transcripts. Results were then interpreted in the context of the research goals, as is done with inductive approaches [19,52]. Our report of gender differences in the results relies on the summative analysis results and interpretation. Throughout the paper, we refer to father participants as "Fa#" and mother participants as "Mo#".

Limitations

All participants identified as currently having or previously having a partner of the opposite gender. Though we did not recruit heterosexual parents in any of the studies, our recruitment either did not reach or did not appeal to same-sex partners with children, a significant gap that needs to be addressed in future work. We did not ask participants their household income, but no participants reported facing severe financial strain. We oversampled families in which the parents were married: 86% of our participants were married whereas U.S. Census data [47] reports that 71% of families live in a married household. There are also limitations in synthesizing data from multiple studies. While many of our questions were similar across each study, we used three different interview protocols. We considered the context of interview questions to the extent possible in our coding and interpretation of the data.

RESULTS

Results are organized around the three research questions: what mothers and fathers post about children online, how mothers and fathers negotiate sharing policies, and how the perceived affordances of SNSs help them to do this work.

Gender Roles and Managing Disclosure

Both mothers and fathers in our sample said that mothers did the majority of disclosure management work, which included deciding what to share, negotiating sharing policies with partners, and posting content online. The summative content analysis revealed 66 instances where participants said the mother managed posting content about children to SNSs more than the father did, but only 14 instances where participants reported that the father posted more than the mother.

Both mothers and fathers shared child-related content online, especially photos; however, many reported that mothers share more and more often than fathers. For example, Fa03 said that while he posted photos, his wife often posted them daily:

> My wife does a lot more of that…she posts a lot more of what the kids are dressed up like. I do it occasionally, but she'll do it like a daily posting, 'cause we have three girls. So if the youngest is smiling, she'll take a picture of that….so my middle child started scout girls as a Daisy and she took a picture of her in her outfit and posted it. Fa03

Mothers of younger children posted pictures that were "cute" or "captured a really sweet moment." They posted pictures of their children eating different types of food, wearing various outfits, or meeting family and friends. They also posted milestone pictures that highlighted their child's development. A number of fathers told us they posted about their children's activities, particularly those related to sports. Fa29 said:

> If it's my daughter accomplishing something like a [soccer] goal, or in ballet of her performing, or in voice, doing a recital in front of the town in our local little fair… I'll look for things that kinda capture the audience size, or capture the competition. Fa29

Fa12 stayed at home with the first of his three children, and he remained involved in their activities after returning to work. He posted photos of them at sporting activities to Facebook. Fa23 posted photos of his son's little league baseball team and of baseball games he attended with his son. Fa26 posted when his son overcame obstacles in sports. Fa24, a single father, said that he shared many "Hey, I'm so proud of you" moments on Facebook. But he also shared photos of him and his daughter, saying "I think everybody likes that daddy-daughter thing."

Managing Suggestive Content

Fathers described concerns about sharing images of their children—especially their daughters—in ways that could be interpreted as sexually suggestive. Some fathers had actually experienced this: for example, Fa29 had shared a photo of his daughter on Facebook perched on one foot and a Facebook Friend made a sexually suggestive comment about the pose depicting an exotic dancer. Fa29 told us:

> I actually nearly de-friended the guy over it… I basically had to tell him that was awful... It was something that made me feel uncomfortable and something that [even] if I remove it, other people have seen it. I didn't want to make it an issue… I said, "My shotgun would say otherwise", I think that's exactly how I said it. I try to use humor to defuse and to balance, because it's both positive and it's like using a smart-ass response to keep somebody in place. Fa29

Fa35 reported that he would share photos of his 10-year-old daughter as long as they did not exceed a specific "threshold." When asked to define threshold, he replied "something that I felt was over-sexualized for a 10-year-old... Shorts were too short, and making the duck-lip expression kind of thing, I wouldn't post that." Mo05 reported her husband's concern about suggestive content:

> I learned a lesson. [My son] was lying in our bathroom naked one night reading a book. And I took a picture of it and I mailed it to, I sent it to [husband] and he wrote me back and was like,

> "Never, ever, ever, send me photos of a naked child, even if it's our own, to my work phone." Mo05

Evaluating Audience Expectations

Fathers reported that they considered their Facebook audiences to be a broad, heterogeneous group including professional networks who were not interested in seeing pictures of children. Many fathers said they did not want to share too many—or sometimes any—photos of their children to this broad audience. One father said:

> I have a group of military friends and I have a group of [local] friends and most of them have... absolutely different viewpoints of the world... and I'm caught in the middle. So I don't post stuff so as not to upset either of the crowds. Fa03

Fa08 noted that his Facebook audience contained professional colleagues whereas his wife's was mostly friends and family. As a result, they mostly posted pictures to her network:

> The people I am friends with on Facebook [are] in an extremely heterogeneous group: from colleagues to childhood friends and people from college; most of them would not give a damn about my daughter. My wife's Facebook group is much smaller; she has close friends and family... She does post photos of [daughter] on Facebook and she usually gets a lot of responses. Fa08

In contrast, mothers described their Facebook audiences as a mix of close family and friends as well as a variety of weaker ties (e.g., high school friends) and acquaintances. Though many mothers also had professional connections in their Facebook audience, they did not report this as a constraining factor.

Negotiating what is Appropriate to Post

Negotiating Posting Preferences with Partners

Although mothers manage more of the work in posting content, both mothers and fathers reported that they discussed—and sometimes negotiated—with one another about what content to share. When parents had different perspectives, they had to consider their partners' desires when deciding what to share about their children or about one another:

> My husband is becoming less of a Facebook user. Just professionally I think he doesn't want as much out there... Um, so he will say "Don't tag me in that. [So when I share a picture, I ask myself] is my husband going to be upset? Mo04

This was especially the case when fathers disapproved of sharing on SNSs. Mothers developed self-censorship mechanisms to try to prevent problems:

> My husband... doesn't like social network kinds of stuff... I just don't post as much. I mean, I edit myself. Like I told you, like, I'll start to write something and say, "Eh, like, does the world really need to know that? Probably not." Mo06

Though our sample of divorced or single parents was relatively small, we observed some greater tensions when ex-partners needed to negotiate with one another. Fa31's ex-wife did not want Fa31 to share any content about their child online. Though they did not argue about it, they had different opinions about whether it was acceptable to post photos of their child online. Importantly, because his ex-wife did not post photos of their son, Fa31 worried that he would never see photos except when she showed them to him in person. Another participant who had separated from his child's mother relied on his father's Facebook friendship with his ex-partner to see pictures of their child because he was no longer Facebook Friends with her.

Managing Disclosure by Extended Family and Others

In addition to negotiating with their husbands, mothers took an active role in negotiating SNS sharing policies with extended family members. This negotiation took one of two forms: formal rules, which were typically sent to close family members to establish expectations about appropriate photo-sharing behaviors, and informal rules, which involved handling contingencies arising from family members sharing photos of children. Parents who used formal rules often communicated this information to family members and friends during later stages of their pregnancy or when they announced the birth of the child. For example, Fa16 and his wife had decided that others should not be allowed to share photos of their child online, and Fa16's wife sent an email to the family to that effect:

> Before [our son] was born, we actually talked in great detail about what we wanted to share. So we came to an agreement, and I think it's held up... It was mostly, we were thinking about photos. And the basic deal with it, that she and I could basically choose what photos to share. But third parties, like [grand]parents, were not allowed to share photos without asking us. Fa16

Some mothers and fathers wanted to control what people they did not know could see about their child. They took steps to contain how much information was shared about their child by asking family members—particularly grandparents—to limit the kinds of photos they shared or limit who they shared them with. In cases where family members might not know how to take certain steps (e.g., using privacy settings on Facebook), participants settled by asking those people to be cautious about what kinds of photos they shared. One mother explained:

> I have my mother who shares photos of [granddaughter] once in a while and, um, my mother-in-law will share once in a while. I've kind of asked them to be careful with that only because I can't really control who's seeing it if they share it on their Facebooks. Mo15

Though many parents did not want their children tagged online so that Facebook or Google would not know the identity of their child, a small number of parents *wanted* their children to be tagged to ensure that they knew what was shared about their child. Mo09 created a Facebook account for her child and permitted family members to post photos of her son only if they tagged his Facebook account:

> Like people other than my husband, um, would post photos of [my son]. Even his grandparents would… In the beginning, they asked if it was okay. And I just explained to them my only concerns and just to keep those concerns in mind, and they can post. As long as they tag [my son]. Because when they tag [my son], I can see it. I can check it. Mo09

However, sharing rules became more complicated if spouses had different opinions, and family members violated one spouse's preferences but not the other's.

> [My husband's] side of the family is much more active in Facebook than my side of the family is even though [my husband] hates it and I am okay with it. So it's usually his aunt and his sister who are bugging me for photos on Facebook... when other people, like my sister or sister-in-law post photos of [my daughter] and tag me in it to Facebook, I don't, like, untag us.... But, I mean, I think everybody knows that my husband hates Facebook. Mo06

Mo14 found that controlling other people's sharing was more difficult than expected. Mo14's sister-in-law posted a picture of Mo14's daughter's face to Facebook against her wishes. Mo14 decided not to ask her to take it down to avoid hurt feelings and family conflict. Mo08's husband's aunt took a picture of Mo08's son in the shower and emailed it to Mo08, saying she wanted to post the photo online. In response, Mo08 said she "flipped out on my husband and said, tell her not to, even, you know, no." Mo08 believed pictures that showed nudity should not be posted online, and should only be shared with family.

Finally, some parents decided it was too difficult to control what content about their children appeared online, and they stopped trying. For example, while Mo05 did not have a problem with family members sharing photos of her son, she discovered that her son's babysitter had made a photo of her son her public cover photo on Facebook. Mo05 and her husband did not want the babysitter to know they had looked at her Facebook page, and they wanted to maintain a positive relationship with the babysitter. They decided not to pursue the matter further rather than "making it awkward and Friending her or talking to her about it."

Perceived Affordances of Social Network Sites

Most participants in our dataset had Facebook accounts and had shared at least some photos of their children on Facebook. However, parents raised concerns about oversharing and maintaining control of the content that they shared. Concerns about oversharing reflected parents' beliefs about what their audience would want to see, while concerns about control reflected their desire to keep certain types of content more private than others. Parents took advantage of a range of SNSs and online services that they perceived to have particular affordances for sharing and maintaining control. Specifically, participants reported using Dropbox, Google+, LiveJournal, Flickr, Shutterfly, Snapfish, Instagram, and iCloud when they wanted to use a site to share to smaller or more private audiences than they had on Facebook.

Managing Oversharing

Participants were concerned about sharing too many photos of their children to their Facebook audience. Parents were sensitive to overburdening their networks with photos and believed that the number of photos their Facebook Friends would want to see was probably fewer than family members, such as grandparents, would want to see. To overcome this concern, parents turned to other online platforms. Blogs enabled parents to share more about their children without "overloading" or "blowing up" their Facebook page. For example, Fa16 indicated that while he or his wife might share one photo on Facebook, they would share the rest of the "action shots" on their blog, which the grandparents followed. He said his wife's preferences contributed to this approach.

> She is significantly more concerned than I am about oversharing and overposting. She shared the concern [that] people on Facebook may not want to see as many baby photos as people viewing the blog. Fa16

Most parents noted that if a photo was really good, they would share it on Facebook:

> Our friends and family don't have to see everything that we do there. Some of the best photos, we'll put up on Facebook so our friends and our family can see them. [The rest of the photos], they're just on our computer or on a hard drive. Oh, Shutterfly is another big thing. My wife puts a lot of our photos in Shutterfly. Fa13

Differentiating SNSs Based on Audience

A few parents were opposed to sharing photos of their children on Facebook regardless of the content of the photo or perceived audience on the site. For example, Fa09 said:

> Facebook is not private. So we're not going to make anything public about our son. Also, I'm pretty active on Twitter and I would never tweet a picture of my son. We do share photos with family via iOS photo which from my perception is more private, but Facebook is pretty much public. So I don't want... My son should decide that for himself. Fa09

Other parents expressed concerns that broad audiences should not see certain types of content, particularly if it could be interpreted as suggestive. Fa22 did not want his or his wife's Facebook Friends to see photos of his daughter at gymnastics where she wore tights. While he had business friends and "actual, real friends" (as he called them) on Facebook, his wife had a large network of people she knew in grade school whom she "hadn't talked to in 20 years." He felt "leery" about her sharing online to this broad audience.

While other parents echoed a similar view of posts on Facebook being "public", most still posted some photos and status updates about their children. Fa20 shared photos that he did not deem public in a private platform:

> With Facebook, I am very aware that anything I put on it is very public, fully public. I wouldn't put something on Facebook unless I consider it fully public. With LiveJournal, I have some degree of actual protection. Of course, with my personal Dropbox, I have as much protection as I want… I do not plan to keep up with Facebook legal and interface updates. Fa20

Fa37 noted that while he did a lot of blogging, his wife did most of the Facebook postings; they both understood that the blog was more public and should contain fewer pictures. Fa23, a single father, also shared more pictures of his daughter on Facebook than on his blog. Some mothers and fathers said they did not share the locations or names of their children online, and many more expressed caution about how and where they shared this kind of information.

When participants wanted to share more photos (e.g., an entire set of vacation photos) or more private photos (e.g., vacation photos of family members in swimsuits at the beach), they often shared these on different platforms with a narrower audience. Fa10, for example, had posted more than 200 photos of his daughter to Flickr. He kept that account private and gave grandparents the login credentials. He said that he would not share a photo of his six-year-old daughter in a swimsuit on Facebook, though he would share it on Flickr. He also would not share photos on Facebook of his children fighting or if their bedroom if it was "super messy."

Eighteen parents indicated they used Instagram to share photos. While some parents said they used Instagram to share photos in much the same way as Facebook, others noted that they used their Instagram to share photos with specific audiences. Specifically, some said they shared "cute" and the "best" photos on Facebook whereas they might share funny photos on Instagram:

> There was a cute picture that I took with my phone of my daughter playing in the snow, very innocently. So I put that on Facebook. There's a picture of her with a pretty evil look on her face throwing a snowball, that one I put on Instagram... I use Facebook mostly for close friends and family. I use Instagram for kind of a different set of friends, people who I share interests with or [who] have a similar sense of humor. Fa10

Fa11 told us he used Instagram because he was "sick of" all of the advertisements on Facebook and he had more control on Instagram where he could be "restrictive" about what he shared about his children. Ma13 created a separate Instagram account for her daughter and preferred to share photos of her daughter's activities to a network of close family and friends with rather than her large Facebook network, where she felt certain pictures like beach photos would not be culturally appropriate. Fa12 defined private pictures as those that depicted a trip to a beach with his family or features of their home, and similarly chose to share those only in a private Flickr gallery.

Fa23, who shared child-related content on his smaller Google+ network rather than Facebook, also considered how Google+ integrated with other services that extended family used.

> Our Google+ networks are a small fraction of what our Facebook network is… We have explicitly told [grandparents], "Hey, if you want to have access to photos and videos of your granddaughter quickly, why don't you just start a Google+ account since you guys have Gmail addresses anyway and it'll be integrated?" We perceive Google+ as more secure and we have more control over and, we try to be very discreet about who we share it with. Fa23

DISCUSSION

The Work to Manage Children's Identities Online

Parents face a significant and time-intensive responsibility of deciding how to balance their desire to post content about their children with the implications for their children's future digital identities. The current generation of parents had a clean slate when they first went online—the next generation will inherit a persistent online identity created for them by their parents, likely started before they are even born. Parents must consider their children's age and social, emotional, and physical development—a concern especially expressed by fathers of young daughters.

Our results suggest that many parents manage the work of sharing information about their children online by assigning de facto roles to one parent. Participants were always able to articulate who did the sharing and what kinds of sharing they did, though the roles tended to emerge organically. In the same way that one parent often does the cooking or the dishes, our results suggest that one parent takes on the primary responsibility of sharing about children online. Women often held this responsibility, perhaps because they are more active SNS users [5], or perhaps because their roles as primary caregiver are extended into these online spaces. Regardless, tensions emerged when one parent posted a picture that violated the other parent's personal preferences for what is appropriate to share. Additional stressors arose if extended family members violated parents' sharing preferences.

When existing approaches break down, parents must engage in articulation work to develop new approaches for managing disclosure management online. This work includes many of the strategies described Lampenin et al. [21]. Specifically, parents employed preventative strategies such as explicitly announcing to extended family their preferences for sharing child-related content online, using alternative software services, or by creating separate profiles for their child. Corrective strategies included interpreting a disclosure as non-serious or asking others to delete content on their personal profiles. Parents, particularly fathers, also adopted the lowest common denominator approach [17] as opposed to mothers who considered their networks to be denser and more pruned.

We refer to this emerging work as the "third shift", a concept building off Hoschchild's "second shift" that highlights the unacknowledged time and work that parents expend, typically in unpaid and unacknowledged labor [16]. Similar to the first and second shifts—paid labor and homemaking, respectively—the third shift expands itself into parents' already busy days. Much like the labor involved in managing and organizing family photos [37,39], mothers took the lead in doing the work of posting content online, as well as managing disclosure about their children, though fathers also actively did these behaviors. For both parents, the third shift of parenting online spans across work and home life, facilitated by constant access provided by mobile devices and SNSs. Mazmanian and Erickson describe the "constant availability" that is increasingly expected of workers and which coincidences with the technologies that enable it [27]. Together, this line of research portrays a broader pattern of expectations placed on Internet users that requires them to be available, active, and vigilant about their online identities.

Parents, and SNS users more generally, are presented with a new kind of demand on their time, one that requires participation online to be able to receive a number of benefits in the form of social and emotional support online [12,15,30,41]. Self-disclosure, in particular, is related to receiving these benefits. However, these benefits correspond with self-disclosure in the form of revealing information about oneself to others [48]; here, self-disclosure is inextricably tied to sharing about the child's identity as well. In the case of children, parents must tradeoff the benefits of receiving social support with the potential risks of revealing too much or inappropriate information about their children. For example, disclosing stigmatized behaviors like mental health issues can compromise a child's identity and privacy and can lead to judgment of the parents themselves [2]. These tradeoffs exist for a number of interpersonal relationships online; couples, friends, and coworkers all have to engage in disclosure and identity management behaviors [21]. Unfortunately, users lack clear norms for posting content [46] about other people, and thus have to perform the work of deciding—and often negotiating with one or more others—what is appropriate to share. In the case of our work, as children grow up, this negotiation evolves to include their own privacy and identity preferences (an important area for future work). New theoretical frameworks are needed to explain what happens when parents' self-disclosure desires conflict with the disclosure interests—or best interests—of the child. More generally, SNS users are actively posting content online, and in doing so, often sharing identities with other people. This requires new theoretical frameworks to understand how people manage this third shift of work while spending time online.

Design Opportunities for Managing Children's Identities

Our results show a need for design approaches that facilitate parental disclosure management. Currently on Facebook, individuals (usually) "own" just one account—their own. This is a technical features that offers affordances [54] for users to control who can see what content. However, there are few affordances for shared accounts among multiple owners. New technologies will be needed to help children perform their own disclosure management. Parents currently help their children create Facebook accounts [7] and set rules about technology use [50]. These practices are often driven by parents' concerns and interest in teaching their children how to become thoughtful and responsibility technology users. Yet, parents do not engage in practices to transfer the content they themselves have created to their children. Our work suggests three areas of design opportunities for supporting this kind of disclosure management:

- Joint accounts: SNSs could create joint sharing features that allow one or more users to create an account and share responsibility of it. Such an account would allow parents to jointly control privacy settings and manage content.
- Silent tagging: Parents could engage in "silent tagging" practices so that profiles and content are stored for later use, if a child decides she wants her identity to be attached to this content.
- Retroactive identity management: Children could be given the opportunity to more easily and powerfully alter their online presence, after it has been established by their parents.

Policy and Education Decisions

A risk related to the proposed design ideas is that Facebook (or other SNSs) would own more content about young children. Furthermore, current Internet policies such as COPPA are generally thought to be poorly conceived and ineffective (see [7]). New government regulation might be needed to give parents more rights and agency over their children's online identities at a younger age, but to also ensure children's own rights as they come of age to take over ownership of their online identities. Indeed, recent policy developments show increasing public appetite for the ability to manage digital footprints. The California legislature passed a law in 2013 that requires websites to allow minors to delete content they have posted [42] and the "right to be forgotten" in Europe allows people to request that search engines remove links to particular content from search results [44]. In addition to policy changes, more education and support is needed for parents. A significant portion of parenting now revolves around family technology use [7,31,50]. Policy makers, researchers, and media focus on children's behavior and risks, but focus less on how to help their parents. Organizations like Common Sense Media are working to educate parents; we argue that greater scholarly attention should be directed to support these efforts.

CONCLUSION

Parents share personal information about their children online and must decide what is appropriate to share and negotiate these decisions with their partner. We refer to this work as parental disclosure management. Mothers share content online and take on the responsibility of managing sharing more than fathers do. Fathers are more restrictive about sharing to their broad networks and are concerned about sharing content that could be perceived as sexual. Both mothers and fathers work to leverage perceived affordances of SNSs to minimize oversharing on Facebook and to maintain appropriate privacy levels when they do share. Results surface a third shift of online work that parents take on to manage their family life. Designing new kinds of social media affordances will be critical to help parents manage family identities online. Future work should also investigate how children feel about their online identity being created and curated for them.

ACKNOWLEDGEMENTS

We thank the National Science Foundation (HCC #1318143) for support. Any opinion, findings, and conclusions or recommendations expressed in this material are those of the authors and do not necessarily reflect the views of the National Science Foundation.

REFERENCES

1. Ames, M., Eckles, D., Naaman, M., Spasojevic, M., and Van House, N. Requirements for mobile photoware. In Proc. *Personal and Ubiq. Comp. 14*, 2 (2010), 95–109.
2. Ammari, T., Schoenebeck, S.Y., and Morris, M.R. Accessing Social Support and Overcoming Judgment on Social Media among Parents of Children with Special Needs. In *Proc. ICWSM,* AAAI, (2014).
3. Balaam, M., Robertson, J., Say, R., et al. Motherhood and HCI. *CHI Workshop*, (2013).
4. Bartel Sheehan, K. An investigation of gender differences in on-line privacy concerns and resultant behaviors. *J. of Int. Marketing 13*, 4 (1999), 24–38.
5. Bartholomew, M.K., Schoppe-Sullivan, S.J., Glassman, M., Kamp Dush, C.M., and Sullivan, J.M. New Parents' Facebook Use at the Transition to Parenthood. *Family Relations 61*, 3 (2012), 455–469.
6. Besmer, A. and Richter Lipford, H. Moving beyond untagging: photo privacy in a tagged world. In *Proc. CHI '10*, ACM (2010), 1563–1572.
7. Boyd, D., Hargittai, E., Schultz, J., and Palfrey, J. Why parents help their children lie to Facebook about age: Unintended consequences of the 'Children's Online Privacy Protection Act'. *First Monday 16*, 11 (2011).
8. Brush, A.J.B., Inkpen, K.M., and Tee, K. SPARCS: exploring sharing suggestions to enhance family connectedness. In *Proc. CSCW*, ACM (2008), 629-638.
9. Cherlin, A. *The Marriage-Go-Round: The State of Marriage and the Family in America Today.* Knopf, 2009.
10. Egelman, S., Brush, AJ, & Inkpen, K. Family Accounts: A new paradigm for user accounts within the home environment. In *Proc. CSCW*, ACM (2008), 669–678.
11. Ellison, N.B., Steinfield, C., and Lampe, C. Connection strategies: Social capital implications of Facebook-enabled communication practices. *New Media & Society 13*, 6 (2011), 873–892.
12. Eriksson, H. and Salzmann-Erikson, M. Supporting a caring fatherhood in cyberspace – an analysis of communication about caring within an online forum for fathers. *Scand. J. of Caring Sci. 27*, 1 (2013), 63–69.
13. Fletcher, R. and StGeorge, J. Heading Into Fatherhood-Nervously: Support for Fathering From Online Dads. *Qual. Health Res. 21*, 8 (2011), 1101–1114.
14. Gibson, J. *The theory of affordances*. Hilldale, 1977.
15. Gibson, L. and Hanson, V.L. Digital motherhood: how does technology help new mothers? In *Proc. CHI 2013*, ACM (2013), 313–322.
16. Hochschild, A.R. and Machung, A. *The Second Shift: Working Parents and the Revolution at Home.* Viking, 1989.
17. Hogan, B. The presentation of self in the age of social media: Distinguishing performances and exhibitions online. *Bull. of Sci., Tech. & Soc. 30*, 6 (2010), 377–386.
18. Hoy, M.G. and Milne, G. Gender Differences in Privacy-Related Measures for Young Adult Facebook Users. *J. of Interactive Advertising 10*, 2 (2010), 28–45.
19. Hsieh, H.-F. and Shannon, S.E. Three approaches to qualitative content analysis. *Qualitative Health Research 15*, 9 (2005), 1277–1288.
20. Kim Parker and Wendy Wang. *Modern Parenthood.* Pew Research, 2013.
21. Lampinen, A., Lehtinen, V., Lehmuskallio, A., and Tamminen, S. We're in it together: interpersonal management of disclosure in social network services. In *Proc. CHI '11*, ACM (2011), 3217–3226.

22. Lincoln, Y.S. and Guba, E.G. Designing a naturalistic inquiry. *Naturalistic inquiry*, (1985), 221–249.
23. Litt, E. Knock, Knock. Who's There? The Imagined Audience. *Journal of Broadcasting & Electronic Media 56*, 3 (2012), 330–345.
24. Livingstone, S. and Helsper, E. Parental Mediation of Children's Internet Use. *Journal of Broadcasting & Electronic Media 52*, 4 (2008), 581–599.
25. Livingstone, S. and Helsper, E. Balancing opportunities and risks in teenagers' use of the internet: the role of online skills and internet self-efficacy. *New Media & Society 12*, 2 (2010), 309–329.
26. Madden, M. Privacy management on social media sites. *Pew Research Center*, 2012.
27. Mazmanian, M. and Erickson, I. The Product of Availability: Understanding the Economic Underpinnings of Constant Connectivity. In *Proc, CHI*, ACM (2014), 763–772.
28. Mickelson, K.D. Seeking social support: parents in electronic support groups. In S. Kiesler, ed., *Culture of the Internet*. LEA, 1997, 157–178.
29. Miller, A.D. and Edwards, W.K. Give and Take: A Study of Consumer Photo-sharing Culture and Practice. In *Proc. CHI 2007*, ACM (2007), 347–356.
30. Morris, M.R. Social Networking Site Use by Mothers of Young Children. In *Proc. CSCW 2014*, ACM (2014) 1272-1282.
31. Nelson, M.K. *Parenting Out of Control: Anxious Parents in Uncertain Times*. NYU Press, 2010.
32. Neustaedter, C., Yarosh, S., and Brush, A.J. *Designing for families*. In *CHI EA 2009*, ACM, 2009, 2735-2738.
33. Norman, D. *The Design of Everyday Things*. Doubleday, New York, 1990.
34. Norman, D.A. Affordance, Conventions, and Design. *interactions 6*, 3 (1999), 38–43.
35. Pauwels, L. A private visual practice going public? Social functions and sociological research opportunities of Web-based family photography. *Visual Studies 23*, 1 (2008), 34–49.
36. Petronio, S. *Boundaries of Privacy: Dialectics of Disclosure*. SUNY Press, 2002.
37. Petronio, S. Communication privacy management theory: What do we know about family privacy regulation? *Journal of Family Theory & Review 2*, 3 (2010), 175–196.
38. Rose, G. Family photographs and domestic spacings: a case study. *Trans. of the Institute of British Geographers 28*, 1 (2003), 5–18.
39. Sarkadi, A. and Bremberg, S. Socially unbiased parenting support on the Internet: a cross-sectional study of users of a large Swedish parenting website. *Child care health and development 31*, 1 (2005), 43–52.
40. Sarvas, D. and Frohlich, P.. The Future of Domestic Photography. Springer London, 2011, 139–177.
41. Schoenebeck, S.Y. The Secret Life of Online Moms: Anonymity and Disinhibition on YouBeMom.com. In *Proc. ICWSM 2013*, AAAI (2013).
42. Sengupta, S. Sharing, With a Safety Net. *The New York Times*, 2013. http://www.nytimes.com/2013/09/20/technology/bill-provides-reset-button-for-youngsters-online-posts.html.
43. Smith, Aaron. 6 new facts about Facebook. *Pew Research Center*. http://www.pewresearch.org/fact-tank/2014/02/03/6-new-facts-about-facebook/.
44. Streitfeld, D. European Court Lets Users Erase Records on Web. *The New York Times*, 2014. http://www.nytimes.com/2014/05/14/technology/google-should-erase-web-links-to-some-personal-data-europes-highest-court-says.html.
45. Thomas, D.R. A General Inductive Approach for Analyzing Qualitative Evaluation Data. *American Journal of Evaluation 27*, 2 (2006), 237–246.
46. Uski, S. and Lampinen, A. Social norms and self-presentation on social network sites: Profile work in action. *New Media & Soc.*, (2014), 1461444814543164.
47. Vespa, J., Lewis, J.M., and Kreider, R.M. *America's Families and Living Arrangements: 2012*. U.S. Bureau of the Census, 2013.
48. Vitak, J. and Kim, J. "You Can't Block People Offline": Examining How Facebook's Affordances Shape the Disclosure Process. In *Proc. CSCW*, ACM (2014), 461–474.
49. Wang, Y., Norcie, G., Komanduri, S., Acquisti, A., Leon, P.G., and Cranor, L.F. "I Regretted the Minute I Pressed Share": A Qualitative Study of Regrets on Facebook. In *Proc. SOUPS*, ACM (2011), 10:1–10:16.
50. Yardi, S. and Bruckman, A. Social and Technical Challenges in Parenting Teens' Social Media Use. In *Proc. CHI*, ACM, (2011), 3237–3246.
51. Yarosh, S., Chew, Y.C., and Abowd, G.D. Supporting Parent–Child Communication in Divorced Families. *Int'l J. of Human Comp. Studies 27*, 2 (2009), 192–203.
52. Zhang, Y. and Wildemuth, B. Qualitative analysis of content. *Applications of social research methods to questions in info. and library science*, (2009), 308–319.
53. Zhao, X., Schwanda Sosik, V., and Cosley, D. It's Complicated: How Romantic Partners Use Facebook. In *Proc. CHI '12*, ACM (2012), 771–780.
54. Zhao, Y., Liu, J., Tang, J., and Zhu, Q. Conceptualizing perceived affordances in social media interaction design. *Aslib Proceedings 65*, 3 (2013), 289–303.

Understanding and Supporting Fathers and Fatherhood on Social Media Sites

Tawfiq Ammari, Sarita Schoenebeck
School of Information
University of Michigan
{tawfiqam,yardi}@umich.edu

ABSTRACT
Fathers are taking on more childcare and household responsibilities than they used to and many non-profit and government organizations have pushed for changes in policies to support fathers. Despite this effort, little research has explored how fathers go online related to their roles as fathers. Drawing on an interview study with 37 fathers, we find that they use social media to document and archive fatherhood, learn how to be a father, and access social support. They also go online to support diverse family needs, such as single fathers' use of Reddit instead of Facebook, fathers raised by single mothers' search for role models online, and stay-at-home fathers' use of father blogs. However, fathers are constrained by privacy concerns and perceptions of judgment relating to sharing content online about their children. Drawing on theories of fatherhood, we present theoretical and design ideas for designing online spaces to better support fathers and fatherhood. We conclude with a call for a research agenda to support fathers online.

Author Keywords
Fathers; social media; Internet; parents.

ACM Classification Keywords
H.5.m. Information interfaces and presentation (e.g., HCI): Miscellaneous.

INTRODUCTION
Since 2012, fathers have gathered at the Dad 2.0 Summit, an annual conference for father bloggers to interact with one another and with marketers and advertisers [40]. Following in the footsteps of Mom 2.0, founded in 2008, Dad 2.0 has brought mainstream attention to the growing presence of fathers and fathering online. These fathers are actively involved in raising their children and tend to despise the consumer marketing-perpetuated trope of the "hapless, bumbling" father [40]. As a result of their online activism, major companies like Huggies have pulled advertisements that discredited fathers, usually after facing online backlash [46]. Despite fathers' active engagement on sites like Facebook, Twitter, Blogger, and Reddit [7,30], little research has investigated what they are doing and why. HCI research in particular has focused on mothers in recent years [5,17,32,39], but fathers remain overlooked. Furthermore, while extensive research has documented online behavior on sites like Facebook, it is not known to what extent this resonates with fathers' experiences.

CHI 2015, April 18 - 23 2015, Seoul, Republic of Korea

ACM 978-1-4503-3145-6/15/04...$15.00
http://dx.doi.org/10.1145/2702123.2702205

This paper argues that we are at a critical juncture for studying and promoting fatherhood. Fathers' roles have steadily evolved over time from moral mentor and breadwinner to caregiver and emotional supporter [18,44]. Though still imbalanced with mothers, fathers take on more childcare and household responsibilities than they used to [24]. Problematically, the focus on mothers and motherhood in academic research could inadvertently perpetuate the unequal focus on mothers as primary caregivers—undercutting some of the very premises motherhood research is looking to address. The Internet offers a promising platform for supporting fathers and fatherhood, an area we explore in this work.

We conducted an interview study with 37 fathers about their family life, their roles as fathers, and their Internet use as it relates to fatherhood. We find that fathers have a variety of motivations for using social media, which vary according to the particular settings and context of their family life. These include documenting and archiving fatherhood, learning how to be a father, and accessing social support—including emotional support—from other fathers. However, they are inhibited by perceptions of judgment and stigma, and they express privacy concerns about sharing online. Drawing on prior work on the social construction of fatherhood and determinants of involved fathers, we present theoretical and design ideas to demonstrate how online platforms might be better designed to support fathers. We conclude with a call for more research toward understanding the lives of fathers and for leveraging technology to promote equity among parents.

RELATED WORK
We draw on theories about the social construction of fatherhood, what factors correspond to involved fathers, and prior work on parents online. We also describe differences between mothers and fathers online and offline.

Throughout, we consider what prior work and our own studies mean for diverse families beyond a typical two-parent household that has often been assumed in studies of the family. This approach builds on a CHI 2013 workshop that explored what it means to design for diverse family structures and which advocated for more research towards this goal [23].

Social Construction of Fatherhood

Traditional perspectives on fatherhood have defined fathers as authority figures, breadwinners, and emotionally distant [29]. Fathers were expected to play an instrumental role in the family, ensuring the family was taken care of and order was kept; in contrast, mothers were expected to play the expressive role, nurturing the emotional wellbeing and development of the family [19,44]. Feminist movements uprooted these notions, advocating for equality in the workplace, and in the home in terms of childcare and household responsibilities. Notions of "new fatherhood" reflect changes in household behavior and expectations about how fathers should behave [18]; indeed, the amount of work fathers do at home has increased, though imbalances still exist [24]. However, change has been slow, in part because cultural products (e.g., laws and norms for paternity leave in most countries) tend to be conservative in their representations, reinforcing existing stereotypes rather than innovating in representations of gender relations [18].

One framework for understanding how we might promote new kinds of notions of fatherhood is the concept of schemas. Schemas are information structures in memory that help people to organize past experiences and to respond to new situations [3]. Schemas can refer to stereotypes about how people behave (e.g., mothers stay home to raise children), scripts that contain a set of expectations about what will happen (e.g., parents will take their children to a restaurant and order from a children's menu), social roles (e.g., mothers feel that they *should* stay home to raise a child), or worldviews (e.g., families where a parent stays home to raise the child will do better at raising their children) [8,19,38]. Parenting schemas in particular refer to conceptions about the caregiving role and how to function in that role, conceptions of a child (i.e., how they should develop), and conceptions about one's own child in particular [3]. Parenting schemas help parents to process information about how they have behaved in the past and how they might behave in the future.

However, the roles of fathers and fatherhood are slow-changing, and fathers may be stuck in an overly rigid or poorly formed schema about how they should act. Fatherhood schemas are shaped by individual experiences parents have in their own families, by ongoing interactions with other people in their lives, and most importantly, the socially constructed roles which guide how parents do or should behave. However, many schemas are adaptive and flexible and can help parents identify problems when they happen [3]. Developing schemas about what it means to be a good father requires understanding the components of involved fathers and fathering. In this work, we explore how fathers turn to social media sites to explore, learn, and reconsider their existing conceptions of fatherhood.

Determinants of Involved Fathers

To understand fatherhood, it is useful to reflect on what it means to be an "involved father", a term used by major government and non-profit initiatives for fathers. Lamb, a preeminent fatherhood scholar, proposes four areas for measuring father involvement: motivation, skills and self-confidence, social support, and institutional practices [28].

Motivation is shaped by fathers' conceptions of fatherhood based on cultural background, current social conditions, and upbringing [28]. Some factors correlate to increased involvement, including class (lower class fathers spend more time with their children), age (fathers spend more time with younger children), child's gender (fathers spend more time with male children), and maternal employment (fathers spend more time with children if their partner is employed) [28]. However, fathers may also be motivated by peer or societal pressure to be active in their children's lives, or they may seek to overcome a lack of such involvement from their own fathers [20,43]. Even if fathers are motivated to be involved in their children's lives, they may be limited by real or perceived lack of skills. Both mothers and fathers develop skills "on the job" [27] and they learn about parenting from the people around them, through their own experiences as children, and through social learning processes by observing other parents [6].

Though little evidence suggests that fathers are differently-abled than mothers at child-rearing, if they are denied exposure (e.g., babysitting as a teenager), they may be socialized to feel less competent as adults. Father involvement requires a supportive network of friends, work colleagues, and family [26,27]. While most industrialized societies today advocate for high father involvement in family life, both mothers and fathers experience employment pressure related to child-rearing, and mothers have been consistently shown to pay an extra penalty in the workplace [9]. Institutional barriers to involved fatherhood also persist. In particular, many companies offer little or no paternity leave to fathers, and where companies do offer paternity leave, social norms may inhibit fathers from actually taking the leave [35]. However, there is a growing body of government and non-profit organizations dedicated to supporting fathers, such as the National Fatherhood Initiative [11,33] in the U.S. and the Fatherhood Institute [14] in the UK. This research builds on these initiatives, focusing on understanding ways that technologies might also support fathers.

Parents Online

Parents are a fast-growing demographic of social media users. Very little prior work in HCI has studied fathers online, though some work exists outside the field.

Johansson and Hammarén analyzed eight blogs by young, single Swedish fathers and described pictures of fathers and children, discussions of changing identities, and the challenges they faced as fathers [22]. An Australian study of a small chat room for new fathers showed they request and share social support using humor and self-disclosure [16]. A second study of the same dataset showed that fathers observed a lack of social spaces, support, and services for new fathers [42]. A Scandinavian study of new fathers in an online forum described their efforts to support one another and concerns they shared about being a new parent [13]. A second study of the same dataset focused on what they called "healthcare parental support" (HCPS) [37]. Fathers felt supported by HCPS, but they also felt disregarded and invisible, especially in relation to the mother. An intervention called the New Fathers Network improved first-time fathers' self-efficacy and satisfaction during the first eight weeks after their child's birth [21]. An intervention to support fathers of children with brain tumors demonstrated improvements in coping and grappling with challenges [34]. Together, these point to small but promising opportunities for supporting fathers.

Within HCI literature, we see that both mothers and fathers post statuses and photos of their new babies on Facebook, though mothers do this slightly more often than fathers [7]. Mothers have been a particular focus in HCI research, such as a CHI 2013 workshop on HCI and motherhood [5]. Mothers use Facebook to maintain their identity as more than just mothers during the early days of new motherhood [17]. New mothers use Facebook and Twitter to share about their child after birth and their posts are slightly more positive after a child's birth [32]. A subset of mothers are active on anonymous sites to share and receive support about topics they might not feel comfortable sharing in face-to-face interactions or on non-anonymous sites like Facebook [39]. Prior work shows that offline social networks offer important methods, techniques, and support for mothers [12]. Mothers in dense offline networks exhibit more competence in mothering roles than mothers in loosely knit offline networks [1]. However, parenting philosophies tend to be controversial, and when shared openly, can be contradictory. If provided without additional support, such information can actually undermine a mother's confidence in raising her child [1]. Prior work has not explored how fathers use social media, nor has it examined their attitudes about the role of social media in their lives; this work addresses that gap.

METHODS

We conducted semi-structured interviews with 37 fathers about their use of social media. Most of the interviews were conducted with fathers in the U.S. (n=31) but also from Canada, Australia, Germany, Sweden, Taiwan and Jordan (one father from each). We recruited fathers by contacting organizations for fathers, posting advertisements on organizations' Facebook pages (with their permission), and

	Marital Status	Degree, Employment		Partner Degree, Employment		*	**
F01	Married	CO	FT	BA	PT	2	4,8
F02	Div (non-resident)	CO	FT	HS	PT	1	3
F03	Married	CO	FT	BA	SAHM	3	½, 4, 6
F04	Married	GS	FT	BA	PT	2	½,3
F05	Married	CO	FT	BA	FT	3	10,12,21
F06	Married	CO	FT	MA	FT	2	4, 9
F07	Married	GS	FT	MA	SAHM	1	1
F08	Married	GS	FT	MSW	FT	1	2
F09	Married	GS	FT	HS	SAHM	1	3
F10	Married	CO	FT	BA	PT	3	6, 14, 15
F11	Married	GS	FT	BA	FT	2	4, 7
F12	Married	GS	FT; SAHD	BA	FT	3	9, 12, 15
F13	Married	CO	FT	BA	SAHM	2	2, 4
F14	Married	GS	FT	MD	FT	2	10, 13
F15	Married	HS	SAHD	PhD	FT	2	7, 10
F16	Married	GS	FT	BA	SAHM	1	2
F17	Married	GS	FT	PhD	FT	2	6, 9
F18	Married	HS	FT	HS	SAHM; Homeschool	2	6, 7
F19	Married	CO	FT	BA	SAHM	1	2
F20	Married	CO	FT	BA	SAHM; Homeschool	2	3, 5
F21	Div (resident)	GS	FT	MA	FT	1	21
F22	Married	HS	FT	HS	PT	4	5, 7, 11, 14
F23	Div (custody of 1)	CO	FT	BA	NA	2	14, 17
F24	N/A (split custody)	HS	FT	NA	NA	1	7
F25	Married	GS	FT	MA	FT	2	7, 15
F26	Separated	CO	FT	BA	FT	1	7
F27	Married	CO	FT	BA	FT	1	1
F28	Married	HS	FT	MSW	FT	2	6, 10
F29	Married	GS	FT	BA	FT	2	4, 11
F30	Married	GS	FT	M.Ed	FT	2	12, 15
F31	Div (split custody)	HS	PT	BA	NA	1	8
F32	Div (primary custody)	GS	FT	NA	NA	4	7, 8, 10, 11
F33	Married	GS	FT	PhD	SAHM	2	13, 18
F34	Married	CO	FT	BA	SAHM	5	10, 13, 15, Missing
F35	Div (split custody)	CO	FT	Cert	FT	1	10
F36	Married	CO	FT	BA	Student	2	3, 3
F37	Married	CO	FT	Assc	SAHM	3	1.5, 4, 8

Table 1. Participant and partner demographics. *Number of children. ** Ages of children. SAH[D/M]=Stay-at-home-[dad/mom].; CO: College Education; GS: Graduate School; HS: High School

posting to online platforms like Twitter. The recruitment message requested participants who were fathers and who used the Internet; most participants used the Internet for a variety of purposes, which included fathering. Through online recruitment, snowball, and word-of-mouth techniques, we gained traction and scheduled interviews with all of the participants who expressed interest over the subsequent weeks. A substantial minority of participants—13 out of 37—were active father bloggers. Their stories are woven throughout the results. The content of their blogs however, was not used in the analysis.

Interviews were conducted between Oct 2013 and February 2014. Most fathers were married at the time of the interview (n=30); the remaining seven were separated or divorced. Six had high school diplomas or a GED, 16 had bachelor's degrees, and the remaining 15 had advanced degrees. Two participants were stay-at-home-fathers (SAHDs), one worked part-time, and the other 34 worked full-time. Their partners were equally educated: four had high school diplomas, two had an associate's degree, 18 had bachelor's degrees, and the remaining 15 had advanced degrees. However, partners (mothers) worked in paid professions less than participants (fathers); 11 were stay-at-home-mothers (SAHMs), five worked part-time, and the remaining 21 worked full-time (compared to 34 of the fathers). Most fathers were heavy users of social media. They used Facebook (n=35), Twitter (n=24), Instagram (n=10), Pinterest (n=9), and Reddit (n=6).

The shortest interview length was 20 minutes (unanticipated language barriers made the interview difficult to execute), and the longest interview was 90 minutes. The median time was 47 minutes. Most interviews were conducted over the telephone (n=19) and Skype (n=12); a smaller number were in-person (n=6). The interview began with background questions about who lived in the home with the father (if anyone), their employment, and the children in the home (if any). We asked fathers about their roles as fathers, about their parenting philosophies, and about their social media and Internet use. The last section focused on perceptions of stigma and judgment; we asked what they would post online or not and why, and experiences of judgment they might have felt online or offline. We also asked whether they felt that mothers and fathers used the Internet differently related to parenting. We transcribed the interviews and coded them using an inductive process [40]. We conducted multiple passes over the codes, iterating until we began to see broader patterns in the data. The research team discussed the codes between each pass and developed themes after the final coding. We describe fathers' lives from their own perspectives in the Results; we synthesize and interpret their stories in the context of differences between fathers and mothers and parenting more broadly in the Discussion. Most of the respondents either had a college or graduate education (n=32). This is higher than the national average for holders of a college degree or more (27%) [36]. Future work in this area should investigate the use of social media by fathers with lower SES.

RESULTS

Results are organized around three overarching themes: use of social media to learn how to be a father, how diverse experiences influence social media use, and perceived barriers to sharing online. Many fathers' experiences overlap across these three themes; taken together, they shed light on opportunities and limitations of social media for supporting fathers and fatherhood.

Motivations for Using Social Media

Learning how to be a Father

Fathers turned to online sites like Facebook to ask parenting questions and read parenting information from other parents. Social media sites served as filters for fathers to see parenting content without necessarily having to go look for it. F12 told us: "social media acts as a content curator for me." F13 similarly noted:

> It's mostly your friends or people that are part of your friends on Facebook. So, [if] someone's talking about the new way to get your kids to fall asleep earlier tonight... and your kid was one that wasn't sleeping well, I'm sure you would look twice at it and think about it, be influenced by it. F13

The extent to which fathers looked for information online varied with their experience and parenting styles. For example, F04 relied on online posts when he was a new father; now that he had his own "parenting philosophy," he was more likely to aggregate conversations online into a "cohesive viewpoint" that was aligned with his existing philosophies. F26 also aggregated multiple viewpoints into his parenting philosophy:

> Just hearing all the stories from countless [fathers], just we listen to hundreds of podcasts and [read] thousands of blog posts just on any given year and I mean you can't not be a better father after having consumed as much fatherhood content. F26

Fathers also used social platforms to learn about what kinds of activities they could do with their children. F02 and F29 both followed other parents on Pinterest to find activities they could do with their young children. F07 kept track of activities that other parents in his Facebook network shared. F01, a non-resident father, Skyped regularly with his daughter and looked online for examples of what to do to maintain a child's attention on Skype.

Participants also looked to other parents, to learn from their mistakes. Some observed other parents' parenting decisions, and if they felt they were bad or wrong decisions, took care to avoid those decisions themselves. F15 said he had rarely been influenced enough to change his parenting style based on other fathers' posts on social media, but he did sometimes read a story and think to himself 'boy, I would never do that with my kids.' F35 said he "cringed" when he saw other parents criticizing their children publicly online and had become more aware of criticisms he might post about his own children. Fathers also sought affirmation of their own parenting styles when they interacted with other parents. However, in many cases, parenting styles differed, and these differences manifested on Facebook:

> I've had friends of mine who had fights about [cry-it-out versus co-sleeping] before on [Facebook]... One friend would be trying the cry-it-out method with his kid…and another one would be like 'how could I let my baby cry?' Each parent is clinging on the faint hope that they are not screwing up their kid and if they need to bitch a little about it on their Facebook page to feel good about that, I am totally for that. F07

Fathers described the positive benefits of being able to compare themselves to other parents, not because they enjoyed seeing other parents fail, but because they felt reassured knowing that other parents faced similar challenges. For example, F07 said he felt more secure when he saw other parents in his network going through the same problems he and his wife experienced:

> [I'm] glad other parents go through [parenting problems]… so, it's kind of like…positive social comparison… so it's normal to feel stressed out about stuff like that. F07

F06 had a Facebook friend who posted regularly about his son's autism on Facebook. Whenever F06 felt frustrated about raising his four-year-old, he recalled posts about his friend's son and felt he gained better perspective.

Documenting and Archiving Fatherhood

Participants were interested in documenting their lives as fathers, both to share their experiences with other fathers as well as to create a record they could return to when their children were older:

> When I'm home alone with the kids, I'll be talking to myself quite a bit... I have a great time with my kids. I'm like, "You know something? Let me start putting this down on paper, or on the computer". I just felt like I have something to share. I enjoy it, and if nothing else, eventually as the kids get older, it'll be something for them to look at and read and hopefully get a laugh out of. F22

Father bloggers were motivated to blog by their interest in documenting, archiving, and sharing their lives as fathers. They also described blogging as a platform that facilitates more detailed expression. F19 described his experience:

> Facebook, Instagram... everything is sound bites these days… So [the blog is] really almost just a public journal of things that I'm either thinking about, things that I might want to express, and it also serves as a tool for my son to go back and read one day so that he knows where his father's mind was at during a certain point in his life. F19

Two participants, F12 and F37, had created aggregate sites for fathers to cross-post and comment on one another's blogs. Both were motivated to do this by the lack of sites for fathers online, feeling that there was an abundance of sites for mothers, but not enough for fathers. F12, a SAHD for the first of his three children, lamented the lack of fathering material during that time especially:

> Everything that was online was branded for moms. And we felt like men were taking on a completely new role, in terms of, caretaking and involvement in the home. And it just wasn't being reflected in what was being published online and we felt like there was a real opening to help, to serve the dad audience. F12

F37 had created a popular site that aggregated and cross-posted posts from other father bloggers. F37 felt that though more fathers were doing childcare, they were still sharing a disproportionately small amount about their lives as fathers compared to mothers. Furthermore, though his site had considerable father blogger engagement, he felt men were predominantly still interested in content areas related to sports, news, technology, and health rather than parenting.

Fathers felt that humor was an appropriate way of communicating online. One father, F22, was critical of fathers who were too negative:

> It's almost like "Jeez man, lighten up already". Okay, if you're gonna have a blog, write something funny, like do a review about some product that's good for parents. Don't sit there and complain because a diaper commercial has women in it instead of men. It seems like some of the dads are just really... Aside from going on their own accomplishments, it seems like they whine a lot more than the women do. F22

Though F22's critical tone was not pervasive, it did surface a point of disagreement among the fathers who blogged about the role of advertising and monetizing their blogs. Some father bloggers felt that the attention mother bloggers received from advertisers should also be given to father bloggers. F12 had considered connecting with brands that might sponsor his blog; however, other fathers perceived the prospect of monetization to be a threat to the authenticity of their online presence. F19 felt that the Dad 2.0 Summit involved a lot of "pandering" where sponsors tried to influence father bloggers in particular ways. Though not unique to fathers, this reveals a tension father bloggers experience between a pure documentation of their experiences of fatherhood online versus integrating this motivation with an external agenda, one that will impact how authentically fathers are able to express themselves.

Accessing Social Support

Six participants belonged to closed Facebook groups for fathers. They felt these were safe and private spaces to discuss challenges or to vent about parenting as well as marriage, focusing on the relationship with the spouse in addition to child-rearing questions. One, for instance, described a personal incident he had shared with the group:

> My wife and I got in a very heated debate on the home front, verbal battle argument, borderline kind of physical abuse happening there. And long story short, that night ended up locking myself in a car because I wanted to isolate myself from my very family, for my own safety. While I was in that car, whipped out my smart phone, got on the private Facebook, said, "Hey, guys. I'm dealing with this. My wife and I are [in a] highly... combative situation on the home front, I've locked myself in my car. [chuckle] I'll be staying here until 6:00 AM. What do I do? I can't deal with this shit. [code removed]

F37 emphasized that other fathers in his Facebook group were very understanding. He would turn to them without hesitation "if I'm looking for some help or some suggestions." Older fathers who had raised their children through adulthood remained in such groups to provide social support for younger fathers. For example, though F21's son was now an adult, F21 remained in a Facebook group and gave one example of recently offering advice to a father who was granted sole custody of his three-year-old child. Though some fathers in our study reported being members of Facebook groups for fathers or participating in offline groups for fathers, the majority did not report participation in either of these.

Diverse Experiences and Social Media Uses

Though many participants in our sample fit into a normative family arrangement of a husband and wife and one to three children [10,11,24,35], a number of them were in, or had come from, particularly diverse family arrangements. This section focuses on single fathers, fathers raised by single mothers, and stay-at-home-fathers. Their stories echo the motivations for using social media presented in the prior section; however, they also described particular motivations based on their diverse experiences and contexts. Though the sample size of each is small, telling their stories is important for understanding the diversity of fathers' experiences online.

Single Fathers

Three participants used Reddit to connect with other fathers and discuss fatherhood. All three were no longer in a relationship with their children's mother. They turned to specific subreddits relative to their own lives. For example, F32 was a single father who posted pictures of his children to Facebook but preferred not to ask parenting questions there; instead, he went to general parenting subreddits as well as the single parenting subreddit because he wanted to find information in an "anonymous type of site." F31 had joint custody of his son with his ex-wife. Since his recent divorce, F31 felt that his activity on Facebook had decreased and he was sharing less there than he used to. He had also turned to parenting subreddits, though he typically lurked rather than posting questions himself:

> I look through there and I've seen what other single dads are... Well, not single dads, but people co-parenting with a partner, and try and get a feel for sort of how other people are dealing with these situations... it's just interesting to get their perspective and see the things that they've had to deal with. F31

F02 was also recently divorced. The dissolution was related to his decision to leave the faith that he and his ex-wife had been born into. He joined a subreddit for other individuals who had left the same faith. Though the subreddit was not meant explicitly for single parents, many of its members were facing divorce or broken families because one partner had decided to leave the faith.

> You know, people talk about their family and divorce and going through divorce, the trauma of leaving religion and things like that and they would help relate and talk about that what they have gone through... that experience when they leave the religion and the family breaks up, you know, divorce, and then antagonism between them and other family members. I relate where I can. F02

He suggested that Reddit provided a "peaceful place to post an opinion, as opposed to Facebook where I already know that I am very different from that group of people." Reddit's anonymity provided an advantage over Facebook in the context of the complex social relationships he had with other members of his family and friends, all of whom were still practicing followers of the same religion.

Fathers Raised by Single Mothers

Three participants lacked a father figure themselves and had turned to the Internet in order to find father role models. "I am an accident", explained F18. "My biological father was a big-time junkie, and he was here and there, in and out":

> The Internet, for better or for worse, taught me how to be a man, how to interview for a job, how to propose to a girl, how to change a diaper. I mean these things... I went to the Internet just looking for help, and like I said, for better or for worse, you take the good with the bad. That's how I learned how to be the man I am today. They've really helped me become a good dad, 'cause I didn't have a good example growing up. And that was a scary thing about having kids is: how are you supposed to be a good dad when you didn't have one? F18

F37 was also raised in an environment where his biological father was unavailable to him. Joining a father blogger group provided him with an opportunity to discuss his parenting problems with other fathers and to ask questions.

> So when [my brothers and I] became fathers, a lot of us were just kind of taking it day by day, making it up as we went along. I don't even know if my brothers ever asked advice from anybody. So feeling I'm not alone when I suddenly found myself joining a father blogger group, stories, anecdotes, comments back and forth, made me feel like I was not so alone. I had people, if I posted something that I was worried about with my children or a concern or frustrated with, immediately, I had other fathers saying "I know exactly how you feel." F37

F24's father was similarly unavailable to him. F24 described a troubled childhood that included drug addictions and an unplanned pregnancy. He experienced a major transformation when he became active in a church: he "began to seek out other men's groups. I needed to get some strong Christian men around me." He was the only single father in his men's group and started a blog for single Christian fathers in which he described his own life and the experiences of other father bloggers online. He created a Facebook page for single fathers as well and described a community that had coalesced around shared experiences.

Stay-at-Home-Fathers

Two participants, F12 and F15, had been or were currently SAHDs, and they used social media sites to find other SAHDs they could talk with and relate to. Both described experiencing biases against fathers both offline and online. F12 described going to Starbucks, where women would say things like "oh, you're giving mom a break, how nice" and would talk to the baby instead of to him. F15 told us he "needed a social life. I needed to get out of the house and talk to other adults." The first online parenting group he joined was overwhelmingly composed of mothers, so he focused on finding fathers groups specifically. He echoed the importance of fathers groups for socializing—and socialization—for both him and his children before they became of school age.

Other fathers who were not SAHDs themselves also valued the roles that SAHDs played online. F37 worked full-time but said:

> Well, some of these guys have been stay-at-home-dads for a number of years. They day-in and day-out have to deal with everything that I don't. I feel like I'm more well-equipped… because these guys have all done it before. There's plenty of them that have done, that are empty-nesters that, or kids who are teens, and then there's new dads. So you have someone, some other people who will always pitch in and say, "I know what you're going through, maybe try this." or "This is what I did and it worked. Not saying it's for you, but maybe give it a try." F37

F04 joined Facebook groups for fathers and attended social meetups with fathers and their children, though his reliance on both online and offline social gatherings decreased when his children went to school. After going to daycare or school, children made their own friends and participants reported a decreased reliance on online groups.

Barriers to Sharing Online: Privacy and Judgment

Fathers were sensitive about sharing too much information online that might violate their children's privacy or that might subject them to stigma and judgment from other parents. Some responded to these concerns by selectively posting on one platform versus another (e.g., Facebook versus blogs). F37 explained:

> On my dad blog… I kind of try to be careful how much I put out my children's photos for the world to see, but I have my closed, private social media sites that I post to as well for family and friends. F37

Fathers were especially sensitive about sharing information about their young children online. They engaged in protective behaviors like searching for their child's name on Google to see if pictures of their child might come up. Others used pseudonyms to obscure their child's identity. F26 was going through a divorce at the time of the interview and was now second-guessing some of the posts he had shared publicly about his separation. He was not concerned about his ex-wife seeing them, but instead that his son might see them when he got older. F28 had posted publicly about a long-standing conflict he was facing with his children's school where he had shared his opinions and documentation of events. His wife felt he should not be blogging about school conflicts but he was less certain:

> Could [my children] be retaliated against? It's a big concern, but I feel like we have to do the right thing, and we have to set the right example that we're standing up for what we believe in. F28

Fathers also expressed privacy concerns regarding their own profiles. F17 had considered joining a public Facebook community page called the Orange Rhino Challenge which calls on parents to "Yell Less and Love More." The goal of the challenge is to decrease the number of times a parent yells at his children. F17 told us he was taking the challenge (successfully), but he decided against "liking" the community page on Facebook because it would publicly display to his network that he yelled at his children. F11 similarly noted that he would not want to post his "flaws as a parent."

Fathers refrained from offering advice to other parents to avoid backlash about controversial topics. They tended to avoid divisive topics like sleep training, vaccinations, and breastfeeding. F04 felt that anything someone posts related to parenting would create "a fan and an enemy," so he kept his parenting posts to a minimum. He felt that as a result,

Facebook had become the "softened" version of his identity. Others shared this perspective:

> I've never said anything like, "Oh, we're letting our son cry it out tonight." I've seen many conversations on Facebook…you know, I am against spanking and I did say that on Facebook and people feel judged when I say it and that can be a very sticky place to maneuver, so I try to avoid it because ruffling feathers in the social media space… Facebook is this funny place and where I gotta huge range of contacts… F06

F11 felt his parenting style could probably be inferred through some of his posts, but he would not explicitly share his parenting philosophies in a Facebook status. Thus, people might judge the way that he parented, but they would not have a mechanism to directly confront him about it. Fathers described a variety of ways that parents might judge one another online using general, vague, or indirect language to criticize other parents' approaches:

> Like they won't mention it as in saying that you are doing the wrong thing, but they will mention it by justifying what they are doing ….that they are doing the right thing…which by logical extension means that what we are doing is wrong. F07

Not all fathers shared the experiences of judgment on Facebook, however. Some fathers, such as F09 and F12, reported having relatively homogeneous networks—usually family and close friends—so they felt comfortable expressing parenting opinions there, but this perception was less common among participants.

DISCUSSION

Differences between Mothers and Fathers Online

Fathers use social media to document and archive fatherhood and to access social support, similar to mothers [17,32,39]. However, two differences emerge. First, fathers used social media to "learn how to be a good father", a practice that was especially critical for fathers who felt they did not have good father role models themselves. In contrast, mothers do not frame their motivations as "learning how to be a good mother" [17,45], though they do seek validation of motherhood, a subtle difference. To illustrate, consider how a search of books for new fathers (e.g., search Amazon for "fathers parenting") surfaces books that are referred to as "guides", "manuals" or "advice"; this phenomenon is rarely observed as indicated by the same search for mothers books. This difference may emerge from early socialization processes through which mothers are expected to take to motherhood naturally [19]. Fathers are left believing that they must learn how to be a father, regardless of whether there are actual differences between what a mother or father knows when they become a parent.

Second, fathers report a dearth of sites for fathers online. Indeed, the overwhelming popularity of sites for mothers (BabyCenter.com says 1 out of 5 new moms globally are BabyCenter users [4]) indicates that their perceptions are accurate. This phenomenon is pervasive offline as well; LaRossa describes how Parenting Magazine created a "Fathers Column" in the 1930s in response to interest for fathers. Yet, this single column indicated that the rest of the magazine was by default designed for mothers [29]. Almost a century later, this trend continues with the June 2014 issue containing a "For Fathers Only" section focused on fathers. This highlights a prevalent theme in participants' narratives: mothers and motherhood are overemphasized in parenting platforms online. Though not the focus of this analysis, it is interesting to note the contrast between mothers as the dominant group of social media users as compared to fathers as the stereotypically dominant user in other technological contexts such as video games or more recently, the maker movement [41].

Opportunities of Social Media for Supporting Fathers

This section explores ideas for promoting a research agenda to better support fathers online.

Developing Schemas of How to Be a Father

Fathers enter fatherhood with particular schemas about childrearing that draw on socialization they have experienced throughout their own upbringing. Prior work describes the process of searching for information online as a "search schema." Search schemas that are developed about a particular domain could be shared with others with similar needs [25]. Social media sites could explore designs that promote fathering schemas paired with search schemas to help fathers find higher quality information about fatherhood, as well as to find other fathers with similar needs. Consider some examples: fathers experiencing marital problems may avoid the stigma of Facebook, but not realize there are private Facebook groups or anonymous subcommunities on Reddit they could turn to for support. Fathers looking to advocate for fathers' rights could turn to blogging communities to find like-minded fathers. Both of these examples counter traditional norms and expectations of family life; developing search schemas for finding support might expose fathers to other fathers' struggles, validating their experiences through positive social comparisons [15].

Reducing Perceived Stigma through Anonymity

Perhaps the biggest threat to the support of fathers online—and parents more generally—is the strong perception of judgment described by fathers in our study and echoed in prior work [2,31,39]. Public sharing in social media platforms can threaten fathers' self-image, especially those experiencing stigmatized life changes such as a recent divorce. Anonymous venues where fathers can feel comfortable sharing might help overcome the perceived stigma and judgment a father experiences on real-name sites. When acting anonymously, fathers can post controversial or unpopular parenting philosophies and have an easier time ignoring comments if they are met with judgment; an approach that would be difficult on a personal Facebook profile. However, some limitations exist. The private, anonymous nature of these platforms can make them hard to find, especially given the shortage of fathering sites online. Second, these kinds of interactions inhibit fathers from receiving persistent social support through the strong ties available in Facebook groups or father blogger groups. Furthermore, parents tend to screen for content and people that expresses similar belief systems and orientations [12]. Balancing access to diverse parenting perspectives while maintaining access to affirmation and support is an important goal.

Increasing Visibility of Audience Norms and Expectations

One approach for overcoming perceptions of judgment or even perceived stigma is to help posters understand what their audience might expect—and want—to see, so they can adjust what they post and to whom accordingly. Parenting philosophies are personal, complicated, and nuanced, and sharing them online can isolate a poster from an audience who does not share their views. Furthermore, social media users' inability to anticipate an audience's expectations and reactions can make it especially difficult for parents to know how their posts will be received. Prior work shows that parents of children with special needs feel less judged online than offline, but nuanced notions of what is acceptable (e.g., humor) versus not acceptable (e.g., violence) challenge parents to find the right balance of what to post [2]. Future work could explore audience perceptions of appropriateness in order to help fathers—and mothers—craft their parenting posts to supportive audiences. For example, if certain categories of posts are known to be controversial (e.g., sleep training), fathers might decide to share them to a smaller audience of close father friends. If they desire feedback from a broad audience, they might turn to a site like Reddit where they can manage threats to their self-image more judiciously. The acceptability of different types of posts could be evaluated using norms elicitation protocols [2] through a survey or crowd approach; this would enable fathers to understand whether they are likely to be judged for different posts to different audiences.

CONCLUSION: TOWARDS A RESEARCH AGENDA FOR SUPPORTING FATHERS

Many non-profit and government organizations have pushed for changes in fathers' attitudes and in policies to support fathers [10]. Efforts to develop new parenting schemas about fathers' roles in their children's lives require that fathers be provided with information, support, and buy-in to these roles. Our results show that fathers' motivations for using social media include documenting and archiving fatherhood, learning how to be a father, and accessing social support from other fathers. Fathers coming from diverse family environments rely on online spaces to find fathers in similar experiences. However, fathers lament the lack of spaces online to support fathers and fatherhood. Future work should explore how to provide fathers with online platforms where they can access information and support. We take an advocacy stance, arguing for more research that aims to understand fathers' social lives and how they might be better supported through computing technologies.

ACKNOWLEDGEMENTS

We thank the National Science Foundation (HCC #1318143) for support. Any opinion, findings, and conclusions or recommendations expressed in this material are those of the authors and do not necessarily reflect the views of the National Science Foundation.

REFERENCES

1. Abernethy, V.D. Social network and response to the maternal role. *International Journal of Sociology of the Family*, (1973), 86–92.
2. Ammari, T., Schoenebeck, S.Y., and Morris, M.R. Accessing Social Support and Overcoming Judgment on Social Media among Parents of Children with Special Needs. In *Proc. ICWSM*, (2014).
3. Azar, S.T., Nix, R.L., and Makin-Byrd, K.N. Parenting schemas and the process of change. *Journal of Marital and Family Therapy 31*, 1 (2005), 45–58.
4. BabyCenter. babycenter.com/help-about-company.
5. Balaam, M., Robertson, J., Say, R., et al. Motherhood and HCI. *CHI Workshop*, (2013).
6. Bandura, A. *Social Learning Theory.* General Learning Press, New York, 1977.
7. Bartholomew, M.K., Schoppe-Sullivan, S.J., Glassman, M., Kamp Dush, C.M., and Sullivan, J.M. New Parents' Facebook Use at the Transition to Parenthood. *Family Relations 61*, 3 (2012), 455–469.
8. Biddle, B.J. *Role theory: Expectations, identities, and behaviors.* Academic Press, New York, 1979.
9. Budig, M.J. and England, P. The Wage Penalty for Motherhood. *American Sociological Review 66*, 2 (2001), 204–225.
10. Cabrera, N. and Peters, H.E. Public Policies and Father Involvement. *Marr. & Fam. Rev. 29*, 4 (2000), 295–314.
11. Cabrera, N., Tamis-LeMonda, C.S., Bradley, R.H., Hofferth, S., & Lamb, M.E. Fatherhood in the Twenty-First Century. *Child Dev. 71*, 1 (2000), 127–136.
12. Cochran, M.M. and Brassard, J.A. Child development and personal social networks. *Child development*, (1979), 601–616.
13. Eriksson, H. and Salzmann-Erikson, M. Supporting a caring fatherhood in cyberspace–an analysis of communication about caring within an online forum for fathers. *Scand. J. of Caring Science 27*, 1 (2013), 63–69.

14. Fatherhood Institute. www.fatherhoodinstitute.org/.
15. Festinger, L. A theory of social comparison processes. *Human relations 7*, 2 (1954), 117–140.
16. Fletcher, R. and StGeorge, J. Heading Into Fatherhood — Nervously: Support for Fathering From Online Dads. *Qualitative Health Research 21*, 8 (2011), 1101–1114.
17. Gibson, L. and Hanson, V.L. Digital motherhood: How Does Technology Help New Mothers? In *Proc. CHI '13*, ACM (2013), 313–322.
18. Gregory, A. and Milner, S. What is "New" about Fatherhood?: The Social Construction of Fatherhood in France and the UK. *Men & Masc. 14*,5 (2011), 588–606.
19. Hays, S. *The Cultural Contradictions of Motherhood.* Yale University Press, 1996.
20. Himsel, A.J. and Goldberg, W.A. Social Comparisons and Satisfaction with the Division of Housework Implications for Men's and Women's Role Strain. *Journal of Family Issues 24*, 7 (2003), 843–866.
21. Hudson, D.B., Campbell-Grossman, C., Fleck, M.O., Elek, S.M., and Shipman, A. Effects of the New Fathers Network on first-time fathers' parenting self-efficacy and parenting satisfaction during the transition to parenthood. *Issues in Comprehensive Pediatric Nursing 26*, 4 (2003), 217–229.
22. Johansson, T. and Hammarén, N. 'Imagine, just 16 years old and already a dad!'The construction of young fatherhood on the Internet. *International Journal of Adolescence and Youth*, (2012), 1–16.
23. Kazakos, K., Bales, E., Neustaedter, C., Yarosh, S., Kaye, J. "Jofish," and Kirk, D. Exploring the Diversity of Families: Designing Technologies for the Contemporary Family Life. In *CHI '13 Extended Abstracts* (2013), 3255–3258.
24. Kim Parker and Wendy Wang. *Modern Parenthood.* Pew Research, 2013.
25. Kittur, A., Peters, A.M., Diriye, A., and Bove, M. Standing on the Schemas of Giants: Socially Augmented Information Foraging. In *Proc. CSCW '14,* ACM (2014), 999–1010.
26. Lamb, M.E. The History of Research on Father Involvement. *Marr. & Fam. Rev. 29*, 2-3 (2000), 23–42.
27. Lamb, M.E., Pleck, J.H., Charnov, E.L., and Levine, J.A. Paternal behavior in humans. *American zoologist*, (1985), 883–894.
28. Lamb, M., Pleck, J.H., Charnov, E.L., and Levine, J.A. A biosocial perspective on paternal behavior and involvement. 111-142. In *Parenting across the life span: Biosocial dimensions*. 1987, 111–142.
29. LaRossa, R. *The Modernization of Fatherhood: A Social and Political History.* Univ. of Chicago Press, 1997.
30. Marketing to Moms Coalition. *State of the American Mom 2012.* 2013.
31. Mickelson, K.D. Seeking social support: parents in electronic support groups. In S. Kiesler, ed., *Culture of the Internet*. LEA, 1997, 157–178.
32. Morris, M.R. Social Networking Site Use by Mothers of Young Children. In *Proc. of CSCW '14*, ACM, (2014), 1272-1282.
33. *National Fatherhood Initiative.* www.fatherhood.org/
34. Nicholas, D.B., Chahauver, A., Brownstone, D., Hetherington, R., McNeill, T., and Bouffet, E. Evaluation of an online peer support network for fathers of a child with a brain tumor. *Social Work in Health Care 51*, 3 (2012), 232–245.
35. Rehel, E.M. When Dad Stays Home Too Paternity Leave, Gender, and Parenting. *Gender & Society*, (2013), 0891243213503900.
36. Ryan, C.L. and Siebens, J. Educational attainment in the United States: 2009. *US Census Bureau,* (2012).
37. Salzmann-Erikson, M. and Eriksson, H. Fathers sharing about early parental support in health-care - virtual discussions on an Internet forum. *Health & Social Care in the Community 21*, 4 (2013), 381–390.
38. Schank, R.C. and Abelson, R.P. *Scripts, Plans, Goals, and Understanding: An Inquiry Into Human Knowledge Structures.* Psychology Press, 2013.
39. Schoenebeck, S.Y. The Secret Life of Online Moms: Anonymity and Disinhibition on YouBeMom.com. In *Proc. ICWSM 2013*, (2013).
40. Seligson, H. Fathers Seek Advertising That Does Not Ridicule. *The New York Times*, 2013. http://www.nytimes.com/2013/02/24/business/fathers-seek-advertising-that-does-not-ridicule.html.
41. Sivek, S.C. "We Need a Showing of All Hands" Technological Utopianism in MAKE Magazine. *Journal of Communication Inquiry 35*, 3 (2011), 187–209.
42. StGeorge, J.M. and Fletcher, R.J. Fathers Online: Learning About Fatherhood Through the Internet. *The Journal of Perinatal Education 20*, 3 (2011), 154–162.
43. Tuffin, K., Rouch, G., and Frewin, K. Constructing adolescent fatherhood: responsibilities and intergenerational repair. *Culture, health & sexuality 12*, 5 (2010), 485–498.
44. White, N.R. About Fathers: Masculinity and the Social Construction of Fatherhood. *Journal of Sociology 30*, 2 (1994), 119–131.
45. Zhao, S. Parental education and children's online health information seeking: Beyond the digital divide debate. *Social Science & Medicine 69*, 10 (2009), 1501–1505.
46. We're Dads, Huggies. Not Dummies. *Change.org.* www.change.org/p/we-re-dads-huggies-not-dummie

Look, My Baby Is Using an iPad! An Analysis of YouTube Videos of Infants and Toddlers Using Tablets

Juan Pablo Hourcade, Sarah L. Mascher, David Wu and Luiza Pantoja
University of Iowa
14 MacLean Hall, Iowa City, IA 52242 USA
{juanpablo-hourcade,sarah-mascher,luiza-supertipantoja}@uiowa.edu,
davidwu583@gmail.com

ABSTRACT
We know very little about the use of computers by children under the age of three. While few children in that age range used computers before the advent of smartphones and tablets, these devices have made computers much more accessible to infants and toddlers. In this paper, we provide a window into how these children are using tablets through an analysis of relevant YouTube videos. A majority of children aged 12 to 17 months in the videos in our dataset showed at least moderate ability to use the tablets. For children aged two, it was over 90 percent who displayed at least moderate ability. Our analysis also includes trends in interaction styles, child and device positioning, social aspects, and app genres. These findings point both to opportunities for research and starting points for design.

Author Keywords
Baby; infant; toddler; young child; iPad; tablet; Android; mobile device; touchscreen.

ACM Classification Keywords
H.5.m. Information interfaces and presentation (e.g., HCI): Miscellaneous.

INTRODUCTION
We know very little about the use of computers by children under the age of three. The historical reasons are that interactions through widely available hardware required the use of an indirect pointing device or keyboard until a few years ago, which could still be challenging at age three or four [10, 11, 12, 27, 29]. Tablets have lifted this restriction, as interacting through touch matches the motor abilities of much younger children [6].

CHI 2015, April 18–23, 2015, Seoul, Republic of Korea.

ACM 978-1-4503-3145-6/15/04…$15.00.
http://dx.doi.org/10.1145/2702123.2702266

We also know that parents are providing children with access to tablets [8]. A quick search on YouTube yields scores of videos of infants and toddlers using tablets. What we do not know is how children are making use of these devices, and whether they can make meaningful use of them.

These are important questions to ask because those early years of life are crucial to children's development [13]. Adding interactive computing to children's lives at such young ages could lead to significant shifts in children's interactions with the world around them.

To begin to answer these questions, and inspired by Anthony et al.'s study of YouTube videos showing touchscreen use by people with motor impairments [3], we decided to follow a similar route and study YouTube videos of infants and toddlers using tablets. The videos provided us with examples of real-world use of the devices and helped us identify patterns of use by age group.

Based on our analysis, a majority of children aged 12 to 17 months in the videos in our dataset showed at least moderate ability to use the tablets. For children aged two, it was over 90 percent who displayed this ability level. Our analysis also includes trends in interaction styles, child and device positioning, social aspects, and app genres.

In the following sections we first discuss related research, including developmental milestones, child development theories, and existing research on computer and television use by young children. We then present the research questions, method, and results of the study, followed by a discussion of the results and future work, and the conclusion.

RELATED RESEARCH

Developmental Milestones
To better understand infants and toddlers and how they may use computers it is useful to refer to developmental milestones. The United States Centers for Disease Control (CDC) is one of many agencies and associations throughout the world to publish these. They are collections of typical

behaviors by age, and mostly intended for parents to quickly identify any developmental delays.

Below, we present relevant developmental milestones for key age groups, based on a brochure from the CDC [6]. These correspond to the age groups we used in our analysis of the videos.

By six months of age, children are typically able to recognize familiar faces, play with others, and respond to emotions. They can recognize their name, respond to sounds by making sounds, and can vocalize vowel sounds. They are curious about items around them, often reaching for them, or bringing them to their mouth. They can support their weight on their legs when standing, and begin to sit without support.

When they reach one year of age, children typically show behaviors related to attachment to primary caregivers, such as crying when they leave, and being nervous around strangers. They can respond to simple spoken requests, can use simple gestures, such as waving goodbye, and begin to say simple words such as "mom" or "dad". They explore objects by interacting with them in various ways (e.g., hitting, shaking), look at the right picture or object when it is named, copy gestures, and can poke with the index finger. This suggests they would be able to perform simple interactions with a touchscreen device.

At 18 months, children typically become more social in their behavior, for example, being able to say several single words, handing objects to others as part of play, showing affection to loved ones, and using pointing gestures to bring attention to something. They know about the purpose of common objects, participate in pretend play, and are able to scribble on their own. In terms of gross motor skills, they are typically able to walk alone, and can also drink from a cup and eat with the help of a spoon. The use of purposeful pointing and scribbling suggests more advanced interactions with touchscreen devices may be possible.

By their second birthday, children typically copy behavior they see in parents and older children, and can get excited when playing in a space where there are other children. They can recognize the names of familiar people and objects, follow simple instructions, speak using short sentences, and repeat words. They may be able to sort items by shape and color, play simple make-believe games, begin to show hand preference, and can name items in a picture book. In terms of skills that would impact touchscreen use, they are typically able to make copies of straight lines and circles.

Child Development

How do children change as they go through these milestones? Child development researchers study change in children. Perhaps the best-known theories on child development come from Jean Piaget, who developed the idea of adaptation, where learning and development occur as children adapt to their environment. Socio-cultural approaches, such as those developed by Lev Vygotsky made a greater emphasis on the social aspects of learning and the tools available in the environment, and argue that learning and development have to be understood within a particular socio-cultural context [9].

More recent systems approaches (e.g., connectionism) to development connect Piagetian and socio-cultural approaches with what we know about the biology of the brain [31].

One of the main emphases of these systems approaches is the notion of embodiment [31]. They see learning and development occurring through interactions between the brain, the body, and the environment (including other people). When we learn to complete a task, we learn how to do it with our bodies, using the resources available in the environment. As learning, change, and development occur, the brain, the body, and the environment learn, change, and develop together.

These approaches also bring a "biological systems" view of the brain, with small components working together to accomplish tasks, and knowledge representations, behaviors, and skills emerging over time [31]. Emerging skills, for example, are likely to show a great deal of variability initially, with the best alternatives becoming more likely over time. This also links to the concept of plasticity, where it is much easier to change behavior and learn new skills for younger people (they also show greater variability in behavior) but it is more challenging later in life.

How does all this link to tablets? Tablets have opened up a significant opportunity for change in early childhood environments. They may be the most malleable tools infants and toddlers have ever been able to use. The problem is that we know very little about how they are being used, and what impact they are having on children.

Screens, Computers, and Young Children

There are some clues as to what to expect from infants and toddlers' use of tablets based on what we know from the literature on young children (generally aged three and older) and their use of computers, and what we know about children and television.

A first question to ask would be how much time children spend in front of screens. An Australian study of thousands of children who were randomly sampled found that two to three year old children spent a mean of almost two hours a day of screen time during weekdays in 2006, but there were no reports of videogame or computer time for that age group. For three to four year olds, weekday videogame and computer time averaged 6 and 17 minutes a day respectively in 2007 [30]. Note that this study predates the wide adoption of tablets.

What impact is this screen time having on children? Bavelier et al. [4] provide a useful review of the literature. Their conclusion is both reasonable and not surprising in that children's use of technology can have positive, neutral, or negative impacts, depending on what technology is used, and how it is used. Sweetser et al. [30] delved further into the different kinds technology by distinguishing between passive screen time, and active screen time. Among types of active screen time, they mentioned physically active screen time, which includes playing videogames that involve children moving (e.g., Nintendo Wii). They also discussed cognitively active screen time, which involves the use of cognitive skills as part of games or other activities.

Young Children and Computers

In terms of specifically studying the impact of computers on young children's learning and cognition, a group from Wayne State University has conducted the most thorough examinations. They have done so through studies with children enrolled in Head Start, a United States program that provides early childhood education, health, and nutrition to low-income children aged three to five. Their findings have been positive both in correlational and controlled studies.

Their first study involved administering a battery of tests to 122 children and combining that information with surveys filled out by caregivers. The researchers found that children who had access to a computer performed better on measures of school readiness and cognitive development, after controlling for children's developmental stage and family socioeconomic status [18].

Since that evidence was correlational, they then conducted a study in which they manipulated computer use by providing half the children with 15 to 20 minutes of access to appropriate educational software a day, while the other half participated in the Head Start curriculum. After six months, the group using computers performed significantly better on a school readiness test [19].

This was followed by a study with 136 children that delved into what type of home computer use was most beneficial. In this correlational study, children whose parents reported active involvement in their computer use scored higher on cognitive measures than children whose parents reported non-active involvement [21].

The final study from this group of researchers was also correlational and involved 200 children. They found that using a computer correlated with some aspects of cognitive development after controlling for parental education and income [7].

Reflecting on the reasons why computers benefited children, the Wayne State University research group [20] speculated it was due to computers helping children benefit from a variety of learning experiences, being interactive, and contributing to problem solving and learning. In addition, they argued that computers can motivate children, and often involve interactions with others.

Other researchers who conducted similar studies include Castles et al. [5], who found a positive correlation between computer use and letter knowledge even after controlling for cognitive and environmental factors, based on a survey and testing of 1539 four year old children. Plowman et al. [23, 24] studied the use of computers in the homes of similarly aged children (three to four years old). They did so through a survey of over 300 families and 24 case studies. Through their study, they identified areas where parents could have typically provided more support for their children: acquiring basic interaction skills, building confidence and independence in the use of computers, learning how to use them to learn about topics such as mathematics and language, and understanding the role of technology in everyday life. Tablets could potentially lower some of these barriers.

The main criticisms and controversy with regard to the impact of computers on young children comes mostly from speculation of possible negative impacts [1, 9, 20]. They include the possibility that computers could lead to social isolation, that they could be used for entertainment instead of educational activities, that they could affect the development of perceptual and motor skills, provide access to inappropriate content, lead to physical injury (e.g., if a computer falls), or obesity due to lack of physical activity.

Within the human-computer interaction community there has been little research conducted with very young children. The earliest studies on young children's computer use came from researchers who then worked at *Sesame Workshop*. They were interested in the most appropriate input devices for children as young as three years old, and conducted experiments that generally supported the use of the mouse and the trackball [27, 29] over other input devices. At the time, tablet-like devices were not easily available.

More recently, Raffle et al. worked on systems to enable remote communication between young children and family members. One of the systems, *Family Story Play*, supported dialogic reading activities between children and grandparents [25]. The system included a paper book, two screens, and sensors. They continued their work with *StoryVisit*, a system with a similar goal as *Family Story Play*, but one that relied fully on software [26]. Through an evaluation, the researchers found the most engaged age group to be three-year-old children. The company *Kindoma* then used similar ideas for their apps.

The existing literature suggests that young children may benefit from using computers under the right circumstances. At the same time, it is clear that we know very little about the use of computers by children under the age of three, and even less for children under the age of two.

Television Studies
Another area of research that has some relevance to young children's use of computers is what we know about the impact of viewing television. Obviously, most interactions with computers are likely to be more active than those with television, but they share some of the concerns raised by critics of young children's use of computers. The results of studies suggest that the effect of television is highly dependent on the type of programs watched and how children watch them.

An example of this came from a study by Linebarger and Walker [17] who surveyed parents every three months about their children's television viewing from the time the children were six months old, until the age of 30 months. The sample included 51 children. After controlling for parental education, home environment, and the children's cognitive performance, they found, not surprisingly, that different programs had different impacts. In particular, children who viewed *Dora the Explorer, Blue's Clues, Arthur, Clifford,* and *Dragon Tales* had greater vocabularies and higher expressive language scores. On the other hand, watching *Teletubbies* correlated with fewer vocabulary words and lower expressive language scores. The common characteristics of the shows that led to better results included child-directed speech, elicitation of responses, object labeling, and/or a coherent storybook-like framework.

A similar, but much larger, study by Schmidt et al. [28] did not delve into actual shows, but followed 872 children with reports on television viewing habits at six months, one year, and two years of age. They then conducted an evaluation of language and visual motor skills at age three. They found that after adjusting for maternal age, income, education, picture vocabulary test, marital status, child's age, gender, birth weight, breastfeeding, race/ethnicity, primary language and speech, that television viewing was not associated with language or visual motor skills at age three.

Another large study by Zimmerman et al. [32] consisted of a single survey of 1008 parents of children aged 2 to 24 months. They found that after adjusting for sex, age, number of siblings, premature birth, hours per week in daycare, parental presence, income, race/ethnicity, and state of birth, viewing of baby-oriented videos (e.g., *Baby Einstein*) was correlated with a significantly lower score in Communicative Development Inventory score for children aged 8 to 16 months. Other types of content did not have a significant impact.

To summarize, there is more information about the impact of television on infants and toddlers than about the impact of computers. In particular, the research literature points at a complex set of factors that influence whether television has a positive or negative impact. Of particular note is that certain types of shows are more likely to lead to cognitive gains. This nuanced view stands in contrast to the recommendations by the American Academy of Pediatrics of avoiding screen time for children under the age of two [2].

RESEARCH QUESTIONS
Given the significant lack of empirical data on the use of computers by children under the age of three, the main research question we sought to answer in this paper is how infants and toddlers are using tablets. We decided to focus on tablets because we believe they have made computers accessible to the youngest children in ways that were not possible with keyboards and indirect pointing devices.

More specifically we wanted to answer the following questions about infants and toddlers and tablets:

- Can they make meaningful use of tablets?
- What type of interactions are they using?
- How do they position the device and themselves?
- Are they using tablets together with others?
- What type of apps are they using?
- How do the answers to these questions change for different age groups?

METHOD

Identifying Relevant Videos
We used YouTube's search to identify relevant videos. To begin with, we searched for combinations of a word related to a young child (baby, infant, toddler, kid, child) and the word "iPad". As an alternative, we also searched for the same child-related terms and the word "tablet" instead of "iPad". We also used a translation tool to substitute the term "baby" for its equivalent in several other languages (French, Spanish, Portuguese, German, Japanese, Korean).

For each search, we looked through the first 200 results, or all results if less, and added any videos that appeared relevant (i.e., may involve a child under three years old using a tablet) based on search result information to a playlist that helped us easily identify duplicates. As we watched the videos, we often saw listings of related videos or playlists that provided additional, relevant results. We added these videos to the playlist if they were not already present.

While watching the videos on the playlist, we also ran into situations where we learned that the video did not fit our criteria – there were no children in our desired age range using a tablet – and we removed these videos. We also removed videos if they did not include the age of the child and we could not see enough of the child to determine age, if we could not see what the child was doing with the device, or if the device was not a tablet.

Coding Videos
Two members of the research team gathered basic information about the videos including URL, title, YouTube username, and length. Then, one member coded each video for the age of the child (with a best guess if not specified), gender, ability to use the tablet and app(s) (from

1 to 5 based on the ability to control and comprehend), languages used, emotions displayed by the child, context, number of people participating other than the child, physical position of the device, physical position of the child, use of fingers, use of hands, use of gestures, and genre of app used.

More specifically, the ratings for ability indicated the following:

1- No or very low ability (i.e., randomly touches the device)
2- Low ability (i.e., purposeful actions, but no full understanding of app(s); little accuracy)
3- Moderate ability (i.e., some difficulty with basic interactions, but able to use app(s); needs assistance to get to child-oriented app(s))
4- High ability (e.g., able to navigate to app(s), and use app(s), but occasionally makes mistakes)
5- Very high ability (e.g., has no problem navigating to and using app(s))

We were particularly concerned with the validity of our coding of age and ability. To address this concern, a second rater went through all the videos and coded the age, as well as noted whether a guess was required. For 66 percent of videos, the rater was able to get the age of the child from the video through the title, the description, or by having access to one of the former in another video featuring the same child (and adjusting the age based on the date of the video). For agreement at the 6 six month grouping level used in our statistical analysis, the intraclass correlation coefficient [14] was .871 for individual measures (reliability of scale=.931), p<.001.

To ensure the validity of our coding of children's ability, a second rater watched four randomly selected videos for each of the five points in the scale. Then, the rater rated another 55 randomly selected videos (no overlap). The intraclass correlation coefficient was .655, and the reliability scale was .792 (p<.001).

DATASET DESCRIPTION

Video Characteristics

The dataset consisted of 208 videos. Their median length was 93 seconds (minimum=13, first quartile=51, third quartile=160, maximum=1420).

Child Characteristics

The children included 57 under the age of 12 months (17 under six months), 43 between 12 and 17 months old, 49 between 18 and 23 months old, and 59 who were 24 to 29 months old. For convenience, we have organized our analysis around these four age groups.

While gender was roughly evenly divided, there were more girls than boys in the videos through 23 months of age, with a sharp change in favor of boys in videos featuring children aged 24 months and older (see Figure 1). In fact, the distribution for the oldest age group was roughly two-to-one in favor of boys.

Devices Used

An overwhelming majority of devices used in the videos were Apple iPads, with only 27 videos featuring other tablets.

Context

YouTube users filmed almost all their videos at home, with only one video filmed in an office. A majority of the videos featured English as the only language, with 30 featuring another language.

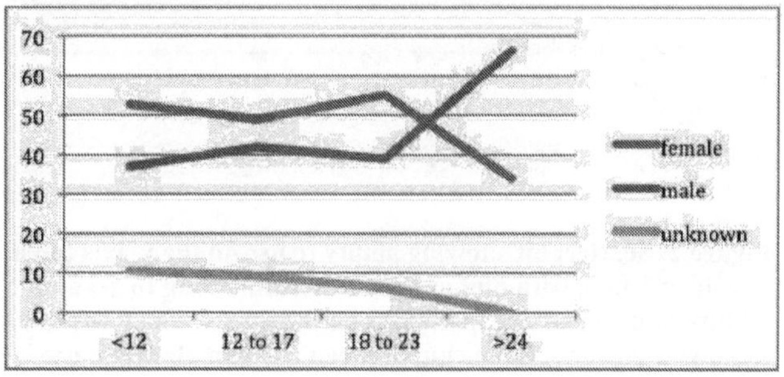

Figure 1. Percent of participants by gender and age group, in months.

RESULTS

We analyzed the data using SPSS 21. Our goal was to understand the changes that typically occur with age in the way children use these devices. For a majority of variables, we analyzed them by age group (<12 months, 12-17 months, 18-23 months, and 24-29 months). To learn if age group had a statistically significant effect on a variable we used logistic regression if the variable was categorical (e.g., the position of the device), and non-parametric correlations for ordinal variables.

Ability to Use

We coded ability to use on a scale of 1 to 5, with 1 being no or very low ability, and 5 being very high ability to comprehend and control the device and app(s) being used. Figure 2 shows a scatterplot, with age in months on the x-axis, and ability to use on the y-axis. A power trendline was the best fit to the relationship, yielding an R^2 value of .51.

Figure 3 shows a clearer picture of the distributions of ability to use by age group. It shows a pattern going from having about 90 percent of children under 12 months of age at levels 1 or 2, with a similar percentage at levels 3 to 5 for the group between 24 and 29 months of age.

Interaction Styles

Number of Hands

One of our main interests was to learn about how children interacted with the devices. The first variable we analyzed was how many hands children used to interact with the device. This analysis yielded a clear trend, with use of two hands more common for younger children, and one hand more common for older children (see Figure 4). A Spearman correlation between age group and the number of hands used was statistically significant ($p<.001$, correlation coefficient =-.286).

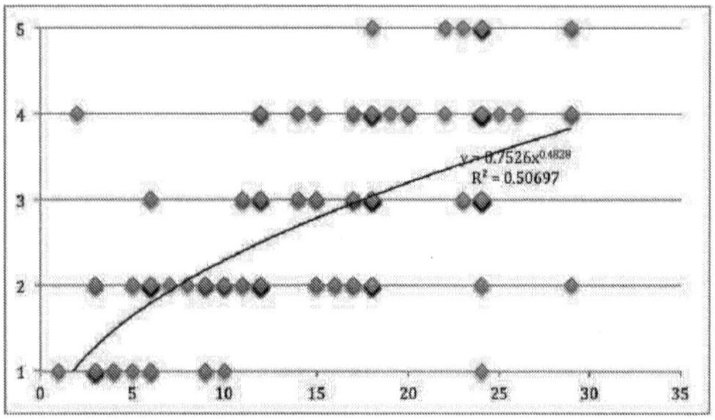

Figure 2. Scatterplot showing ability to use on the y-axis (on a scale of 1 to 5, with higher scores corresponding to greater ability to use) and age in months on the x-axis. The trendline shows a power relationship between age and ability to use.

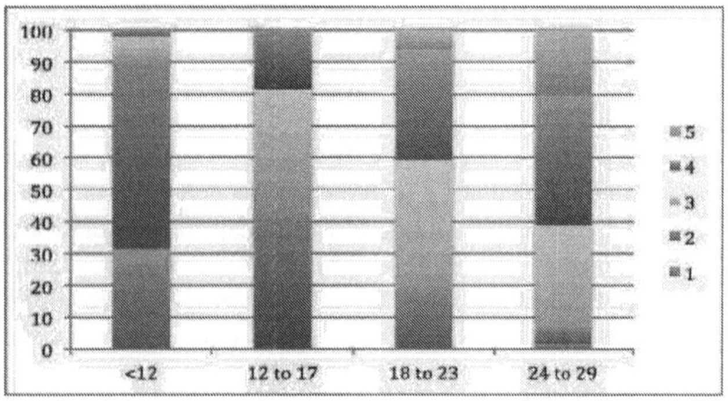

Figure 3. Percentage of children reaching a particular level of ability to use (on a scale of 1 to 5, with higher scores corresponding to better ability to use), by age group in months.

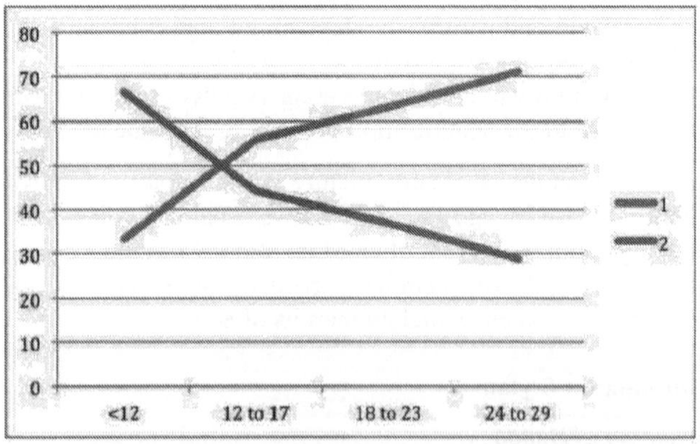

Figure 4. Percentage of children (on the y-axis) using one or two hands (lines) by age group in months (on the x-axis).

Use of Fingers and Gestures

We then analyzed how children used their hands, including how many fingers they used, and what type of gestures they used. Figure 5 shows clear trends. The more salient ones involve a sharp decrease with age in the use of the full hand, multiple fingers, and hitting the device. This is accompanied by a sharp increase in single finger interactions by tapping. There is also a slow, but steady increase in the use of dragging gestures. The only gesture that follows an odd path is swiping, which increases for children between 12 and 17 months of age, and then decreases again.

Based on logistic regressions, all variables fit the model ($p<.001$ in all cases), meaning that age group had a significant effect on them.

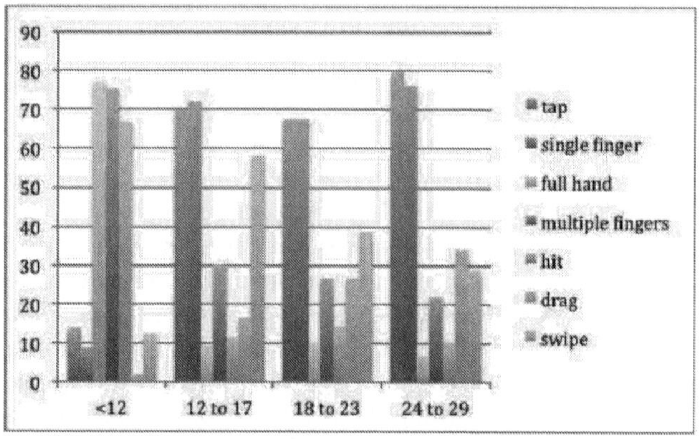

Figure 5. Percentage of children (on the y-axis) who made particular use of their hand or fingers by age group in months (on the x-axis).

Device Position

In terms of device position, we classified this into four separate categories: held by child, held by an adult, lying flat on a surface, or propped up by some object. In many videos, especially for older children, we saw more than one way of holding the device in the same video. Figure 6 shows one clear trend with older children more likely to hold the device ($p<.005$ for the model). The other variable that showed statistical significance was whether the device was held by an adult ($p<.05$ for the model). Both having the device flat or propped up held relatively steady, although having devices flat on a surface was roughly twice as popular.

Child Position

We classified children's positions while interacting with the device into standing or walking, sitting, and lying down. In this case, there were no clear trends, except for the fact that sitting was the most popular position. See Figure 7. Age group only had a statistically significant effect on lying down based on logistic regression ($p<.005$).

Other People in Video

We analyzed the number of people who appeared in videos, other than the child and the person filming. We only counted people who had an active role in the activity (e.g., we did not count people who happened to walk by in the background). Figure 8 shows how between 30 and 50 percent of the time there is another person participating in the activity. In this case, logistic regression did not yield statistically significant effects.

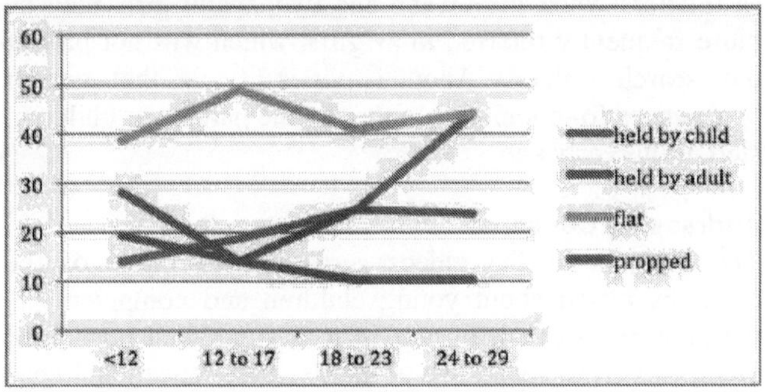

Figure 6. Percentage of videos (on the y-axis) featuring a particular device position (lines) by age group in months (on the x-axis).

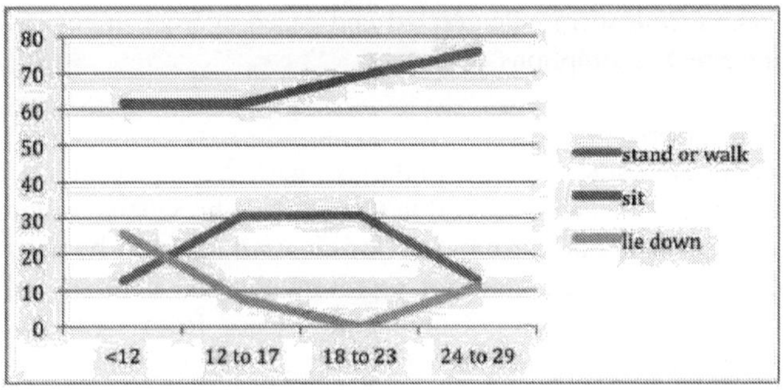

Figure 7. Percentage of videos (on the y-axis) with the child in a particular position (lines) by age group in months (on the x-axis).

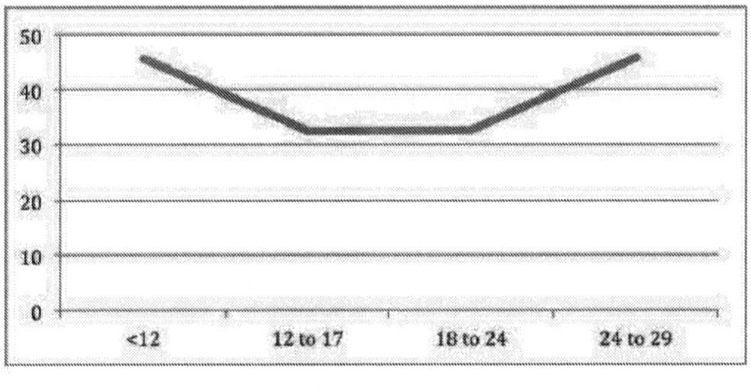

Figure 8. Percentage of videos (on the y-axis) in which another person other than the child and the person filming played an active role in the activity by age group in months (on the x-axis).

App Genres

When we were able to see the screen, we classified the genre of the app(s) the child used. The genres we observed were: games, educational, video, music, pictures, and lifestyle (e.g., potty training, image distraction for babies). Logistic regression yielded a statistically significant effect of age group for all genres, except for video and pictures ($p<.001$ for music, $p<.005$ for games and educational, $p<.05$ for lifestyle).

Figure 9 illustrates these trends. Music was the most popular genre for the youngest age group, but the popularity of this genre drops to about ten percent of cases for older children. Games and educational apps see the opposite trend, from being a distant second and third for the youngest group, to dominating the videos in the dataset for the oldest group.

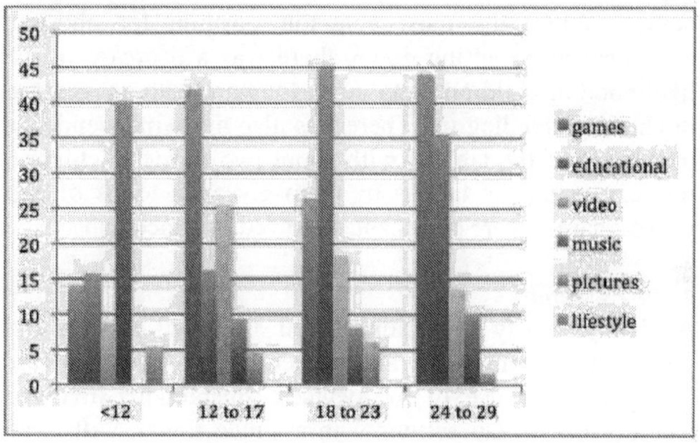

Figure 9. Percentage of videos (on the y-axis) featuring a particular app genre by age group in months (on the x-axis).

Emotions

Emotions displayed by children in the videos were overwhelmingly neutral (in 190 of the videos), with the remaining videos split between 15 displaying positive, and three displaying negative emotions.

DISCUSSION

Characterization by age group

The analysis of YouTube videos presented in this paper provides us with a sense of how infants and toddlers are using tablets. Below we discuss typical characteristics of use for each age group, which may be useful as starting points for designs.

Under 12 Months

A majority of children under 12 months (90 percent) in our sample did not display a moderate ability to use the app(s) they were using on a tablet. Their most common form of interaction was hitting the tablet with a full hand, using multiple fingers. They were almost twice as likely to use both their hands, than only one hand. Tablets were most often laid flat for them to use, with an adult holding the tablet coming second in terms of device position. Most of the children this age (almost 90 percent) used the tablet while sitting or lying down. Almost half used the device together with another person. In terms of app genres, music apps were the most popular for this age group, enabling children to use gross motor control to generate sounds.

12 to 17 Months
Children in this age range were much more likely to display a moderate ability to use the devices, with over half of the children we observed at this level. This coincides with a significant shift from interacting with full hands by hitting the device, to interacting with a single finger by tapping on it. There was also a shift from primary use of two hands to interact, to using only one hand slightly more often than two. Device positioning was similar to the younger age group, except for a decrease in adults holding the device, and an increase in the likelihood that children will hold the device. While the most common position for children continued to be sitting down, there was a decrease in the likelihood of children lying down together with an increase in children standing up. There was also more independence in the use of the tablets, with about two thirds of children this age using the tablets by themselves. In terms of app genres, games were dominant, followed by video apps.

18 to 23 Months
A clear majority of children aged 18 to 23 months old (about 80 percent) were able to achieve at least moderate ability in their use of the devices. Interactions involved again primarily tap actions with a single finger, with drag interactions rising significantly. There was also an increased likelihood of using only one hand instead of two (about two-to-one ratio). As in every other age group, devices were most likely to be lying flat. For this age group there was an increase in the likelihood of children holding the device, as well as the device being propped up. Children's positions and the participation of others in the tablet activities stayed similar to the levels for children 12 to 17 months of age. In terms of apps, there was a significant increase in the use of educational apps for this age group, which were followed in popularity by games.

24 to 29 Months
Over 90 percent of the children in our sample who had turned two years old showed at least moderate ability to control and comprehend the app(s) they used. We continued seeing most interactions occur through single-finger taps, with a continued increase of drag interactions, and even more dominance of one hand. In terms of device position, there was an increase in the likelihood that children would hold the tablet, which together with having it lying flat was the most common position. There were no major changes in children's positions, although there was a slight increase in the number of people other than the child participating in the use of the tablet. In terms of apps, games and educational apps were by far the most popular.

Gender
A surprise we had when analyzing the data was the dramatic shift in gender balance from having a slim majority of videos featuring girls through 23 months of age, to having a two-to-one ratio of boys-to-girls for children aged 24 months and older. This distribution is inconsistent with previous studies looking at access to computers and frequency of use by gender for preschool children [18]. It could also be due to boys being more frequently referred to as toddlers when they reach age two, while girls may be more frequently referred to as girls, which was not part of our search criteria. Another possibility is that gender preferences for computers, either by the parents or children, start at this early age.

Addressing Concerns
The analysis of the videos suggests that many of the concerns raised about young children and computers [1] may not be justified. In particular, a significant portion of videos involved social use of the devices, educational apps were similarly popular to games, and many of the apps appeared to enable children to practice perceptual and motor skills. While tablets could still be used in ways that may lead to negative outcomes, recommendations of no screen time seem exaggerated and based at least in part on incorrect assumptions.

Limitations
There are some obvious limitations with the approach used to obtain the data analyzed in this paper. The videos posted on YouTube come from a set of children selected by their caregivers, which may not represent the full diversity of users. Since we did not obtain the videos from a random sample of the population, the results of inferential statistics should be taken with caution, while focusing on the descriptive statistics. It is also worth keeping in mind alternative approaches, such as surveys and direct observation, would have also involved self-selection or non-response, and may not have included the geographic and cultural diversity we found in our sample.

We can also consider whether the behavior in the videos was atypical for the featured children, and whether the children are atypical. The first concern should be alleviated by the length of the videos, with the median at 1m33s. If children had amazing luck in using an iPad, showing unusual performance, it would be unlikely to happen for that long. In terms of the children having atypical abilities, they did not do anything that is not within developmental milestones.

It is also possible that caregivers may have avoided posting videos featuring children who are frustrated at not being able to use their devices. That said, we did see a clear progression by age in the type of interactions children were capable of successfully performing.

Perhaps the main limitation given the questions in this topic is that our research methodology did not enable us to track children over time to understand the impact of their use of tablets on their development. However, such a study would have been significantly more costly than this one, and we consider this to be a useful first step in learning about the topic.

Another obvious limitation is that this was not a controlled study. We were not able to control what the children did with the devices, where they did it, how they went about interacting with the devices, or who was there with them. On the other hand, there is an advantage in seeing how these devices are used in real-world circumstances, something that is often difficult to replicate in a laboratory study.

A final limitation is that we focused on tablets, while there is also use of smartphones. We thought for a first study it would be better to focus on one screen size. We also considered that tablets may be more appropriate for younger children, as larger screens could also include larger targets that are more appropriate for their developing motor skills.

FUTURE WORK

To complement this study, it would be a good idea to conduct a longitudinal survey based on a random sample of birth records for a particular geographic area, to obtain a different kind of sample and better understand the likelihood of children of a certain age using tablets, how they are using them, and how it affects their development.

It would also be useful to more deeply study the use of apps and see how often they include the factors related to success in television shows (i.e., child-directed speech, elicitation of responses, object labeling, and/or a coherent storybook-like framework) [17].

Beyond that, there is a clear opportunity to explore the design of apps for very young children, starting as early as 12 to 17 months of age. The evidence presented in this paper suggests a majority children in this age group and older can understand and use basic apps. The research question is how to design them such that they have similar characteristics to beneficial television shows, while helping children build communication, visual, and motor skills, and increase their connections to their caregivers (see a similar call by Lieberman et al. [15]).

CONCLUSION

We conducted a study of YouTube videos showing infants and toddlers using tablets. Our analysis of the videos provides a window into how they are using these devices. While most of the children under age one struggled to make meaningful use of the tablets, a majority of children aged 12 to 17 months showed moderate ability. In addition, more than 90 percent of children aged two reached this level of ability.

Our study also provides an account of interaction styles, device and child positioning, and social aspects of tablet use. Designers could use this information as starting points in the design of apps for these age groups.

REFERENCES

1. Alliance for Childhood. (2001). Fool's Gold: A Critical Look at Computers in Childhood. Retrieved from http://www.allianceforchildhood.org/publications
2. American Academy of Pediatrics. (n.d.). Media and Children. Retrieved September 15, 2014, from http://www.aap.org/en-us/advocacy-and-policy/aap-health-initiatives/Pages/Media-and-Children.aspx
3. Anthony, L., Kim, Y., & Findlater, L. (2013). Analyzing user-generated youtube videos to understand touchscreen use by people with motor impairments. In *Proceedings of the SIGCHI Conference on Human Factors in Computing Systems*. 1223-1232. Retrieved from http://dl.acm.org/citation.cfm?id=2466158
4. Bavelier, D., Green, C. S., & Dye, M. W. G. (2010). Children, Wired: For Better and for Worse. *Neuron, 67*(5), 692–701.
5. Castles, A., McLean, G. M., Bavin, E., Bretherton, L., Carlin, J., Prior, M., … Reilly, S. (2013). Computer use and letter knowledge in pre-school children: A population-based study. *Journal of Paediatrics and Child Health, 49*(3), 193–198. doi:10.1111/jpc.12126
6. CDC. (n.d.). Milestone Moments. Retrieved from http://www.cdc.gov/ncbddd/actearly/pdf/parents_pdfs/milestonemomentseng508.pdf
7. Fish, A. M., Li, X., McCarrick, K., Butler, S. T., Stanton, B., Brumitt, G., … Partridge, T. (2008). Early Childhood Computer Experience and Cognitive Development among Urban Low-Income Preschoolers. *Journal of Educational Computing Research, 38*(1), 97–113.
8. Hernandez, A. (2014). Toddlers and Tablets: Emerging Apps Take Cues from Learning Science. *Education Next, 14*(1). Retrieved from http://www.questia.com/library/journal/1G1-352376588/toddlers-and-tablets-emerging-apps-take-cues-from#/
9. Hourcade, J. P. (2008). Interaction Design and Children. *Foundations and Trends in Human–Computer Interaction, 1*(4), 277–392. doi:10.1561/1100000006
10. Hourcade, J. P., Bederson, B. B., Druin, A., & Guimbretière, F. (2004). Differences in Pointing Task Performance Between Preschool Children and Adults Using Mice. *ACM Trans. Comput.-Hum. Interact., 11*(4), 357–386. doi:10.1145/1035575.1035577
11. Hourcade, J. P., Crowther, M., & Hunt, L. (2007). Does Mouse Size Affect Study and Evaluation Results?: A Study Comparing Preschool Children's Performance

with Small and Regular-sized Mice. In *Proceedings of the 6th International Conference on Interaction Design and Children* (pp. 109–116). New York, NY, USA: ACM. doi:10.1145/1297277.1297300

12. Hourcade, J. P., Perry, K. B., & Sharma, A. (2008). PointAssist: Helping Four Year Olds Point with Ease. In *Proceedings of the 7th International Conference on Interaction Design and Children* (pp. 202–209). New York, NY, USA: ACM. doi:10.1145/1463689.1463757
13. Johnston M.V., Nishimura A., Harum K., Pekar J., and Blue ME. (2001). Sculpting the developing brain. *Advances in Pediatrics, 48*, 1-38.
14. Kottner, J., Audige, L., Brorson, S., Donner, A., Gajewski, B. J., Hróbjartsson, A., ... & Streiner, D. L. (2011). Guidelines for reporting reliability and agreement studies (GRRAS) were proposed. *International journal of nursing studies, 48*(6), 661-671.
15. Lieberman, D. A., Bates, C. H., & So, J. (2009). Young Children's Learning With Digital Media. *Computers in the Schools, 26*(4), 271–283. doi:10.1080/07380560903360194
16. Lieberman, D. A., Fisk, M. C., & Biely, E. (2009). Digital Games for Young Children Ages Three to Six: From Research to Design. *Computers in the Schools, 26*(4), 299–313. doi:10.1080/07380560903360178
17. Linebarger, D. L., & Walker, D. (2005). Infants' and Toddlers' Television Viewing and Language Outcomes. *American Behavioral Scientist, 48*(5), 624–645. doi:10.1177/0002764204271505
18. Li, X., & Atkins, M. S. (2004). Early Childhood Computer Experience and Cognitive and Motor Development. *Pediatrics, 113*(6), 1715–1722.
19. Li, X., Atkins, M. S., & Stanton, B. (2006). Effects of Home and School Computer Use on School Readiness and Cognitive Development Among Head Start Children: A Randomized Controlled Pilot Trial. *Merrill-Palmer Quarterly, 52*(2), 239–263.
20. McCarrick, K., & Li, X. (2007). Buried Treasure: The Impact of Computer Use on Young Children's Social, Cognitive, Language Development and Motivation. *Association for the Advancement of Computing in Education (AACE) Journal, 15*(1), 73–95.
21. McCarrick, K., Li, X., Fish, A., Holtrop, T., Bhavnagri, N. P., Stanton, B., … Partridge, T. (2007). Parental Involvement in Young Children's Computer Use and Cognitive Development. *NHSA Dialog, 10*(2), 67–82. doi:10.1080/15240750701436410
22. Plowman, L., McPake, J., & Stephen, C. (2008). Just picking it up? Young children learning with technology at home. *Cambridge Journal of Education, 38*(3), 303–319. doi:10.1080/03057640802287564
23. Plowman, L., & Stephen, C. (2005). Children, play, and computers in pre-school education. *British Journal of Educational Technology, 36*(2), 145–157.
24. Plowman, L., Stevenson, O., Stephen, C., & McPake, J. (2012). Preschool children's learning with technology at home. *Computers & Education, 59*(1), 30 – 37. doi:http://dx.doi.org/10.1016/j.compedu.2011.11.014
25. Raffle, H., Ballagas, R., Revelle, G., Horii, H., Follmer, S., Go, J., … Spasojevic, M. (2010). Family Story Play: Reading with Young Children (and Elmo) over a Distance. In *Proceedings of the SIGCHI Conference on Human Factors in Computing Systems* (pp. 1583–1592). New York, NY, USA: ACM. doi:10.1145/1753326.1753563
26. Raffle, H., Revelle, G., Mori, K., Ballagas, R., Buza, K., Horii, H., … Spasojevic, M. (2011). Hello, is Grandma There? Let's Read! StoryVisit: Family Video Chat and Connected e-Books. In *Proceedings of the SIGCHI Conference on Human Factors in Computing Systems* (pp. 1195–1204). New York, NY, USA: ACM. doi:10.1145/1978942.1979121
27. Revelle, G. L., & Strommen, E. F. (1990). The Effects of Practice and Input Device Used on Young Children's Computer Control. *Collegiate Microcomput., 8*(4), 33–41.
28. Schmidt, M. E., Rich, M., Rifas-Shiman, S. L., Oken, E., & Taveras, E. M. (2009). Television Viewing in Infancy and Child Cognition at 3 Years of Age in a US Cohort. *Pediatrics, 123*(3), e370–e375. doi:10.1542/peds.2008-3221
29. Strommen, E. F., Revelle, G. L., Medoff, L. M., & Razavi, S. (1996). Slow and steady wins the race? Three-year-old children and pointing device use. *Behaviour & Information Technology, 15*(1), 57–64. doi:10.1080/014492996120409
30. Sweetser, P., Johnson, D. M., Ozdowska, A., & Wyeth, P. (2012). Active versus passive screen time for young children | QUT ePrints. *Australasian Journal of Early Childhood, 37*(4), 94–98.
31. Thelen, E., & Bates, E. (2003). Connectionism and dynamic systems: are they really different? *Developmental Science, 6*(4), 378–391. doi:10.1111/1467-7687.00294
32. Zimmerman, F. J., Christakis, D. A., & Meltzoff, A. N. (2007). Associations between Media Viewing and Language Development in Children Under Age 2 Years. *The Journal of Pediatrics, 151*(4), 364 – 368. doi:http://dx.doi.org/10.1016/j.jpeds.2007.04.071

Apparition: Crowdsourced User Interfaces That Come To Life As You Sketch Them

Walter S. Lasecki
Computer Science Department
University of Rochester
wlasecki@cs.rochester.edu

Juho Kim
CSAIL
MIT
juhokim@mit.edu

Nicholas Rafter
Independent Researcher
nicholas.rafter@gmail.com

Onkur Sen
Computer Science Department
Stanford University
onkursen@gmail.com

Jeffrey P. Bigham
HCI and LT Institutes
Carnegie Mellon University
jbigham@cmu.edu

Michael S. Bernstein
Computer Science Department
Stanford University
msb@cs.stanford.edu

ABSTRACT
Prototyping allows designers to quickly iterate and gather feedback, but the time it takes to create even a Wizard-of-Oz prototype reduces the utility of the process. In this paper, we introduce crowdsourcing techniques and tools for prototyping interactive systems in the time it takes to describe the idea. Our Apparition system uses paid microtask crowds to make even hard-to-automate functions work immediately, allowing more fluid prototyping of interfaces that contain interactive elements and complex behaviors. As users sketch their interface and describe it aloud in natural language, crowd workers and sketch recognition algorithms translate the input into user interface elements, add animations, and provide Wizard-of-Oz functionality. We discuss how design teams can use our approach to reflect on prototypes or begin user studies within seconds, and how, over time, Apparition prototypes can become fully-implemented versions of the systems they simulate. Powering Apparition is the first self-coordinated, real-time crowdsourcing infrastructure. We anchor this infrastructure on a new, lightweight write-locking mechanism that workers can use to signal their intentions to each other.

Author Keywords
Rapid prototyping; crowdsourcing; human computation

ACM Classification Keywords
D.2.2 Design Tools and Techniques

INTRODUCTION
The effort required to produce an interactive prototype is a clear limiting factor in effective design practice. Prototyping grounds an iterative process of creation and reflection [28], where the prototype becomes a mechanism for continuous course correction and ideation. This process, which David Kelley terms "enlightened trial and error", is most effective when prototypes can be fluidly produced and evaluated. However, even the most rapid interactive prototype construction (e.g., Wizard-of-Oz prototyping) is easily an order of magnitude slower than envisioning through a sketch.

CHI 2015, April 18–23 2015, Seoul, Republic of Korea

ACM 978-1-4503-3145-6/15/04 $15.00
http://dx.doi.org/10.1145/2702123.2702565

Sensing this disparity, foundational work nearly 20 years ago suggested that designers might be able to author interactive prototypes simply by sketching [14]. However, while these systems can transform simple elements such as rectangles into buttons, they stop short of capturing the full variety of interactive elements and behaviors a designer might envision. If a designer wants to create a simple video game character, make them follow a cursor, and destroy enemies by jumping on them, they are facing hours in a code editor.

In this paper, we introduce tools and techniques for prototyping interactive systems in the time it takes to simply describe the idea visually and verbally. Our system, called *Apparition*, uses paid crowds to make even hard-to-automate functions work immediately without the need for one-off control implementations, allowing fluid prototyping of interfaces containing interactive elements, complex animations, and intelligent feedback. As users sketch their interface and describe it aloud in natural language, crowd workers refine interface elements, add animations, and control the prototype's responses. Visual elements replace sketches within 8 seconds on average, and interactive behaviors function in 3 seconds. The speed of such prototypes makes it possible to create an interactive prototype moments after thinking of the idea.

For Apparition to work, a group of microtask workers must coordinate a complex set of goals and dependencies in real-time. *Apparition is the first crowdsourcing system to enable self-managing, real-time crowd coordination.* Unfortunately, direct approaches yield blocking behaviors where multiple workers all attempt the same task and conflict while other tasks remain untouched. Introducing managers slows the system beyond real-time responses. We introduce a lightweight write-locking mechanism that lets workers signal to others which elements they are editing and roles they are fulfilling.

Envisioned Interaction
Lavanya is a developer at a small startup that is creating a new real-time strategy game. She has just had an idea for a

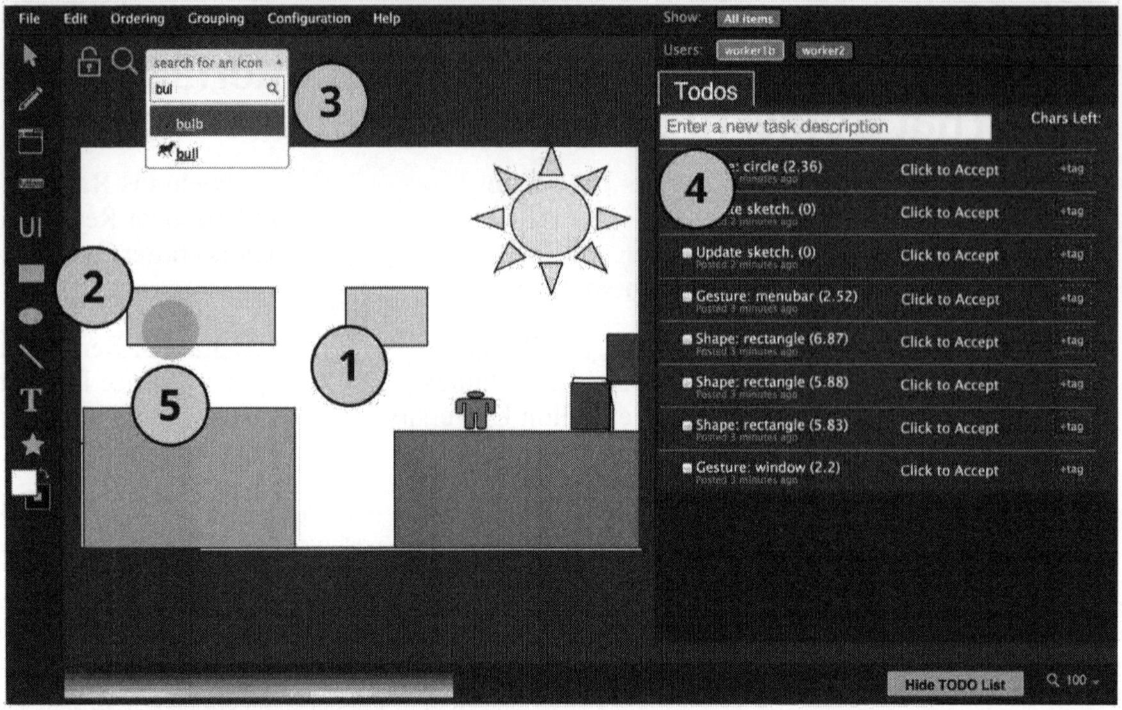

Figure 1. Apparition allows designers to quickly create functional interface prototypes using sketches and verbal descriptions. (1) A collaborative canvas where the user(s) and workers can draw. (2) Drawing tools and icons to quicken workers' creation of UI elements. (3) A search function to help workers find relevant icons. (4) A to-do list that shows what has been drawn by the user but not yet converted to UI elements. Workers can "accept" tasks to signal what they are currently working on. (5) "In-progress" markers for workers to show where they are currently working to avoid conflicts.

new enemy character. Lavanya flags her coworker Ellen to tell her about the idea, but Ellen is unsure whether the character will fit the feel of the game. In response, Lavanya opens Apparition and begins to quickly sketch out a scenario.

As Lavanya sketches a version of the game UI, her sketches are immediately converted into properly aligned interface elements. In less than a minute, Lavanya has sketched a rough version of the game's UI, complete with a handful of enemy characters. "See, these creatures run away when I get too close," Lavanya explains, "they find some distance and then start following me again." As she describes her idea in more detail, the new enemy characters on screen begin to look and act as she describes. Ellen then pulls out her tablet, connects to the same Apparition session as Lavanya, draws a few of her own characters, and sees how the system responds in various situations. When Ellen finds situations that were underspecified, Lavanya describes aloud how the approach would work, and the system-controlled characters change their behavior to match. Impressed, Ellen tells Lavanya she should demo this approach at the team meeting later that afternoon.

While Lavanya prepares her talk, she puts Apparition into "Bake In" mode, which continues to improve the prototype without further end-user intervention. A few hours later, when demoing the system to the team, Lavanya notes that the workers have replaced the early images with more refined assets. The previously described behaviors are still in effect but are continuously refined as people ask questions and make suggestions. Team members can copy the interface and branch, comparing ideas side-by-side.

Outline and Contributions

Apparition works to make near-instant prototyping possible by using human computation to power interactions that automated systems cannot yet handle alone. Apparition users can fluidly prototype designs by sketching and speaking on a shared canvas. If its automatic sketch recognition algorithm recognizes UI elements, Apparition replaces them with higher-fidelity representations [14]. For all other elements — friend lists, game characters, map interfaces — paid crowd workers coordinate the transformation of each sketch into the desired prototype element. Given more time to "bake in," the prototype visuals continue to develop. Users can speak desired behaviors, *e.g.*, "when I click the button, the friend list slides over and the map pops up," and crowd workers Wizard-of-Oz the behavior the next time the action is triggered in real-time.

We make the following contributions in this paper:

- The first crowdsourcing system where workers self-coordinate to complete a complex task in real-time.
- The concept of intelligent prototyping tools powered by an on-demand, self-coordinating crowd.
- Methods and tools for coordinating large groups of people on simultaneous control and creation tasks.
- Apparition, a tool that lets crowds of online human workers collectively help users create working interface prototypes from sketches and verbal descriptions in seconds.
- Validation of our approach through examples of the types of prototyping that Apparition makes possible.

We begin with a discussion of the background and related work in design, prototyping, and crowdsourcing. We then discuss how Apparition works and demonstrate that it can quickly create accurate, functional prototypes. We conclude with a discussion of our results and future directions of research made possible by releasing Apparition.

BACKGROUND

Apparition builds on 20 years of Wizard-of-Oz prototyping tools and demonstrates how paid crowds can form a scalable, always-available set of wizards. It also extends the literature from static screenshots to functional prototypes with dynamic, intelligent behaviors. In this section, we discuss prior work in UI sketching, prototyping, and crowdsourcing.

Easier Prototyping with Sketching and Wizard-of-Oz

Tools such as Balsamiq (www.balsamiq.com) or JustInMind (www.justinmind.com) allow designers to create interfaces without requiring the same significant intervention during testing that paper prototypes do. However, these applications require training and a large amount of effort to create, making them impractical during the earliest stages of design [14].

Systems such as SILK [14] and DENIM [20] reduce the overhead of prototyping by recognizing designers' sketches as interface elements. Designers can then create a linked storyboard defining appropriate state transitions for different interactions. While this is effective, the scope of elements they recognize is limited and interactions can only result in individual state updates.

d.tools [9] allows designers to begin with a rapid prototype created from visual statecharts and move towards implementation versions by adding code to parts of the statechart. d.note[8] allows users to revise both appearance and behavior by annotating screenshots and storyboards. Apparition allows similar revisions of behaviors and appearance in real-time during interaction via speech and sketching.

The advantages of multi-modal interaction, *e.g.*, combining sketching with spoken natural language descriptions, have been studied in diverse settings and contexts [3]. Natural language provides a means of capturing many types of information that is difficult or unnatural to capture in sketches, *e.g.*, temporal relationships, behaviors, and spatially disjoint elements [3]. By integrating voice, these selection, scoping, and description issues become single-interaction tasks rather than multi-step processes. Apparition uses multimodality to expedite the creation process for the end-user and clarify meaning for crowd workers. We aim for a process like describing a system to a co-located colleague.

Designing behaviors is difficult partly because of limitations in tools available to designers—a vast majority of 267 interviewed designers found programming behaviors more difficult than visual design [26]. More importantly, behaviors targeted by these designers were too diverse to embed into any one system with a fixed set of supported features. Apparition addresses this problem by leveraging human intelligence with spoken language to support highly diverse sets of behaviors with just a simple description. These designers also struggled to fully communicate their desired behaviors with the developers building the system. One goal of Apparition is to allow designers to easily create a "living spec" that developers interact with to better understand the designers' intended behaviors.

Wizard-of-Oz control simulates complex functionality in prototypes [11] – a human "wizard" provides feedback or control to simulate difficult-to-implement features. For instance, to test whether a chat-based support tool will help users better find information on a webpage, an instant messenger tool might be built into the site so that users can communicate with a designer instead of an automated system.

Tools such as SketchWizard [5] make Wizard-of-Oz prototyping easier by allowing the end-user to create pen sketches, and a wizard behind the scene converts their sketch into geometric shapes and elements. Because of the speed and accuracy needed to keep up with even within-lab use cases, situational planning and practice is needed for wizards to support trials with users in real-time. In contrast, Apparition provides a canvas and coordination tools that allow many crowd workers to share the work of keeping up with user interactions in live sessions and demonstrations. Thus, Apparition provides open-ended support without prior planning or setup.

Apparition's ability to use speech also extends the expressiveness of the interfaces and behaviors that can be prototyped. Turvy [24] used Wizard-of-Oz to control an intelligent agent that users could instruct in natural language. Turvy let researchers see how users would really interact with their agent, leading to insights that can aid in the development and automation of a released system. Prior work has also explored Wizard-of-Oz conversational interaction, including combining the input of human wizards and machines [7, 18, 27].

While quicker and easier than a full implementation, these Wizard-of-Oz powered systems are generally one-off and can still require significant development effort. Apparition overcomes that by providing a set of broadly-applicable tools and techniques for coordinating multiple workers so that complex, concurrent actions are supported with relative ease.

Crowdsourcing and Real-Time Human Computation

Human computation engages people as part of a process to solve problems that automated approaches cannot handle alone. Crowdsourcing, where an open call is made to a population to elicit responses, effectively accesses human intelligence for computational tasks. Workers can be recruited on demand from platforms such as Amazon Mechanical Turk and engaged for short time periods to complete a task. However, this process has the caveat that workers are unknown to task requesters and might be of low quality or even malicious in rare cases.

Most work has focused on coordinating workers by dividing work into small microtasks [21] or well-specified ongoing roles [16]. Prior work has also explored how crowds themselves might be used to recursively generate these workflows [13] with some end-user oversight. In constrast, Apparition must be able to create new roles and tasks as soon as the user describes an intent, so real-time coordination for defining and adopting these roles is our goal.

Real-Time Crowdsourcing
Real-time human computation has been explored in systems like VizWiz [2], which showed that the crowd could answer visual questions in less than 30 seconds, and Adrenaline [1], which formalized the retainer model for bringing a group of crowd workers together in two seconds. Systems like Legion [17] have explored how a synchronous crowd can work together effectively once recruited (in that case to collectively control existing user interfaces). Apparition allows the end-user to work with the crowd to produce an artifact.

Chorus [18] engaged a group of workers in a conversational interaction with a user, using an incentive mechanism and memory space to encourage the crowd to act as a single consistent individual. Workers powering Apparition must also be consistent because prototypes must reliably function in the same way over multiple interactions with end-users.

Crowdsourcing for Drawing and Rapid Evaluation
Crowdsourcing inherently provides access to individuals with diverse skills, which provides guidance to users during the design process [22] and improves specific skills like drawing. Limpaechter *et al.* collected sketch data from a crowd of players of their DrawAFriend game and used the resulting model to correct user-drawn lines in real-time [19].

Foundry [23] allows end-users to create "flash teams", computer-mediated teams of expert crowd workers that were able to complete complex tasks such as design prototyping and animation that are produced by experts, rather than microtask workers, from the crowd.

Glance [15] uses the crowd to help users explore video datasets by quickly marking arbitrary user-specified events. This divide-and-conquer process is common in crowdsourcing because it allows the inherent parallelism of the crowd to help solve problems faster. Apparition uses a similar division of labor to make complex, parallel control tasks possible, but unlike prior work in crowdsourcing, it supports worker self-coordination and task-finding in real-time.

While existing Wizard-of-Oz approaches rely on a single user who is an expert with a particular system, crowdsourcing has the potential to provide an on-demand workforce that can be hired for exactly the amount of time needed to power an interaction. Crowds also have the potential for supporting more complex, parallel actions than single controllers could.

APPARITION
Apparition's goal is to let designers create prototypes, complete with visual elements and behaviors, in real-time as they freely sketch and describe their ideas. To do this, Apparition connects the designer to a crowd of paid microtask workers who collectively translate the designer's intentions into a functional prototype in real time.

The primary challenges are:
- supporting synchronous editing of interface mockups
- avoiding repetitive work and production blocking
- allowing the crowd to upgrade the interface over time
- remembering behaviors so that the interfaces are immmediately Wizard-of-Oz'ed

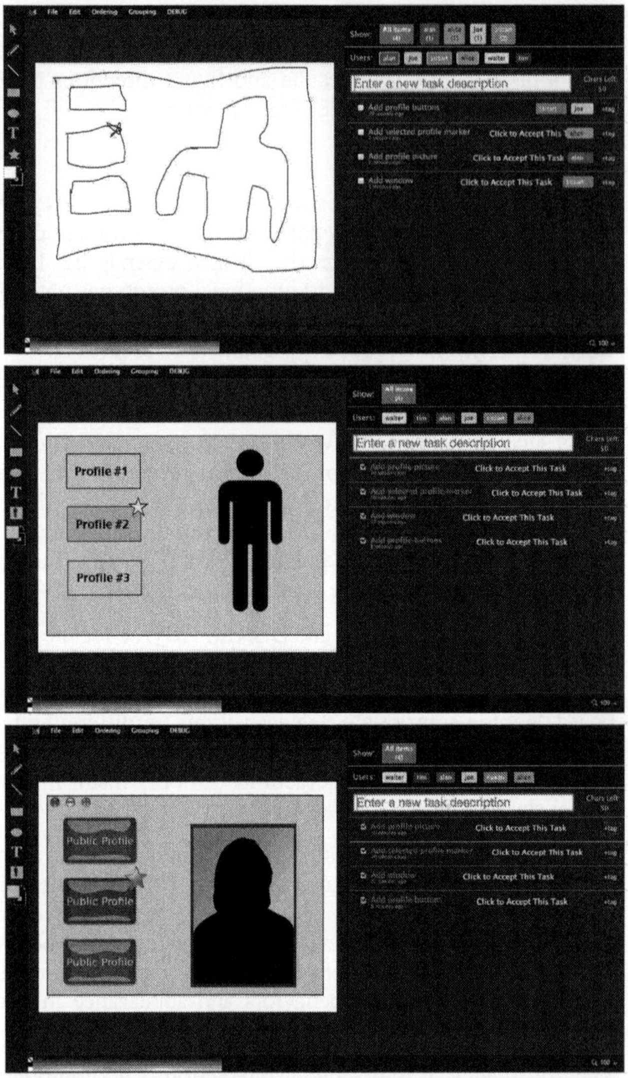

Figure 2. Designers roughly sketch their interface while describing it in natural language (top). As they do, crowd workers collaboratively update the interface into a low-fidelity prototype (middle). Over time, the crowd workers further improve its quality (bottom). As these interfaces are created, they are immediately functional, even when adding complex behaviors via collective Wizard-of-Oz control by the crowd.

System Architecture Design
Apparition can be run from any device with a web browser, making it possible to generate interfaces in settings where generating high-fidelity UIs is currently impossible, such as from a mobile device. Audio is streamed from the user to each crowd worker using Adobe Media Server. Users can pause the audio stream at any point they wish (for privacy).

Designers begin by sketching a low-fidelity version of their interface using either a pen and tablet or a mouse. Automatic gesture recognition identifies user strokes when possible (similar to SILK's approach [14]). This is done using a specially trained $1 Recognizer [29]. If the recognizer cannot confidently classify and convert the sketch into the UI element it represents, Apparition asks workers to produce a higher fidelity rendering in real-time by using simple visual prototyping tools provided to them.

To bring the interface to life, behaviors can be animated by moving, adding, and removing elements on the canvas. Natural language descriptions help the crowd fill in details of both the interface layout and behaviors despite minimal content in the initial sketch. Thus, designers can quickly iterate on their ideas without having to sketch each version in detail.

While beyond the scope of this paper, it is worth noting that our approach can even work without the user directly sketching their idea on real media (*e.g.*, paper or whiteboard). From a verbal description or gestures viewed via a webcam to help ground the layout, workers can still get a rough idea of what the designer intends and render it.

Below, we describe operational aspects of Apparition and discuss features that allow workers to coordinate effectively to create prototypes within seconds of when users initially sketch them. These design decisions were made over the course of building Apparition during informal evaluation sessions with dozens of in-person volunteers, workers from Mechanical Turk and oDesk, and other contributors.

Canvas

Apparition's canvas is a version of SVG-Edit (code.google.com/p/svg-edit), a browser-based vector graphic editor, that we modified to support multiple users. Our synchronized version uses Meteor (www.meteor.com), a JavaScript framework that allows us to quickly share information between clients. Each worker connects to an active session and can see the actions of others as they work. The core tool is similar to Google Draw, but it includes custom features making it possible to coordinate groups of workers creating, editing, and animating simultaneously — something Google Draw was not designed to do.

Apparition improves efficiency of workers with a library of standard interface elements. The most common of these are provided as top-level elements in a toolbar (seen on the left-hand side of Figure 1). For the larger set of less frequently used elements, we provide a search tool suggesting UI elements based on partial, related, or non-exact element names, for example "profile", "tab", or "star." Search helps prevent workers from spending too long browsing for an element that does not actually exist.

Roles

Apparition synchronizes canvases so that designer(s) and crowd workers always see the current design. Roles can also be defined for different user groups. The information shown and synchronized can be modified to best fit the needs of each type of user. For example, designers may not need to see worker to-do items (discussed later) or workers' in-progress elements, so these are synchronized after completion. Conversely, a user's input is shown immediately to workers.

Workers can also see who is online, and each worker has a globally consistent and unique color assigned to them. This color code applies to all interactions that a worker has with the system, so other users can get a sense of what actions are being performed by a single individual. This helps with semantic grouping and understanding what tasks others are performing — key elements in maintaining coordination.

ENABLING REAL-TIME WORKER COORDINATION

No one worker can keep up with a designer who is sketching and describing interfaces in real time. Once a worker has converted each sketch element or behavior task—each of which can take several seconds—the designer has long since moved on. For people, understanding is not typically the roadblock in this setting, but rather creating the grounded representation of the described concepts quickly enough. In early versions of Apparition, workers fell prey to diffusion of responsibility [4], and all would wait for someone else to pick up each task. Making Apparition responsive required a method for coordinating workers around very open-ended, potentially subjective tasks such that they do not conflict or repeat work.

To solve this problem, Apparition uses a write-lock coordination mechanism that allows workers to self-manage task delegation in real time.

Naive coordination fails

To coordinate workers and ensure that no task is missed, even when the designer is speaking quickly, Apparition uses a to-do list that synchronizes short messages from the system and workers to other workers. The intention is for this to-do list to populate automatically as the designer works. Using a partially-automated to-do list prevents the latency issues associated with completely manual curation of this set and any resulting duplicated work.

Apparition automatically groups nearby sets of sketches into a single unit and assigns them as a to-do item in the list. By mousing over the to-do item, workers can see which canvas elements are being referenced. Workers can claim to-dos and add new ones if desired. In addition, sketches that the gesture recognizer captures with only medium confidence are automatically converted into to-do entries. This approach strikes a balance between the benefits of automatic guessing and the risks of introducing errors.

Unfortunately, our early observations were that this approach produced significant conflict. Workers focused on their self-defined tasks and often missed looking at the to-do list on the side of the screen at a critical time. This resulted in blocking actions where multiple workers would try to complete the same task — in the worst case, accidental conflicts caused work to be undone.

Ad hoc leaders with delegation power can be extremely effective for short-lived teams [12]. Thus, we tried specifying some workers as "managers" who could create tasks and assign others to tasks. However, requiring that a worker first tag and route a task introduced unacceptable latency.

Write locks enable effective distributed coordination

The to-do list was insufficient because workers placed their primary attention on the actual canvas. In other words, it was not a problem of the input jobs, but a problem with write-locking the actual "data".

To overcome this, we added a form of informal write-locking where workers can click a location and drop an "in-progress" marker that tells other workers that they are working in that general vicinity (Figure 3). These markers do not actually

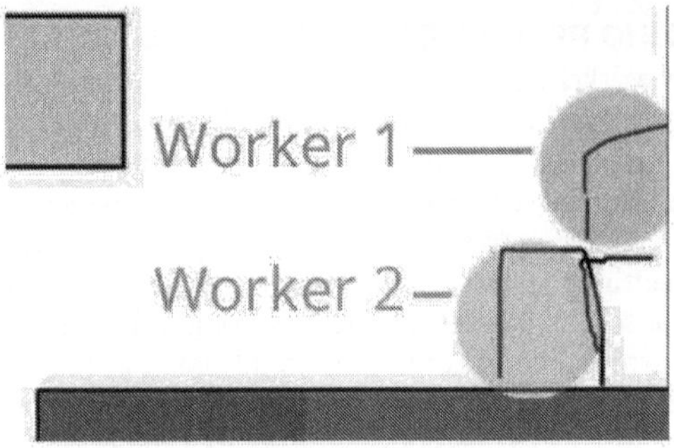

Figure 3. An example of Mechanical Turk workers using "in-progress" markers in a live trial. Each worker's marker is a different color (here, green for worker 1 and blue for worker 2) translucent to interface elements and editing actions and can be added in two clicks. By making it easy for workers to signal to others what they are working on, production blocks and repeated work are avoided.

prevent any edits within the designated region, but they allow a worker to signal to others that they are working on a task associated with this area. Markers can be tied to specific to-do entries, or they can be used in place of them when no text is needed to describe the task that they are performing based on context. At most one of these markers is visible for any worker at a time, and placing a new one automatically removes the prior one. While they are displayed on top of all canvas elements, markers are partially transparent and completely un-selectable, preventing them from blocking others who are currently editing canvas content.

Because we typically expect fewer than 10 workers to be present simultaneously, these markers also do not clutter the interface as it is being edited. They also do not appear to end-users, who only see the results generated by workers, not the coordination elements they use.

Using these markers, workers self-manage and implicitly or explicitly claim elements of the to-do list. This increases parallelism and reduces conflicts.

Supporting Concurrent Editing: Replace-at-Layer

One significant hurdle to concurrent editing in small regions of the document arises from element layering. The most common practice of visual design tools with respect to layering is to have the layer index of an element be determined by the temporal ordering of creation (as seen in Adobe Photoshop, Google Draw, etc.). This means that if a window is sketched and then a button is drawn, the button will be one layer above the window. This is a natural interaction in single-user settings — but when a crowd of workers is simultaneously editing a single region of the canvas, replacing a window sketch by adding a window element to the canvas results in the window element arriving as the top-most selectable and visible item, covering up any other elements that other workers might be attending to. This leads to a production block for everyone working in that area, and in practice, often leads to errors being introduced by workers performing actions not meant for the now-topmost window.

To overcome this, we added a *replace-at-layer* feature that lets workers select a sketched figure, create a replacement element, and then replace the sketch with the new element at the same layer index in a single operation. This means that workers can create elements behind others in a single click.

To prevent mistaken operations, replace-at-layer first checks for spacial proximity to see if the new element overlaps with the same approximate region (in our case 150% of the size of the original sketch). We also require the worker to explicitly select the element they wish to replace first, as a separate selection action, so that the automatic selection of an element after initial creation will not be used to trigger a replacement (so that sequential creation operations can be done seamlessly). An optional replacement confirmation message can also be enabled if a safety check is desired. Once we have determined that the worker intends to replace a given element, we find that element's location in the display stack, remove the initial sketched element, and then add the worker's newly-created element at the same relative location (above and below the same content as the original sketch).

Protecting Against Malicious Workers

During initial trials, we saw that reliability might be a concern, as it often is with crowdsourcing tasks. We ran five trials with three workers in each. In three of five trials, one worker moved elements out of place, negatively impacting the final result. In two of these cases, that worker was the last one to edit the prototype.

To address potential worker confusion, we added tutorials and examples. To flag malicious or contrarian workers from disproportionately impacting a task, we looked at the history of workers' operations. If a worker is performing a specific action repeatedly over time, the system flags them as potentially malicious. For example, a user removing many elements created by others (where no other worker finds that those elements need to be removed) might be deleting useful elements. On the other hand, a worker creating a large set of elements when others are not might be spamming.

INCREASING FIDELITY AND ADDING BEHAVIORS

In this section, we explore how Apparition can move beyond quick mock-ups and static interfaces by making these interfaces improve themselves over time and come alive.

From Mock-Up to Polished Prototype

Apparition's real-time nature means that the level of detail of the immediately-available interface is limited — we don't want workers to spend extensive amounts of time worrying over small details. However, over time, workers can refine elements to create a more polished version. This additional time might arise when the user leaves for a period of time, such as for lunch, overnight, or over a weekend. As such, we assume that this additional interface refinement can operate as an asynchronous offline process.

To draw on prior work that has shown parallel prototyping leads to more creativity [6], we use a branch-and-merge algorithm similar to Multiverse [25]. When users set the system to "bake in" mode, they select time and cost bounds and Apparition automatically begins to create parallel copies (typically 3-5 per round) of the current interface. Each of these copies is distributed to multiple crowd workers who work to improve the existing prototype either synchronously or asynchronously (in our experiments, we allow for either depending on workers' arrival time). For context, workers are also able to access the original user descriptions of the interface (via audio and screen recording).

Once several different workers (typically 5-8) have contributed to each prototype, the final results of each are shown to a new group of workers to select the best version. The winning version is then copied into multiple universes for the next iteration and those are again redistributed to new workers. This iterative process continues as many times as the time and cost bounds will permit. At the end, the result is a single "best" refinement of the original mock-up. For example, in Figure 2, we can see the initial sketch in the top frame, the immediately-available version in the middle, and a more polished version that was created a few moments later, after workers had time to find graphic resources on the web.

Prototyping Interactive Behaviors

We have described how Apparition allows designers to quickly see an improved version of the interface they describe, and given more time, see an even higher-fidelity version if they choose. But interfaces are not static artifacts.

Apparition allows designers to describe the desired behavior of their prototype out loud, and then immediately interact with a working version of their interface. Workers hear the description of the correct action and then can immediately Wizard-of-Oz the behavior as needed. To modify or correct results, the end-user can simply describe them verbally and click if direct reference to an object is needed.

The to-do list can again be used by workers to coordinate roles in supporting repeated interaction. For simple behaviors, such as popping up a window, workers might be able to accept multiple tasks, while for more complex behaviors, such as controlling a character in a video game so that it hides from the player as they move, a worker might need to focus on only that task. Once a worker has assigned themselves to a task, they can continue to monitor it until they choose to leave or hand off responsibility.

Showing User Interactions

When describing to-be-supported actions in natural language, users often will use language that requires supporting context to understand [10]. For example, if a user says "When I click *here*, the value of the counter will increase," the position referenced by "here" must be specified. While this is done naturally in communication between co-located individuals, Apparition supports this using a shared visualization of user interaction on the canvas. When a user clicks a position on the canvas, the point where they clicked is displayed as a dot animation to all workers. The animation lasts $\sim$2 seconds, but when paired with speech, it provides a clear signal to workers. Support for swipes and other gestures using line animations can also be added. These gestures support not only referential phrases, but also interactions with the interface that are not mentioned in speech directly.

Adding Constraints

While Apparition's prototypes are meant to be dynamic, users might want to specify that some sub-component of their system is complete, while wanting others to be improved or iterated on. Apparition lets users specify elements which should be "locked" in place as immutable either at the beginning of any round during the UI refinement process or during editing in a live setting where animations might otherwise move a given element. When a canvas-wide lock mode is toggled, these elements are made immutable for both workers and users to prevent these locked elements from being modified during interactions.

However, freezing an element in place is not always the right constraint. In some situations, users might wish for an element to simply remain in a certain region or have a certain range of motion during animation. For example, a user may want to bound a map pin to stay within the map. To allow for this, users can define bounding boxes around elements that restrict the motion of that element to a specific region when lock mode is activated.

In combination, locks and bounding boxes help workers create accurate animations and effects with minimal effort. For example, to create an accurate slider animation, a line or bar can be locked in place, and a handle element can be restricted to a narrow horizontal region on top of that line (Figure 4). Then, when the canvas is locked, workers are only able to move the handle of the slider along the axis, and only within the bounds of the corresponding line element. This avoids jitter and makes the animating worker's task simple.

EXPERIMENTS

To verify Apparition's ability to create interface prototypes in real time, we first selected a set of five common interface types to mock up and had a UX designer create napkin sketches of each as a starting point. We added appropriate behaviors to each, resulting in the following data set:

- **Map viewer**: Contains – zoom bar, divider bar, main window, and selector buttons (x3). Behaviors – zoom in (x3), zoom out (x3), click to change window contents (x4).
- **Profile manager**: Contains – divider bar (x2), main window, and selector buttons (x6). Behaviors – zoom in (x3), zoom out (x3), click to change window contents (x4).
- **Document editor**: Contains – main window, option buttons (x2), back arrow, and selector buttons (x5). Behaviors – button click to change window contents (x3), button click to change button color (x6).
- **Platformer game (*e.g.*, Super Mario Bros.)**: Contains – game character, separated ground (x2), large floating block, small floating block, stacked boxes (x3), and sun. Behaviors – move to clicked location (x4).
- **Real-time strategy game**: Contains – player character, enemy characters (x3), radar, control menus (x2), divider bar, menu button. Behaviors – follow player character with 3 enemies (x2), follow player character with 3 enemies (x3).

We recruited 46 workers from Amazon Mechanical Turk using LegionTools [15], a tool for quickly recruiting and directing synchronous crowds of workers. We ran 10 trials, two for

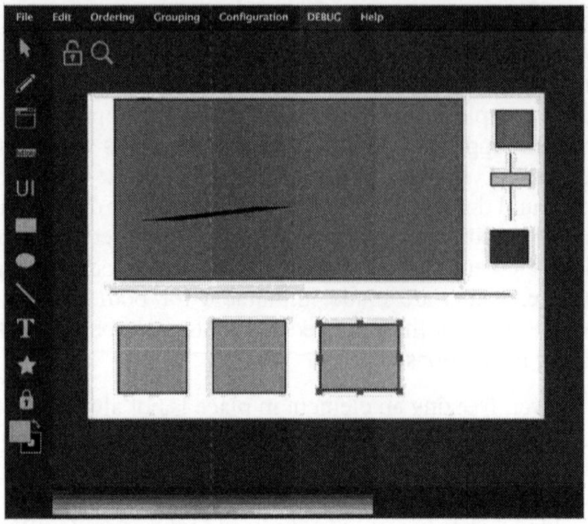

Figure 4. An example of an interface being created during one of our trials. End-user input consisted exclusively of a pencil tool and natural language speech, which workers converted to UI elements.

each of our five example interfaces (with 23 workers in each half). Trials were moderated by a researcher who acted as the end-user and tried to re-create the mockups we obtained from the UX designer. Each trial lasted approximately 5 minutes for workers, including the tutorial, and paid \$0.95 (\$19/hour). We limited our tasks to U.S.-based workers with an approval rate of at least 90%. We recruited 3-6 synchronous workers to convert the interface that they were shown. The task consisted of both a *creation and editing* phase, as well as a *behaviors and actions* phase. In half of the trials, workers did not have access to "in-progress" markers, while in the rest they did.

We measure precision using the number of actions taken that were intended by the requester and recall using the number of actions intended by the requester that the crowd completed. If, after a short while, the request had to be repeated or highlighted to workers, the first request was counted as a miss and the second question counted as a separate instance.

8 Seconds from Sketches to Interfaces

Creating and editing interface elements includes all steps taken by workers to convert sketches to real elements, create or remove elements from verbal cues, change an element's static position, resize elements, and change their color. These actions had a median latency of 8.3 seconds (mean 10.9s, $sd = 6.2$s), with 90.8% precision and 97.6% recall.

Workers React with Behaviors in 3 Seconds

Behaviors and animations include any element placement, coloration, dynamic movement, or visibility that is an effect of interacting directly with the interface (*e.g.*, clicking a button), rather than a direct user request to change the state of the interface. Performing these actions had a median latency of just 3 seconds (mean 3.6s, $sd = 2.3$s), and achieved 92.9% precision and 90.5% recall.

In-Progress Markers Prevented Production Blocking

We found that workers were very willing to use in-progress markers when they were available: 72.2% of all workers used markers during the live session, and they were used in all sessions in which they were available. An average of 7 markers were placed per trial (median 7.5s, $sd = 6.67$s), making the average per-worker usage 2.7 times per session.

Markers helped workers avoid redundant or conflicting work, which appeared to result in fewer scenarios where no worker completed a task because they were unsure of if others were already doing it. This resulted in a significant improvement from 82.3% recall in the trials without markers, to 97.0% ($p < .05$) in the trials with them. While marker use also resulted in higher precision (94.8% with markers versus 90.4% without them), this difference was not significant ($p > .5$). Latency was also not detectably impacted ($p > .8$).

Markers were almost exclusively used for creation tasks, specifically when the creation task was grounded by a sketch. This means that it overlaps significantly with the use case of the to-do list. However, as expected, we observed that the usage of the to-do list was almost entirely replaced by markers in three of our five trials with markers. In only one case was a marker used to denote ownership over a behavior.

DISCUSSION

Our evaluation suggests that Apparition can keep pace with designers, transforming each sketch element within eight seconds into a higher-fidelity representation. Once created, the prototype quickly reacts to user input. The result: a user could step up to a tablet, sketch a game of Super Mario Brothers, and start playing it within seconds.

We envision designers receiving feedback far more quickly than they can using methods like paper prototypes. Apparition allows iteration within a brainstorming session or meeting and allows users to immediately see how their changes would affect the interface, reducing the need to speculate. This may result in more helpful feedback from early users. The crowd itself can also provide feedback. Prior work has explored how individuals can get feedback from crowd workers during the design process [22].

Apparition can be used with non-microtask crowds as well. For example, in a design meeting, designers themselves may act as crowd workers to help flesh out their own or others' ideas and view the resulting interactions. More reliable expert workers can also be recruited from contract-work sites, such as oDesk or Elance. These workers can be especially helpful when producing higher-fidelity versions of the desired interface. These workers can include graphic artists and designers, as well as programmers who implement functionality that the end-user designer did not but that still requires only an amount of effort reasonable for the targeted fidelity.

Deleting Content

One of our concerns when designing Apparition was that malicious or confused workers might delete parts of the interface while the user was designing. To prevent this, we designed a tool to detect unilateral actions such as deletes and catch potentially-malicious workers. However, our trials encountered no examples of malicious workers deleting valid content. Instead, there were two instances where a worker

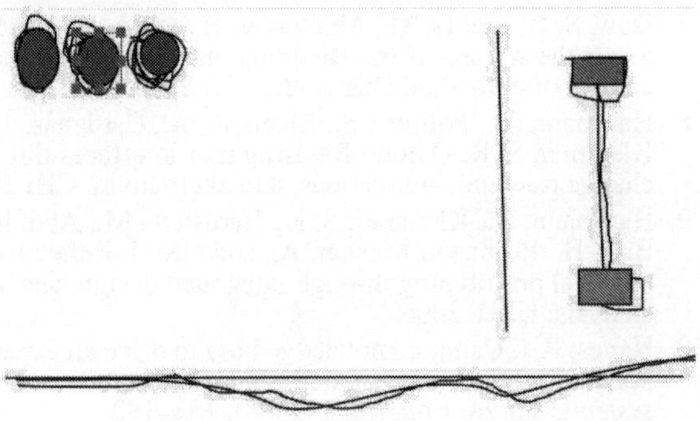

Figure 5. In some of our trials, workers hesitated to delete content. This resulted in valid elements being drawn on top of, but not replacing, user sketches (possibly because workers were not comfortable deleting what the user created). Future versions of the system will automate approaches to replacement.

mistakenly added content. From the usage, both cases appeared to be caused by accidentally selecting a tool, and then trying to select content (resulting in an element created along the intended drag path).

Interestingly, we found that workers' hesitation to delete content caused many more issues. In extreme cases (Figure 5), these remaining sketches detract from the visual aesthetic of the prototype and create problems with motion-based behaviors by leaving a sketched copy of the element in its original location, adding to clutter.

Our element replacement tool was meant to overcome some of this. While it helped in several settings, it was calibrated to work only when the system was extremely confident in the placemen. Even then, it prompted for confirmation. In future versions, we will slightly loosen these restrictions and explore methods for intelligently determining appropriate replacement situations based on the locations and sizes of the elements, input from the gesture recognizer.

Remembering Interface Behaviors

As part of our UI behavior and animation experiments, we asked workers to perform simple actions based on user input. Because these actions are defined in natural language and not repeatable, workers are required to remember what behavior was requested. For instance, if told that a certain action should be performed in response to a certain button being clicked, the crowd is expected to remember the association. To test how well the crowd can collectively remember behaviors, we conducted a small set of tests that asked the crowd to perform a behavior that was requested K interactions ago.

In our sample of 16 one-, two-, and "many"-ago interactions (with 3, 8, and 5 examples respectively), we found that the crowd was able to recall the correct behaviors and apply it in 81% of cases. Interestingly, the "many" cases were all performed correctly. This suggests that the crowd can reasonably recall behaviors that users describe, though longer-term memory will require methods for letting the crowd store information for future use either by themselves or others.

Communication

One common piece of feedback that we got from workers was that they wanted to chat with the requester and other workers. Providing this feedback and between-worker communication channel will likely help workers better understand the task early on but runs the risk of distracting workers and slowing down response times [18]. Some workers were initially confused by the task, but others found the task to be easy to understand given prior experience with graphical editing tools. Over time, workers without this experience may learn how to complete our tasks. Nevertheless, this experience is common enough to be useful among workers on Mechanical Turk.

Limitations

Our study focused on demonstrating that the collaboration environment that Apparition provides allows crowd workers to create prototypes within seconds. Our study did not use external design participants as end-users so that we could control the settings and designs more carefully. In the future, our goal is to release Apparition, allowing us to explore how real-world use of intelligent prototyping systems can impact the design process.

FUTURE WORK

Our results with Apparition demonstrate that it is possible to supply synchronous crowds with relatively light-weight coordination tools and enable them to create interfaces and behaviors within seconds of their original description. Future improvements will aim to make the process appear more seamless to end-users by letting crowd workers prepare changes before making them visible, while preventing redundant work by leveraging the fact that workers actively use markers.

Programming Crowd Functions

Complex behaviors can also rely on a series of descriptions given by a user. However, we assume that the crowd is dynamic and that workers come and go — no one worker can be relied upon to be available for a fixed span of time. To ensure that behaviors are retained even as the crowd changes, we need workers to be able to record the instructions for how to respond to input. Capturing this knowledge can be thought of as 'programming' a crowd function – it defines an atomic task that can be completed by any worker who arrives in the future. Currently, the to-do task description serves this role, but ongoing work will allow workers richer ways to pass on knowledge. For instance, they may annotate the canvas with animation paths or even point to recordings of past responses.

Automatically Capturing Behaviors

Many behaviors are associated with actions that are repeated over time. We want to be able to not only allow the crowd to simulate these behaviors, but also to learn when these behaviors should occur. The simplest way to do this is to identify how a crowd worker responded to a user's input (such as selection), and ask them if this should always be the response. If so, then we can record the set of actions they take in response by bounding the sequence by the user input in the beginning and the worker marking the to-do item complete at the end.

Ongoing work will allow Apparition to replay action sequences automatically when the appropriate input is received. Workers and designers can mark this automatic action as incorrect if a situation arises where it is not appropriate. We will explore automatically finding the differences in the state of the interface so that we can intelligently decide when to execute recorded sequences.

Transitioning to Code

We are also exploring ways to add code directly. Since we know the element type, we can begin to automatically add Javascript event listeners, allowing designers to add real code with low overhead. For example, if a designer edits a button element, we will show a pop-up window that lets them enter code for a 'click' event handler. Elements can also be easily referenced from code. This allows basic functions to be implemented on-the-fly as desired, while more complex functions are handled by the crowd.

Application developers can then use the partially crowd-powered version of the system as a "living specification" when creating production code. The existing code can be used as a reference, and the notes that crowd workers have made about behaviors can help clarify issues that might be otherwise missed from a traditional paper writeup. Finally, developers can use the crowd-powered version of the interface to answer questions about use cases that might have been otherwise missed or unclear from the documentation.

CONCLUSION

We have presented Apparition, a system that allows designers to create working interface prototypes in real-time by sketching and describing its functionality in natural language. The prototypes created by Apparition are over 90% accurate to the user's intent, and the system can respond to create elements within 8 seconds and prototype behaviors within 3 seconds of the user describing it. Apparition will allow designers to create prototypes fast enough to iterate within single design sessions, improving the feedback they receive.

ACKNOWLEDGEMENTS

The authors would like to thank Geza Kovacs and Patrick Baudisch for inspiring this idea. This work was funded by National Science Foundation Awards #IIS-1149709, #IIS-1218209, #IIS-1351131, Google, an Alfred P. Sloan Foundation Fellowship, and a Microsoft Research Ph.D. Fellowship.

REFERENCES

1. Bernstein, M. S., Brandt, J. R., Miller, R. C., and Karger, D. R. Crowds in two seconds: Enabling realtime crowd-powered interfaces. UIST 2011.
2. Bigham, J. P., Jayant, C., Ji, H., Little, G., Miller, A., Miller, R. C., Miller, R., Tatarowicz, A., White, B., White, S., and Yeh, T. Vizwiz: nearly real-time answers to visual questions. UIST 2010.
3. Cohen, P. R. The role of natural language in a multimodal interface. UIST 1992.
4. Darley, J. and Latane, B. Bystander intervention in emergencies: diffusion of responsibility. J. Pers. Soc. Psych. 8(4) (1968): 377.
5. Davis, R. C., Saponas, T. S., Shilman, M., and Landay, J. A. Sketchwizard: Wizard of oz prototyping of pen-based user interfaces. UIST 2007.
6. Dow, S. P., Glassco, A., Kass, J., Schwarz, M., Schwartz, D. L., and Klemmer, S. R. Parallel prototyping leads to better design results, more divergence, and increased self-efficacy. *ACM Trans. Comput.-Hum. Interact. 17*, 4 (2010), 18:1–18:24.
7. Dow, S. P., Mehta, M., MacIntyre, B., and Mateas, M. Eliza meets the wizard-of-oz: Blending machine and human control of embodied characters. CHI 2010.
8. Hartmann, B., Follmer, S., Ricciardi, A., Cardenas, T., and Klemmer, S. R. D.note: Revising user interfaces through change tracking, annotations, and alternatives. CHI 2010.
9. Hartmann, B., Klemmer, S. R., Bernstein, M., Abdulla, L., Burr, B., Robinson-Mosher, A., and Gee, J. Reflective physical prototyping through integrated design, test, and analysis. UIST 2006.
10. Hayes, P. J. Using a knowledge base to drive an expert system interface with a natural language component. *Expert systems: the user interface* (1988), 153–182.
11. Kelley, J. F. An iterative design methodology for user-friendly natural language office information applications. *ACM Trans. Inf. Syst. 2*, 1 (1984), 26–41.
12. Klein, K., Ziegart, J., Knight, A., Xiao, Y. Dynamic Delegation: Shared, Hierarchical, and Deindividualized Leadership in Extreme Action Teams. Admin. Sci. 2006.
13. Kulkarni, A., Can, M., Hartmann, B. Collaboratively Crowdsourcing Workflows with Turkomatic. CSCW 2012,
14. Landay, J. A., and Myers, B. A. Interactive sketching for the early stages of user interface design. CHI 1995.
15. Lasecki, W. S., Gordon, M., Koutra, D., Jung, M. F., Dow, S. P., and Bigham, J. P. Glance: Rapidly coding behavioral video with the crowd. UIST 2014.
16. Lasecki, W. S., Miller, C. D., Sadilek, A., Abumoussa, A., Kushalnagar, R. and Bigham, J. P. Real-time Captioning by Groups of Non-Experts. UIST 2012.
17. Lasecki, W. S., Murray, K., White, S., Miller, R. C., and Bigham, J. P. Real-time crowd control of existing interfaces. UIST 2011.
18. Lasecki, W. S., Wesley, R., Nichols, J., Kulkarni, A., Allen, J. F., and Bigham, J. P. Chorus: A crowd-powered conversational assistant. UIST 2013.
19. Limpaecher, A., Feltman, N., Treuille, A., and Cohen, M. Real-time drawing assistance through crowdsourcing. *ACM Trans. Graph. 32*, 4 (2013), 54:1–54:8.
20. Lin, J., Newman, M. W., Hong, J. I., and Landay, J. A. Denim: Finding a tighter fit between tools and practice for web site design. CHI 2000.
21. Little, G., Chilton, L. B., Goldman, M., Miller, R.C. TurKit: human computation algorithms on mechanical turk. UIST 2010.
22. Luther, K., Tolentino, J., Wu, W., Pavel, A., Bailey, B., Agrawala, M., Hartmann, B., and Dow, S. P. Structuring, Aggregating, and Evaluating Crowdsourced Design Critique. CSCW 2015.
23. Retelny, D., Robaszkiewicz, S., To, A., Lasecki, W. S., Patel, J., Rahmati, N., Doshi, T., Valentine, M., and Bernstein, M. S. Expert Crowdsourcing with Flash Teams. UIST 2014.
24. Maulsby, D., Greenberg, S., and Mander, R. Prototyping an intelligent agent through wizard of oz. CHI 1993.
25. Murray, K. I. Multiverse: Crowd algorithms on existing interfaces. CHI EA 2013.
26. Myers, B., Park, S., Nakano, Y., Mueller, G., and Ko, A. How designers design and program interactive behaviors. VLHCC 2008.
27. Rossen, B., and Lok, B. A crowdsourcing method to develop virtual human conversational agents. *Int. J. Hum.-Comput. Stud. 70*, 4 (2012), 301–319.
28. Schon, D. The reflective practitioner. 1984. Basic Books.
29. Wobbrock, J. O., Wilson, A. D., and Li, Y. Gestures without libraries, toolkits or training: A $1 recognizer for user interface prototypes. UIST 2007.

Zensors: Adaptive, Rapidly Deployable, Human-Intelligent Sensor Feeds

Gierad Laput[1] Walter S. Lasecki[2] Jason Wiese[1] Robert Xiao[1] Jeffrey P. Bigham[1] Chris Harrison[1]

[1] HCI Institute, Carnegie Mellon University
5000 Forbes Avenue, Pittsburgh, PA 15213
{glaput, jwwiese, brx, jbigham, chris.harrison}
@cs.cmu.edu

[2] ROC HCI, University of Rochester
500 Joseph C. Wilson Boulevard
Rochester, NY 14627
wlasecki@cs.rochester.edu

ABSTRACT

The promise of "smart" homes, workplaces, schools, and other environments has long been championed. Unattractive, however, has been the cost to run wires and install sensors. More critically, raw sensor data tends not to align with the types of questions humans wish to ask, e.g., do I need to restock my pantry? Although techniques like computer vision can answer some of these questions, it requires significant effort to build and train appropriate classifiers. Even then, these systems are often brittle, with limited ability to handle new or unexpected situations, including being repositioned and environmental changes (e.g., lighting, furniture, seasons). We propose *Zensors*, a new sensing approach that fuses real-time human intelligence from online crowd workers with automatic approaches to provide robust, adaptive, and readily deployable intelligent sensors. With Zensors, users can go from question to live sensor feed in less than 60 seconds. Through our API, Zensors can enable a variety of rich end-user applications and moves us closer to the vision of responsive, intelligent environments.

Author Keywords: Smart environments; sensing; human computation; computer vision; machine learning; end-user programming;

ACM Keywords: H.5.2. [Information interfaces and presentation]: User interfaces – Input devices and strategies.

INTRODUCTION

For decades, "intelligent" environments have promised to improve our lives by inferring context, activity and events in diverse environments, ranging from public spaces, offices, and labs, to homes and healthcare facilities. To achieve this vision, smart environments require sensors, and lots of them. However, installation continues to be expensive, special purpose, and often invasive (e.g., running power).

An even more challenging problem is that sensor output rarely matches the types of questions humans wish to ask. For example, a door opened/closed sensor may not answer the user's true question: "are my children home from school?" A restaurateur may want to know how many patrons need their beverages refilled, and graduate students want to know, "is there free food in the kitchenette?" Unfortunately, these sophisticated, multidimensional and often contextual questions are not easily answered by the simple sensors we deploy today. Although advances in sensing, computer vision (CV) and machine learning (ML) have brought us closer, systems that generalize across these broad and dynamic contexts do not yet exist.

CHI 2015, April 18 - 23 2015, Seoul, Republic of Korea

ACM 978-1-4503-3145-6/15/04 $15. http://dx.doi.org/10.1145/2702123.2702416

In this work, we introduce *Zensors*, a new sensor approach that requires minimal and non-permanent sensor installation and provides human-centered and actionable sensor output. To achieve this, we fuse answers from crowd workers and automatic approaches to provide instant, human-intelligent sensors, which end users can set up in under one minute.

To illustrate the utility of Zensors, we return to our restaurant example. John, the proprietor, finds a disused smartphone or tablet and affixes it to the wall of his restaurant. He installs and launches our Zensors app, which uses the front facing camera to provide a live overview of the restaurant. John presses the "new sensor" button and circles the bar countertop, thus specifying a region of interest. John can then enter a plain text question, for example: *"how many drinks are almost empty?"*

By pressing "go", the sensor is activated and starts providing real-time data, in this case numerical. John can now use *e.g.*, a companion app to see a real time visualization of how many drinks need to be refilled, or use an end user programming tool to have the system automatically message a co-worker requesting help if the number exceeds ten. Within a few minutes, John could similarly set up sensors for: *"does table four need to be cleaned?", "are customers wearing their coats inside?", "is a check sitting on the table?"* and other questions relevant to the dining experience.

Unbeknownst to John, his sensors are initially powered by crowd workers interpreting his plain text question, providing immediate human-level accuracy, as well as rich, human-centered abstractions. However, using crowd workers can be costly and difficult to scale, and so ideally it is only used temporarily – answers from the crowd are recorded and used as labels to bootstrap automatic processes. More specifically, our system begins training and testing image-based machine learning classifiers, testing against the ground truth provided by the crowd labels. If the classifiers begin to achieve human-like accuracies, they begin to vote alongside crowd responses. Eventually, if sufficiently robust, the classifiers can take full control. This human-computer handoff is seamless and invisible to end-users; as far as users like John are concerned, they have a sensor with human-level accuracy from minute one and onward. Even when the classifiers do not achieve the needed level of accuracy, we have designed savings measures into our crowd-based method to conserve costs. Through our API, Zensors enables a variety of applications that help realize the potential of smart environments. This abstracts the complexity of crowdsourcing, computer vision and machine learning, enabling developers to treat our "zensors" just as they would traditional electro-mechanical sensors.

We designed Zensors to achieve five key criteria 1) answer diverse natural language "sensor" questions, 2) with reasonably high-accuracy, 3) while being easy enough to be used by non-experts, 4) requiring zero training, and 5) receive live data within seconds. We are unaware of a single prior computer vision system that achieves these five properties.

We make the following contributions in this work:

- Zensors, a new approach and architecture for hybrid crowd-ML powered sensors, with an API to enable access to sensor data streams.
- A proof-of-concept mobile application for easy, end-user authoring of on-demand intelligent sensors.
- A tool for end-user programming of case-based events that turn sensor output into meaningful actions.
- A study that demonstrates the accuracy and reliability of Zensors in a variety of settings.
- Evidence that our human-powered sensors can be used to train computer vision approaches in situ, leading to an automatic handoff in most cases.

RELATED WORK

Our work touches on several areas including crowd-driven annotation, computer vision, and more generally, smart environments and activity sensing. We now summarize key related work in these respective domains.

Crowd-Driven Annotation

Crowdsourcing allows systems to access human intelligence through online marketplaces such as Mechanical Turk. For example, the ESP Game asked workers to label images with keywords in order to make the web more accessible [24]. VizWiz [3] asks crowd workers to answer visual questions for blind users with a latency of under a minute. However, both VizWiz and the ESP Game have difficulty scaling because they elicit un-typed, natural language responses to non-repeated images, making it difficult for machine learning algorithms to learn key patterns with high accuracy.

Marcus et al. [20] explored how to perform SQL query estimations that computers cannot do alone, e.g., answer how many people in a database of images were of a certain gender. In their system, users could pre-define functions that specified crowd tasks, which were used to find an answer estimation for query filtering. CrowdDB [10] explored a similar crowdsourcing concept, using the crowd to fill in missing data and overcome the closed-world assumption held in traditional DBs. In both of these examples, the language the user must use to pose queries is a slight variant of SQL, and the crowd's input is used to estimate relationships and missing data over large, pre-existing datasets. In contrast, Zensors turn a live stream of images into an easily accessible structured data stream.

Tohme [13] use the crowd to improve accessibility information in maps by asking workers to label curbs in Google StreetView images. Unlike Zensors, Tohme addressed a single, specific question, using a specialized interface to facilitate labeling. Tohme also included a computer vision component that enabled it to learn how to identify curbs in specific areas over time. They demonstrated that this automated approach could be successful. However it, too, relied on the detailed object segmentation and labeling information obtained from workers through the custom interface (and in combination with GPS and other metadata from Google Maps). Zensors, by contrast, targets general-purpose domains in which no additional information is available, and answers a broad range of user-defined questions.

VATIC [25] uses the crowd to annotate video with labels and object bounding boxes. Glance [17] annotates spans of time with user-requested event labels within minutes by leveraging the ability of large sets of crowd workers to concurrently complete an otherwise time-consuming task. Both VATIC and Glance are approaches for analyzing previously recorded, fixed-length video. By contrast, Zensors is focused on real-time analysis of still images, and offers the potential for handing sensor labeling off from the crowd to machine learning algorithms.

Legion:AR [18] recruits the crowd to provide activity labels using data from live video and RFID tags. It uses an active learning approach to request crowd labels for partial streams of live video. While this solution is related to Zensors, the crowd architecture is different. Legion:AR does not use computer vision, only attempts automatic activity recognition via RFID tags, and collects open-ended questions and answers, not *typed* values (i.e., data type). More specifically, Legion:AR collects open-ended plain text answers, in contrast to the structured labels of Zensors. Further, Legion:AR gathers multiple workers into a single session for a long duration, having them synchronously generate multiple incomplete sets of labels that are merged into a final stream—a configuration that costs tens of dollars for a few minutes. Legion:AR monitors an *instrumented* space (RFID scanners, Kinects), and was not designed to be a *generalizable* sensing platform.

Image- and Video-Based Sensors

The field of computer vision has largely developed in pursuit of extracting meaning from images without the need for human assistance. Today, there exist robust and automatic approaches for applications as diverse as face detection [28] and traffic monitoring [15]. Most related to our present work are video-based, end-user sensing systems, such as the techniques proposed in Crayons [8] and the Eyepatch system [21]. Light Widgets [9] allowed users to create virtual interactive elements on everyday surfaces through video-based sensing. Other systems, e.g. Slit-Tear Visualizations [23], aim to help users better recognize environmental events. These systems often rely on users annotating images to provide training data or demarcate regions of interest. Researchers have also explored crowd-based approaches for improving computer vision techniques [7,26], which could be used to enhance systems such as our own.

Smart Environments

A broad body of work in the HCI and UbiComp communities has outfitted home, work and public environments and objects in those environments with sensors to detect various activities in the environment [1]. The Context Toolkit [22] utilized data from numerous sensors to make contextual inferences about a place (e.g. what is going on in a space, or how many people are around). In a project to support aging-in-place, Lee and Dey created an augmented pillbox that detected whether or not an older adult had taken their pills for a given day [19]. In another example, the AwareOffice project [29] outfitted various office artifacts with diverse sensors to detect their state, including: whiteboard pen (writing or not), eraser (wiping whiteboard), chair (in use or free), window & door (open/closed).

While there are clearly many benefits of dedicated hardware sensors in UbiComp smart environments, there are many drawbacks that limit their use. Compared to Zensors, these approaches are fairly heavyweight, requiring one sensor per item that is being sensed. In contrast, by segmenting the view from a single camera to evaluate the current state of many objects, Zensors offers this same functionality with just a single device. Furthermore, Zensors enables almost anyone to answer arbitrary questions about their environment, without requiring the hardware/software technical skills needed to implement traditional sensor approaches.

APPLICATION SPACE

To help us understand the expanse of questions and functionalities enabled by a human-intelligent, camera-driven sensing system, we recruited 13 interaction designers and solicited their input in a structured ideation session.

First, participants were split into four groups, and each group was asked to enumerate scenarios that would greatly benefit from a "super smart environment sensor." After fifteen minutes, groups were asked to share their ideas with one another. Immediately after, four groups were merged into two, and the new teams were asked to discuss potential issues from the ideas mentioned prior. Next, all groups were asked to examine the area of "camera-based sensing." Specifically, we asked them to generate and categorize "questions" that they might want to ask from a "highly intelligent" camera-based sensing system. Finally, using input from the previous round, we asked participants to "program" image-based sensing applications (using a mockup software we provided) inspired from the questions they previously explored. In total, the session lasted 90 minutes. All participants were briefed at the end of the session, and were compensated for their time.

Data gathered from the session were analyzed using affinity-diagramming techniques. From this, several themes emerged from the categories of questions generated by each group, including optimization of domestic tasks (e.g., "what food in my fridge will go bad if I don't cook them the next day?"), health (e.g., "who is experiencing the most severe depression right now?"), public space monitoring (e.g., "how many cars are in this parking lot?"), and item finding (e.g., "where did I last leave my keys?"). These questions were also tied to a strong set of contexts and environments: including the home, urban and public spaces, educational institutions (e.g., "are students interested in the topic?"), health facilities, and supply chains (e.g., "what items should I restock from my inventory?"). When asked about issues concerning the deployment of "super smart environment sensing," participants cited consent and privacy (e.g., data storage), as well as technical feasibility (e.g., sensing capabilities, computation) as chief concerns. Altogether, these results draw out the expansive set of applications that would otherwise be hard or impossible to implement with CV-based technologies alone.

COMPARISION TO COMPUTER VISION

Additionally, we wanted to understand the work requirements and economic implications of building smart environment sensing using existing software engineering approaches. Intuitively, one or more experienced programmers would be able to implement most of our proposed intelligent sensors. But, how long would it take, and at what cost?

We conducted informal interviews with nine freelance developers from oDesk.com, a popular online workplace. To recruit capable candidates, we created a targeted job posting (titled "Image-Based Sensing System"), asking experienced software developers to build a computer vision-based automatic "bus detection" system. The job posting included illustrative details and clear task requirements (e.g., system should perform with at least 90+% accuracy), along with a labeled image set (e.g., a view of a bus stop on a city street).

Interested candidates were asked a series of follow-up questions, most notably: "how long do you think the project will take?", "what is your hourly rate?" and "how many hours will you expect to work per week?" Candidates were encouraged to ask follow-up questions. All interviews were conducted online using oDesk's internal messaging system. Afterwards, participants were debriefed (e.g., we clarified the true intent of the job posting), and were paid $25.

Across all users, the average estimated project cost was \$3,044 (SD=\$2,113), with an average completion time of 4.5 weeks (SD=2.2 weeks), excluding time spent for data collection. While these results are anecdotal – given that none of the developers went ahead and actually built the system – we do believe it illustrates the significant complexity, cost and development time of special purpose computer-vision-driven sensing systems.

ZENSORS

We now describe how Zensors provides end-users with intelligent sensing capabilities, leveraging both crowdsourcing and machine learning. Figure 1 provides an illustrated overview of the architecture.

System Architecture

First, a mobile application serves as the primary end-point for creating and modifying sensors. Users highlight a region of the camera image and an associated question, *e.g.*, "how many parking spots are available?" As images stream from the device's front-facing camera, our system intelligently decides when to push requests to the crowd.

Next, crowd workers process these requests through a web-based interface. To reduce noise and reject malicious workers, several answers are collected per image, then fused together using quality-control algorithms (*e.g.*, voting) to determine the best response for a given instance. Finally, the responses gathered from the crowd are stored into a back-end database. These responses provide immediate, human-intelligent answers to the questions asked by users, and also serve as a corpus for training computer-vision based, machine learning classifiers.

Sensors from Images

Leveraging cameras as multi-purpose sensors. From mobile phones, security cameras, and Kinects in people's living rooms, cameras are everywhere. They continue to become more powerful, while remaining small. More importantly, time-series data from cameras offers rich contextual information about an activity or environment far more than what basic sensors (e.g., proximity) can provide. One can ask several multi-dimensional questions from camera images across a time period, such as "how many people are smiling?", "is it sunny?" or "is the table messy?", all of which provide useful information in learning about the context or activity within an environment. Thus, the cost, availability, and information bandwidth that cameras offer make them an ideal "multi-purpose" commodity sensor.

Repurposing old mobile devices as sensor hosts. Users upgrade their devices on average once every two years [27]. It is not uncommon for people to have a slew of older smart devices stashed in a drawer or closet. Although older, these devices are capable computers, typically featuring one or more cameras, a touchscreen, and wifi connectivity. This is the ideal platform for rapidly deployable, image-based sensing. Users simply download our Zensors app onto the devices, which allows them to create or modify sensors. Users then "stick" the device in a context of their choosing.

WiFi Cameras. Zensors can also utilize stand-alone wifi-enabled cameras, costing as little as \$30 today. In this case, a web interface can be used to define sensors (Figure 3).

Privacy Preservation

Image Subregions. Contextual information from cameras creates an inherent tradeoff between information and privacy [4,5,14]. A naïve approach would utilize the entire raw image. However, this can easily violate privacy, especially when personally identifying information is present, or when images depict people in sensitive situations. To partially mitigate this issue, our system asks users to select an arbi-

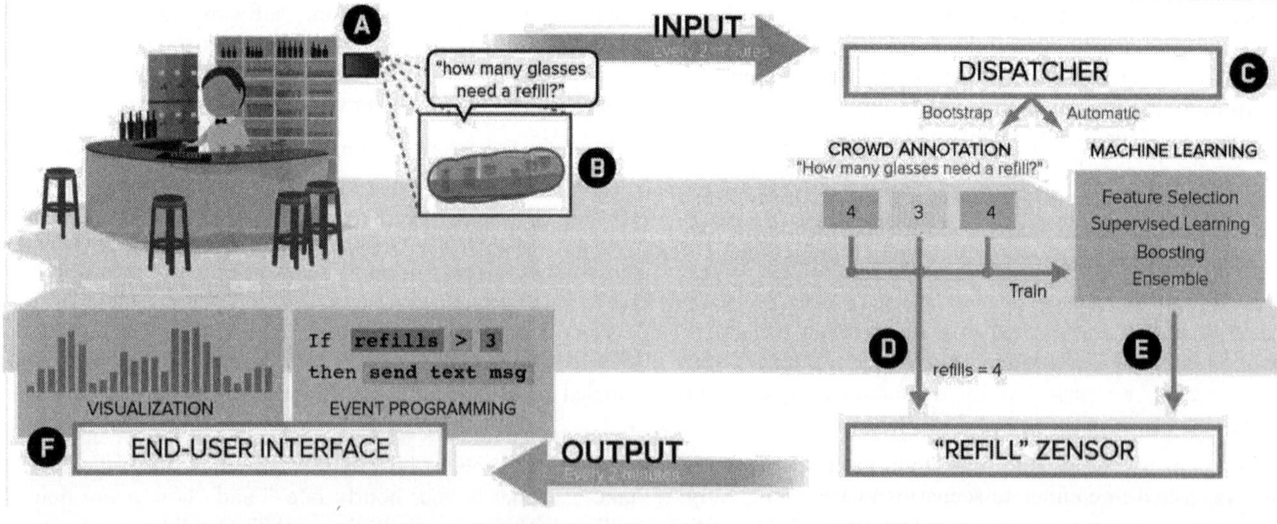

Figure 1. Zensors architecture. A bartender repurposes a tablet as a sensor host, affixing it to the wall behind the bar (A). Using the live view from the front facing camera, he selects a region of the scene and asks, "how many glasses need a refill?" (B). Periodically, the device takes snapshots, and forwards this data to a dispatcher (C). Initially, the dispatcher uses crowd workers to power the sensor, providing immediate human-level accuracy (D). In the background, answers from the crowd train a computer-vision-based, machine learning classifier (E). As it approaches crowd-level accuracy, the system employs a hybrid crowd-ML scheme to power the sensor stream. Sensor output can drive end-user applications, such as a real time visualizer (F, left) or event-based end-user programmable system (F, right).

trarily shaped subregion relating to the question they wish to ask; image data outside the subregion is masked away. This approach helps users to strike a balance between privacy and information content, and as a positive side effect, it reduces file size, removes unnecessary image elements, and simplifies the sensing effort for both human raters and computer vision techniques.

Image Obfuscation. For users wishing to add an additional level of privacy, we offer several image obfuscation techniques. These are applied to images on the device before they are sent to the cloud. Image obfuscation and privacy has been previously researched, and therefore we integrated the guidelines suggested by Hudson [14] and Boyle [4,5]. Users can choose to leave the image subregion unaltered, or select from four obfuscation methods: light blur, heavy blur, median filter, and edge filter (Figure 2).

Creating New Sensors

Sensor Questions. Every sensor starts with a question. Users create a new sensor by selecting a region of the image, and entering a plain text question. For example, in Figure 1, the bartender highlights the bar area, and asks, "how many glasses need a refill?" Questions define the "capabilities" of a sensor, and thus, the quality of answers depends on several factors, such as the question's context and relevance.

Data Types. To further add context and relevance, our system requires users to define a data type when creating new sensors. Data types curb variance and constrain the range of possible values returned by a sensor (i.e., the answer to the sensor's question), and facilitate simple automated processing of the data stream. To this end, we categorize questions into four example data types:

`YesNo` – This type of question can be answered by either *yes* or *no*. It is analogous to an ON/OFF sensor mechanism. Examples include: "is the door open or closed?", "is there food in the kitchen?", or "can you see a bus in this image?"

`Number` – Number data types are intended for questions that require counting. Numbers are continuous and are bound between a minimum and maximum range. Examples include: "how many cars do you see in the parking lot? (*min*=0, *max*=30)", and "what percentage of the water tank is full? (*min*=0, *max*=100)"

`Scale` – Scale data types are analogous to Likert-scale questions. Answers belong to discrete values specified within an increasing/decreasing scale. For this data type, users are required to supply scale-value pairs. Examples include: "how messy is this table? (1= Clean, 2=Average, 3= Messy)", or "how happy does the person look? (1=Very Sad, 2=Sad, 3=Neutral, 4=Happy, 5=Very Happy)"

`MultipleChoice` – When creating multiple-choice questions, users are required to specify the list of choices. Unlike scale data types, choice order is irrelevant. Examples include: "what type of food do you see? (None, Indian, Thai, Asian, Salad, Bagels, Other)" and "what are people doing? (reading, using computers, eating, other)".

Figure 2. In addition to subregion masking, users can select image obfuscation methods if desired. From top to bottom: raw image, light blurring, heavy blurring, median filter, and edge masking.

Frequency. When creating sensors, users need to specify the frequency at which sensor readings are taken. Depending on the question, frequency readings can range from near real-time (e.g., every one or two seconds for questions like "is the refrigerator door open? [`YesNo`]"), to extended periods (e.g., once per day for: "what product is advertised on the billboard? [`MultipleChoice`])."

Web Interface. Along with the mobile application, we built a companion web interface for sensor management (Figure 3). Users link one or more sensors to a web account, where they can create, modify, and synchronize sensors across all of their devices. The web UI also makes it possible to create new sensors remotely. For example, users can "stick" a sensor device at an elevated vantage point (e.g., for viewing an entire parking lot), and then manage and create sensors without having to physically touch the device.

Similar Image Detection and Rejection

Sensor image streams often have periods of little variation (*e.g.,* buildings after closing hours, outdoor scenes at night). Thus, to avoid soliciting redundant (and thus costly) responses from the crowd on highly similar images, we collapse runs of similar images. We calculate image similarity using a simple technique. First, we count the number of pixels that have changed from the previous frame using their RGB values and a predetermined *pixel difference threshold.* If the number of changed pixels in an image exceeds a certain *image area percentage threshold,* we consider the image to be different. Although this algorithm worked well for our purposes, we note that more sophisticated approaches (see e.g., [16]) could be used.

To determine optimal parameters, we performed a brute force optimization experiment. We compiled a corpus of roughly 6000 time-stamped images taken from multiple pilot sensor streams. We then manually labeled whether or not an image was the same as the previous image, providing a ground truth set. We then ran our image similarity algorithm, seeded with all combinations of the following thresholds: 2% to 40% *pixel difference threshold,* in 2% increments, and 0.1% to 5.0% *image area percentage threshold,* in 0.1% increments. This produced 130 result sets, which we compare to our ground truth using Jaccard's distance metric. By using a *pixel difference* and *image area* threshold of 10% and 1.0% respectively, a Jaccard distance of .64 is achieved. On average, this process removes roughly 40% of images – a significant saving.

Sensing with the Crowd

Images streamed from sensor devices are stored in a database. Crowd workers process un-answered instances through a web-based interface seen in Figure 4. The interface varies slightly based on the question/response type. Each sensor instance is answered (i.e., labeled) by several different crowd workers; we use voting to determine the best response (at present, we use three workers, but other numbers are possible). The resulting value is then saved in the database and the instance is considered answered and ready for sharing with end users or powering applications.

Our goal is to ensure workers are presented with a simple task that they can answer quickly. As such, we present one image to each worker and collect a single response. If workers are unable to answer an image-based question, they can mark it as an exception ("I can't tell" button, Figure 4), which informs the system that there is something amiss with the sensor itself (e.g., occlusion, insufficient lighting, poorly defined question). In addition, workers are prompted to provide textual descriptions when exceptions occur. This approach provides actionable user feedback to help remedy the problem.

To recruit users fast enough to receive answers in real time, we use LegionTools [17], a toolkit for quickly recruiting workers from Mechanical Turk using a web-based interface.

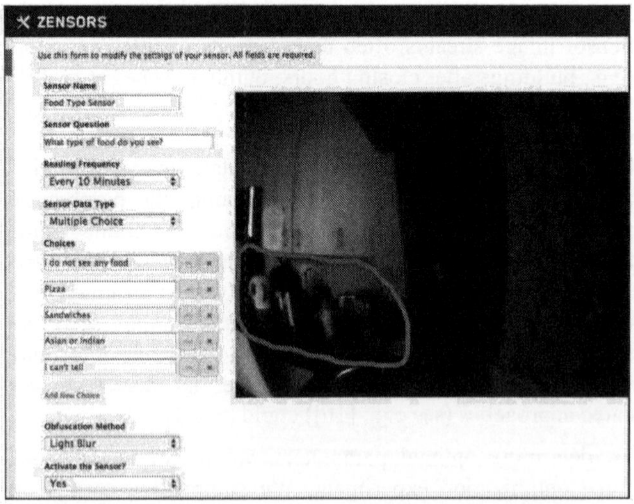

Figure 3. Users create and synchronize Zensors across all of their devices using a web API, allowing them to manage sensors without physical device interaction.

It leverages a retainer model [2], which pre-recruits workers so they are ready to respond to a task within as little as two seconds. When sensors are crowd-powered, this sets the lower-bound on our system latency.

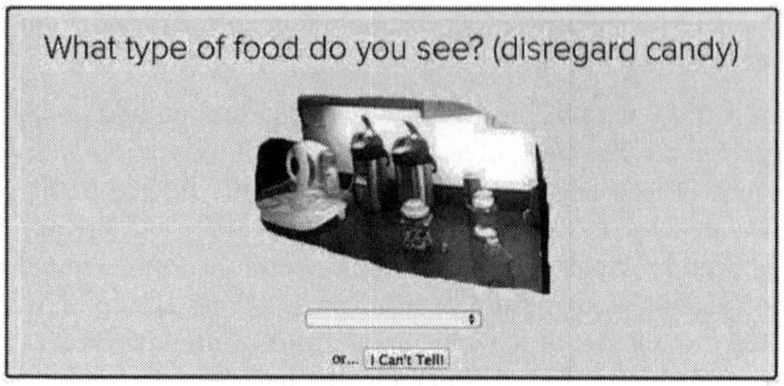

Figure 4. Our Mechanical Turk interface, which lets workers answer the question or raise an exception.

Training Automated Sensors

Solutions using crowd-power alone can be costly and difficult to scale (i.e., more sensors requires more people). Zensors reduces its reliance on crowd workers over time by using crowd-provided answers to train machine learning classifiers, which are fast and inexpensive. However, even after machine learning has taken over processing sensors feeds, crowd workers are still needed to provide a periodic human-accuracy baseline to ensure high accuracy. Here, we describe the machine learning framework for our prototype deployment.

The classifier is trained on all the input data to date, except for the most recent full day of data, which is set aside for evaluation. For sensors that produce data infrequently, the test set can be extended to one week or more to ensure there are sufficient test instances.

Histogram equalization is applied to each image to reduce the effect of lighting variances. Then, each input image is processed into a large number of global features. Additionally, each sensor image (which is itself a subregion of the larger original image) is broken into a grid of sub-images. In addition to a 1x1 grid (simply the image unchanged), we also use 4x4, 7x7 and 10x10. Each of these variously-sized sub-images is then converted to a luminance image, and the mean, standard deviation and mean-squared error across the window are used as numerical features. This produces a total of 332 image features. Feature selection is used as a post-process to extract exemplar features for a given sensor feed. Of course, much more advanced computer vision and scene understanding approaches exist that are beyond the scope of this work.

We use correlation-based feature selection [12] to select features from the training set, coupled with a backtracking best-first attribute searcher. Both algorithms are implemented in the Weka [11] machine learning toolkit. This selection process typically chooses between 10 and 30 features. Of note, the feature sets for different sensors rarely overlap.

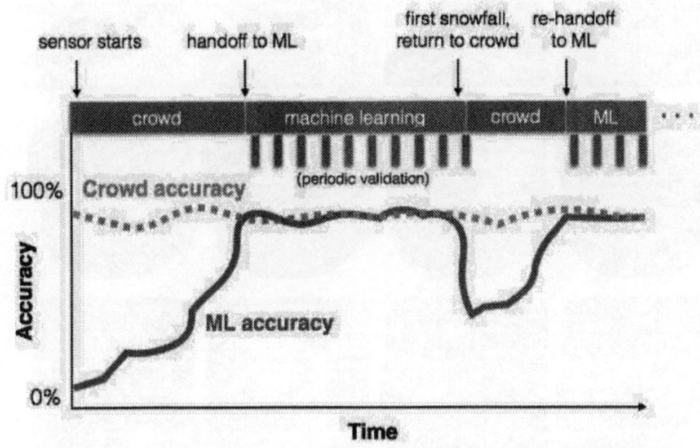

Figure 5. Sensors can toggle between the crowd and machine learning to adapt to environment changes. Note that end users and applications only ever see the max of the crowd and ML accuracies.

We then train classifiers depending on the type of sensor. A "pre-classifier" is first trained to distinguish between exceptions and non-exceptions, to ensure that the main classifier is not polluted by incorrect data. For continuous (numeric or scale) sensors, we train a support vector machine regression classifier using the SMOReg algorithm. For discrete sensors (yes/no, multiple choice), we use a one-versus-one multiclass quadratic-kernel SVM trained with the SMO algorithm, and for simple binary sensors we train a single SVM. The SVM was chosen as the basic classifier because of its ease of training and predictable behavior, though other classification approaches are certainly possible and valid. A more robust version of this system would maintain a library of feature extractors and classification algorithms, selecting those exhibiting the best performance for a given sensor.

Machine Learning Handoff

As the training corpus grows from crowd labeled instances, the accuracy of the machine learning classifiers typically improves. Once the accuracy of the machine learning exceeds a predefined threshold (e.g., 95%) for several days, the sensor hands off classification tasks to the machine learning algorithm. It is also possible to do a soft handoff, where the relative weighting between crowd and machine learning labels shifts over time.

Periodic Ground Truth Validation and Adaptation

To ensure continued sensor accuracy after the handoff to machine learning, the system periodically submits small batches of fresh sensor data to the crowd for labeling. This is used to benchmark the classifier accuracy. If accuracy is sufficiently robust, the machine learning can continue to power the sensor. However, if the accuracy has fallen below a threshold, the system can revert to crowd-power. This serves two immediate purposes: 1) the sensor immediately regains human-intelligence level accuracy, and 2) the system can incorporate new labels in its training for a hopeful future handoff.

In this way, Zensors can automatically handle infrequent changes (such as the first snow fall in a parking lot; Figure 5) that would prove challenging for most computer-vision-driven systems (which are first trained and then deployed). This ability to seamlessly toggle between crowd and automatic approaches, without sensor interruption, makes our approach highly adaptive and robust.

End-User Programming

We built a basic end-user programming tool that lets users design event-based notifications using data from one or more sensors (e.g., "send an email when the stove is ON *and* ZERO people are in the house"). These directives can be chained together as set of conjunctions ("and" clauses), or for alternative responses ("or" clauses). Multiple chains can be defined to represent different configurations. These disjunctions of conjunctions comprise a fully expressive set of logical terms.

This interface works similar to the popular *If This Than That* tool (ifttt.com) – users can select a sensor, select a value and comparison operator, and then select an action type from the set of supported APIs. Our current implementation allows users to select from an email, text message, audio, or chat alert. For each alert type, users are able to define a custom message, which can also display the current value of the sensor by using a specially marked variable.

Implementation and API

As a proof of concept, our Zensors mobile application was developed on Android, and deployed on a fleet of DOPO 9" Internet tablet M975, each costing less than $50. Our web UI, backend server, and end-user programming interfaces were implemented using PHP, MySQL, jQuery, d3.js, node.js, and socket.io. For our machine-learning component, we used the Weka toolkit [11]. We also provide a web API that allows services and end-user applications to leverage sensor data. As a proof of concept, we built two applications using this facility: our end user programming tool, described in the previous section, and a basic data visualization tool – both can be seen in our Video Figure.

PROTOTYPE DEPLOYMENT

The goal of our prototype deployment was to illustrate that even with a basic approach, the Zensors architecture can achieve high accuracy, at low cost, quickly, and author-able by end users using plain text queries..

We deployed 16 sensors across four diverse environments: a home kitchen, office kitchenette, building food court, and parking lot (see Figure 6 for four examples). Sensor questions ranged from "is this café door open?" to "what type of food is on the counter?" A range of reporting frequencies (from once per minute to twice per hour) and deployment durations (10 days to 3 weeks) were represented by our sample sensor set. We also manually labeled images from seven sensors to create a ground-truth dataset for later experiments. These "expert" labels have the advantage of superior context understanding as well as being able to view the entire dataset, not just a small snapshot.

Accuracy of the Crowd

To analyze how well our sensors can quickly provide accurate sensing data, we measured the precision, recall, and latency of our aggregated crowd responses. Figure 7 shows the accuracy of crowd workers' ratings, using expert labels as the ground truth. Cohen's kappa [6] is calculated to mitigate the effects of skewed class distribution (e.g., the leftover food sensor returned "no" over 75% of the time). Crowd accuracy reaches as high as 96.8% (kappa score 0.859), with mean accuracy 77.4% (median 76.0%). The crowd performed very well on three sensors (accessible parking spots occupied, number of cars in parking lot, and dishwasher door), moderately well on one sensor (leftover food), and poorly on three sensors (food type, line length sensor, countertop messy).

The food type sensor required users to distinguish between seven types of cuisine ("I do not see any food", "Pizza", "Sandwiches", "Cake or pastries", "Asian or Indian", "Salad", "Bagels or doughnuts", "Other cuisine or I can't tell") based on a very low-resolution image, while the line length sensor and countertop sensors both involved subjective judgments (e.g. "is the line orderly", "how messy is the countertop"). By contrast, quantitative questions ("is there food here", "is the door closed", "how many cars are there") generally had superior performance.

In designing questions to be posed to the crowd, operators may make assumptions that are not obvious to crowd workers, leading to incorrect results. In one example, workers were asked to identify the presence of food on a kitchen countertop. The countertop has a permanent candy jar, which the experimenters assumed would not be classified as food, yet several crowd workers marked the otherwise-empty countertop as having food. Based on the observed results, the question was amended to explicitly exclude candy, after which the expected results were obtained.

Estimating Live Accuracy

This experiment sought to estimate the accuracy of a sensor, over the course of its deployment, as viewed "live" by its operator. For each sensor, we defined ten time periods each covering one-tenth of the data, numbered t=0.1 through t=1.0. To estimate live accuracy at time t, we trained on all data up to time t, and then tested on all data from time t to time $t+0.3$ (i.e. we tested on a sliding window of 30% of the data). The results for three representative sensors are shown in Figure 7, compared against the crowd accuracies. In many cases, a relatively small portion of the data is needed to reach crowd-level accuracies.

Assessing Future Accuracy Post ML Handoff

Alternatively, it is equally important to assess what the accuracy of a sensor would be going forward, assuming a ML handoff occurs at time t. To assess this, we simulate a complete ML handoff at each time increment. All data up to that point is used for training, while all future data is used for testing. We stop this analysis when less than 30% of the data is available for testing, to avoid noisy results from insufficient test data. These results are summarized in Figure 8, compared against the overall crowd accuracies. The accuracies follow similar curves to the curves of Figure 7, suggesting that live classification accuracy may be able to predict future post-handoff classification accuracy.

Figure 6. Sensor image time series. Associated questions top to bottom "do you see a parked car?", "how many dishes in the sink?", "do you see a dishwasher door?", and "how orderly is the line?"

Similar Image Rejection in Practice

As described previously, our system sends labeling requests to the crowd only when there is a sufficient visual change between consecutive images, otherwise the last sensor value is simply copied forward. In our deployment, we found that our image similarly mechanism rejected an average of 61.2% of images (SD=17.2%, minimum=40.5%, maximum=93.7%).

Sensors that Fail

It is important to acknowledge that some of our sensors failed to produce reliable output. We initially hypothesized that failure would primarily be due to shortcomings in our computer vision implementation. However, we found that our classifiers work well in practice, with six of our seven sensors (for which we had expert labels, and thus a ground truth) getting to within 90% of crowd accuracy when we trained on half of the crowd-labeled data (mean 98.1%, SD=14.4%; tested on the second half). Instead, we found that the classification bottleneck for several of the sensors was caused by the poor accuracy of the crowd answers (as compared against our ground truth). For these underperforming sensors, we found a common theme: the sensor questions were subjective or required additional context.

For example, one sensor asked, "how orderly is the line?" (Figure 6) with three possible answers: "no people visible in image", "people present, but no obvious organization", and "people standing in a line". Because this is subjective (e.g., relative to local cultural norms) we found that crowd workers provided widely varying answers. Another sensor was

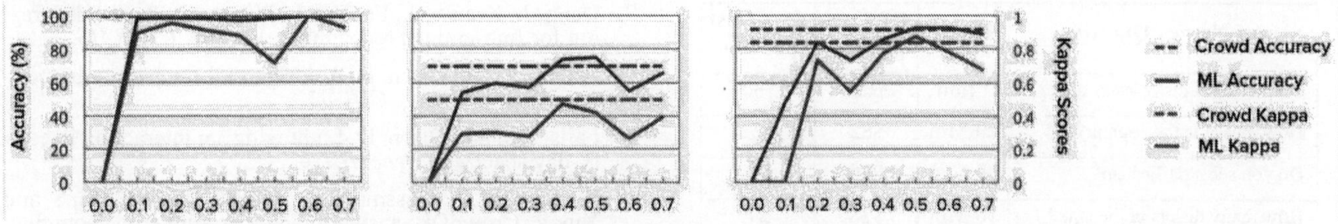

Figure 7. "Live" accuracy evaluation of three sensors. This is the accuracy of a sensor over the course of its deployment, as viewed "live" by its operator. X-axes represent training set cutoff time *t*. Left: "do you see a dishwasher door." Middle: "how messy is the counter." Right: "which parking spots are occupied."

tasked with sensing whether a dishwasher was opened or closed (see Figure 6 for some example images). In piloting, the question was defined as "is the dishwasher door open?" However, this appeared to confuse crowd workers, reducing sensor accuracy. We hypothesize that this problem was caused by the fact that most of the time, no dishwasher was visible in the closed state. When presented with the question of "is the dishwasher door open?", the crowd presumably wondered "what dishwasher?". We found that rephrasing the question to be more context-free – "Do you see a dishwasher door?" – significantly boosted accuracy.

There are a number of ways to alleviate "bad" sensor questions. One approach is to suggest example questions or provide structured question templates (e.g., "do you see a _____ [in/on] the _____?"), helping end-users formulate questions with less ambiguity. Additionally, the "I can't tell" button in the crowd interface (see "sensing with the crowd" section) could allow the system to flag sensors causing confusion and suggest the question or image subregion be modified. Another approach is for the crowd labeling interface to provide exemplar images, one for each possible answer (e.g., show examplars of both dishwasher door states). Finally, we can also show crowd workers a random set of previously collected sensor images that hopefully better capture the full range of possible states (e.g., orderly line to chaotic), so they can make better relative judgments.

Zensors Economics

The HITs we use for Zensors paid 2 cents each, a pay rate chosen to be above the U.S. minimum wage even for slower workers. This means, e.g., that a sensor that takes images every 10 minutes would cost roughly $100 per month (assuming an average similar image rejection rate) to be fully human-powered (30 days * 24 hours * 6 images per hour * 40% different images * $0.02 * 3 workers). To offer a concrete example, our median sensor in terms of images captured was the dishwasher door sensor, which triggered every minute. It captured 528 non-similar images over a 7-day deployment, which translates to $135/month in costs assuming only human-power.

For many of our sensors, we found that our automatic classification pipeline could reasonably approximate the crowd's answers using the first week as training data. Once there is sufficient agreement between crowd and machine learning, we can decrease the number of human workers from three to two, and eventually to one (and recruit more workers when there is significant disagreement). This means we can reduce the price by 67% even before the machine learning is fully trained, without reducing accuracy. To get to a point where machine learning can shoulder the entire load, we found that our test sensors took between 90 and 687 data points (depending on polling rate and setting). This means that we can train an automated sensor for as little as $5.40 (and our worst sensor for $41).

One of the strengths of Zensors is its ability to use human-intelligence to handle previously unseen scenarios. As such, even if a handoff to ML is possible, there is a continued cost to validate that the automated system is still working By periodically having the crowd spot-check the output of sensors, we can detect e.g., errors and scene changes, switching back to human-power (and thus training) if needed. This periodic validation can run at different intensities. Validating e.g., 1 in every 50 sensor instances would cost roughly $1/50^{th}$ the typical human-powered cost, which is perhaps a few dollars per month.

When ML Handoff is Not Possible

Finally, there may be cases where the system cannot attain a full ML handoff (e.g., poor image resolution, noisy training data, or simply a hard question incompatible with CV ap-

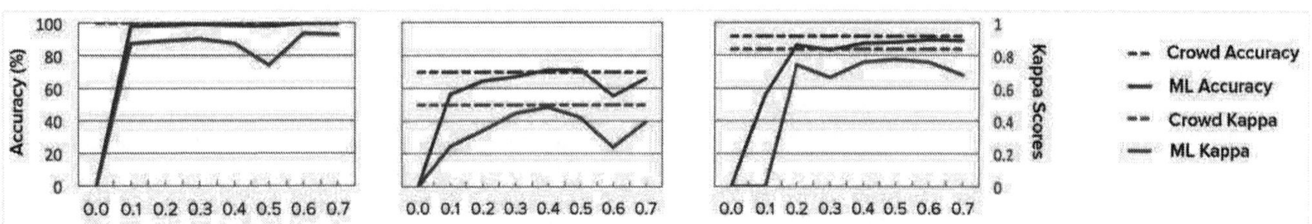

Figure 8. "Future" accuracy evaluation of three sensors. This is the accuracy of the sensor assuming ML handoff at time *t*. X-axes represent ML handoff time *t*. Left: "do you see a dishwasher door." Middle: "how messy is the counter." Right: "which parking spots are occupied."

Sensor Name / Question	Freq,	CP Cost per Mo.	Exp. Cost per Mo.
Do you see a dishwasher door?	1 min	$135	$35
How messy is the counter?	10 Min	$82	$22
Do you see a parked car?	30 Min	$30	$8
How many dishes in the sink?	10 Min	$28	$7
How many cars do you see?	30 Min	$43	$12
What type of food do you see?	10 Min	$87	$23

Table 1. Estimated monthly costs if sensors were fully crowd-powered (CP cost), as well as expected cost (Exp. Cost) assuming ML handoff after week one and continued periodic validation.

proaches). As a result, the system will need to rely on a fully crowd-powered approach for an indefinite period, which can be relatively expensive; Table 1 offers some example costs from our deployment. However, even if ML handoff never occurs, it is important to note that end users and applications only ever see human-accuracy level answers.

CONCLUSION

Zensors enables easy end-user creation of arbitrary sensors for any visually observable property. Zensors uses crowd-powered answers to produce near-instant sensor readings with high accuracy while requiring no explicit training. Once enough data labels have been collected, Zensors can seamlessly hand-off image classification to machine learning utilizing computer-vision-derived features. Our formative design exercises highlight the potential that Zensors holds for enabling a broad variety of applications beyond those available using contemporary electro-mechanical sensors. We conclude with results from our prototype deployment, which suggest our approach is feasible, accurate and can be cost effective.

ACKNOWLEDGEMENTS

This work was supported by Yahoo! InMind, National Science Foundation award #IIS-1149709, NSERC of Canada, an Alfred P. Sloan Foundation Fellowship, and fellowships from Microsoft Research, Disney Research, and Qualcomm.

REFERENCES

1. Abowd, G. D. and Mynatt, E. D. Designing for the human experience in smart environments. *Smart environments: technologies, protocols, and applications* (2004).
2. Bernstein, M.S., Brandt, J., Miller, R.C., Karger, D.R. Crowds in two seconds: enabling realtime crowd-powered interfaces. In *Proc. UIST '11*.
3. Bigham, J. P., et al. VizWiz: nearly real-time answers to visual questions. In *Proc. UIST '10*.
4. Boyle, M. and Greenberg, S. The language of privacy: Learning from video media space analysis and design. *ACM ToCHI*, 2005.
5. Boyle, M., Edwards, C., Greenberg, S. The effects of filtered video on awareness and privacy. In *Proc. CSCW '00*.
6. Cohen, J. A coefficient of agreement for nominal scales. Educational and Psychological Measurement 20(1), 1960.
7. Deng, J., Krause, J., Fei-Fei, L. Fine-grained crowdsourcing for fine-grained recognition. In *Proc. CVPR '13*.
8. Fails, J.A. and Olsen, D. A design tool for camera-based interaction. In *Proc. CHI '03*.
9. Fails, J.A. and Olsen, D. Light widgets: interacting in every-day spaces. In *Proc. IUI '02*.
10. Franklin, M. J., Kossmann, D., Kraska, T., Ramesh, S. and Xin, R. CrowdDB: answering queries with crowdsourcing. In *Proc. SIGMOD '11*.
11. Hall, M., Frank, E., Holmes, G., Pfahringer, B., Reutemann, P., Witten, I. H. The WEKA data mining software: an update. ACM SIGKDD explorations, 11(1) '09.
12. Hall, M.A., Correlation-based Feature Subset Selection for Machine Learning. 1998.
13. Hara, K., Sun, J., Moore, R., Jacobs, D., Froehlich, J.E. Tohme: Detecting Curb Ramps in Google Street View Using Crowdsourcing, Computer Vision, and Machine Learning. In *Proc. UIST '14*.
14. Hudson, S.E. and Smith, I. Techniques for addressing fundamental privacy and disruption tradeoffs in awareness support systems. In *Proc. CSCW '96*.
15. Kastrinaki, V., Zervakis, M., Kalaitzakis, K. A survey of video processing techniques for traffic applications. *Image and Vision Computing* 21(4), 2003.
16. Khan, M., Acharya, B. and Verm, S. Comparison between different illumination independent change detection techniques. In *Proc. ICCCS '11*.
17. Lasecki, W., Gordon, M., Koutra, D., Jung, M., Dow, S., Bigham, J. Glance: Rapidly Coding Behavioral Video with the Crowd. In *Proc. UIST '14*.
18. Lasecki, W.S., Song, Y., Kautz, H., and Bigham, J.P. Real-time crowd labeling for deployable activity recognition. In *Proc. CSCW '13*.
19. Lee, M. L., Dey, A. K. Sensor-based observations of daily living for aging in place. *Pers. Ubiquit. Comp.*, 2014, 1-17.
20. Marcus, A., Karger, D., Madden, S., Miller, R., Oh, S. Counting with the crowd. In *Proc. VLDB '12*.
21. Maynes-Aminzade, D., Winograd, T., Igarashi, T. Eyepatch: prototyping camera-based interaction through examples. In *Proc. UIST '07*.
22. Salber, D., Dey, A. K., Abowd, G. D. The context toolkit: aiding the development of context-enabled applications. In *Proc. CHI '99*.
23. Tang, A., Greenberg, S., and Fels, S. Exploring video streams using slit-tear visualizations. *Proc. AVI '08*.
24. von Ahn, L. and Dabbish, L.. Labeling images with a computer game. In *Proc. CHI '04*.
25. Vondrick, C., Patterson, D., and Ramanan, D. Efficiently Scaling Up Crowdsourced Video Annotation. *International Journal of Computer Vision*.
26. Wah, C. Crowdsourcing and its applications in computer vision. University of California, San Diego. 2006.
27. Walton, A. Life Expectancy of a Smartphone. Retrieved from chron.com, September 21, 2014.
28. Zhao, W., Chellappa, R., Phillips, P. and Rosenfeld, R. Face recognition: A literature survey. *ACM Comput. Surv.* 35(4), 2003.
29. Zimmer, T., & Beigl, M. AwareOffice: Integrating Modular Context-Aware Applications. In *Proc. ICDCSW'06*.

Exploring Privacy and Accuracy Trade-Offs in Crowdsourced Behavioral Video Coding

Walter S. Lasecki
Computer Science Department
University of Rochester
wlasecki@cs.rochester.edu

Mitchell Gordon
Computer Science Department
University of Rochester
m.gordon@rochester.edu

Winnie Leung
HCI Institute
Carnegie Mellon University
winniel@andrew.cmu.edu

Ellen Lim
HCI Institute
Carnegie Mellon University
eslim@andrew.cmu.edu

Jeffrey P. Bigham
HCI and LT Institutes
Carnegie Mellon University
jbigham@cs.cmu.edu

Steven P. Dow
HCI Institute
Carnegie Mellon University
spdow@cs.cmu.edu

ABSTRACT

Coding behavioral video is an important method used by researchers to understand social phenomenon. Unfortunately, traditional hand-coding approaches can take days or weeks of time to complete. Recent work has shown that these tasks can be completed quickly by leveraging the parallelism of large online crowds, but using the crowd introduces new concerns about accuracy, reliability, privacy, and cost. To explore these issues, we conducted interviews with 12 researchers who frequently code behavioral video, to investigate common practices and challenges with video coding. We find accuracy and privacy to be the researchers' primary concerns. To explore this more concretely, we used sample videos to investigate whether crowds can accurately recognize instances of commonly coded behaviors, and show that the crowd yields accurate results. Then, we demonstrate a method for obfuscating participant identity with a video blur filter, and find, as expected, that workers' ability to identify participants decreases as blur level increases. The workers' ability to accurately and reliably code behaviors also decreases, but not as steeply as the identity test. This trade-off between coding quality and privacy protection suggests that researchers can use online crowds to code for some key behaviors in video without compromising participant identity. We conclude with a discussion of how researchers can balance privacy and accuracy on their own data using a system we introduce called Incognito.

Author Keywords

Data analysis; subjective coding; crowdsourcing; video

ACM Classification Keywords

H.5.1 Multimedia Information Systems: Video

INTRODUCTION

Social science and interaction researchers must often interpret video data to gain insight about human behavior in a specific situation or interaction. Even with great advances in computer vision, computers cannot automatically identify and interpret the nuances of most human behavior. The most common way to extract meaning from video data is to have one or more human analysts manually *code* it – identify specific events, and mark their time of occurrence. This process is known to be very time-consuming, adding significant overhead to analyzing video data [14].

Recent work has introduced methods for coding behavioral video using online crowds [5, 16, 24, 23]. These systems use online crowdsourcing platforms such as Mechanical Turk to recruit groups of people who can help complete coding tasks with less effort for researchers [23, 24], and in some cases, far more quickly by leveraging the parallelism available on such platforms [16]. However, the shift from using coders who are

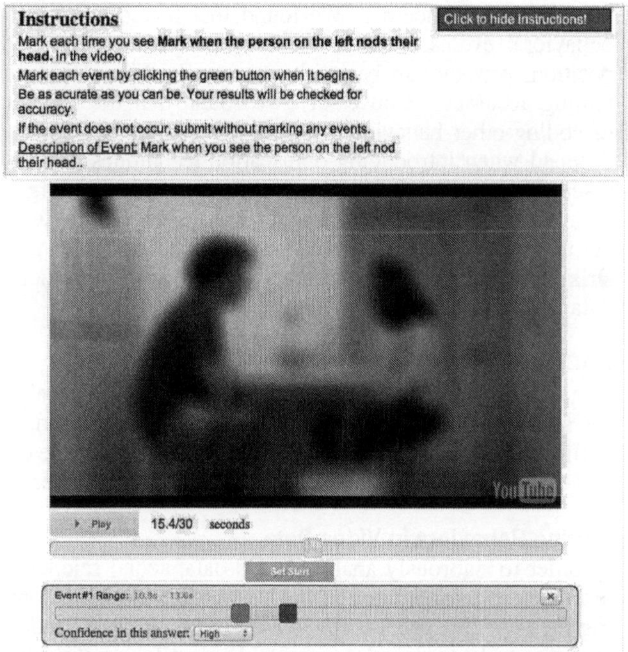

Figure 1: Our studies explore the trade-off between the level of obsfucation and coding accuracy. This figure shows the interface used by workers recruited through Amazon Mechanical Turk to identify behaviors in obfuscated video.

CHI 2015, April 18–23 2015, Seoul, Republic of Korea

ACM 978-1-4503-3145-6/15/04 $15.00
http://dx.doi.org/10.1145/2702123.2702605

part of a research team, to untrained, relatively anonymous online workers, presents a new set of potential concerns.

In this paper, we report on interviews conducted with 12 experienced behavioral researchers to understand common practices with video coding, and to uncover their concerns with using crowd-powered systems to code video data. The two primary concerns they had with using the crowd revolved around maintaining the *accuracy* of behavioral judgements and protecting the *privacy of study participants*. To explore this tradeoff, we investigate the accuracy of using online crowds to analyze five commonly coded behaviors. Our results show that crowd workers produce high precision (median 89.5%) and recall (median 78.4%) in comparison to expert-coded behavioral judgements.

We explored how image blurring might be used to address these privacy concerns. We found that for some types of behavioral events, such as touching of the face and body position, privacy can be safely preserved while also maintaining accuracy. Conversely, we found that the accuracy of coding other behaviors, such as eye contact and smiling, dropped when introducing obfuscation techniques. To help researchers explore the tradeoffs of online video coding for their data, we created a software tool called Incognito, which automatically samples obfuscation techniques and attempts to strike a balance between accuracy and privacy for particular data and constraints.

BACKGROUND

Our work explores the intersection of behavioral data analysis for social sciences and crowdsourcing. In this section, we outline the work in these areas that has motivated our use case and made crowd-powered coding of video data possible.

Coding Behaviors in Video Data

In order to rigorously analyze video data, social science researchers in a wide range of fields use behavioral video coding [9, 14]. This process involves training multiple "coders" (usually student research assistants) to identify specific events in a video in a consistent manner [2]. This often takes days or weeks for complex events, and requires determining the specific events of interest in advance, and then generating a corresponding training curriculum. To ensure trained coders are consistent amongst one another, segments of video content are redundantly coded and compared against each other to find the inter-rater agreement [10]. If this is sufficiently high, the coders are trusted to complete other portions of the video independently. To avoid missing event occurrences, practitioners recommend that coders make several passes through the video data and *code one event type at a time*. This increases reliability at the cost of significant additional time required to code a video.

Designing the coding scheme can also be a challenge. Analysts may use a bottom-up approach, in which the coding scheme is constructed from behavioral features observed during careful viewing and re-viewing of the video, or a top-down approach, in which it is derived from theory. Most commonly, some mix of these two methods is used [25]. However, data-driven exploration of video data is difficult using conventional techniques because of the time needed to look for events in large video data sets (consisting of tens or hundreds of hours of video, or more), and the time and monetary cost of recruiting and training a team of coders to perform each stage of the exploratory analysis.

Tools such as ANVIL [15], Datavyu [1], VACA [8], and VCode [12] have been developed to provide interfaces for easily annotating events in video. Despite the availability of such tools, the time required to code behavioral video remains high because it remains a linear process that grows with the total size of the video data set.

Annotating Video Using the Crowd

Crowdsourcing has been used on tasks that rely on human judgment and that are difficult for automated systems. For example, Soylent [3] uses the crowd to edit or shorten writing, VizWiz [4] answers questions about photographs quickly, and Legion [17] follows natural language commands to intelligently control a GUI.

The crowd has also been leveraged in the context of activity recognition systems. For instance, VATIC [24] allows crowd workers to tag where objects appear in a scene. While the crowd provides annotations, it is not designed to respond quickly to the end-user. Similarly, Legion:AR [18] explores crowd labeling of *low-level* actions and even activity structure [20] in video for assistive home monitoring: workers are asked to watch a video stream and provide labels as events happens live; an automated system then learns from these labels for future occurrences. Legion:AR does not process video any faster than an individual can, and is designed for use *not* by a human analyst, but by a Hidden Markov Model-based system.

DiSalvo *et al.* [11] added game elements to an annotation task to get the crowd to mark where an object appears. "Guess What?" is a game that allows the crowd to help annotate affective behaviors in video. Prior work has shown that using the crowd for affective behavioral coding can collectively be comparable to an expert coder in accuracy [5].

Online crowdsourcing platforms, such as Mechanical Turk, provide a means of easily hiring and distributing small tasks to large sets of crowd workers. Glance [16] uses this on-demand access to a highly parallelizable workforce to dramatically cut the time it takes to get video coded by the crowd to a few seconds or minutes, instead of the hours or days achieved by the quickest previous approaches. This paper extends prior work by investigating how behavioral researchers might leverage the crowd for video coding and what concerns they may have in doing so.

PRACTITIONER INTERVIEWS

While Gottman's techniques provide a basic intro for individual coders, we wanted a better understanding for how behavioral researcher and their teams practically deal with coding video. Also, given the emerging technology for leveraging online crowds for video analysis, we wanted researchers' perspective on the potential benefits and concerns with this approach. To understand if and how crowdsourcing could be

ID	Role	Research area/topics	Behavioral codes
1	Grad student	Rapport in learning settings	Eye gaze, gesture, non-verbal behaviors
2	Faculty	Relationships and stress	Eye gaze, non-verbal behavior
3	Faculty	Group negotiations	Contents of speech (bargaining behavior, reciprocation behavior, etc)
4	Grad student	Rapport & cultural differences	Rapport & cultural differences
5	Faculty	Conflict in groups	Contradictions, aggressiveness, turns in speech
6	Grad student	Classroom culture, turn-taking	Eye contact, gestures, turn-taking
7	Faculty	Couples coping with diabetes	Non-verbal behaviors, emotions
8	Grad student	Communication in person / online	Eye gaze, non-verbal behaviors, rapport judgements
9	Faculty	Learning in classrooms, cultural difference	Deep v. shallow explanations
10	Faculty	Internet, deception	Turn taking, nonverbal gesture, length of hesitation
11	Grad student	Hormonal stress response	Emotions, physical effects
12	Grad student	Rapport between friends versus strangers, self disclosure	Head nods, smiles, eye-gaze, verbal interactions

Table 1: A summary of interview participants, their research areas, and common behavioral codes used in their research.

used as part of a behavioral video coding process, we interviewed twelve researchers with experience in coding video using conventional approaches. All participants have coded at least 100 hours of video data in the past. The researchers comprised 6 faculty members and 6 graduate students from a range of domains across HCI, psychology, and sociology (see Table 1). We recruited participants from an academic university through email and word-of-mouth; no renumeration was offered. Interviews lasted from 30 minutes to an hour. We asked the researchers to describe their current practices around video coding, including how they create their annotation coding schemes, how they record and manage video, and how they analyze video data. We were particularly interested in surfacing common behavioral events and issues that occur while coding video. Finally, we opened a discussion about leveraging online crowdsourcing for video coding and asked participants to reflect on potential benefits and concerns.

All interviews were audio recorded and transcribed. To analyze the data, we went back through the interviews, took down notes, printed out the data, clustered them using open-coding techniques and affinity analysis to find common practices and recurring themes.

Findings

Our findings explore the current state of video coding practice for behavioral researchers and the primary concerns with a crowdsourced approach to this process.

A time consuming process

The current process of video coding is quite time intensive. As P1 claims "it can take ten times the recording time to annotate (the data)." Most researchers reported that the coding process for a particular study can typically take an entire semester or more. One professor commented that "sometimes I can't finish coding in a semester. It might take a year to finish coding one system (P2). Another professor talked about how he collects data during the school year so that he can hire several full-time coders during the summer. Many faculty hire undergraduate research assistants at relatively inexpensive hourly rates, however they report issues with finishing the coding around the students' schedules.

Wide variety of contexts and behaviors

Participants use video coding for a variety of domains and research questions (Table 1). Eight out of twelve participants generally explore research questions about communication and relationships between people, ranging from couples dealing with stress to group negotiations. Two researchers focus on classrooms and group settings; they use video coding because provides a means to "be as unobtrusive as possible" (P9). The final two of our participants look specifically at how people interact with and through technology (e.g., online tutors, Skype calls). Across all the projects, the researchers often coded their video data for non-verbal gestures, facial expressions, eye contact, and turns of speech. To capture these behaviors on video, the researchers typically rely on a single camera positioned so that it can see participants' faces and upper torso.

Developing and refining coding schemes

Behavioral researchers either start with an existing coding scheme or develop one from extant theory. P4 remarked that "the annotation scheme comes out of a mix of two things: the first thing is what does the data look like, what physical data would you code for if you wanted to, and the other is literature, what other people have already." Nearly all participants talked about referencing existing coding manuals from prior literature and tailor them for their own projects. As P3 notes, "we never code for something unless we have a strong motivational hypothesis." Once researchers establish this theoretical grounding, they must develop a coding manual, validate it with their data, and calculate inter-reliability between multiple coders. Sometimes this process never pans out; P3 described trying to code for rapport "we went through (a coding scheme) like six times and eventually decided it was too difficult." For P7, this process "took us probably 6 weeks ... and we started out with a set of codes." The coding manual often goes through many iterations before inter-reliability is achieved, and only then does formal video coding begin.

Preparing people to be video coders

All researchers discussed their processes for training video coders typically undergraduates to use their tailored coding manuals. First video coders read and familiarize themselves with what can often be an extensive coding scheme. One researcher made a "cheat sheet" (P7) so that she could use an abbreviated version of the massive coding manual. P2 discussed how she instructs coders to "watch the video once without doing anything" and then after coding a small portion of the overall data, they "come back and compare with previous coding data and justify ratings." Researchers vary in terms of how they segment and distribute video among a coder team. Several interviewees reported that they typically give the graduate student final authority to meet and resolve disagreements or disparity in coding. After a team of coders achieves inter-coder reliability (typically measured using either Cohen's or Krippendorff's kappa), they can finally begin to individually code segments of video.

Reactions to online video coding with crowds

In general, researchers showed interest in the idea of using online crowds as part of a video coding service, especially if it allowed them to iterate faster on their research questions. P2 discussed how such a service could amenable to "sequential coding" since the video could be broken into chunks. P1 hypothesized that "emotional constructs may be easier for (online workers)." A crowd-based video coding service would need to evaluate efficacy for a range of behavioral events.

Concerns with quality/reliability

In general, the researchers questioned the quality and reliability of data obtained from crowd workers. Many of those interviewed look at non-verbal gestures, which are typically subtle and require either extensive training or a solid grounding in theory. As P6 said "the more interesting gestures are the ones that might have ambiguity." P5 talked about the "subtleties in the way people negotiate" and that coders need to develop "a deeper level of understanding" when coding. P9 noted that she would consider whether online video coders "havent been thinking about these things for a while." Although, P3 noted that "we want people who don't know the theory, because you don't want them to guess the hypotheses and potentially influence their coding." Likewise, P4 mentioned that "annotators did not need to know about the science."

Several researchers brought up the issue of training. Considering the arduous process of training undergrad RAs, P9 wondered how the crowd would be trained:

> If I need ten thousand workers and it takes two hours to train each one, I don't know if you get into issues with the financial costs or the consistency or quality of doing that for each person.

Researchers provided a number of ideas for training. For example, P5 suggested having a tutorial for crowd workers and developing clear, detailed directions for each video. Both P5 and P7 suggested using payment bonuses to reward workers who reach a certain level of accuracy. P6 suggested as a first step to "pick something very easy to code such as eyebrow raises and body movements."

Issues around segmenting data

Some researchers were concerned with how long a clip would have to be for crowdsourcing workers to be able to code reliably. One researcher who does research on conflict and negotiation discussed how "crowdworkers will need to see at least a couple of minutes... the context would be important." (P5) Likewise, a professor noted:

> "An arbitrary time-based unit of chunking wouldnt work because it breaks up the natural units in the thing that you would want to code, they can be speech based or activity based" (P10).

One researcher suggested that such a system could automatically stagger and overlap the clips to avoid this problem.

Concerns with participant privacy and IRB

Additional concerns regarding online video coding revolved around how to protect participants' privacy and whether universities' institutional review boards (IRB) would approve. All participants commented that it would be necessary to obtain specific permission from the participants to upload videos. One participant noted that "The IRB should be okay with this study if the participants know ahead of time that the data would be shared" (P10). However, the IRB needs sufficient evidence that the process is safe and will keep the identity of the participants confidential. P6 suggested that a service would need to "convince the IRB that the process is legitimate and safe (by) first using publicly available data where identity doesn't matter."

Discussion of Interview Study

The interviews provided greater context around the process researchers go through when coding video data. We learned more about the common strategies and pain points during this process. We also discovered concerns around reliability, video segmentation, and participant privacy that researchers may have with crowdsourcing the video coding process.

We uncovered an interesting potential tradeoff between protecting participant identity and achieving high-quality results. Based on this, we conducted a series of experiments (1) to explore the quality and reliability of using online crowds to code a range of behaviors in video, and (2) to understand if and how obfuscation methods affect the ability to identify behaviors and if these adequately protect participants' identities.

ANSWER QUALITY

The first question we set out to study based on the results of our survey was: "can the crowd accurately answer questions that real researchers want answered?" To test this, we selected the 5 most commonly discussed behaviors mentioned by the researchers we interviewed to have coded by the crowd. For each of the following behaviors, we recorded a video using a volunteer participant who agreed to have their image shared with web workers. Each behavior is listed along with the instruction that we provided to workers:

(a) No Blur (b) Level 6 (c) Level 5 (d) Level 4 (e) Level 3

Figure 2: Examples of the blur levels we used in our experiments. At level 3 almost no personally identifying features can be made out. However, most broad motions can still be made out. As the blur level decreases, more fine-grained features can be identified. Beyond level 6, the effects of blurring are not easily detectable. Level 10 is no blur.

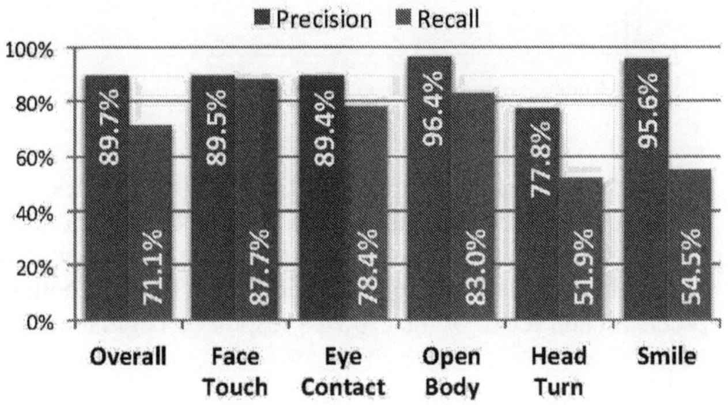

Figure 3: Precision and recall rates for each of the 5 most commonly coded types of events from our interviews with researchers. Note that while the overall scores are high, the `Head Turn` and `Smile` events showed lower recall due to ambiguity in the description given to workers – a common issue for both crowd-powered and traditional coding methods.

- `Eye Contact:` Mark when the person facing the camera makes eye contact with the interviewer.
- `Open Body:` Mark when the person facing the camera has an open body position. This means that they are leaning back in chair/away from evaluator and spreading their limbs apart. [1]
- `Smiling:` Mark when the person facing the camera is smiling.
- `Face Touch:` Mark when the person facing the camera is touching their face.
- `Head Position:` Mark when the person facing the camera turns their head away from the camera/interviewer.

These actions comprise important actions for researchers and span both objective and gestalt, accounting for a wide range of the possible types of actions that researchers may wish to code for with the crowd.

Our interviews with behavioral researchers also revealed that most video is recorded in a lab setting and contains a single person being filmed. The most common camera angle is front-on (often over the shoulder of the evaluator). The side-on angle is also often used, but to limit this study to a reasonable amount of trials, we will focus on the more common front-on angle. As these videos are filmed in a lab setting, they are typically well-lit and high quality. Therefore, we simulated a video recording in a lab setting, and using an actor filmed from a front-on, over the evaluator's shoulder angle.

[1]This is defined in the literature as the face/body leaning back in chair/away from evaluator and spreading their limbs apart.

Experiments

We recruited 89 workers from Mechanical Turk to perform the coding. Figure 3 shows the performance of each of the 5 event types over our video, which was segmented into 6 pieces each with each piece coded by three unique workers. Overall, the crowd averaged a precision of 89.7% (median 89.5%, SD=7.4), and recall of 71.1% (median 78.4%, SD =16.6). Closer inspection shows that not all tasks performed equally well, as would be expected. In this case, the `Head Turn` and `Smile` had 51.9% (SD=43.5) and 54.5% (SD=31.1) recall rates respectively, compared to the other behaviors which averaged 80.1% (SD=4.63) recall between them. This might be due to the fact that the instructions for `Head Turn` and `Smile` are minimal, and while the events seem reasonably intuitive, the ground truth example included even very subtle events that were technically part of the code's definition. The disagreement (low kappa score) between crowd workers at these points likely would mean that in real settings, the system would alert the researcher to the potential ambiguity.

Quality Discussion

One potential reason for this disparity in two of the five cases is that these two behaviors were also the least specifically described of the five. Due to this, workers might have been unclear on a number of the cases that were included in both conditions, leading to the lower recall, while still maintaining relatively high accuracy (77.8% (SD=39.0) for `Head Turn` and 95.6% (SD=8.2) for `Smile`). This reasoning is also supported by prior work that found more vague behavioral descriptions led to less worker agreement and higher error rates.

PROTECTING PRIVACY

Protecting the privacy of study participants was the other primary concern identified by our interview participants. Ensuring this protection is important for running an ethical study with fully informed users, recruiting participants who might be uncomfortable with their likeness being distributed to web workers, and properly informing IRBs of risk.

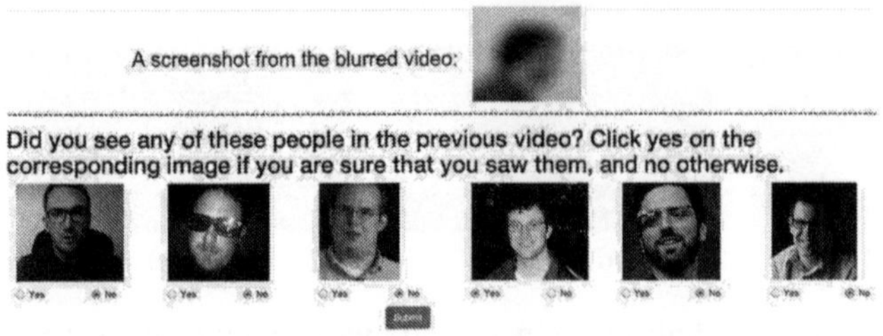

Figure 4: Our study of participant privacy in crowdsourced behavioral video coding used a lineup tool to test whether or not crowd workers were able to recognize individuals (shown in the bottom line-up) based on the content of the video they were asked to code (an image of the video is shown at the top of this figure, but was not shown to workers).

Related Work

Prior work gives us a means of combating these privacy concerns, though it comes with the risk of reducing the ability of workers to identify certain actions with the same accuracy. These approaches have not directly been focused on preserving privacy in study settings.

Identifying Personal Identity Visually

Gauging people's ability to recognize persons from visual information has been well studied in the past. For example, law enforcement often relies on witnesses recognizing individuals from suspect lineups. The Police Chiefs Association of Santa Clara County published a document containing guidelines as to how to correctly conduct a police-style witness identification lineup [22]. Guidelines include information such as "individuals may not appear exactly as they did on the date of the incident as head and facial hair are subject to change" and "photos/persons will be presented in random order." We used the guidelines in this document when creating our identification lineup tool in order to ensure its accuracy.

Many researchers have studied the accuracy level of these police-style lineups. Henderson et al. conducted multiple studies where participants were first shown a mock robbery CCTV video, then shown photos of the two robbers and seven similar looking people [13]. In one study, they were shown low quality CCTV footage, where the participant's accuracy in correctly identifying the robber was 28%. In a later study, different participants were shown higher quality footage shot by a documentary crew, and their accuracy increased to 76%. In addition, Bruce et. al conducted a study where images of a target were grabbed from a video and shown to participants. Participants accurately identified the target in a video 79% of time when shown a straight on image of the target and 70% of the time when shown an image of the target where the head angle varied by 30 degrees [7]. Both of these studies show that this method is a reasonably accurate way to determine whether someone can be identified visually. Their accuracy rates compare similarly to ours, as we discuss later.

Obscuring Information in Video

Prior work has examined multiple methods for obfuscating people's identity in video while maintaining awareness of actions, such as applying a blur or pixelation filter. Boyle discusses how blurring proved to be more effective at obscuring identity than pixelation [6], and presents 10 different levels of filtering (10 being no blur, 1 being the highest blur level), representing a spectrum of magnitudes for which the effect can be applied. Boyle et al. explore what can protect privacy while letting a large portion of people still identify very course-grain information in an office space, such as how many people or objects are in a room. They do not explore what impact it has on people's ability to recognize events that researchers are interested in when coding video, which often include very subtle behaviors. The office setting used by Boyle et al. is also very robust to errors: there is no critical issue caused by relatively low recognition rates, unlike in the behavioral video coding setting we explore in this work.

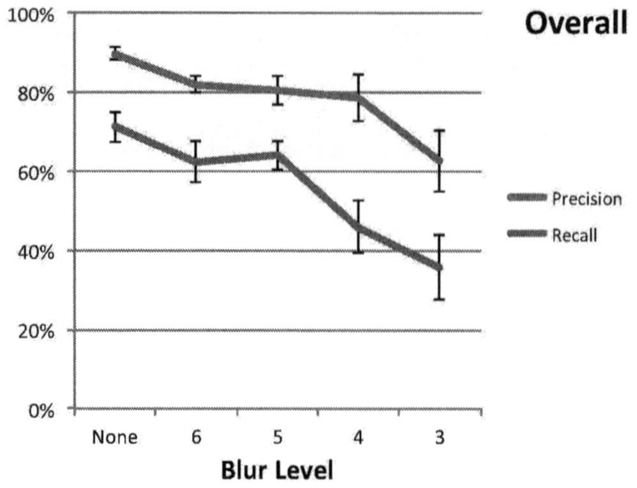

Figure 5: Overall average results from all five of the events we coded for over the unaltered video and 4 levels of added blur. Error bars show the standard deviation. As the severity of the blur filter is increased (from level 6 to level 3), both the precision and recall of the crowd's responses begin to fall.

In our initial experiments, we chose to replicate Boyle's blur filter and the exact increments of magnitude for each level. Boyle's blur uses a box filter, meaning that a pixel's filtered color is the mean of the neighborhood of pixels surrounding it. Unlike the discrete regions seen with a pixelation filter, the image smoothly changes from one region to the next. Boyle implemented this algorithm such that each level corresponded to a fixed box size that divides into their video's resolution. Our implementation is similar, however it can accept any resolution of video and adjust the box size accordingly.

Prior work has considered how to preserve identity while hiding possibly embarrassing actions in a telecommuting setting [21]. They found that blurring is not an effective privacy tool for home-based video conferencing. This work attempted to hide the actions that were occurring, rather than hide the identities of who is doing them. Our work looks to do the opposite, and so showing that actions can still be identified in a blurry video suggests our approach may be feasible.

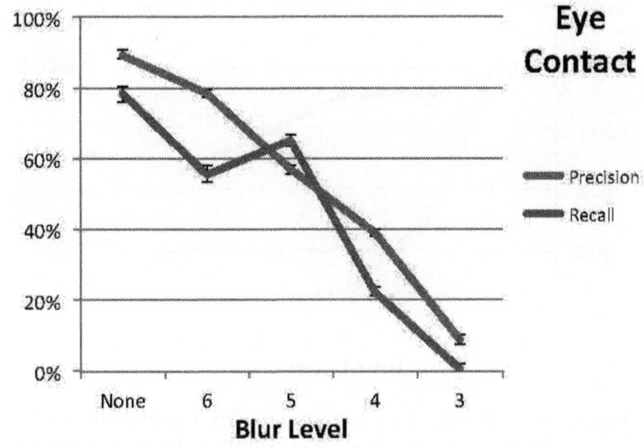

Figure 6: Results from the 'eye contact' event we coded for over the unaltered video and 4 levels of added blur with standard deviation error bars shown. Since identifying eye contact requires recognizing fine-grained movements, both the precision and recall of the crowd's responses fall dramatically as the severity of the blur filter is increased from level 6 to level 3. The 'eye contact' event was the most highly affected by blur of the 5 events we coded.

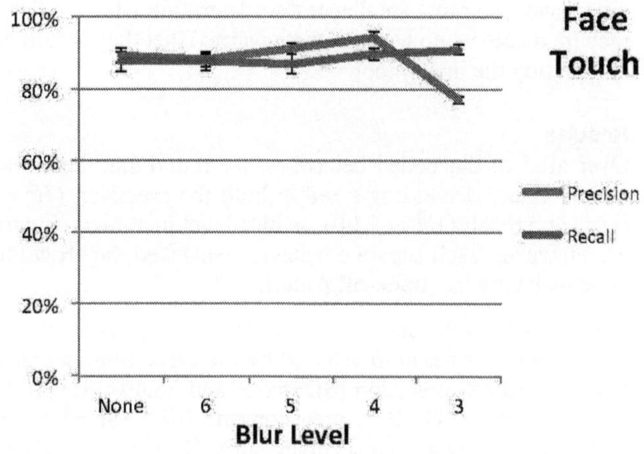

Figure 7: Results from the 'face touch' event we coded for over the unaltered video and 4 levels of added blur with standard error bars shown. Since identifying when someone touches their face requires recognizing relatively drastic movements, both the precision and recall of the crowd's responses are almost unaffected as the severity of the blur filter is increased from level 6 to level 3. The 'face touch' event was the least effected by blur of the 5 events we coded.

Exploring Privacy-Quality Trade-Offs

Since no existing approach can reduce the visual identifiably of participants without also potentially interfering with the identifiably of those participants' behaviors, we want to establish what type and severity of impact privacy filters have on accuracy. We focus on visual privacy in these studies since we found it is most often the focus of researchers' inquiries. To discover how privacy and accuracy can be traded off, we designed our experiment using video of the commonly coded behaviors that we used in our earlier quality experiments.

Experimental Setup

Our study was evaluated using Amazon Mechanical Turk with 553 unique workers. Tasks paid between 19 and 21 US cents. No worker coded a video or completed the facial identification task more than once. This ensured that workers did not become more accurate at identification after having multiple attempts and views of the person to learn from. For example, we want to avoid situations such as letting a worker who coded a video clip with a low amount of blur go on to later code the same clip with a higher amount of blur – the worker would likely be more accurate than they otherwise should have been.

Video Obfuscation Approach

As we discussed earlier in our related work section, Boyle et al. [6] looked at using 10 levels of blur to obfuscate sensitive information in video, and found it to be fairly effective when compared to other techniques such as pixellation. Additionally, blur can serve well as a catch-all for a large variety of actions. Building on this work, we replicated Boyle's levels of blur and chose to code video on levels 3, 4, 5, 6, and 10 (unblurred). We chose these levels because they represented the range of reasonable amounts of blur that would be used with our video. Because our video contained rather large, zoomed in objects, any level of blur higher than 6 would have been indistinguishable from coding an un-blurred video. Likewise, any level of blur lower than 3 would have been too blurry to reveal any interesting results. Figure 2 shows examples of the different blur levels we selected for our tests.

We also ran an exploratory test of a second obfuscation method that exposed only a partial window of the video. Coding for some actions requires only a small, non-identifiable portion of the human body to be visible, e.g., coding for smiling requires that the mouth be visible, but the rest of the video could be heavily obfuscated without affecting accuracy. Masking all but a window could allow sensitive areas to be hidden while retaining accurate coding. We tested this for smiling with an un-obfuscated window around the mouth.

Testing the Visual Identifiably of Participants

To measure how well workers could visually identify the participant used on our videos, we selected 5 images of different people with similar appearances. The image of the participant was chosen to be a clear, direct image, but not one directly from the video workers watched – this prevents higher-level information such as clothing color or type from biasing worker's ability to recognize the participant. Our lineup task interface is shown in Figure 4.

After each worker has finished coding a video segment, they are forwarded to a line-up tool (Figure 4) that asks them to identify the person they saw in the video from a set 6 randomly ordered images. This is similar to common police lineups used to let witnesses fairly identify potential suspects.

For most tests, we did not give workers any warning or indication that they would be completing the lineup task after coding a video. However, since a potentially malicious worker might have the intention of remembering who they saw in the video, we also ran a smaller test to determine whether accuracy increases when workers were warned that they would be completing the lineup tool.

Results

Over all 5 of our coded behaviors, we found that there was a clear linear decreasing trend in both the precision (R^2 = 0.84) and recall (R^2 = 0.90), as blur level increased (Figure 5). However, each separate behavior we asked the crowd to code had a distinct trade-off pattern.

Figure 6 shows the accuracy curve for our 'eye contact' action, which was the *most* affected by increased blur, decreasing from 89.4% precision (SD=5.61) and 78.4% (SD=10.6) recall to 8.9% (SD=21.7) precision and 0.6% (SD=1.5) recall. Figure 7 shows the accuracy curve for our 'face touch' action, which was the *least* affected by increased blur, going from 89.5% (SD=9.1) precision and 87.7% (SD=12.2) recall to 77.2% (SD=38.3) precision and 91.1% (SD=12.8) recall. Figure 8 shows the accuracy curves for the remaining 3 behaviors we coded.

These accuracy results demonstrate two intuitive but important points: coding accuracy is affected by privacy filtering, and the type of behaviors being coded for impact the size of this effect. Our next goal is to see how workers' ability to identify participants in the video is impacted as the privacy filter is applied at different levels.

The number of workers who are able to identify our participant from a lineup containing theirs and other images quickly falls from 90.9% with no blur applied, to just 31.3% when even a light blur filter is applied, down to near zero recall for higher levels of blur (Figure 9). Note that over many examples, we don't necessarily expect high-blur cases to converge to the rate of random selection (16.7%) because they are able to tell us that they are not sure they recognize the participant in any of the images. Interestingly, we saw almost no fluctuation in the number of false positives (incorrect identifications) marked by workers (2 or 3 in our experiments).

To test whether allowing the worker to know they were going to be asked to identify the participant after their task posed an issue, we ran 2 additional tests which alerted workers that they would be asked to spot the worker from a lineup after their coding task. This is an important effect to measure because malicious workers in future tasks will likely know in advance that they plan to steal the information [19]. We tested this at the two extremes of our prior data to check for any detectable effect: blur level 3, and no blur (level 10). We found the recall rate 85.7% for no blur, and 7.7% for level 3 blur – both of these values are nearly identical to the un-alerted cases. This suggests that preparation is not what is preventing workers from accessing and recalling this information later.

Privacy Discussion

The results from our unfiltered baseline trials closely match the accuracy levels found in [16], where the researchers selected their own set of example videos. This provides additional confirmation that our setup matched the relevant prior work. For effective privacy preservation in a task where we

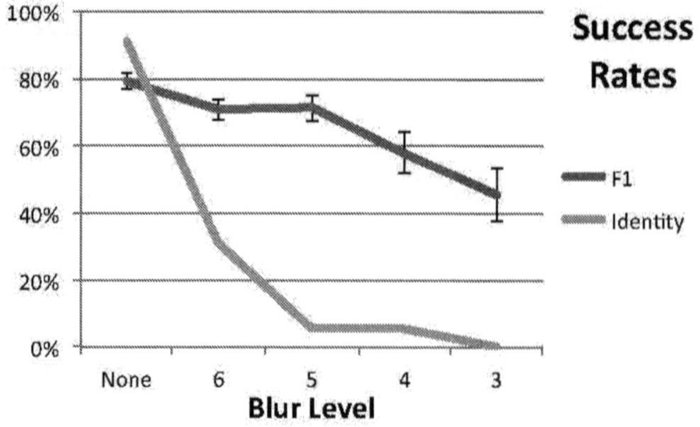

Figure 9: The output of Incognito. The green line (bottom) shows the identity recall rates as the blur level is increased. The purple line (top) shows the average F1 score of the coding results generated by the crowd. Using this, researchers can find the setting-specific optimal trade-off point between privacy protection and coding accuracy for their data.

still want to collect data, the most important aspect of this data is that the decay rates between the identity recall rates and behavioral coding quality over blur level is not one-to-one. Instead, personally identifiable information is easier to obscure with a simple filter than the behavioral information being coded.

Figure 9 shows both the identity recognition rates, as well as the overall F1 scores[2] of the behavioral coding results. The gap between video coding accuracy and identity recognition accuracy widens as the blur becomes greater. This shows that while it is possible to code for types of actions for which precise vision isn't necessary, identity recognition from a blurry video becomes impossible.

INCOGNITO

Our work aims to demonstrate the viability of crowd-powered video coding in realistic use cases. While we exemplify this with a set of common use-cases, we are interested in making it possible for researchers to guarantee their participant pool that their data will be handled in way that will respect their privacy, even if crowd-based video coding approaches are used, in the specific setting of the research project.

To let researchers explore how privacy may be protected in their specific use cases, we created Incognito. Incognito allows researchers to record example videos of behaviors they would like to code, and then test what level of privacy protection filters are sufficient for their use case and what impact it will have on the accuracy of the crowd-generated coding results. The initial participants used for this calibration can be drawn from a smaller pool of participants willing to share potentially identifiable information, or can be drawn from the researchers themselves.

[2] An F1 score is a commonly used measure that combines both precision and recall into one value. We use it here because it makes it easier to see the trade-off between the two response rate values.

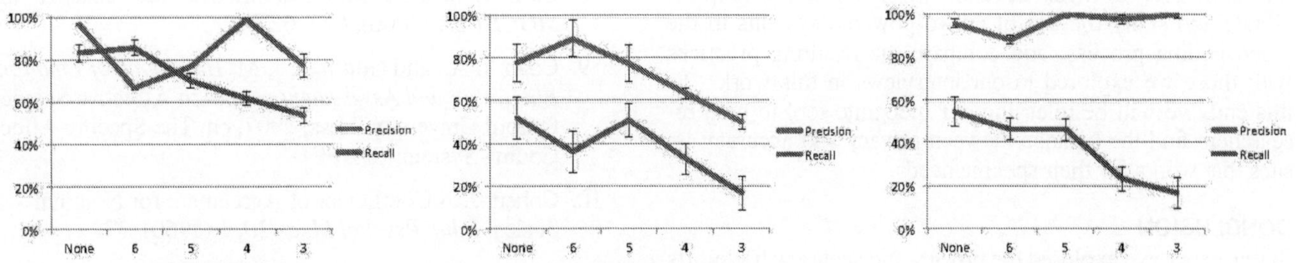

(a) Open Body (b) Head Turn (c) Smile

Figure 8: Results from the other three videos in our experiments over increasing blur level, with standard error bars shown. In (c) we see the the results from coding `Smile` differ from the others: while recall falls with high blur levels, precision remains high. This suggests that the types of instances of smiling that are being obscured by blur are limited to a subtle subset, where more obvious examples, *e.g.*, when a wide smile shown teeth, are still discernible by crowd workers.

Usage

To use Incognito, a researcher first provides a set of example videos that show the events and behaviors they wish to code. Incognito then applies a video filter, and then uses our worker interface (Figure 1) to test the crowd's ability to find each event using the filter. Crowd workers can mark one or more segment of the video as containing a specified action, and submit their task when they have finished.

If the filter used can be applied in multiple ways or at multiple intensity levels (such as level of blurring, or mask padding), Incognito can measure the effect of each level and provide researchers with a trade-off curve in terms of precision and recall rate (or F1 score, as shown in Figure 9) over filter level. To ensure that the results are not biased by workers seeing the same content form a prior example (especially important since Incognito will typically operate on a small set of preliminary data), the system recruits a distinct group of workers for each trial it runs.

Reducing Identity Recollection

After each worker has finished coding a video segment, they are then forwarded to the line-up tool (Figure 4), just as in our study. The set of images use in the lineup must be provided by the researcher and should contain roughly 3-6 non-participant images, and then 1 image of the participant that is not directly drawn from the video that workers will see.

Based on the overall identification rate, Incognito can determine if privacy will be sufficiently preserved (based on a specified privacy requirement) at a given level, or that more levels need to be run. Alternatively, the determination will be left to researchers, in which case the final information on event versus identification recall rate and accuracy are provided to researchers to inform their decision (Figure 9). This information can help researchers determine how to discuss privacy issues with their review board and participants.

Analyzing Results

To read the output of Incognito, researchers can find the maximum level of potential privacy risk they are willing to accept *e.g. to satisfy the requirement "no more than 5% of workers should be able to identify any of the participants from video."* on the X-axis, then check the accuracy results on the Y-axis to see if the crowd can perform well enough to produce usable output for the type of video data the researcher intends to code. For example, in Figure 9, blur level 4 would prevent all but around 5% of workers from being able to identify participants, but it will not work if the researcher had to catch at least 2/3rds of all instances of the behavior in question – in that case they could only use level 5 or higher. However, from the results, they would also know that the change from blur level 4 to blur level 5 only results in an additional 0.22% of workers being able to identify participants in the study. In exchange, overall coding accuracy (in terms of F1 score) jumps 13.2%, from 58.0% to 71.2%. Thus, in this case, the minor decrease in privacy level is probably worth the increase in speed and accuracy.

FUTURE WORK

In the future, our results motivate a wide range of work related to how crowdsourcing approaches can be used in real behavioral data analysis settings.

Other Approaches to Filtering Information

As we discussed in the Related Work section, there are many ways to obfuscate video content. While we studied blurring because it is general purpose, easy to implement, and easy to replicate in future studies, we are also interested in the effects other filters have.

For example, we also collected data using a masking filter that completely hid all but a given section of the video a researcher believes they need for their event. We masked all but the participant's mouth to code for `Smile` events in the data, achieving 73.2% precision and 50.3% recall. While these results are lower than the ones we saw when using the blur filter, it speaks to the importance of visual context for workers. Future work will investigate factors such as this, which remain to be fully explored in the context of crowd-powered behavioral video coding.

Real-World Usage Studies

Our results suggest that participant privacy can be preserved well enough to begin considering crowd-powered approaches for use in real settings. In future work, we aim to help facilitate and study the use of crowd-powered systems in the video coding process, and compare the resulting practices with those we explored in our interviews in this work. To this end, we will be releasing our Incognito tool to help researchers find the balance between privacy and accuracy issues that works for their specific needs.

CONCLUSION

In this paper, we explored the privacy and accuracy trade-offs in crowdsourced behavioral coding of video. Through interviews with 12 researchers experienced in coding behaviors, we identified many common themes and types of behaviors that are coded for across different settings and tasks. We also found that the primary concerns researchers had with crowd-powered approaches to video coding were the response quality and protecting the privacy of participants. To investigate these issues, we ran experiments with 636 crowd workers recruited from Mechanical Turk. Our first experiment demonstrated that the crowd is able to answer the 5 most common types of behaviors that are coded with nearly 90% accuracy. We then discussed methods for protecting participant privacy in video, and ran a set of experiments to show the trade-off that occurs when video quality is degraded to help prevent workers from being able to identify participants. Our results show that for many types of behaviors there are opportunities to protect participants identity almost entirely, while still being able to get highly accurate answers from the crowd. Finally, we introduced Incognito to let researchers explore trade-offs between accuracy and privacy in their own data.

ACKNOWLEDGEMENTS

This work was supported by National Science Foundation awards #IIS-1217929, #IIS-1149709, #IIS-1208382, #IIS-1217096, Google, an Alfred P. Sloan Foundation Fellowship, and a Microsoft Research Ph.D. Fellowship

REFERENCES

1. Datavyu. http://datavyu.org/.
2. Bakeman, R., and Gottman, J. M. *Observing interaction: An introduction to sequential analysis.* Cambridge University Press, 1986.
3. Bernstein, M. S., Little, G., Miller, R. C., Hartmann, B., Ackerman, M. S., Karger, D. R., Crowell, D., and Panovich, K. Soylent: a word processor with a crowd inside. In *UIST* (2010), 313–322.
4. Bigham, J. P., Jayant, C., Ji, H., Little, G., Miller, A., Miller, R. C., Miller, R., Tatarowicz, A., White, B., White, S., and Yeh, T. Vizwiz: nearly real-time answers to visual questions. In *UIST* (2010), 333–342.
5. Borsboom, B. Guess who?: A game to crowdsource the labeling of affective facial expressions is comparable to expert ratings, 2012.
6. Boyle, M., Edwards, C., and Greenberg, S. The effects of filtered video on awareness and privacy. In *CSCW* (2000), 1–10.
7. Bruce, V. Fleeting images of shade: Identifying people caught on camera. *The Psychologist* (1998), 331–338.
8. Burr, B. Vaca: A tool for qualitative video analysis. In *SIGCHI EA* (2006), 622–627.
9. Coan, J. A., and Gottman, J. M. *Handbook of Emotion Elicitation and Assessment.* Series in Affective Science. Oxford University Press, 2007, ch. The Specific Affect Coding System (SPAFF).
10. Cohen, J. A Coefficient of Agreement for Nominal Scales. *Educ Psychol Meas 20*, 1 (1960), 37.
11. Di Salvo, R., Giordano, D., and Kavasidis, I. A crowdsourcing approach to support video annotation. In *VIGTA* (2013), 8:1–8:6.
12. Hagedorn, J., Hailpern, J., and Karahalios, K. G. Vcode and vdata: Illustrating a new framework for supporting the video annotation workflow. In *AVI* (2008), 317–321.
13. Henderson, Z., Bruce, V., and Burton, A. M. Matching the faces of robbers captured in video. *Applied Cognitive Psychology* (2001), 445–464.
14. Heyman, R. E., Lorber, M. F., Eddy, J. M., West, T., Reis, E. H. T., and Judd, C. M. *Handbook of Research Methods in Social and Personality Psychology.* Cambridge University Press, 2014, ch. Behavioral observation and coding.
15. Kipp, M. ANVIL- a generic annotation tool for multimodal dialogue. *Eurospeech* (2001), 1367–1370.
16. Lasecki, W. S., Gordon, M., Koutra, D., Jung, M. F., Dow, S. P., and Bigham, J. P. Glance: Rapidly coding behavioral video with the crowd. In *UIST* (2014).
17. Lasecki, W. S., Murray, K. I., White, S., Miller, R. C., and Bigham, J. P. Real-time crowd control of existing interfaces. In *UIST* (2011), 23–32.
18. Lasecki, W. S., Song, Y. C., Kautz, H., and Bigham, J. P. Real-time crowd labeling for deployable activity recognition. In *CSCW* (2013).
19. Lasecki, W. S., Teevan, J., and Kamar, E. Information extraction and manipulation threats in crowd-powered systems. In *CSCW* (2014).
20. Lasecki, W. S., Weingard, L., Ferguson, G., and Bigham, J. P. Finding dependencies between actions using the crowd. In *SIGCHI* (2014), 3095–3098.
21. Neustaedter, C., and Greenberg, S. Balancing privacy and awareness in home media spaces. In *UBICOMP* (2003).
22. Police Chiefs Association of Santa Clara County. Line-up protocol for law enforcement.
23. Riek, L. D., O'Connor, M. F., and Robinson, P. Guess what? a game for affective annotation of video using crowd sourcing. In *ACII* (2011), 277–285.
24. Vondrick, C., Patterson, D., and Ramanan, D. Efficiently scaling up crowdsourced video annotation. *Int J of Comput Vision* (2012), 1–21.
25. Weingart, L. R., Olekalns, M., and Smith, P. L. Quantitative coding of negotiation behavior. *Int Negotiation 3*, 9 (2005), 441–456.

Crowdsourcing Stereotypes: Linguistic Bias in Metadata Generated via GWAP

Jahna Otterbacher
Graduate Program in Social Information Systems
Open University of Cyprus
jahna.otterbacher@ouc.ac.cy

ABSTRACT
Games with a Purpose (GWAP) is a popular approach for metadata creation, enabling institutions to collect descriptions of digital artifacts on a mass scale. Creating metadata is challenging not only because one must recognize the artifact; the description must then be encoded into natural language. Language behaviors are influenced by many social factors, particularly when we are asked to describe other people. We consider labels for images of people generated via the ESP Game. While ESP has been shown to produce relevant labels, critics claim they are obvious and stereotypical. Based on theories of *linguistic biases*, we examine whether there are systematic differences in the ways players describe images of men versus women. Our first analysis considers images of people generally, and reveals a tendency for women to be described with subjective adjectives. A second analysis compares images depicting men and women within each of six occupational roles. Images of women receive more labels related to appearance, whereas those depicting men receive more occupation-related labels. Our work exposes the presence of gender-based stereotypes through linguistic biases, illustrates the forms in which they manifest, and raises important implications for those who design systems or train algorithms using data produced via GWAP.

Author Keywords
Crowdsourcing; Games with a Purpose; gender; linguistic bias; metadata; stereotypes; subjective language

ACM Classification Keywords
I.2.6. [Learning]: Knowledge acquisition. H.5.2. [User Interfaces]: Natural language.

Stereotypes, they're sensual, cultural weapons. That's the way that we attack people. At an artistic level, stereotypes are terrible writing. –*Junot Diaz*

INTRODUCTION
Crowdsourcing systems enlist human intelligence and perceptual capabilities in solving problems that cannot be fully automated [10]. *Games with a Purpose* (GWAP) has become a well-established approach in crowdsourcing, enticing people to participate by making tasks fun. GWAP is being used to solve large-scale computational problems, from translating texts into one language from another, to detecting suspicious activities recorded on security cameras [35]. At the same time, manually labeled datasets collected via GWAP provide crucial resources for the machine learning of such complex human judgments.

The creation of multimedia metadata is a task for which GWAP is a natural choice. As digital repositories grow in size and number, so does the need for quality metadata to facilitate resource discovery [25]. Several popular GWAP have been developed for multimedia annotation tasks (e.g., the ESP Game [36], the Metadata Games suite[1]), attesting to the potential of GWAP to meet the increasing needs for metadata. In recent years, GWAP is being rapidly adopted in the cultural heritage domain [24], enabling institutions such as libraries, archives and museums to harness the public's knowledge of their growing collections of digital images and artifacts. Thus, not surprisingly, researchers have raised the question of the quality and utility of metadata resulting from GWAP (e.g., [17, 34]).

While there are no universal guidelines for measuring metadata quality, the criteria most often mentioned in the literature are *accuracy, completeness* and *consistency* [25]. It is generally agreed that human performance on metadata generation tasks is still superior to that of machines [21]. But are humans accurate, complete and consist when describing multimedia? Are we objective when describing multimedia artifacts in which other people are represented, such as digital photographs? In such cases, we might wonder if social stereotypes are triggered and if so, how often they are reflected in descriptive metadata.

In the current work, we consider the possibility that social stereotypes are conveyed through systematic differences in the labels chosen to describe digital images of people. As will be explained, we study the labels generated via the ESP Game, the first and arguably most influential GWAP system for crowdsourcing image metadata creation. The task of metadata generation is fundamentally a communication process. Images embody rich but implicit

CHI 2015, April 18 - 23 2015, Seoul, Republic of Korea .

ACM 978-1-4503-3145-6/15/04...$15.00.
http://dx.doi.org/10.1145/2702123.2702151

[1] http://www.metadatagames.org

information about the subject(s) they depict. The task of the annotator is to make this implicit information explicit, through the choice of natural language tags, a set of words that describe the image. The goal of a GWAP then, is to provide the context and motivation for players (i.e., annotators) to complete this task. While much research on GWAP considers how tasks are gamified, and the incentives that are provided to the players [19,29], the current work sheds light on a challenge for GWAP that has not yet been discussed in the literature: the possibility for *linguistic biases* to appear in the data produced.

Language, Stereotypes and Image Labeling

In our interactions, we often craft messages carefully in order to have a desired interpretation, or to make a positive impression. However, the words we choose to express ourselves reveal a great deal of information that we may not intend to communicate, such as our emotional state, to which social group(s) we belong, and our relationships to others [32]. Of particular relevance to the current work is the tendency to inadvertently choose words that reveal *stereotypes* and prejudices toward particular social groups.

Stereotypes are the perceptions and beliefs that we hold about groups of people. While the term often evokes a negative connotation, it is important to note that from the perspective of social psychology, stereotypes serve at least three useful functions [23]. First, they can be viewed as cognitive devices aiding explanation, allowing us to categorize similarities and differences between ourselves and others. Secondly, stereotypes are heuristics; they save us time and effort. If we know that someone belongs to a particular social group, we can infer additional information about her. Finally, stereotypes are shared beliefs that promote cohesion within a given group. Through the cultivation of a stereotype, members within the group become more similar to one another, while differentiating themselves from other groups.

In short, we all hold social expectations of other people, and it is natural for us to express them. Despite this, stereotypes can also serve as "guides to misunderstanding," if they lead us to attend to particular characteristics or information while filtering out other details [23]. For example, we might assume that an attractive, blond woman is unintelligent based on her looks alone, without considering other aspects of her behavior and personality. Although we do not yet fully understand the extent to which the application of stereotypes in our social behaviors is under conscious control [18], it does appear that it is somewhat context-dependent [31,33]. In particular, people may be more likely to invoke stereotypes when engaging with an interlocutor, when their behavior has a communicative purpose [22].

The question at hand then, is to what extent social stereotypes make their way into the metadata generated for images of people. The use of natural language labels that maintain stereotypes potentially negatively impacts the *accuracy* dimension of metadata quality. Accuracy implies the correct "description and representation of data and resource content" [25]. Since stereotypes are not shared universally, stereotypical descriptions might not be the most accurate. Therefore, extensive use of stereotypes in image labels might lead to future problems in accessing the image in a database or via a Web search engine.

Furthermore, there are social consequences that should be considered. If stereotypes are embedded in a technology, they may be perpetuated in society [37]. For instance, when searching the Web for images of "doctor," users could be presented, via a search engine, with images of men, whereas in a search for "nurse" they are presented with those depicting women. With repeated occurrences, this could affect how young girls view their future career prospects, and more generally, what is expected of their gender. Baker and Potts [1] note that while we should be careful in making generalizations about the effects that such embedded stereotypes have on the users of a given technology, we should certainly be concerned about the fact that few technologies offer a means to voice objections to stereotypes. After searching for images on Google for "doctor," there is no means, such as a flagging mechanism or a rating function, for the user to protest the fact that she is presented with few images of women doctors.

Goals of the Current Work

We investigate whether *gender stereotypes* make their way into labels generated for images via linguistic biases. Since linguistic biases have not been previously explored in the context of crowdsourcing, our goal is to see if they exist, and in which forms. This study lays the necessary groundwork for understanding the relationship between the stimulus (i.e., image), social cues (i.e., how the task is gamified) and the quality of the resulting metadata.

Although no longer active, the ESP Game project has had, and continues to have, a tremendous impact on GWAP research. In addition, its inventors have released a dataset of images and labels. Thus, it provides an appropriate setting for studying the transmission of stereotypes through linguistic biases in image labels. Therefore, we address the following research questions:

- How often do we observe the use of abstract or subjective language in the labels assigned to images?
- Do we observe linguistic biases? Are images of men and women systematically described in a more/less abstract or subjective manner?

RELATED WORK

In this section, we describe the ESP Game in more detail. We then review literature on the expression of stereotypes through linguistic biases. This serves to ground our approach to identifying abstract and subjective language in the labels assigned to images of women and men.

The ESP Game

The ESP Game was designed to accomplish the task of labeling images collected on the Web [36]. Randomly assigned pairs of players are shown a series of images, and must agree on as many descriptive labels as possible in 2.5 minutes. During each round, players are shown an image, and are asked to "think like each other," providing their best guess as to what their partner will type. Partners earn points whenever they agree on a word that describes the image, receiving a bonus if and when they have reached agreement on 15 images. In order to incentivize players to venture beyond extremely general terms (e.g., man), the game eventually lists taboo words that players may not use.

Despite that players are not explicitly asked to provide accurate descriptions of images, and that their motivation is to have fun rather than to help solve a problem, ESP's inventors have demonstrated that the resulting labels are useful and relevant [36]. In order to ensure quality, a label should be agreed upon by a minimum number of partners before the word is associated with the image. The inventors also claim that since many players see and describe the same image, ESP labels are often better than those resulting from the work of an individual annotator.

As mentioned, ESP has had tremendous influence on the development of GWAP and human computation, and has been discussed and critiqued extensively in the literature. Perhaps its most frequently discussed criticism is its tendency to produce obvious labels. Robertson and colleagues showed that given the first label for an image, a statistical language model could assign additional, appropriate labels for the majority of images [29]. In other words, data of comparable quality could be generated with little human effort and no access to the image. Likewise, Ho and colleagues [19] noted the lack of diversity in labels. They argued in favor of adding a competitive element. A third player was introduced, who had the goal of preventing the partners from agreeing. This pushed players to generate less obvious labels. Both studies clearly claim that a more diverse set of labels is necessary for effective image retrieval; however, neither mentions the potential impact of social stereotypes in labeling.

Social Stereotypes and Linguistic Biases

Psychologists and communication scientists have become increasingly convinced that the manner in which we use language plays a key role in the transmission and maintenance of social stereotypes [22,30]. This happens via subtle cues that can go unnoticed. While people typically refrain from using derogatory language concerning a given group (e.g., blatantly sexist terms or racial slurs), their *linguistic biases* often give away the stereotypes that influence them. Linguistic bias can be defined as a systematic asymmetry in the way that one uses language, as a function of the social group of the person(s) being described [3]. We consider two linguistic patterns that may reveal social expectations: the use of abstract versus concrete language, and the use of subjective words.

Abstract versus concrete language

When describing people and their behaviors, the use of more abstract versus concrete language conveys information about social expectations. The more expectancy-incongruent a person and her behavior appears to us, the more likely we are to describe the person with more concrete language, without extrapolating beyond the particular context [22]. In contrast, the more comfortable we are with the person, in the sense that she does not violate our expectations, the more likely we are to use more abstract language, making causal inferences about her identity, disposition or behaviors [13]. The origin of this bias is believed to be cognitive; prototypes or stereotypical scenes are simply easier for humans to process [40].

For instance, when presented with an image of an individual dressed in white holding a syringe, an annotator might choose a verb (e.g., inject), a noun (e.g., doctor) or an adjective (e.g., caring) as labels. "Inject" simply describes the concrete behavior observed at a point in time. However, "doctor" indicates that the annotator has made an inference as to the subject's occupation and who she is. Even further abstract is the description of "caring," as here, the annotator ventures to say something about the subject's disposition.

We consider the proportion of labels assigned to an image that are *adjectives,* which are indicative of a relatively more abstract description. Linguists have long discussed the possibility that a word's part-of-speech is intricately linked to underlying cognitive functions, and may even affect how a speaker or listener views a situation or person [6]. As compared to verbs, labels that are adjectives or nouns may suggest that the annotator is making inferences about a person – who she is or her disposition – rather than simply describing concrete, observed behaviors. It can also be noted that in many seminal works on stereotypes (e.g., [9]), participants are asked to describe what they perceive as the key attributes of a given social group using adjectives.

In contrast to previous studies, in which manual analyses gauged the extent to which language used to describe people was abstract [13], we consider the proportion of adjectives in a given image's labels. As will be explained in the methodology, our part-of-speech tagger can disambiguate adjectives from other words with a high degree of accuracy, even when taken out of context (i.e., tagging isolated word-labels). While this is a somewhat crude approach to measuring abstraction, by automating the process, we are able to study the systematic differences in the choices of labels in a large corpus of images. It will tell us how often ESP players describe *how someone is* (adjective) versus *what someone is doing* (verb) in an image, or *what or who the subject is* (noun).

Subjective words

The use of subjective words (e.g., beautiful, nice, ugly, bad) is a means through which we convey beliefs or opinions about a person. In recent years there has been much interest in the automatic detection of sentiment, or polarity, of words. The technology has many practical applications; for instance, the use of subjective adjectives in texts has been shown to provide salient clues as to the overall sentiment of the text [28]. As will be explained, we use the Subjectivity Lexicon [39] to identify words in labels that are subjective, and whether they carry positive or negative sentiment.

METHODOLOGY

Dataset

We obtained the "Small ESP Game Dataset,"[2] which contains labels assigned to 100,000 images. To identify which images depict people, we ran the labels through the Linguistic Inquiry and Word Count (LIWC) software [26]. We relied on the LIWC scores on the attributes "humans," "friends," and "family" (subcategories of LIWC's social psychological processes), finding the subset of images for which the labels contained words in any of these categories. This process resulted in a set of 46,392 images of people.

Next, we used WordNet[3] [12] to obtain the hyponyms for the words "man" and "male," and "woman" and "female," respectively. We then searched the people images to identify those for which the labels contained words referring to "man/male" but not words for "woman/female," and vice versa. This process resulted in 18,916 images depicting one or more men, and 14,628 images depicting one or more women. We did not consider images that feature both men and women.

Pre-processing of Labels

Part-of-speech (POS) tagging

Labels were run through the CLAWS POS tagger [16]. The C5 tagset[4] was requested, which was used to tag Version 2 of the British National Corpus (BNC). While this is the smaller of the two available tagsets, our analysis does not rely on the more fine-grained categories. Rather, we identified labels that are adjectives, nouns or verbs, of any subcategory. In particular, we considered all three subcategories of adjectives (unmarked, comparative and superlative), all four subcategories of nouns (those neutral for number, singular, plural and proper nouns), and all 25 subcategories of verbs (all tenses, aspects and modalities).

Since the validity of our findings hinges on the performance of the POS tagger, we performed a spot check to interpret its accuracy in tagging labels. A judge was given 100 randomly selected images from the dataset, and was asked to identify all adjectives, nouns and verbs in the images' labels. The manually annotated data was compared against the automatically produced POS tags, resulting in an overall error rate of 3.22%. In comparison, the reported error rate when tagging words in full texts on the BNC[5] is 1.15%.

The automatic identification of adjectives is of particular importance, since they are used in more abstract descriptions of people [3]. The error analysis revealed that adjectives can be distinguished from other POS in the labels quite accurately (error rate of 1.45%; recall of 1; precision of 0.985). This performance does not differ significantly from that on full texts (error rate of 1.35% on the BNC). That which troubles the tagger is disambiguating verbs from nouns (e.g., smile, laugh, frown). Indeed, without additional information, one cannot know what the annotator intended. Our observed error rate on tagging nouns in the image labels is 1.47% and on verbs is 32.1%. However, even on full texts, verbs are difficult to tag accurately (15% error rate on the BNC). Given the performance of the POS tagger, our analysis focuses on the proportion of descriptive labels that are adjectives.

Identification of subjective words

We used Wilson, Wiebe and Hoffman's [39] Subjectivity Lexicon to identify labels that convey sentiment. This resource is a list of over 8,000 English words. Each word is associated with a *type* (strongly or weakly subjective), its POS, and its *prior polarity*. Words with weak subjectivity convey sentiment in certain, but not all, contexts, while strong subjective words most always convey sentiment. A word's prior polarity refers to whether it evokes positive or negative sentiment, regardless of context. It should be noted that some words in the lexicon are associated with both or neutral polarity. We have not considered such words; since we are analyzing labels rather than full texts, we found it prudent to focus on the clearest signals of subjectivity and polarity. Examples of are shown in Figure 1.

		Type	
		Strong	**Weak**
Prior Polarity	**Positive**	Happy	Light
	Negative	Ugly	Fat

Figure 1: Examples of subjective adjectives.

Analysis 1

Our first analysis examines how language used to describe images of people differs by gender. Here, we consider the general trends in language use, by comparing the following characteristics of labels between the set of 18,916 images of men and the set of 14,628 images of women:

- The proportion of assigned labels that are *adjectives*.

[2] http://www.cs.cmu.edu/~biglou/resources/

[3] http://wordnetweb.princeton.edu/perl/webwn

[4] http://ucrel.lancs.ac.uk/claws5tags.html

[5] http://ucrel.lancs.ac.uk/bnc2/bnc2error.htm

- The proportion of adjective labels that are *strongly subjective.*
- The proportion of subjective adjective labels that have *positive/negative prior polarity.*
- The most frequent strongly subjective adjectives.

Categorizing people, or images of people, by perceived social attributes is often messy, and can result in the "torquing" of one's identity [4] (p. 223). Recognizing the complicated relationship between sex, gender and the concepts of masculinity and femininity [2], we further separated the images of people by perceived sexual orientation. Specifically, we identified the subset of images with one or more of the following labels: gay, homosexual, lesbian. This resulted in four sets of images, based on ESP players' perceptions of the subjects' genders and sexual orientations, and the above comparisons were made between the four groups. We were not able to explore the labels used to describe images of people of additional genders / sexual orientations as they did not appear with adequate frequencies in the dataset. Appropriate statistical tests were used to detect linguistic biases (two-sample t test for comparisons between two groups; ANOVA followed by Tukey HSD [20] for comparisons between the four groups).

Analysis 2

Analysis 1 demonstrated that gender is strongly correlated to linguistic bias in the ESP game, when we consider all images in the dataset. However, the kinds of images posted to the Web of men and women are likely to differ (i.e., they are depicted in different contexts, such that we expect differences in their descriptions). Therefore, the second analysis takes a closer look at the language used to describe men and women in more specific, comparable contexts. In particular, we compare the labels of images that have been associated with six occupations, as detailed in Table 1.

Occupation label(s)	Men	Women
Athlete	70	11
Doctor	80	40
Singer	555	404
Soldier / Army	245	8
Teacher	29	26
Waiter / waitress	10	10

Table 1: Number of images with occupation labels.

Our intent was to include occupations for which there are gender stereotypes in many cultures. For instance, when someone mentions a doctor or a teacher, in the absence of additional information, we likely assume that the person being described is a man / woman, respectively. As can be seen, for many occupations there are few images in the data that depict women. We considered only occupations for which there were at least eight relevant images.

To examine what ESP players attended to when describing images of people of the six occupations, we carried out a manual analysis. The author served as the first judge, while master-level Mechanical Turkers[6] provided a second judgment on each label-occupation pair. For each pair, judges answered the following yes/no questions:

- Could this word be used to describe the physical appearance of [an athlete]?
- Could this word describe the disposition or character of [an athlete]?
- Does this word describe something about the occupation of [athlete]?

To assess the level of interjudge agreement, Cohen's Kappa [7] was computed over all labels. There was a high level of agreement on the labels related to physical appearance and disposition (κ = 0.69 and 0.78). For occupation labels, agreement was lower, but still better than chance (κ = 0.38). The major discrepancy between Judge 1's labels and those of the Turkers was that Turkers included the names of celebrities as being occupation-related terms (e.g., Britney Spears for singer, Venus Williams for athlete), while Judge 1 did not. Having established the robustness of the task, annotations provided by Judge 1 were used in the analysis.

RESULTS: ANALYSIS 1

We observe systematic asymmetries in label choices as a function of the gender of the person(s) depicted in images. As shown in Table 2, ESP players assign nearly the same number of labels to images of men and women. While the effect size is modest (as gauged by Cohen's *d* [8]), there is evidence that images of women are more likely to be labeled with adjectives as compared to men.

Table 3 demonstrates a striking difference in the use of *subjective words* to describe images of women versus men. When we consider the proportion of labels that are *strong* clues of subjectivity according to the Subjectivity Lexicon, we observe that the proportion of subjective labels used to describe women is nearly double that of men. Of these strong subjective labels, we considered the proportion that has positive prior polarity. Table 4 demonstrates significant

	Men	Women	t	p-value	d
Labels	14.99	14.83	3.195	.0014	0.036
Adj	0.1754	0.2026	23.32	<.001	0.261

Table 2: Total # of labels; prop. of labels that are adjectives.

	Men	Women	t	p-value	d
Adj	0.03650	0.08609	28.96	<.001	0.324

Table 3: Proportion of labels that are strongly subjective.

[6] http://www.mturk.com

	Men	Women	t	p-value	d
Adj	0.4539	0.8165	27.32	<.001	0.350

Table 4: Strongly subjective labels with positive polarity.

Rank	Men	Women
1	Happy (385)	Sexy (2,425)
2	Ugly (225)	Happy (549)
3	Sad (201)	Ugly (254)
4	Angry (132)	Sad (241)
5	Drunk (124)	Cute (117)
6	Scary (107)	Beautiful (84)
7	Funny (103)	Fun (67)
8	Cute (88)	Drunk (58)
9	Mad (74)	Scary (51)
10	Fun (63)	Little (40)

Table 5: Most frequent, strongly subjective adjectives.

differences by gender; the majority of subjective adjectives used to label images of women is positive, while less than half of the adjectives describing images of men is positive.

Finally, we considered the most frequent, strongly subjective adjectives (Table 5). It is interesting to note that all describe either physical appearance (e.g., sexy, ugly, cute) or disposition or character (e.g., angry, happy, fun). Of the top 10 subjective adjectives for men, only two describe appearance, while for women half describe appearance. In fact, 2,425 images of women (16.6%) were associated with the most frequent, subjective label of "sexy." In comparison, "sexy" was used to describe only 20 images (0.1%) depicting men in the dataset.

In summary, labels used to describe images of women contain strongly subjective adjectives, more so than those associated with images of men. In addition, ESP players often describe women's physical appearances. Even without reviewing the images that were shown to players, it is clear that players often use subjective language that expresses their opinions, particularly of a woman's looks.

Label Choice, Gender and Sexual Orientation

When considering the perceived sexual orientation of people depicted in images (i.e., whether or not ESP players associated the image with the labels "gay," "lesbian" or "homosexual"), we observe that the effect of sexual orientation on the use of subjective adjectives is not as strong as that of gender. As shown in Table 6, images of gay men and women tend to be assigned 1.5 to 2 more labels as compared to images that do not depict gay men and women. In addition, the images of gay men and women are likely to have a greater proportion of labels that are adjectives. ESP players are more likely to describe *how* someone is, if they believe he or she is gay.

Considering the effect of sexual orientation on the proportion of adjective labels that is strongly subjective (Table 7), the main effect is not significant. Regarding the proportion of strongly subjective labels that has positive polarity (Table 8), the ANOVA reveals a significant negative effect for sexual orientation. However, Tukey HSD reveals no differences between the two groups of women, nor between the gay women and either group of men. Rather, images of women who are not perceived as gay are labeled with more positive adjectives as compared to men generally. Thus, we again observe the association between gender and the use of positive adjectives. In all ANOVAs, the effect of gender on the choice of words used to describe images is highly significant.

Table 9 presents a qualitative comparison of the strongly subjective adjectives that are most frequently used to describe each of the four social groups. Here, there is an interesting trend. Half of the subjective adjectives used to

	Men		Women		ANOVA F			p-value			d
	Not Gay	Gay	Not Gay	Gay	SO	Gender	SO*G	SO	Gender	SO*G	
Labels	14.96	17.41	14.82	16.98	73.4	7.7	0.15	<.001	<.01	0.70	0.529
Adj	0.1749	0.2186	0.2025	0.2413	29.7	564.8	0.081	<.001	<.001	0.777	0.385

Table 6: Labels used to describe images of people by sexual orientation (SO) and gender.

	Men		Women		ANOVA F			p-value			d
	Not Gay	Gay	Not Gay	Gay	SO	Gender	SO*G	SO	Gender	SO*G	
Adj	0.0364	0.04484	0.0862	0.0453	2.277	883.9	0.001	0.131	<.001	<.05	NA

Table 7: Proportion of adjective labels that are strongly subjective by sexual orientation (SO) and gender.

	Men		Women		ANOVA F			p-value			d
	Not Gay	Gay	Not Gay	Gay	SO	Gender	SO*G	SO	Gender	SO*G	
Adj	0.4530	0.4853	0.8170	0.7083	7.664	898.3	0.731	.0057	<.001	0.392	-.427

Table 8: Proportion of strongly subjective adjective labels that carry positive polarity, by sexual orientation (SO) and gender.

Rank	Men		Women	
	Not	Gay	Not	Gay
1	Happy	Drunk	Sexy	Happy
2	Ugly	Happy	Happy	Sexy
3	Sad	Ugly	Ugly	Drunk
4	Angry	Cute	Cute	Sad
5	Drunk	Fun	Beautiful	Funny
6	Scary	Weird	Fun	Fun
7	Funny	Tired	Drunk	
8	Cute	Sexy	Scary	
9	Mad	Scary	Little	
10	Fun	Handsome	Desperate	

Table 9: Strongly subjective adj.: not gay vs. gay.

describe gay men and women who are not gay, are associated with appearance. In addition, 7 of 10 frequent adjectives for these groups are the same. However, the most frequent subjective adjectives used to describe gay women and men who are not gay, primarily refer to an individual's disposition. If we accept that gender stereotypes are both descriptive and prescriptive [11], this suggests similar social expectations of heterosexual women and gay men.

RESULTS: ANALYSIS 2

Analysis 1 revealed a consistent gender effect: ESP players tend to label images of women with strongly subjective labels, which often concern physical appearance. The 46,392 images analyzed were collected from around the Web for use in the ESP Game. Given that images were selected randomly, a wide variety is likely represented. However, perhaps there are salient differences in the types of images featuring men and women shared on the Web (e.g., pictures of physically attractive women but unremarkable men). Analysis 2 was designed to test whether the gender bias discovered in Analysis 1 holds up in more comparable contexts, where a label related to an occupation has been assigned. In addition, it allows us to see if the trends identified by our automated analyses are consistent with the findings of a robust manual analysis.

Labels Describing Physical Appearance

In the annotation task, judges were asked to identify labels that describe subjects' physical appearance. To this end, they included labels indicating body parts, items of clothing, as well as objective (e.g., blond hair) and subjective (e.g., beautiful) observations of ESP players. We expect images depicting women to receive a larger proportion of labels related to appearances. This is true for four occupations (singer, army soldier, teacher, and waiter/waitress), as shown in Table 10, which details the proportion of labels for images of men (top) and women (bottom), p-values for the z-test to compare the two proportions, and Cohen's *d*. For the remaining two occupations (athlete, doctor) images of men actually received a greater proportion of labels related to appearance. Table 11 provides a qualitative comparison of frequently used labels, with strongly subjective words in bold. ESP players do describe men's physical characteristics and the clothing they wear. For images of women, we observe that even for the occupations of athlete and doctor, players assign labels that concern objective observations (e.g., hair color, uniform) as well as those conveying sentiment (e.g., hot, model).

Labels Describing Disposition

Judges were also asked to indicate which labels concern subjects' disposition or character traits. Since such traits are not visible, this indicates cases where ESP players have made inferences about the subject – who or how she is as a

	N	Appearance	p-val	d	Disposition	p-val	d	Occupation	p-val	d
Athlete	1164	0.2784	<.001	-.504	0.005154	NA	NA	0.4003	0.470	NA
	194	0.1340			0.01546			0.4278		
Doctor	1258	0.2599	0.048	-.131	0.01510	0.841	NA	0.2234	0.252	NA
	576	0.2170			0.01389			0.1997		
Singer	8981	0.1819	<.001	0.418	0.007794	0.136	NA	0.3933	<.001	-.478
	6101	0.3219			0.005737			0.2142		
Soldier / Army	4237	0.1343	<.001	0.417	0.008261	0.001	0.787	0.3481	0.0658	NA
	149	0.2483			0.03356			0.2752		
Teacher	508	0.1339	<.001	0.352	0.005906	NA	NA	0.4114	<.001	-.401
	424	0.2264			0.004717			0.2524		
Waiter	204	0.1569	<.001	0.489	0.009804	NA	NA	0.3382	0.0163	-.316
	161	0.3106			0.006211			0.2236		

Table 10: Proportion of labels that concern appearance, disposition and occupation by gender [men / women]

	Men	Women
Athlete	Face, hair, eyes, nose, hand	Legs, **smile**, shoes, model, hair
Doctor	Face, hair, eyes, nose, hand	Hair, hand, face, Asian, blonde
Singer	Hair, face, shirt, hat, nose	Hair, face, blonde, model, **hot**
Soldier / Army	Hat, helmet, old, uniform, face	Hat, face, uniform, **smile**, shirt
Teacher	Hair, suit, hand, shirt, **smile**	Hair, face, shirt, glasses, **smile**
Waiter	**Smile**, face, Asian, tie, shirt	Hair, **smile**, bra, bikini, breasts

Table 11: Most frequent words describing appearance.

	Men	Women
Athlete	Sports, football, game, basketball, soccer	Sport, runner, tennis, running, race
Doctor	Hospital, medicine, stethoscope, medical, scientist	Nurse, hospital, patient, **sick**, medical
Singer	Music, sing, microphone, band, rock	Music, sing, CD, microphone, album
Soldier / Army	**War**, military, gun, helmet, uniform	**War**, police, uniform, military, helmet
Teacher	School, class, students, chalk, teach	School, kids, class, children, room
Waiter	Restaurant, food, eat, dinner, table	Food, tray, plate, table, eat

Table 12: Most frequent words describing occupation.

person. We were curious to see if labels reflect gender-based stereotypes (e.g., women doctors are "caring"; men athletes are "tough"). The only occupation for which we found a greater incidence of labels related to disposition for women is Army soldier. Here, we find labels related to feelings (e.g., sad, happy) as well as national origin (e.g., Korean, Chinese). For men, we find labels related to character and preferences (e.g., tough, gay) as well as national origin. But, overall, such labels are rarely used.

Labels Relating to Occupation

Finally, judges identified labels related to each occupation. The goal was to see if women would be described using less "professional" vocabulary. As observed in Table 12, there is much overlap in occupation-related labels that describe images of men and women. However, we indeed find that men receive greater proportions of such labels for three occupations: singer, teacher and waiter/waitress. These occupations are arguably woman-dominated, with women often sexualized in these roles. Women are described by their physical appearances, rather than occupation. Another observation is that while "nurse" does not occur at all in the images of men, it is assigned to half of the images of women doctors, indicative of the stereotype that women can be nurses but men are doctors.

DISCUSSION

We observed evidence of gender-based linguistic bias in the labels generated via the ESP Game. In Analysis 1, we saw that players use adjectives to describe *how* someone is more often in the case of images of women versus men. We also saw differences in the extent to which subjective language is used, with *subjective adjectives* more often used to describe women. In the sub-analysis in which images were classified by gender and perceived sexual orientation, the gender effect was most salient. However, there were interesting similarities in the descriptions of women perceived as being heterosexual and men perceived to be gay, again suggesting that social stereotypes influence ESP players' choices for descriptive labels.

The results of Analysis 2 also support the finding of gender-based linguistic bias. For most occupations we considered, women received a greater proportion of labels describing their physical appearance. This was especially true of stereotype-congruent images depicting women in "feminine" occupations, where players described physical attributes and used fewer occupation-related labels.

Our observations are certainly not surprising. Gender stereotypes are deeply engrained in society and are linked not only to traditional social roles but also to gender-related power inequalities [11]. Such stereotypes dictate not only what our social expectations are but also offer prescriptive attributes of what we should be [27]. Compared to men, women are noted as being physically attractive (belief) and therefore they should be attractive (prescription). Through label choices, ESP players convey these expectations.

Still, we should question both the social and practical implications. If we assume that the ultimate goal of ESP is to produce *accurate* metadata, we might interpret the prevalence of stereotype-reinforcing labels as evidence of a values-based conflict in the game design [14]. The social cues and incentives built into the game (e.g., use of taboo labels, the mechanism by which players earn points) have resulted in the generation of labels expressing prevalent gender stereotypes. Given that games are cultural artifacts, it is worth reflecting on whether or not their embedded values could or should reflect human values (e.g., gender equality) or simply technical ones (e.g., efficient, low-cost production of metadata) [15]. Given the already widespread use of GWAP to crowdsource metadata creation, and its growing popularity in the cultural heritage domain [24], this question is worth serious consideration.

IMPLICATIONS

We have not yet teased apart the relationships between the stimulus for ESP players' input, the social cues provided by the game, and the resulting output. However, per our current goals, we have provided evidence of gender-based linguistic biases in the metadata produced from GWAP, which raises serious concerns, particularly for system designers, as well as the machine learning community.

Designers of technologies that take as input data generated via GWAP, must keep in mind that any values, such as the expression of social stereotypes, which are embedded into this data, will be carried downstream into their applications. In addition, our work highlights the fact that the detection of such problems can be challenging. It is easy to automatically detect and filter out undesirable language, such as racist or sexist terms, but the expression of stereotypes through linguistic biases is a much more subtle means of perpetuating ideas about particular social groups.

Likewise, values reflected in labels produced by GWAP will be "inherited" by algorithms trained on them. In their study of the perpetuation of stereotypes through the auto-complete function in Google's search form, Baker and Potts [1] describe humans as shaping technology in their own image, "having taught stereotypes to search engines and even trained them to hastily present these as results of 'top relevance'" (p. 201). It is easy to envision a number of supervised learning tasks performed on the ESP dataset, which would result in an algorithm perpetuating gender stereotypes (e.g., automatic detection of images depicting doctors, singers or teachers based on features of the image, guided by players' assigned labels). On a practical note, this runs contrary to the goals and promise of GWAP. We want to use it to harness human intelligence and creativity, but as alluded to in the opening quote by Junot Diaz, stereotypical thinking is just plain boring.

FUTURE WORK

Which social cues and incentives, when embedded into a GWAP, result in fewer stereotypical labels and more diverse descriptions of multimedia artifacts? Should linguistic biases, which contribute to the transmission and maintenance of stereotypes in society, be discouraged, and if so, how? Future work must address these questions.

The current work was not a controlled experiment. In future study, image content could be manipulated such that images are identical except for the subject, varying his/her social group. In addition, as linguistic biases may be less likely to occur when players have fewer social cues [22], one could manipulate cues from none at all (i.e., a one-player game) to open communication with one's partner in a two-player game. Such a study will allow us to understand the relation between social cues, and the triggering of biased language.

In conclusion, linguistic biases – systematic differences in the words used to describe people, as a function of their social groups – are an important consideration for metadata generation via GWAP. While language facilitates the expression of information we intend to convey, it can also reflect prevalent stereotypes. The ESP Game has demonstrated the potential of crowdsourcing to solve many AI-hard problems, but we must further explore the tensions between the social cues and incentives provided by a GWAP, and the quality of the data that is generated.

ACKNOWLEDGMENTS

The author is grateful to three anonymous reviewers as well as the two ACs who provided very thorough comments on the paper's first draft.

REFERENCES

1. Baker, P. and Potts, A. "Why do white people have thin lips?" Google and the perpetuation of stereotypes via auto-complete search forms. *Critical Discourse Studies 10,* 2 (2013), 187-204.
2. Bem, S.L. Gender schema theory: a cognitive account of sex typing. *Psychological Review 88*, 4 (1981), 354-364.
3. Beukeboom, C.J. Mechanisms of linguistic bias: How words reflect and maintain stereotypic expectancies. In: Laszlo, J., Forgas, J. and Vincze, O. (eds.), *Social Cognition and Communication (*pp. 313-330). New York, NY: Psychology Press, 2013.
4. Bowker, G.C. and Star, S.L. *Sorting Things Out: Classification and its Consequences.* The MIT Press, Cambridge, MA, 2000.
5. Brahnam, S. and De Angeli, A. Gender affordances of conversational agents. *Interacting with Computers 24*, (2012), 139-153.
6. Brown, R.W. Linguistic determinism and the part of speech. *The Journal of Abnormal and Social Psychology 55*, 1 (1957), 1-5.
7. Cohen, J. A coefficient of agreement for nominal scales. *Education and Psychological Measurement 20*, (1960), 37-46.
8. Cohen, J. *Statistical power analysis for the behavioral sciences.* Erlbaum, Hillsdale NJ, 1988.
9. Devine, P.G. and Elliot, A.J. Are racial stereotypes really fading? The Princeton trilogy revisited. *Personality and Social Psychology Bulletin 21*, 11 (1995), 1139-1150.
10. Doan, A., Ramakrishnan, R. and Halevy, A.Y. Crowdsourcing systems on the World-Wide Web. *Communications of the ACM 54*, 4 (2011), 86-96.
11. Eagly, A.H. *Sex differences in social behavior: a social-role interpretation.* Erlbaum, Hillsdale, NJ, 1997.
12. Fellbaum, C. WordNet and wordnets. In: Brown, K. et al. (eds.), *Encyclopedia of Language and Linguistics, Second Edition, (*pp. 665-670). Oxford: Elsevier, 2005.

13. Fiedler, K. and Semin, G. On the causal information conveyed by different interpersonal verbs: the role of implicit sentence context. *Social Cognition 6*, 1 (1988), 21-39.

14. Flanagan, M., Howe, D.C. and Nissenbaum, H. Values at play: design tradeoffs in socially-oriented game design. In *Proc. CHI 2005*, ACM Press (2005), 751-760.

15. Flanagan, M. and Nissenbaum, H. A game design methodology to incorporate social activist themes. In *Proc. CHI 2007*, ACM Press (2007), 181-190.

16. Garside, R., and Smith, N. A hybrid grammatical tagger: CLAWS4, in Garside, R., Leech, G., and McEnery, A. (eds.) *Corpus Annotation: Linguistic Information from Computer Text Corpora*. London: Longman (1997), 102-121.

17. Gligorov, R., Hildebrand, M., van Ossenbruggen, J., Schreiber, G. and Aroyo, L. On the role of user-generated metadata in audio visual collections. In *Proc. ACM K-CAP,* ACM Press (2011), 145-152.

18. Greenwald, A.G. and Banaji, M.R. Implicit social cognition: Attitudes, self-esteem and stereotypes. *Psychological Review 102*, 1 (1995), 4-27.

19. Ho, C-J, Chang, T-H, Lee, J-C, Hsu, J.Y. and Chen, K-T. 2009. KissKissBan: a competitive human computation game for image annotation. In *Proc. of the ACM SIGKDD Workshop on Human Computation* (HCOMP '09), ACM, New York, NY, USA, 11-14.

20. Jaccard, J., Becker, M.A., and Wood, B. Pairwise multiple comparison procedures: a review. *Psychological Bulletin 96*, 3 (1984), 589-596.

21. Jeon, J., Lavrenko, V. and Manmatha, R. Automatic image retrieval using cross-media relevance models. In *Proc. SIGIR*, ACM Press (2003), 119-126.

22. Maass, A., Salvi, D., Arcuri, L, and Semin, G. Language use in intergroup contexts: the Linguistic Intergroup Bias. *Journal of Personality and Social Psychology 57*, 6 (1989), 981-993.

23. McGarty, C., Yzerbyt, V.Y. and Spears, R. *Stereotypes as explanations: the formation of meaningful beliefs about social groups.* Cambridge University Press, Cambridge, UK, 2002.

24. Oomen, J. and Aroyo, L. Crowdsourcing in the cultural heritage domain: opportunities and challenges. In *Proc. C&T 2011*, ACM Press (2011), 138-149.

25. Park, J.-R. Metadata quality in digital repositories: a survey of the current state of the art. *Cataloging & Classification Quarterly 47*, (2009), 213–228.

26. Pennebaker, J.W., Booth, R.J and Francis, M.E. Linguistic Inquiry and Word Count (LIWC): A computerized text analysis program. *LIWC.net*, 2007.

27. Prentice, D.A. and Carranza. What women and men should be, shouldn't be, are allowed to be and don't have to be: the contents of prescriptive gender stereotypes. *Psychology of Women Quarterly 26*, (2002), 269-281.

28. Rittman, R., Wacholder, N., Kantor, P., Ng, K.B., Strzalkowski, T., and Sun, Y. Adjectives and indicators of subjectivity in documents. In Proc. 67th ASIS&T Annual Meeting vol. 41 (2004), 349-359.

29. Robertson, S. Vojnovic, M. and Weber, I. Rethinking the ESP game. In *CHI '09 Extended Abstracts on Human Factors in Computing Systems* (CHI EA '09). ACM, New York, NY, USA, 3937-3942.

30. Rubin, M., Paolini, S. and Crisp, R. Linguistic description moderates the evaluations of counterstereotypical people. *Social Psychology 44*, (2013), 289-298.

31. Smith, E.R. and Semin, G.R. Situated social cognition. *Current Directions in Psychological Science* 16, 3 (2007), 132-135.

32. Tausczik, Y.R. and Pennebaker, J. The psychological meaning of words: LIWC and computerized text analysis methods. *Journal of Language and Social Psychology 29*, 1 (2010), 24-54.

33. ter Doest, L., Semin, G.R. and Sherman, S.J. Linguistic context and social perception: Does stimulus abstraction moderate processing style? *Journal of Language and Social Psychology 31*, 3 (2002), 195-229.

34. Thogersen, R. Data quality in an output-agreement game: A comparison between game-generated tags and professional descriptors. *Collaboration and Technology, Lecture Notes in Computer Science 8224,* (2013), 126-142.

35. von Ahn, L. Games with a purpose. *Computer 39*, 6 (2006), 92-94.

36. von Ahn, L. and Dabbish, L. Labeling images with a computer game. In *Proc. CHI 2004*, ACM Press (2004), 319-326.

37. Wajcman, J. Feminist theories of technology. *Cambridge Journal of Economics* (2009), 1-10.

38. Wigboldus, D.H.J., Spears, R. and Semin, G.R. When do we communicate stereotypes? Influence of the social context on the Linguistic Expectancy Bias. Group Processes & Intergroup Relations 8, 3 (2005), 215-230.

39. Wilson, T., Wiebe, J. and Hoffman, P. Recognizing contextual polarity in phrase-level sentiment analysis. Proc. HLT/EMNLP 2005, Association for Computational Linguistics (2005).

40. Winkielman, P., Halberstadt, J., Fazendeiro, T. and Catty, S. Prototypes are attractive because they are easy on the mind. *Psychological Science 17*, 9 (2006), 799-806.

Tiree Energy Pulse: Exploring Renewable Energy Forecasts on the Edge of the Grid

Will Simm[1], Maria Angela Ferrario[2], Adrian Friday[1], Peter Newman[1], Stephen Forshaw[3], Mike Hazas[1] and Alan Dix[4]
[1]School of Computing and Communications, [2]Management School, [3]LICA, Lancaster University, UK
[4]Tiree Tech Wave, Tiree, UK and University of Birmingham, UK
{w.simm, m.ferrario, a.friday, p.newman, s.forshaw, m.hazas}@lancaster.ac.uk, alan@hcibook.com

ABSTRACT
In many parts of the world, the electricity supply industry makes the task of dealing with unpredictable spikes and dips in production and demand invisible to consumers, maintaining a seemingly unlimited supply. A future increase in reliance on time-variable renewable sources of electricity may lead to greater fluctuations in supply. We engaged remote islanders as equal partners in a research project that investigated through technology-mediated enquiry the topic of synchronising energy consumption with supply, and together built a prototype renewable energy forecast display. A number of participants described a change in their practices, saving high energy tasks for times when local renewable energy was expected to be available, despite having no financial incentive to do so. The main contributions of this paper are in: 1) the results of co-development sessions exploring systems supporting synchronising consumption with supply and 2) the findings arising from the deployment of the prototype.

Author Keywords
Social innovation; Sustainability; Energy; Electricity; Forecast; Renewable Energy

ACM Classification Keywords
H.5.m. Information Interfaces and Presentation (e.g. HCI): Miscellaneous

INTRODUCTION
In modern times we are used to an electricity supply system which allows us as consumers access to as much energy as we want, any time we want it for relatively low cost. Much of this electricity is sourced from burning a carbon rich diet of coal, oil and gas which has fuelled industrial development and economies. The future of this energy supply is looking rather less reliable. Borrowing from M. King Hubbert's peak theory [4], peak gas in UK was reached in the year 2000[1]. Much of UK's nuclear capacity is reaching end of life over the next decade, requiring renewal [25]. Diminishing reserves of fossil fuels, and thus vulnerability to volatile costs, and a need to meet stringent targets to de-carbonise the energy supply may mean increasing reliance on renewable energy in the coming decades. Unless storage of energy becomes viable to avoid blackouts becoming normality [23] we will need to synchronise our consumption with the availability of this resource.

ACM 978-1-4503-3145-6/15/04 ...$15.00.
http://dx.doi.org/10.1145/2702123.2702285

Figure 1. Tiree Energy Pulse located device.

In this work researchers have spent 250 person days living and working in this new energy context through fieldwork on an island at the edge of the electricity grid, with its own community-owned wind turbine. Through a series of technology mediated interactions, including interviews, field visits and workshops, we worked with various stakeholders to explore the design of new technologies to promote awareness of variable and intermittent supply. One branch of this work resulted in developing a display called 'Tiree Energy Pulse' (TEP, shown in Figure 1) designed for and with Tiree islanders that presents the *energy 'pulse'* of the island, integrating a local renewable energy production forecast with a local

[1]UK gas and electricity crisis looming:
http://www.resilience.org/stories/2005-08-27/uk-gas-and-electricity-crisis-looming

weather forecast. Over a period of five weeks researcher-developers worked with a group of community-developers who acted as the participant stakeholders in the development process. Since the community-developers were embedded in the process they took real ownership of the system they were contributing to. While we deployed and developed this display with no expectation of change, this paper presents our findings which detail the actions around intermittent renewable energy and practices in relation to the presence of the display in their homes.

Through this study we are observing the effect of giving people the information about local renewable energy availability. This may involve shifting the usual time of doing energy intensive tasks (laundry, running the dishwasher, cooking, heating etc.) to times when local renewable energy is available, or simply placing in mind an awareness of when renewable energy is available. In all except one household who had their own micro-generation, there was no financial incentive at all. In contrast to most prior studies the participants were not paid for participation nor for shifting their energy usage. Our intention was not to encourage them to lower demand, rather give them the tools to be able to synchronise with the cycles of naturally occurring renewable energy.

The key contributions of this paper are firstly A) developing a renewable energy forecast with domestic consumers which has been under-explored in HCI literature, and in particular with no financial incentive, secondly B) observations on this which have implications for how we might design such systems in the future.

Context

"Eco-forecasting" of the type we investigate presents expected future state to users. This gives opportunity for the person to make a change—to delay or reconfigure performances *before* they are carried out. This is in contrast to "eco-feedback", which allows people to see only their past—which cannot be changed, and may require significant interpretation of practices to apply to changes in the future.

Using less energy is accepted as appropriate to reduce environmental impact, however renewable energy also provides opportunity to raise (or shift) demand in times of plenty. Currently grid systems struggle to handle the peaks in supply from renewable energy: in 2014 in the UK alone, wind turbine operators were paid over £53 million to constrain output[2] at times of excess. Eco-forecasting provides the tools to plan, helping to maximise this opportunity.

Tiree Context

Tiree is a small island off the west coast of Scotland, with approximately 650 inhabitants spread thinly in farm crofts and small clusters of homes. Tiree is 'on the edge' of the UK's infrastructure, connected to the electricity grid by a fragile sub-sea cable and reliant on a subsidised ferry service and airport for transport and other supplies. This community on the edge provides an ideal environment to foster innovation that may be generalisable beyond the island. Ferrario et al. [8] explore the energy situation in Tiree more completely, but for context a summary is provided here.

Tiree has a community owned wind turbine, an Enercon E-44 rated at 910 kW known locally as 'Tilley'. Tiree Trust operate Tilley through a wholly owned subsidiary which sells electricity to the UK grid on a feed-in tariff, and the money is used to fund community projects. Along with private solar panels and wind turbines, renewable sources are capable of supplying ⅔ of island peak demand, although this energy is only available *on supply*—when the wind is blowing and the sun is shining, not typically aligning with peak demand. Excess energy is exported to the mainland grid, incurring associated transmission losses.

The exposed location means islanders suffer several power cuts from storm damage annually and recently the sub-sea cable to the mainland failed completely, requiring replacement. During periods of disconnection from the mainland grid, the island relies on a diesel fuelled power station to cover the approximately 1–1.5MW of nominal demand—and Tilley is braked to tickover at 50kW, as the island infrastructure cannot respond quickly to the variation in supply as the wind rises and falls. In many respects, the energy supply on Tiree is less secure, more intermittent, and contains a greater mix of renewable sources than the mainland.

Global Context

In 2009, the world relied on renewable sources for around 13.1% of its primary energy supply[3]. Renewable sources accounted for 19.5% of global electricity generation and 3% of global energy consumption for road transport in the same year. However with most renewable energy supplies comes a new challenge—how to balance the grid when renewable sources of energy are so time variant: wind power is only available when windy, solar energy when the sun is shining. Using energy when it is available helps mitigate this problem.

Our work has increasing relevance in the UK through problems with electricity supply due to ageing infrastructure and delayed plant replacement. Dynamic peak pricing already impacts large energy consumers in the UK, and although politically sensitive, consultations have been made with domestic consumers regarding demand side response [11]. Infrastructure that can support this is being rolled out in the form of smart metering by 2020[4]. In Australia time of use pricing is already used, with Strengers finding there is a strong social inclination to respond to problems in supply [21], here eco-forecasting may further support this. Presenting localised energy forecasts in locations that suffer rolling blackouts and brownouts, e.g. in parts of Asia[5] may help domestic consumers to plan and make best use of energy when it is available. Similar Eco-Forecasting designs to TEP might also prevail in western locations that, like Tiree, have a high concen-

[2]Renewable Energy Foundation: Balancing Mechanism Wind Farm Constraint Payments
`http://www.ref.org.uk/constraints/indextotals.php`

[3]IEA Statistics `http://www.iea.org/statistics/`

[4]Policy: Helping households to cut their energy bills
`https://www.gov.uk/government/policies/helping-households-to-cut-their-energy-bills/supporting-pages/smart-meters`

[5]Electricity in Vietnam: A heavy load `http://econ.st/1rusUUo`

tration of wind or solar energy such as the Pacific Northwest of the USA and parts of Scandinavia.

RELATED WORK

There is much written about presenting consumers with the amount they are consuming, with smart metering, home energy displays and all manner of visualizations pitched to encourage people to change what they do, in ways that reduce energy demand. The success of these devices is apparently limited, with consumption changing little [22].

Eco-Feedback

The centralisation of generation, grid balancing mechanisms, market forces and tariff construction have hidden the complex and sometimes fragile energy production and distribution process from most people. Making energy and the degree of usage more visible and easily interpreted by consumers is a goal of eco-feedback. Pierce and Paulos [16] summarise the state of eco-feedback within the HCI literature and argue a need to move beyond visualizing consumption. The effectiveness of portraying consumption is limited, it is understood that that energy use is the result of supporting everyday practices (showering, laundering and keeping warm), which are mediated by social, cultural, technical and institutional dynamics, rather than as a series of rational informed choices [22]. Rather than consumption, our focus is the times of the day which renewable energy is expected to be available.

Yang et al. [27] studied the use of a learning thermostat in 19 households and distilled a set of design implications for Eco-Interaction systems. In the first few months of intervention, user interaction had a large impact as the system built a schedule. Long term, the device required less frequent interaction and user interest waned, reducing the effectiveness of the devices as the user schedule evolved. In their implications Yang et al. suggest that employing mixed initiative designs, providing actionable recommendations, and stimulating reassessment may be starting points for designing more effective eco-interactions in the future. In this veign, TEP is designed to invite reflection and augments the existing practice of weather forecasting.

Eco-Forecasting

Extending weather prediction to forecast the availability of renewable energy has also been a focus of prior work [14, 19]—and indeed is fundamental to energy markets for balancing supply against demand. While these forecasts are used extensively by energy markets and grid operators, they are rarely presented directly to domestic consumers. Where renewable energy forecasting has been used with consumers, these forecasts have frequently been combined with other factors to estimate the likely cost of energy to encourage demand shifting [2] or automate household tasks [13]. We frame our system in terms of energy availability, rather than in financial terms.

Costanza et al. [2] specifically examined laundry routines, and propose a smart grid approach with real-time pricing asking participants to book a time slot for their laundry. Price forecasts were derived from weather and demand forecasts, assuming renewable energy is cheaper and this price would change as forecasts were updated. The information was presented to the participant as a likely price, with the source of the energy masked by the algorithm. They found that consumers were prepared to shift their laundry with an associated financial incentive, however no comment was made about motivations to synchronize with local renewable energy.

Bourgeois et al. [1] studied the routines of households with their own solar micro-generation. These households effectively get free energy when the sun shines and have invested in the generation technology—so are significantly motivated to make best use of this energy. Charts of historical production and forecasts (derived from cloud-cover weather forecasts) for the coming days' production as a fraction of the maximum output were emailed to participants every three days as a mechanism to allow users to plan household tasks. A washing machine that automatically selects the optimal time (within a user selected period) to start based on forecast data was also deployed. TEP in contrast offers a live forecast display of community scale renewables, where there is no individual financial reward.

There are online sources that show the live state of the UK grid[6]. The energy mix from this data is presented to users by Earth Notes' "GB Grid Intensity"[7], where the data is presented as a traffic light system. They also give advice to consumers about the carbon content of energy at the current point in time, encouraging them to shift consumption to times of higher renewable availability.

Schrammel et al. [20] proposed an ambient display of future renewable energy availability in the form of a wearable watch design concept. This design augments a clock face with an overlay of the next 12/24 hours of renewable energy forecast, and live and historical household consumption. This design was created following a workshop with end users, but was sadly neither implemented nor trialled.

Shifting Demand

A key concern of the electricity grid is to balance supply of energy to meet demand. This demand levelling is a concern of the grid operators [12]. Through the drive to reduce carbon output to meet carbon targets, time varying renewable sources will in future make up more of the energy mix and increase the complexity of this problem.

Pierce and Paulos [17] found that by displaying the live state of local renewable energy in two households, people would be willing to shift laundry to times of plentiful supply. Participants also reconfigured some practices to make use of energy when it is available—such as celebratory meals. They did not include forecasting in their display—however one of their participants suggested this.

Scottish Hydro's *Total Heating Total Control* (THTC), uses remote controlled electric storage heaters to synchronise use

[6]UK Balancing Mechanism reporting
`http://www.bmreports.com`

[7]`http://www.earth.org.uk/_gridCarbonIntensityGB.html`

with available off peak electricity [7]. Dynamic peak pricing (DPP) in Australia combines punitively priced electricity at times of very high predicted load, together with a range of notifications (SMS, Phone, in-home-display, email) to temporarily reduce the use of electricity (mainly due to air conditioning) on particularly hot days [21].

For households with their own micro-generation, there is a financial motivation to shift demand to make best use of their generation and minimise the cost of buying grid energy. In a study of attitudes towards micro-generation, researchers presented data driven probes exploring how to get the best out of micro-generation [18], and found households questioning their consumption and shifting demand to times of peak generation, however they did not explore energy forecasts.

Community Engagement in Energy

How households engage and communicate around home practices and strategies for shifting consumption when compared with one another was described by Dillahunt et al.'s 'social-energy' study [6]. Although we did not encourage households to compare energy use, tools like TEP have the potential to enable households to come together and discuss strategies for shifting consumption in a similar manner. Dillahunt et al. [5] also focus specifically on energy-reliant practices in households that did not pay for their energy, thus removing financial incentive. Despite this, they found participants were motivated to save energy, citing protecting the environment and an aversion to waste as motivations.

On the Isle of Eigg in Scotland which is powered totally by off-grid community owned renewable sources, households are subject to a 5kW cap. Households are asked to voluntarily reduce their electricity demand when renewable sources are running low using a traffic light system in community areas [26]. Here they do not give forecasts of when energy is likely to be in abundance or forecast periods of low supply.

METHODS

This work was conducted as part of the *OnSupply project*, a nine-month (November 2014–July 2014), sub-project of the Catalyst! project [24]. OnSupply brought together in partnership a multidisciplinary team of academics, residents of Tiree, and community leaders Tiree Trust. The main goal of the OnSupply partnership was to investigate if and to what extent digital technology can help people synchronise to the dynamic nature of renewable energy sources.

We follow Speedplay [9], an interdisciplinary management approach for the rapid prototyping of digital tools with a social innovation remit. This paper concentrates on the Speedplay *Build Step*, where a prototype is built in collaboration with a core user group engaged as equal partners, through an agile process where we deliver working software from the outset and capture participant feedback on the system developed as build iterations progress. In contrast to traditional prototyping, here the build step integrates ongoing community engagement and domain understanding into the process.

Most prior studies of this type of domestic intervention [2, 3, 17] deliver a complete working technology designed by researchers to homes and then study the use of it. Speedplay ensures that our participants are an intrinsic part of the design of the technology from an early stage–they were involved in ideating, designing, building and evaluating features as the technology was iterated. A key aspect of this was that we were able to capture a wealth of information about the impact the technology was having in the home, and that participants take considerable ownership of the resulting prototype and its refinements.

Tiree Energy Pulse—Emergence

This work builds on our prior work [8, 10, 15] which explored opportunities for designing ICT to support synchronisation with renewable energy supply. This work comprised of series of workshops that took place as a 'technology mediated enquiry' over a period of 8 months, engaging community members on Tiree throughout. These workshops were used as a means of eliciting requirements for a future energy scenario which relies on renewable sources—and the results of these workshops directly informed the inception and design of the TEP system.

Through this work [8] it is suggested that the opportunities at a community level for synchronising everyday life with supply are *opportunistic exploitation*—having mechanisms that can take advantage of energy when it is in plentiful supply and cannot be electrically stored, and *collaborative load management* where the technologies that help the community to predict and plan for future availability. One of the major themes elicited through a game workshop and refined through physical prototyping [15] was *forecasting*—presenting the likely future availability of energy.

The initial ideas for TEP arose from a subsequent physical prototyping workshop, where a physical prototype was used as a provocation to inspire the participants into thinking about what may be possible in ambient displays in future. This prototype, called the 'Datarium' comprised a 3D printed bulb-like plant with leaves that move and change colour with the live and forecast state of renewable energy on the island. Two of the recurrent themes that emerged out of this were (i) a desire for more clear information on the live and forecast state of renewable energy than presented by Datarium, and (ii) participants likened the Datarium to a 'tamagotchi' digital creature, and liked the idea that it gave advice and required interaction and action to survive.

Tiree experiences amongst the highest persistent wind speeds in the UK as well as boasting one of the highest annual hours of sunlight in the UK. The weather on Tiree has a massive impact on daily life and routine on Tiree and because of this we decided to augment existing performances of checking the weather forecast with our renewable energy forecast. Our intention was to augment an existing practice with a mixed initiative design to increase engagement [27].

Tiree Energy Pulse—Description

The name 'Tiree Energy Pulse' represents an attempt to show the *energy pulse* of the island, natural energy overlaid with electrical energy generated directly from nature, to present an opportunity to synchronise with natural energy cycles. TEP

Participant	No. Calls	Attended Workshops	Discussion Group	Household Inhabitants	Heating / Hot Water	Electricity Tariff	Cooking	Dryer
Janet	2	Yes	Present	2	Oil	Conventional (RE supplier)	Bottled Gas	Yes & used
Tony	2	No	Present	4	Air source heat pump	Conventional	Bottled Gas	Broken
Sarah	2	Yes	Interviewed	1	Coal Fire & Electric	Economy 7 (TOU)	Electric	Once a year!
Linda	2	No	Not present	2	Electric, Multifuel / Solar	Own turbine with feed-in tariff	Electric	Not used
Trish	0	Yes	Not present	2	Electric / Solar Water	Conventional	Electric	None
David	1	No	Not present	2	Electric Storage & Multifuel Stove	Total Control	Electric / Multifuel	None
Margaret	2	Yes	Present	2	Electric Convection / Electric	Conventional	Electric	None
Natalie	1	No	Present	2	Wet Electric / Electric	Economy 7 (TOU)	Electric	None

Table 1. Participants to the study (names changed). All have and use a washing machine and all except Sarah have and use a dishwasher.

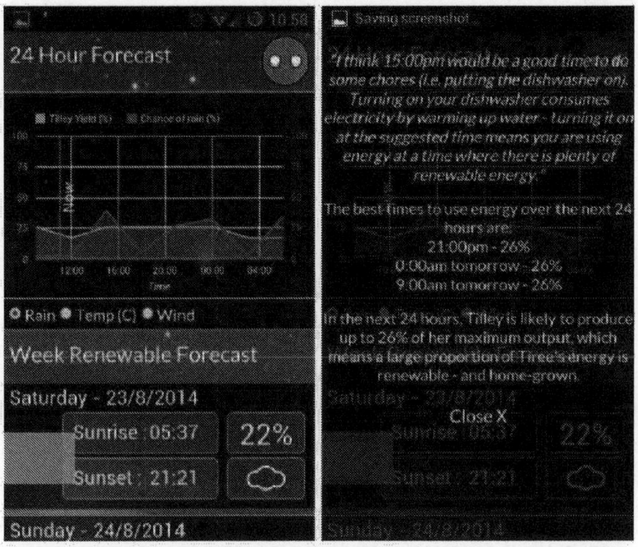

Figure 2. Tiree Energy Pulse Screenshot. Blinky is the red circle in the left screenshot and when clicked gives the advice shown on the right.

is a located display of a renewable energy forecast which was deployed to the homes of the participants as shown by Figure 1. The display shows a line chart showing the day ahead forecast of Tilley's output, overlaid with weather forecast data such as temperature and chance of rainfall. As the display is scrolled, it gives a week-ahead energy and weather forecast split by day. In the top-right is 'Blinky' (named by participants), who when pressed will give a text summary of the energy situation and give actionable suggestions to when might be a good time to do high energy and weather dependant tasks such as laundry. Since TEP was built as a flexible web app, TEP can be viewed on the supplied located display, or on a participant's own smartphone, tablet or computer.

The first version of TEP was built by the research team and the induction for participants provided the first round of feedback. As the five week development period progressed a number of features were refined and added as a direct result of participant feedback. A screen shot of the last version of TEP is shown by Figure 2, and the major features and the evolution of TEP are described below.

Day Ahead Energy Forecast

The primary display area was used to show a day-ahead forecast of the energy produced by Tilley. When the app is viewed with a landscape screen (as in the located device in Figure 1) this takes up the whole screen. To produce a forecast of Tilley's electricity generation, a weather forecast was obtained from the MET office DataPoint API[8] for Tiree airport. The wind speed forecasts from this were used to look up the corresponding turbine output from the manufacturer supplied datasheet[9]. The energy forecast was presented as a fraction of the peak output of Tilley, rather than electrical units which partipants did not find easy to interpret. Although the forecasts are presented as likely representations of future energy availability, any forecast has error to some degree [14]. In this study our focus is not the accuracy of the forecasts supplied, rather we observe the reaction to giving people this information that they did not have before—the forecast was presented as being as likely to be correct as a weather forecast.

Five day forecasts

The participant can scroll down to see a week ahead energy forecast. Since space is limited the five day forecast data was shown in a lower resolution (daily forecast rather than hourly). This also provided an alternative representation of similar data which the participants could comment on. The same algorithm was used as the day ahead forecast to give the week ahead energy forecast, again annotated with weather forecast data but here using conventional weather symbols.

Blinky

Blinky suggests the best time to do energy intensive tasks. Blinky emerged from the 'datarium' workshop described earlier where in discussion participants likened a physical representation of energy to a 'tamagotchi' that required regular interaction—Janet: *"I think its really cute (...) it would be good if it talked to you"* and Margaret: *"Maybe when lots of energy is being used, maybe its, you know, unhappy"*.

Blinky is located in the top right of the display and the colour of Blinky's face represents the energy outlook for the next 24 hours—red for low turbine output changing through to green for high turbine output. This is calculated from an average of the next 24hrs forecast data, not a live figure. When selected, Blinky pops up a message suggesting the best times in the next twenty-four hours to do energy intensive tasks—so Blinky highlights the peaks in turbine output. Blinky also suggests the best time to do specific tasks—a period of high turbine output (to power washing machine), followed with

[8]Datapoint `http://www.metoffice.gov.uk/datapoint`
[9]Enercon Product Overview
`http://www.enercon.de/p/downloads/ENERCON_PU_en.pdf`

low precipitation (for drying washing without using a dryer) will result in Blinky suggesting a good time to do laundry.

TEP Development and Participant Engagement

TEP was continuously developed over a period of five weeks with regular contact points with participants. The participants were drawn from the pool of full-time Tiree residents who had taken part in earlier activities and shown an interest in the process. An email was sent out and 8 participants (and hence 8 households) came forward to commit to the process and represented different demographics with people involved in roles such as community leadership, teachers, retirees, and remote tech industry workers. Table 1 lists the participants, along with the times they were contacted after the induction, household infrastructure used for common domestic tasks, and electricity tariff information. Note that names have been changed so participants remain anonymous. Although we did not pay our participants, Linda owns a domestic turbine and benefits from 'free' electricity when it is producing, so is the only participant with a financial incentive to synchronize tasks with renewable supply. Regarding selection bias, an environmentally aware mind-set is prevalent in inhabitants, perhaps arising through the exposed realities of island life, but we would not necessarily characterise all as being sustainably minded.

Deployment

A researcher visited Tiree 16–18 June 2014 to conduct inductions to TEP. Out of 8 participants 6 inductions were conducted face to face and 2 were done over the telephone.

TEP was deployed on an Android smartphone, with a stand designed to hold the phone horizontally, and left plugged in at a location of the participant's choice. The setup is shown by Figure 1 and a screenshot in Figure 2. The device was to be located in the home so mobile connectivity was not required.

TEP was pitched to participants as 'a device to give an at-a-glance view of the renewable energy situation right now and near forecast, with the aim of providing information to sync up with supply'. It was made clear that TEP was in an embryonic stage and it was a first prototype that is far from perfect or a final product. The development process was described to the participants—that they would be involved in proposing, defining and evaluating features through feedback telephone interviews in the coming weeks. Participants were given a participant information sheet and consent form, and the first follow up call was scheduled.

The TEP device was connected to the participant's WiFi for Internet access, and the unique participant ID recorded. The features of the app were described to the participant on the device, and the web app brought up on the participants own smartphone and other devices (tablets, laptops). The participant was given time to familiarise with TEP and notes were taken on their initial reaction to the presentation of information. The device was located in the participants household and a photo taken. A number of potential new features were discussed with the participant to inform future development.

A discussion followed, with the aim of discovering the the perceived high energy tasks in the home, how and when the decision was made to carry out those tasks. The participant's energy tariff (time of use, total control, standard) was recorded. We asked them what they knew about Tilley, and the energy mix on the island.

Phone Contact

Over the period of the study, each participant was called by telephone to capture feedback on the usage of TEP and development of features (again, see the table in Figure 1 for a summary of contact). The number of calls varied according to level of participant engagement and participant's availability. One participant contributed by email. Prompts for the telephone conversations included: number of uses and when it was used; for what purpose it was used; which devices were used to view TEP; location of device; clarity of information display and existing features; proposed new features; and finally a short brainstorm of future features was held.

Discussion Group

Before the discussion group, researchers planned a set of guiding questions centred on the *use, usefulness, usage* and *future vision* of TEP. These were used as prompts—the discussion was open to change direction; so the discussion was not limited and it ranged much wider. The usage traces for each participant present were displayed and participants asked to guess which was theirs to see if they used TEP as they thought. Unfortunately half of the participants could not make the discussion group, 4 of the 8 were present.

FINDINGS

Here we summarise the findings that emerged, drawn mainly from the discussion group but also from the consultations during the development period. We broadly split findings into categories, looking at the different uses of TEP, how it fit into the household ecosystem, changes in household practices and a review of the interface elements.

Uses of TEP

TEP combined a local energy forecast with a local weather forecast in one view. Some participants primarily used TEP for the energy forecast to help plan tasks- Natalie: *"I was basically using it as a way to estimate what was good to do, like lots of washing on today and whether was going to be windy enough to get it dry"*, and some used it purely for the weather forecasts - Tony: *"I find it more useful as weather app"*. When used for weather forecasts the energy forecast is implicit - Natalie: *"I think it was quite nice to have something where you go to check the weather in principle and then it makes you think, all right this is Tilleys production today"* so the participant gets the energy information as well, even if they did not specifically look for it or do not plan on doing anything with it. The weather overlay was well received so it remained for the duration of the study.

David, Sarah, Linda, Natalie and Tony all used TEP on supplied located Android devices positioned in their kitchens. Margaret used her own iPhone smartphone as a located device (left on her desk), whereas Trish preferred to use her own iPhone mobile smartphone, and Janet used her own (mobile) iPad tablet. The system was largely platform agnostic so a preference for alternative platforms was not a problem.

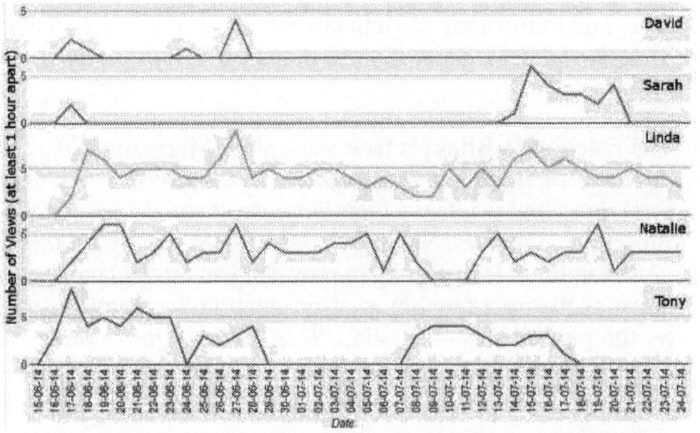

Figure 3. Usage traces for participants using located Android devices.

For those that used the Android device we supplied, we were able to track the number of views of the TEP forecast the participant's household made. Unfortunately we were not able to track the usage of iPhone and iPad devices. The usage traces for those that used the supplied Android devices are shown in Figure 3. Here a 'reloads' or views of TEP are only counted if they are at least 1 hour apart. Sarah was called away on a work trip for part of the study accounting for her early lack of use. David also took a holiday early in the study, was not available for telephone calls and perhaps lost interest in the study. What is especially interesting from the plots is that Tony indicated he did not use the located device much, however somebody else in his household did use the device fairly regularly. Over the short period of this study it was not really possible to say if the users got into a routine, however it is apparent that Linda, Natalie and Sarah (when she was in the country) did look at TEP a number of times every day.

TEP in the Household Energy Ecosystem

In the short period of the study, participants developed practices to maximise usage on days where local renewables were abundant. Their only motivation in this was to make better use of local renewable energy when it is available. Margaret: *"if it is a windy day, you know and Tilley is producing, you could justify that you could do the washing AND the tumble drying because Tilley is producing a lot!"* and *"when blinky goes green I think 'free run'—I can run the washing machine, now I can do the dishes"*. Margaret prioritised her tasks—so at times of high local renewable energy production Margaret would do the low priority loads: *"I do the pet laundry because I always save that for the green. The pet laundry isn't as important as the human laundry, the dog's walking round without a clean bed is fine, but us walking round without clean clothes is another thing. So on green days I'm like 'strip the bed, strip the tables', do the dog's laundry and we can run the dishwasher all the time, we sort of see the green days as 'yeah go for it'"*.

The two energy intensive tasks that were highlighted by the participants to be negotiable and acceptable to shift timing to some extent were laundry and using dishwashing machines—Margaret: *"I could run it today, or leave it and run it twice tomorrow when the wind is really up"*. For Margaret, some of these 'negotiable' tasks were season-dependant: *"I think that would be something that I would be doing more in winter because in the summer I do not like leaving dirty plates because you get flies, but in the winter when you do not get the flies, I'd be more inclined to take wait and take advantage of energy supply from Tilley"*.

Margaret reported gaining an 'energy instinct', TEP giving her the information required to correlate the 'feeling' of nature to the potential production: *"The feel of the wind versus how much energy is produced (...) so you are looking at it (TEP) and you know that Tilley is going to produce, e.g 10% and after a while you can go outside you can feel the wind level"*. Sarah also reported this connection: *"When I use it, it makes me more aware, certainly of what I'm doing"*.

Changes in Household Practice

Some participants felt motivated to make better use of local renewable energy—Margaret: *"well I feel a bit PROUD! Yes I am using Tilley's energy instead of a power station"*. For Margaret and Natalie, checking TEP before doing laundry became routine. Natalie checked TEP each morning: *"I would think to go and check in the morning to be honest to see what was to happen and that dictated whether I was going to put the washing on or not"* and *"there was no real need to do it today and knowing if I did it another day meant a better use of local energy, that is a good reason to do it because I do not have any other factor for that decision making process"*. Margaret delayed her washing: *"today is sunny BUT in two days is sunny AND windy, so we can wait for those days"*. These are both households without children and they acknowledged this might make it harder- Margaret: *"I have laundry building up but because we do not have a family and we have got a week's worth of clothes we can wait two days."*.

For Tony, the pressures of family life (ever mounting piles of washing) meant it was not possible to integrate the energy mix into routines: *"if you've got a young family you tend to get things done as they pile up, [TEP] probably did not change our pattern of usage"*, however there was an indication that it might be possible to change routine if the motivation was strong enough *"if you really really really try to get into a new routine it is possible, definitely possible, but I suppose it is convenience, you do what makes your life easier"*.

Janet reported genuinely wanting to synchronise with renewable energy, and reported checking TEP every three days. However she didn't feel it meshed with the other drivers of the task: *"I am not very good with routines, so I wasn't going to do it (washing) at certain times, but when we were running out (of clothes)"*. Janet felt a sense of 'guilt' that she did not manage to not change her irregular routines to synchronise, and did not understand why it did not happen: *"for somebody that is chaotic this could be actually a GOOD thing to have something that tells you when to do it, so I cannot quite work out why I didn't"*.

Sarah felt she already 'minimised' her consumption, aiming to be as efficient as possible in her energy use. This was on her own timescales without consideration to synchronising with renewable energy. Despite reporting that TEP gave her more of a sense of the potential power generated in nature, in terms of taking action, Sarah highlighted there is a disconnect between the concepts of local energy generation and paying for it via a grid mix "*It doesn't affect what I do or switch on, because I'm not getting my energy from that source*".

Before TEP was introduced Linda already synchronised household tasks to the generation of her own turbine. Rather than use any digital display, she simply looks out of the window to see her turbine, and delays tasks such as washing and dishwashing until it is turning. In periods of low wind, she turns off her large electric 'Rayburn' stove as it is so well insulated it stays hot for long periods. However Linda's husband noted "*especially in the summer time when you don't have as much wind, you can only put off a job for so long*". The energy forecast provided by TEP did prove useful to them—Linda: "*it did change my planning, because I thought 'there's rain coming' go put the washer on, put the kettle on and have cup of tea*", and Linda's husband: "*if you need to do a job in the next couple of days, and you see that tomorrow is just as bad as today, you might as well do it today*".

TEP Interface

Throughout the study, we got feedback on TEP's interface and how it was used. participants felt they could interpret the information displayed by the chart easily and identify periods of high renewable energy availability - however there was some difficulty relating to the figures. Participants wanted to (or felt they should) understand what that meant in terms of familiar device consumption - Margaret: "*something like here we are producing enough to power 200 washing machines would make much more sense, although I like looking at the graph, I'm not sure I actually understand (in terms of) things that tie into everyday life*".

It was felt the 'located' rather than mobile nature of the TEP device supplied led to more use than it would viewing on a personal smartphone or browser—Natalie: "*yeah, I dont think I would have had look at it either if it was on my PC, it is just handy to have that thing there*" and Margaret: "*I could check it on my PC, go through my bookmarks, find the link, that little bit of extra time and effort that you do not feel like bothering, (...) when I see this (TEP device) I think 'oh yea! Lets check the weather'*".

Users liked that it is a tailored, local forecast that required no setting up—Natalie: "*so it is the fact that is local and it tells what is happening at my front door, rather than me having to try to find that information from a larger Internet space where there are lots of different things happening. This is what is happening here and it tells me immediately*".

Janet, Margaret and Sarah suggested push notifications could tell a user when a particular combination of weather and turbine output was expected, and that might prompt action- Margaret: "*you could set it when the weather/wind is such and such, ping me sort of thing*" and Janet would like to customize alerts: "*I would need a sound, but you could choose (the type of alert)*" and Sarah: "*I'm going to keep mulling it over to to motivate myself to use it more—I think push notifications would be useful*". Bourgeouis et al. [1] explored alerts of this type, and found their participants preferred to get advance notification of peak generation so they had time to plan and act.

Blinky

The reaction to Blinky's face was split—Margaret: "*just seeing the little thing it makes it more FUN! because you see this little thing and you feel a little bit guilty if you do not check on Blinky for a day*" vs. Natalie: "*it feels weird calling it Blinky*"; however, the role of Blinky in providing an 'at-a-glance' summary of the next few hours of production was well received by the participants—Natalie: "*It is quite useful to have that extra way of digesting the information*" and Margaret: "*when blinky goes green I think 'free run'*".

IMPLICATIONS

Here we discuss how our findings hold implications for the design of future domestic renewable energy forecasting systems, and for the sustainable HCI community.

Augmenting Existing Practice

TEP presented an energy forecast overlaid with weather forecast data, as a deliberate attempt to augment existing daily routines, and offer additional intrinsic value. The motivation for doing this was that much of life on Tiree is planned around the quickly changing weather using forecasts, and the forms of renewable energy currently available on Tiree (wind, solar) are intrinsically linked with the weather. Here bringing the two forecasts together helps plan a task such as laundry, which requires electricity to power the machine and dry weather to hang out washing. Both weather and energy forecast data are required to synchronise this task with renewable energy availability.

A number of our users liked to use TEP as a weather forecast—it presents data in an alternative way (wind speed line chart, temperature, chance of rain) to conventional weather forecasts (symbols), perhaps leading to novelty in the forecast and preference to existing services.

An implication for the future design of such systems is to consider how we might augment existing performances (like checking the weather), rather than requiring participants to adapt to completely new ones (like annotating an eco-feedback trace). For our case, we believe this resulted in increased engagement.

Building Understanding and Variation of Practices

We learnt there was a variety of energy intensive household activities and appliances. A number of our participants did not really understand the amount of energy consumed by different devices—for example we were asked if the computer used more, or less energy overall than the freezer. Every device has a power rating, however that is the maximum power consumed—easily understandable for a kettle, which always consumes that power when turned on but a little more difficult to interpret for a freezer which is not always running its compressor. Here we believe a wider understanding about relative consumption, and what constitutes an energy intensive action, is required before participants can be expected to change.

In the household there are tasks and sub-tasks with differing time sensitive priorities which may have negotiable timescales. For example one participant prioritised human laundry over her pet's laundry indicating that some tasks may be broken down further with some planning.

One of our participants hinted at seasonal variance in household practices. This has a big effect on synchronising with renewable energy—since the energy produced also varies seasonally. Clearly, more domestic heating is required in the winter, which aligns well with higher wind speeds in winter. But the feasibility of delays to other performances (such as Margaret considering delaying dishwashing, only in colder weather) should be considered.

Here the implications are to equip participants with the knowledge about the relative consumption of devices, and that prioritising tasks and seasonal variation should play a better part in negotiating practices.

Towards an 'Energy Awareness'

One of the interesting components of this study was to peel back the layers that hide energy production from consumption. In the same way that meat is bought neatly packaged on the supermarket shelf with little evidence of where it came from and the process it went through, the sources of energy are invisible to consumers.

In those that engaged the most with TEP, we found they had begun to develop an 'energy awareness'. Through observing the energy forecast a connection was made when later leaving the house and feeling the strength of the wind. Here a correlation between the 'feel' of the wind and the likely output of Tilley was made. Perhaps in the future this will mean to some extent TEP will become somewhat redundant, as that connection between weather and energy become implicit.

Transitioning Everyday Practice

This project was never presented to participants as a way to 'save money' or an attempt to 'persuade' them to change. The desire to make better use of local resources was already embedded to different extents in our participants before we came along. Given the energy forecast data, some participants apparently changed routines fairly easily, and they were able to describe these shifts.

Others did not change practice. For Tony, despite absorbing the forecast information, it was clearly much more difficult to change routine because of the number of tasks and the constraints of everyday life in a busy household. Janet had a strong desire to synchronise her tasks with Tilley's production, but she did not really plan her tasks in advance, for example doing laundry only when needed. She would arrive at the time laundry was needed and felt 'guilty' if TEP was indicated it was a 'bad time' but would have to do the laundry anyway. Here it is important to design interventions to avoid 'problematising' and blaming individuals.

Our participants reported that a financial incentive would contribute towards motivating them to synchronise with local renewable supply, and future tariff markets may exploit this to make better use of renewable energy. Our reason for not including a financial incentive here was to avoid abstraction away from the source of the energy—we wanted this study to be about synchronising with natural cycles of renewable energy supply (a long term societal benefit) rather than saving money (a short term personal benefit). That is not to say the two are incompatible.

The implication from this is that we found the motivation to make better use of resources already existed in our participants *without any financial incentive*, aligned with Dillahunt et al.'s finding of an 'aversion to waste' [5]. Not everybody was able to act on the information presented by TEP, and devices like the 'best use' washing machine by Bourgeouis et al. [1], can take their own action.

User Interface

In TEP we tried a number of interfaces, the detailed hourly line charts, the aggregate daily bar charts, the colouring of Blinky representing the coming hours, and the text based actionable recommendations provided by clicking on Blinky. We found different people preferred different representations, with layers of detail exposed through interaction. All users liked the tailored, local forecast which required no setting up or startup procedure. Participants found the figures TEP displayed were not easily related to house household consumption or specific devices. One interface we did not explore that we feel would warrant further exploration was that of push alerts, that would interrupt the user and notify periods of high or low production.

Our implication here is that interfaces need to be simple to operate with low user effort, yet present sufficient complexity of data to support decision making if that is the intention. An area for further investigation is how this type of forecast information in electrical units can be made relevant to and presented in a manner that is easily interpreted by domestic consumers.

CONCLUDING REMARKS

Tiree Energy Pulse explored the presentation of community wind turbine production in domestic homes on the wild edge of the UK infrastructure. The key contributions of this work are in: 1) the results of co-development sessions exploring systems supporting synchronising consumption with supply and 2) the findings arising from the deployment of the TEP prototype in the home.

Tiree has an unique energy situation that means consumers are somewhat disconnected from community energy production by the operation of energy markets in the UK. But the island has great potential to be an exemplar of practice which is more closely tied to its supporting energies. Our engagement in this unique situation has given rise to a potentially much broader set of community-scale interventions that we wish to explore in future work.

ACKNOWLEDGEMENTS

We are grateful to the islanders of Tiree and Tiree Development Trust for their participation. We gratefully acknowledge our funders EPSRC via Citizens Transforming Society: Tools for Change (CaTalyST!) ref. #EP/I033017/1. Our thanks also to Yolande Strengers for helping us to consider the importance of our participants' existing weather forecasting routines in our thinking.

REFERENCES

1. Bourgeois, J., Van Der Linden, J., Kortuem, G., Price, B. A., and Rimmer, C. Conversations with my washing machine: an in-the-wild study of demand shifting with self-generated energy. In *Proc. UBICOMP*, ACM (2014), 459–470.
2. Costanza, E., Fischer, J. E., Colley, J. A., Rodden, T., Ramchurn, S. D., and Jennings, N. R. Doing the laundry with agents: a field trial of a future smart energy system in the home. In *Proc. CHI*, ACM (2014), 813–822.
3. Costanza, E., Ramchurn, S. D., and Jennings, N. R. Understanding domestic energy consumption through interactive visualisation: a field study. In *Proc. UBICOMP*, ACM (2012), 216–225.
4. Deffeyes., K. S. *Hubbert's peak: the impending world oil shortage*. Princeton Univ. Press, 2008.
5. Dillahunt, T., Mankoff, J., Paulos, E., and Fussell, S. It's not all about green: Energy use in low-income communities. In *Proc. UBICOMP*, ACM (2009), 255–264.
6. Dillahunt, T. R., and Mankoff, J. Understanding factors of successful engagement around energy consumption between and among households. In *Proc. CSCW*, ACM (2014), 1246–1257.
7. Edberg, O., and Naish, C. Energy Storage and Management Study. Tech. rep., AEA Technology PLC, October 2010.
8. Ferrario, M. A., Forshaw, S., Newman, P., Simm, W., Friday, A., and Dix, A. On the edge of supply: designing renewable energy supply into everyday life. In *ICT for Sustainability 2014 (ICT4S-14)*, Atlantis Press (2014).
9. Ferrario, M. A., Simm, W., Newman, P., Forshaw, S., and Whittle, J. Software engineering for'social good': integrating action research, participatory design, and agile development. In *Proc. ICSE*, ACM (2014), 520–523.
10. Forshaw, S., Newman, P., Ferrario, M. A., Simm, W., Friday, A., and Coulton, P. Stimulating a Dialogue on Renewable Energy Through Making. In *Proc. DIS*, ACM (2014).
11. Frontier Economics and Sustainability First. Demand side response in the domestic sector-a literature review of major trials. Tech. rep., Department of Energy & Climate Change, 2012.
12. Guy, S., and Marvin, S. Transforming urban infrastructure provision—the emerging logic of demand side management. *Policy Studies 17*, 2 (1996), 137–147.
13. Liu, X., Ivanescu, L., Kang, R., and Maier, M. Real-time household load priority scheduling algorithm based on prediction of renewable source availability. *Consumer Electronics, IEEE Trans. on 58*, 2 (2012), 318–326.
14. Morales, J. M., Conejo, A. J., Madsen, H., Pinson, P., and Zugno, M. Renewable energy sourcesmodeling and forecasting. In *Integrating Renewables in Electricity Markets*. Springer, 2014, 15–56.
15. Newman, P., Forshaw, S., Simm, W., Ferrario, M. A., Whittle, J., and Friday, A. Seeding the design process for future problems.
16. Pierce, J., and Paulos, E. Beyond energy monitors: interaction, energy, and emerging energy systems. In *Proc. CHI*, ACM (2012), 665–674.
17. Pierce, J., and Paulos, E. The local energy indicator: designing for wind and solar energy systems in the home. In *Proc. DIS*, ACM (2012), 631–634.
18. Price, B. A., van der Linden, J., Bourgeois, J., and Kortuem, G. When looking out of the window is not enough: Informing the design of in-home technologies for domestic energy microgeneration. In *ICT for Sustainability (ICT4S)*, ETH Zurich (February 2013), 73–80.
19. Roulston, M. S., Kaplan, D. T., Hardenberg, J., and Smith, L. A. Using medium-range weather forcasts to improve the value of wind energy production. *Renewable Energy 28*, 4 (2003), 585–602.
20. Schrammel, J., Gerdenitsch, C., Weiss, A., Kluckner, P. M., and Tscheligi, M. Fore-watch–the clock that tells you when to use: Persuading users to align their energy consumption with green power availability. In *Ambient Intelligence*. Springer, 2011, 157–166.
21. Strengers, Y. Air-conditioning Australian households: The impact of dynamic peak pricing. *Energy Policy 38*, 11 (2010), 7312–7322.
22. Strengers, Y. A. Designing eco-feedback systems for everyday life. In *Proc. CHI*, ACM (2011), 2135–2144.
23. Trentmann, F. Disruption is normal: blackouts, breakdowns and the elasticity of everyday life. In *Time, Consumption, and Everyday Life*, E. Shove, F. Trentmann, and R. Wilk, Eds. Oxford, UK: Berg, Oxford, 2009, 67–84.
24. Whittle, J., Ochu, E., Ferrario, M. A., Southern, J., and McNally, R. Beyond research in the wild: Citizen-led research as a model for innovation in the digital economy. In *Proc. Digital Futures* (2012).
25. World Nuclear Association. Nuclear Power in the United Kingdom, February 2014.
26. Yadoo, A., Gormally, A., and Cruickshank, H. Low-carbon off-grid electrification for rural areas in the united kingdom: Lessons from the developing world. *Energy Policy 39*, 10 (2011), 6400–6407. Sustainability of biofuels.
27. Yang, R., Newman, M. W., and Forlizzi, J. Making sustainability sustainable: Challenges in the design of eco-interaction technologies. In *Proc. CHI*, ACM (2014), 823–832.

Designing Persuasive Technology to Manage Peak Electricity Demand in Ontario Homes

Valerie Sugarman and Edward Lank
Cheriton School of Computer Science
University of Waterloo, Waterloo, ON, Canada
{vsugarman, lank}@uwaterloo.ca

ABSTRACT

When it comes to environmental sustainability, the time that electricity is consumed matters. For example, using an air conditioner on a hot summer afternoon as the power grid is strained necessitates the use of more polluting sources to meet demand. In this paper, we analyze end-user response to two utility-driven conservation programs in Ontario, Canada: Time-of-Use pricing and the peaksaver program. We find that time-of-use pricing encourages shifting some electricity demand, but only when it is convenient. We also find that while potentially effective at a larger scale, the peaksaver program in its current form is unattractive to participants. These results are discussed in the context of Fogg's Behavior Model for Persuasive Design, which allows us to explore the design space for improvement to these programs and ground our design implications for the design of technologies to encourage reduction of peak electricity demand.

Author Keywords: Sustainability; Peak Electricity Load; Persuasive Technology; Design

ACM Classification Keywords

H.5.m. Information interfaces and presentation (e.g., HCI): Miscellaneous.

INTRODUCTION

One area of interest to HCI researchers has been the study of tools, interfaces, and devices that can encourage a reduction in electricity consumption. In this area, we find studies of in-home displays [8,12], prototypes of the smart grid [7] and use of smart thermostat control [21,34], among others.

Alongside research deployments to encourage reduced electricity use, electrical utilities are also very concerned about when electricity is consumed. On a daily basis, the demand for electricity varies from low during overnight hours to higher during the day. Summer heat waves can cause extremely high demand to be placed on the electrical grid, with residential cooling account for nearly 22% of the peak demand [17]. Failure to meet this peak demand can cause disruptions in electricity availability – brownouts, rolling black outs, or even wide-spread power outages. In order to avoid this, utilities manage supply to ensure that they meet peak demand. There are side-effects and trade-offs from the possible solutions. One option is to simply have larger power plants with surplus generating capacity. The downside is that power plants are most efficient when they are being run consistently at their full capacity. Alternatively, special generating plants can be constructed solely to be used during times of particular need – which could be as infrequently as a few hours per year [35].

To reduce the varying demand for electricity and the attendant financial and environmental costs of that varying demand, several electrical utility companies have devised programs to encourage more optimally timed consumption of electricity. The two specific program types we focus on in this paper are:

- **Variable pricing schemes**, where electricity rates vary consistently depending on time-of-day. The goal of variable pricing is to encourage behavior change on the part of the consumer, to use less electricity at daily peak times.
- **Critical peak load programs**, where participants opt-in and allow the utility to selectively control their home air conditioning units. This allows the utilities to lower the demand for electricity at critical peak times.

The end goal of both research-led and industry-led programs is to persuade consumers to change their habits with respect to the consumption of electricity. In the HCI research community, we are familiar with technologies to encourage behavior change, such as BJ Fogg's work on persuasion and behavior [9]. Many designers and researchers have explored how deployed technology can be leveraged to encourage positive action in communities of end-users [e.g. 6].

This paper presents a set of design implications for persuasive technology to encourage or enable a reduction in electricity demand from households at these peak times. To develop these, we conducted interviews with 18 people who were automatically enrolled or opted in to the versions of the industry-led programs in Ontario, Canada, in order to understand the impact of these programs on their day to day practices. These findings were then analyzed using Fogg's Behavior Model for Persuasive Design [11], along with consideration of other models of behavior change to see where these programs are missing opportunities and how

CHI 2015, April 18 - 23, 2015, Seoul, Republic of Korea

ACM 978-1-4503-3145-6/15/04 $15.00
http://dx.doi.org/10.1145/2702123.2702364

they can be improved. Along with the widespread availability of smartphones and internet-enabled thermostats, we begin to explore ways that programs can evolve to better satisfy end users and lead to reduced demand at peak load times.

The remainder of this paper is organized as follows. In the next section, we discuss related work. We then describe the methodology of the study and present results of the interviews. We conclude by presenting a series of design recommendations that arise from our interview findings and existing knowledge of behavior change.

BACKGROUND AND RELATED WORK

Behavior Change

In his exploration of persuasive technology, Fogg introduced a Behavior Model for Persuasive Design (FBM) [11]. FBM proposes that in order for a target behavior to take place, three criteria are necessary. Firstly, the person must be sufficiently *motivated*. Secondly, the person must have the *ability* to execute the behavior. Thirdly, if the first two criteria are met, there must be some sort of *trigger* to actually suggest the behavior at an opportune moment. Fogg places the first two aspects as axes demonstrating a tradeoff between *motivation* and *ability* (see Figure 1).

Even if a person's *motivation* is low, if you can make the target behavior very easy to do (high *ability*) then it is likely a *trigger* will succeed in prompting the desired behavior. Successful persuasive design will increase the position on of the axes, or will provide opportune *triggers*. FBM allows for a structured analysis of programs and technologies.

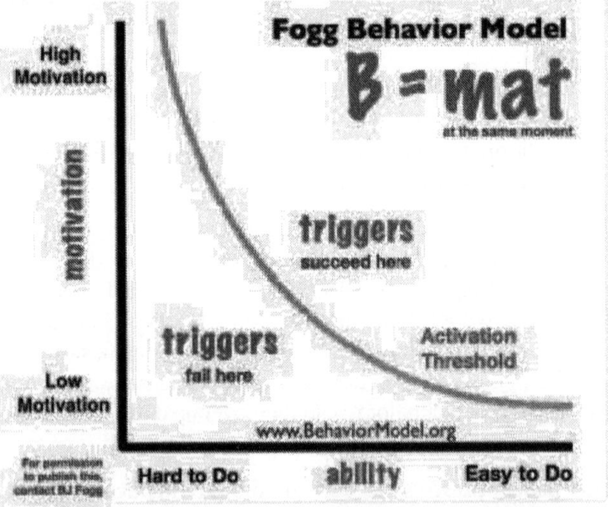

Figure 1 - Fogg's Behavior Model (© BJ Fogg) [10]

Other models of behavior change have been used in HCI research, including the stage-based, or Transtheoretical Model (TTM) of behavior change [5], and work has been done to help bridge the gap between behavior change research in HCI and established Behavioral Theory [16]. He et al. incorporate the TTM and acknowledge that it is necessary to target eco-feedback design interventions to the individual because of the different stage and unique circumstances they are in [15]. We include some discussion of targeting interventions based on TTM in our design implications. However, most HCI work using the TTM focuses almost exclusively on motivation. We argue that FBM offers a more holistic perspective, through the additional consideration of how technology can increase ability and be used as triggers.

Many other theories of behavior modification exist. Classical concepts such as operant conditioning (positively reinforcing or punishing certain behaviors) are considered throughout this work, particularly with respect to the monetary incentives. Operant conditioning is part of the larger discussion of increased motivation, ability and triggers. However, operant conditioning through positive reinforcement can lead to the "over-justification effect" [22] where the incentives or rewards reduces intrinsic motivation. Countering the over-justification effect is self-perception theory, which argues that attitudes are influenced by behavior. Other theories abound: balance theory, cognitive dissonance theory, social comparison theory, discursive practices, etc. At heart, these theories examine how attitudes and behaviors are linked, and these theories are implicitly incorporated into FBM. As Fogg notes, motivation includes pleasure/pain, hope/fear, and social acceptance/rejection, and ability includes time, effort, cognitive complexity, social deviance, and habitual vs. non-routine behaviors. Many of the psychological theories of the link between attitude and behavior or of behavior change can be mapped onto these dimensions of FBM.

Sustainability in the HCI Community

Creating a sustainable future requires contributions from a large set of disciplines – engineering, green design, and renewable generation, among others. Even within the HCI community, there is discussion of what role HCI can best serve in this research community, and how to best go about it [14,19]. Prototyping the smart grid is becoming increasingly common in recent HCI work [7,27,34], and Costanza et al. propose that HCI in particular is well positioned to prototype and study interfaces for the increasingly complicated electricity system now, while they are still being developed [7].

Going Beyond Eco-Feedback

Brynjarsdóttir et al. provide a review of HCI research in persuasive technology for sustainability from 2009 to 2011, and argue that much of the research done so far has been focused on making users "more aware" of their consumption through feedback, which is taking a limited view of the problem [3]. Pierce and Paulos express similar views in another review of HCI research that emphasizes electricity consumption feedback [25], and also suggest that investigating demand response technologies could be particularly interesting from an HCI perspective, given the deeper behavior change that would be required. With a few exceptions [2,32], this area has been relatively unexplored.

Focus on the Human and Everyday Practice

Strengers gives a name to the practice of designing for increasing awareness: designing for "Resource Man" [33]. This fictional character is interested in technology, educated, motivated to manage his resource consumption in a fully rational way, and stereotypically male. She argues that design geared toward Resource Man will ultimately fail because it neglects lived experiences. Brynjarsdóttir et al. [3], similarly, note that much research in sustainability has been grounded in a "modernist" approach, i.e. the assumption that once quantified and provided with expert-level advice, individuals will act rationally to improve their practices. They also argue that we need to refocus on lived experiences both with respect to the individual and to the collective. Some recent research (e.g. [18,26]) has explored domestic interactions as a mechanism for understanding constraints on behaviors within households. Our goal, similarly, is to examine the lived experiences of households subject to both variable pricing schemes and critical peak load programs as a first step to a broader perspective.

FBM and Sustainability

Brynjarsdóttir et al. [3], in their survey of sustainability in HCI, note that much HCI research in sustainability leverages Fogg's ideas of persuasion and technology to encourage sustainability. However, they also note that, of the papers that they surveyed, *"almost half"* had no evaluation, and that the *"typical duration of a field study is 3-4 weeks, which is likely not long enough to go beyond novelty effects"*.

In this paper, FBM is leveraged to guide the analysis and re-design of two demand management programs that have been deployed for several years. In our analysis, we find that FBM frames data on these programs' successes and failures while retaining a link to past research in designing new persuasive technologies to promote conservation. As a result, it serves both as a reflective tool on the efficacy of existing programs [13] and as a tool to guide redesign of different aspects of these programs.

CASE STUDY CONTEXT

The research presented in this paper is based on a case study of two specific programs that are currently implemented in Ontario, Canada. Currently, the baseline electricity needs of Ontario are met by nuclear and large hydroelectric power stations. The peak demand is generally met with natural gas powered plants, as well as some smaller hydroelectric plants [36]. Thus, reducing peak demand in Ontario can directly lead to reduced greenhouse gas emissions. The existing programs are a variable pricing scheme for electricity, i.e. time-of-use pricing (TOU), and a program for mitigating the severity of critical peak usage, the peaksaver program (peaksaver).

These specific programs in Ontario, Canada were chosen as a case study in addressing power consumption for a number of reasons:

- Ontario experiences notable peaks in electricity consumption – both daily and at critical times;
- There exist specific programs that are well defined to address these peaks, and these programs have existed for a number of years;
- Other researchers have used these programs and the Ontario context to perform quantitative analysis of the costs and benefits of these programs, which provides complimentary data to our analysis.

Beyond the pragmatic reasons outlined above, there are issues of social sustainability surrounding power generation in Ontario. In 2013, political decisions to relocate new power plants to pacify voters during an election campaign resulted in almost $1 billion in costs to Ontario taxpayers. Essentially, power consumption in Ontario is an issue of active public discourse, increasing public awareness of both the environmental, economic, and social problems surrounding electricity production and consumption and programs designed to address these problems.

INTERVIEWS

While in this work we build from existing models of behavior change, we first need to know more about the existing practices surrounding shifting electricity consumption to off-peak times. While studies have focused on electricity consumption as a whole [15,26], peak demand and shifting usage has not been a major focus.

Method

The study consisted of 18 semi-structured interviews that took place in person, by phone or by Skype. Participants received a $20 gift card to an online retailer for their time.

Participants were recruited through email lists, online classified ads throughout Ontario, word of mouth, and posters at local community centers and libraries. Participants were pre-screened before being interviewed in order to ensure a variety of participants with respect to age, who they live with, what type of dwelling they inhabit, whether they have central air conditioning, the type of thermostat they use, and involvement and knowledge about the peaksaver program. See Table 1 for a summary.

Table 1 - Background Data of Interview Participants

Age	20s: 6 30s: 7 40s: 5
Gender	Female: 13 Male: 5
Air Conditioning	Central Air Conditioning: 14 Portable or window: 4
Lives with	Partner only: 6 Partner and children: 5 Parents (with or without siblings): 3 Roommates: 3 Alone: 1
Peaksaver	Enrolled: 3 Previously enrolled: 1

The interviewer had a set of topics and some starter questions to discuss, but the interviews were also open ended in order to learn more about specific habits, devices and programs of the participants. The topics included:

- Usage of air conditioning;
- Control of the thermostat;
- Awareness and consideration of TOU pricing when making consumption decisions;
- Awareness and consideration of peak load times
- Thoughts about various existing demand response programs and pricing schemes; and
- Awareness and consideration of the peaksaver program.

Interviews lasted between 30 minutes and 1 hour. All interviews were audio recorded and then transcribed for analysis. Affinity diagramming done by two researchers, using incremental, open coding was used to group codes into 95 clusters. A cross cutting analysis linked these clusters into 4 themes. A subset of these themes and clusters are presented in this work in the context of the two Ontario programs.

TIME-OF-USE PRICING

Details and Related Work

While many variants of differential pricing of electricity exist, Ontario's TOU pricing scheme varies the price of electricity throughout the day at three different levels (off-peak - 7.5 ¢/kWh, mid-peak - 11.2 ¢/kWh and on-peak - 13.5¢/kWh as of Sept. 2014) on a consistent schedule. This schedule changes twice per year (summer versus winter). Overnight (7pm to 7am) is always off-peak, as are weekends and holidays. In practice, the overall financial benefits for many consumers from shifting usage due to TOU pricing are small, particularly when considering that paying for electricity makes up only about 1.8% of average total household expenditure in Ontario [28]. As of May 2014, 95.9% of households and small business paid these variable rates for electricity in Ontario [24].

The scope of Ontario TOU pricing has led to research on the programs as a whole. At a macro level, Strapp et al. found that TOU pricing does encourage some shifting, and there is often a small net conservation effect when the shifted consumption is less than the peak period reduction [31]. Rowlands and Furst found that bills changed by less than 5% in either direction as a result of the adoption TOU pricing in Ontario [29]. Adepetu et al. criticize the existing distribution of hours and prices as being neither optimal nor effective at reducing the mean peak-to-average ratio of demand [1].

Outside of the Ontario context, Strengers examined smart metering demand management programs in Australia [32], which included the use of In-Home-Displays (IHDs) along with a critical peak/TOU pricing scheme. She notes that the decisions people make about using resources for the comfort and cleanliness of their homes is much more complex than a rational decision about optimizing resource consumption or cost. Specifically, programs and technologies that seek to foster behavior change should allow for the tensions between convenience/comfort and cost [32]. Many of our findings echo this.

There are a variety of technologies that support consumers in adapting to TOU pricing. Research on programmable thermostats indicates that the challenge of programming these devices limits their impact [23]. Direct feedback through IHDs can reduce overall consumption by 5-15% in the short term [8].

Findings

Money Incentivizes Easy Shifting

There was a common sentiment of why not shift usage if it saves a bit of money and is convenient. The consensus was that the off-peak times are a convenient time to do laundry and run the dishwasher for those with a regular weekday working schedule.

On the other hand, many participants noted that, without the potential to save money, they might not consider load shifting, and that the money causes them to act. For P4, *"if it works in your schedule, any money is worth it"*, since *"money is a tangible thing, where you're like 'I'll wait that extra hour'"*. Although we probed, we found little evidence that participants were motivated by sustainability, or other concerns when shifting day to day usage.

Not all Shifting is Easy

The ease of shifting any one activity varied across participants. P17 worked from home, and found it convenient to do laundry at lunch time. She was fully aware that it cost a little more, but felt that *"I'm also like, I don't want to do this tonight, when I'm tired, so, I'll pay the extra"* combined with justifying the small expense by saving money in other ways. Cooking was an interesting example for participants too, and behavior fell on a continuum which varied from never shifting despite TOU pricing (P2), to saving long roasting for the weekends but using the stovetop on weeknights (P10, P11, P5), to P7 who stated that *"I've actually sat there like ok we're going to make dinner. Ok like I could start cooking at 6, but I'll just wait until 7"*. A number of our participants had gas ranges, so this discussion did not apply.

Considering TOU in Home Cooling is Uncommon

One of the most important aspects of peak electricity demand is the use of air conditioners during hot, humid summers in Ontario. Only two participants directly mentioned making explicit changes in home comfort using the thermostat because of TOU pricing or consideration of daily peaks. These included purchasing a programmable thermostat for use with both air conditioning and electric heat (P10) and pre-cooling the house to avoid using the air conditioner during peak hours (P2). Other participants had programmable thermostats, but either did not program them or did not consider TOU in the process. Most focused only on the overall cost of using their air conditioner. Many also noted that they were more concerned about the temperature in their home for the comfort of family members - children and older parents at home during the day - or guests and pets, as opposed to themselves. This resonates with Fogg's inclusion of social acceptance as an important contributor to the motivation axis [11], as well as Strengers' findings [32].

The Impact of Shifting is Unclear

P5 explains she has *"a hard time visualizing what my little impact of not doing my load of laundry in the, during the day has on the broader system, although I recognize that if everyone was doing their laundry during the middle of the day it might be a bit of an issue"*. Without some awareness of the broader impacts of collective action, our participants, instead, weigh the cost versus inconvenience to them.

PEAKSAVER PROGRAM

Details and Related Work

The peaksaver program [37] is an opt-in program, designed to address critical peaks in electricity consumption. Residents of single-family homes with central air conditioning are offered a free internet-connected, programmable thermostat. In exchange, the utility installs a controller on the air conditioner. During critical peak load times, the target temperature of the air conditioner is either increased by up to 2°C or cycled off for 15 to 30 minutes every hour for up to four hours of the day. These occurrences are limited to weekdays, and a maximum of 10 times per year.

Examining specifically the peaksaver program in Ontario, Singla and Kehsav suggest that there are not enough people participating in the program on a voluntary basis to significantly impact consumption [30]. They devise a scheme that would pay participants up to $2 per degree hour that they increased the setpoint of their thermostat in the summer (for central air conditioning) and demonstrate that this scheme would still reduce operating costs in Ontario by $688 million in the next 20 years, by reducing the need for the construction of new power plants.

Strengers' studied critical peak pricing in Australia, with day ahead notice by email or phone call [32]. In this scheme, prices increased by 10 to 20 times on hot weekday afternoons, to better match the real time price of electricity at those times. She found that those who participated in the critical peak pricing program were more likely to sacrifice comfort in the short term specifically because of the high cost of power at critical peaks.

The option of paying consumers for signing up has been leveraged by Nest through a program called "Rush Hour Rewards" [38]. These "Rush Hours" are simply an analogy for peak load times. With this enabled, the Nest thermostat pre-cools the home, then ensures that the air conditioner runs only intermittently during peak times. The user can override the Rush Hour if desired.

Findings

Few Understand Critical Peak Load

Having some awareness of critical peak load times and their significance is the first step towards having some non-zero motivation to reduce usage at times of critically high demand for electricity. For our participants, even this awareness is missing. Some participants were able to identify that peak load times correspond to heat waves, but did not make the connection to the impact on electricity demand in the moment.

Taking Action is Hard

When asked directly about taking action or changing behavior at peak load times, there was a common sentiment among many of the participants that they were already doing the best they could to reduce electricity consumption at all times (generally because of cost), and there was not much that they could change and still live their life comfortably at critical peak times. Some were aware of the environmental impact and the small monetary cost from TOU, but comfort in their home took priority. P11 explains that *"I realize that I probably shouldn't be and I realize that you know, there's probably, every other person in this apartment building is probably doing the same thing, but I do want to be comfortable"*. For P8, *"being so hot, like it kind of trumps, like the amount, or the cost that you know you'll have to pay later"*. Some participants did take action as required: P5 and P7, who had only portable air conditioning units, discussed going to work in order to be in the air conditioning there.

One issue that arose during our discussions with participants is that many people do not have any control over the temperature at work, and the choices made by their workplace did not correspond with what they might choose in their own home, either for comfort or financial reasons. P7 suggests that even at critical peak times, *"I don't change any of my habits at work"* because it's *"totally financially motivated, which makes me kind of sad"*. P4 laments the lack of control at work, and was frustrated that it makes her own efforts at conservation seem negligible. P15 recalls *"I hated it going in to work and I had to dress like it was winter inside. It doesn't need to be that cold"*. Some participants expressed similar feelings of preferring open windows or a higher temperature in the home, but were overruled by roommates or family members.

Others May Not Do Their Part

This idea of collective action was also significant when we discussed rolling blackouts or brownouts because of insufficient supply. P9 noted that *"we would try to reduce [consumption] but then we'd also probably get kind of annoyed when other people don't [...] we'd want that conservation to go on not just from us, we'd want it to be everybody"*. Similarly, P11 suggested that *"if only one person changes their behavior and no one else does, then it really doesn't help"*. The perceived threat and inconvenience of blackouts was a much bigger motivator for some more than others. For example, P17 explained that a previous blackout *"certainly put a monkey wrench in my day to day existence"*. On the other hand, P18 figured *"we're not going to be the only ones in the blackout, so it wouldn't really affect our usage"*, and says *"to me a blackout wouldn't be such a big deal"*.

A number of participants also commented on the practices of neighbors or relatives being noticeably inefficient in general. One participant knew others who had *"a really bad habit of running their air conditioning and leaving their windows open"*. The question then becomes how to design solutions that reach those people too.

Peaksaver

Three of our participants were currently a part of the peaksaver program: P1, P3 and P17. P16 participated but when she switched energy providers, that provider did not offer the peaksaver program. P1 learned about peaksaver through an ad in the newspaper promising a free programmable thermostat, but it became clear in the interview that he was not aware of the fact that the utility had the option to cycle down his central air conditioner during peak times. P1 was actually quite averse to the idea of utility being able to control his home air conditioning unit. The others learned about the program through the mail - either an insert with the electricity bill or a separate flyer. They had a much stronger grasp of what the program entailed, and joined for the purpose of putting less strain on the grid. As P3 put it *"it didn't seem like a big sacrifice"* and she suggested that *"I don't even think it really should be optional"*. We also found that, with the exception of P16, participants were unaware of changes to their air conditioning, and noticed no difference to their comfort level, which supports claims made in advertising materials. P16 noticed it was a little warmer in the house, but *"I totally understood that, made a lot of sense"*. This difference was likely because she set the air conditioning to 24 or 25 degrees, which was a higher baseline temperature than the others.

Participants who were not enrolled in peaksaver may have heard something about the program, but, because of limited motivation, had not bothered to learn more. For these participants, we described the program and gauged their reactions, finding a continuum of opinion from being actively averse to the idea of someone else controlling some aspect of their home, to not having a direct problem with utility control but not seeing enough benefit to themselves to bother making the effort to join. Many participants noted that there was some aspect of "big brother" that they found distasteful. With more appropriate incentives, even those who were extremely opposed to the idea of someone else having control over their home might consider it. P12 suggested if a rebate occurred *"that would be a different story"* and would *"relax my concern of someone else being able to control it"*. P9, who was quite concerned initially, expressed *"if it was going to save money, then definitely"*.

With two days' notice, participants can opt out of peaksaver for a 48 hour period. We probed the issue of control and opt out with our participants. Some participants indicated that if they were to join, they would fully commit to the program, such as P4 who states that if she joined, *"I wouldn't want to go through the hassle of like opting out"*. On the other hand, being able to opt out in the moment, or in some way override the system in the moment, would be absolutely required for others to even consider joining. P9 would want ultimate control out of concern for her family *"maybe somebody has a kid who as a fever [...] as long as it's like, in the end, I've got the ultimate control over it, then that would be ok"*.

One positive aspect that interviewees brought up about the peaksaver program was that it supports collective action. P5 says she likes that it works on *"a collective rather than an individual basis"*. Additionally, P8 thinks it makes sense since *"it's not guaranteed that I or another person would make the changes"* and it *"at least guarantees some action taken"*. P17 likes that the change is done for her - *"I don't have to think about it. Just one more thing off my list"*.

DESIGN IMPLICATIONS (DI)

There are a number of design implications that we identified from our findings, which are supported by relevant related work. The intertwined concepts of motivation, ability and triggers from FBM were used to develop these. Specifically, we considered each theme identified from the affinity diagram and analyzed what our participants were telling us about their habits, and whether it effectively increased or decreased ability or motivation, or whether it was indicative of existing or missing triggers. We gathered what we could learn from existing practices (e.g. shifting usage as a result of TOU pricing) and what barriers were in place to making more dramatic shifts in behavior at critical peak load times.

Motivation

The core motivators identified by Fogg are:

- Pleasure/pain: which focuses on the immediate response;
- Hope/fear: which focuses on the anticipated future outcome of the behavior; and
- Social acceptance/rejection: which focuses on social norms.

DI: Communicate the Impact of Peak Load

It is clear from our interviews that most people are rarely aware of the times that the electricity grid is strained, and are even less aware of the impact that peak load demand has on neither the construction of new power plants nor the environmental consequences. One potential area for persuasive technology to help is in increasing this type of knowledge. These should build from existing knowledge of motivational techniques [20].

This design implication targets the core motivator of hope/fear. Ideally one could instill a hope for a better world, and that should be the focus. On the other hand, in reality, many of our participants were especially motivated by the fear of imminent blackouts. This DI targets those in the early stages of the TTM, who are not yet aware of the benefits of taking action.

DI: Harness Collective Action

Our participants noted both not being able to comprehend the impact of their individual behavior (such as shifting laundry) and the worry that they would be the only ones making sacrifices during peak load times. Both of these impacted their motivation to make changes, and could be addressed by demonstrating collective action. For daily peaks, this could be communicated at the time of making a decision to use an appliance. As the internet-of-things expands to include common household objects, these objects could communicate information about current consumption.

Collective action can particularly be harnessed to address critical peak times. Social media tools can be used to communicate who is making cutbacks within a social circle. They can be used to anonymously communicate the net effect of cutbacks to the masses. They can be used to allow occupants of a large building to collaborate to increase the temperature during times of acute demand. In our work, we found the lack of awareness of collective participation and collective effect sapped motivation. Participants cannot always make extreme efforts to conserve, but for those infrequent critical peaks, collective action holds the promise to both motivate and serve as a trigger. The work of Boucher et al. capitalizes on this need [2].

DI: Give Consumers Ultimate Control

We found a number of participants who were not opposed to the small or imperceptible reduction in comfort from peaksaver, but the specific implementation details turned them off – specifically the idea of an outsider having control, with limited ability to opt out in the moment. Giving consumers ultimate control over adjustments and thus the ability to opt out in the moment using the thermostat would reduce this fear. One concern of the designers of peaksaver was that people could in theory opt out en masse at the times when changes were most needed. However, in practice, peaksaver participants were unaware of the changes, so this is unlikely to be the case.

Nest is already working with a limited number of utility companies to offer rebates, or even a free Nest thermostat for signing up for their Rush Hour Rewards program, which does not preclude opting out in the moment.

DI: Allow Flexibility and Customization

As others have noted, it is essential to target behavior change interventions to what stage the participant is in the TTM [5,15]. Even beyond this, there is a need for further flexibility and ability for customization tailored to the individual, since they have different thresholds for comfort and willingness to contribute to the greater good, as well as perceptions of social norms.

While in general our participants understood that a small change in temperature would not have a large impact on their home comfort, the primary motivation for cooling the home was for the pleasure of being cool on a hot day. Further flexibility would allow users to cycle down their air conditioning only to the extent that they are comfortable with it, for a proportionally smaller reward. If this increased flexibility means that more people would sign up, even if the individual impact was small, collective impact would still have an important impact on peak load.

Ability

According to Fogg, lowering any of time, money, physical effort, mental effort, social deviance or non-routine aspects of an action increases its simplicity and therefore increases the ability of a person to perform the task. If any one of these elements are lacking for a specific person, then the behavior is not simple for that person. The simplicity of the behavior is assessed at the time that it is triggered, based on these criteria.

DI: Allow Users to Set it and Forget It, or Customize and Optimize

Even the simple implementation of TOU pricing was not fully understood by most of our participants. Many people were unable or unwilling to invest the time or "brain cycles" in learning the details of this program, including the actual price differential, or the mid-peak and on-peak hours, beyond the 7pm threshold to off-peak. On the other hand, some made very deliberate choices about running home comfort systems and appliances with respect to these prices. New appliances are increasingly coming with timers in order to make it easy to consume at off-peak times. In a fully connected future, these appliances could even connect to the grid directly and run at the best time given the constraints of the user.

In the same vein, the fact that peaksaver made the changes automatically was appealing to a number of our participants, since they did not have to think about making the changes themselves. There are also those who have demonstrated a desire to be more actively engaged in managing their resource consumption and home comfort, and be able to customize systems to their individual needs. While Strengers cautions us of designing *only* for Resource Man, designers should be careful not to alienate these users.

DI: Use Appropriate Incentives

Many participants were reluctant to forgo the comfort of air conditioning on hot days. In these cases, the small monetary savings of TOU pricing were particularly ineffective. For some, no feasible amount of money would be enough to convince them, but others were willing to make changes for appropriate monetary incentives. Still others indicated that the hypothetical financial reward was not necessary, and they were happy to do their part. An additional concern is how to handle the problem that putting a monetary value on a behavior can actually have negative spillover on other environmentally conscious activities because of putting a price on it [20].

The existing one-time gift of a thermostat for the long-term commitment of participation in peaksaver seemed disproportionate to many of our participants. While different participants have different levels of price-sensitivity, in order to expand the reach of utility driven air conditioning demand response programs, more appropriate incentives are required.

DI: Offer Suggestions of How to Reduce Consumption at Peak Times (And Make These Easy To Do)

Our participants simply did not know of reasonable ways to reduce their consumption at critical peak times, which correlated with [32]. In order for behavior change to occur, it is necessary for them to not have to think too hard about what to do, or work too hard to do it, or in Fogg's words, decrease the brain cycles and physical effort required. Thus, easy to do suggestions are required, such as:

- Using the barbecue to avoid heating up the house (and causing the air conditioner to work harder);
- Cooking in advance of a heatwave and using the microwave or toaster oven to reheat;
- Spending time in larger groups at places that are already air conditioned instead of at home.

These behaviors were gathered from those who do not have central air conditioning at home, as necessities for keeping cool. Admittedly, they do have higher motivation to find ways to keep cool since they do not have the simple option of turning on the air conditioning. But there are alternative ways to keep cool that could help reduce peak demand, including closing windows blinds, the use of ceiling, circulating or portable fans which were mentioned by a number of our participants to reduce their need for air conditioning in order to save money. Making these suggestions of other ways to keep cool without much discomfort, and with lower cost, may be beneficial to those who did not take these actions already. Exploring the automation of some of these lower tech solutions in order make them easy for those that do have the option is one path going forward.

Taking these suggestions to the next level, families could plan a group barbeque and consolidate their need for air conditioning, with the added benefit of increasing a sense of community and social action at these critical peak times. Issues of sustainability around food preparation has also been studied within the HCI community [4]. Making this behavior part of accepted social practice and pitching in to help with this problem is where the design challenge lies. Taking more intensive action at the more infrequent critical peak load times is where efforts should be directed, given the increased impact [30]. This could also help overcome the fatigue noted by our participants.

Triggers

Fogg describes three types of triggers:

- Spark: Trigger with a motivational element;
- Facilitator: Trigger that also makes the behavior easier to do;
- Signal: Notification or reminder.

These types of triggers should be used appropriately to help increase whichever of the elements is lacking.

DI: Integrate Triggers

To provide some small trigger, some participants did post the TOU schedule in the kitchen or laundry room to remind themselves of peak times. Additionally, certain IHDs do provide feedback about the current price level. However, these IHDs require the user to engage with the display to be informed, i.e. they are separated in space from the location of the instantaneous decision. An alternative trigger could be a set of small displays attached on or near the controls of electricity-intensive appliances that signal whether it is an appropriate time to use the appliance, combined with an increasingly common delayed-start feature. Such ubiquitous devices would be more appropriate triggers as they are in-the-moment, localized awareness mechanisms that are visible as a decision is being made.

Participants were often unaware of critical peak times, and so lack any form of trigger to alter their behavior in-the-moment. The most obvious trigger, particularly for critical peaks, is some form of simple notification such as an email or text message. While we had difficulty finding scientific studies on the effectiveness of basic email of text message notifications, it is also worthwhile to note that the use of a generic notification is sufficiently undirected that it may be ineffective as a trigger if motivation and ability are not high enough [11]. Utilities are proficient at predicting demand days in advance of critical peak periods, and could easily notify customers in advance to increase consumers' ability to plan, which has been shown to be feasible for some [7].

DI: Consider Sparks and Facilitators

Critical peaks are particularly amenable to sparks and facilitators, because they are sufficiently infrequent that the spark or facilitator will not become so commonplace that they become irksome.

Networked thermostats could be used to spark behavior change in a variety of ways. Given the ability of utilities to pay up to $2 per degree hour for savings during these periods [30], one could imagine using the network interface to provide significant incentives to consumers. Imagine a smartphone interface where, by leaving your house and idling your air conditioner, you obtained a free cold drink at a local cafe, as indicated by a coupon on your smartphone. If the interface included a simple button to raise the temperature, the interface combines the positive attributes of a spark and facilitator to promote high-impact, low-frequency behavior change, particularly important during critical peak periods. However, those who choose to forgo central air conditioning should not be unduly punished. Additionally, designers need to be careful that this system does not encourage excess car use, which could undermine potential benefits.

DISCUSSION

In their survey and critique of sustainability research, Brynjarsdóttir et al. [3] identify oversights in past sustainability research in its narrow definition of sustainability, its focus on the individual, its assumption of rationalism, its neglect of lived experiences, and its neglect of dynamics. While we do not claim to address all issues with past research in sustainability, we note that applying FBM to an analysis of two real-world demand management programs does provide data on the lived experiences of participants with these programs and the dynamics of behavior of participants with respect to these programs over time. In exploring experiences with these two demand management programs, our design implications – particularly the first two motivational implications – also touch on the rationalism of participants and on collective versus individual actions and decisions.

One characteristic of past research on sustainability is a strong focus on awareness mechanisms. Brynjarsdóttir et al. [3] in particular claim that most systems *"aim to provide information and raise awareness, in the hopes that this will lead in some way to altered behavior"*. Strengers [31], too, notes that individuals may frequently not be aware of possible actions they can take to conserve power in-the-moment. Within our design implications, we address these under the theme of Ability, noting that offering concrete suggestions and enabling those suggestions is an important aspect of addressing critical peaks, in particular.

While we focus on the implementation of the programs in Ontario, other regions have both similar and different problems. Many of the design implications that come out of this work could be generalized or adapted. As discussed by Boucher et al. [5] there are other reasons for occasional, more unpredictable short-term changes in demand. Inclement weather can cause damage to distribution systems, or incidents at generating facilities can constrict supply. In such cases, centralized control by the utility is the preferred solution, since there is not enough time for people to become informed and to react. Renewable energy sources, such as solar and wind power are often constrained on the supply side, so having systems and technologies for temporarily reducing demand can again reduce the need to rely on more polluting sources. We would argue that our work provides a path toward broader participation in demand management programs like peaksaver, and that the broader participation in these programs extends beyond simply addressing critical demand peaks.

It is important to consider that even air conditioning demand management programs would only be part of the solution. Some utilities have adapted the peaksaver to include cycling down pool pumps, but it could also be expanded to pool heaters, and even electric hot water heaters in homes. For very short term peaks, such as those caused by accidents, even refrigerators or chest freezers could be cycled down by a few percent without negative consequences. Other researchers in areas like engineering are working on other types of solutions including reducing waste in the grid, better efficiencies in generation, and better electricity storage.

CONCLUSION

In this paper, we use Fogg's Behavior Model to analyze conservation programs implemented by electrical utilities in Ontario, Canada. While we find that these programs do have some net positive effect, we also identify several shortcomings of existing programs. We use these shortcomings, coupled with an application of Fogg's Behavior Model to identify a series of design implications for persuasive technology. It is our belief that, by adapting programs and the design of new technologies to align with the design implications we provide, the programs can promote more optimally-timed consumption of electricity and foster the participation of more electricity consumers.

ACKNOWLEDGMENTS

Funding provided by the Natural Science and Engineering Research Council of Canada (NSERC) and the Networks of Centres of Excellence for Graphics, Animation and New Media (NCE-GRAND).

REFERENCES

1. Adepetu, A., Rezaei, E., Lizotte, D., and Keshav, S. Critiquing Time-Of-Use Pricing in Ontario. *IEEE SmartGridComm Symposium*, (2013).
2. Boucher, A., Cameron, D., and Jarvis, N. Power to the people: dynamic energy management through communal cooperation. In *Proc. DIS '12*, ACM (2012), 612–620.
3. Brynjarsdóttir, H., Håakansson, M., Pierce, J., Baumer, E., DiSalvo, C., and Sengers, P. Sustainably unpersuaded: how persuasion narrows our vision of sustainability. In *Proc. CHI '12*, ACM (2012).
4. Clear, A.K., Hazas, M., Morley, J., Friday, A., and Bates, O. Domestic food and sustainable design: a study of university student cooking and its impacts. In *Proc. CHI '13*, ACM (2013), 2447–2456.
5. Consolvo, S., McDonald, D.W., and Landay, J.A. Theory-driven design strategies for technologies that support behavior change in everyday life. In *Proc. CHI '09*, ACM (2009), 405–414.
6. Consolvo, S., McDonald, D.W., Toscos, T., et al. Activity Sensing in the Wild: A Field Trial of Ubifit Garden. In *Proc. CHI '08*, ACM (2008), 1797–1806.
7. Costanza, E., Fischer, J.E., Colley, J.A., Rodden, T., Ramchurn, S.D., and Jennings, N.R. Doing the laundry with agents: a field trial of a future smart energy system in the home. In *Proc. CHI '14*, ACM (2014).

8. Darby, S. *The Effectiveness of Feedback on Energy Consumption.* Environmental Change Institute, University of Oxford, 2006.
9. Fogg, B.J. Persuasive technology: using computers to change what we think and do. *Ubiquity 2002*, December (2002), 5.
10. Fogg, B.J. [Graphic illustration of the Fogg Behavior Model]. *BJ Fogg's Behaviour Model*, 2007. http://behaviormodel.org/.
11. Fogg, B.J. A behavior model for persuasive design. In *Proc. Persuasive '09*, ACM (2009), 40:1–40:7.
12. Froehlich, J., Findlater, L., and Landay, J. The design of eco-feedback technology. In *Proc. CHI '10*, ACM (2010), 1999–2008.
13. Greenberg, S. and Buxton, B. Usability evaluation considered harmful (some of the time). *Proceedings of the SIGCHI Conference on Human Factors in Computing Systems*, ACM (2008), 111–120.
14. Haakansson, M. and Sengers, P. No Easy Compromise: Sustainability and the Dilemmas and Dynamics of Change. In *Proc. DIS '14*, ACM (2014).
15. He, H.A., Greenberg, S., and Huang, E.M. One size does not fit all: applying the transtheoretical model to energy feedback technology design. In *Proc. CHI '10*, ACM (2010), 927–936.
16. Hekler, E.B., Klasnja, P., Froehlich, J.E., and Buman, M.P. Mind the theoretical gap: interpreting, using, and developing behavioral theory in HCI research. In *Proc. CHI '13*, ACM (2013), 3307–3316.
17. HydroOne. Electricity Demand in Ontario. 2003. http://www.ontarioenergyboard.ca/documents/directive_dsm_HydroOne211103.pdf.
18. Katzeff, C. and Wangel, J. Social Practices, Households, and Design in the Smart Grid. In L.M. Hilty and B. Aebischer, eds., *ICT Innovations for Sustainability*. Springer International Publishing, 2015, 351–365.
19. Knowles, B., Blair, L., Hazas, M., and Walker, S. Exploring Sustainability Research in Computing: Where We Are and Where We Go Next. In *Proc. UbiComp '13*, ACM (2013), 305–314.
20. Knowles, B., Blair, L., Walker, S., Coulton, P., Thomas, L., and Mullagh, L. Patterns of Persuasion for Sustainability. In *Proc. DIS '14*, ACM (2014).
21. Koehler, C., Ziebart, B.D., Mankoff, J., and Dey, A.K. TherML: Occupancy Prediction for Thermostat Control. In *Proc. UbiComp '13*, ACM (2013).
22. Lepper, M.R., Greene, D., and Nisbett, R.E. Undermining children's intrinsic interest with extrinsic reward: A test of the" overjustification" hypothesis. *Journal of Personality and social Psychology 28*, 1 (1973), 129.
23. Meier, A. How people actually use thermostats. (2012).
24. Ontario Energy Board. Backgrounder – May 1 electricity price change. 2014. http://www.ontarioenergyboard.ca/oeb/_Documents/Press%20Releases/bg_RPP_TOU_20140416.pdf.
25. Pierce, J. and Paulos, E. Beyond energy monitors: interaction, energy, and emerging energy systems. In *Proc. CHI '12*, ACM (2012), 665–674.
26. Pierce, J., Schiano, D.J., and Paulos, E. Home, habits, and energy: examining domestic interactions and energy consumption. In *Proc. CHI '10*, ACM (2010).
27. Rodden, T.A., Fischer, J.E., Pantidi, N., Bachour, K., and Moran, S. At home with agents: exploring attitudes towards future smart energy infrastructures. In *Proc. CHI '13*, ACM (2013), 1173–1182.
28. Rowlands, I.H. Demand response in Ontario: exploring the issues. *A report for the Independent Electricity System Operator (IESO) of Ontario*, (2008).
29. Rowlands, I.H. and Furst, I.M. The cost impacts of a mandatory move to time-of-use pricing on residential customers: an Ontario (Canada) case-study. *Energy Efficiency 4*, 4 (2011), 571–585.
30. Singla, S. and Keshav, S. Demand response through a temperature setpoint market in Ontario. In *Proc. SmartGridComm '12*, (2012), 103–108.
31. Strapp, J., King, C., and Talbott, S. *Ontario Smart Price Pilot: Final Report.* 2007.
32. Strengers, Y. Smart metering demand management programs: challenging the comfort and cleanliness habitus of households. In *Proc. OZCHI '08*, (2008).
33. Strengers, Y. *Smart Energy Technologies in Everyday Life: Smart Utopia?* Palgrave Macmillan, New York, 2013.
34. Yang, R., Newman, M.W., and Forlizzi, J. Making sustainability sustainable: Challenges in the design of eco-interaction technologies. In *Proc. CHI '14*, ACM (2014), 823–832.
35. Smoothing the Peaks. *IESO.* https://www.ieso.ca/imoweb/siteshared/smoothing_the_peaks.asp?sid=ic.
36. IESO Ontario's Supply Mix. *IESO.* http://www.ieso.ca/Pages/Ontario%27s-Power-System/Supply-Mix/default.aspx.
37. peaksaver PLUS®. http://www.hydroone.com/MyHome/SaveEnergy/Pages/Peaksaver.aspx.
38. What is Rush Hour Rewards? http://support.nest.com/article/What-is-Rush-Hour-Rewards.

Eco-Forecasting for Domestic Electricity Use

Jesper Kjeldskov, Mikael B. Skov, Jeni Paay, Dennis Lund, Tue Madsen, Michael Nielsen
Department of Computer Science / Research Centre for Socio+Interactive Design
Aalborg University, Aalborg East, Denmark
{jesper, dubois, jeni}@cs.aau.dk

ABSTRACT
Over the past decade we have seen an increased awareness about domestic energy consumption and a growing focus on eco-feedback displays. In this paper we explore the concept of providing *forecasts* in such displays as a supplement to information about past usage. Our prototype, eForecast, extends the display of past electricity usage with forecasts about expected usage, electricity price, availability of wind power, and expected demand drops and peaks. Building on previous eco-feedback display research, our approach specifically enables people to use electricity at more opportune times – when it is cheap, green, or when there is an abundance of capacity. We evaluated eForecast in real world use in three domestic households for 22 weeks, where we explored potentials and limitations of forecasting for shifting electricity consumption. In this way, families were able to act in a more sustainable way – without necessarily reducing the amount of electricity consumed.

Author Keywords
Sustainability; forecasting; energy consumption; domestic

ACM Classification Keywords
H.5.m. Information interfaces and presentation (e.g., HCI): Miscellaneous.

INTRODUCTION
Sustainability has in recent years become an area of interest in CHI research exploring, amongst others, the design and use of "eco-feedback displays" for informing people about their consumption of various precious resources, such as water and electricity. The motivation behind eco-feedback displays is that by making the consumption of resources more evident and accessible, people are able to reflect on their usage, and possibly reduce it. This potentially leads to monetary savings for the individual consumer and to better environmental sustainability for society. While such eco-feedback displays offer a lot of functional advantages over traditional out-of-sight metering of utilities, such as being able to see when and where resources were used, the information provided is generally retrospective. This means that little input is given on how to act in order to become, or remain, environmentally sustainable. While several studies have reported positive user reactions to such eco-feedback displays, research has not yet shown clear evidence that they reliably cause people to actually take action or change behaviour [10]. Another limitation of the traditional eco-feedback approach is that the underlying goal of *reduction* only addresses one side of the challenge of sustainability. While it is, of course, good to lower our use of resources, for some types of them, such as electricity from renewable energy sources, the challenge facing us is also a matter of being able to use it *at the right time*.

CHI 2015, April 18 - 23 2015, Seoul, Republic of Korea
Copyright 2015 ACM 978-1-4503-3145-6/15/04...$15.00
http://dx.doi.org/10.1145/2702123.2702318

One problem with "green" electricity like wind turbines or solar panels is that the level of supply is not controllable or constant but relies on weather conditions. Therefore there is sometimes a low level of supply, while at other times more electricity is produced than being used. Since no technology exists for efficiently storing large amounts of electricity, this surplus of energy is simply lost. This leaves a currently underexplored potential for improved sustainability. If we can enable people to *shift* [8] some of their electricity consumption to more favourable times, then we can also reduce the use of electricity generated from conventional fuels – even without necessarily reducing our absolute consumption. In order to do this, however, people need to know when those favourable times are, when their pattern of usage is not ideal, and when it would be good to act differently. This is very different from what is currently provided by retrospective eco-feedback systems.

Here we present a case study in this new area, looking at eco-feedback displays for domestic electricity use from the angle of *forecasting* by exploring the ability to provide relevant information about the near future. Electricity is a particularly interesting case for this because several factors influence if usage is favourable or not. While the use of renewable electricity sources (e.g. wind) is obviously preferable for the environment, it is also preferable to avoid large peaks in demand, as this will challenge the capacity, and hence the sustainability, of the power grid. From the consumer's perspective, time-based electricity prices also make it preferable to use power when it is cheap. For this case we have developed an eco-forecasting display with information about availability of green energy sources, capacity in the grid, the price, and evaluated in domestic settings. We describe the design of the system, details of the deployment, and present and discuss our findings.

BACKGROUND

Previous work on sustainability within CHI falls primarily within what Mankoff et al. [5] refer to as sustainability *through* design, aiming to deploy technology facilitating sustainable behaviour. Much of this work focuses on "eco-feedback" to help people reduce resource consumption or environmental impact by showing information about usage and behaviours in the past [2]. Froelich et al. [3] did an evaluation of eco-feedback displays for water usage at fixture level in North America examining design elements such as data and time granularity. The study showed great interest in this level of data detail, but also that additional information would be needed to facilitate changes, such as comparisons over time, and with others, for contextualizing performance. Also focussing on water use, Pathmanathan et al. [6] investigated eco-feedback on mobiles for promoting water conservation in Australia. This study found that while information about past water usage might reveal patterns, and be useful as context for future usage, it is not in itself sufficient for enabling people to behave environmentally sustainably in the present or near future. In a similar study, Kjeldskov et al. [4] investigated eco-feedback on domestic electricity use in Denmark, finding that in order to help people change behaviour, or continue good behaviour, other information than retrospective is needed, in particular, cues on how to act in the present and near future. Also focussing on domestic energy consumption, based on interviews and surveys, Pierce et al. [8] present a vocabulary of terms capturing actions and strategies of energy conservation including *shifting* it. In [7] this is extended with a review of energy related work in which the idea of using energy differently by, for example, shifting consumption informed by demand response system is further discussed. Also influencing the eco-feedback research agenda Strengers [10] shows how domestic energy use is deeply embedded in non-negotiable everyday practices and not reflected well by the view on families as potential "micro-resource managers". Together, these works have contributed to defining as well as broadening the scope of interactive system design for eco-feedback and sustainability.

Responding to these insights on eco-feedback, Yang et al. [11] studied people's interactions with conventional eco-intelligent thermostats in domestic households, and propose the use of *eco-feedforward* to communicate actionable suggestions and their expected impact. Also aiming at being prospective rather than retrospective, Costanza et al. [1] explore the use of a washing machine agent, using data on future electricity price, combined with chargeable batteries, to minimize the cost of a wash. Similarly, Schrammel et al. [9] discuss the use of basic power generation forecasts for helping users align energy consumption with availability.

Forecasting

Building on this related work, our approach to eco-feedback displays is to use *forecasting* as a form of prospective eco-feedforward that enables people to act more favorably in their use of resources. By forecasting we refer to the process of making assertions about occurrences that have not yet happened, or whose actual outcomes have not yet been observed. Forecasting is used for many purposes, such as climate, energy, economics, production planning etc. and comes in several variants, for example naive, time-series-based, judgmental, and causal methods. In the context of facilitating sustainable domestic electricity use, several forecasts may be of value. Weather forecasting can inform us about imminent availability of wind and sun power, demand forecasting can tell us about forthcoming capacity, and electricity market models can give us a rather precise picture of the hourly electricity price within the next 24 hours. Data on past electricity use can inform forecasts about expected patterns of consumption in the future.

eFORECAST

Our prototype, eForecast, is similar to the idea in [9] but extends this with several sources of forecasts and a system deployment. We designed and created eForecast to present recent usage, expected usage, electricity price, availability of wind power, and expected peaks in demand. eForecast is designed to run on an always-on tablet that can be placed in a suitable place in the home e.g. on a shelf or mounted on the wall. eForecast is not meant to include a lot of detail about past electricity usage. Instead the aim here is to empower people to respond to some of the external factors that influence the sustainability of electricity use.

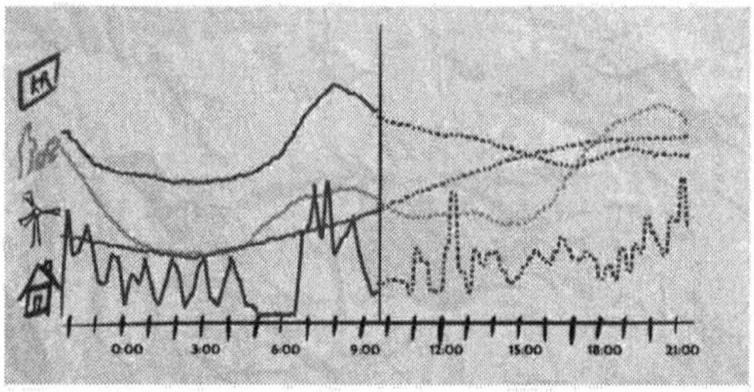

Figure 1. Screenshot: historical data (solid lines) and forecast (dotted lines) for the household's consumption (blue), wind power (green), grid capacity (yellow) and price (red)

eForecast consists of six different screens, which the user can swipe between. Four of these screens display different visualizations of the household's recent electricity usage combined with forecasts from external sources. The fifth screen shows all forecasts combined (Figure 1). The vertical line in the middle indicates current time, with the last 12 hours represented on the left (solid line), and the forecast for the next 12 hours on the right (dotted line). In this example it can be seen that the household has an expected peak of electricity use just after 12:00 and an increase in use after 19:00 (blue), and that there will be an increase in available wind power during the afternoon, leveling out after 18:00 (green). Price will go down until 17:00 (red), and demand is expected to go up after 15:00 (yellow). It can also be seen that there is a "sweet spot" between 16-17:00 where price and demand is low while the availability of wind power is high. Based on this, one might attempt to delay the 12-13:00 peak in use by a few hours.

Figure 2. Clock with eco-forecast.

In order to provide people with a simple overview, a dedicated screen displays a clock with a simplified indication of upcoming time-periods where it would be favorable to use electricity – either because it is green, cheap, or in good capacity. This is illustrated in Figure 2.

Implementation

eForecast has two components: a client application that displays the data to the user, and a server that collects and manages data from different sources. Electricity use data is collected from a home automation system, ZenseHome, which contains real-time measurements from the individual power outlets in the house. This is used to record, display and predict usage in 15-minute intervals. Electricity price data is collected using web scraping of Northern Europe's leading power market, Nord Pool Spot, where electricity pricing is negotiated at least 12 hours in advance. Data on the expected availability of wind power is based on weather forecasts from the Open Weather Map weather service. The expected demand on the power grid is calculated on the basis of data about similar households' combined patterns of consumption, taking into account the day of the week, and the month of the year. The household's expected energy demand is calculated in the same manner but based on their own history of use.

EVALUATION

We tested eForecast in a longitudinal trial deployment with three Danish households over the spring and summer of 2014. Our main aim of the trial deployment was to test the approach of providing eco-feedback forecast information in real world domestic settings, and to gain qualitative feedback from users. For this purpose it was important for us that the households had the eForecast system in their home for enough time to avoid the initial news effect, and let it possibly be integrated into their daily lives.

Participants

We recruited three families in the region to participate in a longitudinal study of domestic electricity use. The families all had the ZenseHome system installed in their house required for collecting usage data, but had no eco-feedback system. Household 1 was a married couple in their thirties with 3 children aged 4 and 1 (twins). Household 2 was a married couple in their early forties with no children. Household 3 was a married couple in their forties with two children aged 10 and 16. The families came from different towns, and did not know each other. They were all middle-class households, with both parents in permanent jobs.

Procedure

The trial deployment lasted 22 weeks, and involved 12 1-hour semi-structured interviews (4 with each family). To sustain interest in the system we introduced the screens in steps. At the beginning of the study the only screens enabled were individual forecasts on price, wind power and capacity. After two weeks we enabled the combined forecast (Figure 1) and after four weeks we enabled the clock-based forecast (Figure 2). The interviews were conducted by three researchers and focused on the families' perceptions and use of the system, and on their electricity use behavior and understanding. We asked them questions about how they interpreted the information presented; how it fitted their picture of electricity use in the household; how electricity usage was tied to their daily routines; what usage they would and wouldn't be able to shift; if, how and when the system had enabled them to shift electricity use; and what factors had played a role in this. The interviews were recorded, transcribed, and coded for thematic analysis.

Findings

All participating families enjoyed using the system, and kept using it throughout the duration of the deployment. We logged a total of 631 user interactions, distributed over the 22-week period. For creating the eco-forecasts, the system gathered approximately 2.4 million electricity consumption entries, 4058 price data entries, and 1475 wind data entries. The interviews showed that forecasting in the eco-feedback display facilitated not only insight on consumption patterns, but also awareness and understanding of the context of electricity use, and some of the factors that may contribute to improved sustainability. People were generally intrigued by the idea that they could contribute to sustainability not only by reducing electricity use but also by using it at particular times. They were also attracted to the idea that those times could be seen from the relatively simple forecasts provided through the system. Hence, although we could not measure quantitatively significant changes in consumption patterns, the study showed that forecasting did indeed enable people to identify opportunities for shifting electricity use to more favorable times.

All families reported that they were able to understand the forecasts, and that the forecasting element gave them an added value over traditional backward looking eco-feedback displays. For this, it was expressed that the screen with combined forecasts was most useful because this view allowed people to consider different forecasted tendencies up against each other, for example, when electricity was going to be *both* green *and* cheap. In relation to this, the forecast information on the clock screen was sometimes too simplistic on its own, as it did not reveal this level of detail, but only gave an overall indication of upcoming favorable times for electricity usage. This meant that people had to check the detailed forecast view in order to fully understand why the clock had marked out a particular time period as good for using electricity. However, it was also reported that the system was often left displaying the clock screen, rather than the graphs, because this screen was useful more generally, and provided a central and easily accessible point of entry to the eco-forecast. In discussing the different forecasts in relation to each other, all families expressed that the greatest motivational factor for shifting electricity use was reduced costs. While they all understood the positive environmental effects of using green electricity, they expressed that since they were paying the same for power independent of origin and grid capacity, they were entitled to use it when it suited *them* best, and not when it would be best for the utility provider. To motivate people shifting electricity use to more sustainably favorable times, there needed to be an economical reward.

Use of the system also prompted discussions about what appliances and devices the families would be able to use flexibly in light of eco-forecasts. All families expressed that during the study they had found some appliances so tightly coupled to the family's daily routines, for example for cooking and for entertainment, that they were very difficult to shift in time. It was reported as particularly difficult to shift electricity use in the mornings of weekdays (e.g. the use of coffee machines and toasters) because people were typically on a tight schedule to get to work or school then. The use of other appliances, like dishwashers, washing machines, and battery chargers for mobile devices, was however considered very flexible, as they would typically run in the background, and not be part of an activity. Being out of focus, however, these also presented new challenges: although enabling the families to see opportune times for using electricity, it was reported that when planning to move the running of an "electricity-hungry" appliance to a later time (like a dishwasher or washing machine), they sometimes forgot to actually set it off when that time came.

DISCUSSION AND CONCLUSIONS

The contribution of this work is a pilot study of the concept of forecasting in eco-feedback displays, and insights about potentials and challenges of this in relation to facilitating sustainability in domestic electricity use. We have presented a prototype system, eForecast, designed and deployed to investigate potentials for shifting parts of a household's electricity usage to more favorable times. Our study confirms some of the thoughts in [7, 8, 9] that eco-forecasting has potentials for enabling people to shift some of their electricity use, and that people understand and like this idea. They would, however, expect a financial reward for their effort. At the same time, our results also confirm the findings in [8] and [10] that shifting domestic electricity use is challenging. Electricity use in the home is closely related to family activities that are often highly routine-bound within certain time constraints, and non-negotiable [10]. The value of eco-forecasting for shifting this electricity consumption depends on the family's flexibility within their daily routines, and the challenges and opportunities of influencing these routines needs to be investigated. However, in line with [1] our results also show that the biggest potential gain from eco-forecasts is from time shifting of appliances that can be de-coupled from daily routines. In our study these were particularly identified as dishwashers, washing machines, and computer chargers, but in the future this could also include electric heat pumps and charging of electric cars. For these types of appliances we found that the challenge is not so much about domestic routines, but more about bridging between eco-forecast and appliance control, for example, telling the washing machine to run, or the electric car to charge, when electricity is green and in capacity. This challenge is both a matter of partial automation, and of interaction design.

ACKNOWLEDGEMENTS

This work is a part of TotalFlex funded by Energinet.dk

REFERENCES

1. Costanza, E., Fisher, J.E., Colleu, J.A., Rodden, T., Ramchurn, S.D., Jennings N.R. Doing the Laundry with Agents: a Field Trial of a Future Smart Energy System in the Home. *Proc. CHI'14,* ACM (2014), 823-832
2. Froehlich, J., Findlater, L., and Landay, J. The design of eco-feedback technology. *Proc. CHI'10,* ACM (2010), 1999–2008
3. Froehlich, J., Findlater, L., Ostergren, M., Ramanathan, S., Peterson, J., Wragg, I., Larson, E., Fu, F., Bai, M., Patel, S. and Landay, J. A. The design and evaluation of prototype eco-feedback displays for fixture-level water usage data. *Proc. CHI'12,* ACM (2012), 2367–2376
4. Kjeldskov, J., Skov, M. B., Paay, J. and Pathmanathan, R. Using mobile phones to support sustainability: A field study of residential electricity consumption. *Proc. CHI'12,* ACM (2012), 2347–2356
5. Mankoff, J. C., Blevis, E., Borning, A., Friedman, B., Fussell, S. R., Hasbrouck, J., Woodruff, A., and Sengers, P. Environmental sustainability and interaction. *Ext. Abstracts of CHI'07,* ACM (2007), 2121–2124
6. Pathmanathan, R., Pearce, J., Kjeldskov, J. and Smith, W. Using Mobile Phones for Promoting Water Conservation. *Proc. OzCHI'11,* ACM (2011), 243-252
7. Pierce, J. and Paulos, E. Beyond Energy Monitors: Interaction, Energy, and Emerging Energy Systems. *Proc. CHI'12.* ACM (2012), 665-674
8. Pierce, J., Schiano, D., and Paulos, E. Home, Habits, and Energy: Domestic Interactions and Energy Consumption. *Proc. CHI'10.* ACM (2011), 1985-1994
9. Schrammel, J., Gerdenitsch, C., Weiss, A., Kluckner, P., and Tscheligi, M. FORE-Watch - The Clock that Tells You When to Use. *Proc AmI'11,* LNCS (2011), 157-166
10. Strengers, Y. Designing eco-feedback systems for everyday life. *Proc. CHI'11,* ACM (2011), 2135–2144
11. Yang, R., Newman, M.W., and Forlizzi, J. Making Sustainability Sustainable: Challenges in the Design of Eco-Interaction Technologies. *Proc. CHI'14,* ACM (2014), 823-832

Beyond Eco-Feedback: Adding Online Manual and Automated Controls to Promote Workplace Sustainability

Ray Yun[1,2], Azizan Aziz[1], Peter Scupelli[1], Bertrand Lasternas[1], Chenlu Zhang[1], Vivian Loftness[1]

[1] Carnegie Mellon University, Pittsburgh, PA, USA
{ryun, azizan, scupelli, blastern, chenluz, loftness} @cmu.edu

[2] Hongik University, Seoul, Korea
ryun@hongik.ac.kr

ABSTRACT
Whereas eco-feedback has been widely studied in HCI and environmental psychology, online manual control and automated control have been rarely studied with a focus on their long-term quantitative impact and usability. To address this, an intervention was tested with eighty office workers for twenty-seven weeks. Through the long-term field test, it was found that the addition of online controls in the feedback intervention led to more energy savings than feedback only and worked better for light and phone usage than computer and monitor usage. The addition of automated control led to the greatest savings but was less effective for efficient users than inefficient ones.

Author Keywords
Sustainability; behavior change; energy dashboard, energy feedback; online control; automated control; workplace

ACM Classification Keywords
H.5.2 [Information Interfaces And Presentation]: User Interfaces – Graphical user interfaces (GUI);

INTRODUCTION
Commercial buildings consume at least 18% of the total electrical energy used in the United States [1] and over $2.8 billion is wasted every year due to computers being left on during the night and weekends [2]. Yet up to 30-40% of the plug-load energy consumption can be reduced by behavior change [3, 4]. HCI and environmental psychology researchers have developed eco-feedback systems (e.g., [14, 15]) and proved their positive effectiveness by measuring energy savings from the intervention (e.g., [7, 19]). Online control technology for individual electric devices has become available recently and allows users to simply control their devices remotely through web or mobile applications [8]. This technology has rarely been studied in the HCI field [17], but its savings impact was measured for a month and documented in the NREL report [8]. While previous studies have focused on either feedback or control only, this paper includes the addition of online control to feedback intervention and compares its long-term effectiveness towards sustainability. Fogg [12] argues in his behavior theory that when an intervention that simplifies the target behavior is added to the motivational intervention (e.g., eco-feedback), the target behavior is more likely to occur. We hypothesize that the addition of online controls results in more energy savings than employing feedback alone. As Froehlich et al. [5] and Brynjarsdottir et al. [6] point out, we noticed many HCI studies on energy behavior have a small sample size (an average of 11 participants) and a short study length (an average of 2.5 weeks), and measure behavior change effectiveness without having a control group and baseline data. To address this limitation, we conducted a bigger-scale, long-term field study. The study targeted office workers because they are not typically responsible for paying for electricity and tend to care little about saving energy at work [13].

CHI 2015, April 18 - 23 2015, Seoul, Republic of Korea
Copyright 2015 ACM 978-1-4503-3145-6/15/04$15.00
http://dx.doi.org/10.1145/2702123.2702268

INTELLIGENT DASHBOARD FOR OCCUPANTS (ID-O)
To investigate the effectiveness of the addition of online control to feedback intervention, the Intelligent Dashboard for Occupants (ID-O, Figure 1) was developed, equipped with the most commonly used feedback features (self-monitoring, advice, comparison) [18] and online controls (manual and automated). To enable monitoring and control of each desktop technology's electricity usage through the ID-O, a Plugwise device is employed (www.plugwise.com).

Feedback

Self-monitoring
The ID-O offers views of each device's data usage in real time with different time ranges (day, week, month) and chart types (bar, area, line), so people can view their energy consumption from various angles. By hovering over a data point in a chart, users can view the numeric values and related statistics, and by projecting the past data onto a chart, they can understand their previous consumption (e.g. a week ago) and predict their future performance.

Advice

The ID-O provides energy tips users can follow immediately with predicted energy savings based on the PIER report [9] and suggestions to replace their energy hog device with an energy-efficient one such as an Energy Star™ product for a long-term savings. For example, when the system detects energy waste (e.g., the task light had been left on during the night last week), the advice text alerts the users by displaying the recommendation in red font.

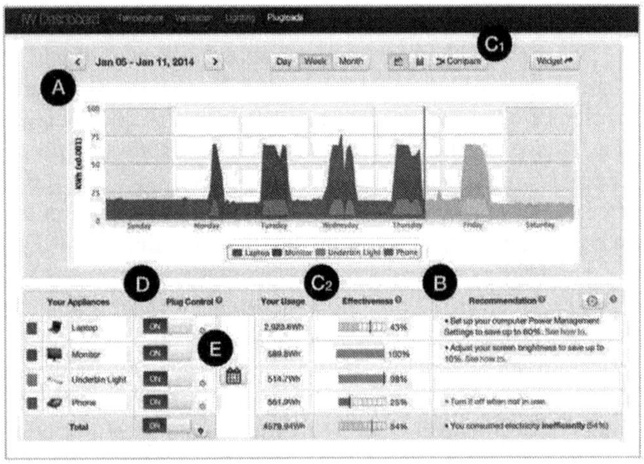

Figure 1. Screenshot of ID-O. A) self-monitoring, B) advice, C1) peer-comparison, C2) self-comparison, D) online remote (manual) control, E) automated control (calendar)

Comparison

Peer- and self-comparison were developed to inspire the users to more energy-effective behavior. With the peer compare mode, the ID-O provides a linear energy display: the user's energy consumption, the office average, and the best person in the office. With the comparison chart, users can monitor their energy performance compared with others'. For self-comparison, an individual's behavior effectiveness index is calculated as the ratio between the optimal use of the appliance and the total energy consumption over the measured period [10]. The dashboard displays behavior effectiveness with a colored bar and the percentage number to indicate poor (red), average (yellow) and good behavior (green). This performance index was developed to support user behavior regardless of the quality of technology they have been given, since most office workers do not choose their own energy efficient products. However, they do have the power to improve the performance of whatever equipment they have been given through settings and time management.

Online Remote (Manual) Controls

The dashboard provides online remote controls for office devices. This allows workers to remotely turn off their devices by pressing the control buttons. If ID-O users group some of the items together, group-control is also possible.

Automated Controls

A calendar control feature was developed to allow users to set up a schedule to turn on and off the devices. The calendar contains a drag-able scheduler which allows users to select the devices and control types (on/off) and then drag the item(s) to the timetable to set the day and time for those control settings during a typical week.

The above-described features were iteratively refined through field-testing with twenty-one subjects and a lab study with thirty-five participants. The detailed screenshots, system structure description and preliminary studies can be found at [11,16].

METHODS

Four groups of twenty were formed to investigate the interventions about *feedback, manual control* and *automated control.* The participants were recruited from one department (realty services) in a large company and all reported being full-time workers who spend most of their time on the computer. Four Plugwise™ devices were installed at each of the 80 workstations to monitor user actions and energy use of their laptops, monitor, phone and task light (where existing). The participants were randomly assigned to a group (twenty people per group) and their baseline energy use data was collected for fourteen weeks. After this, three of the four groups were given one of three dashboard systems (Figure 2). The first group (Group A) was not provided a dashboard interface and served as a "control" group. The second group (Group B) was provided with three feedback features only (self-monitoring, advice, comparison), the third group (Group C) was provided with the three feedback features and on-line controls, and the last group (Group D) was provided with the feedback features, on-line control, and automated/calendar controls.

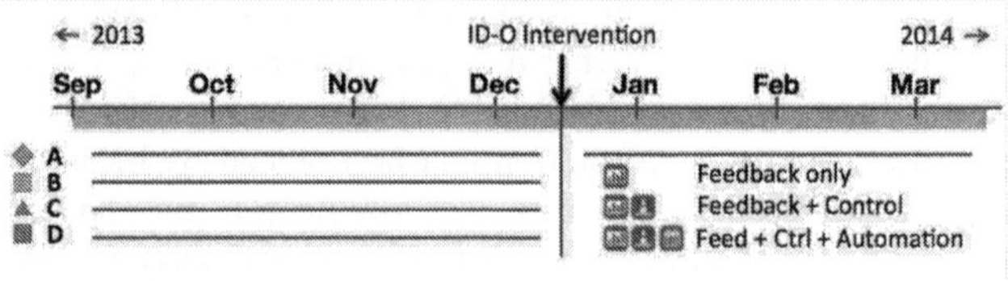

Figure 2. The study timeline with four test groups

RESULTS

Addition of online controls leads to more savings

Figure 3 illustrates the weekly average electricity consumption per group before and after the ID-O. Group A without a dashboard showed a 7% energy reduction but no statistical difference between pre- and post-intervention was found. Group B with feedback only saved 13% ($t[14]=2.44$, $p<.03$); adding on-line control resulted in a 25% energy savings for Group C ($t[15]=2.56$, $p<.03$), and Group D equipped with all the above plus the automated calendar controller achieved a 38% savings ($t[15]=2.93$, $p<.01$). No statistically significant differences between the groups were found.

The more features offered, the more savings that were achieved. As hypothesized, adding online manual and automated control contributed to greater savings. Group A's energy reduction was caused by two big savers with 35% and 25% savings. They may have been affected by peer discussions about energy usage and savings with the dashboard users. Nineteen participants were excluded in this analysis due to the participants' refusal to participate, relocation, irregular work schedule or meter mal-functioning.

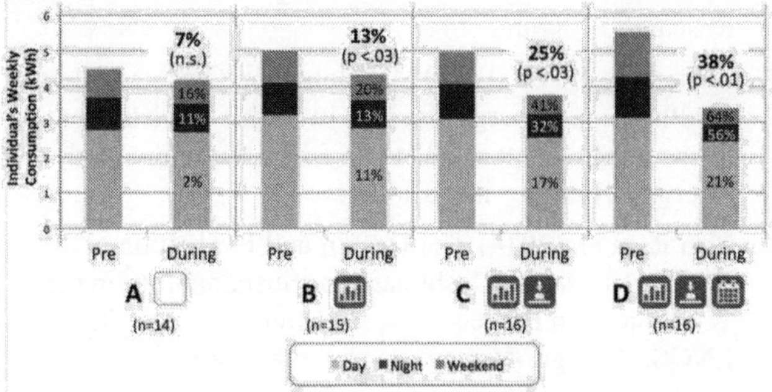

Figure 3. Overall weekly average consumption per group

Online controls work better for light and phone usage

Computers, monitors, lights and phones were the typical devices used in the workplace. The biggest energy usage difference was shown with lighting. Dashboard users in Groups A, B, C and D showed 28%, 36%, 52% and 75% savings respectively. The greatest savings came from calendar users on nights and weekends – 97% and 93% respectively, showing a huge potential for the calendar intervention. One of Group A's big savers introduced in the previous section saved 46% for lighting and contributed to Group A's 28% saving (n=6). Regarding phone usage, Group A did not show a difference, whereas the dashboard users (Groups B, C, D) achieved 15%, 17%, and 47% energy savings. While the dashboard for Group B lacked control features for phones, people used a power strip to turn them on and off. Again, the greatest savings came from the calendar users during nights (73%) and weekends (67%). Regarding computer usage, savings were 8%, 11%, 10% and 16% for Groups A to D respectively. The manual and automated control features were recommended for use only in logout (sleep) mode. The savings for the computer usage were limited due to the company's corporate policy for computer maintenance purposes. Thus, the control features were not actively used here, and only 2 participants in Group D used the calendar for their computers, and they showed 45% and 51% savings. Regarding the monitors, unlike the other devices, these did not lead to large savings during the weekends and nights. It turned out that most of the monitors were already energy-efficient products that went into sleep mode automatically when not in use. No statistically significant differences per devices were found between the groups before the interventions were given to the groups.

Automated control less effective for efficient users

To investigate how the dashboard influenced users with different behavior efficiency, individual users' behavior effectiveness index was considered (see *comparison* section). The addition of the automation feature contributed to a low effectiveness of energy savings for the users who originally consumed energy efficiently, but a high effectiveness for the ones who wasted energy ($r = 0.762$, $n = 12$, $p = 0.004$, Figure 4). This may be because automation lets people depend on the feature, and the savings are only made to the extent that the system allows. In contrast, the feedback and manual control features did not show any correlation with the user's consumption effectiveness. People in those groups put effort towards understanding their consumption and reducing energy waste, regardless of their previous efficiency. However, since this requires the user's time and effort, not everyone showed an increase in savings.

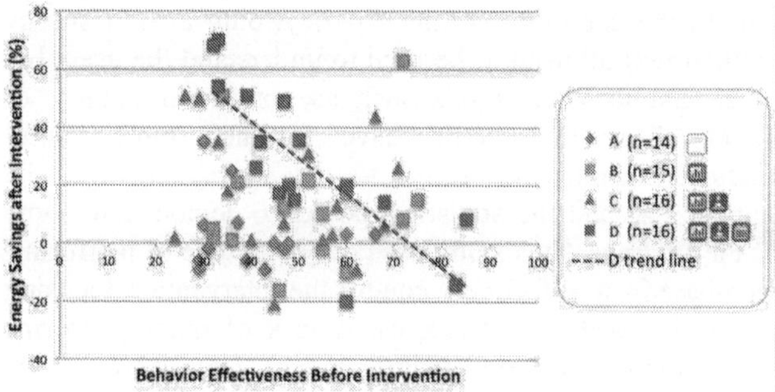

Figure 4. Correlation between individuals' behavior effectiveness before the dashboard intervention (x axis) and the energy savings achieved after the intervention (y axis)

User issues were the main barriers to using the ID-O

After the dashboard intervention, a survey with questions about the system's usability was conducted. One of the questions asked which features were useful for saving energy, and participants selected "very useful or "useful" for all the features. Another question addressed the possible issues that the users could have experienced (not user-friendly, hard to access, not useful, mal-functioning, too busy to use, forgot to use) and asked for their agreement on each. It was found that the user issues (too busy to use, forgot to use) were the barriers to over a third of the respondents, whereas the system issues (not user-friendly, hard to access, not useful, mal-functioning) became the barriers to under 10% of the users. For office workers, putting extra effort into energy savings at work is the main barrier since it is not their primary task and responsibility.

Some of the participants pointed out that the user issues could be resolved with easier access to the system. (e.g., *"Because it was not something that was automatically visible to me, I did not go out of my way to use it due to my busy schedule."*) Some users pointed out that it is not easy to reset the calendar for every trip. (e.g., *"The calendar function should be able to be overridden if one is on vacation or out of the office."*) To overcome this, the next version of the calendar needs to allow users to have multiple schedules or link to occupancy sensors to automate controls.

CONCLUSION

This paper has explored the effectiveness of online manual and automated control intervention strategies towards sustainability in the workplace. The different combinations of the UI interventions were designed and tested with eighty office workers for twenty-seven weeks. Our long-term field study revealed a quantifiable energy savings impact, its correlation with user efficiency, and the usability of the online control features. The individuals' energy savings were significantly correlated with their dashboard access time ($r=0.53$, $n=45$, $p<0.001$) and this suggests the dashboard intervention played an important role in achieving energy conservation.

Due to the corporate partner's policy, only a short survey method was allowed to be used to understand the users but other qualitative methods such as contextual inquiry or direct observation could have revealed more useful findings. Limited responses to the survey reduced the sample size and the statistical power to demonstrate some of the findings. This study used only one type of platform - web-based - to effectively control the intervention focusing on "web-based" UI strategies. A mix of other platforms (e.g. mobile, desktop widget, kiosk) may increase the dashboard's impact on sustainability in the workplace.

ACKNOWLEDGMENTS

This study was supported by the Energy Efficient Buildings Hub Consortium (EEBHub.org, a U.S. DOE Innovation Hub, Subtask 6.4) under the U.S. Department of Energy Award Number EE0004261.

REFERENCES

1. EIA, U. (2011). Annual energy review. Energy Information Administration, US Department of Energy: Washington, DC, online at www.eia.doe.gov/emeu/aer.
2. 1E PC Energy Report (2009). PC Energy Report 2009, USA, United Kingdom, Germany
3. Energy Star, (2009). Fast Facts on Energy Use.
4. NBI (2012) "Managing Your Office Equipment Plug Load"
5. Froehlich, J. et al. (2010). The design of eco-feedback technology. CHI '10 (pp. 99–2008). ACM.
6. Brynjarsdottir et al. (2012). Sustainably unpersuaded: how persuasion narrows our vision of sustainability. CHI '12 (pp. 947-956). ACM.
7. Kappel, K., & Grechenig, T. (2009, April). Show-me: water consumption at a glance to promote water conservation in the shower. In *Proceedings of the 4th international conference on persuasive technology* (p. 26). ACM.
8. Metzger, I et al. (2012). *Plug-Load Control and Behavioral Change Research in GSA Office Buildings.* NREL/TP-7A40-55780. Golden, CO: National Renewable Energy Laboratory.
9. Mercier, C., & Moorefield, L. (2011). Commercial office plug load savings and assessment: Final report. Produced by ECOVA and Supported Through the California Energy Commission's Public Interest Energy Research Program.
10. Lasternas, B. et al. (2014). Behavior Oriented Metrics for Plug Load Energy Savings in Office Environment. In Proceedings of the 2014 ACEEE Summer Study on Energy Efficiency in Buildings.
11. Yun R. et al. (2014) The Design and Evaluation of Intelligent Energy Dashboard for Sustainability in the Workplace. In Proceedings, HCI International 2014, LNCS: Springer-Verlag.
12. Fogg, B. J. (2009, April). A behavior model for persuasive design. InProceedings of the 4th international Conference on Persuasive Technology (p. 40). ACM.
13. Foster, D., Lawson, S., Wardman, J., Blythe, M., & Linehan, C. (2012). "Watts in it for me?": design implications for implementing effective energy interventions in organisations. CHI '12 (pp. 2357–2366). ACM.
14. Erickson, T. et al. (2013, April). The dubuque electricity portal: evaluation of a city-scale residential electricity consumption feedback system. CHI '13 (pp. 1203-1212). ACM.
15. Froehlich, J et al. (2009, April). UbiGreen: investigating a mobile tool for tracking and supporting green transportation habits. CHI '09 (pp. 1043-1052). ACM.
16. Yun R. et al. (2013). Toward the Design of a Dashboard to Promote Environmentally Sustainable Behavior among Office Workers. In Persuasive Technology (pp. 246-252). Springer Berlin Heidelberg.
17. Yun, R. et al. (2013). Sustainability in the Workplace: Nine Intervention Techniques for Behavior Change. In Persuasive Technology (pp. 253-265). Springer Berlin Heidelberg.
18. Ehrhardt-Martinez, K et al. J.A.S.: Advanced Metering Initiatives and Residential Feedback Programs: a meta-review for household electricity-saving opportunities. Washington, D.C. (2010)
19. Carrico, A. R., & Riemer, M. (2011). Motivating energy conservation in the workplace: An evaluation of the use of group-level feedback and peer education. *Journal of environmental psychology*, *31*(1), 1-13.

Understanding the Role of Thermography in Energy Auditing: Current Practices and the Potential for Automated Solutions

Matthew Louis Mauriello[1], Leyla Norooz[2], Jon E. Froehlich[1]
Makeability Lab | Human-Computer Interaction Lab (HCIL)
Department of Computer Science[1], College of Information Studies[2]
University of Maryland, College Park
{mattm401, leylan, jonf}@umd.edu

ABSTRACT

The building sector accounts for 41% of primary energy consumption in the US, contributing an increasing portion of the country's carbon dioxide emissions. With recent sensor improvements and falling costs, auditors are increasingly using thermography—infrared (IR) cameras—to detect thermal defects and analyze building efficiency. Research in *automated* thermography has grown commensurately, aimed at reducing manual labor and improving thermal models. Though promising, we could find no prior work exploring the professional auditor's perspectives of thermography or reactions to emerging automation. To address this gap, we present results from two studies: a semi-structured interview with 10 professional energy auditors, which includes design probes of five automated thermography scenarios, and an observational case study of a residential audit. We report on common perspectives, concerns, and benefits related to thermography and summarize reactions to our automated scenarios. Our findings have implications for thermography tool designers as well as researchers working on automated solutions in robotics, computer science, and engineering.

Author Keywords

Energy audits; thermography; robotics; formative inquiry; design probes; Sustainable HCI; human-robotic interaction

ACM Classification Keywords

H.5.m. Information interfaces and presentation (*e.g.*, HCI)

INTRODUCTION

The building sector accounts for 41% of primary energy consumption in the US, far more than any other sector, and contributes an increasing portion of total carbon dioxide emissions—40% in 2009 compared to 33% in 1980 [46]. One reason for these high emissions is building age. Residential buildings, for example, constitute 95% of all buildings in the US and are on average over 50 years old [51]. Most were constructed using energy inefficient designs and their materials have degraded over time. To address these issues, renovations and retrofits of existing building stock has become a pressing need. The US Department of Energy (DOE), for example, has set a goal of reducing housing energy use by up to 70% [37]

Figure 1: We developed five automated thermography scenarios inspired by the research literature (*e.g.*, [6,10,35,41]) to help elicit reactions to envisioned automated solutions. Above, a screen capture from our unmanned aerial vehicle (UAV) design probe. See supplementary video.

As a response, professional energy auditing has seen a resurgence of interest [25,39]. Audits help identify building inefficiencies through walk-through inspections, on-site measurements, and computer simulations [45]. The DOE recommends home energy audits because of their impact on reducing energy usage (*e.g.*, 5-30% reductions in monthly utility bills) and increasing structural safety [49]. With recent improvements in handheld sensor technology and falling costs, auditors are increasingly using thermography—infrared (IR) scanning with thermal cameras—to detect thermal defects and air leakage [2,8,28,47].

Work in *automated* thermography has also grown markedly in the past three years, encompassing disciplines from computer science and robotics to environmental and civil engineering. Researchers have primarily explored technical approaches for automatically transforming thermal images into higher fidelity 3D representations of buildings [17,20,29,31,38] and employing robots for data collection [6,10,13,30,35,41]. However, user studies of these tools have not been performed. And while some work exists on examining client reactions to thermography in general (*e.g.*, [18,25]), perceptions of thermography use from the *auditor's* perspective has received little attention. As the primary users of thermography, this perspective is important both to the design of current thermal scanners and analysis software as well as to this growing area of automated thermography.

CHI 2015, April 18 - 23 2015, Seoul, Republic of Korea

ACM 978-1-4503-3145-6/15/04…$15.00
http://dx.doi.org/10.1145/2702123.2702528

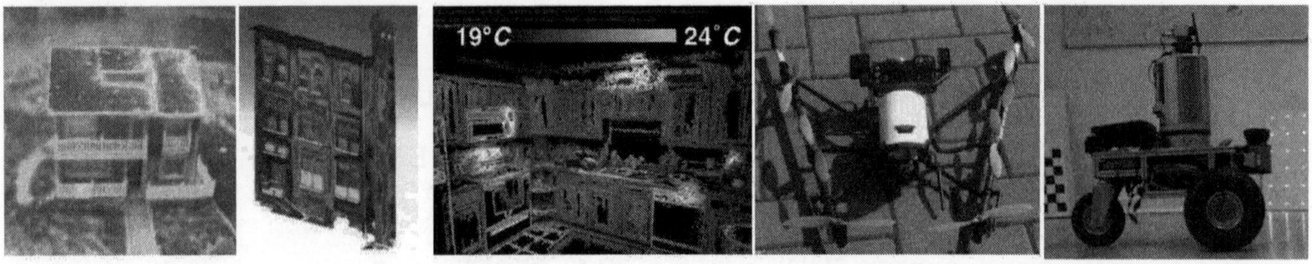

Figure 2: Example automated thermography from the literature: (a) UAV-based thermography [30]; (b) a textured 3D façade model [41] (c) 3D thermographic reconstruction of a kitchen [20] (d) a UAV equipped with a thermal camera [41]; (e) the Irma3D indoor thermal mapper robot [6]

In this paper, we investigate current energy auditing practices and the role of thermography therein. We also critically assess the potential for automated thermographic methods. Our research questions include: How is thermography currently being used by auditors? What benefits and drawback do auditors identify when envisioning the use of robotics for thermographic data collection? What are the implications for the design of these automated thermography tools?

To address these questions, we conducted two studies: a semi-structured interview study with 10 professional energy auditors that included five design probes, and an observational case study of one on-site residential audit. For the design probes, we developed five scenarios of automated thermography based on the research literature—*e.g.*, indoor robotic thermography [6,10] and large-scale urban thermography using unmanned aerial vehicles (UAVs) [13,30,35,41]. The scenarios were designed to provoke and ground discussion and critically assess how automated thermography may be used in the future. The interviews provide insight into current auditing procedures, the benefits and challenges of thermography, and reactions to our design probes, while the observation helps contextualize our findings and further emphasizes the complexities of energy auditing.

Inspired by the recent call to action from within HCI [43] to better understand practical efforts towards sustainability and to question the (over)promise of purely technological solutions, this paper contributes the first human-centered investigation of thermographic automation. Our contributions include: (i) an assessment of energy auditing and thermography's role therein through semi-structured interviews and a complementary observational study; (ii) a critical examination of the potential for emerging automated thermographic solutions through the use of five custom a design probes; and (iii) a set of reflections and guidelines to help inform the design of future energy auditing and thermographic tools. As interdisciplinary work, our findings have implications not just for the design of emerging thermographic tools but also those research communities focused specifically on automated methods and human robotic interaction, which span computer science, building science, and civil engineering.

BACKGROUND AND RELATED WORK

We describe background related to energy auditing and thermography as well as research in automated methods and links to Sustainable HCI.

Building Energy Audits

As noted in the introduction, energy audits are becoming increasingly common. For example, recent legislation mandates building audits every 5-10 years in some cities [1]. Most energy audit programs extend from a physical-technical-economic model (PTEM) of energy consumption [23]; the dynamics of human behavior are not typically incorporated [24]. Residential audits are administered by utilities or government contractors and involve a range of evaluations from blower door tests[1] [48] to thermography [47]. This data is entered into software tools and processed by computational models to predict the effects of potential retrofits. Finally, client-facing reports are produced with efficiency recommendations.

Studies of energy auditing focus largely on potential environmental benefits [3] and/or on the building owner perspective [23,24]. For example, in a large-scale study of homeowner experiences, Ingle *et al.* [25] found that physical face-to-face discussion with auditors was critically important *("the most informative part of the whole process"*, p. 13) and that the use of infrared thermography was "particularly compelling" because it made invisible energy flows and leakage problems more tangible (p. 16). This latter point seems crucial. In an experimental study of 87 homes, Goodhew *et al.* [18] found that those households who saw thermal imagery from their audits were nearly five times more likely to install retrofits. Thus, thermography is not just a measurement approach but a way of communicating findings to clients.

Studies of the auditors themselves are much rarer. One exception is a recent study by Palmer *et al.* [39], who surveyed 459 auditors and explored common audit practices, shared challenges, and the degree to which homeowners took action on efficiency recommendations. Though thermography was not their primary focus, they found that 63% of auditors surveyed used infrared imaging "fairly often" or "always" (the primary impediment was equipment cost). Our studies offer a complementary

[1] A blower door is a powerful fan mounted on an exterior door that lowers indoor air pressure causing outside air to flow through unsealed cracks and openings; these air leaks appear as salient streaks with the infrared camera [48]

Figure 3: Screen captures from the UAV-based thermography video design probe (Scenario 4). See supplementary materials for full video.

qualitative perspective along with a specific emphasis on thermography and emerging automated solutions.

Thermography Use

Energy auditors use thermography to measure surface temperatures of walls, roofs, ceilings, floors, and other parts of a building's envelope to detect heat loss, air leakage, moisture buildup, and to locate hidden infrastructure (*e.g.*, water pipes) [8,28]. Before surveying, the thermographer must assess environmental conditions such as weather, wind, HVAC operations, and direction/intensity of the sun—all of which can affect or prevent proper scans. For example, the ISO standard requires a minimum temperature differential of 10° C between the interior and exterior to properly detect thermal irregularities [26,50]. In addition, to increase air flow between the building envelope and the outdoors, blower door tests are commonly used in conjunction with thermography [47,48]. While the DOE recommends thermographic-based energy audits [47], criticisms include that it remains a qualitative method subject to the expertise of the auditor and lacks special software tools, algorithms, and audit guidelines [50].

Automating Thermography

Recent automated thermography efforts have focused on two areas (Figure 2): transforming thermal images into 3D-reconstructions of buildings (*e.g.*, [17,20,29,31,38]) and employing robots and vehicles to scale up data collection (*e.g.*, [6,10,13,30,34,35,41]). Researchers argue that traditional 2D thermal images: (i) do not include geometry and spatial relationships, which are important for interpreting thermography [20,29]; (ii) are unordered, messy, and difficult to organize [17,20]; (iii) and require time-consuming and labor intensive post-hoc analysis [17,20,38]. Thermographic 3D reconstruction is cast as a solution to these problems and as a means of enabling better modeling that should reduce auditor error and subjectivity [17,29].

Typically, the 3D-models are built either by computational photography methods—*e.g.*, structure-from-motion (SFM) [17,20,35]—or through the use of precise range scanners such as LiDAR, which are texture-mapped with thermal images [31,36,38]. Both require large amounts of data. Thus, researchers are increasingly using robots for data collection, including ground-based rovers for indoor thermography (*e.g.*, [6,10]) and UAVs for outdoor thermography (*e.g.*,[13,30,35,41]). The robots are equipped with a suite of sensors such as thermal and optical cameras, laser scanners, and GPS. These "massive data acquisition" systems [30] are described as advantageous because they reduce manual labor, can survey otherwise inaccessible areas of buildings (*e.g.*, high floors, rooftops), and collect more precise data. They can also enable or facilitate new types of analyses (*e.g.*, surveying and comparing thermal performance from large numbers of buildings [34]).

Given the technical complexity of this work, most research thus far focused on technology evaluations (*e.g.*, accuracy of geometric models [20]) rather than user studies. Indeed, we could find no prior work that explored the auditor perspective of these emergent methods, that attempted to elicit user feedback to early models/designs, or that tried to demonstrate that 3D reconstructions enabled auditors to better detect building defects or energy inefficiencies compared with their 2D counterparts. In this paper, we begin to address these gaps.

Sustainable HCI

Since its emergence at CHI in 2007 [5], sustainability HCI research has matured and evolved. Although much of the early work focused on persuasive technology aimed at promoting environmentally sustainable behaviors (*e.g.*, see reviews [14,16]), more recent work has called for and explored a broadened scope including politics [15], socioeconomics [11,12], energy infrastructure [42], and sociological perspectives [9,44]. Researchers have also reflected on the tension between HCI—typically a design- and innovation-oriented discipline—and research where findings may imply non-technology solutions (*e.g.*, the implication is *not* to design [4,40]). As formative work, our research shares similar aims to other qualitative Sustainable HCI studies (*e.g.*, [12,19,52]), that is, to understand current practices in an area and identify what role HCI may play.

Finally, we take inspiration from two recent "call to action" articles [33,43] that outline limitations of Sustainable HCI and articulate paths forward, such as the need to draw from and study work outside of HCI, to pursue practical as well as fanciful research, and to address broader topics. We provide the first HCI-based examination of the everyday practices and views of energy auditors and the potential disconnects between the technology-driven research in automated thermography and the complexities, nuances, and practical demands of performing audits in the field.

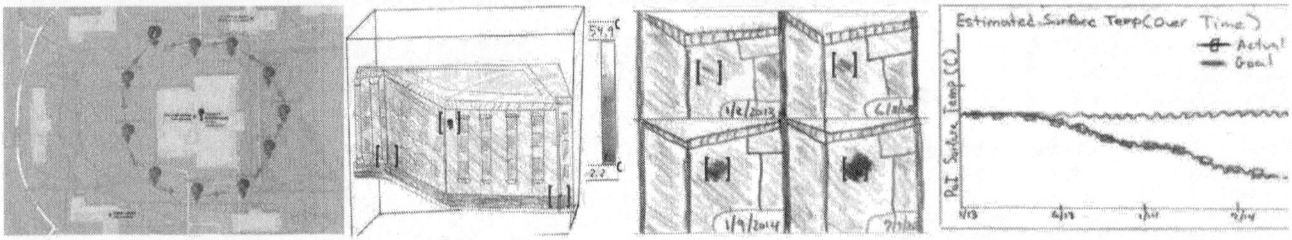

Figure 4: Screen excerpts from our interactive mid-fidelity prototype built in Axure. (a) Users input a rough thermography route for the UAV. (b) The analysis software automatically identifies anomalous thermal signatures (red brackets) on a 3D-reconstruction. (c) The auditor can zoom in and see how this area of the building has changed over time (every few months). (d) A co-located temporal graph of the estimated surface temperature is also provided.

STUDY 1: INTERVIEW STUDY AND DESIGN PROBES

To investigate the role of thermography in energy auditing and to elicit feedback about emerging automated methods, we conducted a two-part study with 10 professional auditors: a semi-structured interview and design probes.

Automated Thermography Design Probes

The design probes included five scenarios using three different mediums: (i) three written narrative scenarios (~150 words) of increasing complexity that described thermographic 3D reconstruction and robotic data collection, (ii) a short video mockup of a UAV performing a thermal audit, and (iii) an interactive medium-fidelity prototype demonstrating how automation control and analysis software of a thermographic UAV may work in the future. Each probe was inspired by recent work in automated thermography and was designed to provoke discussion, ground conversation, and elicit feedback. The probes used 2nd-person narration to help our participants envision the scenarios. The full probes are included in our supplementary materials and summarized below.

Scenario 1 (Text): Residential Audit. The first text probe described a residential audit using a UAV.

As you arrive at a home, meet with the client, and assess the home's interior, a UAV collects exterior thermographic data and builds a 3D thermal model of the building in real-time. You investigate the 3D model (all building sides and the roof) via an interactive application on your tablet/smartphone. You can also browse anomalous thermal signatures, which can be shared with your client. The UAV automatically returns to a docking station on your vehicle after completing its scans.

Scenario 2 (Text): Automated Audit of a Large Campus. The second probe positioned the participant as a facilities manager at a large campus site such as a university or government facility with many buildings.

You are responsible for a small fleet of thermography UAVs. The UAVs fly around semi-autonomously collecting thermal data about each building on your campus. When abnormalities are detected, the UAVs are programmed to more closely examine these areas and provide high resolution reports of potential problems. The UAVs reduce labor costs compared with manual assessments, can investigate otherwise inaccessible areas of buildings (e.g., high exterior floors), and enable historical reports showing thermal performance over time.

Scenario 3 (Text): Large-scale Urban Audit. The final text probe had the participant work as a government employee in charge of analyzing the energy efficiency of a large urban center with skyscrapers, office buildings, and other structures.

You have real-time access to utility usage for each building as well as indoor and outdoor thermographic robots. The ground-based robots are permanently deployed at the larger buildings (e.g., skyscrapers) and communicate with the UAVs to provide interior/exterior thermal scans. As with Scenario 2, the UAVs function semi-autonomously and special software compares utility usage with thermal data over time.

Scenario 4 (Video): UAV-based Thermography. The ~41 second video probe showed a semi-autonomous UAV collecting thermographic data of a campus building and performing real-time analysis. We created the video using a Parrot AR Drone 2.0 UAV, which is equipped with a 720p 30fps optical video camera. *Adobe After Effects* was used to create the robot's interface and to apply a "thermal filter" to the video stream (Figures 1 and 3).

Scenario 5 (Medium-Fidelity Prototype): UAV Control and Analysis Interface. For the final probe, we presented a medium-fidelity interactive software prototype that scaffolded the participant through the process of establishing a new survey project, including: scheduling a semi-autonomous UAV data collection flight and analyzing the collected data both spatially and temporally. This analysis procedure included: automated generation of a 3D model with a thermal overlay, an overview of interactive features, an automated point-of-interest analysis, and a comparison of historical data. The prototype was created in Axure using a combination of hand-drawn sketches and built-in widgets (Figure 4). For consistency, a research assistant operated the prototype for all participants.

In summary, the probes depicted a range of automated thermography scenarios, which varied in technological complexity, autonomy, and scope. Each scenario emphasized at least one new data collection approach along with some new analysis not currently possible with handheld IR cameras (*e.g.*, the ability to see thermal signatures change over long periods of time).

Method

Participants

We recruited ten professional energy auditors (8 current, 2 former; 1 female) through email lists, word-of-mouth, and social media from across the US. Our recruitment materials

ID	EMPLOYER	AUDIT EXPR. (YRS)	AGE	GENDER	THERMOGRAPHY TRAINING
P1	Former	1	25	Male	Training Course
P2	Private	20	61	Male	Level 3
P3	Former	6	30	Male	College Course
P4	Private	11	57	Male	Level 2
P5	Private	6	41	Male	Level 2
P6	Private	7	51	Male	Level 1
P7	Government	2	36	Female	None
P8	Private	4	64	Male	Level 2
P9	Private	3	30	Male	None
P10	Government	7	53	Male	Training Course

Table 1: Study 1 participant (professional auditor) demographics.

specified that participants needed professional experience using thermal cameras for building energy audits. Our participants ranged in age (M=44.8 years old; SD=14.2), audit experience (M=6.7 years; SD=5.5), and location—six states were represented in total (Table 1). All participants reported the same number of years performing energy audits as performing thermography with the exception of P6 (7 years energy auditing, 4 with thermography). For thermography training, five participants received certification training through professional organizations (*e.g.*, Infrared Training Center, The Snell Group, and similar organizations), two participants received on-the-job training through a company sponsored program, and one had taken a college course. Two reported no official training. To enable geographic diversity, half the interviews were conducted remotely via Skype with screen sharing to view the design probes. For the co-located interviews, participants read printouts of the text scenarios and used a researcher's laptop for the video and mid-fi prototype.

Procedure

Each session lasted an average of 93 minutes (SD=19.47) and included a background questionnaire, semi-structured interview, and design probes. The semi-structured approach allowed us to dynamically pursue themes we had not identified *a priori*. All participants were asked a similar set of questions, but new topics emerged in accordance with a participant's background, skills, and experience. The design probes immediately followed the interviews. Participants were asked to "think aloud" and evaluate each scenario. The researcher provided guidance at the start of the video and throughout the mid-fi prototype. Our objective was to identify aspects of the probe that participants were interested in and uncover concerns. At the completion of the session, participants were compensated $20.

Data and Analysis

The sessions were audio recorded, transcribed, and coded for themes of interest. As exploratory work, we pursued an iterative analysis approach using a mixture of inductive and deductive codes [7,22]. We created two codebooks—one for each part of the study—which initially derived from the research literature, our study protocol, and post-interview discussions amongst the research team. The unit of analysis was an answer (or stream of answers) for a specific topic in Part One and a full reaction to each probe in Part Two. Our iterative coding approach was similar for both.

Part One Analysis. Codes included: views on thermography (*e.g.*, misconceptions, procedures, automation), impact (*e.g.*, uses, benefits, findings), and challenges (*e.g.*, application, clients, interpretation). A random transcript was selected and coded by two researchers. To calculate inter-rater reliability (IRR), we used Krippendorff's alpha (α=0.64; SD=0.43; *total disagreements*=7 out of 120 decisions). Krippendorff's [27] suggests that scores below alpha < 0.667 be discarded or recoded. In our case, 4 of the 10 codes were < 0.667. The two researchers met, resolved all 7 disagreements, and updated the codebook accordingly. Both researchers then independently coded a second random interview, establishing IRR (α=0.85, SD=0.24). Finally, the first researcher coded the remaining interviews.

Part Two Analysis. For Part Two, we started with 11 codes including: types of use (*e.g.*, traditional thermography, alternative applications), interests (*e.g.*, automation, data, features), concerns (*e.g.*, technical feasibility, data quality) and reactions to scenarios (*e.g.*, positive, neutral, and negative). IRR was established after two iterations (final α=0.80; SD=0.27). However, the neutral reaction code was difficult to reach agreement on and was removed before the 2nd code pass. Again, disagreements were resolved through consensus. The remaining eight probe transcripts were coded by a single researcher.

Findings

We present frequent patterns and emergent themes.

Part One: Existing Practices

We summarize five themes related to the current practices, concerns, and desires of thermography practitioners. Though our interviews asked about general auditing practices, our focus here is on thermography.

Required Knowledge. Our participants highlighted the expertise needed to assess thermographic data, including: an understanding of building materials and construction (6 participants), an understanding of the physics of heat and airflow (5), applied training and experience (4), and an awareness of environmental conditions (3). As P2 states: *"the thing that is absolutely the most critical is to understand how heat behaves and interacts with different materials."* Participants emphasized that simply pointing a thermal camera at a structure was insufficient: *"you have to keep the environment in mind or else you're going to make a judgment call and it's going to be wrong" (P7).*

Thermography Benefits. Despite the admitted complexity, all participants (10) expressed that thermography provided at least some benefit to the audit process. Reaffirming prior work (*e.g.*, [18,25]), 7 participants thought that thermography was useful as a communication tool for interacting with clients: *e.g.*, P1 reflected, *"how do you explain convective heat flow? If you have an image you can go and look... sometimes it's tough in words."* In addition, as a form of non-destructive testing, thermal cameras allow auditors to assess areas that are hidden or difficult to access.

P10 gave a poignant example from an audit where he had trouble believing a client's complaint:

> *"But we gave her the camera, [and] she went right into the bedroom ...directly over her bed between the two ceiling joists was about a four foot strip with no insulation."*

Participants also found thermography useful as a diagnostic (6) or verification tool (5). For example, P6 said, *"I use [thermography] as a screening tool to then target the areas that you want to focus on."* For verification, thermography was used to confirm a suspicion or to check that a retrofit (*e.g.,* new insulation) was completed correctly. P7 stated, *"...you can survey large areas very quickly and... it should help you target areas to further investigate."*

Client Interactions. Participants emphasized that an energy audit is a social process as much as it is a technical one. Most participants felt that client interactions were crucial to a successful audit (9), including information gathering at the audit's onset, understanding client perceptions and motivations, and establishing trust. Some clients were wary that auditors were attempting to sell them retrofit materials. This attitude, P5 conjectured, *"...stems from people selling [thermography] as a silver bullet. You've got people that say it can do more than it does."* To overcome these issues, energy auditors strategically include the client in the audit process, asking residents to identify problems with them:

> *"...give the customer the thermal camera. And have them look around, and have them say 'oh my look at that', 'what's that', which is very engaging and opens them up to a discussion about the dynamic of what's happening in the house, or the wall, or the attic."* (P10).

In terms of client motivations for scheduling an audit, comfort was the most frequently mentioned. Cost savings and environmental concern were also mentioned, though less common (*e.g.,* P8 recalled only one household who was concerned with their "*carbon footprint*" over 4 years).

Thermography Challenges. All participants expressed concerns about thermography, including the difficulty of interpretation (8), untrained or undereducated practitioners (7), and equipment sensitivity (6). Interpretation was viewed as difficult because of the influence of confounding factors such as weather, shading, nearby buildings, and building materials. Given these complexities, thermography was characterized as a highly *subjective* process (similar to [50]), as captured by P2:

> *"The reality is that you can have three guys with the same camera, looking at the same thing, and have three totally different reports" (P2).*

Weather could also be frustrating because of the required interior-to-exterior temperature differential: *"unless there's a really big temperature swing you're not going to see much with the thermal camera" (P1).* However, high end equipment has the potential to mitigate some weather conditions, as stated by P5: *"if you've got the right camera the time of year [or day] really doesn't matter."* While having adequate equipment is important, participants emphasized that having a better camera only helps to a degree; it will not make practitioners better interpreters.

Desire for Automation. Before moving into the design probes (so as to limit bias), we asked our participants how they might automate an energy audit with or without thermography. Eight participants expressed interest in automation including: data collection (6), assessment (5), and report generation (2). For data collection, participants mentioned thermal cameras mounted to cars that survey neighborhoods quickly to identify locations with *"visual thermal patterns that may be indicative of energy issues"* (P4). Similarly, P10 suggested a thermographic overlay in Google Earth that would allow inspection of entire areas and identify *"building stock that is inefficient."*

For automating assessment, three participants mentioned 3D reconstruction, two mentioned better energy models or simulations, and two mentioned reducing or eliminating subjectivity. For example, P9 thought a dream tool would be a thermography report that *"could interface with a 3D model of the [audited] home."* P4 thought automation should eliminate subjectivity: *"make it independent of the auditor... my interpretation should not be different from yours."* For report automation, participants mentioned efficiency and reducing the tedium of manual preparation, P6 states: *"The biggest problem in dealing with the volume of work is creating reports."* Still, some participants expressed concerns with automation, such as P2, *"how do you get the software to understand what the [auditor] otherwise understands."*

Part One Summary. Our findings reaffirm and extend past explorations of energy audits (*e.g.,* [18,25,39]). Thermal tools should be designed both for expert users (the auditors) and for client interactions. In terms of automation, our participants were most interested in automating data collection and assessment followed by report generation. However, these automated solutions should remain visually oriented to facilitate client interactions and will need to address the same challenges that manual approaches have to overcome (*e.g.,* establishing temperature differentials).

Part Two: Design Probes

We first summarize overall reactions to our probes before describing common themes, suggestions, and concerns.

Overall Reactions. Our design probes elicited mixed reactions. Though most (9) reacted positively to the mid-fi prototype (Scenario 5) and to the multi-building and urban scenarios (Scenarios 2 and 3), only 2 participants found value in the UAV-based residential audit (Scenario 1) and reactions were equally split to the video (Scenario 4). P5 reacted negatively to all scenarios, feeling that it would be hard to acquire *"actionable data"* and expressing concerns for data quality: *"doing an exterior flyby is not going to be a replacement for an actual audit of a building."* He was most positive about automating interior scans.

Scenario 1. Most participants (7) reacted negatively to the UAV-based residential audit, expressing doubt that meaningful data could be acquired from exterior scans without, for example, blower door tests as well as concerns for cost and data overload. For the two participants that reacted positively, they mentioned its ability to examine inaccessible places, save time, and generate 3D models.

Scenario 2. In contrast, 9 participants reacted positively to the UAV-based multi-building scenario, largely because of opportunities such as tracking degradation over time and examining inaccessible areas and equipment (*e.g.*, HVAC). Still, participants expressed concerns about cost and the need for the system to have more information on building materials and construction for proper analysis.

Scenario 3. Similar to Scenario 2, most participants (9) were positive about the large-scale urban monitoring system, including the connections between thermography and utility data, the automatic anomaly detection, and "push" notifications. Participants also mentioned that this system could be used to check on LEED certified buildings that are supposed to be performing efficiently. Primary concerns included handling reflective surfaces and the "heat island effect" (where built structures like pavement cause increased ambient temperatures).

Scenario 4. Half of the participants (5) reacted positively to the video probe of a UAV surveying a campus building. Identified benefits included the ability to reach inaccessible areas ("*terrific for large buildings,*" P6), and as a tool for performing rapid preliminary investigations. Concerns included feasibility, the need for more information than is available from an exterior thermal scan, and the autonomy of the UAV (how it was controlled).

Scenario 5. Finally, most participants (9) reacted positively to the mid-fi prototype, citing its ability to provide geometrical (3D) model data, historical analysis, and automation scheduling. Participants suggested that the software tool should incorporate energy analysis from metering, information about building construction, and combined interior/exterior views.

Below, we briefly describe the key benefits and concerns identified across the five scenarios.

Automated Data Collection. Most participants (9) agreed that there was the potential to save time and money with automated data collection "*You can get the UAV to film a whole side of the building at once and then you can zoom in on the sections you want to see.*" (P8). However, there was general recognition that simply performing thermography was not sufficient—more data was necessary such as utility usage, weather, and information on building materials. Still, most participants thought UAV-based or other automated methods would be sufficient for preliminary analysis—though P5 thought it would create too many false positives.

Historical Analysis. Most participants (9) mentioned the benefits of historical analysis, which are really only feasible via automated data collection due to labor/time costs. As P7 highlights: "*...If you said, 'Hey, for four months, we've had this. Let's look and see how it could be fixed.' I like that idea.*" Typically, thermal scans do not include temporality (*i.e.*, the ability to look back in time and observe changes).

Model Generation. A majority of participants (6) saw value in automatically generating 3D building models with accurate geometry because it increases the utility of the collected data, enables faster analysis, and the resulting geometry could be exported into other tools:

> *"You spend a lot of time building this model, just measuring the outside of the house, counting the windows and the doors, and looking around. Then, you take that data load it into your modeling program... this would streamline that" (P10).*

Automatic Anomaly Detection. While most participants (8) accepted the "anomaly detection" in our scenarios without comment, 2 provided critical feedback related to the complications of filtering out noise, removing false positives, and the difficulty of interpreting the data:

> *"How do you get rid of the noise and have actionable data so that you save labor? ...I think you're going to expend a vast amount of labor in chasing down false positives" (P5).*

Data Quality. Half (5) of our participants raised concerns about data quality including the feasibility of using automated exterior scans to acquire useful thermal data across environmental conditions (*e.g.*, weather, sun direction). P8 questioned whether exterior scans could yield meaningful data at all:

> *"I don't see this as being very useful at this point primarily because the use that I've been able to make of [external] thermography is limited." (P8)*

Data Overload. Three participants expressed concerns about data overload: "*I don't see the value at this initial moment ...there's some new generation tools but it's still just too much data*" (P6). Others thought the 3D reconstructions would allow for better organization of the data leading to better interpretations.

Feasibility. Feasibility concerns included technological viability, robustness, and cost. Robustness and maintenance costs were potential barriers to adoption: "*I don't know that many fiscal managers would be able to justify the system*" (*P3*). Additionally, some participants (4) raised concerns about the need to have control over the environment because, "*you have to set up a pressure difference to be able to identify air infiltration... a UAV can't do that" (P1).*

Fear and Privacy. Though only mentioned by three participants, there was reasonable concern about how robotic thermography may frighten people or impinge on privacy: "*If [people are] in the building, they'd feel a little bit frightened*" (P3). P7 mentioned that UAVs may collect unintentional data: "*though you're focused on your clients' residence, you're going to get some of the neighbors*" (P7).

Part Two Summary. Our findings highlight important concerns with automated solutions described in the literature but which have previously not been discussed or acknowledged such as issues of data quality, data overload, technical feasibility, privacy, and problems of overreliance on automated exterior scans. Still, participants were positive with the general idea of automation especially 3D reconstruction, historical/temporal analysis, anomaly detection, and the potential for time savings.

STUDY 2: OBSERVATIONAL CASE STUDY

To contextualize our Study 1 findings we conducted an observational case study of a residential energy audit.

Method

We recruited a senior energy auditor from the Maryland Energy Administration's list of certified practitioners. The participant was male, age 50 and had 5 years of energy auditing experience Informal thermography training was provided by his employer. For the observation, the auditor selected an appointment he considered a *"typical audit"* and received client permission for our presence. The audit took place in a mid-sized home and lasted ~100 minutes. One researcher shadowed the auditor, taking field notes and photographs. Due to weather conditions, thermography was *not* used; however, the auditor spoke to the researcher about how/why he would ordinarily use thermography. Following the audit, the participant completed a 30-minute debrief and was compensated $20. We thematically analyzed field notes from the observation and debrief session [7] looking for patterns that confirmed, extended, or differed from Study 1.

Findings

We present our observational findings around three areas: procedure, using thermography, and challenges.

Audit Procedure. The auditor said that he generally spends 2 hours in the field, plus 4-5 hours for report generation and follow-up confirming Study 1's finding that *report generation* is effortful and time consuming. The audit procedure included meeting the client, establishing rapport, and determining reasons for the audit. The client joined the auditor for an initial walkthrough, which the auditor later explained was critical to enhancing client understanding and buy-in. During the walkthrough, the auditor took pictures of areas of interest and performed both a combustion test (*e.g.*, checking appliances) and a blower door test. Here, the auditor indicated he would normally use his thermal camera. Finally, the auditor met with the client to explain findings and suggested changes explained in terms of cost savings. The next day, the auditor created and sent his report to the client using in-house software.

Thermography. Though thermography was not used, the auditor did not think thermography would have altered his overall efficiency recommendations to his client. He described using thermography for confirmation, client communication, and to help work crews perform retrofits. Again, the visual nature of thermography was key to "*help[ing] explain complex things*." He described a client base motivated by utility bills: "*Many people expect the bill to be wrong, not to have an issue in the home*." The thermographic images helped overcome that misconception.

Primary Challenges. The auditor described two technical challenges: establishing proper conditions for thermography and the effort required to generate a report.

DISCUSSION

As the first qualitative, human-centered inquiry into both conventional and emerging thermographic processes and tools, our findings help reveal challenges, highlight energy audits as a social-technical process, and inform future work. Below, we reflect on our findings, provide design considerations, and discuss limitations and future work.

Conventional Thermography

Auditors were generally positive about the role of thermography in energy auditing, particularly as a communication and diagnostic tool—but stressed that it required skill and expertise to use. Here, we focus on three aspects of conventional thermography that have implications for design and future research.

Social Process. As in [25], energy auditing was portrayed as a social process as much as a technical one. Auditors emphasized the importance of understanding their client's needs and reasons for a home assessment, gaining trust and credibility, and being able to explain identified problems and their implications. To help establish trust and communicate findings, auditors allowed clients to operate their thermal cameras. This "role reversal" places increased emphasis on the thermal camera while deemphasizing the interpretative role of the auditor. In this way, the thermal camera becomes a sort of "inscription device" [32] that translates the complex or the contested into material fact but potentially obscures the full complexities of the instrument, the techniques required for proper use, and the skills necessary for interpretation. To support this social process and role reversal, how can future tools be designed to accommodate both expert and novice users (clients)? How can tools better support auditor-client interaction, both in real-time during the audit as well as post-hoc in the report generation process?

Subjectivity. Though thermography relies on sophisticated technology, the interpretation of its output is fundamentally subjective. Our participants desired greater objectivity in how to apply and interpret thermography but barriers included a lack of universal standards, varying levels of training in the auditing community, poor guidelines, and the inherent complexity of the task (echoing [50]). Participants with higher levels of training in our study (Level 2 or 3) felt that they had superior interpretative skills than those without. However, more work is needed to study how training and experience affects interpretation, how interpretations vary across thermographers for the same audit site (extending [21]), how these differences manifest in energy efficiency recommendations, and how tools can be better designed to aid analysis and reduce subjectivity.

Ethical Concerns. Subjectivity is also a concern in a transactional context where thermography is used not only to identify problems but also to make a sale. As noted in our findings, some clients are skeptical of auditor motives, particularly when the auditor works for a home improvement company (as 3 did in our study). In these cases, auditors may consciously or unconsciously be biased in their interpretations. If future thermographic tools can reduce subjectivity, ethical concerns may be mitigated.

Automated Thermography

Our five design probes allowed us to explore thermographer reactions to various automation scenarios, including indoor and outdoor robotic data collection, 3D reconstruction, automatic anomaly detection, and advanced temporal analyses. We discuss challenges, privacy and policy implications, and a call-to-action.

Challenges. Though 9 of 10 participants reacted positively to one or more design probe(s), our findings surfaced important concerns regarding data quality, data overload, fear and privacy, and technical feasibility—none of which have been studied in the automation literature. For automated data collection, in particular, our auditors were concerned with the lack of environmental control compared with manual audits (*e.g.,* to establish pressure differentials), how to manage this large amount of data, and general data quality issues (*e.g.,* filtering). However, most were interested in how this "big data" may transform and enable new analyses (*e.g.,* historical comparisons). For 3D reconstructions, our auditors noted that thermal data alone, though useful, is insufficient—better models would include information about building materials, weather conditions during the scan, utility data, and even occupant behaviors.

Privacy and Policy. Though mentioned by only a few participants, the use of remote, automated data collection has privacy and policy implications. For example, if buildings can easily be scanned at scale, how may this change the way governments assess and regulate building energy efficiency and/or award and monitor "green" certifications (*e.g.,* LEED)? New business models are emerging (*e.g.,*[34]) based on automated thermography that sell exterior scan data and analyses to utility companies to help determine which houses "leak the most energy" and target energy-efficiency programs. Because exterior thermal scans can be performed remotely (*e.g.,* from the street or air), should a building's thermal profile be considered public data? Can building owners opt-out of scans?

Moving Forward. As a pursuit framed purely as a technical challenge, the automation literature has been, unsurprisingly, focused on engineering. However, our findings further highlight thermography as a socio-technical problem where the interplay between auditor, client, and thermal camera plays a crucial role (*e.g.,* in building trust, communicating results). Future automation work should consider existing thermographic practices and engage in human-centered design with both auditors and clients to improve and validate their tools. As others have argued, the Sustainable HCI community needs to be more engaged in these emerging areas, especially those that are not necessarily consumer-facing. Thermography is a growing area that will likely become more popular as governmental institutions increasingly recommend thermographic-based energy audits and thermal devices become more prevalent (even as smartphone attachments[2] and low-cost sensors[3]).

Limitations

There are four primary limitations to this work. First, we interviewed professional energy auditors who specialize in residential buildings. Reported practices and reactions to the design probes may differ from those of commercial and industrial energy auditors. Second, our design probes primarily emphasized UAV-based exterior data collection, anomaly detection, historical analysis, and 3D reconstruction. Future work should more closely examine other parts of the automation pipeline (*e.g.,* indoor robotic, data collection, report generation). Third, our study method relied on self-report from semi-structured interviews, complemented by a single observation of an energy audit (without thermography). More thorough and longer-term ethnographic fieldwork of energy auditors may yield new insights. Finally, we acknowledge the potential dichotomy in asking professional auditors about scenarios that could be perceived as replacing or undercutting their jobs; however, none commented on feeling supplanted. Instead, auditors expressed interest in automation because of its potential to increase their efficiency, enable new types of analyses, improve building models/simulations, and allow for greater coverage (*e.g.,* entire neighborhoods).

CONCLUSIONS

This paper contributes the first human-centered investigation of thermographic automation. Through semi-structured interviews and a complementary observational case study, we assessed energy auditing practices and thermography's role therein. Through five design probes, we critically examined emerging automated thermographic solutions and identified important challenges/concerns. Our findings have implications not just for the design of emerging thermographic tools but also for researchers focused on automation and human robotic interaction.

REFERENCES

1. Association of Energy Engineers. Certified Energy Auditor. 2014. http://www.aeecenter.org/i4a/pages/index.cfm?pageid=3365.
2. Balaras, C.A. and Argiriou, A.A. Infrared thermography for building diagnostics. *Energy and Buildings 34*, 2 (2002), 171–183.
3. Bardhan, A., Jaffee, D., Kroll, C., and Wallace, N. Energy efficiency retrofits for U.S. housing: Removing the bottlenecks. *Regional Science and Urban Economics 47*, (2014), 45–60.
4. Baumer, E.P.S. and Silberman, M.S. When the Implication is Not to Design (Technology). *Proc. of CHI'11*, 2271–2274.
5. Blevis, E. Sustainable Interaction Design: Invention & Disposal, Renewal & Reuse. *Proc. of CHI'07*, 503–512.

[2] FLIR ONE: http://www.flir.com/flirone/
[3] FLiR Dev Kit: https://www.sparkfun.com/products/13233

6. Borrmann, D., Nüchter, A., Dakulovic, M., et al. The Project ThermalMapper—Thermal 3D mapping of indoor environments for saving energy. *Proc. of SYROCO'12*, 1-8.
7. Braun, V. and Clarke, V. Using thematic analysis in psychology. *Qualitative Research in Psychology 3*, 2 (2006), 77–101.
8. Brooks, P. Testing Building Envelopes with Infrared Thermography: Delivering the "Big Picture." *Interface, the Technical Journal of RCI July*, (2007).
9. Brynjarsdottir, H., Håkansson, M., Pierce, J., *et al.* Sustainably Unpersuaded: How Persuasion Narrows Our Vision of Sustainability. *Proc. of CHI'12*, 947–956.
10. Demisse, G.G., Borrmann, D., and Nuchter, A. Interpreting thermal 3D models of indoor environments for energy efficiency. *Proc. of ICAR'13*, 1–8.
11. Dillahunt, T., Mankoff, J., Paulos, E., and Fussell, S. It's Not All About "Green": Energy Use in Low-income Communities. *Proc. of UbiComp'09*, 255–264.
12. Dillahunt, T., Mankoff, J., and Paulos, E. Understanding Conflict Between Landlords and Tenants: Implications for Energy Sensing and Feedback. *Proc. of UbiComp'10*, 149–158.
13. Dios, J.R.M.-D. and Ollero, A. Automatic Detection of Windows Thermal Heat Losses in Buildings Using UAVs. *2006 World Automation Congress*, IEEE (2006), 1–6.
14. DiSalvo, C., Sengers, P., and Brynjarsdóttir, H. Mapping the Landscape of Sustainable HCI. *Proc. of CHI'10*, 1975–1984.
15. Dourish, P. HCI and environmental sustainability: the politics of design and the design of politics. *Proc. of DIS'10*, 1–10.
16. Froehlich, J., Findlater, L., and Landay, J. The Design of Eco-feedback Technology. *Proc. of CHI'10*, 1999–2008.
17. Golparvar-Fard, M. and Ham, Y. Automated Diagnostics and Visualization of Potential Energy Performance Problems in Existing Buildings Using Energy Performance Augmented Reality Models. *J. of Computing in Civil Engineering 28*, 1 (2014), 17–29.
18. Goodhew, J., Pahl, S., Auburn, T., and Goodhew, S. Making Heat Visible: Promoting Energy Conservation Behaviors Through Thermal Imaging. *Environment and Behavior*, (2014).
19. Håkansson, M. and Sengers, P. Beyond Being Green: Simple Living Families and ICT. *Proc. of CHI'13*, 2725–2734.
20. Ham, Y. and Golparvar-Fard, M. An automated vision-based method for rapid 3D energy performance modeling of existing buildings using thermal and digital imagery. *Advanced Engineering Informatics 27*, 3 (2013), 395–409.
21. Helcke, G.A., Conti, F., *et al.* A detailed comparison of energy audits carried out by four separate companies on the same set of buildings. *Energy and Buildings 14*, 2 (1990), 153–164.
22. Hruschka, D.J., Schwartz, D., *et al.* Reliability in Coding Open-Ended Data: Lessons Learned from HIV Behavioral Research. *Field Methods 16* , 3 (2004), 307–331.
23. Ingle, A., Moezzi, M., Lutzenhiser, L., and Diamond, R. How well do home energy audits serve the homeowner? *Proc. of ACEEE Summer Study on Energy Efficiency in Buildings'12*.
24. Ingle, A., Moezzi, M., Lutzenhiser, L., and Diamond, R. Better home energy audit modelling: incorporating inhabitant behaviours. *Building Research & Info. 42*, 4 (2014), 409–421.
25. Ingle, A., Moezzi, M., Lutzenhiser, L., et al. Behavioral Perspectives on Home Energy Audits: The Role of Auditors, Labels, Reports, and Audit Tools on Homeowner Decision Making. 2013, 1–396. http://goo.gl/74iRfR.
26. *ISO 6781:1983: Thermal Insulation-Qualitative detection of thermal irregularities in building envelopes-IR method.* 2012.
27. Krippendorff, K.. Content Analysis: An Introduction to Its Methodology. *Sage Publications, Inc.*, (2003).
28. Kylili, A., Fokaides, P.A., Christou, P., and Kalogirou, S.A. Infrared thermography (IRT) applications for building diagnostics: A review. *Applied Energy 134*, (2014), 531–549.
29. Lagüela, S., Armesto, J., Arias, P., and Herráez, J. Automation of thermographic 3D modelling through image fusion and image matching techniques. *Automation in Constr. 27*, (2012), 24–31.
30. Lagüela, S., Diaz-Vilarino, L., *et al.* Aerial oblique thermographic imagery for the generation of building 3D models to complement Geographic Information Systems. *Proc. of QIRT'14*.
31. Lagüela, S., Martínez, J., Armesto, J., and Arias, P. Energy efficiency studies through 3D laser scanning and thermographic technologies. *Energy and Buildings 43*, 6 (2011), 1216–1221.
32. Latour, B. and Woolgar, S. *Laboratory Life: The Construction of Scientific Facts.* Princeton University Press, 1986.
33. Mankoff, J. HCI and sustainability: a tale of two motivations. *interactions 19*, 3 (2012), 16–19.
34. Matheson, R. Drive-By Heat Mapping. *MIT News*, 2015. http://goo.gl/ZxFDff.
35. Mauriello, M.L. and Froehlich, J.E. Towards Automated Thermal Profiling of Buildings at Scale Using Unmanned Aerial Vehicles and 3D-reconstruction. *Poster Proc. UbiComp'14*, 119–122.
36. Moghadam, P. and Vidas, S. HeatWave: the next generation of thermography devices. *SPIE Sensing Technology + Applications*, International Society for Optics and Photonics (2014), 91050F.
37. Norberg-Bohm, V. and White, C. *Building America Program Evaluation.* 2004.
38. Oreifej, O., Cramer, J., and Zakhor, A. Automatic Generation of 3D Thermal Maps of Building Interiors. *ASHRAE Trans.*, (2014).
39. Palmer, K., Walls, M., Gordon, H., and Gerarden, T. Assessing the energy-efficiency information gap: results from a survey of home energy auditors. *Energy Efficiency 6*, 2 (2012), 271–292.
40. Pierce, J. Undesigning Technology: Considering the Negation of Design by Design. *Proc. of CHI'12*, 957–966.
41. Previtali, M., Barazzetti, L., *et al.* Thermographic Analysis from UAV Platforms for Energy Efficiency Retrofit Applications. *J. Mob. Multimed. 9*, 1-2 (2013), 66–82.
42. Rodden, T., Fischer, J., Pantidi, N., Bachour, K., and Moran, S. At Home with Agents: Exploring Attitudes Towards Future Smart Energy Infrastructures. *Proc. of CHI'13*, 1173–1182.
43. Silberman, M.S., Nathan, L., Knowles, B., et al. Next steps for sustainable HCI. *interactions 21*, 5 (2014), 66–69.
44. Strengers, Y.A.A. Designing Eco-feedback Systems for Everyday Life. *Proc. of CHI'11*, 2135–2144.
45. Thumann, A. and Younger, W.J. *Handbook of Energy Audits.* The Fairmont Press, Inc., 2008.
46. US Department of Energy. *Buildings Energy Data Book.* 2011.
47. US Department of Energy. Thermographic Inspections. 2012. http://energy.gov/energysaver/articles/thermographic-inspections.
48. US Department of Energy. Blower Door Tests. 2012. http://energy.gov/energysaver/articles/blower-door-tests.
49. US Department of Energy. Home Energy Audits. 2014. http://energy.gov/articles/askenergysaver-home-energy-audits.
50. Vavilov, V.P. A pessimistic view of the energy auditing of building structures with the use of infrared thermography. *Russian Journal of Nondestructive Testing 46*, 12 (2011), 906–910.
51. Wang, C., Cho, Y.K., and Gai, M. As-Is 3D Thermal Modeling for Existing Building Envelopes Using a Hybrid LIDAR System. *Journal of Computing in Civil Engineering 27*, 6 (2013), 645–656.
52. Woodruff, A., Hasbrouck, J., and Augustin, S. A Bright Green Perspective on Sustainable Choices. *Proc. of CHI'08*, 313–322.

Keepin' it Real: Challenges when Designing Sports-Training Games

Mads Møller Jensen[1], Majken K. Rasmussen[1], Florian 'Floyd' Mueller[2], Kaj Grønbæk[1]

[1]Dept. Computer Science
Aarhus University, Denmark
{mmjensen, mkirkegaard, kgronbak}@cs.au.dk

[2]Exertion Games Lab
RMIT University, Melbourne, Australia
floyd@exertiongameslab.org

ABSTRACT
Using game elements and mechanics in sports training holds great potential for increasing player enjoyment, but also introduces a risk of reducing training relevance. This paper describes a novel training installation for individual handball training, called "The Bouncer", and the design process behind three training games. In order to investigate how game elements can affect the training experience, we conducted a study with 10 experienced amateur handball players, eliciting responses regarding the training relevance of the games. Based on the study and our design insights, we propose three challenges that designers of interactive sports-training games need to consider: 1) Maintaining relevance when translating physical elements into digital representations. 2) Choosing an appropriate level of sensing as game input. 3) Introducing points in training exercises without reducing sport relevance. For the three challenges, we propose strategies to help future designers of training games.

Author Keywords
Interactive sports-training games; exertion interfaces; sports; handball; exergames; human-computer interaction;

ACM Classification Keywords
H.5.m. Information interfaces and presentation (e.g., HCI): Miscellaneous.

INTRODUCTION
Most players recognize the importance of training, but would readily agree that playing the actual sport is significantly more fun and engaging, than training for it. Using technology to support sports training has received interest from both the sport science and HCI community, where a range of different examples of using technology to aid training in sport have been developed (e.g. [6,21]).

CHI 2015, April 18 - 23 2015, Seoul, Republic of Korea
Copyright 2015 ACM 978-1-4503-3145-6/15/04…$15.00
http://dx.doi.org/10.1145/2702123.2702243

However, few have addressed increasing the engagement in training by adding game elements as a way to motivate players to carry out the necessary training. We believe that designing training as games can motivate players to train, and shift training from being repetitive and boring to being engaging and fun. However, as pointed out by Jensen et al. [10], designing training as games requires designers to be sensitive to elements from the sport, as design decisions can lead to inexpedient behavior. By inexpedient, we mean actions that are inappropriate, undesirable or illegal in relation to the sport. Thus, designers of training games are faced with the challenge of utilizing game elements in an appropriate way that balances the use of engaging elements to make the training interesting, while keeping it real and relevant to the sport.

Our research seeks to add to the limited knowledge of designing interactive sports-training games by providing insights on how game elements can be used to increase engagement in sports training and how they affect sport relevance. In this paper, we articulate characteristic challenges that designers of training games will encounter, and propose strategies for approaching them.

Figure 1. The Bouncer

The paper is structured as follows: We start by looking at related work that combines technology and sport. Then we present the Bouncer, an interactive training installation, and the design process behind three training games. We present a study with 10 experienced amateur handball players, resulting in findings regarding the handball relevance of the training games. Based on the study and our design insights, we propose three characteristic challenges that designers of interactive sports-training games need to consider: 1) Maintaining relevance when translating physical elements into digital representations. 2) Choosing an appropriate level of sensing as game input. 3) Introducing points in training exercises without reducing sport relevance. For each of the three challenges, we propose strategies aimed at helping designers to create training games with a high relevance to sport training.

RELATED WORK

Three specific areas that combine sport and technology have informed our research: Exertion games, training systems, and interactive sport-training games. These areas focus on encouraging physical engagement, training sport relevant skills, and combining games and training, respectively. We have limited our scope of exertion games and training systems to screen-based examples, as we have used a screen-based approach in our work.

Exertion games: Focus on physical engagement

Exertion games refer to games that use bodily activity as input to facilitate engagement. Exertion games are not focused on training a sport, but often use elements from sports in their design. Within exertion games, screens have been used to facilitate physical games between multiple players, who are either distributed in different location, e.g. Table Tennis for Three [17], Breakout for Two [14], and Remote Impact [15], or playing in the same space, e.g. Splashball [8]. In these games, players interact through a screen, using a ball or their body, and the game provides a virtual space where the players' physical actions have an impact, e.g. by awarding points to players for smashing virtual bricks. Exertion games have also been popular at sports museums, enabling visitors to situate themselves in a sports context, such as shooting a soccer penalty (National Sports Museum, Melbourne), or scoring a goal in hockey (Hockey Hall of Fame, Toronto). While the setup of these installations might resemble a training situation, they are not training visitors' sport abilities. However, by applying game-like settings, the installations engage visitors in sports-related experiences. These examples of exertion games illustrate different ways of transferring physical elements into a virtual space in order to create an engaging experience.

Training systems: Focus on sport relevance

Training systems refer to interactive systems that facilitate training of different sport-specific skills. An example is using a large screen as a video mirror for training martial arts, thereby allowing athletes to perform and evaluate spin kicks; a move that is difficult to practice using a regular mirror [6]. Several systems explore using screens to create virtual environments for athletes to train their perceptual and decision-making skills isolated from the sport [13]. An example is the decision-making training system for cricket by Hopwood et al. [9], where cricket players are placed in front of a life-size video projection of batters striking virtual balls from different fielding positions. Similar examples exist from handball training [1,22], where goalkeepers' reactions are trained by using a virtual space and virtual ball-throwers. This enables goalkeepers to train important decision-making and reaction skills. Examples of screen-based training interfaces also include the numerous variants of golf simulators, e.g. [23], where screens are used to display a digital golf course that the players hit actual golf balls towards, allowing training of swing technique in a controlled environment. These training systems illustrate various ways of training specific skills, e.g. decision-making, using virtual environments.

Interactive sports-training games: Combining engagement and sport relevance

Interactive sports-training games focus on training systems that use game elements and mechanics in their design. Examples of interactive sport-training games, include the trampoline training games presented by Holsti et al. [7]. The system mixes jumping-height training on a trampoline with controlling a virtual character on a screen. The player's movements are tracked and displayed on the screen, enabling a platform style game where the player has to jump higher and higher to succeed. Football Lab is a football-training installation that trains players' ball-handling skills [10]. A player is placed in a small football field surrounded by sensor-mounted rebounders that call for the ball using lights and sound, and players are rewarded with points depending on how many passes they make during a game. TacTowers [4] is an example of an interactive handball-training game, which embeds the training of micro tactics and kinesthetic empathy in an interactive context through different games. The games aim to train the players' ability to "read" each other's intensions, and are played by two players without a ball. These interactive sports-training games illustrate different ways of combining relevant skill training and engaging gameplay, often by focusing on isolated skills, e.g. micro tactics or ball handling.

THE BOUNCER: TRAINING GAMES FOR HANDBALL

Inspired by existing work, we developed an interactive installation, supporting individual handball training, called "The Bouncer". We decided on screen-based interaction as the outset for our design, as 1) existing work indicate that using a screen supports the training of perception and decision-making skills (e.g. [1,9,13]), and 2) a screen enables a virtual space for incorporating game elements and mechanics (e.g. [14,15,17]).

Handball was chosen, as it is a popular team sport in Europe. Handball is a fast paced, high scoring game that is played by two teams of six court players and one goalkeeper. The game is played between two 3x2 meter goals, which are surrounded by a 6-meter zone, where only the defending goalkeeper is allowed. Players can score by throwing the ball past the goalkeeper and into the goal.

Technical description of The Bouncer

The Bouncer installation consists of a 270x270 cm frame strung with wire (called an M-station [24]) that has the ability to return an impacting ball with 95% of its speed. The M-station is fitted with 8 piezoelectric sensors that provide signals to a positioning algorithm running on an Atmel Xmega microcontroller. The algorithm detects the impacting balls and calculates the impact time and coordinates using a best-fit approach with an accuracy of approx. 10 cm. The micro controller sends data to a computer, and the computer's screen is projected onto a surface placed behind the M-station (see Figure 1).

THE PROCESS OF DESIGNING A TRAINING GAME

The following section presents the design process behind three games for The Bouncer. The aim of the design process was to design an engaging handball-relevant training game that would allow players to train individually.

In order to ensure handball relevance of our training games, we invited three graduate students in sports science to a brainstorming workshop. The students had theoretical and practical knowledge about coaching and playing various sports, two of them specifically in handball. The workshop lasted 2 hours and took place in front of The Bouncer, enabling the participants to explain and externalize their ideas by acting them out, using the installation. Three simple demo games were designed to kick-start the ideation process, and exemplify some of the possibilities offered by the installation, such as training handball penalty shots, hit accuracy and reaction time.

Especially two findings from the initial workshop influenced alterations to the installation and the design of the training games: First, the game should be more than target shooting training, and second, the installation needed additional sensing to encourage relevant movements.

Increasing handball relevance: beyond hitting a target

The workshop suggested that a training game should go beyond hitting targets and include other aspects, e.g. changing direction, reaction time, or decision-making, supported by previous research, emphasizing that aspects such as decision-making and cognitive skills should be addressed in training situations [11]. The demo games focused primarily on static target shooting, and our participant found that approach too simplistic for handball training. This is in line with the idea of balancing training between *part practice* and *whole practice* [12], as focusing on a specific and isolated part of a sport helps to limit stimuli of the players' senses, but too narrow a focus can complicate the process of implementing the learning outcomes back into the actual game. The most prevalent idea that arose during the workshop was the prospect of training decision-making abilities while being in the air during shot execution. Many handball players, especially when pressured, revert to their *habitual shot*, instead of surveying the situation in order to make a shot decision. A habitual shot is the shot that players like the most and often tend to shoot in stressful situations. Furthermore, research encourage incorporating option generation, cognitive processing and decision making in training, as these abilities are found to be different between elite and amateur players [19]. Consequently, we wanted to design the games in a way where targets only appear to the players when they jump in order to train their in-air decision-making skills.

Increasing handball relevance: adding a sensor

The workshop also emphasized that additional sensors in the game space were required to enforce handball relevant movements. The demo games rarely required the players to move more than few meters, and that is in contrast to actual handball, where players are in constant motion, often jumping whilst shooting towards goal. In order to address this issue and enable the design of training games that encouraged handball relevant movements, we needed to change the game space. Consequently, we incorporated an additional sensor, a large touch plate (50x150cm), which was placed on the ground, 6 m from the M-station. The

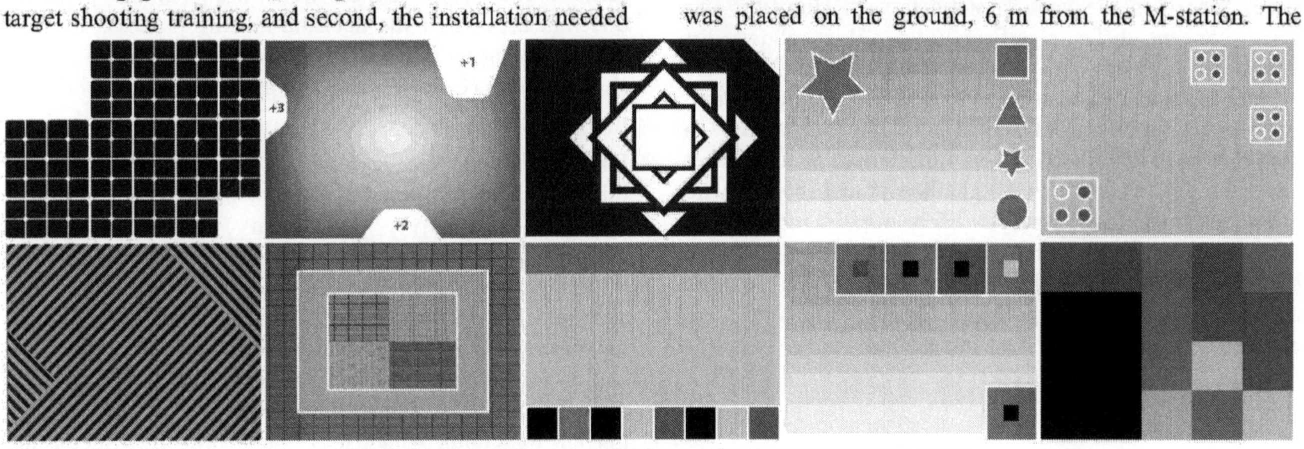

Figure 2. Examples of graphics used for the Wizard of Oz test

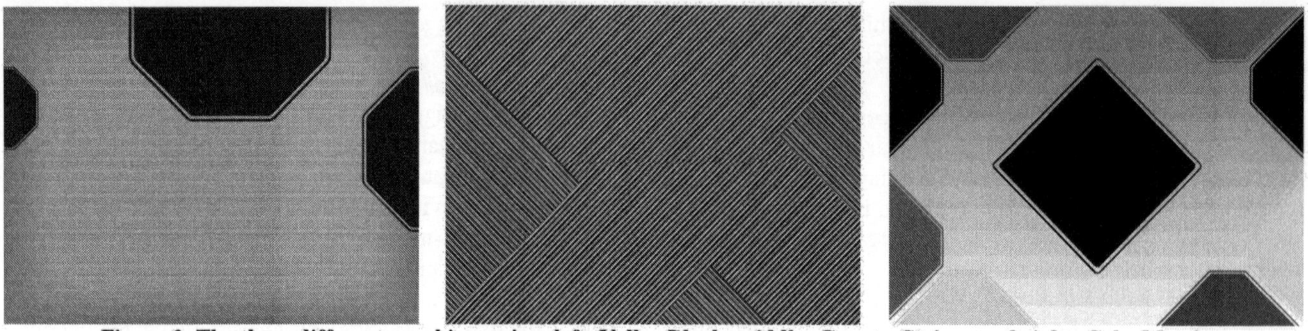

Figure 3. The three different graphic version, left: YellowBlack, middle: CounterStripes and right: ColorMatch

sensor was used to detect when a player jumps in order to change the graphics displayed and reveal the targets to hit. Moreover, in order to enforce handball-relevant movement patterns, we decided that training games should consist of multiple jumps and shots and have a high intensity.

Our final game concept

Bringing these elements together formed our game concept: A player starts 12 meter away from the screen with a ball. The game starts after a 5 seconds countdown, where the player then runs toward the screen and jumps off the touch plate. As the player's foot connects with the touch plate, the graphics on the screen changes, displaying different targets to hit. This forces the player to make decisions on where to hit, while being in the air. When the ball has been thrown, the player sprints back to the starting point, collects a new ball and runs towards the screen again. This continues for 40 seconds, and the aim of the game is for the player to get as many points as possible by hitting the appearing targets.

Relation to regular handball training

We are aware that jump shots and shot-time decision-making only represent a small part of handball, and training with The Bouncer should be considered as *part-progressive practice* [12]. Therefore, it should be part of a training session, where the elements trained are understood in relation to the sport as a whole. Training with The Bouncer is similar to traditional handball training, where in a typical shooting exercise, the players would run towards goal and shoot either to score on a goalkeeper or to hit cones or jersey placed in the goal as static targets. However, our game concept differ significantly, as 1) it allows for individual training with dynamic targets, and 2) forces players to make decisions in air based on their perception. Both are opportunities not present in traditional training. On the other hand The Bouncer has a limitation, as it does not cover the relationship between goalkeeper and shooter, who often anticipate and react to each other's movements. However, our intension has not been to cover all aspects, but instead to make the training independent of the opposing goalkeeper's skill level, and truly force the players to make their decisions in air.

Designing the training game graphics

Having settled on the basic game concept, we explored different graphic versions for the virtual targets (see Figure 2). The different graphics were tested using the Wizard of Oz method in order to ascertain their difficulty, handball relevance, and decision-making demands.

By experimenting with different graphics, we found that different graphical representations emphasized different aspects of the decision-making process. For example, we found that some level of cognitive load in the graphics made the game more engaging, however, overly complex graphics made the games too difficult, as players were unable to perceive the targets, make decisions and throw the ball, while being in the air. The use of abstract graphics also made it possible to create different sized targets, giving different scores, thus, introducing another game mechanic to the training game. This led us to design three different games based on the same game concept, in order to explore how they altered players' perception of the training games' handball relevance while considering engagement.

The three new training games (see Figure 3) were: 1) *YellowBlack*, which had three targets in three varying sizes, where the largest target had the lowest score, and the smallest the highest score, 2) *CounterStripes*, which also had three targets and the same scoring as YellowBlack, but displayed the targets more subdued, and 3) *ColorMatch*, which had 8 colored targets located around a center, with the point-giving targets determined by the color in the center. The three games were designed to highlight different aspects of the decision-making process, such as; choosing a target between different options (YellowBlack), shifting focus (ColorMatch), and pushing players' ability to locate targets (CounterStripes).

For each of the three games, we developed two different difficulty levels in order to see how players coped with an increased cognitive load. In YellowBlack and CounterStripes, the level was increased by removing the largest target within the first second after the targets appeared. The rationale was to simulate a goalkeeper luring the player to shoot at a certain location in order to anticipate and save the shot, as suggested by goalkeeper training manuals, e.g. [25]. By removing the largest target we forced players to rethink where they should hit, thus, increasing the cognitive demand. In ColorMatch the difficulty was increased by having eight different colors, rather than four, giving the players only one target to locate and hit.

USER STUDY

We conducted a study of the three games in order to explore how proficient handball players experienced the different training games, as well as how the graphics affected the handball relevance.

Participants

For this study, we recruited 10 participants (8 male and 2 female) aged between 24 and 27, with an average age of 25 years. We recruited the participants by engaging with a local handball club as well as Aarhus University´s School of Sports Science's social forum. The participants had an average handball experience of 16 years, and they were active amateur players, who trained 2-4 times per week, except one, who only played occasionally after having played 4 times a week for 7 years. The combined participants covered all of the different positions in handball: Wing, backcourt, pivot and goalkeeper.

Procedure

After the participants had warmed up, they were introduced to the system and the structure of the study. The study consisted of playing each of the three games on the two levels of difficulty. Before each game the participants could choose whether they wished to see a live demonstration of the game or try it out in a slow pace. Each of the 6 games lasted for 40 seconds and was followed by a semi-structured interview. We restricted the study to 6 repetitions due to the high intensity of the training exercise. We mixed the order in which the participants played the training games by applying a Latin square to minimize the influence of fatigue, maturation of the participants and carry-over effects, giving each game equal terms of evaluation. Each study took between 60 and 90 minutes, and each participant received a $40 gift certificate for participating in the study.

Data Collection and Analysis

We used video recordings from three different angles in order to compare whether the movements of the participants altered when playing the games. The interviews were audio recorded and transcribed. We used a coding process to structure the transcriptions and identify key concepts in the data. These concepts were then placed in an affinity diagram and through an iterative sorting process we derived dominant themes from the study. These themes, which summarize and conclude the collected data, will be presented as findings in the following section.

EXPERIENCES WITH THE BOUNCER

All participants stated that they enjoyed training with The Bouncer. They had a high level of exertion throughout the games and were focused on their score and performance. Although, increasing the engagement and enjoyment of the training had been a focus in our design, the relevance of the handball training had higher priority as The Bouncer was created to be a handball-training tool. All participants stated that the training games had relevance for their handball training, supported by comments such as, *"It's a good mix between throwing and hitting targets, plus you have to force yourself to stay in the air"* (P1), and, *"it creates a coupling between reacting to something quickly, as you would have to with a goalkeeper, which makes it a great tool"* (P9).

The following sections present findings from the study categorized by the three dominant themes that emerged from the data: Movement patterns, perceptual reactions, and context characteristics

Movement patterns

Movement patterns relate to the way players move, and cover the execution of technique-related skills, e.g. throwing and jumping in handball.

Finding 1: Exploring different movement strategies

All of the players experimented with different ways of jumping in order to get more time in the air to survey the screen and locate the targets. 7 of the participants stated that they tried to jump higher, as the graphics got more complicated. One participant noted, *"I am focusing a lot more on getting to the plate and in the air now, instead of the speed"* (P9), as he went on to play ColorMatch. Another participant realized during a game that he had to jump higher to locate the targets: *"In the beginning I was just jumping and shooting [...] but in the end I found that I had to stay in the air to locate the targets"* (P6). Figure 4 illustrates how one of the players altered the style of his

Figure 4. Example of altering the jump

jump, from a forward to a more upwards jump. In relation to handball, he answered, *"It is better to jump up than forward, but you should be able to do both, dependent on the situation"* (P4). Although both ways of jumping are useful in handball, jumping upward seems to improve players' ability to survey the screen. However, consulting the video showed no significant difference between the jump types in terms of time in the air.

Rather than focusing on jumping higher, 4 participants stated that they experimented with slowing down to get more precision, *"We were told to get as many points at possible, so I thought I would take fewer shots with higher precision. But if I had increased the intensity I might have gotten more points, so I will try that next"* (P3) and *"I slowed down a little so I had a more energy in the air to sort out where the colors were"* (P4). In general, the game forced the players to find a balance between intensity and precision, because as one participant noted, *"as soon as the intensity goes up, the technique goes down"* (P10).

Finding 2: Movement patterns are affected by fatigue

Fatigue and stress caused by the high tempo also impacted the players' jumping abilities, as one stated, *"I could feel the lactic acid here in the end. It gets harder to jump high enough in order to get time enough to think"* (P10). Others noted that fatigue impacted their shooting abilities, stating that they go to their habitual shot, if the were unable to locate the targets. This was emphasized as a positive element of the training game, e.g. by one players, who noted, *"There are many, who has habitual shots, so if you can remove that from a player, also when he is tired, I believe that would optimize his abilities as a player"* (P4). Thus, the high intensity of the game increased the training relevance, by creating a situation of fatigue, similar to the last period of handball matches, where players often tend to fall back to their habitual shot due to exhaustion. Training in this specific physical state might help the players to make better decisions in these situations.

Finding 3: Facilitating self insights of movement patterns

Playing the training games provided the participants with knowledge about themselves and their habits: 7 players commented on their shooting habits, e.g. *"I found that I start looking at the top and then at the bottom [of the screen], and that made me aware that I prefer to shoot up there"* (P8). One player noted that playing the game *"gives you a better overview, so you don't just do you habitual shot. And you do get pressured, maybe not physically in the air, but mentally"* (P6). In summary, because the games dictated where players could score, it provided them with insights on their habits, and helped raise reflection on areas where they could improve.

Finding 4: Altering relevant actions to improve score

All the players wanted to get high scores in the games, however, the strategies they employed to perform well were not always conforming to how they would act when playing handball. When asked what he did differently from the last game, one participant answered, *"I slowed down"* (P3). The interviewer questioned the proficiency in relation to handball to which he answered, *"in the last round, which was not so good, I did as I would do if I played handball, so now I chose a tactic, where I did not do as I would do when playing handball"*, and elaborated, *"I did it because of this game. It is probably not a good idea in relation to handball"*. However, when asked how the game then succeeded as a training game, he answered, *"It might be that I would become a better handball player by doing it this way"*. Thus, it is not apparent if altering the way players normally move is positive or negative.

Perceptual reaction

Perceptual reaction refers to the way players are able to perceive a situation and react accordingly.

Finding 5: Perception of abstract representations impact the level of difficulty

The graphics of the games provided different levels of difficulty in terms of perceiving the targets. All participants regarded the complexity of YellowBlack as being easier than the other two. One player described the difference between CounterStripes and YellowBlack as, *"It was much easier to focus (in YellowBlack) than in the striped one. The stripes really confused me, because it was the same colors all the way round, but they were just divided. When I was shown the game, in the beginning I couldn't even see where the targets were, so it was difficult compared to this one, where the targets were clearly marked"* (P6). However, despite the unanimous agreement that YellowBlack was easier than CounterStripes, surveying the data from the games showed that the average hit percentage was higher in CounterStripes (93,3%) than YellowBlack (78,7%). The discrepancy might be caused by the larger target sizes in CounterStripes, or because players tended to shoot more after the big targets in CounterStripes. This was evident as the average hit score was lower in YellowBlack (119 points per shot) compared to CounterStripes (98 points per shot) despite the higher average hit rate.

The graphics of ColorMatch required the players to combine two tasks, namely to identify the color to hit and locate a corresponding target. While this might seem as an easy task when standing still, it showed to be a difficult task to perform in air, as one player noted, *"I was surprised that it was so difficult to locate the colors. When I was just observing the first few times, I thought it was easy to see where they were, but when you hang in the air, there is suddenly not that much time. It was more difficult than I thought"* (P4). Many players admitted to panic in the air, e.g. *"when there is a color you have to hit, and you can't find it, then I ended up shooting right in the center"* (P3) or *"I ended up shooting at the big one in the center. I certainly think I could learn something from this"* (P5).

Finding 6: Enforced decision making is engaging

In YellowBlack and CounterStripes the different sized targets allowed players to choose different strategies in order to score points. The choice of targets left the players in a dilemma, which was phrased by one player as, *"should I go for the easy solution and score, or should I choose the difficult one and maybe miss"* (P6). The players often altered their tactics along the way, aiming for smaller targets if they were unhappy with their score, or if they had gained confidence from a previous game, as one described as, *"the tactic was a bit different now, because I know that I haven't got time for that many rounds, and I know that I can hit the small one. I showed that when I got the 900 point"* (P7). Although most had the intention to hit the small targets, they did not always succeed, and when the large target disappeared in the second level of the games, the players had to reconsider their decisions, e.g. *"when there were three targets to hit, then you felt that the largest one was kind of a buffer, if you couldn't hit the other two, but here you quickly have to eliminate it, and see if you can hit the others"* (P4).

Finding 7: Coherence between the abstract graphical representations and handball training

The three games were perceived differently in regard to handball relevance. The graphics in CounterStripes was hardest for the players to relate to playing handball. One player stated, *"I don't see great transferability to playing handball. As I see it, the goal has a color and the goalkeeper typically has a different color"* (P9). Another pointed out that, *"it was a fun game and it trains you, [...], but I just find it a bit difficult to relate it to handball [...] it demand something else to be able to detect the patterns, whereas in handball, if there is a free space, you can always see it"* (P3), and others viewed the graphics as being a cognitive test, rather than related to handball. However, one player preferred CounterStripes, as *"the yellow and black were sometimes too easy to see, it was too clear, whereas this one (CounterStripes), you had to be more focused"* (P4). Thus, even though the graphics might be hard to relate directly to handball, they can still offer valuable training in terms of cognitive processing and perception.

Where the graphics of YellowBlack and CounterStripes might relate to identifying scoring opportunities in the goal, the graphics in ColorMatch present a less clear link to handball goalkeepers. However, many players related the way of surveying the goal to handball, noting that, *"it's like reacting to how a goalkeeper stands, you look for the free space. Here you look for a colour, so in that sense I think it's transferable"* (P5).

The notion of removing the targets in YellowBlack and CounterStripes was by some related to a goalkeeper luring the player to shoot in a specific place, which he then closed off, as one player noted, *"that an element disappears is a bit like if there is a goalkeeper that closes it off"* (P6). However, one found the situation less relatable, *"I don't know if it makes sense in relation to handball [...] it's just because it's a different sensation, when you look at the goalkeeper, you don't know if she tries to lure you"* (P10).

Finding 8: Abstract representation allows for alternative target shooting training

2 players noted that the abstract representations provided players with an opportunity to train elements that might be difficult to train with a real goalkeeper: *"I can feel that I am being challenged on something you might not always think about, if you play against a goalkeeper, [...] here you are forced to do what you really don't want to do, which may be more difficult against a goalkeeper"* (P5), and *"I definitely think that I could transfer it, the way of thinking, when you are in the air, the execution of your shot, everything, it might sometimes be a bit farfetched on a goalkeeper, [...] here that just how it is"* (P6). The two quotes illustrate how the games trained desirable skills, which might be difficult to train on a handball field. The isolation of decision-making and shot execution enables the players to explicitly focus on developing these skills.

Context characteristics

Context characteristics refer to the context of a game, covering both the physical and the digital game space, and the environment that facilitates a game.

Finding 9: Changing the physical game space could increase relevance

All participants positively received the game space, and they found the distance between the touch plate and the rebounder appropriate for viewing and hitting the targets and ensuring a high tempo in the game. However, 4 participants also noted that in order to increase the handball relevance to their position (backcourt and wing), the distance had to be increased. Two participants also stated that it would improve the game to have a physical obstacle to jump over, *"so you jump upward and not forward"* (P8).

Finding 10: Sensors impact game difficulty and relevance

The participants applauded the touch plate sensor that required a jump in order to trigger the targets, stated as, *"So everything is fun! Also because there are different things to train, so it's not all about precision"* (P10), and, *"The relevance only increases the more handball elements you incorporate: How many can you hit, how hard you are shooting, and maybe how high and far you jump"* (P2). This last comment articulate an opinion that additional sensors would be interesting, supported by 3 other players stating that, *"if you can measure jumping height and shot strength you could evaluate other exercises. For example, if bench pressing makes you shoot harder"* (P9), and, *"it would be a good idea to incorporate shot strength because you tend to get careful and thinking just about hitting and not about shooting as a real handball shot"* (P8). When asked how to increase the difficulty of the games, one participant suggested changing the floor sensor to detect touch off instead of foot contact in order to force players to jump higher.

CHALLENGES WHEN DESIGNING TRAINING GAMES

We now articulate a set of characteristic challenges that should be addressed when designing training games. The challenges are derived based on related work, our experiences with creating The Bouncer as well as insights gained from the study. We present each challenge followed by a strategy for addressing it. The challenges and strategies might be applicable to other areas where balancing engagement and purpose is needed, e.g. serious games.

Challenge 1: Maintaining relevance when translating physical elements into digital representations

Designing training games usually requires translating physical objects or opponents into a digital representation. For example, in The Bouncer a handball goalkeeper is transformed into abstract graphical targets. Another example is Football Lab [10], where co-players are replaced by light and sound signals. Designing these representations poses a challenge of extracting relevant elements from the sport and choosing an appropriate type of representation, without reducing the sport relevance.

A digital representation requires a translation from sport to game. This translation can be literal, such as a virtual goalkeeper simulation, or abstract, as in the games for The Bouncer. Choosing a literal translation poses a range of technical requirements in order to make players perceive it as a useful training tool, as players potentially hold the same expectations for the digital representation as they do for a real goalkeeper. Thus, in order to create a realistic training situation, a simulated goalkeeper would require complex and expensive sensing and interpretation of player movements in order to enable intelligent reactions to the player's actions.

Choosing an abstract representation provides designers with more freedom to utilize game mechanics and elements in their design. Abstract representations also require less extended sensing, as players do not have predetermined expectations. Furthermore, abstract representations enable designers to extract and highlight different elements of a skill, e.g. different aspects of decision-making, as illustrated by our three different games.

Utilize abstract representations and cognitive elements

The challenge of maintaining relevance in the digital representation is therefore not simply a matter of being able to replicate elements of the sports as realistically as possible, but instead a matter of extracting relevant aspects of the game and translate them in an appropriate manner. This relates to Campbell et al.'s [2] view on representation in fitness applications, stating that a good representation; is an abstraction without loss of meaning, is neither too complex nor too shallow, provides context for play and drives player interactions. Our study indicates that although the graphics looked nothing like a goalkeeper, the players found the games relevant to handball and commented that they might even train aspects that would be difficult to train on a handball court in front of a real goalkeeper (finding 8).

Despite the challenges of maintaining sport relevance and creating a recognizable situation to the players, utilizing abstract representations holds a great potential for training games. We believe that applying abstract representations offers an extra level to the training game as it allows for the game to incorporate cognition and decision-making. By using abstract representations with different cognitive or decision-making layers in our three games, players found that the games offered an extra dimension compared to regular target shooting training (finding 8), and that the games allowed them try different decision-making strategies (finding 6). However, some found it easier than others to relate the abstract graphics to playing handball (finding 7).

When choosing an abstract representation over a literal one, we believe it is increasingly important to involve domain experts in order to identify important aspects. We propose to involve sport experts; not only in workshops and tests, but also directly in the design process in order to qualify decisions and enable constant experimentation, iteration and reflection.

Challenge 2: Choosing an appropriate level of sensing as game input

Almost all training games require some level of sensing of the player, which facilitates the interaction between player and game. The challenge when designing training games is choosing the appropriate level of sensing as game input, while ensuring sport relevance and allowing for engaging interactions.

As illustrated by the demo games used at the initial workshop with The Bouncer, games can be built based on sensing a single aspect. In these games, only the ball's impact position was used to facilitate game interactions. However, only sensing one element did not enable the games to encourage handball-like movement patterns, despite being designed with handball in mind. Thus, sensing a single aspect might limit the possibilities of designing training games, where several actions should impact the outcome of a training exercise. Contrary, games can be based on sensing every movement of the player. However, based on our findings we believe that creating training games, where every movement is sensed and dictated by the system, will affect the players' engagement negatively, but perhaps more importantly curtail their opportunity to experiment with different strategies.

Allow for autonomy and physical additions

Technology makes it possible to sense almost every aspect of a player's actions, however, the challenge lies in determining the appropriate level of sensing as game input. Choosing the level of sensing requires a careful balance between the flexibility available from using a few sensors and the possibility of movement guidance enabled by using several sensors. Using only a few sensors allows for embracing ambiguity [5] in the design and assigning more decisions to the player, but entail the risk of introducing inexpedient behavior, as undetected inexpedient behavior might result in a better score. Using multiple sensors could reduce this risk, but simultaneously create a more rigid game space, as it would impose a specific behavior on the players, rather than letting them explore different strategies (finding 1). This corresponds to Park et al.'s notion of selecting key primitives of a sport exercise to fit the purpose of an exertion game, and how these choices influence gameplay and player experiences [18]. For example, sensing shot-power in order to only award powerful shots could potentially increase the handball relevance of The Bouncer (finding 10), but it could simultaneously prevent players from choosing particular types of shots.

It is a delicate balance to determine the right level of sensing, and we suggest that designers should find a balance, which encourages sport-relevant behaviors without hindering the freedom to make choices and try different strategies. We believe that designing for autonomy in training games will increase the engagement of players, supported by game research [20], and therefore games should be designed to encourage optimal movements for the sport, and reward these with the highest score. Instead of increasing the level of sensing, an alternate approach is to make changes to the physical space in order to increase sport relevance. This approach was supported by our study, where players suggested introducing physical obstacles to overcome in the game, rather than adding more sensors (finding 9). However, additional sensors could be used for gathering information about players' performances in order to assist players in self-reflection about their tendencies and abilities (finding 3).

Challenge 3: Introducing points in training exercises without reducing sport relevance

While game elements hold great potential to motivate players to exert themselves in training sessions, it also raises the challenge of avoiding influencing the sport relevance in a negative way.

The game elements in The Bouncer illustrate how introducing competition can motivate players to push their performance. However, our study also highlights the challenge of including a competitive element. The desire to get higher scores caused at least two of the players to make choices, which deviated from their regular handball actions, potentially inducing inexpedient movements. However, omitting points from the game would have removed the motivational, competitive element, as well as left the players without a way to gauge their performance. During the fast paced games it was difficult for the players to evaluate their performances, as returning to collect the next ball had higher priority than evaluating their immediate accuracy. Furthermore, the difficult-dependent amounts of points in YellowBlack and CounterStripes, compelled the players to search and go for the smaller targets, thus pushing themselves harder in terms of precision. We believe that without the differentiating points, players would generally have chosen easier targets, rather than engaging in the decision-making challenge.

Frame the training game and reward optimal performances

Introducing game elements and competition in training exercises introduces a risk of shifting the focus away from the training, as players will focus on getting a high score instead of perfectly executing the exercise-targeted movements. Thus, we believe that when using competitive elements it is important to clearly frame the game as training. By doing this the players will stay in a training mindset, and we believe that is the reason that caused the two players, who did alter their movements, to actually reflect about it (finding 4). This correlates to Chen et al.'s work that shows that framing exertion games as training instead of games made participants increase the duration of use [3].

Rewarding points based on effort and performance enable players to evaluate their own proficiency and compare it to others (finding 10). This relates to Mueller et al.'s understanding of exertion and context, stating that it is important that the mapping of players' gaming skills corresponds to the real world, so they do not over- or under-estimate their physical abilities [16]. Thus, we believe that it is important for the point system to be transparent and award players for making an extra effort. As a result, we recommend designers to ensure that achieving high scores in the game is correlated with performing handball relevant actions, e.g. by rewarding extra points for the optimal execution. This idea addresses Jensen et al.'s design sensitivities for training games [10], suggesting to design games so game optimal movements are not inexpedient or prohibited in the targeted sport. This sensitivity can be approached if designers ensure that perfect movements are generously rewarded in the training game.

LIMITATIONS

Even though our work is based on a design process involving handball experts and our participants related it to their regular training, we cannot ensure that players' handball abilities will improve over time by using the game. We acknowledge that transferability is a challenge for designers of both digital [4,10] and analogue [12] training equipment and exercises, and this is no exception for The Bouncer.

CONCLUSION

In this paper, we presented The Bouncer and 3 handball-training games. We presented a study of the training games, showing that they were engaging to play as well as handball relevant. Based on the study and our design insights, we proposed three challenges that designers of interactive sports-training games will need to consider: 1) Maintaining relevance when translating physical elements into digital representations. 2) Choosing an appropriate level of sensing as game input. 3) Introducing points in training exercises without reducing sport relevance. For each of the three challenges, we proposed strategies to help designers of future training games. With the work presented in this paper, we hope to contribute to improve the quality and design of future training games that engage athletes in their training. Furthermore, we hope that other game designers, who are balancing engagement and purpose, can use our work to support their process.

ACKNOWLEDGEMENT

We would like to thank the KrogagerFoundation, as well as Jacob Andersen and Jesper Nielsen, The Alexandra Institute, Denmark, for their contribution to the development of the hit positioning platform.

REFERENCES

1. Bideau, B., Multon, F., Kulpa, R., Fradet, L., and Arnaldi, B. Virtual Reality Applied to Sports: Do Handball Goalkeepers React Realistically to Simulated Synthetic Opponents? In *Proc. SIGGRAPH 2004*, ACM (2004), 210–216.
2. Campbell, T., Ngo, B., and Fogarty, J. Game Design Principles in Everyday Fitness Applications. In *Proc. CSCW 2008*, ACM Press (2008), 249–252.
3. Chen, F.X., King, A.C., and Hekler, E.B. "Healthifying" Exergames: Improving Health Outcomes Through Intentional Priming. In *Proc. CHI 2014*, ACM Press (2014), 1855–1864.
4. Fogtmann, M.H., Grønbæk, K., and Ludvigsen, M.K. Interaction technology for collective and psychomotor training in sports. In *Proc. ACE 2011*, ACM Press (2011), 13:1–13:8.
5. Gaver, W.W., Beaver, J., and Benford, S. Ambiguity As a Resource for Design. In *Proc. CHI 2003*, ACM Press (2003), 233–240.
6. Hämäläinen, P. Interactive Video Mirrors for Sports Training. In *Proc. NordiCHI 2004*, ACM Press (2004), 199–202.
7. Holsti, L., Takala, T., Martikainen, A., Kajastila, R., and Hämäläinen, P. Body-controlled Trampoline Training Games Based on Computer Vision. In *Proc. CHI '13 EA*, ACM Press (2013), 1143–1148.
8. Hoonhout, J. and Fontijn, W. It's hard, it is fun: throwing balls inside the home. *Paper presented at CHI 2008 Workshop on Exertion Interfaces*, (2008), http://workshopchi.pbwiki.com/f/CHI2008_splashball_exertion_interfaces_uploaded.pdf.
9. Hopwood, M., Mann, D., Farrow, D., and Nielsen, T. Does Visual-Perceptual Training Augment the Fielding Performance of Skilled Cricketers? *International Journal of Sports Science and Coaching 6*, 4 (2011), 523–536.
10. Jensen, M.M., Rasmussen, M.K., and Grønbæk, K. Design Sensitivities for Interactive Sport-training Games. In *Proc. DIS 2014*, ACM Press (2014), 685–694.
11. Lenzen, B., Theunissen, C., and Cloes, M. Situated analysis of team handball players' decisions: An exploratory study. *Journal of Teaching in Physical Education 28*, 1 (2009).
12. McMorris, T. *Acquisition and Performance of Sports Skills*. John Wiley and Sons, 2004.
13. Miles, H.C., Pop, S.R., Watt, S.J., Lawrence, G.P., and John, N.W. A review of virtual environments for training in ball sports. *Computers & Graphics 36*, 6 (2012), 714–726.
14. Mueller, F., Agamanolis, S., and Picard, R. Exertion Interfaces: Sports over a Distance for Social Bonding and Fun. In *Proc. CHI 2003*, ACM Press (2003), 561–568.
15. Mueller, F. "Floyd," Agamanolis, S., Gibbs, M.R., and Vetere, F. Remote Impact: Shadowboxing over a Distance. In *Proc. CHI '08 EA*, ACM Press (2008), 2291–2296.
16. Mueller, F. "Floyd," Edge, D., Vetere, F., et al. Designing Sports: A Framework for Exertion Games. In *Proc. CHI 2011*, ACM Press (2011), 2651–2660.
17. Mueller, F. "Floyd" and Gibbs, M. A table tennis game for three players. In *Proc. OzCHI 2006*, ACM Press (2006), 321–324.
18. Park, T., Yoo, C., Choe, S.P., Park, B., and Song, J. Transforming Solitary Exercises into Social Exergames. In *Proc. CSCW 2012*, ACM Press (2012), 863–866.
19. Raab, M. and Johnson, J.G. Expertise-based differences in search and option-generation strategies. *Journal of Experimental Psychology: Applied 13*, 3 (2007), 158–170.
20. Rigby, S. and Ryan, R.M. *Glued to Games: How Video Games Draw Us in and Hold Us Spellbound*. ABC-CLIO, 2011.
21. Spelmezan, D. An Investigation into the Use of Tactile Instructions in Snowboarding. *MobileHCI 2012*, ACM Press (2012), 417–426.
22. Vignais, N., Bideau, B., Craig, C., et al. Does the Level of Graphical Detail of a Virtual Handball Thrower Influence a Goalkeeper's Motor Response? *Journal of Sports Science & Medicine 8*, 4 (2009), 501–508.
23. X-Golf. http://www.xgolf.com.au/.
24. Munin Sports. http://www.muninsports.com/en/.
25. The Danish Way - DHF. http://www.dhf.dk/Landshold/drenge_talenttraening/thedanishway/the_danish_way_-_english_version.

Flow is Not Enough: Understanding the Needs of Advanced Amateur Runners to Design Motivation Technology

Kristina Knaving*
Department of Applied IT
University of Gothenburg
Gothenburg, Sweden
kristina.knaving@ait.gu.se

Paweł Woźniak*, Morten Fjeld
t2i Interaction Lab
Chalmers University of Technology
Gothenburg, Sweden

Staffan Björk
Department of Applied IT
University of Gothenburg
Gothenburg, Sweden

ABSTRACT
Motivation studies on running are often focused on how to convince non-runners to run, mainly through designing for extrinsic motivations such as health concerns or external reward systems. In contrast, we conducted a structured inquiry into understanding how to design technology for those whom are already committed to running and participate in organized races. Through interviews, focus groups, ethnographic observation, questionnaires, and design-based research over the course of two years, we investigated the needs of the advanced amateur runner community. An analysis of the gathered data led to five design themes – Festival, Competition, Practicalities, Togetherness, and Support – to inform future runner motivation technology. While flow theory appears to be a convenient tool to understand support during a race, we observed a number of other factors that need to be considered. Through combining the themes with previous research, we conclude by presenting nine guidelines for designing technology for this domain.

Author Keywords
Running; Intrinsic motivation; Motivation; Engagement; Design guidelines

ACM Classification Keywords
H.5.2 [Information Interfaces and Presentation]: User Interfaces - User-centered design

INTRODUCTION
Since amateur running comes with low entry costs and wide availability, it has become a key fitness activity included in local and national health strategies. Training programs intended to help people start running are reported in the mainstream press and attract interest from people intrigued

*Equally contributing authors

CHI 2015, April 18 - 23, 2015, Seoul, Republic of Korea.

ACM 978-1-4503-3145-6/15/04...$15.00.
http://dx.doi.org/10.1145/2702123.2702542

Figure 1: The five design themes of the advanced amateur runner experience.

by the sport's health and leisure benefits. Marketing campaigns have been launched to expand national runner communities and convince more people to be part of the running experience. As a consequence, many design efforts in human-computer interaction (HCI) have investigated how to design systems promoting a more active lifestyle. Many commercial products (e.g. mobile phone applications, custom devices, and augmented weighing scales) have been released to remind us of the benefits of the daily run.

In the media, images of happy families dressed in ideal branded clothing while running in perfect weather attract an increasing number of followers. Such persuasive images present running as it can be only some of the time. More importantly, when running is presented in this way it creates a vision that spreads to other fields, such as designing runner support technology. The technologies we see today are presented in the context of situations where running is easy and fun.

Drawing from our research efforts in this area, we introduce a novel take on design for amateur runners. Instead of creating technology for the inspiring run in perfect weather, we wish to design for the more human aspects of running. We propose to shift the focus of design to the less appealing scenarios by understanding users in the field, especially in the unique scenario of a race day. People who already run regularly and participate in races constitute the user group targeted in our inquiry (we call them *advanced amateur runners*). Can technology help the runner smeared in his own spit during the last mile of a marathon? How do we support the runner with interactive systems when they are nervously pacing around the room trying to decide what to do with their time when they are injured? Can we present means to ease the frustrations of families when their lives are starting to be organized according to training programs? What support can we provide when a race is not going as planned?

This paper offers insights into different aspects of advanced amateur running and the potential avenues to explore when designing new technology for runner support. We stray from the persuasive aspects of running technology and, instead, highlight complex real life issues that must be considered when designing for running. We focus on the various aspects of motivation and the role it plays in the lives of runners, their friends, and family. We also investigate interaction scenarios that occur during a race day and everyday training.

Outline of this paper

This paper is organized as follows. First, we discuss a number of works from a variety of research fields that influenced our work and will provide an initial framework for understanding advanced amateur running. We then present the methodology we used to gather data about the user needs of runners. Next, we provide details of the results of our two-year study and discuss the five themes that become apparent from our data. Finally, we provide a set of design considerations for future runner motivation technology. The paper contributes the following: (1) A detailed inquiry resulting in increased understanding of the user needs of advanced amateur runners; (2) a set of design themes emerging from our study, and (3) design guidelines for future runner support technology.

RELATED WORK

The related work section presents both readings that we reviewed prior to our work and literature that later guided us in making sense of the data gathered.

We investigated how motivation is modeled in sports psychology and looked for other ways to understand the running experience. We explored the very nature of the sources of motivation, such as flow and social surroundings, and its role during running. We also reflect on past designs of technology for runners.

Understanding motivation

According to Ryan & Deci [16], motivation can be divided into two categories: intrinsic and extrinsic. Intrinsic motivation occurs when an activity is satisfactory or fun in itself, while extrinsic motivation is based on external goals such as money, health, or social approval. Deci et al. [5] have shown that extrinsic motivation sometimes undermines intrinsic motivation. Furthermore, they have identified four types of extrinsic motivation which are, in increasing order of internalization: external regulation, introjected regulation, identified regulation, and integrated regulation. While external regulation refers to compliance based only on external rewards and punishments, integrated regulation refers to highly internalized extrinsic motivations where the user chooses to perform an activity because the results align with perceived benefits and their self-image. Our work investigates how advanced amateur runners use extrinsic and intrinsic motivation in order to understand how to design runner support technology. Brière et al. [2] designed the Sports Motivation Scale for measuring sports motivation. The scale divides intrinsic motivation into the groups "to know," "to accomplish," and "to experience." It measures external, introjected, and identified regulation, and also adds amotivation. An amotivated individual cannot perceive a relationship between their behavior and that behavior's subsequent outcome. A translated and validated scale questionnaire by Pelletier et al. [15] has been used in our inquiries.

Self Determination Theory (SDT) [17] credits individuals with three innate needs that must be satisfied to achieve well-being and mental health: competence, autonomy, and relatedness. To satisfy the innate needs defined by SDT assists in the internalization of extrinsic motivations, making the activity itself more satisfactory. Bloom et al. [1] investigated how young people develop talent and describe talent's three stages: romance, precision, and integration. Romance occurs when people first develop intrinsic motivations and a love for their chosen field. It is characterized by play, exploration, and fun. Throughout their careers, their subject's passion for their subject was sustained. In our work, we sought to investigate if that passion could be applied to how advanced amateur runners maintain their interest and training habits.

Running and flow

The concept of flow, as coined and defined by Csikszentmihalyi, is a perceived optimal experience of an activity [3]. Flow may be attained when the feedback is perceived as immediate, the goals are clearly understood, and challenges and skills are identified as balanced. When people are in a flow state, they have a sense of control and find the activity intrinsically rewarding. Flow during marathon running has been shown to positively influence future running motivation, although it has not been directly linked to race performance [18]. For us, investigating the role flow could play in designing motivational support for

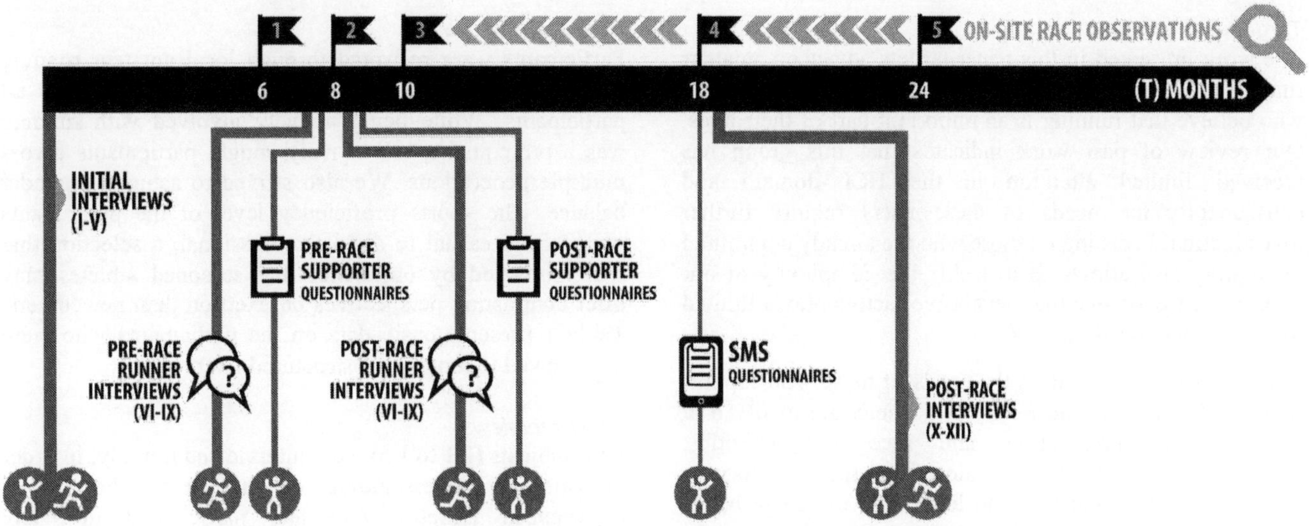

Figure 2. Timeline presenting a summary of all research activities presented in the paper.

runners was an aspect of our inquiry given its relation to motivation.

Running and social connection

Designing interactive artifacts that cater to social connections is a known goal of HCI [13]. Furthermore, it is an established design principle to design artifacts that fit well in human social environments and reflect human values in technology [19]. In a related field, Ying et al. [23] used small ambient devices to support long distance relationships between parents and children, offering an experience different from conventional voice-based communication technology. Mueller et al. [12] applied these lessons to an exertion scenario, for which they created a system that enabled runners to connect to their remote friends and "run together over a distance." An alternative experience is that of a running companion in the form of a drone [9]. TripleBeat [14] focused on enhancing performance during training sessions, and many applications, such as Chick clique [22], were designed to support the formation of running groups amongst friends. McGookin and Brewster investigated enhanced technology support for undirected navigation [10]. In one of the few inquiries that addressed amateur race performance, Curmi et al. [4] focused on the implications of real-time biometric data broadcasting during races. Our work differs from these past efforts by focusing on motivation for runners who are already pursuing a training routine. Furthermore, we explore how running affects not only the lives of these advanced amateur runners, but also those of their friends and family. Finally, we investigate the design requirements for developing solutions that can function within the already established social constructs surrounding advanced amateur runners.

Managing motivation and exertion

Morgan et al. [11] observed what they called the practices of association and dissociation for athletes. An athlete in an associative state focuses on reality even if it is uncomfortable, while an athlete in a dissociative state tries to detach from reality and focus on something else. They found that so-called sub-elite runners by and large prefer to dissociate when running becomes uncomfortable. Shipway et al. [20] researched running communities and found that runners often deal with their reported hardships of training by creating social groups. This inquiry also showed the need for further qualitative research to understand the running phenomenon. Shipway et al. illustrated how an ethnographic inquiry where the researcher engages in running can be used to understand the social psychology of running and inspired our own use of a similar methodology. This was further inspired by how Dourish and Bell [6] illustrated the importance of ethnographic inquiry for understanding the design of future technologies.

DATA GATHERING

Past work motivates our assumption that the nature of the running experience is complex and multifaceted. Hence, designing technological solutions for runner motivation requires a thorough understanding of the design constraints. We took part in a wide range of activities to encompass the perspective of a wide range of runners, focusing on the less-than-optimal situations in running. We were determined to avoid excessive focus on technology and idealistic scenarios, as these are the most prevalent in runner-oriented research.

Our core data consists of interviews and questionnaire responses. Some of the interviews and questionnaires were conducted in the context of a runner support system prototype we developed in order to stimulate responses from runners. Furthermore, we attended five organized races where we took ethnographic notes and conducted interviews with runners and supporters. Lastly, one of the authors replicated Shipway et al.'s [20] methodology by getting involved in a half marathon training program.

Target user group

The work presented in this paper targets advanced amateur runners, i.e. individuals with a seasoned running routine who believe that running is an important part of their lives. Our review of past work indicates that this group has received limited attention in the HCI domain and consequently the needs of these users require further investigation. Focusing on those who are already committed to running also allows us to tackle the complexity of our inquiry, as we assume that persuasive factors play a limited role for experienced runners.

We simultaneously address the needs of those who support runners. The friends and family of a runner are involved in training, race preparation, and race day activities. Consequently, we treat their side of the running story as equally important and strive to learn how to design better supporter technology.

	Code	Gender	Age	Sports	SP
Initial	I-1	M	40-50	RCS	5
	I-2	M	30-40	RT	4
	I-3	M	60-70	RS	4
	I-4	F	40-50	R	3
	I-5	M	20-30	R	1
Prototype	P-6	F	40-50	R	2
	P-7	F+M+M	20-30	R	3
	P-8	M+F	30-40	R	4
	P-9	M	20-30	R	4
Motivation	M-10	F	40-50	R	4
	M-11	F	20-30	R	3
	M-12	M	40-50	R	2

Table 1: Runner interviewees recruited for this work, listed in chronological order. The codes provided point to interview sources (first column). We used a five-step Likert scale for sport proficiency (SP, 1- complete newcomer, 5 – seasoned athlete). R – running, T – triathlon, C – road cycling, S – cross-country skiing. This table only presents the participants of long, semi-structured interviews.

Research activity details

This section presents our activities in a chronological order to give the reader an impression of how our understanding of the domain evolved. Our data consists mainly of interview material (a total of 15 hours), ethnographic notes, and questionnaire answers. Figure 2 provides a chronological overview of our activities.

Participant profile

Participants were recruited through local amateur running clubs and newsletters sent by race organizers to all participants. While being actively involved with running was a prerequisite, we actively sought participants across multiple generations. We also strived to achieve a gender balance. The sports proficiency level of the participants varied from casual to almost professional, a selection that was motivated by our belief that seasoned athletes may offer contrasting perspectives on exertion than newcomers. Table 1 presents basic data on the participants who were interviewed in long, semi-structured interviews.

Initial interviews

Five subjects (I-1 to I-5) were interviewed initially, in order to gain an understanding of the field. These were experienced athletes who had participated in many organized races, thereby fitting within the category of advanced amateur runners. By providing extensive accounts of their race experiences and the role motivation and outside support played in their running, they influenced how the rest of the research was planned.

Interviews and data gathering in the context of a prototype

Inspired by a round of initial interviews on how running and support can be mediated by technology, we built a prototype system that provides interactive remote support for runners. Runners were equipped with a mobile phone and a dedicated device. Using a webpage, this system enabled supporters to send three different support signals: "I'm thinking of you," "Go! Go! Go!" and "C'mon!" The signals were communicated to the runner in the form of ambient light and vibrations. The prototype was tested in a race. Through interviews and discussions among runners and supporters, we collected reflections on the role of support in the running experience. Four runners (P-6 to P-9) and fourteen supporters were involved in testing the system. The prototype generated further data in the form of pre- and post-race interviews with the runners and their supporters. The supporters also completed two questionnaires. The prototype system served as a means of eliciting additional feedback on support. The prototype system served as a means of eliciting additional feedback on support from runners. We were careful while analyzing the data gathered with the prototype to avoid bias and checked whether these results were congruent with other parts of our study.

Motivation-focused inquiry

Next, we asked amateur runners who fit our target user group and have participated in a half-marathon race to rate their motivation using the Sports Motivation Scale [15]. We then recruited three of these runners (M-10 to M12) to conduct structured interviews focused on motivation.

Race-day observations

Finally, in order to gain a deep understanding of supporter motivation and their relationship to runners, we attended five organized races. Short on-the-spot interviews were conducted with random supporters (a total of 25) on each occasion. The interviews were focused on the reasons that brought them to the course of the race and the social value of their support.

MOTIVATIONAL THEMES

Because of the varied nature of the data, we present the results in two ways. First, we present the results of a questionnaire and a selection of insights from interviews about motivation. Second, we describe a number of themes that come to light based on the whole body of work presented here.

We found that while runners reported higher SMS values (see Figure 3) for intrinsic motivations, extrinsic motivations were not far behind. All runners had very low scores for amotivation. These results also highlight the fact that amateur athletes run for many reasons; no runner interviewed in our inquiry relied on just one or two types of motivation. The interviews about motivation also showed how users had more than one strategy for motivation. Notably, most users mostly discussed extrinsic motivations and only mentioned the intrinsic motivations briefly, in spite of ranking them higher on the SMS scale. Mention of intrinsic motivations in the interviews were mainly concerned with flow-like states—as one runner remarked in regard to cheering:

It would help especially if I felt bad or had a difficult stretch. I don't think it would help much in the beginning of the race or when it is going well—then the focus is on going with the flow. (P-7)

The "flow" here is not a direct reference to the concept of flow mentioned earlier. The runners' focus in the interviews was on how to handle less optimal situations, where the only support was extrinsic motivations.

While modeling runner motivation through theoretical constructs from sports psychology such as intrinsic/extrinsic motivation or SDT is a valuable perspective, our inquiry shows that this is insufficient from an interaction design perspective. Consequently, we analyzed our gathered data using inductive coding in order to discover recurring themes. We performed open coding of interview material and matched the data with observations and questionnaires. Five themes emerged, which we will use to present our results: Festival, Competition, Practicalities, Togetherness, and Support. We believe the themes represent the key motivation sources affecting advanced amateur runners. These themes were then considered in the light of literature on motivation, resulting in a number of design guidelines.

Festival

Many participants reported experiencing an organized race as a festive activity, and commented on the unique characteristics of the race day. Understanding events as festivals is a known practice in the social sciences and past research has attempted to understand art exhibitions [21] and music festivals [8] through the lens of festive celebration. Our results show that runners are empowered by the intense atmosphere of the event and they perceive that it is the cause of their improved performance (P-6). During an event, participants said the hardships of an endurance run seem easier to cope with because there are many other runners and supporters with whom to share the experience (P-6, M-10). They appreciate the engagement of everyone around (M-11). One participant (P-6) said: *"I can't help feeling better when I run past an orchestra."* Those who had experienced participation both as supporters and athletes were even more engaged and enjoyed many aspects of the experience, stressing the importance of the festive atmosphere during the race (M-10). As the race event is often important for entire communities, running becomes a domestic conversation topic, even for runners who do not usually discuss running with friends and family (M-11). In the supporter interviews, the festival atmosphere was by far the most important reason for liking one race above other. The gathered data suggests that the uniqueness of the race day is an important consideration for designing technology for runners.

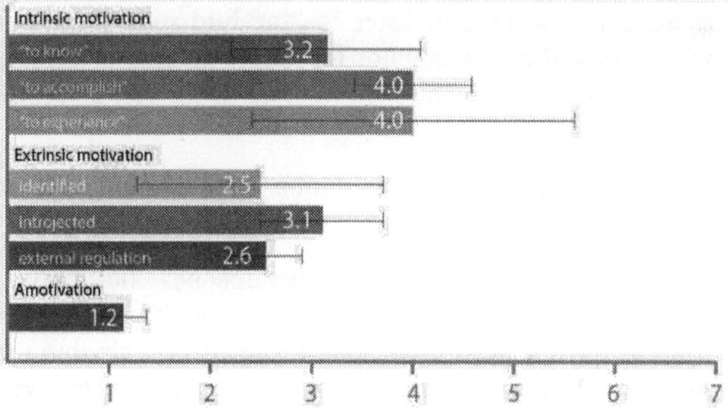

Figure 3: Average results and standard deviation on the Sports Motivation Scale (Likert)

Competition

All of our runner participants reported that competition (internal with themselves or externally with colleagues) played a role in their running experience. We observed an entire spectrum of how important competition was for the running experience. One participant reported that competing with colleagues was his key motivation, despite the physical act of running being an unpleasant experience. His goal was to be the best among his colleagues, and he was often motivated by a need to get even and surpass them (M-12). Another runner was inspired by his workplace running group to start running again despite the perceived hardships, and reported that colleagues made it possible to be goal-oriented (P-6, M-10). Stories of past successful races were considered inspirational (P-6)—competing with oneself was most often mentioned in the context of dealing with pain and physical limitations:

It's hard close to the finish line—your legs hurt, but you fight with yourself and try to keep running. (M-11)

After reaching the finish line some users were happy to have beaten their own limitations (M-10) and some were interested in how their colleagues performed (M-12). When analyzing runner social media, we noticed that most often users would "like" certain routes taken by their friends that were perceived to demand extra effort. The competitive element of running must be taken into consideration in runner-centered technology and the multifaceted nature of competition may require additional design work.

Practicalities

Many interviewees described running as restful, invigorating and helpful for them to recover from stressful and intensive work, like critical care nursing or HR consultanting (P-7, M-10, M-11). Athletes' choice tracks for training were close to home. Routes should be quiet and there should be the possibility to easily vary the length and difficulty of a run without having to plan beforehand. Running in a quiet environment was restful, almost "meditative" as one runner put it, and indeed many runners noted with emphasis that they did not run with headphones because they wanted to listen to "the bird song," a phrase we interpreted as a metaphor for nature sounds in general. However, one user mentioned running in the city as an eye opener:

It's amazing how far you get. I didn't realize how far I run every day. (M-11)

One runner chose to run with headphones, but only in training and never at races. She noted that she preferred to listen to spoken word because it doesn't have a rhythm that might interfere with her own running rhythm. Events were one of the main additional goals the runners set for themselves to motivate regular training runs. They knew it was hard to keep up running and even harder to start running after the winter season. Scheduling a race kept them focused on a goal, and also helped them create a recurring yearly pattern.

Our observations showed that family lives are affected by everyday training. The supporters overwhelmingly cheered for their family members—out of 25 supporters only two were there to cheer on friends. When asked about their role in the training schedule and race events, many supporters noted giving the runner time to run and agreeing to take care of the children. In the race interviews, the majority of supporters also stated it was their idea to attend the race and cheer. This indicates that while runners orchestrate most of their own experience, their friends and family usually enter a voluntary relationship whereby they become part of the running experience.

Togetherness

All of our interviewees discussed and had views on the relationship between runners, but most of them ran alone when training. One runner preferred to leave her phone at home while on a run—it would be impossible for her to ignore a call even though she wouldn't want to answer. Running together often meant having to force oneself to run differently in order to suit another runner's pace. One interviewee (M-10) commented that she liked the idea of running at the same time but separately, and then meeting up afterwards to talk in the sauna—*"but not running together."* She sometimes ran with her son, but noted that they had become used to each other's pace. A supporter at the on-site interviews stated categorically that he doesn't run together with his girlfriend, but then rephrased his statement: *"We don't run together. We use an app so we can see each other."* While they did not run together, they always kept tabs on each other's routes with live tracking, and furthermore they discussed their running with each other. So, even for runners who prefer to run alone, connection with other runners is still important and desirable.

One person (M-12) was unusual in that he clearly stated he preferred to run with company. He had signed up for his last running event with colleagues but was disappointed they had parted early in the race—he hoped that they could have *"separated some hundred meters from the end [...] where I, of course, see myself as the winner."* This runner emphasized his focus on winning, also in other contexts, but what was also clear was that he found support from other runners to be very important for his motivation. He even said—with some surprise, as he had forgotten it—that the reason he continued running, despite being very tired at the end of his last race, was because another runner had encouraged him and told him to keep running.

After Avenyn [street in the second half of the race], I was very tired. [...] I started to walk a couple of steps. Then a woman came up to me, and said: 'You cannot start walking now! I have [been running]... I have been right behind you, I have seen your back the whole race, you are not allowed to give up now. Come on! Let's run.' And then... I couldn't really walk after that.

He noted that the important part here was that she was another runner, and that a bystander at the sidelines would not have made such an impression on him.

Many of the supporters interviewed at the course of the race were or had been runners themselves. When asked about what they enjoyed about standing at the sidelines, they noted how they felt vicarious pleasure and inspiration when seeing other people run. When asked why they weren't running, they often mentioned injuries or noted that someone had to take care of the children. One mother who could no longer run proudly said that her son ran because of her. A daughter said of her father, for whom she was cheering:

He was so inspired when he came and cheered for me—he had almost never even been to [a race] before. And then, after that, he has run every single year and been really focused.

These sentiments were echoed by another runner (M-10), who had been cheering and helping out with a race many years before she entered herself. She described how inspiring it was to meet people that had run in the race for decades; she also noted that she felt good about being able to tell people she had run the race herself.

65% of the supporters at the racecourse interviews considered themselves runners. A man who was there to see his wife run noted:

"Sometimes I cheer her on, sometimes she cheers for me."

There was a strong correlation between being a runner and focusing on inspiration, joy, and motivation as being the best aspects of attending the race and cheering. On the topic of joy, a supporter that also ran noted:

I enjoy the view of them pushing themselves; enjoy the view on their faces when they see the finish line. I think you can see this bit of hope they might reach it.

Another supporter wanted to be inspired:

It is so fun, but also inspiring. I actually like to run... I am just in a slump right now. So maybe I get a little boost.

Support

One initial interviewee (I-1) was very involved in endurance sports. He mentioned a number of running competitions, ultra-marathons, long cross-country ski trips, and bike races, some of which entailed traveling to other countries. When discussing one of the bike races, he noted that because of the lack of spectators, his main source of cheering was from his father who sent him text messages. He could only read these messages when stopping for water, but he felt that the buzzing sound from a message was a great motivator in itself. An interviewee in our initial round (I-3) was just about to run the Gothenburg half marathon. He runs in a number of races in the nearby area, and also participates in cross-country skiing events. He noted that concerning motivation, the next race was an easy race, because there were many people all along the route who cheered on the runners. In contrast, he mentioned a ten-kilometer race close to where he lived. It was a small event with almost no spectators. He reflected on this, remarking that most of the spectators were people he knew. He noted that this was very important motivator for him. He also mentioned an in-between case: at one of the ski races, people who worked at the event sometimes quickly looked up the start numbers for the athletes, and then cheered them by name. This felt much more personal to him than being cheered on by a crowd, and also meant he felt more motivated.

One runner commented that he did not care much for cheering (M-12), and also stated that he found watching races boring—he wanted to participate. In contrast many of the other runners described how they had cheered at the sidelines of races. Another interviewee commented on how, while they did not often talk to others about their training, they often discussed the race with friends and colleagues. The race was a shared experience; even non-runners are supposed to understand and care about it (M-11).

One runner much preferred races to training, as she considered spectators—especially those she knew—as one of the most motivational aspects of running. Not only for the cheering and sentiment involved, but being watched also made her feel motivated to do better: *"... I run faster and care more and try harder when someone is watching."* (P-6).

Some interviewees used the word "pressure" when they described the effect friends and family had on them during a race (P-7, M-11, M-12). They were careful to note that they found the pressure to be positive, but it still made them feel a slight performance anxiety—they did not want to be found lacking in the eyes of others: *"Of course you are influenced by the cheering. You want to do better."*

One runner commented that she liked the idea of broadcasting her run to friends, because it helped them to *"know where I was,"* making it easier for them to find and cheer her on without spending too much time waiting. Her focus was on the supporter's experience, not her own.

Regarding Runkeeper Live, an app that broadcasts runner position to invited friends, one runner stated:

"The thing was that I knew they sat and watched me, and that made me feel a strong urge to, well... they see exactly what I do and when... I have to keep at it" (P-7).

She also noted that this meant the data was very personal for her.

Notably, many of the prototype-based inquiry supporters mentioned how they wanted to be of help to the runner. *"I felt how he ran. I imagined I was helping!"* This was not only a matter of altruism. *"It was exhilarating that the runner could hear my cheering during the run."* A long discussion on a Facebook event page for one of the runners involved in the prototype test also shows that the supporters are engaging in the cheering and determined to overcome temporary technical difficulties in order to cheer at the right moment:

A: Cheer when he's running uphill.
B: I'm giving the medium cheer now.
C: Hit C'mon on the uphill!
[In the meantime, the tracking system experienced glitches due to the overloading of the network]
B: Based on D's calculations, he should be on the uphill. Shall we hit C'mon?

The supporters at the course of the race interviews also focused on the importance of being of help; either through cheering, stating how proud they were or through making it possible for the runner to find the time to run (as evinced by the Practicalities theme). Two supporters also mentioned other races that had information on the runner's position; this was considered an important feature as it meant they would not miss the runner.

GUIDELINES

A general lesson that we can derive from our studies is that one cannot design for all of the complex facets of supporting advanced amateur runners. The majority of factors that have an impact on the race day experience are outside of the control of both runners and their supporters (the weather, the behavior of other runners, the number of people cheering, etc.). As a consequence, these runners try to control all the factors they can, such as clothing, nutrition, and equipment. This is why we believe that, generally, support systems for advanced amateur runners must enable them to craft their experience of the race. They should be flexible enough to cater for on-the-spot decisions, which are inherent of a dynamic experience such as running a race.

Each guideline below is derived from one or more of the themes; guideline descriptions provide the names of related themes. Unless otherwise stated, we believe that the guidelines can be considered for both training and race day design although some guidelines naturally focus on one or the other.

The unique properties of the race day

Our analysis shows that the experiences of the race day differ from what is associated with running during the training period, as depicted in the Festival theme. Runners and supporters are affected by external factors such as the unique festive atmosphere, other runners on the course, and crowds cheering alongside the road. All of these factors create the feeling that the race day is an extraordinary moment. Participants report that their perceptions of time and space are altered by the race day conditions. Consequently, we suggest that future systems highlight the festive atmosphere of the race day.

Guideline 1: *Provide features that play on the festive nature of the race day for both runners and supporters. Use different means to interact with the runner for race days and training in order to keep the race special.*

Internal and external competition

The participants of our study cited both internal and external competition as important factors affecting their running motivation. Competing with oneself (as described in the Competition theme) was cited as often as competing with friends or colleagues. Most participants were blending those sources of motivation. For those designing runner technology, this means that future systems should accommodate both socially and personally motivated goals and achievements.

Guideline 2: *Allow users to define personal and social goals as part of their running experience.*

Facilitating internalization of motivation

Extrinsic motivations can be internalized, as noted by Deci *et al.* [5]. Future runner support technology should explore this and attempt to help users recognize and internalize motivations for running, e.g. by designing for the innate needs defined by Self Determination Theory. As illustrated by the Competition theme, runners in our study reported having learned to use internal competition as a means to motivate themselves. This leads us to believe that these runners would be best served by design for motivational support and for internalizing existing extrinsic motivations, rather than design that would them to develop new motivations. This would require a designer who is careful about considering the preexisting motivations of runners. To paraphrase B. J. Fogg's recent address at the Persuasive Technology Conference: "Do not motivate those who don't want to be motivated" [7].

Guideline 3: *Build systems that strengthen the runners' internal motivations rather than attempting to design technology that only supports separable goals.*

Embracing everyday running

The Practicalities theme shows how important it is for runners to harmoniously integrate running into their everyday lives. We observed how participants integrated running as part of their everyday lives and used running to cope with daily struggles. Events add more meaning to everyday training sessions, but most participants saw the invigorating nature of regular running as the main advantage of the sport. Casual running is used to relax and to think about life, which clearly differs from a race day scenario. The contrasting functions of everyday and race day running imply distinct design constraints for in-run technology.

Guideline 4: *For everyday running, design must support thinking, exploration, and relaxation.*

Be aware of the supporters

As noted in the Supporter theme, support takes on many forms. For the supporters we interviewed, support meant more than just cheering at the sidelines. A majority of our randomly chosen sample of supporters at the races were also runners. In the Togetherness theme, the relationship between runners is important. They understand each other; designs may want to take into account how other runners can inspire and inform each other even when they do not run together.

Supporters preferred large organized races, as those events were careful to create settings that catered to the supporter experience as well. This setting could act as a connection between the runner and the supporters. Inversely, remote supporters do not get a boost from the shared environment. While supporters do have the desire to take an active part in the race, it is difficult for them to maintain focus as they have limited control over the activity and they may have a different perception of space and time than the runner.

Guideline 5: *Manage supporter connection and engagement to ensure that they have the opportunity to provide well-timed feedback.*

The role of flow

It is tempting to design solely with the concept of flow in mind. However, our studies show that while the element of being "in the zone" at the race is indeed important, many of the other factors in the running experience cannot be controlled by either the runner or technology. It is thus impossible to successfully design assuming a constant state of flow. Furthermore, none of our participants explicitly mentioned flow and one of them even dismissed its importance. This makes it even more important to design for situations when the runner is not going with the flow, but rather is bored or struggling. Our results indicate that "out of the zone" moments are when supporters are especially important and needed most. As shown in the Togetherness theme, there are moments when support and being together with fellow runners take precedence over other factors. If a run is perfect all the time, support would be unnecessary. We believe that the complex nature of runner–supporter relationships calls for addressing the experience as a wider phenomenon.

Guideline 6: *When designing for runner support, do not prioritize flow over other constraints.*

Designing for association and dissociation

The Practicalities theme shows that mere details can be decisive for the running experience. In our work, we observed that runners often use association and dissociation as strategies for coping with the hardships of distance running. Many runners use both strategies depending on their affective states and the stage of the race. Proficient use of these strategies makes for experienced amateur athletes. Participants reported using running to relax and detach from their everyday burdens. In contrast, at a race other runners provide motivation and help increase focus when the run is tough. This further suggests that both techniques are prominently used. Some participants indicated that support systems are only needed when effort levels increase. There is a temporal relationship between the need for support from friends and family and use of association/dissociation.

Guideline 7: *When designing interfaces for use while running, take into account how fragile the states of association and dissociation are, and accompanying streams of input/output techniques must thus be adjusted.*

Guideline 8: *Minimize distraction for in-run communication. Use non-intrusive interfaces that can be ignored when the runner is in an associative state.*

Guideline 9: *Provide means for supporters to know when the runner is in a dissociative state needs support the most.*

FUTURE WORK

Even though this paper describes an extensive inquiry spanning almost two years, we can identify some limitations in this work. Firstly, our work was conducted in only two European countries. The cultural aspect may be important in the case of running, especially in terms of how running communities are formed. A noteworthy aspect of our work is that the two countries have significantly different running culture adoption rates. Furthermore, our interviews spanned multiple levels of proficiency in amateur runners, from beginners to seasoned ultra-marathoners. An alternative approach would be to focus on a group with a particular level of advancement. Our literature review was inconclusive on whether this may limit the number of design constraints, e.g. by limiting the number of strategies used by the runners to cope with exertion. Finally, some of the data was elicited using a prototype. We have tried to ensure that this does not overly influence the findings provided in paper, i.e. prototype interviews served to confirm findings from other sources and we did not consider them a standalone data source.

We are convinced that the application area should be explored further from both a design and an ethnographic perspective. We also wonder how our work may affect HCI for endurance sports other than running. Cross-cultural studies are one option, as the ways support is communicated by friends and family are likely to differ between cultures. We aim to continue our work in this area by establishing a closer collaboration with race organizers and analyzing the profiles of those who participate in races. This will allow us to address larger groups of runners, where we hope to identify subgroups with specific design requirements. This may yield a better understanding of current technology use and envision how future runner support technology may look.

CONCLUSIONS

In this paper we presented our insights into how to design engaging motivational technology that caters to advanced amateur runners and those supporting them in their pursuits. Based on data gathered through many means including interviews, design work, questionnaires, and immersion over the course of two years, we discussed the requirements and constraints involved in designing for runner support. We explored intrinsic and extrinsic motivation, the role of emotions and how runners and supporters are engaged on race day. We summarized our work with a set of guidelines for future running technology that takes motivation and engagement into account.

Our findings show that although understanding amateur running through the lens of flow seems at first glance to be a good design tool, applying it would likely severely limit possible exploration. In order to provide a richer understanding of designing runner support technology, five themes were introduced. These can be used as a way to understand the user experience of advanced amateur runners. Runner support technology should transform from the elaborate measurement techniques available now to tools that enable runners and supporters to design their own running experience for both everyday and race day. Concluding, we hope our guidelines and the methodology used here can be reused in the context of other individual endurance sports. We also believe our work can contribute to a larger HCI practice of working with amateur athletes.

ACKNOWLEDGEMENTS

We would like to thank the organizers of the Gothenburg Half Marathon for help, as well as the runners and supporters involved in our study. The work reported in this paper has received funding from "EVINN – Eventbaserad Innovation", an Interreg IVA project funded by the EU and the People Programme (Marie Curie Actions) of the European Union's Seventh Framework Programme /2007-2013/ under REA grant agreement no. 290227.

REFERENCES

1. Bloom, B.S. and Sosniak, L.A. *Developing talent in young people*. Ballantine Books, New York, 1985.
2. Brière, N.M., Vallerand, R.J., Blais, M.R., and Pelletier, L.G. Développement et Validation d'une Mesure de Motivation Intrinsèque, Extrinsèque et d'Amotivation en Contexte Sportif: L'Échelle de Motivation dans les Sports (ÉMS). *International Journal of Sport Psychology 26*, 4 (1995), 465–489.
3. Csikszentmihalyi, M. *Flow: the psychology of optimal experience*. 1990.
4. Curmi, F., Ferrario, M.A., Southern, J., and Whittle, J. HeartLink: open broadcast of live biometric data to social networks. *CHI '13*, ACM (2013), 1749–1758.
5. Deci, E.L., Koestner, R., and Ryan, R.M. A meta-analytic review of experiments examining the effects of extrinsic rewards on intrinsic motivation. *Psychological bulletin 125*, 6 (1999), 627–68; discussion 692–700.
6. Dourish, P. and Bell, G. *Divining a digital future: Mess and mythology in ubiquitous computing*. Cambridge: MIT Press, 2011.
7. Fogg, B.J. Introduction to Persuasive 2014. 2014.
8. Getz, D. The Nature and Scope of Festival Studies. *International Journal of Event Management Research 5*, (2010), 1–47.
9. Graether, E. and Mueller, F. Joggobot: a flying robot as jogging companion. *CHI EA '12*, ACM (2012), 1063–1066.
10. McGookin, D.K. and Brewster, S.A. Investigating and supporting undirected navigation for runners. *CHI EA '13*, ACM Press (2013), 1395.
11. Morgan, W. and Pollock, M. Psychologic characterization of the elite distance runner. *Annals of the New York Academy of Sciences 301*, (1977), 382–403.
12. Mueller, F., Vetere, F., Gibbs, M.R., Edge, D., Agamanolis, S., and Sheridan, J.G. Jogging over a distance between Europe and Australia. *UIST '10*, ACM Press (2010), 189.
13. Mynatt, E.D., Rowan, J., Craighill, S., and Jacobs, A. Digital family Digital family portraits: supporting peace of mind for extended family members. *CHI '01*, ACM Press (2001), 333–340.
14. De Oliveira, R. and Oliver, N. TripleBeat: enhancing exercise performance with persuasion. *Mobile HCI 2008*, ACM (2008), 255–264.
15. Pelletier, L.G., Tuson, K.M., Fortier, M.S., et al. Toward a New Measure of Intrinsic Motivation , Extrinsic Motivation , and Amotivation in Sports : The Sport Motivation Scale (SMS). *English 17*, 1 (1995), 35–53.
16. Ryan, R. and Deci, E. Intrinsic and Extrinsic Motivations: Classic Definitions and New Directions. *Contemporary educational psychology 25*, 1 (2000), 54–67.
17. Ryan, R.M. and Deci, E.L. Self-determination theory and the facilitation of intrinsic motivation, social development, and well-being. *The American psychologist 55*, (2000), 68–78.
18. Schüler, J. and Brunner, S. The rewarding effect of flow experience on performance in a marathon race. *Psychology of Sport and Exercise 10*, 1 (2009), 168–174.
19. Sellen, A., Rogers, Y., Harper, R., and Rodden, T. Human Values in the Digital Age. *Communications of the ACM 52*, 3 (2009), 58–66.
20. Shipway, R., Holloway, I., and Jones, I. Organisations, practices, actors, and events: Exploring inside the distance running social world. *International Review for the Sociology of Sport 48*, 3 (2012), 259–276.
21. Sosnowski, L. Sztuka jako świętowanie. *Estetyka i Krytyka*, 2(5) (2003), 90–105.
22. Toscos, T., Faber, A., An, S., and Gandhi, M.P. Chick clique: persuasive technology to motivate teenage girls to exercise. *CHI EA '06*, ACM (2006), 1873–1878.
23. Ying, F., Li, B., Li, Z., Li, X., Tao, J., and Gao, S. Telepathy Lamp: Remote Affective Interaction Based on Ambient Metaphor for Emotional Caring of the Elderly. *2010 International Conference on System Science, Engineering Design and Manufacturing Informatization*, IEEE (2010), 129–132.

Jogging with a Quadcopter

Florian 'Floyd' Mueller, Matthew Muirhead
Exertion Games Lab
RMIT University
Melbourne, Australia
{floyd, matt}@exertiongameslab.org

ABSTRACT
Jogging is a popular exertion activity. The abundance of jogging apps suggests to us that joggers can appreciate the opportunity for technology to support the jogging experience. We want to take this investigation a step further by exploring if, and how, robotic systems can support the jogging experience. We designed and built a flying robotic system, a quadcopter, as a jogging companion and studied its use with 13 individual joggers. By analyzing their experiences, we derived three design dimensions that describe a design space for flying robotic jogging companions: Perceived Control, Focus and Bodily Interaction. Additionally, we articulate a series of design tactics, described by these dimensions, to guide the design of future systems. With this work we hope to inspire and guide designers interested in creating robotic systems to support exertion experiences.

Author Keywords
Jogging; running; movement-based play; whole-body interaction; sports; quadcopter; robot; exertion

ACM Classification Keywords
H.5.2. [Information Interfaces and Presentation]: User Interfaces - Miscellaneous.

INTRODUCTION
Understanding the role of interactive technology to support physical exertion is a thriving field in HCI. By exertion interactions we mean interactions with technology that require intense physical effort from the user [20]. Supporting exertion is important, as exertion activity can facilitate social, mental and physical health benefits.

One popular exertion activity is jogging, i.e. running at a leisurely pace. The abundance of jogging apps, sports watches and wearable sensors (for example embedded in

Figure 1. What is it like to jog with a quadcopter?

shirts and socks [3]) suggests to us that joggers appreciate the opportunity for technology to support their jogging experience. This trend has been recognized and investigated by research [39] while special interest groups (SIGs) at CHI have also been formed to encourage further developments in this area [23, 24].

We believe that the current range of systems to support jogging is only the beginning of a trend. With sensor advancements, improvement in battery performance and miniaturization, more opportunities will emerge for designers to support people's exertion experiences. Along with technology advancements, there have also been advances in our understanding of the role of bodily aspects from a system's design perspective, most often under the name of embodiment [10, 36]. We take this investigation a step further and wonder if exertion activities like jogging that are so embodiment-focused might benefit from designs with a similar embodiment focus. We see robots as having the potential for such an embodiment focus, and therefore begin by exploring if, and how, robotic systems can support

CHI 2015, April 18 - 23 2015, Seoul, Republic of Korea.

ACM 978-1-4503-3145-6/15/04…$15.00
http://dx.doi.org/10.1145/2702123.2702472

the jogging experience. We therefore designed and built a flying robotic system, a quadcopter, and ask the question: "What is it like to jog with a quadcopter?"

Our quadcopter is an autonomous unmanned vehicle (UAV or drone) that flies around a predetermined jogging path at a fixed speed in order to accompany a jogger. Although more advanced systems that support richer interactions with the jogger have been implemented inside laboratories [14], we believe our quadcopter is the first system that has been successfully deployed in an outdoor setting generating data for an HCI study. We can therefore present the first conceptual understanding of flying robots in relation to outdoor jogging. However, as we studied only one flying robot, our results are naturally limited and incomplete. Nevertheless, our work is grounded in our first-hand experience of designing such a system, including six flying robot design iterations (and associated informal jogging experiences), as such, we believe we can offer first insights into the design of future flying systems supporting jogging. We focus on various flying robots such as quadcopters, helicopters, wing-based robots and augmented blimps as we are interested in supporting joggers outdoors, avoiding trips or falls by floor-based robots. We note that such flying robots are becoming more affordable and hence more accessible, and they seem to be increasingly targeted at supporting sportspeople, for example see [1] (however, so far focus has been on capturing video of the sportsperson rather than directly supporting the sports action). Yet none of them appear to be designed according to HCI principles, as so far no such guidance exists. CHI work has previously highlighted the importance for HCI researchers to study novel technology in its early stages, to guide advances through HCI knowledge [19], as such, our work aims to serve as such early guidance for this emerging field.

We used interview data, video footage and system logs from 13 joggers who jogged with our quadcopter outdoors. With these results, we derived three dimensions that describe a design space for flying robotic jogging companions: Perceived Control, Focus and Bodily Interaction. Additionally, we articulate a series of design tactics, described by these dimensions, to guide the design of future systems. Together with the quadcopter design, they form the central contribution of this paper.

TECHNOLOGY SUPPORTING JOGGING

The use of interactive technology to support jogging experiences is a recent trend, exemplified by popular mobile phone apps like Nike+, Endomondo, Runtastic, TrackMyRun and Runkeeper. They appear to support the jogging experience, however, most of the apps focus on the data analysis *after* the jog, such as how many kilometers have been run. Sports and smart watches such as those offered by Polar, LG and Suunto offer similar functionality, however, their strength is real-time feedback glances at the wrist to gather information about the jog, such as current speed. These devices offer support *during* the jog, however only when the jogger decides to look at the watch.

A few systems support the jogging experience *throughout*; for example, the mobile phone app "Zombies, Run!" [39] delivers a narrative-focused game experience using headphones. This suggests to us that technology can support the jogging experience while it occurs, and recent research has built on this: for example, Curmi et al. have developed a system that allows joggers to share their heart rate during a run with other joggers but also with friends at home, highlighting how technology can support companionship as part of the jogging experience [9]. Another example of a system that draws on jogging companions via means of technology is Jogging over a Distance [28]. It used relative heart rate data to balance participants of different physical abilities, allowing people who would not be able to do so without the technology to jog together [26]. This highlights that technology provides an opportunity to facilitate novel jogging companion experiences.

All systems described above focus on supporting the jogging experience through a screen- or audio-based interface. We want to explore alternative technologies to support the jogging experience. In particular, we are inspired by prior work on human-robot interaction that highlights their potential for companionship [6, 12] and recent developments in our understanding of designing technologies to support exertion activities [31, 38]. Furthermore, prior work has investigated the use of technology for joggers indoors (on treadmills) [30], in contrast we are interested in supporting the outdoor jogging experience [28, 29].

Prior work on the convergence of robotics and sports exists, however, it often focuses on either trying to create robots that "do" the sport (like in the Robocup initiative or attempts to create jogging robots [4]) or utilizing robots to train specific actions, e.g. with ball machines (e.g. [5]) and does therefore not examine the interaction between the human and the robot.

Prior research has demonstrated a quadcopter aimed to support athletes, however the objective with this prior system was to capture athletes' actions via an attached camera [16] for subsequent analysis. The idea to focus on joggers with a quadcopter is also not new: an AR.Drone has been previously used to demonstrate the idea as a design concept [22]. The demo used the in-built camera to read a visual marker on the jogger's T-shirt in order to fly at a fixed distance in front of the jogger, adapting the speed to match the jogger. Due to the light-sensitive technology used, it was targeted at indoor use. Furthermore, no formal user study was conducted, so we do not know much about the quadcopter-jogger interaction.

A QUADCOPTER AS JOGGING COMPANION

Based on our review of existing work and understanding of existing technologies, we set out the following criteria for our quadcopter: a) being autonomous yet manually controllable, b) suitable to be used near people, c) large enough to be seen by joggers, d) open platform, e) long battery life, f) works outdoors and g) could fly as fast as common jogging speeds. In particular, our system needed to be different to the prior work's commercial platform [22] as we wanted our quadcopter to know its absolute speed and position (that required combining high-accuracy GPS with inertial sensors), feature a protective guard system (that we needed to balance against performance requirements) to ensure the safety of the joggers and bystanders, and include a manual override-function in case of any emergency. We quickly realized we needed to build our own system.

Figure 2. The final design of our quadcopter.

We built six different quadcopters guided by our experiences working with joggers [29], designing jogging systems [28], and following related works as well as our personal experiences using commercial jogging systems. Having personally designed and developed these quadcopters resulted in an annotated portfolio [13], with the associated craft knowledge providing insights on the best size for the quadcopter (we experimented between 10-60cm), the preferred speed (maximum speed vs. flying time), optimal propeller orientation being up- or downwards (safety implications) and different protective guards (affecting flying behavior in wind). We found the design in Fig. 2 the best compromise between performance, safety, stability and outdoor flight characteristics suitable for jogging [25]. It consists of four 10-inch propellers, 980kv brushless motors, a 3DR Pixhawk/PX4 controller with Invensense MPU6050 accelerometer/gyroscope and MS5611 barometer, and an off-board uBlox GPS and HMC5883 magnetometer. Our quadcopter measures approximately 55 x 55 x 10 cm while the flight time is approximately 16 minutes depending on wind. We designed the quadcopter to fly approx. 4 meters in front of the jogger at an altitude of 3 meters; however, altitude depends on sensor accuracy and environmental factors.

The quadcopter is able to follow a predetermined path through a set of waypoints that we laid out on a satellite photo. After taking off, the quadcopter will fly to each waypoint using assisted GPS. It should be noted that a quadcopter travelling along waypoints exhibits unique movement characteristics, quite different to, for example, a plane. First, the quadcopter is never completely horizontal in the air, slightly "wobbles" and tilts due to wind and sensor inaccuracies. We call these secondary movements to contrast them with the primary movement along its path. The quadcopter's controller compares GPS data at 5Hz with the next waypoint, and once within its hit zone (qualifying as having arrived at the waypoint), it orients itself towards the next waypoint. We learned that we needed to carefully manage the size of the hit zone, as a too large hit zone can mean the quadcopter's path does not match the jogging path, and a too small hit zone can mean the quadcopter might overshoot the waypoint. Furthermore, we also needed to consider the waypoint density, as adding a waypoint meant that the quadcopter spends some time reorienting itself at the waypoint, which affects overall speed. However, too few waypoints restrict the shape of the terrain that can be covered. A typical flight path for one jogging lap can be seen in Fig. 3, with a high waypoint density at the corners to smooth the turning angles.

Figure 3. The waypoints and quadcopter flight path for a single jogging lap.

STUDY

We conducted a study in order to understand the experience of jogging with a quadcopter. We recruited 13 casual joggers (10 male, 3 female) aged between 24 and 44 years old (average 32.8 years). Our joggers jog on average 7 times per month, 44% of these runs are with other people and their average jogging distance is 6 kilometres for a duration of 34 minutes. The participants were all volunteers and they were not monetarily compensated.

Procedure

Our study took place outside in a park with even terrain; it is often used for sports activities (with suitably short grass) and jogging. Three of the 13 participants jogged with a different quadcopter model due to technical difficulties or varying wind conditions, which we considered in the analysis. We asked participants beforehand at which pace they would like to jog. Most participants knew their jogging pace from the use of jogging apps, if not, we organized a test run to ascertain pace. We also gave participants the opportunity to jog with our system for a couple of minutes. We equipped participants with a GoPro action cam that we attached to their head with the supplied GoPro headstrap in order to record their experience. We then started the quadcopter, which followed a predefined flight path, similar to the circumference of a football field. Participants were free to cut corners or jog on the outside of the circumference. We were positioned at the starting point in order to be able to take manual control of the quadcopter at any time for safety reasons. Participants were free to stop at any time. If participants wanted to jog longer than our batteries lasted, the quadcopter, upon running out of power, was programmed to fly back to the starting point where we exchanged the batteries. Each run was between 15 and 40 minutes long, with an average of 26 minutes.

Data Collection and Analysis

At the end of the jog, we interviewed participants while they were still exhausted. Our interviews were audio-recorded and semi-structured; we focused on the participants' experience, asking questions such as: "what was it like to jog with a quadcopter?" and "did the quadcopter affect your jogging experience and if so, how?" Most interviews lasted around 30 minutes. We then watched the action cam recording together, asking the joggers to comment on their relived experience.

We included our participants in the data analysis process as we wanted to have a rich account of how the experience unfolded throughout the run from their perspective. We found interviews during the run not to be feasible, hence we opted for the approach of interviewing straight afterwards, while still exhausted, complemented with watching a video from a first person perspective. We imported the data into qualitative data analysis software (NVivo). We transcribed both, the initial interview and action cam comments. Coding was done by the first author who has extensive experience in open-coding interview data; the goal was to derive key themes that were further distilled through affinity diagrams into the results below.

JOGGING WITH A QUADCOPTER

Participants expressed that they enjoyed taking part in the study. They described it as a *"very interesting"* experience and enquired if they could use the quadcopter in their future jogs. We now describe the different elements that came together for our participants in making jogging with our quadcopter an engaging experience, and also highlight elements that did not work for our joggers.

Quadcopter as a pace keeper: Pace keeping

As the quadcopter's speed was determined by the jogger, it was not surprising that all participants engaged with the quadcopter at some point by using it for pace keeping. This was particularly prevalent along the straight parts of the path: *"...and then it started to feel like a pace keeper. [...] I think there is something great in [the quadcopter] that it forces you to go a certain pace, pushes you a bit further." [P10]*

Pace keeping was appreciated by our joggers who found it difficult to keep a constant pace without technology: *"If I was running by myself, I think my pace would vary a bit more, this is a more set pace." [P7]*

One participant explained how he used his watch's pace keeper previously: it requires a deliberate look at the display, whereas the quadcopter allowed for a more continuous way of being aware of his pace: *"You start to take this [pace keeping] in quite passively, as your pace, cause it's in front of you and you sort of, you get in tune with it, so your pace is almost subconsciously controlled." [P5]*

Quadcopter as a pace keeper: Peer pressure from the quadcopter

The joggers also felt they needed to keep jogging if the quadcopter keeps on flying, and compared this form of pressure to their positive experiences when jogging with peers: *"If you jog with someone, you have the motivation to keep running, because the other person is still running, and its similar to that because you know it keeps going a certain pace, and you have to keep your pace up all the way around, so it's a good way to stay motivated." [P7]*

"I think ultimately there was a level of engagement. You felt you had to be responsible for its actions, because in theory you had programmed it go along a certain route, so you had to keep with it, so you felt responsible for it." [P2]

Quadcopter as a pace keeper: Finding a way to jog together

Inducing joggers to change the way they jogged was perceived as detrimental to their experience as it did not match their expectations. However, our joggers noted how, over time, they *"figured out"* how to jog with the quadcopter: *"...started to find a jogging pattern with it, started to arc around it when it hit a hard corner, or arc inside of it [...] after maybe the 3rd lap or so, started to find my rhythm with it, started working with it a bit better..." [P10]*

Quadcopter as a pace keeper: The quadcopter dictating the path

Our participants said they were disappointed that they did not have more control over the path, lamenting a lack of autonomy [32]: *"I felt the experience was more of a training exercise, we are running a track, a circuit, I didn't get to run wherever I like. [...] I had to maintain a circuit, so I didn't get as much control over my path." [P10]*

Quadcopter as a pace keeper: Perceived performance improvement

Participants applauded that the system resulted in a perception of an improved jogging performance, meaning participants thought the quadcopter *"made"* them jog longer and faster than they would have without: *"The best thing was it did make me exercise more!" [P5]*

"[...] without the [quadcopter], I would have slowed down more, but the [quadcopter] perhaps motivated me to keep a faster pace as my jog continued." [P10]

Safety

The quadcopter was designed with the safety of the jogger in mind. We also instructed our participants to not touch it to reduce risk and explained the dangers that come with any flying object, borrowing language from quadcopter safety manuals and legislations. This focus on safety made it into the interview statements, where participants expressed that the safety aspects affected their jogging experience: *"So safety was one thing that felt a bit weird, but once overcoming that, then it became interesting." [P10]*

Participants sometimes experienced the quadcopter being seemingly *"out of control"*, for example when the quadcopter diverted from its path when caught by wind or through sensor inaccuracies. Although slight path variations do not necessarily have to be safety issues, any perception of compromised safety affected the participants' experiences negatively: *"The worst [was] when it nearly rotated 90 degrees and I wasn't sure what is going to happen with it, thought it might run into me." [P10]*

"[Pointing at an instance where the quadcopter diverted from its path] At that point I don't trust it." [P10, action cam interview]

Safety: Safety concerns drawing attention

The safety concerns drew the jogger's attention to the quadcopter, which affected their jogging experience: *"But it definitely did take some of my attention away from the experience as I was worried about focusing on [the quadcopter], so for safety and pace, keep an eye on it I guess." [P3]*

The quadcopter as a companion: Movements caused by wind

Our participants experienced secondary movements, often in the form of little jiggles and slight variations from the flight path that were the result of wind and sensor inaccuracies. Our joggers perceived some of these secondary movements as means of communication, i.e. they thought the quadcopter wanted to tell them something: *"Also the movements of the robot, I think it did this motion, I think it was the wind [...] it was trying to tell me some message, it felt a bit like there was some communication [...] I wouldn't say I did feel a human touch thing going on, but I had a slight feeling of, well it could have communicated to me, well those actions felt like 'slow down!' [laughs]." [P5]*

In response, they thought of the quadcopter as a companion: *"I am not sure of wind or whatever, but it started to wobble, and it started to crisscross in front of me, and I quite liked it, because it reminded me that I am running with something, I like running with a buddy, [...] it gave it a bit of personality, a bit of character, I think what was cool about it, in that moment, cause it was like 'Hey, follow me!' [laughs][...] It was playful, I liked that! [...] That kinda injected some character into it, cause I am thinking if I am following it, [...] and it was completely static, it would feel really sterile, completely like a training tool. Whereas at least like that it was like, I don't know, like having a buddy." [P3]*

The quadcopter as a companion: The quadcopter being in the way

The quadcopter's actions also affected how our joggers jogged: sometimes by simply being in the way when it diverted from its path due to wind and sensor inaccuracies. As a result, the joggers had to slow down in order not to run into it or be underneath it (we told them not to be underneath it due to safety): *"My pace was a bit slower here because I felt I needed to slow down because [the quadcopter] felt like it was slower, to not be underneath it." [P1, action cam interview]*

"Sometimes it stops a bit, and then you have to stop a bit until it corrects course." [P7]

Desire for control: Joggers seeking more, but not complete control over the quadcopter

A desire to be more in control of the quadcopter was another dominant theme that came out of the data: *"It's more than a coach than my peer, because it's not negotiating a pace with me, we are not communicating, it has some kind of authority combined with sort of a removedness, I can't communicate with it." [P10]*

"The worst thing is just that it was not adapting to any of my actions, it was just a robot doing it's thing, and I felt that I wanted it to react more to what I was doing." [P5]

One reason why the joggers wanted to be more in control is for safety reasons: *"I didn't mind I can't manipulate it like some subservient robot, but was bothered I couldn't at least communicate like 'watch out!'" [P10]*

Our joggers also expressed that they did not want complete control, but rather some control over the quadcopter: *"Even if I could not set the speed, like it was treating more of a negotiation, like 'No, [jogger's name], we are going 12k's', I'd like that if it were encouraging me, so if I at least, maybe it says 'Come on, let's try 12' 'Yeah, alright', and I'd say 'No, no, I definitely can't', and then 'Alright, we do 8' that would be cool, I'd feel like it was working with me, maybe negotiating [...] the speed." [P3]*

"[...] having some kinda discussion about [the pace] would be good. Not completely control it, or set the speed, that would kinda devalue it." [P10]

Quadcopter draws attention: Attention pull of quadcopter affecting the ability to unwind

Participants expressed that the attention the quadcopter demanded reduced the opportunity to use the jog to unwind: *"[...] it definitely did take some of my attention away from the experience as I was worried about focusing on [the quadcopter] I didn't get to look around or think to myself, being very mindful of [the quadcopter], but again, as I got more acquainted with [the quadcopter], that came down a bit, I was less distracted by it, or less preoccupied, I wouldn't say it was distracting, but it was engaging maybe. [...] I feel [by] more practicing with [the quadcopter], I would get more familiar with it and pay less attention to it." [P10]*

Quadcopter draws attention: Spectators

As our participants were jogging in a public park, there were opportunities where other park users could observe them jogging with the quadcopter: *"And the best experience, [...] I come around that corner, a woman or young lady noticed, she was in awe, that was kinda cool I'm jogging with a robot, and people think it's rad." [P10]*

However, the same jogger noted: *"[...] I felt a bit awkward with a camera on my head and jogging with a robot." [P10]*

Quadcopter draws attention: Distraction from the discomfort of exercise

Participants applauded that the system changed their focus away from the discomfort of exercise, distracting them from associated fatigue: *"It distracted me from getting tired." [P5, action cam interview]*

"You have something in front of you floating in front of you, distracts you, so it's easier to get through the workout. Distracting in a good way, made the run a bit easier [...] similar to having someone running along side you, chatting, similar sort of, taking your mind of the physical activity, and sort of focusing somewhere else." [P7]

Quadcopter draws attention: Altitude directing focus

The quadcopter attracted the jogger's attention, in particular, the altitude of the quadcopter influenced what joggers focused on and that in turn affected how they perceived their jog: *"I preferred it when it was higher up, the distraction, taking your mind of your tired legs, if you are looking up, at the sky, you forget you have all this distance to run, whereas when it drops you see how far you have left to run, when you look down you don't close your head when you are tired, if you look up, and there is the sky and everything and you are not thinking about the distance in front of you." [P7]*

DESIGNING ROBOTS FOR JOGGING

Based on our analysis, we found that the key to facilitating an engaging robot-supported jogging experience is to find the right balance between supporting the jogger towards a satisfying athletic performance and considering the jogger's abilities and intentions. In this sense, the designer helps participants enter the "flow zone", in which skill and challenge levels are aligned [8]. We begin by articulating the design of flying robots for jogging through a set of dimensions: Perceived Control, Focus and Bodily Interaction. Based on our study, we present broad aspects of these dimensions, describing a design space. To aid designers in navigating this space, we also use these dimensions to articulate a set of design tactics. These are based on our craft knowledge of designing our quadcopter and our study. We note that the design dimensions are to be understood as a proposal based on this initial study, while future investigations, such as longitudinal studies, may provide further insights that might lead to revising these design dimensions. In fact, this first study can provide the grounding for future studies and help to design these.

Dimension 1: Perceived Control

Every robot needs some kind of control. Our study suggests that a careful balance of who is in control of the robot and how is it perceived is a key aspect of a system's design. "Perceived Control" is therefore our first dimension and deals with who is in control of the robot. We identified three broad aspects of how a robot could be controlled and how this is perceived, and in turn, how it affects the jogging experience:

Robot in Perceived Control: The robot being in perceived control means that the jogger perceives an autonomous system with no sensed input from the jogger. Technically, our robot was in control, as it did not sense the jogger, however, our participants perceived some sense of control coming not from the robot, which we explain next.

Jogger in Perceived Control: Our joggers perceived some of the movements of the quadcopter in response to wind and sensor inaccuracies as the quadcopter trying to communicate in response to their jogging movements. As the joggers set the initial pace at the beginning of the study, they perceived to be in control of the quadcopter at least to some extent themselves.

Third-Person in Perceived Control: We as designers were also partially in control by having laid out the course for the robot to follow. Furthermore, we had one instance where a jogger perceived that we temporarily took over manual control with our remote controller, which suggests to us that designers should also consider having a third-person take control of the robot. In our case, we were ready to do so for safety reasons, but our interviews suggest that participants can also see value in a coach having control over the robot, for example to offer remote guidance in a tele-training scenario [35].

This dimension also highlights that perceived control facilitated our joggers' experience with the quadcopter in three key ways: firstly as a tool, when they used it for pace keeping; secondly as a safety issue when it was seemingly out of control; and thirdly as a companion during their jogging activity. The first two aspects remind us of the ready-to-hand and present-at-hand concepts previously appropriated by HCI [10] to describe how the same technology can be experienced as invisible when the focus is on the task, but also quite disruptive when a breakdown occurs. Our work shows that in an exertion context, technology can additionally be experienced as companion, in particular, our joggers perceived the quadcopter both as a companion and as a tool within the same exertion activity.

To facilitate this experience of a companion, designers do not necessarily need to design specific control aspects, as the perception of control might suffice: our quadcopter showed that robots do not necessarily need to sense the jogger to be considered a companion, utilizing simple wind movements can already contribute to a sense that the robot is a "buddy". This aligns with prior work on social robots that highlights that people can experience a social connectedness with them [6, 12], here we extend this work by highlighting that perceived control matters in contributing to a social exertion experience.

Dimension 2: Focus

A jogger's attention can be on the jog, trying to focus on the path ahead or paying attention to how the body responds to the physical activity. A jogger's attention can also be away from the jog, used to unwind and distract oneself from the discomfort of exercise. With the addition of a robot, a jogger now has another opportunity to shift focus elsewhere. Our study suggests that designers need to carefully consider the jogger's attention in regards to the robot and the jog. "Focus" is concerned with the extent to which the robot is designed to demand focus. We identified the following key ways how designers can direct focus to and away from the robot:

Size: The size of the robot affects the attention it can draw; in our study, the jogger needed to see the robot, therefore fist-size quadcopters, which we also experimented with, we deemed not suitable as they are much more difficult to locate and track at a distance. A larger quadcopter can draw more attention, however, designers need to consider size in relation to battery performance and therefore flight time.

Altitude: Another way designers can direct attention is by considering the altitude of the flying robot. On the one hand, a high altitude directs the jogger's attention away from the path and tired legs (but might invite tripping), distracting from the discomfort of exercise, on the other hand if the altitude is lower, joggers can focus on the path but might also pay more attention to any fatigue.

Proxemics: Considering the distance between the jogger and the robot is another way designers can direct focus. This draws on the notion of proxemics, the interpersonal distance between people [15], but has also been shown to apply between people and robots [11]. Our study demonstrated that if the quadcopter gets too close to the jogger, it immediately shifts any focus, even if it is just from a safety perspective. Designers should therefore consider how they could use this interpersonal distance to direct any focus between the robot and the jog.

Dimension 3: Bodily Interaction

Our study highlighted the potential of the robot's actions to affect the jogger's actions. This dimension is therefore concerned with the bodily interaction between the robot and the jogger: it describes the extent to which the robot's actions affect the jogger's actions.

One pole of the dimension is where the designer minimizes the effect the robot's actions have on the jogger's actions (where the robot becomes a spectator), the other pole is where the designer tries to actively affect the jogger's actions through the robot's actions (for example if the quadcopter would use its propellers to create a draft that propels the jogger forward). We see a unique potential for robots to affect the jogger's bodily actions but also note that this dimension could be complemented with other, more cognitive-focused approaches (such as robots that cheer the jogger on). We identified the following key ways designers can use the robot's actions to affect the jogger's actions:

Contending for Space: Both the jogger and the robot have a physical body that share the same physical space, and unlike virtual avatars, they cannot occupy the same location at the same time. So when our quadcopter flew into the way of the jogger, the jogger had to yield. As the quadcopter was contending for space, participants had to sometimes slow down and step to the side, changing the way they ran. So one way to affect the jogging action is by utilizing the robot's actions to contend for space.

Bodily Directing Jogger's Actions: Designers can use the robot's actions to guide a person's actions, in our case the quadcopter directed where the joggers jogged through the path it set. Robots can either subtly direct a person's actions, such as the pace setting in our study, or they can direct a person's actions to a more physical extent, for example we can envision a physiotherapy application in which a robot physically directs a person's limbs.

Robot Exerts: Another way the robot's actions affected the jogger's actions was through the quadcopter "exerting": flying requires a significant amount of energy (just like jogging), which was visible to the jogger through the propellers turning very fast, the amount of noise and the fact that we needed to change batteries from time to time. As the robot as well as the jogger was exerting, a shared exertion experience [28] emerged, which motivated our joggers to jog for longer.

Tactics for Designing Robots for Jogging

We now present 5 design tactics we derived from our craft knowledge of designing, building and studying the use of our quadcopter system. These design tactics are aimed at guiding designers navigate the design space in order to make good choices when designing flying robots for jogging. We describe them using the dimensions.

Tactic 1: Support "Contending for Space" to facilitate movement variety

If joggers are not completely in control of the robot (Dimension 1), designers have the opportunity to design the robot's movements so that there are opportunities to contend for space (Dimension 3) with the jogger. Usually if a robot contends for space with a human it is seen as undesirable, however, our study suggests that in the context of jogging, this can be exploited to facilitate movement variety.

In "Run, Zombies!" a narrative and contending for virtual space turns the jog into interval training [39]. It highlights for us the power of technology to change the character of jogging experiences. Our work extends this by pointing out that designers can use robots to support contending for physical space, facilitating movement variety.

Tactic 2: Use robot to direct focus away from discomfort of exercise

Exertion activities often involve some moments where the participant experiences discomfort as a result of the exercise. Prior work showed that designers can employ technology to distract from this discomfort of exercise, contributing positively to the experience [28]. Here we point to the robot as design opportunity to direct focus away from the body (Dimension 2), which could result in a distraction away from discomfort. However, designers should consider the right time when to direct focus away from discomfort: we believe designers could benefit from knowing when these discomforts occur (informed by, for example, biosensors), as they could then aim to alter the focus of attention, for example by changing the altitude of the quadcopter.

Tactic 3: Utilize, not fight the robot's secondary movements

Most robots exhibit some sort of secondary movements when they are moving. Secondary movements [21] are movements that do not directly relate to the robot's goal [17], in our case secondary movements were those movements caused by wind and sensor inaccuracies. Engineers usually try to minimize these secondary movements (for example by creating better sensors), in contrast, our study suggests that these secondary movements have the potential to contribute positively to the jogging experience: our joggers reported that they draw focus (Dimension 2), which some of them perceived as entertaining and can even read as communication attempts, resulting in the quadcopter being described as having some "character".

Prior work on secondary movements highlight their expressive and performative potential to support movement-based interactions by humans [18, 34], here we extend this work by suggesting that these secondary movements can also be exploited in robots to support joggers.

Tactic 4: Utilize the shared space to support movement

We also recommend to designers to utilize the shared space that hosts both the robot's actions and the jogger's actions (Dimension 3) to support movement. In our study, the use of the quadcopter as physical pace keeper acting within the same space worked very well for our participants: it provided them with a continuous awareness of their target pace that was easy to comprehend because both the robot and jogger were moving in the same physical space.

This contrasts with screen-based pace keeping watches: our robot was situated in the same physical space and therefore always available (Dimension 2) and therefore did not require a deliberate interaction such as looking at the watch. Furthermore, the robot communicated the desired pace by moving through the same space (in contrast to a mapped virtual space or a number that demands cognitive load), as such it was much easier to understand how much the jogger needs to speed up (in contrast to a numerical display asking for a 0.4 min/km increase for example).

Using embodied systems to support movement in the same space has been previously discussed in embodied interaction research [36] and human-robot interaction [37]. Our work extends this by highlighting the opportunity of autonomous robots to support exertion actions by utilizing the shared space.

Tactic 5: Exploit mutual exertion investment

Sports science found that investing exertion with others changes one's pain threshold and can therefore lead to working out harder [7]. Although we did not measure athletic performance in our study, our joggers appreciated that the quadcopter was also "working out", resulting in a perceived performance enhancement. We noticed our joggers perceived the quadcopter to also be exerting mainly through what we initially thought were "shortcomings" in our design: the motors were quite loud, the quadcopter does not maintain hovering stability, and the battery needs to be changed from time to time. At the beginning, we thought we needed to "fix" these shortcomings through an engineering approach, however, we became quickly aware that our participants appreciated them as they attracted attention (Dimension 2) to the fact that the quadcopter also exerted during the activity, which contributed to the emergence of a shared exertion experience that our joggers appreciated.

In consequence, we suggest that designers exploit the fact that robots invest physical effort – that they "exert" to operate. In other words, if designers design for exertion, a suitable approach might be considering an exerting technology, as it can offer an opportunity to complement the exertion character of the human's experience with the potential result of facilitating a shared exertion experience.

LIMITATIONS

One limitation of our work is the fact that we were always in eyesight in order to be able to manually take control of the quadcopter if safety needs had arisen. The presence of researchers is quite different to our joggers' usual jogging experiences. Furthermore, our joggers only jogged once with the system. Nevertheless, we believe our in-the-wild [33] insights can serve as valuable starting points towards future investigations when participants can be outfitted with quadcopters without supervision.

Another limitation is that our quadcopter did not sense the jogger nor the terrain, i.e. we had to lay out a path that did not involve trees or other obstacles and the jogger did not have the opportunity to change the path or alter the jog in any other way. Our participants lamented this lack of autonomy. However, we showed that even a restricted quadcopter system can support the jogging experience. With advancements in technology, future studies that consider these additional aspects will provide further insights.

CONCLUSION

We have presented the first study of a flying robot as jogging companion. We analyzed the participants' experiences and found key elements that made jogging with a flying robot an engaging experience. With these key elements, we derived a set of dimensions that create a design space for flying robots supporting jogging experiences. We then used these dimensions to articulate tactics for the design of future systems. As this work is the first investigation around quadcopter-jogger interactions, we see our dimensions as a starting point towards future studies. In particular, we think studies where people jog with a quadcopter multiple times might provide further insights. Nevertheless, we believe our dimensions and associated tactics could also be beneficial for the design of robots in other sports, in particular parallel [27] exertion activities, i.e. exertion activities in which participants are not physically interfering with one another, such as cycling, cross-country skiing and rowing. For example, designers could use Tactic 1 in a cycling scenario, where a flying robot is moving close to the cyclist, "occupying" the space while using its propellers to create a draft, providing a psychological and maybe even physical boost. Similarly, Tactic 2 could be applied to long-distance cross-country skiing, where a flying robot with an embedded display could show motivating messages when participants get tired, directing focus away from the discomfort of exercise. In a rowing scenario, Tactic 3 could be used to design a flying robot that would hover just above the water's surface, utilizing secondary movements caused by water movement, adding a performative element to the experience.

We believe our dimensions and associated tactics could also support coaching, for example we can envision future quadcopters supporting "fun runs" as pace keepers and coaches utilizing them to support their training targets. This is not that far in the future, as some sports clubs already utilize quadcopters (however, up to now only for birds-eye video analysis afterwards [2]). Our dimensions might also contribute insights to the design of sports technologies such as watches and jogging apps from an embodiment perspective, highlighting opportunities for designers. Our work might also inform the design of other exertion-focused systems such as the Wii, Sony Move and Kinect that in the future might incorporate small robotic toys as part of the game experience (this is not that far off as flying robotic toys are already popular with children). Lastly, our work might be beneficial to support the design of a range of actuator-based systems that aim to support bodily activity, for example clinical programs that use interactive moving parts to support movement rehabilitation.

Overall, our work aims to inspire other designers to utilize robotic systems to support exertion activities. By doing so, we believe we can not only enhance our understanding of the design of engaging sports activities, but also our knowledge of the coming together of exertion activities with exerting systems, and how they can draw from each other to further the field of embodied interactions.

Our results also highlight the potential of robots to *support* human action (contrasting the approach of *replacing* human action as popularized by robotic vacuum cleaners) that humans like to engage in, such as jogging. In other words, our work contributes to a trend of using robots to support playful human activities. In particular, we believe our work can sensitize designers to the fact that exertion activity can benefit from exerting systems and vice versa, and we see the current research as the first step in this promising direction.

In summary, we hope our work is able to inspire and guide designers interested in creating robotic systems to support exertion experiences and hence ultimately contribute to further participation in physical activity, supporting more people to profit from the many benefits of exertion.

ACKNOWLEDGEMENTS

We thank all joggers and everyone who helped with this project. Florian 'Floyd' Mueller thanks the Australian Research Council Fellowship DP110101304.

REFERENCES

1. Airdog. http://www.airdog.com/.
2. Drone flying takes off as a popular hobby. http://www.theage.com.au/digital-life/digital-life-news/drone-flying-takes-off-as-a-popular-hobby-20140709-zst12.html.
3. Sensoria Fitness. http://www.sensoriafitness.com/.

4. U-M researcher honored for MABEL, the jogging robot. http://ns.umich.edu/new/multimedia/videos/20819-u-m-researcher-honored-for-mabel-the-jogging-robot.
5. Baca, A. and Kornfeind, P. Rapid feedback systems for elite sports training. *Pervasive Computing, IEEE, 5* (4). (2006), 70-76.
6. Breazeal, C. Toward sociable robots. *Robotics and autonomous systems, 42* (3). (2003), 167-175.
7. Cohen, E.E.A., Ejsmond-Frey, R., Knight, N. and Dunbar, R.I.M. Rowers' high: behavioural synchrony is correlated with elevated pain thresholds. *Biology Letters, 6* (1). (2010), 106.
8. Csikszentmihalyi, M. *Flow: The psychology of optimal performance*. New York: Harper and Row, 1990.
9. Curmi, F., Ferrario, M.A. and Whittle, J. BioShare: a research tool for analyzing social networks effects when sharing biometric data. In *Companion Proc. DIS 2014*, ACM Press (2014), 101-104.
10. Dourish, P. *Where the Action Is: The Foundations of Embodied Interaction*. Boston, USA: MIT Press, 2001.
11. Eresha, G., Haring, M., Endrass, B., Andre, E. and Obaid, M. Investigating the influence of culture on proxemic behaviors for humanoid robots. In *RO-MAN, 2013 IEEE*, (2013), IEEE, 430-435.
12. Fong, T., Nourbakhsh, I. and Dautenhahn, K. A survey of socially interactive robots. *Robotics and autonomous systems, 42* (3). (2003), 143-166.
13. Gaver, W. What should we expect from research through design? In *Proc. CHI 2012*, ACM Press, 937-946.
14. Graether, E. and Mueller, F. Joggobot: a flying robot as jogging companion. In *Proc. CHI 2012 Extended Abstracts*, ACM Press (2012), 1063-1066.
15. Greenberg, S., Marquardt, N., Ballendat, T., Diaz-Marino, R. and Wang, M. Proxemic interactions: the new ubicomp? *ACM Interactions, 18* (1). (2011), 42-50.
16. Higuchi, K., Shimada, T. and Rekimoto, J., Flying sports assistant: external visual imagery representation for sports training. In *Proc. Augmented Human 2011*, ACM Press (2011), 1-4.
17. Hoffman, G. and Ju, W. Designing Robots With Movement in Mind. *Journal of Human-Robot Interaction, 3* (1). (2014), 89-122.
18. Hornecker, E. and Buur, J. Getting a grip on tangible interaction: a framework on physical space and social interaction. In *Proc. CHI 2006,* ACM Press, 437-446.
19. Lieberman, H. Out of many, one: reliable results from unreliable recognition. In *Proc. CHI 2002 Extended Abstracts*, ACM Press (2002), 728-729.
20. Mueller, F., Agamanolis, S. and Picard, R., Exertion Interfaces: Sports over a Distance for Social Bonding and Fun. In *Proc. CHI 2003,* ACM Press, 561-568.
21. Mueller, F., Edge, D., Vetere, F., Gibbs, M.R., Agamanolis, S., Bongers, B. and Sheridan, J.G. Designing Sports: A Framework for Exertion Games. In *Proc. CHI 2011,* ACM Press (2011), 2651-2660.
22. Mueller, F., Graether, E. and Toprak, C. Joggobot: jogging with a flying robot. In *Proc. CHI 2013 Extended Abstracts*, ACM Press (2013), 2845-2846.
23. Mueller, F., Khot, R.A., Chatham, A.D., Pijnappel, S., Toprak, C.C. and Marshall, J. HCI with sports. In *Proc. CHI 2013 Extended Abstracts*, ACM Press, 2509-2512.
24. Mueller, F., Marshall, J., Khot, R.A., Nylander, S. and Tholander, J. Jogging with technology: interaction design supporting sport activities. In *Proc. CHI 2014 Extended abstracts*, ACM Press (2014), 1131-1134.
25. Mueller, F., Muirhead, M. Understanding the Design of a Flying Jogging Companion. In *Adjunct Proc. UIST 2014*, ACM Press (2014), 81-82.
26. Mueller, F., Vetere, F., Gibbs, M., Edge, D., Agamanolis, S., Sheridan, J. and Heer, J. Balancing exertion experiences. In *Proc. CHI 2012,* ACM Press (2012), 1853-1862.
27. Mueller, F., Vetere, F., Gibbs, M.R., Agamanolis, S. and Sheridan, J. Jogging over a Distance: The Influence of Design in Parallel Exertion Games. In *ACM SIGGRAPH 2010*, 2010, ACM.
28. Mueller, F., Vetere, F., Gibbs, M.R., Edge, D., Agamanolis, S. and Sheridan, J.G. Jogging over a distance between Europe and Australia. In *Proc. UIST 2010*, ACM Press (2010), 189-198.
29. O'Brien, S. and Mueller, F. Jogging the distance. In *Proc. CHI 2007*, ACM Press (2007), 523-526.
30. Park, T., Yoo, C., Choe, S.P., Park, B. and Song, J., Transforming solitary exercises into social exergames. In *Proc. CSCW 2012,* ACM Press (2012), 863-866.
31. Pijnappel, S. and Mueller, F. Designing interactive technology for skateboarding. In *Proc. TEI 2014*, ACM Press (2014), 141-148.
32. Rigby, S. and Ryan, R. *Glued to games*. Praeger, 2011.
33. Rogers, Y. Interaction design gone wild: striving for wild theory. *interactions, 18* (4). (2011), 58-62.
34. Sheridan, J. and Bryan-Kinns, N. Designing for Performative Tangible Interaction. *Journal of Arts and Technology. 1* (3/4). (2008), 288-308.
35. Sheridan, J. and Mueller, F. Fostering Kinesthetic Literacy Through Exertion Games. In *Workshop on Whole-Body Interactions at CHI 2010.*
36. van Dijk, J., van der Lugt, R. and Hummels, C. Beyond distributed representation: Embodied cognition design supporting socio-sensorimotor couplings. In *Proc. TEI 2014,* ACM Press (2014), 181-188.
37. Wallis, M., Popat, S., McKinney, J., Bryden, J. and Hogg, D.C. Embodied conversations: performance and the design of a robotic dancing partner. *Design Studies, 31* (2). (2010), 99-117.
38. Walmink, W., Wilde, D. and Mueller, F. Displaying heart rate data on a bicycle helmet to support social exertion experiences. In *Proc. TEI 2014,* ACM Press (2014), 97-104.
39. Witkowski, E. Running from zombies. In *Proc. Interactive Entertainment 2013,* ACM Press (2013), 1-8.

ClimbSense - Automatic Climbing Route Recognition using Wrist-worn Inertia Measurement Units

Felix Kosmalla
German Research Center for Artificial Intelligence (DFKI)
felix.kosmalla@dfki.de

Florian Daiber
German Research Center for Artificial Intelligence (DFKI)
Lancaster University
florian.daiber@dfki.de

Antonio Krüger
German Research Center for Artificial Intelligence (DFKI)
krueger@dfki.de

ABSTRACT
Today, sports and activity trackers are ubiquitous. Especially runners and cyclists have a variety of possibilities to record and analyze their workouts. In contrast, climbing did not find much attention in consumer electronics and human-computer interaction. If quantified data similar to cycling or running data were available for climbing, several applications would be possible, ranging from simple training diaries to virtual coaches or usage analytics for gym operators.

This paper introduces a system that automatically recognizes climbed routes using wrist-worn inertia measurement units (IMUs). This is achieved by extracting features of a recorded ascent and use them as training data for the recognition system. To verify the recognition system, cross-validation methods were applied to a set of ascent recordings that were assessed during a user study with eight climbers in a local climbing gym. The evaluation resulted in a high recognition rate, thus proving that our approach is possible and operational.

Author Keywords
Climbing; sports technologies; inertial sensors; machine learning.

ACM Classification Keywords
H.5.2 User Interfaces: Input devices and strategies

INTRODUCTION
Tracking of sports like running and cycling with smartphones and special sport devices is becoming increasingly popular [10]. These devices allow the recognition of tracks ran or distances cycled. In contrast, it is only possible to assess the routes which were climbed during a climbing session by hand. Common methods are noting the climbed routes and their difficulty levels in a book, spreadsheet, or low fidelity smartphone apps. Existing methods and applications for climbing tracking lack user-friendliness and additional value. Ladha et al. [11] developed a system which assess

CHI 2015, April 18 - 23 2015, Seoul, Republic of Korea
Copyright is held by the owner/author(s). Publication rights licensed to ACM.
ACM 978-1-4503-3145-6/15/04...$15.00
http://dx.doi.org/10.1145/2702123.2702311

Figure 1. ClimbSense wearable sensors to automatically detect climbed routes with wrist-worn Inertia Measurement Units.

the user's climbing style and performance by analyzing accelerometer readings assessed by sensors which were worn on both wrists during an ascent.

In this paper we introduce ClimbSense, a system that is able to record and automatically recognize the route which a user climbed during a climbing session (see Figure 1). A climbing gym usually provides a large amount of different climbing routes that consist of several artificial holds mounted to the climbing walls. One particular route consists of a certain set of holds and only these are allowed to be used as either a hand- or foothold (see Figure 2). Climbing routes usually do not have one single possible sequence of movements to master an ascent, which makes it hard to recognize the climbed routes. In our approach the climber is tracked by wrist-worn Inertia Measurement Units (IMUs). A corpus of climbing data was collected in an initial user study which should investigate the general feasibility of an automatic route recognition system. Eight climbers of different skill levels participated in the study. The features that were extracted from the collected data were used as training data for the recognition system. Our recognition approach is based on feature extraction and string comparison. To verify the recognition system, cross-validation methods were applied to a set of the corpus data. This evaluation resulted in a recognition rate of 90.19% ($SD = 5.39$).

We envision the following scenario that shows the potential of automatic climbing route recognition using wrist-worn IMUs reaching from self tracking for training and coaching to analytics for climbing gym maintenance. Our ClimbSense approach does not fully implement this vision yet. However, an automatic route recognition and tracking system, as it is described in this paper, could be the first step towards such applications.

Figure 2. A climbing route consists of a certain set of holds (often denoted by color). Only these holds are allowed to be used during an ascent.

Scenario

When Paul enters the climbing gym, his phone notifies him that, according to his training plan, today is a cardio day. Since Paul uses his sensor armbands that automatically record every ascent he does, the system adapts to him. It knows that Paul usually climbs in the grades around VII+[1] and likes overhanging routes with big holds. Thanks to crowd sourced information every route is tagged with information about the holds, if dynamic moves are required or which inclination the wall has.

The system suggests a cardio training, which requires Paul to climb five different routes with three repetitions, within 30 minutes. To make things easier, five routes are proposed which are one level easier as Pauls average climbing skill. The routes which Paul climbed in the past were automatically assessed by his climbing wrist bands. Pauls climbing partner Sarah, who also uses the system, is also doing cardio training. After an exhausting training session, Paul and Sarah sit in the lounge and compare each others training progress on their smartphones. The system summarizes the last months sessions and visualizes the training progress. Back in the climbing gym office, Michael, the manager of the gym opens the dashboard of the climbing gym management software. The dashboard displays operating numbers like the number of routes, the average route age, and the route distribution. Thanks to the climbing history data he automatically receives from his customers, he can compare the present difficulty distribution with the skill levels of his customers. He sees that many new customers started climbing which require routes in the easier difficulty levels. To counterbalance, he schedules ten new routes for beginners that should be created during the next route setting session.

To sum up, this paper contributes a method to detect features in individual recordings of climbing route ascents based on absolute arm orientations which are assessed by wrist worn IMUs. A modified edit distance algorithm makes it possible to compare two recordings of ascents and returns a measure of similarity. Furthermore we cast a vision of how this technique could be used to enhance the climbing experience for both, climbers and climbing gym operators.

RELATED WORK

Our work builds on methods for (1) sports and activity tracking and (2) climbing technologies and research.

Activity Tracking

Today, a number of devices and smartphone apps are available which enable the user to track various parts of her live. This ranges from sports tracking, through activity tracking, to sleep cycle logging. These examples show that not only sports can be tracked, but also daily activities such as counting steps, recording sleep cycles, and calculating the number of calories burned. Many of these trackers incorporate a corresponding smartphone app that visualize the recorded data, rewards the user with achievements, acts like a mobile coach, or makes it possible to share data within social networks.

The motivations for users to track activities are diverse. According to Rooksby et al. [18] the reasons for activity tracking could be directive, documentary or diagnostic, but also motivated by collectable rewards or simply for the sake of the fetishized gadget. Ojala and Saarela [14] have shown that sharing also plays an important role for the motivation of the users. By interviews they identified seven main categories that motivated them to use the online communities.

Besides consumer-ready devices and services, a variety of research exists on activity recognition and tracking. Kranz et al. [10] introduced GymSkill, an app-based personal trainer which assesses the exercises performed on a balance board. They proposed an assessment algorithm that relies on the accelerometer of a smartphone and evaluated it with the assessment of a professional coach as ground truth. Swimming as a sport got also some attention in research. Daukantas et al. [5] made a first step towards measuring swimming performance of butterfly strokes with inertial sensors attached to the swimmers' spine. Their work reveals several problems when trying to assess the moving speed from acceleration data. Stamm et al. [20, 19] also tried to measure the swimming velocity with

[1] For climbing, many different grading systems exist varying according to country. The UIAA grading system is used within the scope of this work because the participants were familiar with this system. The grade reach from I (easy) to XII- (hard). Average skilled and sportive people might quickly reach the V range while climbing a VI requires some training. Climbing in grades above VII make a regular and rigor training regime necessary.

the help of an accelerometer that was attached the to swimmers sacrum. An evaluation indicated a good match between the proposed accelerometer-based velocity profile and a tethered speed probe. Kooyman et al. [9] presented a gyroscope-driven system to improve motor skills while performing a golf putt. A user study showed that experienced and inexperienced participants improved their putting performance after using the feedback GUI. Morris et al. [13] introduced RecoFit, a system for automatic tracking of repetitive exercises. They used an arm worn IMU to recognize fitness exercises. In an evaluation study 20 participants had to perform two rounds of a four-exercise course which resulted in an average recognition accuracy of 99.3%.

The proposed papers suggest that the usage of accelerometers and gyroscopes attached to the sport device or the user herself is a common and proven method for activity tracking. In addition to the research in tracking technology, the related work showed that using a tracking system could improve the performance of the user. We envision this for climbing and assume that a virtual climbing coach could be built that is based on the climbing data, in terms of the determination of climbed routes, assessed by the system proposed in this paper.

Climbing and HCI

Sport climbing can be performed indoors as well as outdoors and requires protection such as harnesses and ropes. Indoor climbing gyms provide the climber with a variety of routes in different difficulty levels. Artificial holds are mounted to the climbing wall which allows a large variety in different route styles and difficulties. A climber can decide whether she wants to climb *top rope* or *lead*. In the first case, the climber is tied on a rope that leads from the bottom to the top, passing through carabiners and is held fast by a second person, the belayer, with the help of a belay device. In case of a fall the belayer prevents the climber from hitting the ground. *Lead climbing* describes the type of sport climbing where the rope is carried up by the climber who has to clip the rope into carabiners. Bouldering is another discipline of climbing which requires neither a rope nor a harness. Bouldering is climbing in low heights that is performed indoors as well as outdoors. Artificial bouldering walls are surrounded by thick mats that prevent a climber from severe injuries in case of a fall. As of recently, climbing got some attention in research maybe because of its growing popularity. Climbing-related research includes work on technology aided route creation, instrumented climbing walls, and automated skill assessment.

Pfeil et al. [16] propose a climbing route designer that aims to enable even non-expert route setter to create quality climbing routes. An informal user study showed some limitations that were explained by the missing specification of certain climbing moves and feedback on why a move fails. They concluded that this system could be used by experienced and novice climbers to design routes for children. Daiber et al. [4] investigated handheld augmented reality for collaborative boulder training. They present a mobile augmented reality application to define, document and share boulder problems. Kajastila and Hämäläinen [8] also explored augmented reality for climbing walls but they directly augmented the wall with a projector. A preliminary Wizard-of-Oz study with six interaction prototypes and structured interviews showed that users liked the system.

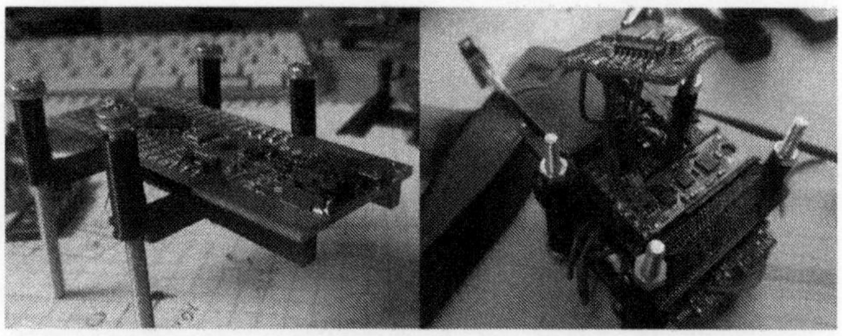

Figure 3. Mounting for the sensor modules. Left: Arduino Fio. Right: SDCard writer and sensor stick.

There are various possibilities to track a climber such as body-worn sensors, image processing, or instrumented climbing walls. Liljedahl et al. [12] proposed Digiwall, which consists of holds that can sense the climber's position with built-in capacitive sensors and provide subtle feedback with LEDs. The focus of this work is gaming, competitions, and challenges that can be rather used for playful activities than rigorous training. A very similar instrumentation was done by Ouchi et al. [15] whereas the goal of their work was to model play behavior of children. The used climbing holds that incorporated a LED and a strain gauge. Their work aims to improve the design of age-appropriate and safer playground equipment. Aladdin and Kry [1] proposed an instrumented climbing wall for static pose reconstruction. They use holds equipped with 6-axis force torque sensors that were used to reconstruct the climber's pose during an ascent. An evaluation showed that dynamic motions and higher errors coincide. Fuss and Niegl [6] also used torque sensors in instrumented climbing holds to measure the performance of a climber. Data collected on three climbing events was be segmented into the three phases of contact: set-up phase, crank phase, and lock off.

While the previous methods required an instrumented climbing wall, Ladha et al. [11] used wrist worn accelerometer sensors to assess the climbing performance of the user. An evaluation of the system during a climbing competition resulted in a positive correlation between the predicted and the actual score of the participants.

Although our system is closely related to the work of Ladha et al. [11] we follow a slightly different approach. The purpose of our system is not to assess the skills of the climber, but rather to automatically detect which routes she is climbing during a session. We further used sensor-fused orientation information and accelerometer data of a 9 degrees of freedom (DOF) IMU instead of accelerometer-only data. Our approach is motivated by self-tracked sports activities and thus requires no additional instrumentation of the environment. Other approaches that instrument the climbing wall (e.g. with RFID/NFC technology) instead of the climber are indeed possible, but we think that instrumenting solely the climber is the better option.

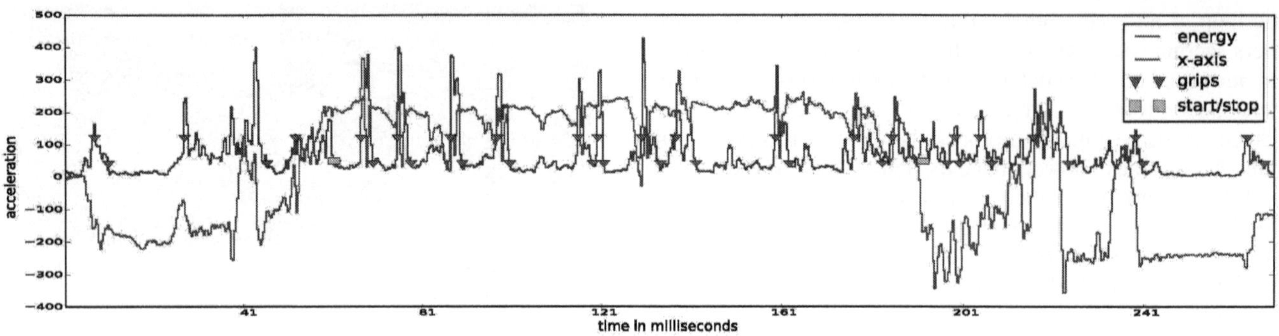

Figure 4. Recorded data (left hand) of an ascent. Blue: sum of standard deviations, green: mean of x-axis acceleration, red triangles: thresholds for move segmentation, pink squares: start and stop of climbing sequence.

CLIMBING DATA COLLECTION

Wrist-worn inertia measurement units (IMUs) were used to automatically recognize climbed routes. After introducing the hardware prototype a data collection study with eight climbers of different skill levels is presented. The aim of this study was to collect a corpus of climbing data to extract features as training data for the recognition system.

Climbing Sensor Hardware

Commercial accelerometer driven products like the fitbit or the Nike+ FuelBand do not provide access to the raw data collected by the device [3]. The missing API of commercial devices and the need for additional data like the orientation of the sensor required to build a custom prototype.

The prototype uses a Razor 9DOF Sensor Stick containing a triple-axis gyroscope, a triple-axis accelerometer, and a triple-axis magnetometer. This sensor allowed to assess the orientation. A microSD card writer was used to store the sensor readings during the climbing sessions. Both components were driven by an Arduino Fio v3 with an ATmega32U4 chip and a rechargeable battery. The sensor box could record approximately three hours of climbing with a fully charged battery.

Since the sensor should be worn on the wrist, a 3D model of a housing was designed using OpenScad[2] and printed with an Ultimaker[3] 3D printer. As it can be seen in Figure 3, stackable frames were used to hold the individual modules in place. This setup also allows later extensions of the prototype by muscle or heart rate sensors. The frames were held in place by off-the-shelf nuts and bolts inside a custom built housing. This housing had the dimensions of 7cm $\times$ 3.5cm $\times$ 5cm. A leather strip with Velcro was used to fix the sensor boxes on the wrist of the climber (see Figure 5): The sensor bands have to be tightly attached to the wrist to avoid slipping of the box during a climb.

Participants and Task

Eight climbers with different skill levels participated in the study, were one participant was female. In average the participants climbed for 7.25 years ($SD = 7.12$), ranging from four to 24 years. The participants' skill levels ranged from IV to $VIII+$ (UIAA). Seven of the participants were right-handed. Furthermore the height ($M = 177.38cm$, $SD = 9.40$) and arm span ($M = 183.25$, $SD = 10.61$) of the participants was assessed. To build a data corpus, the participants were asked to climb a set of 5 predefined routes. The difficulty of the routes ranged from $IV-$ to $VI+$ and they contained dynamic and static moves, and different hold types. All routes had the same height and roughly the same number of holds. The routes were straight with no to little overhang. Each route varied in terms of holds in different forms and difficulty to grip which resulted in a broad variety of climbing styles. Most of the routes had more holds than necessary, allowing varying ascents and thus, resulting in differing recordings for every ascend. Furthermore, all routes were top-rope routes. Beside the general security aspect, top-roping allowed the participants to fully concentrate on climbing. The participants were asked to climb each route two times. No participant climbed any of the selected routes before. Both ascents were recorded. Since not every participant was able to climb every route during the recording sessions, the average number of recording per route was 10 ($SD = 3.53$). As a result, in total 50 recordings could be achieved.

[2]`http://www.openscad.org/`

[3]`https://www.ultimaker.com`

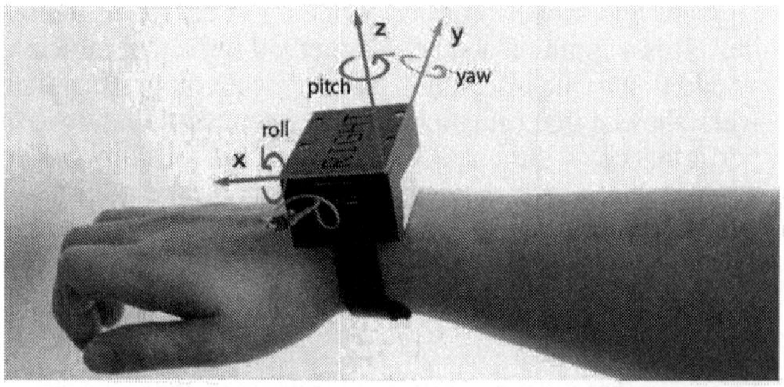

Figure 5. Sensor box attached to wrist. The attached button is used to manually mark timestamps in the recorded data. The x-axis runs parallel to the arm which is later used to determine if the arm is pointing up- or downward. Yaw, pitch, and roll corresponds to the y-, z-, and x-axis.

Procedure

To assess the climbing data, the following procedure was performed for each climb. First, the participant had to put on the wristbands. Since the recognition of the route relies on the orientations of the arms, it was necessary to put on the sensors in the same way for each recording (details on the recognition see below). The sensors had labels to distinguish between the left and right hand. Figures 1 and 5 show the sensors, worn by participants. After the participant tied herself in, the recording was started by simultaneously pressing the external buttons of the sensor boxes. This was necessary since the current prototype does not contain clock modules for synchronization. Additionally the climbing tasks were video captured for later analysis. The video footage was mainly used to compare the collected sensor data with the actual movements of the climber.

Each recording of the ascents lasted about 30 minutes per participant. The participants were allowed to take breaks as often as they wanted. When the participant had finished the route she was lowered. As a final step the recording was stopped by switching of the sensor boxes. The sensor data for each ascent was automatically written in a separate file on the internal SDCard. These files were finally uploaded via an API into the analytics toolkit. We developed the analysis toolkit with the help of the Django web framework [4] which made it easy to implement both, GUIs and CLIs, to access the functions of our system. The analytics toolkit is responsible for the storage and processing of the collected climbing data.

Results

To analyze the recordings, the data was preprocessed by the analytics toolkit. First the orientation of the sensors was calculated with a sensor fusion algorithm[17] using the direction cosine[5]. The algorithm calculates a robust orientation of the device based on the data from the magnetometer, the gyroscope, and the accelerometer. In a second step the data stream was segmented with a sliding window procedure: each window covered $280ms$ of data with $20ms$ overlap on each side. Next, the average and the standard deviation of the three accelerometer values was calculated for each window. The sum of the standard deviations served as a description for the movement energy within the borders of a window.

When visually analyzing the plots from the data described above, the climbing sequence and the individual grips of the hands could be easily identified (see Figure 4). Most of the time during an ascent both hands are pointing upwards. This results in a mostly positive value of the acceleration in the x-axis (green). Transitions from one hold to another can be identified by the peaks of the standard deviation (blue). The valleys in-between the peaks indicate the gripping of a climbing hold.

CLIMBSENSE SYSTEM

The automatic route recognition introduced in this section is based on the assumption that a route can be characterized by a sequence of arm orientations, asessed in the moment of gripping a hold. Our system relies on the assumption that some of the recordings collected during training are similar to the recording to be recognized. Since the setup of a route usually limits the number of possibilities on how a route can be climbed, this assumption should be fulfilled. We chose the arm orientations in the moment of gripping a hold as characterization, since the determination of absolute movement based on the available accelerometer data is hard. This is due to errors based on the double integration of accelerometer readings [22]. Especially during movements like fast hand switching or shaking the hands for relief, using the absolute arm orientations in holding position as opposed to interpreting movements, is a viable approach.

Every aspect of processing and data management is covered by the analytics toolkit. Each recording of an ascent is stored in a so-called recording dataset. This includes the raw data obtained from the sensors as also the processed data, i.e. the extracted features of the ascent.

The process of the route recognition consists of the following steps: (0) preprocessing, (1) climb segmentation and grip detection, (2) feature extraction, and (3) matching. After segmenting the climb within a recording, grips are detected and the arm orientations of each grip are extracted. The orientations are discretized and considered as a sequence of symbols, i.e. a string. Since each route can now be characterized by a string, the identification of new unrecognized recordings is achieved by applying a weighted Levenshtein edit distance [2].

(0) Preprocessing

As mentioned above, preprocessing includes the calculation of the orientation based on a sensor fusion algorithm which uses the sensor readings from the accelerometer, gyroscope, and magnetometer [17]. A sliding window procedure is applied and parameters such as the average acceleration and the standard deviation are calculated. The following steps are applied on the resulting windows.

(1) Climb Segmentation and Grip Detection

After preprocessing the recorded data, the climbing sequence was extracted from each recording dataset. Each recording dataset only contains one climbing sequence. This also includes standing on the ground, the ascent itself, and lowering.

From the accelerometers point of view, a climbing sequence is defined as a sequence of alternations between low and high movement. These alternations arise when gripping a hold and the transition from one hold to another. Analog to this definition, the segmentation of individual movements is achieved by applying two thresholds t_{low} and t_{high} on the energy (i.e. the sum of the standard deviations) for each window. An alternation between those two thresholds indicates a movement that is set as property of the window (*is_gripping_window*). A second pair of thresholds is applied to the x-axis (parallel to the climber's arm) acceleration indicating whether the arm is pointing down (t_{down}) or up (t_{up}). After identifying the movements and arm position in the dataset for the left and right hand, the climbing sequence is narrowed down by observing both arms simultaneously. For this, both window sequences (left hand and right hand) are iterated and flagged with *both_hands_down* or *both_hands_up* whenever in two corresponding windows (two windows correspond if they share the same timestamp) the arms are pointing up or down.

[4] https://www.djangoproject.com/

[5] https://github.com/ptrbrtz/razor-9dof-ahrs

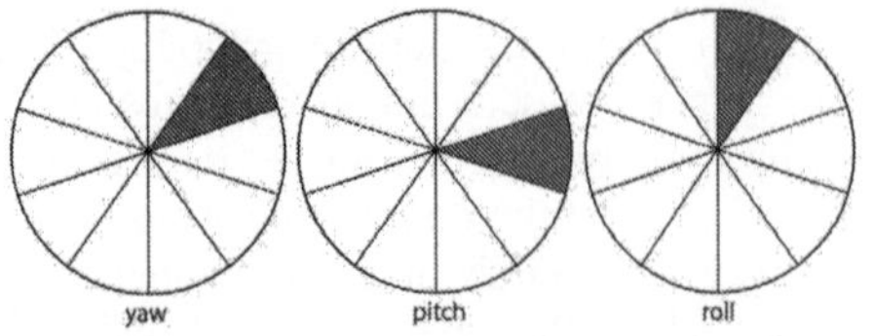

Figure 6. Segmentation of the orientation $yaw = 50°$, $pitch = 125°$, $roll = 10°$. One segment spans an interval of $[i \times 36, (i+1) \times 36 - 1]$. For the sake of simplicity, the number of segments was reduced to 10.

The thresholds for climb segmentation and grip detection were determined in an iterative procedure on data recorded during a pilot study. For this, the actual number of grips was manually transcribed from all videos. Based on this, an average number of grips was calculated for each route. An interval ranging from a relatively low to a relatively high energy was assigned to each threshold. After iterating over all values within these intervals, the script returned the "best" combination of thresholds. The "best" combination is defined as the set of thresholds which result in the smallest delta between the actual number and the detected number of grips. During the later measurement of the recognition performance, data different from the data assessed in the pilot study was used.

In a final step, the climbing sequence within the recording is marked by applying the definition above. Figure 4 shows a plot of a route's recording with the hold transitions and the boundaries of the climbing sequence indicated as red triangles and pink squares. This results in two sequences of groups of windows which were marked as gripping windows. These sequences are then used to extract the features of this ascent.

(2) Feature Extraction

The method of gesture recognition as proposed by [21] uses a codebook to convert the direction vectors which were calculated from accelerometer data into symbols. A codebook is basically a mapping from a set of values to one single value or symbol. A sequence of those symbols forms a string. This string is then considered a word, which can be used to calculate the Levenshtein distance [2] between two "stringified" gestures.

We adapted this method for the route recognition process. Instead of direction vectors, arm orientations, which arise during the ascent of a route, are used. These orientations are fetched whenever a hand grips a hold. An orientation is converted, with the help of a codebook into a symbol representing the yaw, pitch and roll angles. The codebook is generated as follows. First, a circle is divided into 30 segments. The resulting $12°$ circular segments represent a satisfying tradeoff between generalization and sufficient discriminability. This step has to be executed three times, one time for each of the three angles (yaw, pitch, roll).

The following example illustrates this procedure: To convert a specific orientation of the sensor box, the matching segment for each angle is chosen. Supposing the orientation $yaw = 50$, $pitch = 125$, $roll = 10$ the resulting segments for the three axis would have the indices 4, 10, and 0 (see Figure 6). By using this method an orientation of a sensor box can be coded into one of $30 \times 30 \times 30 = 27.000$ resulting symbols. During recognition each orientation is assigned to a combination of segment indices.

(3) Matching

In a final step of the route recognition process, the route is determined based on the calculated strings. The general approach is to compare the incoming dataset with each of the training datasets that are stored in the database for each individual route. As comparison, a weighted Levenshtein distance is used. The weighted Levenshtein distance used by the system is defined by the following equation.

$$m = |u|, \quad n = |v|$$
$$D_{i,0} = i, 1 \le i \le m, \quad D_{0,j} = j, 1 \le j \le n$$
$$D_{i,j} = \min \begin{cases} D_{i-1,j-1} & +0 \text{ if } u_i = v_j \\ D_{i-1,j-1} & +0.1 \times SymDist(u_i, v_j) \\ D_{i,j-1} & +1 \textit{ (Insertion)} \\ D_{i-1,j} & +0.1 \textit{ (Deletion)} \end{cases}$$
$$1 \le i \le m, 1 \le j \le n$$

$SymDist$ depicts the distance between two symbols, i.e. two orientations and is used when applying a substitution. The symbol distance has to be included in the calculation, since the system should allow a certain degree of deviation. This need arises, since an ascent is not always performed in the same way. Skipping of holds or different grip positions produce a variation in every ascent, which is compensated by this method. The distance between two symbols is calculated by adding the encoded angle distance of all three axis, e.g. $dist([0,0,0],[0,1,2]) = 0 + 1 + 2 = 3$. Since there are always two possibilities to transition from one angle to another, the shortest difference has to be chosen. As an example, consider a circle from its center two lines arise. Both of these lines have an outer and an inner angle. As a result, the distance between the two symbols $[0,0,0]$ and $[29,0,0]$ is 1 and not 29.

To generate the final result, the incoming dataset has to be compared to the training datasets which are available for each route. For this, the Levenshtein distances between the strings for the left hand and the strings for the right hand are summed up, which results in a score for the pair of the two datasets (incoming and training). The smaller the score is the higher is the probability that the route is recognized correctly. Thus, the pair with the lowest score is chosen as the winner.

ANALYSIS

The recognition performance of the algorithm was evaluated based on the data corpus collected in the user study. For this, the recorded data was used as both, training and testing data using cross validation methods.

Grip Detection

The first step in the route recognition process is the detection of grips. To evaluate the grip detection of the system, five sample recordings were randomly chosen. For each sample the number of grips was assessed manually by inspecting the video recording. This number served as a ground

Ascent	LH_V	RH_V	LH_D	RH_D	S_V	S_D	Δ
1	10	10	11	8	20	19	1
2	10	10	11	11	20	22	2
3	9	9	10	9	18	19	1
4	9	10	10	12	19	22	3
5	9	10	12	12	19	24	5

Table 1. Grip detection. A random sample of 5 ascents was analyzed. Ground truth based on video recordings and detected number of grips. LH: left hand, RH: right hand, $_V$: video, $_D$: detected, S: sum, Δ: delta.

Route	actual no. of holds	min	max	mean	SD
Route 1	16	21	32	27	2.78
Route 2	21	26	39	32	4.30
Route 3	18	21	34	25	4.32
Route 4	16	19	28	22	3.62
Route 5	17	16	31	22	3.60

Table 2. Statistics w.r.t the number of detected grips for all routes used in the study. The table shows that the number of actual holds correlates with the average number of detected holds per climb.

truth and was compared to the number of automatically recognized grips. This measure was chosen since the number of grips during an ascent varies from climber to climber but correlates with the number of holds mounted to the wall. Table 1 shows the result of this assessment. For each ascent the actual number of holds per hand was transcribed from the video and compared to the number of detected grips. The number of actual grips ranged from nine to ten while the recognized number of grips ranged from eight to twelve. Except for one record, the difference between the actual number of grips and the detected number of grips fluctuated between one and three. One record differed in five grips.

Furthermore, the minimum, maximum, and average number of detected holds was calculated for each route. This was done for the whole data corpus. Additionally, the number of holds attached to the wall was included in this analysis. Table 2 shows the results. The actual number of holds per route ranged from 16 to 21, while the average detected number of grips ranged from 16 to 39. Although the average difference between the actual number of holds and the average number of detected grips was 8.0 a correlation could be identified. A computation of the Pearson correlation resulted in 0.788 which shows a significant relation between the detected number of grips and the actual number of holds mounted on the climbing wall. The standard deviations of the average number of detected grips ranged from 2.78 to 4.32.

Route Recognition

To evaluate the route recognition exhaustive and non-exhaustive cross validation methods were applied: *leave-one-out cross-validation* (LOOCV) and *2-fold cross validation.* (2FCV). When applying LOOCV to every recording dataset, the system tries to recognize the route based on all 49 remaining recordings. For this, the evaluation script iterates over all recordings and queries the analytics toolkit, which responds with a route id. Since all recordings, including the testing data, are linked with the corresponding route, the number of correctly recognized routes can be divided by the number of processed routes. This results in the recognition rate. The results of this validation method indicate how good the system works, when a relatively large number of recordings per route are available.

Leave-one-out cross-validation

This LOOCV is executed two times with a slightly different training set. In the first run the training set contains all records except the one record which is used for testing. To validate if the recognition is influenced by the fact that the training set and also the testing set both contain records of the same person, the following method was applied. Whenever a dataset was used for testing which was recorded by participant A, all records from this participant were removed from the training set. This test should reveal whether the recognition system is influenced by user dependence, or if a *general* corpus of foreign training data is sufficient.

Applying the LOOCV over the complete dataset resulted in a recognition rate of 100%. When using only "foreign" training records, i.e. the training dataset does not contain recordings of the user whose dataset is to be recognized, a recognition rate of 100% was achieved.

Two-fold cross-validation

To investigate how good the system performs when only a small number of recordings per route is available a 2FCV was applied. In a 2FCV the available data is divided into two groups of the same size. One group is used as training data, while the other one is used for testing. In the case of the recognition system, the datasets can not be simply divided into two parts. This is due to the fact that it could not be assured that every route is equally represented in each group. For this, the two sets (*training* and *testing* data) are compiled as follows. The recording datasets of all routes are shuffled and afterwards split into two parts. These two parts are then appended to the *training* group, respectively the *testing* group. The resulting groups are then analyzed with the 2-fold cross-validation described above. This step was performed 100 times to get a more meaningful result.

As for the LOOCV, the 2FCV is also applied in two modes. In the first run the training dataset was not modified and contained a random set of recordings, except the ones that were used for testing. In the second run, the training dataset was modified as follows. At first, all participants which created records used in the training set were identified. Then, all records of these participants were removed from the testing dataset to ensure a user-independent recognition.

The application of the 2FCV resulted in an average recognition rate of 93.11% ($SD = 5.52$). When observing only foreign training records the average recognition rate was 90.19% ($SD = 5.39$).

One Handed Recognition

Motivated by the growing popularity of smartwatches, the validation methods described above were also applied on a modified implementation of the recognition system. The implementation was modified in such a way, that it would only consider either the left or the right hand for training and recognition. This could be easily achieved since both, the data for the left and the right hand were gathered separately. The current implementation of the climb segmentation, that is, identifying the ascent within a recording, uses the sensor data of both hands. Since the grip detection relies on the correct segmentation of the ascent, an evaluation of the grip detection using only one hand was not performed.

Applying the cross-validation methods on only the left and only the right hand resulted in different recognition rates. The leave-one-out cross-validation scored with 84% for the left hand and 94% for the right hand (see Table 3). Using only user independent data sets resulted in recognition rates of 68% and 94%. It can be seen that using only the data from the right hand resulted in a recognition rate almost as good as using both hands.

When applying a 2-fold cross-validation similar observations could be made. Using only data from the left hand resulted in an average recognition rate of 73.15% ($SD = 6.95$) (see Table 4). Applying the 2FCV on only data of the right hand resulted in an average recognition rate of 89.46% ($SD = 4.99$). When considering only user independent records recognition rates of 69.19% ($SD = 6.36$) for the left hand and recognition rates of 87.46% ($SD = 5.4$) could be achieved.

The the chance recognition rate for all validation methods was 20% and lies below the recognition rates our system could achieve.

	LOOCV		
	Left	*Right*	*Both*
complete	84.0%	94.0%	100%
user independent	68.0%	94.0%	100%

Table 3. Summarized evaluation results of the LOOCV. Using only data of the right hand results in higher recognition rates as when only using data of the left hand.

DISCUSSION

Grip Detection

When analyzing the grip detection performance, it can be seen that randomly picked samples (see Table 1) showed good results. The difference between the actual number of attached holds and the number of detected holds can be explained with various possible climbing styles. First, a usual technique is to grip a hold with both hands (also known as matching). This is used whenever the next hold is too far away or difficult to grip. Very fast transitions from one hold to another or the movement away and then again back to hold may also result in detection errors. Extensive use of momentum during an ascent may also influence the efficiency of the detection. Another reason for the varying number of holds is the fact that some climbers do not use every single hold that is available. Additionally, it is also possible to use the wall itself as support, which could be falsely detected as gripping. Also sometimes climbers use a single hold for a really short amount of time, using the momentum to ease the transition to the next hold. All these reasons may lead to a false detection of grips.

	2FCV					
	Left		*Right*		*Both*	
	Mean	*SD*	*Mean*	*SD*	*Mean*	*SD*
C	73.15%	6.95	89.46%	4.99	93.11%	5.52
U	69.19%	6.36	87.46%	5.40	90.19%	5.39

Table 4. Summarized evaluation results of the 2FCV. *C*: complete dataset, *U* user independent. As in the LOOCV, only data of the right hand results in higher recognition rates as when only using data of the left hand.

This can be also seen when investigating Table 2. Although the standard deviation of the average number of detected grips is relatively low, there are sometimes outliers. This can be noticed in the maximum number of detected grips in route 2. When investigating the video recording of the corresponding dataset, it could be seen that the participant struggled a lot during her first ascent. This resulted in changing the grip of her hands multiple times before continuing with the climb. As a result, the system detected more grips than a "normal" ascent would require. An implication of that would be, that the recognition performs good at routes which are climbed confidently, but may fail when the climbers struggles during the ascent.

Route Recognition

The evaluation results suggest that automatic route recognition based on wrist worn IMUs is possible and operative. The very good recognition rate of 100% when applying the LOOCV may have several reasons. First, a large number of training records per route are available. Whether this would be the case in a productive environment is discussed later on. Additionally, a relatively small number of routes is used. This needs to be investigated further in the future.

As it can be seen in the difference between the LOOCV and the 2FCV, a larger number of recordings per route are beneficial for the recognition process. When applying the 2FCV on an unfiltered training set, a higher recognition rate than in the other run could be observed. The (filtered) training set used in the second run of the 2FCV only relies on records from participants which were not included in the testing dataset. The cause for the difference between the runs on the filtered and unfiltered dataset could not be definitely identified. One reason could be the resulting smaller number of training data sets. A small training dataset increases the probability of false recognitions. In future work, we plan an extensive study to gain more insights regarding this issue. The second reason would be the difference in climbing styles between the participants which are responsible for the *training* data sets and the participants which are responsible for the *testing* data sets. As it can be seen in the high recognition rate of the LOOCV, a higher number of training datasets would solve this problem.

One Handed Route Recognition

Using only one hand for recognition and training leads to additional promising insights. It could be observed that when using only data from the right hand, higher scores could be achieved as when only data from the left hand was used. This could be due to the fact that most of the participants were right-handed. We conclude that gripping with the dominant hand resulted in more precise movement and in less jitter of the limb. With this, a better recognition of the orientation could be achieved and thus, a more expressive sequence of orientations is used for the recognition process. The fact that the LOOCV for only one limb still performs well may be a result of the large number of records per route. This assumption is encouraged when considering the results of the 2FCV for only one limb. Smaller training sets result in lower recognition rates.

The results suggest that in future work the application of smartwatches for route recognition should be investigated in more detail. Using future sports bands that allow access to the raw data could also be used for the recognition and would make special wrist bands for climbing recognition unnecessary.

Prerequisites

Currently the system relies on the assumption that each recording contains exactly one ascent. In the current prototype, this is achieved by turning the devices on before the climb, and switching them of after lowering. The ultimate goal would be to integrate a climb segmentation which would recognize each climb within a recording of a complete climbing session. This could be established like described in [11].

Another prerequisite is the existence of a sufficient amount of training data. Initial training data could be assessed by the route setter herself. After setting the new route, she could climb the route a couple of times which would suffice for a basic training data set. Another option would be crowdsourcing. A corresponding smartphone application could be used to link recordings of the wristbands to the manual logging of climbed routes. As motivation for the linking of recordings with routes, an achievement system could be deployed. The user could gain achievements like badges or coupons for free admittance in the climbing gym. Considering the scenario described above, the gym operator would also profit from knowing which routes are being climbed. This would justify the expenses of the coupons.

Limitations

The current implementation of the system limits the recognition to routes which were fully climbed, i.e. climbed from the bottom to the top without falling or resting. Routes which are only climbed partially are not recognized, since the system would not find a match to a partial route. This is due to the fact that the edit distance, which is the similarity measure, is also influenced by the different number of recognized grips during two ascents. A comparison between an incomplete route and the training set would result in a higher edit distance per se. Depending on the intended use of the system, e.g. only as list of completed routes in a climbing gym, this might not be flaw. In fact, a common training method for endurance training is to climb a well known, but hard route multiple times [7].

To recognize the route of a newly recorded ascent, the recording has to be compared to each training dataset. Although this process requires more resources as more routes are available in the system, this is not a big concern. Since a real-time recognition is not necessary, the recognition process can be performed offline in a server structure. Systems like Strava and their segment recognition prove that this is a viable solution.

Shaking the arms for relief, fast switching of holds, chalking (i.e. applying magnesium carbonate to the hands to remove perspiration and thus reduce slipping), or clipping the rope in a belay might evoke irritations of the grip detection. This results in too many or too few orientations represented by an ascent. As a result, the edit distances derivates from the actual value. To overcome this issue, additional machine learning could be applied to recognize and discard non-transition movements like the ones listed above. With this technique grips could be identified better and non-transition movements could be discarded. This would result in a better segmentation, which would give better route recognition rates.

CONCLUSION AND OUTLOOK

This paper introduced ClimbSense, a system that is able to record and automatically recognize the route which a user is climbing. The climber is tracked by wrist-worn IMUs. A corpus of climbing data was collected in a user study with 8 climbers of different skill levels. The features which were extracted from the collected data were used as training data for the recognition system. To verify the recognition system, cross-validation methods were applied to a set of the corpus data. The analysis of the recognition system showed promising results. Eight participants climbed five routes, resulting in 50 recorded data sets. These datasets were used for a combination of two cross-validation methods. The leave-one-out cross-validation resulted in a recognition rate of 100%. A 2-fold cross-validation was performed 100 times and resulted in a recognition rate of 93.11%. Considering the good performance of the recognition process when using the data of only one limb, the use of smartwatches as tracking device should be investigated in more detail. In general, the recognition could be improved in future work by an extended user study. Further machine learning methods could be applied to obtain a better grip detection. A better grip detection might also result in a higher recognition rate.

Since the recognition relies on training data, two concepts were introduced to obtain training records. One option would be, that the setter of the route could climb the route a couple of times, while wearing the wristbands. As an alternative, the training sets could be compiled through crowd sourcing. Climbers could wear the wristbands and link recording with routes with the help of a smartphone application. By improving the one handed recognition, open fitness tracker or smart watches could be used to crowdsource the training data. Furthermore, using future generations of smart watches makes it obsolete to carry a smartphone around. Incentives for the use of the application could be given by virtual achievements or coupons for drinks.

Although the results of the evaluation are satisfying, there are aspects that need more attention in future works. First, a larger number of routes have to be included in the evaluation. This would give insights into how well the system scales. With an increasing number of routes, the detection of movements and grips has to be refined. Currently the system does not distinguish between transitions from one hold to another and other movements like clipping, shaking the arms for relief or chalking. These movements could be detected using machine learning methods. To get closer to the goal of making this system consumer ready, climb segmentation as in [11] would be desirable. Currently only recordings containing one single ascent can be processed. Furthermore the system only detects complete ascents of a route. Falls, resting on the rope or partially climbed routes will certainly result in recognition failures.

Including performance assessment into the system would make it possible to detect user problems that arise at specific routes. These problems could be deducted by the stability and power the user shows during an ascent. With the help of these data and the knowledge of available routes, the system could make suggestions that would tackle the climber's weaknesses and helps her to improve her climbing skills.

Another way of extending the system would be the implementation of a real-time recognition. Currently the user would have to upload the data into the online portal to receive the results of her climbing session. With the immediate knowledge about the already climbed routes a virtual climbing coach could adapt to the user and suggest routes which fit into the current state of training. This would be especially helpful for smartwatches. In fact, smartwatches or wrist-worn activity trackers could replace special sensors like the ones used in this paper. This is shown by the promising results of the one handed route recognition evaluation.

ACKNOWLEDGMENTS

This research project is partially supported by the Deutsche Forschungsgemeinschaft (DFG KR3319/8-1).

REFERENCES

1. Aladdin, R., and Kry, P. Static pose reconstruction with an instrumented bouldering wall. In *Proc. VRST* (2012), 177–184.
2. Cormen, T. H., Leiserson, C. E., and Rivest, R. L. *Introduction to Algorithms , Second Edition*, vol. 7. The MIT Press, 2001.
3. Curmi, F., Ferrario, M. A., and Whittle, J. Sharing real-time biometric data across social networks. In *Proc. DIS* (2014), 657–666.
4. Daiber, F., Kosmalla, F., and Krüger, A. BouldAR - Using Augmented Reality to Support Collaborative Boulder Training. In *Proc. CHI EA* (2013), 949–954.
5. Daukantas, S., Marozas, V., and Lukosevicius, A. Inertial sensor for objective evaluation of swimmer performance. In *Proc. BEC* (2008), 321–324.
6. Fuss, F. K., and Niegl, G. Instrumented climbing holds and dynamics of sport climbing. In *The Engineering of Sport 6*, E. F. Moritz and S. Haake, Eds. Springer New York, 2006, 57–62.
7. Horst, E. J. *How to Climb 5.12*, 2nd ed. Falcon, 2003.
8. Kajastila, R., and Hämäläinen, P. Augmented climbing: Interacting with projected graphics on a climbing wall. In *Proc. CHI EA* (2014), 1279–1284.
9. Kooyman, D. J., James, D. A., and Rowlands, D. D. A feedback system for the motor learning of skills in golf. *Procedia Engineering 60*, 0 (2013), 226 – 231.
10. Kranz, M., Möller, A., Hammerla, N., Diewald, S., Plötz, T., Olivier, P., and Roalter, L. The mobile fitness coach: Towards individualized skill assessment using personalized mobile devices. *Pervasive and Mobile Computing 9*, 2 (2013), 203–215.
11. Ladha, C., Hammerla, N. Y., Olivier, P., and Plötz, T. Climbax: Skill assessment for climbing enthusiasts. In *Proc. UbiComp* (2013), 235–244.
12. Liljedahl, M., Lindberg, S., and Berg, J. Digiwall: An interactive climbing wall. In *Proc. ACE* (2005), 225–228.
13. Morris, D., Saponas, T. S., Guillory, A., and Kelner, I. Recofit: Using a wearable sensor to find, recognize, and count repetitive exercises. In *Proc. CHI* (2014), 3225–3234.
14. Ojala, J., and Saarela, J. Understanding social needs and motivations to share data in online sports communities. In *Proc. MindTrek* (2010), 95–102.
15. Ouchi, H., Nishida, Y., Kim, I., Motomura, Y., and Mizoguchi, H. Detecting and modeling play behavior using sensor-embedded rock-climbing equipment. In *Proc. IDC* (2010), 118–127.
16. Pfeil, J., Mitani, J., and Igarashi, T. Interactive climbing route design using a simulated virtual climber. In *SA Sketches* (2011), 2:1–2:2.
17. Premerlani, W., and Bizard, P. Direction cosine matrix imu: Theory. *DIY Drones.[Online] http://goo.gl/cCGNXB* (2009).
18. Rooksby, J., Rost, M., Morrison, A., and Chalmers, M. C. Personal tracking as lived informatics. In *Proc. CHI* (2014), 1163–1172.
19. Stamm, A., James, D., and Thiel, D. Velocity profiling using inertial sensors for freestyle swimming. *Sports Engineering 16*, 1 (2013), 1–11.
20. Stamm, A., Thiel, D. V., Burkett, B., and James, D. A. Towards determining absolute velocity of freestyle swimming using 3-axis accelerometers. *Procedia Engineering 13*, 0 (2011), 120 – 125.
21. Stiefmeier, T., Roggen, D., and Tröster, G. Gestures are strings: efficient online gesture spotting and classification using string matching. *Proc. BodyNets* (2007).
22. Thong, Y., Woolfson, M., Crowe, J., Hayes-Gill, B., and Jones, D. Numerical double integration of acceleration measurements in noise. *Measurement 36*, 1 (July 2004), 73–92.

Towards Multimodal Affective Feedback : Interaction between Visual and Haptic Modalities

Akshita
IIIT-Hyderabad, India
akshita@research.iiit.ac.in

Harini Sampath
IIIT-Hyderabad, India
harini@research.iiit.ac.in

Bipin Indurkhya
IIIT-Hyderabad, India
bipin@iiit.ac.in

Eunhwa Lee
Samsung Electronics,
Republic of Korea
eunhwa.lee@samsung.com

Yudong Bae
Samsung Electronics,
Republic of Korea
yd21c.bae@samsung.com

ABSTRACT
We explored how emotional cues presented in visual and haptic modalities interact. We constructed an affective haptic dataset, and used the emotional visual stimuli from the International Affective Picture System (IAPS). Participants were asked to rate the visual stimuli, haptic stimuli and visual-haptic stimuli. Analysis of the results indicated that the presence of haptic stimulus affects the arousal of the visual stimulus, but does not affect the valence significantly. We further explored this interaction in terms of the intensity, frequency, waveform and rhythm of the haptic stimuli. Finally, we generated a set of guidelines on visual-haptic interaction that could be used to design multimodal affective feedback.

Author Keywords
Multimodal affective feedback, Haptics, Visual Haptic Interaction

ACM Classification Keywords
H.5.m. Information Interfaces and Presentation (e.g. HCI): Miscellaneous

INTRODUCTION AND RELATED WORK
Current research in affective computing has concentrated predominantly on providing machines with the ability to *recognize emotions* expressed by its users and adapt accordingly. For instance, *AutoTutor* is a cognitive tutor that can detect emotions based on activity pattern and alter the content presented to the students if it detects that the student is bored [13]. Another example is *iSeT:* a system designed to detect emotions from facial expressions, which is aimed at helping individuals with autism in understanding the emotional state of their communication partner [14].

However, the ability to *generate* emotionally intelligent feedback is equally important for an immersive user experience. In this research, our focus is on affective *visual-haptic* feedback. In particular, we are interested in understanding how affective cues presented in the haptic modality interact with the affective cues that visuals convey. This knowledge could be used to design accompanying haptic stimuli that enhance or tone down the emotions conveyed by visuals. For example, one could enhance the thrill conveyed by the visuals in a game, or provide a calming effect in a news app when the article contains unpleasant and shocking images.

CHI 2015, April 18 - 23 2015, Seoul, Republic of Korea.

ACM 978-1-4503-3145-6/15/04...$15.00
http://dx.doi.org/10.1145/2702123.2702288

Multisensory Integration
Human interaction with the real world is inherently multimodal. We seamlessly integrate information from multiple input channels to form a unified coherent percept. In Cognitive Science, multi-sensory integration is investigated using the conflict paradigm [9], where incongruent cues about one particular aspect of the environment are presented in two modalities. Some of the classic experiments include the Ventriloquist effect [1], which shows that the spatial location of auditory stimuli is influenced by the synchronous visual stimuli. Participants hear flashes of sound bursts and see flashes of light, synchronous with the sound bursts, originating from spatially distinct sources. They are asked to point towards the source of the sound bursts while ignoring the light flashes. Results show that pointing typically shifts towards the location of light flashes.

Similarly, the Rubber-hand illusion [4, 23] illustrates how the tactile perception can be influenced by visual input. Participants watch a rubber hand being stroked, while their actual hand, hidden from their view, is also stroked synchronously. Most participants report feeling sensations on the rubber hand. This illusion arises because the human brain mislocalizes the tactile percept based on the visual percept.

The parchment skin illusion [20] shows the interaction between audio and tactile stimuli. Participants are asked to rub their palms. This sound is recorded and modified by accentuating frequencies above 2KHz and played back to the participants through headphones, who report that their skin is very dry like a parchment paper.

When two different cues are presented in two modalities, the cue presented in one modality could enrich or inhibit the cue presented in the other modality, or they could interact to produce a completely novel percept. It has been hypothesized that humans tend to act as maximum-likelihood integrators and combine information from multiple sensory modalities in a statistically optimal fashion [15].

Multimodal Affect Integration

Similar results have been reported when participants integrate emotional cues from multiple modalities. For example, the Emotional McGurk Effect [10] illustrates how humans integrate facial expressions and prosody cues to perceive affect. Participants are provided with static faces exhibiting multiple emotions along with speech sounds varying in prosody conveying different emotions. Results on emotion identification show sometimes a visual bias, sometimes an auditory bias, and sometimes a new, emergent emotion [8].

Multimodal feedback

Multimodal interfaces have been inspired by the vision that an interface that affords multimodal input and output would allow intuitive real-world-like interactions [24]. Such interfaces are particularly well suited for mobile devices where a small screen size and the operating conditions (e.g. in buses/trains, while driving) render unimodal visual interaction insufficient. For instance, Hoggan et al [18] investigated the accuracy of text entry with fingers in a mobile device with and without haptic feedback. They found that the addition of haptic feedback improved accuracy. A multimodal interface has to combine inputs from multiple modalities (e.g. gaze, speech, touch input, mouse input) to extract information, and encode information into multiple modalities (e.g., visual, auditory, haptic) to provide feedback to users. Research in multimodal feedback has considered how to optimally present the same cues redundantly in multiple modalities to enhance reliability, and how to present different cues in different modalities to enhance the amount of information transferred.

Some researchers have studied how best to design multimodal feedback. Brewster et al [19] investigated the use of audio-tactile icons to represent information. They presented participants with auditory, tactile and audio-tactile icons to convey multiple types of information - confirmations, errors, warnings and progress updates. The auditory and haptic icons were generated by varying rhythm, texture, spatial location, duration and tempo. Participants preferred the combined audio-tactile icons in general, and ranked them especially higher for presentation of errors and warning information. Burke et al [7] conducted a meta-analysis of 43 studies comparing visual-haptic and visual-auditory to visual-feedback alone. Their results showed that multimodal feedback reduces reaction time, and improves performance compared to unimodal feedback. They also found that visual-auditory feedback was more effective when a single task was being performed and visual-tactile feedback was more effective in multitasking conditions.

Multimodal Affective Feedback

Research on how best to design multimodal affective feedback has been relatively sparse. Bonnet et al [3] studied the role of haptic feedback in recognizing the emotions in facial expressions. Participants were asked to recognize facial expressions of a virtual character. Haptic feedback was presented using a haptic arm. In the presence of haptic feedback, participants were able to better recognize anger, disgust, pride, love and envy. However, the presence of haptic feedback negatively affected the identification of surprise, sympathy, interest and fascination. Facial expression is just one class of images that we encounter, but most research investigating visual-haptic affect has concentrated on this class [2, 3].

In our research, we investigated a more general problem of how the presence of an emotion-eliciting haptic stimulus affects the perception of arousal and valence of a visual stimulus. We began by constructing a database of affective visual and haptic stimuli with known affective responses. Then we constructed a multimodal affective visual-haptic stimuli set, in which both the congruent and the conflicting emotional cues were presented in the visual and haptic modalities. Participants were asked to provide valence and arousal ratings for the visual-haptic stimuli. Analysis of these ratings provided clues on how these two modalities interact in the affective dimension. Following this, we conducted another experiment to investigate how the haptic-stimuli parameters, namely intensity, frequency, waveform and rhythm, affect the arousal of the multimodal visual-haptic stimuli.

EXPERIMENT I - DATASET CONSTRUCTION

The goal of this experiment was to construct affective visual and haptic datasets that could be used further in our study. We used the circumplex model [25], in which affective experiences are characterized in a two-dimensional space parametrized by valence (how pleasant or unpleasant is the experience) and arousal (how exciting or calming is the experience). For instance, being relaxed would be a pleasant and calming experience (High Valence, Low Arousal) while being bored would be an unpleasant and calming experience (Low Valence, Low Arousal).

Experiment I(a) : Affective Visual Dataset

The International Affective Picture System (IAPS) [21] is a well-cited dataset containing 1182 images with associated valence and arousal ratings. We chose a representative sample of 120 images from IAPS containing all the categories (object, people, scene and animals) and emotion ratings uniformly distributed over the original dataset ($\chi^2 = 12.06, p < 0.05$).

The experiments described in this paper were conducted with Indian population. Cultural differences in emotion perception has long been acknowledged in emotion literature [21]. However, the IAPS dataset has not been explicitly evaluated on Indian participants. Hence we conducted a pilot study to verify if the IAPS ratings reported in literature were reproducible with our set of participants.

Participants

Eight participants (four male and four female) in the age group of 18 to 35 years took part in this study.

Procedure

Each participant was presented with 12 images chosen from the representative subset of IAPS dataset. At the start of the experiment, participants were explained the concepts of valence and arousal. Each image was then presented for 6 seconds. Participants were given 10 seconds to provide valence and arousal ratings on a 9-point Self-Assessment Manikin

(SAM) [5] scale. The SAM scale (Fig. 1) is a Likert scale designed specifically for obtaining valence and arousal ratings. A gap of 4 seconds was provided between successive images, and a blank screen was presented during this interval.

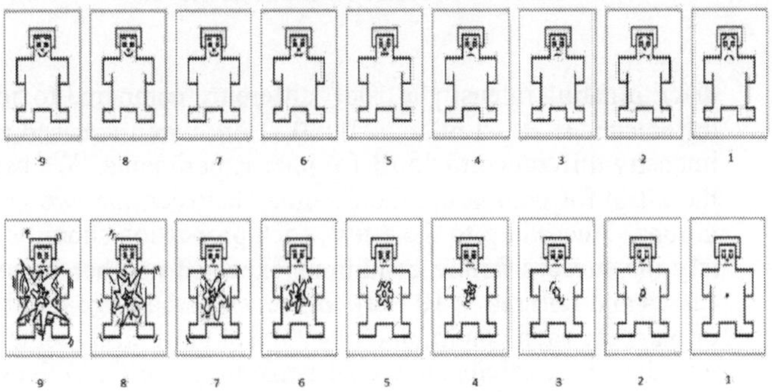

Figure 1: Valence - Arousal SAM Scale.

Results

We computed the mean valence and arousal ratings for each image and compared them with the ratings reported in literature [21]. We found that there was no statistically significant difference between the two ratings for valence ($t = 0.05, p = 0.95$) or arousal ($t = 0.75, p = 0.45$). This confirms that the IAPS dataset is appropriate for use with our target population.

Experiment I(b): Affective Haptic Dataset

The term haptic feedback refers to a wide variety of touch-related sensations. The major types used in the design of haptic interfaces include the kinesthetic feedback used in telerobotics and the vibrotactile stimulations provided by the contemporary mobile phones. The kind of vibrations generated by mobile devices work by stimulating mechanoreceptors of the skin, and are of interest in our research. In the rest of this paper, we use the term *haptic* to refer to these tactile-mechanical sensations.

Unlike the visual domain, there are no standardized haptic datasets available. The only work that addresses this issue explores how various haptic rhythms [26] affect the emotional response of users. Hence, we followed the steps outlined below to construct a haptic dataset.

1. Based on the existing literature, we identified four dimensions of haptic stimuli, and varied them systematically to construct a haptic dataset.
2. We refined this dataset by conducting perceptual discrimination experiments to obtain a final dataset.
3. We obtained affective ratings from participants for the stimuli in this dataset through a grouping experiment. These ratings were used in subsequent experiments.

These three steps are explained in more detail below.

ViviTouch Haptic Actuator

In our studies, we used the ViviTouch haptic actuator from Artificial Muscle Inc. The device is illustrated in Fig. 2a. It

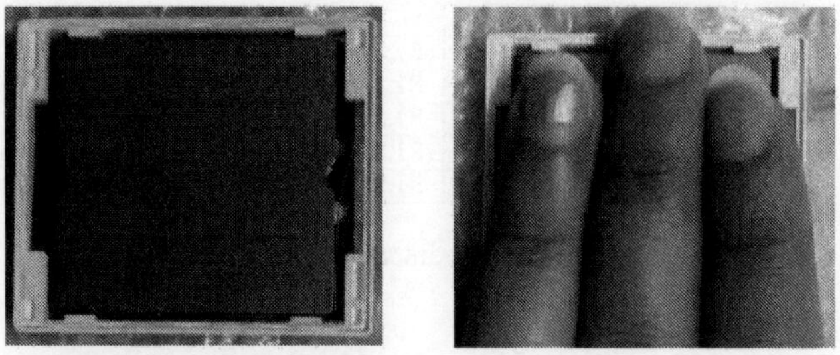

(a) Vivitouch™ haptic actuator. (b) Participant touching the device.

Figure 2: Experiment setup showing Haptic Actuator.

can output frequencies from DC to 200 Hz. The bandwidth of this device was a critical factor that governed the design of our haptic dataset.

Step 1 - Dimensions and choice of parameters

Research on human haptic perception has established six dimensions along which vibrotactile stimuli can be varied: Intensity, Frequency, Waveform, Duration, Rhythm and Spatial Location [16, 6, 17]. Intensity refers to the magnitude of the vibration, which is defined as the square of its amplitude. Intensity is expressed in sensation levels (SL), which is the amplitude level relative to the threshold of detection. A 55 dB sensation level is considered painful by most users [16]. Untrained users can discriminate around 15 levels of intensity, but can absolutely identify only three levels in the perceivable range. A difference threshold of upto 2.5 dB has been reported in the literature. In our initial dataset design, to be conservative, we chose three intensity levels at 5 dB difference: 20 dB, 25 dB and 30 dB SL .

Frequency refers to the rate of vibration. The usable range of frequency for human skin is from 10 to 400 Hz: the maximum sensitivity is between 200 Hz to 300 Hz peaking at about 250 Hz. Users can identify three to five different frequency levels [27]. However, the device we used had a maximum output frequency of 200 Hz. We had two choices to sample the frequency - sample close to the 200 Hz range where the perceptual sensitivity is highest or sample uniformly across the spectrum. We chose the second sampling option to obtain a more expressive dataset, and used four frequency levels of 55Hz, 95 Hz, 135 Hz, and 175 Hz.

The waveform of a haptic signal is perceived as its texture. Sine waves are perceived as having a smooth texture, while pulse is perceived as having a rough structure [16, 6]. We chose four waveform types - sine, sawtooth, pulse and noise. We expected that users would perceive sine as the smoothest and noise as the roughest.

Rhythms are constructed by on-off bursts or notes. It has been found that participants tend to identify rhythms mostly by note length and unevenness [28]. It can be seen that rhythm is the parameter that offers the most flexibility. The rhythm set we used in our experiment, shown in Fig. 3, is inspired by the one used by Seifi et al. [26]. The grey block indicates an *on* burst and the white block indicates an *off* burst. Each on or off burst is 62.5 ms long. A rhythm bar has eight such bursts

Type	Parameter Varied	Sample stimuli pair	
Type I	Rhythm	R1,Sine,20dB,55Hz	R6,Sine,20dB,55Hz
Type II	Waveform	R1,Sine,20dB,55Hz	R1,Pulse,20dB,55Hz
Type III	Intensity	R1,Sine,20dB,55Hz	R1,Sine,25dB,55Hz
Type IV	Frequency	R1,Sine,20dB,55Hz	R1,Sine,20dB,175Hz
Type V	None	R1,Sine,20dB,55Hz	R1,Sine,20dB,55Hz

Table 1: Stimuli for discrimination experiment.

and is 500 ms long. Haptic stimuli of two-seconds duration were constructed by repeating a rhythm bar four times.

Spatial location refers to the location of the body that is stimulated. The hand offers the best spatial resolution, while the abdomen has very poor resolution. In our experiments, participants were asked to place their hand on the haptic actuator as shown in Fig. 2b. A potentially useful location to explore is the wrist (for a device like the smart-watch), but we left this for future research.

Step 2 - Discrimination experiments

Though we chose values for each parameter based on the results from existing literature, different haptic actuators can lead to different results. Hence, we conducted an experiment to identify if participants could perceive the stimuli in this haptic dataset with the ViviTouch haptic actuator. Our evaluation criteria was that all the haptic-dataset stimuli should be perceptually discriminable. This was to ensure that we could obtain a dataset without any redundant stimuli that would be perceived similar.

Participants

Eleven participants (seven male and four female) in the age group of 18 to 30 years participated in this experiment.

Procedure

We created five types of paired stimuli from the haptic dataset. Within each type, one parameter of the haptic stimuli was varied between the two stimuli constituting a pair, while the other parameters were held constant. For instance, in Type I, rhythm was varied, while the other parameters were held constant. In Type V, both the stimuli in a pair were identical, so that we could assess the reliability of responses from the participants. All the types are illustrated in Table 1. A total of 110 pairs of stimuli were used.

The two stimuli in a pair were presented sequentially separated by an interval of 500ms. The presentation order was randomized. Participants were asked to make a decision whether the two stimuli in a pair were similar or different. Participants completed the task in two sessions, each lasting 15 to 20 minutes, with a break of five minutes in between.

Results

A reliability factor was calculated for each participant as the accuracy obtained for Type V (identical pair) stimuli. This was greater than 85% ($Mean(SD)$: 95(5.57)) for all the participants, ensuring that they all were able to judge the haptic stimuli.

The overall accuracy obtained when discriminating for intensity was low (18%). Participants were significantly better at discriminating intensity at 10dB difference compared to 5dB difference ($z = -1.86, p = 0.06$). Hence we increased the intensity difference to 15dB for later experiments. We used the z-test for comparing the accuracy between the two conditions. According to the z-test, each proportion should satisfy the success-failure condition: expected number of successes and failures > 10 [12]. Since we had a large number of pairs for each condition ($n > 25$) and our null-hypothesis was that the participants would perform at the chance level ($accuracy = 50\%$), each proportion should independently satisfy this condition, which they did in our case.

All participants reported difficulty perceiving the noise waveform: the discrimination accuracy for these stimuli pairs was 9%. Hence we removed the noise stimuli from the dataset and used only the sine, sawtooth and pulse waveforms for later experiments. At 175hz, the discrimination accuracy for all the waveforms was significantly lower ($z = -3.6, p < 0.01$) compared to other frequencies. Hence, we removed this frequency level and used three evenly-spaced frequency levels: 55hz, 110hz and 165hz.

We conducted a follow-up study using the same procedure as above with five participants (Age: 22 to 32 years) with the modified parameters. Participants were able to discriminate between all stimuli pairs, with 100% accuracy. The final haptic dataset consisted of 10*3*3*2 = 180 stimuli files and is shown in Table 2.

Parameter	Number of Levels (Values)
Rhythm	10 (Fig.3)
Waveform	3 (Sine, Saw-tooth and Pulse)
Frequency	3 (55Hz, 110Hz and 165Hz)
Intensity	2 (20dB SL and 35dB SL)

Table 2: Modified Parameter Levels.

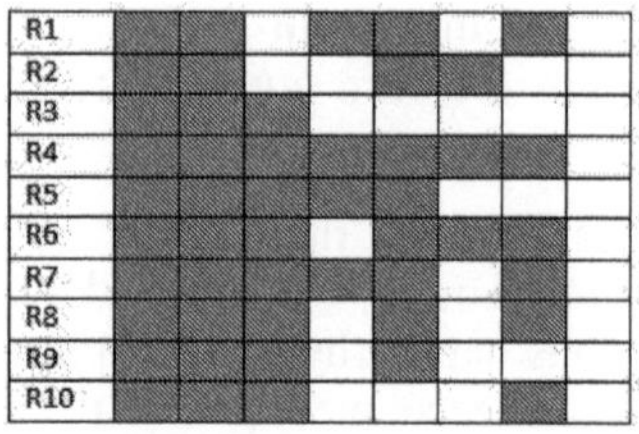

Figure 3: Rhythm Set. Grey blocks are *on* bursts and white blocks are *off* bursts.

Step 3 - Obtaining affective Ratings for Haptic Dataset

Our next goal was to obtain affective ratings for all the stimuli in the haptic dataset. We conducted a pilot study in which we asked two participants to rate the haptic stimuli on a nine-point SAM scale. The participants reported that this scale was too fine-grained, which was attributed to the abstract nature of the haptic stimuli. Hence we used a coarser 3x3 scale, and asked the participants to group the haptic stimuli into nine groups based on the emotion elicited (Fig. 4). A similar procedure has been used in literature for obtaining affective ratings for haptic stimuli [26].

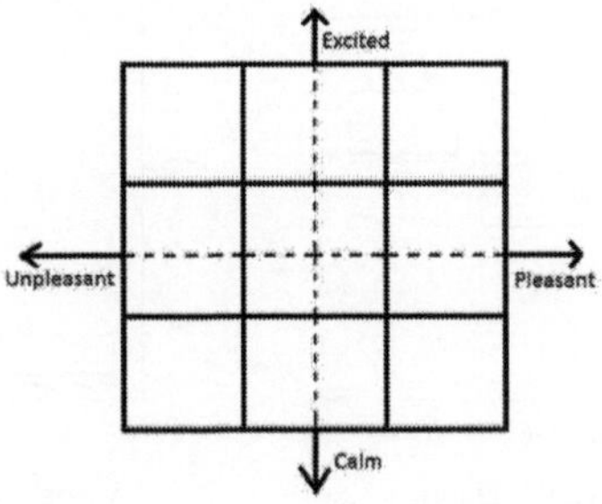

Figure 4: Participants had to group the haptic stimuli into one of these nine valence-arousal groups.

Participants
Sixteen participants (nine male and seven female) in the age group of 18 to 35 years took part in this study.

Procedure
We used the 180-stimuli haptic dataset that was created as explained above. Participants were presented with the screen shown in Fig. 5. The bottom panel had numbered buttons. Selecting a button caused the haptic actuator to be activated by the corresponding stimulus. Participants could drag the numbered button to any grey area to categorize the presented stimulus according to the emotion they felt. Participants could play the haptic stimulus as often as they wanted. They could also change the group of a stimulus by dragging the corresponding button from one grey area to another. Once all the stimuli on the screen were categorized, participants could obtain the next set of stimuli by clicking on 'Next' . The task was finished once all the stimuli were grouped, and the participant was satisfied with her or his grouping: the participant could then press 'Done' on the last screen. This task was conducted in two sessions, each lasting 55 minutes, and a break of five minutes was given in between. The presentation order was randomized for each participant.

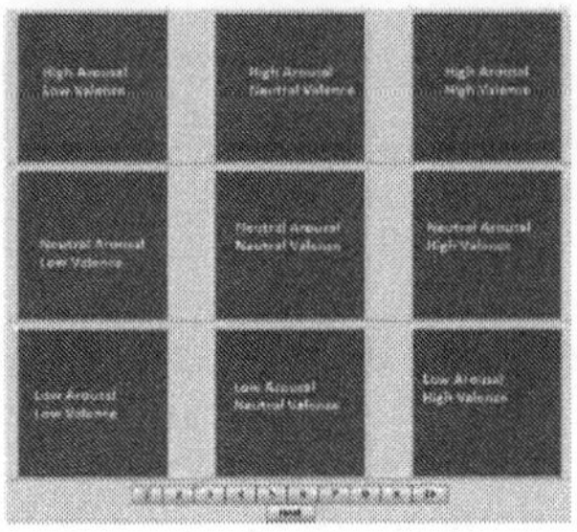

Figure 5: Interface for obtaining affective ratings for Haptic Dataset. Selecting a numbered button in the lower panel generated the haptic stimuli. Participants had to drag this to one of the nine affective groups to classify it.

Results - Factors affecting ratings
Since we used a within-subjects design to obtain the ratings, we used the Friedman test to analyze the effects of the haptic dimensions on haptic ratings. Given the non-normal nature of our ranking results, we used a Wilcoxon signed-rank test with Bonferroni correction for the posthoc analysis.

Intensity had a significant effect on arousal ($Q = 101.9, p < 0.001$) and valence ($Q = 95.8, p < 0.001$). Arousal ratings for 35dB stimuli were significantly higher than those for 20dB stimuli. However, valence ratings for 20dB stimuli were higher than those for 20dB stimuli.

Frequency had no significant effect on arousal ($Q = 3.62, p = 0.16$) but a significant effect on valence ($Q = 28.9, p < 0.001$). The valence ratings obtained for 55Hz stimuli were significantly lower than the valence ratings obtained for 165Hz.

Waveform had a significant effect on both valence ($Q = 15.2, p < 0.001$) and arousal ($Q = 8.4, p = 0.01$). The posthoc analysis revealed that the arousal ratings obtained for sine and sawtooth were significantly lower than pulse, but the corresponding valence ratings were significantly higher than pulse. There was no significant effect of rhythm on valence ($Q = 2.55, p = 0.97$) or arousal ($Q = 3.63, p = 0.163$).

EXPERIMENT II: HIGH-LEVEL EXPLORATION OF VISUAL-HAPTIC INTERACTION

The goal of this experiment was to understand how emotions elicited in visual and haptic modalities interact. We considered this as *high-level* exploration as we did not consider the low-level features of haptic stimuli. As mentioned above, the existing literature provides strong evidence for an interaction between visual and haptic modalities. So we hypothesized that there would be an interaction in the affective cues presented using these modalities as well. To capture this, we posited the null hypothesis that the visual-haptic ratings will not be different from either the visual or the haptic ratings (already known in our datasets) alone.

Participants
Nineteen participants (eleven male and eight female), aged between 18 and 52 years took part in this experiment.

Stimuli
All the affective stimuli (visual and haptic) were chosen from the datasets created in Experiment I. Stimuli with valence (arousal) ratings less than 4.5 were considered as having low valence (arousal). Ratings between 4.5 to 5.5 were considered neutral and stimuli with ratings higher than 5.5 were considered as having high valence (arousal).

The visual and haptic stimuli were paired under both conflicting and supporting conditions. In the supporting condition, the visual and haptic stimuli conveyed congruent affective information. In the conflicting condition, the visual and haptic stimuli conveyed incongruent affective information. This is illustrated in Table 3. If valence was the dimension of interest in a given pair, then arousal was maintained as neutral, and vice-versa. In all, 40 pairs of visual-haptic pairs were used.

Procedure
Each of the 40 visual-haptic stimuli pairs was presented to the participants for six seconds (the visual and haptic stimuli were presented simultaneously). The participants were then asked to rate the valence and arousal for the visual-haptic

Condition	Visual Stimuli	Haptic Stimuli	Number
Supporting	Low Valence	Low Valence	5
	High Valence	High Valence	5
	Low Arousal	Low Arousal	5
	High Arousal	High Arousal	5
Conflicting	Low Valence	High Valence	5
	High Valence	Low Valence	5
	Low Arousal	High Arousal	5
	High Arousal	Low Arousal	5

Table 3: Visual-Haptic Stimuli Pair Design.

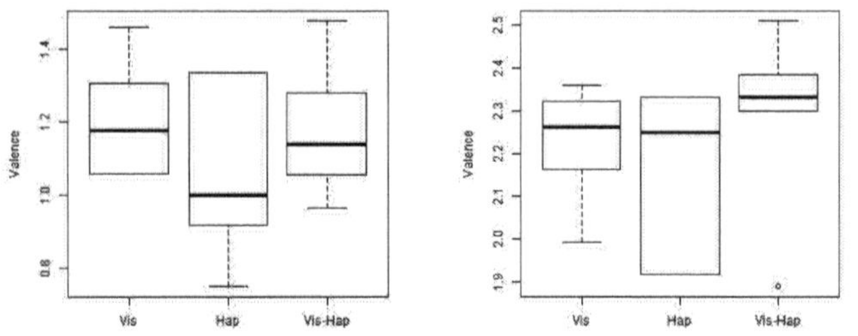

(a) Visual : Low ; Haptic - Low (b) Visual : High ; Haptic - High

Figure 6: Supporting Valence. No significant difference between Visual-only and Visual-Haptic or Haptic-only and Visual-Haptic valence.

stimulus on a SAM scale. The presentation order was randomized and counter-balanced. Participants completed the task in two sessions, each lasting 15 minutes, with a break of five minutes in between.

Results

We compared the ratings obtained for the visual, haptic and visual-haptic conditions. The visual and haptic ratings were obtained from the respective datasets (Experiment I) and the visual-haptic ratings were provided by the participants in this experiment (Experiment II). Since different sets of participants provided ratings for each of these conditions, we used the non-parametric Mann-Whitney test which compares independent groups. Also, to visualize the haptic and visual ratings on a similar scale, the visual and visual-haptic ratings were mapped to a three-point scale. Ratings closer to 1 represent low valence/arousal and ratings closer to 3 represent high valence/arousal.

Supporting Case - Valence

When both the visual and haptic valence were low, we did not find any significant difference between the valence ratings for the combined visual-haptic stimuli and the valence ratings for the visual stimuli ($U = 10, z = 0.4178, p = 0.67$) or the haptic stimuli ($U = 9, z = -0.62, p = 0.52$). Similarly, when both the visual and haptic valence were high, there was no statistically significant differences between the visual and visual-haptic ($U = 8, z = -0.83, p = 0.40$) and between the haptic and visual - haptic conditions ($U = 8, z = -0.83, p = 0.40$). Both these cases are illustrated in Fig. 6.

Supporting Case - Arousal

When the arousal of the visual and haptic stimuli were both low, there was no significant difference between the arousal ratings obtained for haptic and visual-haptic stimuli ($U = 6.5, z = -1.14, p = 0.25$). But the arousal difference between the visual and visual-haptic stimuli was significant ($U = 1, z = -2.29, p = 0.021$). Similar effect was observed when the arousal of visual and haptic stimuli was high. There was no significant difference between the haptic and visual-haptic ($U = 9, z = -0.62, p = 0.52$), but there was a significant difference between the visual and visual-haptic stimuli ($U = 0, z = -2.50, p = 0.012$). These cases are illustrated in Fig. 7.

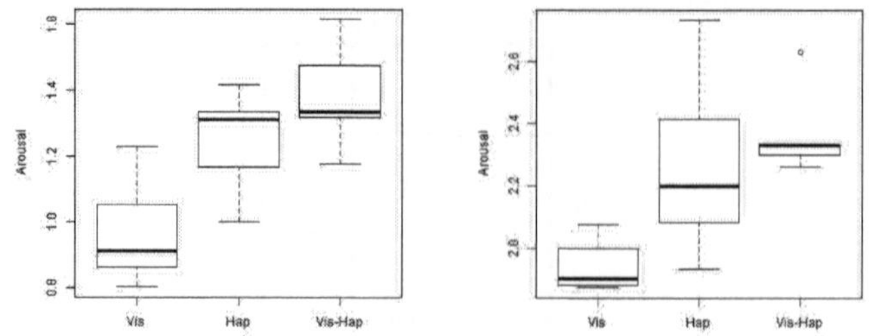

(a) Visual : Low ; Haptic - Low (b) Visual : High ; Haptic - High.

Figure 7: Supporting Arousal. Visual-Haptic arousal was significantly higher than visual-only arousal.

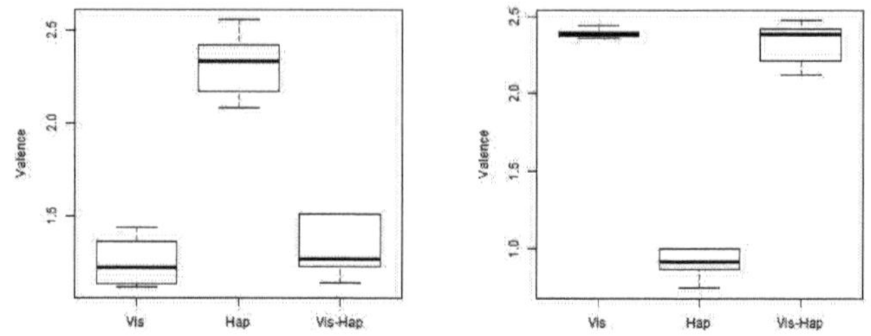

(a) Visual - Low ; Haptic - High (b) Visual - High ; Haptic - Low.

Figure 8: Conflicting Valence : Visual-Haptic valence was not statistically different from visual-only valence.

Conflicting Case - Valence

We did not find any significant differences between the valence ratings obtained for visual stimuli and visual-haptic stimuli when the visual stimuli was of low valence ($U = 7, z = -1.044, p = 0.3$) or high valence ($U = 12, z = 0, p = 1$). But we found significant differences between the ratings obtained for haptic stimuli and visual-haptic stimuli when the haptic stimuli was of low valence ($U = 0, z = -2.5, p = 0.012$) or of high valence ($U = 0, z = 2.5, p = 0.012$). This showed that the valence ratings obtained for visual-haptic stimuli resemble closely the valence ratings of visual stimuli and are very different from the valence ratings of the haptic stimuli. This is illustrated in Fig. 8.

Conflicting Case - Arousal

In both the conflicting cases for arousal, we found that the arousal ratings obtained for the visual-haptic stimuli were higher than the arousal ratings of the visual stimuli. When low-arousal visual stimuli and high-arousal haptic stimuli were combined, the arousal ratings of the visual-haptic stimuli were significantly higher than those of the visual stim-

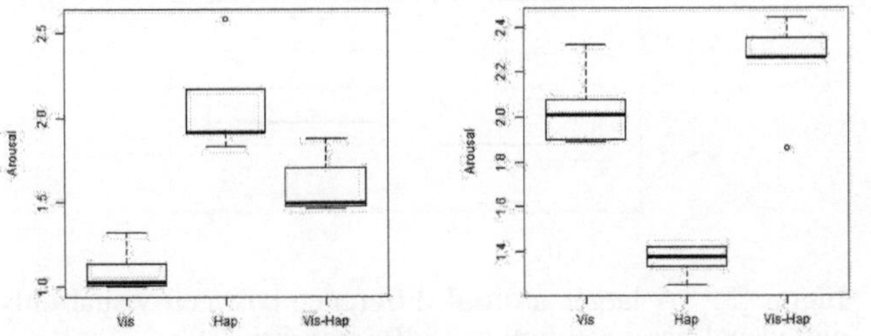

(a) Visual : Low ; Haptic - High. (b) Visual : High ; Haptic - Low.

Figure 9: Conflicting Arousal. Visual-Haptic arousal was significantly higher than visual-only arousal.

uli ($U = 0, z = -2.5, p = 0.012$) and significantly lower than the arousal ratings of the haptic stimuli ($U = 1, z = 2.29, p = 0.02$). When high-arousal visual stimuli was combined with low-arousal haptic stimuli, the arousal ratings of the visual-haptic stimuli were significantly higher than those of the haptic stimuli ($U = 0, z = -2.5, p = 0.012$) but not significantly different than those of the visual stimuli ($U = 1, z = -2.29, p = 0.021$). These results are illustrated in Fig. 9.

Summary

In the supporting-valence condition, there was no significant difference between the valence ratings obtained for multimodal visual-haptic stimuli and unimodal visual or unimodal haptic stimuli. In the conflicting-valence condition, the valence ratings of the visual-haptic stimuli were similar to those of the visual stimuli. In both the supporting and the conflicting conditions for arousal, the arousal ratings of the multimodal visual-haptic stimuli were higher than those of the unimodal visual stimuli. In other words, simultaneous presence of haptic stimuli increases the arousal of the visual stimuli. It is noteworthy that this increase in arousal is observed even when the arousal of the visual stimuli is high and that of the haptic stimuli is low.

EXPERIMENT III: ROLE OF LOW-LEVEL HAPTIC FEATURES ON VISUAL-HAPTIC AROUSAL

Experiment II showed that though the valence of a visual-haptic stimulus is dominated by its visual aspect, its arousal is significantly affected by the haptic component. This suggests that adding an appropriate haptic stimulus to a give visual stimulus would allow us to modulate the arousal rating of the combined visual-haptic stimulus. In order to facilitate such modulation, it is necessary to understand in more depth how the low-level features of haptic stimuli — intensity, frequency, waveform and rhythm — affect the arousal of visual-haptic stimuli. Recall that our study in Experiment 1(b) to create an affective haptic dataset indicated that the valence and arousal ratings of a haptic stimulus are affected by its low-level features. Hence, we expected that these features would contribute to the arousal of the visual-haptic pair as well. So we designed a follow-up experiment to explore this affect: the null hypothesis was that any change in the haptic feature values (intensity, frequency, waveform, rhythm) will not result in any change in the arousal-difference between visual and visual-haptic ratings: e.g. arousal difference with 20dB haptic stimuli will be same as arousal difference with 35dB haptic stimuli.

Participants

Twenty-four participants (twelve male and twelve female), aged between 18 and 35 years took part in this experiment.

Stimuli

We chose three groups (VisL, VisN, VisH) of stimuli from the IAPS dataset, each group having 54 images with low, neutral or high arousal ratings, respectively. The valence ratings were kept close to neutral (≈ 5). This is shown in Table 4.

Group	No. of Images	Valence Ratings	Arousal Ratings
VisL	54	≈ 5	Low (< 4.5)
VisN	54	≈ 5	Medium ($4.5 - 5.5$)
VisH	54	≈ 5	High (> 5.5)

Table 4: Visual Stimuli Used.

We chose 108 haptic stimuli from the affective haptic dataset we had created. These stimuli were classified into two groups (HapL, HapH) of 54 stimuli each. The stimuli in HapL had 20dB SL intensity and HapH had 35dB SL intensity. The other parameters were similar for both the groups. We used six rhythms (R1, R3, R4, R6, R8, R10), three frequencies (55Hz, 110Hz, 165Hz) and three waveforms (Sine, Sawtooth, Pulse). The distribution of these parameters is illustrated in Table 5.

Rhythm	Frequency	Waveform
R1, R3, R4, R6, R8, R10	55 Hz	
R1, R3, R4, R6, R8, R10	110 Hz	Sine
R1, R3, R4, R6, R8, R10	165 Hz	
R1, R3, R4, R6, R8, R10	55 Hz	
R1, R3, R4, R6, R8, R10	110 Hz	Sawtooth
R1, R3, R4, R6, R8, R10	165 Hz	
R1, R3, R4, R6, R8, R10	55 Hz	
R1, R3, R4, R6, R8, R10	110 Hz	Pulse
R1, R3, R4, R6, R8, R10	175 Hz	

Table 5: Haptic Stimuli for Exp. III. These 54 stimuli were presented with 20dB intensity for HapL and with 35dB intensity for HapH.

For generating multimodal visual-haptic stimuli, we paired the visual and haptic stimuli as shown in Table 6. In all, 324 visual-haptic stimuli were created.

Participant Group	Visual Group	Haptic Group	No. of Pairs
Group A	VisL	HapL	54
Group A	VisN	HapL	54
Group A	VisH	HapL	54
Group B	VisL	HapH	54
Group B	VisN	HapH	54
Group B	VisH	HapH	54

Table 6: Visual Haptic Pairing. VisL, VisN, VisH has low, neutral and high arousal respectively. HapL had intensity of 20dB and HapH had intensity of 35dB.

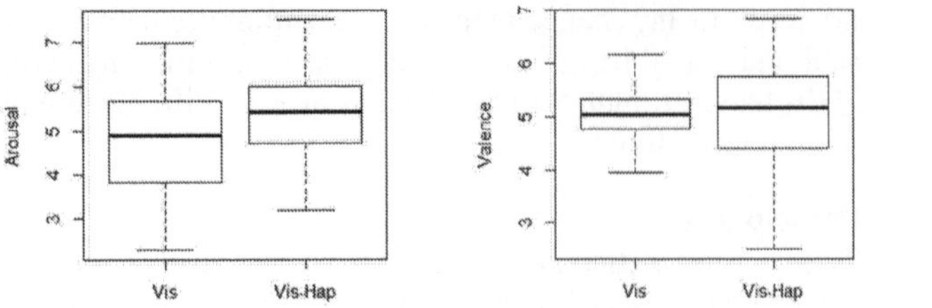

(a) Arousal ratings were significantly higher for visual-haptic stimuli compared to visual-only stimuli.

(b) No significant difference in valence ratings between visual-only and visual-haptic stimuli.

Figure 10: Arousal and Valence in Low-Level Experiment.

Procedure

The participants were randomly assigned into two groups - Group A and Group B. Each group had twelve participants (six male and six female). Group A and Group B were presented with the visual-haptic stimuli created with HapL and HapH groups respectively as illustrated in Table 6. Participants were presented with the visual, haptic and visual-haptic stimuli and asked to provide valence and arousal ratings on the SAM scale. Participants completed the task in three sessions, each lasting about 35 minutes, with two breaks (two minutes each) in between the sessions. The presentation order was randomized within each session.

Results

We conducted a Wilcoxon signed rank test to compare the valence and arousal ratings for the visual-only and visual-haptic group. There was a statistically significant difference in the arousal ratings obtained for visual-haptic and visual stimuli ($p < 0.001$) but there was no significant difference in the valence ratings ($p = 0.151$). These results were consistent with those from Experiment II. This is illustrated in Figs. 10a and 10b.

Factors affecting arousal difference

We analyzed the difference in arousal ratings obtained for the multimodal visual-haptic stimuli and the unimodal visual stimuli to find out which of the haptic parameters have the most impact on this difference. Our response variable was ordinal and we needed to analyze the effect of the haptic parameters and their interactions on the response variable. Since commonly used nonparametric statistics like Kruskal-Wallis and Friedman tests do not allow for studying interaction effects, we used the Aligned Rank Transform (ART)[29]. ART aligns and averages ranks and after this preprocessing, common ANOVA procedures and posthoc analysis can be applied to the processed data.

Intensity

Intensity had a significant effect on the arousal difference: the difference obtained at 35 dB was significantly higher than the difference obtained at 20 dB ($F = 27.47, p < 0.001$). This is illustrated in Fig. 11. The highest arousal difference was obtained for the low-arousal images as shown in Fig. 12. Hence, we included the arousal category of the image also as a factor in further analysis.

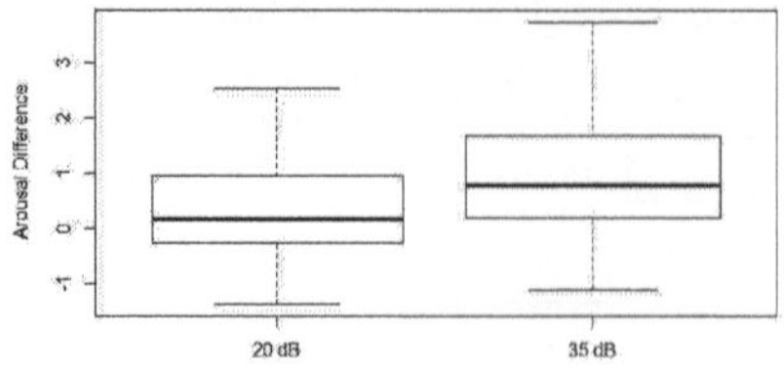

Figure 11: A larger arousal difference between visual-only and visual-haptic stimuli at 35dB intensity,.

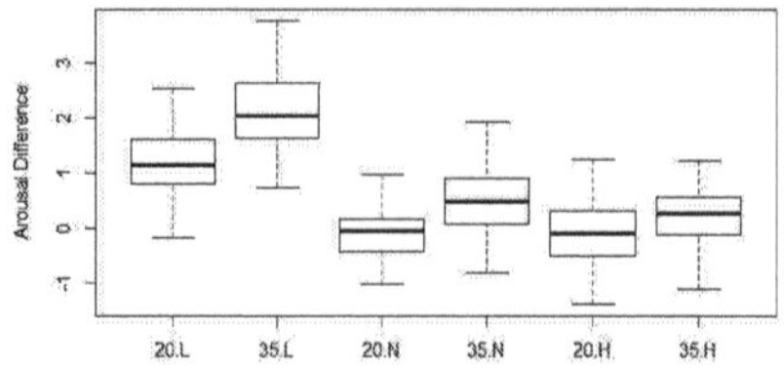

Figure 12: The largest difference between visual-only and visual-haptic arousal was observed for low-arousal images.

Frequency

Frequency had no significant main effect on the arousal difference ($F = 0.89, p = 0.63$). There was a statistical trend to have a significant interaction between intensity and frequency ($F = 3.077, p = 0.08$). There was also a significant interaction between frequency and arousal category ($F = 4.23, p < 0.05$). Posthoc analysis using Tukey's test showed that frequency contributed to increase in arousal difference in low-arousal images most (Fig. 13). There was also a significant interaction effect between frequency, intensity and category ($F = 6.4, p < 0.01$). Posthoc analysis revealed that for low-arousal images at 20dB intensity, there was a trend for arousal increase to be significantly higher at 55 Hz compared to at 110 Hz ($p = 0.08$) or at 165 Hz ($p = 0.071$). At high intensity, arousal increase at 110 Hz ($p < 0.05$) and at 165 Hz ($p < 0.05$) was significantly higher than at 55 Hz.

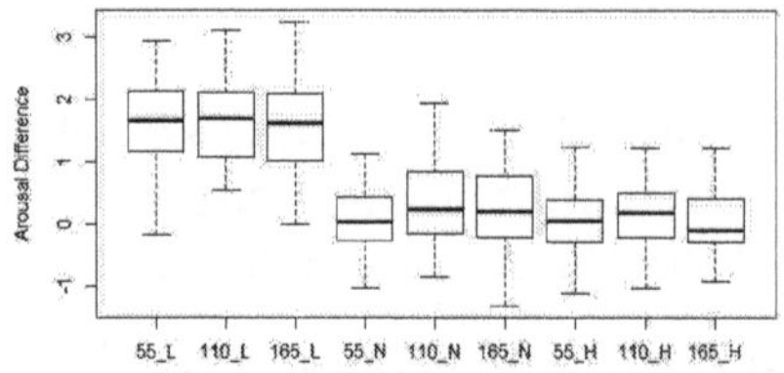

Figure 13: Frequency contributed to increase in arousal difference in low-arousal images most.

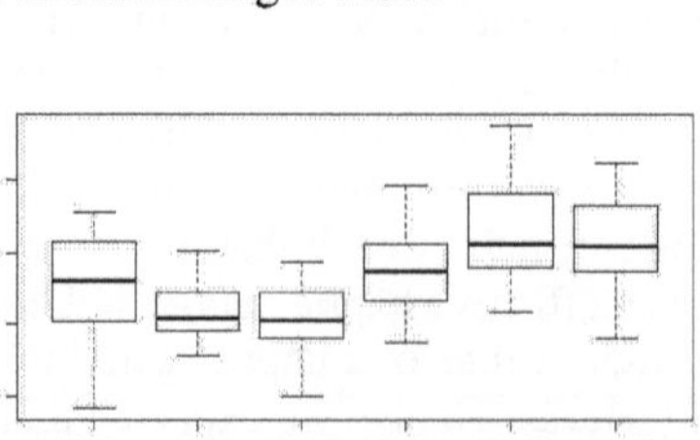

Figure 14: Significant interaction was observed between intensity and frequency.

Waveform

Waveform had no significant main effect on the arousal difference ($F = 1.663, p = 0.4$). Visual analysis showed that at high intensity, the arousal difference contributed by the pulse waveform was marginally higher than that for the sine and sawtooth waveforms (Fig. 15). However, this interaction effect was not statistically significant ($F = 1.792, p = 0.168$).

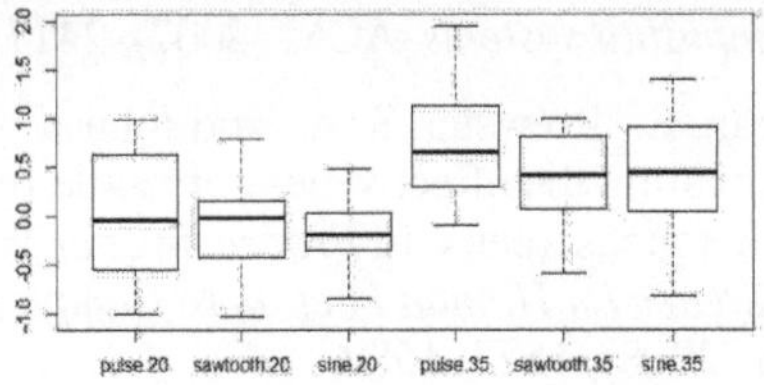

Figure 15: Waveform was not a significant predictor of arousal difference between visual and visual-haptic stimuli.

Rhythm

Rhythm also had no significant effect on the arousal difference ($F = 4.08, p = 0.53$) as illustrated in Fig.16. There were no significant interaction effects between rhythm and intensity ($F = 1.775, p = 0.171$) or among rhythm, intensity and category ($F = 1.391, p = 0.25$).

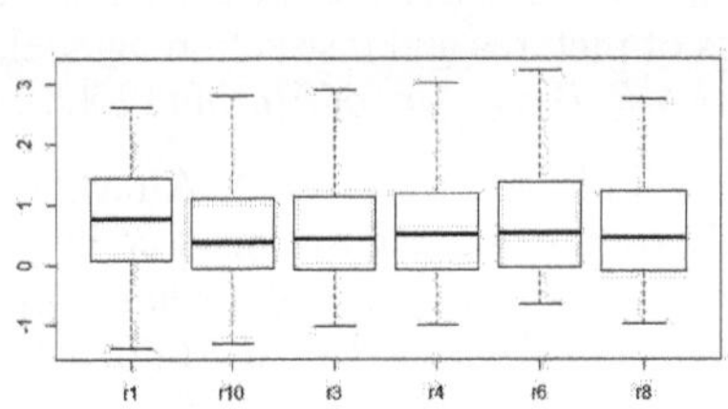

Figure 16: Rhythm was not a significant predictor of arousal difference between visual-only and visual-haptic stimuli.

GUIDELINES

Summarizing the results from our experiments, we provide a few guidelines on how affective cues in visual and haptic modalities interact and how the features of the haptic stimuli contribute to this interaction.

1. The valence rating for a visual-haptic stimulus is dominated by the valence rating of its visual component: e.g. combining a low-valence visual stimulus with a high-valence haptic stimulus yields a low-valence visual-haptic stimulus.

2. Addition of haptic stimulus generally increases the arousal rating of the visual stimulus. Even adding a low-arousal haptic stimulus to a visual stimulus results in a visual-haptic stimulus with a higher arousal rating than that of the visual-only stimulus.

3. A high-intensity haptic stimulus (35 dB) is more effective in increasing the arousal of a given visual stimulus compared to a low-intensity (20 dB) stimulus. More specifically, for low-arousal visual images, adding a haptic stimuli with high intensity (35 dB) and high frequency (110 Hz or 165 Hz) results in a significant increase in the arousal.

4. Waveform and Rhythm do not contribute significantly to the difference in arousal between visual-only stimuli and the corresponding visual-haptic stimuli.

DISCUSSION

Although we explored how the haptic-stimuli parameters contribute to an increased arousal of the multimodal visual-haptic stimuli, we have not explored how the visual-stimuli parameters impact the valence of the visual-haptic pair. This is partly due to the difficulty in characterizing the visual affect in terms of low-level features. Research in neuroscience and emotion-based image retrieval has focused on identifying the low-level visual features that affect the emotional response to a stimuli. Many low-level visual features [22, 11] have been identified for impacting emotions in images: spatial frequency, edge strength, complexity of image, color, texture, composition. Most of these studies try to classify images based on emotion keywords (e.g. sad, happy) and the effect of these features on valence and arousal of the image is not clear. We propose to explore this issue further in our future work.

CONCLUSION AND FUTURE WORK

We have investigated the interaction between affective cues presented in visual and haptic modalities. We found that in a visual-haptic stimulus, the visual component dominates the valence while its haptic component affects the arousal. The followup experiment investigating the effect of low-level haptic features on arousal shows that high-intensity haptic stimuli contributes most to increasing the arousal; and the low-arousal visual images were affected most by the addition of haptic stimuli. These results provide guidelines for interaction designers to generate multimodal visual and haptic feedback considering the affective dimension.

At present, a limitation of our work is the specificity of the results to the haptic actuator used. Though the results from the high-level exploration are generic, the low-level features are dependent on the hardware used. The frequency range of the haptic actuator (0 Hz to 200 Hz) used in our experiments covers only a part of the spectrum to which human skin is sensitive (10 Hz - 400 Hz); this deserves further exploration. We plan to replicate our study with other haptic devices in the future.

We also plan to explore if the valence of a visual image can be parametrized in terms of some combinations of low-level visual features. This would allow us to explore how these low-level features affect the valence of visual-haptic stimuli. We are also interested in exploring the affective interactions between audio-haptic and audio-visual stimuli. The audio-haptic pair is particularly interesting as it is easier to identify low-level features of audio stimuli (e.g. pitch, tempo, intensity) along the similar dimensions of haptic stimuli.

ACKNOWLEDGEMENTS

This research was supported in part by a grant under the Samsung Global Research Outreach (GRO) Program.

REFERENCES

1. Bertelson, P., and Radeau, M. Cross-modal bias and perceptual fusion with auditory-visual spatial

discordance. *Perception & psychophysics 29*, 6 (1981), 578–584.

2. Bickmore, T. W., Fernando, R., Ring, L., and Schulman, D. Empathic touch by relational agents. *Affective Computing, IEEE Transactions on 1*, 1 (2010), 60–71.
3. Bonnet, D., Ammi, M., and Martin, J.-C. Improvement of the recognition of facial expressions with haptic feedback. In *Haptic Audio Visual Environments and Games (HAVE), 2011 IEEE International Workshop on*, IEEE (2011), 81–87.
4. Botvinick, M., and Cohen, J. Rubber hands feel touch that eyes see. *Nature 391*, 6669 (1998), 756–756.
5. Bradley, M. M., and Lang, P. J. Measuring emotion: the self-assessment manikin and the semantic differential. *Journal of behavior therapy and experimental psychiatry 25*, 1 (1994), 49–59.
6. Brewster, S. A., and Brown, L. M. Non-visual information display using tactons. In *CHI'04 extended abstracts on Human factors in computing systems*, ACM (2004), 787–788.
7. Burke, J. L., Prewett, M. S., Gray, A. A., Yang, L., Stilson, F. R., Coovert, M. D., Elliot, L. R., and Redden, E. Comparing the effects of visual-auditory and visual-tactile feedback on user performance: a meta-analysis. In *Proceedings of the 8th international conference on Multimodal interfaces*, ACM (2006), 108–117.
8. Collignon, O., Girard, S., Gosselin, F., Roy, S., Saint-Amour, D., Lassonde, M., and Lepore, F. Audio-visual integration of emotion expression. *Brain research 1242* (2008), 126–135.
9. De Gelder, B., and Bertelson, P. Multisensory integration, perception and ecological validity. *Trends in cognitive sciences 7*, 10 (2003), 460–467.
10. De Gelder, B., and Vroomen, J. The perception of emotions by ear and by eye. *Cognition & Emotion 14*, 3 (2000), 289–311.
11. Delplanque, S., Ndiaye, K., Scherer, K., and Grandjean, D. Spatial frequencies or emotional effects?: A systematic measure of spatial frequencies for iaps pictures by a discrete wavelet analysis. *Journal of neuroscience methods 165*, 1 (2007), 144–150.
12. Diez, D. M., Barr, C. D., and Cetinkaya-Rundel, M. *OpenIntro statistics*. CreateSpace, 2012.
13. D'mello, S., and Graesser, A. Autotutor and affective autotutor: Learning by talking with cognitively and emotionally intelligent computers that talk back. *ACM Transactions on Interactive Intelligent Systems (TiiS) 2*, 4 (2012), 23.
14. El Kaliouby, R., and Goodwin, M. S. Iset: Interactive social-emotional toolkit for autism spectrum disorder. In *Proceedings of the 7th international conference on Interaction design and children*, ACM (2008), 77–80.
15. Ernst, M. O., and Banks, M. S. Humans integrate visual and haptic information in a statistically optimal fashion. *Nature 415*, 6870 (2002), 429–433.
16. Geldard, F. A. Some neglected possibilities of communication. *Science* (1960).
17. Hoggan, E., and Brewster, S. New parameters for tacton design. In *CHI'07 extended abstracts on Human factors in computing systems*, ACM (2007), 2417–2422.
18. Hoggan, E., Brewster, S. A., and Johnston, J. Investigating the effectiveness of tactile feedback for mobile touchscreens. In *Proceedings of the SIGCHI Conference on Human Factors in Computing Systems*, ACM (2008), 1573–1582.
19. Hoggan, E. E., and Brewster, S. A. Crossmodal icons for information display. In *CHI'06 extended abstracts on Human factors in computing systems*, ACM (2006), 857–862.
20. Jousmäki, V., and Hari, R. Parchment-skin illusion: sound-biased touch. *Current Biology 8*, 6 (1998), R190–R191.
21. Lang, P. J., Bradley, M. M., and Cuthbert, B. N. International affective picture system (iaps): Affective ratings of pictures and instruction manual. *Technical Report A-8, University of Florida* (2008).
22. Machajdik, J., and Hanbury, A. Affective image classification using features inspired by psychology and art theory. In *Proceedings of the international conference on Multimedia*, ACM (2010), 83–92.
23. Pavani, F., Spence, C., and Driver, J. Visual capture of touch: Out-of-the-body experiences with rubber gloves. *Psychological Science 11*, 5 (2000), 353–359.
24. Reeves, L. M., Lai, J., Larson, J. A., Oviatt, S., Balaji, T., Buisine, S., Collings, P., Cohen, P., Kraal, B., Martin, J.-C., et al. Guidelines for multimodal user interface design. *Communications of the ACM 47*, 1 (2004), 57–59.
25. Russell, J. A. A circumplex model of affect. *Journal of personality and social psychology 39*, 6 (1980), 1161.
26. Seifi, H., and MacLean, K. E. A first look at individuals' affective ratings of vibrations. In *World Haptics Conference (WHC), 2013*, IEEE (2013), 605–610.
27. Sherrick, C. E. A scale for rate of tactual vibration. *The Journal of the Acoustical Society of America 78*, 1 (1985), 78–83.
28. Ternes, D., and Maclean, K. E. Designing large sets of haptic icons with rhythm. In *Haptics: perception, devices and scenarios*. Springer, 2008, 199–208.
29. Wobbrock, J. O., Findlater, L., Gergle, D., and Higgins, J. J. The aligned rank transform for nonparametric factorial analyses using only anova procedures. In *Proceedings of the SIGCHI Conference on Human Factors in Computing Systems*, ACM (2011), 143–146.

Emotions Mediated Through Mid-Air Haptics

Marianna Obrist[1], Sriram Subramanian[2], Elia Gatti[3], Benjamin Long[4], Thomas Carter[4]
m.obrist@sussex.ac.uk | sriram@cs.bris.ac.uk | GattiE@adf.bham.ac.uk | info@ultrahaptics.com
[1]School of Engineering and Informatics, University of Sussex, UK
[2]Department of Computer Science, University of Bristol, UK
[3]CNCR, c/o School of Psychology, University of Birmingham, UK
[4]Ultrahaptics Limited, Bristol, UK

ABSTRACT
Touch is a powerful vehicle for communication between humans. The way we touch (*how*) embraces and mediates certain emotions such as anger, joy, fear, or love. While this phenomenon is well explored for human interaction, HCI research is only starting to uncover the fine granularity of sensory stimulation and responses in relation to certain emotions. Within this paper we present the findings from a study exploring the communication of emotions through a haptic system that uses tactile stimulation in mid-air. Here, haptic descriptions for specific emotions (e.g., happy, sad, excited, afraid) were created by one group of users to then be reviewed and validated by two other groups of users. We demonstrate the non-arbitrary mapping between emotions and haptic descriptions across three groups. This points to the huge potential for mediating emotions through mid-air haptics. We discuss specific design implications based on the spatial, directional, and haptic parameters of the created haptic descriptions and illustrate their design potential for HCI based on two design ideas.

Author Keywords
Emotions; Touch; Mid-Air; Emotional Tactile Experiences; UltraHaptics; Emotion-Haptics-Mapping.

ACM Classification Keywords
H.5.m. Information interfaces and presentation (e.g., HCI).

General Terms
Human Factors; Design.

INTRODUCTION
Affect and emotions are important areas of research for human-computer-interaction. There is a growing trend to design interactive systems that elicit and support emotions beyond facial and vocal channels [17,13,9,7]. In particular, communicating and mediating emotions through touch is an area of research that opens up new design opportunities for emotion-related communication [8]. This is evidenced in recent work on the integration of touch during phone conversations for enhancing the emotional expressiveness in long-distance relationships [13], the design of a wearable system that allows different types of social touch [9], and the increased number of studies on understanding the rich expressiveness of tactile sensations linked to the increasing availability of haptic systems [7,12].

CHI 2015, April 18–23, 2015, Seoul, Republic of Korea.
Copyright 2015 © ACM 978-1-4503-3145-6/15/04...$15.00.
http://dx.doi.org/10.1145/2702123.2702361

Park et al. [13], for instance, showed that sharing a tactile vocabulary enabled couples to express and understand emotions over distance. For positive emotions participants used weak touches, while negative emotions were often expressed through hard, fast, and continuous touches. Huisman and Frederiks [9] specifically focused their design on six emotions, expressed through a tactile sleeve mounted on the forearm and equipped with different vibration motors. They identified different types of touch for each emotion (e.g., stroking for love, squeezing for fear), but also reported participants' difficulty in differentiating the intensity of the expressions on the worn sleeve. These results suggest the potential for communicating emotions through touch but do not inform sufficiently which or how specific emotions can be mediated through haptic feedback.

In this paper we bridge this knowledge gap by using a novel methodology that was adopted from the crowdsourcing community [1]. Their Find-Fix-Verify approach splits complex crowd intelligence tasks into a series of generate and review stages to produce more reliable results. Instead of relying on a single crowd worker to complete a complex task, different sets of workers are recruited to complete parts of the complex task. Thus, this process prevents single errant crowd workers from contributing too much, too little, or introducing errors into the data collected. We conducted a user study by applying this principle in a lab-based environment to "Generate, Select and Verify" the mapping between specific emotions and haptic stimuli. We used the UltraHaptics system [4] that conveys haptics using acoustic radiation forces through mid-air.

In our study, a first group of participants created their own *haptic descriptions* for standardized emotional stimuli taken from the International Affective Picture System database [10]. These descriptions were reviewed and ranked by a second group (eliminating half of them) and the remaining descriptions were played back to and rated by an independent third group. Through this process, we showed that the mapping between emotions and haptics is not random and that self-expressiveness can be successfully combined with objective tactile parameters. The main contributions of this paper are (a) the demonstration of a non-arbitrary mapping of emotions through haptic stimuli sensed through a mid-air haptic system, (b) identification of mappings of freely expressed haptic descriptions derived from participants interpretation of the emotional state to the controlled emotional stimuli from the standardized IAPS datasets, and (c) derivation of design opportunities for mediating emotions through mid-air haptics based on three main characteristics: *spatial* (i.e., location), *directional* (i.e., movement), and *haptic* (i.e., frequency, intensity, duration) parameters.

RELATED WORK

Touch is extensively and richly used in everyday life. While it is often assumed that the use of touch in communicating is primarily relevant for the blind and deaf, it is just as relevant for us all. In particular, the way we touch embraces specific meanings and mediates certain emotions, which are well explored and understood in social sciences [5], but not within HCI and the design of user interfaces.

Manipulate, map and influence emotions through touch

Communicating emotions (and in general abstract concepts) through haptic feedback has become an exciting challenge. Psychologists and designers have investigated the relationship between haptics and emotions by following three main approaches: (i) manipulating haptic stimuli to express emotions, (ii) mapping stimuli to emotional terms, and (iii) influencing emotions through haptic stimuli. The results highlight how it is possible to connect haptic stimuli with users' emotional reactions.

Bailenson [1] for example has shown the manipulation of haptic stimuli to express emotions. His findings show that people are able to express and recognize emotions by using a force feedback device that simulated a handshake. Smith and MacLean [17] confirmed strangers' ability to express and recognize each others' specific emotions using a purely haptic link. Salmien et al. [15], in contrast, studied the mapping of haptic stimuli to emotional stimuli and showed how a simple haptic stimulus (the rotation of a cylinder at different speed and at different frequency intervals) could be interpreted as having emotional ratings stable across participants specifically asked to rate it on the dimensions of pleasantness, approachability, dominance, and arousal. Despite the fact that these stimuli are highly controlled, and the emotional rating relatively easy to understand, from a sensorial point of view this kind of study has the drawback of limiting the stimuli to be related with the participants' emotions, with a consequent loss of flexibility.

Gatti et al. [6] also tried to influence the emotional states of participants through haptic stimuli. Their findings suggest that haptic interaction has an effect on the interpretation of emotional stimuli at a secondary emotion's stage, that is at a stage where users merge their primary physiological emotional reaction with the information from the context, giving rise to complex interpreted emotional states. In their experiments, two different groups of users were asked to evaluate emotional pictures while interacting with a Phantom haptic device. Each group experienced a different degree of friction while moving the robotic arm of the device. There was no effect of the haptic interaction on the physiological recording, but there was an effect on the participants' evaluation of the pictures (in particular on their arousal dimension) suggesting that haptic stimulation, despite not providing an emotional activation by itself (therefore eliciting physiological parameters underpinning primary emotions), can play a role when the user is explicitly asked to focus on his/her own emotional state.

In terms of HCI research this result suggests that interaction designers might work with haptic stimulation in order to communicate emotions between two or more users, or even to mediate the emotional response, rather than use it to elicit an emotional reaction per se.

Use of emotion-related haptic interaction in HCI

Hertenstein et al. [8] showed that even strangers can communicate distinct emotions when communicating solely through touch. One person touched a stranger's forearm, trying to convey one of 12 emotions, which then had to be recognized by the other person (the two people did not see each other, interacting only through touch). Their data suggests that anger, fear, disgust, love, gratitude, and sympathy were decoded at greater than chance level, and they discuss the findings for emotion-related communication. Huisman and Frederiks [9] built on this by exploiting these findings from human-human interaction for computer-mediated communication. They developed TaSST, a tactile sleeve for social touch, focusing on the forearm by integrating different vibration motors. Based on an initial study with 16 participants they identified different types of touch for each emotion (e.g., stroking for love, squeezing for fear) and demonstrate how technology could be designed for emotional expressiveness through touch.

As introduced before, Park et al. [13] explored the role of touch during phone conversations for long-distance relationships. They developed POKE, a device that enables the callers to share touches during the conversation. Touch was sent and received through a device's inflatable surface and a skin-like touch input button over a conventional phone. Their findings from a one-month study show that sharing a tactile vocabulary over distance was useful for expressing and understanding emotions. For positive emotions weak touches were delivered, while negative emotions were often expressed through hard, fast, and continuous touches. The findings also show that the voice, the sound of the voice, in this particular use case played an important role to understand the tactile stimulation.

Overall, these examples highlight the rich potential of touch for communicating emotions. Most recently Nummenmaa et al. [11] presented maps of bodily sensations associated with different emotions. They demonstrate the validity of emotion specific activation maps across west European and East Asian samples in five experiments and conclude "emotions are represented in the somatosensory system as culturally universal categorical somatotopic maps" ([11], p. 646). With respect to our research, the question is to what extent can these emotions be mapped towards technological features that create tactile sensations through mid-air.

Emotions mediated through mid-air haptics

Haptic feedback has recently received a boost through the increased attention on ultransonic haptic feedback, which is a promising means of creating tactile sensations in mid-air without encumbering the user with an actuator [18,4]. Haptic systems such as UltraHaptics ([4], see Figure 1) is an example using this new technique of focusing air pressure waves on the human hand from an array of ultrasound transducers. One or more focal points on the hand can be stimulated and each stimulus can be modulated by changing its frequency, duration and intensity.

While Obrist et al. [12] explored the variety of tactile experiences created through such a haptic system, Wilson at al. [18] studied the perception, in particular the localization and motion across the hand, for UltraHaptics. There is however no study yet done that investigates the communication potential of touch in mid-air to mediate specific emotions. Hashimoto and Kajimoto [7] conducted an initial study projecting emotional information through tactile sensations on the palm using air pressure. Through changing the frequency of the vibration they demonstrated the perception of 'soft' feelings and living things in participants' hands. With a low frequency range (1 to 30Hz) participants perceived small living creatures such as a small bird or hamster, while with a medium frequency (3 to 30Hz) they imagined a dog or cat. With a high frequency range (30 to 300Hz) participants reported sensations similar to vibrating motors or solenoids. Although they show that rich tactile sensations could stimulate participants' imagination their link to emotions per se was still weak.

Considering the increased attention on haptic stimuli in relation to emotions, it is vital to systematically investigate this design opportunity for use in HCI. We help to address this challenge by devising the first controlled study of its kind using the UltraHaptics system.

THE STUDY

The purpose of this study is twofold. (1) As the main objective, we assess the non-arbitrary communication of emotions through haptic stimuli delivered by UltraHaptics, a haptic system that uses mid-air stimulation for creating tactile sensations. Insights from this work will help to further understand haptic communication and proving the efficacy of the UltraHaptics device in conveying emotional meanings. (2) As a secondary objective, we propose to investigate the connection between haptic stimuli and emotions by associating freely expressed haptic descriptions to controlled emotional stimulation from standardized emotional stimuli. In this way, participants will be able to represent their emotions using a vast range of emotional stimuli. However, the ambiguity of what they are actually representing will be limited by the use of well-defined affective pictures.

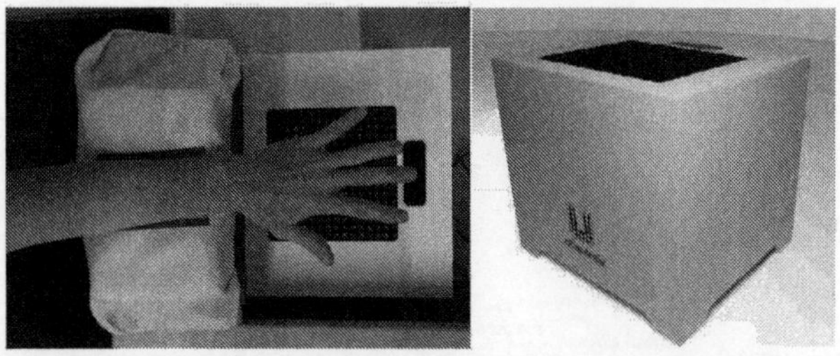

Figure 1. The UltraHaptics system used in our study, where participants positioned their left hand above the array (20cm distance) on a soft structure to keep the hand position steady.

Study design and procedure

We applied the "Find-Fix-Verify" pattern, introduced by Bernstein [1], which splits complex tasks into a series of generate and review stages to produce reliable results. Although Bernstein and colleagues introduced this approach to handle complex tasks through crowdsourcing, we considered it a very good fit for our study. Considering the complexity of emotions and expressiveness through touch the collection of independent descriptions and their subsequent judgement is beneficial to produce valid results.

Three groups of participants took part in the experiment. Each group consisted of ten participants (n=30). Five emotional pictures representing valence (pleasure) and arousal extracted from the International Affective Picture System (IAPS) and with reference to the IAPS manual [10] were used in our study. Positive valence and low arousal was represented by a scene from nature, calm scenery with trees [picture #7211], while positive valence and high arousal was represented through adventure sport, a scene from water rafting [picture #8370]. Negative valence and low arousal was represented through grief, a graveyard scene [picture #9001], while negative valence with high arousal was illustrated by human threat showing a car on fire [picture #8485]. As a neutral picture we selected a simple wall clock [picture #7211]). The choice of this set of pictures was carefully considered based on the picture classification established by Bradley and Lang [3] (see Figure 2, integrating our selection of pictures). Please note that the terms of use of the IAPS dataset do not allow one to publish the images in an article, thus we refer to the pictures through their numbers (#) through which they can be identified in the IAPS database.

Each participant in the ***first group*** was presented with 2 out of the 5 emotional pictures and asked to create a haptic description by modulating the frequency, intensity, and duration of the ultrasound stimulation. The pictures were pseudo-randomly assigned to participants, so that we could obtain four haptic descriptions for each of the five selected emotional pictures. The meaning of the haptic description

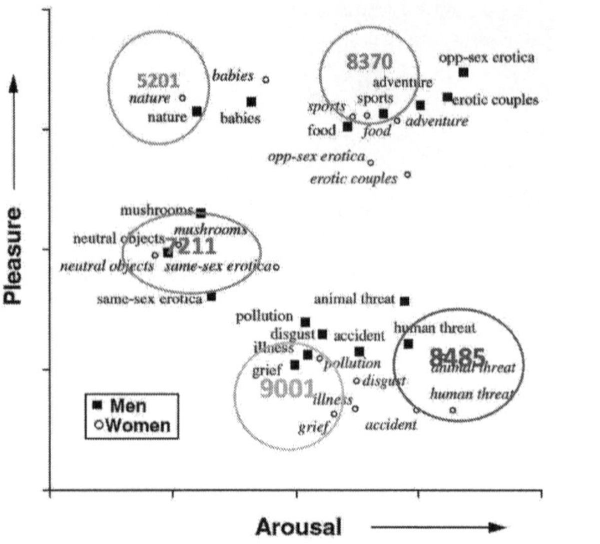

Figure 2. Selected emotional pictures from the IAPS identified by their # and allocated based on the classification [3] in low and high arousal, low and high pleasure (emotional valence).

was explained to the participants by the experimenter at the beginning of the study as follows:

"Abstract artists express their emotions through colours and shapes, while musicians express them through music. You will be shown two pictures, which might elicit emotions in you. Please try to describe those emotions by varying the parameters of the tactile stimulation from the device: the frequency, intensity, duration, and the position on your palm. Ideally, another person experiencing the tactile stimulation you create will think "this is anger!" or "this is communicating happiness!" depending on the emotion you want to express. Please remember that the haptic description should ***represent the emotions*** *that the picture is eliciting in you, rather than being a description* ***of the picture itself****."*

After the explanation, participants were introduced to the system by playing a test stimulus consisting of 4 focal points and a diagonal pattern precisely focused on the participant's palm. This was used to make sure the position of the participant's hand was correctly placed above the array of transducers. Then participants familiarized themselves with the device for some minutes, interacting with a graphical interface for controlling the device and its properties (see Figure 3, bottom left). When ready, they were asked to create the haptic description of the emotion each picture elicited in them. Participants created the haptic descriptions by leaning the non-dominant hand (left hand) on a structure posed over the haptic device (see Figure 1), to allow a comfortable and steady position of the hand for the stimulation by UltraHaptics. The focal point of the device in the z dimension (height) was fixed, so that the participants only had to experience the haptic stimuli on the palm along the x and y dimensions (4x4 areas on the palm).

The choice of using the non-dominant hand was made in order to allow participants to set up the haptic description with ease using their dominant hand. Prior work has shown no differences between dominant and non-dominant hand from a perceptual point of view [18]. Participants wore noise-cancelling headphones, playing pink noise, to mask any sound from the device and to remove any audio cues. The participants specified the characteristics of the haptic description using the graphical interface that is presented in more detail in the next subsection (see Figure 3).

The haptic description for each picture was designed as a haptic stimulus along six pre-defined fields that could be filled and extended with more fields if wished, but not more than 12 in total. The haptic stimulation for each field could be varied with the parameters of location on the palm (12 areas), intensity (from low, medium, high), and frequency (with five options from 16Hz to 265Hz). Each individual pre-defined field had a set duration of 200ms, which could be modified by participants as well.

The ***second group*** of 10 participants' task was to confirm the appropriateness of the haptic descriptions created by the first group by ranking the four haptic descriptions for each of the five emotional pictures. From these rankings the overall best and second best haptic description (i.e., haptic stimuli: Stim1 and Stim2) for each picture were chosen. In order to do so, participants rested the non-dominant hand on the support structure as for the first group. Before starting with the task, they were also able to familiarise themselves with the haptic system following the same procedure as participants from group one. Following the ranking, the first two descriptions in terms of appropriateness for each picture were selected, achieving a total of 10 haptic descriptions to be taken further into the next review stage.

A ***third group*** of participants were then presented with the five emotional pictures in a randomized order along with the 10 haptic descriptions from group two. Participants in this group also followed the same hand positioning and went through the same device familiarization procedure as the earlier two groups. When presented with each picture, the participants of this third group experienced one after another all the 10 selected haptic descriptions, also in a randomized order. After each haptic description, the participant was asked to rate on a Likert scale from 1 to 7 (7 was the maximum level of appropriateness) the fit of the haptic description with the emotion elicited by the picture.

At the end of each test session, each participant in all three groups were presented with a short questionnaire, in which they were asked for each picture to name one to three emotions that could describe the feeling they had while looking at the pictures, and to complete the Self-Assessment Manikin [3] for the emotional assessment of each picture. Participants from the third group were additionally asked how difficult it was for them to map the haptic stimuli and the emotions elicited through the pictures, as well as how confident they were with their final ratings. Presented with all 10 haptic descriptions their rating provided the final verification of the initial creations and selections from the previous groups. All participants also shared some final thoughts on their experience with the system and the mapping between touch and emotions.

Figure 3. ***Top Row:*** **The study design involving 3 groups (10 participants in each group) for creating, ranking, rating the haptic descriptions.** ***Bottom Row:*** **the interfaces used for the 3 groups, the black boxes indicate the position of the emotional pictures.**

The interface to design the haptic description

Participants were allowed to design their haptic descriptions of the emotional pictures by interacting with a graphical user interface (see Figure 3, bottom row). The interface was programmed so that the participants were able to decide about the position of the stimulus they wanted to deliver on the hand (palm) by clicking on one of the 16 areas (4x4) in the position grid. By using sliders they were subsequently able to adjust the frequency and the intensity range of the stimulus presented on the selected location. Participants could then decide to change the duration of the stimulation (in milliseconds). The default was set at 200ms. By clicking on the button "Play stimulus" participants were able to experience the stimulus they had just designed.

It is important to note that the whole haptic description of the emotional pictures could be composed of a sequence of up to six stimuli, rather than by just one stimulus in a single location. In order to create a train of stimulations in different locations, participants clicked into each of the pre-defined fields and they could also add more fields through a right click "Add stimulus". Participants were told that they had no obligation to fill all the six pre-defined fields. By clicking on the play button in the timeline participants were able to experience the whole haptic description they had created.

Once the position, frequency, intensity and duration for each field were decided, the haptic description was saved and all values were reset to zero to continue with the next picture following the same procedure.

Participants

A total of 30 participants took part in the study, 10 for each group with no participant belonging to more than one group. In each group 5 female and 5 male participants were recruited to ensure gender balance. The average age of participants was 33 years (± 9.46). Participants were recruited through University mailing lists and social media so as to have a broad variety of participants. None of the participants had ever used or interacted with a haptic system conveying tactile stimuli in mid-air. Therefore, they were all newly introduced to this interaction concept in this study. They received a small monetary compensation for their participation in the 30-minute session.

Data analysis

We analyzed all the data collected for each group individually summarizing the ratings from the Likert scales and the qualitative feedback on the performed tasks. Additionally we examined the detailed characteristics of the created haptic descriptions identifying the main parameters used in relation to the stimulated emotion (valence and arousal). By doing so we were able to extract insights into the spatial, directional, and haptic features of the created haptic descriptions. However, the main data analysis focused on the ratings obtained by the third group of participants, in order to verify the validity of the mid-air tactile stimulation in conveying emotional meaning. We tested whether participants of the third group scored the haptic descriptions selected by participants of the second group as the most appropriate in describing the picture they were created for. Moreover, we further explored correlations among 'appropriateness' ratings in order to gather more insights about the human ability in communicating emotions through tactile feedbacks.

RESULTS

The average ratings of the pictures based on the self-assessment Manikin showed a clear match between the emotions intended by the picture from the IAPS database across all three groups. Thus we can be sure that the mapping is based on a solid foundation. In the following we present the main findings and the analysis performed from each stage of the user study.

Group 1: creating the haptic descriptions

Participants in the first group were each tasked to create haptic descriptions for two emotional pictures. Overall, the task was perceived as very challenging reflected in the average difficulty rating of 3.7 (± 1.95) on a scale from 1 to 7 (were 1 is very difficult to 7 not difficult at all). It took on average 10 minutes for the participants to create one haptic description, and the session lasted about 30 minutes in total.

All 10 participants perceived the positional control on the palm as the most useful parameter to create the haptic description. Thus the usefulness of the position was rated with 6 and 7 on a scale from 1 to 7 (1 is not useful at all, 7 is very useful). The usefulness of the intensity was also rated high with 7 by eight participants, one participant gave intensity a 5 and one only a 2 arguing that *"the intensity wouldn't affect the emotion"* [P10] (it is worth noting that P10's creation were not chosen by group two as appropriate to represent the elicited emotions). Finally the frequency range was perceived as the least useful parameter for the creation of the haptic descriptions. Half of the participants still rated it with a 7, one with 6, two participants with 5, one 4, and one with 3 out of a scale from 1 to 7. With respect to the position on the palm, and the combination with intensity and frequency, we noticed a distinction between the inner and outer part of the palm as well as the low and high intensity and frequency ranges in relation to arousal elicited through the emotional pictures.

When participants explained their final haptic description at the end of the study, they also talked about the direction and movement of their creations. One participant explained the creations for picture #8485 and picture #8370; both with high arousal, but different valence, the first a negative [car on fire] and the second [water rafting] a positive emotion. *"I used a not predictable pattern for the fire picture, spreading around the palm. That is not a pattern to be easily comfortable with. In contrast to that, the pattern for the other picture with the water rafting is predictable and anticipation is possible"* [P7]. The participant further explained that the predictable pattern was expressing the excitement (positive emotion), rather than the panic and fear inherent in the other picture.

Another participant confirmed this strategy in creating the haptic description for picture #8485 as well *"I was creating a random pattern to express the panic. Here the order is not important but the pattern"* [P9]. In contrast to that, when creating the haptic description for picture #9001 [graveyard] the rationale was: *"the pattern is slow and gently progressing, there are not many changes of the position, apart from the last position, which is different and far away from the progression and has a high frequency in contrast in order to express the unexpectedness at a graveyard"* [P9]. One participant specifically mentioned that the *"frequency and intensity ranges are only useful at the extreme, I couldn't be bothered with the middle ranges, only 16Hz and 256Hz are needed, and high and low intensity"* [P8]. This comment becomes relevant looking at the final results from group three at the verification of emotional pictures in the high and low valence ratings.

Overall, 20 haptic descriptions (four for each of the five emotional pictures) were created by group one.

Group 2: ranking the haptic descriptions

Participants in the second group were presented with all five emotional pictures (one after another, randomized) along with the four haptic descriptions for each picture. They could play through the different stimuli as often as they wanted until they were certain which one fitted best and second best the emotion elicited by the picture shown. At the end of this review and selection stage 10 out of the 20 haptic descriptions were selected and ranked best (Stim1) and second best (Stim2) for each picture.

Participants rated the difficulty of this task on average with 3.75 (± 1.98) on a scale from 1 to 7, which is similar to the average rating by group one. Participants initially expressed difficulty in finding the mapping between emotions and haptics, but realized along the way that it was actually not so difficult overall. Two participant expressed it as follows: *"To begin with it is an alien thing, you don't do it normally, think about your hand and emotions"* [P6]; *"I don't have an existing mental model of my palm and emotions"* [P3]. Based on participants' feedback we could identify similarities between group one and two in the rationales of their choices. One participant said, that *"the chaotic patterns felt more unpleasant to me"* [P1], which fits the intention described above about the unpredictable pattern for expressing panic, to convey negative emotions. Another participant made the following metaphor: *"the middle part of my palm is more sensitive ("accepting things" - it is like the belly, that you can only touch if you know each other well, very intimate) versus the edges of the palm which is more casual like a touch on a shoulder"* [P3]. This links back to the discussion in group one on the inner and outer part of the palm conveying more or less sensitive emotions.

Participants found it easier to find a mapping of haptic descriptions and emotional stimuli for high arousal pictures than for those with low arousal. The neutral stimulus represented through a wall clock was the most difficult as it had two possible interpretations, either it was perceived as positive (time to go home) or negative (time pressure). Although participants were instructed to focus on the emotions, one participant expressed the challenge of suppressing the visual influence *"I tried to focus on the haptic stimulus but the visual was overpowering"* [P3].

Overall, participants perceived the location on the palm and the combinations of the areas as the most useful parameter to select the haptic stimulus for an emotion, followed by intensity as parameter and least useful the frequency that couldn't really be distinguished when playing the stimuli. One participant summarized it as such: *"the palm areas were the most useful feature, followed by the intensity on which I could pick up on quickly"* [P5].

At the end of this stage, we found that six participants from group one were the creators for the 10 selected stimuli, out of which both creations from four participants were chosen [P2, P5, P6, P7], plus one each from P4 and P9. These selected 10 stimuli were further presented to group three.

Group 3: rating the selected haptic descriptions

Participants in the final group were presented with the final 10 haptic descriptions, which they had to rate against the five emotional pictures on a scale from 1 to 7 (1 is not appropriate at all, 7 is very appropriate – 'appropriateness' ratings). In particular participants were presented with each one of the five pictures in a randomized order (one at time). While being presented with each picture participants experienced on their hand sequentially the 10 selected haptic stimuli. They were instructed to rate from 1 to 7 "*How appropriate the presented haptic description is for the emotion elicited by the picture on the screen?*"

Similarly to the previous two groups the difficulty level of the task received an average rating of 3.5 (± 1.17). The confidence level of participants' ratings was however quite high with an average rating of 5.8 (± 1.13) on a scale from 1 to 7 (1 is not confident at all, 7 very confident). Further we used the R software for the data analysis and statistics. As a first step in analyzing the data, we ensured that there was no difference between "appropriateness" ratings between haptic descriptions meant to describe the same emotional stimulus. To this aim, a paired t-test was performed. Ratings for the "best" describing haptic description did not differ from ratings for the "second best" haptic description. No difference was found between the two groups ($t = -0.85$, p-value = 0.39).

As a second step, a multiple factors repeated measure ANOVA was performed in order to assess the factors influencing the appropriateness ratings from the subject of the third group. A normality test was performed allowing us to assume a normal distribution of the data ($p>.05$). Ratings were tested depending on: *the emotional pictures.* This factor had five levels, one for each of the pictures used, and *the haptic stimuli:* The type of haptic description, that is, whether the haptic description was intended to describe picture one, two, three, four or five. Please note that this level encompassed the ratings from both the best and the second best selected haptic descriptions, since no difference between them was shown by the previous t-test. This choice was made to allow us to have more data points per cell, therefore increasing the statistical power of the analysis (power for an effect size of 0.75 at a level of significance of 0.01 was estimated as 0.67 for the unmerged data, and as 0.99 for pooled in data). It is important to point out, however, that this analysis is considered only as a preliminary step in connecting tactile stimuli and emotional interpretation. Pooling together data only allowed us to draw a clear picture of the results. Further experiments (i.e., acquiring data from more participants) will allow us to consider best and second best descriptions separately.

Results of the ANOVA showed no main effects of the displayed picture, nor a main effect of the haptic stimulus. However, the main reason for the ANOVA was to assess the interaction between our two independent variables, given that we were interested in assessing if haptic descriptions were rated differently depending on the emotional stimuli they were presented with. The ANOVA showed an effect of the interaction between displayed picture and haptic stimulus, indicating that participants rated each haptic description differently depending on the picture displayed on the screen ($F= 7.0219$, $p<0.001$). Simple effect analysis was used to better understand the nature of the interaction. In particular, a series of paired t-test (Bonferroni corrected) were performed. Results from these comparisons are summarised in the bar plot in Figure 4a, that shows the differences between the haptic descriptions for each picture. Haptic descriptions intended to represent picture #8370 are marked as "the outer left grey bar", followed by the ones intended to represent picture #9001 and so on marked with decreasing grey scales.

In general, participants tended to assign significantly higher 'appropriateness' ratings to the descriptions when they were presented together with the picture the haptic description were intended for, therefore proving that communication of emotional meanings by means of mid-air stimulation was effective. However, participants' ratings for the haptic description for picture #8485 were always similar to the ones for picture #8370. Also ratings for haptic descriptions for pictures #9001, #7211, #5201 showed high correlations among them (see correlation plot in Figure 4b, the numbers 1 to 5 refer to the five pictures and the five haptic descriptions respectively to the order shown in Figure 4a).

One possible explanation for that is that participants were relatively good at interpreting the arousal conveyed by the haptic descriptions (which was, for example, similar for pictures #8370 and #8485), but not so good when it came to interpreting the valence of the emotion inspiring the haptic description (opposite for picture #8370 and #8485).

To better investigate the relations between the ratings related to each class of haptic descriptions (that is: haptic descriptions intended to describe each specific emotional picture), a metric multidimensional scaling (MDS) on two dimensions was applied (pooled together from each participant).

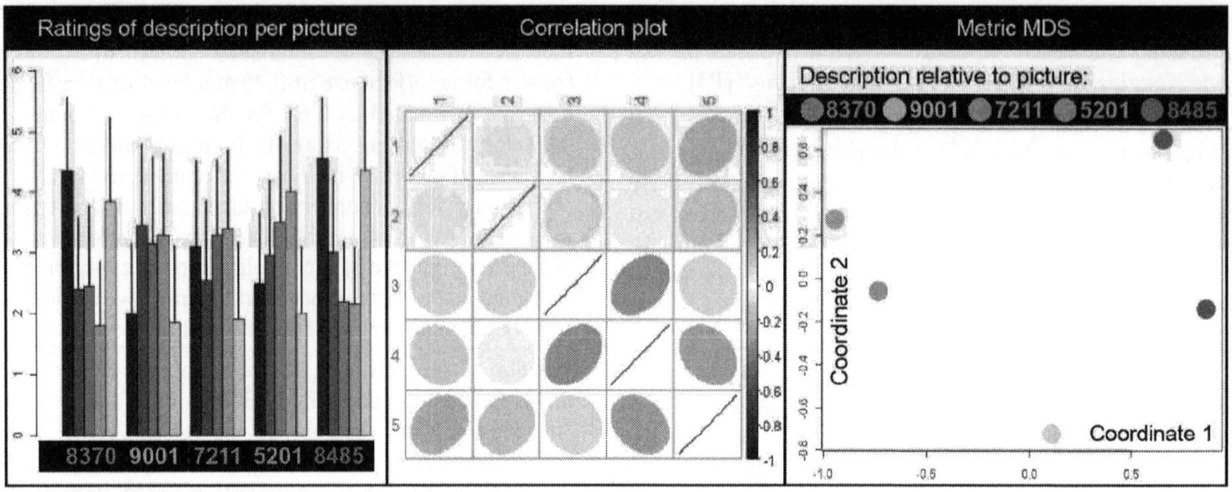

Figure 4: (a) Shows the differences in interaction between each picture and the haptic descriptions. (b) Correlation plot for the ratings for the haptic descriptions for each picture; the strength and direction of the correlation is represented by the color of the ellipses. (c) MDS representation for the haptic descriptions meant to describe the emotional pictures (see details of Figure in text).

The correlation plot from Figure 4b was transformed into a similarity matrix representing the distance among the different haptic descriptions in a two dimensional space. The number of spatial dimensions was set at two based on a scree-plot evaluation; a scree-plot displays the proportion of the total variation in a dataset that is explained by each of the components from the principal component analysis. The results from the MDS (Figure 4c) show that two dimensions were enough to represent the data. Interestingly, the representation of the 'appropriateness' ratings of the haptic descriptions strongly resembled the one achieved by Bradley and Lang [3] for the ratings concerning the *actual emotional* pictures (shown in Figure 2). This further attests that it is possible to convey emotional meanings by means of mid-air tactile stimulation.

Overall, our findings suggest that the haptic descriptions match well the intended emotions (arousal and valance) elicited through the standardized pictures. Our findings however also show that people find it easier to recognize emotional arousal and harder to deal with emotional valence when going through the mapping between the haptic descriptions and their appropriateness for the elicited emotion. These specific insights provide an initial basis for exploring the emotional design space for haptics in mid-air.

DESIGN IMPLICATIONS

In this section we discuss how our findings can guide the design for emotions through mid-air haptics. To do so, we discuss the specific *'spatial'*, *'directional'*, and *'haptic'* parameters represented in the selected haptic descriptions. 'Spatial' refers to the particular location on the palm, while 'directional' refers to the direction of the movement of the haptic description. The 'haptic' parameters refer to the frequency, intensity range, and the duration of the haptic stimulation. We further linked them to *valence* and *arousal*.

Spatial parameters

Our findings suggest that for a positive emotion through haptic stimulation one might want to stimulate the area around the thumb, the index finger and the middle part of the palm. These are areas selected most by participants in group one to create descriptions for the two positive pictures (#8370 and #5201). If one wants to elicit negative emotions (represented by picture #9001, #8485) the area around the little finger (pinky) and the outer parts of the palm become a relevant design space. Finally, to design for a neutral emotional stimulus, e.g., to regulate a previous extreme emotion, the haptic stimulation could target the upper end of the palm (junction between palm and fingers), which was the area dominating the two haptic descriptions of the neutral stimulus (Stim1 and Stim2 for picture #7211).

While our final dataset contains only ten haptic descriptions (two for each picture), we are confident that there is some strength in this spatial distinction as it was shown across all three groups. The meaning of the different areas on the palm is further supported by participants' feedback. Areas perceived as pleasant and associated with positive feelings are located in the middle of the palm and near the thumb. One participant in group two, for instance, described it as such *"the area around the thumb is the more active area, an area I feel more in control, in contrast to the other end of my palm"* [G2,P5]. Participants confirmed that the middle part of the palm is the most pleasant, positive, and intimate part (e.g., [G1,P4] [G1,P5] [G2,P3] [G3,P5]). In group two a participant made the comparison with a person's belly '*that you can only touch if you know each other well, very intimate'* in contrast '*the edges of the palm which is more casual like a touch on a shoulder'* [P3]. This mapping of positive and negative emotions on the hand can be further explored based on the direction of the haptic stimulation.

Directional parameters

In our haptic descriptions we can also identify implications for how to direct a haptic stimulus. If you want to design for positive emotions a vertical movement of the stimulus towards the person is suggested [found in all four haptic descriptions for positive emotions; Stim1 and Stim2 for picture #8370, and Stim1 and Stim2 for picture #5201]. Such stimulation could start at the area around the thumb and move on towards the middle of the palm, or the wrist. In contrast, to design the movement of a negative haptic stimulation our findings suggest directing the stimulus away from the palm towards the fingers [found in Stim1 and Stim2 for picture #8485, Stim1 for picture #9001]. With regard to a neutral stimulation the directional parameter in both haptic stimuli were moving horizontally along the top end of the palm (junction to the fingers). We observed both directions of movement (L→R & R→L).

The interesting design opportunity here is not only the clear change from a vertical to a horizontal stimulation pattern for neutral images but also the selected starting position. While all participants rated the picture as neutral in the self-assessment manikin questionnaire, which confirms that it elicits the intended emotion (being neutral), two of the four participants in group one interpreted the elicited emotion as more positive, while the other two interpreted it as leaning towards negative. The visual stimulus used for this emotion was a simple wall clock. P6 described the emotion elicited by the picture as *"Walk home: calm, happy"* (Stim1 for #7211), while P2 described the elicited emotion as *"Time: pressure, tasks, work"* (Stim1 for #7211). The implication is twofold: first it confirms the positive / negative mapping on the palm (described in the spatial parameters), and second it highlights the cross-sensory influence of the visual stimulus on the emotion and consequently on the haptic stimulus, which demands more attention around multi- and cross-sensory system design.

Haptic parameters

Here we provide guidance on haptic parameters that elicit specific emotions. For high positive arousal one might select high frequency ranges (128 and 256Hz) combined with a high intensity (found in Stim1 for picture #8370). Stim2 for the same picture had more variety in the use of haptic parameters and explored a broader range of combinations (between 16 to 128Hz frequency range) with a variation from low, medium, and high intensities. In the end, Stim1 received higher ratings on appropriateness by group three, which suggests the use of higher frequency and intensity ranges for positive emotions with high arousal.

Looking at pictures with negative arousal, we see a similar pattern for high frequency and intensity (Stim2 for #8485 was created with only 256Hz frequency, while Stim1 for the same picture used only 16Hz; both however used high intensity). The Stim2 for picture #8485 was created by P5 in group one and the choice for a low frequency was explained as such: *"I chose low for unpleasant and high for pleasant, as lower frequencies are for more energetic emotions, like a base in music"* [G1, P5]. This difference in the interpretation of the use of the frequency range is a powerful design element to allow expressiveness. In the end, Stim2 was rated higher in the appropriateness for the emotion by group three, which shows the preference for high frequency ranges for negative emotions with high arousal. The design challenge in the high arousal range [#8370 and #8485] is to carefully combine the haptic parameters with the spatial and directional parameters to make a distinction between positive and negative arousal.

The design implications for the emotional stimuli with low arousal and the neutral stimuli are less clear as they represent a larger variety of design possibilities around frequency and intensity range. While all frequency ranges are possible, for the selection of the intensity our haptic descriptions provide some guidance. For positive emotions with low arousal [picture #5201] a low intensity is useful as it provides a calm and comforting sensation (e.g., [G1,P6; G1,P4; G2,P4; G2,P7; G3,P5; G3,P10]). However for a negative emotion with low arousal, the intensity is moving more towards medium intensity [Stim1 #9001] to better express the presence of negativity but not as alarming as in high arousal. Finally a neutral emotion is either to be stimulated with low or medium intensity depending on the interpretation of the elicited emotion.

Finally, the duration of the haptic stimulation suggest that for pictures with high arousal, short and quick stimuli are useful (there were no changes in any of the four haptic descriptions for #8370 and #8485, both used 200ms). For emotions with low arousal and neutral stimuli a longer stimulation time is recommended (as seen for Stim1 for picture #7211, Stim2 for picture #7211, and Stim2 for picture #5201) while for a neutral emotional stimulation, one could design breaks in the haptic stimulation as we saw in both haptic descriptions for picture #7211.

DESIGN OPPORTUNTIES

By showing the efficacy of mid-air haptics in conveying emotional meanings, a new design spectrum is opened up for emotional design. Below we describe two design ideas (use cases) combining the insights gained from our study.

One-to-many communication

This is an idea inspired by Kaoss Pads' products and interfaces that allow performers to change parameters in an effect setting (e.g., Korg.com), such as sound effects in a musical performance (e.g., [14]). Creating an emotional tactile stimulation, for instance when clubbing, and in combination with music is a possible design idea for mediating emotions through mid-air. The UltraHaptics system can render multiple focal points at distance of up to 2m while still maintaining the receiver's distinct sensation. *Scenario:* Imagine a high-pitched summer song in a room full of people dancing. Now they raise their hands into the air as DJ Hapster offers them some emotional stimulation in mid-air: it starts at the upper end of the palm, runs along the palm, then into the middle of the palm and back to the upper edges creating a predictable loop and a positive feeling of excitement and stability. The DJ is using high frequencies (128 to 256Hz) with high intensity to create emotional arousal. The DJ is creating the haptic stimulus by moving along the thumb and middle part of palm. If one doesn't like the stimulus, hands can be put down.

One-to-one communication

This is an idea inspired by the increased interest in wearable technology within HCI, and in particular enhancing objects near our body (e.g., jewellery, cuffs, cloths, and other objects) with technology [16]. Creating an emotional tactile stimulation for an individual or connecting two individuals (e.g., couples in [13]) is a design idea for mediating emotions through mid-air. In contrast to the previous use case, this one is more discrete in its design and customizable for one-to-one communication. *Scenario:* Imagine a couple that just had a fight in the morning before going to work. She is sitting in a meeting wearing her bracelet that transmits haptic emotional messages from her partner. When she receives a new stimulus, she pulls out the string from her bracelet and connects it to her ring finger (as she is still angry, and does not want him to get near her index finger). Her partner created a haptic stimulus using a combination of 16 and 32Hz frequencies with low intensity, so that she realises he is not angry anymore. She moves the string to her index finger, receives the comforting stimulus along her right part of the hand into the middle of the palm.

These are two simplified scenarios illustrating the potential of mediating emotions through mid-air haptics. We can further expand the scope of this research by exploring tactile emotional stimulation beyond the hand, inspired by promising recent work on the emotion-body map [11].

CONCLUSIONS

Our findings show that communicating through mid-air haptics is not arbitrary and that participants were able to express and recognize tactile stimulation to convey emotional meanings. Haptic emotional descriptions were created by one set of users and validated by a different set of users, showing evidence for successful emotional communication between people through haptics. These insights open up new opportunities for interaction design in different contexts. We discussed various design directions and two design scenarios in particular showing the added value for one-to-many and one-to-one communications.

ACKNOWLEDGEMENTS

This work is supported by the EC within the 7th framework programme through the European Research Council (Starting Grant Agreement 278576).

REFERENCES

1. Bailenson, J. N., Yee, N., Brave, S., Merget, D., and Koslow, D. Virtual interpersonal touch: Expressing and recognizing emotions through haptic devices. In *HCI,* 22(3), (2007) 325-353.
2. Bernstein, M.S., Little, G., Miller, R.C., Hartmann, B., Ackerman, M.S., Karger, D.R., Crowell, D., and Panovich, K. Soylent: a word processor with a crowd inside. In *Proc. UIST '10.* ACM, (2010) 313-322.
3. Bradley, M.M. and Lang, P.J. Measuring emotion: The self-assessment manikin and the semantic differential. In *J. Beh. Ther and Exp. Psych..* 25(1), (1994) 49-59.
4. Carter, T., Seah, S. A., Long, B., Drinkwater, B., and Subramanian, S. UltraHaptics: multi-point mid-air haptic feedback for touch surfaces. In *Pro. UIST'13*, ACM, (2013) 505-514.
5. Classen, C. (2005). *The book of touch.* Berg Publishers.
6. Gatti, E., Caruso, G., Bordegoni, M., and Spence, C. Can the feel of the haptic interaction modify a user's emotional state?. In *World Haptics,* 2013 247-252.
7. Hashimoto, Y., and Kajimoto, H. A novel interface to present emotional tactile sensation to a palm using air pressure. In *Proc. CHI '08* ACM, 2703-2708.
8. Hertenstein, M. J., Holmes, R., McCullough, M., and Keltner, D. The communication of emotion via touch. In *Emotion* 9 (4), (2009) 566-573.
9. Huisman, G., and Frederiks, A.D. Towards tactile expressions of emotion through mediated touch. In *Proc. CHI '13.* ACM, 1575-1580.
10. Lang, P.J., Bradley, M. M., and Cuthbert, B. N. International Affective Picture System (IAPS): Affective ratings of pictures and instruction manual. *Technical Report A-6.* Univ. of Florida (2005).
11. Nummenmaa, L., Glerean, E., Hari, R., and Hietanen, J. K. Bodily maps of emotions. In *Proceedings of the National Academy of Sciences* 111, (2013) 646–651.
12. Obrist, M., Seah, S. A., and Subramanian, S. Talking about tactile experiences. In *Proc. CHI'13.* 1659-1668.
13. Park, Y-W, Baek, K-M, and Nam, T-J. The roles of touch during phone conversations: long-distance couples' use of POKE in their homes. In *Proc. CHI '13.* ACM, (2013) 1679-1688.
14. Patten, J., Recht, B., and Ishii, H. Audiopad: a tag-based interface for musical performance. In *Proc. NIME'02,* (2002) Singapore, 1-6.
15. Salminen, K., Surakka, V., Lylykangas, J., Raisamo, J., Saarinen, R., Raisamo, R., Rantala, J., and Evreinov, G. Emotional and behavioral responses to haptic stimulation. In *Proc. CHI'08*, ACM, 1555-1562.
16. Seymour, S. *Fashionable Technology: The Intersection of Design, Fashion, Science, and Technology.* Springer.
17. Smith, J., and MacLean, K. Communicating emotion through a haptic link: Design space and methodology. In *IJHCS* 65(4), (2007) 376-387
18. Wilson, G., Carter, T., Subramanian, S., and Brewster, S.A. 2014. Perception of ultrasonic haptic feedback on the hand: localisation and apparent motion. In *Proc. CHI '14.* ACM, (2014) 1133-1142.

In the Heat of the Moment: Subjective Interpretations of Thermal Feedback During Interaction

Graham Wilson[1], Gavin Davidson & Stephen Brewster[1]
Glasgow Interactive Systems Group
School of Computing Science
University of Glasgow, Glasgow G12 8QQ
[1]{first.last}@glasgow.ac.uk

ABSTRACT
Research has shown that thermal feedback can be an engaging and convincing means of conveying experimenter-predefined meanings, e.g., material properties or message types. However, thermal perception is subjective and its meaning in interaction can be ambiguous. Interface designers may not be sure how users could naïvely interpret thermal feedback during interaction. Little is also known about how users would choose thermal cues to convey their own meanings. The research in this paper tested subjective interpretations of thermal stimuli in three different scenarios: social media activity, a colleague's presence and the extent of use of digital content. Participants were also asked to assign their own thermal stimuli to personal experiences, to help us understand what kinds of stimuli people associate with different meanings. The results showed strong agreement among participants concerning what warmth (presence, activity, quality) and cool mean (absence, poor quality). Guidelines for the design of thermal feedback are presented to help others create effective thermal interfaces.

Author Keywords
Thermal feedback; interaction design; mobile interaction.

ACM Classification Keywords
H.5.2. User Interfaces – Haptic IO.

INTRODUCTION
Thermal stimulation is an inherent aspect of sensory experience, with strong links to social (e.g., physical closeness) [2,14] and emotional (e.g., "warm and loving") phenomena [20]. Thermal feedback in HCI may be capable of improving user experience by bridging the gap between data and their underlying social or emotional content. It has been used in HCI to convey information [1,21], improve materiality [5,16] or for communication [14,18]. However, most research has either been technological, developing new ways of providing thermal feedback [1], or perceptual, testing how well participants can detect or identify thermal stimuli [21,22]. There are few examples of applications where thermal feedback is tested in real-world interactions to see how users interpret it. Researchers have started to measure subjective views on potential meanings or uses for thermal feedback [3,14,18], but they have been in limited scenarios and provide few details about the specific stimuli used. Research is required to understand interpretations of thermal feedback in a range of familiar scenarios if it is to be effectively utilized in everyday interfaces.

Existing research also tends to prescribe meaning for the thermal feedback, attaching specific information to the stimuli used. Little is known about how users naturally and freely interpret thermal changes in a variety of interaction environments, which is key for the design of effective thermal UIs. This paper extends previous research by measuring the subjective meanings attributed to thermal stimuli in real-world examples. We let participants assign their own subjective meanings to stimuli and choose their own stimuli to represent personal experiences, to help us understand how people would interpret and use thermal feedback during interaction. We also tested different data types, including categories, range data and experiences, to provide a broader understanding of how thermal feedback is understood. The paper makes the following novel contributions: 1) Testing four real-world interactions not yet investigated with thermal feedback; 2) Testing associations of thermal feedback to different information/data types; 3) Recording how participants inherently interpret and assign thermal feedback; 4) Providing clear design guidelines.

We chose four scenarios to test interpretations of thermal cues: 1) conveying social media activity, 2) conveying physical presence, 3) conveying application usage and 4) a restaurant experience scenario. Thermal feedback has strong inherent emotional and social cues and so it may be useful for enhancing uses where these cues are central. Therefore, these scenarios were chosen because they are common and familiar, and they are related to social/emotional experiences, so allowing us to measure the corresponding associations of thermal feedback.

RELATED RESEARCH
Thermal feedback was first used in HCI to improve the materiality of objects in virtual reality, by mimicking different patterns of thermal conductivity [6,7]. Since then, the most common use case has been to augment media or communi-

CHI 2015, April 18 - 23 2015, Seoul, Republic of Korea

ACM 978-1-4503-3145-6/15/04...$15.00
http://dx.doi.org/10.1145/2702123.2702219

cation with emotional or social content. There is evidence of an inherent link between biological temperature and social emotion, as Williams and Bargh [20] found a connection between physical warmth and interpersonal warmth.

Nakashige *et al.* [15] combined images of food with warm, neutral or cold stimuli and found that foods presented with the correct corresponding temperature (e.g., warmth with soup) were rated as more delicious than those that were not. Both Salminen *et al.* [17] and Halvey *et al.* [3] measured participants' emotional responses to thermal stimuli. Salminen *et al.* looked at the stimuli in isolation, while Halvey *et al.* studied the effect of combining stimuli with audio and visual media. Both found that thermal stimuli influenced emotional state but the results were slightly different. Halvey *et al.* found warm stimuli were more pleasant than cool, while Salminen *et al.* found no difference in pleasantness. Warm stimuli did generally lead to higher arousal in both studies, compared to cool. Wilson *et al.* [23] also reported that warm stimuli were more intense and less comfortable than neutral and cold stimuli. These emotional studies did not measure any perceived meaning in the stimuli, only the participants' resulting affective state.

Researchers have looked at using thermal stimulation in interpersonal communication. Iwasaki *et al.* [8] augmented a mobile device with galvanic skin response (GSR) sensors to convey the emotional state of another user, with higher emotional arousal resulting in warmer feedback. Gooch [2] also showed that providing warm stimuli around the abdomen (to mimic a "hug") during instant messaging between physically separate users could increase feelings of social presence, although the effect was quite weak.

These studies all presented participants with the researchers' own choice of stimuli, sometimes with a prescribed meaning, before measuring participant responses to them. But how would participants naturally interpret meaning from ambiguous thermal changes, and how would they convey their own intentions through thermal feedback? Understanding this is key if thermal displays are to be effective on a large scale. Lee and Lim [13,14] have investigated participants' own subjective perceptions of thermal sensations in general [13] and specifically in the context of interpersonal communication [14]. In the latter study, they also asked participants to design their own feedback choices along three dimensions: temperature, duration and rate of temperature change. Participants tended to treat the warm-cold dichotomy as two opposites of meaning, with stronger changes representing the degree of difference.

Participants stated that there were specific temperatures that were appropriate for particular phenomena, suggesting a believed universality in interpretation. However, the results did not necessarily support this. In general, warmth was used for positive meanings, such as physical attraction or enjoyment, while cold represented negative meaning, such as the presence of a stranger. However, some participants used cold to represent positive aspects, such as refreshment.

Suhonen *et al.* [18] tasked pairs of participants with discussing something happy, something sad or angry and something emotionally neutral (restaurants). They allowed users to send warm or cold stimuli based on their own intentions and recorded what meaning they attached to the stimuli. Like Lee and Lim [14], warm sensations were generally used to convey positive and pleasant feelings or experiences (in both the happy and sad/angry scenarios) but across a wide range of interpretations, including emphasising happy memories, social closeness, empathy, gratitude and good food/restaurants. However, some participants used heat to indicate anger or annoyance. In contrast, cold was regularly associated with negative factors, such as nervousness, sadness, pain or anger. Cold represented a poor choice of restaurant. The meaning of stimuli, and the valence attached, depended on the valence of the context (discussion topic), which is in line with Lee and Lim's [14] suggestion that emotional state influences interpretation.

These papers are important as they give some insight into how naïve participants would use and interpret thermal feedback in the real world, outside of prescribed experimental stimuli. However, there are several limitations. Neither Lee and Lim [14] nor Suhonen *et al.* [18] report on the specific thermal feedback designs used in their studies, in terms of temperatures, rates of change or durations, so it is not known how the participants' intentions map to specific thermal stimuli. This information is needed to design appropriate feedback in the future. Also, the feedback designs and interpretations are limited to only interpersonal communication. In this paper we present an investigation into how interpretations vary across different scenarios and in relation to different subject matter, and outline specific thermal feedback design guidelines based on the results.

EXPERIMENTS

This section describes the four experimental scenarios designed to measure the subjective interpretation of thermal feedback: social media activity, physical presence, content deletion and restaurant experience. Like Lee and Lim [14], we did not dictate specific mappings of feedback to meaning. In each example, we present a range of thermal stimuli and ask participants what meaning or information they take from the stimulus. 15 participants (3 F) aged 18 to 31 (mean = 22.7) took part in all scenarios in a random order and were paid £6 for a 60min session. *A priori* sample size computation indicated 15 was sufficient for valid analysis.

Thermal Apparatus

The thermal stimulation was provided by the Peltier-based device used by Wilson *et al.* [21,22] (Figure 1). It is controlled over Bluetooth and can be set between -20°C and 45°C, accurate to 0.1°C. We used two 2cm^2 Peltier modules and changed temperatures at a rate of 3°C/sec to maximise the sensation [23]. For all four scenarios, the Peltiers were sitting on a desk facing up for the participants to rest the palm of their hand on top, supported by a padded rest (Figure 2). The Peltiers were controlled by either a PC (in the restaurant scenario) or a mobile phone (other scenarios). While we chose to stimulate the palm, arm locations are similarly sensitive [23], so wearable devices, such as smart watches, may be suitable stimulators for mobile interaction. Mobility influences thermal perception [21,22,23] so this will be tested in future research.

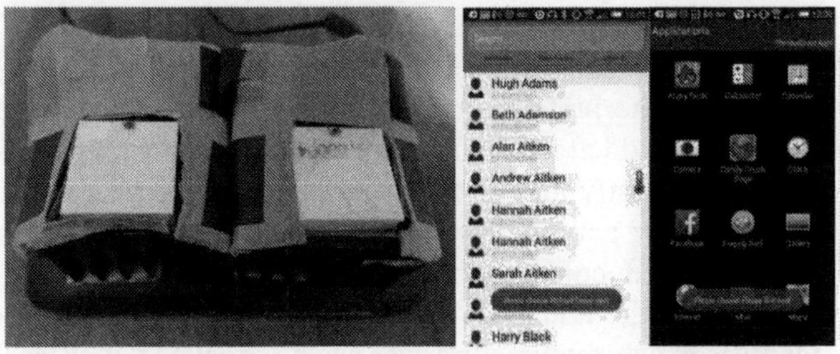

Figure 1: Peltier devices (left) and Contact List/Content Deletion interfaces (right). Cardboard covered the heatsinks.

Lee and Lim [14] allowed their participants to vary three parameters of thermal change: temperature delta ($t\Delta$, the change from skin temperature), rate of temperature change (ROC) and duration. Unfortunately, they did not report what range of ROC or durations were used, nor what specific designs participants chose. Perceptual research suggests that increasing any one of these factors would cause an increase in the intensity of the sensation [10,23]. Further, immediate perception of thermal stimuli is not guaranteed [4,11,23] so the duration and ROC may not be reliably perceivable in realistic scenarios [4,22,23]. We chose to limit our stimuli to changes in $t\Delta$, which will influence intensity but will not require the accurate perception of other factors.

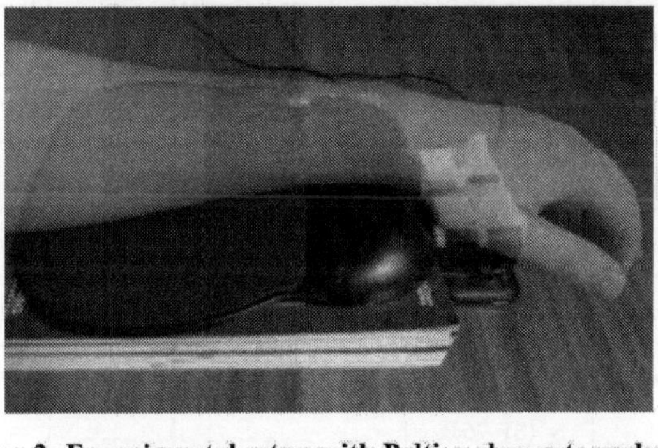

Figure 2: Experimental setup with Peltier elements under the palm and the padded armrest for comfort.

Experimental Setup

Thermal perception is different to audio, visual and tactile perception in that it is bipolar: the skin rests at a homeostatic neutral temperature and can be warmed or cooled from there [9]. Other modalities are unipolar, changing from no stimulus to increasing levels of stimulus. A resting state (in between trials) for audio, visual and tactile stimuli involves the absence of a stimulus. This is not possible for thermal feedback, as the stimulator and skin always have a temperature, and so the resting state for thermal feedback is skin temperature. For all interactions, the Peltiers were returned to a neutral temperature of 30°C between each trial: thermal research commonly uses a similar set starting temperature for controlled comparison between stimuli and 30°C is within the skin's natural range of resting temperatures [9]. In the social media, presence/availability and content deletion scenarios, 30°C was also included as an experimental stimulus (as it is a valid potential interaction cue), so participants were made aware that any lack of change during a trial was intentional and they were to treat the stimulus like any other. The specific temperatures used in each scenario are described below, but they all ranged from 22°C to 38°C. This range was chosen because it is safe, comfortable, reliably perceivable and centered on neutral 30°C skin temperature [9,12,23]. These temperatures have also elicited emotional responses in previous research [3,17,18].

For all four scenarios, the participant was sat at a desk in an office. On the desk were the armrest, Peltier devices, an Android mobile phone and a computer monitor and mouse. The participants rested their non-dominant hand on the armrest so that the palm of their hand made good contact with the two Peltier modules. The hand remained in contact with the Peltiers throughout each scenario but was removed during rest periods between scenarios. For the social media, physical availability and content deletion scenarios, the participant interacted with the mobile phone (which controlled the Peltiers) with their dominant hand to receive experimental instructions and provide input via the touchscreen GUI. For the restaurant experience scenario, the participant used the mouse to interact with an interface shown on the monitor while a PC controlled the Peltiers. A PC was used because the task required participants to type text and search and/or scroll long lists to find bars and restaurants, and they were presented with images and text describing the establishments. This interface would have been more cluttered and cumbersome on a small screen.

Online Activity: Phone Contact List

This scenario investigated the use of thermal feedback to provide an immediate overview of online activity, by conveying the recency of an individual's social media activity from their entry in a contact list application. The purpose was to see how participants relate temperature to temporal activity. As the contact list is scrolled, the user can hold a finger over an individual's contact to receive thermal feedback relating to how recently the person has posted on social media. We presented a range of temperatures and asked participants to state how recently the person was active.

Stimuli & Measures

Nine thermal stimuli were used: 22°C to 38°C in 2°C intervals. 1°C changes can be difficult to perceive [23], so a 2°C change was chosen as the smallest usable delta. These nine temperatures were each assigned to two different contact names and all 18 names were used as targets for the experimental trials. This meant that each stimulus was responded to twice but the participant was not necessarily aware of it, reducing any bias. For each trial, the Peltiers would be changed to one of the temperatures and remain there until a response was submitted. The Peltiers were then returned to 30°C for 10 seconds in preparation for the next trial. Participants were told that the thermal feedback represented how long ago the person was active on social media, but not how the temperature related to time. Once the target name and accompanying temperature were presented, the user was asked the question *"how long ago was this person on social media?"* A text box for a number value and a drop-down menu to indicate the time frame were presented: "seconds", "minutes", "hours", "days", "weeks", "months" or "years". This scenario used categorical data representing seven time frames to investigate how consistently thermal stimuli were attributable to 1) a set range of categories and 2) time.

Procedure

The interface (Figure 1, right) presented the participant with an alphabetical contact list of names and the experimental software requested each of the 18 target names in a random order, one per trial. In a given trial, the software would present the text *"Please choose [name] next"*. The participant would then have to scroll the list to find the name and long-press it (touch for 1 second), at which point the Peltiers would change temperature from neutral to the accompanying temperature. The interface then presented the experimental question along with the text box and drop-down menu for user input. Once the user had responded, he/she pressed a "submit" button, after which the Peltiers were returned to 30°C for 10 seconds before the next trial began.

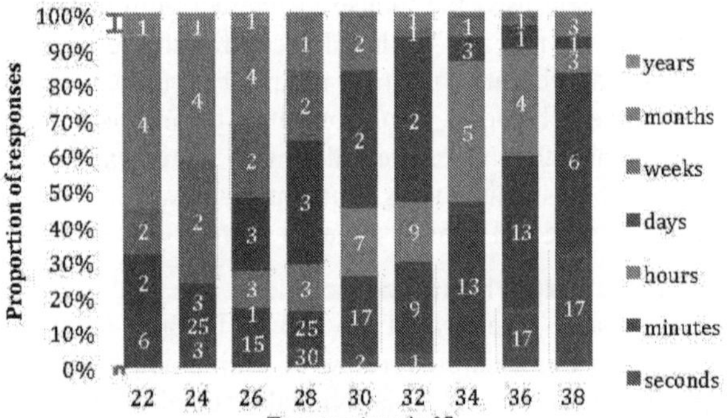

Figure 3: Bars show the proportion of responses that attributed each time frame to each thermal stimulus in the Contact List scenario. The numbers within each bar show the average enumeration of that time frame, e.g., 17 seconds.

Results & Initial Discussion

Figure 3 shows the proportion of responses that attributed each time frame to each of the nine thermal stimuli. These data do not take into account the number value enumerating the time frame, such as the 3 in "3 weeks", but the data were organized so that responses such as "14 days" were counted as a response in "weeks" rather than "days". The results show that participants generally attributed colder stimuli to longer time frames (older activity), such as days, weeks and months, and attributed warmer stimuli to shorter time frames (more recent activity) such as minutes or hours. The average value enumerating each time frame (the 3 in "3 weeks") is shown in white within each bar in Figure 3. The cooler stimuli were perceived as representing between 3 seconds and 1 year ago, while the warmer temperatures were interpreted as being between 17 seconds and 3 months ago. Overall, the colder the feedback temperature, the older the social media activity is perceived as being.

As seen in Figure 3, ~90% of responses interpreted the warm temperatures (34-38°C) as representing activity ≤ 1 day ago. For the warmest temperatures (36°C and 38°C), most were interpreted as being just seconds or minutes ago. There is a sudden shift where the neutral temperatures (28-32°C) are mostly interpreted as representing days ago. This trend of older activity continues as the majority of responses interpreted colder temperatures (22-26°C) as meaning weeks, months and even years since the last activity. To identify which temperature was most associated with each time frame, Friedman tests were run on the number of responses for each temperature within each time frame, e.g., compare the number of times "seconds" were attributed to each temperature. Following a significant Friedman test, *post hoc* Wilcoxon tests with Bonferroni adjusted p-values ($p<0.0014$) were used for pairwise comparisons. Any significant differences would indicate the most associated temperature(s). Effect size was calculated on the Wilcoxon tests using $r = Z/\sqrt{N}$, where Z is the Wilcoxon Z statistic and N is the total number of samples. Effect sizes were interpreted as $r = 0.1$ (small), $r = 0.3$ (medium) and $r = 0.5$ (large). A summary of the statistical analysis, including recommended feedback design, is shown in Table 1.

Number of responses attributing each temperature to time frames				
Time Frame	**Friedman Test (n) = df**	**Significant Pairwise Comparisons**	***Best Conveyed By***	*Suggested Alternative*
Seconds	$\chi^2(8)=43.10$, $p<0.001$	None	~	*38°C*
Mins	$\chi^2(8)=80.69$, $p<0.001$	34°C, 36°C, 38°C > 22-28°C	***> 34°C***	~
Hours	$\chi^2(8)=54.31$, $p<0.001$	34°C > 22°C, 24°C	***34°C***	~
Days	$\chi^2(8)=66.95$, $p<0.001$	32°C > 24°C	***32°C***	~
Weeks	$\chi^2(8)=43.89$, $p<0.001$	None	~	*24°C*
Months	$\chi^2(8)=76.0$, $p<0.001$	22°C > 30-38°C	***22°C***	~
Years	Not significant	None	~	*22°C*

Table 1: Summary of statistical analysis on the Contact List data. The table includes the "best" temperature for conveying each time frame and suggested alternative temperatures.

For the "seconds" data, there was a significant effect of temperature on the number of responses, but no pairwise comparisons reached the adjusted p-value, suggesting no individual temperature can reliably convey seconds. There was a significant effect within the "minutes" data with several significant pairwise comparisons: all three of 22°C, 24°C and 26°C had significantly fewer "minute" responses than 34°C, 36°C and 38°C (all medium effect sizes: $r =$

0.31 to 0.35). 28°C had significantly fewer than 34°C (r = 0.3) and 38°C (r = 0.31). This shows that warmer temperatures (≥34°C) are much more associated with a minute time frame than cooler temperatures, but no singular warm temperature is best suited to representing minutes. A significant effect was found within the "hours" data, with the 34°C stimulus having significantly more "hour" responses than 22°C (r = 0.38) and 24°C (r = 0.38). As 34°C was the only value significantly higher, it might best represent hours.

Following a significant effect within the "days" data, only 32°C had significantly more responses than 24°C (r = 0.31), suggesting 32°C is good for representing days. While there was a significant effect in the "weeks" data, no pairwise comparisons reached significance, suggesting no individual temperature conveys weeks reliably. A significant effect was found within the "months" data, as 22°C had significantly more responses than 30-38°C (r = 0.40 to 0.42), suggesting it is best at representing months. Finally, there was no significant effect of temperature on the "years" data.

Overall there is a greater sense of recency attributed to warmer stimuli. A pattern that goes against this trend is the somewhat U-shaped relationship between temperature and the number of "seconds" responses. The number decreases from 38°C (33% of responses) to 34°C (0%) before increasing again, with 16% of responses interpreting the coldest temperature (22°C) as representing seconds. Therefore, responses for 22°C ranged from seconds to years. Similarly, 6% of 38°C responses were months, giving a range of seconds to months for the hottest temperature. It may be that, for some participants, extreme temperatures can be interpreted as either extreme value within the relevant range.

Physical Presence: Augmented Office Door Handle

This scenario investigated how participants relate temperature to the presence and availability of a colleague in an office environment. Here we envision a smart office with an augmented door handle capable of warming up and cooling down (Figure 4). An individual wants to speak with a coworker but is unsure of his/her availability. If the inside of the office cannot be seen, the physical presence of the person is unknown. An un-answered knock on the door could mean that 1) they are away, 2) they are in but do not want to be disturbed or 3) they simply did not hear the knock.

For this scenario, we imagined conveying the co-worker's presence through thermal feedback when the visitor touched the augmented door handle. We chose a set of five 'availability' categories that cover a range of situations: 1) "Out of department", 2) "Back soon", 3) "In. Please knock", 4) "Available for short times" and 5) "Extremely busy". These were modelled on the paper indicators commonly used on office doors where a marker indicates the appropriate category of busyness. During the study, participants felt different stimuli and had to interpret their meaning as one of the five categories. While we prescribed the categories, we did not attach specific stimuli to them: participants applied their own interpretation to each stimulus.

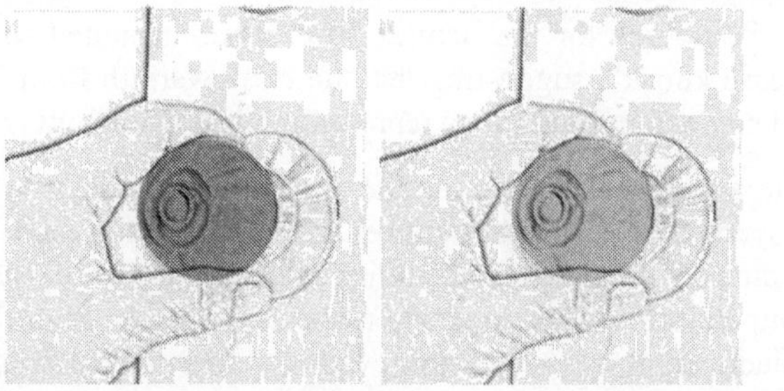

Figure 4: An augmented door handle could use thermal feedback to convey the presence or absence of the person inside.

Stimuli & Measures

Five stimuli were used: 22°C, 26°C, 30°C, 34°C and 38°C and each was presented twice, one per trial and participants were told that the thermal feedback represented the person's "availability". After the Peltier temperature had been changed, the mobile device presented a screen with the request: *"Choose which option best suited that temperature?"* There was a drop-down menu showing the five availability categories for participant responses. This scenario also used categorical data, but to test how thermal feedback is mapped to the physical presence of a person.

Procedure

During each trial, the software would set the Peltiers to the random target temperature before presenting the request to choose the corresponding meaning. Participants chose the availability category they felt was best represented by the thermal stimulus before pressing "submit". The Peltiers returned to 30°C for 10 seconds before the next trial began.

	Absence		*Presence*		
°C	Out of Dept.	Back soon	In. Please knock	Short times	Extremely busy
38	3	1	1	4	21
34	1	5	11	9	4
30	2	6	20	2	0
26	13	9	4	3	1
22	19	4	3	0	4
Best	<26°C	26°C	30°C	34°C	38°C

Table 2: Frequency counts for each label attributed to each thermal stimulus during the Physical Presence scenario. Shading shows most common (green) to least common (white). The "best" temperature for conveying each state is also shown.

Results & Initial Discussion

The results showed a strong degree of agreement among participants as to how temperature related to the presence of the colleague, which is inherently linked to his/her availability (see Table 2). In accord with previous research [2,14], the warm temperatures were interpreted as conveying the presence of the colleague but with greater warmth indicating less availability (while present). In contrast, cool temperatures were interpreted as absence, with greater cold indicating a greater degree of unavailability (absent for longer). The results for the moderate warm (34°C) are mostly split between "In. Please knock" (37%) and "Available for short times" (30%). There is a similarity in the practical meaning of these two categories, as both could mean that the visitor is welcome to enter. However, 67% of the responses for the neutral 30°C were attributed to "In. Please knock", suggesting that the extra warmth from 34°C led some to interpret it as representing less availability.

The same analysis as for the Contact List task was employed: comparing the number of responses for each temperature within each availability category, to identify which temperature was particularly associated with it. Significant Friedman tests were followed by Bonferroni-adjusted ($p<0.005$) Wilcoxon pairwise comparisons and effect size r calculations. There was a significant effect of temperature on the number of responses under all five categories ($p <= 0.001$). For the "Out of Department" responses, both 22°C and 26°C had significantly more responses than 30°C, 34°C and 38°C ($r = 0.36$ to 0.49), showing that the coolest temperatures were uniquely associated with the person being away. For the "Back Soon" data, 26°C had significantly more responses than 38°C ($r = 0.4$), suggesting that cool temperatures are more associated than particularly warm ones. The "In. Please Knock" data showed that 30°C had significantly more responses than all other temperatures ($r = 0.34$ to 0.49), and 34°C had significantly more than 38°C ($r = 0.36$) and 22°C ($r = 0.32$). Moderate temperatures are, therefore, particularly associated with presence and availability. For "Short times" 34°C had significantly more responses than 22°C (large effect size: $r = 0.5$), suggesting moderate warmth represents this state of moderately busy presence. Finally, 38°C had significantly more responses than all other temperatures under "Extremely Busy" (large effect sizes: $r = 0.53$ to 0.59), showing that the warmest temperature uniquely represented the highest busyness.

Ordinal data: Content Deletion

Temperature has a strong association with safety and danger in our environment: burning fire, comfortable warmth and freezing cold. For this scenario we wanted to investigate how thermal feedback might be interpreted in a situation that related to dangerous or risky interaction. There are a number of computing functions that result in permanent and irrevocable changes to the system, such as deleting content, upgrading an operating system or reverting to a factory state. Operating systems often force the user to reflect on the potential severity of the action and confirm their desire to carry it out through a dialogue box. However, the severity is likely to depend on the significance of the content being altered. Deletions, for example, may not matter if the content in question is unused or unwanted. If it is frequently used, the deletion is potentially more dangerous.

In this scenario, we looked at how thermal feedback might relate to the severity of deletions in the context of removing applications from a mobile phone, by using the feedback to convey the amount of use the application has had (although the principle could be applied to any digital content). When the participants long-pressed an icon (the action used in Android and iOS to allow deletions) they were provided with thermal feedback indicating the amount of use of the associated application. Different interactions require different data types, so a second motivation for this study was to measure interpretation of thermal feedback along an ordinal scale (in this case magnitude of usage), as the previous scenarios measured allocation of stimuli into categories.

Stimuli & Measures

The same nine stimuli from the Contact List scenario were used again. Each temperature was assigned to two of 18 application icons, each of which was a target during the experiment. Like the Contact List, this meant that each temperature was tested twice, but the user was not primed by a previous response. The participants were told that the thermal feedback represented how much the relevant application had been used but not how the temperature related to usage. The study followed a *magnitude estimation* design, where the participants were asked to attribute numbers to each stimulus that represented the magnitude of application usage. In perceptual research, magnitude estimation studies typically test only heat or cold perception and not both directions in one study [12]. In these cases, the stimulator rests at neutral skin temperature and changes to varying degrees of warmth *or* cold, but not both. The participant then attributes magnitude values to those varying degrees. As we wanted to examine interpretations of both within the same application, we changed the design: we made neutral indicate a moderate amount of use and allowed participants to attribute stimuli along a spectrum of greater or lesser use.

Before the experiment started, the Peltiers were set to 30°C and participants were told that it represented a middle amount of usage and was given the magnitude value of 50. After each stimulus, the user was asked *"how much has this application been used?"* Participants were instructed to respond with a value that represented their perceived magnitude of usage by typing numbers into a text box. At this point, we only had a number attributed to each temperature but we would not necessarily know whether that number represented more or less usage than the middle 50. For example, 70 could represent more usage (e.g., a greater amount) or less usage (e.g., it was used longer ago). Therefore, the application also asked participants, via a drop-down box, whether their value represented a greater or lesser extent of usage than the middle value of 50. In contrast to the first two scenarios, this used a participant-defined, continuous range. While we dictated the middle value, participants could attribute any number to the stimuli, including negative numbers and large positive numbers. This scenario allowed us to see how thermal feedback is mapped to a continuous range of data, representing an overall "amount", which could be applied in other scenarios, such as navigation distance or e-fitness targets.

Procedure

The procedure was very similar to the Contact List scenario, however the experiment GUI (Figure 1, right) showed 18 icons in an arrangement similar to both Android and iOS. During each trial, the experimental software presented the instruction *"Please select [application] next"* and users were told to long-press the icon to delete it. Each of the 18 icons was a target, one per trial. Upon long-pressing, the software changed the Peltiers to the relevant temperature and participants were presented with the text box and drop-down menu. After pressing "submit", the Peltier was returned to 30°C and the next trial began after 10 seconds.

Results & Initial Discussion

The geometric mean magnitude values for each temperature are shown in Figure 5. There was a significant positive correlation between stimulus temperature and perceived usage magnitude using Pearson's product-moment correlation coefficient (r (7) = 0.989, $p<0.01$). Perceived usage increased as stimulus temperature increased. Every participant indicated that higher values indicated a higher level of usage, which suggests that warmth is interpreted as representing high usage and cold temperature low usage. While there is a strong correlation, the pattern is slightly different for warm and cold stimuli. Warm temperatures (>30°C) increase in usage magnitude linearly, but magnitudes for cooler temperatures (<30°C) drop more quickly before levelling out at 24°C.

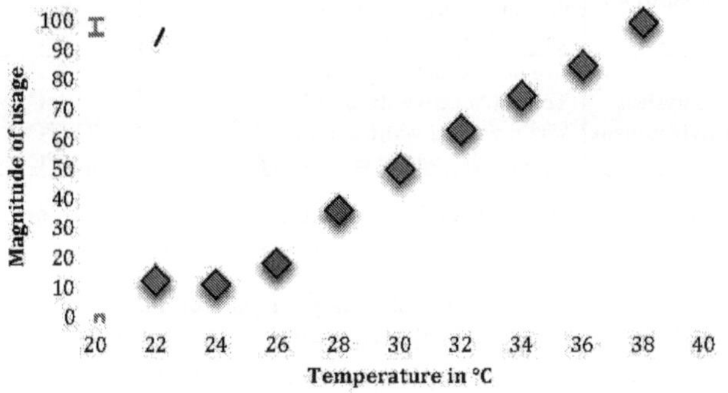

Figure 5: Geometric mean of magnitude values given for each temperature during the application deletion task (r = 0.989).

A repeated-measures ANOVA on normalized magnitude values showed a significant effect of temperature on usage magnitude ($F_{(6,232)} = 68.044$, $p<0.001$). *Post hoc* Bonferroni pairwise comparisons showed that 22°C, 24°C and 26°C were not significantly different from each other, but all other temperature comparisons differed significantly ($p<0.05$ for all adjacent temperatures except 32°C vs. 34°C; $p<0.001$ for all other comparisons including 32°C vs. 34°C). Effect sizes were all r = 0.3 or above. This shows that all warm temperatures had significantly different perceived magnitude values, but there was no difference between temperatures below 28°C.

It may be that participants perceived cold as representing a more singular state of "little use", while degrees of warmth meant degrees of use. While users can have some difficulty differentiating degrees of change in thermal feedback, this affects warm temperatures much more than cold [4,22,23]. This is, therefore, less likely to have affected perception of the cold stimuli and the linear, significant increases in perceived usage above 30°C would suggest that this did not happen to the warm stimuli either. While the mapping of warmth to greater usage is not particularly surprising, the finding that users can reliably appreciate up to 7 temperature levels is a new finding in thermal feedback research. From the results, it appears as though thermal feedback could effectively convey amount of usage. As mentioned above, application usage and importance are related, and so thermal feedback may also be useful in supporting users to reflect on the importance of their actions in different applications. These could include agreeing to share personal information or opening potentially suspicious emails/links.

Subjective Experience: Restaurant Ratings

In the previous examples, we presented the participants with set thermal stimuli and asked for their interpretations of those signals. Previous research has also provided set stimuli for users to interpret. Only Lee and Lim [14] have asked participants how they would convey their own information or intentions by choosing their own feedback designs, and this was limited to interpersonal communication. However, Lee and Lim provided no details about the actual stimuli participants' chose. Here we take a step further by asking participants to convey their personal opinions on familiar bars or restaurants by setting thermal stimuli to a desired temperature. We report and discuss the specific temperatures associated with each type of response.

Restaurant review sites are widely used and the numerical rating, typically from 1 (bad) to 5 (excellent), is an established means of quickly identifying "good" or "bad" places to go. However, individual reasons for liking or disliking an establishment include many social/emotional aspects, such as the quality of food, the service or the atmosphere. Temperature and food are inherently linked, e.g., soup is generally hot and soft drinks are generally cold, and thermal stimuli are appreciated in food-based media [15]. On a hedonic level, hot drinks may be enjoyable on a cold day, while cold drinks may be enjoyable on a hot day. The link between language and temperature to describe social settings is also strong: 'warm and welcoming' service; being given the 'cold shoulder'; an establishment is 'cool and trendy'. This makes choosing appropriate thermal feedback to represent restaurants/bars difficult.

We wanted to understand how people would use temperature to convey their own experiences of bars and restaurants. This could relate to overall quality, or some other social or hedonic element. By looking at the relationships between thermal stimuli and meaning across different participants, we can see if there are any patterns that could be used to inform the design of thermal feedback. In this scenario, participants were asked to assign a temperature to places that they liked, disliked and were indifferent to, and provide an explanation of their temperature mapping. In this way, we would see how temperature was used across places of varying subjective quality.

Stimuli & Measures

This scenario was different from the others, as no predefined thermal stimuli were presented to participants. Instead, a list of 395 bars and restaurants from Glasgow were shown on the PC monitor. Participants were asked to search the list for six bars or restaurants that they had visited (all participants were from the city): two that they liked, two that were average and two that they did not like. Three data points were collected for each of the places: a user-selected temperature that represented his/her experience along with some text that explained their temperature choice. Finally, an indication of whether they thought the bar/restaurant was "good", "average" or "bad" was entered. The temperature was set through a slider, which changed the Peltier temperature in real-time. The possible temperatures were 22°C (far-left position) to 38°C (far right) at a resolution of 0.1°C. No numerical value for the temperature was shown.

Procedure

This experiment ran on a PC, with the participant sat at a desk, with a monitor, keyboard and mouse in front of them along with the Peltier devices and armrest. They were asked to search for each of the six bars/restaurants either by typing relevant text into a search bar or scrolling the alphabetical list. When an establishment was selected, the monitor showed a screen including the name and representative image along with the input slider, text box and drop-down menu. The participants were asked to set the temperature of the Peltiers in response to the question *"What temperature would you associate with this place?"* They were told they were free to base their feedback on any aspect of their experience. Once the temperature had been set, they were asked to type their reasoning for the stimulus, or what it represented, before indicating whether they thought the place was "good", "average" or "bad" from the drop-down menu.

Rating	★☆☆☆☆	★★☆☆☆	★★★☆☆	★★★★☆	★★★★★
Temp	25°C	27.5°C	30°C	32.5°C	35°C

Table 3: Recommended temperatures for conveying the star rating of bars and restaurants using thermal feedback

Results & Initial Discussion

The average (min and max) temperature attributed to the three overall quality ratings "good", "average" and "bad" were 34.8°C (24.5°C, 38.0°C), 29.8°C (25.6°C, 32.7°C) and 25.4°C (22.0°C, 35.2°C), respectively. A Friedman test on the average representative temperature showed a significant effect of quality (χ^2 (2)=38.89, $p<0.001$). *Post hoc* Bonferroni-adjusted ($p<0.0167$) Wilcoxon tests showed that all three ratings were significantly different from each other. There were no numerical values shown next to the slider in the GUI, yet participants naturally chose almost equally spaced values centred on the neutral temperature of 30°C (±5°C). The average temperatures attached to the good, average and bad establishments could be extended to represent the common 1-5 star ratings, as shown in Table 3. While ~35°C was chosen to represent "good", in some mobile scenarios, stimuli between 32-35°C might be difficult to tell apart [21,22], so the 4- and 5-star temperatures could instead be ~34°C and 38°C, to facilitate differentiation.

Analysing the attribution of temperatures to experiences, we identified five categories of meaning: 1) the overall rating or quality (e.g., warm for good; 76 responses), 2) hedonic/emotional meaning (e.g., nice atmosphere; 16 responses), 3) social aspects (e.g., friendly people; 10 responses) and representing the thermal properties of 4) the food/drinks consumed (e.g., hot coffee; 5 responses) or 5) the physical environment (e.g., cold at night; 8 responses). A summary of responses is in Table 4, including the temperatures participants chose to represent their experiences.

Response Category	Subjective Experiences	Associated Temperature
Quality or Rating	"Good restaurant, so warm temperature"	35°C
	"The food was ok so…neutral temperature"	30°C
	"Good food"	34.1°C
	"Not a fan. Not at all!"	26.3°C
Hedonic or Emotion	"Nice atmosphere"	36.5°C
	"[Poor] atmosphere"	24.6°C
	"[Good] because [the coffee] smells nice"	33.1°C
	"Really cute…place"	36.5°C
Social	"Friendly place…it's easy to meet people"	35.2°C
	"Hot girls" (interesting people)	34.1°C
Food, Drink	"Gave me a cold pie"	23.4°C
	"Very spicy…map…temperature [to] heat"	36.3°C
	"I mainly go for cold food"	24°C
	"They sell hot coffee"	33.1°C
Physical Environment	"I've only been at night when it's cold"	28.8°C
	"You get hot from dancing"	34.1°C
	"You'd go on a warm summer evening"	32.7°C
	"I went…in…winter and I was freezing"	22.2°C

Table 4: Selected subjective responses, grouped by category. Includes the thermal feedback representing the experience.

It was clear that the vast majority of participants attributed the thermal stimulus to the overall quality or rating of the establishment, in line with the average temperatures for the overall ratings. Thermal feedback in a restaurant experience scenario appears to be used to represent the overall quality. Given the response consistency, there may be a strong link between thermal feedback and enjoyment. The second most common meaning attributed to thermal stimuli was hedonic or emotional comments. Nine responses commented on using temperatures to convey the atmosphere or mood in the place. For all responses, colder temperatures were used for poor atmosphere and warmer temperatures for good.

Several of the experiences relating to atmosphere were joined by social comments on the quality or *"friendliness"* of the service received from staff. Generally, the quality of service correlated with the overall quality rating, so warm temperatures were used for good service and cold for bad. The quality, atmosphere and social attributes all gel with the results from the two previous scenarios, where warmth is characteristic of physical or social warmth. Eight responses used the temperature to represent a corresponding environmental temperature, while the remaining responses related to the physical characteristics of the food, such as poor cold food or nice hot coffee.

It is noteworthy that the two restaurant experience categories that represent real, concrete features (food or environmental responses) numbered so few, while the vast majority fall under abstract or subjective categories (quality, hedonic, social). This suggests that, at least in relation to a restaurant experience, thermal feedback is not seen a descriptive or representative signal, one that conveys an actual state. It is an excitatory, emotional signal for conveying high-level impressions. Thermal feedback has been shown to be effective and convincing in mimicking object/surface thermal properties in virtual reality [5,16]. However, this was not a common usage for thermal feedback by participants here.

DISCUSSION & FEEDBACK GUIDELINES

In all four scenarios there was a strong uniformity in the participants' interpretation of thermal feedback, in slight contrast to previous research [14,18]. In general, our results suggest that warm feedback represents 1) the presence of life or activity and 2) emotional positivity, while cold feedback represents the opposite: 1) the absence of people and activity and 2) emotional negativity. When asked how recently a person had been active on social media, warm temperatures (34-38°C) were consistently interpreted as meaning very recent activity (no more than a few hours), while cold temperatures (22-26°C) were interpreted as meaning much older activity (weeks and months). This could be interpreted as a *temporal* social closeness, rather than a *physical* social closeness. This relationship of warmth to presence and cold to absence was also found in the office availability scenario. There was strong agreement that warm temperatures (34-38°C) indicated presence in the office and cold temperatures (22-26°C) indicated absence. Stronger warmth was also interpreted as meaning the person had a higher level of unavailability ("Extremely busy", compared to "Available for short times"), while stronger cold meant that the individual was away for longer. Another view on the social media and presence data could be that a person's activity level could be indicated along an axis from *no activity* (cold 22°C) to *most activity* (warm 38°C).

The results from the first three scenarios throw up an interesting comparison to previous research on the perception or identification of predefined thermal changes for conveying information in HCI. Research has shown that our ability to identify a virtual material from its thermal conductivity (change in temperature over time) alone can be poor, ranging from 16% to 100%, even when choosing between only 4-5 possible materials [5,6,7]. The identification of more explicitly structured thermal feedback (e.g., 2 to 3 set levels of warmth) is more accurate, at around 75-100% for 4-5 levels or alternatives [19,21,22]. Both the social media and content deletion scenarios had reliable patterns of responses. Excluding the neutral temperatures (30-32°C), each of the remaining 7 stimuli in the social media scenario had a different pattern of time frames being attributed to them. The deletion scenario showed significant differences in perceived magnitude between all but the 3 lowest temperatures, which suggests participants could differentiate 7 levels. This includes 4 different levels of warmth, where identifying only 2 has been challenging previously [21,22].

We did not test absolute identification, and participants were not told how many stimuli were used (or how far apart they were). However, it is unlikely that participants could identify each stimulus uniquely, due to the lack of explicit structure and the relatively large number of stimuli. What our results suggest, however, is that participants were still able to reliably perceive, and appraise differently, up to 7 levels of thermal change, indicating an inherent or subconscious appreciation of several extents of temperature change. This is a larger number than users have been able to consciously identify in previous research. The implication for thermal interface design is that, while users may not be able to deliberately identify many levels, perhaps due to comparison-induced uncertainty, they can be relied on to appreciate and make use of several different thermal states. In this case, thermal feedback may be better suited as an ambient or supplemental feedback method than a primary means of conveying specific information.

The restaurant experience scenario resulted in a narrower range of responses than we had anticipated, given the open-ended nature of how participants could choose the stimuli and assign meaning to them. 66% of all the meanings attached to the thermal stimuli related simply to the overall quality of the establishment. This strong uniformity suggests that, within the restaurant scenario, thermal feedback has a clear meaning and widespread interpretation. This is helpful for interaction designers as they can be confident in how the feedback will be interpreted: the higher rated the place, the hotter the feedback should be. Warmth (>30°C) could also be used to indicate a friendly or social atmosphere. It should be noted that the framing of the scenario, asking participants to choose good, average and bad places, could have unintentionally guided them towards a quality-based perspective. However, they were explicitly told that the stimulus could represent any aspect of their experience.

Feedback Design Guidelines

High degree of common interpretation

Participants interpreted thermal feedback in a consistent manner, with very similar views on the meaning of both warm and cool changes. Previous research has generally shown a similar consistency [14,18]. Therefore, despite the variable nature of thermal perception [9,23], thermal feedback designs can be created with a good degree of reliability in how they will be interpreted by different users.

Warmth means social and physical presence

Warmth (>32°C) should be used to convey the physical or social presence of other people, while cool (<30°C) should be used to convey the absence of people or usage. Greater or lesser degrees, respectively, of presence, activity and positivity can be conveyed through increasing the extent of heat or cold. This could include the digital presence of someone online, the physical presence of a friend nearby (using location aware services) or a friendly, social occasion, such as calendar events. A number of different social/spatial states could also be conveyed through thermal feedback: spatial proximity in navigation, website traffic or the number of social media posts on a topic.

Temperature maps to quality

The quality or rating of content can be conveyed through temperature, with cool (~22-25°C) indicating the lowest quality and warmth (~35-38°C) indicating the highest.

Thermal feedback can convey risk-related status

When a user attempts to alter data, thermal feedback can reliably convey how used (and perhaps important) the content is. This could help to impose upon the user the risk of permanent alterations to their information.

Users can appreciate multiple levels of ambient feedback

While unique identification of thermal stimuli is challenging, users are able to appraise and make use of multiple (in our case up to 7) different feedback temperatures. Feedback designs can therefore reliably utilize different temperatures, but should do so in an ambient or supportive manner.

CONCLUSIONS

This paper presented studies that investigated how participants interpret thermal feedback in the context of four different types of information: online social activity, physical presence, digital content usage and experiential content. Participants reliably interpreted multiple levels of thermal feedback in consistent ways, attributing similar meanings to warm and cool changes. Warmth indicated 1) more recent social media activity, 2) physical presence and busyness, 3) higher content use and 4) positive experiences at bars or restaurants. Cooler stimuli conveyed the opposite. The results provide new insight into what inherent meaning thermal feedback has in HCI contexts and our design guidelines suggest how it might be effectively utilized in interfaces.

REFERENCES

1. Gallo, S., Cucu, L., Thevenaz, N., Sengul, A., and Bleuler, H. Design and control of a novel thermo-tactile multimodal display. *Proc. HAPTICS 2014*, pp 75–81.
2. Gooch, D. & Watts, L. Communicating social presence through thermal hugs. *Proc. SISSE 2010*, pp 11–19.
3. Halvey, M., Henderson, M., Brewster, S., Wilson, G., and Hughes, S. Augmenting Media with Thermal Stimulation. *Proc. HAID 2012*, pp 91–100.
4. Halvey, M., Wilson, G., Brewster, S., and Hughes, S. "Baby It's Cold Outside": The Influence of Ambient Temperature and Humidity on Thermal Feedback. *Proc. CHI 2012*, pp 715–724.
5. Ho, H.-N. and Jones, L. Contribution of thermal cues to material discrimination and localization. *Perception & Psychophysics 68*, 1, pp 118–128.
6. Ho, H.-N. and Jones, L. Development and evaluation of a thermal display for material identification and discrimination. *ACM TAP*, 4 (2) 2007, Article 13.
7. Ino, S., Shimizu, S., Odagawa, T., *et al.* A tactile display for presenting quality of materials by changing the temperature of skin surface. *Proc. IEEE Robot and Human Communication*, pp 220–224.
8. Iwasaki, K., Miyaki, T., and Rakimoto, J. AffectPhone: A Handset Device to Present User's Emotional State with Warmth/Coolness. *Proc. BIOSTEC 2010*, pp 1–6.
9. Jones, L. and Berris, M. The Psychophysics of Temperature Perception and Thermal-Interface Design. *Proc. HAPTICS 2002*, pp 137–142.
10. Kenshalo, D., Holmes, C., and Wood, P. Warm and Cool Thresholds as a Function of Temperature Change. *Perception & Psychophysics 3*, 2A, pp 81–84.
11. Kenshalo, D., Nafe, J., and Brooks, B. Variations in Thermal Sensitivity. *Science 134*, 1, pp 104–105.
12. Lautenbacher, S. and Rollman, G. Sex differences in responsiveness to painful and non-painful stimuli are dependent upon the stimulation method. *Pain 53*, 1, pp 255–264.
13. Lee, W. and Lim, Y. Thermo-Message: Exploring the Potential of Heat as a Modality of peripheral Expression. *Proc. CHI 2010 Ext. Abs.*, pp 4231–4236.
14. Lee, W. and Lim, Y. Explorative research on the heat as an expression medium: focused on interpersonal communication. *Personal and Ubiquitous Computing 16*, pp 1039–1049.
15. Nakashige, M., Kobayashi, M., Suzuki, Y., *Tamaki, H., and Higashino, S.* "Hiya-Atsu" media: augmenting digital media with temperature. *Proc. CHI 2009 Ext. Abs.*, pp 3181–3186.
16. Richter, H., Hausen, D., Osterwald, S., and Butz. Reproducing Materials of Virtual Elements on Touchscreen using Supplemental Thermal Feedback. *Proc. ICMI 2012*, pp 385–392.
17. Salminen, K., Surakka, V., Raisamo, J., *et al.* Emotional Responses to Thermal Stimuli. *Proc. ICMI 2011*, pp 193–196.
18. Suhonen, K., Muller, S., Rantala, J., *et al.* Haptically Augmented Remote Speech Communication: A Study of User Practices and Experiences. *Proc. NordiCHI 2012*, pp 361–369.
19. Wettach, R., Behrens, C., Danielsson, A., and Ness, T. A thermal information display for mobile applications. *Proc. MobileHCI 2007*, pp 182–185.
20. Williams, L. and Bargh, J. Experiencing physical warmth promotes interpersonal warmth. *Science 322*, 1, pp 606–607.
21. Wilson, G., Brewster, S., Halvey, M., and Hughes, S. Thermal Icons: Evaluating Structured Thermal Feedback for Mobile Interaction. *Proc. MobileHCI 2012*, pp 309–312.
22. Wilson, G., Brewster, S., Halvey, M., and Hughes, S. Thermal Feedback Identification in a Mobile Environment. *Proc. HAID 2013*, Article 2.
23. Wilson, G., Halvey, M., Brewster, S., and Hughes, S. Some Like it Hot? Thermal Feedback for Mobile Devices. *Proc. CHI 2011*, pp 2555–2564.

EnviroPulse: Providing Feedback about the Expected Affective Valence of the Environment

Deltcho Valtchanov, Mark Hancock
University of Waterloo
Waterloo, Ontario, Canada
{dvaltchanov,mark.hancock}@uwaterloo.ca

ABSTRACT
Interacting with nature is beneficial to a person's mental-state, but it can sometimes be difficult to find environments that will induce positive affect (e.g., when planning a run). In this paper, we describe *EnviroPulse*—a system for automatically determining and communicating the expected affective valence (EAV) of environments to individuals. We describe a prototype that allows this to be used in real-time on a smartphone, but *EnviroPulse* could easily be incorporated into GPS systems, mapping services, or image-based systems. Our work differs from existing work in affective computing in that, rather than detecting a user's affect directly, we automatically determine the EAV of the environment through visual analysis. We present results that suggest our system can determine the EAV of environments. We also introduce real-time affective visual feedback of the calculated EAV of images, and present results from an informal study suggesting that real-time visual feedback can be used for induction of affect.

Author Keywords
Human Factors; Affective Computing; Mobile Interfaces

INTRODUCTION
Over the past forty years, psychologists have demonstrated strong and consistent evidence that interacting with nature is highly important for psychological and physical well-being [10,26]. This principle, known as *biophilia,* is based on empirical evidence demonstrating that interactions with the natural world improve cognitive abilities (e.g., the ability to sustain attention, vigilance, etc.) and reduce stress and its associated negative effects (e.g., high blood pressure, increased stress hormones, and diminished autoimmune response) [26,27]. In the absence of this interaction with the natural world, the chronic stress leads to increases in mental disorders (e.g., anxiety disorders, attention deficit disorders, etc.), stronger negative emotions such as fear and anger,

CHI 2015, April 18 - 23 2015, Seoul, Republic of Korea

ACM 978-1-4503-3145-6/15/04...$15.00
http://dx.doi.org/10.1145/2702123.2702510

Figure 1. An individual viewing her environment through her phone's camera before she takes a picture.

and diminished life satisfaction [10]. Unfortunately, while many people (61%) recognize that stress is a serious problem, only a small number (35%) know how to effectively reduce it [2]. As a result, 78 percent say their stress has increased or stayed the same in the past five years [2].

In human-computer interaction (HCI), the importance of identifying and alleviating stress has been recognized, and various different sensing and mobile intervention technologies have been developed to combat the "stress epidemic" [19]. The field of affective computing has already demonstrated that technology can be used to detect and respond to emotional states [12]. People's emotions can be detected through facial features [12], gestures [4], and physiological measures [20]. Computational methods have also been described for determining the aesthetics of an image specifically [8]. However, the majority of this research has focused on responding to current emotional state, rather than on providing feedback about the likely impact of the environment on that emotion.

In this paper we present *EnviroPulse,* a technology derived from research on the psychological impact of environments, images, and videos to support a novel kind of affective computing. Rather than focusing on real-time detection of a person's affect [12], *EnviroPulse* automatically calculates an expected affective valence (EAV) score for the environment through visual analysis of image and video input in real-time. It can be used to direct people toward places and scenery that promote better psychological well-being (rather than acting as a barrier to them). For example, it can be used to crawl through Google Street View data to develop affective valence maps of the world. Using this, map-

Figure 2. (left) A person using our prototype smartphone camera app to get real-time feedback about the psychological impact of the environment. (right) A zoomed in view (darkened background) of the detailed visual feedback provided with multiple bars.

ping services, such as Google and Bing maps can be augmented with an "affective valence" layer (much like the traffic layers) to show users which locations and routes are most psychologically positive. *EnviroPulse* can also be incorporated into gaming, camera, GPS, and augmented reality smartphone applications to provide real-time analysis of the environment using the smartphone's camera (Figure 2). In order to test *EnviroPulse*, both "in the wild" and in the lab, we describe a prototype and how it is integrated into a smartphone camera app to allow for real-time feedback about a photo or video being captured. Our prototype provides information about the expected affective valence (EAV) of visual data, allowing the smartphone to be used as a "smart window" into the environment (Figure 2) by panning the camera around to find environments that are psychologically positive, and potentially photo-worthy. In order to communicate the EAV score of the environment to the user, we implemented four types of visual feedback of affective valence: two that present factual information via bar graph and data glyph, and two that *induce* emotion and provide individuals with immediate emotional feedback.

We therefore provide three contributions: (1) we designed and developed *EnviroPulse*, a prototype algorithm and interface for the real-time automated analysis of the expected affective valence of images and video, optimized to run on smartphone hardware; (2) we present empirical results from a validation study which suggests that *EnviroPulse* achieves moderate accuracy for determining the affective valence of environments, and offers greater and more reliable accuracy than the average independent human observer; and (3) we describe the design of four versions of real-time visual feedback of EAV, two traditional and two based on psychological literature on human shape and contour preference, to display the affective analysis from our algorithm (i.e., whether something is stressful or calming/pleasant), which we tested in an informal study.

RELATED WORK

The areas of research most pertinent to our work are the HCI literature on *mobile augmented reality* and *affective computing*, and the *psychology of scene and colour perception and preference*.

Mobile Augmented Reality

Using mobile devices, such as smartphones, to create augmented reality (AR) or mixed reality is a practice that is growing in popularity and complexity as mobile computing power continues to improve [28]. Augmented reality in smartphones can take many forms, including reading barcodes or QR codes from the camera view to give details about a product, labeling nearby landmarks in the camera view, or overlaying interactive visualizations on top of the live video of the real environment [21].

Mobile augmented reality typically uses the smartphone's camera and wireless connection combined with other sensors such as the GPS, accelerometer, and compass to compare the individual's location and image data to a database and pull relevant information (e.g., nearby coffee shops) [21,24]. For example, the smartphone app *Layar* overlays information on top of the video feed coming from the smartphone's camera when a barcode or template image is recognized by the software [21]. The development of augmented reality apps has not been limited to simply displaying information. By overlaying information on top of the video feed from the smartphone's camera, mobile augmented reality apps transform smartphones into windows through which individuals can view an augmented version of their environment. In this paper, we use this idea of smartphones as windows to an augmented version of the environment, and display information that may not be immediately obvious: the expected affective impact of the environment on the individual.

Affective Computing

In the field of affective computing, an effort has been made to detect and respond to emotional states of users [12]. Such methods have been used to categorize media using the viewer as a source of information for valence and arousal by monitoring the viewer's facial expressions [12]. Some work has also focused on applying psychological models of valence and arousal to categorize media along the two-dimensional space of valence (positive or negative) versus arousal (high or low) [11,31]. Similarly, computational methods have also been described for determining the aesthetics of images [8].

The field of affective computing has also explored how this affective data may be visualized and communicated to the user via affective visualizations. For example, recent research by Zhang et al. [31] has shown evidence that affective states prompted by movies may be presented in a simple "affective visualization" which uses four colours to depict the four quadrants of high vs. low arousal and positive vs. negative valence. However, the authors explicitly note that affective visualizations ought to be more intuitive and informative than they currently are.

We propose an alternative to these methods for determining and representing affect in technology. Our *EnviroPulse* prototype builds on this work by using an algorithm that can estimate the affect prompted by an environment, rather than sensing it from the user [11,12, 31]. We also attempt to create informative affective visual feedback that can communicate the expected affective impact of the environment.

Psychology of Scene Perception and Preference

Our work combines the wealth of research on the human scene preference and the affective (emotional) influence of individuals' surroundings (i.e., where they live, work, go to relax, etc.) with modern advancements in smartphone technology. We take into account a diverse set of literature looking at (1) visual reward circuits in the human brain that preferentially respond to some types of scenes [5], (2) how the human brain processes visual characteristics of scenes [27], and (3) the way that images of the environment may be analyzed and related to the activation of neural circuits responsible for positive and negative emotions [14,17,27].

Previous research has demonstrated that humans prefer environments (and images) that contain curved shapes and contours, over those that contain jagged contours or pointed shapes [1,3]. This research has found that jagged objects are perceived as more threatening, activating brain areas associated with fear and threat processing [3].

Similarly, research on scene perception has found that urban environments, such as New York City traffic, prompt higher stress levels compared to their natural counterparts (e.g., Central Park) [26,27]. Research on how images of cities influence the viewer's emotional state suggests that urban environments are more stressful than natural environments because they contain more jagged patterns and shapes [26]. Urban environments which contain smooth contours and round shapes are perceived as less threatening, and may even be perceived as similarly pleasant to some natural environments [27]. This line of research has also found that, as visual complexity (density of shapes and contours) in images increases beyond an ideal threshold, the emotional response to the images become more negative and stressful [27]. This finding is consistent with research on the dose-response curve for the impact of tree cover density on stress reduction [13]. It is important to note that these perceptual and neural mechanisms are believed to be "automatic" and consistent across individuals and populations in the absence of disorders [1,3,5,14,17,26,27].

Psychology of Colour Perception and Preference

To get a more complete picture of human preference for scenes and shapes, we also consulted literature on human colour perception and colour preference. Studies investigating the effects of colour on emotions have discovered several factors that influence how humans respond to colours.

Humans have strong preferences for colour hues ranging from blue to green, a strong to moderate aversion for colour hues ranging from green to yellow and yellow to red, and a moderate preference for colours ranging from red to blue (Figure 3, left) [18,25].

When analyzing the effects of colour brightness and colour and saturation on perceived pleasure, researchers have found that brighter (non-white) and more saturated colours are more calming and pleasurable (Figure 3, right). In contrast, darker colours were more likely to elicit feelings of anger, hostility, or aggression. We integrate these findings on scene and colour preference into a prototype for real-time detection of affect induced by an image or video. It should be noted that researchers exploring the effects of colour on emotion highlight that their findings are relevant only in situations in which colours are reasonable (e.g., blue meat would not be preferred even though blue is a highly preferred colour) [18,25].

ENVIROPULSE: ANALYSING AFFECT IN IMAGES

We developed *EnviroPulse*, an algorithm for determining the affective response that is likely to be induced by an environment. In this section, we describe the algorithm that could be incorporated into any system that involves images of the environment, such as mapping services or GPS systems, and then describe the design of an interface for a smartphone camera app that can sense and communicate the affect of photographs and videos.

Implementation

We conceptualized our *EnviroPulse* algorithm using research on the automatic and psychophysiological factors that shape human scene perception and affective responses to visual stimuli [1,3,5,14,25,26,27]. The algorithm is designed to automatically determine the expected affective valence of images and videos across populations. In this section, we highlight some of the challenges in aggregating this research and developing a computational algorithm for real-time visual analysis. We then describe the details of our algorithm.

Emotional Response Factors

We aggregated psychological findings from a variety of research on human scene and colour preference to create six composite curves representing the six factors believed to be responsible for automatic emotional responses to scenes and environments: *shape*, *contour*, *complexity*, *colour hue*,

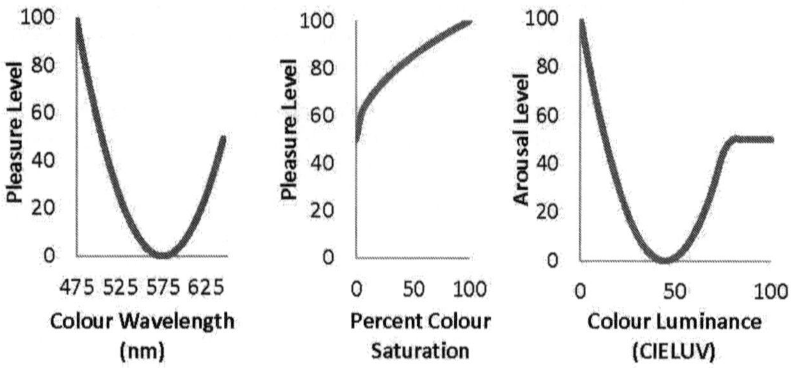

Figure 3. Curves of mappings used in our algorithm from colour space to pleasure and arousal levels. Previous work [25] shows that people prefer (left) blue-green (~475-500 nm) and red (~650 nm), and dislike yellow (~570 nm) and (middle) high colour saturation and that (right) luminance can be used to estimate arousal levels.

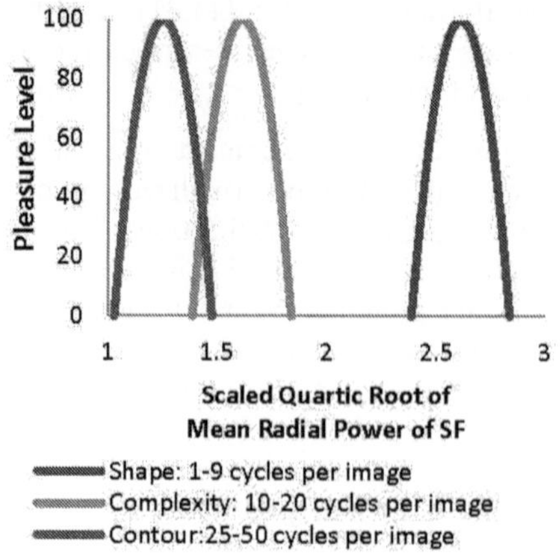

Figure 4. Curves informed by psychology research relating affective responses to shape, complexity and contour with the spatial frequencies of an image.

colour saturation, and *colour brightness* (Figure 3-4) [1,3,25,27]. The composite curves (Figure 3-4) represent both the aggregation of past findings from different sources [1,3,25,27], and our interpretation of these findings, resulting in a novel representation of emotional response factors. This was in part because the psychology literature on human preference presents its findings based on relative subjective categorical scales (e.g., 1 = not pleasant, 4 = moderately pleasant, 7 = highly pleasant). Since the measurement scales differed across researchers and experiments, and were categorical in nature, we had to convert such results into an absolute metric that would allow for cross-research aggregation. We did this by mapping results from previous literature on human preference onto quadratic, and square-root functions, which have been previously shown to represent human responses to a variety of cognitive and emotional situations and stimuli [13,25,27].

Expected Affective Valence (EAV) Score

Our *EnviroPulse* prototype captures the pleasure and arousal associated with changes in the six psychological factors using individual scores for each factor. Each of the scores is computed in parallel and is then combined into one expected affective valence (EAV) score. Each score is calculated using a quadratic function or its inverse, and is normalized between 0 and 1. The equations were extrapolated from previous work [9,14,25,27] and are of the form:

$$y = \left(\frac{x-a}{b}\right)^2,$$

where the score can be either y (quadratic), x (root), or 1-y (inverted quadratic).

Based on Valdez and Mehrabian's theory of colour's contribution to affective response [25], whose findings have been recently been replicated by Palmer and Schloss [18], colour wavelength (quadratic, $a = 575$, $b = 100$) and saturation (root, $a = 0.5$, $b = 0.05$) are computed for each pixel and averaged to create a colour pleasure score, which is "calmed" using a colour arousal score computed using luminance (inverted quadratic, $a = 45$, $b = 45$; or the constant 0.5, neutral, if luminance is above 80, white), again averaged across all pixels. This combined equation becomes:

$$color\ score = color\ pleasure \cdot color\ arousal$$

To compute theoretical pleasure levels for the content in the scene, a scaled discrete Fourier transform is used on a grayscale version of the scene to extract the average radial power of each of the three ranges of spatial frequencies (Figure 3, [9,14,16,27]). A score for each of *shape* (inverted quadratic, $a = 2.614$, $b = 0.225$), *complexity* (inverted quadratic, $a = 1.61627$, $b = 0.225$), and *contour* (inverted quadratic, $a = 1.255$, $b = 0.225$) is calculated, and their average is used to provide an overall *content score*.

The colour score and content score are then combined into the EAV score using weights inferred from the variance and regression analysis in Valdez and Mehrabian [25], and Valtchanov [27], as follows:

$$EAV\ Score = 0.3 \cdot colour\ score + 0.7 \cdot content\ score$$

Scores of 40 or below represent a negative affective impact, while scores from 40–60 represent a neutral affective impact, and scores of 60 or greater represent a positive affective impact. We used this procedure for calculating the emotional impact of incoming image data, to label scenes as psychologically positive, neutral, or negative, which we then make available in real-time through visual feedback.

Incorporating EnviroPulse into Image-Based Software

The EAV score can be calculated for any image, and therefore can be incorporated into any image- or camera-based technology. For instance, the EAV score could be calculated for all images on Google Street View, allowing Google Maps to provide feedback about the likely affective impact of a walking route. *EnviroPulse* could also be incorporated into wearable head-mounted technology, such as

Google Glass, warning of danger when a person is spending too much time in dense city environments. We next describe a specific design that incorporates *EnviroPulse* into a smartphone camera application to provide real-time feedback about the expected average emotional response to the environment, and the images/video currently being captured.

AFFECTIVE VISUAL FEEDBACK IN A CAMERA APP

To demonstrate how *EnviroPulse* can be used in an interface, we implemented a smartphone camera application that uses EAV score to measure the emotional valence of the image/video feed coming from the smartphone's camera. This required that the result of the analysis be presented in a rapid, comprehensive, and intelligible manner to the individual using a smartphone. We wanted to avoid simply presenting the overall EAV score in a numerical format, since we expected that it would encourage users to always try to achieve the highest rating. Instead, we made it possible to recognize how moving the smartphone camera around (i.e., changing in the visible scene) results in more positive or negative scores along the six emotional response factors. Visualizing the multiple dimensions that determine EAV will not only help explain the score, but allow more freedom to establish photography or videography that captures a wider spectrum of emotional response, rather than assuming that what this prototype rates as "positive" relates to the desired outcome.

In order to accomplish this, we consulted past attempts at affective visualizations [6,31] and the psychological literature related to affect induction [26,29], as well as literature in multi-dimensional visualizations [15], to inform the design of four versions of real-time visual feedback. We designed four examples of visual feedback of the calculated EAV score because we wanted to investigate whether factual or affective visual feedback could better communicate the estimated affective valence of an environment. Our first two versions use a traditional approach of communicating the information by simply presenting the facts in bar or glyph forms, and our second two versions make use of our algorithmic knowledge of affect to *induce* the affect more abstractly through waves and shapes.

Factual Visual Feedback

To communicate the information contained within our analysis prototype, we first considered the six scores as separate dimensions in a multi-dimensional visualization, and used traditional information visualization techniques for displaying these multiple dimensions: *bars* and *glyphs*.

Multiple Bars

We used *multiple bars* (Figure 5, top-left), similar to a bar chart, which projects from a centred neutral label toward either a negative or positive label anchor while altering its colour along a red to white to green gradient to indicate the negative, neutral, or positive valence of the environment. We used both a single bar to indicate the overall score at the bottom of the display, and a series of six bars to represent the multiple dimensions used to determine the score (shape, contour, complexity, colour hue, colour saturation, and colour brightness). The colour scheme was chosen based on the commonly used social symbols of red indicating threat (e.g., red traffic lights, red stop sign, warning labels on drugs, etc.) and green indicating something positive (e.g., green traffic lights, nature/vegetation, etc.) since it is a highly pleasant colour [25].

Glyphs

We also designed visual feedback based on star *glyphs* [15] (Figure 5, bottom-left), which displays scores of the environment along six axes representing the measured dimensions used to calculate affective valence. Much like *multiple bars*, it gradually shifts between red, white, and green to represent the overall negative, neutral or positive valence.

Affective Visual Feedback

Since the foundation of our prototype is based on the principle that a person's affect can be estimated from knowledge of several essential features of an image, our second approach to visualizing this information was to communicate our affective analysis using the affective channel, rather than the more traditional approach of simply displaying the facts. We compared the representations of valence used in the Self-Assessment Manikin (SAM) [6] with previous literature in psychology on affective responses to shapes and contours, and found that the SAM exploits well-documented relationships between affect and shapes and contours [1,3,22,27]. Similar to the SAM graphic, we used the relationship between shapes, contours, colours and affect to generate two affective versions.

We recognize that there is some redundancy in displaying affect about an image by inducing affect through visual feedback (this affect will be induced by the environment or image itself). However, it is worth noting that participants in the studies on human affective responses to scenes [26] took up to 10 minutes to fully feel the effect of the environment. The techniques used in our affective visual feedback were shown to induce these responses in seconds.

Affective Waves

We presented visual feedback through a *wave* (Figure 5, top-right), which alters its contour type (smooth vs. jagged), amplitude (low vs. high), pulse rate (short vs. long), and colour (red to white to green representing negative to neutral to positive overall valence). This design was inspired by Poffenberger and Barrows' [22] research on the affective responses to waves, which demonstrated that jagged waves were found to be agitating, while smooth waves were found to be calming; waves with higher amplitudes were found to be more arousing compared to those with lower amplitudes; and waves with short periods were found to be more unnerving than those with longer periods. *Affective wave* was coded so that stressful negative environments produced jagged, tall, rapid red waves while calming positive environments produced smooth, short, wide green waves.

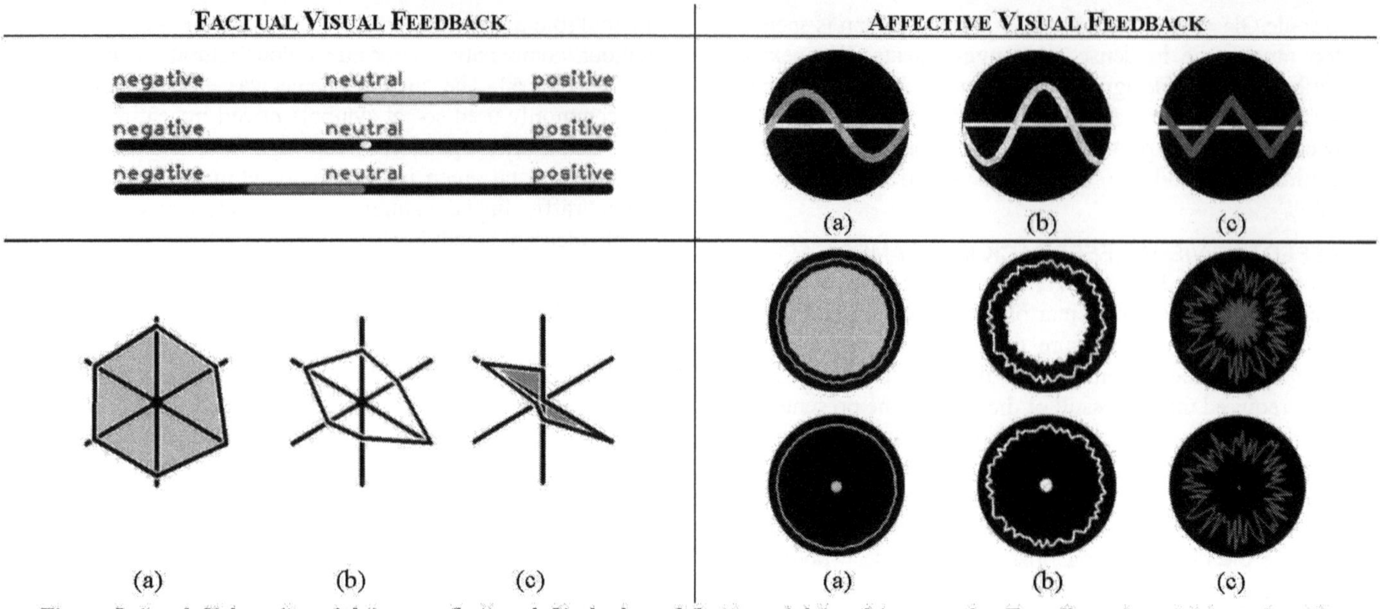

Figure 5. (top-left) bar, (top-right) wave, (bottom-left) glyph, and (bottom-right) pulsing amoeba. For all versions, (a) is moderately positive, (b) is neutral, and (c) is moderately negative and colour changes along a gradient from green, to white, to red, respectively.

Pulsing Amoeba

We also present visual feedback through a *pulsing amoeba* (Figure 5, bottom-right), which alters its contour type (smooth/jagged), its pulse rate (short/long), and its colour (red to white to green, representing negative to neutral to positive valence). For negative stressful environments the amoeba's shape tenses up and shifts toward being jagged and spiked, while the radiating pulse (its "heart rate") dramatically increases and changes to bright red, resembling a warning light. For positive calming environments, the amoeba relaxes and its shape shifts toward a smooth circular contour while its pulse rate slows significantly and its colour changes to green. The pulse occurs from the centre toward the outside, and then retracts back toward the centre.

EVALUATION OF SCENE ANALYSIS ALGORITHM

To determine if our *EnviroPulse* prototype gives estimates of affective valence that are consistent with human responses to environments, we conducted a validation study: our prototype's estimations of the affective valence of images were compared to previous empirical data from human participants. In a previous set of studies by Valtchanov [27], participants viewed photographs of low and high density cities, rural villages, parks, savannah landscapes, forests, beaches, mountains, and lakes while physiological measurements were taken. Participants in these studies also answered questionnaires which assessed the affective impact of viewing each photograph. For our validation study, we used *EnviroPulse* to analyze the photographs used in this past research and compared these scores to those given by participants in the study.

It is important to note that while the research by Valtchanov [27] was partially used to inform the design of *EnviroPulse,* our algorithm uses a composite of several other studies [1,3,9,15,25] to create a new metric for scene analysis: We use six response factors that we have inferred from research [1,3,9,14,25,27], compared to the single response factor that is described by Valtchanov [27]. Since this is the first time these factors have been combined into a single equation for determining EAV of visual stimuli, it required validation.

Validation Experiment Setup

Sixty-five photographs of environments (e.g., cities, parks, forests, mountains, etc.) that were previously used in studies by Valtchanov [27], were projected onto a screen, one at a time, for 3 seconds each. An Android smartphone running our custom camera application with *EnviroPulse* was mounted onto a tripod in front of the screen, such that the smartphone's camera had a complete view of the projected image (Figure 6). Photographs were presented for 3 seconds to allow the smartphone's camera to adjust to changes in luminance and focus between images. Our camera app analyzed each photograph and assigned it an affective score.

EnviroPulse versus Human Perception

We compared the affective scores of the 65 photographs given by our algorithm to the averaged affective scores given by 53 participants (26 male, 27 female) for the same images in Valtchanov [27] using an independent samples t-test. Scores given by our algorithm were on a scale from 0 (highly negative) to 50 (neutral) to 100 (highly positive), while scores from studies by Valtchanov [27] were on a scale from -6 (highly negative) to 0 (neutral) to +6 (highly positive). To allow for comparison, both scores were standardized to the same scale of 0 to 100. The test revealed that the affective scores given by our algorithm were not significantly different from those given by human participants ($t(128) = 0.38$, $p = .70$, $SE = 2.70$). This promising result suggested that our algorithm's analysis was giving similar affective scores to human participants.

In order to measure if *EnviroPulse* correctly categorized the photographs based on valence, we computed the agreement between the valence category assigned by our prototype and that given by the average of the participants in Valtchanov [27] for each of the photographs using Cohen's Kappa (K), a statistic that measures the proportion of agreement above chance [30]. There was moderate agreement ($K = 0.51$, $p < .001$) between the valence category assigned by our algorithm and that assigned by human participants for each image (Figure 7). *EnviroPulse's* categorization was identical to the categorization given by the average participant in 72.8% of cases (81.3% of the negative images, 62.2% of the neutral images, and 75.0% of the positive images). *EnviroPulse's* accuracy was similar to other, more complex, automated algorithms that extract up to 15 image features when determining image aesthetics [8], validating our approach. The moderate accuracy of our algorithm, and past attempts [8,23], reflects the difficulty of automating image analysis to determine subjective preference [8,23].

To gain perspective on the meaning of our achieved level of agreement between human data and EnviroPulse, we investigated how accurately the participants in the study could estimate other participants' affect scores. This was done by computing K values between participants from Valtchanov [27] and the average across all participants. On average, independent human observers were worse at estimating the response of the overall population ($K = 0.36$) compared to our *EnviroPulse* prototype ($K = 0.51$). This promising result suggests that individuals may be unaware of the impact the environment has on them, and that many individuals could benefit from *EnviroPulse's* analysis of the environment.

INFORMAL STUDY ON AFFECTIVE VISUAL FEEDBACK

The validation study provided evidence that our scene analysis algorithm was able to discern the affective valence of environments using a smartphone camera. This indicated that we had succeeded in implementing past psychological findings on scene, shape, contour, and colour preference into a prototype that could calculate the valence of a scene with moderate reliability. We next examined whether our four versions of visual feedback could successfully communicate the outcome of this calculation to individuals in a simple, rapid, and meaningful manner. We used the Android SDK (version 2.3 or higher) to develop the animated visual feedback and implemented them into our Android camera application. A detailed view of the six emotional response factors used to calculate the overall affective valence of the scene was optionally displayed (using *multiple bars*) for all four types of visual feedback.

Participants

We deployed an *EnviroPulse* camera app to a group of 9 individuals (7 male, 2 female) of mixed academic expertise. Four had a background in engineering and human-computer interaction, and the other 5 had a background in psychology. All participants installed our *EnviroPulse* camera app onto their Android smartphones (including Galaxy S3, Nexus 4, Galaxy Nexus, Galaxy Note) and were asked to casually use it over the course of two weeks.

Figure 6. Smartphone mounted on tripod analyzing projected photographs of various environments.

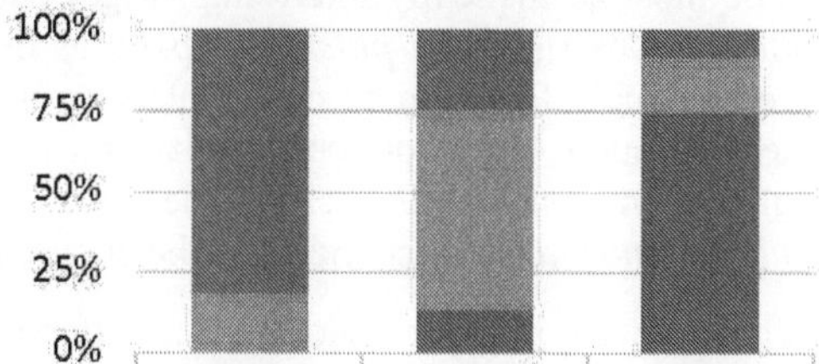

Participant Rating of Environment:	Negative [0,40]	Neutral (40,60)	Positive [60,100]
	EnviroPulse Rating of Environment:		
Negative [-6.0,-1.2]	**81.3%**	24.3%	8.3%
Neutral (-1.2, 1.2)	18.8%	**62.2%**	16.6%
Positive [1.2,6.0]	0.0%	13.5%	**75.0%**

Figure 7. Agreement between expected affective valence score from *EnviroPulse* and ratings from participant data [27].

Interview Responses

Participants were individually interviewed about their experience with our augmented camera app after they had used it for two weeks. During the interview, they were shown a video of the app analyzing different environments using the four types of visual feedback, and then asked about the different states of affective valence (e.g., jagged rapidly pulsing red amoeba vs. smooth slowly pulsing green amoeba).

Participant Impressions on Ease of Use

Participants were asked about which version they found easiest to understand. All participants unanimously agreed that it was the dynamically coloured bar. Participants reported that it was easy to understand because it projected from neutral (centre of the screen) to negative (left) or positive (right), combined with an "intuitive" colour (red for negative valence, and green for positive valence). Participants reported that this made it easy to quickly understand whether their environment was negative or positive based on the direction, size, and colour of the bar.

Participants were asked to rank the four types of feedback in terms of their intuitiveness. Overall participants rated them as follows: 1) *bar,* 2) *pulsing amoeba*, 3) *wave*, 4) *glyph.* This ranking appeared to follow the amount of information presented. The *bar* and *pulsing amoeba* presented only the overall affective valence of the scene, while the *wave* presented two (arousal and affect), and the *glyph* presented the scores for the six emotional response factors (i.e., shape, contour, complexity, colour hue, colour saturation, and luminance). While it may be a coincidence, it is possible that the complexity of the displayed data impacted how "intuitive" participants found the visual feedback to be. It is possible that feedback with more information may become preferred over time.

Participant Impressions on Aesthetics

Participants were asked which visual feedback they found to be most aesthetically interesting. Eight out of nine participants described the *pulsing amoeba* as being the most "captivating". Participants commented on how they liked the continuous pulse of the amoeba and how it changed with the environment. Participants described feeling like the *pulsing amoeba* was responding to the environment.

When viewing the video showing the different states of the *pulsing amoeba*, four of the participants spontaneously noted how the jagged and rapidly pulsing red-coloured state of the amoeba (i.e., the form it takes when the environment would induce a negative response) felt "threatening and unpleasant". Similarly, three of the participants spontaneously commented that the smooth, slowly pulsing, green state of the amoeba was "soothing and aesthetically pleasant to look at". These were exciting comments, since they indicated that we were successfully eliciting affect by manipulating the shape, contours, and colour of the visual feedback in accordance with previous research [3,22]. When participants were asked to rank the feedback in terms of aesthetics, they were ranked as follows: 1) *pulsing amoeba*, 2) *wave*, 3) *bar*, 4) *glyph.* These results were interesting since they indicated that the two versions employing principles from the shape preference literature were rated higher in aesthetic appeal. While further studies would be required to empirically validate these findings, these early results suggest that it may be possible to create affective visual feedback using design rules based on psychological research [3,22].

Participant Impressions on Accuracy of EnviroPulse

Participants were asked about whether they felt the score given by the camera app matched how they felt about the environment. None of the participants reported feeling like the tool was incorrectly assessing the affective valence of their environment (e.g., when walking, their office, the local park, etc.). All participants were informed that they were testing an early version of the tool that may show inaccurate analyses, in an attempt to prompt mistrust in its accuracy, but this did not change their minds. Based on *EnviroPulse's* moderate accuracy for assessing a wide range of environments, it is possible that participants did not encounter a situation where they would disagree with it.

DISCUSSION

In this paper, we explored the possibility of developing technology that can automatically determine the expected affective valence of the environment using the psychological correlates of scene, shape, contour, and colour perception [1,3,22,25,27] in order to enable novel interaction methods. We also investigated the use of affective visual feedback, which can potentially induce affect, as a method for communicating the expected affective valence of the environment. We believe that by using design principles inspired by research on human scene, shape, and contour perception [1,3,22,27], it is possible to create technology that is effective and efficient in affective analysis and visualization. With a camera application that incorporates *EnviroPulse*, such as the one we developed and deployed to participants, any individual with a smartphone can use their phone's camera to get a real-time affective analysis of their immediate environment and then see the results on their screen. However, there are many more possible applications of *EnviroPulse* outside of integration into camera apps.

Applications of EnviroPulse

Unlike the current reactive technologies which attempt to measure a person's affect and respond to it, *EnviroPulse* is a technology which determines the expected affective valence of an image or video, and can be incorporated into existing technologies in a variety of novel ways:

EnviroPulse can be used to crawl through street-view data from mapping services, such as Google and Bing maps, to create a "affective valence" layer (much like the traffic layers) to show users which locations and routes are most psychologically beneficial. This could be integrated into existing computerized mental-health interventions developed by the HCI community [19] to help reduce chronic stress by pre-emptively directing users through psychologically positive environments.

The affective layers for maps could be integrated into virtual assistants (e.g., Siri and Google Now), allowing them to suggest pleasant nearby areas, or display stored photos from scenic locations when given emotional input (e.g., "I'm feeling stressed", "I want to find a happy place").

Using *EnviroPulse,* photo, video, and augmented reality applications could also begin to sense the affective valence of the surrounding environment, creating awareness and potentially prompting engagement with the environment in a positive stress-reducing manner.

Lastly, mobile games could be augmented with *EnviroPulse* to guide players toward psychologically beneficial environments. For example, a "virtual pet" can be made to desire environments that are psychologically positive, becoming happier when the player shows it such an environment via the smartphone camera. *EnviroPulse* is the core technology necessary in any of these systems to sense the expected affective valence of real-world environments.

Limitations and Improvements of EnviroPulse

Our validation study indicates that *EnviroPulse* may be better at estimating the valence of an environment compared to the average human observer, and that it is comparable to previous attempts to automatically determine subjective visual aesthetics of images [8]. The moderate accuracy of our algorithm reflects the difficult problem of automatically computing subjective preference without individualized user data such as age, gender, et cetera [8,23].

Thus, in order to increase accuracy when determining the affective valence of environments using our prototype or similar automated approaches [8], additional individualized data must be considered. Past literature indicates that people use a combination of bottom-up perceptual mechanisms (similar to those used by *EnviroPulse*) and top-down cognitive mechanisms (such as past experience and expectations) when responding to an environment [27,28]. Our focus on implementing mathematical interpretations of the automatic bottom-up perceptual mechanisms for affective responses has allowed us to automatically analyze and categorize the affective valence of scenes in real-time using a smartphone. However, it is evident determining subjective preference with higher accuracy will require that the system is seeded with user statistics over time.

We believe that *EnviroPulse*, and other similar systems, should learn from the individual and dynamically adjust calculations for preference based on user input. By doing this, *EnviroPulse* could reweight the six emotional response factors to provide a more personalized experience. For example, if someone has a negative association with a particular type of environment, the characteristics of the environment could be associated with negative affect: A sandy beach on a sunny day may be a perceptually pleasant sight for most individuals [27], but someone who gets sunburned easily may experience negative affect (i.e., fear of sunburn/pain). In this case, the combination of blue water and yellow/white sand co-occurring could be associated with a personalized assessment of all beach environments by the system, without influencing positive assessments of other environments that contain blue water and other terrain.

Investigation of Affective Visual Feedback

We have presented an informal study describing the opinions of a small group of individuals on four types of visual feedback, two of which presented factual information (via bars and glyph), and two of which communicated affective information through psychological phenomena. While future work would benefit from a more in-depth study with a higher number of participants, there are several informative insights that can be gleaned from the current results. The first, and possibly most important, is that individuals from varied backgrounds are open to new styles of visual feedback when it comes to presenting affective data. Participants in our informal study were most excited and interested in the *pulsing amoeba* and *wave* visual feedback, even though they were not the easiest to interpret. This brings forth an interesting problem: affective visual feedback may be more engaging, but they may not necessarily be the most informative nor easiest to understand, suggesting that there may be a trade-off between affective visual feedback and simpler or more common feedback (e.g., bar graphs).

The affective feedback (e.g., *pulsing amoeba* and *wave)* used in our informal study attempted to incorporate design principles inspired by psychology. Participants suggested that we should make opposite ends of the spectrum (i.e., positive vs. negative) more exaggerated for the affective visual feedback. For example, for the *pulsing amoeba*, participants suggested that it should pulse slower (0.2 Hz) than it does currently (0.5 Hz) for a psychologically positive environment and quicker (2 Hz) than it currently does (1 Hz) for a psychologically negative environment. There are currently no guidelines for developing optimal affective visual feedback that are guaranteed to induce the desired affect in participants. This means that it is very difficult to develop feedback that induces affect reliably and accurately. We have taken early steps into developing affective feedback by consulting psychological literature on affective responses to shape and contours [3,22]. We believe that affective visualizations require more rigorous investigation and refinement before they can be effectively used to communicate emotional data.

CONCLUSION AND FUTURE WORK

In this paper, we presented our design and development of *EnviroPulse*, a prototype technology and interface for the analysis of the affective valence of environments. We presented empirical results which suggest that *EnviroPulse* achieves moderate accuracy for determining the affective valence of environments, and offers greater and more reliable accuracy than the average independent human observer. The accuracy of our technology is similar to other technologies for determining semi-subjective phenomena, such as aesthetics [8]. We also investigated the use of factual versus affective visual feedback to communicate the affective analysis from *EnviroPulse* (i.e., whether something is stressful or calming/pleasant), through an informal study.

In the future, we plan to improve the accuracy of *EnviroPulse* by integrating user-specific profiles that capture user input over time. We are also working on implementing real-time sound analysis into *EnviroPulse* (by using input from the phone's microphone), since there is strong evidence in psychology literature that sound and music can have profound influences on physiological, cognitive and behavioural responses to environments [26,29]. We believe that adding sound analysis and user-specific profiles to our prototype will significantly enhance accuracy and reliability.

Acknowledgements

We would like to thank the Natural Sciences & Engineering Council of Canada (NSERC), the Social Sciences & Humanities Research Council (SSHRC) and its IMMERse network, and the University of Waterloo Games Institute.

REFERENCES

1. Amir, O., Biederman, I., & Hayworth, K.J. The neural basis for shape preferences. *Vision research 51*, 20 (2011), 2198-2206.
2. American Psychological Association, *Stress in America 2013*, http://www.apa.org/news/press/releases/stress/
3. Bar, M., & Neta, M. Visual elements of subjective preference modulate amygdala activation. *Neuropsychologia 45,* 10 (2007), 2191-2200.
4. Baltrusaitis, Tadas, et al. Real-time inference of mental states from facial expressions and upper body gestures. In *Automatic Face & Gesture Recognition and Workshops (FG 2011),* IEEE Press, (2011), 909-914.
5. Biederman, I., & Vessel, E.A. Perceptual pleasure and the brain. *American Scientist 94*, 3 (2006), 249-255.
6. Bradley, M.M., & Lang, P.J. Measuring emotion: the self-assessment manikin and the semantic differential. *J BEHAV THER EXP PSY 25*, 1 (1994), 49-59.
7. Coyne, R. Nature vs. Smartphones. *Interactions, 21,5* (2014), 24-31.
8. Datta, R., Joshi, D., Li, J., & Wang, J. Z. Studying aesthetics in photographic images using a computational approach. In *Computer Vision–ECCV* (2006), 288-301
9. Fernandez, D., & Wilkins, A.J. Uncomfortable images in art and nature. Perception 37, 7 (2008), 1098-1113.
10. Gullone, E. The biophilia hypothesis and life in the 21st century: Increasing mental health or increasing pathology? *Journal of Happiness Studies*, *1*,3 (2000), 293-322.
11. Hanjalic, A. Extracting moods from pictures and sounds: Towards truly personalized TV. *IEE Signal Processing Magazine, 23*, 2 (2006), 90-100.
12. Hernandez, J., Hoque, M.E., and Picard, R.E. Mood Meter: large-scale and long-term smile monitoring system. In *ACM SIGGRAPH 2012 Emerging Technologies*, ACM Press (2012), 1.
13. Jiang, B., Chang, C. Y., & Sullivan, W. C. A dose of nature: Tree cover, stress reduction, and gender differences. *Landscape and Urban Planning, 132* (2014), 26-36.
14. Juricevic, I., Land, L., Wilkins, A., & Webster., M.A. Visual discomfort and natural image statistics. *Perception 39,* 7 (2010), 884-899.
15. Lie, A. E., Kehrer, J., & Hauser, H. Critical design and realization aspects of glyph-based 3D data visualization. In *Proc. 25th Spring Conference on Computer Graphics*, ACM Press (2009), 19-26.
16. Oliva, A., & Torralba, A. Modeling the shape of the scene: A holistic representation of the spatial envelope. *Int. Journal of Computer Vision 42*, 3 (2001), 145-175.
17. O'Hare, L., & Hibbard, P. B. Spatial frequency and visual discomfort. *Vision Research 51,* 15, (2011), 1767-1777.
18. Palmer, S. E., & Schloss, K. B. An ecological valence theory of human color preference. In *Proc. National Academy of Sciences, 107*, 19, (2010), 8877-8882.
19. Paredes, P., Gilad-Bachrach, R., Czerwinski, M., Roseway, A., Rowan, K., & Hernandez, J. PopTherapy: Coping with Stress through Pop-Culture. In Proc *Pervasive Technologies for Healthcare*, (2014).
20. Poh, M.Z., Kim, K., Goessling, A.D., Swenson, N.C., Picard, R.W., *Heartphones: Sensor Earphones and Mobile Application for Non-obtrusive Health Monitoring.* In Proc. *IEEE International Symposium on Wearable Computers*, (2009) 153-154.
21. Pence, H.E. Smartphones, smart objects, and augmented reality. *REF LIB 52*, (2010): 136-145.
22. Poffenberger, A.T., and Barrows, B.E. The Feeling Value of Lines. *Journal of Applied Psychology 8*, 2 (1924), 187-205.
23. Quercia, D., Schifanella, R., & Aiello, L.M. The shortest path to happiness: Recommending beautiful, quiet and happy routes in the city. In *Proc. Hypertext and social media*, ACM Press (2014), 116-125.
24. Sandor, C., Dey, A., Cunningham, A., Barbier, S., Eck, U., Urquhart, D., Marner, M.R., Jarvis, G., and Rhee, S. Egocentric space-distorting visualizations for rapid environment exploration in mobile mixed reality. In *Virtual Reality Conference (VR) 2010*, IEEE Press (2010), 47-50.
25. Valdez, P., & Mehrabian, A., Effects of color on emotions. *Journal of Experimental Psychology: General 123*, 4 (1994), 394-409.
26. Valtchanov, D., & Ellard, C. Physiological and affective responses to immersion in virtual reality: Effects of nature and urban settings. *JCR 3*, 4 (2010), 359-373.
27. Valtchanov, D., Exploring the Restorative Effects of Nature: Testing A Proposed Visuospatial Theory. (Doctoral dissertation). U of Waterloo, ON, CA, 2013.
28. van Krevelen, D.W.F., & Poelman, R. A survey of augmented reality technologies, applications and limitations. *International Journal of Virtual Reality 9,* 2 (2010), 1-19.
29. Västfjäll, D. Emotion induction through music: A review of the musical mood induction procedure. *Musicae Scientiae 5*, 1 (2002), 173-211.
30. Viera, A.J., & Garrett, J.M. Understanding Interobserver Agreement: The Kappa Statistic. *Family Medicine 37*, 5 (2005), 360-363.
31. Zhang, S., Huang, Q., Jiang, S., Gao, W., & Tian, Q. Affective visualization and retrieval for music video. *Multimedia, IEEE Transactions on Multimedia 12*, 6 (2010), 510-522.

Expanding and Refining Design and Criticality in HCI

James Pierce[1], Phoebe Sengers[2], Tad Hirsch[3], Tom Jenkins[4], William Gaver[5], Carl DiSalvo[4]

[1] HCI Institute Carnegie Mellon University jjpierce@cs.cmu.edu

[2] Information Science Cornell University sengers@cs.cornell.edu

[3] School of Art, Div. of Design University of Washington thirsch@uw.edu

[4] School of Literature, Media, and Communication Georgia Institute of Technology cdisalvo@gatech.edu tom.jenkins@gatech.edu

[5] Interaction Research Studio, Goldsmiths, University of London w.gaver@gold.ac.uk

ABSTRACT

The term 'critical design' is on the upswing in HCI. We analyze how discourses around 'critical design' are diverging in Design and HCI. We argue that this divergence undermines HCI's ability to learn from and appropriate the design approaches signaled by this term. Instead, we articulate two ways to broaden and deepen connections between Design and HCI: (1) develop a broader collective understanding of what these design approaches can be, without forcing them to be about 'criticality' or 'critical design,' narrowly construed; and (2) shape a variation of design criticism to better meet Design practices, terms, and ways of knowing.

Author Keywords

Critical design, speculative design, design thinking, design criticism, expanded design practice, critical theory

INTRODUCTION

There was a time when one had to argue for including designerly ways of knowing in human-computer interaction (HCI) research [21,37,55]. When design was included, it was as instrumentalized problem-solving. Anything else was considered superfluous, or, worse, art. That time is past. Now it is commonplace for keywords in design papers to include all manner of qualifiers: ludic, reflective, critical.

In particular, over the past several years, 'critical design' has received increasing attention in the HCI research community. While this signals a welcomed interest in new modes of design practice and possibilities for engaging designed products, we believe that the attachment to 'critical design' is problematic and there is a need for other articulations of criticality in HCI design, including design practices that eschew the very term 'critical.' Put awkwardly, we need additional ways of talking about and doing criticality through design, without being tied to 'critical design.' While this may sound like a semantic issue, it reflects deeper issues around design and criticism.

CHI 2015, April 18–23, 2015, Seoul, Republic of Korea.

ACM 978-1-4503-3145-6/15/04…$15.00.
http://dx.doi.org/10.1145/2702123.2702438

In this paper, we analyze how discourses around 'critical design' are diverging in Design and HCI (we use "Design" here to refer to the discipline as taught in arts-inflected design programs). This divergence undermines our ability in HCI to learn from, adapt, appropriate, and innovate the very design approaches signaled by enthusiasm for 'critical design'. It does so by channeling exchanges with HCI through a narrow range of Design and design criticism practice. Instead, we lay out two ways to broaden and deepen the connections between Design and HCI: (1) by developing a broader collective understanding of what these new design approaches can be, without forcing them to be about 'criticality' or 'critical design,' narrowly construed; and (2) by shaping a variation of design criticism that better meets Design practices, terms, and ways of knowing.

CRITICAL DESIGN I: DESIGN

The term "critical design" was coined by Tony Dunne and Fiona Raby in the mid-90s. Since then, they have brought the term to the attention of the Design community and beyond through publications, exhibitions and designs. Dunne & Raby describe critical design in various, related ways [18,19,20]. For example, they position critical design against a standard "affirmative design" [19, p. 58], which they see as mindlessly supporting the cultural status quo. In contrast, they describe critical design as creating "products for the mind,"[19, p. 64], i.e. design proposals that question the role of design in shaping our everyday reality. For instance, the Electro-Draught Excluder, part of the Placebo Project series [19], purports to screen people from electromagnetic energy to which they might be sensitive. The device would not literally work: instead it is presented to question how products both raise fears and ameliorate them. Dunne & Raby see such proposals as fulfilling a critical function by "[e]ncourag[ing] the viewers to ask themselves why the values embodied in the proposal seem 'fictional' or 'unreal', and to question the social and cultural mechanisms that define what is real or fictional." (p. 63)

Critical designs frequently project a strange user whose needs and desires seem odd, but which are, upon reflection, plausible if uncomfortable. For example, Toran's "Object for Lonely Men" [53] describes a series of designs for after a break-up, replacing the lost partner with products replicating perverse aspects of the relationship: a plate-throwing robot mimics the effects of arguments; a motorized housing steals the sheets at night; a smoking device shares a cigarette after a night of lonely sex. The intended "user" of the proposal, which is often based on and evokes a somewhat fictionalized lifeworld, appears to be not the user of the product itself but rather the reading audience of educated designers and other sophisticates who have the background and orientation to appreciate the form of tantalizing intellectual pleasure they embody.

Whereas in HCI we often think of "design" as necessarily entailing a "functioning" device that can be deployed and tested, in critical design designed objects are often not implemented to be functional or actually used in everyday context. Instead, they are prototyped with a sophisticated finish that suggests they already exist. In cases where they are implemented and deployed in everyday contexts, this use appears to often be oriented towards 'performing' the objects rather than assessing users' experiences with them.

Within design studies and design research, critical design has served the purpose of reinvigorating discussions of design as a method of cultural provocation [38]. Some scholars take critical design as a starting point for discussing how social issues and political themes might enter design practice [40]. There have also been calls for a "post-critical design" that addresses limits of critical design, including its potential to reinforce rather than question and confront the status quo [16]. Even Dunne & Raby appear to be moving away from 'critical design' to 'speculative design' [18].

Of late, discussions are emerging about issues with and limits of speculative and critical design (SCD). Over the spring and summer of 2014 a lively debate has emerged around speculative and critical design as a colonialist practice, seemingly only concerned with Western problems of privilege (see [42], [52] and online discussion that erupted following [51]).

CRITICAL DESIGN II: HCI

While Dunne & Raby's critical design work has long been a (perhaps underground) source of inspiration for HCI [e.g. 30,48], the popularity of the term "critical design" itself has recently skyrocketed. Perhaps the most significant and influential recent use of the term in HCI is a series of works by Jeffrey Bardzell, Shaowen Bardzell, and their collaborators towards a design criticism of critical design. This work was originally rooted in an interest in Dunne & Raby's approach as a methodology to embody cultural criticism in design, coupled with concerns that the approach requires additional methodological and conceptual articulation to be accessible to HCI researchers [5,6].

In [5] Bardzell & Bardzell address this problem through a theoretical analysis of what it means to be critical, which they use to correct a series of conceptual problems they identify with Dunne & Raby's articulation of critical design. To do so, they analyze ideas about criticality from two traditions in criticism: critical theory and metacriticism. They synthesize both to articulate how these traditions can be understood to jointly frame what it means to be "critical." Based on this framing, they propose a new definition of 'critical design' intended to more accurately describe how criticality manifests in design:

> [A] *design research project may be judged 'critical' to the extents that it proposes a perspective-changing holistic account of a given phenomenon, and that this account is grounded in speculative theory, reflects a dialogical methodology, improves the public's cultural competence, and is reflexively aware of itself as an actor — with both power and constraints — within the social world it is seeking to change.* (p. 3304).

They demonstrate how projects that are not Dunne & Raby style critical design could nevertheless be understood as 'critical design' under this new definition. In follow-on work to this paper, they and their collaborators build on this redefinition to develop reading practices that allow one to identify whether a particular design is critical and how it accomplishes that through design choices [4] and propose an iterative methodology for developing a general theory and canon of critical design exemplars [24].

In sum, Bardzell & Bardzell address both potential and shortcomings of Dunne & Raby-style critical design by developing a new form of design criticism for critical design in HCI, and in the process intentionally alter what critical design means. The stated aims of this design criticism are to help HCI researchers/practitioners, curators, the general public, and other stakeholders to establish what critical design is and to provide pedagogical support for researchers and practitioners outside of the art-influenced design tradition to do critical design.

Indeed, it does seem that critical design is gaining purchase in HCI, given the increasing number of papers that speak directly to critical design, as well as sessions termed "critical design" at CHI and DIS. This includes papers explicitly adapting ideas about critical design to new domains, such as Feinberg et al's use of provocative designs to identify and undermine standard assumptions in meta-data design [22,23] and Wilde et al's use of craft practices to raise issues around embodiment and disability [54]. Other works not explicitly using this term but folded under the "critical design" label at these conferences include Odom's design of a device that challenges users' expectations for speed of interaction [41] and Pierce's design studies that shift design from expanding possibilities to restricting them [45]. These works signal an apparently increasing trend in HCI to collect and develop critically oriented design work under the banner of critical design.

A TALE OF TWO CRITICAL DESIGNS

In this section, we will argue that despite the proliferation of academic works aiming to bring critical design from Design into HCI, the terms of discussion in these two communities are diverging. In this section, we will explain significant differences in how each community understands (1) what critical design is, (2) where it fits into the space of conceptually related practices, and (3) the kinds of knowledge practices required to make sense of them. What is at stake may at first appear to be a simple matter of terminology, but these differences both lead to and are symptomatic of a wider range of divergences about the actual and potential relationships between criticality and design. Our goal here, then, is both to surface these differences and explain why they make a difference.

Critical design ≠ critical design

As may be clear from the above discussion, there is a significant difference in the referent of the term 'critical design' in Design and in its latest uptake in HCI. In HCI, 'critical design' refers to a broad array of practices, ranging from the original practices pursued by Dunne & Raby, to the criticism-inspired definition of Bardzell & Bardzell, to an apparent broader identification of critical design to refer to any use of design that draws, or appears to draw, from a critical perspective. In Design, critical design is a highly specific term, referring to a known school of design particularly associated with Dunne, Raby and their students and disciples and associated with the Design Interactions programs at the Royal College of Art, London. This design school not only shares the programmatic philosophy mentioned previously but also has a cohesive visual and thematic aesthetic, easily recognized in the designed objects created under this rubric by Dunne & Raby and their followers. Critical design often draws on dark and uncomfortable subject matter. It brings this subject matter into an everyday context to create a tension, sometimes through black humor. Aesthetically it is quite polished and borrows the sleek and seductive visual and form language from fine art traditions and high-end design and advertising.

Critical design is not a formal organization, like the Situationist International, which formally endorsed or expelled want-to-be adherents. Nevertheless, it is strongly associated with particular actors at a particular historical moment expressing particular views on design and drawing on particular stylistic features. Thus, from a Design perspective the best it seems we could hope for in HCI in adopting critical design is to be derivative of the original. To build on its attitudes and methods in ultimately new ways would render the new approaches by definition, and without critique, "not critical design." This aspiration also appears dated; in design studies critical design is discussed as potentially past its peak and there are calls for a "post-critical design" [16]. Even Dunne & Raby seem to be abandoning 'critical' in favor of 'speculative' [18].

While it is possible to argue that these Design concerns are not relevant to HCI, the redefinition of critical design also has a significant impact within our field on its ability to reflect on, learn from and critique the Dunne & Raby approach. By redefining critical design, we make it difficult if not impossible to refer coherently and precisely to the design practice that originated the term, which remains a key touchpoint for HCI discourse. In the process, we undermine, rather than enhance, HCI practitioners' ability to understand and build on that specific design practice. In order to keep terms clear here, for the rest of our argument we will use *critical design*™ to refer to the Dunne & Raby school and *criticism through design* to refer to the Bardzell & Bardzell criticism-based redefinition. We return to the question of labels for broader uses of 'critical design' later.

Critical design™ ≠ critical theory + design

A second significant difference between the two communities is how they frame the intellectual heritage of critical design™. Bardzell & Bardzell argue for a significant conceptual linkage between critical theory and critical design™. In [5] they open the section "Origins and goals of critical design" with discussion of the Frankfurt School, a strand of critical theory emphasizing a Marxist-inflected cultural critique of consumer society. While acknowledging that Dunne & Raby deny a close link, Bardzell & Bardzell argue that the vocabulary and concepts they use to describe the critical function of their work reveal an affinity to the Frankfurt School. Both frame society in terms of systemic structures of domination of which participants are normally largely unaware, and highlight the role of the critic/critical designer to reveal how those structures work and to provide conceptual alternatives. In doing so critical design™ emphasizes the search for unexpected meanings hidden under the surface of apparently neutral cultural phenomena that is the hallmark of critical theory. Bardzell & Bardzell thus see critical design™ as sharing the goals of critical theory, while embodying them in a new form: that of design research.

This connection then grounds and potentially legitimates the move from critical design™ to what we are terming criticism through design. Their redefinition hinges on working through what it means to be 'critical.' They do so through a masterful synthesis of a broad swath of critical literature from critical theory (philosophy), English-language literary criticism, and analytic aesthetics. Thus criticism through design is intentionally and explicitly linked to, indeed defined by, a humanities tradition whose epistemological hallmark is the construction of consistent and compelling textual arguments.

Within Design, the relationships between critical theory and critical design™ are seen as more tenuous and circuitous. There is certainly a shared sensibility between critical design™ and critical theory along the lines Bardzell & Bardzell suggest, but to the degree that Dunne & Raby draw on critical theory, they do so strategically and sporadically, using piecemeal concepts for inspiration and explanation, rather than attempting to construct a complete and internally consistent argument. As a design practice, critical design™ is perhaps better understood in relation to (1) recent design approaches that expand design methods, tactics and strategies beyond generating consumer products (e.g. research through design [26,56], speculative design [18], ludic design [28], reflective design [48], design fiction [e.g., 8,9,], contestational design [32], slow design [31,41], counterfunctional design [45], and adversarial design [15]),

(2) a 100-year history of avant-garde approaches, including Dada, Situationism, and tactical media [46], that "game the system" by integrating playful forms of critique with the design of arts 'objects,' variously understood [13], and (3) activist approaches to Design specifically, and making more generally, that aim to question and reframe the social role of institutional practices of design (e.g. Design for the real world [43], social practice art [35], critical making [47]).

In other words, **there is a 'critical' tradition in design and the arts that is largely independent of critical theory and metacriticism**. If we frame 'being critical' as necessarily and exclusively understood through these textual traditions, we make it more difficult to understand where critical design™ is coming from, we blinker from view Design perspectives besides Dunne & Raby's of what criticality can and should do in design practice, and we may incorrectly assume that the only way to understand the meaning of design is through the forms and traditions of humanistic criticism.

Knowledge ≠ knowledge

A third significant difference arising between Design and HCI has to do with the forms of knowledge that are considered helpful for doing design. This is not our own insight; Bardzell, Bardzell, and their collaborators start by arguing that the forms of knowledge publically available about critical design™ are not adequately detailed for non-Design practitioners to learn from [6]. In [5], Bardzell & Bardzell criticize Dunne & Raby's writings about critical design™ for their lack of coherence and direction:

> Their primary strategy [to explain their approach] is to offer dozens if not hundreds of examples of designs that they argue serve a critical function. These examples... are thematically organized around provocative ideas. In many cases, these readings are supplemented with brief allusions to critical thinkers and design intellectuals.... [As an example, a chapter from *Hertzian Tales*] is a soup of ideas: dozens of challenging designs, a dizzying array of Marxist, semiotic, and architectural theorists follow on each other fast and furious, with little explication or development. (p. 3300)

In [5], they build on criticism's theoretical firepower to clarify concepts they see as muddled or insufficiently grounded in critical design™. They move on in later works [24] to begin developing critical design criticism, or "a general theorization of critical design" (p. 357), which they suggest will make criticism through design more accessible to new practitioners. This movement "towards a systematic theory of critical design" [24, p. 368] draws in particular on the forms of knowledge from literary and aesthetic analysis and emphasizes the development of strong, coherent, rational arguments. For example, in [4] they and their collaborators describe design, by analogy to critical judgments, as "depending on judgments accompanied by arguments that seek assent" (p. 1953).

By this standard, Dunne & Raby's manifestos indeed fare poorly, particularly in the context of humanist disciplines whose *raison d'etre* is clear and consistent argumentation. Their works do not effectively answer the ontological questions Bardzell & Bardzell see as key to being able to do critical design: What is critical design? How can you tell if a design is critical or affirmative? Is critical design art? Dunne & Raby do have answers to these questions, but, as Bardzell & Bardzell point out, it is not difficult to argue against those answers [4,5]. Seeking insight, but finding claims that quickly appear contradictory or nonsensical, it is no wonder that critical design™ may appear an "elitist mystery" [6, p. 290] missing a clear method or approach.

Yet, Dunne & Raby's writings appear a fairly clear articulation of method if we take their claims not as *ontological* statements ("this object is inherently critical") but as *tactical* statements about considerations to bring into design. Thus, for example, the statement that critical design™ is not art is not intended as an unsupportable claim that under no circumstances can an object created through critical design™ ever be thought of as an art object. Rather it is tactical advice that critical design™ proposals more effectively provoke thought if we present them as real products rather than if we frame them as art objects for safe and distanced contemplation. Similarly, the statement that critical design™ is different from affirmative design does not entail a dubious philosophical distinction between two distinct categories of designed objects. Rather, it rallies designers (somewhat heavy-handedly) to shift attention from purportedly supporting the status quo to questioning the realities design creates. The "soup of ideas" that defies conceptions of linear argumentation is exactly what Dunne & Raby have on offer: a grab-bag of provocative concepts and ideas which designers can draw on to inspire their own design work, without an obligation for rationalization. The work, we would argue, is deliberately polyphonic, because it is oriented to supporting (situated) *doing of*, not (formally) *knowing about*.

What is more, critical design™ is explicitly oriented towards *undermining* ontological certainty. Ambivalence plays a key role in the aesthetics and tactics of critical design™ as a way to set up situations that demand reflection, including at times ambiguity about whether a design proposal even *is* critical design™ (this strategy is also common in tactical media [46]). For example, Auger and Loizeau's Audio Tooth [2] is a design proposal for an artificial tooth implanted with an audio receiver allowing persons to receive and send telephone calls directly through their skulls. While their description refers to an intention to stimulate dialogue about "the possibilities of biotechnology and it's potential impact on society and culture," it is presented on the authors' website in language that suggests a promo commercial from a tech incubator and includes without comment several links to media coverage of the Audio Tooth as an affirmative product (including a Time Magazine award as one of the best inventions of 2002 [1]). The ambiguous framing of Audio Tooth (is it critical? Is it not?) is not a question to be settled but an issue the design intentionally raises, as this somewhat cryptic comment suggests: "The Audio Tooth Implant was pitched at a level where its desirability and believability would be acceptable in terms of the contemporary attitude in society" [2].

Does this mean it is a mistake for design criticism to construct clear arguments about Design and to seek to answer ontological questions about the relationship between criticality and design? No; this seems a worthy endeavor speaking to a longer history of aesthetic criticism. However, we must be clear-eyed that because of its different epistemological register—one that emphasizes clarity over generativity, argument over inspiration, ontology over tactics—this work is unlikely to inform or speak directly to current Design practice, including the goal of bootstrapping new practitioners into a (critical) Design sensibility.

A WAY FORWARD: CRITICALITY AND/OR DESIGN

Stepping back, these considerations lead us to three key claims. First, **critical design™ is not the same, and does not need to be the same**, as either criticism through design or the broader range of design practices sometimes collected under this banner in HCI. Second, **critical design™ is only one of a wide range of related practices** from Design and beyond that provide important perspectives distinct from critical theory that we could learn from. Third, if the goal is to inform, inspire, and pass on the sensibilities of Design practice, we need **forms of design criticism that are more focused on clarifying tactics and less on resolving ontology**.

We recognize and welcome the growing interest in critical design and design criticism in HCI. In formulating our argument, our goal is to foster the flourishing in HCI of innovative design practices and analysis aimed at uncovering new possible relationships between criticality and design. **The key claim of this paper is that the best way to do so is to systematically open the gate for broader and deeper exchanges between new modes of Design practice and HCI** than the current terms of the discussion support. These deeper exchanges will enable a wider range of sources of inspiration in HCI; a deeper understanding of what designers in both fields are trying to do, actually doing, and how; and a culture that supports deep and thoughtful innovation and appropriation rather than imitation. Such an opening can be created, we believe, through two significant shifts in the terms of the discussion.

First, we argue for abandoning 'critical design,' both the term and the Design practice, as the primary touchpoint for discussions in HCI of design practices that embody, or could be read as embodying, some form of critical stance. One of the potential attractions of critical design™ is that it challenges many of the central assumptions of user-centered design (UCD): for example, that designs should be based on empirical, average, or acceptable user needs, or that the hallmark of quality for a design concept is how well a designed object functions in an empirically circumscribed setting. Yet these refusals to play by the rules of UCD are not exclusive to critical design™; as we will argue in more detail later, there is a significant range of new design practices in both Design and HCI that provide alternatives to user-centered design by explicitly allowing for an authorial voice and by reframing how 'users' are understood. So, **one way we should open the gate to Design is by recognizing, understanding, and drawing on this wider range of practice.**

Second, there is a tension between the need for standard concepts to use for analysis and judgment, and the contingency of design. Arguably, the various areas of design thrive on practices and things that are provisional, partial and incomplete [27,50]. It is not that we cannot and should not analyze and critique critical moves in design—we must. But, at the same time, we need to recognize the dynamism and contingency of design and provide the space necessary for new modes of criticality to constantly re-develop. Put another way, setting boundaries and standards through processes of classification and categorization can thwart rather than incite criticality. The very character of critical work is that if it is to stay critical, it must be inventive. This is true both of the objects of design and the theories that interrogate those objects. Thus, **we should also open the gate by embracing rather than attempting to resolve the provisionality, partiality, incompleteness, and openness of Design practice**: in short, the mess.

What does this mean in practice? In the remainder of the paper, we embark on two complementary programs of action to open the gates between HCI and expanded practices of design. The first is to widen and deepen our collective understanding of these new design approaches. The second is to shape a variation of design criticism that can bridge between these discourses by aligning better with Design practice, knowledge and discourse. These projects overlap, but do not coincide; neither design nor criticism need be a handmaid of the other. In practice we expect (and hope this work supports) a range of practices.

DESIGN: EXPANDING & REFINING PRACTICE IN HCI

Our feeling is that the term "critical design" is currently being used as a sort of catchall for emerging design practice within HCI that extends well beyond both critical design™ and criticism through design. It seems to us, therefore, that use of the term "critical design" should be retired, or at least curtailed. In saying this, we in no way wish to dampen growing enthusiasm for work that questions, provokes or expresses adverse or adversarial propositions set in opposition to the status quo. However, we need to recognize and articulate differences among practices within HCI that combine "criticality" and "design" without force-fitting them into a 'critical design' straitjacket. We also need to recognize work that has affinities with "critical design" but without always relying on "critical" and its cognates, terms that can obscure the ultimately generative, productive and positive goals of such work.

Before suggesting alternatives to "critical design," though, we must first ask ourselves why there has been such interest in the work. After considering the work that the "critical design" label is doing in HCI, we will be in a better position to suggest approaches that support emerging design practices while avoiding the problems with critical design.

Recognize design authorship

In reviewing works coming under the banner of 'critical design,', it seems to us that HCI may be drawn to the term because it evokes practices that diverge radically from the user-centered design (UCD) paradigm. The use of "critical design" as a label could be a symptom of a new perspective for HCI; if so, a defining implicit tenet is that designers should not only be *allowed* an authorial voice, they should be *encouraged* to embrace, develop and enact one. By **design authorship,** we mean that design explicitly and significantly embodies intentions or ideas arising from a concern or curiosity of the designer. The product or service is a clear expression of the "voice" of the designer and her interpretation of social or cultural themes and concerns. While all design to some extent "embodies" such concerns and intentions, what's unique here is that this is explicitly acknowledged and presented as such.

Design authorship may serve critical ends, for example by revealing hidden assumptions or challenging and aiming to change the status quo. But while authorship is a significant feature of critical practice, it can also be at play in works that do not fit under even the most expansive definition of 'critical design.' As the iPhone—emerging from Apple's distinctly non-user-centered design approach—has dramatically shown, design authorship may usefully serve other ends, too: e.g. innovation and disruption.

Nonetheless, design authorship should be of interest to an HCI community oriented to critical reflection regardless of where it occurs because of its implicit challenge to UCD. Acknowledging design authorship diverges from some UCD approaches that see product designs as ideally emerging from a priori analysis of user needs. Projects exhibiting design authorship provide fertile ground for a critical reinterpretation of such work, even if explicitly "not critical design". For example, hailed as an exemplar of research through design [56] and 'critical design' [24], the Drift Table has been described by its authors as a way of exploring "ludic" activities "motivated by curiosity, exploration, and reflection rather than externally defined tasks" [28, p. 885]. Yet concerns over ludic design are not motivated *a priori* by formal user studies. Instead they seem to arise from the designers' own intuitions of what others may find to be of interest. What the 'critical' label here obscures is that the Drift Table is only tangentially 'critical.' It is more centrally authorial. And if we step back from the 'critical' label we find myriad examples in HCI of this sort of design to consider and draw from—old and new (e.g., [9,11,22,23,28,29,30,31,32,34,36,41,45,48,49]).

That said, acknowledging design authorship in no way demands a rejection of user-centered design. Users are and should remain an important consideration. But even as HCI has generally moved away from exclusively valorizing utility and efficiency (evidenced by the rise of experience design and "third wave HCI" [10]), the specter of the user has arguably remained as a mythic guard against poor system design, or worse, the indulgences of designers. What expanded design practices help us to see is that people are more than "users." When designers are allowed a clear voice, they are liberated to speak about topics and issues that are difficult to address in a UCD framework. For example, they can address experiences and stances that are particular, idiosyncratic, even alien or unacceptable. The authorial voice opens the possibility of new relationships with 'users', not as potential consumers of utilitarian products to solve their needs, but as collaborators in discovering new meanings and values in the things they design. Expanded design practices thus open us to new ideas about what designers are, who "users" can be, and how designers and users can speak to each other.

Expand our terminology

Despite its allure, the term "critical design" is too specific to serve as a label for the emergence of design practices that exhibit a "critical voice" in some form. Going forward we see three options. First, we could find a different label to indicate this movement. This appeals in that it recognizes what does seem to be an emerging area of design in HCI that adopts an authorial voice, distinguishing itself from traditional UCD. The problem is that finding a single label for such diverse practices is difficult in practice, and perhaps overly restrictive and reifying in principle as well.

Second, we could simply recognize all these practices as Design. An advantage of this is to acknowledge that the processes, materials, outcomes, traditions and ways of thinking and acting associated with "critical design" have a firm basis in the traditions of Design practice. In addition, insisting that these practices are Design is a powerful way to infiltrate, inform, and converse with other Design practices, as it denies the temptation to pigeonhole them as "other" or to label these approaches as "special".

Third, and the option we lean towards, is simultaneously to recognize these emerging approaches and practices as Design, while developing a more varied, evolving, and provisional set of labels to describe, develop and advocate for them—including "adversarial,"[15] "reflective,"[48] "ludic,"[28] "speculative,"[18] "design fiction,"[9] and, yes, "critical". This permits a more nuanced discussion of the many approaches to design being explored and maps more closely to Design discourses outside of CHI.

CRITICISM: EXPANDING & REFINING PRACTICE IN HCI

Clearly, endorsing a broad range of perspectives that have affinities with "critical design" and the term "critical" requires articulating differences between such perspectives, especially the specific ways in which "criticality" is and is not at work, and the variety of strategies used. This is, at core, a question of design criticism.

Interest in design criticism in HCI, including ours, arises in part because of concerns that knowledge of critical design or other forms of expanded design practice is out of reach for HCI researchers and practitioners from non-Design backgrounds. One model for increasing the reach of expanded design practice in HCI is to develop recognizably HCI variants of Design methods. In such a model a job of design criticism is to translate Design concepts and methods into a familiar HCI vernacular. While this can be useful and effective, such a model keeps the traffic between Design and HCI narrow. It places design critics or other translators as bottlenecks between the disciplines and leaves 'untranslated' Design practices out of reach. Instead, we believe the pedagogical goal of design criticism should be to promote literacy of design texts and objects that will let people move from reading 'digested' versions to being able to access the originals, incorporate them into their own work, and thereby develop their own authorial voice. Further, we hope and expect that design criticism could be an aid to experienced designers, for example by providing inspiration for new forms of design. In addition, we will argue that expanded design practices shift the objects and practices of design to a degree that requires adaptation of design criticism to adequately analyze it. In this section, then, we lay out how to approach design criticism to better meet the practices, knowledge, and terms arising in the expanded modes of design practice described previously.

A design criticism that is provisional, open, incomplete, and even a bit messy (like design!)

If design criticism within HCI is to contribute to or help draw practitioners into Design practices, then we believe its philosophical orientations must better align with those of Design. In particular, design criticism would benefit from theoretical foundations that tend toward being provisional, generative, and ontologically agnostic. Yet the stance most prevalent in the current design criticism discourse in HCI appears to be metacritical. This stance tends to see 'criticality' as an attribute that can be embodied (or not) in objects and aims to clarify what designs are ontologically. Put far too simply, the metacritical approach seeks to tidy things up into orderly categories. But there are epistemological traditions within the history of critical thought that question the value and politics of establishing ontological certainty. These traditions provide alternative modes of critique and knowledge production perhaps better matched to design practice, for example by being less concerned with "stating what is" than with "informing what could be." They tend to embrace provisionality, incompleteness, and even disorder.

One such orientation is schizoanalysis, which eschews reducing things to generalizations and instead focuses attention on tracing connections and transformations [17]. Schizoanalysis takes a tactical approach to knowledge: "A concept is a brick. It can be used to build the courthouse of reason. Or it can be thrown through the window." [38, p. xii]. One way we could draw on this sensibility in design criticism is to orient less towards taxonomies and classification schemes and more to tracing the rhizomatic lines that lead from one design project to another. A concept can be used to rationalize why one design is better than another. Or it can be used to design something else.

Another such theory is the feminist concept of performativity [12], which, simply put, recognizes that knowledge practices not only uncover but simultaneously construct the things they study. Performativity would lead us to ask not 'is a design critical?' or even 'how is a design critical?' but 'how does a design become 'critical'?' and 'how do the questions we ask in design and design criticism shape and alter what 'critical' can be?' It recognizes and seeks to do justice to the way in which 'observers' (critics) become entangled with 'the observed' (design). Feminist scholars have used performativity for rethinking science [3]; [34] use related ideas to rethink HCI design.

Not "great works" but dynamic, provisional exemplars

Another area in which a move to complexification could be beneficial is in the question of which design projects we should take as standard reference points for embodying criticality in design. Ferri et al [24] suggest establishing a canon of critical designs to improve design literacy in the HCI community. They articulate goals and benefits of a canon including setting normative values around critical design and elevating a set of "exemplars" to guide discourse and pedagogy and to shape future design practices. Yet as they also remind us, canons often become the subject of intense debate over what they include and exclude and have been criticized for reproducing "aristocratic" power relations. To these concerns we add the tendency for canons to act as a sort of thoughtless 'shorthand' for a field's self-conception that undermines vigorous, dynamic discourse and cross-fertilization.

We suggest a more provisional and vibrant approach to design scholarship and criticism, in which sets of exemplars are marshaled contextually in support of particular analytic or interpretive frames on design ([29] is a well-known example in HCI). The meaning and relevance of these frames, and the examples they contain, is subject to continual reassessment and reinterpretation by communities of interest. These are not canons in a classic sense; they are dynamic and what Ferri et al might term implicit canons [24]. This is clearly a much more provisional approach to design scholarship that leaves questions of definition open to ongoing interpretation and contestation. This is intentional. It recognizes and aims to communicate the voice of the critic in shaping the "canon." Through its construction it communicates to the reader not that there is one "right way" to do or think about design but rather many stances one can take on design and how to perform it.

Reveal what designs are and how they operate

Particularly in the case of the expanded design practices we are talking about here, questions arise as to the definition of "the work," "the design," or "the thing" that designers produce and whether it should be limited to a material object, or extended to include how that design is being positioned. One example of such positioning is the 'paratext,' or materials produced by the designers, curators, or other stakeholders arguing for the intended interpretation of the design. Particularly for designs that are intended primarily as forms of knowledge production or even critical interventions, it can be difficult to understand how the design is intended strategically *as* critical, and to judge its success at that intention, without analyzing the discourse against and within which the design is placed and how it is intended to intervene. Particularly for expanded design practices that embody an authorial voice, then, the positionality and paratext of the design is an explicit part of the design work that should be examined and critiqued.

Sometimes, designers aim through such paratexts to argue for a meaning of the designed object as "expositor" or "positioner." This is by far the most common approach at CHI, for example in design case studies. In certain cases, most of the design work is arguably not even 'in' the object itself but in the way the design is positioned. In such cases, paratexts can be seen as part of a tactical intervention within a discourse. For example, news reports in 1993 reported concerned parents buying talking GI Joe dolls and Teen Talk Barbies who had had their voice boxes switched, so that Teen Talk Barbie might say "vengeance is mine" [25]. This was reported as the action of the Barbie Liberation Organization, which was said to have placed 300-500 such dolls in stores for purchase. Yet it is unknown whether the voice boxes were ever switched; the "concerned parents" phoning journalists may have been the artists themselves. While it is tempting to treat either the representational image of a modified Barbie doll as "the design" or "the thing", it is arguably the paratext surrounding it and its tactical effects to manipulate the news media into reporting a particular interpretation that is more interesting, especially as it relates to criticality. Indeed, this example shows how ambiguity concerning where a design ends and paratext begins can be part of both the design intention and outcome. In such cases, the job of criticism may not be to resolve such ambiguity but to appreciate what a design might be and what it is doing, to analyze the degree and modes of success of its tactics, and to open this all up for reflection and discussion.

Develop a participatory design criticism

A classic model of criticism splits the critic and the author into separate discursive universes: authors are responsible for creating texts, while critics are responsible for judging their social and cultural meanings. Authors may object to being mischaracterized, yet have little recourse. In contrast, a design criticism in HCI must be, and already is, participatory. By this we mean critics, designers and other stakeholders are necessarily in dialogue in adjudicating how to understand design. This is for several reasons.

First, designers are always already critically reading and arguing for the meaning of design. Partially this is through the production of paratexts, as described earlier; when design artifacts are presented and positioned within art galleries or research publications, these presentations make both explicit and implicit claims about the meanings of the works. In HCI, for example, we have examples of two hybrid roles: the designer-as-critic, i.e. the designer who explains the meaning and implications of their own work [e.g. 28] and the critic-as-designer, who writes about (others') design, often with a curatorial approach, from the perspective of a designer [e.g. 15]. If we take a critic as a arguing for an interpretation, then designers have already become critics (though not necessarily good ones, particularly not by the standards of criticism originating within the humanities) as soon as they take a stance on the cultural meaning of their or other designers' work [e.g., 43].

For design practices that leverage authorial viewpoints, we note, this happens even before a paratext is produced, since the designed objects themselves act, in a sense, as statements. As [6] point out, design practices that take on a critical intention can be thought of as critique by other (non-textual) means. Research through design discourse describes the idea of design thinking "embodied in" an artifact [26, p. 5], or design knowledge residing "within" an artifact [14, p. 6; 56, p. 310]. In this sense, a design expresses a critical understanding in a manner somewhat analogous to a critical text, even though it is not expressed in the forms, language, or logic of traditional criticism.

But even all of this aside, it's crucial to note that in HCI we are in a somewhat unique interdisciplinary situation. While literary critics may get together without authors, art historians without artists, and anthropologists without subjects, in HCI we would structurally hope and expect that critics and designers will be in the same room speaking to each other. This suggests that the model of critics and designers in separate interpretive universes will in any case fail in HCI. Thus a design criticism that is to aid in bridging between HCI and expanded design practices needs to be generally accountable to and enrolled in both discourses.

So does this make designers authorities on their own work, and not allow critics to disagree? No. Critics should and must generate their own interpretations. But what it does suggest is that the issue of the designer's intention needs to be handled carefully. While in traditional literary criticism it is acceptable, indeed perhaps preferable, to bracket what an author intended a work to mean or do, in a participatory or dialogic model of design criticism one can disagree with but not outright ignore an authorial intention. In this model, we need to recognize that designers have a stake in how their designs are placed, and to the extent that a reading disagrees with a designer's explicit placement, the critic has at least as much responsibility to their reading's effects as anthropologists have with their subjects.

CONCLUSION: FOSTER FLUID TRANSITIONS BETWEEN DESIGN, DESIGN STUDIES, AND HCI

We have articulated two ways to broaden the communication between Design and HCI to support analysis and innovation of what has been loosely collected under the term 'critical design.' One is to **articulate the broad range of design practices that convey an authorial voice with critical dimensions** as an alternative to (but not a replacement of) user-centered design. The second is to **shape a variation of design criticism that better meets Design ways of speaking and knowing** as an alternative to (but not a replacement of) design criticism oriented to ontology and taxonomy.

We are deeply aware of the need to make emergent design practices accessible to a CHI audience. Doing away with a single umbrella term leaves the intellectual waters quite muddied, and while we believe that this is ultimately a good thing, it is also desirable that people who are excited by new design work should be able to approach it without significant formal design training. One approach is to use CHI's tutorial track to offer courses in emergent design practices for those with a passing interest in such matters. Another approach is to create broader literacy in Design by continuing to produce and acknowledge works that articulate design thinking, processes and practices for HCI [e.g., 34]. A third route is to continue to import literature and other knowledge from Design outside of HCI.

These issues bring our attention back to the relationships between the communities and discourses of HCI and those of Design that exist outside of (and predate) HCI. We believe it is a problem when conversations about design within HCI become illegible to designers outside the HCI community. To be clear, we do not expect that CHI will or even should appeal to all design practitioners. However, a growing number of academic designers, design researchers and practicing designers/artists are active in other scholarly and intellectually rigorous communities. They have much to offer and to gain from deeper involvement with HCI. To the extent we seek to develop a "culture of design" in HCI, the ways we talk about design should be familiar to, connect with, and draw on these more general design scholars.

Despite its longstanding interest in technical pursuits and the behavioral sciences, the disciplines of Design are solidly grounded in the Arts and Humanities. As such, design brings a distinct set of concerns to bear on the specification, production, use and understanding of interactive products. These include concerns with aesthetics and a consideration of technology products as cultural artifacts; an interest in situated practices and immediate effects that are not always easily generalized; and a willingness to champion authorial intent that might at times ignore or even thwart audience's (or users') desires and expectations. Design also employs a plurality of ways of expressing its concerns, including narrative styles that may prefer thematics to categories, and non-textual or more visual and tangible formats.

Accommodating design within CHI is not trivial. The ways designers produce and disseminate knowledge are often different from, and perhaps confounding to, engineers and behavioral scientists, as well as social scientists and humanities scholars. Embracing design practice and discourse may require us to rethink, for example, how we conduct peer review, select and prioritize publication formats, and set conference registration fees. The good news is that the CHI community appears ready and willing to take some of these challenges on. We are heartened by recent experiments with pictorial publication formats, annotated portfolios [11], and the emergence of "research through design" [27,44,56]. We believe these efforts will be strengthened with the development of a richer design discourse within CHI to which we hope these considerations contribute.

ACKNOWLEDGMENTS

We thank the reviewers for their instructive comments. Support provided by Intel STC for Social Computing, NSF #1217685, NSF #1451465, and ERC #226528.

REFERENCES

1. Anonymous. 2002. Best inventions of 2002. Time Magazine.http://www.time.com/time/2002/inventions/toc.html. Last accessed Sept 21, 2014.
2. Auger, J. & J. Loizeau. 2001. Audio Tooth Implant. http://www.auger-loizeau.com/index.php?id=7 Last accessed Sept 21, 2014.
3. Barad, K. 2007. *Meeting the universe halfway*. Duke UP.
4. Bardzell, J., Bardzell, S. & Stolterman, E. Reading Critical Designs: Supporting Reasoned Interpretations of Critical Design. Proc. CHI '14.
5. Bardzell, Jeffrey, and Shaowen Bardzell. What Is "Critical" About Critical Design?" Proc. CHI '13.
6. Bardzell, S., Bardzell, J., Forlizzi, J. Zimmerman, J., & Antanitis, J. 2012. Critical Design and Critical Theory: The Challenge of Designing for Provocation. In Proc. DIS '12.
7. Bardzell, S.,Gross, S., Wain, J. Toombs, A. & Bardzell, J. 2011. The Significant Screwdriver. Proc. BCS-HCI '11.
8. Bleaker, J. "Design Fiction: A Short Essay on Design, Science, Fact and Fiction."
9. Blythe, M. Research Through Design Fiction: Narrative in Real and Imaginary Abstracts. Proc. CHI '14.
10. Bødker, S. 2006. When second wave HCI meets third wave challenges. In Proc. NordiCHI '06.
11. Bowers, J. The Logic of Annotated Portfolios: Communicating the Value of 'Research Through Design.' Proc. DIS '12.
12. Butler, J. 1989. *Gender trouble.* Routledge.
13. Costa Pederson, C. 2012. *Gaming the system*. Unpublished doctoral dissertation, Cornell Art History.
14. Cross, N. 1999. "Design research: A discipline conversation." Design Issues 15(2):5-10.
15. DiSalvo, C. 2012. *Adversarial Design*. MIT Press.
16. DiSalvo, C. moderator. Feature Discussion Session 4: Is there a Post-Critical Design?

https://www.designresearchnetwork.org/drn/content/feature-discussion-session-4%3A-there-post-critical-design%3F

17. Deleuze, G. & F. Guattari. B. Massumi, trans., *A thousand plateaus*. U. Minnesota P, 1987.

18. Dunne, A. & Raby, F. Speculative Everything: Design, Fiction, and Social Dreaming. The MIT Press, 2013.

19. Dunne, A., & F. Raby. 2002. Design Noir: The Secret Life of Electronic Objects. Birkhauser.

20. Dunne, A. 2008. *Hertzian Tales*. MIT Press.

21. Fallman, D. 2003. Design-oriented human-computer interaction. Proc. CHI '03.

22. Feinberg, M., Carter, D., & Bullard, J. Always Somewhere, Never There: Using Critical Design to Understand Database Interactions. Proc. CHI '14.

23. Feinberg, M., Carter, D., & Bullard, J. A Story Without End: Writing the Residual into Descriptive Infrastructure. Proc. DIS '14.

24. Ferri, G., Bardzell, J., Bardzell, S. & Louraine, S. Analyzing Critical Designs: Categories, Distinctions, and Canons of Exemplars. Proc. DIS '14.

25. Firestone, David. 1993. While Barbie Talks Tough, G.I. Joe Goes Shopping. NY Times, December 31, 1993.

26. Frayling, C. 1993. Research in art and design. Royal College of Art Research Papers, Vol. 1, No. 1, 1993/4.

27. Gaver, W. What Should We Expect from Research Through Design? Proc. CHI '12.

28. Gaver, W., Bowers, J. Boucher, A., Gellerson, H., Pennington, S., Schmidt, A., Steed, A., Villars, N., & Walker, B. The Drift Table: Designing for Ludic Engagement. In CHI '04 EA.

29. Gaver, William W., Jacob Beaver, and Steve Benford. "Ambiguity As a Resource for Design." Proc. CHI '03.

30. Gaver, W. & A. Dunne. 1999. Projected realities. In Proc. CHI '99, 600-607.

31. Hallnäs, L. & Johan Redström. 2001. Slow Technology – Designing for Reflection. *Personal Ubiquitous Comput.* 5, 3 (January 2001), 201-212.

32. Hirsch, T. 2008. Contestational Design : Innovation for Political Activism. Unpublished PhD Thesis, MIT.

33. Hirsch, T. & Henry, J. TXTmob: Text Messaging for Protest Swarms." In CHI '05 EA.

34. Jarvis, N., D. Cameron, & A. Boucher. 2012. Attention to detail. In *Proc NordiCHI '12*, 11-20.

35. Lacy, S. 1994. *Mapping the Terrain: New Genre Public Art.* Seattle, WA: Bay Press Critical making:

36. Leahu , L. & P. Sengers. 2014. Freaky: performing hybrid human-machine emotion.Proc. DIS '14, 607-616.

37. Löwgren, J. 1995. Applying design methodology to software development. Proc. DIS'95, 87-95.

38. Malpass, M. 2013 Between Wit and Reason: Defining Associative, Speculative, and Critical Design in Practice, Design and Culture(5):3, 333-365

39. Massumi, B. Translator's forward. In [A Thousand Plateaus - just cross-ref the references], pp ix-xv.

40. Mazé, R., & Redström, J. 2007. Difficult forms: Critical practices of design and research. Proc. of IASDR'07.

41. Odom, W., Sellen, A., Banks, R., Kirk, D., Regan, T., Selby, M., Forlizzi, J., & Zimmerman, J. Designing for Slowness, Anticipation and Re-Visitation: A Long Term Field Study of the Photobox. Proc. CHI '14.

42. Oliveira, P. Cheat Sheet for a Non (or Less) Colonialist Speculative Design. Medium. Accessed September 22, 2014. https://medium.com/@pedroliveira_/cheat-sheet-for-a-non-or-less-colonialist-speculative-design-9a6b4ae3c465.

43. Papanek, V. J. 1972. *Design for the Real World*. New York: Bantam Books.

44. Pierce, J. 2014. On the Presentation and Production of Design Research Artifacts in HCI. Proc. DIS '14

45. Pierce, J. & Paulos, E. 2014. Counterfunctional Things: Exploring Possibilities in Designing Digital Limitations. Proc. DIS '14

46. Raley, R. 2009. *Tactical Media*. U. Minnesota Press

47. Ratto, M. "Critical Making: Conceptual and Material Studies in Technology and Social Life." *Information Society* 27, no. 4 (2011): 252-60.

48. Sengers, P., Boehner, K., David, D., & Kaye, J. Reflective Design. Proc CC '05.

49. Sengers, P. & Gaver, B. Staying Open to Interpretation: Engaging Multiple Meanings in Design and Evaluation. Proc. DIS '06

50. Schon, D. The Reflective Practitioner: How Professionals Think in Action. New edition edition. New York: Ashgate Publishing Limited, 1995.

51. Thackara, J. "Republic of Salivation (Michael Burton and Michiko Nitta)." Design and Violence. Accessed September 22, 2014. http://designandviolence.moma.org/republic-of-salivation-michael-burton-and-michiko-nitta/.

52. Tonkinwise, C. 2014. How We Intend to Future: Review of Anthony Dunne and Fiona Raby, Speculative Everything: Design, Fiction, and Social Dreaming. *Design Philosophy Papers* 12(2): 169-188.

53. Toran, N. 2001. Object for Lonely Men. http://noamtoran.com/NT2009/projects/object-for-lonely-men

54. Wilde, D., Underwood, J. & Pohlner, R.PKI: Crafting Critical Design. Proc. DIS '14.

55. Wolf, T., Rode, J., Sussman, J. & Kellogg, W. 2006. Dispelling "design" as the black art of CHI. Proc. CHI '06, 521-530.

56. Zimmerman J, Stolterman E, & Forlizzi J. 2010. An analysis and critique of research through design: toward a formalization of a research approach. Proc. DIS 2010.

Immodest Proposals: Research Through Design and Knowledge

Jeffrey Bardzell
Informatics and Computing
Indiana University
Bloomington, IN 47408
jbardzel@indiana.edu

Shaowen Bardzell
Informatics and Computing
Indiana University
Bloomington, IN 47408
selu@indiana.edu

Lone Koefoed Hansen
Aesthetics and Communication
& PIT Research Centre
Aarhus University, Denmark
koefoed@cavi.au.dk

ABSTRACT
This paper offers theoretical support for research through design (RtD) by arguing that to legitimize and make use of research through design as *research*, HCI researchers need to explore and clarify how RtD objects contribute to knowledge. One way to pursue this goal is to leverage knowledge-producing tactics of the arts and humanities traditions of aesthetics, key among which is a community-wide and ongoing critical analysis of aesthetic objects. Along these lines, we argue that while the *intentions* of the object's designer are important and annotations are a good mechanism to articulate them, the *critical reception* of objects can be equally generative of RtD's knowledge impacts. Such a scholarly critical reception is needed because of the potential inexhaustibility of design objects' meanings, their inability to be paraphrased adequately. Offering a multilevel analysis of the (critical) design fiction Menstruation Machine by Sputniko!, the paper explores how design objects co-produce knowledge, by working through complex design problem spaces in non-reductive ways, proposing new connections and distinctions, and embodying design ideas and processes across time and minds.

Author Keywords
Research through design; HCI; criticism; epistemology

ACM Classification Keywords
H.5.m. Information interfaces and presentation (e.g., HCI): Miscellaneous.

INTRODUCTION
Research through design (RtD), the practice of using design thinking, processes, and products as an inquiry methodology, has garnered considerable attention in both HCI and design discourses [e.g., 3,4,6,9,11,12,15,20,22,28,29,32,37, 40,41,42]. As an emerging practice, there remains some contradiction and confusion about what it is and what it should be, which might [41] or might not be [22] a problem in itself. Whether or not a unifying theory is the answer, our position is that to support the theoretical development of RtD as a research practice, to support the community's uptake of its knowledge contributions, and to support more HCI researchers and practitioners trying out this practice, at a minimum more research needs to be done to explore and to evaluate the *epistemic* potentials for RtD to contribute to knowledge in HCI. Design is both a noun and a verb as [18] writes; here, we focus on the noun—*design as objects*.

We begin by observing that while RtD as a practice is in itself knowledge producing [1], so too can design objects produce knowledge. However, what this means is unclear in the research literature. Is the knowledge outcome of an RtD object a special form of communication, one that is superior in some sense to verbal discourse? Is it these objects' job to reveal true propositions about the world? To reveal the potentials of design materials? To reify design arguments? To express emotional or subjectively felt experiences of the artificial world and its apparent trajectory? To critique assumptions imbued in everyday designs? To reveal alternative ways of being to motivate us to pursue them?

We investigate RtD in its relation to the production of knowledge; specifically, *how design objects are knowledge producers both for those that encounter them and those that design them.* In the arts and humanities, the ability of objects to produce knowledge is well understood, and the aim of this paper is to characterize how we might understand the kind of knowledge that RtD objects produce, how they produce it, and how we engage with it. We begin by characterizing the discourses on RtD in HCI vis-à-vis its knowledge objectives. We observe that there is demand for "good analytical skills to carve out core and recognizable important new concepts" [37, p14], but less on what the analytical skills actually look like or do. To respond we turn to hermeneutical practice in aesthetics, which is based on the view that a central value of the arts is that art objects and phenomena co-produce meaning (as opposed to understanding aesthetics as primarily related to beauty, emotional expression, or aesthetic pleasure). In principle, this goes back

CHI 2015, April 18 - 23 2015, Seoul, Republic of Korea
Copyright 2015 ACM 978-1-4503-3145-6/15/04···$15.00
http://dx.doi.org/10.1145/2702123.2702400

to the eighteenth-century German philosopher Baumgarten and has been explored throughout the twentieth century in both continental and analytic aesthetics (see [26,30,36] for accounts of these histories). Following these traditions, we argue that all objects can be critiqued from a critical and aesthetic perspective, but that some objects are far more complex than others, thus offering an (in principle) inexhaustible) source of knowledge production; this view offers strong theoretical support for RtD in HCI. Also, RtD's influential formulation in Frayling [20] appears to be committed to this argument, which is currently (and sadly) underdeveloped in HCI. We also argue that the success of RtD hinges not only on the development of a substantial collection of outstanding exemplars (as has already been proposed in HCI and RtD research [22,40] and in art-and-technology research centers such as V2 and SymbioticA), but also on the development of a hermeneutic community capable of actively critiquing and interpreting the significance of these exemplars for HCI and design.

To explore how a detailed critique might work when we understand objects as knowledge producers offering to the viewer the possibility to engage in meaning-making practices unfolding a range of complex and multifaceted views, we offer a multilevel analysis of a (critical) design fiction, the Menstruation Machine by Sputniko! (aka Hiromi Ozaki) [35]. Drawing on the analytic practices in the arts and aesthetics, we connect this analysis back to the issue of research through design and the contribution to knowledge that certain design exemplars are able to make.

RESEARCH THROUGH DESIGN AND KNOWLEDGE

Although the terminology has since been redefined [32] and added to [11], Frayling's highly influential working paper "Research in Art and Design" [20] is typically cited as the source of the term "research through design," though others from the RCA investigated the links and overlaps between practitioners and researchers [1], and though the practice had active precursors prior to the publication of Frayling's paper [40]. In it, Frayling critiques a false dichotomy between research and art/design—that the former is cognitive and the latter is expressive—concluding that since many of the motivations and practices of the two are alike, there is a more productive distinction of the relations between research and art and design [20, p.5], including the following (corresponding to a nearly identical triplet in [1]):

Research into art and design: historical research, aesthetic and perceptual research, and research into theoretical perspectives on art and design (i.e., traditional art historical and critical-humanist approaches to art and design).

Research through art and design: materials research (i.e., "customising a piece of technology to do something no one had considered before"), and the explicit and detailed use of an art/design research diary.

Research for art and design: research "where the end product is an artefact—where the thinking is [...] *embodied in the artefact*, where the goal is not primarily communicable knowledge in the sense of verbal communication."

This is a dense passage in a short but dense article, and some confusions have emerged. What HCI researchers call "research through design" most closely maps onto what Frayling in fact called "research for design" (cf. [32]). Additionally, Frayling's use of "research into/through/for art and design" is commonly edited in HCI research to skip the "art and" part, as if Frayling had no interest in art and was only theorizing design research. However, the similarities between art and design were foundational to his essay.

One consequence of eliding "art and" from Frayling's distinctions is to bury his commitment to art as a mode of knowledge and understanding, in which the artist, like the designer and the researcher, is determined to explore and investigate (i.e. research) the world through interrogating, designing, organizing, and making—"research through practitioner action" is [1]'s term for this. The designer as well as the artist is, Frayling writes, a "creator of meaning" and, like the researcher, this happens in "an orderly way" and thus in a "cognitive idiom" (p3). The point of Frayling's paper is to argue that "research for art and design" (i.e., what HCI calls HCI "research through design") is not merely an expressive mode where objects are personal expressions of the creator's mind, devoid of cultural and societal significance. Instead, Frayling seeks to establish it as "a tradition which stands outside the artefact at the same time as standing within it" (p5), a view that echoes [Archer]'s "shed[ding] light on [something] by attempting to construct something" (p11) as well as resembles contemporary art theories arguing that art participates in culture/society by commenting on it or looking at it from a particular position.

We will follow HCI in referring to "research through design," even though in Frayling it is referred to as "research for art and design," but we will not follow HCI in suppressing the role of art and the way that artists operate "quite consciously—in a cognitive idiom" (p3) because this understanding of how artists work—and thus of how art objects produce meaning as part of an aesthetic and cultural exchange with the viewer—provides theoretical resources that can contribute to research through design in HCI today.

Knowledge is unfolded in objects

As a field, HCI must answer what sorts of knowledge outcomes can come from objects in (art and) design projects; if we can't, we cannot legitimize RtD as a way of doing HCI research. Naming it design-oriented research, Fallman [15] argues that it "should include 'problem setting' as an important part, the possibility of exploring possibilities outside of the current paradigm (p231). Stolterman and Wiberg [37] describe how a concept design "carries and manifests all the combined knowledge that has influenced the design" (p104). Such knowledge is available to designers as well as to the user, we might add; in these objects, paradigms are being challenged, complex ideas are being explored.

Similarly, [38] argues: "art has a crucial democratic significance. Artists can experiment with the politics of things: they draw attention to a matter, turn it into an experience, rewrite it [...] enable people to see through the [hidden] political role of things and play with it" (p26-7). Again, some objects can shift our perspective on and understanding of a situation, not by prescribing a particular way of looking, but by drawing attention to existing practices by designing something that questions them. This is a more open ended version of a similar view by [40] for whom "RtD is a type of research practice focused on improving the world by making new things that disrupt, complicate or transform the current state of the world." This research approach speculates on what the future could and should be" by producing "design exemplars." The knowledge contribution of RtD is to offer concrete exemplars of preferred alterity, which are generative of further design thinking.

Research through design, then, is a thing-making practice whose objects can offer a critique of the present and reveal alternative futures, while remaining grounded in empirical science, behavioral theory, contemporary technological possibility, and socio-cultural practices. Similarly, [7,12,13] all argue that some objects lend themselves to an encounter aimed at reflecting on contemporary technology discourses as much as it is aimed at providing a sensual experience. In other words, as [7] write, "works of digital art are experiments in interaction design" (p24) that "invite us to reimagine and redefine our contexts" (p28).

Gaver [22] offers another view of RtD: "instead of being extensible and verifiable, theory produced by research through design tends to be provisional, contingent and aspirational. [..] an endless string of design examples is precisely at the core of how design research should operate, and [..] the role of theory should be to annotate those examples rather than replace them" (p938). For Gaver, design exemplars are prioritized over theory. This suggests that rather than viewing RtD projects as instrumentally serving better HCI or design theory, the goal should be to build the strongest possible collection of design exemplars and then to annotate the exemplars to help bring forward *their* knowledge contributions. It also suggests that the corpus of research becomes not a collection of papers (as in the ACM Digital Library) but rather a corpus of designs, with texts existing to explain them—a portfolio of annotated designs, much like artists exhibit their work in galleries, attaching manifestos and artists' statements to the exhibition. [21] go as far as to argue that digital artifacts themselves "should stand as peer-reviewable forms of research, worthy of professional credit and contestable as forms of argument" (p407). These calls echo structures found in other aesthetic practices where critics, peers, and buyers assess the objects in reviews, critiques, exhibitions, and concert bookings.

While we acknowledge important differences among the authors cited above, we want to stress several commonalties to the formulations offered. We note that none of these formulations frame RtD as contributing to HCI theory in the scientific sense of the word 'theory.'. Instead, common to all of the formulations is that RtD offers non-verbal design proposals in the form of artifacts, which support design thinking: the interplay of object and tradition in a way that opens up practice [20]; the ability of experimental objects to aid designers wrestling with the boundaries of design problem setting and framing [7,15]; the ability of experimental objects to provide material images of a speculative future [13,40]; and the role of objects to encode knowledge and to become themselves the primary research corpus, moving the verbal into a supportive role [22,37].

Knowledge is unfolded in the interpretation of objects

Having emphasized the designer's understanding of the object, in the following we argue that the *critical reception* of objects can also articulate and develop its knowledge impacts. Although we all already perform critiques as part of daily practice, there is little culture of sustained critical analysis of objects in HCI. If there are too few exemplars of RtD in HCI, there are even fewer exemplars of scholarship on these exemplars [17,27]. Yet in the arts and humanities, both types of exemplars are common, to the point of dominating those discourses. The role of critique in those discourses is to remove barriers to appreciation [10], and collectively they help artists and critics alike think more generatively and creatively about the arts, including genres, materials, forms, meanings, and society more broadly, including social and political change. Recalling [1], we argue that RtD in HCI would benefit from this.

How aesthetic appreciation has such epistemic power has been theorized in the arts and humanities. In Anglo-American aesthetics, [23] writes that literature (by extension, art) "can be seen as in some significant respect *informative* of extra-textual reality [...], declar[ing] to the reader something about the way her world is" (p82). In addition, art can also "illuminate experience by making us more sensitively aware of what it [experience] contains" [25, p71]. In continental aesthetics, Seel [36] develops a theory of "aesthetic appreciation" (or 'interpretations'): first, aesthetic appreciation is an experience of "appearing" in that the object cannot be determined completely. The object is perceived in its "constitutive indeterminacy," i.e., we deliberately do not search for one meaning but search "with greater attentiveness to what is indeterminable in them" (p54). The attraction lies in never being done with the reading. Second, aesthetic appreciation results from a complex interplay between the work, the spectator, and the (cultural) context. While there is potentially no end to the ways that an object can be interpreted, an interpretation is also conditioned by knowledge of the type of object materially and formally, its histories of production and reception, and commonly understood categories and meanings (cf. Gadamer's "horizons of understanding," Iser's "modulating operations," and in design literature Coyne's notion of design criticism as constrained by a community of practice).

In other words, an important value of art is its contribution to understanding, which comes through a meaningful encounter. Art is thus a meaning-making practice with meaning-making objects, and, like science, it helps us understand the world. It differs from science, though, in the ways by which it informs us about the world: oversimplifying, this view holds that whereas art chiefly improves our thinking (e.g., by enhancing our perceptiveness, imagination, intellectual sensitivity, ability to make fine discriminations, etc.), science chiefly extends our knowledge through the discovery of new facts and explanations [23,24,38]. Following this, we offer the pragmatic claim that taking seriously the reading and interpretation of complex design objects provides resources to support RtD. Designers are tasked with understanding the relationships between present and near-future technological possibility and future ways of being, such that design solutions can be introduced.

What we are arguing here is that such a job is epistemically akin to one of the roles played by the artist, as described by aesthetic philosopher Eldridge [14]: "The special pertinence of [..] artistic achievement is that human life continually presents materials about which we do not know exactly how to feel and judge. [...] We can wish to have our puzzlement worked through and clarified, and successful art will do this in a way that does not resolve the puzzlement into a dogmatic moral, but which clarifies its complex particularities" (p226). It is not difficult to paraphrase Eldridge from the standpoint of design. Technology and technology-mediated behaviors are the materials "about which we [as designers] do not know how to feel and judge." And a successful RtD object might be understood as an object that helps us work through and clarify a given puzzling problem space, not to resolve it into a dogmatic theory, but rather to clarify its complex particularities (e.g., the specific contours of the design problem, to paraphrase Fallman).

The role of the work of art or RtD is not to present us with new facts about the world, but rather to enrich our capabilities of perceiving and interpreting the world, that is, "viewing the world through art, rather than checking art against the world" as [25] writes, before asking "Does this make us alive to new aspects of this sort of occasion?" (p68-70). When [40] write of RtD that "The knowledge produced functions as a proposal, not a prediction" [40], they are getting at the same idea as [25]: the knowledge role of the object is not to offer an accurate representation of the world (past, present, or future) but rather to "make us alive to new aspects of" a human domain of interest. The key difference is that whereas works of art serve these purposes for a public, RtD serves these purposes for designers. RtD makes designers "more alive" to the design situation, who, like artists, also must work with a view of human experience in its widest sense: "visual, aural, and tactile, as well as practical, emotional, and intellectual." And just as works of art are better at this than verbal discourses, so good RtD exemplars are rightly prioritized over verbal discourse.

Knowledge is unfolded in interpretative communities

The notion that design exemplars are the primary body of knowledge, and that verbal discourse does not stand over that body but rather serves to remove barriers to the understanding of how these exemplars serve design thinking, is present in all of our primary RtD sources. And it is specifically this role of the verbal to which we now turn. Consider the following argument by American philosopher Goodman [24] on theme and variation in architecture and other arts: "Establishment and modification of motifs, abstraction and elaboration of patterns, differentiation and interrelation of modes of transformation, all are processes of constructive search; and the measures applicable are not those of passive enjoyment but those of cognitive efficacy: delicacy of discrimination, power of integration, and justice of proportion between recognition and discovery. Indeed, one typical way of advancing knowledge is by progressive variation upon a theme" (p261). A passage like this provides strong theoretical support for Gaver's call for portfolios. It is through collections of multiple exemplars that themes and variations become visible, and progressive variation upon a theme is a typical way of advancing knowledge, e.g., Goldsmiths' interrogation of themes of ludic interaction and ambiguity over the years. Annotation of course can help render themes, variations, and their interpreted significances visible to broader audiences, helping to articulate and disseminate knowledge—but knowledge that is primarily *in* the designs themselves. This is why professor in Architecture Flyvbjerg [18] calls for more case-study research, arguing that "the Kuhnian insight that a scientific discipline without a large number of thoroughly executed case studies is a discipline without systematic production of exemplars, and a discipline without exemplars is an ineffective one."

But here we argue that annotated portfolios, important as they are, are not enough. For not only does a given design studio perform progressive variations on a theme to generate knowledge: the whole design community does. To scope this inquiry to individual studios is to obfuscate the collective achievements of the community at-large. Likewise, the notion of annotations also has an important limitation: in [8,22], the studio itself annotates its own portfolio. But imagine if our knowledge of modernist painting were limited to what Matisse said about Matisse, what Picasso said about Picasso, and so forth? If the HCI and design research and practitioner communities are to leverage the growing numbers of RtD objects into more generalizable knowledge, these communities will need to collectively practice the role that Gaver ascribes to annotation, which is to remove the barriers of appreciation of individual and collections of exemplars for the broader community through writing about designs.

There have already been calls for more criticism in HCI (e.g., [1,5,16] as well as examples of it in action [17,27] though often without using the term [7,12,31]), but while it has often used RtD as its objects of inquiry, the connection has been tacit. Advocating for an expansion of design criticism alongside the development of RtD exemplars and annotated portfolios maintains the hierarchy of design exemplars over verbal explications, a hierarchy that has been in place in the humanities for centuries. But we stress that we need more than first-person annotations of exemplars by their own designers, although they remain very welcome.

THE MENSTRUATION MACHINE

To explore the benefits of critical analysis of RtDs, we offer a critique of one such exemplar: Menstruation Machine (MM hereafter) by Sputniko! [35]. In it, we summarize available interpretations of this design and argue that they have significant defects, offering our own analysis of how MM significantly contributes to design research. In doing so, we move the burden of identifying RtD knowledge contributions from solely the designer toward a more community-distributed model—a hermeneutic community, as has been tried and proven in the arts and humanities. MM (Figure 1) is a 2010 (critical) design fiction by Sputniko!, also known as Hiromi Ozaki, a Japanese artist then at the RCA and now at MIT. It is a metal chastity belt-like device, which simulates menstruation for its wearer. The device is accompanied by a 3-minute music video and the following short artist statement (quoted in full):

> It's 2010, so why are humans still menstruating? The pill free interval was devised in the early days of the contraceptive pill only because it was felt that women would find having a 'period' more acceptable—however, out of all mammals only humans, apes and bats need to bleed monthly for their reproductive cycle. What does Menstruation mean to humans? Who might choose to have it, and how might they have it?
>
> Fitted with a blood dispensing mechanism and lower-abdomen-stimulating electrodes, the Menstruation Machine simulates the pain and bleeding of an average 5 day menstruation process of a human. Menstruation Machine (Takashi's Take) is a music video about a boy 'Takashi', who builds the machine in an attempt to dress up as a female, biologically as well as aesthetically, to fulfill his desire to understand what it might feel like to be a truely kawaii (cute) girl. He determinedly wears the machine to hang out with his kawaii friend in Tokyo, but...

(MIS-)READING MENSTRUATION MACHINE

We have shown this design in several design and health informatics courses in the U.S. and Europe, and we ask students what they think this design means. The response is among the strongest we have ever seen to such prompts, even when we take a step back and explain the particular nature of the speculative and critical design tradition at RCA [13]. What initially emerges is what we call a functionalist reading of MM, which states that the device helps men empathize with women concerning menstruation. The main view is that by facilitating this, men would be more motivated to 'solve' the 'problems' of menstruation. One graduate student appreciated the design's 'tactic,' which he said is to take something that he as a man has no access to (menstruation) and convert it into a design challenge. Further, a debate about this design was held in 2014 at MoMA

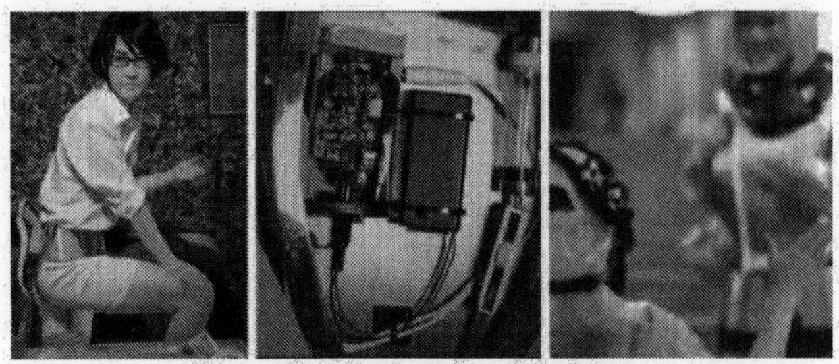

Figure 1: Menstruation Machine

and documented online [39]. The debate centered around the *authenticity* of MM's simulation, casting epistemological doubt on any empathy that arises from it. The debate asked questions such as: Is empathy in design a good thing? How do you know as a designer when you have 'real empathy'? Does MM falsely promise to give men an experience that they can't really have? These are important questions with implications for design practice and education. Yet they also carry forward the assumption that—despite the speculative backdrop—MM's primary purpose is to create empathy among men by providing a simulated female experience. All three readings are predicated on a radical difference between men and women, and the 'function' of the MM is to simulate for one side the experience of the other.

The strengths of these functionalist readings are that they focus on what seems to be the most salient feature of the design—its ability to simulate menstruation—and that the design makes us imagine new scenarios in which men might want to use this device and why. As a functionalist and even a critical design, this reading asserts, it prompts us to imagine new scenarios of use and clearly supports design thinking in the domain of gender, the body, and technology.

But this type of reading also raises a number of doubts. It assumes that the device is for men. Neither the designer in her statement nor the design itself says that the design is "for men": there is no reason it cannot be used by women, trans individuals—anyone. It seems revealing that everyone—even feminist scholars at MoMA—in one way or another take for granted that the design is to be read in terms of gender binaries and gender essentialism. Another doubtful feature of this reading is its assumption that design is always also problem-solving; that the device might be ironic, satiric, or otherwise polysemous seems to be secondary or even excluded as a possibility. Finally, it is important to note that none of these readings take seriously the device's very sophisticated aesthetics. Yet the design, the artist statement, and the music video all collectively present a highly sophisticated and stylized way of being (which includes a futuristic, urbanized, Japanese, youthful, gender-bending, electronic, high fashion, special night out)—an ironic oversight indeed for a debate staged at MoMA.

Collectively, the functionalist reading suggests some common assumptions concerning electronic devices: that they are above all functional; that they solve problems; that they reinforce but don't problematize social norms such as gender; that they do not attempt to offer cultural commentary. This is a very limiting view of an object's power. If collections of RtD exemplars are to have impact on the research community, we will collectively need to up our game.

RE-READING MENSTRUATION MACHINE

We now offer our own reading of Menstruation Machine, informed by critical practices in art, philosophy, and design.

A Descriptive Account of Menstruation Machine

We begin with a *description* of MM's aesthetics, that is, how are we supposed to understand its role as a specific style or way of being? With its polished steel and finished form, its visual language connotes technology, high-end product design, and futuristic fashion. It hides its machinery but also makes no secret that it is a machine, like an Apple product. In the music video, it also fits seamlessly with the Japanese kawaii (cute girl) aesthetic (e.g., the protagonist's rainbow-colored hair, glamour make-up, clothes made with metallic textiles, pop baseball cap, and designer purse). In the statement that accompanies the design (reproduced above), she asks, "What does menstruation mean to humans?" Thus, she avoids making the commitment to gender essentialism by asserting that this is a design for men. She does not ask about what it's like to experience simulated menstruation, but rather, what does menstruation *mean*? She also foregrounds the presentation's aesthetics, devoting a third of her statement to the music video.

The video presents MM in an aestheticized way, using the medium of the music video: MTV style editing, techno soundtrack, song lyrics, a simple narrative, a rock'n'roll protagonist. It introduces MM as part of the protagonist's impressive fashion; MM manages to look entirely of a piece with the rest of the outfit. The protagonist's putting on the device is shown alongside makeup, doing her hair, and putting on her outfit: everything here suggests that this is a particularly special night out, an experience to be cherished. The protagonist's narrative is cross-cut with footage of the technology of the device, revealing its technical guts and functions, almost like a stylized technology demonstration. Finally, the lyrics of the song are important, because they do not merely communicate the experience of cross-dresser wearing the machine—but rather *taunt* the protagonist, and by extension the viewer, to try it in the first place: "You can learn / If you really dare" and "I thought you really really really really want to know how it feels," tellingly adding, "Right?" The music video dares us to enter its fictive world, and the protagonist should be read not as standing in for a man who wants to know what it's like to menstruate, but as anyone in our world who wishes to enter a world where this is a common consumer device—including the pains ("It hurts, doesn't it?") and new perspectives ("Tell me what you can see / Can you ever feel the same?") it brings.

In professional criticism, the role of a descriptive account such as this is to get the critic and her readers on the same page. While another critic or reader will likely point to other details, everyone can agree that these details are there. But by pulling these details into view, we have also taken the first analytic step, because this selection of details has implications for how we read the device—if nothing else, the details we have provided undermine the legitimacy of the functionalist reading by demonstrating that that reading contradicts the artist's explicit intentions and fails to account for a very high number of concrete details that are undeniably part of the device and its presentation to us.

Menstruation Machine's Propositional Content

MM expresses cultural as well as physiological aspects of menstruation and makes them manifest in a physical form. As previously stated, audience responses vary but frequently include laughter, puzzlement, disgust, and even dismissiveness, due to the device's clash with some of the cultural connotations to menstruation (for instance that it is 'a curse'). One way of understanding the effects of the device is that it addresses cultural discourses on menstruation by providing an interpretation of its effects, proposing that menstruation is not only (or even primarily) a physiological event, but has cultural, social and personal effects as well. Following ethnographer Mol's study of medical practices [33], we might say that MM proposes that menstruation is ontologically multistable; it is far from merely a 'simple' physiological event but must be understood from several, equally important, perspectives. These include links between menstruation and age, in the cases of menarche and menopause; menstruation as a taboo, even impure or disgusting; menstruation as controllable; views of menstruation as a super power that connects Earth and fertile women; and the menopausal woman as vulnerable according to women's magazines. All of these accounts propose that menstruation is a powerful and exclusively female phenomenon, something that MM is possibly circumventing.

So when MM brings menstruation with its blood and pain to the forefront of the design, menstruation becomes a choice but also a desirable, visible, festive, optional, on-demand, and fetishized event, that is no longer exclusively available to women. In addition, MM makes menstruation a spectacle for onlookers: it is a highly desirable object made of polished chrome. All of this seems to go counter what we expect of a technology that mediates menstruation, and it seems to get at issues of gender, the body, and technology. But what is the contribution of MM to design knowledge?

In the following we undertake an analysis to clarify ways that MM contributes to design knowledge, pointing as well to ways that such an analytical strategy might serve as a way to strengthen RtD's research impacts. Specifically, we explicate and analyze the propositional content of the device. If RtD objects function as design proposals, we can ask, *what exactly does Menstruation Machine propose?* To answer this, we identify a handful of propositions made by the design, and we analyze them as knowledge contributions. By 'proposition' we mean a claim that is offered as 'true' in the sense of correctly picking out some feature of the world. Propositions in science, philosophy, and other disciplines are commonly organized into hierarchies in support of one another, reaching for more general or higher level propositions. So to analyze a design in this way is first to generate a number of propositions that the design seems to make, and second to assess what that group of propositions aggregates into. This is, of course, a critical practice, and we make no claim that others would derive the same set of propositions as if these and only these were objectively present in the design, but we do believe that others would accept that our outcome here is at least reasonable. We number each proposition for easy reference in our analysis, but this list is not intended to be read as ordered.

1. Menstruation is a design material. [34] define design materials as "what a designer puts together in compositional relationships, creating real things. Materials are used to bring a design into existence in the world, to make it *appear* in a *real* sense" (p227). Design materials are not limited to physical materials but also include abstract material ("a process, or a symbol, or system") and "to people as social, cultural, and spiritual material." MM proposes that menstruation can be a design material, both in the physical sense of milliliters of blood and electric force required to induce cramps, and in the semantic sense of its various cultural significations. More subversively, it proposes that a cultural taboo can be a design material.

2. Menstruation is desirable. This is the design's most obvious and most critical proposition, the one that everyone instantly grasps and feels compelled to respond to. But as we have shown in our analysis so far, there's more than one way to unpack the desirability of menstruation. We might say: It is desirable for men to experience menstruation, so that they can improve their empathy towards women. Or: It is desirable for transgender women to have this device to feel 'more' feminine. It is visually desirable as an accessory for kawaii ("cute girl") fashion. It is desirable to have devices that can simulate sex-specific physiological experiences. It is intellectually and pedagogically desirable to illustrate Judith Butler's difficult concept of "performativity," giving this concept more intellectual traction. This list could go on, not least because of its ability to scale from very specific statements to very general ones—all of which invite us to imagine a world where a phenomenon colloquially known as 'the curse' is re-construed as desirable.

3. Menstruation can be simulated with a device. People can experience what it is like for another person to menstruate. The device proposes that anyone can experience a menstrual cycle (measured physiologically). This is not limited to men, but could include, for instance, premenstrual girls, postmenopausal women, or, for that matter, a menstruating woman who wants to double the symptoms. But this proposition implies some unexpected propositions as well, including the idea that menstruation can be turned on or off at will, since consumer devices have this ability.

4. Menstruation is a physiological event. The design operationalizes its menstrual simulation in strictly physiological and even medicalized terms. Doing so is part of its point—see proposition 2 above. Still, it doesn't accommodate crucial physiological aspects like menstruation's connection to pregnancy (e.g., the skipped period's implications for an unwanted pregnancy) or the feeling of bonding when periods of women living together, synchronize. The connotation that nature works in mysterious ways is left out of the design, even if it focuses on physiology.

5. Technological innovation is regressively gendered. The designer explicitly makes this point, "I wanted to illustrate how technology doesn't necessarily evolve fairly" and contrasts the approval processes of drugs for birth control versus erectile dysfunction. Part of the design's impact is that it normalizes a sexually marginalized position, and the act of doing so could be interpreted as shedding light on the fact that the opposite is closer to the norm. In this way, it encourages designers more generally to imagine design problem spaces from the perspective of those who are sexually (or otherwise) marginalized, that is, to normalize their world by inscribing their norms matter of factly in design.

6. A feminine performance is not "real" unless it has the possibility of a full menstrual experience. This proposition comes through most explicitly in the video, which is centrally about the performance of the feminine. Specifically, the video proposes that to be a kawaii involves more than a visual performance: one also has to *experience* menstruation, and this experience must in some sense be transformative: "I thought you really really really really want to know how it feels" and "Can you ever feel the same?" This proposition rules out, for example, wearing a pair of pants with simulated blood dyed into the crotch. This proposition also exists in some tension with Proposition 4, that menstruation is physiological, because the video suggests that menstruation for the protagonist is much more than that.

Analysis of Menstruation Machine's Propositions

For reasons of space, we stop enumerating propositions at six, though we could easily extend the list to include many more, such as "A menstrual simulator should achieve medically precise accuracy," which reflects the strong medicalization of the device and its design process as presented in various supporting documents, suggesting that this is not 'merely' an art project even if it is based in the speculative design paradigm. We turn instead to an analysis of these propositions. Again, in philosophy and science, propositions are generally structured to support higher-level claims or propositions. However, though MM may be a 'design proposal,' it does not paraphrase straightforwardly into a coherent argument along the lines of science or philosophy. We've only stated six inferred propositions, and already we see that they exist in tension with one another. Further analysis will reveal more tension.

Let us situate MM's propositions in relation to the debate in gender studies about gender essentialism. *Gender essentialism* is the view that men and women have irreducibly different experiences of their bodies that cannot be reconciled under a single universal 'human,' with diverse implications for the social sciences, policy, institutions, etc. The view is controversial in gender studies, but it is beyond the scope of this paper to rehearse the various positions. We raise it here because one of the central propositions of MM is that menstruation can be experienced by anyone who wears MM, a position that on the surface appears to reject gender essentialism—or to design a way out of it. Moreover, as we saw in the debate on this design at MoMA, a concern was raised that the device makes a promise—to help men feel empathy for women—that it can't deliver, an essentialist objection.

Let us analyze the propositions to see whether the device is essentialist. Proposition 1 (menstruation as design material) is gender non-essentialist, because the material—bleeding and muscle contractions—are experienced by all humans. Proposition 2 (m. as desirable) makes no commitment one way or another as phrased, but its various unpackings do. For example, the unpacking that says menstruation is desirable because it helps men empathize with a female experience is essentialist, while the unpacking that says it's desirable because it exemplifies Butler's concept of "performativity" is not. Proposition 3 (m. as simulatable) also does not commit to an essentialist position, because it makes menstruation portable and therefore separable from women's bodies. Proposition 4 (m. as physiological) medicalizes menstruation while denying its cultural connotations; if we follow feminists in analytically distinguishing between (socially constructed) gender and (biological) sex, Proposition 4 gravitates towards biological sex and thus towards an essentialist position. Proposition 5 (technological innovation is regressively gendered) frames technological innovation in a way that categorically distinguishes between men and women; it is essentialist. Proposition 6 (feminine performance is only real if m.) is also essentialist, because it suggests that to be subjectively 'real,' a feminine experience has to include the experience of menstruation. In sum, the propositions are all over the map on the essentialism issue, and some of them are even internally ambivalent.

With our proposition-driven account of MM, we above all wanted to experimentally try out the possibility of verbally articulating ways that designs function as 'proposals' open to interpretative inquiry. Specifically, we wanted to bring into view the propositions that constitute the design as a proposal, as a way of gaining insight into how they might contribute to design thinking. Identifying the propositions also continued to undercut the functionalist reading by revealing a number of aspects of the design *qua* proposal unrelated to or even contradicting the functionalist one.

FROM DESIGNS TO KNOWLEDGE

The above reading of MM suggests that design can serve as an open-ended cultural and social commentary as well as a commentary on the role of design thinking in making technologies for particular purposes. In doing so, it reveals that there is much more to be understood about a design than the functionalist reading. This expansion of interpretive understanding is crucial, because a perspective limited to functionality is not very useful for RtD objects whose purpose, among other things, is to work on having fewer blind spots in design research, or, as [15] puts it "exploring possibilities outside of current paradigms." Let us return, then, to the question of how RtD might contribute to HCI research.

Designs as Reified Arguments?

One possibility is that the knowledge offered by an RtD object is one particular argument. Proposing a way of linking design objects to research and thus knowledge production, [21] argue that RtD objects "reify arguments," which in addition to contributing to knowledge can even anticipate and preempt criticisms. While such an idea is provocative, they do not drill down to the level of propositions and chains of reasoning to show what that would look like, or even establish convincingly that such a thing is possible. Our experiment in analyzing MM through individual propositions gave us an opportunity to take a run at it.

But our proposition-driven account did *not* in the end provide a single, straightforward answer to what MM is or means, and we remain dubious that a design like MM can, by itself, "reify an argument," at least not in the way that we understand an argument. While we presented sufficient evidence to reject the functionalist view, we were not able to replace it with an alternative view at that level of simplicity. Rather, we demonstrated that the propositions do not by themselves resolve neatly into a single coherent research *argument*, even though the design materials do resolve neatly into a single coherent design *form*.

The point that an RtD's formal coherence does not manifest or signify an underlying coherence of argument is crucial to a theoretical understanding of RtD as a research methodology. It explains why design exemplars, rather than annotations or critiques of them such as this one, are primary: like art, RtDs are polysemous and even inexhaustible. "It helps men empathize with women" captures the meaning of MM as well as "action is the chief end of existence" captures the meaning of *Hamlet*, which is to say: not well at all. We are skeptical that we can expect this type of object to provide an interesting, cogent, verbally paraphrasable research argument. Our analysis showed that MM, rather than making an argument, instead opens a discussion of complex cultural and social norms such as gender and taboos and on how these are affected by the design of particular technologies.

Conceptual Polysemy and Design Understanding

If the knowledge provided by an RtD object cannot necessarily be viewed as a scientific explanation, a reified argument, or the sum of its functional meanings, then how does it contribute to design research, knowledge, or understanding? Let us return to MM: once we started working with possible meanings or propositions, it became clear that MM is multistable and polysemous, offering perspectives from many angles. Instead of offering a coherent position on the issue of gender essentialism, we found it self-contradictory. But this logical inconsistency does not imply a cognitive failure of the work: As our analysis shows and as Seel's concept of an object's "constitutive indeterminacy" [36] suggests, we look to the RtD in a way analogous to the way that aesthetics says we look to art: to "work through and clarify" an area of human life "about which we do not know exactly how to feel and judge" [14]; to "make us alive to new aspects of this sort of occasion" [25]; to develop through theme and variation finer "delicacy of discrimination, power of integration, and justice of proportion between recognition and discovery" [24].

In saying this we agree with but also extend Stolterman and Wiberg [37], who write of concept-driven designs,

> The key here is that the concept carries and manifests all the combined knowledge that has influenced the design. It is in this way that *knowledge is embodied in the artifact*; it is not necessarily expressed in words or other descriptions, even though such descriptions do complement and strengthen the experience and understanding of the concept design. (p104)

The artifact embodies a considerable amount of combined knowledge. However, it embodies more than the combined knowledge that has influenced the design, which presumably could be elucidated via annotation; it also comes to embody the combined knowledge of those who engage it seriously and analytically once it is released into the world. In this way, over time the object that merits such attention will continue to accrete new meanings, entering into complex relationships with prior understood meanings, the mastery of which will eventually come to define RtD collections of exemplars in relation to a hermeneutic community of practice. This hermeneutic community of practice, comprising designers and researchers alike, will share an expert analytical vocabulary and sensibility to co-produce meanings with RtD objects, whose symbolic functioning is too semantically, syntactically, and pragmatically dense to paraphrase, to decode, or to interpretatively pin down or exhaust.

But Did She Intend It?

It is highly improbable that Ozaki intended viewers of her design to use it to engage debates in aesthetics and philosophy of science about what constitutes "knowledge." What evidence we have of her intentions suggests that MM was a speculative design, specifically intended to reimagine the meanings of menstruation using design, rather than text, as the medium of inquiry. And often RtD has more pragmatic goals—to explore the expressive or functional capabilities of a new material, say, or to help a designer creatively explore a problem domain. As MM was surely successful within the scope of its intended speculations about menstruation, so can RtD projects be successful in their pragmatic goals without immediately aspiring to scientific or philosophical contributions [22].

But as we hope has become clear, our objective here has not been to decode Sputniko!'s intentions or even to unpack "all the combined knowledge that has influenced the design." It has been, rather, to seek to identify and communicate ways that MM can contribute to HCI and design knowledge *beyond* the immediate contexts and goals within and for which it was undertaken. Specifically, we have argued that the design can be understood to interrogate relations among technology, design, gender, taboo, and the body, without reducing these issues to a universal theory, bullet list of "design implications," or dogma—and that this interrogation is a form of knowledge production.

As we, in a design critical role, begin to develop these understandings, introduce new connections, propose new links between design materials and cultural meanings, and so on, the device comes to mean more than Ozaki intended. This is no more a criticism of Ozaki than it is a criticism of Shakespeare to say that *Hamlet* has remained relevant across centuries and world cultures by transforming in significance in ways he could never have begun to imagine, let alone sanction. But this also means that design annotations, while an important contribution to RtD and design knowledge more generally, is the beginning, not the end, of the articulation of a design's contributions to knowledge.

MM neither serves to *make* nor to *illustrate* a single or particular argument: it does much more work than that. By entering into a polysemous dialogue with existing design languages, cultural norms, user experiences, and research literature—which are publicly available to design researchers and not locked in the private mind of the designer—MM can co-produce new design understandings, if we have the ability to read it. This latter skill is why competence in design criticism is so important for HCI: without it, it will be difficult to bridge between the compositional, formal, semantic, and experiential composition of the design and the conceptual nature of design research. In Seel's words, in order for the object to "appear," it needs to enter a qualified and engaged dialogue with an interpretative community.

ACKNOWLEDGEMENTS

This research has been funded by Aarhus University's interdisciplinary research centre for Participatory Information Technology, The Intel Science and Technology Center for Social Computing, and the National Science Foundation (#1002772). Thanks also to Jodi Forlizzi, Erik Stolterman, and our reviewers for their constructive criticisms..

REFERENCES

1. Archer, B. (1995). The Nature of Research. *Co-design, interdisciplinary journal of design*, Jan 1995, 6-13.
2. Bardzell, J. (2011). Interaction criticism: An introduction to the practice. *Interacting with computers*, 23(6), 604-621.
3. Bardzell, J., and Bardzell, S. (2013). What is critical about critical design?. In *Proc. of CHI'13*. ACM.

4. Bardzell, J., Bardzell, S., and Stolterman, E. (2014). Reading critical designs: Supporting reasoned debates about critical designs. In *Proc. of CHI'2014*. ACM.
5. Bertelsen, O., and Pold, S. (2004). Criticism as an approach to interface aesthetics. In *Proc. of NordiCHI'04*. ACM.
6. Blythe, M. (2014). Research through design fiction: Narrative in real and imaginary abstracts. In *Proc. of CHI'2014*. ACM.
7. Bolter, J. D. and Gromala, D. (2003). *Windows and Mirrors: Interaction Design, Digital Art, and the Myth of Transparency*. The MIT Press.
8. Bowers, J. (2012). The logic of annotated portfolios: Communicating the value of "Research through Design." In *Proc. of DIS2012*. ACM.
9. Carroll, J. M. & Kellogg, W. A. (1989) Artifact as theory-nexus: hermeneutics meets theory-based design. In *Proc. of CHI '89*, 7-14. ACM.
10. Carroll, N. (2009). *On Criticism*. Routledge.
11. Dalsgaard, P. (2010). Research in and through design: An interaction design research approach. In *Proc. of OzCHI '10*. ACM.
12. DiSalvo, C. (2012). Spectacles and Tropes: Speculative Design and Contemporary Food Cultures. *The Fibreculture Journal 2012 (20)*, 109-122.
13. Dunne, A. and Raby, F. (2013). *Speculative Everything*. The MIT Press.
14. Eldridge, R. (2003). *An Introduction to the Philosophy of Art*. Cambridge: Cambridge University Press.
15. Fallman, D. (2003). Design-oriented human-computer interaction. In *Proc. of CHI'03*. ACM.
16. Feinberg, M., Carter, D., & Bullard, J. Always somewhere, never there: Using critical design to understand database interactions. Proc. CHI'14, ACM, 1941-1950.
17. Fernaeus, Y. and Vallgårda, A. (2014) Ajna: negotiating forms in the making of a musical cabinet. In *Proc. of DIS'14*. ACM.
18. Flusser, V. (1995) On the Word Design: An Etymological Essay. *Design Issues*, 11(3), 50-53.
19. Flyvbjerg, B. (2006). Five Misunderstandings about case-study research. *Qualitative Inquiry 12*(2), 219-245.
20. Frayling, C. (1993/4). Research in art and design. *Royal College of Art Research Papers 1*(1), 1-5.
21. Galey, A. & Reuker, S. (2010). How a prototype argues. *Literary and Linguistic Computing 25*(4), 405-24.
22. Gaver, W. (2012). What should we expect from research through design? In *Proc. of CHI'12*. ACM.
23. Gibson, J. (2007). *Fiction and the Weave of Life*. Oxford: Oxford University Press.
24. Goodman, N. (1976). *Languages of Art*. Hackett.
25. Graham, G. (2005). *Philosophy of the Arts*. 3rd ed. Routledge.
26. Guyer, P. History of Modern Aesthetics. In J. Levinson, ed., 2003, *The Oxford Handbook of Aesthetics*, Oxford University Press, 25-62.
27. Hansen, L.K. (2011) The Interface at the Skin. In Andersen, C.U. and Pold, S. (eds.) *Interface Criticism. Aesthetics Beyond Buttons*. Aarhus University Press.
28. Hansen, L. K. and Kozel, S. (2007) Embodied imagination: a hybrid method of designing for intimacy. *Digital Creativity*, 18 (4), 207-220.
29. Koskinen, I., Zimmerman, J., Binder, T., Redstrom, J., & Wensveen, S. (2011). *Design research through practice: From the lab, field, and showroom*. Elsevier.
30. Kyndrup, M. (2008). Den æstetiske relation. Gyldendal.
31. Löwgren, J. (2009). Toward an articulation of interaction esthetics. *New Review of Hypermedia and Multimedia* 15(2), 129-146
32. Ludvigsen, M. (2006). Designing for social interaction: physical, co-located social computing. PhD Dissertation, Center for Interactive Spaces, Aarhus.
33. Mol, A. (2002). *The Body Multiple: Ontology in Medical Practice*. Duke University Press: Durham.
34. Nelson, H. and Stolterman, E. (2013). *The Design Way*. 2nd ed. The MIT Press.
35. Ozaki, H. (2010). Menstruation Machine. http://www.di10.rca.ac.uk/hiromiozaki/menstruation-machine.html (accessed 20 Sept 2014)
36. Seel, M. (2005). *Aesthetics of Appearing*. Stanford University Press.
37. Stolterman, E., and Wiberg, M. (2010). Concept-driven interaction design research. *Human–Computer Interaction, 25*(2), 95-118.
38. Verbeek, P.-P. (2012). Politics at Issue. On Art and the Democratization of Things. In Boomgaard, J. et al. (eds.), *Open 24: Politics of Things*. nai010, Rotterdam.
39. Yang, H. (2014). Review of MoMA Design and Violence Debate. http://yanghanzi.com/2014/04/13/to-what-extent-can-design-transcend-human-experience-boundaries/ (accessed 20 Sept 2014)
40. Zimmerman, J. & Forlizzi, J. (2014) Research through design in HCI. In Olson, J. & Kellogg, W., eds., *Ways of Knowing in HCI*, Springer.
41. Zimmerman, J., Forlizzi, E., Evenson, S. (2007). Research through design as a method for interaction design research in HCI. In *Proc. of CHI'07*. ACM.
42. Zimmerman, J., Stolterman, E., & Forlizzi, J. (2010). An analysis and critique of Research through Design. In *Proc. of DIS'10*. ACM.

Making Multiple Uses of the Obscura 1C Digital Camera: Reflecting on the Design, Production, Packaging and Distribution of a Counterfunctional Device

James Pierce[1,2], Eric Paulos[2]

[1] Carnegie Mellon University
HCI Institute
jjpierce@cs.cmu.edu

[2] University of California Berkeley
Berkeley Center for New Media
eric@paulos.net

ABSTRACT

This paper describes and explains details of the design, production and packaging of a counterfunctional device: The Obscura 1C Digital Camera. We further describe a small-scale distribution of Obscura 1C packages into everyday contexts. The paper then reflects on the various types of conceptual, imaginary and firsthand uses made of the Obscura 1C. These include its uses for everyday audiences as a unique camera and as a conceptually usable device. But we also prioritize uses particular to the HCI and design audience. These include using the Obscura 1C to articulate the concepts of inhibitive interfaces, counterfunctionality, and enabling limitations. The Obscura 1C is further used to articulate how abstract ideas can be translated into material forms, to rethink the role of packaging in user studies, and to draw attention to how discursive design objects are packaged and presented.

Author Keywords

Design, research through design, limitations

INTRODUCTION

This paper describes and explains details of the design, production and packaging of an experimental product: The Obscura 1C Digital Camera. We further discuss a small-scale experimental distribution of the Obscura 1C packages for everyday audiences. However, here we do not empirically assess everyday use of the Obscura 1C. Rather we focus on how multiple forms of firsthand, imaginary and conceptual use are made of the device—both for this audience and everyday audiences. The Obscura 1C has been designed to allow the device to "speak for itself". We introduce it accordingly. See Figure 1.

The text from the front of the packaging reads:

"OBSCURA 1C DIGITAL CAMERA / COUNTERFUNCTIONAL DEVICE SERIES."

Text on the reverse side of the packaging reads:

> "**Obscura 1C Digital Camera** captures photo, video and audio recordings. In order to access the media files recorded, you must physically break apart the concrete enclosure to reveal the micro SD memory card buried inside. Obscura inhibits access to its contents to offer a digital experience based on uncertainty, patience and surprise."

The Obscura 1C is part of a larger constellation of devices we have designed under the theme of counterfunctionality. Previously we presented the concept of counterfunctionality as a design-oriented concept of creating new functionality by inhibiting or removing common or expected features of a technology [22]. This paper contributes insights and concepts that can inform a clustering of exploratory and critically-oriented HCI research including design-oriented investigations of slow [20,21], reflective [27], adversarial [5] and ludic technologies [9,12], and empirical studies of non-use [2]

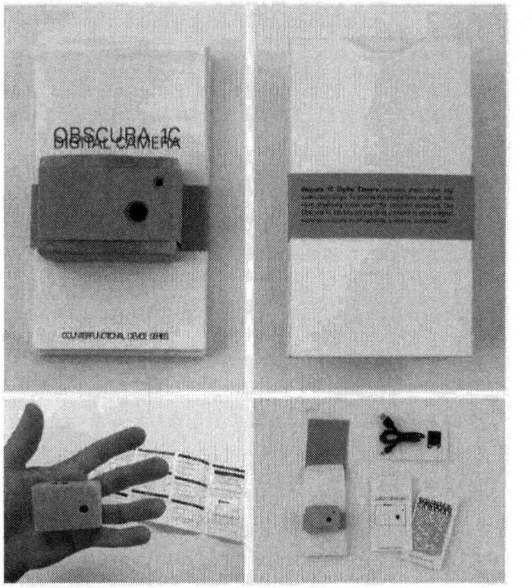

Figure 1. The Obscura 1C Digital Camera package.

CHI 2015, April 18–23, 2015, Seoul, Republic of Korea.

http://dx.doi.org/10.1145/2702123.2702405

and busyness [17]. This paper also contributes a detailed example of how design artifacts and their exposition can uniquely contribute HCI research knowledge.

Our original intention in writing this paper was to focus on the Obscura 1C as a concrete artifact that translates the abstract concepts of inhibitive interfaces, counterfunctionality, and enabling limitations. However it quickly became apparent that we needed to help establish a context for this type of work and justify our decision to present a well-developed, field-deployable product in the absence of a traditional user study. Despite recent works in HCI that propose and demonstrate viable alternatives (e.g., [16,19,21]), design-oriented research at CHI still tends to carry the expectation of a "functional prototype" deployed or tested with study participants. We further recognized that in establishing this context for itself, this work could contribute to broader discussions of the use of prototypes and research through design artifacts [23,30].

Consequently, this paper exhibits a somewhat unusual structure. First we disambiguate three important types of "use", and note prior work that emphasizes imaginary and conceptual uses of prototypes. We then describe the design, production, packaging and distribution of the Obscura 1C in detail. The concluding discussion explains how use is variously made of the Obscura 1C, including its usefulness in thinking about packaging and design artifacts.

DISAMBIGUATING USE

In HCI, we use the words "use", "user" and "function" all the time. Yet phrases such as "end user", the "use of a working system" and "functional prototypes" are used with mostly implicit meanings. The result is that it can be difficult to appreciate other uses/users of prototypes and design artifacts more generally. These include the various uses we as researchers make of "functional" and "non-functional" prototypes. (What exactly *is* the difference, then?) This section disambiguates 3 types of use of design artifacts: **(1) firsthand use, (2) imagined firsthand use,** and **(3) conceptual use**. These are offered as heuristic rather than precise analytic categories. (And we omit reference to relevant thought from media studies, philosophy, etc.)

Arguably all use of artifacts begins with some sort of *firsthand use*. For example, using a digital camera to take pictures (a use which most readers will have experienced firsthand). Or actually using the Obscura 1C to take pictures (which presumably very few if any readers have done).

A second type of use makes use of the first. *Imagined firsthand use* involves imagining firsthand use of an artifact. For example, imagining using your digital camera now, or looking at photographs of the Obscura 1C here and imagining smashing it apart (Figure 1, Appendix).

The third type of use makes use of the second. *Conceptual use* has a basis in imagined firsthand use. In this paper, imagined uses of the Obscura 1C will be used to help verbally articulate concepts such as "counterfunctionality", "enabling limitation", and "conceptual use".

As these last examples demonstrate, an imagined or conceptual use can be taken as a firsthand use. As is hopefully becoming clear, thinking about use recursively in this way can become confusing. Fortunately there is an obvious first choice for establishing firsthand use: everyday use. Since our goal here is heuristic insight rather than analytic precision, we offer a simple operational notion of everyday use as use within an everyday context and with emphasis on familiar, routine, and embodied interactions. "Firsthand everyday use" then refers not only to the familiar firsthand use of everyday things, but also to the firsthand uses of the novel artifacts that HCI researchers deploy and study within everyday contexts such as homes, workplaces and public places.

IMAGINARY AND CONCEPTUAL USE IN PRIOR WORKS

While CHI places a heavy emphasis on empirical studies of firsthand use, this is not the only type of use that is made of prototypes and other design artifacts in HCI. Here we briefly point to some relevant prior works that exemplify a focus on imagined and conceptual uses of design artifacts and, in each case, without the use of a traditional user study. One area of prior work has presented the processes and material outcomes of research through design to reveal techniques, strategies and concepts. A key example is Jarvis et al.'s recent photo-essay paper that depicts details of their design process constructing Indoor Weather Stations [16]. Other examples include Odom et al.'s discussion of the Photobox [21] and Valgaarda's presentation of PLANKS and computational composites [28]. Related to this is Neustaedter and Sengers' observation that prior works have made use of autobiographical studies of systems by their creators [19]. Another area demonstrates that visual/representational artifacts can be presented as polished, final outcomes of a research through design process. A key example is Aipperspach, Hooker, and Woodruff's illustrated design concept booklets [1]. Other related examples include the uptakes of design fiction (e.g., [3,31]) and critical and speculative design (e.g., [6]).

THE COUNTERFUNCTIONAL BACKDROP

Translating between verbal criticism and material things

The inspiration and motivation for this work originates from social and cultural critiques of technology. The types of criticism most directly related to the Obscura 1C center on issues (here negatively framed) such as disengagement, boredom, overload and distraction. Key writings related to these themes include recent essays from areas adjacent to HCI discussing the value of simple communication tools in an age of digital overload [15], the benefits of deleting and forgetting in an age where Facebook and Google remember everything [18], and the literal and metaphorical lack of sleep amidst a 24/7 culture [4]. Writings outside of academic discourse also inspire and elucidate counterfunctional design. An evocative, if not critical, example is a recent collection of essays entitled

"Photographs Not Taken" [26]. Yet another relevant set of works are popular culture writings such as those keyworded with "disconnecting", "unplugging" and "digital detox". Paralleling these writings are a number of recent works in HCI that engage issues of busyness and overwork [20], simple living [13], conflicting cultural discourse surrounding the smart phone [14], and the voluntary non-use and removal of technologies such as Facebook [2].

But we need to be clear about what our reasons for drawing on criticism are, and what they are not. Our goal here is not to directly defend or debate such critiques, but rather to translate critical arguments into material, thingly forms. To make an analogy with user-centered design, we are approaching the intellectual critiques of writers and scholars as we might approach the shortcomings and complaints raised in a usability study or contextual inquiry: as positive design opportunities worth exploring.

Counterfunctionality and Enabling Limitations

Counterfunctionality is the idea that new functionality can emerge (often counterintuitvely) from directly opposing or inverting ordinary or expected functionality. We have previously described the concept of a counterfunctional thing as a "thing that exhibits features that counter some of its own 'essential functionality' while nonetheless retaining familiarity as 'essentially that thing'" [22, p. 375].

As a way of doing design, counterfunctionality articulates a process that involves first identifying common positive features of a particular technology and then designing around the absence or restriction of these features. In the case of the Obscura 1C, a positive and desirable feature that is identified is the immediate access to digital images and video. An ordinary point-and-shoot camera is then redesigned to severely inhibit this positive feature by literally encasing the camera and SD card in cement.

When framed as way of approaching the design process, counterfunctionality has similarities with Gaver, Beaver and Benford's strategy to "block expected functionality to comment on familiar products" [12, p. 239] and Sengers and Gaver's strategy of "stimulating interpretations by blocking expected ones" [26, p. 103]. One key difference lies in our focus on offering counterfunctionality as a salient positive feature of a thing. Put another way, "limitation" is presented to users as a positive design offering. Another key difference is that the counterfunctional things we design function in part to draw attention to themselves and the concepts they embody and articulate. In this way our counterfunctional cameras also function discursively as conceptual focusing devices.

Related to counterfunctionality is the concept of enabling limitations. This concept articulates a more general feature of human-technology relations and directly builds on philosopher of technology Peter-Paul Verbeek's work on technological mediation [29]. Drawing on the work of Latour, Akrich and Ihde, Verbeek describes how the details of a technology work to both invite and inhibit human interaction, and amplify and reduce human perception.

The concept of enabling limitations shows how objectively negative features of a design (what things *don't* do, c.f. [29]) may contribute to the subjective experience of something positively enabling (a useful or desirable feature). What may initially be considered a technological limitation may also enable new positive possibilities. Conversely, the concept of limiting possibilities articulates how seemingly neutral options can in fact be limiting, even disabling. Consider an everyday example. Electronic hypertext enables the reader to immediately read related texts with the click of a link. Print is much more limited in this capacity. Yet through the lens of limiting possibilities, hyperlinks can be seen as at times distracting the reader from the immediate text. And when seen through the lens of enabling limitations, printed books limit the reader's ability to reference other texts but enable reading without the distracting *potential* to do so. A book can be read as an inadvertent counterfunctional thing. Twitter, Snapchat and phonograph records are some other noteworthy examples to consider for this type of analysis using enabling limitations.

THE OBSCURA 1C DIGITAL CAMERA

In this section we describe in detail the design, production, packaging and distribution of the Obscura 1C.

The Obscura 1C Origins and Its Variational Context

Obscura 1C as focal point

The Obscura 1C has slowly and iteratively developed over the course of approximately one and a half years. Its development has been part of a broader research program designing counterfunctional devices. Instead of viewing the Obscura 1C as the final outcome of this process, it is best viewed as focal point among an array of counterfunctional camera variants. Some of these variants have been presented in prior published works in forms ranging from

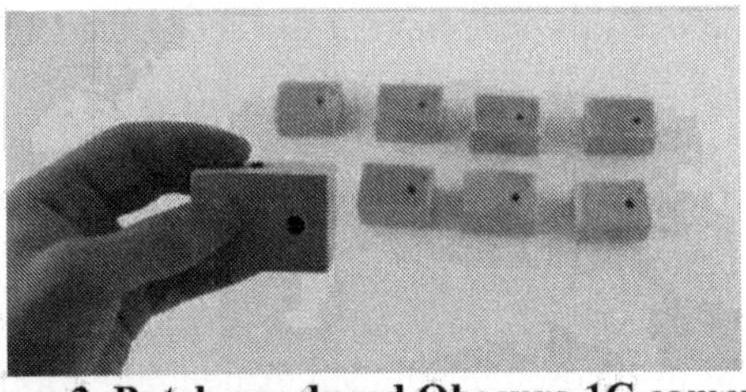

Figure 2. Batch-produced Obscura 1C cameras.

Figure 3. Experimental distribution at a boutique vintage shop (left) and community resale shop (right)

simple illustrations and text [24] to physical model and interactive prototypes [22]. We refer to the strategy of generating, refining and formally presenting a range of design variations constrained and held together by a common theme as a *variational design approach*. Below we summarize our prior published work while highlighting important insights leading up to the Obscura 1C package.

Capsule Camera prototypes
The Obscura 1C originated with the concept for an Unviewable Image camera, which quickly led to the variation of a Smash Camera (see [24, p. 133]). This was later renamed and reformed as the Capsule Camera, which was one of 8 counterfunctional camera prototypes presented to participants in [22]. Among these 8 prototypes, the Capsule Camera was decided to be among the most likely to be adopted and used firsthand by everyday users.

Inhibitive Camera Enclosures
In [22] we also presented form studies of "inhibitive interfaces." These consisted of a concrete camera similar to the Obscura 1C and a wooden camera, which we have continued to develop as the Obscura 1W (Figure 5-5b). As designers we found this concrete camera to be an interesting and provocative form to tangibly interact with firsthand. Photographs of the smashed cameras have also functioned well as emblematic images (see Appendix), which in turn help convey the concepts of inhibitive interfaces, counterfunctionlity, and enabling limitations.

Pictorial Counterfunctional Camera variants
In [24] we presented a selection of counterfunctional camera variants in the form of schematic illustrations and textual descriptions. Footnotes offered additional commentary of a conceptual nature. This work was published in the new Pictorial format at the DIS conference (a format being introduced to CHI 2016.) This work shows the power of representational design artifacts to do conceptual work. This pictorial publication was subsequently revised and translated into a product brochure included in the Obscura 1C package (Figure 5).

Operational Prototypes and Batch Production
Following Gaver et al [9], we adopted a batch-prototyping production process. To date we have batch-produced approximately 20 Obscura 1C cameras and plan to produce more. The ability to batch-produce the cameras at low-cost was a primary consideration in our design. The total cost of materials for each camera is approximately $20.

Early operational prototypes included a display that counted up with each image taken ("0001", "0002", etc.). Plans were also made to include a viewfinder. While we have successfully built and continue to develop versions with displays, we ended up proceeding with a simpler version for batch production. This version makes use of an inexpensive digital camera costing approximately $10. To produce the Obscura 1C, the camera electronics are removed and sealed in protective thermoplastic (HMA) and acrylic support pieces. This is then cast in Rocktite™ patching cement using a custom mold. (Technically, the Obscura 1C is cast in cement, not concrete.) The cast forms are then roughly sanded only to deburr the sharp edges, leaving a distinctly hand-cast look and feel. Next, laser-cut button assemblies are installed. Finally, the cameras are tested prior to physically removing the data pins from the USB charging port—effectively sealing off access to the SD memory card buried inside. The Obscura 1C cameras currently take several hours each to construct. However, we are already developing ways to streamline this process.

Cost, ease of production, and robustness of the end product were the main reasons we opted for a version that did not include a numerical display or viewfinder. This also required us to rely on a low-quality image sensor producing grainy images reminiscent of security camera videos.

Interestingly, while these decisions were initially viewed as worthwhile tradeoffs, they were quickly reconstituted as additional counterfunctional features and advertised as such in the product packaging. The lack of a display and viewfinder added elements of uncertainty and surprise, while the lower resolution camera created images perceptually distinct from normal digital photos (cf. Ultra-Low Resolution Cameras, Figure 5-2b, and [24 p., 136]).

The Complete Obscura 1C Package
In addition to producing a set of operational Obscura 1C cameras, we designed and produced a complete set of packaging and instructional material for distribution. This complete Obscura 1C package (Figure 4), rather than the camera alone, constitutes the core material design outcome of this work. A great deal of thought and care went into the design of the packages. This included concern with the usability and "out of the box experience". This also included concern the device's "conceptual usability".

The high-level goal of the packaging design is summed up with the notion of allowing the devices to "speak for themselves". More precisely what this means is that the packages contain material that both verbally and non-verbally communicate key aspects of its functionality: how to operate it, what its intended and envisioned uses are, and the practical and conceptual intentions of its creators. This in turn helps the devices to be taken more seriously as products similar to, yet distinct from, everyday commercial products. This also allows the devices to be presented for everyday firsthand use without the in-person scaffolding of most user studies, such as a site visits, in-person conversations, data gathering forms and tools, financial compensation, and concomitant social expectations.

Interacting with the Obscura 1C packages
In terms of visual and tactile interaction, the packaging was designed to fulfill several straightforward design criteria:

a. *Showcase the actual cameras*. We especially wanted to showcase the unique material use of concrete. Further we wanted to juxtapose the uniquely hand-crafted forms of the cameras with the modern reproducible aesthetic of the

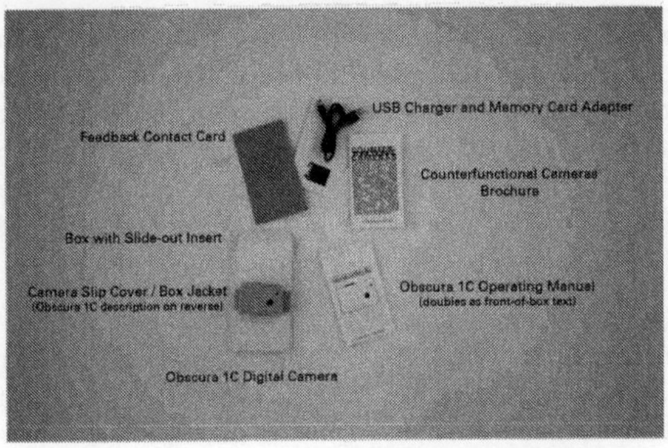

Figure 4. Obscura 1C packages and contents.

packaging graphics and with Electronics as a product genre.

b. *Invite browsing of the instruction manual.* This is especially important because Obscura 1C offers unfamiliar functionality. Easy access to the manual helps explain them.

c. *Stack upright for display.* We wanted the devices to be displayable at storefronts. But we also did not want to rely on hang-tab or other specialized retail display machinery.

The name: Obscura 1C

Names and titles are an important and often initial point of contact for retail products, experimental designs and artistic works alike. Given the emphasis on the representational and conceptual functions of the Obscura 1C, it's worth devoting space to explain the design of its name.

Previously the concept underlying the Obscura 1C has been encapsulated in several differently named forms. However in its present form a new name was desired to help suggest representational and conceptual functions. Obscura 1C serves this function well. Most familiarly to camera geeks, the Obscura 1C references the camera obscura, the technological predecessor to the modern camera. Obscura is a Latin word meaning "dark". Yet phonetically, and stripped if its Latin context, "obscura" has a crisp, modern ring to it. Further, "obscurus" is the etymology of "obscure", which means both to visually conceal and to intellectually make difficult to understand. This name is doubly fitting since the Obscura 1C literally inhibits access to its visual contents, yet the purpose of this may be somewhat intellectually obscure. Taken together, these three references—the perceptual obscurity of the image, the intellectual obscurity of the conceptual intent, and the somewhat obscure historical reference to the camera obscura—have been designed with the possibility (not to be confused with likelihood) of prompting deeper intellectual engagement with the device.

The "1C" portion of the naming references the popular Apple iPhone 5s and 5c. We use 1C as an abbreviation for "version 1, concrete model". This direct reference to the iPhone is, in part, a subtle joke. The source of the joke lies in the Obscura 1C describing itself as a "counterfunctional device" in opposition to the celebrated and "seemingly endless possibilities [of 'digital technologies']" (Figure 5-1a, 5-1b). Such "endless possibilities" are of course exemplified by the elegantly multifunctional iPhone. But at the same time this iPhone reference is serious in that the Obscura 1C is also designed so it can be taken as a legitimate, functional counterpart to everyday electronics.

At face value, then, the name "Obscura 1C" can be taken as an attempt to associate with a product genre composed of sleek, modern electronic products. But on closer inspection, the reference may create a humorous tension. Is this product presenting itself in a literal, serious manner? Is it trying to sell itself like the iPhone? Or, is it rather trying to ostensibly associate in order to ultimately distance itself from this genre of products? This orchestrated ambiguity mirrors the multiple, overlapping intentions underlying the product. It can be taken as simply a novel and unusual product. Or it can also be engaged with at a deeper conceptual level as a conceptually counterfunctional device.

Clearly this manner of closely reading the Obscura 1C is something that even many academics or designers are unlikely to do. But attention to this linguistic detail is important for several reasons. First, the ambiguous semantic function of the name is "useable" even if only one or two of the references is noted in passing. Second, this discussion emphasizes the possible rhetorical and discursive functions of design artifacts *for this audience* (even of artifacts intended for everyday firsthand use). We expand on this point in the concluding discussions. The following section extends this line of thinking into non-verbal realms.

The hybrid visual and form languages of the Obscura 1C

The visual and form languages of the complete Obscura 1C package draws on those of several product genres:

See Figure 4.

The final packages are designed to present themselves in a way that, if read carefully—and with the proper expertise—can be verbally translated as follows: "You can take me as a mass-market retail product. Or conversely, you can take me as a one-off art project. (But in actuality, I'm an experimental design product produced in limited quantities—a product that intentionally plays into the genres of both mass-market consumer products and artistic productions." We develop out this translation more below.

The visual and physical form of the Obscura 1C packaging references 5 key product genres:

a. *Sleek, modern product design exemplified by Apple.* Examples: The name "Obscura 1C"; lots of whitespace and a modern sans-serif logotype on the cover (Figure 5-8a).

b. *Lower-end consumer electronics & instruction manuals.* Examples: The layout and language of the manual, such as black headers and a "Caution" message (Figure 5-4a).

c. *Artist's books* (a genre where the particular codec form dovetails with the artistic intention). Examples: The use of high-quality archival paper for the manual and brochure; the tongue-in-cheek uses of the Frequently Asked Questions format (Figure 5-6a); the negative leading of the Obscura 1C logotype and brochure cover (which plays into both "obscurity" and "counterfunctionality").

d. *Zines* (self-published, typically low-cost print publications). Examples: All of the packaging elements can be created with accessible everyday tools without relying on offset printing, injection molding, 3D printing, etc.

e. A *one-off, hand-crafted object* aesthetic of the camera body, which creates a juxtaposition with the industrial aesthetic of everyday cameras and consumer electronics. Examples: The rough, hand-deburred edges of the slightly imperfect rectangular concrete camera bodies.

Each of these product genre references can become an interpretive focus, offering a single stable interpretation of the Obscura 1C (e.g., as a sleek modern product, a hand-crafted artistic object, a zine-like DIY consumer product alternative, etc.). Alternatively, the juxtaposition of these competing genres can encourage a closer reading of the conceptual intent underlying the Obscura 1C package.

Instruction manual & Counterfunctional Cameras brochure

The instruction manual was designed to fulfill the following design criteria: (1) double as the text and graphics for the front of the package, (2) explain the camera operation to support everyday firsthand use, and (3) succinctly describe with minimal jargon the concepts underlying the Obscura 1C and the Counterfunctional Device Series. A brochure of additional Counterfunctional Cameras was also included inside the package box. The document references the genre of a promotional product brochure, and suggests that these might be actual product offerings. However this is left uncertain to encourage representational and conceptual readings. In the spirit of allowing these materials to "speak for themselves", and as a way of simulating the firsthand Obscura 1C package experience, we visually reproduce these materials here: See Figure 5.

Obscura 1C Package Distribution and Exchange

To date we have distributed 10 complete Obscura 1C packages to non-acquaintances. Our primary goal has been to experiment firsthand with different forms of distribution and exchange. We approach this both as exploratory prototyping (with ties to packaging and service design) and as a means of demonstrating "proof of distribution concept". To be clear, our distribution was explicitly not for data collection, although we offer some revealing empirical observations that have been inadvertently gleaned.

Craigslist Ads

Our initial distribution was through San Francisco Bay Area Craigslist classified ads posted to the "Free" and "For Sale, Photo+Video" sections. (A one-time posting of each ad received 20 and 2 responses, respectively; several "Free" respondents offered to purchase cameras.) Ads included images of the Obscura 1C package and contents. An excerpt of the 270-word ad text reads:

> We are offering a limited number of unique digital cameras as part of an experimental design program. Our aim is to create and distribute unconventional, alternative consumer products. ... If you'd like to acquire an Obscura 1C, send us a message with a few words telling us why you'd like to have one of these devices.

6 Obscura 1C packages were distributed to people that each indicated an envisioned use that we anticipated or else found surprising. Some Obscura 1C were delivered in-person (3 were sold for $20 each). Others were anonymously mailed or left at home addresses. Below are inquiries from some individuals we then offered cameras to:

> Hi, I'm super interested in buying one of these cameras. I love film photography so the idea of something digital giving a film like experience (delayed gratification etc.) is really interesting...

> I would love to have a camera. I think I'd want to use it as a sort of time capsule, but I would probably not last very long without smashing it. This whole idea looks like a whole lot of fun.

> ... sounds like an awesome project. ... we'll be working on a startup from home. I think it would be awesome to have an Obscura Camera in our main work room periodically documenting our work.

> Perfect! Reminds me of being a kid in Montana, saving money to buy one roll of film. Then carefully planning out 12 shots and waiting 2 weeks for the film to be processed and mailed back. You have a great idea here..

Other experimental distribution outlets

Other distribution outlets we have experimented with include local retail partnerships, community bulletin boards, and guerilla tactics such as "droplifting" (leaving a product in a retail store). See Figure 3.

MAKING USES OF THE OBSCURA 1C

The concluding discussion reflects on how use is intended to be made, has been made, and is actively being made of the Obscura 1C—in the hands and minds of researchers, designers and a more diverse set of everyday users.

Making everyday, firsthand uses of the Obscura 1C

The Obscura 1C was designed to be used in everyday contexts by non-experts in the areas of HCI or Design (or Art or Philosophy). A goal was to get these devices into the hands and everyday lives of people that would hopefully enjoy them and the experience they offered. We carefully designed packages with instructional material to allow the

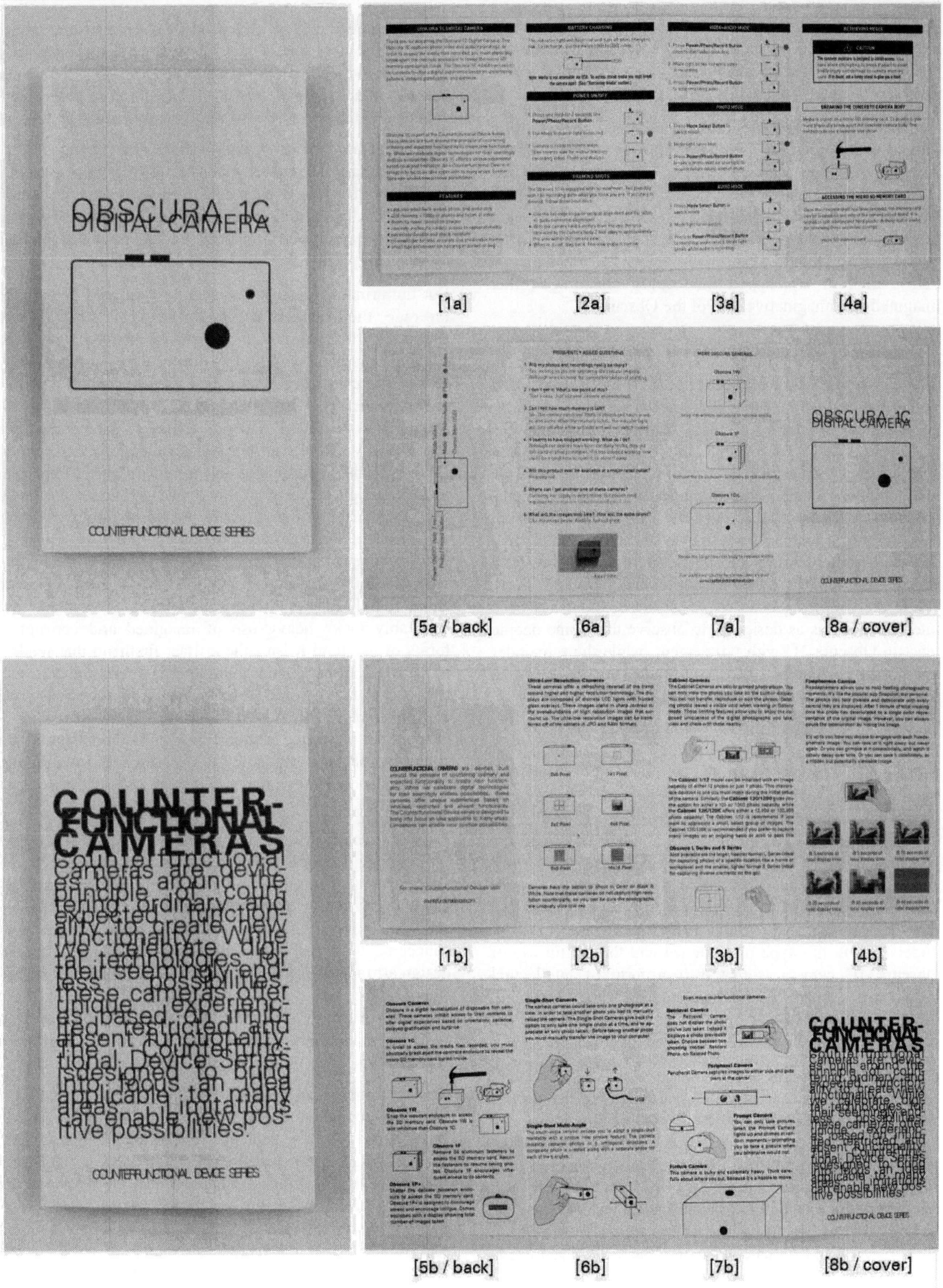

Figure 5. Obscura 1C Operating Manual (top) and Counterfunctional Cameras brochure (bottom).

devices to "speak for themselves" and be encountered in a manner more akin to retail product offerings than formal research studies. The packaging also functioned to advertise and promote the Obscura 1C.

Yet the types of everyday use we designed for were not limited to the firsthand use of the cameras to take pictures and eventually be smashed to bits. We also designed the Obscura 1C packages so users could imagine firsthand uses of other counterfunctional cameras, such as the Retrieval Camera, Fixedephemera Camera, Cabinet Cameras, and the Obscura 1W, 1F, and 1P+ (Figure 5; or, see supplemental PDF). In turn we hoped this might encourage other imagined and imaginative uses of the Obscura 1C.

We further designed the Obscura 1C to be a "conceptually usable" device. Specifically we wanted to encourage a form of everyday intellectual engagement with the idea that limitations can be enabling, and that the seemingly endless possibilities of digital devices can be limiting (c.f. [2,4,17,15,18,25]). For example, the phrase "limitations can enable new positive possibilities" is featured in both the instruction manual and Counterfunctional Cameras brochure. Verbally stated, this idea can be quite obscure even to the academically inclined. The Obscura 1C was designed with precisely the intention of articulating this abstract concept in a usable, embodied, concrete form. While the following observation is anecdotal, it has been interesting for us as designers to observe that some people react to Obscura 1C with puzzlement, while the remainder react with enthusiasm (Similar findings are discussed in [22]; See also [27] on the appropriate level of "strangeness" for reflective design).

It is also important to note that this type of intellectual engagement was designed as an optional rather than required feature of Obscura 1C. We imagine that many will use the Obscura cameras *without* the sort of intellectual considerations we've outlined here for this audience. However we *do* expect that most will use the device firsthand in a manner similar to a "time capsule" or a "disposable camera" (as the people we've given and sold the devices to have indicated.) And one way of understanding this type of sustained and thoughtful use of Obscura 1C camera is that it *is* a form of intellectual engagement with "counterfunctionality" and "enabling limitations"—regardless of whether these concepts are rigorously engaged with in a precise, verbal manner.

Of course, it's not only possible but in fact likely that many aspects of our Obscura 1C package did not work as well as we envisioned and hoped. But our goal of distributing the cameras here was never to offer compelling empirical evidence of this sort (not in the present work at least). Instead what we offer is a "proof of concept" of these uses that rests primarily on the imagined and conceptual use we have created within the context of this paper. The empirical support we have offered concerning others' firsthand use is limited, anecdotal, and inadvertently gleaned rather than carefully collected. Yet independent of empirical evidence of firsthand use, our detailed design case presented here serves as a model for how a product can function in the ways outlined above. (Even if it doesn't quite work firsthand in the ways that we, and you, may imagine it to.)

Why didn't you empirically study others' firsthand use?

At this point the reader may be asking this question. Wouldn't a user study only help to substantiate our claims? To begin with, space limitations of the 10-page CHI format would have prohibited us from having these discussions alongside reporting the details of a user study.

But the primary logic behind this decision was actually to leverage the absence of a user study. While we've prevented the reader and ourselves the authors from engaging firsthand with findings from a rigorous user study, we've also created *real* imagined and conceptual use here in this paper. This lends support to a multi-part argument about the value of design artifacts independent of scientifically established empirical validations. Succinctly: (1) imagined and conceptual use are very real and important uses of design artifacts; (2) imagined and conceptual uses can most certainly benefit from but do not strictly require empirical support from user studies (c.f. [19]); (3) everyday firsthand use is not always the most important or interesting type of use to *directly* design for, reflect upon, or write about (c.f. [1,28]); (4) empirical studies of firsthand use inevitably make heavy use of imagined and conceptual forms of use (and it isn't the artifact firsthand that readers of a CHI paper experience, but rather it is reproductions and references in the forms of images, descriptions and concepts, c.f. [23]); and (5) the process alone of making a product for everyday firsthand use leads to insights and concepts that are valuable to the research community, again, independent of a user study (c.f. [16,21]).

To be clear, *this is not an argument against user studies.* Rigorous empirical investigation and evaluation of artifacts is a unique strength of CHI and should continue to be championed, as recent longitudinal and large-scale studies have done [8,9,19]. What we are instead arguing is that we need to better acknowledge the representational and conceptual work that field-deployed and empirically studied design artifacts are also and always doing. Further, we need to recognize that *certain* representational and conceptual functions of design artifacts can be detached from or need only be minimally supported by user studies and field deployments.

Making Conceptual Uses of the Obscura 1C for HCI

We now focus on conceptual uses of the Obscura 1C specifically for this audience composed of researchers, designers and other practitioners interested in HCI and interaction design. These conceptual uses are based not on you the reader's firsthand use of the Obscura 1C, or on rigorous empirical data of outside participants' firsthand use. Rather these conceptual uses have a basis in the imaginary uses we have helped to create within the context of this paper through representations and reproductions of the Obscura 1C (supported by the author's firsthand experiences). Here we outline five conceptual uses.

(a) **Obscura 1C as inhibitive interface.** The Obscura 1C helps make the following abstract concept concrete: An interface can inhibit desirable interactions in ultimately desirable ways (see also: Appendix).

(b) **Obscura 1C as counterfunctional design**. If an inhibitive interface is a design tactic, the design strategy is counterfunctionality. Our detailed discussion of the Obscura 1C illustrates a design process that involves identifying common positive features of a technology and then designing around the absence or inhibition of these features. As a material design outcome, the Obscura 1C shows how useful, desirable functionality can emerge counterintuitively through this process.

(c) **Obscura 1C as enabling limitation.** As discussed earlier, the Obscura 1C concretely illustrates the concept that inhibited or absent functionality (negative functionality) can in fact enable positive functionality. This concept builds directly on technological mediation theory, which describes how technologies both invite and inhibit human action [29]. In the case of the Obscura 1C, inhibited access to digital images enables positive experiences of delayed gratification, surprise and intrigue. Technologies as diverse as Twitter, Snapchat, vinyl records, printed newspapers and various HCI exemplars such as Photobox [21] and Drift Table [11] offer further insights when analyzed through the concept of enabling limitations.

(d) **Obscura 1C as designing digital limitations.** Generalizing further, yet back toward design, the Obscura 1C serves as a focal point among a wider array of counterfunctional cameras that give shape to a design space of *designing digital limitations*. While this space is highly motivated in theory (e.g., [2,4,13,14,15,17,18,25]), it remains practically underexplored through design.

(e) **Obscura 1C as critique/philosophy translated.** One way to understand conceptual use of the Obscura 1C is that it serves as an example of "higher-level" concepts. While this is a useful way to see things, we prefer to also engage with the Obscura 1C as a translation from verbal concepts to material things. Such material translations—as "ideas lodged in things" [6, p. 124]—are not necessarily reductions or "dumbing down" but rather should be seen as "equals to, or even improvements over, the original—precisely to the extent that they depart from it" [6, p. 118]. Even as we make conceptual use of the Obscura 1C here, we should not lose touch (even if it is an imagined touch) with the device's embodied and embedded firsthand uses. For it is precisely these departures from abstract concepts that make material things so concretely compelling.

Making Extended Use of Packaging for Everyday Use

The Obscura 1C demonstrates a level of concern with packaging and instructional material that is unique within HCI. This in turn suggests ways that the HCI community could benefit from closer attention to the design of packaging for prototypes and user studies. The Obscura 1C also generally speaks to the particular forms through which research through design knowledge is produced, presented and disseminated.

Packaging for user studies

Producing packaged devices that "speak for themselves" can be useful in a number of ways. First, packaging and instructional material can help to clearly and consistently explain aspects of a prototype such as its operation, possible uses, and underlying intentions. Conversely, packaging and instructional material can help the research team maintain an ambiguous or mysterious stance regarding aspects of use, operation, and intention (e.g., mailing the devices allowed us to avoid having to further explain in-person their intended uses). Packaging can also open up new functional possibilities. Here we made use of additional "representational products" using the format of a product brochure (Figure 5). Finally, packaging can be used to promote the product to users in a manner akin to retail products. This can help the research team to find a target market of users with a strong desire or curiosity about using the product, or that demonstrate some specific type of understanding of it. Conversely, the research team can also seek out users that describe envisioned uses that may be at odds with those that were envisioned or intended by the designers (a tactic we have also made use).

Users studies as packaging

At a broader conceptual level, the Obscura 1C helps us to see that *all* user studies are forms of packaging, distribution and exchange with parallels but key differences to things the circulate within the machinery of retail markets. If we agree that even the most seemingly minor details of a product's design matter, then surely similar is the case for the details of its packaging, distribution and exchange. Although this is an empirical question, it is not difficult to imagine how some very different findings could result when a prototype no longer requires the direct human scaffolding of research teams to deliver the product, fix it when it breaks, ask questions about how it is experienced, promise financial compensation, and create various concomitant forms of social expectation for engagement.

Packaging discursive design objects

The Obscura 1C also helps us to appreciate design artifacts as ways of packaging up intellectual ideas or research through design knowledge (c.f. [23,30]). The audience of these packages could be the special discursive audience of CHI (cf. [10]) or the packaging could be for the public more broadly constructed (cf. [5]).

CONCLUSION & FUTURE DIRECTIONS

This paper has described and explained details of the design, production, packaging and distribution of the Obscura 1C Digital Camera. Here we have prioritized conceptual and imaginary use over of empirically evaluated firsthand use. A number of new concepts have been articulated: counterfunctionality, inhibitive interfaces, enabling limitations, and designing digital limitations. We've also articulated methodologically oriented concepts of conceptual use, material/conceptual translation, criticism as design opportunity, user studies as packaging, and packaging discursive design objects.

In future work we intend to present refinements of these concepts—verbally, materially, and empirically. Here, our main goal and hope is that these formal concepts and general ideas can inspire and provoke new ways of thinking about and doing design-oriented work in HCI. To the extent that these concepts here may appear fragmentary and under-articulated in words, we hope this can be appreciated as reflective of forms of knowledge production we would like to better acknowledge and develop for design-oriented HCI research: knowledge as design thinking residing "within" artifacts [30, p. 51]; as "ideas lodged in things" [6, p. 124]; and as devices that can partially "speak for themselves".

ACKNOWLEDGEMENTS

Financial support for this work was provided in part by NSF grant #IIS-1451465. All images © James Pierce.

APPENDIX (CODA)

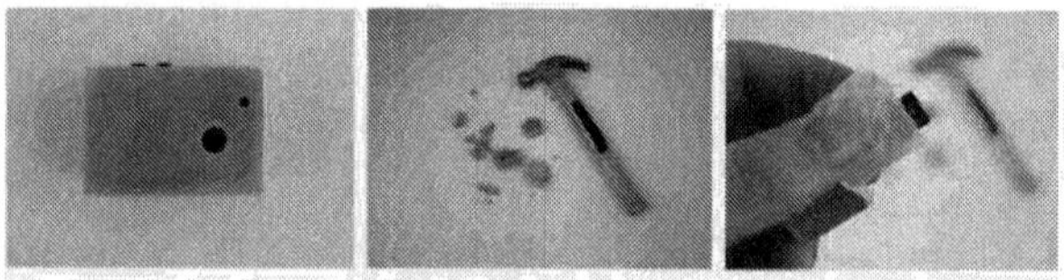

REFERENCES

1. Aipperspach, R., Hooker, B. &Woodruff, A. The Heterogeneous Home. Proc. UbiComp '08.
2. Baumer, E., Adams, P., Khovanskaya, V., Liao, T., Smith, M., Sosik, V. & Williams, K. 2013. Limiting, leaving, and (re)lapsing: an exploration of facebook non-use practices and experiences. Proc. CHI '13.
3. Blythe, Mark. Research through design fiction: Narrative in real and imaginary abstracts. Proc. CHI '14.
4. Crary, J. 2013. *24/7: Late Capitalisms and the Ends of Sleep*. Verso.
5. DiSalvo, C. 2012. *Adversarial Design*. MIT Press.
6. Dworkin, C. 2013. *No Medium*. The MIT Press.
7. Dunne, A. & Raby, F. 2013. *Speculative Everything*. MIT Press.
8. Erickson, T. et al. The Dubuque Electricity Portal: Evaluation of a City-Scale Residential Electricity Consumption Feedback System. Proc. CHI '13.
9. Gaver,W., Bowers, J., Boehner, B., Boucher, A., Cameron, D., Hauenstein, M., Jarvis, N. & Pennington, S. 2013. Indoor Weather Stations: Investigating a Ludic Approach to Environmental HCI Through Batch Prototyping. Proc. CHI '13.
10. Gaver, W. & Bowers, J. Annotated Portfolios. Interactions 19, no. 4 (July 2012): 40–49.
11. Gaver, W., Bowers, J., Boucher, A., Gellerson, H., Pennington, S., Schmidt, S., Steed, A., Villars, N. & Walker, B. 2004. The drift table: designing for ludic engagement. CHI EA '04.
12. Gaver, W., Beaver,J. and Benford,S. 2003. Ambiguity as a resource for design. Proc. CHI '03.
13. Håkansson, M. & Sengers, P. 2013. Beyond being green: simple living families and ICT. Proc. CHI '13.
14. Harmon, E. & Mazmanian, M. 2013. Stories of the Smartphone in everyday discourse: conflict, tension and instability. Proc. CHI '13.
15. Harper, R. 2012. *Texture: Human Expression in the Age of Communications Overload*. MIT Press.
16. Jarvis, N., Cameron, D., Boucher,A. Attention to Detail: Annotations of a Design Process. Proc. NordiCHI '12.
17. Leshed, G. & Sengers, P. 2011. "I lie to myself that I have freedom in my own schedule": productivity tools and experiences of busyness. Proc. CHI '11.
18. Mayer-Schönberger, V. Delete the Virtue of Forgetting in the Digital Age. Princeton. Princeton Press, 2009.
19. Neustaedter, C. & Sengers, P. Autobiographical Design in HCI Research: Designing and Learning Through Use-It-Yourself. Proc. DIS '12.
20. Odom, W., Selby, M., Sellen, A. Kirk, D. Banks, R. & Regan, T. Photobox: On the Design of a Slow Technology. Proc. DIS '12.
21. Odom, W., Selby, M., Sellen, A., Kirk, D., Banks, R. & Regan, T. 2012. Photobox: on the design of a slow technology. Proc. DIS '12.
22. Pierce, J. & Paulos, E. 2014. Counterfunctional Things: Exploring Possibilities in Designing Digital Limitations. Proc. DIS '14.
23. Pierce, J. 2014. On the presentation and production of design research artifacts in HCI research. Proc. DIS '14.
24. Pierce, J. & Paulos, E. Some Variations on a Counterfunctional Digital Camera. Proc. DIS '14.
25. Sengers, P. 2011. What I learned on Change Islands: reflections on IT and pace of life. interactions, 18(2).
26. Sengers, P. & Gaver, B. Staying Open to Interpretation: Engaging Multiple Meanings in Design and Evaluation. Proc. DIS '06.
27. Sengers, P., Boehner, K., David, D., & Kaye, J. Reflective Design. Proc. CC '05.
28. Vallgaarda, A. 2008. PLANKS: A Computational Composite. Proc. NordiCHI '08.
29. Verbeek, P.-P. 2005. What Things Do: Philosophical Reflections on Technology, Agency, and Design. Penn State University Press.
30. Wakkary, R., Desjardins, A., Hauser, S. & Maestri, L. 2008. A Sustainable Design Fiction: Green Practices. TOCHI, 20, no. 4, 23:1–23:34.
31. Zimmerman J, Forlizzi J, and Evenson, S. 2007 Research through design as a method for interaction design research in HCI. Proc. CHI'07.

Pause Moment Experience in SNS Communication

Jae-eul Bae[a] **Youn-kyung Lim**[a] **Jin-bae Bang**[b] **Myung-suk Kim**[a]

[a]Department of Industrial Design, KAIST, Daejeon, Korea, Republic of
{thereisabird, younlim, mskim}@kaist.ac.kr
[b] KAKAOLAB, Seoul, Korea, Republic of
jinbae.bang@gmail.com

ABSTRACT

The evolution of SNS applications has focused on the increasing pace of communication. Accordingly, adopting *pause moment design* for the SNS domain becomes significant, considering its worth for mental well-being and diversity of experience. Nonetheless, the vision is currently controversial, as it is lacking in attempts to examine the worth of pause moment design for SNS communication. Therefore, we discussed the benefits of pause moment design as an SNS application, based on the case of Ripening Room. From observation, we have identified three benefits of pause moment design; preserving room for solitude, expanding time experience, and providing additional indirect cues for communication. Nevertheless, the benefits also imply limitations of the current design, thus require following attempts to adopt a pause moment design for the SNS domain.

Author Keywords

Pause moment design; SNS; slow technology.

ACM Classification Keywords

H.5.m. Information interfaces and presentation (e.g., HCI): Miscellaneous

INTRODUCTION

Since their introduction, social networking sites (SNS) have evolved to become a dominant form of communication, to make our interaction more convenient, immediate, and persistent, by quickening the pace of such exchanges. Does the fast pace of communication in SNS applications, however, cause us to have a desirable online experience? This doubt resonates with the branches of HCI movements that reconsider slowness in our lives with technology.

A *pause moment* in the experience of interactive systems has been re-illuminated for its worth in allowing us to rest from the flow of experience and be in the mode of reflection [6, 8]. By slowing down the pace of interaction, a pause moment allows us to look for the qualities of life besides efficiency and productivity [18] and to pursue our true well-being [10]. With this notion, assigning some pause moments in the flow of interaction has become considered as one of the alternative strategies of designing interactive systems [3].

The significance of a pause moment design can also reach the design of SNS applications. Increasing the pace of communication in SNSs has perhaps taken away something from us that we needed for our well-being; that is, the opportunity to reflect on and reveal true values [9]. Moreover, it becomes an inevitable doubt, with the problematic situation that current SNSs are facing (e.g., regrets of ranting excessive sentiments and privacy exposure [19, 23]).

Accordingly, the application of pause moment design seems reasonable to consider for developing SNS applications. Nonetheless, current clues still seem to focus on negative prospects for pause moment design in SNS domain. SNS users' desires are known to be oriented to the convenience, immediacy and synchronicity of communication [12, 16], thereby forecasting SNS users' disfavor on slowed pace of communication by pause moment design.

Therefore, we believe that our research, which attempts to investigate and discuss the worth of pause moment design as an alternative and supplementary design philosophy for today's SNS applications, can be worthwhile and make some contribution to this interesting research space. For our investigation, we adopted Ripening Room (RR) [2], an SNS application developed according to the pause moment design.

RIPENING ROOM

RR is a micro-blogging website equipped with the basic features of current SNS applications, such as building social connections and sharing content. The feature of pause moment design in RR is ripening time, a delay period between generating and sharing content. The *ripening time* is customizable between zero and 48 hours before a post or a comment is shared throughout the social network. During that time, the contents of posts/comments are visible only to their own user, who can privately reflect upon and revise content with the pause moment. Meanwhile, the posts/comments in ripening time are still visible to other users, except their content—instead, it shows a message that says the material "is under ripening," and provides information about its ripening time (when it began and its duration), while other users are also allowed to leave

CHI 2015, April 18 - 23 2015, Seoul, Republic of Korea
Copyright 2015 ACM 978-1-4503-3145-6/15/04 $15.00
http://dx.doi.org/10.1145/2702123.2702435

comments for the post. When a user deletes the whole content of a post or a comment, it preserves the trace of the article (the empty post/comment). Those features allow for the *sharing of a pause moment* for users in RR. As an SNS application, RR allows users to not only have a pause moment, but also to share the moment with others in a distinguished way from a practical application of a delay moment for SNSs (e.g., a timer nudge in [24]).

The previous empirical observation on users' experience and the behavior of self-expression in RR had revealed that the ripening time worked as a moment for reflection into one's emotions and thoughts (e.g., controlling sentiments) [2]. However, as the study only focused on the individual's experience of self-reflection in self-expression, the user's experience of SNS communication in RR was not sufficiently discussed in the previous work. Accordingly, the benefit of RR as an SNS application still remained unclear.

METHOD AND PROCEDURE

Social Network Composition

We recruited 29 university students (22 males and 9 females) between the ages of 17 to 21 ($M= 18.38$, $SD= 0.78$) in South Korea as participants and formed a single social network (hereafter coded as P1, P2 ...). They were from the same club of a university and shared varying levels of intimacy among each other, according to the length of their affiliation period. The number of participants was decided by the number of expected audience members for common SNS users between 10 and 50 [14]. Based on the background, we could expect that the network size would provide the sense of the presence of a social network in order to create a realistic simulation of an actual SNS application. Further, with this particular social group, we expected to observe an amplified impact of a pause moment design for SNS communication within the short period of observation. As a group of close peers is naturally more sensitive to the consequences of the current trend of SNS communication (e.g., the exposure of private information or the spreading of a rumor), the impact of a pause moment design was expected to be contrasted with their current SNS communication experience.

Empirical Test and Analysis

We asked the participants to use RR instead of any other SNSs, except during inevitable circumstances, for 4 weeks. This was intended to lead the participants to reflect their desire of SNS use intensively on RR. We explained to them how RR works, but provided no guidelines regarding its purposes. It was to give the participants maximum liberty while observing their response to pause moment design, based on their natural desire and perception of SNS communication. We observed the participants' behaviors of using RR from the use logs, and also collected the experience of using RR through post-interviews after four weeks. The interviews were semi-structured based on the following foci.

- Which and what stories (thoughts, emotions, opinions, etc.) did the participants want to publish and share in RR?
- What are the pros and cons of using RR for communication among members in the social network?
- Were there any significantly impressive experiences while using RR? How is it different from other ordinary SNSs?

All users' reports about their experience in RR and activity logs were coded, and the codes were grouped according to their similarity and relevance to each other. The groups were reorganized, regrouped, separated or discarded by three researchers throughout iterative discussions that focused on their meaning and significance as an SNS experience. We ultimately obtained the most interesting and notable patterns of experience which emerged among the experience in RR from the finalized groups of codes.

FINDINGS AND IMPLICATION

We distinguished three patterns of experience in RR. Based on the users' evaluation of the experiences, as well as related literature, we discussed the value and limitations of a pause moment design in SNS applications.

Preserved Room for Solitude in Public Online Space

The ripening feature was evaluated to be provocative for sentimental moods (*"I felt an obligation in RR to be reflective and sentimental more than usual" – P13*). This aspect of experience has been considered to promote the expression of one's emotions and thoughts [2]; however, in the sense of SNS communication, the benefits of such aspects were undiscussed in the earlier study on RR.

A simple assumption is that it encourages the sharing of deeper emotions in SNS, which is beneficial for the development of intimacy [17]. However, it becomes doubtful as the participants mentioned that they didn't have much desire to share their deeper emotion (*"If I used RR to talk about my anxiety or sentiments, then I would think it is very helpful [...] but I didn't have such feelings for the last four weeks" – P5*). Accordingly, it is hard to simply state that a pause moment design is valuable for the expression of emotions in SNS.

Nonetheless, the sentimental aspect of a ripening design still seems to be beneficial for several reasons. One implied benefit is that, as the ripening feature lets its users have a private moment for reflection, it led the participants to have a moment of solitude [8] by providing the option for them not to share (*"Writing down my feeling [in RR] helped me to be relieved. There was no need to share my anger with others, so I deleted the writings during ripening time." – P3)*. In the sense of solitude moment for our lives, it would provide more sincere comfort for our mental well-being.

Another benefit of the preserved chances for solitude in SNS is that they support the settlement of conflict among users' desires of self-disclosure and the management of social images. Self-disclosure in SNS, especially when it is about sentiments, is one of the significant sources of regret

[19, 23] and the disfavor of others [7]. Accordingly, it can be understood that the participants could have a sufficient moment to reflect on one's sentiments, as well as options to share them or not, to make a more desirable choice. Such a benefit of the ripening process resonates with the other cases of nudging for a slower pace of sharing in SNS in order to prevent regret and curtail the spread of rumors (e.g., [22, 24]).

The chances to be solitary in RR were also appreciated by a few participants to control potential audiences in SNS. That is, the decision to establish the timing of content publication enabled the management of the target audience (as P11 said, *"I wrote some posts [with sentiments] and made them ripen until midnight, hoping that not too many, but still a few of my friends, would read them."*). Such appropriation of the ripening feature is especially notable, as it is distinguished from the previously reported strategies of managing publics' access on one's self-disclosure in SNSs [20, 25]; for example, owning multiple profiles and managing social groups.

After all, the reflective and emotional aspect of the pause moment design includes the controversial issue, in terms of sharing emotions throughout a social network, yet it seems worthwhile to preserve room for solitude in RR. Moreover, the few cases of appropriation of the solitude moments imply the considerable approach of supporting users' self-disclosure for the more desirable experience in SNS.

Expanded Time Experience

Today's leading SNS applications privilege the experience of the "present" [13, 15] by their features [11], such as the latest on the top in the timeline and interfaces for instant publication. On the contrary, RR seems to stretch the experience of time to the past and the future; that is, the experience of reminiscence and reflection for the future, which are not well supported in the current SNS applications since their time experience is limited to the present. The ripening feature reminded users of the past moment when a post was made. The participants considered the moment of reminding as the experience of everyday reminiscences (*"It was just an ordinary post about my day [...] I had no need to ripen it for 23 hours. [...] in the next day, when I read it again, I had a little pleasure from looking back to yesterday" – P4*). Also, encouraged by the ripening feature, the participants were able to think about and anticipate their future status and events and reflect on them in their activities while using RR, e.g. sending a letter to oneself in the future (posting as *"[to himself] I suppose you are regretting in this moment, when you are reading it [after ripening is over]" – P27*), or sending a prepared message (*"I hope you are surprised when this message is opened. Happy birthday!" – P16 to P21, whose birthday was the following day*).

Moreover, such reflected thoughts were considered as thoughtful and considerate to other users (*"It was fun and insightful to see my friends posting their expected regret or anxiety for the future" – P7*) to improve personal image and also a sense of satisfaction from communication with each other's thoughtfulness (*"[When I saw P16's surprising message] I thought that he was thoughtful, while many people are depending on Facebook's notification for them [to acknowledge friends' birthdays]" – P21*).

However, a delay moment in sharing content raised the problem of accessibility, as the posts move down toward the past of the timeline while ripening proceeded (*"I'd revise my post once again, but it was hard to find in the timeline." – P8, "I didn't like that my posts go below in the timeline without anyone reading them" – P16*). Despite there were only 29 participants, the problem of a delay moment in the stream of user-generated content seemed crucial.

The issue might be treated as the usability problem of RR; however, the anxiety of the participants for falling behind the stream of SNS communication due to the delay moment extends the issue beyond the simple usability problem (*"If my friends cannot empathize with my feelings now, after all, what it is for?" – P29*). The observation also resonates with the reported evidence of the avoidance of being "out-of-date" [11] and the important feelings of co-presence and interactive reciprocity [12] in current SNSs.

Pause Moment as Indirect Cue in Online Communication

Throughout a few cases, we found that sharing the process of ripening was somehow considered as an exchange of a kind of indirect cues among the participants. Some participants mentioned that a longer ripening time for posts raised their curiosity and concerns about the content or the writer (*"When I saw P11 was ripening a post for 23 hours, I thought 'What on earth kind of serious story requires such long ripening time?'" – P13*). Such tensions, shaped by curiosities and concerns, sometimes made for funny or surprising circumstances (e.g., a surprising congratulation post for a birthday; fooling friends with empty posts – *"I totally believed that he had to say something in RR!" – P24*).

The ways that ripening time worked were similar to the physical cues in real-world communication, such as subtle nuances in facial expressions before people begin to speak. In other words, RR is given with a kind of alternative cue that supplements the absence of physical cues in online communication [21]. Moreover, the existence of such a novel, ambiguous cue in online communication inspires users to be more engaged in the process of revealing and refining meanings within the communication, in order to lead users to mindful experience [9] of communication in SNS.

However, it is the attractiveness of the online space's [21] absence of physical cues that increases communication loads [5]. Accordingly, in SNSs, the appearance of a new kind of cue that is created by a pause moment should be considered as presenting both sides of a coin, as it can also raise the burden of communication for some users. For example, the nuance of a cue was sometimes considered negative or oppressive (*"When the comment from my friend was done ripening, the comment was empty. Then I felt unpleasant, because the original comment could be something bad." – P25*). Further, the inconsistency between the perceived cue and the exact content is also considered exhaustive (*"It is exhaustive to see the other user ripening for a long time for nothing." – P21*). Accordingly, those findings suggest that it requires a considerate approach for designing a pausing feature for communication in an SNS.

CONCLUSION AND DISCUSSION

Formerly, a pause moment design, as a branch of slow technology [10] or a design for reflection [3], had been considered as applicable for communication in a close relationship, rather than in a bigger social network, due to its reflective and sentimental nature. This research, however, has proved that the pause moment design is also worth applying to SNSs, as the design preserves the moment for emotional, reflective, and reminiscent experience in communication and also enriches communication with the expanded time experience and indirect cues.

Nevertheless, this study found limitations of the current pause moment design for SNS; for example, increasing the anxiety of falling behind and the problem of accessibility to delayed posts. However, the limitations should be considered a source of insights for further exploration for an improved strategy of a pause moment design for SNS, rather than an unsolvable problem. For example, a shortcut link to a post during/after a pause moment, which is not provided in the current RR interface, is one possible option to improve its accessibility problem to delayed posts.

This study also implies a cultural bias, as the pause moment design is significantly related to the emotional and indirect aspect of communication. Moreover, the age of users becomes significant, as it is an influential factor for the network size and intensity of activities in SNS [1] and user's desire to receive immediate responses [4], which are related to the issue of delayed communication. The expected biases remained undiscovered in this study, as our participants only cover university students in South Korea. Hence, further research is required to examine the worth of a pause moment in SNS communication in different cultures and generations.

REFERENCES

1. Arjan, R., et al. Age differences in online social networking. *Extended Abst. on CHI'08*. ACM, (2008).
2. Bae, J., et al. Ripening room: designing social media for self-reflection in self-expression. *Proc. DIS 2014. ACM,* (2014).
3. Bagnara, S., and Pozzi, S. Design for reflection. *Work: A Journal of Prevention, Assessment and Rehabilitation 41* (2012), 1108-1113.
4. Boyd, D. Why youth (heart) social network sites: The role of networked publics in teenage social life. *MacArthur foundation series on digital learning–Youth, identity, and digital media* (2007), 119-142.
5. Burgoon, J.K., Walther, J.B. Nonverbal expectancies and the evaluative consequences of violations. *Human Communication Research 17*, 2 (1990), 232-265.
6. Danzico, L. Adding By Leaving Out: The Power of the Pause, *Interactions 17*, 4 (2010), 55-57.
7. Forest, L., and Wood, J. When Social Networking Is Not Working Individuals With Low Self-Esteem Recognize but Do Not Reap the Benefits of Self-Disclosure on Facebook. *Psychological Science* (2012).
8. Fullerton, B. Designing for Solitude. *Interactions, 17*, 6 (2010), 6-9.
9. Grosse-Hering, B., et al. Slow design for meaningful interactions. *Proc. CHI 2013*. ACM (2013).
10. Hallnäs, L., and Redström, J. Slow technology–designing for reflection. *Personal and ubiquitous computing 5*, 3 (2001), 201-212.
11. Harper, R., Whitworth, E. and Page, R. Fixity: Identity, time and durée on Facebook. In *Proc. IR 13*, 0 (2012).
12. Kaplan, A., and Haenlein, M. Users of the world, unite! The challenges and opportunities of Social Media. *Business horizons 53*, 1 (2010), 59-68.
13. Keightley, E. Introduction: time, media, modernity. In *Time, Media and Modernity*. Basingstoke: Palgrave Macmillan, pp. 1–24.
14. Manago, A., Taylor, T. and Greenfield, P. Me and my 400 friends: the anatomy of college students' Facebook networks, their communication patterns, and well-being. *Developmental psychology 48*, 2 (2012), 369.
15. Page, R. Re-examining narrativity: Small stories in status updates, *Text & Talk 30* (2010), 423-444.
16. Pai, P., and Arnott, C. User adoption of social networking sites: Eliciting uses and gratifications through a means-end approach.*ComputersinHumanBehavior29*,3 (2013).
17. Reis, H. T., and Shaver, P. Intimacy as an interpersonal process. In *Handbook of personal relationships* (1988).
18. Sengers, P. What I learned on Change Islands: reflec-tions on IT and pace of life. *Interactions 18*, 2 (2011).
19. Sleeper, M., et al. i read my Twitter the next morning and was astonished: a conversational perspective on Twitter regrets. *Proc. CHI 2013*. ACM, (2013).
20. Stutzman, F., and Hartzog, W. Boundary regulation in social media. *Proc. CSCW 2012*. ACM (2012).
21. Walther, B. *Computer-mediated communication: impersonal, interpersonal, & hyperpersonal interaction* (1996).
22. Wang, Qi, et al. Think twice before reposting it: Promoting accountable behavior on Sina Weibo. *Proc. of CSCWD 18th*. IEEE, (2014).
23. Wang, Y., et al. I regretted the minute I pressed share: A qualitative study of regrets on Facebook. *Proc. Sym. on Usable Privacy and Security*. ACM, (2011).
24. Wang, Y., et al. Privacy nudges for social media: an exploratory Facebook study. *Proc. WWW 2013*. (2013).
25. Wisniewski, P., Lipford, H., and Wilson, D. Fighting for my space: Coping mechanisms for SNS boundary regulation. Proc. CHI 2012. ACM, (2012)

Author Index

www.ingramcontent.com/pod-product-compliance
Ingram Content Group UK Ltd.
Pitfield, Milton Keynes, MK11 3LW, UK
UKHW051417290926
15471UKWH00009B/1656

9 781450 337748